Quantitative Methods
for Business

PEARSON

We work with leading authors to develop the strongest learning experiences, bringing cutting-edge thinking and best learning practice to a global market. We craft our print and digital resources to do more to help learners not only understand their content, but to see it in action and apply what they learn, whether studying or at work.

Pearson is the world's leading learning company. Our portfolio includes Penguin, Dorling Kindersley, the Financial Times and our educational business, Pearson International. We are also a leading provider of electronic learning programmes and of test development, processing and scoring services to educational institutions, corporations and professional bodies around the world.

Pearson Custom Publishing enables our customers to access a wide and expanding range of market-leading content from world-renowned authors and develop their own tailor-made book. You choose the content that meets your needs and Pearson Custom Publishing produces a high-quality printed book.

Every day our work helps learning flourish, and wherever learning flourishes, so do people.

To learn more please visit us at: www.pearsoncustom.co.uk

PEARSON CUSTOM PUBLISHING

Quantitative Methods for Business

Compiled from:

Basic Business Statistics: Concepts and Applications
Twelfth Edition
by Mark L. Berenson, David M. Levine and Timothy C. Krehbiel

Business Math
Ninth Edition
by Cheryl Cleaves, Margie Hobbs and Jeffrey Noble

PEARSON

Harlow, England • London • New York • Boston • San Francisco • Toronto • Sydney • Auckland • Singapore • Hong Kong
Tokyo • Seoul • Taipei • New Delhi • Cape Town • Sao Paulo • Mexico City • Madrid • Amsterdam • Munich • Paris • Milan

Pearson Education Limited
Edinburgh Gate
Harlow
Essex CM20 2JE

And associated companies throughout the world

Visit us on the World Wide Web at:
www.pearsoned.co.uk

This Custom Book Edition © Pearson Education Limited 2012

Compiled from:

Basic Business Statistics: Concepts and Applications
Twelfth Edition
by Mark L. Berenson, David M. Levine and Timothy C. Krehbiel
ISBN 978-0-273-75318-6
© Pearson Education Limited 2012

Business Math
Ninth Edition
by Cheryl Cleaves, Margie Hobbs and Jeffrey Noble
ISBN 978-0-13-510817-8
© 2012 Pearson Education, Inc., publishing as Prentice Hall, 1 Lake Street, Upper Saddle River, New Jersey, 07458.

All rights reserved. No part of this publication may be reproduced, stored in a retrieval system, or transmitted in any form or by any means, electronic, mechanical, photocopying, recording or otherwise, without either the prior written permission of the publisher or a licence permitting restricted copying in the United Kingdom issued by the Licensing Agency Ltd, Saffron House, 6–10 Kirby Street, London EC1N 8TS.

ISBN 978 1 78134 180 3

Printed and bound in Italy.

Contents

The following chapters are from:
Basic Business Statistics: Concepts and Applications
Twelfth Edition
by Mark L. Berenson, David M. Levine and Timothy C. Krehbiel

1	Introduction	2
2	Organizing and Visualizing Data	26
3	Numerical Descriptive Measures	94
4	Basic Probability	144
5	Discrete Probability Distributions	180
6	The Normal Distribution and Other Continuous Distributions	216
7	Sampling and Sampling Distributions	248
8	Confidence Interval Estimation	278
9	Fundamentals of Hypothesis Testing: One-Sample Tests	324
13	Simple Linear Regression	364

The following chapters are from:
Business Math
Ninth Edition
by Cheryl Cleaves, Margie Hobbs and Jeffrey Noble

11	Simple Interest and Simple Discount	420
13	Compound Interest, Future Value, and Present Value	458
14	Annuities and Sinking Funds	494
16	Mortgages	534
19	Insurance	562

1 Introduction

USING STATISTICS @ Good Tunes & More

1.1 Why Learn Statistics

1.2 Statistics in Business

1.3 Basic Vocabulary of Statistics

1.4 Identifying Types of Variables
  Measurement Scales

1.5 Statistical Applications for Desktop Computing

1.6 How to Use This Book
  Checklist for Getting Started

USING STATISTICS @ Good Tunes & More Revisited

CHAPTER 1 EXCEL GUIDE

EG1.1 Getting Started with Excel

EG1.2 Entering Data and Variable Type

EG1.3 Opening and Saving Workbooks

EG1.4 Creating and Copying Worksheets

EG1.5 Printing Worksheets

EG1.6 Worksheet Entries and References

EG1.7 Absolute and Relative Cell References

EG1.8 Entering Formulas into Worksheets

EG1.9 Using Appendices D and F

CHAPTER 1 MINITAB GUIDE

MG1.1 Getting Started with Minitab

MG1.2 Entering Data and Variable Type

MG1.3 Opening and Saving Worksheets and Projects

MG1.4 Creating and Copying Worksheets

MG1.5 Printing Parts of a Project

MG1.6 Worksheet Entries and References

MG1.7 Using Appendices D and F

Learning Objectives

In this chapter, you learn:

- How businesses use statistics
- The basic vocabulary of statistics
- The types of data used in business
- How to use Microsoft Excel and/or Minitab with this book

USING STATISTICS

@ Good Tunes & More

Managers at Good Tunes & More, a consumer electronics retailer, are looking to expand their chain to take advantage of recent store closings by their competitors. These managers have decided to approach local banks for the funding needed to underwrite the expansion. The managers know that they will have to present information about Good Tunes & More that will convince the bankers that the retailer is a good candidate for expansion.

The managers ask you to help prepare the supporting documents to be submitted to the bankers. To this end, they give you access to the retailer's sales transactions for the past five years. What should you do with the data? To help find a starting point for the task, you decide to learn more about statistics.

1.1 Why Learn Statistics

Statistics is the branch of mathematics that transforms numbers into useful information for decision makers. Statistics lets you know about the risks associated with making a business decision and allows you to understand and reduce the variation in the decision-making process.

Statistics provides you with methods for making better sense of the numbers used every day to describe or analyze the world we live in. For example, consider these news stories:

- **"More Clicks to Escape an Email List"** (*The New York Times*, **March 29, 2010, p. B2**) A study of 100 large online retailers reported that 39% required three or more clicks to opt out of an email list in 2009, compared to 7% in 2008.
- **"Green Power Purchases Targeted to Wind, Solar"** (**P. Davidson,** *USA Today*, **April 1, 2009, p. 3B**) Approximately 55% of green power sales was for wind energy.
- **"Follow the Tweets"** (**H. Rui, A. Whinston, and E. Winkler,** *The Wall Street Journal*, **November 30, 2009, p. R4**) In this study, the authors used the number of tweets that mention specific products to make accurate predictions of sales trends.

Do these numbers represent useful information? How can you decide? Statistical methods help you understand the information contained in "the numbers" and determine whether differences in "the numbers" are meaningful or are just due to chance.

Why learn statistics? First and foremost, statistics helps you make better sense of the world. Second, statistics helps you make better business decisions.

1.2 Statistics in Business

In the business world, statistics has these important specific uses:

- To summarize business data
- To draw conclusions from those data
- To make reliable forecasts about business activities
- To improve business processes

The statistical methods you use for these tasks come from one of the two branches of statistics: descriptive statistics and inferential statistics.

> DESCRIPTIVE STATISTICS
>
> **Descriptive statistics** are the methods that help collect, summarize, present, and analyze a set of data.
>
> INFERENTIAL STATISTICS
>
> **Inferential statistics** are the methods that use the data collected from a small group to draw conclusions about a larger group.

Many of the tables and charts found in a typical presentation are the products of descriptive methods, as are statistics such as the mean or median of a group, which you may have encountered previously. (The mean and median are among the concepts discussed in Chapter 3.) When you use statistical methods to help choose which investment from a set of investments might lead to a higher return or which marketing strategy might lead to increased sales, you are using inferential methods.

There are four important uses of statistics in business:

- To visualize and summarize your data (an example of using descriptive methods)
- To reach conclusions about a large group based on data collected from a small group (an example of using inferential methods)

- To make reliable forecasts that are based on statistical models for prediction (inferential methods)
- To improve business processes using managerial approaches such as Six Sigma that focus on quality improvement

To use descriptive and inferential methods correctly, you must also learn the conditions and assumptions required for using those methods. And since many of the statistical methods used in business must be computerized in order to be of practical benefit, you also need to know how computers can help you apply statistics in the business world.

To help you develop and integrate these skills, which will give you a basis for making better decisions, every chapter of *Basic Business Statistics* begins with a Using Statistics scenario. Each scenario describes a realistic business situation in which you are asked to make decisions that can be enhanced by applying statistical methods. For example, in one chapter you must decide the location in a supermarket that best enhances sales of a cola drink, while in another chapter you need to forecast sales for a clothing store.

In the scenario on page 33, you need to answer the following questions: What data should you include to convince bankers to extend the credit that Good Tunes & More needs? How should you present those data?

Because Good Tunes & More is a retailer, collecting data about the company's sales would be a reasonable starting point. You could present the details of every sales transaction for the past few years as a way of demonstrating that the business is thriving. However, presenting the bankers with the thousands of transactions would overwhelm them and not be very useful. You need to summarize the details of each transaction in some useful way that will give the bankers the information to (perhaps) uncover a favorable pattern about the sales over time.

One piece of information that the bankers would presumably want to see is the yearly dollar sales totals. Tallying and totaling sales is a common summary task. When you tally sales—or any other relevant data about Good Tunes & More that you choose to use—you follow standard business practice and tally by a business period, such as by month, quarter, or year. When you do so, you end up with multiple values: sales for this year, sales for last year, sales for the year before that, and so on.

Knowing more about statistics will definitely help you prepare a better presentation for the bankers! And the best way to begin knowing more about statistics is to learn the basic vocabulary of statistics.

1.3 Basic Vocabulary of Statistics

Seven terms—*variable, data, operational definition, population, sample, parameter,* and *statistic* (singular)—identify the fundamental concepts of the subject of statistics. Learning about and making sense of the statistical methods discussed in later chapters is nearly impossible if you do not first understand the meaning of these words.

Variables are characteristics of items or individuals. They are what you analyze when you use a statistical method. For the Good Tunes & More scenario, sales, expenses by year, and net profit by year are variables that the bankers would want to analyze. When used in everyday speech, *variable* suggests that something changes or varies, and you would expect sales, expenses, and net profit to have different values from year to year. These different values are the *data* associated with a variable or, more simply, the "data to be analyzed."

> **VARIABLE**
>
> A **variable** is a characteristic of an item or individual.
>
> **DATA**
>
> **Data** are the different values associated with a variable.

Variables can differ for reasons other than time. For example, if you conducted an analysis of the composition of a large lecture class, you would probably want to include the variables class standing, gender, and major field of study. These variables would also vary because each student in the class is different. One student might be a sophomore, a male, and an accounting major, while another might be a junior, a female, and a finance major.

Variable values are meaningless unless their corresponding variables have **operational definitions**. These definitions are universally accepted meanings that are clear to all associated with an analysis. Even though the operational definition for sales per year might seem clear, miscommunication could occur if one person were to refer to sales per year for the entire chain of stores and another to sales per year per store. Even individual values for variables sometimes need to be defined. For the class standing variable, for example, what *exactly* is meant by the words *sophomore* and *junior*? (Perhaps the most famous examples of vague definitions have been election disputes, such as the one that occurred in Florida during the 2000 U.S. presidential election that involved the definitions for "valid" and "invalid" ballots.)

The subject of statistics creates useful information from either populations or samples.

POPULATION
A **population** consists of all the items or individuals about which you want to reach conclusions.

SAMPLE
A **sample** is the portion of a population selected for analysis.

A *population* consists of all the items or individuals about which you want to reach conclusions. All the Good Tunes & More sales transactions for a specific year, all the customers who shopped at Good Tunes & More this weekend, all the full-time students enrolled in a college, and all the registered voters in Ohio are examples of populations.

A *sample* is the portion of a population selected for analysis. From the four examples of populations just given, you could select a sample of 200 Good Tunes & More sales transactions randomly selected by an auditor for study, a sample of 30 Good Tunes & More customers asked to complete a customer satisfaction survey, a sample of 50 full-time students selected for a marketing study, and a sample of 500 registered voters in Ohio contacted by telephone for a political poll. In each of these examples, the transactions or people in the sample represent a portion of the items or individuals that make up the population.

Parameter and *statistic* complete the basic vocabulary of statistics.

PARAMETER
A **parameter** is a measure that describes a characteristic of a population.

STATISTIC
A **statistic** is a measure that describes a characteristic of a sample.

The average amount spent by all customers who shopped at Good Tunes & More this weekend is an example of a parameter because this amount refers to the amount spent in the entire population. In contrast, the average amount spent by the 30 customers completing the customer satisfaction survey is an example of a statistic because it refers only to the amount spent by the sample of 30 customers.

1.4 Identifying Types of Variables

Identifying the characteristic of an item or individual to study and assigning an operational definition to that characteristic is only part of the variable definition process. For each variable, you must also establish the type of values it will have.

Categorical variables (also known as **qualitative variables**) have values that can only be placed into categories such as yes and no. "Do you currently own bonds?" (yes or no) and the level of risk of a bond fund (below average, average, or above average) are examples of categorical variables.

Numerical variables (also known as **quantitative variables**) have values that represent quantities. Numerical variables are further identified as being either discrete or continuous variables.

Discrete variables have numerical values that arise from a counting process. "The number of premium cable channels subscribed to" is an example of a discrete numerical variable because the response is one of a finite number of integers. You subscribe to zero, one, two, or more channels. "The number of items purchased" is also a discrete numerical variable because you are counting the number of items purchased.

Continuous variables produce numerical responses that arise from a measuring process. The time you wait for teller service at a bank is an example of a continuous numerical variable because the response takes on any value within a *continuum*, or an interval, depending on the precision of the measuring instrument. For example, your waiting time could be 1 minute, 1.1 minutes, 1.11 minutes, or 1.113 minutes, depending on the precision of the measuring device used. (Theoretically, no two continuous values would ever be identical. However, because no measuring device is perfectly precise, identical continuous values for two or more items or individuals can occur.)

At first glance, identifying the variable type may seem easy, but some variables that you might want to study could be either categorical or numerical, depending on how you define them. For example, "age" would seem to be an obvious numerical variable, but what if you are interested in comparing the buying habits of children, young adults, middle-aged persons, and retirement-age people? In that case, defining "age" as a categorical variable would make better sense. Again, this illustrates the earlier point that without operational definitions, variables are meaningless.

Asking questions about the variables you have identified for study can often be a great help in determining the variable type you want. Table 1.1 illustrates the process. Note that the "answers" to the questions are labeled *responses*. The word *responses* is sometimes used in statistics to refer to the values of a variable.

TABLE 1.1
Types of Variables

Question	Responses	Data Type
Do you currently have a profile on Facebook?	❏ Yes ❏ No	Categorical
How many text messages have you sent in the past week?	____	Numerical (discrete)
How long did it take to download a video game?	____ seconds	Numerical (continuous)

Measurement Scales

The values for variables can themselves be classified by the level of measurement, or measurement scale. Statisticians use the terms *nominal scale* and *ordinal scale* to describe the values for a categorical variable and use the terms *interval scale* and *ratio scale* to describe numerical values.

Nominal and Ordinal Scales Values for a categorical variable are measured on a nominal scale or on an ordinal scale. A **nominal scale** (see Table 1.2) classifies data into distinct categories in which no ranking is implied. Examples of a nominal scaled variable are your favorite soft drink, your political party affiliation, and your gender. Nominal scaling is the weakest form of measurement because you cannot specify any ranking across the various categories.

TABLE 1.2

Examples of Nominal Scales

Categorical Variable	Categories
Do you currently have a Facebook profile?	❏ Yes ❏ No
Types of investments	❏ Stocks ❏ Bonds ❏ Other ❏ None
Internet email provider	❏ Gmail ❏ Windows Live ❏ Yahoo ❏ Other

An **ordinal scale** classifies values into distinct categories in which ranking is implied. For example, suppose that Good Tunes & More conducted a survey of customers who made a purchase and asked the question "How do you rate the overall service provided by Good Tunes & More during your most recent purchase?" to which the responses were "excellent," "very good," "fair," and "poor." The answers to this question would constitute an ordinal scaled variable because the responses "excellent," "very good," "fair," and "poor" are ranked in order of satisfaction. Table 1.3 lists other examples of ordinal scaled variables.

TABLE 1.3

Examples of Ordinal Scales

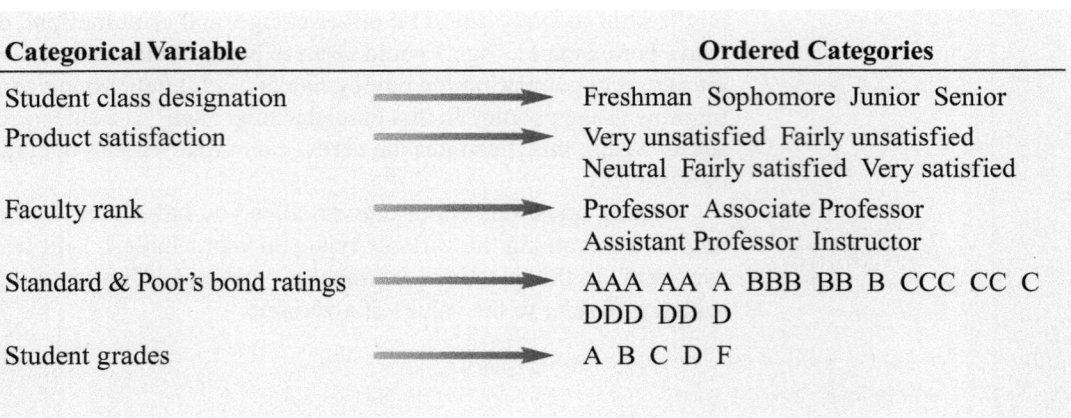

Categorical Variable	Ordered Categories
Student class designation	Freshman Sophomore Junior Senior
Product satisfaction	Very unsatisfied Fairly unsatisfied Neutral Fairly satisfied Very satisfied
Faculty rank	Professor Associate Professor Assistant Professor Instructor
Standard & Poor's bond ratings	AAA AA A BBB BB B CCC CC C DDD DD D
Student grades	A B C D F

Ordinal scaling is a stronger form of measurement than nominal scaling because an observed value classified into one category possesses more of a property than does an observed value classified into another category. However, ordinal scaling is still a relatively weak form of measurement because the scale does not account for the amount of the differences *between* the categories. The ordering implies only *which* category is "greater," "better," or "more preferred"—not by *how much*.

Interval and Ratio Scales Values for a numerical variable are measured on an interval scale or a ratio scale. An **interval scale** (see Table 1.4) is an ordered scale in which the difference between measurements is a meaningful quantity but does not involve a true zero point. For example, a noontime temperature reading of 67 degrees Fahrenheit is 2 degrees warmer than a noontime reading of 65 degrees. In addition, the 2 degrees Fahrenheit difference in the noontime temperature readings is the same as if the two noontime temperature readings were 74 and 76 degrees Fahrenheit because the difference has the same meaning anywhere on the scale.

TABLE 1.4

Examples of Interval and Ratio Scales

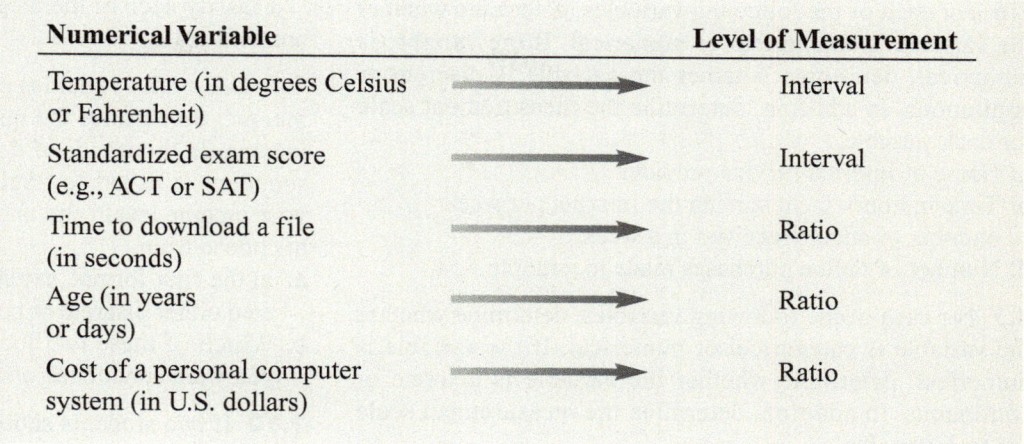

A **ratio scale** is an ordered scale in which the difference between the measurements involves a true zero point, as in height, weight, age, or salary measurements. If Good Tunes & More conducted a survey and asked the amount of money that you expected to spend on audio equipment in the next year, the responses to such a question would be an example of a ratio scaled variable. As another example, a person who weighs 240 pounds is twice as heavy as someone who weighs 120 pounds. Temperature is a trickier case: Fahrenheit and Celsius (centigrade) scales are interval but not ratio scales; the "zero" value is arbitrary, not real. You cannot say that a noontime temperature reading of 4 degrees Fahrenheit is twice as hot as 2 degrees Fahrenheit. But a Kelvin temperature reading, in which 0 degrees means no molecular motion, is ratio scaled. In contrast, the Fahrenheit and Celsius scales use arbitrarily selected 0-degree beginning points.

Data measured on an interval scale or on a ratio scale constitute the highest levels of measurement. They are stronger forms of measurement than an ordinal scale because you can determine not only which observed value is the largest but also by how much.

Problems for Section 1.4

LEARNING THE BASICS

1.1 Four different beverages are sold at a fast-food restaurant: soft drinks, tea, coffee, and bottled water.
a. Explain why the type of beverage sold is an example of a categorical variable. *They are names, not quantifiable*
b. Explain why the type of beverage sold is an example of a nominal scaled variable. *There is no ranking*

1.2 Coffee is sold in three sizes at a fast-food restaurant: small, medium, and large. Explain why the beverage size of coffee is an example of an ordinal scaled variable. *Because they ranked smallest to largest*

1.3 Suppose that you measure the time it takes to download a video from the Internet.
a. Explain why the download time is a continuous numerical variable. *Because it takes a value in continuum*
b. Explain why the download time is a ratio scaled variable. *Because there is a natural zero point*

APPLYING THE CONCEPTS

SELF Test 1.4 For each of the following variables, determine whether the variable is categorical or numerical. If the variable is numerical, determine whether the variable is discrete or continuous. In addition, determine the measurement scale.
a. Number of telephones per household *numerical → discrete*
b. Length (in minutes) of the longest telephone call made in a month *numerical → continuous*
c. Whether someone in the household owns a Wi-Fi-capable cell phone *categorical → nominal*
d. Whether there is a high-speed Internet connection in the household *categorical → ordinal*

1.5 The following information is collected from students upon exiting the campus bookstore during the first week of classes.
a. Amount of time spent shopping in the bookstore *numerical → continuous*
b. Number of textbooks purchased *discrete*
c. Academic major *categorical → nominal ordinal*
d. Gender *categorical → nominal*
Classify each of these variables as categorical or numerical. If the variable is numerical, determine whether the variable is discrete or continuous. In addition, determine the measurement scale for each of these variables.

1.6 For each of the following variables, determine whether the variable is categorical or numerical. If the variable is numerical, determine whether the variable is discrete or continuous. In addition, determine the measurement scale for each variable.
a. Name of Internet service provider
b. Time in hours spent surfing the Internet per week
c. Number of emails received in a week
d. Number of online purchases made in a month

1.7 For each of the following variables, determine whether the variable is categorical or numerical. If the variable is numerical, determine whether the variable is discrete or continuous. In addition, determine the measurement scale for each variable.
a. Amount of money spent on clothing in the past month
b. Favorite department store
c. Most likely time period during which shopping for clothing takes place (weekday, weeknight, or weekend)
d. Number of pairs of shoes owned

1.8 Clients interested in trading on the Kuwait Stock Exchange (KSE) must supply the following information on their applications:
a. Monthly salary
b. Number of jobs in past 10 years
c. Nationality
d. Marital status

Classify each of the responses by type of data and measurement scale.

1.9 One of the variables most often included in surveys is income. Sometimes the question is phrased "What is your income (in thousands of dollars)?" In other surveys, the respondent is asked to "Select the circle corresponding to your income level" and is given a number of income ranges to choose from.
a. In the first format, explain why income might be considered either discrete or continuous.
b. Which of these two formats would you prefer to use if you were conducting a survey? Why?

1.10 If two students score a 90 on the same examination, what arguments could be used to show that the underlying variable—test score—is continuous?

1.11 The director of market research at a large department store chain wanted to conduct a survey throughout a metropolitan area to determine the amount of time working women spend shopping for clothing in a typical month.
a. Describe both the population and the sample of interest. Indicate the type of data the director might want to collect.
b. Develop a first draft of the questionnaire needed in (a) by writing three categorical questions and three numerical questions that you feel would be appropriate for this survey.

1.5 Statistical Applications for Desktop Computing

Advances in computing during the past 40 years have brought statistical applications to the business desktop. Statistical functionality is so commonplace today that many simple statistical tasks once done exclusively with pencil and paper or hand calculators are now done electronically, with the assistance of statistical applications.

Excel and Minitab are examples of desktop applications that people use for statistics. Excel is the Microsoft Office data analysis application that evolved from earlier electronic spreadsheets used in accounting and financial applications. Minitab, a dedicated statistical application, or **statistical package**, was developed from the ground up to perform statistical analysis as accurately as possible. Versions of Minitab run on larger computer systems and can perform heavy-duty corporate analyses involving very large data sets. Excel and Minitab are two very different programs, and their differences have led to an ongoing debate as to which program is more appropriate for use in an introductory business statistics course. Proponents of each program point to their program's strengths: Minitab as a complete statistical solution; Excel as a common desktop tool found in many business functional areas (and in many different business school courses).

Although you are probably more familiar with Excel than with Minitab, both programs share many similarities, starting with their shared use of **worksheets** (or spreadsheets) to store data for analysis. Worksheets are tabular arrangements of data, in which the intersections of rows and columns form **cells**, boxes into which you make entries. In Minitab, the data for each variable are placed in separate columns, and this is also the standard practice when using Excel. Generally, to perform a statistical analysis in either program, you select one or more columns of data and then apply the appropriate command.

Both Excel and Minitab allow you to save worksheets, programming information, and results as one file, called a **workbook** in Excel and a **project** in Minitab. In Excel, workbooks are collections of worksheets and chart sheets. You save a workbook when you save "an Excel file" (as either an **.xls** or **.xlsx** file). In Minitab, a project includes data worksheets, all the results shown in a **session window**, and all graphs created for the data. Unlike in Excel, in Minitab you can save individual worksheets (as **.mtw** worksheet files) as well as save the entire project (as an **.mpj** project file).

You can use either Excel or Minitab to learn and practice the statistical methods learned in this book. The end of each chapter, except for the last chapter, presents guides that contain detailed instructions for applying Microsoft Excel and Minitab to the statistical methods taught in the chapter. These Excel and Minitab Guides use some of the downloadable files discussed in Appendix C to illustrate the step-by-step process by which you apply a method. The Excel Guides additionally offer a choice of techniques—all leading to the same results—that allow you to use Excel either in a semi-automated way to get quick results or as a "sandbox" in which you construct results from scratch or from model templates. This is further explained in Section EG1.1 of the Chapter 1 Excel Guide.

1.6 How to Use This Book

This book organizes its material around the four important uses of statistics in business (see Section 1.2). Chapters 2 and 3 present methods that summarize business data to address the first use listed. Chapters 4 through 12 discuss methods that use sample data to draw conclusions about populations (the second use). Chapters 13 though 16 review methods to make reliable forecasts (the third use). Chapter 17 introduces methods that you can use to improve business processes (the fourth use). In addition, Chapter 2 introduces a problem-solving approach that will help you learn individual methods and help you apply your knowledge beyond the statistics course. Chapter 18 further illustrates this approach and also summarizes the methods discussed in earlier chapters.

As explained in Section 1.2, each chapter begins with a scenario that establishes a business situation to which you can apply the methods of the chapter. At the end of each chapter, you revisit the scenario to learn how the methods of the chapter could be applied in the scenario. Following the revisited scenario, you will find such sections as Summary, Key Terms, Key Equations, and Chapter Review Problems that help you review what you have learned.

Following this review material in most chapters, you will find a continuing case study that allows you to apply statistics to problems faced by the management of Ashland MultiComm Services, a residential telecommunications provider. Most chapters continue with a Digital Case, in which you examine information in a variety of media forms and apply your statistical knowledge to resolve problems or address issues and concerns of the case. Many of these cases will help you think about what constitutes the proper or ethical use of statistics. ("Learning with the Digital Cases" on page 45 introduces you to this unique set of business cases.) Finally, at the very end of each chapter, except for the last chapter, are the Excel Guides and Minitab Guides discussed in Section 1.5.

Don't worry if your instructor does not cover every section of every chapter. Introductory business statistics courses vary in their scope, length, and number of college credits. Your chosen functional area of specialization (accounting, management, finance, marketing, etc.) may also affect what you learn in class or what you are assigned or choose to read in this book.

Checklist for Getting Started

To make the best use of this book, you need to work with Excel or Minitab and download and use files and other electronic resources that are available from the companion website (discussed fully in Appendix C). To minimize problems you may face later when using these resources, review and complete the Table 1.5 checklist. When you have checked off all the tasks necessary for your own work, you will be ready to begin reading the Chapter 1 Excel or Minitab Guide and using the supplemental material in Appendices B, C, D, F and G, as necessary.

When you have completed the checklist, you are ready to begin using the Excel Guides and Minitab Guides that appear at the end of chapters. These guides discuss how to apply

TABLE 1.5

Checklist for Getting Started with *Basic Business Statistics*

- ❏ Select which program, Excel or Minitab, you will use with this book. (Your instructor may have made this decision for you.)
- ❏ Read Appendix A if you need to learn or review basic math concepts and notation.
- ❏ Read Appendix B if you need to learn or review basic computing concepts and skills.
- ❏ Download the files and other electronic resources needed to work with this book. Read Appendix C to learn more about the things you can download from the companion website for this book. (This process requires Internet access.)
- ❏ Successfully install the chosen program and apply all available updates to the program. Read Appendix Section D.1 to learn how to find and apply updates. (This process requires Internet access.)
- ❏ If you plan to use PHStat2 with Excel, complete the special checklist in Appendix Section D.2. If you plan to use the Analysis ToolPak with Excel, read and follow the instructions in Appendix Section D.5.
- ❏ Skim Appendices F and G to be aware of how these appendices can help you as you use this book with Excel or Minitab.

Excel and Minitab to the statistical methods discussed in the chapter. The Excel Guides and Minitab Guides for this chapter (which begin on pages 47 and 52, respectively) review the basic operations of these programs and explain how Excel and Minitab handle the concept of type of variable discussed in Section 1.4.

Instructions in the Excel Guides and Minitab Guides and related appendices use the conventions for computer operations presented in Table 1.6. Read and review Appendix B if some of the vocabulary used in the table is new to you.

TABLE 1.6

Conventions for Computing Operations

Operation	Examples	Interpretation
Keyboard keys	**Enter** **Ctrl** **Shift**	Names of keys are always the object of the verb *press*, as in "press **Enter**."
Keystroke combination	**Crtl+C** **Crtl+Shift+Enter**	Some keyboarding actions require you to press more than one key at the same time. **Crtl+C** means press the **C** key while holding down the **Ctrl** key. **Crtl+Shift+Enter** means press the **Enter** key while holding down the **Ctrl** and **Shift** keys.
Click object	Click **OK**. Click **All** in the **Page Range** section.	A *click object* is a target of a mouse click. When click objects are part of a window that contains more than one part, the part name is also given, e.g., "in the **Page Range** section." Review Appendix Section B.2 to learn the verbs this book uses with click objects.
Menu or ribbon selection	**File → New** **Layout → Trendline → Linear Trendline**	A sequence of menu or ribbon selections is represented by a list of choices separated by the → symbol. **File → New** means first select **File** and then, from the list of choices that appears, select **New**.
Placeholder object	Select *variablename*	An italicized object means that the actual object varies, depending on the context of the instruction. "Select *variablename*" might, for one problem, mean "select the **Yearly Sales** variable" and might mean "select the **Monthly Sales** variable" for another.

USING STATISTICS @ Good Tunes & More Revisited

In the Using Statistics scenario at the beginning of this chapter, you were asked to help prepare documents to support the Good Tunes & More expansion. The managers had decided to approach local banks for funding the expansion of their company, and you needed to determine what type of data to present and how to present those data. As a first step, you decided to summarize the details of thousands of transactions into useful information in the form of yearly dollar sales totals.

SUMMARY

Learning about statistics begins with learning the seven terms that are the basic vocabulary of statistics. With this vocabulary, you can begin to understand how statistics helps you make better sense of the world. Businesses use statistics to summarize and reach conclusions from data, to make reliable forecasts, and to improve business processes.

You learned some of the basic vocabulary used in statistics and the various types of data used in business. In the next two chapters, you will study data collection and a variety of tables and charts and descriptive measures that are used to present and analyze data.

KEY TERMS

categorical variable
continuous variable
data
descriptive statistics
discrete variable
inferential statistics
interval scale
nominal scale
numerical variable
operational definition
ordinal scale
parameter
population
qualitative variable
quantitative variable
ratio scale
sample
statistic
statistical package
statistics
variable

CHAPTER REVIEW PROBLEMS

CHECKING YOUR UNDERSTANDING

1.12 What is the difference between a sample and a population?

1.13 What is the difference between a statistic and a parameter?

1.14 What is the difference between descriptive statistics and inferential statistics?

1.15 What is the difference between a categorical variable and a numerical variable?

1.16 What is the difference between a discrete numerical variable and a continuous numerical variable?

1.17 What is an operational definition, and why are operational definitions so important?

1.18 What are the four measurement scales?

APPLYING THE CONCEPTS

1.19 Visit the official website for either Excel or Minitab, **www.office.microsoft.com/excel** or **www.minitab.com/products/minitab**. Read about the program you chose and then think about the ways the program could be useful in statistical analysis.

1.20 On January 19, 2009, passengers arriving from Europe at Dubai International Airport were surveyed. Surveys were distributed on the planes to all passengers arriving. Of the 13,727 responses received, 80% indicated that the passengers were visiting the country for business and 48% were visiting for business and tourism. The report also noted that 20% of the passengers surveyed were on work visas, and 15.8% indicated that they were visiting relatives.
a. Describe the population of interest.
b. Describe the sample that was collected.

c. Describe a parameter of interest.
d. Describe the statistic used to estimate the parameter in (c).

1.21 The Gallup organization releases the results of recent polls at its website, **www.gallup.com**. Visit this site and read an article of interest.
a. Describe the population of interest.
b. Describe the sample that was collected.
c. Describe a parameter of interest.
d. Describe the statistic used to describe the parameter in (c).

1.22 A Gallup poll conducted in February 2010 for countries of the Middle East indicated that 30% of people in Lebanon had both a mobile phone and home Internet access, and 80% had mobile service only. (Data extracted from **www.gallup.com/poll/121652/cell-phones-outpace-internet-access-middle-east.aspx**, July 13, 2010.) The results were based on face-to-face interviews with approximately 1,000 adults aged 15 and older.
a. Describe the population of interest.
b. Describe the sample that was collected.
c. Is 30% a parameter or a statistic? Explain.
d. Is 80% a parameter or a statistic?

1.23 According to its home page, "Swivel is a website where people share reports of charts and numbers. Businesses use swivel to dashboard their metrics. Students use Swivel to find and share research data." Visit **www.swivel.com** and explore a data set of interest to you.
a. Describe a variable in the data set you selected.
b. Is the variable categorical or numerical?
c. If the variable is numerical, is it discrete or continuous?

1.24 Access the following link on the official statistics page of the New Zealand Census: **www.stats.govt.nz/Census/2006CensusHomePage/QuickStats/AboutAPlace/SnapShot.aspx?type=region&ParentID=&tab=Culturaldiversity&id=1000001**.
a. Give an example of a categorical variable included in this survey.
b. Give an example of a numerical variable included in this survey.

1.25 The Australian Survey of Student Engagement filed an executive summary report in 2009 (see **www.teaching-learning.utas.edu.au/student-and-graduate-feedback/survey-results**). The report indicated that 35 institutions participated in the survey, which had a population of 104,137 first-year students and 119,392 third-year students at the bachelor degree level from both Australia and New Zealand. Samples of 1,523 first-year students and 1,509 third-year students were taken, with a target of 606 responses. Demographic data collected on these students included class (freshman, sophomore, junior, senior), age, gender, and major.
a. Describe the population of interest.
b. Describe the sample that was collected.
c. Indicate whether each of the four demographic variables mentioned is categorical or numerical.
d. For each of the four demographic variables mentioned, indicate the measurement scale.

1.26 A manufacturer of home appliances was planning to survey households in the United Kingdom to determine purchasing habits. Among the variables to be collected were the following:
   i. The primary place of purchase for home appliances
   ii. The number of home appliances purchased
   iii. The brand of the home appliances purchased
   iv. The total amount of money spent for the purchase of the appliances
a. For each of the four items listed, indicate whether the variable is categorical or numerical. If it is numerical, is it discrete or continuous?
b. Develop five categorical questions for the survey.
c. Develop five numerical questions for the survey.

1.27 A sample of 62 undergraduate students answered the following survey:
1. What is your gender? Female _____ Male _____
2. What is your age (*as of last birthday*)? _____
3. What is your current registered class designation?
   Freshman _____ Sophomore _____ Junior _____ Senior _____
4. What is your major area of study?
   Accounting _____
   Computer Information Systems _____ Economics/Finance _____
   International Business _____ Management _____
   Retailing/Marketing _____
   Other _____ Undecided _____
5. At the present time, do you plan to attend graduate school?
   Yes _____ No _____ Not sure _____
6. What is your current cumulative grade point average? _____
7. What is your current employment status?
   Full time _____ Part time _____ Unemployed _____
8. What would you expect your starting annual salary (*in $000*) to be if you were to seek full-time employment immediately after obtaining your bachelor's degree? _____
9. For how many social networking sites are you registered? _____
10. How satisfied are you with the food and dining services on campus? _____
        1 2 3 4 5 6 7
    Extremely   Neutral   Extremely
    unsatisfied   satisfied
11. About how much money did you spend this semester for textbooks and supplies? _____
12. What type of computer do you prefer to use for your studies?
    Desktop _____ Laptop _____
    Tablet/notebook/netbook _____
13. How many text messages do you send in a typical week? _____
14. How much wealth (income, savings, investment, real estate, and other assets) would you have to accumulate

(in millions of dollars) before you would say you are rich? _____
a. Which variables in the survey are categorical?
b. Which variables in the survey are numerical?
c. Which variables are discrete numerical variables?

The results of the survey are stored in **UndergradSurvey**

1.28 A sample of 44 graduate students answered the following survey:
1. What is your gender? Female _____ Male _____
2. What is your age (*as of last birthday*)? _____
3. What is your current major area of study?
   Accounting _____
   Economics/Finance _____
   Management _____
   Retailing/Marketing _____
   Other _____ Undecided _____
4. What is your current graduate cumulative grade point average? _____
5. What was your undergraduate major?
   Biological Sciences _____ Business _____
   Computers _____
   Engineering _____
   Other _____
6. What was your undergraduate cumulative grade point average? _____
7. What is your current employment status?
   Full time _____ Part time _____ Unemployed _____
8. How many different full-time jobs have you held in the past 10 years? _____
9. What do you expect your annual salary (*in $000*) to be immediately after completion of your graduate studies if you are employed full time? _____
10. About how much money did you spend this semester for textbooks and supplies? _____
11. How satisfied are you with the MBA program advisory services on campus?

            1   2   3   4   5   6   7
    Extremely   Neutral   Extremely
    unsatisfied   satisfied
12. What type of computer do you prefer to use for your studies?
    Desktop _____ Laptop _____ Tablet/notebook/netbook _____
13. How many text messages do you send in a typical week? _____
14. How much wealth (income, savings, investment, real estate, and other assets) would you have to accumulate (in millions of dollars) before you would say you are rich? _____
    a. Which variables in the survey are categorical?
    b. Which variables in the survey are numerical?
    c. Which variables are discrete numerical variables?

The results of the survey are stored in **GradSurvey**

END-OF-CHAPTER CASES

At the end of most chapters, you will find a continuing case study that allows you to apply statistics to problems faced by the management of the Ashland MultiComm Services, a residential telecommunications provider. You will also find a series of Digital Cases that extend many of the Using Statistics scenarios that begin each chapter.

LEARNING WITH THE DIGITAL CASES

People use statistical techniques to help communicate and present important information to others both inside and outside their businesses. Every day, as in these examples, people misuse these techniques. Identifying and preventing misuses of statistics, whether intentional or not, is an important responsibility for all managers. The Digital Cases help you develop the skills necessary for this important task.

A Digital Case asks you to review electronic documents related to a company or statistical issue discussed in the chapter's Using Statistics scenario. You review the contents of these documents, which may contain internal confidential as well as publicly stated facts and claims, seeking to identify and correct misuses of statistics. Unlike a traditional case study, but like many business situations, not all of the information you encounter will be relevant to your task, and you may occasionally discover conflicting information that you have to resolve in order to complete the case.

To assist your learning, each Digital Case begins with a learning objective and a summary of the problem or issue at hand. Each case directs you to the information necessary to reach your own conclusions and to answer the case questions. You can work with the documents for the Digital Cases offline, after downloading them from the companion website (see Appendix C). Or you can work with the Digital Cases online, chapter-by-chapter, at the companion website.

DIGITAL CASE EXAMPLE

This section illustrates learning with a Digital Case. To begin, open the Digital Case file **GTM.pdf**, which contains contents from the Good Tunes & More website. Recall that the privately held Good Tunes & More, the subject of the

Using Statistics scenario in this chapter, is seeking financing to expand its business by opening retail locations. Because the managers are eager to show that Good Tunes & More is a thriving business, it is not surprising to discover the "our best sales year ever" claim in the "Good Times at Good Tunes & More" section on the first page.

Click the **our best sales year ever** link to display the page that supports this claim. How would you support such a claim? With a table of numbers? A chart? Remarks attributed to a knowledgeable source? Good Tunes & More has used a chart to present "two years ago" and "latest twelve months" sales data by category. Are there any problems with the choices made on this web page? *Absolutely*!

First, note that there are no scales for the symbols used, so it is impossible to know what the actual sales volumes are. In fact, as you will learn in Section 2.8, charts that incorporate symbols in this way are considered examples of *chartjunk* and would never be used by people seeking to properly use graphs.

This important point aside, another question that arises is whether the sales data represent the number of units sold or something else. The use of the symbols creates the impression that unit sales data are being presented. If the data are unit sales, does such data best support the claim being made, or would something else, such as dollar volumes, be a better indicator of sales at the retailer?

Then there are those curious chart labels. "Latest twelve months" is ambiguous; it could include months from the current year as well as months from one year ago and therefore may not be an equivalent time period to "two years ago." But the business was established in 1997, and the claim being made is "best sales year ever," so why hasn't management included sales figures for *every* year?

Are Good Tunes & More managers hiding something, or are they just unaware of the proper use of statistics? Either way, they have failed to properly communicate a vital aspect of their story.

In subsequent Digital Cases, you will be asked to provide this type of analysis, using the open-ended questions in the case as your guide. Not all the cases are as straightforward as this example, and some cases include perfectly appropriate applications of statistics.

REFERENCES

1. McCullough, B. D., and D. Heiser, "On the Accuracy of Statistical Procedures in Microsoft Excel 2007," *Computational Statistics and Data Analysis*, 52 (2008), 4568–4606.
2. McCullough, B. D., and B. Wilson, "On the Accuracy of Statistical Procedures in Microsoft Excel 97," *Computational Statistics and Data Analysis*, 31 (1999), 27–37.
3. McCullough, B. D., and B. Wilson, "On the Accuracy of Statistical Procedures in Microsoft Excel 2003," *Computational Statistics and Data Analysis*, 49 (2005), 1244–1252.
4. *Microsoft Excel 2010* (Redmond, WA: Microsoft Corporation, 2010).
5. Minitab *Release 16* (State College, PA: Minitab, Inc., 2010).
6. Nash, J. C., "Spreadsheets in Statistical Practice—Another Look," *The American Statistician*, 60 (2006), 287–289.

CHAPTER 1 EXCEL GUIDE

EG1.1 GETTING STARTED with EXCEL

You are almost ready to use Excel if you have completed the Table 1.5 checklist and reviewed the Table 1.6 conventions for computing on page 42. Before going further, decide how you plan to use Excel with this book. The Excel Guides include *In-Depth Excel* instructions that require no additional software and *PHStat2* instructions that use PHStat2, an add-in that simplifies using Excel while creating results identical to those you would get using the Excel instructions. Table EG1.1 lists the advantages and disadvantages of each type of instruction. Because of the equivalency of these two types, you can switch between them at any time while using this book.

TABLE EG1.1

Types of Excel Guide Instructions

In-Depth Excel Instructions
Provides step-by-step instructions for applying Excel to the statistical methods of the chapter. **Advantages** Applicable to all Excel versions. Creates "live" worksheets and chart sheets that automatically update when the underlying data change. **Disadvantages** Can be time-consuming, frustrating, and error prone, especially for novices. May force you to focus on low-level Excel details, thereby distracting you from learning statistics.
PHStat2 **Instructions**
Provides step-by-step instructions for using the PHStat2 add-in with Excel. (To learn more about PHStat2, see Appendix G.) **Advantages** Creates live worksheets and chart sheets that are the same as or similar to the ones created in the *In-Depth Excel* instructions. Frees you from having to focus on low-level Excel details. Can be used to quickly double-check results created by the *In-Depth Excel* instructions. **Disadvantages** Must be installed separately and therefore requires an awareness about installing software on your system. (See Appendix D for the technical details.) Not compatible with OpenOffice.org Calc 3.

If you want to develop a mastery of Excel and gain practice building solutions from the bottom up, you will want to use the *In-Depth Excel* instructions. If you are more of a top-down person, who first wants quick results and then, later, looks at the details of a solution, you will want to maximize your use of the *PHStat2* instructions. At any time, you can switch between these methods without any loss of comprehension. Both methods lead to identical, or nearly identical, results. These results are mostly in the form of reusable workbooks. These workbooks, as well as the workbooks you can download (see Appendix C) are yours to keep and reuse for other problems, in other courses, or in your workplace.

When relevant, the Excel Guides also include instructions for the Analysis ToolPak, an optional component of Excel that Microsoft distributes with many versions of Excel, although not with the current version of Mac Excel.

The Excel Guide instructions feature Windows Excel versions 2010 and 2007 and note their differences, when those differences are significant. The instructions have been written for maximum compatibility with current versions of Mac Excel and OpenOffice.org Calc, an Excel work-alike. If you use either Mac Excel or OpenOffice.org Calc, you will be able to use almost all the workbooks discussed in the *In-Depth Excel* instructions. If you use the older Windows-based Excel 2003, you can use the *PHStat2* instructions as is and can download from this book's companion website the *Using Excel 2003 with Basic Business Statistics* document that adapts the *In-Depth Excel* instructions for use with Excel 2003.

The rest of this Excel Guide reviews the basic concepts and common operations encountered when using Excel with this book.

EG1.2 ENTERING DATA and VARIABLE TYPE

As first discussed in Section 1.5, you enter the data for each variable in a separate column. By convention, you start with column A and enter the name of each variable into the cells of the first row, and then you enter the data for the variable in the subsequent rows, as shown in Figure EG1.1.

FIGURE EG1.1
An example of a data worksheet

	A	B	C	D	E	F	G	H	I
1	Fund Number	Type	Assets	Fees	Expense Ratio	Return 2009	3-Year Return	5-Year Return	Risk
2	FN-1	Intermediate Government	7268.1	No	0.45	6.9	6.9	5.5	Below average
3	FN-2	Intermediate Government	475.1	No	0.50	9.8	7.5	6.1	Below average
4	FN-3	Intermediate Government	193.0	No	0.71	6.3	7.0	5.6	Average

Excel infers the variable type from the data you enter into a column. If Excel discovers a column containing numbers, for example, it treats the column as a numerical variable. If Excel discovers a column containing words or alphanumeric entries, it treats the column as a non-numerical (categorical) variable. This imperfect method works most of the time in Excel, especially if you make sure that the categories for your categorical variables are words or phrases such as "yes" and "no" and are not coded values that could be mistaken for numerical values, such as "1," "2," and "3." However, because you cannot explicitly define the variable type, Excel occasionally makes "mistakes" by either offering or allowing you to do nonsensical things such as using a statistical method that is designed for numerical variables on categorical variables.

When you enter data, never skip any rows in a column, and as a general rule, also avoid skipping any columns. Pay attention to any special instructions that occur throughout the book for the order of the entry of your data. For some statistical methods, entering your data in an order that Excel does not expect will lead to incorrect results.

Most of the Excel workbooks that you can download from this book's companion website (Appendix C) and use with the Excel Guides contain a DATA worksheet that follows the rules of this section. Any of those worksheets can be used as additional models for the method you use to enter variable data in Excel.

EG1.3 OPENING and SAVING WORKBOOKS

You open and save workbooks by first selecting the folder that stores the workbook and then specifying the file name of the workbook. In Excel 2010, you select **File → Open** to open a workbook file or **File → Save As** to save a workbook. In Excel 2007, you select **Office Button → Open** to open a workbook file or **Office Button → Save As** to save a workbook. **Open** and **Save As** display nearly identical dialog boxes that vary only slightly among the different Excel versions. Figure EG1.2 shows the Excel 2010 Open and Save As dialog boxes.

FIGURE EG1.2
Excel 2010 Open and Save As dialog boxes

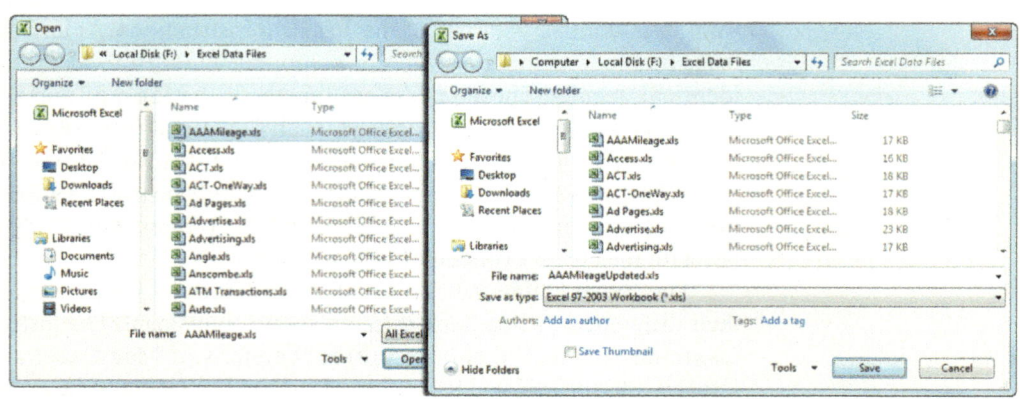

You select the storage folder by using the drop-down list at the top of either of these dialog boxes. You enter, or select from the list box, a file name for the workbook in the **File name** box. You click **Open** or **Save** to complete the task. Sometimes when saving files, you may want to change the file type before you click **Save**. If you want to save your workbook in the format used by Excel 2003 and earlier versions, select **Excel 97-2003 Workbook (*.xls)** from the **Save as type** drop-down list (shown in Figure EG1.2) before you click **Save**. If you want to save data in a form that can be opened by programs that cannot open Excel workbooks, you might select either **Text (Tab delimited) (*.txt)** or **CSV (Comma delimited) (*.csv)** as the save type.

When you want to open a file and cannot find its name in the list box, double-check that the current **Look in** folder is the folder you intend. If it is, change the file type to **All Files (*.*)** to see all files in the current folder. This technique can help you discover inadvertent misspellings or missing file extensions that otherwise prevent the file from being displayed.

Although all versions of Microsoft Excel include a **Save** command, you should avoid this choice until you gain experience. Using Save makes it too easy to inadvertently overwrite your work. Also, you cannot use the Save command for any open workbook that Excel has marked as read-only. (Use Save As to save such workbooks.)

EG1.4 CREATING and COPYING WORKSHEETS

You create new worksheets by either creating a new workbook or by inserting a new worksheet in an open workbook. To create a new workbook, select **File → New** (Excel 2010) or **Office Button → New** (Excel 2007) and in the pane that appears, double-click the **Blank workbook** icon.

New workbooks are created with a fixed number of worksheets. To delete extra worksheets or insert more sheets, right-click a sheet tab and click either **Delete** or **Insert** (see Figure EG1.3). By default, Excel names a worksheet serially in the form Sheet1, Sheet2, and so on. You should change these names to better reflect the content of your worksheets. To rename a worksheet, double-click the sheet tab of the worksheet, type the new name, and press **Enter**.

FIGURE EG1.3

Sheet tab shortcut menu and the Move or Copy dialog box

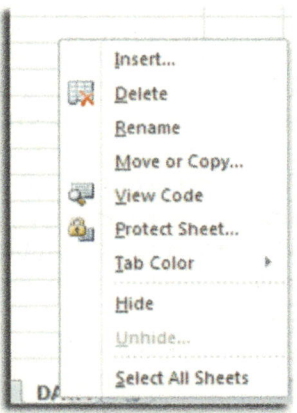
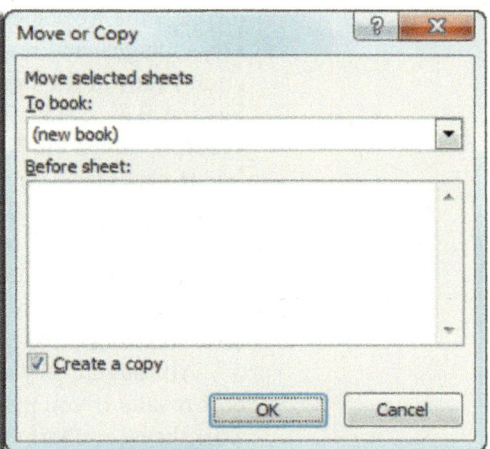

You can also make a copy of a worksheet or move a worksheet to another position in the same workbook or to a second workbook. Right-click the sheet tab and select **Move or Copy** from the shortcut menu that appears. In the **To book** drop-down list of the Move or Copy dialog box (see Figure EG1.3), first select **(new book)** (or the name of the pre-existing target workbook), check **Create a copy**, and then click **OK**.

EG1.5 PRINTING WORKSHEETS

To print a worksheet (or a chart sheet), first open to the worksheet by clicking its sheet tab. Then, in Excel 2010, select **File → Print**. If the print preview displayed (see Figure EG1.4) contains errors or displays the worksheet in an undesirable manner, click **File**, make the necessary corrections or adjustments, and repeat **File → Print**. When you are satisfied with the preview, click the large **Print** button.

FIGURE EG1.4

Excel 2010 and Excel 2007 (inset) Print Preview (left) and Page Setup dialog box (right)

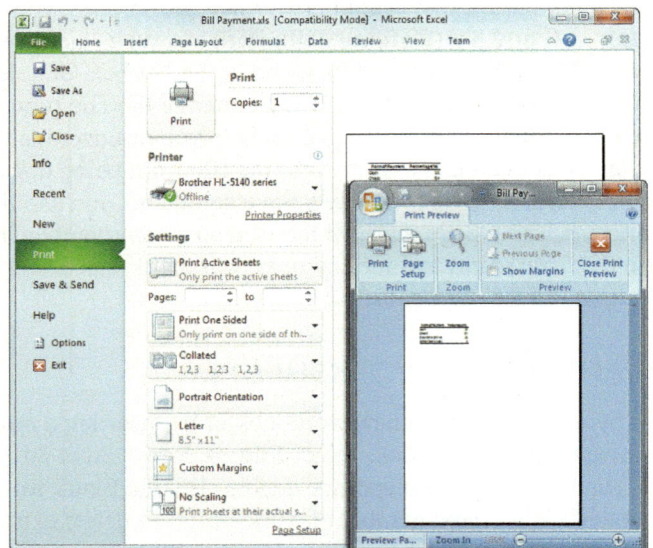
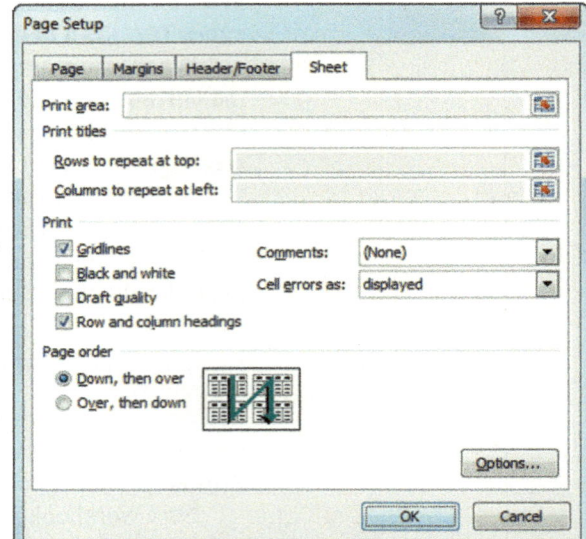

In Excel 2007, the same process requires more mouse clicks. First click **Office Button** and then move the mouse pointer over (but do not click) **Print**. In the Preview and Print gallery, click **Print Preview**. If the preview displayed (see Figure EG1.4) contains errors or displays the worksheet in an undesirable manner, click **Close Print Preview**, make the necessary changes, and reselect the print preview. After completing all corrections and adjustments, click **Print** in the Print Preview window to display the Print dialog box (shown in Appendix Section B.3). Select the printer to be used from the **Name** drop-down list, click **All** and **Active sheet(s)**, adjust the **Number of copies**, and click **OK**.

If necessary, you can adjust print formatting while in print preview by clicking the **Page Setup** icon (Excel 2007) or the **Page Setup** link (Excel 2010) to display the Page Setup dialog box (the right panel of Figure EG1.4). For example, to print your worksheet with gridlines and numbered row and lettered column headings (similar to the appearance of the worksheet on-screen), click the **Sheet** tab in the Page Setup dialog box, check **Gridlines** and **Row and column headings**, and click **OK**.

Although every version of Excel offers the (print) **Entire workbook** choice, you get the best results if you print each worksheet separately when you need to print out more than one worksheet (or chart sheet).

EG1.6 WORKSHEET ENTRIES and REFERENCES

When you open to a specific worksheet in a workbook, you use the cursor keys or your pointing device to move a **cell pointer** through the worksheet to select a specific cell for entry. As you type an entry, it appears in the formula bar, and you place that entry in the cell by either pressing the **Tab** key or **Enter** key or clicking the checkmark button in the formula bar.

In worksheets that you use for intermediate calculations or results, you might enter **formulas**, instructions to perform a calculation or some other task, in addition to the numeric and text entries you otherwise make in cells.

Formulas typically use values found in other cells to compute a result that is displayed in the cell that stores the formula. With formulas, the displayed result automatically changes as the dependent values in the other cells change. This process, called **recalculation**, was the original novel feature of spreadsheet programs and led to these programs being widely used in accounting. (Worksheets that contain formulas are sometimes called "live" worksheets to distinguish them from "dead" worksheets—worksheets without any formulas and therefore not capable of recalculation.)

To refer to a cell in a formula, you use a **cell address** in the form *SheetName!ColumnRow*. For example, **Data!A2** refers to the cell in the Data worksheet that is in column A and row 2. You can also use just the *ColumnRow* portion of a full address, for example, **A2**, if you are referring to a cell on the same worksheet as the one into which you are entering a formula. If the sheet name contains spaces or special characters, for example, **CITY DATA** or **Figure_1.2**, you must enclose the sheet name in a pair of single quotes, as in **'CITY DATA'!A2** or **'Figure_1.2'!A2**.

When you want to refer to a group of cells, such as the cells of a column that store the data for a particular variable, you use a **cell range**. A cell range names the upper-leftmost cell and the lower-rightmost cell of the group using the form *SheetName!UpperLeftCell:LowerRightCell*. For example, the cell range **DATA!A1:A11** identifies the first 11 cells in the first column of the **DATA worksheet**. Cell ranges can extend over multiple columns; the cell range **DATA!A1:D11** would refer to the first 11 cells in the first 4 columns of the worksheet.

As with a single cell reference, you can skip the *SheetName!* part of the reference if you are referring to a cell range on the current worksheet and you must use a pair of single quotes if a sheet name contains spaces or special characters. However, in some dialog boxes, you must include the sheet name in a cell reference in order to get the proper results. (In such cases, the instructions in this book include the sheet name; otherwise, they do not.)

Although not used in this book, cell references can include a workbook name in the form **'[*WorkbookName*] *SheetName*'! *ColumnRow*** or **'[*WorkbookName*] *SheetName*'! *UpperLeft Cell: LowerRightCell*.** You might discover such references if you inadvertently copy certain types of worksheets or chart sheets from one workbook to another.

EG1.7 ABSOLUTE and RELATIVE CELL REFERENCES

Many worksheets contain columns (or rows) of similar-looking formulas. For example, column C in a worksheet might contain formulas that sum the contents of the column A and column B rows. The formula for cell C2 would be **=A2 + B2**, the formula for cell C3 would be **=A3 + B3**, for cell C4, **=A4 + B4**, and so on down column C. To avoid the drudgery of typing many similar formulas, you can copy a formula and paste it into all the cells in a selected cell range. For example, to copy a formula that has been entered in cell C2 down the column through row 12:

1. Right-click cell **C2** and click **Copy** from the shortcut menu. A movie marquee–like highlight appears around cell C2.
2. Select the cell range **C3:C12**. (See Appendix B if you need help selecting a cell range.)
3. With the cell range highlighted, right-click over the cell range and click **Paste** from the shortcut menu.

When you perform this copy-and-paste operation, Excel adjusts the cell references in formulas so that copying the formula **=A2 + B2** from cell C2 to cell C3 results in the formula **=A3 + B3** being pasted into cell C3, the formula **=A4 + B4** being pasted into cell C4, and so on.

There are circumstances in which you do not want Excel to adjust all or part of a formula. For example, if you were copying the cell C2 formula **=(A2 + B2)/B15**, and cell B15 contained the divisor to be used in all formulas, you would not want to see pasted into cell C3 the formula **=(A3 + B3)/B16**. To prevent Excel from adjusting a cell reference, you use an **absolute cell reference** by inserting dollar signs ($) before the column and row references. For example, the absolute cell reference **$B$15** in the copied cell C2 formula **=(A2 + B2)/$B$15** would cause Excel to paste **=(A3 + B3)/$B$15** into cell C3. (For ease of reading, formulas shown in the worksheet illustrations in this book generally do not include absolute cell references.)

Do not confuse the use of the U.S. dollar symbol in an absolute reference with the formatting operation that displays numbers as U.S. currency values.

EG1.8 ENTERING FORMULAS into WORKSHEETS

You enter formulas by typing the equal sign (=) followed by a combination of mathematical and data-processing operations. For simple formulas, you use the symbols +, −, *, /, and ^ for the operations addition, subtraction, multiplication, division, and exponentiation (a number raised to a power), respectively. For example, the formula **=DATA!B2 + DATA!B3 + DATA!B4** adds the contents of cells B2, B3, and B4 of the DATA worksheet and displays the sum as the value in the cell containing the formula.

You can also use **worksheet functions** in formulas to simplify formulas. To use a worksheet function in a formula, either type the function as shown in the instructions in this book or use the Excel Function Wizard feature to insert the function. To use this feature, select **Formulas → Insert Function** and then make the necessary entries and selections in one or more dialog boxes that follow.

If you enter formulas in your worksheets, you should review and verify those formulas before you use their results. To view the formulas in a worksheet, press **Ctrl+`** (grave accent). To restore the original view, the re´sults of the formulas, press **Ctrl+`** a second time. (A "formulas view" accompanies most of the worksheet illustrations in this book.)

EG1.9 USING APPENDICES D and F

Appendices D and F contain additional Excel-related material that you may need to know, depending on how you use this book. If you plan to use PHStat2, make sure you have read Sections D.1 through D.3 in Appendix D. If you would like to learn formatting worksheet details such as how to make the contents of cells appear boldfaced or how to control the number of decimal places displayed, read Sections F.1 and F.2 in Appendix F.

CHAPTER 1 MINITAB GUIDE

MG1.1 GETTING STARTED with MINITAB

You are almost ready to use Minitab if you have completed the Table 1.5 checklist and reviewed the Table 1.6 computing conventions on page 42. Before using Minitab for a specific analysis, you should practice using the Minitab user interface.

Minitab project components appear in separate windows *inside* the Minitab window. In Figure MG1.1 these separate windows have been overlapped, but you can arrange or hide these windows in any way you like. When you start Minitab, you typically see a new project that contains only the session area and one worksheet window. (You can view other components by selecting them in the Minitab **Window** menu.) You can open and save an entire project or, as is done in this book, open and save individual worksheets.

FIGURE MG1.1

Minitab main worksheet with overlapping session, worksheet, chart, and Project Manager windows

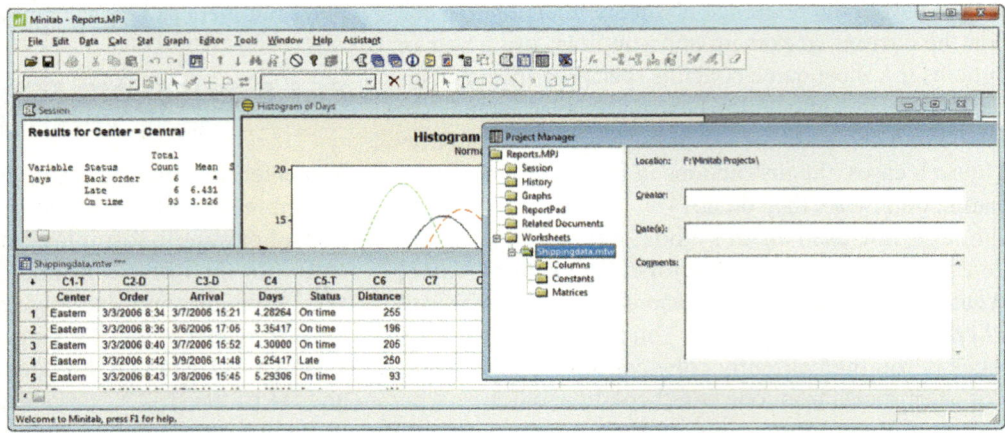

MG1.2 ENTERING DATA and VARIABLE TYPE

As first discussed in Section 1.5, you enter the data for each variable in a separate column. By convention, you start with the first column, initially labeled **C1** by Minitab, and enter the name of each variable into the cells of the unnumbered, shaded first row and then the data for the variable into the numbered rows, as shown in Figure MG1.1.

Minitab infers the variable type from the data you enter in a column. If Minitab discovers a column containing numbers, it treats the column as a numerical variable. If Minitab discovers a column containing words or alphanumeric entries, it treats the column as "text" variable (appropriate for use as a categorical variable). If Minitab discovers a column containing entries that can be interpreted as dates or times, it treats the column as a date/time variable, a special type of numerical variable. This imperfect method works most of the time in Minitab, especially if you make sure that the categories for your categorical variables are words or phrases such as "yes" and "no."

When Minitab identifies a text or date/time variable, it appends a "-T" or "-D" to its column heading for the variable. For example, in Figure MG1.1 above:

- C1-T and C5-T mean that the first and fifth columns contain text variables.
- C2-D and C3-D mean that the second and third columns contain date/time variables.
- C4 and C6 mean that the fourth and sixth columns contain numerical variables.

Because Minitab explicitly defines the variable type, unlike in Excel, your ability to do nonsensical things (such as use a statistical method that is designed for numerical variables on categorical data) is limited. If Minitab misinterprets your data, you can attempt to change the variable type by selecting **Data → Change Data Type** and then selecting the appropriate change from the submenu.

When you enter data, never skip any rows in a column. Minitab interprets skipped rows as missing values. You can use the Minitab workbooks that you can download from this book's companion website (see Appendix C) as models for the method you use to enter variable data in Minitab.

MG1.3 OPENING and SAVING WORKSHEETS and PROJECTS

You open and save Minitab worksheet or project files by first selecting the folder that stores a workbook and then specifying the file name of the workbook. To open a worksheet, you select **File → Open Worksheet**. To open a project, you select **File → Open Project**. To save a worksheet, you select **File → Save Current Worksheet As**. To save a project, you select **File → Save Project As**.

Both pairs of open and save commands display nearly identical dialog boxes. Figure MG1.2 shows the Minitab 16 Open Worksheet and Save Current Worksheet As dialog boxes.

FIGURE MG1.2

Minitab 16 Open Worksheet and Save Current Worksheet As dialog boxes

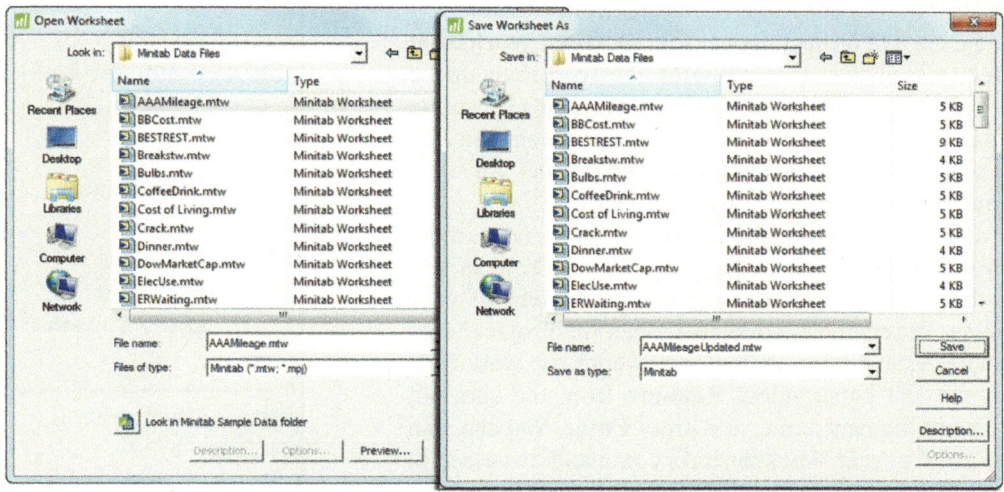

Inside the open or save dialog boxes, you select the storage folder by using the drop-down list at the top of either dialog box. You enter or select from the list box a file name for the workbook in the **File name** box. You click **Open** or **Save** to complete the task. Sometimes when saving files, you might want to change the file type before you click **Save**. If you want to save your data as an Excel worksheet, select **Excel 97-2003** from the **Save as type** drop-down list before you click **Save**. If you want to save data in a form that can be opened by programs that cannot open Excel workbooks, you might select one of the **Text** or **CSV** choices as the **Save as type** type.

When you want to open a file and cannot find its name in the list box, double-check that the current **Look in** folder is the folder you intend. If it is, change the file type to **All (*.*)** to see all files in the current folder. This technique can help you discover inadvertent misspellings or missing file extensions that otherwise prevent the file from being displayed.

When you save a project, you can click **Options** in the Save Project As dialog box and then specify which parts of the project you want to save in a Save Project - Options dialog box (not shown).

Although Minitab includes **Save Current Worksheet** and a **Save Project** commands (commands without the "**As**"), you should avoid this choice until you gain experience. Using Save makes it too easy to inadvertently overwrite your work. Also, you cannot use the Save command for any open workbook that Minitab has marked as read-only. (Use Save As to save such workbooks.)

Individual graphs and a project's session window can also be opened and saved separately in Minitab, although these operations are never used in this book.

MG1.4 CREATING and COPYING WORKSHEETS

You create new worksheets by either creating a new project or by inserting a new worksheet in an open project. To create a new project, select **File → New** and in the New dialog box, click **Minitab Project** and then click **OK**. To insert a new worksheet, also select **File → New** but in the New dialog box click **Minitab Worksheet** and then click **OK**.

A new project is created with one new worksheet. To insert another worksheet, select **File → New** and in the New dialog box click **Minitab Worksheet** and then click **OK**. You can also insert a copy of a worksheet from another project into the current project. Select **File → Open Worksheet** and select the *project* that contains the worksheet to be copied. Selecting a project (and not a worksheet) causes an additional dialog box to be displayed, in which you can specify which worksheets of that second project are to be copied and inserted into the current project.

By default, Minitab names a worksheet serially in the form Worksheet1, Worksheet2, and so on. You should change these names to better reflect the content of your worksheets. To rename a worksheet, open the Project Manager window (see Figure MG1.1), right-click the worksheet name in the left pane, select **Rename** from the shortcut menu, type in the new name, and press **Enter**. You can also use the **Save Current Worksheet As** command discussed in Section MG1.3, although this command also saves the worksheet as a separate file.

MG1.5 PRINTING PARTS of a PROJECT

To print a worksheet, a graph, or the contents of a session, first select the window that corresponds to the object you want to print. Then select **File → Print** *object*, where *object* is either **Worksheet**, **Graph**, or **Session Window**, depending on which object you first selected.

If you are printing a graph or a session window, selecting the **Print** command displays the Print dialog box. The Print dialog box contains settings to select the printer to be used, what pages to print, and the number of copies to produce. If you need to change these settings, change them before clicking **OK** to create your printout.

If you are printing a worksheet, selecting **Print Worksheet** displays the Data Window Print Options dialog box (see Figure MG1.3). In this dialog box, you specify the formatting options for your printout (the default selections should be fine), enter a **Title**, and click **OK**. Minitab then presents the Print dialog box discussed in the previous paragraph.

FIGURE MG1.3

Data Window Print Options dialog box

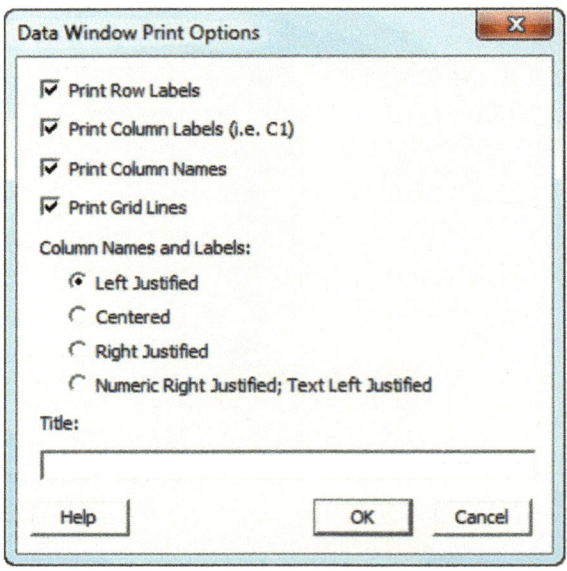

If you need to change the paper size or paper orientation of your printout, select **File → Print Setup** before you select the Print command, make the appropriate selections in the dialog box that appears, and click **OK**.

MG1.6 WORKSHEET ENTRIES and REFERENCES

You refer to individual variables in one of two ways. You can use their column number, such as C1 in Figure MG1.1 on page 52, that appears at the top of a worksheet. Or you can use the variable name that you entered into the cells of the unnumbered, shaded second row, such as Center or Order (in Figure MG1.1). For most statistical analyses, Minitab presents a list of column numbers and their corresponding variable names (if any) from which you make selections. For a variable name such as **Return 2009**, that contain spaces or other special characters, Minitab displays the name using a pair of single quotation marks—for example, **'Return 2009'**—an'd you need to include those quotation marks any time you type such a variable name in a Minitab dialog box.

For clarity and to minimize errors, this book generally refers to columns by their variable names. In later chapters, you will see that Minitab allows you to refer to several consecutive columns by using a hyphen. For example, either **C1-C6** or **Center-Distance** would refer to all six columns of the Shipping data worksheet shown in Figure MG1.1.

MG1.7 USING APPENDICES D and F

Appendices D and F contain additional Minitab-related material of a general nature. Consult these appendices if you have a question about using Minitab that is not answered in the Minitab Guides of this book.

2 Organizing and Visualizing Data

USING STATISTICS @ Choice Is Yours, Part I

2.1 Data Collection

ORGANIZING DATA

2.2 Organizing Categorical Data
The Summary Table
The Contingency Table

2.3 Organizing Numerical Data
Stacked and Unstacked Data
The Ordered Array
The Frequency Distribution
The Relative Frequency Distribution and the Percentage Distribution
The Cumulative Distribution

VISUALIZING DATA

2.4 Visualizing Categorical Data
The Bar Chart
The Pie Chart
The Pareto Chart
The Side-by-Side Bar Chart

2.5 Visualizing Numerical Data
The Stem-and-Leaf Display
The Histogram
The Percentage Polygon
The Cumulative Percentage Polygon (Ogive)

2.6 Visualizing Two Numerical Variables
The Scatter Plot
The Time-Series Plot

2.7 Organizing Multidimensional Data
Multidimensional Contingency Tables
Adding Numerical Variables

2.8 Misuses and Common Errors in Visualizing Data

USING STATISTICS @ Choice Is Yours, Part I Revisited

CHAPTER 2 EXCEL GUIDE

CHAPTER 2 MINITAB GUIDE

Learning Objectives

In this chapter, you learn:

- The sources of data used in business
- To construct tables and charts for numerical data
- To construct tables and charts for categorical data
- The principles of properly presenting graphs

USING STATISTICS

@ Choice Is Yours, Part I

The Choice Is Yours investment service helps clients with their investment choices. Choice Is Yours evaluates investments as diverse as real estate, direct private equity investments, derivatives, and various specialized types of mutual funds. You've been hired to assist clients who seek to invest in mutual funds, which pool the money of many individual clients and invest the money in a mix of securities and other investments. (To learn more about mutual funds, visit **investopedia.com/university/mutualfunds**.)

Because mutual funds that are highly invested in common stocks have had mixed returns recently, Choice Is Yours wants to examine mutual funds that focus on investing in certain types of bonds. Company analysts have selected a sample of 184 such funds that they believe might interest clients. You have been asked to present data about these funds in a way that will help customers make good investment choices. What facts about each bond mutual fund would you collect to help customers compare and contrast the many funds?

A good starting point would be to collect data that would help customers classify mutual funds into various categories. You could research such things as the amount of risk involved in a fund's investment strategy and the type of bonds in which the mutual fund primarily invests. Of course, you would want to learn how well the fund performed in the past, and you would want to supply the customer with several measures of each fund's past performance. (Although past performance is no assurance of future performance, past data could give customers insight into how well each mutual fund has been managed.)

As you further think about your task, you realize that the data for all 184 mutual funds would be a lot for anyone to review. You have been asked to present data about these funds in a way that will help customers make good investment choices. How can you review and explore such data in a comprehensible manner? What facts about each fund would you collect to help customers compare and contrast the many funds?

The challenge you face in Part I of the Choice Is Yours scenario is to examine a large amount of data and reach conclusions based on those data. You can make this business task more manageable by breaking it into these five steps:

- **Define** the variables that you want to study in order to solve a business problem or meet a business objective
- **Collect** the data from appropriate sources
- **Organize** the data collected by developing tables
- **Visualize** the data by developing charts
- **Analyze** the data by examining the appropriate tables and charts (and in later chapters by using other statistical methods) to reach conclusions.

These five steps, known by the acronym **DCOVA** (for **D**efine, **C**ollect, **O**rganize, **V**isualize, and **A**nalyze), are used throughout this book as the basis for statistical problem solving (see Reference 2). In Chapter 1, you already learned that defining a variable includes developing an operational definition and identifying the type of variable. In this chapter, you will learn more about the steps involved in collecting, organizing, visualizing, and analyzing the data.

To help illustrate the DCOVA approach, this chapter frequently uses for its examples the sample of 184 mutual funds that specialize in bond investments mentioned in Part I of the Choice Is Yours scenario. (To examine this sample, open Bond Funds, one of the data files you can download for use with this book as explained in Appendix C.) By the end of the chapter, you will be able to answer the questions posed in the scenario. For example, you will be able to answer questions that compare two categories of bond funds, such as "Is there a difference in the returns of intermediate government bond funds and short-term corporate bond funds?" or "Do intermediate government bond funds tend to be less risky investments than short-term corporate bond funds?"

2.1 Data Collection

Once you have defined your variables, you may need to collect the data for those variables. Examples of **data collection** include the following:

- A marketing analyst who needs to assess the effectiveness of a new television advertisement
- A pharmaceutical manufacturer that needs to determine whether a new drug is more effective than those currently in use
- An operations manager who wants to improve a manufacturing or service process
- An auditor who wants to review the financial transactions of a company in order to determine whether the company is in compliance with generally accepted accounting principles

When you collect data, you use either a **primary data source** or a **secondary data source.** You are using a primary data source when you collect your own data for analysis, and you are using a secondary source if the data for your analysis have been collected by someone else. Data collection almost always involves collecting data from a sample because collecting data from every item or individual in a population is typically too difficult or too time-consuming. (See Chapter 7 to learn more about sample selection methods.)

Organizations and individuals that collect and publish data often use their data as a primary source and may let others use those data as a secondary source. For example, the U.S. federal government collects and distributes data in this way for both public and private purposes. The Bureau of Labor Statistics collects data on employment and also distributes the monthly consumer price index. The Census Bureau oversees a variety of ongoing surveys regarding population, housing, and manufacturing and undertakes special studies on topics such as crime, travel, and health care.

Data sources are created in one of four ways:

- As data distributed by an organization or individual
- As outcomes of a designed experiment

- As responses from a survey
- As a result of conducting an observational study

Market research companies and trade associations distribute data pertaining to specific industries or markets. Investment services such as Mergent (**www.mergent.com**) provide financial data on a company-by-company basis. Syndicated services such as Nielsen provide clients with data that enables client products to be compared with those of their competitors. On the other hand, daily newspapers are secondary sources that are filled with numerical information regarding stock prices, weather conditions, and sports statistics obtained from primary sources.

Conducting a designed experiment is another source of data. For example, one such experiment might test several laundry detergents to compare how well each detergent removes a certain type of stain. Developing proper experimental designs is a subject mostly beyond the scope of this book because such designs often involve sophisticated statistical procedures. However, some of the fundamental experimental design concepts are discussed in Chapters 10 and 11.

Conducting a survey is a third type of data source. People being surveyed are asked questions about their beliefs, attitudes, behaviors, and other characteristics. For example, people could be asked their opinion about which laundry detergent best removes a certain type of stain. (This could lead to a result different from a designed experiment seeking the same answer.) One good way to avoid data-collection flaws when using such a survey is to distribute the questionnaire to a random sample of respondents. (Chapter 7 explains how to collect a random sample.) A bad way would be to rely on a business-rating website that allows online visitors to rate a merchant. Such websites cannot provide assurance that those who do the ratings are representative of the population of customers—or that they even *are* customers.

Conducting an observational study is the fourth data source. A researcher collects data by directly observing a behavior, usually in a natural or neutral setting. Observational studies are a common tool for data collection in business. For example, market researchers use focus groups to elicit unstructured responses to open-ended questions posed by a moderator to a target audience. You can also use observational study techniques to enhance teamwork or improve the quality of products and services.

Problems for Section 2.1

APPLYING THE CONCEPTS

2.1. According to its home page, "Swivel is a website where people share reports of charts and numbers. Businesses use Swivel to dashboard their metrics. Students use Swivel to find and share research data." Visit **www.swivel.com** and explore a data set of interest to you. Which of the four sources of data best describes the sources of the data set you selected?

2.2. Visit the website of the Gallup organization, at **www.gallup.com**. Read today's top story. What type of data source is the top story based on?

2.3. A supermarket chain wants to determine the best placement for the supermarket brand of soft drink. What type of data collection source do you think that the supermarket chain should use?

2.4. Visit **www.turkstat.gov.tr/PreHaberBultenleri.do?id=6355** and examine the "Household Labour Force Survey for the Period of August 2010 (July, August and September 2010)" press release from the Turkish Statistical Institute. What type of data source is the information presented in Table 1 in this press release?

ORGANIZING DATA

After you define your variables and collect your data, you organize your data to help prepare for the later steps of visualizing and analyzing your data. The techniques you use to organize your data depend on the type of variable (categorical or numerical) associated with your data.

2.2 Organizing Categorical Data

Starting with this section, the sections of the Excel and Minitab Guides duplicate the sections in the main chapter. For example, to learn how to use Excel or Minitab to organize categorical data, see either Section EG2.2 or MG2.2.

You organize categorical data by tallying responses by categories and placing the results in tables. Typically, you construct a summary table to organize the data for a single categorical variable and you construct a contingency table to organize the data from two or more categorical variables.

The Summary Table

A **summary table** presents tallied responses as frequencies or percentages for each category. A summary table helps you see the differences among the categories by displaying the frequency, amount, or percentage of items in a set of categories in a separate column. Table 2.1 shows a summary table (stored in **Bill Payment**) that tallies the responses to a recent survey that asked adults how they pay their monthly bills.

TABLE 2.1

Types of Bill Payment

Form of Payment	Percentage (%)
Cash	15
Check	54
Electronic/online	28
Other/don't know	3

Source: *Data extracted from "How Adults Pay Monthly Bills,"* USA Today, *October 4, 2007, p. 1.*

From Table 2.1, you can conclude that more than half the people pay by check and 82% pay by either check or by electronic/online forms of payment.

EXAMPLE 2.1

Summary Table of Levels of Risk of Bond Funds

The 184 bond funds involved in Part I of the Choice Is Yours scenario (see page 57) are classified according to their risk level, categorized as below average, average, and above average. Construct a summary table of the bond funds, categorized by risk.

SOLUTION From Table 2.2, you can see that about the same number of funds are below average, average, and above average in risk. This means that 69.57% of the bond funds are classified as having an average or above average level of risk.

TABLE 2.2

Frequency and Percentage Summary Table Pertaining to Risk Level for 184 Bond Funds

Fund Risk Level	Number of Funds	Percentage of Funds (%)
Below average	56	30.43%
Average	69	37.50%
Above average	59	32.07%
Total	184	100.00%

The Contingency Table

A **contingency table** allows you to study patterns that may exist between the responses of two or more categorical variables. This type of table cross-tabulates, or tallies jointly, the responses of the categorical variables. In the simplest case of two categorical variables, the joint responses appear in a table such that the category tallies of one variable are located in the rows and the category tallies of the other variable are located in the columns. Intersections of the rows and columns are called **cells**, and each cell contains a value associated with a unique pair of responses for the two variables (e.g., Fee: Yes and Type: Intermediate Government in Table 2.3). Cells can contain the frequency, the percentage of the overall total, the percentage of the row total, or the percentage of the column total, depending on the type of contingency table being used.

In Part I of the Choice Is Yours scenario, you could create a contingency table to examine whether there is any pattern between the type of bond fund (intermediate government or short-term corporate) and whether the fund charges a fee (yes or no). You would begin by tallying the joint responses for each of the mutual funds in the sample of 184 bond mutual funds (stored in Bond Funds). You tally a response into one of the four possible cells in the table, depending on the type of bond fund and whether the fund charges a fee. For example, the first fund listed in the sample is classified as an intermediate government fund that does not charge a fee. Therefore, you tally this joint response into the cell that is the intersection of the Intermediate Government row and the No column. Table 2.3 shows the completed contingency table after all 184 bond funds have been tallied.

TABLE 2.3

Contingency Table Displaying Type of Fund and Whether a Fee Is Charged

	FEE		
TYPE	Yes	No	Total
Intermediate government	34	53	87
Short-term corporate	20	77	97
Total	54	130	184

To look for other patterns between the type of bond fund and whether the fund charges a fee, you can construct contingency tables that show cell values as a percentage of the overall total (the 184 mutual funds), the row totals (the 87 intermediate government funds and the 97 short-term corporate bond funds), and the column totals (the 54 funds that charge a fee and the 130 funds that do not charge a fee). Tables 2.4, 2.5, and 2.6 present these contingency tables.

Table 2.4 shows that 47.28% of the bond funds sampled are intermediate government funds, 52.72% are short-term corporate bond funds, and 18.48% are intermediate

TABLE 2.4

Contingency Table Displaying Type of Fund and Whether a Fee Is Charged, Based on Percentage of Overall Total

	FEE		
TYPE	Yes	No	Total
Intermediate government	18.48	28.80	47.28
Short-term corporate	10.87	41.85	52.72
Total	29.35	70.65	100.00

government funds that charge a fee. Table 2.5 shows that 39.08% of the intermediate government funds charge a fee, while 20.62% of the short-term corporate bond funds charge

TABLE 2.5

Contingency Table Displaying Type of Fund and Whether a Fee Is Charged, Based on Percentage of Row Total

	FEE		
TYPE	Yes	No	Total
Intermediate government	39.08	60.92	100.00
Short-term corporate	20.62	79.38	100.00
Total	29.35	70.65	100.00

TABLE 2.6

Contingency Table Displaying Type of Fund and Whether a Fee Is Charged, Based on Percentage of Column Total

	FEE		
TYPE	Yes	No	Total
Intermediate government	62.96	40.77	47.28
Short-term corporate	37.04	59.23	52.72
Total	100.00	100.00	100.00

a fee. Table 2.6 shows that of the funds that charge a fee, 62.96% are intermediate government funds. From the tables, you see that intermediate government funds are much more likely to charge a fee.

Problems for Section 2.2

LEARNING THE BASICS

2.5 A categorical variable has three categories, with the following frequencies of occurrence:

Category	Frequency
A	13
B	28
C	9

a. Compute the percentage of values in each category.
b. What conclusions can you reach concerning the categories?

2.6 A sample of 50 students attending a university graduation ceremony was asked, "Should the university consider improving its technology infrastructure?" The results of the survey were as follows (Y = Yes; N = No; W = Without Opinion):

Males					Females				
N	W	N	N	Y	N	N	N	Y	N
N	Y	N	N	N	N	N	Y	N	N
Y	N	Y	W	N	Y	W	W	N	Y
W	W	N	W	Y	W	N	W	Y	W
N	Y	N	Y	N	W	Y	Y	N	Y

a. Tally the data into a contingency table in which the two rows represent the gender categories and the three columns represent the response categories.
b. Construct contingency tables based on percentages of all 50 responses, based on row percentages, and based on column percentages.

APPLYING THE CONCEPTS

2.7 The Transportation Security Administration reported that from January 1, 2008, to February 18, 2009, more than 14,000 banned items were collected at Palm Beach International Airport. The categories were as follows:

Category	Frequency
Flammables/irritants	8,350
Knives and blades	4,134
Prohibited tools	753
Sharp objects	497
Other	357

a. Compute the percentage of values in each category.
b. What conclusions can you reach concerning the banned items?

2.8 The Energy Information Administration reported the following sources of electricity in the United States in 2008:

Source of Electricity	Net Electricity Generation (millions of megawatt-hours)
Coal	1,994.4
Hydroelectric	248.1
Natural gas	876.9
Nuclear	806.2
Other	184.7

Source: Energy Information Administration, 2008.

a. Compute the percentage of values in each category.
b. What conclusions can you reach concerning the sources of electricity in the United States in 2008?

2.9 Federal obligations for benefit programs and the national debt were $63.8 trillion in 2008. The cost per household ($) for various categories was as follows:

Category	Cost per Household ($)
Civil servant retirement	15,851
Federal debt	54,537
Medicare	284,288
Military retirement	29,694
Social Security	160,216
Other	2,172

Source: Data extracted from "What We Owe," *USA Today*, May 29, 2009, p. 1A.

a. Compute the percentage of values in each category.
b. What conclusions can you reach concerning the benefit programs?

2.10 The following table is based on a survey of 600 college seniors regarding their undergraduate major and whether they plan to go to graduate school.

	UNDERGRADUATE MAJOR		
Graduate School	Business	Engineering	Total
Yes	170	110	280
No	182	138	320
Total	352	248	600

a. Construct contingency tables based on total percentages, row percentages, and column percentages.
b. What conclusions can you draw from these analyses?

2.11 Each day at a large hospital, several hundred laboratory tests are performed. The rate at which these tests are done improperly (and therefore need to be redone) seems steady, at about 4%. In an effort to get to the root cause of these nonconformances, tests that need to be redone, the director of the lab decided to keep records over a period of one week. The laboratory tests were subdivided by the shift of workers who performed the lab tests. The results are as follows:

LAB TESTS PERFORMED	SHIFT		Total
	Day	Evening	
Nonconforming	16	24	40
Conforming	654	306	960
Total	670	330	1,000

a. Construct contingency tables based on total percentages, row percentages, and column percentages.
b. Which type of percentage—row, column, or total—do you think is most informative for these data? Explain.
c. What conclusions concerning the pattern of nonconforming laboratory tests can the laboratory director reach?

2.12 Does it take more time to get yourself removed from an email list than it used to? A study of 100 large online retailers revealed the following:

	NEED THREE OR MORE CLICKS TO BE REMOVED	
YEAR	Yes	No
2009	39	61
2008	7	93

Source: Data extracted from "Drill Down," *The New York Times*, March 29, 2010, p. B2.

What do these results tell you about whether more online retailers were requiring three or more clicks in 2009 than in 2008?

2.3 Organizing Numerical Data

You organize numerical data by creating ordered arrays or distributions. The amount of data you have and what you seek to discover about your variables influences which methods you choose, as does the arrangement of data in your worksheet.

Stacked and Unstacked Data

In Section 1.5, you learned to enter variable data into worksheets by columns. When organizing numerical data, you must additionally consider if you will need to analyze a numerical variable by subgroups that are defined by the values of a categorical variable.

For example, in Bond Funds you might want to analyze the numerical variable **Return 2009**, the year 2009 percentage return of a bond fund, by the two subgroups that are defined by the categorical variable **Type**, intermediate government and short-term corporate. To perform this type of subgroup analysis, you arrange your worksheet data either in stacked format or unstacked format, depending on the requirements of the statistical application you plan to use.

In **Bond Funds**, the data has been entered in **stacked** format, in which the all of the values for a numerical variable appear in one column and a second, separate column contains the categorical values that identify which subgroup the numerical values belong to. For example, all values for the **Return 2009** variable are in one column (the sixth column) and the values in the second column (for the **Type** variable) would be used to determine which of the two **Type** subgroups an individual **Return 2009** value belongs to.

In **unstacked** format, the values for each subgroup of a numerical variable are segregated and placed in separate columns. For example, **Return 2009 Unstacked** contains the **IG_Return_2009** and **STC_Return 2009** variable columns that contain the data of **Return 2009** in unstacked format by the two subgroups defined by **Type,** intermediate government (IG) and short-term corporate (STC).

While you can always manually stack or unstack your data, Minitab and PHStat2 both provide you with commands that automate these operations. If you use Excel without PHStat2, you *must* use a manual procedure.

None of the data sets used in the examples found in the Excel and Minitab Guides require that you stack (or unstack) data. However, you may need to stack (or unstack) data to solve some of the problems in this book.

The Ordered Array

An **ordered array** arranges the values of a numerical variable in rank order, from the smallest value to the largest value. An ordered array helps you get a better sense of the range of values in your data and is particularly useful when you have more than a few values. For example, Table 2.7A shows the data collected for a study of the cost of meals at 50 restaurants located in a major city and at 50 restaurants located in that city's suburbs (stored in **Restaurants**). The unordered data in Table 2.7A prevent you from reaching any quick conclusions about the cost of meals.

TABLE 2.7A

Cost per Person at 50 City Restaurants and 50 Suburban Restaurants

City Restaurant Meal Cost									
62	67	23	79	32	38	46	43	39	43
44	29	59	56	32	56	23	40	45	44
40	33	57	43	49	28	35	79	42	21
40	49	45	54	64	48	41	34	53	27
44	58	68	59	61	59	48	78	65	42
Suburban Restaurant Meal Cost									
53	45	39	43	44	29	37	34	33	37
54	30	49	44	34	55	48	36	29	40
38	38	55	43	33	44	41	45	41	42
37	56	60	46	31	35	68	40	51	32
28	44	26	42	37	63	37	22	53	62

In contrast, Table 2.7B, the ordered array version of the same data, enables you to quickly see that the cost of a meal at the city restaurants is between $21 and $79 and that the cost of a meal at the suburban restaurants is between $22 and $68.

When you have a data set that contains a large number of values, reaching conclusions from an ordered array can be difficult. For such data sets, creating a frequency or percentage distribution and a cumulative percentage distribution (see following sections) would be a better choice.

TABLE 2.7B

Ordered Arrays of Cost per Person at 50 City Restaurants and 50 Suburban Restaurants

City Restaurant Meal Cost									
21	23	23	27	28	29	32	32	33	34
35	38	39	40	40	40	41	42	42	43
43	43	44	44	44	45	45	46	48	48
49	49	53	54	56	56	57	58	59	59
59	61	62	64	65	67	68	78	79	79
Suburban Restaurant Meal Cost									
22	26	28	29	29	30	31	32	33	33
34	34	35	36	37	37	37	37	37	38
38	39	40	40	41	41	42	42	43	43
44	44	44	44	45	45	46	48	49	51
53	53	54	55	55	56	60	62	63	68

The Frequency Distribution

A **frequency distribution** summarizes numerical values by tallying them into a set of numerically ordered **classes**. Classes are groups that represent a range of values, called a **class interval**. Each value can be in only one class and every value must be contained in one of the classes.

To create a useful frequency distribution, you must think about how many classes are appropriate for your data and also determine a suitable *width* for each class interval. In general, a frequency distribution should have at least 5 classes but no more than 15 classes because having too few or too many classes provides little new information. To determine the **class interval width** (see Equation 2.1), you subtract the lowest value from the highest value and divide that result by the number of classes you want your frequency distribution to have.

DETERMINING THE CLASS INTERVAL WIDTH

$$\text{Interval width} = \frac{\text{highest value} - \text{lowest value}}{\text{number of classes}} \tag{2.1}$$

Because the city restaurant data consist of a sample of only 50 restaurants, between 5 and 10 classes are acceptable. From the ordered city cost array in Table 2.7B, the difference between the highest value of $79 and the lowest value of $21 is $58. Using Equation (2.1), you approximate the class interval width as follows:

$$\text{Interval width} = \frac{58}{10} = 5.8$$

This result suggests that you should choose an interval width of $5.80. However, your width should always be an amount that simplifies the reading and interpretation of the frequency distribution. In this example, an interval width of $10 would be much better than an interval width of $5.80.

Because each value can appear in only one class, you must establish proper and clearly defined **class boundaries** for each class. For example, if you chose $10 as the class interval for the restaurant data, you would need to establish boundaries that would include all the values and simplify the reading and interpretation of the frequency distribution. Because the cost of a city restaurant meal varies from $21 to $79, establishing the first class interval as from $20 to less than $30, the second from $30 to less than $40, and so on, until the last class interval is from $70 to less than $80, would meet the requirements. Table 2.8 is a frequency distribution of the cost per meal for the 50 city restaurants and the 50 suburban restaurants that uses these class intervals.

TABLE 2.8

Frequency Distributions of the Cost per Meal for 50 City Restaurants and 50 Suburban Restaurants

Cost per Meal ($)	City Frequency	Suburban Frequency
20 but less than 30	6	5
30 but less than 40	7	17
40 but less than 50	19	17
50 but less than 60	9	7
60 but less than 70	6	4
70 but less than 80	3	0
Total	50	50

The frequency distribution allows you to reach conclusions about the major characteristics of the data. For example, Table 2.8 shows that the cost of meals at city restaurants is concentrated between $40 and $50, while for suburban restaurants the cost of meals is concentrated between $30 and $50.

For some charts discussed later in this chapter, class intervals are identified by their **class midpoints**, the values that are halfway between the lower and upper boundaries of each class. For the frequency distributions shown in Table 2.8, the class midpoints are $25, $35, $45, $55, $65, and $75 (amounts that are simple to read and interpret).

If a data set does not contain a large number of values, different sets of class intervals can create different impressions of the data. Such perceived changes will diminish as you collect more data. Likewise, choosing different lower and upper class boundaries can also affect impressions.

EXAMPLE 2.2

Frequency Distributions of the 2009 Return for Intermediate Government and Short-Term Corporate Bond Mutual Funds

In the Using Statistics scenario, you are interested in comparing the 2009 return of intermediate government and short-term corporate bond mutual funds. Construct frequency distributions for the intermediate government funds and the short-term corporate bond funds.

SOLUTION The 2009 returns of the intermediate government bond funds are highly concentrated between 0 and 10, whereas the 2009 returns of the short-term corporate bond funds are highly concentrated between 5 and 15 (see Table 2.9).

For the bond fund data, the number of *values* is different in the two groups. When the number of *values* in the two groups is not the same, you need to use proportions or relative frequencies and percentages in order to compare the groups.

TABLE 2.9

Frequency Distributions of the 2009 Return for Intermediate Government and Short-Term Corporate Bond Funds

2009 Return	Intermediate Government Frequency	Short-Term Corporate Frequency
−10 but less than −5	0	1
−5 but less than 0	13	0
0 but less than 5	35	15
5 but less than 10	30	38
10 but less than 15	6	31
15 but less than 20	1	9
20 but less than 25	1	1
25 but less than 30	1	1
30 but less than 35	0	1
Total	87	97

The Relative Frequency Distribution and the Percentage Distribution

When you are comparing two or more groups, as is done in Table 2.10, knowing the proportion or percentage of the total that is in each group is more useful than knowing the frequency count of each group. For such situations, you create a relative frequency distribution or a percentage distribution instead of a frequency distribution. (If your two or more groups have different sample sizes, you *must* use either a relative frequency distribution or a percentage distribution.)

TABLE 2.10

Relative Frequency Distributions and Percentage Distributions of the Cost of Meals at City and Suburban Restaurants

COST PER MEAL ($)	CITY Relative Frequency	CITY Percentage (%)	SUBURBAN Relative Frequency	SUBURBAN Percentage (%)
20 but less than 30	0.12	12.0	0.10	10.0
30 but less than 40	0.14	14.0	0.34	34.0
40 but less than 50	0.38	38.0	0.34	34.0
50 but less than 60	0.18	18.0	0.14	14.0
60 but less than 70	0.12	12.0	0.08	8.0
70 but less than 80	0.06	6.0	0.00	0.0
Total	1.00	100.0	1.00	100.0

The **proportion**, or **relative frequency**, in each group is equal to the number of *values* in each class divided by the total number of values. The percentage in each group is its proportion multiplied by 100%.

COMPUTING THE PROPORTION OR RELATIVE FREQUENCY

The proportion, or relative frequency, is the number of *values* in each class divided by the total number of values:

$$\text{Proportion} = \text{relative frequency} = \frac{\text{number of values in each class}}{\text{total number of values}} \quad (2.2)$$

If there are 80 values and the frequency in a certain class is 20, the proportion of values in that class is

$$\frac{20}{80} = 0.25$$

and the percentage is

$$0.25 \times 100\% = 25\%$$

You form the **relative frequency distribution** by first determining the relative frequency in each class. For example, in Table 2.8 on page 66, there are 50 city restaurants, and the cost per meal at 9 of these restaurants is between $50 and $60. Therefore, as shown in Table 2.10, the proportion (or relative frequency) of meals that cost between $50 and $60 at city restaurants is

$$\frac{9}{50} = 0.18$$

You form the **percentage distribution** by multiplying each proportion (or relative frequency) by 100%. Thus, the proportion of meals at city restaurants that cost between $50 and $60 is 9 divided by 50, or 0.18, and the percentage is 18%. Table 2.10 presents the relative frequency distribution and percentage distribution of the cost of meals at city and suburban restaurants.

From Table 2.10, you conclude that meals cost slightly more at city restaurants than at suburban restaurants. Also, 12% of the meals cost between $60 and $70 at city restaurants as compared to 8% of the meals at suburban restaurants; and 14% of the meals cost between $30 and $40 at city restaurants as compared to 34% of the meals at suburban restaurants.

EXAMPLE 2.3

Relative Frequency Distributions and Percentage Distributions of the 2009 Return for Intermediate Government and Short-Term Corporate Bond Mutual Funds

In the Using Statistics scenario, you are interested in comparing the 2009 return of intermediate government and short-term corporate bond mutual funds. Construct relative frequency distributions and percentage distributions for these funds.

SOLUTION You conclude (see Table 2.11) that the 2009 return for the corporate bond funds is much higher than for the intermediate government funds. For example, 31.96% of the corporate bond funds have returns between 10 and 15, while 6.90% of the intermediate government funds have returns between 10 and 15. Of the corporate bond funds, only 15.46% have returns between 0 and 5 as compared to 40.23% of the intermediate government funds.

TABLE 2.11
Relative Frequency Distributions and Percentage Distributions of the 2009 Return for Intermediate Government and Short-Term Corporate Bond Mutual Funds

	INTERMEDIATE GOVERNMENT		SHORT-TERM CORPORATE	
2009 RETURN	**Proportion**	**Percentage**	**Proportion**	**Percentage**
−10 but less than −5	0.0000	0.00	0.0103	1.03
−5 but less than 0	0.1494	14.94	0.0000	0.00
0 but less than 5	0.4023	40.23	0.1546	15.46
5 but less than 10	0.3448	34.48	0.3918	39.18
10 but less than 15	0.0690	6.90	0.3196	31.96
15 but less than 20	0.0115	1.15	0.0928	9.28
20 but less than 25	0.0115	1.15	0.0103	1.03
25 but less than 30	0.0115	1.15	0.0103	1.03
30 but less than 35	0.0000	0.00	0.0103	1.03
Total	1.0000	100.00	1.0000	100.00

The Cumulative Distribution

The **cumulative percentage distribution** provides a way of presenting information about the percentage of values that are less than a specific amount. For example, you might want to know what percentage of the city restaurant meals cost less than $40 or what percentage cost less than $50. You use the percentage distribution to form the cumulative percentage distribution. Table 2.12 shows how percentages of individual class intervals are combined to form the cumulative percentage distribution for the cost of meals at city restaurants. From this table, you see that none (0%) of the meals cost less than $20, 12% of meals cost less than $30, 26% of meals cost less than $40 (because 14% of the meals cost between $30 and $40), and so on, until all 100% of the meals cost less than $80.

Table 2.13 summarizes the cumulative percentages of the cost of city and suburban restaurant meals. The cumulative distribution shows that the cost of meals is slightly lower in suburban restaurants than in city restaurants. Table 2.13 shows that 44% of the meals at suburban restaurants cost less than $40 as compared to 26% of the meals at city restaurants; 78% of the

TABLE 2.12

Developing the Cumulative Percentage Distribution for the Cost of Meals at City Restaurants

Cost per Meal ($)	Percentage (%)	Percentage of Meals Less Than Lower Boundary of Class Interval (%)
20 but less than 30	12	0
30 but less than 40	14	12
40 but less than 50	38	26 = 12 + 14
50 but less than 60	18	64 = 12 + 14 + 38
60 but less than 70	12	82 = 12 + 14 + 38 + 18
70 but less than 80	6	94 = 12 + 14 + 38 + 18 + 12
80 but less than 90	0	100 = 12 + 14 + 38 + 18 + 12 + 6

meals at suburban restaurants cost less than $50 as compared to 64% of the meals at city restaurants; and 92% of the meals at suburban restaurants cost less than $60 as compared to 82% of the meals at city restaurants.

TABLE 2.13

Cumulative Percentage Distributions of the Cost of City and Suburban Restaurant Meals

Cost ($)	Percentage of City Restaurants With Meals Less Than Indicated Amount	Percentage of Suburban Restaurants With Meals Less Than Indicated Amount
20	0	0
30	12	10
40	26	44
50	64	78
60	82	92
70	94	100
80	100	100

EXAMPLE 2.4

Cumulative Percentage Distributions of the 2009 Return for Intermediate Government and Short-Term Corporate Bond Mutual Funds

In the Using Statistics scenario, you are interested in comparing the 2009 return for intermediate government and short-term corporate bond mutual funds. Construct cumulative percentage distributions for the intermediate government and short-term corporate bond mutual funds.

SOLUTION The cumulative distribution in Table 2.14 indicates that returns are much lower for the intermediate government bond funds than for the short-term corporate funds. The table shows that 14.94% of the intermediate government funds have negative returns as compared to 1.03% of the short-term corporate bond funds; 55.17% of the intermediate government funds have returns below 5 as compared to 16.49% of the short-term corporate bond funds; and 89.65% of the intermediate government funds have returns below 10 as compared to 55.67% of the short-term corporate bond funds.

TABLE 2.14

Cumulative Percentage Distributions of the 2009 Return for Intermediate Government and Short-Term Corporate Bond Funds

2009 Return	Intermediate Government Percentage Less Than Indicated Value	Short-Term Corporate Percentage Less Than Indicated Value
−10	0.00	0.00
−5	0.00	1.03
0	14.94	1.03
5	55.17	16.49
10	89.65	55.67
15	96.55	87.63
20	97.70	96.91
25	98.85	97.94
30	100.00	98.97
35	100.00	100.00

Problems for Section 2.3

LEARNING THE BASICS

2.13 Construct an ordered array, given the following data for a sample of $n = 7$ radar readings in km/hr on one of the major highways in Dubai:

   138   104   103   125   101   108   124

2.14 Construct an ordered array, given the following data from a sample of $n = 7$ representing the total minutes of mobile telephone usage during a seven-week period.

   88   78   78   73   91   78   85

2.15 The GMAT scores from a sample of 50 applicants to an MBA program indicate that none of the applicants scored below 450. A frequency distribution was formed by choosing class intervals 450 to 499, 500 to 549, and so on, with the last class having an interval from 700 to 749. Two applicants scored in the interval 450 to 499, and 16 applicants scored in the interval 500 to 549.
a. What percentage of applicants scored below 500?
b. What percentage of applicants scored between 500 and 549?
c. What percentage of applicants scored below 550?
d. What percentage of applicants scored below 750?

2.16 A set of data has values that vary from 11.6 to 97.8.
a. If these values are grouped into nine classes, indicate the class boundaries.
b. What class interval width did you choose?
c. What are the nine class midpoints?

APPLYING THE CONCEPTS

2.17 The file **BBCost** contains the total cost ($) for four tickets, two beers, four soft drinks, four hot dogs, two game programs, two baseball caps, and parking for one vehicle at each of the 30 Major League Baseball parks during the 2009 season. These costs were

164,326,224,180,205,162,141,170,411,187,185,165,151,166,114
158,305,145,161,170,210,222,146,259,220,135,215,172,223,216

Source: Data extracted from **teammarketing.com**, April 1, 2009.

a. Organize these costs as an ordered array.
b. Construct a frequency distribution and a percentage distribution for these costs.
c. Around which class grouping, if any, are the costs of attending a baseball game concentrated? Explain.

2.18 ✓SELF Test The file **Utility** contains the data in the next column about the cost of electricity during July 2010 for a random sample of 50 one-bedroom apartments in a large city.
a. Construct a frequency distribution and a percentage distribution that have class intervals with the upper class boundaries $99, $119, and so on.
b. Construct a cumulative percentage distribution.
c. Around what amount does the monthly electricity cost seem to be concentrated?

Raw Data on Utility Charges ($)

96	171	202	178	147	102	153	197	127	82
157	185	90	116	172	111	148	213	130	165
141	149	206	175	123	128	144	168	109	167
95	163	150	154	130	143	187	166	139	149
108	119	183	151	114	135	191	137	129	158

2.19 One operation of a mill is to cut pieces of steel into parts that will later be used as the frame for front seats in an automobile. The steel is cut with a diamond saw and requires the resulting parts to be within ± 0.005 inch of the length specified by the automobile company. Data are collected from a sample of 100 steel parts and stored in **Steel**. The measurement reported is the difference in inches between the actual length of the steel part, as measured by a laser measurement device, and the specified length of the steel part. For example, the first value, −0.002, represents a steel part that is 0.002 inch shorter than the specified length.
a. Construct a frequency distribution and a percentage distribution.
b. Construct a cumulative percentage distribution.
c. Is the steel mill doing a good job meeting the requirements set by the automobile company? Explain.

2.20 A manufacturing company produces steel housings for electrical equipment. The main component part of the housing is a steel trough that is made out of a 14-gauge steel coil. It is produced using a 250-ton progressive punch press with a wipe-down operation that puts two 90-degree forms in the flat steel to make the trough. The distance from one side of the form to the other is critical because of weatherproofing in outdoor applications. The company requires that the width of the trough be between 8.31 inches and 8.61 inches. The widths of the troughs, in inches, are collected from a sample of 49 troughs and stored in **Trough** and shown here:

8.312	8.343	8.317	8.383	8.348	8.410	8.351	8.373
8.481	8.422	8.476	8.382	8.484	8.403	8.414	8.419
8.385	8.465	8.498	8.447	8.436	8.413	8.489	8.414
8.481	8.415	8.479	8.429	8.458	8.462	8.460	8.444
8.429	8.460	8.412	8.420	8.410	8.405	8.323	8.420
8.396	8.447	8.405	8.439	8.411	8.427	8.420	8.498
8.409

a. Construct a frequency distribution and a percentage distribution.
b. Construct a cumulative percentage distribution.
c. What can you conclude about the number of troughs that will meet the company's requirements of troughs being between 8.31 and 8.61 inches wide?

2.21 The manufacturing company in Problem 2.20 also produces electric insulators. If the insulators break when in use, a short circuit is likely to occur. To test the strength of the insulators, destructive testing in high-powered labs is carried out to determine how much *force* is required to break the insulators. Force is measured by observing how many pounds must be applied to the insulator before it breaks. Force measurements are collected from a sample of 30 insulators and stored in Force and shown here:

1,870 1,728 1,656 1,610 1,634 1,784 1,522 1,696
1,592 1,662 1,866 1,764 1,734 1,662 1,734 1,774
1,550 1,756 1,762 1,866 1,820 1,744 1,788 1,688
1,810 1,752 1,680 1,810 1,652 1,736

a. Construct a frequency distribution and a percentage distribution.
b. Construct a cumulative percentage distribution.
c. What can you conclude about the strength of the insulators if the company requires a force measurement of at least 1,500 pounds before the insulator breaks?

2.22 The file Bulbs contains the life (in hours) of a sample of 40 100-watt light bulbs produced by Manufacturer A and a sample of 40 100-watt light bulbs produced by Manufacturer B. The following table shows these data as a pair of ordered arrays:

Manufacturer A					Manufacturer B				
684	697	720	773	821	819	836	888	897	903
831	835	848	852	852	907	912	918	942	943
859	860	868	870	876	952	959	962	986	992
893	899	905	909	911	994	1,004	1,005	1,007	1,015
922	924	926	926	938	1,016	1,018	1,020	1,022	1,034
939	943	946	954	971	1,038	1,072	1,077	1,077	1,082
972	977	984	1,005	1,014	1,096	1,100	1,113	1,113	1,116
1,016	1,041	1,052	1,080	1,093	1,153	1,154	1,174	1,188	1,230

a. Construct a frequency distribution and a percentage distribution for each manufacturer, using the following class interval widths for each distribution:

Manufacturer A: 650 but less than 750, 750 but less than 850, and so on.
Manufacturer B: 750 but less than 850, 850 but less than 950, and so on.

b. Construct cumulative percentage distributions.
c. Which bulbs have a longer life—those from Manufacturer A or Manufacturer B? Explain.

2.23 The following data (stored in Drink) represent the amount of soft drink in a sample of 50 2-liter bottles:

2.109 2.086 2.066 2.075 2.065 2.057 2.052 2.044 2.036 2.038
2.031 2.029 2.025 2.029 2.023 2.020 2.015 2.014 2.013 2.014
2.012 2.012 2.012 2.010 2.005 2.003 1.999 1.996 1.997 1.992
1.994 1.986 1.984 1.981 1.973 1.975 1.971 1.969 1.966 1.967
1.963 1.957 1.951 1.951 1.947 1.941 1.941 1.938 1.908 1.894

a. Construct a cumulative percentage distribution.
b. On the basis of the results of (a), does the amount of soft drink filled in the bottles concentrate around specific values?

VISUALIZING DATA

When you organize your data, you sometimes begin to discover patterns or relationships in your data, as examples in Sections 2.2 and 2.3 illustrate. To better explore and discover patterns and relationships, you can visualize your data by creating various charts and special "displays." As is the case when organizing data, the techniques you use to visualize your data depend on the *type of* variable (categorical or numerical) of your data.

2.4 Visualizing Categorical Data

The chart you choose to visualize the data for a single categorical variable depends on whether you seek to emphasize how categories directly compare to each other (bar chart) or how categories form parts of a whole (pie chart), or whether you have data that are concentrated in only a few of your categories (Pareto chart). To visualize the data for two categorical variables, you use a side-by-side bar chart.

The Bar Chart

A **bar chart** compares different categories by using individual bars to represent the tallies for each category. The length of a bar represents the amount, frequency, or percentage of values falling into a category. Unlike with a histogram, discussed in Section 2.5, a bar chart separates the bars between the categories. Figure 2.1 displays the bar chart for the data of Table 2.1 on page 60, which is based on a recent survey that asked adults how they pay their monthly bills ("How Adults Pay Monthly Bills," *USA Today*, October 4, 2007, p. 1).

FIGURE 2.1
Bar chart for how adults pay their monthly bills

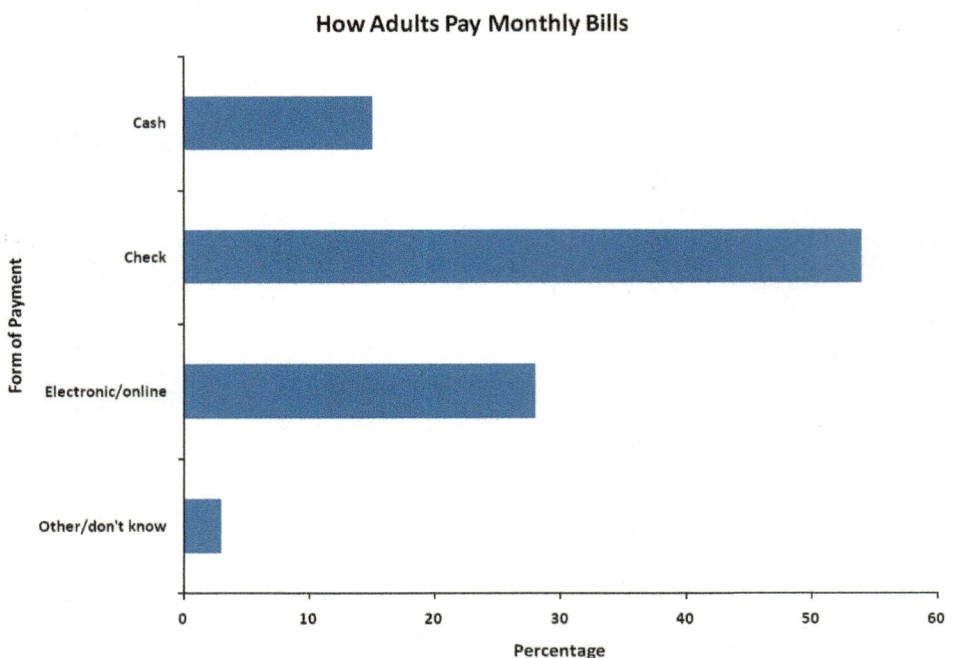

Reviewing Figure 2.1, you see that respondents are most likely to pay by check or electronically/online, followed by paying by cash. Very few respondents mentioned other or did not know.

EXAMPLE 2.5

Bar Chart of Levels of Risk of Bond Mutual Funds

In Part I of the Choice Is Yours scenario, you are interested in examining the risk of the bond funds. You have already defined the variables and collected the data from a sample of 184 bond funds. Now, you need to construct a bar chart of the risk of the bond funds (based on Table 2.2 on page 60) and interpret the results.

SOLUTION Reviewing Figure 2.2, you see that average is the largest category, closely followed by above average, and below average.

FIGURE 2.2
Bar chart of the levels of risk of bond mutual funds

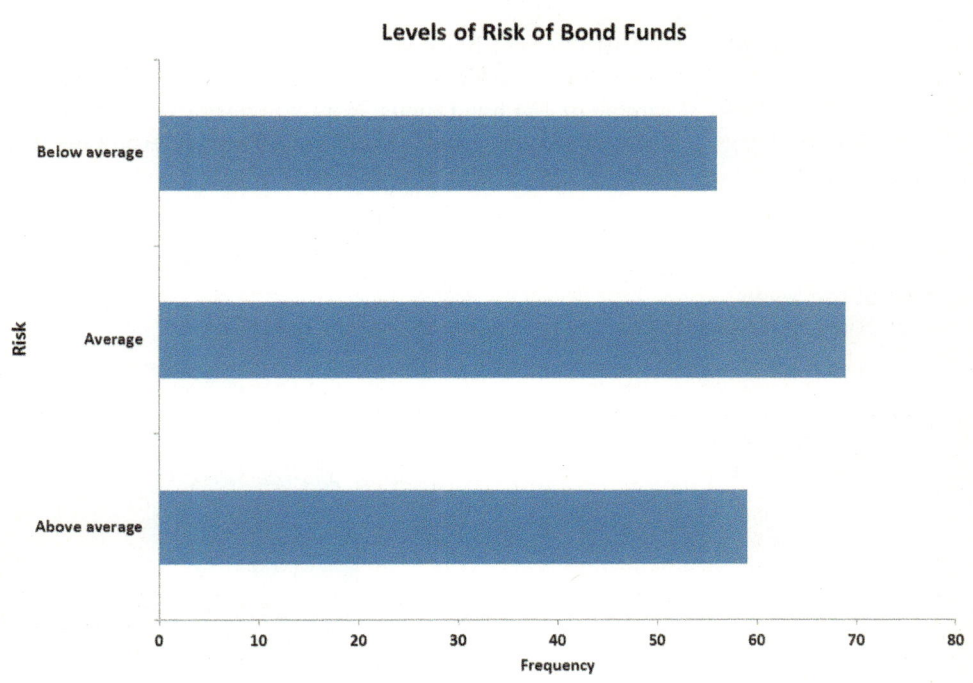

The Pie Chart

A **pie chart** uses parts of a circle to represent the tallies of each category. The size of each part, or pie slice, varies according to the percentage in each category. For example, in Table 2.1 on page 60, 54% of the respondents stated that they paid bills by check. To represent this category as a pie slice, you multiply 54% by the 360 degrees that makes up a circle to get a pie slice that takes up 194.4 degrees of the 360 degrees of the circle. From Figure 2.3, you can see that the pie chart lets you visualize the portion of the entire pie that is in each category. In this figure, paying bills by check is the largest slice, containing 54% of the pie. The second largest slice is paying bills electronically/online, which contains 28% of the pie.

FIGURE 2.3
Pie chart for how people pay their bills

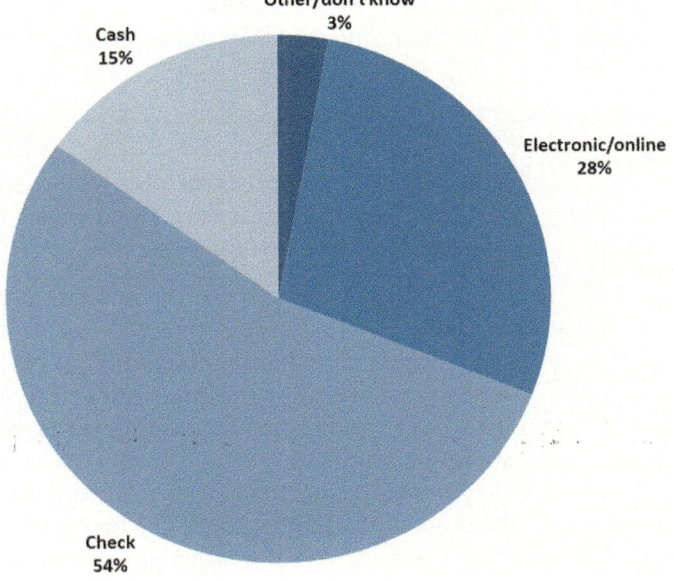

EXAMPLE 2.6

Pie Chart of Levels of Risk of Bond Mutual Funds

FIGURE 2.4
Pie chart of the levels of risk of bond mutual funds

Figure 2.4 shows a pie chart created using Minitab; Figure 2.3 shows a pie chart created using Excel.

In Part I of the Choice Is Yours scenario, you are interested in examining the risk of the bond funds. You have already defined the variables to be collected and collected the data from a sample of 184 bond funds. Now, you need to construct a pie chart of the risk of the bond funds (based on Table 2.2 on page 60) and interpret the results.

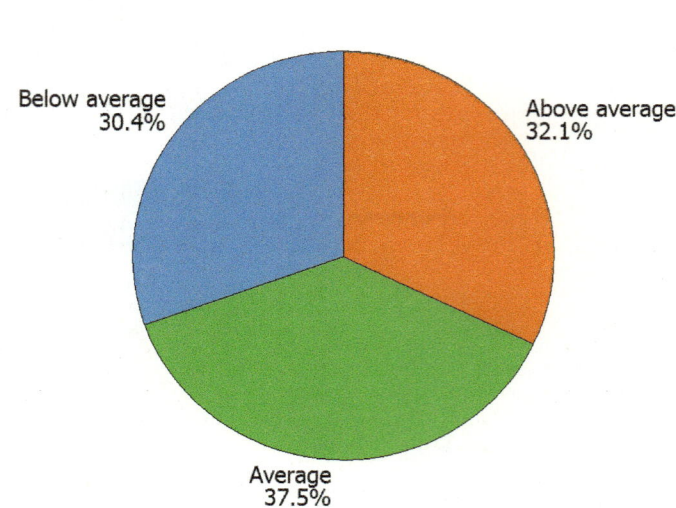

SOLUTION Reviewing Figure 2.4, you see that approximately a little more than one-third of the funds are average risk, about one-third are above average risk, and fewer than one-third are below-average risk.

The Pareto Chart

In a **Pareto chart**, the tallies for each category are plotted as vertical bars in descending order, according to their frequencies, and are combined with a cumulative percentage line on the same chart. A Pareto chart can reveal situations in which the Pareto principle occurs.

> **PARETO PRINCIPLE**
> The **Pareto principle** exists when the majority of items in a set of data occur in a small number of categories and the few remaining items are spread out over a large number of categories. These two groups are often referred to as the "vital few" and the "trivial many."

A Pareto chart has the capability to separate the "vital few" from the "trivial many," enabling you to focus on the important categories. In situations in which the data involved consist of defective or nonconforming items, a Pareto chart is a powerful tool for prioritizing improvement efforts.

To study a situation in which the Pareto chart proved to be especially appropriate, consider the problem faced by a bank. The bank defined the problem to be the incomplete automated teller machine (ATM) transactions. Data concerning the causes of incomplete ATM transactions were collected and stored in ATM Transactions . Table 2.15 shows the causes of incomplete ATM transactions, the frequency for each cause, and the percentage of incomplete ATM transactions due to each cause.

TABLE 2.15
Summary Table of Causes of Incomplete ATM Transactions

Cause	Frequency	Percentage (%)
ATM malfunctions	32	4.42
ATM out of cash	28	3.87
Invalid amount requested	23	3.18
Lack of funds in account	19	2.62
Magnetic strip unreadable	234	32.32
Warped card jammed	365	50.41
Wrong key stroke	23	3.18
Total	724	100.00

Source: Data extracted from A. Bhalla, "Don't Misuse the Pareto Principle," *Six Sigma Forum Magazine*, May 2009, pp. 15–18.

Table 2.16 presents a summary table for the incomplete ATM transactions data in which the categories are ordered based on the frequency of incomplete ATM transactions present (rather than arranged alphabetically). The percentages and cumulative percentages for the ordered categories are also included as part of the table.

TABLE 2.16
Ordered Summary Table of Causes of Incomplete ATM Transactions

Cause	Frequency	Percentage (%)	Cumulative Percentage (%)
Warped card jammed	365	50.41%	50.41%
Magnetic strip unreadable	234	32.32%	82.73%
ATM malfunctions	32	4.42%	87.15%
ATM out of cash	28	3.87%	91.02%
Invalid amount requested	23	3.18%	94.20%
Wrong key stroke	23	3.18%	97.38%
Lack of funds in account	19	2.62%	100.00%
Total	724	100.00%	

Figure 2.5 shows a Pareto chart based on the results displayed in Table 2.16.

FIGURE 2.5
Pareto chart for the incomplete ATM transactions data

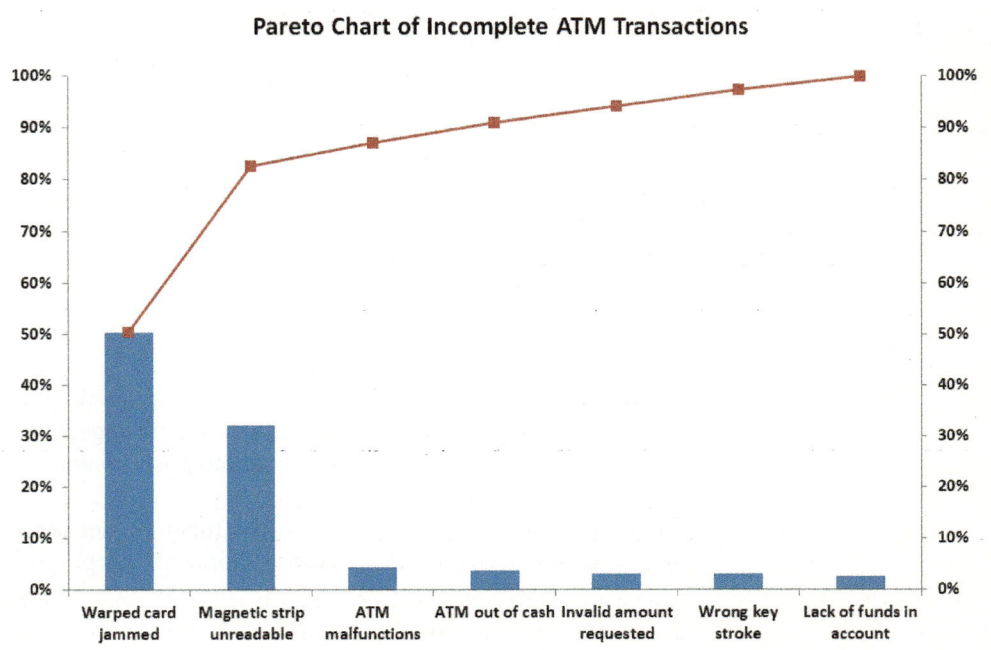

A Pareto chart presents the bars vertically, along with a cumulative percentage line. The cumulative line is plotted at the midpoint of each category, at a height equal to the cumulative percentage. In order for a Pareto chart to include all categories, even those with few defects, in some situations, you need to include a category labeled *Other* or *Miscellaneous*. In these situations, the bar representing these categories should be placed to the right of the other bars.

Because the categories in a Pareto chart are ordered by the frequency of occurrence, you can see where to concentrate efforts to improve the process. Analyzing the Pareto chart in Figure 2.5, if you follow the line, you see that these first two categories account for 82.73% of the incomplete ATM transactions. The first category listed is warped card jammed (with 50.41% of the defects), followed by magnetic strip unreadable (with 32.32%). Attempts to reduce incomplete ATM transactions due to warped card jammed and magnetic strip unreadable should produce the greatest payoff. The team should focus on finding why these errors occurred.

EXAMPLE 2.7
Pareto Chart of Types of Bill Payment

Construct a Pareto chart of the types of bill payment (see Table 2.1 on page 60)

FIGURE 2.6
Pareto chart of bill payment

Figure 2.6 shows a Pareto chart created using Minitab; Figure 2.5 shows a Pareto chart created using Excel.

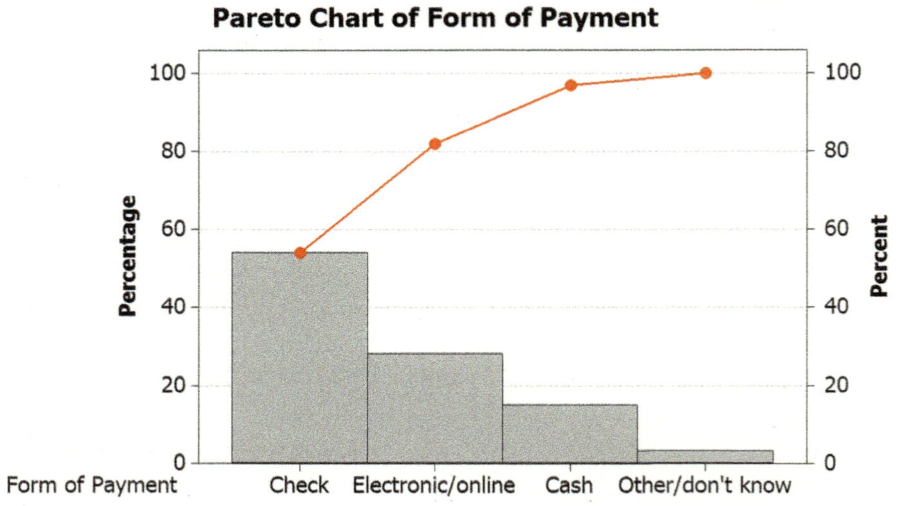

Pareto Chart of Form of Payment

In Figure 2.6, check and electronic/online account for 82% of the bill payments and check, electronic/online, and cash account for 97% of the bill payments.

The Side-by-Side Bar Chart

A **side-by-side bar chart** uses sets of bars to show the joint responses from two categorical variables. Figure 2.7 uses the data of Table 2.3 on page 61, which shows the frequency of bond funds that charge a fee for the intermediate government bond funds and short-term corporate bond funds.

Reviewing Figure 2.7, you see that a much higher percentage of the intermediate government bond funds charge a fee than the short-term corporate bond funds.

FIGURE 2.7
Side-by-side bar chart of fund type and whether a fee is charged

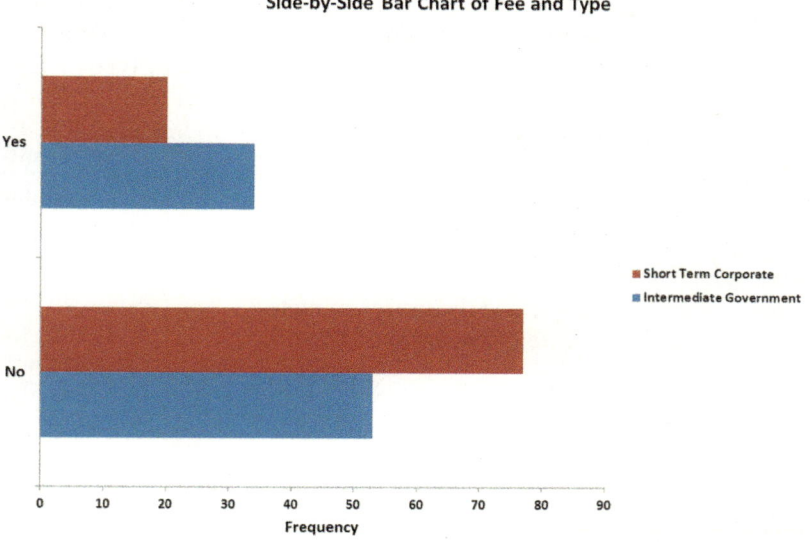

Problems for Section 2.4
APPLYING THE CONCEPTS

2.24 (SELF Test) A survey asked 1,264 women who were their most trusted shopping advisers. The survey results were as follows:

Shopping Advisers	Percentage (%)
Advertising	7
Friends/family	45
Manufacturer websites	5
News media	11
Online user reviews	13
Retail websites	4
Salespeople	1
Other	14

Source: Data extracted from "Snapshots," *USA Today*, October 19, 2006, p. 1B.

a. Construct a bar chart, a pie chart, and a Pareto chart.
b. Which graphical method do you think is best for portraying these data?
c. What conclusions can you reach concerning women's most trusted shopping advisers?

2.25 Carbon dioxide emission is the leading cause of climate change and is a result of industrial activities in different countries producing heat-trapping gases in the atmosphere. The following table shows data compiled using statistics from the Energy Information Administration. The data shows the emission percentage of total carbon dioxide emissions from all sources of fossil fuel burning and consumption for the seven countries with highest carbon dioxide emissions.

Country	Emission Percentage
China	35.9%
United States	32.0%
Russia	9.5%
India	8.2%
Japan	6.7%
Germany	4.6%
Canada	3.2%

Source: U.S. Energy Information Administration (2008).

a. Construct a bar chart, a pie chart, and a Pareto chart.
b. Which graphical method do you think is best for portraying these data?

2.26 The Energy Information Administration reported the following sources of electricity in the United States in 2010:

Source of Electricity	Percentage (%)
Coal	44
Hydroelectric	7
Natural gas	24
Nuclear	20
Other	5

Source: Energy Information Administration, 2010.

a. Construct a Pareto chart.
b. What percentage of power is derived from coal, nuclear, or natural gas?
c. Construct a pie chart.
d. For these data, do you prefer using a Pareto chart or the pie chart? Why?

2.27 An article discussed radiation therapy and new cures from the therapy, along with the harm that could be done if mistakes were made. The following tables represent the results of the types of mistakes made and the causes of mistakes reported to the New York State Department of Health from 2001 to 2009:

Radiation Mistakes	Number
Missed all or part of intended target	284
Wrong dose given	255
Wrong patient treated	50
Other	32

a. Construct a bar chart and a pie chart for the types of radiation mistakes.
b. Which graphical method do you think is best for portraying these data?

Causes of Mistakes	Number
Quality assurance flawed	355
Data entry or calculation errors by personnel	252
Misidentification of patient or treatment location	174
Blocks, wedges, or collimators misused	133
Patient's physical setup wrong	96
Treatment plan flawed	77
Hardware malfunction	60
Staffing	52
Computer software or digital information transfer malfunction	24
Override of computer data by personnel	19
Miscommunication	14
Unclear/other	8

Source: Data extracted from W. Bogdanich, "A Lifesaving Tool Turned Deadly," *The New York Times,* January 24, 2010, pp. 1, 15, 16.

c. Construct a Pareto chart for the causes of mistakes.
d. Discuss the "vital few" and "trivial many" reasons for the causes of mistakes.

2.28 The following table indicates the percentage of residential electricity consumption in the United States, organized by type of appliance in a recent year:

Type of Appliance	Percentage (%)
Air conditioning	18
Clothes dryers	5
Clothes washers/other	24
Computers	1
Cooking	2
Dishwashers	2
Freezers	2
Lighting	16
Refrigeration	9
Space heating	7
Water heating	8
TVs and set top boxes	6

Source: Data extracted from J. Mouawad, and K. Galbraith, "Plugged-in Age Feeds a Hunger for Electricity," *The New York Times,* September 20, 2009, pp. 1, 28.

a. Construct a bar chart, a pie chart, and a Pareto chart.
b. Which graphical method do you think is best for portraying these data?
c. What conclusions can you reach concerning residential electricity consumption in the United States?

2.29 A study of 1,000 people asked what respondents wanted to grill during barbecue season. The results were as follows:

Type of Food	Percentage (%)
Beef	38
Chicken	23
Fruit	1
Hot dogs	6
Pork	8
Seafood	19
Vegetables	5

Source: Data extracted from "What Folks Want Sizzling on the Grill During Barbecue Season," *USA Today,* March 29, 2009, p. 1A.

a. Construct a bar chart, a pie chart, and a Pareto chart.
b. Which graphical method do you think is best for portraying these data?
c. What conclusions can you reach concerning what folks want sizzling on the grill during barbecue season?

2.30 A sample of 500 shoppers was selected in a large metropolitan area to learn more about consumer behavior.

Among the questions asked was "Do you enjoy shopping for clothing?" The results are summarized in the following table:

ENJOY SHOPPING FOR CLOTHING	GENDER		
	Male	Female	Total
Yes	136	224	360
No	104	36	140
Total	240	260	500

a. Construct a side-by-side bar chart of enjoying shopping and gender.
b. What conclusions do you reach from this chart?

2.31 Each day at a large hospital, several hundred laboratory tests are performed. The rate at which these tests are done improperly (and therefore need to be redone) seems steady, at about 4%. In an effort to get to the root cause of these nonconformances, tests that need to be redone, the director of the lab decided to keep records over a period of one week. The laboratory tests were subdivided by the shift of workers who performed the lab tests. The results are as follows:

LAB TESTS PERFORMED	SHIFT		
	Day	Evening	Total
Nonconforming	16	24	40
Conforming	654	306	960
Total	670	330	1,000

a. Construct a side-by-side bar chart of nonconformances and shift.
b. What conclusions concerning the pattern of nonconforming laboratory tests can the laboratory director reach?

2.32 Does it take more time to get yourself removed from an email list than it used to? A study of 100 large online retailers revealed the following:

	NEED THREE OR MORE CLICKS TO BE REMOVED	
YEAR	Yes	No
2009	39	61
2008	7	93

Source: Data extracted from "Drill Down," *The New York Times*, March 29, 2010, p. B2.

a. Construct a side-by-side bar chart of year and whether you need to click three or more times to be removed from an email list.
b. What do these results tell you about whether more online retailers were requiring three or more clicks in 2009 than in 2008?

2.5 Visualizing Numerical Data

Among the charts you use to visualize numerical data are the stem-and-leaf display, the histogram, the percentage polygon, and the cumulative percentage polygon (ogive).

The Stem-and-Leaf Display

A **stem-and-leaf display** allows you to see how the data are distributed and where concentrations of data exist. The display organizes data into groups (the stems) row-wise, so that the values within each group (the leaves) branch out to the right of their stem. For stems with more than one leaf, the leaves are presented in ascending order. On each leaf, the values are presented in ascending order. For example, suppose you collect the following lunch costs ($) for 15 classmates who had lunch at a fast-food restaurant:

5.40 4.30 4.80 5.50 7.30 8.50 6.10 4.80 4.90 4.90 5.50 3.50 5.90 6.30 6.60

To construct the stem-and-leaf display, you use whole dollar amounts as the stems and round the cents, the leaves, to one decimal place. For the first value, 5.40, the stem would be 5 and its leaf would be 4. For the second value, 4.30, the stem would be 4 and its leaf 3. The completed stem-and-leaf display for these data is

```
3 | 5
4 | 38899
5 | 4559
6 | 136
7 | 3
8 | 5
```

EXAMPLE 2.8

Stem-and-Leaf Display of the 2009 Return of the Short-Term Corporate Bond Funds

FIGURE 2.8

Stem-and-leaf display of the return in 2009 of short-term corporate bond funds

Figure 2.8 shows a stem-and-leaf display created using Minitab and modified so that each stem occupies only one row. The leaves using PHStat2 will differ from Figure 2.8 slightly because PHStat2 and Minitab use different methods.

In Part I of the Choice Is Yours scenario, you are interested in studying the past performance of the short-term corporate bond funds. One measure of past performance is the return in 2009. You have already defined the variables to be collected and collected the data from a sample of 97 short-term corporate bond funds. Now, you need to construct a stem-and-leaf display of the return in 2009.

SOLUTION Figure 2.8 illustrates the stem-and-leaf display of the return in 2009 for short-term corporate bond funds.

```
Stem-and-Leaf Display: Return 2009_Short Term Corporat

Stem-and-leaf of Return 2009_Short Term Corporat   N  = 97
Leaf Unit = 1.0

  1    -0  8
 (53)   0  11222223334444455555555566666666677777788888889999999
 43     1  0000001111112222222333333333444555566679
  3     2  4
  2     2  9
  1     3  2
```

Analyzing Figure 2.8, you conclude the following:

- The lowest return in 2009 was –8.
- The highest return in 2009 was 32.
- The returns in 2009 were concentrated between 0 and 20.
- Only one fund had a negative 2009 return, and three funds had 2009 returns 20 and above.

The Histogram

A **histogram** is a bar chart for grouped numerical data in which you use vertical bars to represent the frequencies or percentages in each group. In a histogram, there are no gaps between adjacent bars. You display the variable of interest along the horizontal (X) axis. The vertical (Y) axis represents either the frequency or the percentage of values per class interval.

Figure 2.9 displays frequency histograms for the cost of meals at city restaurants and suburban restaurants. The histogram for city restaurants shows that the cost of meals is concentrated between approximately $40 and $50. Very few meals at city restaurants cost more than

FIGURE 2.9

Histograms for the cost of restaurant meals at city and suburban restaurants

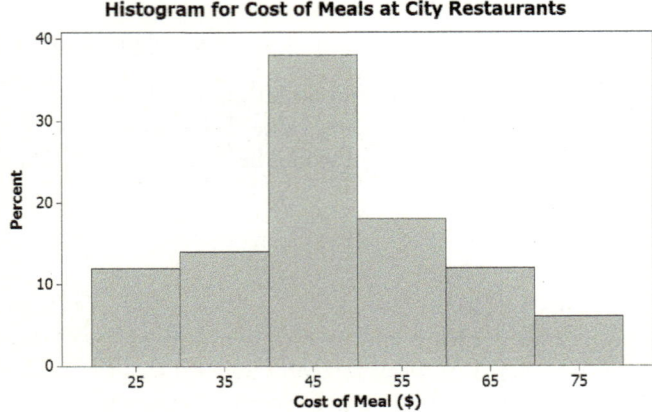
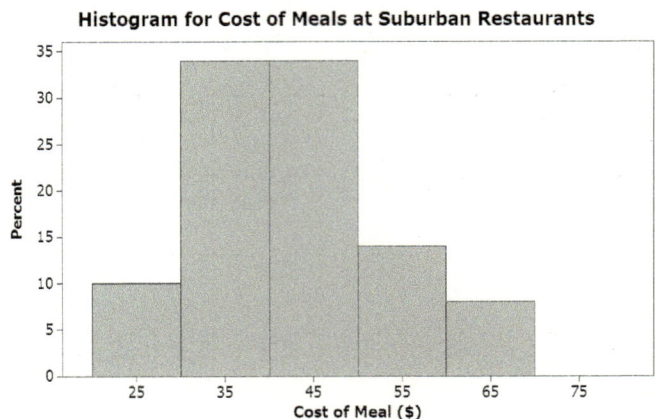

$70. The histogram for suburban restaurants shows that the cost of meals is concentrated between $30 and $50. Very few meals at suburban restaurants cost more than $60.

EXAMPLE 2.9

Histograms of the 2009 Return for the Intermediate Government and Short-Term Corporate Bond Funds

In Part I of the Choice Is Yours scenario, you are interested in comparing the past performance of the intermediate government bond funds and the short-term corporate bond funds. One measure of past performance is the return in 2009. You have already defined the variables to be collected and collected the data from a sample of 184 bond funds. Now, you need to construct histograms for the intermediate government and the short-term corporate bond funds.

SOLUTION   Figure 2.10 displays frequency histograms for the 2009 return for the intermediate government and short-term corporate bond funds.

FIGURE 2.10

Frequency histograms of the 2009 return for the intermediate government and short-term corporate bond funds

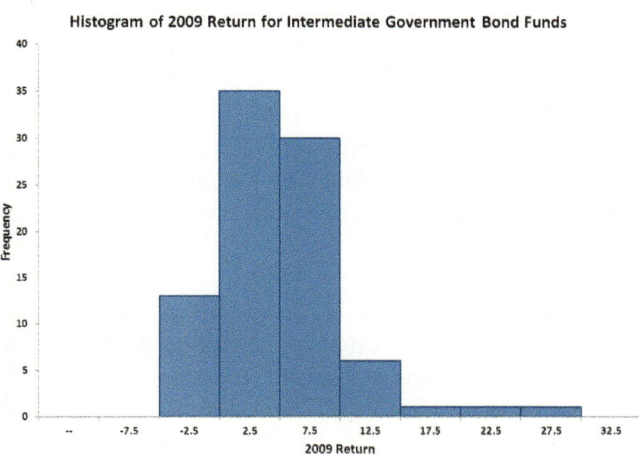
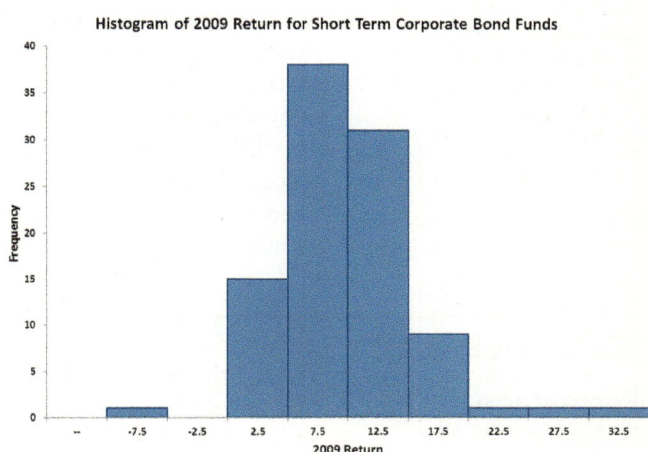

Figure 2.10 shows histograms created using Excel and PHStat2; Figure 2.9 shows histograms created using Minitab.

Reviewing the histograms in Figure 2.10 leads you to conclude that the returns were much higher for the short-term corporate bond funds than for the intermediate government bond funds. The return for intermediate government bond funds is concentrated between 0 and 10, and the return for the short-term corporate bond funds is concentrated between 5 and 15.

The Percentage Polygon

If you tried to construct two or more histograms on the same graph, you would not be able to easily interpret each histogram because the bars would overlap. When there are two or more groups, you should use a percentage polygon. A **percentage polygon** uses the midpoints of each class interval to represent the data of each class and then plots the midpoints, at their respective class percentages, as points on a line.

Figure 2.11 displays percentage polygons for the cost of meals at city and suburban restaurants.

Reviewing the two polygons in Figure 2.11 leads you to conclude that the highest concentration of the cost of meals at city restaurants is between $40 and $50, while the cost of meals at suburban restaurants is evenly concentrated between $30 and $50. Also, city restaurants have a higher percentage of meals that cost $60 or more than suburban restaurants.

FIGURE 2.11

Percentage polygons of the cost of restaurant meals for city and suburban restaurants

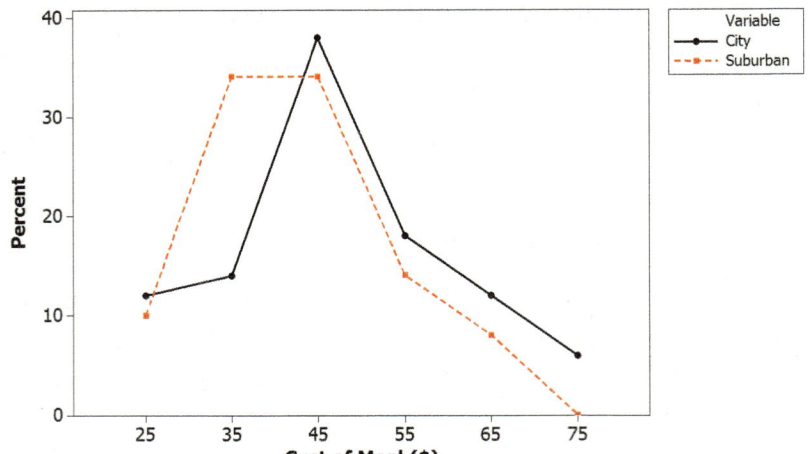

The polygons in Figure 2.11 have points whose values on the X axis represent the midpoint of the class interval. For example, look at the points plotted at $X = 65$ ($65). The point for the cost of meals at city restaurants (the higher one) represents the fact that 12% of the meals at these restaurants cost between $60 and $70. The point for the cost of meals at suburban restaurants (the lower one) represents the fact that 8% of meals at these restaurants cost between $60 and $70.

When you construct polygons or histograms, the vertical (Y) axis should show the true zero, or "origin," so as not to distort the character of the data. The horizontal (X) axis does not need to show the zero point for the variable of interest, although the range of the variable should include the major portion of the axis.

EXAMPLE 2.10

Percentage Polygons of the 2009 Return for the Intermediate Government and Short-Term Corporate Bond Funds

In Part I of the Choice Is Yours scenario, you are interested in comparing the past performance of the intermediate government bond funds and the short-term corporate bond funds. One measure of past performance is the return in 2009. You have already defined the variables and collected the data from a sample of 184 bond funds. Now, you need to construct percentage polygons for the intermediate government bond and short-term corporate bond funds.

SOLUTION Figure 2.12 displays percentage polygons of the 2009 returns for the intermediate government bond and short-term corporate bond funds.

FIGURE 2.12

Percentage polygons of the 2009 return for the intermediate government bond and short-term corporate bond funds

Figure 2.12 shows percentage polygons created using Excel; Figure 2.11 shows percentage polygons created using Minitab.

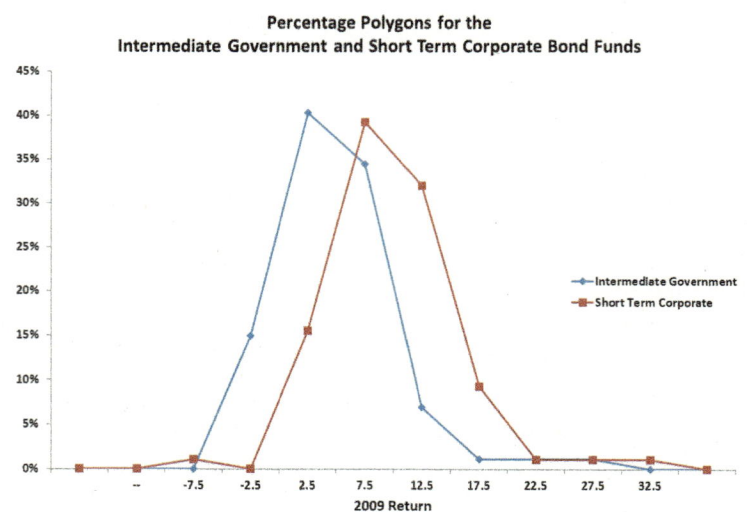

Analyzing Figure 2.12 leads you to conclude that the 2009 return of short-term corporate funds is much higher than for intermediate government bond funds. The polygon for the short-term corporate funds is to the right (the returns are higher) of the polygon for the intermediate government bond funds. The return for intermediate government funds is concentrated between 0 and 10, whereas the return for the short-term corporate bond funds is concentrated between 5 and 15.

The Cumulative Percentage Polygon (Ogive)

The **cumulative percentage polygon**, or **ogive**, uses the cumulative percentage distribution discussed in Section 2.3 to display the variable of interest along the X axis and the cumulative percentages along the Y axis.

Figure 2.13 shows cumulative percentage polygons for the cost of meals at city and suburban restaurants.

FIGURE 2.13
Cumulative percentage polygons of the cost of restaurant meals at city and suburban restaurants

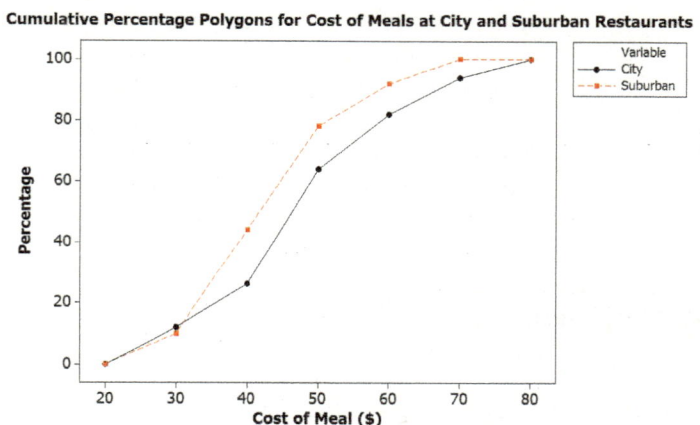

Reviewing the curves leads you to conclude that the curve of the cost of meals at the city restaurants is located to the right of the curve for the suburban restaurants. This indicates that the city restaurants have fewer meals that cost less than a particular value. For example, 64% of the meals at city restaurants cost less than $50, as compared to 78% of the meals at suburban restaurants.

EXAMPLE 2.11

Cumulative Percentage Polygons of the 2009 Return for the Intermediate Government and Short-Term Corporate Bond Funds

In Part I of the Choice Is Yours scenario, you are interested in comparing the past performance of the intermediate government bond funds and the short-term corporate bond funds. One measure of past performance is the return in 2009. You have already defined the variables and collected the data from a sample of 184 bond funds. Now, you need to construct cumulative percentage polygons for the intermediate government bond and the short-term corporate bond funds.

SOLUTION Figure 2.14 on page 84 displays cumulative percentage polygons for the 2009 return for the intermediate government bond and short-term corporate bond funds.

FIGURE 2.14

Cumulative percentage polygons of the 2009 return of intermediate government bonds and short-term corporate bond funds

Figure 2.14 shows cumulative percentage polygons created using Excel; Figure 2.13 shows cumulative percentage polygons created using Minitab.

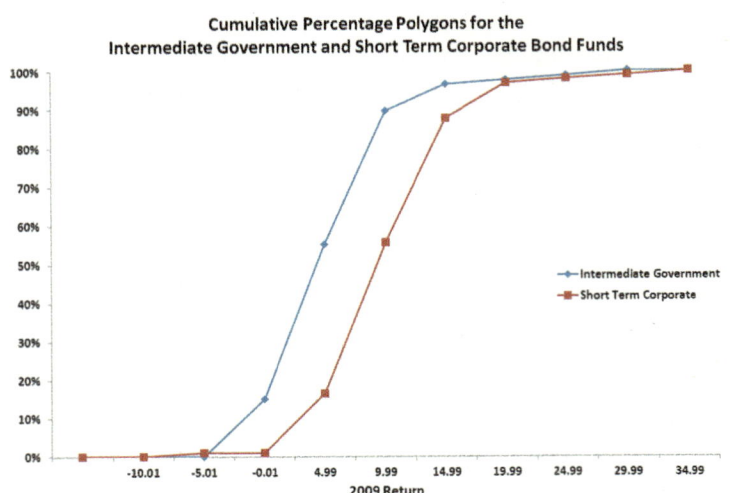

Reviewing the cumulative percentage polygons in Figure 2.14 leads you to conclude that the curve for the 2009 return of short-term corporate bond funds is located to the right of the curve for the intermediate government bond funds. This indicates that the short-term corporate bond funds have fewer 2009 returns that are lower than a particular value. For example, 14.94% of the intermediate government bond funds had negative (returns below 0) 2009 returns as compared to only 1.03% of the short-term corporate bond funds. Also, 55.17% of the intermediate government bond funds had 2009 returns below 5, as compared to 16.49% of the short-term corporate bond funds. You can conclude that, in general, the short-term corporate bond funds outperformed the intermediate government bond funds in 2009.

Problems for Section 2.5

LEARNING THE BASICS

2.33 Construct a stem-and-leaf display, given the following data from a sample of midterm exam scores in finance:

    54 69 98 93 53 74

2.34 Construct an ordered array, given the following stem-and-leaf display from a sample of $n = 7$ midterm exam scores in information systems:

5	0
6	
7	446
8	19
9	2

APPLYING THE CONCEPTS

2.35 The following stem-and-leaf display represents the amount of time, in minutes (with leaves in tenths of a minute), for a sample of 20 customers who used an express checkout stand at a local supermarket in Kuwait:

1	00123478
2	011122339
3	12
4	1

a. Construct an ordered array for these data.
b. Which of these two displays seems to provide more information? Discuss.
c. Comment on the shape of the distribution, indicating where the data are mostly concentrated.

SELF Test 2.36 The file **BBCost** contains the total cost ($) for four tickets, two beers, four soft drinks, four hot dogs, two game programs, two baseball caps, and parking for one vehicle at each of the 30 Major League Baseball parks during the 2009 season.

Source: Data extracted from **teammarketing.com,** April 1, 2009.

a. Construct a stem-and-leaf display for these data.
b. Around what value, if any, are the costs of attending a baseball game concentrated? Explain.

2.37 The file **DarkChocolate** contains the cost per ounce ($) for a sample of 14 dark chocolate bars:

0.68	0.72	0.92	1.14	1.42	0.94	0.77
0.57	1.51	0.57	0.55	0.86	1.41	0.90

Source: Data extracted from "Dark Chocolate: Which Bars Are Best?" *Consumer Reports,* September 2007, p. 8.

a. Construct an ordered array.
b. Construct a stem-and-leaf display.
c. Does the ordered array or the stem-and-leaf display provide more information? Discuss.
d. Around what value, if any, is the cost of dark chocolate bars concentrated? Explain.

2.38 The file Utility contains the following data about the cost of electricity during July 2010 for a random sample of 50 one-bedroom apartments in a large city:

```
96  171 202 178 147 102 153 197 127  82
157 185  90 116 172 111 148 213 130 165
141 149 206 175 123 128 144 168 109 167
 95 163 150 154 130 143 187 166 139 149
108 119 183 151 114 135 191 137 129 158
```

a. Construct a histogram and a percentage polygon.
b. Construct a cumulative percentage polygon.
c. Around what amount does the monthly electricity cost seem to be concentrated?

2.39 As player salaries have increased, the cost of attending baseball games has increased dramatically. The following histogram visualizes the total cost ($) for four tickets, two beers, four soft drinks, four hot dogs, two game programs, two baseball caps, and parking for one vehicle at each of the 30 Major League Baseball parks during the 2009 season that is stored in BBCost.

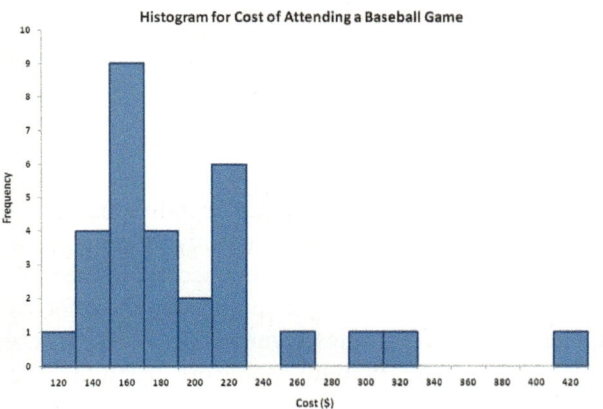

What conclusions can you reach concerning the cost of attending a baseball game at different ballparks?

2.40 The following histogram visualizes the data about the property taxes per capita for the 50 states and the District of Columbia, stored in PropertyTaxes.

What conclusions can you reach concerning the property taxes per capita?

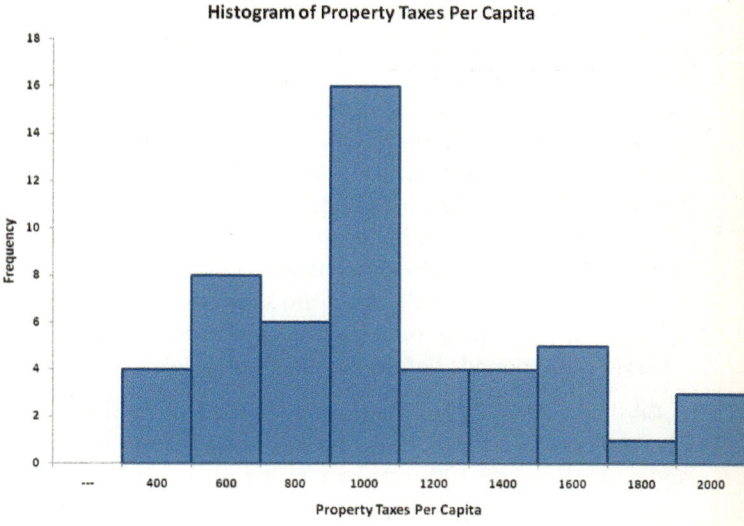

2.41 One operation of a mill is to cut pieces of steel into parts that will later be used as the frame for front seats in an automobile. The steel is cut with a diamond saw and requires the resulting parts to be within ±0.005 inch of the length specified by the automobile company. The data are collected from a sample of 100 steel parts and stored in Steel. The measurement reported is the difference in inches between the actual length of the steel part, as measured by a laser measurement device, and the specified length of the steel part. For example, the first value, −0.002, represents a steel part that is 0.002 inch shorter than the specified length.
a. Construct a percentage histogram.
b. Is the steel mill doing a good job meeting the requirements set by the automobile company? Explain.

2.42 A manufacturing company produces steel housings for electrical equipment. The main component part of the housing is a steel trough that is made out of a 14-gauge steel coil. It is produced using a 250-ton progressive punch press with a wipe-down operation that puts two 90-degree forms in the flat steel to make the trough. The distance from one side of the form to the other is critical because of weatherproofing in outdoor applications. The company requires that the width of the trough be between 8.31 inches and 8.61 inches. The widths of the troughs, in inches, are collected from a sample of 49 troughs and stored in Trough.
a. Construct a percentage histogram and a percentage polygon.
b. Plot a cumulative percentage polygon.
c. What can you conclude about the number of troughs that will meet the company's requirements of troughs being between 8.31 and 8.61 inches wide?

2.43 The manufacturing company in Problem 2.42 also produces electric insulators. If the insulators break when in use, a short circuit is likely to occur. To test the strength of the insulators, destructive testing in high-powered labs is carried out to determine how much *force* is required to break the insulators. Force is measured by observing how many pounds must be applied to the insulator before it breaks. Force measurements are collected from a sample of 30 insulators and stored in Force.

a. Construct a percentage histogram and a percentage polygon.
b. Construct a cumulative percentage polygon.
c. What can you conclude about the strengths of the insulators if the company requires a force measurement of at least 1,500 pounds before the insulator breaks?

2.44 The file Bulbs contains the life (in hours) of a sample of 40 100-watt light bulbs produced by Manufacturer A and a sample of 40 100-watt light bulbs produced by Manufacturer B. The table in the next column shows these data as a pair of ordered arrays:

Use the following class interval widths for each distribution:

Manufacturer A: 650 but less than 750, 750 but less than 850, and so on.
Manufacturer B: 750 but less than 850, 850 but less than 950, and so on.

Manufacturer A					Manufacturer B				
684	697	720	773	821	819	836	888	897	903
831	835	848	852	852	907	912	918	942	943
859	860	868	870	876	952	959	962	986	992
893	899	905	909	911	994	1,004	1,005	1,007	1,015
922	924	926	926	938	1,016	1,018	1,020	1,022	1,034
939	943	946	954	971	1,038	1,072	1,077	1,077	1,082
972	977	984	1,005	1,014	1,096	1,100	1,113	1,113	1,116
1,016	1,041	1,052	1,080	1,093	1,153	1,154	1,174	1,188	1,230

a. Construct percentage histograms on separate graphs and plot the percentage polygons on one graph.
b. Plot cumulative percentage polygons on one graph.
c. Which manufacturer has bulbs with a longer life—Manufacturer A or Manufacturer B? Explain.

2.45 The data stored in Drink represents the amount of soft drink in a sample of 50 2-liter bottles:
a. Construct a histogram and a percentage polygon.
b. Construct a cumulative percentage polygon.
c. On the basis of the results in (a) and (b), does the amount of soft drink filled in the bottles concentrate around specific values?

2.6 Visualizing Two Numerical Variables

Often you will want to explore possible relationships between two numerical variables. You use a scatter plot as a first step to visualize such relationships. In the special case where one of your variables represents the passage of time, you use a time-series plot.

The Scatter Plot

Often, you have two numerical measurements about the same item or individual. A **scatter plot** can explore the possible relationship between those measurements by plotting the data of one numerical variable on the horizontal, or X, axis and the data of a second numerical variable on the vertical, or Y, axis. For example, a marketing analyst could study the effectiveness of advertising by comparing advertising expenses and sales revenues of 50 stores. Using a scatter plot, a point is plotted on the two-dimensional graph for each store, using the X axis to represent advertising expenses and the Y axis to represent sales revenues.

Table 2.17 presents the revenues and value (both in millions of dollars) for all 30 NBA professional basketball teams that is stored in NBAValues. To explore the possible relationship between the revenues generated by a team and the value of a team, you can create a scatter plot.

TABLE 2.17
Values and Revenues for NBA Teams

Team	Value	Revenues	Team	Value	Revenues
Atlanta	306	103	Milwaukee	254	91
Boston	433	144	Minnesota	268	96
Charlotte	278	96	New Jersey	269	92
Chicago	511	168	New Orleans	267	95
Cleveland	476	159	New York	586	202
Dallas	446	154	Oklahoma City	310	111
Denver	321	115	Orlando	361	107
Detroit	479	171	Philadelphia	344	115
Golden State	315	113	Phoenix	429	148
Houston	470	160	Portland	338	121
Indiana	281	97	Sacramento	305	109
Los Angeles Clippers	295	102	San Antonio	398	133
Los Angeles Lakers	607	209	Toronto	386	133
Memphis	257	88	Utah	343	118
Miami	364	126	Washington	313	110

Source: Data extracted from **www.forbes.com/lists/2009/32/basketball-values-09_NBA-Team-Valuations_Rank.html**.

For each team, you plot the revenues on the X axis and the values on the Y axis. Figure 2.15 presents a scatter plot for these two variables.

FIGURE 2.15
Scatter plot of revenue and value

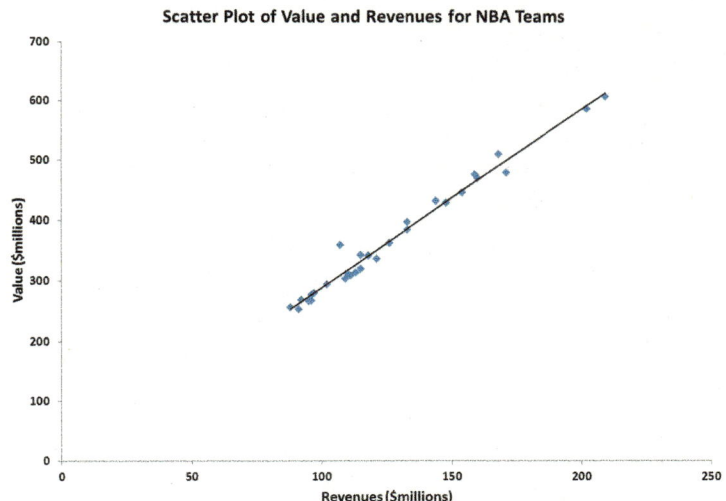

Reviewing Figure 2.15, you see that there appears to be a very strong increasing (positive) relationship between revenues and the value of a team. In other words, teams that generate a smaller amount of revenues have a lower value, while teams that generate higher revenues have a higher value. Notice the straight line that has been superimposed on the plotted data in Figure 2.15. For these data, this line is very close to the points in the scatter plot. This line is a linear regression prediction line that will be discussed in Chapter 13. (In Section 3.5, you will return to this example when you learn about the covariance and the coefficient of correlation.)

Other pairs of variables may have a decreasing (negative) relationship in which one variable decreases as the other increases. In other situations, there may be a weak or no relationship between the variables.

The Time-Series Plot

A **time-series plot** plots the values of a numerical variable on the Y axis and plots the time period associated with each numerical value on the X axis. A time-series plot can help explore trends in data that occur over time. For example, Table 2.18 presents the combined gross (in millions of dollars) of movies released from 1996 to 2009 that is stored in MovieGross. To better visualize this data, you create the time-series plot shown in Figure 2.16.

From Figure 2.16, you see that there was a steady increase in the combined gross of movies between 1996 and 2009. During that time, the combined gross increased from under $6 billion in 1996 to more than $10 billion in 2009.

TABLE 2.18

Combined Gross of Movies

Year	Combined Gross
1996	5,669.20
1997	6,393.90
1998	6,523.00
1999	7,317.50
2000	7,659.50
2001	8,077.80
2002	9,146.10
2003	9,043.20
2004	9,359.40
2005	8,817.10
2006	9,231.80
2007	9,685.70
2008	9,707.40
2009	10,675.60

Source: Data extracted from www.the-numbers.com/movies, February 16, 2010.

FIGURE 2.16

Time-series plot of combined gross of movies per year from 1996 to 2009

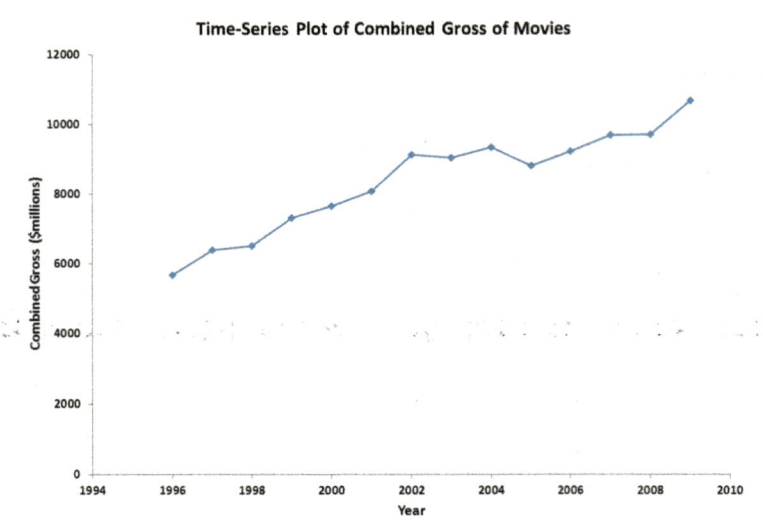

Problems for Section 2.6

LEARNING THE BASICS

2.46 The following is a set of data from a sample of $n = 11$ items:

X:	7	5	8	3	6	0	2	4	9	5	8
Y:	1	5	4	9	8	0	6	2	7	5	4

a. Construct a scatter plot.
b. Is there a relationship between X and Y? Explain.

2.47 The following is a series of annual sales (in millions of dollars) over an 11-year period (2000 to 2010):

Year:	2000	2001	2002	2003	2004	2005	2006	2007	2008	2009	2010
Sales:	13.0	17.0	19.0	20.0	20.5	20.5	20.5	20.0	19.0	17.0	13.0

a. Construct a time-series plot.
b. Does there appear to be any change in annual sales over time? Explain.

APPLYING THE CONCEPTS

2.48 *SELF Test* Movie companies need to predict the gross receipts of individual movies once the movie has debuted. The following results, stored in **PotterMovies**, are the first weekend gross, the U.S. gross, and the worldwide gross (in millions of dollars) of the six Harry Potter movies that debuted from 2001 to 2009.

Title	First Weekend	U.S. Gross	Worldwide Gross
Sorcerer's Stone	90.295	317.558	976.458
Chamber of Secrets	88.357	261.988	878.988
Prisoner of Azkaban	93.687	249.539	795.539
Goblet of Fire	102.335	290.013	896.013
Order of the Phoenix	77.108	292.005	938.469
Half-Blood Prince	77.836	301.460	934.601

Source: Data extracted from www.the-numbers.com/interactive/comp-Harry-Potter.php.

a. Construct a scatter plot with first weekend gross on the X axis and U.S. gross on the Y axis.
b. Construct a scatter plot with first weekend gross on the X axis and worldwide gross on the Y axis.
c. What can you say about the relationship between first weekend gross and U.S. gross and first weekend gross and worldwide gross?

2.49 The file **VeggieBurger** contains data on the calories and total fat (in grams per serving) for a sample of 12 veggie burgers.

Source: Data extracted from "Healthful Burgers That Taste Good," *Consumer Reports*, June 2008, p 8.

a. Construct a scatter plot with calories on the X axis and total fat on the Y axis.
b. What conclusions can you reach about the relationship between the calories and total fat in veggie burgers?

2.50 College basketball is big business, with coaches' salaries, revenues, and expenses in millions of dollars. The file **College Basketball** contains the coaches' salary and revenue for college basketball at 60 of the 65 schools that played in the 2009 NCAA men's basketball tournament (data extracted from "Compensation for Division 1 Men's Basketball Coaches," *USA Today*, April 2, 2010, p. 8C; and C. Isadore, "Nothing but Net: Basketball Dollars by School," money.cnn.com/2010/03/18/news/companies/basketball_profits/).

a. Do you think schools with higher revenues also have higher coaches' salaries?
b. Construct a scatter plot with revenue on the X axis and coaches' salaries on the Y axis.
c. Does the scatter plot confirm or contradict your answer to (a)?

2.51 College football players trying out for the NFL are given the Wonderlic standardized intelligence test. The file **Wonderlic** contains the average Wonderlic scores of football players trying out for the NFL and the graduation rate for football players at selected schools (data extracted from S. Walker, "The NFL's Smartest Team," *The Wall Street Journal*, September 30, 2005, pp. W1, W10).

a. Construct a scatter plot with average Wonderlic score on the X axis and graduation rate on the Y axis.
b. What conclusions can you reach about the relationship between the average Wonderlic score and graduation rate?

2.52 How have stocks performed in the past? The following table presents the data stored in **Stock Performance** that shows the performance of a broad measure of stocks (by percentage) for each decade from the 1830s through the 2000s:

Decade	Performance (%)
1830s	2.8
1840s	12.8
1850s	6.6
1860s	12.5
1870s	7.5
1880s	6.0
1890s	5.5
1900s	10.9
1910s	2.2
1920s	13.3
1930s	−2.2
1940s	9.6
1950s	18.2
1960s	8.3
1970s	6.6
1980s	16.6
1990s	17.6
2000s*	−0.5

* Through December 15, 2009.

Source: Data extracted from T. Lauricella, "Investors Hope the '10s" Beat the '00s," *The Wall Street Journal,* December 21, 2009, pp. C1, C2.

a. Construct a time-series plot of the stock performance from the 1830s to the 2000s.
b. Does there appear to be any pattern in the data?

2.53 According to the U.S. Census Bureau, the average price of a new home declined in 2008 and 2009. The file New Home Prices contains the average price paid for a new home from 1990 to 2009 (extracted from **www.census.gov**, March 15, 2010).
a. Construct a time-series plot of new home prices.
b. What pattern, if any, is present in the data?

2.54 The following table uses the data in Solar Power to show the yearly amount of solar power installed (in megawatts) in the United States from 2000 through 2008:

Year	Amount of Solar Power Installed
2000	18
2001	27
2002	44
2003	68
2004	83
2005	100
2006	140
2007	210
2008	250

Source: Data extracted from P. Davidson, "Glut of Rooftop Solar Systems Sinks Price," *USA Today,* January 13, 2009, p. 1B.

a. Construct a time-series plot for the yearly amount of solar power installed (in megawatts) in the United States.
b. What pattern, if any, is present in the data?

2.55 The file Audits contains the number of audits of corporations with assets of more than $250 million conducted by the Internal Revenue Service (data extracted from K. McCoy, "IRS Audits Big Firms Less Often," *USA Today,* April 15, 2010, p. 1B).
a. Construct a time-series plot.
b. What pattern, if any, is present in the data?

2.7 Organizing Multidimensional Data

In this chapter, you have learned methods for organizing and visualizing a single variable and methods for jointly organizing and visualizing two variables. More and more, businesses need to organize and visualize more than two variables to mine data to discover possible patterns and relationships that simpler explorations might miss. While any number of variables can be used, subject to limits of computation and storage, examples of more than three or four variables can be hard to interpret when simple tables are used to present results. Both Excel and Minitab can organize multidimensional data but the two applications have different strengths: Excel contains **PivotTables**, a type of interactive table that facilitates exploring multidimensional data, while Minitab has specialized statistical and graphing procedures (that are beyond the scope of this book to fully discuss).

Multidimensional Contingency Tables

A **multidimensional contingency table** tallies the responses of three or more categorical variables. In the simplest case of three categorical variables, each cell in the table contains the tallies of the third variable organized by the subgroups represented by the row and column variables.

Consider the Table 2.3 contingency table, which displays the type of fund and whether a fee is charged for the sample of 184 mutual funds. Figure 2.17 presents this table as an Excel PivotTable. Adding a third categorical variable, Risk, to the PivotTable, forms the new multidimensional PivotTable shown in Figure 2.18. The new table reveals that following patterns that cannot be seen in the original Table 2.3 contingency table:

- Although the ratio of fee–yes to fee–no bond funds for the intermediate government category seems to be about 2 to 3 (34 to 53), the ratio for above-average-risk intermediate government bond funds is about 1 to 1 (15 to 14) while the ratio for below average-risk funds is less than 1 to 3 (6 to 20).
- While the group "short-term corporate funds that charge a fee" has nearly equal numbers of above-average-risk, average-risk, and below-average-risk funds (7, 7, and 6), the group "intermediate government bond funds that charge a fee" contains many fewer below-average-risk funds (6) than average risk (13) or above-average (15) ones.
- The pattern of risk tallies differs between the fee–yes and fee–no funds in each of the bond fund categories.

Using methods presented in later chapters, you can confirm whether these first impressions are statistically significant.

FIGURE 2.17
Excel PivotTable version of the Table 2.3 contingency table

	A	B	C	D
1	PivotTable of Type and Fees			
2				
3	Count of Fees	Fees		
4	Type	Yes	No	Grand Total
5	Intermediate Government	34	53	87
6	Short Term Corporate	20	77	97
7	Grand Total	54	130	184

FIGURE 2.18
Excel and Minitab multidimensional contingency table of type, risk, and fees

	A	B	C	D	E
1	Multidimensional Contingency Table of Type, Risk, and Fees				
2					
3	Count of Fees		Fees		
4	Type	Risk	Yes	No	Grand Total
5	⊟ Intermediate Government	Above average	15	14	29
6		Average	13	19	32
7		Below average	6	20	26
8	Intermediate Government Total		34	53	87
9	⊟ Short Term Corporate	Above average	7	23	30
10		Average	7	30	37
11		Below average	6	24	30
12	Short Term Corporate Total		20	77	97
13	Grand Total		54	130	184

```
Tabulated statistics: Type, Risk, Fees

Rows: Type / Risk    Columns: Fees

                                     No   Yes   All
Intermediate Government
              Above average          14    15    29
              Average                19    13    32
              Below average          20     6    26
Short Term Corporate
              Above average          23     7    30
              Average                30     7    37
              Below average          24     6    30
All
              All                   130    54   184

Cell Contents:       Count
```

Adding Numerical Variables

Multidimensional contingency tables can contain numerical variables. When you add a numerical variable to a multidimensional analysis, you use categorical variables or variables that represent units of time for the rows and columns that will form the subgroups by which the numerical variable will be analyzed.

For example, Figure 2.19 on page 92 shows a table that cross classifies fees and type in which the cell amounts are the sums of the asset variable for each subgroup, and Figure 2.20 on page 92 shows the same table formatted to show percentages of assets. Comparing Figure 2.21—the table shown in Figure 2.17 but formatted for percentage of the overall total—to Figure 2.20 shows that the percentage of assets for the intermediate government funds by fee category does not mimic the fees category percentages.

FIGURE 2.19
Excel and Minitab multidimensional contingency table of type, fees, and sums of assets

	A	B	C	D
1	Contingency Table of Type, and Fees, and Sums of Assets			
2				
3	Sum of Assets	Fees		
4	Type	Yes	No	Grand Total
5	Intermediate Government	26252.7	56692.2	82944.9
6	Short Term Corporate	16842.1	67772.3	84614.4
7	Grand Total	43094.8	124464.5	167559.3

```
Tabulated statistics: Type, Fees

Rows: Type    Columns: Fees

                            No      Yes     All

Intermediate Government   56692   26253   82945
Short Term Corporate      67772   16842   84614
All                      124465   43095  167559

Cell Contents:  Assets  :  Sum
```

FIGURE 2.20
Multidimensional contingency table of type of fund, fee category, and percentages of assets

	A	B	C	D
1	Contingency Table of Type, and Fees, and Percentages of Assets			
2				
3	Sum of Assets	Fees		
4	Type	Yes	No	Grand Total
5	Intermediate Government	15.67%	33.83%	49.50%
6	Short Term Corporate	10.05%	40.45%	50.50%
7	Grand Total	25.72%	74.28%	100.00%

FIGURE 2.21
Contingency table of type and percentages of fees

	A	B	C	D
1	Contingency Table of Type and Percentages of Fees			
2				
3	Count of Fees	Fees		
4	Type	Yes	No	Grand Total
5	Intermediate Government	18.48%	28.80%	47.28%
6	Short Term Corporate	10.87%	41.85%	52.72%
7	Grand Total	29.35%	70.65%	100.00%

When you include a numerical variable, you typically compute one of the numerical descriptive statistics discussed in Sections 3.1 and 3.2. For example, Figure 2.22 shows a multidimensional contingency table in which the mean, or average 2009 rate of return for each of the subgroups, is computed.[1] This table reveals, among other things, that although there was virtually no difference in the 2009 return depending on whether a fee was charged, for funds with above-average risk, the return was much higher (4.89) for intermediate government funds that charged a fee than for funds that did not charge a fee (1.41).

[1] See Section 3.1 to learn more about the mean.

FIGURE 2.22
Excel and Minitab multidimensional contingency table of type, risk, fees, and the mean 2009 rates of return

	A	B	C	D	E
1	Contingency Table of Type, Risk, Fees and Means of 2009 Return				
2					
3	Average of Return 2009		Fees		
4	Type	Risk	Yes	No	Grand Total
5	⊟Intermediate Government	Above average	4.89	1.41	3.21
6		Average	3.39	3.74	3.60
7		Below average	5.98	7.17	6.90
8	Intermediate Government Total		4.51	4.42	4.45
9	⊟Short Term Corporate	Above average	15.99	12.42	13.25
10		Average	9.87	9.66	9.70
11		Below average	6.53	5.63	5.81
12	Short Term Corporate Total		11.01	9.23	9.60
13	Grand Total		6.92	7.27	7.16

```
Tabulated statistics: Type, Risk, Fees

Rows: Type / Risk    Columns: Fees

                                    No       Yes       All

Intermediate Government
              Above average        1.407    4.887    3.207
              Average              3.737    3.392    3.597
              Below average        7.170    5.983    6.896
Short Term Corporate
              Above average       12.417   15.986   13.250
              Average              9.663    9.871    9.703
              Below average        5.629    6.533    5.810
All
              All                  7.267    6.917    7.164

Cell Contents:  Return 2009  :  Mean
```

Problems for Section 2.7

APPLYING THE CONCEPTS

 2.56 For this problem, use the data in BondFunds2008.
a. Construct a table that tabulates type, fees, and risk.
b. What conclusions can you reach concerning differences among the types of mutual funds (intermediate government and short-term corporate), based on fees (yes or no) and the risk factor (low, average, and high)?
c. Compare the results of (b) with those shown in Figure 2.18.

2.57 For this problem, use the data in Mutual Funds.
a. Construct a table that tabulates category, objective, and fees.
b. What conclusions can you reach concerning differences among the categories of mutual funds (large cap, medium cap, and small cap), based on objective (growth and value) and fees (yes and no)?

2.58 For this problem, use the data in Mutual Funds.
a. Construct a table that tabulates category, fees, and risk.
b. What conclusions can you reach concerning differences among the categories of mutual funds (large cap, medium cap, and small cap), based on fees (yes and no) and the risk factor (low, average, and high)?

2.59 For this problem, use the data in Mutual Funds.
a. Construct a table that tabulates category, objective, fees, and risk.
b. What conclusions can you reach concerning differences among the categories of mutual funds (large cap, medium cap, and small cap), based on objective (growth and value), the risk factor (low, average, and high), and fees (yes and no)?
c. Which table do you think is easier to interpret, the one in this problem or the ones in Problems 2.56 and 2.57? Explain.

2.8 Misuses and Common Errors in Visualizing Data

Good graphical displays clearly and unambiguously reveal what the data convey. Unfortunately, many graphs presented in the media (broadcast, print, and online) are incorrect, misleading, or so unnecessarily complicated that they should never be used. To illustrate the misuse of graphs, the chart presented in Figure 2.23 is similar to one that was printed in *Time* magazine as part of an article on increasing exports of wine from Australia to the United States.

FIGURE 2.23

"Improper" display of Australian wine exports to the United States, in millions of gallons

Source: Based on S. Watterson, "Liquid Gold—Australians Are Changing the World of Wine. Even the French Seem Grateful," Time, November 22, 1999, p. 68.

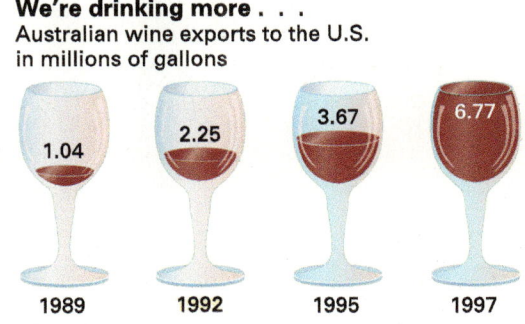

In Figure 2.23, the wineglass icon representing the 6.77 million gallons for 1997 does not appear to be almost twice the size of the wineglass icon representing the 3.67 million gallons for 1995, nor does the wineglass icon representing the 2.25 million gallons for 1992 appear to be twice the size of the wineglass icon representing the 1.04 million gallons for 1989. Part of the reason for this is that the three-dimensional wineglass icon is used to represent the two dimensions of exports and time. Although the wineglass presentation may catch the eye, the data should instead be presented in a summary table or a time-series plot.

In addition to the type of distortion created by the wineglass icons in the *Time* magazine graph displayed in Figure 2.23, improper use of the vertical and horizontal axes leads to distortions. Figure 2.24 presents another graph used in the same *Time* magazine article.

FIGURE 2.24

"Improper" display of amount of land planted with grapes for the wine industry

Source: Based on S. Watterson, "Liquid Gold—Australians Are Changing the World of Wine. Even the French Seem Grateful," Time, November 22, 1999, pp. 68–69.

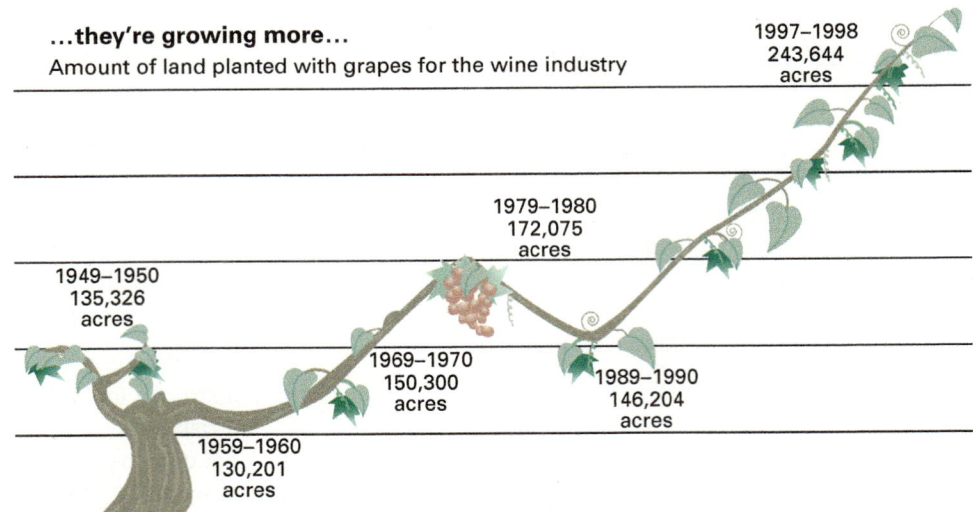

There are several problems in this graph. First, there is no zero point on the vertical axis. Second, the acreage of 135,326 for 1949–1950 is plotted above the acreage of 150,300 for 1969–1970. Third, it is not obvious that the difference between 1979–1980 and 1997–1998 (71,569 acres) is approximately 3.5 times the difference between 1979–1980 and 1969–1970 (21,775 acres). Fourth, there are no scale values on the horizontal axis. Years are plotted next to the acreage totals, not on the horizontal axis. Fifth, the values for the time dimension are not properly spaced along the horizontal axis. For example, the value for 1979–1980 is much closer to 1989–1990 than it is to 1969–1970. Other types of eye-catching displays that you typically see in magazines and newspapers often include information that is not necessary and just adds excessive clutter. Figure 2.25 represents one such display.

FIGURE 2.25

"Improper" plot of market share of soft drinks

Source: Based on Anne B. Carey and Sam Ward, "Coke Still Has Most Fizz," USA Today, May 10, 2000, p. 1B.

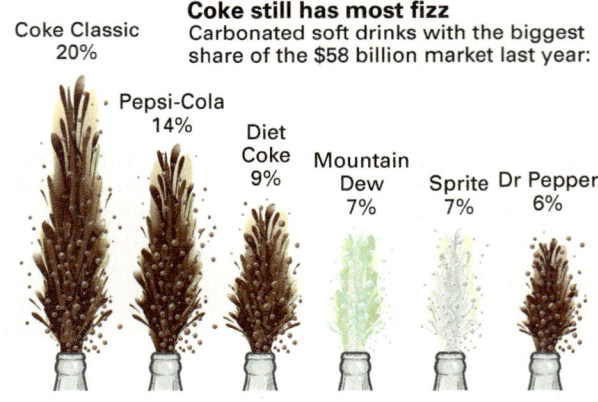

The graph in Figure 2.25 shows the products with the largest market share for soft drinks. The graph suffers from too much clutter, although it is designed to show the differences in market share among the soft drinks. The display of the fizz for each soft drink takes up too much of the graph relative to the data. The same information could be better conveyed with a bar chart or pie chart.

The following are some guidelines for developing good graphs:

- A graph should not distort the data.
- A graph should not contain **chartjunk**, unnecessary adornments that convey no useful information.
- Any two-dimensional graph should contain a scale for each axis.
- The scale on the vertical axis should begin at zero.

- All axes should be properly labeled.
- The graph should contain a title.
- The simplest possible graph should be used for a given set of data.

Often individuals unaware of how to construct appropriate graphs violate these guidelines. Some applications, including Excel, tempt you to create "pretty" charts that may be fancy in their designs but that represent unwise choices. For example, making a simple pie chart fancier by adding exploded 3D slices is unwise as this can complicate a viewer's interpretation of the data. Uncommon chart choices such as doughnut, radar, surface, bubble, cone, and pyramid charts may look visually striking, but in most cases they obscure the data.

Problems for Section 2.8

APPLYING THE CONCEPTS

2.60 (Student Project) Bring to class a chart from either a website, newspaper, or magazine published this month that you believe to be a poorly drawn representation of a numerical variable. Be prepared to submit the chart to the instructor with comments about why you believe it is inappropriate. Do you believe that the intent of the chart is to purposely mislead the reader? Also, be prepared to present and comment on this in class.

2.61 (Student Project) Bring to class a chart from either a website, newspaper, or magazine published this month that you believe to be a poorly drawn representation of a categorical variable. Be prepared to submit the chart to the instructor with comments about why you consider it inappropriate. Do you believe that the intent of the chart is to purposely mislead the reader? Also, be prepared to present and comment on this in class.

2.62 (Student Project) According to its home page, Swivel is "Swivel is a website where people share reports of charts and numbers. Businesses use Swivel to dashboard their metrics. Students use Swivel to find and share research data." Go to **www.swivel.com** and explore some of the various graphical displays.
a. Select a graphical display that you think does a good job revealing what the data convey. Discuss why you think it is a good graphical display.
b. Select a graphical display that you think needs a lot of improvement. Discuss why you think that it is a poorly constructed graphical display.

2.63 The following visual display contains an overembellished chart similar to one that appeared in *USA Today*, dealing with the average consumer's Valentine's Day spending ("USA Today Snapshots: The Price of Romance," *USA Today*, February 14, 2007, p. 1B).

a. Describe at least one good feature of this visual display.
b. Describe at least one bad feature of this visual display.
c. Redraw the graph, using the guidelines given on page 94 and above.

2.64 The following visual display contains an overembellished chart similar to one that appeared in *USA Today*, dealing with the estimated number of hours the typical American spends using various media ("USA Today Snapshots: Minding Their Media," *USA Today*, March 2, 2007, p. 1B).

a. Describe at least one good feature of this visual display.
b. Describe at least one bad feature of this visual display.
c. Redraw the graph, using the guidelines given on pages 94–95.

2.65 The following visual display contains an overembellished chart similar to one that appeared in *USA Today*, dealing with which card is safer to use ("USA Today Snapshots: Credit Card vs. Debit Card," *USA Today*, March 14, 2007, p. 1B).

a. Describe at least one good feature of this visual display.
b. Describe at least one bad feature of this visual display.
c. Redraw the graph, using the guidelines given on pages 94–95.

2.66 Professor Deanna Oxender Burgess of Florida Gulf Coast University conducted research on annual reports of corporations (see D. Rosato, "Worried About the Numbers? How About the Charts?" *The New York Times*, September 15, 2002, p. B7) and found that even slight distortions in a chart changed readers' perception of the information. Using Internet or library sources, select a corporation and study the most recent annual report. Find at least one chart in the report that you think needs improvement and develop an improved version of the chart. Explain why you believe the improved chart is better than the one included in the annual report.

2.67 Figures 2.1 and 2.3 show a bar chart and a pie chart for how adults pay their monthly bills (see pages 72 and 73).
a. Create an exploded pie chart, a doughnut chart, a cone chart, or a pyramid chart that shows how adults pay their monthly bills.
b. Which graphs do you prefer—the bar chart or pie chart or the exploded pie chart, doughnut chart, cone chart, and pyramid chart? Explain.

2.68 Figures 2.2 and 2.4 show a bar chart and a pie chart for the risk level for the bond fund data (see pages 73 and 74).
a. Create an exploded pie chart, a doughnut chart, a cone chart, and a pyramid chart that shows the risk level of bond funds.
b. Which graphs do you prefer—the bar chart or pie chart or the exploded pie chart, doughnut chart, cone chart, and pyramid chart? Explain.

USING STATISTICS @ Choice Is Yours, Part I Revisited

In the Using Statistics scenario, you were hired by the Choice Is Yours investment company to assist clients who seek to invest in mutual funds. A sample of 184 bond mutual funds was selected, and information on the funds and past performance history was recorded. For each of the 184 funds, data were collected on eight variables. With so much information, visualizing all these numbers required the use of properly selected graphical displays.

From bar charts and pie charts, you were able to illustrate that about one-third of the funds were classified as having below-average risk, about one-third had average risk, and about one-third had above-average risk. Cross tabulations of the funds by whether the fund charged a fee and whether the fund invested in intermediate government bonds or short-term corporate bonds revealed that intermediate government bond funds are more likely to charge fees. After constructing histograms on the 2009 return, you were able to conclude that the returns were much higher for the short-term corporate bond funds than for the intermediate government bonds. The return for intermediate government bond funds is concentrated between 0 and 10, whereas the return for the short-term corporate bond funds is concentrated between 5 and 15.

With these insights, you can inform your clients about how the different funds performed. Of course, past performance history does not guarantee future performance. In fact, if you look at returns in 2008, stored in BondFunds2008, you will discover that the returns were much *lower* for the short-term corporate bond funds than for the intermediate government bonds!

Using graphical methods such as these is an important first step in summarizing and interpreting data. Although the proper display of data (as discussed in Section 2.8) helps to avoid ambiguity, graphical methods always contain a certain degree of subjectivity. Next, you will need descriptive statistics to further analyze the past performance of the mutual funds. Chapter 3 presents descriptive statistics (e.g., mean, median, and mode).

SUMMARY

Organizing and visualizing data involves using various tables and charts to help draw conclusions about data. In several different chapter examples, tables and charts helped you reach conclusions about how people prefer to pay their bills and about the cost of restaurant meals in a city and its suburbs; they also provided some insights about the sample of bond mutual funds in the Using Statistics scenario.

The tables and charts you use depend on the type of data you have. Table 2.19 summarizes the proper choices for the type of data and the tables and charts discussed in this chapter. In Chapter 3 you will learn about a variety of descriptive statistics useful for data analysis and interpretation.

TABLE 2.19
Selecting Tables and Charts

Type of Analysis	Type of Data	
	Numerical	**Categorical**
Organizing data	Ordered array, frequency distribution, relative frequency distribution, percentage distribution, cumulative percentage distribution (Section 2.3)	Summary table, contingency table (Section 2.2)
Visualizing one variable	Stem-and-leaf display, histogram, percentage polygon, cumulative percentage polygon (ogive) (Section 2.5)	Bar chart, pie chart, Pareto chart (Section 2.4)
Visualizing two variables	Scatter plot, time-series plot (Section 2.6)	Side-by-side bar chart (Section 2.4)
Organizing multidimensional data	Multidimensional tables (Section 2.7)	Multidimensional tables (Section 2.7)

KEY EQUATIONS

Determining the Class Interval Width

$$\text{Interval width} = \frac{\text{highest value} - \text{lowest value}}{\text{number of classes}} \quad (2.1)$$

Computing the Proportion or Relative Frequency

$$\text{Proportion} = \text{relative frequency} = \frac{\text{number of values in each class}}{\text{total number of values}} \quad (2.2)$$

KEY TERMS

- analyze
- bar chart
- cells
- chartjunk
- classes
- class boundaries
- class interval
- class interval width
- class midpoints
- collect
- contingency table
- cumulative percentage distribution
- cumulative percentage polygon (ogive)
- data collection
- DCOVA
- define
- frequency distribution
- histogram
- multidimensional contingency table
- ogive (cumulative percentage polygon)
- ordered array
- organize
- Pareto chart
- Pareto principle
- percentage distribution
- percentage polygon
- pie chart
- PivotTable
- primary data source
- proportion
- relative frequency
- relative frequency distribution
- scatter plot
- secondary data source
- side-by-side bar chart
- stacked
- stem-and-leaf display
- summary table
- time-series plot
- unstacked
- visualize

CHAPTER REVIEW PROBLEMS

CHECKING YOUR UNDERSTANDING

2.69 How do histograms and polygons differ in their construction and use?

2.70 Why would you construct a summary table?

2.71 What are the advantages and disadvantages of using a bar chart, a pie chart, and a Pareto chart?

2.72 Compare and contrast the bar chart for categorical data with the histogram for numerical data.

2.73 What is the difference between a time-series plot and a scatter plot?

2.74 Why is it said that the main feature of a Pareto chart is its ability to separate the "vital few" from the "trivial many"?

2.75 What are the three different ways to break down the percentages in a contingency table?

2.76 How can a multidimensional table differ from a two variable contingency table?

2.77 What type of insights can you gain from a three-way table that are not available in a two-way table?

APPLYING THE CONCEPTS

2.78 The following summary table presents the breakdown of the cost of attending a four-year university degree program:

Revenue Category	Percentage (%)	
Tuition and fees	66.5	
Basic tuition		34.3
Lab use		15.1
Medical insurance		10.0
Technology fees		7.1
Room and board	24.4	
Room		11.3
Meal plan		7.6
Internet		5.5
Personal expenses, including transportation	6.27	
Books and supplies	2.83	

a. Using the four categories tuition and fees, room and board, personal expenses, and book supplies, construct a bar chart, a pie chart, and a Pareto chart.

b. Using the four subcategories of tuition and three subcategories of room and board, along with the personal expenses and book and supplies categories, construct a Pareto chart.

c. Based on the results of (a) and (b), what conclusions can you reach concerning the cost of education? Do any of these results surprise you?

2.79 The following table represents the market share (in number of movies, gross in millions of dollars, and in number of tickets sold in millions) of each type of movie in 2009:

Type	Number	Gross ($ millions)	Tickets (millions)
Based on book/short story	66	2042.9	272.4
Based on comic/graphic novel	6	376.2	50.2
Based on factual book/article	5	280.7	37.4
Based on game	3	9.2	1.2
Based on musical/opera	1	13.7	1.8
Based on play	8	172.0	22.9
Based on real life events	95	334.9	44.7
Based on toy	1	150.2	20.0
Based on TV	7	267.5	35.7
Compilation	1	0.6	0.1
Original screenplay	203	4,335.7	578.1
Remake	18	422.6	56.3
Sequel	20	2,064.2	275.2
Spin-off	1	179.9	24.0

Source: Data extracted from **www.the-numbers.com/market/Sources2009.php**.

a. Construct a bar chart, a pie chart, and a Pareto chart for the number of movies, gross (in millions of dollars), and number of tickets sold (in millions).
b. What conclusions can you reach about the market share of the different types of movies in 2009?

2.80 A survey was conducted from 665 consumer magazines on the practices of their websites. The results are summarized in a copyediting table and a fact-checking table:

Copyediting as Compared to Print Content	Percentage
As rigorous	41
Less rigorous	48
Not copyedited	11

a. For copyediting, construct a bar chart, a pie chart, and a Pareto chart.
b. Which graphical method do you think is best for portraying these data?

Fact Checking as Compared to Print Content	Percentage
Same	57
Less rigorous	27
Online not fact checked	8
Neither online nor print is fact-checked	8

Source: Data extracted from S. Clifford, "Columbia Survey Finds a Slack Editing Process of Magazine Web Sites," *The New York Times*, March 1, 2010, p. B6.

c. For fact checking, construct a bar chart, a pie chart, and a Pareto chart.
d. Which graphical method do you think is best for portraying these data?
e. What conclusions can you reach concerning copy editing and fact checking of print and online consumer magazines?

2.81 The owner of a restaurant that serves Continental-style entrées has the business objective of learning more about the patterns of patron demand during the Friday-to-Sunday weekend time period. Data were collected from 630 customers on the type of entrée ordered and organized in the following table:

Type of Entrée	Number Served
Beef	187
Chicken	103
Mixed	30
Duck	25
Fish	122
Pasta	63
Shellfish	74
Veal	26
Total	630

a. Construct a percentage summary table for the types of entrées ordered.
b. Construct a bar chart, a pie chart, and a Pareto chart for the types of entrées ordered.
c. Do you prefer using a Pareto chart or a pie chart for these data? Why?
d. What conclusions can the restaurant owner reach concerning demand for different types of entrées?

2.82 Suppose that the owner of the restaurant in Problem 2.81 also wanted to study the demand for dessert during the same time period. She decided that in addition to studying whether a dessert was ordered, she would also study the gender of the individual and whether a beef entrée was ordered. Data were collected from 600 customers and organized in the following contingency tables:

DESSERT ORDERED	GENDER		
	Male	Female	Total
Yes	40	96	136
No	240	224	464
Total	280	320	600

DESSERT ORDERED	BEEF ENTRÉE		
	Yes	No	Total
Yes	71	65	136
No	116	348	464
Total	187	413	600

a. For each of the two contingency tables, construct contingency tables of row percentages, column percentages, and total percentages.
b. Which type of percentage (row, column, or total) do you think is most informative for each gender? For beef entrée? Explain.
c. What conclusions concerning the pattern of dessert ordering can the restaurant owner reach?

2.83 The following data represent the pounds per capita of fresh food and packaged food consumed in the United States, Japan, and Russia in 2009.

FRESH FOOD	United States	Japan	Russia
Eggs, nuts, and beans	88	94	88
Fruit	124	126	88
Meat and seafood	197	146	125
Vegetables	194	278	335

PACKAGED FOOD	United States	Japan	Russia
Bakery goods	108	53	144
Dairy products	298	147	127
Pasta	12	32	16
Processed, frozen, dried and chilled food, and ready-to-eat meals	183	251	70
Sauces, dressings, and condiments	63	75	49
Snacks and candy	47	19	24
Soup and canned food	77	17	25

Source: Data extracted from H. Fairfield, "Factory Food," *The New York Times*, April 4, 2010, p. BU5.

a. Construct a bar chart and a pie chart for the different types of fresh foods consumed in the three different countries.
b. Construct a bar chart and a pie chart for the different types of packaged foods consumed in the three different countries.
c. What conclusions can you reach concerning differences between the United States, Japan, and Russia in the fresh foods and packaged foods consumed?

2.84 In 2000, a growing number of warranty claims on Firestone tires sold on Ford SUVs prompted Firestone and Ford to issue a major recall. An analysis of warranty claims data helped identify which models to recall. A breakdown of 2,504 warranty claims based on tire size is given in the following table:

Tire Size	Number of Warranty Claims
23575R15	2,030
311050R15	137
30950R15	82
23570R16	81
331250R15	58
25570R16	54
Others	62

Source: Data extracted from Robert L. Simison, "Ford Steps Up Recall Without Firestone," *The Wall Street Journal*, August 14, 2000, p. A3.

The 2,030 warranty claims for the 23575R15 tires can be categorized into ATX models and Wilderness models. The type of incident leading to a warranty claim, by model type, is summarized in the following table:

Incident Type	ATX Model Warranty Claims	Wilderness Warranty Claims
Tread separation	1,365	59
Blowout	77	41
Other/unknown	422	66
Total	1,864	166

Source: Data extracted from Robert L. Simison, "Ford Steps Up Recall Without Firestone," *The Wall Street Journal*, August 14, 2000, p. A3.

a. Construct a Pareto chart for the number of warranty claims by tire size. What tire size accounts for most of the claims?
b. Construct a pie chart to display the percentage of the total number of warranty claims for the 23575R15 tires that come from the ATX model and Wilderness model. Interpret the chart.

c. Construct a Pareto chart for the type of incident causing the warranty claim for the ATX model. Does a certain type of incident account for most of the claims?
d. Construct a Pareto chart for the type of incident causing the warranty claim for the Wilderness model. Does a certain type of incident account for most of the claims?

2.85 One of the major measures of the quality of service provided by an organization is the speed with which the organization responds to customer complaints. A large family-held department store selling furniture and flooring, including carpet, had undergone a major expansion in the past several years. In particular, the flooring department had expanded from 2 installation crews to an installation supervisor, a measurer, and 15 installation crews. A business objective of the company was to reduce the time between when the complaint is received and when it is resolved. During a recent year, the company received 50 complaints concerning carpet installation. The data from the 50 complaints, stored in **Furniture**, represent the number of days between the receipt of the complaint and the resolution of the complaint:

```
54    5   35  137   31  27  152   2  123  81  74  27
11   19  126  110  110  29   61  35   94  31  26   5
12    4  165   32   29  28   29  26   25   1  14  13
13   10    5   27    4  52   30  22   36  26  20  23
33   68
```

a. Construct a frequency distribution and a percentage distribution.
b. Construct a histogram and a percentage polygon.
c. Construct a cumulative percentage distribution and plot a cumulative percentage polygon (ogive).
d. On the basis of the results of (a) through (c), if you had to tell the president of the company how long a customer should expect to wait to have a complaint resolved, what would you say? Explain.

2.86 The file **DomesticBeer** contains the percentage alcohol, number of calories per 12 ounces, and number of carbohydrates (in grams) per 12 ounces for 139 of the best-selling domestic beers in the United States.
Source: Data extracted from www.Beer100.com, March 18, 2010.
a. Construct a percentage histogram for each of the three variables.
b. Construct three scatter plots: percentage alcohol versus calories, percentage alcohol versus carbohydrates, and calories versus carbohydrates.
c. Discuss what you learn from studying the graphs in (a) and (b).

2.87 The file **CigaretteTax** contains the state cigarette tax ($) for each state as of December 31, 2009.
a. Construct an ordered array.
b. Plot a percentage histogram.
c. What conclusions can you reach about the differences in the state cigarette tax between the states?

2.88 The file **SavingsRate-MMCD** contains the yields for a money market account and a five-year certificate of deposit (CD) for 25 banks in the United States, as of March 29, 2010.
Source: Data extracted from www.Bankrate.com, March 29, 2010.
a. Construct a stem-and-leaf display for each variable.
b. Construct a scatter plot of money market account versus five-year CD.
c. What is the relationship between the money market rate and the five-year CD rate?

2.89 The file **CEO-Compensation** includes the total compensation (in millions of $) of CEOs of 197 large public companies and the investment return in 2009.
Source: Data extracted from D. Leonard, "Bargains in the Boardroom," *The New York Times*, April 4, 2010, pp. BU1, BU7, BU10, BU11.
a. Construct a frequency distribution and a percentage distribution.
b. Construct a histogram and a percentage polygon.
c. Construct a cumulative percentage distribution and plot a cumulative percentage polygon (ogive).
d. Based on (a) through (c), what conclusions can you reach concerning CEO compensation in 2009?
e. Construct a scatter plot of total compensation and investment return in 2009.
f. What is the relationship between the total compensation and investment return in 2009?

2.90 Studies conducted by a manufacturer of Boston and Vermont asphalt shingles have shown product weight to be a major factor in customers' perception of quality. Moreover, the weight represents the amount of raw materials being used and is therefore very important to the company from a cost standpoint. The last stage of the assembly line packages the shingles before the packages are placed on wooden pallets. The variable of interest is the weight in pounds of the pallet which for most brands holds 16 squares of shingles. The company expects pallets of its Boston brand-name shingles to weigh at least 3,050 pounds but less than 3,260 pounds. For the company's Vermont brand-name shingles, pallets should weigh at least 3,600 pounds but less than 3,800. Data are collected from a sample of 368 pallets of Boston shingles and 330 pallets of Vermont shingles and stored in **Pallet**.
a. For the Boston shingles, construct a frequency distribution and a percentage distribution having eight class intervals, using 3,015, 3,050, 3,085, 3,120, 3,155, 3,190, 3,225, 3,260, and 3,295 as the class boundaries.
b. For the Vermont shingles, construct a frequency distribution and a percentage distribution having seven class intervals, using 3,550, 3,600, 3,650, 3,700, 3,750, 3,800, 3,850, and 3,900 as the class boundaries.
c. Construct percentage histograms for the Boston shingles and for the Vermont shingles.
d. Comment on the distribution of pallet weights for the Boston and Vermont shingles. Be sure to identify the percentage of pallets that are underweight and overweight.

2.91 What was the average price of a room at two-star, three-star, and four-star hotels in cities around the world in 2009? The file `HotelPrices` contains the prices in English pounds (about US $1.57 as of October 2010). Complete the following for two-star, three-star, and four-star hotels.

Source: Data extracted from www.hotels.com/press/hotel-price-index-2009-h2.html.

a. Construct a frequency distribution and a percentage distribution.
b. Construct a histogram and a percentage polygon.
c. Construct a cumulative percentage distribution and plot a cumulative percentage polygon (ogive).
d. What conclusions can you reach about the cost of two-star, three-star, and four-star hotels?
e. Construct separate scatter plots of the cost of two-star hotels versus three-star hotels, two-star hotels versus four-star hotels, and three-star hotels versus four-star hotels.
f. What conclusions can you reach about the relationship of the price of two-star, three-star, and four-star hotels?

2.92 The file `Protein` contains calorie and cholesterol information concerning popular protein foods (fresh red meats, poultry, and fish).

Source: U.S. Department of Agriculture.

a. Construct a percentage histogram for the number of calories.
b. Construct a percentage histogram for the amount of cholesterol.
c. What conclusions can you reach from your analyses in (a) and (b)?

2.93 The file `Gas Prices` contains the monthly average price of gasoline in the United States from January 1, 2006, to March 1, 2010. Prices are in dollars per gallon.

Source: "Energy Information Administration," www.eia.doe.gov, March 26, 2010.

a. Construct a time-series plot.
b. What pattern, if any, is present in the data?

2.94 The following data (stored in `Drink`) represent the amount of soft drink in a sample of 50 consecutively filled 2-liter bottles. The results are listed horizontally in the order of being filled:

2.109 2.086 2.066 2.075 2.065 2.057 2.052 2.044 2.036 2.038
2.031 2.029 2.025 2.029 2.023 2.020 2.015 2.014 2.013 2.014
2.012 2.012 2.012 2.010 2.005 2.003 1.999 1.996 1.997 1.992
1.994 1.986 1.984 1.981 1.973 1.975 1.971 1.969 1.966 1.967
1.963 1.957 1.951 1.951 1.947 1.941 1.941 1.938 1.908 1.894

a. Construct a time-series plot for the amount of soft drink on the Y axis and the bottle number (going consecutively from 1 to 50) on the X axis.
b. What pattern, if any, is present in these data?

c. If you had to make a prediction about the amount of soft drink filled in the next bottle, what would you predict?
d. Based on the results of (a) through (c), explain why it is important to construct a time-series plot and not just a histogram, as was done in Problem 2.45 on page 86.

2.95 The S&P 500 Index tracks the overall movement of the stock market by considering the stock prices of 500 large corporations. The file `Stock Prices` contains weekly data for this index as well as the daily closing stock prices for three companies from January 2, 2009, to December 28, 2009. The following variables are included:

WEEK—Week ending on date given
S&P—Weekly closing value for the S&P 500 Index
GE—Weekly closing stock price for General Electric
DISC—Weekly closing stock price for Discovery Communications
AAPL—Weekly closing stock price for Apple

Source: Data extracted from finance.yahoo.com, March 26, 2010.

a. Construct time-series plots for the weekly closing values of the S&P 500 Index, General Electric, Discovery, and Apple.
b. Explain any patterns present in the plots.
c. Write a short summary of your findings.

2.96 (Class Project) Have each student in the class respond to the question "Which carbonated soft drink do you most prefer?" so that the instructor can tally the results into a summary table.

a. Convert the data to percentages and construct a Pareto chart.
b. Analyze the findings.

2.97 (Class Project) Let each student in the class be cross-classified on the basis of gender (male, female) and current employment status (yes, no) so that the instructor can tally the results.

a. Construct a table with either row or column percentages, depending on which you think is more informative.
b. What would you conclude from this study?
c. What other variables would you want to know regarding employment in order to enhance your findings?

REPORT WRITING EXERCISES

2.98 Referring to the results from Problem 2.90 on page 101 concerning the weight of Boston and Vermont shingles, write a report that evaluates whether the weight of the pallets of the two types of shingles are what the company expects. Be sure to incorporate tables and charts into the report.

2.99 Referring to the results from Problem 2.84 on page 100 concerning the warranty claims on Firestone tires, write a report that evaluates warranty claims on Firestone tires sold on Ford SUVs. Be sure to incorporate tables and charts into the report.

TEAM PROJECT

The file **Bond Funds** contains information regarding nine variables from a sample of 184 mutual funds:

  Fund number—Identification number for each bond fund
  Type—Bond fund type (intermediate government or short-term corporate)
  Assets—In millions of dollars
  Fees—Sales charges (no or yes)
  Expense ratio—Ratio of expenses to net assets in percentage
  Return 2009—Twelve-month return in 2009
  Three-year return—Annualized return, 2007–2009
  Five-year return—Annualized return, 2005–2009
  Risk—Risk-of-loss factor of the mutual fund (below average, average, or above average)

2.100 For this problem, consider the expense ratio.
a. Construct a percentage histogram.
b. Using a single graph, plot percentage polygons of the expense ratio for bond funds that have fees and bond funds that do not have fees.
c. What conclusions about the expense ratio can you reach, based on the results of (a) and (b)?

2.101 For this problem, consider the three-year annualized return from 2007 to 2009.
a. Construct a percentage histogram.
b. Using a single graph, plot percentage polygons of the three-year annualized return from 2007 to 2009 for intermediate government funds and short-term corporate funds.
c. What conclusions about the three-year annualized return from 2007 to 2009 can you reach, based on the results of (a) and (b)?

2.102 For this problem, consider the five-year annualized return from 2005 to 2009.
a. Construct a percentage histogram.
b. Using a single graph, plot percentage polygons of the five-year annualized return from 2005 to 2009 for intermediate government funds and short-term corporate funds.
c. What conclusions about the five-year annualized return from 2005 to 2009 can you reach, based on the results of (a) and (b)?

STUDENT SURVEY DATABASE

2.103 Problem 1.27 on the page 44 describes a survey of 62 undergraduate students (stored in **UndergradSurvey**). For these data, construct all the appropriate tables and charts and write a report summarizing your conclusions.

2.104 Problem 2.103 describes a survey of 62 undergraduate students (stored in **UndergradSurvey**).
a. Select a sample of undergraduate students at your school and conduct a similar survey for those students.
b. For the data collected in (a), construct all the appropriate tables and charts and write a report summarizing your conclusions.
c. Compare the results of (b) to those of Problem 2.103.

2.105 Problem 1.28 on the page 45 describes a survey of 44 graduate students (see the file **GradSurvey**). For these data, construct all appropriate tables and charts and write a report summarizing your conclusions.

2.106 Problem 2.105 describes a survey of 44 MBA students (stored in **GradSurvey**).
a. Select a sample of MBA students in your MBA program and conduct a similar survey for those students.
b. For the data collected in (a), construct all the appropriate tables and charts and write a report summarizing your conclusions.
c. Compare the results of (b) to those of Problem 2.105.

MANAGING ASHLAND MULTICOMM SERVICES

Recently, Ashland MultiComm Services has been criticized for its inadequate customer service in responding to questions and problems about its telephone, cable television, and Internet services. Senior management has established a task force charged with the business objective of improving customer service. In response to this charge, the task force collected data about the types of customer service errors, the cost of customer service errors, and the cost of wrong billing errors. It found the following data:

Types of Customer Service Errors

Type of Errors	Frequency
Incorrect accessory	27
Incorrect address	42
Incorrect contact phone	31
Invalid wiring	9
On-demand programming error	14
Subscription not ordered	8
Suspension error	15
Termination error	22
Website access error	30
Wrong billing	137
Wrong end date	17
Wrong number of connections	19
Wrong price quoted	20
Wrong start date	24
Wrong subscription type	33
Total	448

Cost of Customer Service Errors in the Past Year

Type of Errors	Cost ($ thousands)
Incorrect accessory	17.3
Incorrect address	62.4
Incorrect contact phone	21.3
Invalid wiring	40.8
On-demand programming errors	38.8
Subscription not ordered	20.3
Suspension error	46.8
Termination error	50.9
Website access errors	60.7
Wrong billing	121.7
Wrong end date	40.9
Wrong number of connections	28.1
Wrong price quoted	50.3
Wrong start date	40.8
Wrong subscription type	60.1
Total	701.2

Type and Cost of Wrong Billing Errors

Type of Wrong Billing Errors	Cost ($ thousands)
Declined or held transactions	7.6
Incorrect account number	104.3
Invalid verification	9.8
Total	121.7

1. Review these data (stored in AMS2-1). Identify the variables that are important in describing the customer service problems. For each variable you identify, construct the graphical representation you think is most appropriate and explain your choice. Also, suggest what other information concerning the different types of errors would be useful to examine. Offer possible courses of action for either the task force or management to take that would support the goal of improving customer service.

2. As a follow-up activity, the task force decides to collect data to study the pattern of calls to the help desk (stored in AMS2-2). Analyze these data and present your conclusions in a report.

DIGITAL CASE

In the Using Statistics scenario, you were asked to gather information to help make wise investment choices. Sources for such information include brokerage firms, investment counselors, and other financial services firms. Apply your knowledge about the proper use of tables and charts in this Digital Case about the claims of foresight and excellence by an Ashland-area financial services firm.

Open **EndRunGuide.pdf,** which contains the EndRun Financial Services "Guide to Investing." Review the guide, paying close attention to the company's investment claims and supporting data and then answer the following.

1. How does the presentation of the general information about EndRun in this guide affect your perception of the business?

2. Is EndRun's claim about having more winners than losers a fair and accurate reflection of the quality of its investment service? If you do not think that the claim is a fair and accurate one, provide an alternate presentation that you think is fair and accurate.

3. Review the discussion about EndRun's "Big Eight Difference" and then open and examine Mutual Funds, a sample of mutual funds. Are there any other relevant data from that file that could have been included in the Big Eight table? How would the new data alter your perception of EndRun's claims?

4. EndRun is proud that all Big Eight funds have gained in value over the past five years. Do you agree that EndRun should be proud of its selections? Why or why not?

REFERENCES

1. Huff, D., *How to Lie with Statistics* (New York: Norton, 1954).
2. Levine, D. and D. Stephan, "Teaching Introductory Business Statistics Using the DCOVA Framework," *Decision Science Journal of Innovative Education*, January 2011.
3. *Microsoft Excel 2010* (Redmond, WA: Microsoft Corporation, 2010).
4. *Minitab Release 16* (State College, PA: Minitab, Inc., 2010).
5. Tufte, E. R., *Beautiful Evidence* (Cheshire, CT: Graphics Press, 2006).
6. Tufte, E. R., *Envisioning Information* (Cheshire, CT: Graphics Press, 1990).
7. Tufte, E. R., *The Visual Display of Quantitative Information*, 2nd ed. (Cheshire, CT: Graphics Press, 2002).
8. Tufte, E. R., *Visual Explanations* (Cheshire, CT: Graphics Press, 1997).
9. Wainer, H., *Visual Revelations: Graphical Tales of Fate and Deception from Napoleon Bonaparte to Ross Perot* (New York: Copernicus/Springer-Verlag, 1997).

CHAPTER 2 EXCEL GUIDE

EG2.2 ORGANIZING CATEGORICAL DATA

The Summary Table

PHStat2 Use **One-Way Tables & Charts** to create a summary table. For example, to create a summary table similar to Table 2.2 on page 60, open to the **DATA worksheet** of the **Bond Funds workbook**. Select **PHStat → Descriptive Statistics → One-Way Tables & Charts**. In the procedure's dialog box (shown below):

1. Click **Raw Categorical Data**.
2. Enter **I1:I185** as the **Raw Data Cell Range** and check **First cell contains label**.
3. Enter a **Title**, check **Percentage Column**, and click **OK**.

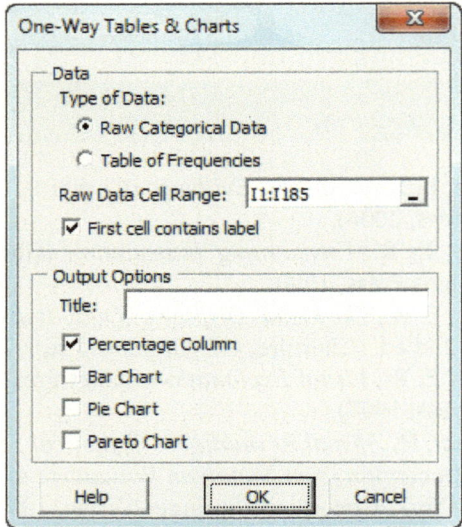

The DATA worksheet contains unsummarized data. For data that have already been tallied into categories, click **Table of Frequencies**.

In-Depth Excel For data that need to be tallied, use the PivotTable feature to create a summary table. (For the case in which data have already been tallied, use the **SUMMARY _SIMPLE worksheet** of the **Chapter 2 workbook** as a model for creating a summary table.)

For example, to create a summary table similar to Table 2.2 on page 60, open to the **DATA worksheet** of the **Bond Funds workbook** and select **Insert → PivotTable**. In the Create PivotTable dialog box (shown at the top of the next column):

1. Click **Select a table or range** and enter **I1:I185** as the **Table/Range** cell range.
2. Click **New Worksheet** and then click **OK**.

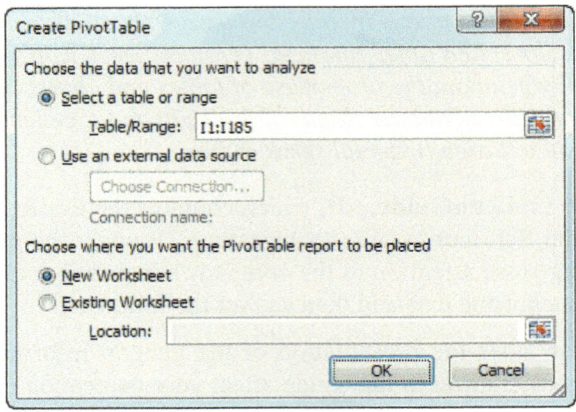

In the PivotTable Field List task pane (shown below):

3. Check **Risk** in the **Choose fields to add to report** box.
4. Drag the checked **Risk** label and drop it in the **Row Labels** box. Drag a second copy of this checked **Risk** label and drop it in the Σ **Values** box. This second label changes to **Count of Risk** to indicate that a count, or tally, of the occurrences of each risk category will be displayed in the PivotTable.

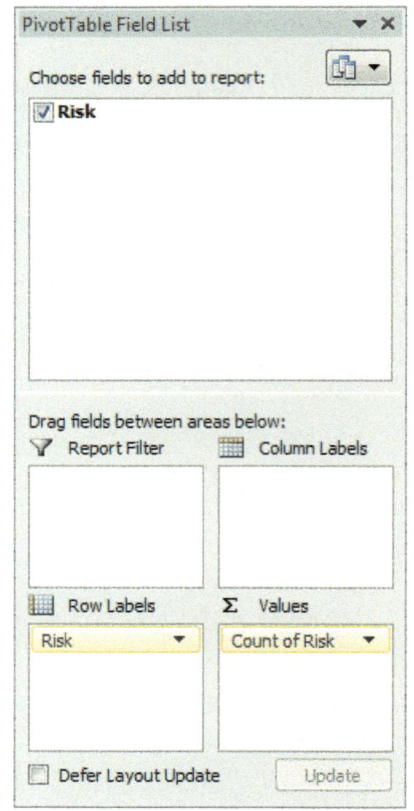

In the PivotTable being created:

5. Right-click and then click **PivotTable Options** in the shortcut menu that appears.

In the PivotTable Options dialog box (shown below):

6. Click the **Layout & Format** tab.
7. Check **For empty cells show** and enter **0** as its value. Leave all other settings unchanged.
8. Click **OK** to complete the PivotTable.

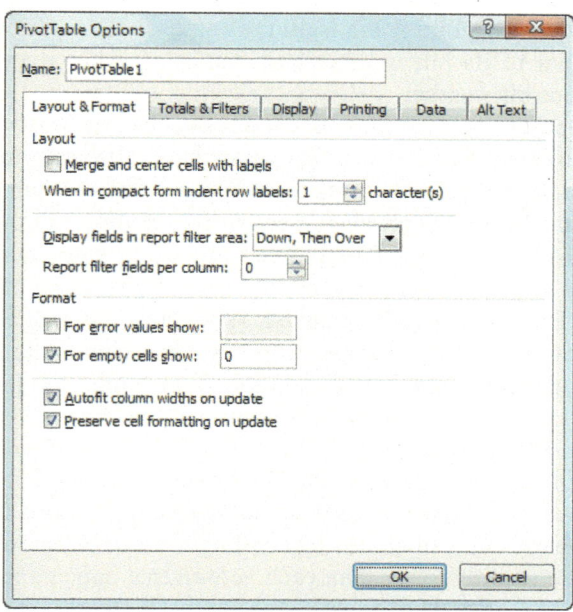

To add a column for the percentage frequency:

9. Enter **Percentage** in cell C4. Enter the formula =B5/B$8 in cell **C5** and copy it down through row 7.
10. Select cell range **C5:E5**, right-click, and select **Format Cells** in the shortcut menu.
11. In the **Number** tab of the Format Cells dialog box, select **Percentage** as the **Category** and click **OK**.
12. Adjust cell borders, if desired (see Appendix F).

The Contingency Table

PHStat2 Use **Two-Way Tables & Charts** to create a contingency table for data that need to be tallied. For example, to create the Table 2.3 contingency table on page 61, open to the **DATA worksheet** of the **Bond Funds workbook**. Select **PHStat** → **Descriptive Statistics** →

Two-Way Tables & Charts. In the procedure's dialog box (shown below):

1. Enter **B1:B185** as the **Row Variable Cell Range**.
2. Enter **D1:D185** as the **Column Variable Cell Range**.
3. Check **First cell in each range contains label**.
4. Enter a **Title** and click **OK**.

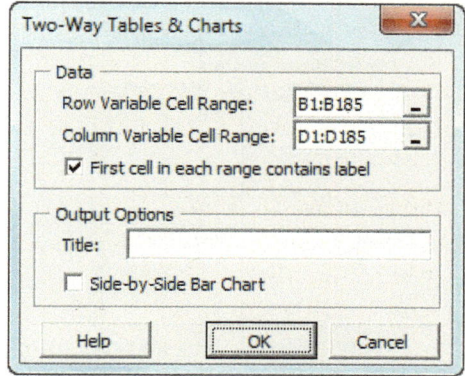

After the procedure creates the PivotTable, rearrange the order of the "No" and "Yes" columns:

5. Click the **Fees** drop-down list in cell B3 and select **Sort Z to A**.

In-Depth Excel For data that need to be tallied, use the PivotTable feature to create a contingency table. (For the case in which data have already been tallied, use the **CONTINGENCY_SIMPLE worksheet** of the **Chapter 2 workbook** as a model for creating a contingency table.) For example, to create the Table 2.3 contingency table on page 61, open to the **DATA worksheet** of the **Bond Funds workbook**. Select **Insert** → **PivotTable**. In the Create PivotTable dialog box:

1. Click **Select a table or range** and enter **B1:D185** as the **Table/Range** cell range. (Although **Type** is in column B and **Fees** is in column D, Excel does not allow you to enter a range comprised of nonadjacent columns.)
2. Click **New Worksheet** and then click **OK**.

In the PivotTable Field List task pane (shown at the top of page 108):

3. Check **Type** and **Fees** in the **Choose fields to add to report** box.
4. Drag the checked **Type** label and drop it in the **Row Labels** box.
5. Drag a second copy of the check **Type** label and drop it in the Σ **Values** box. (This label changes to **Count of Type**.) Then drag the checked **Fees** label and drop it in the **Column Labels** area.

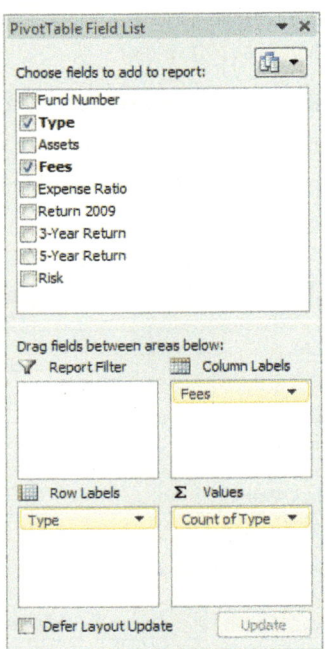

In the PivotTable being created:

6. Click the **Fees** drop-down list in cell B3 and select **Sort Z to A** to rearrange the order of the "No" and "Yes" columns.
7. Right-click and then click **PivotTable Options** in the shortcut menu that appears.

In the PivotTable Options dialog box:

8. Click the **Layout & Format** tab.
9. Check **For empty cells show** and enter **0** as its value. Leave all other settings unchanged.
10. Click the **Total & Filters** tab.
11. Check **Show grand totals for columns** and **Show grand totals for rows**.
12. Click **OK** to complete the table.

EG2.3 ORGANIZING NUMERICAL DATA

Stacked and Unstacked Data

PHStat2 Use **Stack Data** or **Unstack Data** to rearrange data. For example, to unstack the **Return 2009** variable in column F of the **DATA** worksheet of the **Bond Funds** workbook, open to that worksheet. Select **Data Preparation → Unstack Data**. In that procedure's dialog box, enter **B1:B185** (the Type variable cell range) as the **Grouping Variable Cell Range** and enter **F1:F185** as the **Stacked Data Cell Range**. Check **First cells in both ranges contain label** and click **OK**. The unstacked data appears on a new worksheet.

The Ordered Array

In-Depth Excel To create an ordered array, first select the data to be sorted. Then select **Home → Sort & Filter** (in the **Editing group**) **→ Sort Smallest to Largest**.

The Frequency Distribution, Part I

To create a frequency distribution, you must first translate your classes into what Excel calls *bins*. Bins approximate the classes of a frequency distribution. Unlike classes, bins do not have precise lower and upper boundary values. You establish bins by entering, in ascending order, a list of "bin numbers" into a column cell range. Each bin number, in turn, defines a bin: A bin is all the values that are less than or equal to its bin number and that are greater than the previous bin number.

Because the first bin number does not have a "previous" bin number, the first bin can never have a precise lower boundary value, as a first class always has. A common workaround to this problem, used in the examples throughout this book, is to define an extra bin, using a bin number that is slightly lower than the lower boundary value of the first class. This extra bin number, appearing first, will allow the now-second bin number to better approximate the first class, though at the cost of adding an unwanted bin to the results.

In this chapter, Tables 2.8 through 2.11 on pages 66 through 68 use class groupings in the form "*valueA* but less than *valueB*." You can translate class groupings in this form into nearly equivalent bins by creating a list of bin numbers that are slightly lower than each *valueB* that appears in the class groupings. For example, the Table 2.9 classes on page 66 could be translated into nearly equivalent bins by using this bin number list: −10.01 (the extra bin number), −5.01 ("slightly less" than −5), −0.01, −0.01, 4.99 (slightly less than 5), 9.99, 14.99, 19.99, 24.99, 29.99, and 34.99.

For class groupings in the form "all values from *valueA* to *valueB*," such as the set 0.0 through 4.9, 5.0 through 9.9, 10.0 through 14.9, and 15.0 through 19.9, you can approximate each class grouping by choosing a bin number slightly more than each *valueB*, as in this list of bin numbers: (the extra bin number), 4.99 (slightly more than 4.9), 9.99, 14.99, and 19.99.

Use an empty column in the worksheet that contains your untallied data to enter your bin numbers (in ascending order). Enter **Bins** in the row 1 cell of that column as the column heading. Enter your bin numbers before you use the Part II instructions to create frequency distributions.

When you create your own frequency distributions, you can include frequency, percentage, and/or cumulative percentages as columns of one distribution, unlike what is shown in Tables 2.8 through 2.11. Also, when you use Excel, you create frequency distributions for individual categories separately (e.g., a frequency distribution for intermediate government bond funds, followed by one for short-term corporate bond funds). To form worksheets that look like two-category Tables 2.8 through 2.11, you cut and paste parts of separately created frequency distributions. (Examine the **FD_IG** and **FD_STC** worksheets of the **Chapter 2** workbook and then examine the **FD_COMBINED** worksheet to see how frequency distributions for an individual category can be cut and pasted to form one table.)

The Frequency Distribution, Part II

PHStat2 Use **Frequency Distribution** to create a frequency distribution. For example, to create the Table 2.9 frequency distribution on page 66, open to the **DATA** worksheet of the **Bond Funds workbook**. Select **PHStat → Descriptive Statistics → Frequency Distribution**. In the procedure's dialog box (shown below):

1. Enter **F1:F185** as the **Variable Cell Range**, enter **J1:J11** as the **Bins Cell Range**, and check **First cell in each range contains label**.
2. Click **Multiple Groups - Stacked** and enter **B1:B185** as the **Grouping Variable Cell Range**. (In the DATA worksheet, the 2009 returns for both types of bond funds are stacked, or placed in a single column. The column B values allow PHStat2 to unstack the returns for intermediate government funds from the returns for the short-term corporate funds.)
3. Enter a **Title** and click **OK**.

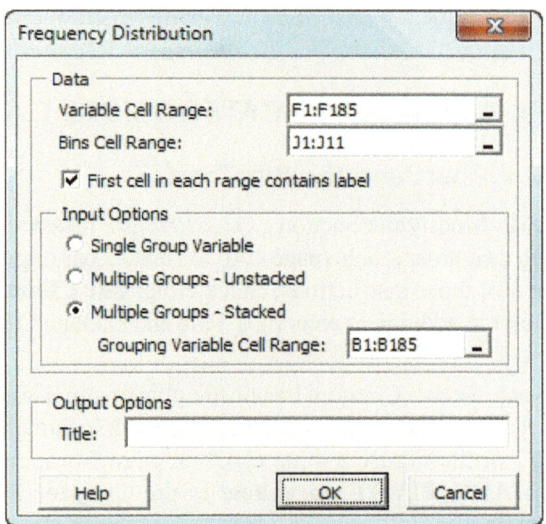

When creating other frequency distributions, if you use a worksheet that contains data for a single group, such as the **IGDATA** or **STCDATA** worksheets, click **Single Group Variable** in step 2. Note that the **Histogram & Polygons** procedure, discussed in Section EG2.5, also creates frequency distributions.

In-Depth Excel Use the **FREQUENCY** worksheet function and a bin number list (see "The Frequency Distribution, Part I" on page 108) to create a frequency distribution. For example, to create the Table 2.9 frequency distribution on page 66, open to and review the **IGDATA** and **STCDATA** worksheets of the **Bond Funds workbook**. Note that the worksheets divide the bond funds sample by fund type and that the two worksheets contain identical bin number lists in column J. With the workbook open to the IGDATA worksheet:

1. Right-click the **IGDATA sheet tab** and then click **Insert** in the shortcut menu. In the Insert dialog box, click the **Worksheet** icon and click **OK** to insert a new worksheet.
2. In the new worksheet, enter a worksheet title in cell **A1**, **Bins** in cell **A3**, and **Frequency** in cell **B3**.
3. Copy the **bin number list** that is in the cell range **J2:J11** of the IGDATA worksheet and paste this list into column A of the new worksheet, starting with cell **A4**.
4. Select the cell range **B4:B13** that will contain the frequency function.
5. Type, but do not press the **Enter** or **Tab** key, the formula **=FREQUENCY(IGDATA!$F$1:$F$88, $A$4:$A$13)**. Then, while holding down the **Ctrl** and **Shift** keys (or the **Apple** key on a Mac), press the **Enter** key. (This combination keystroke enters an "array formula," explained in Appendix F, in the cell range **B4:B13**.)

To create the frequency distribution for short-term corporate bonds, repeat steps 1 through 5 but enter the formula **=FREQUENCY(STCDATA!$F$1:$F$98, $A$4:$A$13)** in step 5. Then cut and paste the results from the two frequency distributions to create a table similar to Table 2.9.

Note that in step 5, you entered the cell range as **IGDATA!$F$1:$F$88** (or **STCDATA!$F$1:$F$98**) and not as **F1:F88** (or **F1:F98**) because the data to be summarized are located on another worksheet, and you wanted to use absolute cell references to facilitate the copying of the frequency column to create a table similar to Table 2.9.

Analysis ToolPak Use **Histogram** with a bin number list (see "The Frequency Distribution, Part I" on page 108) to create a frequency distribution. For example, to create the Table 2.9 frequency distribution on page 66, open to the **IGDATA worksheet** of the **Bond Funds workbook** and select **Data → Data Analysis**. In the Data Analysis dialog box, select **Histogram** from the **Analysis Tools** list and then click **OK**. In the Histogram dialog box (see the top of page 110):

1. Enter **F1:F88** as the **Input Range** and enter **J1:J11** as the **Bin Range**. (If you leave **Bin Range** blank, the procedure creates a set of bins that will not be as well-formed as the ones you can specify.)
2. Check **Labels** and click **New Worksheet Ply**.
3. Click **OK** to create the frequency distribution on a new worksheet.

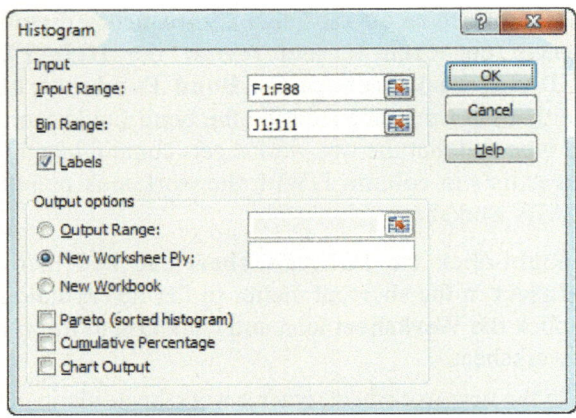

This worksheet contains the frequency distribution for the intermediate government bond funds. To modify this worksheet to include percentage and cumulative percentage distributions:

1. Enter **Total** in cell **A14** and enter **=SUM(B4:B13)** in cell **B14**.
2. Enter **Percentage** in cell **C3** and **Cumulative Pctage** in cell **D3**.
3. Enter **=B4/$B$14** in cell **C4** and copy this formula down through all the rows of the frequency distribution.
4. Enter **= C4** in cell **D4**. Enter **=D4 + C5** in cell **D5** and copy this formula down through all the rows of the frequency distribution.
5. Select the cell range **C4:D13**, right-click, and click **Format Cells** in the shortcut menu.
6. In the **Number** tab of the Format Cells dialog box, select **Percentage** as the **Category** and click **OK**.

If you want a column of relative frequencies instead of percentages, change the cell **C4** column heading to **Rel. Frequencies**. Then select the cell range **C4:C13**, right-click, and click **Format Cells** in the shortcut menu. In the **Number** tab of the Format Cells dialog box, select **Number** as the **Category** and click **OK**.

Analysis ToolPak Use the preceding *In-Depth Excel* instructions to modify a frequency distribution created using the "The Frequency Distribution, Part II" instructions.

In the new worksheet:

4. Select row 1. Right-click row 1 and click the **Insert** shortcut menu. Repeat. (This creates two blank rows at the top of the worksheet.)
5. Enter a title for the frequency distribution in cell A1.

The ToolPak creates a frequency distribution that contains an improper bin labeled **More**. Correct this error as follows:

6. Manually add the frequency count of the **More** row to the count of the preceding bin. (This is unnecessary if the **More** count is 0, as it is in this Table 2.9 example.)
7. Click the worksheet row number for the **More** row (to select the entire worksheet row), right-click on the row, and click **Delete** in the shortcut menu that appears.

Open to the **STCDATA worksheet** and repeat steps 1 through 7 with rows 1 through 98. Then cut and paste the results from the two frequency distributions to create a table similar to Table 2.9.

The Relative Frequency, Percentage, or Cumulative Percentage Distribution

PHStat2 To create these other distributions, first use the *PHStat2* instructions in "The Frequency Distribution, Part II" to create a frequency distribution that contains a column of percentages and cumulative percentages. To create a column of relative frequencies, reformat the percentage column. Select the cells containing the percentages, right-click, and then select **Format Cells** from the shortcut menu. In the **Number** tab of the Format Cells dialog box, select **Number** as the **Category** and click **OK**.

In-Depth Excel To create these other distributions, modify a frequency distribution created using the *In-Depth Excel* instructions in "The Frequency Distribution, Part II" by adding a column for percentages (or relative frequencies) and a column for cumulative percentages. For example, open to the **FD_IG worksheet** of the **Chapter 2 workbook**.

EG2.4 VISUALIZING CATEGORICAL DATA

The Bar Chart and the Pie Chart

PHStat2 Modify the Section EG2.2 *PHStat2* instructions for creating a summary table (page 106) to create a bar or pie chart. In step 3 of those instructions, check either **Bar Chart** and/or **Pie Chart** in addition to entering a **Title** and clicking **OK**.

In-Depth Excel Create a bar or pie chart from a summary table. For example, to create the Figure 2.2 bar chart on page 73 or the Figure 2.4 pie chart on page 74, open to the **SUMMARY_PIVOT worksheet** of the **Chapter 2 workbook** and:

1. Select cell range **A4:B7** (Begin your selection at cell B7 and not at cell A4, as you would normally do).
2. Click **Insert**. For a bar chart, click **Bar** in the **Charts group** and then select the first **2-D Bar** gallery choice (**Clustered Bar**). For a pie chart, click **Pie** in the **Charts group** and then select the first **2-D Pie** gallery choice (**Pie**).
3. Relocate the chart to a chart sheet and adjust chart formatting by using the instructions in Appendix Section F.4 on page 845.

For a pie chart, select **Layout** → **Data Labels** → **More Data Label Options**. In the Format Data Labels dialog box, click **Label Options** in the left pane. In the Label Options right pane, check **Category Name** and **Percentage** and clear the other check boxes. Click **Outside End** and then click **Close**.

For a bar chart, if the horizontal axis scale does not begin with 0, right-click the horizontal (value) axis and click **Format Axis** in the shortcut menu. In the Format Axis dialog box, click **Axis Options** in the left pane. In the Axis Options right pane, click the first **Fixed** option button (for Minimum) and enter **0** in its box. Click **Close**.

The Pareto Chart

PHStat2 Modify the Section EG2.2 *PHStat2* instructions for creating a summary table on page 106 to create a Pareto chart. In step 3 of those instructions, check **Pareto Chart** in addition to entering a **Title** and clicking **OK**.

In-Depth Excel To create a Pareto chart, modify the summary table that was originally created using the instructions in Section EG2.3. In the original table, first sort the table in order of decreasing frequencies and then add a column for cumulative percentage. Use the sorted, modified table to create the Pareto chart.

For example, to create the Figure 2.5 Pareto chart, open to the **ATMTable worksheet** of the **ATM Transactions workbook**. Begin by sorting the modified table by decreasing order of frequency:

1. Select row **11** (the Total row), right-click, and click **Hide** in the shortcut menu. (This prevents the total row from getting sorted.)
2. Select cell **B4** (the first frequency), right-click, and select **Sort** → **Sort Largest to Smallest**.
3. Select rows **10** and **12** (there is no row 11), right-click, and click **Unhide** in the shortcut menu.

Next, add a column for cumulative percentage:

4. Enter **Cumulative Pctage** in cell **D3**. Enter **=C4** in cell **D4**. Enter **=D4 + C5** in cell **D5** and copy this formula down through row 10.
5. Select the cell range **C4:D10**, right-click, and click **Format Cells** in the shortcut menu.
6. In the **Number** tab of the Format Cells dialog box, select **Percentage** as the **Category** and click **OK**.

Next, create the Pareto chart:

7. Select the cell range **A3:A10** and while holding down the **Ctrl** key also select the cell range **C3:D10**.
8. Select **Insert** → **Column** (in the Charts group) and select the first **2-D Column** gallery choice (**Clustered Column**).
9. Select **Format** (under **Chart Tools**). In the Current Selection group, select the entry for the cumulative percentage series from the drop-down list and then click **Format Selection**.
10. In the Format Data Series dialog box, click **Series Options** in the left pane and in the **Series Options** right pane, click **Secondary Axis**. Click **Close**.
11. With the cumulative percentage series still selected in the Current Selection group, select **Design** → **Change Chart Type**, and in the **Change Chart Type** gallery, select the fourth **Line** gallery choice (**Line with Markers**). Click **OK**.

Next, set the maximum value of the primary and secondary (left and right) *Y* axes scales to 100%. For each *Y* axis:

12. Right-click on the axis and click **Format Axis** in the shortcut menu.
13. In the Format Axis dialog box, click **Axis Options** in the left pane and in the **Axis Options** right pane, click the second **Fixed** option button (for Maximum) and enter **1** in its box. Click **Close**.

Relocate the chart to a chart sheet and adjust chart formatting by using the instructions in Appendix Section F.4 on page 845.

When using a PivotTable as a summary table, table sorting is simpler: Right-click the cell that contains the first frequency (cell B5 in the sample worksheet) and select **Sort** → **Sort Largest to Smallest**. However, creating a Pareto chart from a PivotTable with additional columns for percentage and cumulative percentage is much more difficult than creating a chart from a simple summary table. The best workaround is to convert the PivotTable to a simple summary table by copying the category names and frequencies in the PivotTable, along with the additional columns, to an empty worksheet area.

The Side-by-Side Chart

PHStat2 Modify the Section EG2.2 *PHStat2* instructions for creating a contingency table on page 107 to create a side-by-side chart. In step 4 of those instructions, check **Side-by-Side Bar Chart** in addition to entering a **Title** and clicking **OK**.

In-Depth Excel Create a chart based on a contingency table to create a side-by-side chart. For example, to create the Figure 2.7 side-by-side bar chart on page 77, open to the **CONTINGENCY_PIVOT worksheet** of the **Chapter 2 workbook** and:

1. Select cell **A4** (or any other cell inside the PivotTable).
2. Select **Insert** → **Bar** and select the first **2-D Bar** gallery choice (**Clustered Bar**). Relocate the chart to a chart sheet and adjust the chart formatting by using the instructions in Appendix Section F.4 on page 845, but with this exception: When you click **Legend**, select **Show Legend at Right**.

When creating a chart from a contingency table that is not a PivotTable, select the cell range of the contingency table, including row and column headings, but excluding the total row and total column, before selecting **Insert → Bar**.

Occasionally when you create a side-by-side chart, the row and column variables need to be swapped. If a PivotTable is the source for the chart, rearrange the PivotTable by making the row variable the column variable and vice versa. If the chart is not based on a PivotTable, right-click the chart and then click **Select Data** in the shortcut menu. In the Select Data Source dialog box, click **Switch Row/Column** and then click **OK**. (In Excel 2010, you can also use this second method for PivotTable-based charts.)

You may also need to rearrange the order of categories shown on the chart. To flip their positions for a chart based on a PivotTable, click the pull-down list for the categorical variable that needs to be rearranged and select **Sort A to Z**. In this example, after step 2, click the **Fees** pull-down list for the categorical variable that needs to be rearranged and select **Sort A to Z**. To rearrange the order of categories for a chart not based on a PivotTable, physically rearrange the worksheet columns that contain the data for the chart.

EG2.5 VISUALIZING NUMERICAL DATA

The Stem-and-Leaf Display

PHStat2 Use the **Stem-and-Leaf Display** procedure to create a stem-and-leaf display. For example, to create a stem-and-leaf display similar to Figure 2.8 on page 80, open to the **STCDATA worksheet** of the **Chapter 2 workbook**. Select **PHStat → Descriptive Statistics → Stem-and-Leaf Display**. In the procedure's dialog box (shown below):

1. Enter **F1:F98** as the **Variable Cell Range** and check **First cell contains label**.
2. Leave **Autocalculate stem unit** selected.
3. Enter a **Title** and click **OK**.

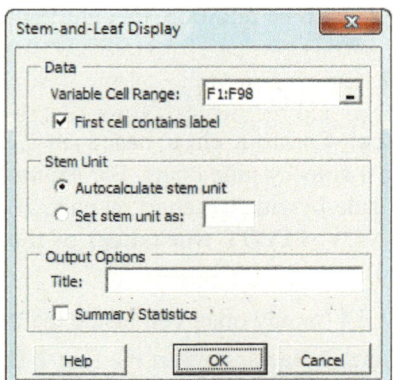

Because Minitab uses a truncation method and PHStat2 uses a rounding method, the leaves of the PHStat2 display differ slightly from Figure 2.8 (created using Minitab).

When creating other displays, use the **Set stem unit as** option sparingly and only if **Autocalculate stem unit** creates a display that has too few or too many stems. (Any stem unit you specify must be a power of 10.)

In-Depth Excel Manually construct the stems and leaves on a new worksheet to create a stem-and-leaf display. Use the **STEM_LEAF worksheet** of the **Chapter 2 workbook** as a guide to formatting your display.

The Histogram

PHStat2 Use the **Histogram & Polygons** procedure to create a histogram from unsummarized data. For example, to create the pair of histograms shown in Figure 2.10 on page 81, open to the **DATA worksheet** of the **Bond Funds workbook**. Select **PHStat → Descriptive Statistics → Histogram & Polygons**. In the procedure's dialog box (shown below):

1. Enter **F1:F185** as the **Variable Cell Range**, **J1:J11** as the **Bins Cell Range**, **K1:K10** as the **Midpoints Cell Range**, and check **First cell in each range contains label**.
2. Click **Multiple Groups - Stacked** and enter **B1:B185** as the **Grouping Variable Cell Range**. (In the DATA worksheet, the 2009 returns for both types of bond funds are stacked, or placed in a single column. The column B values allow PHStat2 to separate the returns for intermediate government funds from the returns for the short-term corporate funds.)
3. Enter a **Title**, check **Histogram**, and click **OK**.

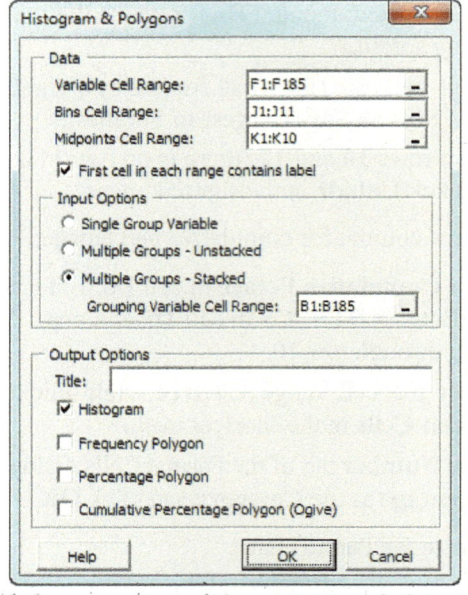

The **Bins Cell Range** and the **Midpoints Cell Range** should appear in the same worksheet as the unsummarized data, as the DATA worksheet of the Bond Funds workbook illustrates. Because a first bin can never have a midpoint (because that bin does not have a lower boundary value defined), the procedure assigns the first midpoint to the second bin and uses "---" as the label for the first bin. Therefore, the **Midpoints Cell Range** you enter must be one cell smaller in size than the **Bins Cell Range**. Read "The Histogram: Follow-up" in the next column for an additional adjustment that you can apply to the histograms created.

In-Depth Excel Create a chart from a frequency distribution. For example, to create the Figure 2.10 pair of histograms on page 81, first use the Section EG2.4 "The Frequency Distribution, Part II" *In-Depth Excel* instructions on page 109.

Follow those instructions to create a pair of frequency distributions, one for the intermediate government bond funds, and the other for the short-term corporate bond funds, on separate worksheets. In each worksheet, add a column of midpoints by entering the column heading **Midpoints** in cell **C3**, '--- in cell **C4**, and starting in cell **C5**, the midpoints **-7.5, -2.5, 2.5, 7.5, 12.5, 17.5, 22.5, 27.5, and 32.5**. In each worksheet:

1. Select the cell range **B3:B13** (the cell range of the frequencies).
2. Select **Insert → Column** and select the first **2-D Column** gallery choice (**Clustered Column**).
3. Right-click the chart background and click **Select Data**.

In the Select Data Source dialog box:

4. Click **Edit** under the **Horizontal (Categories) Axis Labels** heading.
5. In the Axis Labels dialog box, enter the cell range *formula* in the form =*SheetName*!**C4:C13** (where *SheetName* is the name of the current worksheet) and then click **OK** to return to the Select Data Source dialog box.
6. Click **OK**.

In the chart:

7. Right-click inside a bar and click **Format Data Series** in the shortcut menu.

In the Format Data Series dialog box:

8. Click **Series Options** in the left pane. In the Series Options right pane, change the **Gap Width** slider to **No Gap**. Click **Close**.

Relocate the chart to a chart sheet and adjust the chart formatting by using the instructions in Appendix Section F.4 on page 845. Read "The Histogram: Follow-up" for an additional adjustment that you can apply to the histograms created.

Analysis ToolPak Modify the Section EG2.3 Analysis ToolPak instructions for "The Frequency Distribution, Part II" on page 109 to create a histogram. In step 5 of those instructions, check **Chart Output** before clicking **OK**.

For example, to create the pair of histograms in Figure 2.10 on page 81, use the modified step 5 with both the **IGDATA** and **STCDATA** worksheets of the **Chapter 2 workbook** (as discussed on page 109) to create a pair of worksheets that contain a frequency distribution and a histogram. Each histogram will have (the same) two formatting errors that you can correct:

To eliminate the gaps between bars:

1. Right-click inside one of the histogram bars and click **Format Data Series** in the shortcut menu that appears.
2. In the **Series Options pane** of the Format Data Series dialog box, move the **Gap Width** slider to **No Gap** and click **Close**.

To change the histogram bin labels:

1. Enter the column heading **Midpoints** in cell **C3** and enter '--- in cell **C4** (the first bin has no midpoint). Starting in cell **C5**, enter the midpoints −7.5, −2.5, 2.5, 7.5, 12.5, 17.5, 22.5, 27.5, and 32.5, in column C. (The midpoints will serve as the new bin labels in step 3.)
2. Right-click the chart background and click **Select Data**.
3. In the Select Data Source dialog box, click **Edit** under the **Horizontal (Categories) Axis Labels** heading. In the Axis Labels dialog box, enter the cell range *formula* in the form =*SheetName*!**C4:C13** as the **Axis label range** and click **OK**. Back in the Select Data Source dialog box, click **OK** to complete the task.

In step 3, substitute the name of the worksheet that contains the frequency distribution and histogram for *SheetName* and note that the cell range **C4:C13** does not include the column heading cell. Read the next section for an additional adjustment that you can apply to the histograms created.

The Histogram: Follow-up

Because the example used throughout "The Histogram" uses a technique that uses an extra bin (see "The Frequency Distribution, Part I" in Section EG2.4), the histogram created will have the extra, meaningless bin. If you would like to remove this extra bin, as was done for the histograms shown in Figure 2.10, right-click the histogram background and click **Select Data**. In the Select Data Source Data dialog box, first click **Edit** under the **Legend Entries (Series)** heading. In the Edit Series dialog box, edit the **Series values** cell range formula. Then click **Edit** under the **Horizontal (Categories) Axis Labels** heading. In the Axis Labels dialog box, edit the **Axis label range**. For the example used in the previous section, change the starting cell for the **Series values** cell range formula from B4 to B5 and change the starting cell for the **Axis label range** cell range formula from C4 to C5.

The Percentage Polygon

PHStat2 Modify the *PHStat2* instructions for creating a histogram on page 112 to create a percentage polygon. In step 3 of those instructions, click **Percentage Polygon** before clicking **OK**.

In-Depth Excel Create a chart based on a modified percentage distribution to create a percentage polygon. For example, to create the Figure 2.12 percentage polygons on page 82, open to the **CPD_IG worksheet** of the **Bond Funds workbook**. (This worksheet contains a frequency distribution for the intermediate government bond funds and includes columns for the percentages and cumulative percentages in column C and D.) Begin by modifying the distribution:

1. Enter the column heading **Midpoints** in cell **E3** and enter **'---** in cell **E4** (the first bin has no midpoint). Starting in cell **E5**, enter **-7.5, -2.5, 2.5, 7.5, 12.5, 17.5, 22.5, 27.5, and 32.5,** in column E.
2. Select row 4 (the first bins row), right-click, and select **Insert** in the shortcut menu.
3. Select row 15 (the total row), right-click, and select **Insert** in the shortcut menu.
4. Enter **0** in cells **C4, D4** and **C15**.
5. Select the cell range **C3:C15**.

Next, create the chart:

6. Select **Insert → Line** and select the fourth **2-D Line** gallery choice (**Line with Markers**).
7. Right-click the chart and click **Select Data** in the shortcut menu.

In the Select Data Source dialog box:

8. Click **Edit** under the **Legend Entries (Series)** heading. In the Edit Series dialog box, enter the formula **="Intermediate Government"** for the Series name and click **OK**.
9. Click **Edit** under the **Horizontal (Categories) Axis Labels** heading. In the Axis Labels dialog box, enter the cell range formula **=CPD_IG!E4:E15** for the **Axis label range** and click **OK**.
10. Back in the Select Data Source dialog box, click **OK**.

Back in the chart sheet:

11. Right-click the vertical axis and click **Format Axis** in the shortcut menu.
12. In the Format Axis dialog box, click **Number** in left pane and then select **Percentage** from the **Category** list in the Number right pane. Enter **0** as the **Decimal places** and click **OK**.

Relocate the chart to a chart sheet and adjust chart formatting by using the instructions in Appendix Section F.4 on page 845.

Figure 2.12 on page 82 also contains the percentage polygon for the short-term corporate bond funds. To add this polygon to the chart just created, open to the **CPD_STC worksheet**. Repeat steps 1 through 5 to modify this distribution. Then open to the chart sheet that contains the intermediate government polygon. Select **Layout → Legend → Show Legend at Right**. Right-click the chart and click **Select Data** in the shortcut menu. In the Select Data Source dialog box, click **Add**. In the Edit Series dialog box, enter the formula **="Short Term Corporate"** as the **Series name** and enter the cell range formula **=CPD_STC!C4:C15** as the **Series values**. Click **OK**. Back in the Select Data Source dialog box, click **OK**.

The Cumulative Percentage Polygon (Ogive)

PHStat2 Modify the *PHStat2* instructions for creating a histogram on page 112 to create a cumulative percentage polygon, In step 3 of those instructions, click **Cumulative Percentage Polygon (Ogive)** before clicking **OK**.

In-Depth Excel Create a cumulative percentage polygon by modifying the *In-Depth Excel* instructions for creating a percentage polygon. For example, to create the Figure 2.14 cumulative percentage polygons on page 84, use the instructions for creating percentage polygons, replacing steps 4 and 8 with the following:

4. Select the cell range **D3:D14**.
8. Click **Edit** under the **Horizontal (Categories) Axis Labels** heading. In the Axis Labels dialog box, enter the cell range formula **=CPD_IG!A4:A14** for the **Axis label range** and click **OK**.

Later, when adding the second polygon for the short-term corporate bond funds, enter the cell range formula **=CPD_STC!D4:D14** as the **Series values** in the Edit Series dialog box.

EG2.6 VISUALIZING TWO NUMERICAL VARIABLES

The Scatter Plot

PHStat2 Use the **Scatter Plot** procedure to create a scatter plot. For example, to create a scatter plot similar to the one shown in Figure 2.15 on page 87, open to the **DATA worksheet** of the **NBAValues workbook**. Select **PHStat2 → Descriptive Statistics → Scatter Plot**. In the procedure's dialog box (shown below):

1. Enter **C1:C31** as the **Y Variable Cell Range**.
2. Enter **B1:B31** as the **X Variable Cell Range**.
3. Check **First cells in each range contains label**.
4. Enter a **Title** and click **OK**.

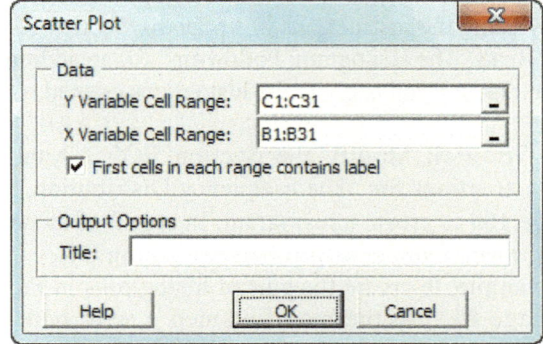

You can also use the **Scatter Plot** output option of the **Simple Linear Regression** procedure to create a scatter plot. Scatter plots created using this alternative will contain a superimposed line like the one seen in Figure 2.15. (See the Excel Guide for Chapter 13 for the instructions for using the Simple Linear Regression procedure.)

In-Depth Excel Use a worksheet in which the column for the X variable data is to the left of the column for the Y variable data to create a scatter plot. (If the worksheet is arranged Y then X, cut and paste the Y variable column to the right of the X variable column.)

For example, to create a scatter plot similar to the one shown in Figure 2.15 on page 87, open to the **DATA worksheet** of the **NBAValues** workbook and:

1. Select the cell range **B1:C31**.
2. Select **Insert → Scatter** and select the first **Scatter** gallery choice (**Scatter with only Markers**).
3. Select **Layout → Trendline → Linear Trendline**.

Relocate the chart to a chart sheet and adjust the chart formatting by using the instructions in Appendix Section F.4 on page 845.

The Time-Series Plot

In-Depth Excel Create a chart from a worksheet in which the column for the time variable data appears to the immediate left of the column for the numerical variable data. (Use cut and paste to rearrange columns, if necessary.)

For example, to create the Figure 2.16 time-series plot on page 88, open to the **DATA worksheet** of the **MovieGross workbook** and:

1. Select the cell range **A1:B15**.
2. Select **Insert → Scatter** and select the fourth **Scatter** gallery choice (**Scatter with Straight Lines and Markers**).

Relocate the chart to a chart sheet and adjust chart formatting by using the instructions in Appendix Section F.4 on page 845.

EG2.7 ORGANIZING MULTIDIMENSIONAL DATA

Multidimensional Contingency Tables

In-Depth Excel Use PivotTables to create multidimensional contingency tables. For example, to create the Figure 2.18 fund type, risk, and fees table on page 91, open to the **DATA worksheet** of the **Bond Funds workbook** and select **Insert → PivotTable**. In the Create PivotTable dialog box:

1. Click **Select a table or range** and enter **A1:I185** as the **Table/Range**.
2. Click **New Worksheet** and then click **OK**.

In the PivotTable Field List task pane (shown below):

3. Drag **Type** in the **Choose fields to add to report** box and drop it in the **Row Labels** box.
4. Drag **Risk** in the **Choose fields to add to report** box and drop it in the **Row Labels** box.
5. Drag **Fees** in the **Choose fields to add to report** box and drop it in the **Column Labels** box.
6. Drag **Fees** in the **Choose fields to add to report** box a second time and drop it in the **Σ Values** box. (This label changes to **Count of Fees**.)

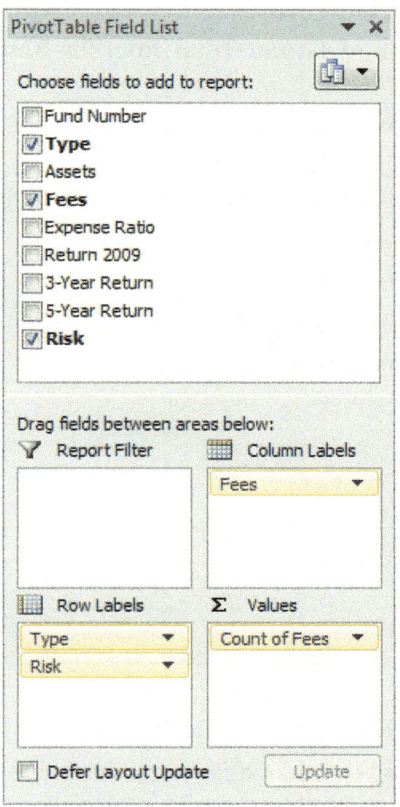

In the PivotTable being created:

7. Click the **Fees** drop-down list in cell B3 and select **Sort Z to A** to rearrange the order of the "No" and "Yes" columns.
8. Right-click and then click **PivotTable Options** in the shortcut menu that appears.

In the PivotTable Options dialog box:

9. Click the **Layout & Format** tab.
10. Check **For empty cells, show** and enter **0** as its value. Leave all other settings unchanged.
11. Click the **Total & Filters** tab.
12. Check **Show grand totals for columns** and **Show grand totals for rows**.
13. Click **OK** to complete the table.

If you create a PivotTable from an **.xlsx** file in Excel 2007 or later, the default formatting of the PivotTable will differ from the formatting of the PivotTables shown in Section 2.7. Also, in step 7 you will always see **Column Labels** as the name of drop-down list and that drop-down list will appear in cell B3.

To display the cell values as percentages, as was done in Figures 2.20 and 2.21 on page 92, click **Count of Fees** in the PivotTable Field List task pane and then click **Value Field Settings** from the shortcut menu. In the Value Field Settings dialog box (shown below):

1. Click the **Show Values As** tab.
2. Select **% of Grand Total** from the **Show values as** drop-down list.
3. Click **OK**.

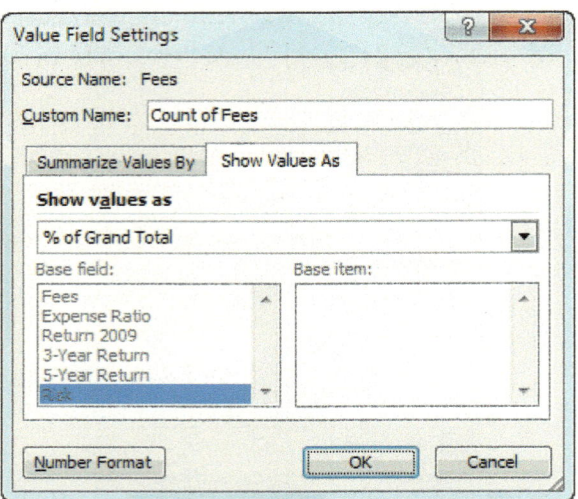

Adding Numerical Variables

In-Depth Excel Add a numerical variable to a PivotTable by dragging a numerical variable label from the **Choose fields to add to report** box to the Σ **Values** box and deleting the **Count of** *categorical variable* label (by dragging the label and dropping it anywhere outside the Σ **Values** box). To display something other than the sum of the numerical variable, click the **Sum of** *numerical variable* and then click **Value Field Settings** and make the appropriate entries in the Value Field Settings dialog box.

For example, to create the Figure 2.22 PivotTable of fund type, risk, and fees, showing averages of the 2009 return (see page 92) from the Figure 2.18 PivotTable, first create the Figure 2.18 PivotTable using steps 1 through 12 of the preceding section. Then continue with these steps:

13. Drag **Return 2009** in the **Choose fields to add to report** box and drop it in the Σ **Values** box. (This label changes to **Sum of Return 2009**.)
14. Drag **Count of Fees** in the Σ **Values** box and drop it anywhere outside that box.
15. Click **Sum of Return 2009** and click **Value Field Settings** from the shortcut menu.

In the Value Field Settings dialog box (shown below):

16. Click the **Summarize Values By** tab and select **Average** from the list. The label **Sum of Return 2009** changes to **Average of Return 2009**.
17. Click **OK**.

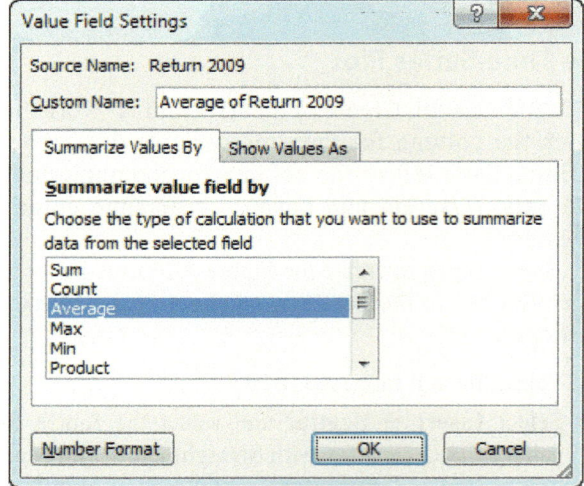

Adjust cell formatting and decimal place display as required (see Appendix F).

CHAPTER 2 MINITAB GUIDE

MG2.2 ORGANIZING CATEGORICAL DATA

The Summary Table

Use **Tally Individual Variables** to create a summary table. For example, to create a summary table similar to Table 2.2 on page 60, open to the **Bond Funds worksheet**. Select **Stat → Tables → Tally Individual Variables**. In the procedure's dialog box (shown below):

1. Double-click **C9 Risk** in the variables list to add **Risk** to the **Variables** box.
2. Check **Counts** and **Percents**.
3. Click **OK**.

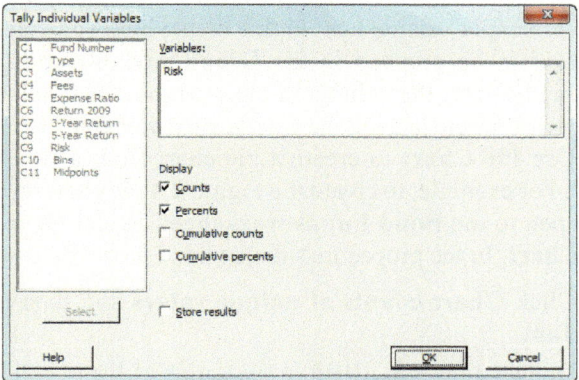

The Contingency Table

Use **Cross Tabulation and Chi-Square** to create a contingency table. For example, to create a contingency table similar to Table 2.3 on page 61, open to the **Bond Funds worksheet**. Select **Stat → Tables → Cross Tabulation and Chi-Square**. In the procedure's dialog box (shown below):

1. Enter **Type** in the **For rows** box.
2. Enter **Fees** in the **For columns** box
3. Check **Counts**.
4. Click **OK**.

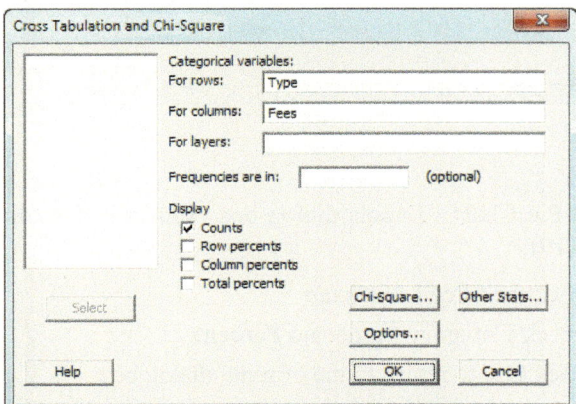

To create the other types of contingency tables shown in Tables 2.4 through 2.6, change step 3 by checking other additional **Display** items.

MG2.3 ORGANIZING NUMERICAL DATA

Stacked and Unstacked Data

Use **Stack** or **Unstack Columns** to rearrange data. For example, to unstack the **Return 2009** variable in column C6 of the **Bond Funds worksheet**, open to that worksheet. Select **Data → Unstack Columns**. In the procedure's dialog box (shown below):

1. Double-click **C6 Return 2009** in the variables list to add **'Return 2009'** to the **Unstack the data in** box and press **Tab**.
2. Double-click **C2 Type** in the variables list to add **Type** to the **Using subscripts in** box.
3. Click **After last column in use**.
4. Check **Name the columns containing the unstacked data**.
5. Check **OK**.

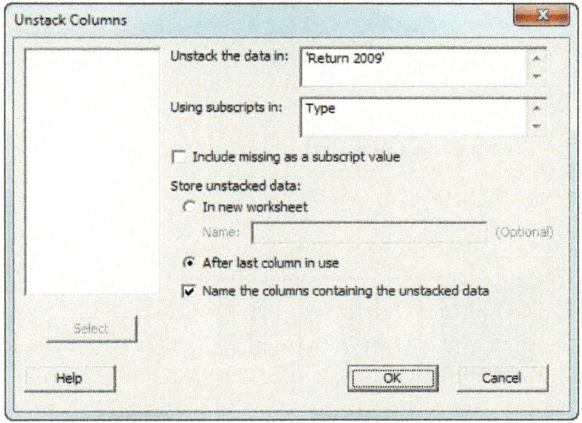

Minitab inserts two new columns, **Return 2009_Intermediate Government** and **Return 2009_Short Term Corporate**, the names of which you can edit.

To stack columns, select **Data → Stack → Columns**. In the Stack Columns dialog box, add the names of columns that contain the data to be stacked to the **Stack the following columns** box and then click either **New worksheet** or **Column of current worksheet** as the place to store the stacked data.

The Ordered Array

Use **Sort** to create an ordered array. Select **Data → Sort** and in the Sort dialog box (not shown), double-click a column name in the variables list to add it to the **Sort column(s)** box and then press **Tab.** Double-click the same column name in the variables list to add it to the first **By column** box. Click either **New worksheet**, **Original column(s)**, or **Column(s) of current worksheet**. (If you choose the third option, also enter the name of the column in which to place the ordered data in the box). Click **OK**.

The Frequency Distribution

There are no Minitab commands that use classes that you specify to create frequency distributions of the type seen in Tables 2.8 through 2.11. (See also "The Histogram" in Section MG2.5.)

MG2.4 VISUALIZING CATEGORICAL DATA
The Bar Chart and the Pie Chart

Use **Bar Chart** to create a bar chart from a summary table and use **Pie Chart** to create a pie chart from a summary table. For example, to create the Figure 2.2 bar chart on page 73, open to the **Bond Funds worksheet**. Select **Graph → Bar Chart**. In the procedure's dialog box (shown below):

1. Select **Counts of unique values** from the **Bars represent** drop-down list.
2. In the gallery of choices, click **Simple**.
3. Click **OK**.

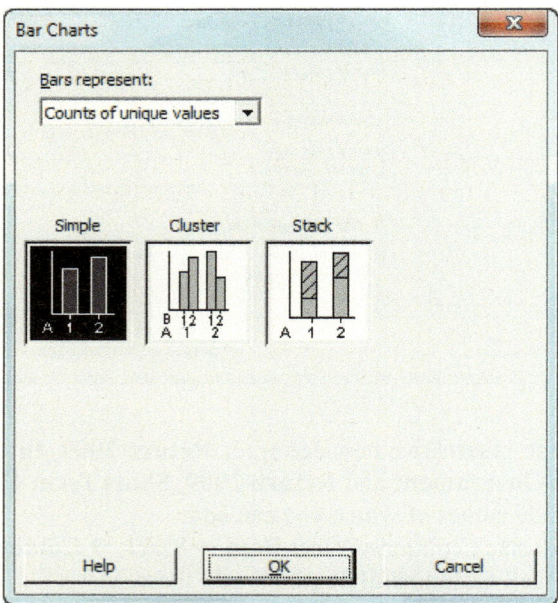

In the Bar Chart - Counts of unique values, Simple dialog box (see the top of the next column):

4. Double-click **C9 Risk** in the variables list to add **Risk** to **Categorical variables**.
5. Click **OK**.

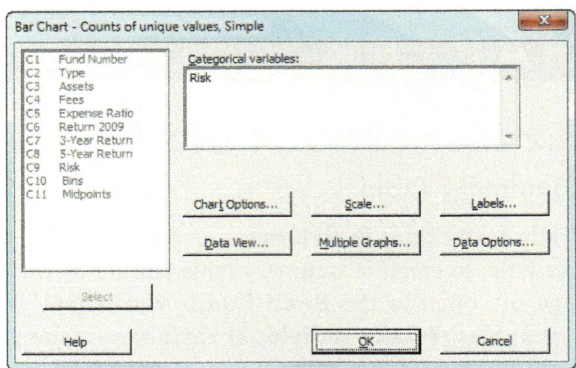

If your data are in the form of a table of frequencies, select **Values from a table** from the **Bars represent** drop-down list in step 1. With this selection, clicking **OK** in step 3 will display the "Bar Chart - Values from a table, One column of values, Simple" dialog box. In this dialog box, you enter the columns to be graphed in the **Graph variables** box and, optionally, enter the column in the worksheet that holds the categories for the table in the **Categorical variable** box.

Use **Pie Chart** to create a pie chart from a summary table. For example, to create the Figure 2.4 pie chart on page 74, open to the **Bond Funds worksheet**. Select **Graph → Pie Chart**. In the procedure's dialog box (shown below):

1. Click **Chart counts of unique values** and then press **Tab**.
2. Double-click **C9 Risk** in the variables list to add **Risk** to **Categorical variables**.
3. Click **Labels**.

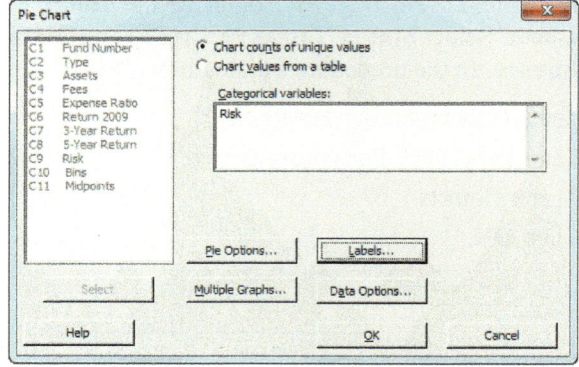

In the Pie Chart - Labels dialog box (shown at the top of page 119):

4. Click the **Slice Labels** tab.
5. Check **Category name** and **Percent**.
6. Click **OK** to return to the original dialog box.

Organizing and Visualizing Data **89**

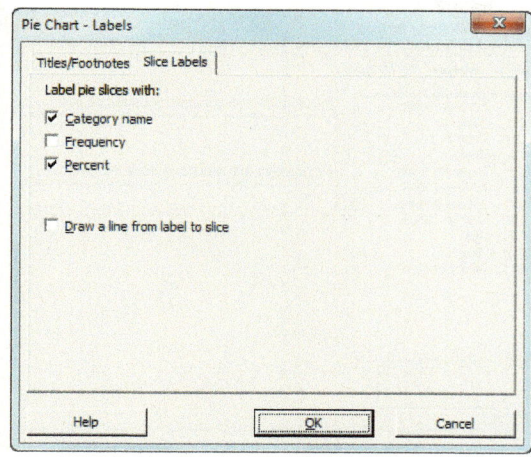

Back in the original Pie Chart dialog box:

7. Click **OK**.

The Pareto Chart

Use **Pareto Chart** to create a Pareto chart. For example, to create the Figure 2.5 Pareto chart on page 75, open to the **ATM Transactions worksheet**. Select **Stat → Quality Tools → Pareto Chart**. In the procedure's dialog box (shown below):

1. Double-click **C1 Cause** in the variables list to add **Cause** to the **Defects or attribute data in** box.
2. Double-click **C2 Frequency** in the variables list to add **Frequency** to the **Frequencies in** box.
3. Click **Do not combine**.
4. Click **OK**.

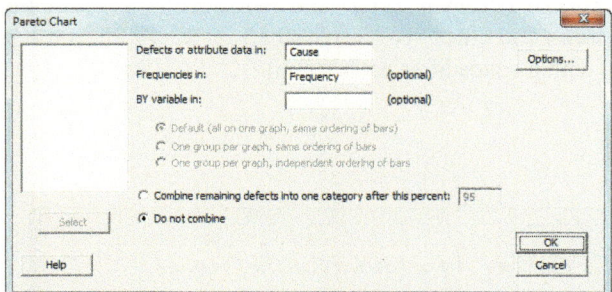

The Side-by-Side Chart

Use **Bar Chart** to create a side-by-side chart. For example, to create the Figure 2.7 side-by-side chart on page 77, open to the **Bond Funds worksheet**. Select **Graph → Bar Chart**. In the procedure's dialog box:

1. Select **Counts of unique values** from the **Bars represent** drop-down list.
2. In the gallery of choices, click **Cluster**.
3. Click **OK**.

In the "Bar Chart - Counts of unique values, Cluster" dialog box (shown below):

4. Double-click **C2 Type** and **C4 Fees** in the variables list to add **Type** and **Fees** to the **Categorical variables (2–4, outermost first)** box.
5. Click **OK**.

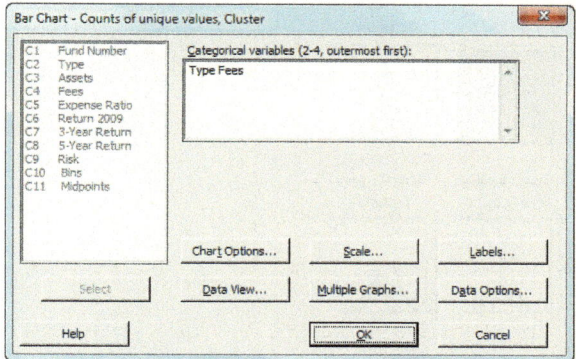

MG2.5 VISUALIZING NUMERICAL DATA

The Stem-and-Leaf Display

Use **Stem-and-Leaf** to create a stem-and-leaf display. For example, to create the Figure 2.8 stem-and-leaf display on page 80, open to the **Bond Funds worksheet**. Select **Graph → Stem-and-Leaf**. In the procedure's dialog box (shown below):

1. Double-click **C6 Return 2009** in the variables list to add **'Return 2009'** in the **Graph variables** box.
2. Click **OK**.

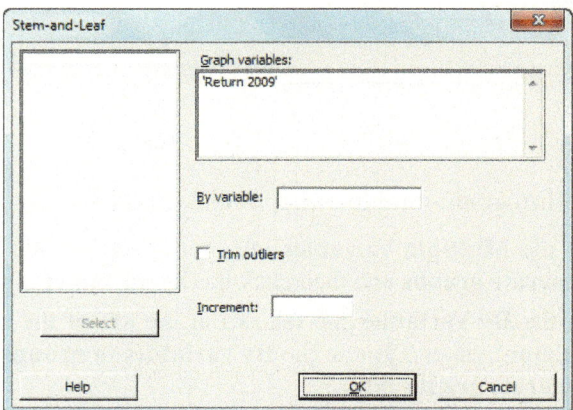

The Histogram

Use **Histogram** to create a histogram. For example, to create the pair of histograms shown in Figure 2.10 on page 81, open to the **Bond Funds worksheet**. Select **Graph → Histogram**. In the Histograms dialog box (shown below):

1. Click **Simple** and then click **OK**.

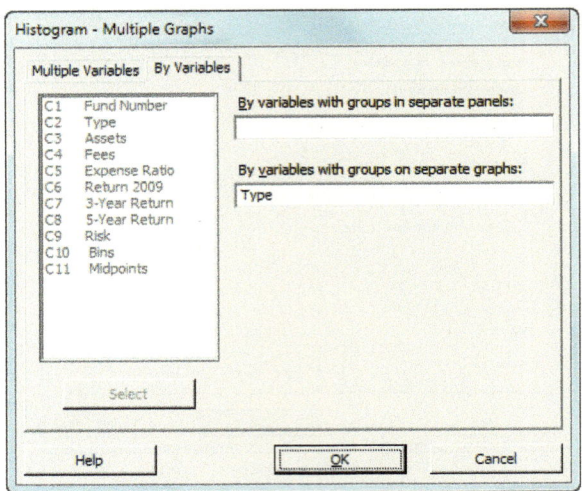

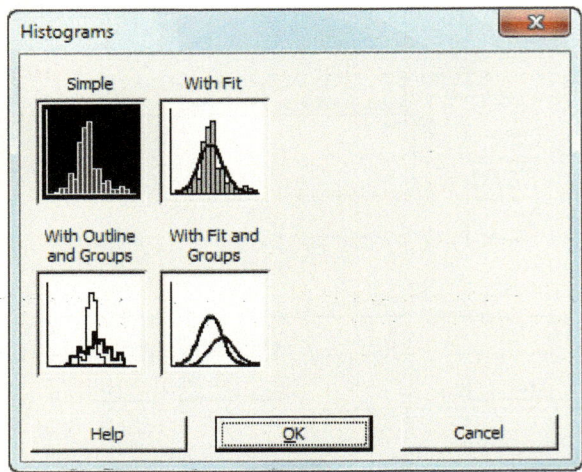

In the Histogram - Simple dialog box (shown below):

2. Double-click **C6   Return 2009** in the variables list to add **'Return 2009'** in the **Graph variables** box.
3. Click **Multiple Graphs**.

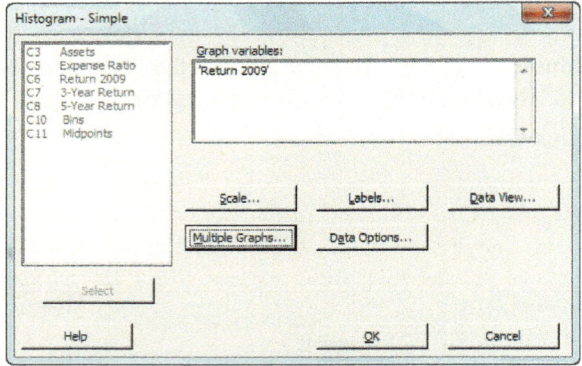

In the Histogram - Multiple Graphs dialog box:

4. In the **Multiple Variables** tab (not shown), click **On separate graphs** and then click the **By Variables** tab.
5. In the **By Variables** tab (shown at the top of the next column), enter **Type** in the **By variables in groups on separate graphs** box.
6. Click **OK**.

Back in the Histogram - Simple dialog box:

7. Click **OK**.

The histograms created use classes that differ from the classes used in Figure 2.10 (and in Table 2.9 on page 66) and do not use the midpoints shown in Figure 2.10. To better match the histograms shown in Figure 2.10, for each histogram:

8. Right-click the X axis and then click **Edit X Scale** from the shortcut menu.

In the Edit Scale dialog box (shown below):

9. Click the **Binning** tab (shown below). Click **Cutpoint** (as the **Interval Type**) and **Midpoint/Cutpoint positions** and enter **-10 -5 0 5 10 15 20 25 30 35** in the box (with a space after each value).

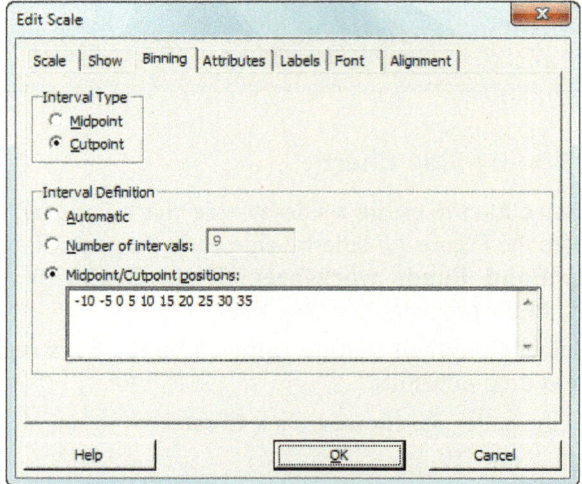

10. Click the **Scale** tab (shown below). Click **Position of ticks** and enter **-7.5 -2.5 2.5 7.5 12.5 17.5 22.5 27.5 32.5** in the box (with a space after each value).
11. Click **OK**.

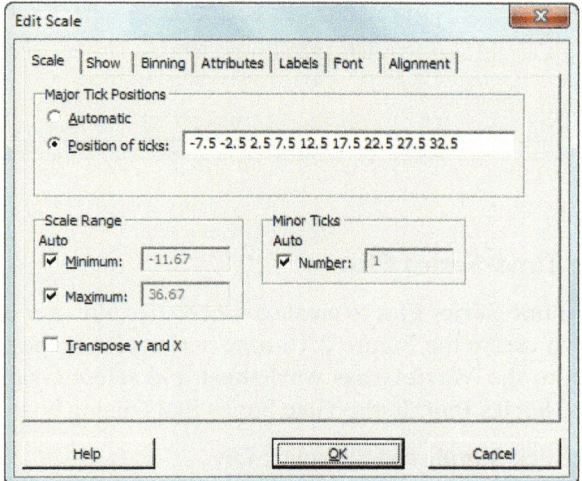

To create the histogram of the 2009 returns for all the bond funds, repeat steps 1 through 11, but in step 5 delete **Type** from the **By variables in groups on separate graphs** box. In the general case, if you have not just created histograms by subgroups (as was done in the example), then follow steps 1 through 4, changing step 4 to "Click **OK**" to create a single histogram that contains all the values of a variable.

To modify the histogram bars, double-click over the histogram bars and make the appropriate entries and selections in the Edit Bars dialog box. To modify an axis, double-click the axis and make the appropriate entries and selections in the Edit Scale dialog box.

The Percentage Polygon

Use **Histogram** to create a percentage polygon. For example, to create the pair of percentage polygons shown in Figure 2.12 on page 82, open to the **Return 2009 Unstacked worksheet**. Select **Graph → Histogram**. In the Histograms dialog box:

1. Click **Simple** and then click **OK**.

In the Histogram - Simple dialog box:

2. Double-click **C1 Intermediate Government** in the variables list to add **'Intermediate Government'** in the **Graph variables** box.
3. Double-click **C2 Short-Term Corporate** in the variables list to add **'Short-Term Corporate'** in the **Graph variables** box.
4. Click **Scale**.

In the Histogram - Scale dialog box:

5. Click the **Y-Scale Type** tab. Click **Percent**, clear **Accumulate values across bins**, and then click **OK**.

Back again in the Histogram - Simple dialog box:

6. Click **Data View**.

In the Histogram - Data View dialog box:

7. Click the **Data Display** tab and then check **Symbols**.
8. Click the **Smoother** tab and then click **Lowness** and enter **0** as the **Degree of smoothing** and **1** as the **Number of steps**.
9. Click **OK**.

Back again in the Histogram - Simple dialog box:

10. Click **OK** to create the polygons.

The percentage polygons created use classes that differ from the classes used in Figure 2.12 (and in Table 2.9 on page 66) and do not use the midpoints shown in Figure 2.12. To better match the polygons shown in Figure 2.12:

11. Right-click the X axis and then click Edit X Scale from the shortcut menu.

In the Edit Scale dialog box:

12. Click the **Binning** tab. Click **Cutpoint** as the **Interval Type** and **Midpoint/Cutpoint positions** and enter **-10 -5 0 5 10 15 20 25 30 35** in the box (with a space after each value).
13. Click the **Scale** tab. Click **Position of ticks** and enter **-7.5 -2.5 2.5 7.5 12.5 17.5 22.5 27.5 32.5** in the box (with a space after each value).
14. Click **OK**.

The Cumulative Percentage Polygon (Ogive)

If you have access to image or photo editing software, use the instructions in the section "The Percentage Polygon" to create a cumulative percentage polygon. In step 5, click **Percent** and check **Accumulate values across bins** before clicking **OK**. At this point, the data points will be plotted (incorrectly) to the midpoints and not the ends of the classes (the cutpoints). With the graph open, select **File → Save Graph As** and save the graph using a **Save as type** format compatible with your image or photo-editing software. Open the software and replace the X axis labels (the midpoints) with the proper cutpoint values.

Otherwise, use **Scatterplot** with columns of data that represent a cumulative percentage distribution to create a cumulative percentage polygon. For example, to create the Figure 2.13 cumulative percentage polygons of the cost of restaurant meals at city and suburban restaurants, open to the **Restaurant Cumulative Percentages worksheet.** Select **Graph** ➜ **Scatterplot**. In the Scatterplots dialog box:

1. Click **With Connect Line** and then click **OK**.

In the Scatterplot - With Connect Line dialog box (shown below):

2. Double-click **C2   City Restaurants** in the variables list to enter **'City Restaurants'** in the **Y variables row 1** cell.
3. Double-click **C1   Cost of Meal** in the variables list to enter **'Cost of Meal'** in the **X variables row 1** cell.
4. Double-click **C3   Suburban Restaurants** in the variables list to enter **'Suburban Restaurants'** in the **Y variables row 1** cell.
5. Double-click **C1   Cost of Meal** in the variables list to enter **'Cost of Meal'** in the **X variables row 2** cell.
6. Click **OK**.

In the chart, right-click the *Y* axis label and then click **Edit Y Axis Label** from the shortcut menu. In the Edit Axis Label dialog box, enter **Percentage** in the **Text box** and then click **OK**.

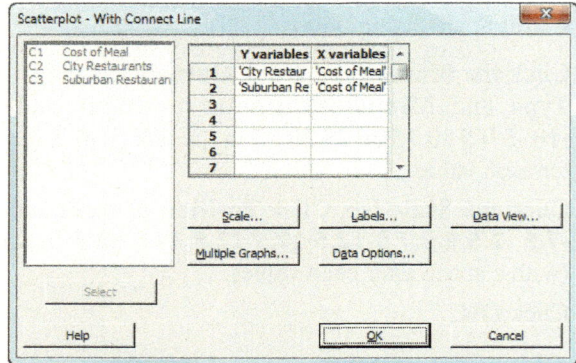

MG2.6 VISUALIZING TWO NUMERICAL VARIABLES

The Scatter Plot

Use **Scatterplot** to create a scatter plot. For example, to create a scatter plot similar to the one shown in Figure 2.15 on page 87, open to the **NBAValues worksheet**. Select **Graph** ➜ **Scatterplot**. In the Scatterplots dialog box:

1. Click **With Regression** and then click **OK**.

In the Scatterplot - With Regression dialog box (shown at the top of the next column):

2. Enter **Value** in the **row 1 Y variables** cell.
3. Enter **Revenue** in the **row 1 X variables** cell.
4. Click **OK**.

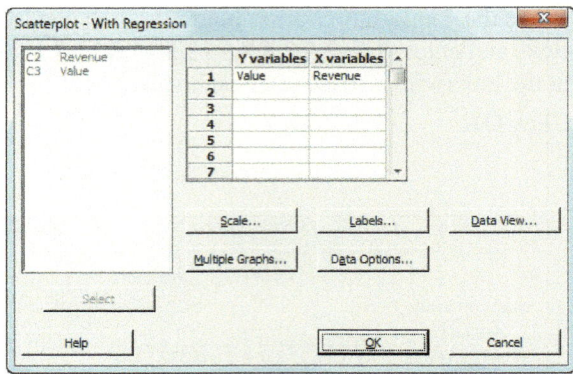

The Time-Series Plot

Use **Time Series Plot** to create a time-series plot. For example, to create the Figure 2.16 time-series plot on page 88, open to the **MovieGross worksheet** and select **Graph** ➜ **Time Series Plot**. In the Time Series Plots dialog box:

1. Click **Simple** and then click **OK**.

In the Time Series Plot - Simple dialog box (shown below):

2. Double-click **C2   Combined Gross** in the variables list to add **'Combined Gross'** in the **Series** box.
3. Click **Time/Scale**.

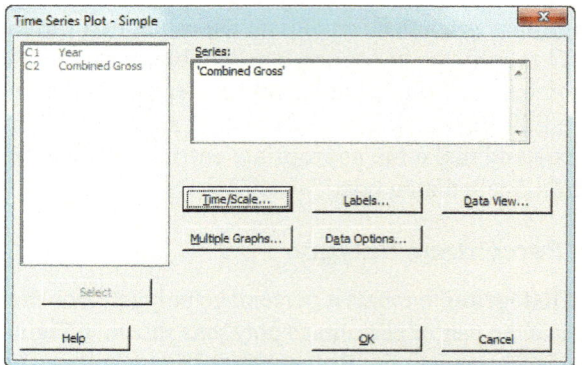

In the Time Series Plot - Time/Scale dialog box (shown at the top of page 123):

4. Click **Stamp** and then press **Tab**.
5. Double-click **C1   Year** in the variables list to add **Year** in the **Stamp columns (1-3, innermost first)** box.
6. Click **OK**.

Back in the Time Series Plot - Simple dialog box:

7. Click **OK**.

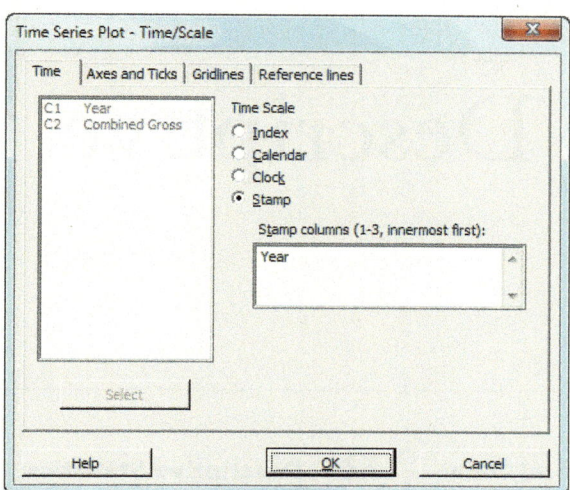

MG2.7 ORGANIZING MULTIDIMENSIONAL DATA

Multidimensional Contingency Tables

Use **Cross Tabulation and Chi-Square** to create a multidimensional contingency table. For example, to create a table similar to the Figure 2.18 fund type, risk, and fees table on page 91, open to the **Bond Funds worksheet**. Select **Stat → Tables → Cross Tabulation and Chi-Square**. In the procedure's dialog box:

1. Double-click **C2   Type** in the variables list to add **Type** to the **For rows** box.
2. Double-click **C9   Risk** in the variables list to add **Risk** to the **For rows** box and then press **Tab**.
3. Double-click **C4   Fees** in the variables list to add **Fees** to the **For columns** box.
4. Check **Counts**.
5. Click **OK**.

To display the cell values as percentages, as was done in Figures 2.20 and 2.21 on page 92, check **Total percents** instead of **Counts** in step 4.

Adding Numerical Variables

Use **Descriptive Statistics** to create a multidimensional contingency table that contains a numerical variable. For example, to create the Figure 2.22 table of fund type, risk, and fees on page 92, showing averages of the 2009 return, open to the **Bond Funds worksheet**. Select **Stat → Tables → Descriptive Statistics**. In the Table of Descriptive Statistics dialog box (shown below):

1. Double-click **C2   Type** in the variables list to add **Type** to the **For rows** box.
2. Double-click **C9   Risk** in the variables list to add **Risk** to the **For rows** box and then press **Tab**.
3. Double-click **C4   Fees** in the variables list to add **Fees** to the **For columns** box.
4. Click **Associated Variables**.

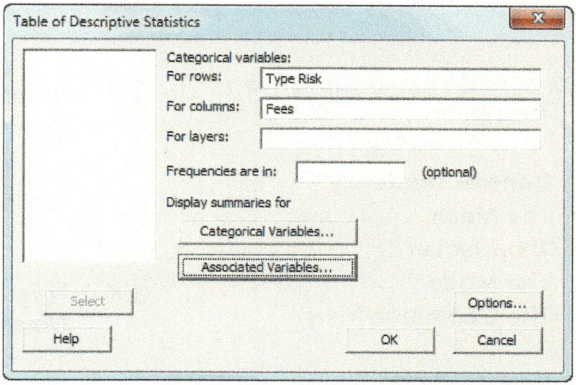

In the Descriptive Statistics - Summaries for Associated Variables dialog box (shown below):

5. Double-click **C6   Return 2009** in the variables list to add **'Return 2009'** to the **Associated variables** box.
6. Check **Means**.
7. Click **OK**.

Back in Table of Descriptive Statistics dialog box:

8. Click **OK**.

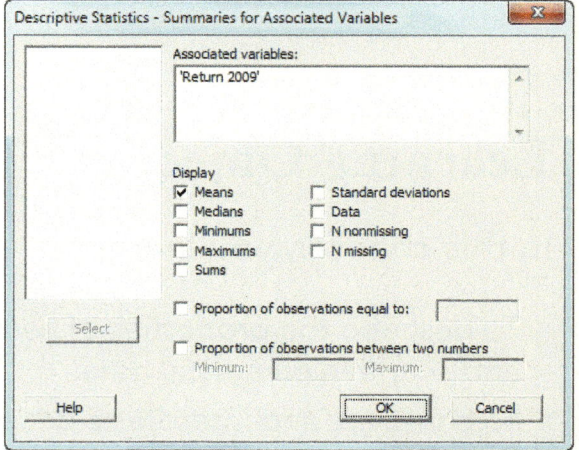

3 Numerical Descriptive Measures

USING STATISTICS @ Choice Is Yours, Part II

3.1 Central Tendency
The Mean
The Median
The Mode
The Geometric Mean

3.2 Variation and Shape
The Range
The Variance and the Standard Deviation
The Coefficient of Variation
Z Scores
Shape

VISUAL EXPLORATIONS: Exploring Descriptive Statistics

3.3 Exploring Numerical Data
Quartiles
The Interquartile Range
The Five-Number Summary
The Boxplot

3.4 Numerical Descriptive Measures for a Population
The Population Mean
The Population Variance and Standard Deviation
The Empirical Rule
The Chebyshev Rule

3.5 The Covariance and the Coefficient of Correlation
The Covariance
The Coefficient of Correlation

3.6 Descriptive Statistics: Pitfalls and Ethical Issues

USING STATISTICS @ Choice Is Yours, Part II Revisited

CHAPTER 3 EXCEL GUIDE

CHAPTER 3 MINITAB GUIDE

Learning Objectives

In this chapter, you learn:

- To describe the properties of central tendency, variation, and shape in numerical data
- To construct and interpret a boxplot
- To compute descriptive summary measures for a population
- To compute the covariance and the coefficient of correlation

USING STATISTICS

@ Choice Is Yours, Part II

The tables and charts you prepared for the sample of 184 bond mutual funds has been useful to the customers of the Choice Is Yours service. However, customers have become frustrated trying to evaluate bond fund performance. Although they know how the 2009 returns are distributed, they have no idea what a typical 2009 rate of return is for a particular category of bond funds, such as intermediate government and short-term corporate bond funds. They also have no idea of the extent of the variability in the 2009 rate of return. Are all the values relatively similar, or do they include very small and very large values? Are there a lot of small values and a few large ones, or vice versa, or are there a similar number of small and large values?

How could you help the customers get answers to these questions so that they could better evaluate the bond funds?

The customers in Part II of the Choice Is Yours scenario are asking questions about numerical variables. When summarizing and describing numerical variables, you need to do more than just prepare the tables and charts discussed in Chapter 2. You also need to consider the central tendency, variation, and shape of each numerical variable.

> **CENTRAL TENDENCY**
> The **central tendency** is the extent to which the data values group around a typical or central value.
>
> **VARIATION**
> The **variation** is the amount of dispersion, or scattering, of values away from a central value.
>
> **SHAPE**
> The **shape** is the pattern of the distribution of values from the lowest value to the highest value.

This chapter discusses ways you can measure the central tendency, variation, and shape of a variable. You will also learn about the covariance and the coefficient of correlation, which help measure the strength of the association between two numerical variables. Using these measures would give the customers of the Choice Is Yours service the answers they seek.

3.1 Central Tendency

Most sets of data show a distinct tendency to group around a central value. When people talk about an "average value" or the "middle value" or the "most frequent value," they are talking informally about the mean, median, and mode—three measures of central tendency.

The Mean

The **arithmetic mean** (typically referred to as the **mean**) is the most common measure of central tendency. The mean is the only common measure in which all the values play an equal role. The mean serves as a "balance point" in a set of data (like the fulcrum on a seesaw). You compute the mean by adding together all the values in a data set and then dividing that sum by the number of values in the data set.

The symbol $\bar{X}$, called *X-bar*, is used to represent the mean of a sample. For a sample containing n values, the equation for the mean of a sample is written as

$$\bar{X} = \frac{\text{sum of the values}}{\text{number of values}}$$

Using the series $X_1, X_2, \ldots, X_n$ to represent the set of n values and n to represent the number of values in the sample, the equation becomes

$$\bar{X} = \frac{X_1 + X_2 + \cdots + X_n}{n}$$

By using summation notation (discussed fully in Appendix A), you replace the numerator $X_1 + X_2 + \cdots + X_n$ with the term $\sum_{i=1}^{n} X_i$, which means sum all the X_i values from the first X

value, X_1, to the last X value, X_n, to form Equation (3.1), a formal definition of the sample mean.

> **SAMPLE MEAN**
> The **sample mean** is the sum of the values in a sample divided by the number of values in the sample.
>
> $$\bar{X} = \frac{\sum_{i=1}^{n} X_i}{n} \tag{3.1}$$
>
> where
>
> $\bar{X}$ = sample mean
> n = number of values or sample size
> X_i = ith value of the variable X
> $\sum_{i=1}^{n} X_i$ = summation of all X_i values in the sample

Because all the values play an equal role, a mean is greatly affected by any value that is greatly different from the others. When you have such extreme values, you should avoid using the mean as a measure of central tendency.

The mean can suggest a typical or central value for a data set. For example, if you knew the typical time it takes you to get ready in the morning, you might be able to better plan your morning and minimize any excessive lateness (or earliness) going to your destination. Following the Define, Collect, Organize, Visualize, and Analyze approach, you first define the time to get ready as the time (rounded to the nearest minute) from when you get out of bed to when you leave your home. Then, you collect the times shown below for 10 consecutive workdays (stored in `Times`):

Day:	1	2	3	4	5	6	7	8	9	10
Time (minutes):	39	29	43	52	39	44	40	31	44	35

The first statistic that you compute to analyze these data is the mean. For these data, the mean time is 39.6 minutes, computed as follows:

$$\bar{X} = \frac{\text{sum of the values}}{\text{number of values}}$$

$$\bar{X} = \frac{\sum_{i=1}^{n} X_i}{n}$$

$$\bar{X} = \frac{39 + 29 + 43 + 52 + 39 + 44 + 40 + 31 + 44 + 35}{10}$$

$$= \frac{396}{10} = 39.6$$

Even though no individual day in the sample actually had the value 39.6 minutes, allotting about 40 minutes to get ready would be a good rule for planning your mornings. The mean is a good measure of central tendency here because the data set does not contain any exceptionally small or large values.

Consider a case in which the value on Day 4 is 102 minutes instead of 52 minutes. This extreme value causes the mean to rise to 44.6 minutes, as follows:

$$\bar{X} = \frac{\text{sum of the values}}{\text{number of values}}$$

$$\bar{X} = \frac{\sum_{i=1}^{n} X_i}{n}$$

$$\bar{X} = \frac{446}{10} = 44.6$$

The one extreme value has increased the mean from 39.6 to 44.6 minutes. In contrast to the original mean that was in the "middle" (i.e., was greater than 5 of the getting-ready times and less than the 5 other times), the new mean is greater than 9 of the 10 getting-ready times. Because of the extreme value, now the mean is not a good measure of central tendency.

EXAMPLE 3.1
The Mean Calories for Cereals

Nutritional data about a sample of seven breakfast cereals (stored in Cereals) includes the number of calories per serving:

Cereal	Calories
Kellogg's All Bran	80
Kellogg Corn Flakes	100
Wheaties	100
Nature's Path Organic Multigrain Flakes	110
Kellogg Rice Krispies	130
Post Shredded Wheat Vanilla Almond	190
Kellogg Mini Wheats	200

Compute the mean number of calories in these breakfast cereals.

SOLUTION The mean number of calories is 130, computed as follows:

$$\bar{X} = \frac{\text{sum of the values}}{\text{number of values}}$$

$$\bar{X} = \frac{\sum_{i=1}^{n} X_i}{n}$$

$$= \frac{910}{7} = 130$$

The Median

The **median** is the middle value in an ordered array of data that has been ranked from smallest to largest. Half the values are smaller than or equal to the median, and half the values are larger than or equal to the median. The median is not affected by extreme values, so you can use the median when extreme values are present.

To compute the median for a set of data, you first rank the values from smallest to largest and then use Equation (3.2) to compute the rank of the value that is the median.

MEDIAN

$$\text{Median} = \frac{n+1}{2} \text{ ranked value} \quad (3.2)$$

You compute the median by following one of two rules:

- **Rule 1** If the data set contains an *odd* number of values, the median is the measurement associated with the middle-ranked value.
- **Rule 2** If the data set contains an *even* number of values, the median is the measurement associated with the *average* of the two middle-ranked values.

To further analyze the sample of 10 times to get ready in the morning, you can compute the median. To do so, you rank the daily times as follows:

Ranked values: 29   31   35   39   39   40   43   44   44   52

Ranks: 1   2   3   4   5   6   7   8   9   10

↑

Median = 39.5

Because the result of dividing $n + 1$ by 2 is $(10 + 1)/2 = 5.5$ for this sample of 10, you must use Rule 2 and average the measurements associated with the fifth and sixth ranked values, 39 and 40. Therefore, the median is 39.5. The median of 39.5 means that for half the days, the time to get ready is less than or equal to 39.5 minutes, and for half the days, the time to get ready is greater than or equal to 39.5 minutes. In this case, the median time to get ready of 39.5 minutes is very close to the mean time to get ready of 39.6 minutes.

EXAMPLE 3.2

Computing the Median From an Odd-Sized Sample

Nutritional data about a sample of seven breakfast cereals (stored in **Cereals**) includes the number of calories per serving (see Example 3.1 on page 128). Compute the median number of calories in breakfast cereals.

SOLUTION Because the result of dividing $n + 1$ by 2 is $(7 + 1)/2 = 4$ for this sample of seven, using Rule 1, the median is the measurement associated with fourth ranked value. The number of calories per serving data are ranked from the smallest to the largest:

Ranked values: 80   100   100   110   130   190   200

Ranks: 1   2   3   4   5   6   7

↑

Median = 110

The median number of calories is 110. Half the breakfast cereals have equal to or less than 110 calories per serving, and half the breakfast cereals have equal to or more than 110 calories.

The Mode

The **mode** is the value in a set of data that appears most frequently. Like the median and unlike the mean, extreme values do not affect the mode. Often, there is no mode or there are several modes in a set of data. For example, consider the following time-to-get-ready data:

29   31   35   39   39   40   43   44   44   52

There are two modes, 39 minutes and 44 minutes, because each of these values occurs twice.

EXAMPLE 3.3
Determining the Mode

A systems manager in charge of a company's network keeps track of the number of server failures that occur in a day. Determine the mode for the following data, which represents the number of server failures in a day for the past two weeks:

$$1\ 3\ 0\ 3\ 26\ 2\ 7\ 4\ 0\ 2\ 3\ 3\ 6\ 3$$

SOLUTION The ordered array for these data is

$$0\ 0\ 1\ 2\ 2\ 3\ 3\ 3\ 3\ 3\ 4\ 6\ 7\ 26$$

Because 3 occurs five times, more times than any other value, the mode is 3. Thus, the systems manager can say that the most common occurrence is having three server failures in a day. For this data set, the median is also equal to 3, and the mean is equal to 4.5. The value 26 is an extreme value. For these data, the median and the mode are better measures of central tendency than the mean.

A set of data has no mode if none of the values is "most typical." Example 3.4 presents a data set that has no mode.

EXAMPLE 3.4
Data with No Mode

The bounced check fees ($) for a sample of 10 banks is

$$26\ 28\ 20\ 21\ 22\ 25\ 18\ 23\ 15\ 30$$

Compute the mode.

SOLUTION These data have no mode. None of the values is most typical because each value appears once.

The Geometric Mean

When you want to measure the rate of change of a variable over time, you need to use the geometric mean instead of the arithmetic mean. Equation (3.3) defines the geometric mean.

GEOMETRIC MEAN

The **geometric mean** is the nth root of the product of n values.

$$\bar{X}_G = (X_1 \times X_2 \times \cdots \times X_n)^{1/n} \tag{3.3}$$

The **geometric mean rate of return** measures the average percentage return of an investment per time period. Equation (3.4) defines the geometric mean rate of return.

GEOMETRIC MEAN RATE OF RETURN

$$\bar{R}_G = [(1 + R_1) \times (1 + R_2) \times \cdots \times (1 + R_n)]^{1/n} - 1 \tag{3.4}$$

where

$$R_i = \text{rate of return in time period } i$$

To illustrate these measures, consider an investment of $100,000 that declined to a value of $50,000 at the end of Year 1 and then rebounded back to its original $100,000 value at the end of Year 2. The rate of return for this investment per year for the two-year period is 0 because the starting and ending value of the investment is unchanged. However, the arithmetic mean of the yearly rates of return of this investment is

$$\bar{X} = \frac{(-0.50) + (1.00)}{2} = 0.25 \text{ or } 25\%$$

because the rate of return for Year 1 is

$$R_1 = \left(\frac{50,000 - 100,000}{100,000}\right) = -0.50 \text{ or } -50\%$$

and the rate of return for Year 2 is

$$R_2 = \left(\frac{100,000 - 50,000}{50,000}\right) = 1.00 \text{ or } 100\%$$

Using Equation (3.4), the geometric mean rate of return per year for the two years is

$$\begin{aligned} \bar{R}_G &= [(1 + R_1) \times (1 + R_2)]^{1/n} - 1 \\ &= [(1 + (-0.50)) \times (1 + (1.0))]^{1/2} - 1 \\ &= [(0.50) \times (2.0)]^{1/2} - 1 \\ &= [1.0]^{1/2} - 1 \\ &= 1 - 1 = 0 \end{aligned}$$

Thus, the geometric mean rate of return more accurately reflects the (zero) change in the value of the investment per year for the two-year period than does the arithmetic mean.

EXAMPLE 3.5

Computing the Geometric Mean Rate of Return

The percentage change in the Russell 2000 Index of the stock prices of 2,000 small companies was -33.79% in 2008 and 27.17% in 2009. Compute the geometric mean rate of return per year.

SOLUTION Using Equation (3.4), the geometric mean rate of return per year in the Russell 2000 Index for the two years is

$$\begin{aligned} \bar{R}_G &= [(1 + R_1) \times (1 + R_2)]^{1/n} - 1 \\ &= [(1 + (-0.3379)) \times (1 + (0.2717))]^{1/2} - 1 \\ &= [(0.6621) \times (1.2717)]^{1/2} - 1 \\ &= [0.8419925]^{1/2} - 1 \\ &= 0.9176 - 1 = -0.0824 \end{aligned}$$

The geometric mean rate of return in the Russell 2000 Index for the two years is -8.24% per year.

3.2 Variation and Shape

In addition to central tendency, every data set can be characterized by its variation and shape. Variation measures the **spread**, or **dispersion**, of values in a data set. One simple measure of variation is the range, the difference between the largest and smallest values. More commonly used in statistics are the standard deviation and variance, two measures explained later in this section. The shape of a data set represents a pattern of all the values, from the lowest to highest value. As you will learn later in this section, many data sets have a pattern that looks approximately like a bell, with a peak of values somewhere in the middle.

The Range

The range is the simplest numerical descriptive measure of variation in a set of data.

> **RANGE**
> The **range** is equal to the largest value minus the smallest value.
>
> $$\text{Range} = X_{\text{largest}} - X_{\text{smallest}} \tag{3.5}$$

To further analyze the sample of 10 times to get ready in the morning, you can compute the range. To do so, you rank the data from smallest to largest:

$$29 \quad 31 \quad 35 \quad 39 \quad 39 \quad 40 \quad 43 \quad 44 \quad 44 \quad 52$$

Using Equation (3.5), the range is $52 - 29 = 23$ minutes. The range of 23 minutes indicates that the largest difference between any two days in the time to get ready in the morning is 23 minutes.

EXAMPLE 3.6

Computing the Range in the Calories in Cereals

Nutritional data about a sample of seven breakfast cereals (stored in **Cereals**) includes the number of calories per serving (see Example 3.1 on page 128). Compute the range of the number of calories for the cereals.

SOLUTION Ranked from smallest to largest, the calories for the seven cereals are

$$80 \quad 100 \quad 100 \quad 110 \quad 130 \quad 190 \quad 200$$

Therefore, using Equation (3.5), the range = $200 - 80 = 120$. The largest difference in the number of calories between any cereals is 120.

The range measures the *total spread* in the set of data. Although the range is a simple measure of the total variation in the data, it does not take into account *how* the data are distributed between the smallest and largest values. In other words, the range does not indicate whether the values are evenly distributed throughout the data set, clustered near the middle, or clustered near one or both extremes. Thus, using the range as a measure of variation when at least one value is an extreme value is misleading.

The Variance and the Standard Deviation

Being a simple measure of variation, the range does not consider how the values distribute or cluster between the extremes. Two commonly used measures of variation that take into account how all the data values are distributed are the **variance** and the **standard deviation**. These statistics measure the "average" scatter around the mean—how larger values fluctuate above it and how smaller values fluctuate below it.

A simple measure of variation around the mean might take the difference between each value and the mean and then sum these differences. However, if you did that, you would find that because the mean is the balance point in a set of data, for *every* set of data, these differences sum to zero. One measure of variation that differs from data set to data set *squares* the difference between each value and the mean and then sums these squared differences. In statistics, this quantity is called a **sum of squares (SS)**. This sum is then divided by the number of values minus 1 (for sample data), to get the sample variance (S^2). The square root of the sample variance is the sample standard deviation (S).

Because this sum of squares will always be nonnegative according to the rules of algebra, *neither the variance nor the standard deviation can ever be negative*. For virtually all sets of data, the variance and standard deviation will be a positive value. Both of these statistics will be zero only if there is no variation in a set of data which happens only when each value in the sample is the same.

For a sample containing n values, $X_1, X_2, X_3, \ldots, X_n$, the sample variance (given by the symbol S^2) is

$$S^2 = \frac{(X_1 - \bar{X})^2 + (X_2 - \bar{X})^2 + \cdots + (X_n - \bar{X})^2}{n - 1}$$

Equation (3.6) expresses the sample variance using summation notation, and Equation (3.7) expresses the sample standard deviation.

SAMPLE VARIANCE

The **sample variance** is the sum of the squared differences around the mean divided by the sample size minus 1.

$$S^2 = \frac{\sum_{i=1}^{n}(X_i - \bar{X})^2}{n - 1} \qquad (3.6)$$

where

$\bar{X}$ = sample mean
n = sample size
X_i = ith value of the variable X
$\sum_{i=1}^{n}(X_i - \bar{X})^2$ = summation of all the squared differences between the X_i values and $\bar{X}$

SAMPLE STANDARD DEVIATION

The **sample standard deviation** is the square root of the sum of the squared differences around the mean divided by the sample size minus 1.

$$S = \sqrt{S^2} = \sqrt{\frac{\sum_{i=1}^{n}(X_i - \bar{X})^2}{n - 1}} \qquad (3.7)$$

If the denominator were n instead of $n - 1$, Equation (3.6) [and the inner term in Equation (3.7)] would compute the average of the squared differences around the mean. However, $n - 1$ is used because the statistic S^2 has certain mathematical properties that make it desirable for statistical inference (see Section 7.4 on page 288). As the sample size increases, the difference between dividing by n and by $n - 1$ becomes smaller and smaller.

In practice, you will most likely use the sample standard deviation as the measure of variation [defined in Equation (3.7)]. Unlike the sample variance, which is a squared quantity, the standard deviation is always a number that is in the same units as the original sample data. The standard deviation helps you see how a set of data clusters or distributes around its mean. For almost all sets of data, the majority of the observed values lie within an interval of plus and minus one standard deviation above and below the mean. Therefore, knowledge of the mean and the standard deviation usually helps define where at least the majority of the data values are clustering.

To hand-compute the sample variance, S^2, and the sample standard deviation, S, do the following:

1. Compute the difference between each value and the mean.
2. Square each difference.
3. Add the squared differences.
4. Divide this total by $n - 1$ to get the sample variance.
5. Take the square root of the sample variance to get the sample standard deviation.

To further analyze the sample of 10 times to get ready in the morning, Table 3.1 shows the first four steps for calculating the variance and standard deviation with a mean ($\bar{X}$) equal to 39.6. (See page 127 for the calculation of the mean.) The second column of Table 3.1 shows step 1. The third column of Table 3.1 shows step 2. The sum of the squared differences (step 3) is shown at the bottom of Table 3.1. This total is then divided by $10 - 1 = 9$ to compute the variance (step 4).

TABLE 3.1

Computing the Variance of the Getting-Ready Times

$\bar{X} = 39.6$

Time (X)	Step 1: $(X_i - \bar{X})$	Step 2: $(X_i - \bar{X})^2$
39	−0.60	0.36
29	−10.60	112.36
43	3.40	11.56
52	12.40	153.76
39	−0.60	0.36
44	4.40	19.36
40	0.40	0.16
31	−8.60	73.96
44	4.40	19.36
35	−4.60	21.16
	Step 3: Sum:	Step 4: Divide by $(n - 1)$:
	412.40	45.82

You can also compute the variance by substituting values for the terms in Equation (3.6):

$$S^2 = \frac{\sum_{i=1}^{n}(X_i - \bar{X})^2}{n - 1}$$

$$= \frac{(39 - 39.6)^2 + (29 - 39.6)^2 + \cdots + (35 - 39.6)^2}{10 - 1}$$

$$= \frac{412.4}{9}$$

$$= 45.82$$

Because the variance is in squared units (in squared minutes, for these data), to compute the standard deviation, you take the square root of the variance. Using Equation (3.7) on page 133, the sample standard deviation, S, is

$$S = \sqrt{S^2} = \sqrt{\frac{\sum_{i=1}^{n}(X_i - \bar{X})^2}{n - 1}} = \sqrt{45.82} = 6.77$$

This indicates that the getting-ready times in this sample are clustering within 6.77 minutes around the mean of 39.6 minutes (i.e., clustering between $\bar{X} - 1S = 32.83$ and $\bar{X} + 1S = 46.37$). In fact, 7 out of 10 getting-ready times lie within this interval.

Using the second column of Table 3.1, you can also compute the sum of the differences between each value and the mean to be zero. For any set of data, this sum will always be zero:

$$\sum_{i=1}^{n}(X_i - \bar{X}) = 0 \text{ for all sets of data}$$

This property is one of the reasons that the mean is used as the most common measure of central tendency.

EXAMPLE 3.7

Computing the Variance and Standard Deviation of the Number of Calories in Cereals

Nutritional data about a sample of seven breakfast cereals (stored in **Cereals**) includes the number of calories per serving (see Example 3.1 on page 128). Compute the variance and standard deviation of the calories in the cereals.

SOLUTION Table 3.2 illustrates the computation of the variance and standard deviation for the calories in the cereals.

TABLE 3.2 Computing the Variance of the Calories in the Cereals

$\bar{X} = 130$

Calories	Step 1: $(X_i - \bar{X})$	Step 2: $(X_i - \bar{X})^2$
80	−50	2,500
100	−30	900
100	−30	900
110	−20	400
130	0	0
190	60	3,600
200	70	4,900
	Step 3: Sum:	Step 4: Divide by $(n-1)$:
	13,200	2,200

Using Equation (3.6) on page 133:

$$S^2 = \frac{\sum_{i=1}^{n}(X_i - \bar{X})^2}{n-1}$$

$$= \frac{(80-130)^2 + (100-130)^2 + \cdots + (200-130)^2}{7-1}$$

$$= \frac{13,200}{6}$$

$$= 2,200$$

Using Equation (3.7) on page 133, the sample standard deviation, S, is

$$S = \sqrt{S^2} = \sqrt{\frac{\sum_{i=1}^{n}(X_i - \bar{X})^2}{n-1}} = \sqrt{2,200} = 46.9042$$

The standard deviation of 46.9042 indicates that the calories in the cereals are clustering within 46.9042 around the mean of 130 (i.e., clustering between $\bar{X} - 1S = 83.0958$ and $\bar{X} + 1S = 176.9042$). In fact, 57.1% (four out of seven) of the calories lie within this interval.

The characteristics of the range, variance, and standard deviation can be summarized as follows:

- The greater the spread or dispersion of the data, the larger the range, variance, and standard deviation.
- The smaller the spread or dispersion of the data, the smaller the range, variance, and standard deviation.

- If the values are all the same (so that there is no variation in the data), the range, variance, and standard deviation will all equal zero.
- None of the measures of variation (the range, variance, and standard deviation) can *ever* be negative.

The Coefficient of Variation

Unlike the measures of variation presented previously, the coefficient of variation is a *relative measure* of variation that is always expressed as a percentage rather than in terms of the units of the particular data. The coefficient of variation, denoted by the symbol CV, measures the scatter in the data relative to the mean.

> **COEFFICIENT OF VARIATION**
>
> The **coefficient of variation** is equal to the standard deviation divided by the mean, multiplied by 100%.
>
> $$CV = \left(\frac{S}{\bar{X}}\right)100\% \qquad (3.8)$$
>
> where
>
> S = sample standard deviation
> $\bar{X}$ = sample mean

For the sample of 10 getting-ready times, because $\bar{X} = 39.6$ and $S = 6.77$, the coefficient of variation is

$$CV = \left(\frac{S}{\bar{X}}\right)100\% = \left(\frac{6.77}{39.6}\right)100\% = 17.10\%$$

For the getting-ready times, the standard deviation is 17.1% of the size of the mean.

The coefficient of variation is especially useful when comparing two or more sets of data that are measured in different units, as Example 3.8 illustrates.

EXAMPLE 3.8

Comparing Two Coefficients of Variation When the Two Variables Have Different Units of Measurement

Which varies more from cereal to cereal, the number of calories or the amount of sugar (in grams)?

SOLUTION Because calories and the amount of sugar have different units of measurement, you need to compare the relative variability in the two measurements.

For calories, from Example 3.7 on page 135, the coefficient of variation is

$$CV_{Calories} = \left(\frac{46.9042}{130}\right)100\% = 36.08\%$$

For the amount of sugar in grams, the values for the seven cereals are

6 2 4 4 4 11 10

For these data, $\bar{X} = 5.8571$ and $S = 3.3877$.

Thus, the coefficient of variation is

$$CV_{Sugar} = \left(\frac{3.3877}{5.8571}\right)100\% = 57.84\%$$

Thus, relative to the mean, the amount of sugar is much more variable than the calories.

Z Scores

An **extreme value** or **outlier** is a value located far away from the mean. The **Z score**, which is the difference between the value and the mean, divided by the standard deviation, is useful in identifying outliers. Values located far away from the mean will have either very small (negative) Z scores or very large (positive) Z scores.

> **Z SCORE**
>
> $$Z = \frac{X - \bar{X}}{S} \tag{3.9}$$

To further analyze the sample of 10 times to get ready in the morning, you can compute the Z scores. Because the mean is 39.6 minutes, the standard deviation is 6.77 minutes, and the time to get ready on the first day is 39.0 minutes, you compute the Z score for Day 1 by using Equation (3.9):

$$Z = \frac{X - \bar{X}}{S}$$
$$= \frac{39.0 - 39.6}{6.77}$$
$$= -0.09$$

Table 3.3 shows the Z scores for all 10 days.

TABLE 3.3

Z Scores for the 10 Getting-Ready Times

	Time (X)	Z Score
	39	−0.90
	29	−1.57
	43	0.50
	52	1.83
	39	−0.09
	44	0.65
	40	0.06
	31	−1.27
	44	0.65
	35	−0.68
Mean	39.6	
Standard deviation	6.77	

The largest Z score is 1.83 for Day 4, on which the time to get ready was 52 minutes. The lowest Z score is −1.57 for Day 2, on which the time to get ready was 29 minutes. As a general rule, a Z score is considered an outlier if it is less than −3.0 or greater than +3.0. None of the times in this case meet that criterion to be considered outliers.

EXAMPLE 3.9

Computing the Z Scores of the Number of Calories in Cereals

Nutritional data about a sample of seven breakfast cereals (stored in Cereals) includes the number of calories per serving (see Example 3.1 on page 128). Compute the Z scores of the calories in breakfast cereals.

SOLUTION Table 3.4 on page 138 illustrates the Z scores of the calories for the cereals. The largest Z score is 1.49, for a cereal with 200 calories. The lowest Z score is −1.07 for a cereal with 80 calories. There are no apparent outliers in these data because none of the Z scores are less than −3.0 or greater than +3.0.

TABLE 3.4
Z Scores of the Number of Calories in Cereals

	Calories	Z Scores
	80	−1.07
	100	−0.64
	100	−0.64
	110	−0.43
	130	0.00
	190	1.28
	200	1.49
Mean	130	
Standard deviation	46.9042	

Shape

Shape is the pattern of the distribution of data values throughout the entire range of all the values. A distribution is either symmetrical or skewed. In a **symmetrical** distribution, the values below the mean are distributed in exactly the same way as the values above the mean. In this case, the low and high values balance each other out. In a **skewed** distribution, the values are not symmetrical around the mean. This skewness results in an imbalance of low values or high values.

Shape also can influence the relationship of the mean to the median. In most cases:

- Mean < median: negative, or left-skewed
- Mean = median: symmetric, or zero skewness
- Mean > median: positive, or right-skewed

Figure 3.1 depicts three data sets, each with a different shape.

FIGURE 3.1
A comparison of three data sets that differ in shape

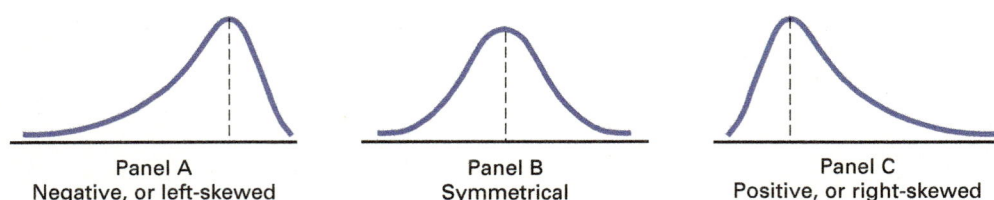

Panel A
Negative, or left-skewed

Panel B
Symmetrical

Panel C
Positive, or right-skewed

The data in Panel A are negative, or **left-skewed**. In this panel, most of the values are in the upper portion of the distribution. A long tail and distortion to the left is caused by some extremely small values. These extremely small values pull the mean downward so that the mean is less than the median.

The data in Panel B are symmetrical. Each half of the curve is a mirror image of the other half of the curve. The low and high values on the scale balance, and the mean equals the median.

The data in Panel C are positive, or **right-skewed**. In this panel, most of the values are in the lower portion of the distribution. A long tail on the right is caused by some extremely large values. These extremely large values pull the mean upward so that the mean is greater than the median.

Skewness and **kurtosis** are two shape-related statistics. The skewness statistic measures the extent to which a set of data is not symmetric. The kurtosis statistic measures the relative concentration of values in the center of the distribution of a data set, as compared with the tails.

A symmetric distribution has a skewness value of zero. A right-skewed distribution has a positive skewness value, and a left-skewed distribution has a negative skewness value.

A bell-shaped distribution has a kurtosis value of zero. A distribution that is flatter than a bell-shaped distribution has a negative kurtosis value. A distribution with a sharper peak (one that has a higher concentration of values in the center of the distribution than a bell-shaped distribution) has a positive kurtosis value.

EXAMPLE 3.10

Descriptive Statistics for Intermediate Government and Short-Term Corporate Bond Funds

In Part II of the Choice Is Yours scenario, you are interested in comparing the past performance of the intermediate government bond and short-term corporate bond funds. One measure of past performance is the return in 2009. You have already defined the variables to be collected and collected the data from a sample of 184 bond funds. Compute descriptive statistics for the intermediate government and short-term corporate bond funds.

SOLUTION Figure 3.2 presents a table of descriptive summary measures for the two types of bond funds, as computed by Excel (left results) and Minitab (right results). The Excel results include the mean, standard error, median, mode, standard deviation, variance, kurtosis, skewness, range, minimum, maximum, sum (which is meaningless for this example), and count (the sample size). The standard error, discussed in Section 7.4, is the standard deviation divided by the square root of the sample size. The Minitab results also include the coefficient of variation, the first quartile, the third quartile, and the interquartile range (see Section 3.3 on pages 143-145).

FIGURE 3.2

Excel and Minitab Descriptive statistics for the 2009 return for the intermediate government and short-term corporate bond funds

	A	B	C
1	Descriptive Statistics for Return 2009		
2		Intermediate Government	Short Term Corporate
3	Mean	4.4529	9.5959
4	Standard Error	0.5747	0.5774
5	Median	4.4000	9.1000
6	Mode	5.7000	6.8000
7	Standard Deviation	5.3606	5.6867
8	Sample Variance	28.7365	32.3389
9	Kurtosis	4.8953	3.7273
10	Skewness	1.4979	0.9002
11	Range	33.4000	40.8000
12	Minimum	-4.8000	-8.8000
13	Maximum	28.6000	32.0000
14	Sum	387.4000	930.8000
15	Count	87	97

```
Variable   Type                       Count   Mean   StDev   Variance   CoefVar
Return 2009 Intermediate Government    87    4.453   5.361   28.736     120.39
           Short Term Corporate        97    9.596   5.687   32.339      59.26

Variable   Type                       Minimum   Q1     Median    Q3     Maximum
Return 2009 Intermediate Government   -4.800   0.900   4.400    6.500   28.600
           Short Term Corporate       -8.800   5.700   9.100   12.950   32.000

                                                                        N for
Variable   Type                       Range    IQR              Mode    Mode
Return 2009 Intermediate Government   33.400   5.600          3.5, 5.7    3
           Short Term Corporate       40.800   7.250     6, 6.7, 6.8, 7.3  3

Variable   Type                       Skewness   Kurtosis
Return 2009 Intermediate Government    1.50       4.90
           Short Term Corporate        0.90       3.73

The data contain at least five mode values. Only the smallest four are shown.
```

In examining the results, you see that there are large differences in the 2009 return for the intermediate government bond and short-term corporate bond funds. The intermediate government bond funds had a mean 2009 return of 4.4529 and a median return of 4.4. This compares to a mean of 9.5959 and a median of 9.1 for the short-term corporate bond funds. The medians indicate that half of the intermediate government bond funds had returns of 4.4 or better, and half the short-term corporate bond funds had returns of 9.1 or better. You conclude that the short-term corporate bond funds had a much higher return than the intermediate government bond funds.

The intermediate government corporate bond funds had a slightly smaller standard deviation than the short-term corporate bond funds (5.3606, as compared to 5.6867). While both the intermediate government bond funds and the short-term corporate bond funds showed right or positive skewness, the intermediate government bond funds were more skewed. The kurtosis of both the intermediate government and the short-term corporate bond funds was very positive, indicating a distribution that was much more peaked than a bell-shaped distribution.

VISUAL EXPLORATIONS: Exploring Descriptive Statistics

Use the Visual Explorations Descriptive Statistics procedure to see the effect of changing data values on measures of central tendency, variation, and shape. Open the **Visual Explorations add-in workbook (Visual Explorations.xla)** and:

1. Select **Add-ins → Visual Explorations → Descriptive Statistics**.
2. Read the instructions in the Descriptive Statistics dialog box and then click **OK** (see the illustration at right).
3. Experiment by entering an extreme value such as 5 into one of the tinted column A cells.

Which measures are affected by this change? Which ones are not? You can switch between the "before" and "after" diagrams by repeatedly pressing **Ctrl+Z** (undo) followed by **Ctrl+Y** (redo) to better see the changes the extreme value has caused in the diagram. (To learn more about Visual Explorations, see Appendix Section D.4.)

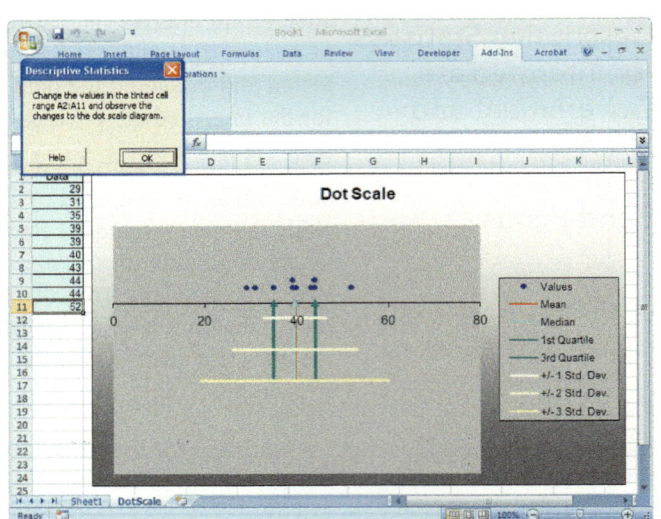

Problems for Sections 3.1 and 3.2

LEARNING THE BASICS

3.1 The following set of data is from a sample of $n = 5$:

  7 4 9 8 2

a. Compute the mean, median, and mode.
b. Compute the range, variance, standard deviation, and coefficient of variation.
c. Compute the Z scores. Are there any outliers?
d. Describe the shape of the data set.

3.2 The following set of data is from a sample of $n = 6$:

  7 4 9 7 3 12

a. Compute the mean, median, and mode.
b. Compute the range, variance, standard deviation, and coefficient of variation.
c. Compute the Z scores. Are there any outliers?
d. Describe the shape of the data set.

3.3 The following set of data is from a sample of $n = 7$:

  12 7 4 9 0 7 3

a. Compute the mean, median, and mode.
b. Compute the range, variance, standard deviation, and coefficient of variation.
c. Compute the Z scores. Are there any outliers?
d. Describe the shape of the data set.

3.4 The following set of data is from a sample of $n = 5$:

  7 −5 −8 7 9

a. Compute the mean, median, and mode.
b. Compute the range, variance, standard deviation, and coefficient of variation.
c. Compute the Z scores. Are there any outliers?
d. Describe the shape of the data set.

3.5 Suppose that the rate of return for a particular stock during the past two years was 10% and 30%. Compute the geometric rate of return per year. (*Note:* A rate of return of 10% is recorded as 0.10, and a rate of return of 30% is recorded as 0.30.)

3.6 Suppose that the rate of return for a particular stock during the past two years was 20% and −30%. Compute the geometric rate of return per year.

APPLYING THE CONCEPTS

3.7 A survey conducted by the American Statistical Association reported the results at the top of page 141 for the salaries of professors teaching statistics in research universities with four to five years in the rank of associate professor and professor.

Title	Median
Associate professor	82,400
Professor	108,600

Source: Data extracted from K. Crank, "Academic Salary Survey," *AmStat News*, December 2009, p. 34.

Interpret the median salary for the associate professors and professors.

3.8 The operations manager of a plant that manufactures tires wants to compare the actual inner diameters of two grades of tires, each of which is expected to be 575 millimeters. A sample of five tires of each grade was selected, and the results representing the inner diameters of the tires, ranked from smallest to largest, are as follows:

Grade X	Grade Y
568 570 575 578 584	573 574 575 577 578

a. For each of the two grades of tires, compute the mean, median, and standard deviation.
b. Which grade of tire is providing better quality? Explain.
c. What would be the effect on your answers in (a) and (b) if the last value for grade Y were 588 instead of 578? Explain.

3.9 According to the U.S. Census Bureau, in February 2010, the median sales price of new houses was $220,500 and the mean sales price was $282,600 (extracted from www.census.gov, March 24, 2010).
a. Interpret the median sales price.
b. Interpret the mean sales price.
c. Discuss the shape of the distribution of the price of new houses.

SELF Test 3.10 The file **FastFood** contains the amount that a sample of nine customers spent for lunch ($) at a fast-food restaurant:

4.20 5.03 5.86 6.45 7.38 7.54 8.46 8.47 9.87

a. Compute the mean and median.
b. Compute the variance, standard deviation, range, and coefficient of variation.
c. Are the data skewed? If so, how?
d. Based on the results of (a) through (c), what conclusions can you reach concerning the amount that customers spent for lunch?

3.11 The file **Sedans** contains the overall miles per gallon (MPG) of 2010 family sedans:

24 21 22 23 24 34 34 34 20 20
22 22 44 32 20 20 22 20 39 20

Source: Data extracted from "Vehicle Ratings," *Consumer Reports*, April 2010, p. 29.

a. Compute the mean, median, and mode.
b. Compute the variance, standard deviation, range, coefficient of variation, and Z scores.
c. Are the data skewed? If so, how?
d. Compare the results of (a) through (c) to those of Problem 3.12 (a) through (c) that refer to the miles per gallon of small SUVs.

3.12 The file **SUV** contains the overall miles per gallon (MPG) of 2010 small SUVs:

24 23 22 21 22 22 18 18 26
26 26 19 19 19 21 21 21 21
21 18 19 21 22 22 16 16

Source: Data extracted from "Vehicle Ratings," *Consumer Reports*, April 2010, pp. 33–34.

a. Compute the mean, median, and mode.
b. Compute the variance, standard deviation, range, coefficient of variation, and Z scores.
c. Are the data skewed? If so, how?
d. Compare the results of (a) through (c) to those of Problem 3.11 (a) through (c) that refer to the miles per gallon of family sedans.

3.13 The file **ChocolateChip** contains the cost (in cents) per 1-ounce serving for a sample of 13 chocolate chip cookies. The data are as follows:

54 22 25 23 36 43 7 43 25 47 24 45 44

Source: Data extracted from "Chip, Chip, Hooray," *Consumer Reports*, June 2009, p. 7.

a. Compute the mean, median, and mode.
b. Compute the variance, standard deviation, range, coefficient of variation, and Z scores. Are there any outliers? Explain.
c. Are the data skewed? If so, how?
d. Based on the results of (a) through (c), what conclusions can you reach concerning the cost of chocolate chip cookies?

3.14 The file **DarkChocolate** contains the cost per ounce ($) for a sample of 14 dark chocolate bars:

0.68 0.72 0.92 1.14 1.42 0.94 0.77
0.57 1.51 0.57 0.55 0.86 1.41 0.90

Source: Data extracted from "Dark Chocolate: Which Bars Are Best?" *Consumer Reports*, September 2007, p. 8.

a. Compute the mean, median, and mode.
b. Compute the variance, standard deviation, range, coefficient of variation, and Z scores. Are there any outliers? Explain.
c. Are the data skewed? If so, how?
d. Based on the results of (a) through (c), what conclusions can you reach concerning the cost of dark chocolate bars?

3.15 Is there a difference in the variation of the yields of different types of investments? The file **SavingsRate-MMCD** contains the yields for a money market account and a five-year certificate of deposit (CD), for 25 banks in the United States, as of March 29, 2010.
Source: Data extracted from **www.Bankrate.com**, March 29, 2010.

a. For money market accounts and five-year CDs, separately compute the variance, standard deviation, range, and coefficient of variation.
b. Based on the results of (a), do money market accounts or five-year CDs have more variation in the yields offered? Explain.

3.16 The file **HotelUK** contains the room price (in $) paid by U.S. travelers in six British cities in 2009:

185   160   126   116   112   105

Source: Data extracted from **www.hotels.com/press/hotel-price-index-2009-h2.html**.

a. Compute the mean, median, and mode.
b. Compute the range, variance, and standard deviation.
c. Based on the results of (a) and (b), what conclusions can you reach concerning the room price (in $) paid by U.S. travelers in 2009?
d. Suppose that the first value was 85 instead of 185. Repeat (a) through (c), using this value. Comment on the difference in the results.

3.17 A bank branch located in a commercial district of a city has the business objective of developing an improved process for serving customers during the noon-to-1:00 P.M. lunch period. The waiting time, in minutes, is defined as the time the customer enters the line to when he or she reaches the teller window. Data are collected from a sample of 15 customers during this hour. The file **Bank1** contains the results, which are also listed here:

4.21   5.55   3.02   5.13   4.77   2.34   3.54   3.20
4.50   6.10   0.38   5.12   6.46   6.19   3.79

a. Compute the mean and median.
b. Compute the variance, standard deviation, range, coefficient of variation, and Z scores. Are there any outliers? Explain.
c. Are the data skewed? If so, how?
d. As a customer walks into the branch office during the lunch hour, she asks the branch manager how long she can expect to wait. The branch manager replies, "Almost certainly less than five minutes." On the basis of the results of (a) through (c), evaluate the accuracy of this statement.

3.18 Suppose that another bank branch, located in a residential area, is also concerned with the noon-to-1 P.M. lunch hour. The waiting time, in minutes, collected from a sample of 15 customers during this hour, is contained in the file **Bank2** and listed here:

9.66   5.90   8.02   5.79   8.73   3.82   8.01   8.35
10.49   6.68   5.64   4.08   6.17   9.91   5.47

a. Compute the mean and median.
b. Compute the variance, standard deviation, range, coefficient of variation, and Z scores. Are there any outliers? Explain.
c. Are the data skewed? If so, how?
d. As a customer walks into the branch office during the lunch hour, he asks the branch manager how long he can expect to wait. The branch manager replies, "Almost certainly less than five minutes." On the basis of the results of (a) through (c), evaluate the accuracy of this statement.

3.19 General Electric (GE) is one of the world's largest companies; it develops, manufactures, and markets a wide range of products, including medical diagnostic imaging devices, jet engines, lighting products, and chemicals. In 2008, the stock price dropped 53.94%, while in 2009, the stock price rose 0.13%.
Source: Data extracted from **finance.yahoo.com**, March 30, 2010.

a. Compute the geometric mean rate of return per year for the two-year period 2008–2009. (Hint: Denote an increase of 0.13% as $R_2 = 0.0013$.)
b. If you purchased $1,000 of GE stock at the start of 2008, what was its value at the end of 2009?
c. Compare the result of (b) to that of Problem 3.20 (b).

3.20 TASER International, Inc., develops, manufactures, and sells nonlethal self-defense devices known as tasers. Marketing primarily to law enforcement, corrections institutions, and the military, TASER's popularity has enjoyed a roller-coaster ride. The stock price in 2008 decreased by 63.31%, and in 2009, the stock price decreased by 17.05%.
Source: Data extracted from **finance.yahoo.com**, March 30, 2010.

a. Compute the geometric mean rate of return per year for the two-year period 2008–2009. (Hint: Denote a decrease of 63.31% as $R_1 = -0.6331$.)
b. If you purchased $1,000 of TASER stock at the start of 2008, what was its value at the end of 2009?
c. Compare the result of (b) to that of Problem 3.19 (b).

3.21 In 2009, all the major stock market indices increased dramatically as they recovered from the world financial crisis that occurred in 2008. The data in the following table (stored in **Indices**) represent the total rate of return (in percentage) for the Dow Jones Industrial Average (DJIA), the Standard & Poor's 500 (S&P 500), and the technology-heavy NASDAQ Composite (NASDAQ) from 2006 through 2009.

Year	DJIA	S&P 500	NASDAQ
2009	18.8	23.5	43.9
2008	−33.8	−38.5	−40.5
2007	6.4	3.5	9.8
2006	16.3	13.6	9.5

Source: Data extracted from **finance.yahoo.com**, April 1, 2010.

a. Compute the geometric mean rate of return per year for the DJIA, S&P 500, and NASDAQ from 2006 through 2009.
b. What conclusions can you reach concerning the geometric mean rates of return per year of the three market indices?
c. Compare the results of (b) to those of Problem 3.22 (b).

3.22 In 2006–2009, the value of precious metals changed rapidly. The data in the following table (contained in the file Metals) represent the total rate of return (in percentage) for platinum, gold, and silver from 2006 through 2009:

Year	Platinum	Gold	Silver
2009	62.7	25.0	56.8
2008	−41.3	4.3	−26.9
2007	36.9	31.9	14.4
2006	15.9	23.2	46.1

Source: Data extracted from **www.kitco.com**, April 1, 2010.

a. Compute the geometric mean rate of return per year for platinum, gold, and silver from 2006 through 2009.
b. What conclusions can you reach concerning the geometric mean rates of return of the three precious metals?
c. Compare the results of (b) to those of Problem 3.21 (b).

3.3 Exploring Numerical Data

Sections 3.1 and 3.2 discuss measures of central tendency, variation, and shape. An additional way of describing numerical data is through an exploratory data analysis that computes the quartiles and the five-number summary and constructs a boxplot. You can also supplement these methods by displaying descriptive statistics across several categorical variables using the multidimensional table technique that Section 2.7 discusses.

Quartiles

Quartiles split a set of data into four equal parts—the **first quartile,** Q_1, divides the smallest 25.0% of the values from the other 75.0% that are larger. The **second quartile,** Q_2, is the median—50.0% of the values are smaller than or equal to the median and 50.0% are larger than or equal to the median. The **third quartile,** Q_3, divides the smallest 75.0% of the values from the largest 25.0%. Equations (3.10) and (3.11) define the first and third quartiles.[1]

[1] The Q_1, median, and Q_3 are also the 25th, 50th, and 75th percentiles, respectively. Equations (3.2), (3.10), and (3.11) can be expressed generally in terms of finding percentiles: $(p \times 100)$th percentile $= p \times (n + 1)$ ranked value, where $p =$ the proportion.

FIRST QUARTILE, Q_1

25.0% of the values are smaller than or equal to Q_1, the first quartile, and 75.0% are larger than or equal to the first quartile, Q_1.

$$Q_1 = \frac{n+1}{4} \text{ ranked value} \qquad (3.10)$$

THIRD QUARTILE, Q_3

75.0% of the values are smaller than or equal to the third quartile, Q_3, and 25.0% are larger than or equal to the third quartile, Q_3.

$$Q_3 = \frac{3(n+1)}{4} \text{ ranked value} \qquad (3.11)$$

Use the following rules to compute the quartiles from a set of ranked values:

- **Rule 1** If the ranked value is a whole number, the quartile is equal to the measurement that corresponds to that ranked value. For example, if the sample size $n = 7$, the first quartile, Q_1, is equal to the measurement associated with the $(7 + 1)/4 =$ second ranked value.
- **Rule 2** If the ranked value is a fractional half (2.5, 4.5, etc.), the quartile is equal to the measurement that corresponds to the average of the measurements corresponding to the two ranked values involved. For example, if the sample size $n = 9$, the first quartile,

In Excel, the QUARTILE function uses different rules to compute quartiles. Use the COMPUTE worksheet of the Quartiles workbook, discussed in Section EG3.3, to compute quartiles using the rules presented in this section.

Q_1, is equal to the $(9 + 1)/4 = 2.5$ ranked value, halfway between the second ranked value and the third ranked value.

- **Rule 3** If the ranked value is neither a whole number nor a fractional half, you round the result to the nearest integer and select the measurement corresponding to that ranked value. For example, if the sample size $n = 10$, the first quartile, Q_1, is equal to the $(10 + 1)/4 = 2.75$ ranked value. Round 2.75 to 3 and use the third ranked value.

To further analyze the sample of 10 times to get ready in the morning, you can compute the quartiles. To do so, you rank the data from smallest to largest:

Ranked values:	29	31	35	39	39	40	43	44	44	52
Ranks:	1	2	3	4	5	6	7	8	9	10

The first quartile is the $(n + 1)/4 = (10 + 1)/4 = 2.75$ ranked value. Using Rule 3, you round up to the third ranked value. The third ranked value for the time-to-get-ready data is 35 minutes. You interpret the first quartile of 35 to mean that on 25% of the days, the time to get ready is less than or equal to 35 minutes, and on 75% of the days, the time to get ready is greater than or equal to 35 minutes.

The third quartile is the $3(n + 1)/4 = 3(10 + 1)/4 = 8.25$ ranked value. Using Rule 3 for quartiles, you round this down to the eighth ranked value. The eighth ranked value is 44 minutes. Thus, on 75% of the days, the time to get ready is less than or equal to 44 minutes, and on 25% of the days, the time to get ready is greater than or equal to 44 minutes.

EXAMPLE 3.11

Computing the Quartiles

Nutritional data about a sample of seven breakfast cereals (stored in **Cereals**) includes the number of calories per serving (see Example 3.1 on page 128). Compute the first quartile (Q_1) and third quartile (Q_3) numbers of calories for the cereals.

SOLUTION Ranked from smallest to largest, the number of calories for the seven cereals are as follows:

Ranked values:	80	100	100	110	130	190	200
Ranks:	1	2	3	4	5	6	7

For these data

$$Q_1 = \frac{(n+1)}{4} \text{ ranked value}$$
$$= \frac{7+1}{4} \text{ ranked value} = \text{2nd ranked value}$$

Therefore, using Rule 1, Q_1 is the second ranked value. Because the second ranked value is 100, the first quartile, Q_1, is 100.

To compute the third quartile, Q_3,

$$Q_3 = \frac{3(n+1)}{4} \text{ ranked value}$$
$$= \frac{3(7+1)}{4} \text{ ranked value} = \text{6th ranked value}$$

Therefore, using Rule 1, Q_3 is the sixth ranked value. Because the sixth ranked value is 190, Q_3 is 190.

The first quartile of 100 indicates that 25% of the cereals have calories that are below or equal to 100 and 75% are greater than or equal to 100. The third quartile of 190 indicates that 75% of the cereals have calories that are below or equal to 190 and 25% are greater than or equal to 190.

The Interquartile Range

The interquartile range is the difference between the third and first quartiles in a set of data.

> **INTERQUARTILE RANGE**
>
> The **interquartile range** (also called **midspread**) is the difference between the third quartile and the first quartile.
>
> $$\text{Interquartile range} = Q_3 - Q_1 \quad (3.12)$$

The interquartile range measures the spread in the middle 50% of the data. Therefore, it is not influenced by extreme values. To further analyze the sample of 10 times to get ready in the morning, you can compute the interquartile range. You first order the data as follows:

29   31   35   39   39   40   43   44   44   52

You use Equation (3.12) and the earlier results above, $Q_1 = 35$ and $Q_3 = 44$:

$$\text{Interquartile range} = 44 - 35 = 9 \text{ minutes}$$

Therefore, the interquartile range in the time to get ready is 9 minutes. The interval 35 to 44 is often referred to as the *middle fifty*.

EXAMPLE 3.12

Computing the Interquartile Range for the Number of Calories in Cereals

Nutritional data about a sample of seven breakfast cereals (stored in Cereals) includes the number of calories per serving (see Example 3.1 on page 128). Compute the interquartile range of the numbers of calories in cereals.

SOLUTION Ranked from smallest to largest, the numbers of calories for the seven cereals are as follows:

80   100   100   110   130   190   200

Using Equation (3.12) and the earlier results from Example 3.11 on page 144, $Q_1 = 100$ and $Q_3 = 190$:

$$\text{Interquartile range} = 190 - 100 = 90$$

Therefore, the interquartile range of the number of calories in cereals is 90 calories.

Because the interquartile range does not consider any value smaller than Q_1 or larger than Q_3, it cannot be affected by extreme values. Descriptive statistics such as the median, Q_1, Q_3, and the interquartile range, which are not influenced by extreme values, are called **resistant measures**.

The Five-Number Summary

A **five-number summary**, which consists of the following, provides a way to determine the shape of a distribution:

$$X_{\text{smallest}} \quad Q_1 \quad \text{Median} \quad Q_3 \quad X_{\text{largest}}$$

Table 3.5 explains how the relationships among these five numbers allows you to recognize the shape of a data set.

TABLE 3.5

Relationships Among the Five-Number Summary and the Type of Distribution

Comparison	Type of Distribution		
	Left-Skewed	Symmetric	Right-Skewed
The distance from $X_{smallest}$ to the median versus the distance from the median to $X_{largest}$.	The distance from $X_{smallest}$ to the median is greater than the distance from the median to $X_{largest}$.	The two distances are the same.	The distance from $X_{smallest}$ to the median is less than the distance from the median to $X_{largest}$.
The distance from $X_{smallest}$ to Q_1 versus the distance from Q_3 to $X_{largest}$.	The distance from $X_{smallest}$ to Q_1 is greater than the distance from Q_3 to $X_{largest}$.	The two distances are the same.	The distance from $X_{smallest}$ to Q_1 is less than the distance from Q_3 to $X_{largest}$.
The distance from Q_1 to the median versus the distance from the median to Q_3.	The distance from Q_1 to the median is greater than the distance from the median to Q_3.	The two distances are the same.	The distance from Q_1 to the median is less than the distance from the median to Q_3.

To further analyze the sample of 10 times to get ready in the morning, you can compute the five-number summary. For these data, the smallest value is 29 minutes, and the largest value is 52 minutes (see page 127). Calculations done on pages 129 and 144 show that the median = 39.5, Q_1 = 35, and Q_3 = 44. Therefore, the five-number summary is as follows:

$$29 \quad 35 \quad 39.5 \quad 44 \quad 52$$

The distance from $X_{smallest}$ to the median (39.5 − 29 = 10.5) is slightly less than the distance from the median to $X_{largest}$ (52 − 39.5 = 12.5). The distance from $X_{smallest}$ to Q_1 (35 − 29 = 6) is slightly less than the distance from Q_3 to $X_{largest}$ (52 − 44 = 8). The distance from Q_1 to the median (39.5 − 35 = 4.5) is the same as the distance from the median to Q_3 (44 − 39.5 = 4.5). Therefore, the getting-ready times are slightly right-skewed.

EXAMPLE 3.13

Computing the Five-Number Summary of the Number of Calories in Cereals

Nutritional data about a sample of seven breakfast cereals (stored in Cereals) includes the number of calories per serving (see Example 3.1 on page 128). Compute the five-number summary of the numbers of calories in cereals.

SOLUTION From previous computations for the calories in cereals (see pages 128 and 144), you know that the median = 110, Q_1 = 100, and Q_3 = 190.

In addition, the smallest value in the data set is 80, and the largest value is 200. Therefore, the five-number summary is as follows:

$$80 \quad 100 \quad 110 \quad 190 \quad 200$$

The three comparisons listed in Table 3.5 are used to evaluate skewness. The distance from $X_{smallest}$ to the median (110 − 80 = 30) is less than the distance (200 − 110 = 90) from the median to $X_{largest}$. The distance from $X_{smallest}$ to Q_1 (100 − 80 = 20) is the more than the distance from Q_3 to $X_{largest}$ (200 − 190 = 10). The distance from Q_1 to the median (110 − 100 = 10) is less than the distance from the median to Q_3 (190 − 110 = 80). Two comparisons indicate a right-skewed distribution, whereas the other indicates a left-skewed distribution. Therefore, given the small sample size and the conflicting results, the shape is not clearly determined.

The Boxplot

A **boxplot** provides a graphical representation of the data based on the five-number summary. To further analyze the sample of 10 times to get ready in the morning, you can construct a boxplot, as displayed in Figure 3.3.

FIGURE 3.3
Boxplot for the getting-ready times

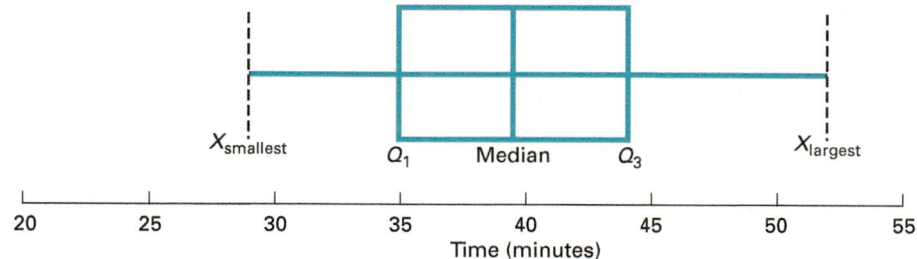

The vertical line drawn within the box represents the median. The vertical line at the left side of the box represents the location of Q_1, and the vertical line at the right side of the box represents the location of Q_3. Thus, the box contains the middle 50% of the values. The lower 25% of the data are represented by a line connecting the left side of the box to the location of the smallest value, $X_{smallest}$. Similarly, the upper 25% of the data are represented by a line connecting the right side of the box to $X_{largest}$.

The boxplot of the getting-ready times in Figure 3.3 indicates slight right-skewness because the distance between the median and the highest value is slightly greater than the distance between the lowest value and the median. Also, the right tail is slightly longer than the left tail.

EXAMPLE 3.14

Boxplots of the 2009 Returns of Intermediate Government and Short-Term Corporate Bond Funds

In Part II of the Choice Is Yours scenario, you are interested in comparing the past performance of the intermediate government bond and short-term corporate bond funds. One measure of past performance is the return in 2009. You have already defined the variables to be collected and collected the data from a sample of 184 bond funds. Construct the boxplot of the 2009 returns for the intermediate government bond and short-term corporate bond funds.

SOLUTION Figure 3.4 contains the five-number summaries and Excel boxplots of the 2009 return for the intermediate government and short-term corporate bond funds. Figure 3.5 displays the Minitab boxplots for the same data. Note that in Figure 3.5 on page 148, several * appear in the boxplots. These indicate outliers that are more than 1.5 times the interquartile range beyond the quartiles.

FIGURE 3.4

Excel five-number summaries and boxplots of the 2009 return for intermediate government bond and short-term corporate bond funds

	A	B	C
1	Five-Number Summary for Return 2009		
2		Intermediate Government	Short Term Corporate
3	Minimum	-4.8	-8.8
4	First Quartile	0.9	5.7
5	Median	4.4	9.1
6	Third Quartile	6.5	12.95
7	Maximum	28.6	32

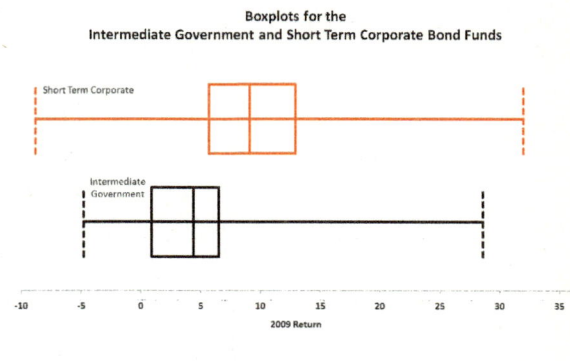

The median return, the quartiles, and the minimum and maximum returns are much higher for the short-term corporate bond funds than for the intermediate government bond funds. The median return for the short-term corporate bond funds is higher than the third quartile return for the intermediate government bond funds. The first quartile return (5.70) for the short-term

FIGURE 3.5
Minitab boxplots of the 2009 return for intermediate government bond and short-term corporate bond funds

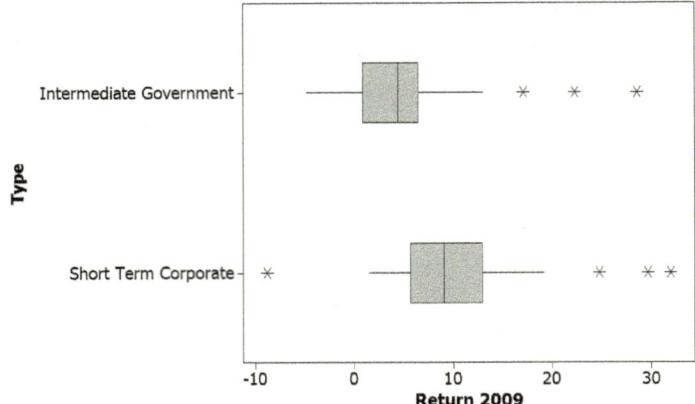

corporate bond funds is higher than the median return (4.40) for the intermediate government bond funds. Both the intermediate government bond and short-term corporate bond funds are right-skewed, with a very long tail in the upper part of the range. These results are consistent with the statistics computed in Figure 3.2 on page 139.

Figure 3.6 demonstrates the relationship between the boxplot and the density curve for four different types of distributions. The area under each density curve is split into quartiles corresponding to the five-number summary for the boxplot.

FIGURE 3.6
Boxplots and corresponding density curves for four distributions

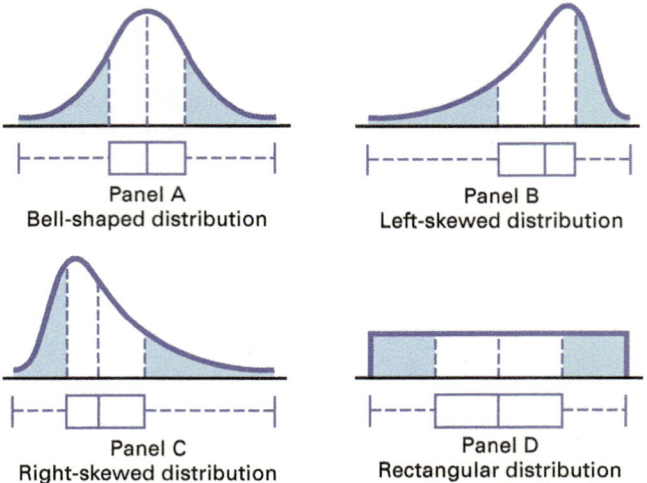

The distributions in Panels A and D of Figure 3.6 are symmetric. In these distributions, the mean and median are equal. In addition, the length of the left tail is equal to the length of the right tail, and the median line divides the box in half.

The distribution in Panel B of Figure 3.6 is left-skewed. The few small values distort the mean toward the left tail. For this left-skewed distribution, there is a heavy clustering of values at the high end of the scale (i.e., the right side); 75% of all values are found between the left edge of the box (Q_1) and the end of the right tail (X_{largest}). There is a long left tail that contains the smallest 25% of the values, demonstrating the lack of symmetry in this data set.

The distribution in Panel C of Figure 3.6 is right-skewed. The concentration of values is on the low end of the scale (i.e., the left side of the boxplot). Here, 75% of all values are found between the beginning of the left tail and the right edge of the box (Q_3). There is a long right tail that contains the largest 25% of the values, demonstrating the lack of symmetry in this data set.

Problems for Section 3.3

LEARNING THE BASICS

3.23 The following is a set of data from a sample of $n = 7$:

$$12 \quad 7 \quad 4 \quad 9 \quad 0 \quad 7 \quad 3$$

a. Compute the first quartile (Q_1), the third quartile (Q_3), and the interquartile range.
b. List the five-number summary.
c. Construct a boxplot and describe its shape.
d. Compare your answer in (c) with that from Problem 3.3 (d) on page 140. Discuss.

3.24 The following is a set of data from a sample of $n = 6$:

$$7 \quad 4 \quad 9 \quad 7 \quad 3 \quad 12$$

a. Compute the first quartile (Q_1), the third quartile (Q_3), and the interquartile range.
b. List the five-number summary.
c. Construct a boxplot and describe its shape.
d. Compare your answer in (c) with that from Problem 3.2 (d) on page 140. Discuss.

3.25 The following is a set of data from a sample of $n = 5$:

$$7 \quad 4 \quad 9 \quad 8 \quad 2$$

a. Compute the first quartile (Q_1), the third quartile (Q_3), and the interquartile range.
b. List the five-number summary.
c. Construct a boxplot and describe its shape.
d. Compare your answer in (c) with that from Problem 3.1 (d) on page 140. Discuss.

3.26 The following is a set of data from a sample of $n = 5$:

$$7 \quad -5 \quad -8 \quad 7 \quad 9$$

a. Compute the first quartile (Q_1), the third quartile (Q_3), and the interquartile range.
b. List the five-number summary.
c. Construct a boxplot and describe its shape.
d. Compare your answer in (c) with that from Problem 3.4 (d) on page 140. Discuss.

APPLYING THE CONCEPTS

3.27 The file **ChocolateChip** contains the cost (in cents) per 1-ounce serving, for a sample of 13 chocolate chip cookies. The data are as follows:

54 22 25 23 36 43 7 43 25 47 24 45 44

Source: Data extracted from "Chip, Chip, Hooray," *Consumer Reports*, June 2009, p. 7.

a. Compute the first quartile (Q_1), the third quartile (Q_3), and the interquartile range.
b. List the five-number summary.
c. Construct a boxplot and describe its shape.

3.28 The file **Dark Chocolate** contains the cost ($) per ounce for a sample of 14 dark chocolate bars:

0.68 0.72 0.92 1.14 1.42 0.94 0.77 0.57 1.51
0.57 0.55 0.86 1.41 0.90

Source: Data extracted from "Dark Chocolate: Which Bars Are Best?" *Consumer Reports*, September 2007, pp. 8.

a. Compute the first quartile (Q_1), the third quartile (Q_3), and the interquartile range.
b. List the five-number summary.
c. Construct a boxplot and describe its shape.

3.29 The file **HotelUK** contains the room price (in $) paid by U.S. travelers in six British cities in 2009:

185 160 126 116 112 105

Source: Data extracted from www.hotels.com/press/hotel-price-index-2009-h2.html.

a. Compute the first quartile (Q_1), the third quartile (Q_3), and the interquartile range.
b. List the five-number summary.
c. Construct a boxplot and describe its shape.

3.30 The file **SUV** contains the overall miles per gallon (MPG) of 2010 small SUVs:

24 23 22 21 22 22 18 18 26
26 26 19 19 19 21 21 21 21
21 18 19 21 22 22 16 16

Source: Data extracted from "Vehicle Ratings," *Consumer Reports*, April 2010, pp. 33–34.

a. Compute the first quartile (Q_1), the third quartile (Q_3), and the interquartile range.
b. List the five-number summary.
c. Construct a boxplot and describe its shape.

3.31 The file **SavingsRate-MMCD** contains the yields for a money market account and a five-year certificate of deposit (CD), for 25 banks in the United States, as of March 29, 2010.
Source: Data extracted from www.Bankrate.com, March 29, 2010.

For each type of account:
a. Compute the first quartile (Q_1), the third quartile (Q_3), and the interquartile range.
b. List the five-number summary.
c. Construct a boxplot and describe its shape.

3.32 A bank branch located in a commercial district of a city has the business objective of developing an improved process for serving customers during the noon-to-1:00 P.M. lunch period. The waiting time, in minutes, is defined as the time the customer enters the line to when he or she reaches the teller window. Data are collected from a sample of 15 customers during this hour. The file **Bank1** contains the results, which are listed at the top of page 150:

```
4.21  5.55  3.02  5.13  4.77  2.34  3.54  3.20
4.50  6.10  0.38  5.12  6.46  6.19  3.79
```

Another bank branch, located in a residential area, is also concerned with the noon-to-1 P.M. lunch hour. The waiting times, in minutes, collected from a sample of 15 customers during this hour, are contained in the file **Bank2** and listed here:

```
9.66   5.90  8.02  5.79  8.73  3.82  8.01  8.35
10.49  6.68  5.64  4.08  6.17  9.91  5.47
```

a. List the five-number summaries of the waiting times at the two bank branches.
b. Construct boxplots and describe the shapes of the distributions for the two bank branches.
c. What similarities and differences are there in the distributions of the waiting times at the two bank branches?

3.33 For this problem, use the data in **Bond Funds2008**.
a. Construct a multidimensional table of the mean 2008 return by type and risk.
b. Construct a multidimensional table of the standard deviation of the 2008 return by type and risk.
c. What conclusions can you reach concerning differences between the type of bond funds (intermediate government and short-term corporate) based on risk factor (low, average, and high)?
d. Compare the results in (a)–(c) to the 2009 returns (stored in **Bond Funds**).

3.34 For this problem, use the data in **Bond Funds2008**.
a. Construct a multidimensional table of the mean three-year return by type and risk.
b. Construct a multidimensional table of the standard deviation of the three-year return by type and risk.
c. What conclusions can you reach concerning differences between the type of bond funds (intermediate government and short-term corporate) based on risk factor (low, average, and high)?
d. Compare the results in (a)–(c) to the three-year returns from 2007–2009 (stored in **Bond Funds**).

3.35 For this problem, use the data in **Bond Funds2008**.
a. Construct a multidimensional table of the mean five-year return by type and risk.
b. Construct a multidimensional table of the standard deviation of the five-year return by type and risk.
c. What conclusions can you reach concerning differences between the type of bond funds (intermediate government and short-term corporate) based on risk factor (low, average, and high)?
d. Compare the results in (a)–(c) to the five-year returns from 2005–2009 (stored in **Bond Funds**).

3.36 For this problem, use the data in **Bond Funds2008**.
a. Construct a multidimensional table of the mean 2008 return by type, fees, and risk.
b. Construct a multidimensional table of the standard deviation of the 2008 return by type, fees, and risk.
c. What conclusions can you reach concerning differences between the type of bond funds (intermediate government and short-term corporate) based on fees (yes or no) and risk factor (low, average, and high)?
d. Compare the results in (a)–(c) to the 2009 returns (stored in **Bond Funds**).

3.4 Numerical Descriptive Measures for a Population

Sections 3.1 and 3.2 presented various statistics that described the properties of central tendency and variation for a sample. If your data set represents numerical measurements for an entire population, you need to compute and interpret parameters for a population. In this section, you will learn about three population parameters: the population mean, population variance, and population standard deviation.

To help illustrate these parameters, first review Table 3.6, which contains the one-year returns for the five largest bond funds (in terms of total assets) as of April 27, 2010 (stored in **LargestBonds**).

TABLE 3.6

One-Year Return for the Population Consisting of the Five Largest Bond Funds

Bond Fund	One-Year Return
PIMCO: Total Rtn;Inst	14.8
American Funds Bond;A	16.5
Dodge Cox Income	16.5
Vanguard Tot Bd;Inv	7.6
Vanguard Int-TmTx;Adm	6.6

Source: Data extracted from *The Wall Street Journal,* April 27, 2010, p. C4.

The Population Mean

The population mean is represented by the symbol μ, the Greek lowercase letter mu. Equation (3.13) defines the population mean.

> **POPULATION MEAN**
>
> The **population mean** is the sum of the values in the population divided by the population size, N.
>
> $$\mu = \frac{\sum_{i=1}^{N} X_i}{N} \qquad (3.13)$$
>
> where
>
> μ = population mean
> X_i = ith value of the variable X
> $\sum_{i=1}^{N} X_i$ = summation of all X_i values in the population
> N = number of values in the population

To compute the mean one-year return for the population of bond funds given in Table 3.6, use Equation (3.13):

$$\mu = \frac{\sum_{i=1}^{N} X_i}{N} = \frac{14.8 + 16.5 + 16.5 + 7.6 + 6.6}{5} = \frac{62.0}{5} = 12.4$$

Thus, the mean percentage return for these bond funds is 12.4.

The Population Variance and Standard Deviation

The **population variance** and the **population standard deviation** are parameters that measure variation in a population. As was the case for the sample statistics, the population standard deviation is the square root of the population variance. The symbol σ^2, the Greek lowercase letter sigma squared, represents the population variance, and the symbol σ, the Greek lowercase letter sigma, represents the population standard deviation. Equations (3.14) and (3.15) define these parameters. The denominators for the right-side terms in these equations use N and not the $(n-1)$ term that is used in the equations for the sample variance and standard deviation [see Equations (3.6) and (3.7) on page 133].

> **POPULATION VARIANCE**
>
> The population variance is the sum of the squared differences around the population mean divided by the population size, N.
>
> $$\sigma^2 = \frac{\sum_{i=1}^{N}(X_i - \mu)^2}{N} \qquad (3.14)$$
>
> where
>
> μ = population mean
> X_i = ith value of the variable X
> $\sum_{i=1}^{N}(X_i - \mu)^2$ = summation of all the squared differences between the X_i values and μ

> **POPULATION STANDARD DEVIATION**
>
> $$\sigma = \sqrt{\frac{\sum_{i=1}^{N}(X_i - \mu)^2}{N}} \qquad (3.15)$$

To compute the population variance for the data of Table 3.6, you use Equation (3.14):

$$\sigma^2 = \frac{\sum_{i=1}^{N}(X_i - \mu)^2}{N}$$

$$= \frac{(14.8 - 12.4)^2 + (16.5 - 12.4)^2 + (16.5 - 12.4)^2 + (7.6 - 12.4)^2 + (6.6 - 12.4)^2}{5}$$

$$= \frac{5.76 + 16.81 + 16.81 + 23.04 + 33.64}{5}$$

$$= \frac{96.06}{5} = 19.212$$

Thus, the variance of the one-year returns is 19.212 squared percentage return. The squared units make the variance difficult to interpret. You should use the standard deviation that is expressed in the original units of the data (percentage return). From Equation (3.15),

$$\sigma = \sqrt{\sigma^2} = \sqrt{\frac{\sum_{i=1}^{N}(X_i - \mu)^2}{N}} = \sqrt{\frac{96.06}{5}} = 4.3831$$

Therefore, the typical percentage return differs from the mean of 12.4 by approximately 4.3831. This large amount of variation suggests that these large bond funds produce results that differ greatly.

The Empirical Rule

In most data sets, a large portion of the values tend to cluster somewhere near the median. In right-skewed data sets, this clustering occurs to the left of the mean—that is, at a value less than the mean. In left-skewed data sets, the values tend to cluster to the right of the mean—that is, greater than the mean. In symmetric data sets, where the median and mean are the same, the values often tend to cluster around the median and mean, producing a bell-shaped distribution. You can use the **empirical rule** to examine the variability in bell-shaped distributions:

- Approximately 68% of the values are within ±1 standard deviation from the mean.
- Approximately 95% of the values are within ±2 standard deviations from the mean.
- Approximately 99.7% of the values are within ±3 standard deviations from the mean.

The empirical rule helps you measure how the values distribute above and below the mean and can help you identify outliers. The empirical rule implies that for bell-shaped distributions, only about 1 out of 20 values will be beyond two standard deviations from the mean in either direction. As a general rule, you can consider values not found in the interval $\mu \pm 2\sigma$ as potential outliers. The rule also implies that only about 3 in 1,000 will be beyond three standard deviations from the mean. Therefore, values not found in the interval $\mu \pm 3\sigma$ are almost always considered outliers.

EXAMPLE 3.15

Using the Empirical Rule

A population of 2 liter bottles of cola is known to have a mean fill-weight of 2.06 liters and a standard deviation of 0.02 liters. The population is known to be bell-shaped. Describe the distribution of fill-weights. Is it very likely that a bottle will contain less than 2 liters of cola?

SOLUTION

$$\mu \pm \sigma = 2.06 \pm 0.02 = (2.04, 2.08)$$
$$\mu \pm 2\sigma = 2.06 \pm 2(0.02) = (2.02, 2.10)$$
$$\mu \pm 3\sigma = 2.06 \pm 3(0.02) = (2.00, 2.12)$$

Using the empirical rule, you can see that approximately 68% of the bottles will contain between 2.04 and 2.08 liters, approximately 95% will contain between 2.02 and 2.10 liters, and approximately 99.7% will contain between 2.00 and 2.12 liters. Therefore, it is highly unlikely that a bottle will contain less than 2 liters.

For heavily skewed data sets and those not appearing to be bell-shaped, you should use the Chebyshev rule, discussed next, instead of the empirical rule.

The Chebyshev Rule

The **Chebyshev rule** (see reference 1) states that for any data set, regardless of shape, the percentage of values that are found within distances of k standard deviations from the mean must be at least

$$\left(1 - \frac{1}{k^2}\right) \times 100\%$$

You can use this rule for any value of k greater than 1. For example, consider $k = 2$. The Chebyshev rule states that at least $[1 - (1/2)^2] \times 100\% = 75\%$ of the values must be found within ± 2 standard deviations of the mean.

The Chebyshev rule is very general and applies to any distribution. The rule indicates *at least* what percentage of the values fall within a given distance from the mean. However, if the data set is approximately bell-shaped, the empirical rule will more accurately reflect the greater concentration of data close to the mean. Table 3.7 compares the Chebyshev and empirical rules.

TABLE 3.7

How Data Vary Around the Mean

	% of Values Found in Intervals Around the Mean	
Interval	Chebyshev (any distribution)	Empirical Rule (bell-shaped distribution)
$(\mu - \sigma, \mu + \sigma)$	At least 0%	Approximately 68%
$(\mu - 2\sigma, \mu + 2\sigma)$	At least 75%	Approximately 95%
$(\mu - 3\sigma, \mu + 3\sigma)$	At least 88.89%	Approximately 99.7%

EXAMPLE 3.16

Using the Chebyshev Rule

As in Example 3.15, a population of 2-liter bottles of cola is known to have a mean fill-weight of 2.06 liters and a standard deviation of 0.02 liters. However, the shape of the population is unknown, and you cannot assume that it is bell-shaped. Describe the distribution of fill-weights. Is it very likely that a bottle will contain less than 2 liters of cola?

SOLUTION

$$\mu \pm \sigma = 2.06 \pm 0.02 = (2.04, 2.08)$$
$$\mu \pm 2\sigma = 2.06 \pm 2(0.02) = (2.02, 2.10)$$
$$\mu \pm 3\sigma = 2.06 \pm 3(0.02) = (2.00, 2.12)$$

Because the distribution may be skewed, you cannot use the empirical rule. Using the Chebyshev rule, you cannot say anything about the percentage of bottles containing between 2.04 and 2.08 liters. You can state that at least 75% of the bottles will contain between 2.02 and 2.10 liters and at least 88.89% will contain between 2.00 and 2.12 liters. Therefore, between 0 and 11.11% of the bottles will contain less than 2 liters.

You can use these two rules to understand how data are distributed around the mean when you have sample data. With each rule, you use the value you computed for $\bar{X}$ in place of μ and the value you computed for S in place of σ. The results you compute using the sample statistics are *approximations* because you used sample statistics $(\bar{X}, S)$ and not population parameters (μ, σ).

Problems for Section 3.4

LEARNING THE BASICS

3.37 Consider a population of 10 weights identical in appearance but having the following weights in grams:

7   5   11   8   3   6   2   1   9   8

a. Compute the population mean.
b. Compute the population standard deviation.

3.38 The following is a set of data for a population with $N = 10$:

7   5   6   6   6   4   8   6   9   3

a. Compute the population mean.
b. Compute the population standard deviation.

APPLYING THE CONCEPTS

3.39 The file **Tax** contains the quarterly sales tax receipts (in thousands of dollars) submitted to the comptroller of the Village of Fair Lake for the period ending March 2010 by all 50 business establishments in that locale:

10.3	11.1	9.6	9.0	14.5
13.0	6.7	11.0	8.4	10.3
13.0	11.2	7.3	5.3	12.5
8.0	11.8	8.7	10.6	9.5
11.1	10.2	11.1	9.9	9.8
11.6	15.1	12.5	6.5	7.5
10.0	12.9	9.2	10.0	12.8
12.5	9.3	10.4	12.7	10.5
9.3	11.5	10.7	11.6	7.8
10.5	7.6	10.1	8.9	8.6

a. Compute the mean, variance, and standard deviation for this population.
b. What percentage of these businesses have quarterly sales tax receipts within ± 1, ± 2, or ± 3 standard deviations of the mean?
c. Compare your findings with what would be expected on the basis of the empirical rule. Are you surprised at the results in (b)?

3.40 Consider a population of 1,024 mutual funds that primarily invest in large companies. You have determined that μ, the mean one-year total percentage return achieved by all the funds, is 8.20 and that σ, the standard deviation, is 2.75.
a. According to the empirical rule, what percentage of these funds are expected to be within ± 1 standard deviation of the mean?
b. According to the empirical rule, what percentage of these funds are expected to be within ± 2 standard deviations of the mean?
c. According to the Chebyshev rule, what percentage of these funds are expected to be within ± 1, ± 2, or ± 3 standard deviations of the mean?
d. According to the Chebyshev rule, at least 93.75% of these funds are expected to have one-year total returns between what two amounts?

3.41 The file **CigaretteTax** contains the state cigarette tax (\$) for each of the 50 states as of December 31, 2009.
a. Compute the population mean and population standard deviation for the state cigarette tax.
b. Interpret the parameters in (a).

3.42 The file **Energy** contains the per capita energy consumption, in kilowatt-hours, for each of the 50 states and the District of Columbia during a recent year.
a. Compute the mean, variance, and standard deviation for the population.
b. What proportion of these states has per capita energy consumption within ± 1 standard deviation of the mean,

within ±2 standard deviations of the mean, and within ±3 standard deviations of the mean?

c. Compare your findings with what would be expected based on the empirical rule. Are you surprised at the results in (b)?

d. Repeat (a) through (c) with the District of Columbia removed. How have the results changed?

3.43 Thirty companies comprise the DJIA. Just how big are these companies? One common method for measuring the size of a company is to use its market capitalization, which is computed by multiplying the number of stock shares by the price of a share of stock. On March 29, 2010, the market capitalization of these companies ranged from Alcoa's $14.7 billion to ExxonMobil's $318.8 billion. The entire population of market capitalization values is stored in `DowMarketCap`.

Source: Data extracted from **money.cnn.com**, March 29, 2010.

a. Compute the mean and standard deviation of the market capitalization for this population of 30 companies.
b. Interpret the parameters computed in (a).

3.5 The Covariance and the Coefficient of Correlation

In Section 2.6, you used scatter plots to visually examine the relationship between two numerical variables. This section presents two measures of the relationship between two numerical variables: the covariance and the coefficient of correlation.

The Covariance

The **covariance** measures the strength of the linear relationship between two numerical variables (X and Y). Equation (3.16) defines the **sample covariance**, and Example 3.17 illustrates its use.

SAMPLE COVARIANCE

$$\text{cov}(X, Y) = \frac{\sum_{i=1}^{n}(X_i - \bar{X})(Y_i - \bar{Y})}{n - 1} \tag{3.16}$$

EXAMPLE 3.17

Computing the Sample Covariance

In Figure 2.15 on page 87, you constructed a scatter plot that showed the relationship between the value and the annual revenue of the 30 teams that make up the National Basketball Association (NBA) (extracted from www.forbes.com/lists/2009/32/basketball-values-09_NBA-Team-Valuations_Rank.html; stored in `NBAValues`). Now, you want to measure the association between the value of a franchise and annual revenue by computing the sample covariance.

SOLUTION Table 3.8 on page 156 provides the value and the annual revenue of the 30 teams. Figure 3.7 on page 156 contains a worksheet that computes the covariance for these data. The Calculations Area section of Figure 3.7 breaks down Equation (3.16) into a set of smaller calculations. From cell F9, or by using Equation (3.16) directly, you find that the covariance is 3,115.7241:

$$\text{cov}(X, Y) = \frac{90{,}356}{30 - 1}$$
$$= 3{,}115.7241$$

The covariance has a major flaw as a measure of the linear relationship between two numerical variables. Because the covariance can have any value, you are unable to use it to determine the relative strength of the relationship. In other words, you cannot tell whether the value 3,115.7241 indicates a strong relationship or a weak relationship. To better determine the relative strength of the relationship, you need to compute the coefficient of correlation.

TABLE 3.8

Values and Annual Revenues of the 30 NBA Teams (in millions of dollars)

Team	Value	Revenue	Team	Value	Revenue
Atlanta	306	103	Milwaukee	254	91
Boston	433	144	Minnesota	268	96
Charlotte	278	96	New Jersey	269	92
Chicago	511	168	New Orleans	267	95
Cleveland	476	159	New York	586	202
Dallas	446	154	Oklahoma City	310	111
Denver	321	115	Orlando	361	107
Detroit	479	171	Philadelphia	344	115
Golden State	315	113	Phoenix	429	148
Houston	470	160	Portland	338	121
Indiana	281	97	Sacramento	305	109
Los Angeles Clippers	295	102	San Antonio	398	133
Los Angeles Lakers	607	209	Toronto	386	133
Memphis	257	88	Utah	343	118
Miami	364	126	Washington	313	110

FIGURE 3.7

Excel worksheet to compute the covariance between the value and the annual revenue of the 30 NBA teams

	A	B	C	D	E	F
1	Covariance Analysis					
2						
3	Revenue	Value	(X-XBar)(Y-YBar)			
4	103	306	1415.2000		Calculations Area	
5	144	433	1174.8000		XBar	126.2000
6	96	278	2687.8000		YBar	367
7	168	511	6019.2000		n-1	29
8	159	476	3575.2000		Σ(X-XBar)(Y-YBar)	90356.0000
9	154	446	2196.2000		Covariance	3115.7241
10	115	321	515.2000			
11	171	479	5017.6000			
12	113	315	686.4000			
13	160	470	3481.4000			
14	97	281	2511.2000			
15	102	295	1742.4000			
16	209	607	19872.0000			
17	88	257	4202.0000			
18	126	364	0.6000			
19	91	254	3977.6000			
20	96	268	2989.8000			
21	92	269	3351.6000			
22	95	267	3120.0000			
23	202	586	16600.2000			
24	111	310	866.4000			
25	107	361	115.2000			
26	115	344	257.6000			
27	148	429	1351.6000			
28	121	338	150.8000			
29	109	305	1066.4000			
30	133	398	210.8000			
31	133	386	129.2000			
32	118	343	196.8000			
33	110	313	874.8000			

The Coefficient of Correlation

The **coefficient of correlation** measures the relative strength of a linear relationship between two numerical variables. The values of the coefficient of correlation range from -1 for a perfect negative correlation to $+1$ for a perfect positive correlation. *Perfect* in this case means that if the points were plotted on a scatter plot, all the points could be connected with a straight line.

When dealing with population data for two numerical variables, the Greek letter ρ (*rho*) is used as the symbol for the coefficient of correlation. Figure 3.8 illustrates three different types of association between two variables.

FIGURE 3.8
Types of association between variables

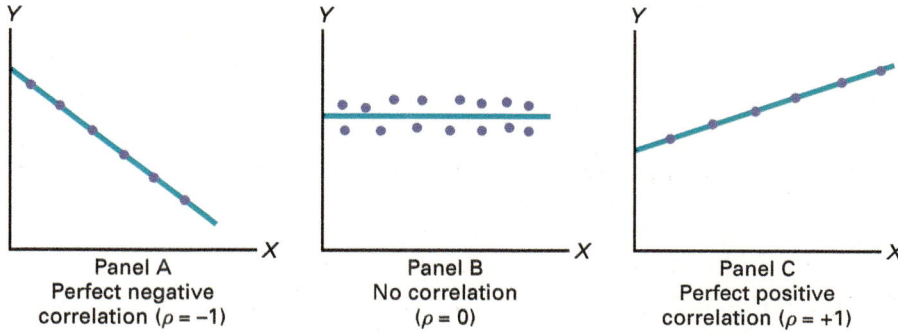

Panel A
Perfect negative correlation ($\rho = -1$)

Panel B
No correlation ($\rho = 0$)

Panel C
Perfect positive correlation ($\rho = +1$)

In Panel A of Figure 3.8, there is a perfect negative linear relationship between X and Y. Thus, the coefficient of correlation, ρ, equals -1, and when X increases, Y decreases in a perfectly predictable manner. Panel B shows a situation in which there is no relationship between X and Y. In this case, the coefficient of correlation, ρ, equals 0, and as X increases, there is no tendency for Y to increase or decrease. Panel C illustrates a perfect positive relationship where equals In this case, Y increases in a perfectly predictable manner when X increases.

Correlation alone cannot prove that there is a causation effect—that is, that the change in the value of one variable caused the change in the other variable. A strong correlation can be produced simply by chance, by the effect of a third variable not considered in the calculation of the correlation, or by a cause-and-effect relationship. You would need to perform additional analysis to determine which of these three situations actually produced the correlation. Therefore, you can say that *causation implies correlation, but correlation alone does not imply causation.*

Equation (3.17) defines the **sample coefficient of correlation (*r*)**.

SAMPLE COEFFICIENT OF CORRELATION

$$r = \frac{\text{cov}(X, Y)}{S_X S_Y} \tag{3.17}$$

where

$$\text{cov}(X, Y) = \frac{\sum_{i=1}^{n}(X_i - \bar{X})(Y_i - \bar{Y})}{n - 1}$$

$$S_X = \sqrt{\frac{\sum_{i=1}^{n}(X_i - \bar{X})^2}{n - 1}}$$

$$S_Y = \sqrt{\frac{\sum_{i=1}^{n}(Y_i - \bar{Y})^2}{n - 1}}$$

128 Quantitative Methods for Business

When you have sample data, you can compute the sample coefficient of correlation, r. When using sample data, you are unlikely to have a sample coefficient of correlation of exactly $+1, 0,$ or -1. Figure 3.9 presents scatter plots along with their respective sample coefficients of correlation, r, for six data sets, each of which contains 100 values of X and Y.

In Panel A, the coefficient of correlation, r, is -0.9. You can see that for small values of X, there is a very strong tendency for Y to be large. Likewise, the large values of X tend to be paired with small values of Y. The data do not all fall on a straight line, so the association between X and Y cannot be described as perfect. The data in Panel B have a coefficient of

FIGURE 3.9
Six scatter plots and their sample coefficients of correlation, r

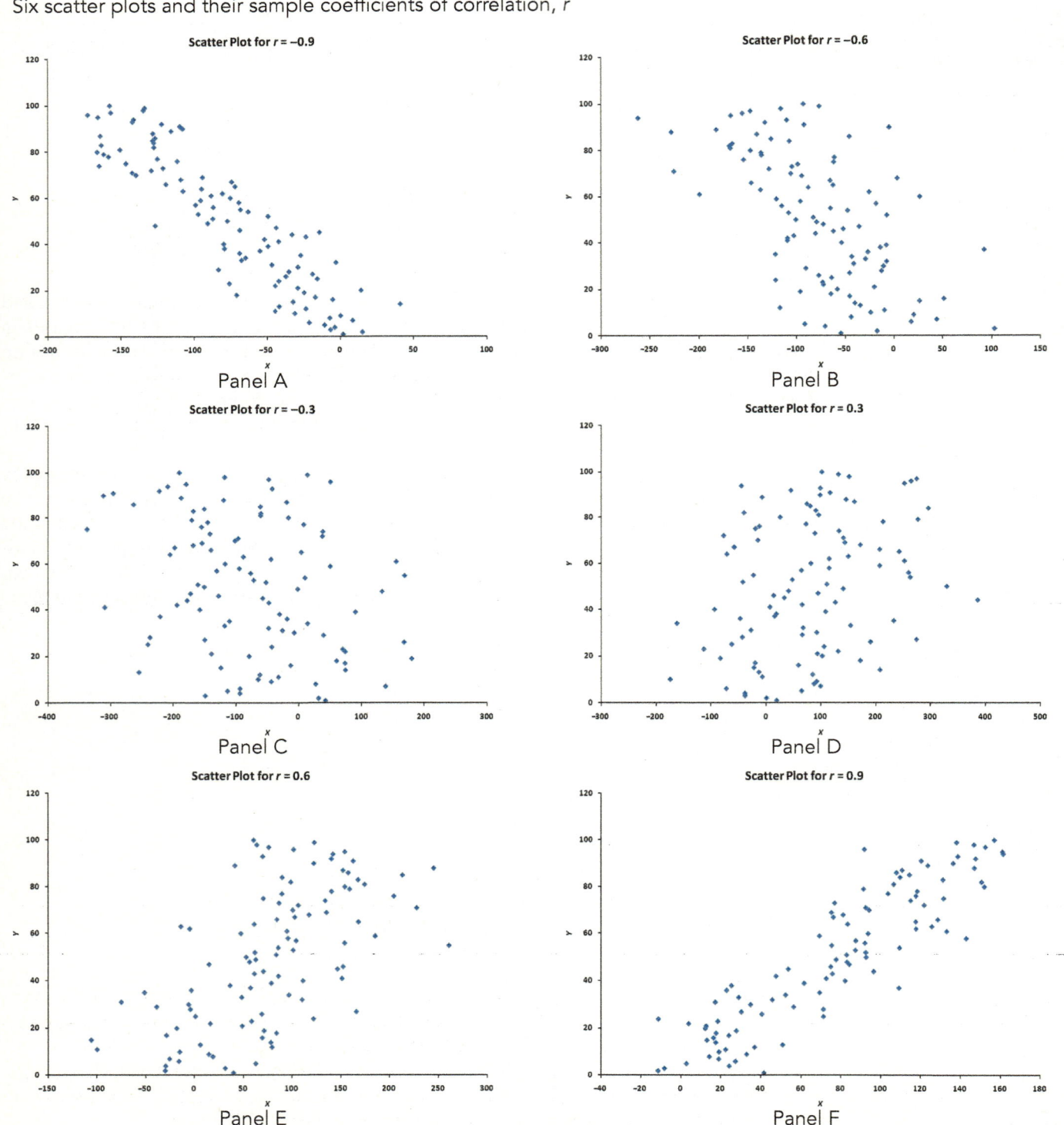

correlation equal to -0.6, and the small values of X tend to be paired with large values of Y. The linear relationship between X and Y in Panel B is not as strong as that in Panel A. Thus, the coefficient of correlation in Panel B is not as negative as that in Panel A. In Panel C, the linear relationship between X and Y is very weak, $r = -0.3$, and there is only a slight tendency for the small values of X to be paired with the large values of Y. Panels D through F depict data sets that have positive coefficients of correlation because small values of X tend to be paired with small values of Y and large values of X tend to be associated with large values of Y. Panel D shows weak positive correlation, with $r = 0.3$. Panel E shows stronger positive correlation with $r = 0.6$. Panel F shows very strong positive correlation, with $r = 0.9$.

EXAMPLE 3.18

Computing the Sample Coefficient of Correlation

In Example 3.17 on page 155, you computed the covariance of the values and revenues of 30 NBA basketball teams. Using Figure 3.10 and Equation (3.17) on page 157, compute the sample coefficient of correlation.

FIGURE 3.10

Excel worksheet to compute the sample coefficient of correlation, r, between the values and revenues of 30 NBA basketball teams

	A	B	C	D	E	F
1	Coefficient of Correlation Calculations					
2						
3	Revenue	Value	(X-XBar)(Y-YBar)		Calculations Area	
4	103	306	1415.2000		XBar	126.2000
5	144	433	1174.8000		YBar	367.0000
6	96	278	2687.8000		$\Sigma(X-XBar)^2$	30550.8000
7	168	511	6019.2000		$\Sigma(Y-YBar)^2$	272410.0000
8	159	476	3575.2000		$\Sigma(X-XBar)(Y-YBar)$	90356.0000
9	154	446	2196.2000		n-1	29
10	115	321	515.2000			
11	171	479	5017.6000		Results	
12	113	315	686.4000		Covariance	3115.7241
13	160	470	3481.4000		S_X	32.4573
14	97	281	2511.2000		S_Y	96.9198
15	102	295	1742.4000		r	0.9905
16	209	607	19872.0000			
17	88	257	4202.0000			
18	126	364	0.6000			
19	91	254	3977.6000			
20	96	268	2989.8000			
21	92	269	3351.6000			
22	95	267	3120.0000			
23	202	586	16600.2000			
24	111	310	866.4000			
25	107	361	115.2000			
26	115	344	257.6000			
27	148	429	1351.6000			
28	121	338	150.8000			
29	109	305	1066.4000			
30	133	398	210.8000			
31	133	386	129.2000			
32	118	343	196.8000			
33	110	313	874.8000			

SOLUTION

$$r = \frac{\text{cov}(X, Y)}{S_X S_Y}$$

$$= \frac{3{,}115.7241}{(32.4573)(96.9198)}$$

$$= 0.9905$$

The value and revenue of the NBA teams are very highly correlated. The teams with the lowest revenues have the lowest values. The teams with the highest revenues have the highest values. This relationship is very strong, as indicated by the coefficient of correlation, $r = 0.9905$.

In general you cannot assume that just because two variables are correlated, changes in one variable caused changes in the other variable. However, for this example, it makes sense to conclude that changes in revenue would cause changes in the value of a team.

Problems for Section 3.5

LEARNING THE BASICS

3.44 The following is a set of data from a sample of $n = 11$ items:

X	7	5	8	3	6	10	12	4	9	15	18
Y	21	15	24	9	18	30	36	12	27	45	54

a. Compute the covariance.
b. Compute the coefficient of correlation.
c. How strong is the relationship between X and Y? Explain.

APPLYING THE CONCEPTS

3.45 A study of 218 students at Ohio State University suggests a link between time spent on the social networking site Facebook and grade point average. Students who rarely or never used Facebook had higher grade point averages than students who use Facebook.

Source: Data extracted from M. B. Marklein, "Facebook Use Linked to Less Textbook Time," **www.usatoday.com**, April 14, 2009.

a. Does the study suggest that time spent on Facebook and grade point average are positively correlated or negatively correlated?
b. Do you think that there might be a cause-and-effect relationship between time spent on Facebook and grade point average? Explain.

SELF Test 3.46 The file **Cereals** lists the calories and sugar, in grams, in one serving of seven breakfast cereals:

Cereal	Calories	Sugar
Kellogg's All Bran	80	6
Kellogg's Corn Flakes	100	2
Wheaties	100	4
Nature's Path Organic Multigrain Flakes	110	4
Kellogg Rice Krispies	130	4
Post Shredded Wheat Vanilla Almond	190	11
Kellogg Mini Wheats	200	10

a. Compute the covariance.
b. Compute the coefficient of correlation.
c. Which do you think is more valuable in expressing the relationship between calories and sugar—the covariance or the coefficient of correlation? Explain.
d. Based on (a) and (b), what conclusions can you reach about the relationship between calories and sugar?

3.47 Movie companies need to predict the gross receipts of individual movies after a movie has debuted. The following results, listed in **PotterMovies**, are the first weekend gross, the U.S. gross, and the worldwide gross (in millions of dollars) of the six Harry Potter movies that debuted from 2001 to 2009:

Title	First Weekend	U.S. Gross	Worldwide Gross
Sorcerer's Stone	90.295	317.558	976.458
Chamber of Secrets	88.357	261.988	878.988
Prisoner of Azkaban	93.687	249.539	795.539
Goblet of Fire	102.335	290.013	896.013
Order of the Phoenix	77.108	292.005	938.469
Half-Blood Prince	77.836	301.460	934.601

Source: Data extracted from **www.the-numbers.com/interactive/comp-Harry-Potter.php**.

a. Compute the covariance between first weekend gross and U.S. gross, first weekend gross and worldwide gross, and U.S. gross and worldwide gross.
b. Compute the coefficient of correlation between first weekend gross and U.S. gross, first weekend gross and worldwide gross, and U.S. gross and worldwide gross.
c. Which do you think is more valuable in expressing the relationship between first weekend gross, U.S. gross, and worldwide gross—the covariance or the coefficient of correlation? Explain.
d. Based on (a) and (b), what conclusions can you reach about the relationship between first weekend gross, U.S. gross, and worldwide gross?

3.48 College basketball is big business, with coaches' salaries, revenues, and expenses in millions of dollars. The file **College Basketball** contains the coaches' salaries and revenues for college basketball at 60 of the 65 schools that played in the 2009 NCAA men's basketball tournament (data extracted from "Compensation for Division 1 Men's Basketball Coaches," *USA Today*, April 2, 2010, p. 8C; and C. Isadore, "Nothing but Net: Basketball Dollars by School," **money.cnn.com/2010/03/18/news/companies/basketball_profits/**).

a. Compute the covariance.
b. Compute the coefficient of correlation.
c. Based on (a) and (b), what conclusions can you reach about the relationship between coaches' salaries and revenues?

3.49 College football players trying out for the NFL are given the Wonderlic standardized intelligence test. The file  contains the average Wonderlic score of football players trying out for the NFL and the graduation rate for football players at selected schools.

Source: Data extracted from S. Walker, "The NFL's Smartest Team," *The Wall Street Journal,* September 30, 2005, pp. W1, W10.

a. Compute the covariance.
b. Compute the coefficient of correlation.
c. Based on (a) and (b), what conclusions can you reach about the relationship between the average Wonderlic score and graduation rate?

3.6 Descriptive Statistics: Pitfalls and Ethical Issues

This chapter describes how a set of numerical data can be characterized by the statistics that measure the properties of central tendency, variation, and shape. In business, descriptive statistics such as the ones you have learned about are frequently included in summary reports that are prepared periodically.

The volume of information available on the Internet, in newspapers, and in magazines has produced much skepticism about the objectivity of data. When you are reading information that contains descriptive statistics, you should keep in mind the quip often attributed to the famous nineteenth-century British statesman Benjamin Disraeli: "There are three kinds of lies: lies, damned lies, and statistics."

For example, in examining statistics, you need to compare the mean and the median. Are they similar, or are they very different? Or, is only the mean provided? The answers to these questions will help you determine whether the data are skewed or symmetrical and whether the median might be a better measure of central tendency than the mean. In addition, you should look to see whether the standard deviation or interquartile range for a very skewed set of data has been included in the statistics provided. Without this, it is impossible to determine the amount of variation that exists in the data.

Ethical considerations arise when you are deciding what results to include in a report. You should document both good and bad results. In addition, when making oral presentations and presenting written reports, you need to give results in a fair, objective, and neutral manner. Unethical behavior occurs when you selectively fail to report pertinent findings that are detrimental to the support of a particular position.

USING STATISTICS @ Choice Is Yours, Part II Revisited

In Part II of the Choice Is Yours scenario, you were hired by the Choice Is Yours investment company to assist investors interested in bond mutual funds. A sample of 184 bond mutual funds included 87 intermediate government funds and 97 short-term corporate bond funds. By comparing these two categories, you were able to provide investors with valuable insights.

The 2009 returns for both the intermediate government funds and the short-term corporate bond funds were right-skewed, as indicated by the boxplots (see Figures 3.4 and 3.5 on pages 147 and 148). The descriptive statistics (see Figure 3.2 on page 139) allowed you to compare the central tendency and variability of returns of the intermediate government funds and the short-term corporate bond funds. The mean indicated that the intermediate government funds returned an average of 4.4529, and the median indicated that half of the funds had returns of 4.4 or more. The short-term corporate bond funds' central tendencies were much higher than those of the intermediate government funds—they had an average of 9.5959, and half the funds had returns above 9.1. The intermediate government funds showed slightly less variability than the short-term corporate funds with a standard deviation of 5.36 as compared to 5.69. An interesting insight is that while 25% of the intermediate government funds had returns of 6.5 or higher ($Q_3 = 6.5$), 75% of the short-term corporate bond funds had returns of 5.7 or higher ($Q_1 = 5.7$). Although past performance is no assurance of future performance, in 2009, the short-term corporate funds greatly outperformed the intermediate government funds. (To see a situation where the opposite was true, open the **Bond Funds2008** file.)

SUMMARY

In this chapter and the previous chapter, you studied descriptive statistics—how you can visualize data through tables and charts and how you can use different statistics to help analyze the data and reach conclusions. In Chapter 2, you were able to visualize data by constructing bar and pie charts, histograms, and other charts. In this chapter, you learned how descriptive statistics such as the mean, median, quartiles, range, and standard deviation are used to describe the characteristics of central tendency, variability, and shape. In addition, you constructed boxplots to visualize the distribution of the data. You also learned how the coefficient of correlation is used to describe the relationship between two numerical variables. Table 3.9 provides a list of the descriptive statistics covered in this chapter.

In the next chapter, the basic principles of probability are presented in order to bridge the gap between the subject of descriptive statistics and the subject of inferential statistics.

TABLE 3.9
Summary of Descriptive Statistics

Type of Analysis	Numerical Data
Describing central tendency, variation, and shape of a numerical variable	Mean, median, mode, quartiles, range, interquartile range, variance, standard deviation, coefficient of variation, Z scores, boxplot (Sections 3.1 through 3.4)
Describing the relationship between two numerical variables	Covariance, coefficient of correlation (Section 3.5)

KEY EQUATIONS

Sample Mean

$$\bar{X} = \frac{\sum_{i=1}^{n} X_i}{n} \quad (3.1)$$

Median

$$\text{Median} = \frac{n+1}{2} \text{ ranked value} \quad (3.2)$$

Geometric Mean

$$\bar{X}_G = (X_1 \times X_2 \times \cdots \times X_n)^{1/n} \quad (3.3)$$

Geometric Mean Rate of Return

$$\bar{R}_G = [(1 + R_1) \times (1 + R_2) \times \cdots \times (1 + R_n)]^{1/n} - 1 \quad (3.4)$$

Range

$$\text{Range} = X_{\text{largest}} - X_{\text{smallest}} \quad (3.5)$$

Sample Variance

$$S^2 = \frac{\sum_{i=1}^{n}(X_i - \bar{X})^2}{n-1} \quad (3.6)$$

Sample Standard Deviation

$$S = \sqrt{S^2} = \sqrt{\frac{\sum_{i=1}^{n}(X_i - \bar{X})^2}{n-1}} \quad (3.7)$$

Coefficient of Variation

$$CV = \left(\frac{S}{\bar{X}}\right) 100\% \quad (3.8)$$

Z Score

$$Z = \frac{X - \bar{X}}{S} \quad (3.9)$$

First Quartile, Q_1

$$Q_1 = \frac{n+1}{4} \text{ ranked value} \qquad (3.10)$$

Third Quartile, Q_3

$$Q_3 = \frac{3(n+1)}{4} \text{ ranked value} \qquad (3.11)$$

Interquartile Range

$$\text{Interquartile range} = Q_3 - Q_1 \qquad (3.12)$$

Population Mean

$$\mu = \frac{\sum_{i=1}^{N} X_i}{N} \qquad (3.13)$$

Population Variance

$$\sigma^2 = \frac{\sum_{i=1}^{N}(X_i - \mu)^2}{N} \qquad (3.14)$$

Population Standard Deviation

$$\sigma = \sqrt{\frac{\sum_{i=1}^{N}(X_i - \mu)^2}{N}} \qquad (3.15)$$

Sample Covariance

$$\text{cov}(X, Y) = \frac{\sum_{i=1}^{n}(X_i - \bar{X})(Y_i - \bar{Y})}{n - 1} \qquad (3.16)$$

Sample Coefficient of Correlation

$$r = \frac{\text{cov}(X, Y)}{S_X S_Y} \qquad (3.17)$$

KEY TERMS

- arithmetic mean
- boxplot
- central tendency
- Chebyshev rule
- coefficient of correlation
- coefficient of variation
- covariance
- dispersion
- empirical rule
- extreme value
- five-number summary
- geometric mean
- geometric mean rate of return
- interquartile range
- kurtosis
- left-skewed
- mean
- median
- midspread
- mode
- outlier
- population mean
- population standard deviation
- population variance
- Q_1: first quartile
- Q_2: second quartile
- Q_3: third quartile
- quartile
- range
- resistant measure
- right-skewed
- sample coefficient of correlation (r)
- sample covariance
- sample mean
- sample standard deviation
- sample variance
- shape
- skewed
- skewness
- spread
- standard deviation
- sum of squares (SS)
- symmetrical
- variance
- variation
- Z score

CHAPTER REVIEW PROBLEMS

CHECKING YOUR UNDERSTANDING

3.50 What are the properties of a set of numerical data?

3.51 What is meant by the property of central tendency?

3.52 What are the differences among the mean, median, and mode, and what are the advantages and disadvantages of each?

3.53 How do you interpret the first quartile, median, and third quartile?

3.54 What is meant by the property of variation?

3.55 What does the Z score measure?

3.56 What are the differences among the various measures of variation, such as the range, interquartile range, variance, standard deviation, and coefficient of variation, and what are the advantages and disadvantages of each?

3.57 How does the empirical rule help explain the ways in which the values in a set of numerical data cluster and distribute?

3.58 How do the empirical rule and the Chebyshev rule differ?

3.59 What is meant by the property of shape?

3.60 How do the covariance and the coefficient of correlation differ?

APPLYING THE CONCEPTS

3.61 The American Society for Quality (ASQ) conducted a salary survey of all its members. ASQ members work in all areas of manufacturing and service-related institutions, with a common theme of an interest in quality. For the survey, emails were sent to 58,614 members, and 7,869 valid responses were received. The two most common job titles were manager and quality engineer. Another title is Master Black Belt, who is a person who takes a leadership role as the keeper of the Six Sigma process (see Section 17.8). An additional title is Green Belt, someone who works on Six Sigma projects part-time. Descriptive statistics concerning salaries for these four titles are given in the following table:

Title	Sample Size	Minimum	Maximum	Standard Deviation	Mean	Median
Green Belt	34	33,000	106,000	18,137	65,679	64,750
Manager	2,128	22,568	182,000	25,078	86,349	84,000
Quality Engineer	1,262	24,000	186,000	19,256	74,314	72,100
Master Black Belt	132	33,000	201,000	24,988	109,481	106,000

Source: Data extracted from J. D. Conklin, "Salary Survey: Seeing Green," *Quality Progress*, December 2009, p. 29.

Compare the salaries of Green Belts, managers, quality engineers, and Master Black Belts.

3.62 In New York State, savings banks are permitted to sell a form of life insurance called savings bank life insurance (SBLI). The approval process consists of underwriting, which includes a review of the application, a medical information bureau check, possible requests for additional medical information and medical exams, and a policy compilation stage, during which the policy pages are generated and sent to the bank for delivery. The ability to deliver approved policies to customers in a timely manner is critical to the profitability of this service to the bank. During a period of one month, a random sample of 27 approved policies was selected, and the following were the total processing times (stored in Insurance):

73 19 16 64 28 28 31 90 60 56 31 56 22 18
45 48 17 17 17 91 92 63 50 51 69 16 17

a. Compute the mean, median, first quartile, and third quartile.
b. Compute the range, interquartile range, variance, standard deviation, and coefficient of variation.
c. Construct a boxplot. Are the data skewed? If so, how?
d. What would you tell a customer who enters the bank to purchase this type of insurance policy and asks how long the approval process takes?

3.63 One of the major measures of the quality of service provided by an organization is the speed with which it responds to customer complaints. A large family-held department store selling furniture and flooring, including carpet, had undergone a major expansion in the past several years. In particular, the flooring department had expanded from 2 installation crews to an installation supervisor, a measurer, and 15 installation crews. The business objective of the company was to reduce the time between when the complaint is received and when it is resolved. During a recent year, the company received 50 complaints concerning carpet installation. The data from the 50 complaints, organized in Furniture, represent the number of days between the receipt of a complaint and the resolution of the complaint:

54   5   35 137 31 27 152   2 123 81 74 27 11
19 126 110 110 29 61   35 94 31 26   5 12   4
165 32 29 28 29 26   25   1 14 13 13 10   5
27   4 52 30 22 36   26 20 23 33 68

a. Compute the mean, median, first quartile, and third quartile.
b. Compute the range, interquartile range, variance, standard deviation, and coefficient of variation.
c. Construct a boxplot. Are the data skewed? If so, how?
d. On the basis of the results of (a) through (c), if you had to tell the president of the company how long a customer should expect to wait to have a complaint resolved, what would you say? Explain.

3.64 A manufacturing company produces steel housings for electrical equipment. The main component part of the housing is a steel trough that is made of a 14-gauge steel coil. It is produced using a 250-ton progressive punch press with a wipe-down operation and two 90-degree forms placed in the flat steel to make the trough. The distance from one side of the form to the other is critical because of weatherproofing in outdoor applications. The company requires that the width of the trough is between 8.31 inches and 8.61 inches. Data are collected from a sample of 49 troughs and stored in Trough, which contains the widths of the troughs in inches as shown here:

8.312 8.343 8.317 8.383 8.348 8.410 8.351 8.373 8.481 8.422
8.476 8.382 8.484 8.403 8.414 8.419 8.385 8.465 8.498 8.447
8.436 8.413 8.489 8.414 8.481 8.415 8.479 8.429 8.458 8.462
8.460 8.444 8.429 8.460 8.412 8.420 8.410 8.405 8.323 8.420
8.396 8.447 8.405 8.439 8.411 8.427 8.420 8.498 8.409

a. Compute the mean, median, range, and standard deviation for the width. Interpret these measures of central tendency and variability.

b. List the five-number summary.
c. Construct a boxplot and describe its shape.
d. What can you conclude about the number of troughs that will meet the company's requirement of troughs being between 8.31 and 8.61 inches wide?

3.65 The manufacturing company in Problem 3.64 also produces electric insulators. If the insulators break when in use, a short circuit is likely to occur. To test the strength of the insulators, destructive testing is carried out to determine how much force is required to break the insulators. Force is measured by observing how many pounds must be applied to an insulator before it breaks. Data are collected from a sample of 30 insulators. The file **Force** contains the strengths, as follows:

1,870 1,728 1,656 1,610 1,634 1,784 1,522 1,696 1,592 1,662
1,866 1,764 1,734 1,662 1,734 1,774 1,550 1,756 1,762 1,866
1,820 1,744 1,788 1,688 1,810 1,752 1,680 1,810 1,652 1,736

a. Compute the mean, median, range, and standard deviation for the force needed to break the insulator.
b. Interpret the measures of central tendency and variability in (a).
c. Construct a boxplot and describe its shape.
d. What can you conclude about the strength of the insulators if the company requires a force measurement of at least 1,500 pounds before breakage?

3.66 The file **VeggieBurger** contains data on the calories and total fat (in grams per serving) for a sample of 12 veggie burgers.

Source: Data extracted from "Healthful Burgers That Taste Good," *Consumer Reports*, June 2008, p 8.

a. For each variable, compute the mean, median, first quartile, and third quartile.
b. For each variable, compute the range, interquartile range, variance, standard deviation, and coefficient of variation.
c. For each variable, construct a boxplot. Are the data skewed? If so, how?
d. Compute the coefficient of correlation between calories and total fat.
e. What conclusions can you reach concerning calories and total fat?

3.67 A quality characteristic of interest for a tea-bag-filling process is the weight of the tea in the individual bags. If the bags are underfilled, two problems arise. First, customers may not be able to brew the tea to be as strong as they wish. Second, the company may be in violation of the truth-in-labeling laws. For this product, the label weight on the package indicates that, on average, there are 5.5 grams of tea in a bag. If the mean amount of tea in a bag exceeds the label weight, the company is giving away product. Getting an exact amount of tea in a bag is problematic because of variation in the temperature and humidity inside the factory, differences in the density of the tea, and the extremely fast filling operation of the machine (approximately 170 bags per minute). The file **Teabags**, as shown below, contains the weights, in grams, of a sample of 50 tea bags produced in one hour by a single machine:

5.65 5.44 5.42 5.40 5.53 5.34 5.54 5.45 5.52 5.41
5.57 5.40 5.53 5.54 5.55 5.62 5.56 5.46 5.44 5.51
5.47 5.40 5.47 5.61 5.53 5.32 5.67 5.29 5.49 5.55
5.77 5.57 5.42 5.58 5.58 5.50 5.32 5.50 5.53 5.58
5.61 5.45 5.44 5.25 5.56 5.63 5.50 5.57 5.67 5.36

a. Compute the mean, median, first quartile, and third quartile.
b. Compute the range, interquartile range, variance, standard deviation, and coefficient of variation.
c. Interpret the measures of central tendency and variation within the context of this problem. Why should the company producing the tea bags be concerned about the central tendency and variation?
d. Construct a boxplot. Are the data skewed? If so, how?
e. Is the company meeting the requirement set forth on the label that, on average, there are 5.5 grams of tea in a bag? If you were in charge of this process, what changes, if any, would you try to make concerning the distribution of weights in the individual bags?

3.68 The manufacturer of Boston and Vermont asphalt shingles provides its customers with a 20-year warranty on most of its products. To determine whether a shingle will last as long as the warranty period, accelerated-life testing is conducted at the manufacturing plant. Accelerated-life testing exposes a shingle to the stresses it would be subject to in a lifetime of normal use via an experiment in a laboratory setting that takes only a few minutes to conduct. In this test, a shingle is repeatedly scraped with a brush for a short period of time, and the shingle granules removed by the brushing are weighed (in grams). Shingles that experience low amounts of granule loss are expected to last longer in normal use than shingles that experience high amounts of granule loss. In this situation, a shingle should experience no more than 0.8 gram of granule loss if it is expected to last the length of the warranty period. The file **Granule** contains a sample of 170 measurements made on the company's Boston shingles and 140 measurements made on Vermont shingles.

a. List the five-number summaries for the Boston shingles and for the Vermont shingles.
b. Construct side-by-side boxplots for the two brands of shingles and describe the shapes of the distributions.
c. Comment on the ability of each type of shingle to achieve a granule loss of 0.8 gram or less.

3.69 The file **Restaurants** contains the cost per meal and the ratings of 50 city and 50 suburban restaurants on their food, décor, and service (and their summated ratings). Complete the following for the urban and suburban restaurants.

Source: Data extracted from *Zagat Survey 2009 New York City Restaurants* and *Zagat Survey 2009–2010 Long Island Restaurants*.

a. Construct the five-number summary of the cost of a meal.

b. Construct a boxplot of the cost of a meal. What is the shape of the distribution?
c. Compute and interpret the correlation coefficient of the summated rating and the cost of a meal.

3.70 The file `Protein` contains calories, protein, and cholesterol of popular protein foods (fresh red meats, poultry, and fish).

Source: U.S. Department of Agriculture.

a. Compute the correlation coefficient between calories and protein.
b. Compute the correlation coefficient between calories and cholesterol.
c. Compute the correlation coefficient between protein and cholesterol.
d. Based on the results of (a) through (c), what conclusions can you reach concerning calories, protein, and cholesterol?

3.71 The file `HotelPrices` contains the average price of a room at two-star, three-star, and four-star hotels in cities around the world in 2009 in English pounds (about US$1.57 as of October 2010). Complete the following for two-star, three-star, and four-star hotels.

Source: Data extracted from www.hotels.com/press/hotel-price-index-2009-h2.html.

a. Compute the mean, median, first quartile, and third quartile.
b. Compute the range, interquartile range, variance, standard deviation, and coefficient of variation.
c. Interpret the measures of central tendency and variation within the context of this problem.
d. Construct a boxplot. Are the data skewed? If so, how?
e. Compute the covariance between the average price at two-star and three-star hotels, between two-star and four-star hotels, and between three-star and four-star hotels.
f. Compute the coefficient of correlation between the average price at two-star and three-star hotels, between two-star and four-star hotels, and between three-star and four-star hotels.
g. Which do you think is more valuable in expressing the relationship between the average price of a room at two-star, three-star, and four-star hotels—the covariance or the coefficient of correlation? Explain.
h. Based on (f), what conclusions can you reach about the relationship between the average price of a room at two-star, three-star, and four-star hotels?

3.72 The file `PropertyTaxes` contains the property taxes per capita for the 50 states and the District of Columbia.
a. Compute the mean, median, first quartile, and third quartile.
b. Compute the range, interquartile range, variance, standard deviation, and coefficient of variation.
c. Construct a boxplot. Are the data skewed? If so, how?
d. Based on the results of (a) through (c), what conclusions can you reach concerning property taxes per capita, in thousands of dollars, for each state and the District of Columbia?

3.73 The file `CEO-Compensation` includes the total compensation (in millions of $) of CEOs of 197 large public companies and the investment return in 2009. Complete the following for the total compensation (in $).

Source: Data extracted from D. Leonard, "Bargains in the Boardroom," *The New York Times*, April 4, 2010, pp. BU1, BU7, BU10, BU11.

a. Compute the mean, median, first quartile, and third quartile.
b. Compute the range, interquartile range, variance, standard deviation, and coefficient of variation.
c. Construct a boxplot. Are the data skewed? If so, how?
d. Based on the results of (a) through (c), what conclusions can you reach concerning the total compensation (in $millions) of CEOs?
e. Compute the correlation coefficient between compensation and the investment return in 2009.
f. What conclusions can you reach from the results of (e)?

3.74 You are planning to study for your statistics examination with a group of classmates, one of whom you particularly want to impress. This individual has volunteered to use Excel or Minitab to get the needed summary information, tables, and charts for a data set containing several numerical and categorical variables assigned by the instructor for study purposes. This person comes over to you with the printout and exclaims, "I've got it all—the means, the medians, the standard deviations, the boxplots, the pie charts—for all our variables. The problem is, some of the output looks weird—like the boxplots for gender and for major and the pie charts for grade point index and for height. Also, I can't understand why Professor Krehbiel said we can't get the descriptive stats for some of the variables; I got them for everything! See, the mean for height is 68.23, the mean for grade point index is 2.76, the mean for gender is 1.50, the mean for major is 4.33." What is your reply?

REPORT WRITING EXERCISES

3.75 The file `DomesticBeer` contains the percentage of alcohol, number of calories per 12 ounces, and number of carbohydrates (in grams) per 12 ounces for 139 of the best-selling domestic beers in the United States.

Your task is to write a report based on a complete descriptive evaluation of each of the numerical variables—percentage of alcohol, number of calories per 12 ounces, and number of carbohydrates (in grams) per 12 ounces. Appended to your report should be all appropriate tables, charts, and numerical descriptive measures.

Source: Data extracted from www.Beer100.com, March 18, 2010.

TEAM PROJECTS

The file **Bond Funds** contains information regarding nine variables from a sample of 184 bond funds:
- Fund number—Identification number for each bond fund
- Type—Type of bonds comprising the bond fund (intermediate government or short-term corporate)
- Assets—In millions of dollars
- Fees—Sales charges (no or yes)
- Expense ratio—Ratio of expenses to net assets
- Return 2009—Twelve-month return in 2009
- Three-year return—Annualized return, 2007–2009
- Five-year return—Annualized return, 2005–2009
- Risk—Risk-of-loss factor of the mutual fund (low, average, or high)

3.76 Complete the following for expense ratio in percentage, three-year return, and five-year return.
a. Compute the mean, median, first quartile, and third quartile.
b. Compute the range, interquartile range, variance, standard deviation, and coefficient of variation.
c. Construct a boxplot. Are the data skewed? If so, how?
d. Based on the results of (a) through (c), what conclusions can you reach concerning these variables?

3.77 You want to compare bond funds that have fees to those that do not have fees. For each of these two groups, use the variables expense ratio, return 2009, three-year return, and five-year return and complete the following.
a. Compute the mean, median, first quartile, and third quartile.
b. Compute the range, interquartile range, variance, standard deviation, and coefficient of variation.
c. Construct a boxplot. Are the data skewed? If so, how?
d. Based on the results of (a) through (c), what conclusions can you reach about differences between bond funds that have fees and those that do not have fees?

3.78 You want to compare intermediate government to the short-term corporate bond funds. For each of these two groups, use the variables expense ratio, three-year return, and five-year return and complete the following.
a. Compute the mean, median, first quartile, and third quartile.
b. Compute the range, interquartile range, variance, standard deviation, and coefficient of variation.
c. Construct a boxplot. Are the data skewed? If so, how?
d. Based on the results of (a) through (c), what conclusions can you reach about differences between intermediate government and short-term corporate bond funds?

3.79 You want to compare bond funds based on risk. For each of these three levels of risk (below average, average, above average), use the variables expense ratio, return 2009, three-year return, and five-year return and complete the following.
a. Compute the mean, median, first quartile, and third quartile.
b. Compute the range, interquartile range, variance, standard deviation, and coefficient of variation.
c. Construct a boxplot. Are the data skewed? If so, how?
d. Based on the results of (a) through (c), what conclusions can you reach about differences between bond funds based on risk?

STUDENT SURVEY DATABASE

3.80 Problem 1.27 on page 44 describes a survey of 62 undergraduate students (stored in **UndergradSurvey**). For these data, for each numerical variable, complete the following.
a. Compute the mean, median, first quartile, and third quartile.
b. Compute the range, interquartile range, variance, standard deviation, and coefficient of variation.
c. Construct a boxplot. Are the data skewed? If so, how?
d. Write a report summarizing your conclusions.

3.81 Problem 1.27 on page 44 describes a survey of 62 undergraduate students (stored in **UndergradSurvey**).
a. Select a sample of undergraduate students at your school and conduct a similar survey for those students.
b. For the data collected in (a), repeat (a) through (d) of Problem 3.80.
c. Compare the results of (b) to those of Problem 3.80.

3.82 Problem 1.28 on page 45 describes a survey of 44 MBA students (stored in **GradSurvey**). For these data, for each numerical variable, complete the following.
a. Compute the mean, median, first quartile, and third quartile.
b. Compute the range, interquartile range, variance, standard deviation, and coefficient of variation.
c. Construct a boxplot. Are the data skewed? If so, how?
d. Write a report summarizing your conclusions.

3.83 Problem 1.28 on page 45 describes a survey of 44 MBA students (stored in **GradSurvey**).
a. Select a sample of graduate students from your MBA program and conduct a similar survey for those students.
b. For the data collected in (a), repeat (a) through (d) of Problem 3.82.
c. Compare the results of (b) to those of Problem 3.82.

MANAGING ASHLAND MULTICOMM SERVICES

For what variable in the Chapter 2 "Managing Ashland MultiComm Services" case (see page 104) are numerical descriptive measures needed?

1. For the variable you identify, compute the appropriate numerical descriptive measures and construct a boxplot.
2. For the variable you identify, construct a graphical display. What conclusions can you reach from this other plot that cannot be made from the boxplot?
3. Summarize your findings in a report that can be included with the task force's study.

DIGITAL CASE

Apply your knowledge about the proper use of numerical descriptive measures in this continuing Digital Case from Chapter 2.

Open **EndRunGuide.pdf**, the EndRun Financial Services "Guide to Investing." Reexamine EndRun's supporting data for the "More Winners Than Losers" and "The Big Eight Difference" and then answer the following:

1. Can descriptive measures be computed for any variables? How would such summary statistics support EndRun's claims? How would those summary statistics affect your perception of EndRun's record?
2. Evaluate the methods EndRun used to summarize the results presented on the "Customer Survey Results" page. Is there anything you would do differently to summarize these results?
3. Note that the last question of the survey has fewer responses than the other questions. What factors may have limited the number of responses to that question?

REFERENCES

1. Kendall, M. G., A. Stuart, and J. K. Ord, *Kendall's Advanced Theory of Statistics*, *Volume 1: Distribution Theory*, 6th ed. (New York: Oxford University Press, 1994).
2. *Microsoft Excel 2010* (Redmond, WA: Microsoft Corporation, 2010).
3. *Minitab Release 16* (State College, PA: Minitab, Inc., 2010).

CHAPTER 3 EXCEL GUIDE

EG3.1 CENTRAL TENDENCY

The Mean, Median, and Mode

In-Depth Excel Use the **AVERAGE** (for the mean), **MEDIAN**, or **MODE** functions in worksheet formulas to compute measures of central tendency. Enter these functions in the form *FUNCTION(cell range of the variable)*. See Section EG3.2 for an example of their use.

Analysis ToolPak Use **Descriptive Statistics** to create a list that includes measures of central tendency. (Section EG3.2 fully explains this procedure.)

The Geometric Mean

In-Depth Excel Use the **GEOMEAN** function in a worksheet formula in the form =**GEOMEAN**$(($1 + (R_1)), (1 + (R_2)), \ldots(1 + (R_n))) - 1$ to compute the geometric mean rate of return. For example, to compute this statistic for Example 3.5 on page 131, enter the formula =**GEOMEAN**$((1 + (-0.3379)), (1 + (0.2717))) - 1$ in any cell.

EG3.2 VARIATION and SHAPE

The Range, Variance, Standard Deviation, Coefficient of Variation, and Shape

In-Depth Excel Use the **COMPUTE worksheet** of the **Descriptive workbook** as a model for computing measures of central tendency, variation, and shape. This worksheet, shown in Figure 3.2 on page 139, computes the descriptive statistics for the 2009 return variable for the intermediate government and short-term corporate bond funds using data found in columns A and B of the **DATA worksheet**. The worksheet uses the **VAR** (sample variance), **STDEV** (sample standard deviation), **MIN** (minimum value), and **MAX** (maximum value) functions to compute measures of variation for a variable of interest. In row 11, the worksheet takes the difference between **MAX** and **MIN** to compute the range. In row 4, the worksheet uses the **COUNT** function to determine the sample size and then divides the sample standard deviation by the square root (**SQRT**) of the sample size to compute the standard error. (See Section 7.4 to learn more about the standard error.)

To add the coefficient of variation to the **COMPUTE worksheet**, first enter **Coefficient of variation** in cell **A16**. Then, enter the formula =**B7/B3** in cell **B16** and then copy it to cell **C16**. Finally, format cells B16 and C16 for percentage display.

Analysis ToolPak Use **Descriptive Statistics** to create a list that contains measures of variation and shape along with central tendency.

For example, to create a worksheet similar to the Figure 3.2 worksheet on page 139 that presents descriptive statistics for the 2009 return for the intermediate government and short-term corporate bond funds (see page 139), open to the **RETURN2009 worksheet** of the **Bond Funds workbook** and:

1. Select **Data** → **Data Analysis**.
2. In the Data Analysis dialog box, select **Descriptive Statistics** from the **Analysis Tools** list and then click **OK**.

In the Descriptive Statistics dialog box (shown below):

3. Enter **A1:B98** as the **Input Range**. Click **Columns** and check **Labels in First Row**.
4. Click **New Worksheet Ply**, check **Summary statistics**, and then click **OK**.

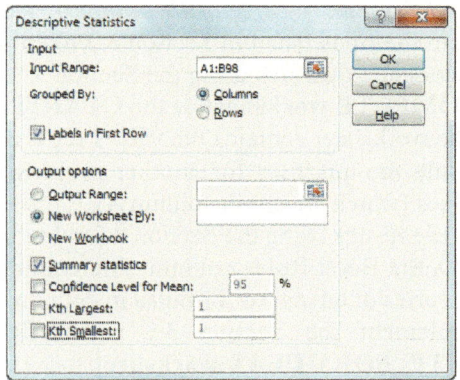

In the new worksheet:

5. Select column C, right-click, and click **Delete** in the shortcut menu (to eliminate the duplicate row labels).
6. Adjust the column headings and cell formatting, using Figure 3.2 as a guide. (See Appendix B for help with these adjustments.)

To add the coefficient of variation to this worksheet, first enter **Coefficient of variation** in cell **A16**. Then, enter the formula =**B7/B3** in cell **B16** and then copy it to cell **C16**. Finally, format cells B16 and C16 for percentage display.

Z Scores

In-Depth Excel Use the **STANDARDIZE** function to compute Z scores. Enter the function in the form **STANDARDIZE***(value, mean, standard deviation)*, where *value* is an X value. Use the **TABLE_3.4 worksheet** of the

Descriptive workbook as a model for computing Z scores. The worksheet uses the AVERAGE and STDEV functions to compute the mean and standard deviation values used in the STANDARDIZE function.

Shape

In-Depth Excel Use the **SKEW** and **KURT** functions to compute skewness and kurtosis, respectively. Enter these functions in the form *FUNCTION(cell range of the variable)*. Use the **COMPUTE worksheet** of the **Descriptive workbook** (discussed earlier in this section) as a model for computing these statistics.

Analysis ToolPak Use **Descriptive Statistics** to compute skewness and kurtosis. The *Analysis ToolPak* instructions given earlier in this section will compute these statistics as well.

EG3.3 EXPLORING NUMERICAL DATA

Quartiles

In-Depth Excel As noted on page 144, the Excel **QUARTILE** function, entered as **QUARTILE***(cell range of data to be summarized, quartile number)*, uses rules that differ from the rules listed in Section 3.3 to compute quartiles. To compute quartiles using the Section 3.3 rules, open to the **COMPUTE worksheet** of the **QUARTILES workbook**. The worksheet contains the values for Example 3.11. To compute the quartiles for another problem, overwrite those values (which appear in column A).

Quartile results using the Section 3.3 rules are shown in column D, the Book Rules column. The column D results rely on a series of advanced formulas in columns G through I to implement the Section 3.3 rules. Open to the **COMPUTE_FORMULAS worksheet** to examine these formulas. (A full explanation of the formulas used in that worksheet is beyond the scope of this book.)

The Interquartile Range

In-Depth Excel Use a worksheet formula that subtracts the first quartile from the third quartile to compute the interquartile range. For example, to compute this statistic for Example 3.12 on page 145, open to the **COMPUTE worksheet** of the **Quartiles workbook** and enter the formula **=D5 – D3** into an empty cell.

The Five-Number Summary and the Boxplot

PHStat2 Use **Boxplot** to create a five-number summary and boxplot. For example, to create the Figure 3.4 five-number summary and boxplot on page 147, open to the **DATA worksheet** of the **Bond Funds workbook**. Select

PHStat → Descriptive Statistics → Boxplot. In the procedure's dialog box (shown below):

1. Enter **F1:F185** as the **Raw Data Cell Range** and check **First cell contains label**.
2. Click **Multiple Groups-Stacked** and enter **B1:B185** as the **Grouping Variable Cell Range**.
3. Enter a **Title**, check **Five-Number Summary**, and click **OK**.

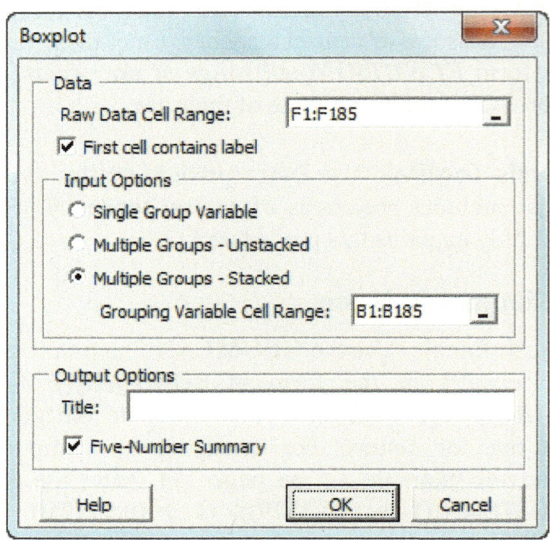

The boxplot appears on its own chart sheet, separate from the worksheet that contains the five-number summary.

In-Depth Excel Use the worksheets of the **Boxplot workbook** as templates for creating a five-number summary and boxplot. Use the **PLOT_DATA worksheet** as a template for creating a five-number summary and a boxplot in one worksheet from unsummarized data. Use the **PLOT worksheet** as a template for constructing a boxplot from a known five-number summary.

Because Excel does not include a boxplot as one of its chart types, creating a boxplot requires the advanced and creative "misuse" of Excel charting features. Open to the **PLOT_FORMULAS worksheet** to examine this "misuse." (A full explanation is beyond the scope of this book.)

EG3.4 NUMERICAL DESCRIPTIVE MEASURES for a POPULATION

The Population Mean, Population Variance, and Population Standard Deviation

In-Depth Excel Use the **AVERAGE** function to compute the population mean. Use the **VARP** and **STDEVP** functions to compute the population variance and standard deviation, respectively. Enter these functions in the form **AVERAGE**(*cell range of the population)*, **VARP**(*cell range of the population)*, and **STDEVP**(*cell range of the population)*.

The Empirical Rule and the Chebyshev Rule

In-Depth Excel Use the **COMPUTE worksheet** of the **Variability workbook** as a template that uses arithmetic formulas to examine the variability in a distribution.

EG3.5 THE COVARIANCE and the COEFFICIENT of CORRELATION

The Covariance

In-Depth Excel Use the **COMPUTE worksheet** of the **Covariance workbook** as a template for covariance analysis. The worksheet contains the Table 3.8 set of 30 values and annual revenues (see page 156). For other problems, overwrite these values and follow the instructions in the worksheet for modifying the worksheet, when you have less than or more than 30 values. (The **COMPUTE_FORMULAS worksheet** shows the formulas used in the COMPUTE worksheet.)

The Coefficient of Correlation

In-Depth Excel Use the **CORREL** function to compute the coefficient of correlation. Enter this function in the form **CORREL**(*cell range of the* **X** *values, cell range of the* **Y** *values*).

Use the **COMPUTE worksheet** of the **Correlation workbook** as a template for the correlation analysis shown in Figure 3.10 on page 159. In this worksheet, the cell F15 formula =CORREL(A4:A33, B4:B33) computes the coefficient of correlation.

CHAPTER 3 MINITAB GUIDE

MG3.1 CENTRAL TENDENCY

The Mean, Median, and Mode

Use **Descriptive Statistics** to compute the mean, the median, the mode, and selected measures of variation and shape. For example, to create results similar to Figure 3.2 on page 139 that presents descriptive statistics for the 2009 return for the intermediate government and short-term corporate bond funds, open to the **Bond Funds worksheet**. Select **Stat → Basic Statistics → Display Descriptive Statistics**. In the Display Descriptive Statistics dialog box (shown below):

1. Double-click **C6 Return 2009** in the variables list to add **'Return 2009'** to the **Variables** box and then press **Tab**.
2. Double-click **C2 Type** in the variables list to add **Type** to the **By variables (optional)** box.
3. Click **Statistics**.

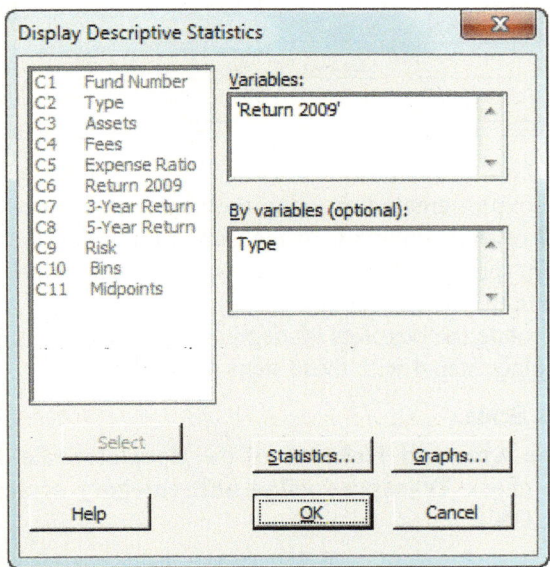

In the Display Descriptive Statistics-Statistics dialog box (shown below):

4. Check **Mean**, **Standard deviation**, **Variance**, **Coefficient of variation**, **First quartile**, **Median**, **Third quartile**, **Interquartile range**, **Mode**, **Minimum**, **Maximum**, **Range**, **Skewness**, **Kurtosis**, and **N total**.
5. Click **OK**.

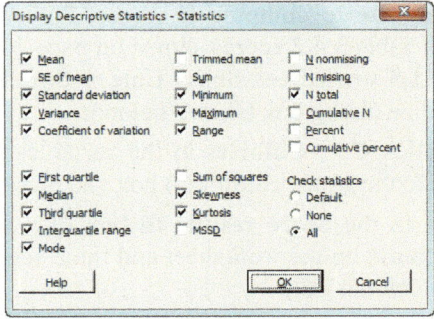

6. Back in the Display Descriptive Statistics dialog box, click **OK**.

The Geometric Mean

Use **Calculator** to compute the geometric mean or the geometric mean rate of return. For example, to compute the geometric mean rate of return for Example 3.5 on page 131, open to the **Investments worksheet**. Select **Calc → Calculator**. In the Calculator dialog box (shown at the top of page 172):

1. Enter **C2** in the **Store result in variable** box and then press **Tab**. (C2 is the first empty column on the worksheet and the result will be placed in row 1 of column C2.)
2. Double-click **Geometric mean** in the **Functions** scrollable list to add **GMEAN(number)** to the **Expression** box.

3. Double-click **C1 Rates of Return** in the variables list to alter the expression to **GMEAN('Rates of Return')**. (If you prefer, you can directly edit the expression as part of the next step.)
4. Edit the expression so that it reads **GMEAN('Rates of Return') – 1**.
5. Click **OK**.

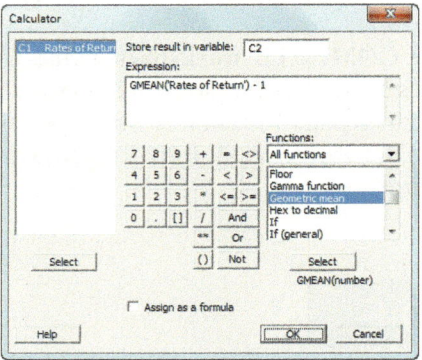

MG3.2 VARIATION and SHAPE

The Range, Variance, Standard Deviation, and Coefficient of Variation

Use **Descriptive Statistics** to compute these measures of variation and shape. The instructions in Section MG3.1 for computing the mean, median, and mode also compute these measures.

Z Scores

Use **Standardize** to compute Z scores. For example, to compute the Table 3.4 Z scores shown on page 138, open to the **CEREALS worksheet**. Select **Calc → Standardize**. In the Standardize dialog box (shown below):

1. Double-click **C2 Calories** in the variables list to add **Calories** to the **Input column(s)** box and press **Tab**.
2. Enter C5 in the **Store results in** box. (C5 is the first empty column on the worksheet and the Z scores will be placed in column C5.)
3. Click **Subtract mean and divide by standard deviation**.
4. Click **OK**.
5. In the new column C5, enter **Z Scores** as the name of the column.

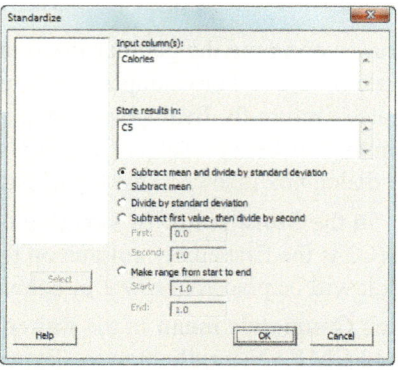

Shape

Use **Descriptive Statistics** to compute skewness and kurtosis. The instructions in Section MG3.1 for computing the mean, median, and mode also compute these measures.

MG3.3 EXPLORING NUMERICAL DATA

Quartiles, the Interquartile Range, and the Five-Number Summary

Use **Descriptive Statistics** to compute these measures. The instructions in Section MG3.1 for computing the mean, median, and mode also compute these measures.

The Boxplot

Use **Boxplot** to create a boxplot. For example, to create the Figure 3.5 boxplots on page 148, open to the **Bond Funds worksheet**. Select **Graph → Boxplot**. In the Boxplots dialog box:

1. Click **With Groups** in the **One Y gallery** and then click **OK**.

In the Boxplot-One Y, With Groups dialog box (shown below):

2. Double-click **C6 Return 2009** in the variables list to add **'Return 2009'** to the **Graph variables** box and then press **Tab**.
3. Double-click **C2 Type** in the variables list to add **Type** in the **Categorical variables** box.
4. Click **OK**.

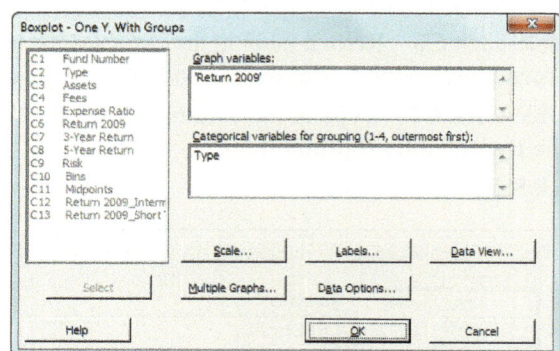

In the boxplot created, pausing the mouse pointer over the boxplot reveals a number of measures, including the quartiles. For problems that involve single-group data, click **Simple** in the **One Y gallery** in step 1.

To rotate the boxplots 90 degrees (as was done in Figure 3.5), replace step 4 with these steps 4 through 6:

4. Click **Scale**.
5. In the **Axes and Ticks** tab of the Boxplot–Scale dialog box, check **Transpose value and category scales** and click **OK**.
6. Back in the Boxplot-One Y, With Groups dialog box, click **OK**.

MG3.4 NUMERICAL DESCRIPTIVE MEASURES for a POPULATION

The Population Mean, Population Variance, and Population Standard Deviation

Minitab does not contain commands that compute these population parameters directly.

The Empirical Rule and the Chebyshev Rule

Manually compute the values needed to apply these rules using the statistics computed in the Section MG3.1 instructions.

MG3.5 THE COVARIANCE and the COEFFICIENT of CORRELATION

The Covariance

Use **Covariance** to compute the covariance. For example, to compute the covariance for the Table 3.8 set of 30 values and annual revenues, open to the **NBAValues worksheet**. Select **Stat → Basic Statistics → Covariance**. In the Covariance dialog box (shown below):

1. Double-click **C2 Revenue** in the variables list to add **Revenue** to the **Variables** box.
2. Double-click **C3 Value** in the variables list to add **Value** to the **Variables** box.

3. Click **OK**.

In the table of numbers produced, the covariance is the number that appears in the cell position that is the intersection of the two variables (the lower-left cell).

The Coefficient of Correlation

Use **Correlation** to compute the coefficient of correlation. For example, to compute the coefficient of correlation for the set of 30 values and annual revenues shown in Figure 3.10 on page 159, open to the **NBAValues worksheet**. Select **Stat → Basic Statistics → Correlation**. In the Correlation dialog box (similar to the Covariance dialog box):

1. Double-click **C2 Revenue** in the variables list to add **Revenue** to the **Variables** box.
2. Double-click **C3 Value** in the variables list to add **Value** to the **Variables** box.
3. Click **OK**.

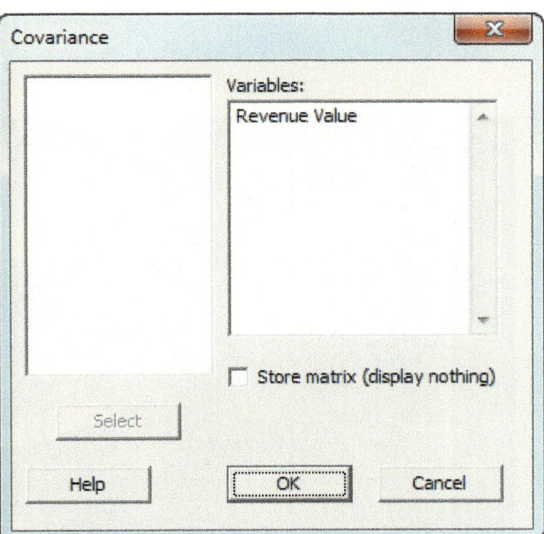

4 Basic Probability

USING STATISTICS @ M&R Electronics World

4.1 Basic Probability Concepts
Events and Sample Spaces
Contingency Tables and Venn Diagrams
Simple Probability
Joint Probability
Marginal Probability
General Addition Rule

4.2 Conditional Probability
Computing Conditional Probabilities
Decision Trees
Independence
Multiplication Rules
Marginal Probability Using the General Multiplication Rule

4.3 Bayes' Theorem

THINK ABOUT THIS: Divine Providence and Spam

4.4 Counting Rules
Counting Rule 1
Counting Rule 2
Counting Rule 3
Counting Rule 4
Counting Rule 5

4.5 Ethical Issues and Probability

USING STATISTICS @ M&R Electronics World Revisited

CHAPTER 4 EXCEL GUIDE

CHAPTER 4 MINITAB GUIDE

Learning Objectives

In this chapter, you learn:

- Basic probability concepts
- Conditional probability
- Bayes' theorem to revise probabilities
- Various counting rules

USING STATISTICS

@ M&R Electronics World

As the marketing manager for M&R Electronics World, you are analyzing the survey results of an intent-to-purchase study. This study asked the heads of 1,000 households about their intentions to purchase a big-screen television sometime during the next 12 months. As a follow-up, you plan to survey the same people 12 months later to see whether they purchased televisions. In addition, for households purchasing big-screen televisions, you would like to know whether the television they purchased had a faster refresh rate (120 Hz or higher) or a standard refresh rate (60 Hz), whether they also purchased a Blu-ray disc (BD) player in the past 12 months, and whether they were satisfied with their purchase of the big-screen television.

You are expected to use the results of this survey to plan a new marketing strategy that will enhance sales and better target those households likely to purchase multiple or more expensive products. What questions can you ask in this survey? How can you express the relationships among the various intent-to-purchase responses of individual households?

In previous chapters, you learned descriptive methods to summarize categorical and numerical variables. In this chapter, you will learn about probability to answer questions such as the following:

- What is the probability that a household is planning to purchase a big-screen television in the next year?
- What is the probability that a household will actually purchase a big-screen television?
- What is the probability that a household is planning to purchase a big-screen television and actually purchases the television?
- Given that the household is planning to purchase a big-screen television, what is the probability that the purchase is made?
- Does knowledge of whether a household *plans* to purchase the television change the likelihood of predicting whether the household *will* purchase the television?
- What is the probability that a household that purchases a big-screen television will purchase a television with a faster refresh rate?
- What is the probability that a household that purchases a big-screen television with a faster refresh rate will also purchase a Blu-ray disc player?
- What is the probability that a household that purchases a big-screen television will be satisfied with the purchase?

With answers to questions such as these, you can begin to make decisions about your marketing strategy. Should your strategy for selling more big-screen televisions target those households that have indicated an intent to purchase? Should you concentrate on selling televisions that have faster refresh rates? Is it likely that households that purchase big-screen televisions with faster refresh rates can be easily persuaded to also purchase Blu-ray disc players?

The principles of probability help bridge the worlds of descriptive statistics and inferential statistics. Reading this chapter will help you learn about different types of probabilities, how to compute probabilities, and how to revise probabilities in light of new information. Probability principles are the foundation for the probability distribution, the concept of mathematical expectation, and the binomial, Poisson, and hypergeometric distributions, topics that are discussed in Chapter 5.

4.1 Basic Probability Concepts

What is meant by the word *probability*? A **probability** is the numeric value representing the chance, likelihood, or possibility that a particular event will occur, such as the price of a stock increasing, a rainy day, a defective product, or the outcome five dots in a single toss of a die. In all these instances, the probability involved is a proportion or fraction whose value ranges between 0 and 1, inclusive. An event that has no chance of occurring (the **impossible event**) has a probability of 0. An event that is sure to occur (the **certain event**) has a probability of 1.

There are three types of probability:

- *A priori*
- Empirical
- Subjective

In ***a priori* probability**, the probability of an occurrence is based on prior knowledge of the process involved. In the simplest case, where each outcome is equally likely, the chance of occurrence of the event is defined in Equation (4.1).

> **PROBABILITY OF OCCURRENCE**
>
> $$\text{Probability of occurrence} = \frac{X}{T} \qquad (4.1)$$
>
> where
>
> X = number of ways in which the event occurs
>
> T = total number of possible outcomes

Consider a standard deck of cards that has 26 red cards and 26 black cards. The probability of selecting a black card is $26/52 = 0.50$ because there are $X = 26$ black cards and $T = 52$ total cards. What does this probability mean? If each card is replaced after it is selected, does it mean that 1 out of the next 2 cards selected will be black? No, because you cannot say for certain what will happen on the next several selections. However, you can say that in the long run, if this selection process is continually repeated, the proportion of black cards selected will approach 0.50. Example 4.1 shows another example of computing an *a priori* probability.

EXAMPLE 4.1

Finding *A Priori* Probabilities

A standard six-sided die has six faces. Each face of the die contains either one, two, three, four, five, or six dots. If you roll a die, what is the probability that you will get a face with five dots?

SOLUTION Each face is equally likely to occur. Because there are six faces, the probability of getting a face with five dots is 1/6.

The preceding examples use the *a priori* probability approach because the number of ways the event occurs and the total number of possible outcomes are known from the composition of the deck of cards or the faces of the die.

In the **empirical probability** approach, the probabilities are based on observed data, not on prior knowledge of a process. Surveys are often used to generate empirical probabilities. Examples of this type of probability are the proportion of individuals in the Using Statistics scenario who actually purchase big-screen televisions, the proportion of registered voters who prefer a certain political candidate, and the proportion of students who have part-time jobs. For example, if you take a survey of students, and 60% state that they have part-time jobs, then there is a 0.60 probability that an individual student has a part-time job.

The third approach to probability, **subjective probability,** differs from the other two approaches because subjective probability differs from person to person. For example, the development team for a new product may assign a probability of 0.60 to the chance of success for the product, while the president of the company may be less optimistic and assign a probability of 0.30. The assignment of subjective probabilities to various outcomes is usually based on a combination of an individual's past experience, personal opinion, and analysis of a particular situation. Subjective probability is especially useful in making decisions in situations in which you cannot use *a priori* probability or empirical probability.

Events and Sample Spaces

The basic elements of probability theory are the individual outcomes of a variable under study. You need the following definitions to understand probabilities.

> EVENT
>
> Each possible outcome of a variable is referred to as an **event**.
> A **simple event** is described by a single characteristic.

For example, when you toss a coin, the two possible outcomes are heads and tails. Each of these represents a simple event. When you roll a standard six-sided die in which the six faces of the die contain either one, two, three, four, five, or six dots, there are six possible simple events. An event can be any one of these simple events, a set of them, or a subset of all of them. For example, the event of an *even number of dots* consists of three simple events (i.e., two, four, or six dots).

> JOINT EVENT
>
> A **joint event** is an event that has two or more characteristics.

Getting two heads when you toss a coin twice is an example of a joint event because it consists of heads on the first toss and heads on the second toss.

> COMPLEMENT
>
> The **complement** of event A (represented by the symbol A') includes all events that are not part of A.

The complement of a head is a tail because that is the only event that is not a head. The complement of five dots on a die is not getting five dots. Not getting five dots consists of getting one, two, three, four, or six dots.

> **SAMPLE SPACE**
>
> The collection of all the possible events is called the **sample space**.
> The sample space for tossing a coin consists of heads and tails. The sample space when rolling a die consists of one, two, three, four, five, and six dots. Example 4.2 demonstrates events and sample spaces.

EXAMPLE 4.2
Events and Sample Spaces

TABLE 4.1
Purchase Behavior for Big-Screen Televisions

The Using Statistics scenario on page 175 concerns M&R Electronics World. Table 4.1 presents the results of the sample of 1,000 households in terms of purchase behavior for big-screen televisions.

PLANNED TO PURCHASE	ACTUALLY PURCHASED		
	Yes	No	Total
Yes	200	50	250
No	100	650	750
Total	300	700	1,000

What is the sample space? Give examples of simple events and joint events.

SOLUTION The sample space consists of the 1,000 respondents. Simple events are "planned to purchase," "did not plan to purchase," "purchased," and "did not purchase." The complement of the event "planned to purchase" is "did not plan to purchase." The event "planned to purchase and actually purchased" is a joint event because in this joint event the respondent must plan to purchase the television *and* actually purchase it.

Contingency Tables and Venn Diagrams

There are several ways in which you can view a particular sample space. One way involves using a **contingency table** (see Section 2.2) such as the one displayed in Table 4.1. You get the values in the cells of the table by subdividing the sample space of 1,000 households according to whether someone planned to purchase and actually purchased a big-screen television set. For example, 200 of the respondents planned to purchase a big-screen television set and subsequently did purchase the big-screen television set.

A second way to present the sample space is by using a **Venn diagram**. This diagram graphically represents the various events as "unions" and "intersections" of circles. Figure 4.1 presents a typical Venn diagram for a two-variable situation, with each variable having only two events (A and A', B and B'). The circle on the left (the red one) represents all events that are part of A.

The circle on the right (the yellow one) represents all events that are part of B. The area contained within circle A and circle B (center area) is the intersection of A and B (written as $A \cap B$), since it is part of A and also part of B. The total area of the two circles is the union of A and B (written as $A \cup B$) and contains all outcomes that are just part of event A, just part of event B, or part of both A and B. The area in the diagram outside of $A \cup B$ contains outcomes that are neither part of A nor part of B.

You must define A and B in order to develop a Venn diagram. You can define either event as A or B, as long as you are consistent in evaluating the various events. For the big-screen television example, you can define the events as follows:

A = planned to purchase B = actually purchased
A' = did not plan to purchase B' = did not actually purchase

In drawing the Venn diagram (see Figure 4.2), you must determine the value of the intersection of A and B so that the sample space can be divided into its parts. $A \cap B$ consists of all 200 households who planned to purchase and actually purchased a big-screen television set.

FIGURE 4.1
Venn diagram for events A and B

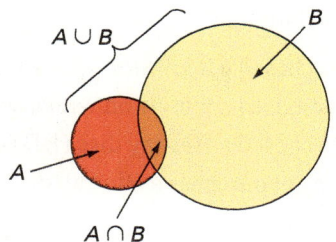

FIGURE 4.2
Venn diagram for the M&R Electronics World example

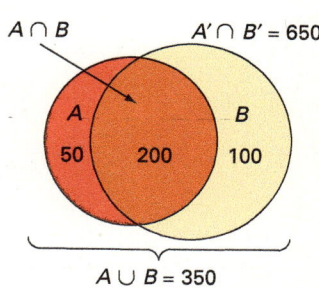

The remainder of event A (planned to purchase) consists of the 50 households who planned to purchase a big-screen television set but did not actually purchase one. The remainder of event B (actually purchased) consists of the 100 households who did not plan to purchase a big-screen television set but actually purchased one. The remaining 650 households represent those who neither planned to purchase nor actually purchased a big-screen television set.

Simple Probability

Now you can answer some of the questions posed in the Using Statistics scenario. Because the results are based on data collected in a survey (refer to Table 4.1), you can use the empirical probability approach.

As stated previously, the most fundamental rule for probabilities is that they range in value from 0 to 1. An impossible event has a probability of 0, and an event that is certain to occur has a probability of 1.

Simple probability refers to the probability of occurrence of a simple event, $P(A)$. A simple probability in the Using Statistics scenario is the probability of planning to purchase a big-screen television. How can you determine the probability of selecting a household that planned to purchase a big-screen television? Using Equation (4.1) on page 176:

$$\text{Probability of occurrence} = \frac{X}{T}$$

$$P(\text{Planned to purchase}) = \frac{\text{Number who planned to purchase}}{\text{Total number of households}}$$

$$= \frac{250}{1{,}000} = 0.25$$

Thus, there is a 0.25 (or 25%) chance that a household planned to purchase a big-screen television. Example 4.3 illustrates another application of simple probability.

EXAMPLE 4.3

Computing the Probability That the Big-Screen Television Purchased Had a Faster Refresh Rate

In the Using Statistics follow-up survey, additional questions were asked of the 300 households that actually purchased big-screen televisions. Table 4.2 indicates the consumers' responses to whether the television purchased had a faster refresh rate and whether they also purchased a Blu-ray disc (BD) player in the past 12 months.

Find the probability that if a household that purchased a big-screen television is randomly selected, the television purchased had a faster refresh rate.

TABLE 4.2

Purchase Behavior Regarding Purchasing a Faster Refresh Rate Television and Blu-Ray Disc (BD) Player

REFRESH RATE OF TELEVISION PURCHASED	PURCHASED BD PLAYER		
	Yes	No	Total
Faster	38	42	80
Standard	70	150	220
Total	108	192	300

SOLUTION Using the following definitions:

$$A = \text{purchased a television with a faster refresh rate}$$
$$A' = \text{purchased a television with a standard refresh rate}$$
$$B = \text{purchased a Blu-ray disc (BD) player}$$
$$B' = \text{did not purchase a Blu-ray disc (BD) player}$$

$$P(\text{faster refresh rate}) = \frac{\text{Number of faster refresh rate televisions}}{\text{Total number of televisions}}$$

$$= \frac{80}{300} = 0.267$$

There is a 26.7% chance that a randomly selected big-screen television purchased has a faster refresh rate.

Joint Probability

Whereas simple or marginal probability refers to the probability of occurrence of simple events, **joint probability** refers to the probability of an occurrence involving two or more events. An example of joint probability is the probability that you will get heads on the first toss of a coin and heads on the second toss of a coin.

In Table 4.1 on page 178, the group of individuals who planned to purchase and actually purchased a big-screen television consist only of the outcomes in the single cell "yes—planned to purchase *and* yes—actually purchased." Because this group consists of 200 households, the probability of picking a household that planned to purchase *and* actually purchased a big-screen television is

$$P(\text{Planned to purchase and actually purchased}) = \frac{\text{Planned to purchase and actually purchased}}{\text{Total number of respondents}}$$

$$= \frac{200}{1{,}000} = 0.20$$

Example 4.4 also demonstrates how to determine joint probability.

EXAMPLE 4.4

Determining the Joint Probability That a Household Purchased a Big-Screen Television with a Faster Refresh Rate and a Blu-ray Disc Player

In Table 4.2, the purchases are cross-classified as having a faster refresh rate or having a standard refresh rate and whether the household purchased a Blu-ray disc player. Find the probability that a randomly selected household that purchased a big-screen television also purchased a television that had a faster refresh rate and purchased a Blu-ray disc player.

SOLUTION Using Equation (4.1) on page 176,

$$P(\text{television with a faster refresh rate and Blu-ray disc player}) = \frac{\text{Number that purchased a television with a faster refresh rate and a Blu-ray disc player}}{\text{Total number of big-screen television purchasers}}$$

$$= \frac{38}{300} = 0.127$$

Therefore, there is a 12.7% chance that a randomly selected household that purchased a big-screen television purchased a television that had a faster refresh rate and a Blu-ray disc player.

Marginal Probability

The **marginal probability** of an event consists of a set of joint probabilities. You can determine the marginal probability of a particular event by using the concept of joint probability just discussed. For example, if B consists of two events, B_1 and B_2, then $P(A)$, the probability of event A, consists of the joint probability of event A occurring with event B_1 and the joint probability of event A occurring with event B_2. You use Equation (4.2) to compute marginal probabilities.

> **MARGINAL PROBABILITY**
>
> $$P(A) = P(A \text{ and } B_1) + P(A \text{ and } B_2) + \cdots + P(A \text{ and } B_k) \quad (4.2)$$
>
> where $B_1, B_2, \ldots, B_k$ are k mutually exclusive and collectively exhaustive events, defined as follows:
>
> Two events are **mutually exclusive** if both the events cannot occur simultaneously.
> A set of events is **collectively exhaustive** if one of the events must occur.

Heads and tails in a coin toss are mutually exclusive events. The result of a coin toss cannot simultaneously be a head and a tail. Heads and tails in a coin toss are also collectively exhaustive events. One of them must occur. If heads does not occur, tails must occur. If tails does not occur, heads must occur. Being male and being female are mutually exclusive and collectively exhaustive events. No person is both (the two are mutually exclusive), and everyone is one or the other (the two are collectively exhaustive).

You can use Equation (4.2) to compute the marginal probability of "planned to purchase" a big-screen television:

$$\begin{aligned} P(\text{Planned to purchase}) &= P(\text{Planned to purchase } and \text{ purchased}) \\ &\quad + P(\text{Planned to purchase } and \text{ did not purchase}) \\ &= \frac{200}{1{,}000} + \frac{50}{1{,}000} \\ &= \frac{250}{1{,}000} = 0.25 \end{aligned}$$

You get the same result if you add the number of outcomes that make up the simple event "planned to purchase."

General Addition Rule

How do you find the probability of event "A or B"? You need to consider the occurrence of either event A or event B or both A and B. For example, how can you determine the probability that a household planned to purchase *or* actually purchased a big-screen television? The event "planned to purchase *or* actually purchased" includes all households that planned to purchase and all households that actually purchased a big-screen television. You examine each cell of the contingency table (Table 4.1 on page 178) to determine whether it is part of this event. From Table 4.1, the cell "planned to purchase *and* did not actually purchase" is part of the event because it includes respondents who planned to purchase. The cell "did not plan to purchase *and* actually purchased" is included because it contains respondents who actually purchased. Finally, the cell "planned to purchase *and* actually purchased" has both characteristics of interest. Therefore, one way to calculate the probability of "planned to purchase *or* actually purchased" is

$$\begin{aligned} P(\text{Planned to purchase } or \text{ actually purchased}) &= P(\text{Planned to purchase } and \text{ did} \\ &\quad \text{not actually purchase}) + P(\text{Did not plan to} \\ &\quad \text{purchase } and \text{ actually purchase}) + P(\text{Planned} \\ &\quad \text{to purchase } and \text{ actually purchased}) \\ &= \frac{50}{1{,}000} + \frac{100}{1{,}000} + \frac{200}{1{,}000} \\ &= \frac{350}{1{,}000} = 0.35 \end{aligned}$$

Often, it is easier to determine $P(A \text{ or } B)$, the probability of the event A or B, by using the **general addition rule**, defined in Equation (4.3).

> **GENERAL ADDITION RULE**
>
> The probability of A or B is equal to the probability of A plus the probability of B minus the probability of A and B.
>
> $$P(A \text{ or } B) = P(A) + P(B) - P(A \text{ and } B) \qquad (4.3)$$

Applying Equation (4.3) to the previous example produces the following result:

$$P(\text{Planned to purchase } or \text{ actually purchased}) = P(\text{Planned to purchase}) + P(\text{Actually purchased}) - P(\text{Planned to purchase } and \text{ actually purchased})$$

$$= \frac{250}{1{,}000} + \frac{300}{1{,}000} - \frac{200}{1{,}000}$$

$$= \frac{350}{1{,}000} = 0.35$$

The general addition rule consists of taking the probability of A and adding it to the probability of B and then subtracting the probability of the joint event A and B from this total because the joint event has already been included in computing both the probability of A and the probability of B. Referring to Table 4.1 on page 178, if the outcomes of the event "planned to purchase" are added to those of the event "actually purchased," the joint event "planned to purchase *and* actually purchased" has been included in each of these simple events. Therefore, because this joint event has been double-counted, you must subtract it to provide the correct result. Example 4.5 illustrates another application of the general addition rule.

EXAMPLE 4.5

Using the General Addition Rule for the Households That Purchased Big-Screen Televisions

In Example 4.3 on page 179, the purchases were cross-classified in Table 4.2 as televisions that had a faster refresh rate or televisions that had a standard refresh rate and whether the household purchased a Blu-ray disc (BD) player. Find the probability that among households that purchased a big-screen television, they purchased a television that had a faster refresh rate or a BD player.

SOLUTION Using Equation (4.3),

$$P(\text{Television had a faster refresh rate } or \text{ purchased a BD player}) = P(\text{Television had a faster refresh rate}) + P(\text{purchased a BD player}) - P(\text{Television had a faster refresh rate } and \text{ purchased a BD player})$$

$$= \frac{80}{300} + \frac{108}{300} - \frac{38}{300}$$

$$= \frac{150}{300} = 0.50$$

Therefore, of those households that purchased a big-screen television, there is a 50.0% chance that a randomly selected household purchased a television that had a faster refresh rate or purchased a BD player.

Problems for Section 4.1

LEARNING THE BASICS

4.1 Two coins are tossed.
a. Give an example of a simple event.
b. Give an example of a joint event.
c. What is the complement of a head on the first toss?

4.2 An urn contains 12 red balls and 8 white balls. One ball is to be selected from the urn.
a. Give an example of a simple event.
b. What is the complement of a red ball?

4.3 Consider the following contingency table:

	B	B'
A	10	20
A'	20	40

What is the probability of
a. event A?
b. event A'?
c. event A and B?
d. A or B?

4.4 Consider the following contingency table:

	B	B'
A	10	30
A'	25	35

What is the probability of
a. event A'?
b. event A and B?
c. event A' and B'?
d. event A' or B'?

APPLYING THE CONCEPTS

4.5 For each of the following, indicate whether the type of probability involved is an example of *a priori* probability, empirical probability, or subjective probability.
a. The next toss of a fair coin will land on heads.
b. Italy will win soccer's World Cup the next time the competition is held.
c. The sum of the faces of two dice will be seven.
d. The train taking a commuter to work will be more than 10 minutes late.

4.6 For each of the following, state whether the events created are mutually exclusive and collectively exhaustive.
a. Registered voters in the United States were asked whether they are registered as Republicans or Democrats.
b. Each respondent was classified by the type of car he or she drives: sedan, SUV, American, European, Asian, or none.
c. People were asked, "Do you currently live in (i) an apartment or (ii) a house?"
d. A product was classified as defective or not defective.

4.7 Which of the following events occur with a probability of zero? For each, state why or why not.
a. A voter in the United States is registered as a Republican and as a Democrat.
b. A voter in the United States is female and registered as a Republican.
c. An automobile is a Ford and a Toyota.
d. An automobile is a Toyota and was manufactured in the United States.

4.8 Does it take more time to be removed from an email list than it used to take? A study of 100 large online retailers revealed the following:

YEAR	NEED THREE OR MORE CLICKS TO BE REMOVED	
	Yes	No
2009	39	61
2008	7	93

Source: Data extracted from "More Clicks to Escape an Email List," *The New York Times*, March 29, 2010, p. B2.

a. Give an example of a simple event.
b. Give an example of a joint event.
c. What is the complement of "Needs three or more clicks to be removed from an email list"?
d. Why is "Needs three or more clicks to be removed from an email list in 2009" a joint event?

4.9 Referring to the contingency table in Problem 4.8, if a large online retailer is selected at random, what is the probability that
a. you needed three or more clicks to be removed from an email list?
b. you needed three or more clicks to be removed from an email list in 2009?
c. you needed three or more clicks to be removed from an email list or were a large online retailer surveyed in 2009?
d. Explain the difference in the results in (b) and (c).

4.10 Do people of different age groups differ in their response to email messages? A survey by the Center for the Digital Future of the University of Southern California (data extracted from A. Mindlin, "Older E-mail Users Favor Fast Replies," *The New York Times*, July 14, 2008, p. B3) reported that 70.7% of users over 70 years of age believe that email messages should be answered quickly, as compared to

53.6% of users 12 to 50 years old. Suppose that the survey was based on 1,000 users over 70 years of age and 1,000 users 12 to 50 years old. The following table summarizes the results:

ANSWERS QUICKLY	AGE OF RESPONDENTS		Total
	12–50	Over 70	
Yes	536	707	1,243
No	464	293	757
Total	1,000	1,000	2,000

a. Give an example of a simple event.
b. Give an example of a joint event.
c. What is the complement of a respondent who answers quickly?
d. Why is a respondent who answers quickly and is over 70 years old a joint event?

4.11 Referring to the contingency table in Problem 4.10, if a respondent is selected at random, what is the probability that
a. he or she answers quickly?
b. he or she is over 70 years old?
c. he or she answers quickly *or* is over 70 years old?
d. Explain the difference in the results in (b) and (c).

4.12 According to a Gallup Poll, the extent to which employees are engaged with their workplace varies from country to country. Gallup reports that the percentage of U.S. workers engaged with their workplace is more than twice as high as the percentage of German workers. The study also shows that having more engaged workers leads to increased innovation, productivity, and profitability, as well as reduced employee turnover. The results of the poll are summarized in the following table:

ENGAGEMENT	COUNTRY		Total
	United States	Germany	
Engaged	550	246	796
Not engaged	1,345	1,649	2,994
Total	1,895	1,895	3,790

Source: Data extracted from M. Nink, "Employee Disengagement Plagues Germany," *Gallup Management Journal*, **gmj.gallup.com**, April 9, 2009.

If an employee is selected at random, what is the probability that he or she
a. is engaged with his or her workplace?
b. is a U.S. worker?
c. is engaged with his or her workplace *or* is a U.S. worker?
d. Explain the difference in the results in (b) and (c).

4.13 What is the preferred way for people to order fast food? A survey was conducted in 2009, but the sample sizes were not reported. Suppose the results, based on a sample of 100 males and 100 females, were as follows:

DINING PREFERENCE	GENDER		Total
	Male	Female	
Dine inside	21	12	33
Order inside to go	19	10	29
Order at the drive-through	60	78	138
Total	100	100	200

Source: Data extracted from www.qsrmagazine.com/reports/drive-thru_time_study/2009/2009_charts/whats_your_preferred_way_to_order_fast_food.html.

If a respondent is selected at random, what is the probability that he or she
a. prefers to order at the drive-through?
b. is a male *and* prefers to order at the drive-through?
c. is a male *or* prefers to order at the drive-through?
d. Explain the difference in the results in (b) and (c).

4.14 A sample of 500 respondents in a large metropolitan area was selected to study consumer behavior. Among the questions asked was "Do you enjoy shopping for clothing?" Of 240 males, 136 answered yes. Of 260 females, 224 answered yes. Construct a contingency table to evaluate the probabilities. What is the probability that a respondent chosen at random
a. enjoys shopping for clothing?
b. is a female *and* enjoys shopping for clothing?
c. is a female *or* enjoys shopping for clothing?
d. is a male *or* a female?

4.15 Each year, ratings are compiled concerning the performance of new cars during the first 90 days of use. Suppose that the cars have been categorized according to whether a car needs warranty-related repair (yes or no) and the country in which the company manufacturing a car is based (United States or not United States). Based on the data collected, the probability that the new car needs a warranty repair is 0.04, the probability that the car was manufactured by a U.S.-based company is 0.60, and the probability that the new car needs a warranty repair *and* was manufactured by a U.S.-based company is 0.025. Construct a contingency table to evaluate the probabilities of a warranty-related repair. What is the probability that a new car selected at random
a. needs a warranty repair?
b. needs a warranty repair *and* was manufactured by a U.S.-based company?
c. needs a warranty repair *or* was manufactured by a U.S.-based company?
d. needs a warranty repair *or* was not manufactured by a U.S.-based company?

4.2 Conditional Probability

Each example in Section 4.1 involves finding the probability of an event when sampling from the entire sample space. How do you determine the probability of an event if you know certain information about the events involved?

Computing Conditional Probabilities

Conditional probability refers to the probability of event A, given information about the occurrence of another event, B.

CONDITIONAL PROBABILITY

The probability of A given B is equal to the probability of A and B divided by the probability of B.

$$P(A|B) = \frac{P(A \text{ and } B)}{P(B)} \tag{4.4a}$$

The probability of B given A is equal to the probability of A and B divided by the probability of A.

$$P(B|A) = \frac{P(A \text{ and } B)}{P(A)} \tag{4.4b}$$

where

$P(A \text{ and } B)$ = joint probability of A and B

$P(A)$ = marginal probability of A

$P(B)$ = marginal probability of B

Referring to the Using Statistics scenario involving the purchase of big-screen televisions, suppose you were told that a household planned to purchase a big-screen television. Now, what is the probability that the household actually purchased the television? In this example, the objective is to find $P(\text{Actually purchased} | \text{Planned to purchase})$. Here you are given the information that the household planned to purchase the big-screen television. Therefore, the sample space does not consist of all 1,000 households in the survey. It consists of only those households that planned to purchase the big-screen television. Of 250 such households, 200 actually purchased the big-screen television. Therefore, based on Table 4.1 on page 178, the probability that a household actually purchased the big-screen television given that he or she planned to purchase is

$$P(\text{Actually purchased}|\text{Planned to purchase}) = \frac{\text{Planned to purchase } and \text{ actually purchased}}{\text{Planned to purchase}}$$

$$= \frac{200}{250} = 0.80$$

You can also use Equation (4.4b) to compute this result:

$$P(B|A) = \frac{P(A \text{ and } B)}{P(A)}$$

where

A = planned to purchase

B = actually purchased

then

$$P(\text{Actually purchased}|\text{Planned to purchase}) = \frac{200/1{,}000}{250/1{,}000}$$
$$= \frac{200}{250} = 0.80$$

Example 4.6 further illustrates conditional probability.

EXAMPLE 4.6

Finding the Conditional Probability of Purchasing a Blu-ray Disc Player

Table 4.2 on page 179 is a contingency table for whether a household purchased a television with a faster refresh rate and whether the household purchased a Blu-ray disc player. If a household purchased a television with a faster refresh rate, what is the probability that it also purchased a Blu-ray disc player?

SOLUTION Because you know that the household purchased a television with a faster refresh rate, the sample space is reduced to 80 households. Of these 80 households, 38 also purchased a Blu-ray disc (BD) player. Therefore, the probability that a household purchased a BD player, given that the household purchased a television with a faster refresh rate, is

$$P(\text{Purchased BD player} \mid \text{Purchased television with faster refresh rate}) = \frac{\text{Number purchasing television with faster refresh rate } and \text{ BD player}}{\text{Number purchasing television with faster refresh rate}}$$

$$= \frac{38}{80} = 0.475$$

If you use Equation (4.4b) on page 185:

A = purchased a television with a faster refresh rate
B = purchased a BD player

then

$$P(B|A) = \frac{P(A \text{ and } B)}{P(A)} = \frac{38/300}{80/300} = 0.475$$

Therefore, given that the household purchased a television with a faster refresh rate, there is a 47.5% chance that the household also purchased a Blu-ray disc player. You can compare this conditional probability to the marginal probability of purchasing a Blu-ray disc player, which is $108/300 = 0.36$, or 36%. These results tell you that households that purchased televisions with a faster refresh rate are more likely to purchase a Blu-ray disc player than are households that purchased big-screen televisions that have a standard refresh rate.

Decision Trees

In Table 4.1 on page 178, households are classified according to whether they planned to purchase and whether they actually purchased big-screen televisions. A **decision tree** is an alternative to the contingency table. Figure 4.3 represents the decision tree for this example.

FIGURE 4.3
Decision tree for M&R Electronics World example

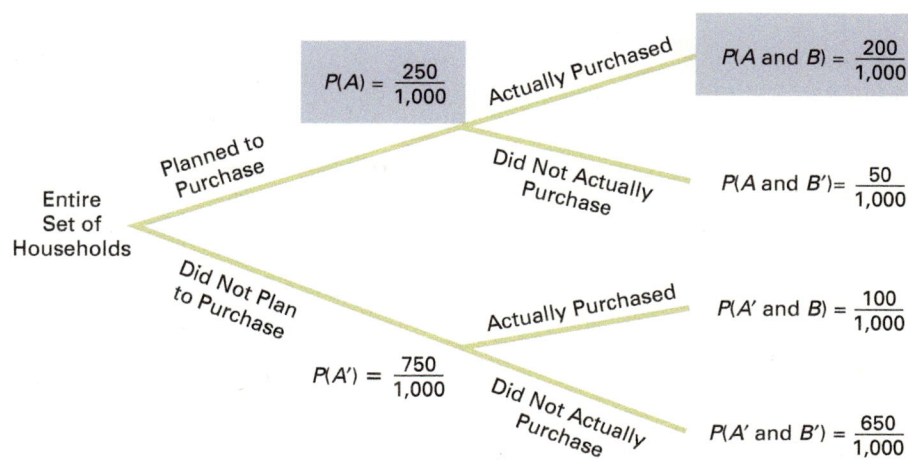

In Figure 4.3, beginning at the left with the entire set of households, there are two "branches" for whether or not the household planned to purchase a big-screen television. Each of these branches has two subbranches, corresponding to whether the household actually purchased or did not actually purchase the big-screen television. The probabilities at the end of the initial branches represent the marginal probabilities of A and A'. The probabilities at the end of each of the four subbranches represent the joint probability for each combination of events A and B. You compute the conditional probability by dividing the joint probability by the appropriate marginal probability.

For example, to compute the probability that the household actually purchased, given that the household planned to purchase the big-screen television, you take P(Planned to purchase *and* actually purchased) and divide by P(Planned to purchase). From Figure 4.3,

$$P(\text{Actually purchased} | \text{Planned to purchase}) = \frac{200/1{,}000}{250/1{,}000}$$

$$= \frac{200}{250} = 0.80$$

Example 4.7 illustrates how to construct a decision tree.

EXAMPLE 4.7

Constructing the Decision Tree for the Households That Purchased Big-Screen Televisions

Using the cross-classified data in Table 4.2 on page 179, construct the decision tree. Use the decision tree to find the probability that a household purchased a Blu-ray disc player, given that the household purchased a television with a faster refresh rate.

SOLUTION The decision tree for purchased a Blu-ray disc player and a television with a faster refresh rate is displayed in Figure 4.4 on page 188. Using Equation (4.4b) on page 185 and the following definitions,

A = purchased a television with a faster refresh rate
B = purchased a Blu-ray disc player

$$P(B|A) = \frac{P(A \text{ and } B)}{P(A)} = \frac{38/300}{80/300} = 0.475$$

FIGURE 4.4

Decision tree for purchased a television with a faster refresh rate and a Blu-ray disc (BD) player

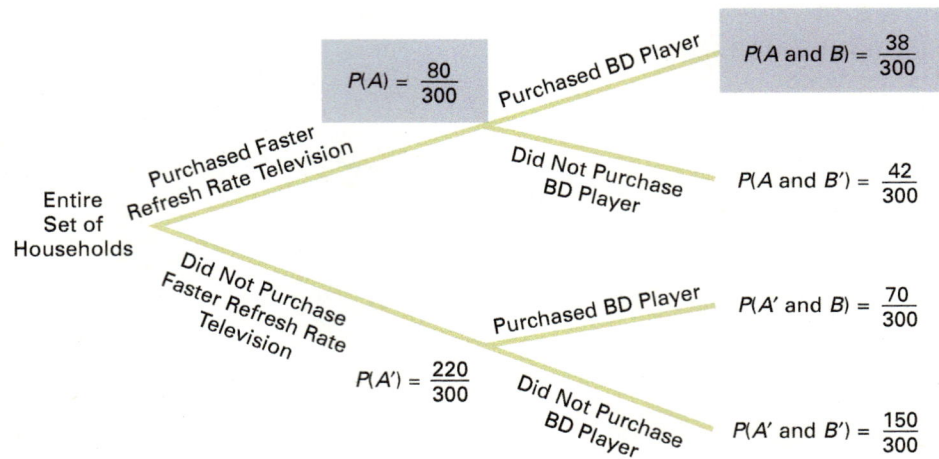

Independence

In the example concerning the purchase of big-screen televisions, the conditional probability is 200/250 = 0.80 that the selected household actually purchased the big-screen television, given that the household planned to purchase. The simple probability of selecting a household that actually purchased is 300/1,000 = 0.30. This result shows that the prior knowledge that the household planned to purchase affected the probability that the household actually purchased the television. In other words, the outcome of one event is *dependent* on the outcome of a second event.

When the outcome of one event does *not* affect the probability of occurrence of another event, the events are said to be independent. **Independence** can be determined by using Equation (4.5).

INDEPENDENCE

Two events, A and B, are independent if and only if

$$P(A|B) = P(A) \tag{4.5}$$

where

$P(A|B)$ = conditional probability of A given B

$P(A)$ = marginal probability of A

Example 4.8 demonstrates the use of Equation (4.5).

EXAMPLE 4.8

Determining Independence

In the follow-up survey of the 300 households that actually purchased big-screen televisions, the households were asked if they were satisfied with their purchases. Table 4.3 cross-classifies the responses to the satisfaction question with the responses to whether the television had a faster refresh rate.

TABLE 4.3

Satisfaction with Purchase of Big-Screen Televisions

TELEVISION REFRESH RATE	SATISFIED WITH PURCHASE?		
	Yes	No	Total
Faster	64	16	80
Standard	176	44	220
Total	240	60	300

Determine whether being satisfied with the purchase and the refresh rate of the television purchased are independent.

SOLUTION For these data,

$$P(\text{Satisfied} | \text{faster refresh rate}) = \frac{64/300}{80/300} = \frac{64}{80} = 0.80$$

which is equal to

$$P(\text{Satisfied}) = \frac{240}{300} = 0.80$$

Thus, being satisfied with the purchase and the refresh rate of the television purchased are independent. Knowledge of one event does not affect the probability of the other event.

Multiplication Rules

The **general multiplication rule** is derived using Equation (4.4a) on page 185:

$$P(A|B) = \frac{P(A \text{ and } B)}{P(B)}$$

and solving for the joint probability $P(A \text{ and } B)$.

GENERAL MULTIPLICATION RULE

The probability of A and B is equal to the probability of A given B times the probability of B.

$$P(A \text{ and } B) = P(A|B)P(B) \tag{4.6}$$

Example 4.9 demonstrates the use of the general multiplication rule.

EXAMPLE 4.9

Using the General Multiplication Rule

Consider the 80 households that purchased televisions that had a faster refresh rate. In Table 4.3 on page 188 you see that 64 households are satisfied with their purchase, and 16 households are dissatisfied. Suppose 2 households are randomly selected from the 80 households. Find the probability that both households are satisfied with their purchase.

SOLUTION Here you can use the multiplication rule in the following way. If

A = second household selected is satisfied
B = first household selected is satisfied

then, using Equation (4.6),

$$P(A \text{ and } B) = P(A|B)P(B)$$

The probability that the first household is satisfied with the purchase is 64/80. However, the probability that the second household is also satisfied with the purchase depends on the result of the first selection. If the first household is not returned to the sample after the satisfaction level is determined (i.e., sampling without replacement), the number of households remaining is 79. If the first household is satisfied, the probability that the second is also satisfied is 63/79 because 63 satisfied households remain in the sample. Therefore,

$$P(A \text{ and } B) = \left(\frac{63}{79}\right)\left(\frac{64}{80}\right) = 0.6380$$

There is a 63.80% chance that both of the households sampled will be satisfied with their purchase.

The **multiplication rule for independent events** is derived by substituting $P(A)$ for $P(A|B)$ in Equation (4.6).

> **MULTIPLICATION RULE FOR INDEPENDENT EVENTS**
>
> If A and B are independent, the probability of A and B is equal to the probability of A times the probability of B.
>
> $$P(A \text{ and } B) = P(A)P(B) \qquad (4.7)$$

If this rule holds for two events, A and B, then A and B are independent. Therefore, there are two ways to determine independence:

1. Events A and B are independent if, and only if, $P(A|B) = P(A)$.
2. Events A and B are independent if, and only if, $P(A \text{ and } B) = P(A)P(B)$.

Marginal Probability Using the General Multiplication Rule

In Section 4.1, marginal probability was defined using Equation (4.2) on page 181. You can state the equation for marginal probability by using the general multiplication rule. If

$$P(A) = P(A \text{ and } B_1) + P(A \text{ and } B_2) + \cdots + P(A \text{ and } B_k)$$

then, using the general multiplication rule, Equation (4.8) defines the marginal probability.

> **MARGINAL PROBABILITY USING THE GENERAL MULTIPLICATION RULE**
>
> $$P(A) = P(A|B_1)P(B_1) + P(A|B_2)P(B_2) + \cdots + P(A|B_k)P(B_k) \qquad (4.8)$$
>
> where $B_1, B_2, \ldots, B_k$ are k mutually exclusive and collectively exhaustive events.

To illustrate Equation (4.8), refer to Table 4.1 on page 178. Let

$P(A)$ = probability of "planned to purchase"
$P(B_1)$ = probability of "actually purchased"
$P(B_2)$ = probability of "did not actually purchase"

Then, using Equation (4.8), the probability of planned to purchase is

$$P(A) = P(A|B_1)P(B_1) + P(A|B_2)P(B_2)$$
$$= \left(\frac{200}{300}\right)\left(\frac{300}{1,000}\right) + \left(\frac{50}{700}\right)\left(\frac{700}{1,000}\right)$$
$$= \frac{200}{1,000} + \frac{50}{1,000} = \frac{250}{1,000} = 0.25$$

Problems for Section 4.2

LEARNING THE BASICS

4.16 Consider the following contingency table:

	B	B'
A	10	20
A'	20	40

What is the probability of
a. $A|B$?
b. $A|B'$?
c. $A'|B'$?
d. Are events A and B independent?

4.17 Consider the following contingency table:

	B	B'
A	10	30
A'	25	35

What is the probability of
a. $A|B$?
b. $A'|B'$?
c. $A|B'$?
d. Are events A and B independent?

4.18 If $P(A \text{ and } B) = 0.4$ and $P(B) = 0.8$, find $P(A|B)$.

4.19 If $P(A) = 0.7$, $P(B) = 0.6$, and A and B are independent, find $P(A \text{ and } B)$.

4.20 If $P(A) = 0.3$, $P(B) = 0.4$, and $P(A \text{ and } B) = 0.2$, are A and B independent?

APPLYING THE CONCEPTS

4.21 Does it take more time to be removed from an email list than it used to take? A study of 100 large online retailers revealed the following:

	NEED THREE OR MORE CLICKS TO BE REMOVED	
YEAR	Yes	No
2009	39	61
2008	7	93

Source: Data extracted from "More Clicks to Escape an Email List," *The New York Times*, March 29, 2010, p. B2.

a. Given that three or more clicks are needed to be removed from an email list, what is the probability that this occurred in 2009?
b. Given that the year 2009 is involved, what is the probability that three or more clicks are needed to be removed from an email list?
c. Explain the difference in the results in (a) and (b).
d. Are needing three or more clicks to be removed from an email list and the year independent?

4.22 Do people of different age groups differ in their response to email messages? A survey by the Center for the Digital Future of the University of Southern California (data extracted from A. Mindlin, "Older E-mail Users Favor Fast Replies," *The New York Times*, July 14, 2008, p. B3) reported that 70.7% of users over 70 years of age believe that email messages should be answered quickly, as compared to 53.6% of users 12 to 50 years old. Suppose that the survey was based on 1,000 users over 70 years of age and 1,000 users 12 to 50 years old. The following table summarizes the results:

	ANSWERS QUICKLY		
AGE OF RESPONDENTS	12–50	Over 70	Total
Yes	536	707	1,243
No	464	293	757
Total	1,000	1,000	2,000

a. Suppose you know that the respondent is between 12 and 50 years old. What is the probability that he or she answers quickly?
b. Suppose you know that the respondent is over 70 years old. What is the probability that he or she answers quickly?
c. Are the two events, answers quickly and age of respondents, independent? Explain.

4.23 What is the preferred way for people to order fast food? A survey was conducted in 2009, but the sample sizes were not reported. Suppose the results, based on a sample of 100 males and 100 females, were as follows:

	GENDER		
DINING PREFERENCE	Male	Female	Total
Dine inside	21	12	33
Order inside to go	19	10	29
Order at the drive-through	60	78	138
Total	100	100	200

Source: Data extracted from www.qsrmagazine.com/reports/drive-thru_time_study/2009/2009_charts/whats_your_preferred_way_to_order_fast_food.html.

a. Given that a respondent is a male, what is the probability that he prefers to order at the drive-through?
b. Given that a respondent is a female, what is the probability that she prefers to order at the drive-through?
c. Is dining preference independent of gender? Explain.

SELF Test 4.24 According to a Gallup Poll, the extent to which employees are engaged with their workplace varies from country to country. Gallup reports that the percentage of U.S. workers engaged with their workplace is more than twice as high as the percentage of German workers. The study also shows that having more engaged workers leads to increased innovation, productivity, and profitability, as well as reduced employee turnover. The results of the poll are summarized in the following table:

	COUNTRY		
ENGAGEMENT	United States	Germany	Total
Engaged	550	246	796
Not engaged	1,345	1,649	2,994
Total	1,895	1,895	3,790

Source: Data extracted from M. Nink, "Employee Disengagement Plagues Germany," *Gallup Management Journal*, **gmj.gallup.com**, April 9, 2009.

a. Given that a worker is from the United States, what is the probability that the worker is engaged?
b. Given that a worker is from the United States, what is the probability that the worker is not engaged?
c. Given that a worker is from Germany, what is the probability that the worker is engaged?
d. Given that a worker is from Germany, what is the probability that the worker is not engaged?

4.25 A sample of 500 respondents in a large metropolitan area was selected to study consumer behavior, with the following results:

ENJOYS SHOPPING FOR CLOTHING	GENDER		
	Male	Female	Total
Yes	136	224	360
No	104	36	140
Total	240	260	500

a. Suppose that the respondent chosen is a female. What is the probability that she does not enjoy shopping for clothing?
b. Suppose that the respondent chosen enjoys shopping for clothing. What is the probability that the individual is a male?
c. Are enjoying shopping for clothing and the gender of the individual independent? Explain.

4.26 Each year, ratings are compiled concerning the performance of new cars during the first 90 days of use. Suppose that the cars have been categorized according to whether a car needs warranty-related repair (yes or no) and the country in which the company manufacturing a car is based (United States or not United States). Based on the data collected, the probability that the new car needs a warranty repair is 0.04, the probability that the car is manufactured by a U.S.-based company is 0.60, and the probability that the new car needs a warranty repair *and* was manufactured by a U.S.-based company is 0.025.
a. Suppose you know that a company based in the United States manufactured a particular car. What is the probability that the car needs warranty repair?
b. Suppose you know that a company based in the United States did not manufacture a particular car. What is the probability that the car needs warranty repair?
c. Are need for warranty repair and location of the company manufacturing the car independent?

4.27 In 38 of the 60 years from 1950 through 2009, the S&P 500 finished higher after the first five days of trading. In 33 of those 38 years, the S&P 500 finished higher for the year. Is a good first week a good omen for the upcoming year? The following table gives the first-week and annual performance over this 60-year period:

	S&P 500'S ANNUAL PERFORMANCE	
FIRST WEEK	Higher	Lower
Higher	33	5
Lower	11	11

a. If a year is selected at random, what is the probability that the S&P 500 finished higher for the year?
b. Given that the S&P 500 finished higher after the first five days of trading, what is the probability that it finished higher for the year?
c. Are the two events "first-week performance" and "annual performance" independent? Explain.
d. Look up the performance after the first five days of 2010 and the 2010 annual performance of the S&P 500 at **finance.yahoo.com**. Comment on the results.

4.28 A standard deck of cards is being used to play a game. There are four suits (hearts, diamonds, clubs, and spades), each having 13 faces (ace, 2, 3, 4, 5, 6, 7, 8, 9, 10, jack, queen, and king), making a total of 52 cards. This complete deck is thoroughly mixed, and you will receive the first 2 cards from the deck, without replacement (the first card is not returned to the deck after it is selected).
a. What is the probability that both cards are queens?
b. What is the probability that the first card is a 10 and the second card is a 5 or 6?

c. If you were sampling with replacement (the first card is returned to the deck after it is selected), what would be the answer in (a)?
d. In the game of blackjack, the face cards (jack, queen, king) count as 10 points, and the ace counts as either 1 or 11 points. All other cards are counted at their face value. Blackjack is achieved if 2 cards total 21 points. What is the probability of getting blackjack in this problem?

4.29 A box of nine gloves contains two left-handed gloves and seven right-handed gloves.
a. If two gloves are randomly selected from the box, without replacement (the first glove is not returned to the box after it is selected), what is the probability that both gloves selected will be right-handed?
b. If two gloves are randomly selected from the box, without replacement (the first glove is not returned to the box after it is selected), what is the probability that there will be one right-handed glove and one left-handed glove selected?
c. If three gloves are selected, with replacement (the gloves are returned to the box after they are selected), what is the probability that all three will be left-handed?
d. If you were sampling with replacement (the first glove is returned to the box after it is selected), what would be the answers to (a) and (b)?

4.3 Bayes' Theorem

Bayes' theorem is used to revise previously calculated probabilities based on new information. Developed by Thomas Bayes in the eighteenth century (see references 1, 2, and 7), Bayes' theorem is an extension of what you previously learned about conditional probability.

You can apply Bayes' theorem to the situation in which M&R Electronics World is considering marketing a new model of televisions. In the past, 40% of the new-model televisions have been successful, and 60% have been unsuccessful. Before introducing the new model television, the marketing research department conducts an extensive study and releases a report, either favorable or unfavorable. In the past, 80% of the successful new-model television(s) had received favorable market research reports, and 30% of the unsuccessful new-model television(s) had received favorable reports. For the new model of television under consideration, the marketing research department has issued a favorable report. What is the probability that the television will be successful?

Bayes' theorem is developed from the definition of conditional probability. To find the conditional probability of B given A, consider Equation (4.4b) (originally presented on page 185 and shown below):

$$P(B|A) = \frac{P(A \text{ and } B)}{P(A)} = \frac{P(A|B)P(B)}{P(A)}$$

Bayes' theorem is derived by substituting Equation (4.8) on page 190 for $P(A)$ in the denominator of Equation (4.4b).

BAYES' THEOREM

$$P(B_i|A) = \frac{P(A|B_i)P(B_i)}{P(A|B_1)P(B_1) + P(A|B_2)P(B_2) + \cdots + P(A|B_k)P(B_k)} \quad (4.9)$$

where B_i is the ith event out of k mutually exclusive and collectively exhaustive events.

To use Equation (4.9) for the television-marketing example, let

event S = successful television   event F = favorable report
event S' = unsuccessful television   event F' = unfavorable report

and

$$P(S) = 0.40 \quad P(F|S) = 0.80$$
$$P(S') = 0.60 \quad P(F|S') = 0.30$$

Then, using Equation (4.9),

$$P(S|F) = \frac{P(F|S)P(S)}{P(F|S)P(S) + P(F|S')P(S')}$$

$$= \frac{(0.80)(0.40)}{(0.80)(0.40) + (0.30)(0.60)}$$

$$= \frac{0.32}{0.32 + 0.18} = \frac{0.32}{0.50}$$

$$= 0.64$$

The probability of a successful television, given that a favorable report was received, is 0.64. Thus, the probability of an unsuccessful television, given that a favorable report was received, is $1 - 0.64 = 0.36$.

Table 4.4 summarizes the computation of the probabilities, and Figure 4.5 presents the decision tree.

TABLE 4.4 Bayes' Theorem Calculations for the Television-Marketing Example

Event S_i	Prior Probability $P(S_i)$	Conditional Probability $P(F\|S_i)$	Joint Probability $P(F\|S_i)P(S_i)$	Revised Probability $P(S_i\|F)$
S = successful television	0.40	0.80	0.32	$P(S\|F) = 0.32/0.50 = 0.64$
S' = unsuccessful television	0.60	0.30	0.18 / 0.50	$P(S'\|F) = 0.18/0.50 = 0.36$

FIGURE 4.5 Decision tree for marketing a new television

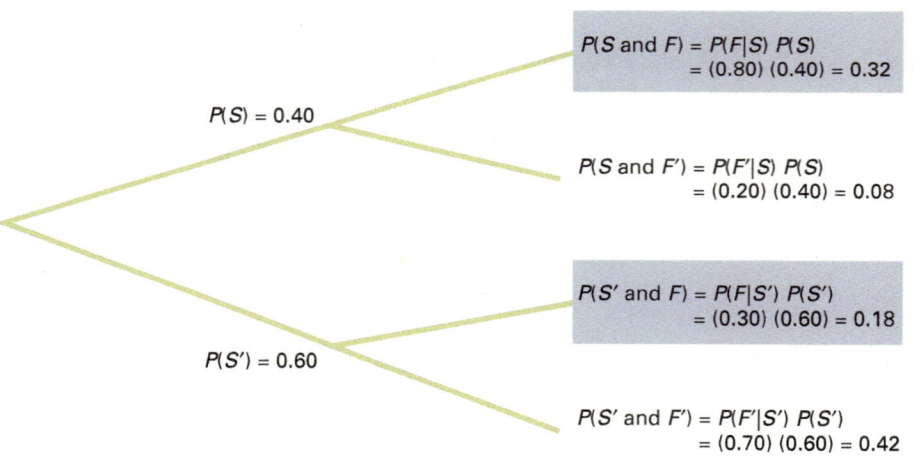

Example 4.10 applies Bayes' theorem to a medical diagnosis problem.

EXAMPLE 4.10

Using Bayes' Theorem in a Medical Diagnosis Problem

The probability that a person has a certain disease is 0.03. Medical diagnostic tests are available to determine whether the person actually has the disease. If the disease is actually present, the probability that the medical diagnostic test will give a positive result (indicating that the disease is present) is 0.90. If the disease is not actually present, the probability of a positive test result (indicating that the disease is present) is 0.02. Suppose that the medical diagnostic test has given a positive result (indicating that the disease is present). What is the probability that the disease is actually present? What is the probability of a positive test result?

SOLUTION Let

event D = has disease event T = test is positive
event D' = does not have disease event T' = test is negative

and

$$P(D) = 0.03 \quad P(T|D) = 0.90$$
$$P(D') = 0.97 \quad P(T|D') = 0.02$$

Using Equation (4.9) on page 193,

$$P(D|T) = \frac{P(T|D)P(D)}{P(T|D)P(D) + P(T|D')P(D')}$$
$$= \frac{(0.90)(0.03)}{(0.90)(0.03) + (0.02)(0.97)}$$
$$= \frac{0.0270}{0.0270 + 0.0194} = \frac{0.0270}{0.0464}$$
$$= 0.582$$

The probability that the disease is actually present, given that a positive result has occurred (indicating that the disease is present), is 0.582. Table 4.5 summarizes the computation of the probabilities, and Figure 4.6 presents the decision tree.

TABLE 4.5
Bayes' Theorem Calculations for the Medical Diagnosis Problem

Event D_i	Prior Probability $P(D_i)$	Conditional Probability $P(T\|D_i)$	Joint Probability $P(T\|D_i)P(D_i)$	Revised Probability $P(D_i\|T)$
D = has disease	0.03	0.90	0.0270	$P(D\|T) = 0.0270/0.0464$ = 0.582
D' = does not have disease	0.97	0.02	0.0194 0.0464	$P(D'\|T) = 0.0194/0.0464$ = 0.418

FIGURE 4.6
Decision tree for the medical diagnosis problem

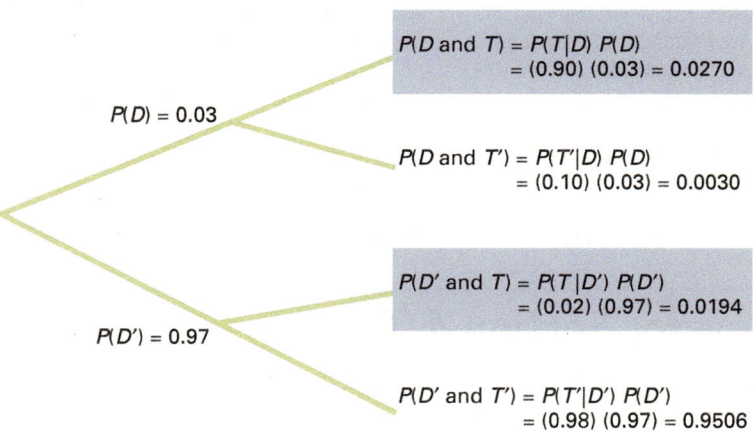

The denominator in Bayes' theorem represents $P(T)$, the probability of a positive test result, which in this case is 0.0464, or 4.64%.

THINK ABOUT THIS: Divine Providence and Spam

Would you ever guess that the essays *Divine Benevolence: Or, An Attempt to Prove That the Principal End of the Divine Providence and Government Is the Happiness of His Creatures* and *An Essay Towards Solving a Problem in the Doctrine of Chances* were written by the same person? Probably not, and in doing so, you illustrate a modern-day application of Bayesian statistics: spam, or junk mail, filters.

In not guessing correctly, you probably looked at the words in the titles of the essays and concluded that they were talking about two different things. An implicit rule you used was that word frequencies vary by subject matter. A statistics essay would very likely contain the word *statistics* as well as words such as *chance*, *problem*, and *solving*. An eighteenth-century essay about theology and religion would be more likely to contain the uppercase forms of *Divine* and *Providence*.

Likewise, there are words you would guess to be very unlikely to appear in either book, such as technical terms from finance, and words that are most likely to appear in both—common words such as *a*, *and*, and *the*. That words would either be likely or unlikely suggests an application of probability theory. Of course, likely and unlikely are fuzzy concepts, and we might occasionally misclassify an essay if we kept things too simple, such as relying solely on the occurrence of the words *Divine* and *Providence*.

For example, a profile of the late Harris Milstead, better known as *Divine*, the star of *Hairspray* and other films, visiting Providence (Rhode Island), would most certainly not be an essay about theology. But if we widened the number of words we examined and found such words as *movie* or the name John Waters (Divine's director in many films), we probably would quickly realize the essay had something to do with twentieth-century cinema and little to do with theology and religion.

We can use a similar process to try to classify a new email message in your in-box as either spam or a legitimate message (called "ham," in this context). We would first need to add to your email program a "spam filter" that has the ability to track word frequencies associated with spam and ham messages as you identify them on a day-to-day basis. This would allow the filter to constantly update the prior probabilities necessary to use Bayes' theorem. With these probabilities, the filter can ask, "What is the probability that an email is spam, given the presence of a certain word?"

Applying the terms of Equation (4.9) on page 193, such a Bayesian spam filter would multiply the probability of finding the word in a spam email, $P(A|B)$, by the probability that the email is spam, $P(B)$, and then divide by the probability of finding the word in an email, the denominator in Equation (4.9). Bayesian spam filters also use shortcuts by focusing on a small set of words that have a high probability of being found in a spam message as well as on a small set of other words that have a low probability of being found in a spam message.

As spammers (people who send junk email) learned of such new filters, they tried to outfox them. Having learned that Bayesian filters might be assigning a high $P(A|B)$ value to words commonly found in spam, such as Viagra, spammers thought they could fool the filter by misspelling the word as Vi@gr@ or V1agra. What they overlooked was that the misspelled variants were even *more likely* to be found in a spam message than the original word. Thus, the misspelled variants made the job of spotting spam *easier* for the Bayesian filters.

Other spammers tried to fool the filters by adding "good" words, words that would have a low probability of being found in a spam message, or "rare" words, words not frequently encountered in any message. But these spammers overlooked the fact that the conditional probabilities are constantly updated and that words once considered "good" would be soon discarded from the good list by the filter as their $P(A|B)$ value increased. Likewise, as "rare" words grew more common in spam and yet stayed rare in ham, such words acted like the misspelled variants that others had tried earlier.

Even then, and perhaps after reading about Bayesian statistics, spammers thought that they could "break" Bayesian filters by inserting random words in their messages. Those random words would affect the filter by causing it to see many words whose $P(A|B)$ value would be low. The Bayesian filter would begin to label many spam messages as ham and end up being of no practical use. Spammers again overlooked that conditional probabilities are constantly updated.

Other spammers decided to eliminate all or most of the words in their messages and replace them with graphics so that Bayesian filters would have very few words with which to form conditional probabilities. But this approach failed, too, as Bayesian filters were rewritten to consider things other than words in a message. After all, Bayes' theorem concerns *events*, and "graphics present with no text" is as valid an event as "some word, X, present in a message." Other future tricks will ultimately fail for the same reason. (By the way, spam filters use non-Bayesian techniques as well, which makes spammers' lives even more difficult.)

Bayesian spam filters are an example of the unexpected way that applications of statistics can show up in your daily life. You will discover more examples as you read the rest of this book. *By the way, the author of the two essays mentioned earlier was Thomas Bayes, who is a lot more famous for the second essay than the first essay, a failed attempt to use mathematics and logic to prove the existence of God.*

Problems for Section 4.3

LEARNING THE BASICS

4.30 If $P(B) = 0.05$, $P(A|B) = 0.80$, $P(B') = 0.95$, and $P(A|B') = 0.40$, find $P(B|A)$.

4.31 If $P(B) = 0.30$, $P(A|B) = 0.60$, $P(B') = 0.70$, and $P(A|B') = 0.50$, find $P(B|A)$.

APPLYING THE CONCEPTS

4.32 In Example 4.10 on page 194, suppose that the probability that a medical diagnostic test will give a positive result if the disease is not present is reduced from 0.02 to 0.01.

a. If the medical diagnostic test has given a positive result (indicating that the disease is present), what is the probability that the disease is actually present?

b. If the medical diagnostic test has given a negative result (indicating that the disease is not present), what is the probability that the disease is not present?

4.33 An advertising executive is studying television viewing habits of married men and women during prime-time hours.

Based on past viewing records, the executive has determined that during prime time, husbands are watching television 60% of the time. When the husband is watching television, 40% of the time the wife is also watching. When the husband is not watching television, 30% of the time the wife is watching television.

a. Find the probability that if the wife is watching television, the husband is also watching television.

b. Find the probability that the wife is watching television during prime time.

4.34 Olive Construction Company is determining whether it should submit a bid for a new shopping center. In the past, Olive's main competitor, Base Construction Company, has submitted bids 70% of the time. If Base Construction Company does not bid on a job, the probability that Olive Construction Company will get the job is 0.50. If Base Construction Company bids on a job, the probability that Olive Construction Company will get the job is 0.25.

a. If Olive Construction Company gets the job, what is the probability that Base Construction Company did not bid?

b. What is the probability that Olive Construction Company will get the job?

4.35 Laid-off workers who become entrepreneurs because they cannot find meaningful employment with another company are known as *entrepreneurs by necessity*. *The Wall Street Journal* reports that these entrepreneurs by necessity are less likely to grow into large businesses than are *entrepreneurs by choice* (J. Bailey, "Desire—More Than Need—Builds a Business," *The Wall Street Journal*, May 21, 2001, p. B4). This article states that 89% of the entrepreneurs in the United States are entrepreneurs by choice and 11% are entrepreneurs by necessity. Only 2% of entrepreneurs by necessity expect their new business to employ 20 or more people within five years, whereas 14% of entrepreneurs by choice expect to employ at least 20 people within five years.

a. If an entrepreneur is selected at random and that individual expects that his or her new business will employ 20 or more people within five years, what is the probability that this individual is an entrepreneur by choice?

b. Discuss several possible reasons why entrepreneurs by choice are more likely than entrepreneurs by necessity to believe that they will grow their businesses.

4.36 The editor of a textbook publishing company is trying to decide whether to publish a proposed business statistics textbook. Information on previous textbooks published indicates that 10% are huge successes, 20% are modest successes, 40% break even, and 30% are losers. However, before a publishing decision is made, the book will be reviewed. In the past, 99% of the huge successes received favorable reviews, 70% of the moderate successes received favorable reviews, 40% of the break-even books received favorable reviews, and 20% of the losers received favorable reviews.

a. If the proposed textbook receives a favorable review, how should the editor revise the probabilities of the various outcomes to take this information into account?

b. What proportion of textbooks receives favorable reviews?

4.37 A municipal bond service has three rating categories (A, B, and C). Suppose that in the past year, of the municipal bonds issued throughout the United States, 70% were rated A, 20% were rated B, and 10% were rated C. Of the municipal bonds rated A, 50% were issued by cities, 40% by suburbs, and 10% by rural areas. Of the municipal bonds rated B, 60% were issued by cities, 20% by suburbs, and 20% by rural areas. Of the municipal bonds rated C, 90% were issued by cities, 5% by suburbs, and 5% by rural areas.

a. If a new municipal bond is to be issued by a city, what is the probability that it will receive an A rating?

b. What proportion of municipal bonds are issued by cities?

c. What proportion of municipal bonds are issued by suburbs?

4.4 Counting Rules

In Equation (4.1) on page 176, the probability of occurrence of an outcome was defined as the number of ways the outcome occurs, divided by the total number of possible outcomes. Often, there are a large number of possible outcomes, and determining the exact number can be difficult. In such circumstances, rules have been developed for counting the number of possible outcomes. This section presents five different counting rules.

Counting Rule 1

Counting rule 1 determines the number of possible outcomes for a set of mutually exclusive and collectively exhaustive events.

> **COUNTING RULE 1**
>
> If any one of k different mutually exclusive and collectively exhaustive events can occur on each of n trials, the number of possible outcomes is equal to
>
> $$k^n \tag{4.10}$$

For example, using Equation (4.10), the number of different possible outcomes from tossing a two-sided coin five times is $2^5 = 2 \times 2 \times 2 \times 2 \times 2 = 32$.

EXAMPLE 4.11
Rolling a Die Twice

Suppose you roll a die twice. How many different possible outcomes can occur?

SOLUTION If a six-sided die is rolled twice, using Equation (4.10), the number of different outcomes is $6^2 = 36$.

Counting Rule 2

The second counting rule is a more general version of the first and allows the number of possible events to differ from trial to trial.

> **COUNTING RULE 2**
>
> If there are k_1 events on the first trial, k_2 events on the second trial, ... , and k_n events on the nth trial, then the number of possible outcomes is
>
> $$(k_1)(k_2)\ldots(k_n) \tag{4.11}$$

For example, a state motor vehicle department would like to know how many license plate numbers are available if a license plate number consists of three letters followed by three numbers (0 through 9). Using Equation (4.11), if a license plate number consists of three letters followed by three numbers, the total number of possible outcomes is $(26)(26)(26)(10)(10)(10) = 17{,}576{,}000$.

EXAMPLE 4.12
Determining the Number of Different Dinners

A restaurant menu has a price-fixed complete dinner that consists of an appetizer, an entrée, a beverage, and a dessert. You have a choice of 5 appetizers, 10 entrées, 3 beverages, and 6 desserts. Determine the total number of possible dinners.

SOLUTION Using Equation (4.11), the total number of possible dinners is $(5)(10)(3)(6) = 900$.

Counting Rule 3

The third counting rule involves computing the number of ways that a set of items can be arranged in order.

> **COUNTING RULE 3**
>
> The number of ways that all n items can be arranged in order is
>
> $$n! = (n)(n-1)\cdots(1) \tag{4.12}$$
>
> where $n!$ is called n factorial, and $0!$ is defined as 1.

EXAMPLE 4.13

Using Counting Rule 3

If a set of six books is to be placed on a shelf, in how many ways can the six books be arranged?

SOLUTION To begin, you must realize that any of the six books could occupy the first position on the shelf. Once the first position is filled, there are five books to choose from in filling the second position. You continue this assignment procedure until all the positions are occupied. The number of ways that you can arrange six books is

$$n! = 6! = (6)(5)(4)(3)(2)(1) = 720$$

Counting Rule 4

In many instances you need to know the number of ways in which a subset of an entire group of items can be arranged in *order*. Each possible arrangement is called a **permutation**.

> **COUNTING RULE 4: PERMUTATIONS**
>
> The number of ways of arranging x objects selected from n objects in order is
>
> $$_nP_x = \frac{n!}{(n-x)!} \tag{4.13}$$
>
> where
>
> n = total number of objects
>
> x = number of objects to be arranged
>
> $n!$ = n factorial = $n(n-1)\cdots(1)$
>
> P = symbol for permutations[1]

[1]On many scientific calculators, there is a button labeled nPr that allows you to compute permutations. The symbol r is used instead of x.

EXAMPLE 4.14

Using Counting Rule 4

Modifying Example 4.13, if you have six books, but there is room for only four books on the shelf, in how many ways can you arrange these books on the shelf?

SOLUTION Using Equation (4.13), the number of ordered arrangements of four books selected from six books is equal to

$$_nP_x = \frac{n!}{(n-x)!} = \frac{6!}{(6-4)!} = \frac{(6)(5)(4)(3)(2)(1)}{(2)(1)} = 360$$

Counting Rule 5

In many situations, you are not interested in the *order* of the outcomes but only in the number of ways that x items can be selected from n items, *irrespective of order*. Each possible selection is called a **combination**.

> **COUNTING RULE 5: COMBINATIONS**
>
> The number of ways of selecting x objects from n objects, irrespective of order, is equal to
>
> $$_nC_x = \frac{n!}{x!(n-x)!} \qquad (4.14)$$
>
> where
>
> n = total number of objects
>
> x = number of objects to be arranged
>
> $n!$ = n factorial = $n(n-1)\ldots(1)$
>
> C = symbol for combinations[2]

[2] On many scientific calculators, there is a button labeled nCr that allows you to compute permutations. The symbol r is used instead of x.

If you compare this rule to counting rule 4, you see that it differs only in the inclusion of a term $x!$ in the denominator. When permutations were used, all of the arrangements of the x objects are distinguishable. With combinations, the $x!$ possible arrangements of objects are irrelevant.

EXAMPLE 4.15

Using Counting Rule 5

Modifying Example 4.14, if the order of the books on the shelf is irrelevant, in how many ways can you arrange these books on the shelf?

SOLUTION Using Equation (4.14), the number of combinations of four books selected from six books is equal to

$$_nC_x = \frac{n!}{x!(n-x)!} = \frac{6!}{4!(6-4)!} = \frac{(6)(5)(4)(3)(2)(1)}{(4)(3)(2)(1)(2)(1)} = 15$$

Problems for Section 4.4

APPLYING THE CONCEPTS

 **4.38** If there are 10 multiple-choice questions on an exam, each having three possible answers, how many different sequences of answers are there?

4.39 A lock on a bank vault consists of three dials, each with 30 positions. In order for the vault to open, each of the three dials must be in the correct position.
a. How many different possible dial combinations are there for this lock?
b. What is the probability that if you randomly select a position on each dial, you will be able to open the bank vault?
c. Explain why "dial combinations" are not mathematical combinations expressed by Equation (4.14).

4.40 a. If a coin is tossed seven times, how many different outcomes are possible?
b. If a die is tossed seven times, how many different outcomes are possible?
c. Discuss the differences in your answers to (a) and (b).

4.41 A particular brand of women's jeans is available in seven different sizes, three different colors, and three different styles. How many different women's jeans does the store manager need to order to have one pair of each type?

4.42 You would like to make a salad that consists of lettuce, tomato, cucumber, and peppers. You go to the supermarket, intending to purchase one variety of each of these ingredients. You discover that there are eight varieties of lettuce, four varieties of tomatoes, three varieties of cucumbers, and three varieties of peppers for sale at the supermarket. If you buy them all, how many different salads can you make?

4.43 A team is being formed that includes four different people. There are four different positions on the teams. How many different ways are there to assign the four people to the four positions??

4.44 In Major League Baseball, there are five teams in the Eastern Division of the National League: Atlanta, Florida,

New York, Philadelphia, and Washington. How many different orders of finish are there for these five teams? (Assume that there are no ties in the standings.) Do you believe that all these orders are equally likely? Discuss.

4.45 Referring to Problem 4.44, how many different orders of finish are possible for the first four positions?

4.46 A gardener has six rows available in his vegetable garden to place tomatoes, eggplant, peppers, cucumbers, beans, and lettuce. Each vegetable will be allowed one and only one row. How many ways are there to position these vegetables in this garden?

4.47 There are eight members of a team. How many ways are there to select a team leader, assistant team leader, and team coordinator?

4.48 Four members of a group of 10 people are to be selected to a team. How many ways are there to select these four members?

4.49 A student has seven books that she would like to place in her backpack. However, there is room for only four books. Regardless of the arrangement, how many ways are there of placing four books into the backpack?

4.50 A daily lottery is conducted in which 2 winning numbers are selected out of 100 numbers. How many different combinations of winning numbers are possible?

4.51 A reading list for a course contains 20 articles. How many ways are there to choose 3 articles from this list?

4.5 Ethical Issues and Probability

Ethical issues can arise when any statements related to probability are presented to the public, particularly when these statements are part of an advertising campaign for a product or service. Unfortunately, many people are not comfortable with numerical concepts (see reference 5) and tend to misinterpret the meaning of the probability. In some instances, the misinterpretation is not intentional, but in other cases, advertisements may unethically try to mislead potential customers.

One example of a potentially unethical application of probability relates to advertisements for state lotteries. When purchasing a lottery ticket, the customer selects a set of numbers (such as 6) from a larger list of numbers (such as 54). Although virtually all participants know that they are unlikely to win the lottery, they also have very little idea of how unlikely it is for them to select all 6 winning numbers from the list of 54 numbers. They have even less of an idea of the probability of winning a consolation prize by selecting either 4 or 5 winning numbers.

Given this background, you might consider a recent commercial for a state lottery that stated, "We won't stop until we have made everyone a millionaire" to be deceptive and possibly unethical. Do you think the state has any intention of ever stopping the lottery, given the fact that the state relies on it to bring millions of dollars into its treasury? Is it possible that the lottery can make everyone a millionaire? Is it ethical to suggest that the purpose of the lottery is to make everyone a millionaire?

Another example of a potentially unethical application of probability relates to an investment newsletter promising a 90% probability of a 20% annual return on investment. To make the claim in the newsletter an ethical one, the investment service needs to (a) explain the basis on which this probability estimate rests, (b) provide the probability statement in another format, such as 9 chances in 10, and (c) explain what happens to the investment in the 10% of the cases in which a 20% return is not achieved (e.g., is the entire investment lost?).

These are serious ethical issues. If you were going to write an advertisement for the state lottery that ethically describes the probability of winning a certain prize, what would you say? If you were going to write an advertisement for the investment newsletter that ethically states the probability of a 20% return on an investment, what would you say?

USING STATISTICS @ M&R Electronics World Revisited

As the marketing manager for M&R Electronics World, you analyzed the survey results of an intent-to-purchase study. This study asked the heads of 1,000 households about their intentions to purchase a big-screen television sometime during the next 12 months, and as a follow-up, M&R surveyed the same people 12 months later to see whether such a television was purchased. In addition, for households purchasing big-screen televisions, the survey asked whether the television they purchased had a faster refresh rate, whether they also purchased a Blu-ray disc (BD) player in the past 12 months, and whether they were satisfied with their purchase of the big-screen television.

By analyzing the results of these surveys, you were able to uncover many pieces of valuable information that will help you plan a marketing strategy to enhance sales and better target those households likely to purchase multiple or more expensive products. Whereas only 30% of the households actually purchased a big-screen television, if a household indicated that it planned to purchase a big-screen television in the next 12 months, there was an 80% chance that the household actually made the purchase. Thus the marketing strategy should target those households that have indicated an intention to purchase.

You determined that for households that purchased a television that had a faster refresh rate, there was a 47.5% chance that the household also purchased a Blu-ray disc player. You then compared this conditional probability to the marginal probability of purchasing a Blu-ray disc player, which was 36%. Thus, households that purchased televisions that had a faster refresh rate are more likely to purchase a Blu-ray disc player than are households that purchased big-screen televisions that have a standard refresh rate.

You were also able to apply Bayes' theorem to M&R Electronics World's market research reports. The reports investigate a potential new television model prior to its scheduled release. If a favorable report was received, then there was a 64% chance that the new television model would be successful. However, if an unfavorable report was received, there is only a 16% chance that the model would be successful. Therefore, the marketing strategy of M&R needs to pay close attention to whether a report's conclusion is favorable or unfavorable.

SUMMARY

This chapter began by developing the basic concepts of probability. You learned that probability is a numeric value from 0 to 1 that represents the chance, likelihood, or possibility that a particular event will occur. In addition to simple probability, you learned about conditional probabilities and independent events. Bayes' theorem was used to revise previously calculated probabilities based on new information. You also learned about several counting rules. Throughout the chapter, contingency tables and decision trees were used to display information. In the next chapter, important discrete probability distributions such as the binomial, Poisson, and hypergeometric distributions are developed.

KEY EQUATIONS

Probability of Occurrence

$$\text{Probability of occurrence} = \frac{X}{T} \qquad (4.1)$$

Marginal Probability

$$P(A) = P(A \text{ and } B_1) + P(A \text{ and } B_2) + \cdots + P(A \text{ and } B_k) \qquad (4.2)$$

General Addition Rule

$$P(A \text{ or } B) = P(A) + P(B) - P(A \text{ and } B) \qquad (4.3)$$

Conditional Probability

$$P(A \mid B) = \frac{P(A \text{ and } B)}{P(B)} \qquad (4.4a)$$

$$P(B \mid A) = \frac{P(A \text{ and } B)}{P(A)} \qquad (4.4b)$$

Independence

$$P(A \mid B) = P(A) \qquad (4.5)$$

General Multiplication Rule

$$P(A \text{ and } B) = P(A|B)P(B) \quad (4.6)$$

Multiplication Rule for Independent Events

$$P(A \text{ and } B) = P(A)P(B) \quad (4.7)$$

Marginal Probability Using the General Multiplication Rule

$$P(A) = P(A|B_1)P(B_1) + P(A|B_2)P(B_2) + \cdots + P(A|B_k)P(B_k) \quad (4.8)$$

Bayes' Theorem

$$P(B_i|A) = \frac{P(A|B_i)P(B_i)}{P(A|B_1)P(B_1) + P(A|B_2)P(B_2) + \cdots + P(A|B_k)P(B_k)} \quad (4.9)$$

Counting Rule 1

$$k^n \quad (4.10)$$

Counting Rule 2

$$(k_1)(k_2)\ldots(k_n) \quad (4.11)$$

Counting Rule 3

$$n! = (n)(n-1)\ldots(1) \quad (4.12)$$

Counting Rule 4: Permutations

$$_nP_x = \frac{n!}{(n-x)!} \quad (4.13)$$

Counting Rule 5: Combinations

$$_nC_x = \frac{n!}{x!(n-x)!} \quad (4.14)$$

KEY TERMS

a priori probability
Bayes' theorem
certain event
collectively exhaustive
combination
complement
conditional probability
contingency table
decision tree
empirical probability
event
general addition rule
general multiplication rule
impossible event
independence
joint event
joint probability
marginal probability
multiplication rule for independent events
mutually exclusive
permutation
probability
sample space
simple event
simple probability
subjective probability
Venn diagram

CHAPTER REVIEW PROBLEMS

CHECKING YOUR UNDERSTANDING

4.52 What are the differences between *a priori* probability, empirical probability, and subjective probability?

4.53 What is the difference between a simple event and a joint event?

4.54 How can you use the general addition rule to find the probability of occurrence of event A or B?

4.55 What is the difference between mutually exclusive events and collectively exhaustive events?

4.56 How does conditional probability relate to the concept of independence?

4.57 How does the multiplication rule differ for events that are and are not independent?

4.58 How can you use Bayes' theorem to revise probabilities in light of new information?

4.59 In Bayes' theorem, how does the prior probability differ from the revised probability?

APPLYING THE CONCEPTS

4.60 A survey by the Pew Research Center ("Snapshots: Goals of 'Gen Next' vs. 'Gen X,'" *USA Today*, March 27, 2007, p. 1A) indicated that 81% of 18- to 25-year-olds had getting rich as a goal, as compared to 62% of 26- to 40-year-olds. Suppose that the survey was based on 500 respondents from each of the two groups.
a. Construct a contingency table.
b. Give an example of a simple event and a joint event.
c. What is the probability that a randomly selected respondent has a goal of getting rich?
d. What is the probability that a randomly selected respondent has a goal of getting rich *and* is in the 26- to 40-year-old group?
e. Are the events "age group" and "has getting rich as a goal" independent? Explain.

4.61 The owner of a restaurant serving Continental-style entrées was interested in studying ordering patterns of patrons for the Friday-to-Sunday weekend time period.

Records were maintained that indicated the demand for dessert during the same time period. The owner decided to study two other variables, along with whether a dessert was ordered: the gender of the individual and whether a beef entrée was ordered. The results are as follows:

DESSERT ORDERED	GENDER		
	Male	Female	Total
Yes	96	40	136
No	224	240	464
Total	320	280	600

DESSERT ORDERED	BEEF ENTRÉE		
	Yes	No	Total
Yes	71	65	136
No	116	348	464
Total	187	413	600

A waiter approaches a table to take an order for dessert. What is the probability that the first customer to order at the table

a. orders a dessert?
b. orders a dessert *or* has ordered a beef entrée?
c. is a female *and* does not order a dessert?
d. is a female *or* does not order a dessert?
e. Suppose the first person from whom the waiter takes the dessert order is a female. What is the probability that she does not order dessert?
f. Are gender and ordering dessert independent?
g. Is ordering a beef entrée independent of whether the person orders dessert?

4.62 Which meal are people most likely to order at a drive-through? A survey was conducted in 2009, but the sample sizes were not reported. Suppose the results, based on a sample of 100 males and 100 females, were as follows:

MEAL	GENDER		
	Male	Female	Total
Breakfast	18	10	28
Lunch	47	52	99
Dinner	29	29	58
Snack/beverage	6	9	15
Total	100	100	200

Source: Data extracted from www.qsrmagazine.com/reports/drive-thru_time_study/2009/2009_charts/whats_your_preferred_way_to_order_fast_food.html.

If a respondent is selected at random, what is the probability that he or she

a. prefers ordering lunch at the drive-through?
b. prefers ordering breakfast or lunch at the drive-through?
c. is a male *or* prefers ordering dinner at the drive-through?
d. is a male *and* prefers ordering dinner at the drive-through?
e. Given that the person selected is a female, what is the probability that she prefers ordering breakfast at the drive-through?

4.63 According to a Gallup Poll, companies with employees who are engaged with their workplace have greater innovation, productivity, and profitability, as well as less employee turnover. A survey of 1,895 workers in Germany found that 13% of the workers were engaged, 67% were not engaged, and 20% were actively disengaged. The survey also noted that 48% of engaged workers strongly agreed with the statement "My current job brings out my most creative ideas." Only 20% of the not engaged workers and 3% of the actively disengaged workers agreed with this statement (data extracted from M. Nink, "Employee Disengagement Plagues Germany," *Gallup Management Journal*, **gmj.gallup.com**, April 9, 2009). If a worker is known to strongly agree with the statement "My current job brings out my most creative ideas," what is the probability that the worker is engaged?

4.64 Sport utility vehicles (SUVs), vans, and pickups are generally considered to be more prone to roll over than cars. In 1997, 24.0% of all highway fatalities involved rollovers; 15.8% of all fatalities in 1997 involved SUVs, vans, and pickups, given that the fatality involved a rollover. Given that a rollover was not involved, 5.6% of all fatalities involved SUVs, vans, and pickups (data extracted from A. Wilde Mathews, "Ford Ranger, Chevy Tracker Tilt in Test," *The Wall Street Journal*, July 14, 1999, p. A2). Consider the following definitions:

A = fatality involved an SUV, van, or pickup
B = fatality involved a rollover

a. Use Bayes' theorem to find the probability that a fatality involved a rollover, given that the fatality involved an SUV, a van, or a pickup.
b. Compare the result in (a) to the probability that a fatality involved a rollover and comment on whether SUVs, vans, and pickups are generally more prone to rollover accidents than other vehicles.

4.65 Enzyme-linked immunosorbent assay (ELISA) is the most common type of screening test for detecting the HIV virus. A positive result from an ELISA indicates that the HIV virus is present. For most populations, ELISA has a high degree of sensitivity (to detect infection) and specificity (to detect noninfection). (See "HIV InSite Gateway to HIV and AIDS Knowledge" at **HIVInsite.ucsf.edu**.) Suppose the probability that a person is infected with the HIV virus for a certain population is 0.015. If the HIV virus is actually present, the probability that the ELISA test will give a positive result is 0.995. If the HIV virus is not actually present, the probability of a positive result from an ELISA is 0.01. If the ELISA has given a positive result, use

Bayes' theorem to find the probability that the HIV virus is actually present.

TEAM PROJECT

The file **Bond Funds** contains information regarding three categorical variables from a sample of 184 bond funds. The variables include

  Type—Bond fund type (intermediate government or short-term corporate)
  Fees—Sales charges (no or yes)
  Risk—Risk-of-loss factor of the bond fund (below average, average, or above average)

4.66 Construct contingency tables of type and fees, type and risk, and fees and risk.
a. For each of these contingency tables, compute all the conditional and marginal probabilities.
b. Based on (a), what conclusions can you reach about whether these variables are independent?

STUDENT SURVEY DATABASE

4.67 Problem 1.27 on page 44 describes a survey of 62 undergraduate students (see the file **UndergradSurvey**). For these data, construct contingency tables of gender and major, gender and graduate school intention, gender and employment status, gender and computer preference, class and graduate school intention, class and employment status, major and graduate school intention, major and employment status, and major and computer preference.
a. For each of these contingency tables, compute all the conditional and marginal probabilities.
b. Based on (a), what conclusions can you reach about whether these variables are independent?

4.68 Problem 1.27 on page 44 describes a survey of 62 undergraduate students (stored in **UndergradSurvey**).

a. Select a sample of undergraduate students at your school and conduct a similar survey for those students.
b. For your data, construct contingency tables of gender and major, gender and graduate school intention, gender and employment status, gender and computer preference, class and graduate school intention, class and employment status, major and graduate school intention, major and employment status, and major and computer preference.
c. Based on (b), what conclusions can you reach about whether these variables are independent?
d. Compare the results of (c) to those of Problem 4.67 (b).

4.69 Problem 1.28 on page 45 describes a survey of 44 MBA students (stored in **GradSurvey**). For these data, construct contingency tables of gender and graduate major, gender and undergraduate major, gender and employment status, gender and computer preference, graduate major and undergraduate major, graduate major and employment status, and graduate major and computer preference.
a. For each of these contingency tables, compute all the conditional and marginal probabilities.
b. Based on (b), what conclusions can you reach about whether these variables are independent?

4.70 Problem 1.28 on page 45 describes a survey of 44 MBA students (stored in **GradSurvey**).
a. Select a sample of MBA students from your MBA program and conduct a similar survey for those students.
b. For your data, construct contingency tables of gender and graduate major, gender and undergraduate major, gender and employment status, gender and computer preference, graduate major and undergraduate major, graduate major and employment status, and graduate major and computer preference.
c. Based on (b), what conclusions can you reach about whether these variables are independent?
d. Compare the results of (c) to those of Problem 4.69 (b).

DIGITAL CASE

Apply your knowledge about contingency tables and the proper application of simple and joint probabilities in this continuing Digital Case from Chapter 3.

Open **EndRunGuide.pdf**, the EndRun Financial Services "Guide to Investing," and read the information about the Guaranteed Investment Package (GIP). Read the claims and examine the supporting data. Then answer the following questions:

1. How accurate is the claim of the probability of success for EndRun's GIP? In what ways is the claim misleading? How would you calculate and state the probability of having an annual rate of return not less than 15%?

2. Using the table found under the "Show Me The Winning Probabilities" subhead, compute the proper probabilities for the group of investors. What mistake was made in reporting the 7% probability claim?

3. Are there any probability calculations that would be appropriate for rating an investment service? Why or why not?

REFERENCES

1. Bellhouse, D. R., "The Reverend Thomas Bayes, FRS: A Biography to Celebrate the Tercentenary of His Birth," *Statistical Science*, 19 (2004), 3–43.
2. Lowd, D., and C. Meek, "Good Word Attacks on Statistical Spam Filters," presented at the Second Conference on Email and Anti-Spam, CEAS 2005.
3. *Microsoft Excel 2010* (Redmond, WA: Microsoft Corp., 2010).
4. *Minitab Release 16* (State College, PA.: Minitab, Inc., 2010).
5. Paulos, J. A., *Innumeracy* (New York: Hill and Wang, 1988).
6. Silberman, S., "The Quest for Meaning," *Wired 8.02*, February 2000.
7. Zeller, T., "The Fight Against V1@gra (and Other Spam)," *The New York Times*, May 21, 2006, pp. B1, B6.

CHAPTER 4 EXCEL GUIDE

EG4.1 BASIC PROBABILITY CONCEPTS

Simple and Joint Probability and the General Addition Rule

PHStat2 Use **Simple & Joint Probabilities** to compute basic probabilities. Select **PHStat → Probability & Prob. Distributions → Simple & Joint Probabilities**. The procedure inserts a worksheet similar to Figure EG4.1 into the current workbook. (Unlike with other procedures, no dialog box is first displayed.) To use the worksheet, fill in the **Sample Space** area with your data.

In-Depth Excel Use the **COMPUTE worksheet** of the **Probabilities workbook** as a template for computing basic probabilities (see Figure EG4.1, below). The worksheet contains the Table 4.1 purchase behavior data shown on page 178. Overwrite these values when you enter data for other problems.

Open to the **COMPUTE_FORMULAS worksheet** to examine the formulas used in the worksheet, many of which are shown in the inset to Figure EG4.1.

FIGURE EG4.1 COMPUTE worksheet of the Probabilities workbook

	A	B	C	D	E
1	Probabilities				
2					
3	Sample Space		ACTUALLY PURCHASED		
4			Yes	No	Totals
5	PLANNED TO PURCHASE	Yes	200	50	250
6		No	100	650	750
7		Totals	300	700	1000
8					
9	Simple Probabilities		Simple Probabilities		
10	P(Yes)	0.25	="P(" & B5 & ")"		=E5/E7
11	P(No)	0.75	="P(" & B6 & ")"		=E6/E7
12	P(Yes)	0.30	="P(" & C4 & ")"		=C7/E7
13	P(No)	0.70	="P(" & D4 & ")"		=D7/E7
14					
15	Joint Probabilities		Joint Probabilities		
16	P(Yes and Yes)	0.20	="P(" & B5 & " and " & C4 & ")"		=C5/E7
17	P(Yes and No)	0.05	="P(" & B5 & " and " & D4 & ")"		=D5/E7
18	P(No and Yes)	0.10	="P(" & B6 & " and " & C4 & ")"		=C6/E7
19	P(No and No)	0.65	="P(" & B6 & " and " & D4 & ")"		=D6/E7
20					
21	Addition Rule		Addition Rule		
22	P(Yes or Yes)	0.35	="P(" & B5 & " or " & C4 & ")"		=B10 + B12 - B16
23	P(Yes or No)	0.90	="P(" & B5 & " or " & D4 & ")"		=B10 + B13 - B17
24	P(No or Yes)	0.95	="P(" & B6 & " or " & C4 & ")"		=B11 + B12 - B18
25	P(No or No)	0.80	="P(" & B6 & " or " & D4 & ")"		=B11 + B13 - B19

EG4.2 CONDITIONAL PROBABILITY

There is no Excel material for this section.

EG4.3 BAYES' THEOREM

In-Depth Excel Use the **COMPUTE worksheet** of the **Bayes workbook** as a template for computing basic probabilities (see Figure EG4.2, at right). The worksheet contains the television-marketing example of Table 4.4 on page 194. Overwrite these values when you enter data for other problems.

Open to the **COMPUTE_FORMULAS worksheet** to examine the simple arithmetic formulas that compute the probabilities which are also shown in the inset to Figure EG4.2.

	A	B	C	D	E
1	Bayes Theorem Calculations				
2					
3			Probabilities		
4	Event	Prior	Conditional	Joint	Revised
5	S	0.4	0.8	0.32	0.64
6	S'	0.6	0.3	0.18	0.36
7			Total:	0.5	

Joint	Revised
=B5 * C5	=D5/$D$7
=B6 * C6	=D6/$D$7
=D5 + D6	

FIGURE EG4.2 COMPUTE worksheet of the Bayes workbook

EG4.4 COUNTING RULES

Counting Rule 1

In-Depth Excel Use the **POWER(*k*, *n*)** worksheet function in a cell formula to compute the number of outcomes given *k* events and *n* trials. For example, the formula **=POWER(6, 2)** computes the answer for Example 4.11 on page 198.

Counting Rule 2

In-Depth Excel Use a formula that takes the product of successive **POWER(*k*, *n*)** functions to solve problems related to counting rule 2. For example, the formula **=POWER(26, 3) * POWER(10, 3)** computes the answer for the state motor vehicle department example on page 198.

Counting Rule 3

In-Depth Excel Use the **FACT(*n*)** worksheet function in a cell formula to compute how many ways *n* items can be arranged. For example, the formula **=FACT(6)** computes 6!

Counting Rule 4

In-Depth Excel Use the **PERMUT(*n*, *x*)** worksheet function in a cell formula to compute the number of ways of arranging *x* objects selected from *n* objects in order. For example, the formula **=PERMUT(6, 4)** computes the answer for Example 4.14 on page 199.

Counting Rule 5

In-Depth Excel Use the **COMBIN(*n*, *x*)** worksheet function in a cell formula to compute the number of ways of arranging *x* objects selected from *n* objects, irrespective of order. For example, the formula **=COMBIN(6, 4)** computes the answer for Example 4.15 on page 200.

CHAPTER 4 MINITAB GUIDE

MG4.1 BASIC PROBABILITY CONCEPTS

There is no Minitab material for this section.

MG4.2 CONDITIONAL PROBABILITY

There is no Minitab material for this section.

MG4.3 BAYES' THEOREM

There is no Minitab material for this section.

MG4.4 COUNTING RULES

Use **Calculator** to apply the counting rules. Select **Calc → Calculator**. In the Calculator dialog box (shown at right):

1. Enter the column name of an empty column in the **Store result in variable** box and then press **Tab**.
2. Build the appropriate expression (as discussed later in this section) in the **Expression** box. To apply counting rules 3 through 5, select **Arithmetic** from the **Functions** dropdown list to facilitate the function selection.
3. Click **OK**.

If you have previously used the Calculator during your Minitab session, you may have to clear the contents of the Expression box by selecting the contents and pressing **Del** before you begin step 2.

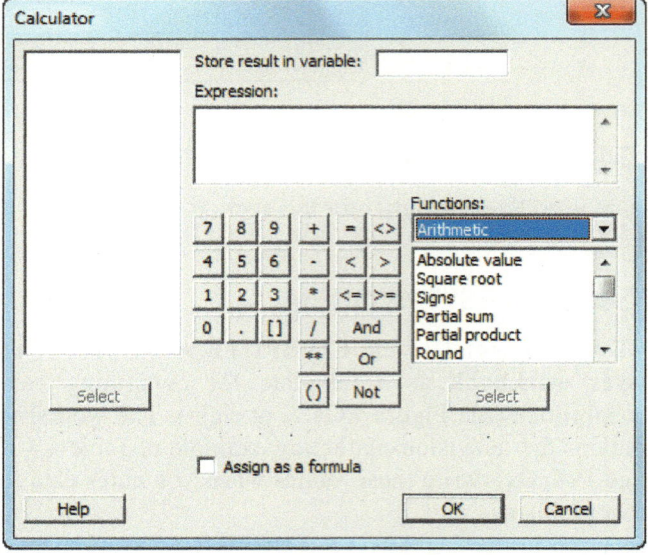

Counting Rule 1

Enter an expression that uses the exponential operator **. For example, the expression **6 ** 2** computes the answer for Example 4.11 on page 198.

Counting Rule 2

Enter an expression that uses the exponential operator **. For example, the expression **26 ** 3 * 10 ** 3** computes the answer for the state motor vehicle department example on page 198.

Counting Rule 3

Enter an expression that uses the **FACTORIAL(n)** function to compute how many ways n items can be arranged. For example, the expression **FACTORIAL(6)** computes 6!

Counting Rule 4

Enter an expression that uses the **PERMUTATIONS(n, x)** function to compute the number of ways of arranging x objects selected from n objects in order. For example, the expression **PERMUTATIONS(6, 4)** computes the answer for Example 4.14 on page 199.

Counting Rule 5

Enter an expression that uses the **COMBINATIONS(n, x)** function to compute the number of ways of arranging x objects selected from n objects, irrespective of order. For example, the expression **COMBINATIONS(6, 4)** computes the answer for Example 4.15 on page 200.

5 Discrete Probability Distributions

USING STATISTICS @ Saxon Home Improvement

5.1 The Probability Distribution for a Discrete Random Variable
Expected Value of a Discrete Random Variable
Variance and Standard Deviation of a Discrete Random Variable

5.2 Covariance and Its Application in Finance
Covariance
Expected Value, Variance, and Standard Deviation of the Sum of Two Random Variables
Portfolio Expected Return and Portfolio Risk

5.3 Binomial Distribution

5.4 Poisson Distribution

5.5 Hypergeometric Distribution

5.6 Online Topic Using the Poisson Distribution to Approximate the Binomial Distribution

USING STATISTICS @ Saxon Home Improvement Revisited

CHAPTER 5 EXCEL GUIDE

CHAPTER 5 MINITAB GUIDE

Learning Objectives

In this chapter, you learn:

- The properties of a probability distribution
- To compute the expected value and variance of a probability distribution
- To calculate the covariance and understand its use in finance
- To compute probabilities from the binomial, Poisson, and hypergeometric distributions
- How the binomial, Poisson, and hypergeometric distributions can be used to solve business problems

USING STATISTICS

@ Saxon Home Improvement

You are an accountant for the Saxon Home Improvement Company, which uses a state-of-the-art accounting information system to manage its accounting and financial operations.

Accounting information systems collect, process, store, transform, and distribute financial information to decision makers both internal and external to a business organization (see reference 7). These systems continuously audit accounting information, looking for errors or incomplete or improbable information. For example, when customers of the Saxon Home Improvement Company submit online orders, the company's accounting information system reviews the order forms for possible mistakes. Any questionable invoices are tagged and included in a daily *exceptions report*. Recent data collected by the company show that the likelihood is 0.10 that an order form will be tagged. Saxon would like to determine the likelihood of finding a certain number of tagged forms in a sample of a specific size. For example, what would be the likelihood that none of the order forms are tagged in a sample of four forms? That one of the order forms is tagged?

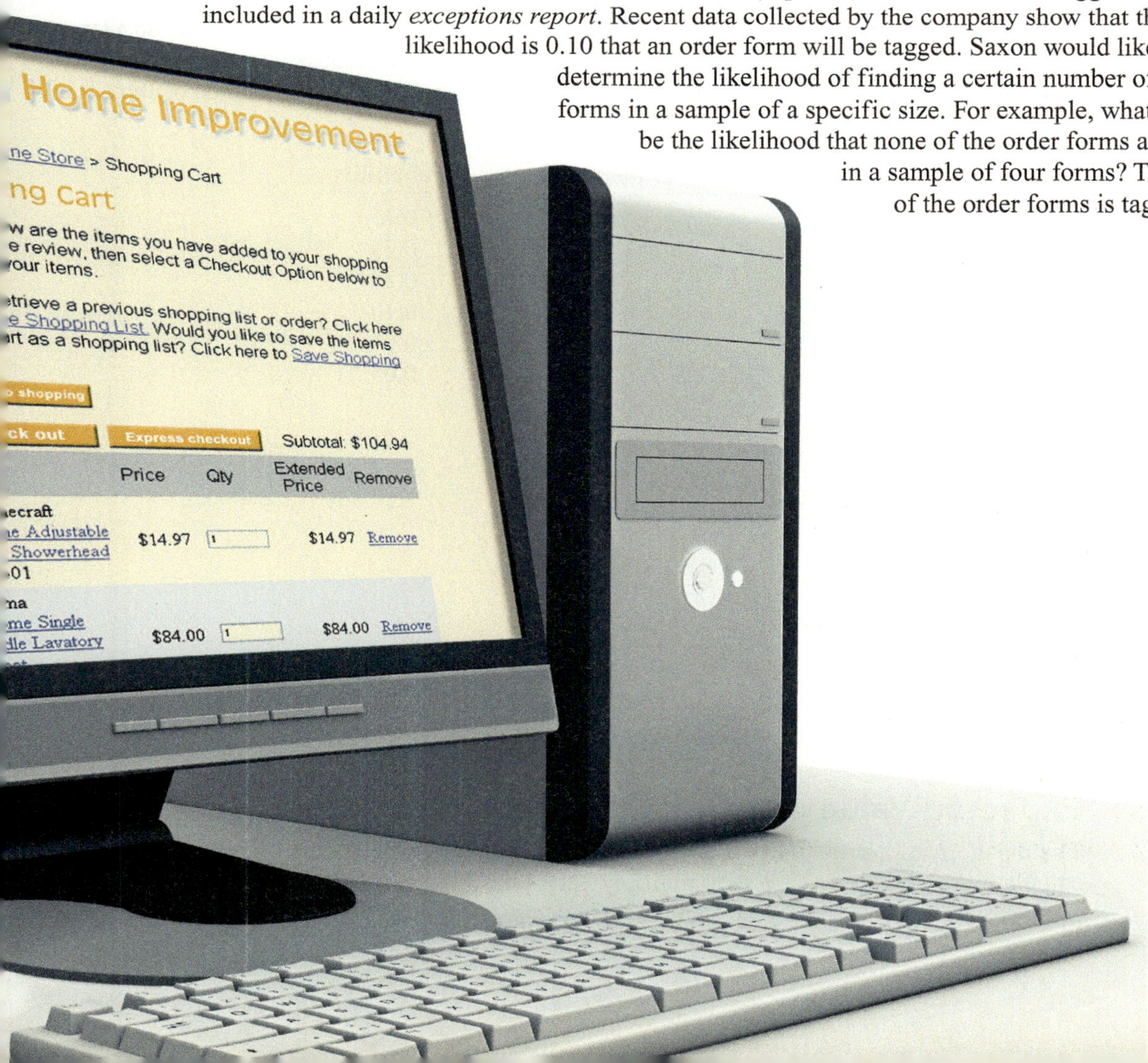

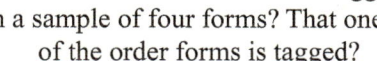

How could the Saxon Home Improvement Company determine the solution to this type of probability problem? One way is to use a model, or small-scale representation, that approximates the process. By using such an approximation, Saxon managers could make inferences about the actual order process. In this case, the Saxon managers can use *probability distributions*, mathematical models suited for solving the type of probability problems the managers are facing.

This chapter introduces you to the concept and characteristics of probability distributions. You will learn how the knowledge about a probability distribution can help you choose between alternative investment strategies. You will also learn how the binomial, Poisson, and hypergeometric distributions can be applied to help solve business problems.

5.1 The Probability Distribution for a Discrete Random Variable

In Section 1.4, a *numerical variable* was defined as a variable that yields numerical responses, such as the number of magazines you subscribe to or your height. Numerical variables are either *discrete* or *continuous*. Continuous numerical variables produce outcomes that come from a measuring process (e.g., your height). Discrete numerical variables produce outcomes that come from a counting process (e.g., the number of magazines you subscribe to). This chapter deals with probability distributions that represent discrete numerical variables.

> PROBABILITY DISTRIBUTION FOR A DISCRETE RANDOM VARIABLE
>
> A **probability distribution for a discrete random variable** is a mutually exclusive list of all the possible numerical outcomes along with the probability of occurrence of each outcome.

For example, Table 5.1 gives the distribution of the number of interruptions per day in a large computer network. The list in Table 5.1 is collectively exhaustive because all possible outcomes are included. Thus, the probabilities sum to 1. Figure 5.1 is a graphical representation of Table 5.1.

TABLE 5.1
Probability Distribution of the Number of Interruptions per Day

Interruptions per Day	Probability
0	0.35
1	0.25
2	0.20
3	0.10
4	0.05
5	0.05

FIGURE 5.1
Probability distribution of the number of interruptions per day

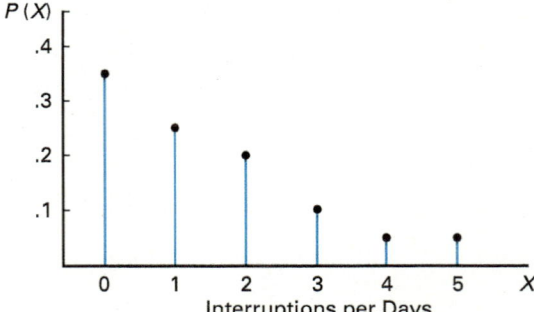

Expected Value of a Discrete Random Variable

The mean, μ, of a probability distribution is the **expected value** of its random variable. To calculate the expected value, you multiply each possible outcome, x, by its corresponding probability, $P(X = x_i)$, and then sum these products.

EXPECTED VALUE, μ, OF A DISCRETE RANDOM VARIABLE

$$\mu = E(X) = \sum_{i=1}^{N} x_i P(X = x_i) \quad (5.1)$$

where

x_i = the ith outcome of the discrete random variable X

$P(X = x_i)$ = probability of occurrence of the ith outcome of X

For the probability distribution of the number of interruptions per day in a large computer network (Table 5.1), the expected value is computed as follows, using Equation (5.1), and is also shown in Table 5.2:

$$\mu = E(X) = \sum_{i=1}^{N} x_i P(X = x_i)$$

$= (0)(0.35) + (1)(0.25) + (2)(0.20) + (3)(0.10) + (4)(0.05) + (5)(0.05)$

$= 0 + 0.25 + 0.40 + 0.30 + 0.20 + 0.25$

$= 1.40$

TABLE 5.2

Computing the Expected Value of the Number of Interruptions per Day

Interruptions per Day (x_i)	$P(X = x_i)$	$x_i P(X = x_i)$
0	0.35	$(0)(0.35) = 0.00$
1	0.25	$(1)(0.25) = 0.25$
2	0.20	$(2)(0.20) = 0.40$
3	0.10	$(3)(0.10) = 0.30$
4	0.05	$(4)(0.05) = 0.20$
5	0.05	$(5)(0.05) = 0.25$
	1.00	$\mu = E(X) = 1.40$

The expected value is 1.40. The expected value of 1.4 for the number of interruptions per day is not a possible outcome because the actual number of interruptions in a given day must be an integer value. The expected value represents the *mean* number of interruptions in a given day.

Variance and Standard Deviation of a Discrete Random Variable

You compute the variance of a probability distribution by multiplying each possible squared difference $[x_i - E(X)]^2$ by its corresponding probability, $P(X = x_i)$, and then summing the resulting products. Equation (5.2) defines the **variance of a discrete random variable**.

VARIANCE OF A DISCRETE RANDOM VARIABLE

$$\sigma^2 = \sum_{i=1}^{N} [x_i - E(X)]^2 P(X = x_i) \quad (5.2)$$

where

x_i = the ith outcome of the discrete random variable X

$P(X = x_i)$ = probability of occurrence of the ith outcome of X

Equation (5.3) defines the **standard deviation of a discrete random variable**.

> **STANDARD DEVIATION OF A DISCRETE RANDOM VARIABLE**
>
> $$\sigma = \sqrt{\sigma^2} = \sqrt{\sum_{i=1}^{N}[x_i - E(X)]^2 P(X = x_i)} \qquad (5.3)$$

The variance and the standard deviation of the number of interruptions per day are computed as follows and in Table 5.3, using Equations (5.2) and (5.3):

$$\sigma^2 = \sum_{i=1}^{N}[x_i - E(X)]^2 P(X = x_i)$$

$$= (0 - 1.4)^2(0.35) + (1 - 1.4)^2(0.25) + (2 - 1.4)^2(0.20) + (3 - 1.4)^2(0.10) + (4 - 1.4)^2(0.05) + (5 - 1.4)^2(0.05)$$

$$= 0.686 + 0.040 + 0.072 + 0.256 + 0.338 + 0.648$$

$$= 2.04$$

TABLE 5.3

Computing the Variance and Standard Deviation of the Number of Interruptions per Day

Interruptions per Day (x_i)	$P(X = x_i)$	$x_i P(X = x_i)$	$[x_i - E(X)]^2 P(X = x_i)$
0	0.35	(0)(0.35) = 0.00	$(0 - 1.4)^2(0.35) = 0.686$
1	0.25	(1)(0.25) = 0.25	$(1 - 1.4)^2(0.25) = 0.040$
2	0.20	(2)(0.20) = 0.40	$(2 - 1.4)^2(0.20) = 0.072$
3	0.10	(3)(0.10) = 0.30	$(3 - 1.4)^2(0.10) = 0.256$
4	0.05	(4)(0.05) = 0.20	$(4 - 1.4)^2(0.05) = 0.338$
5	0.05	(5)(0.05) = 0.25	$(5 - 1.4)^2(0.05) = 0.648$
	1.00	$\mu = E(X) = 1.40$	$\sigma^2 = 2.04$

and

$$\sigma = \sqrt{\sigma^2} = \sqrt{2.04} = 1.4283$$

Thus, the mean number of interruptions per day is 1.4, the variance is 2.04, and the standard deviation is approximately 1.43 interruptions per day.

Problems for Section 5.1

LEARNING THE BASICS

5.1 Given the following probability distributions:

Distribution A		Distribution B	
X	$P(X = x_i)$	X	$P(X = x_i)$
0	0.50	0	0.05
1	0.20	1	0.10
2	0.15	2	0.15
3	0.10	3	0.20
4	0.05	4	0.50

a. Compute the expected value for each distribution.
b. Compute the standard deviation for each distribution.
c. Compare the results of distributions A and B.

APPLYING THE CONCEPTS

SELF Test 5.2 The following table contains the probability distribution for the number of traffic accidents daily in a small city:

Number of Accidents Daily (X)	$P(X = x_i)$
0	0.10
1	0.20
2	0.45
3	0.15
4	0.05
5	0.05

a. Compute the mean number of accidents per day.
b. Compute the standard deviation.

5.3 Recently, a regional automobile dealership sent out fliers to perspective customers, indicating that they had already won one of three different prizes: a Kia Optima valued at $15,000, a $500 gas card, or a $5 Wal-Mart shopping card. To claim his or her prize, a prospective customer needed to present the flier at the dealership's showroom. The fine print on the back of the flier listed the probabilities of winning. The chance of winning the car was 1 out of 31,478, the chance of winning the gas card was 1 out of 31,478, and the chance of winning the shopping card was 31,476 out of 31,478.
a. How many fliers do you think the automobile dealership sent out?
b. Using your answer to (a) and the probabilities listed on the flier, what is the expected value of the prize won by a prospective customer receiving a flier?
c. Using your answer to (a) and the probabilities listed on the flier, what is the standard deviation of the value of the prize won by a prospective customer receiving a flier?
d. Do you think this is an effective promotion? Why or why not?

5.4 In the carnival game Under-or-Over-Seven, a pair of fair dice is rolled once, and the resulting sum determines whether the player wins or loses his or her bet. For example, the player can bet $1 that the sum will be under 7—that is, 2, 3, 4, 5, or 6. For this bet, the player wins $1 if the result is under 7 and loses $1 if the outcome equals or is greater than 7. Similarly, the player can bet $1 that the sum will be over 7—that is, 8, 9, 10, 11, or 12. Here, the player wins $1 if the result is over 7 but loses $1 if the result is 7 or under. A third method of play is to bet $1 on the outcome 7. For this bet, the player wins $4 if the result of the roll is 7 and loses $1 otherwise.
a. Construct the probability distribution representing the different outcomes that are possible for a $1 bet on under 7.
b. Construct the probability distribution representing the different outcomes that are possible for a $1 bet on over 7.
c. Construct the probability distribution representing the different outcomes that are possible for a $1 bet on 7.
d. Show that the expected long-run profit (or loss) to the player is the same, no matter which method of play is used.

5.5 The number of arrivals per minute at a bank located in the central business district of a large city was recorded over a period of 200 minutes, with the following results:

Arrivals	Frequency
0	14
1	31
2	47
3	41
4	29
5	21
6	10
7	5
8	2

a. Compute the expected number of arrivals per minute.
b. Compute the standard deviation.

5.6 The manager of the commercial mortgage department of a large bank has collected data during the past two years concerning the number of commercial mortgages approved per week. The results from these two years (104 weeks) indicated the following:

Number of Commercial Mortgages Approved	Frequeny
0	13
1	25
2	32
3	17
4	9
5	6
6	1
7	1

a. Compute the expected number of mortgages approved per week.
b. Compute the standard deviation.

5.2 Covariance and Its Application in Finance

In Section 5.1, the expected value, variance, and standard deviation of a discrete random variable of a probability distribution are discussed. In this section, the covariance between two variables is introduced and applied to portfolio management, a topic of great interest to financial analysts.

Covariance

The **covariance**, σ_{XY}, measures the strength of the relationship between two numerical random variables, X and Y. A positive covariance indicates a positive relationship. A negative covariance indicates a negative relationship. A covariance of 0 indicates that the two variables are independent. Equation (5.4) defines the covariance for a discrete probability distribution.

COVARIANCE

$$\sigma_{XY} = \sum_{i=1}^{N} [x_i - E(X)][y_i - E(Y)] P(x_i y_i) \qquad (5.4)$$

where

X = discrete random variable X

x_i = ith outcome of X

Y = discrete random variable Y

y_i = ith outcome of Y

$P(x_i y_i)$ = probability of occurrence of the ith outcome of X and the ith outcome of Y

$i = 1, 2, \ldots, N$ for X and Y

To illustrate the covariance, suppose that you are deciding between two different investments for the coming year. The first investment is a mutual fund that consists of the stocks that comprise the Dow Jones Industrial Average. The second investment is a mutual fund that is expected to perform best when economic conditions are weak. Table 5.4 summarizes your estimate of the returns (per $1,000 investment) under three economic conditions, each with a given probability of occurrence.

TABLE 5.4

Estimated Returns for Each Investment Under Three Economic Conditions

$P(x_i y_i)$	Economic Condition	Investment	
		Dow Jones Fund	Weak-Economy Fund
0.2	Recession	$-$300	+$200
0.5	Stable economy	+100	+50
0.3	Expanding economy	+250	-100

The expected value and standard deviation for each investment and the covariance of the two investments are computed as follows:

Let X = Dow Jones fund and Y = weak-economy fund

$E(X) = \mu_X = (-300)(0.2) + (100)(0.5) + (250)(0.3) = \$65$

$E(Y) = \mu_Y = (+200)(0.2) + (50)(0.5) + (-100)(0.3) = \$35$

$Var(X) = \sigma_X^2 = (-300 - 65)^2(0.2) + (100 - 65)^2(0.5) + (250 - 65)^2(0.3)$

$\qquad = 37,525$

$\sigma_X = \$193.71$

$Var(Y) = \sigma_Y^2 = (200 - 35)^2(0.2) + (50 - 35)^2(0.5) + (-100 - 35)^2(0.3)$

$\qquad = 11,025$

$\sigma_Y = \$105.00$

$\sigma_{XY} = (-300 - 65)(200 - 35)(0.2) + (100 - 65)(50 - 35)(0.5)$
$\qquad + (250 - 65)(-100 - 35)(0.3)$

$\qquad = -12,045 + 262.5 - 7,492.5$

$\qquad = -19,275$

Thus, the Dow Jones fund has a higher expected value (i.e., larger expected return) than the weak-economy fund but also has a higher standard deviation (i.e., more risk). The covariance of $-19,275$ between the two investments indicates a negative relationship in which the two investments are varying in the *opposite* direction. Therefore, when the return on one investment is high, typically, the return on the other is low.

Expected Value, Variance, and Standard Deviation of the Sum of Two Random Variables

Equations (5.1) through (5.3) define the expected value, variance, and standard deviation of a probability distribution, and Equation (5.4) defines the covariance between two variables, X and Y. The **expected value of the sum of two random variables** is equal to the sum of the expected values. The **variance of the sum of two random variables** is equal to the sum of the variances plus twice the covariance. The **standard deviation of the sum of two random variables** is the square root of the variance of the sum of two random variables.

EXPECTED VALUE OF THE SUM OF TWO RANDOM VARIABLES

$$E(X + Y) = E(X) + E(Y) \tag{5.5}$$

VARIANCE OF THE SUM OF TWO RANDOM VARIABLES

$$Var(X + Y) = \sigma^2_{X+Y} = \sigma^2_X + \sigma^2_Y + 2\sigma_{XY} \tag{5.6}$$

STANDARD DEVIATION OF THE SUM OF TWO RANDOM VARIABLES

$$\sigma_{X+Y} = \sqrt{\sigma^2_{X+Y}} \tag{5.7}$$

To illustrate the expected value, variance, and standard deviation of the sum of two random variables, consider the two investments previously discussed. If $X =$ Dow Jones fund and $Y =$ weak-economy fund, using Equations (5.5), (5.6), and (5.7),

$$E(X + Y) = E(X) + E(Y) = 65 + 35 = \$100$$

$$\sigma^2_{X+Y} = \sigma^2_X + \sigma^2_Y + 2\sigma_{XY}$$

$$= 37{,}525 + 11{,}025 + (2)(-19{,}275)$$

$$= 10{,}000$$

$$\sigma_{X+Y} = \$100$$

The expected value of the sum of the Dow Jones fund and the weak-economy fund is $100, with a standard deviation of $100. The standard deviation of the sum of the two investments is less than the standard deviation of either single investment because there is a large negative covariance between the investments.

Portfolio Expected Return and Portfolio Risk

Now that the covariance and the expected value and standard deviation of the sum of two random variables have been defined, these concepts can be applied to the study of a group of assets referred to as a **portfolio**. Investors combine assets into portfolios to reduce their risk (see references 1 and 2). Often, the objective is to maximize the return while minimizing the risk. For such portfolios, rather than study the sum of two random variables, the investor weights each investment by the proportion of assets assigned to that investment. Equations (5.8) and (5.9) define the **portfolio expected return** and **portfolio risk**.

PORTFOLIO EXPECTED RETURN

The portfolio expected return for a two-asset investment is equal to the weight assigned to asset X multiplied by the expected return of asset X plus the weight assigned to asset Y multiplied by the expected return of asset Y.

$$E(P) = wE(X) + (1 - w)E(Y) \quad (5.8)$$

where

$E(P)$ = portfolio expected return
w = portion of the portfolio value assigned to asset X
$(1 - w)$ = portion of the portfolio value assigned to asset Y
$E(X)$ = expected return of asset X
$E(Y)$ = expected return of asset Y

PORTFOLIO RISK

$$\sigma_p = \sqrt{w^2\sigma_X^2 + (1 - w)^2\sigma_Y^2 + 2w(1 - w)\sigma_{XY}} \quad (5.9)$$

In the previous section, you evaluated the expected return and risk of two different investments, a Dow Jones fund and a weak-economy fund. You also computed the covariance of the two investments. Now, suppose that you want to form a portfolio of these two investments that consists of an equal investment in each of these two funds. To compute the portfolio expected return and the portfolio risk, using Equations (5.8) and (5.9), with $w = 0.50$, $E(X) = \$65, E(Y) = \$35, \sigma_X^2 = 37{,}525, \sigma_Y^2 = 11{,}025$, and $\sigma_{XY} = -19{,}275$,

$$E(P) = (0.5)(65) + (1 - 0.5)(35) = \$50$$
$$\sigma_p = \sqrt{(0.5)^2(37{,}525) + (1 - 0.5)^2(11{,}025) + 2(0.5)(1 - 0.5)(-19{,}275)}$$
$$= \sqrt{2{,}500} = \$50$$

Thus, the portfolio has an expected return of $50 for each $1,000 invested (a return of 5%) and has a portfolio risk of $50. The portfolio risk here is smaller than the standard deviation of either investment because there is a large negative covariance between the two investments. The fact that each investment performs best under different circumstances reduces the overall risk of the portfolio.

Problems for Section 5.2

LEARNING THE BASICS

5.7 Given the following probability distributions for variables X and Y:

$P(X_iY_i)$	X	Y
0.4	100	200
0.6	200	100

Compute
a. $E(X)$ and $E(Y)$.
b. σ_X and σ_Y.
c. σ_{XY}.
d. $E(X + Y)$.

5.8 Given the following probability distributions for variables X and Y:

$P(X_iY_i)$	X	Y
0.2	-100	50
0.4	50	30
0.3	200	20
0.1	300	20

Compute
a. $E(X)$ and $E(Y)$.
b. σ_X and σ_Y.
c. σ_{XY}.
d. $E(X + Y)$.

5.9 Two investments, X and Y, have the following characteristics:

$$E(X) = \$50, E(Y) = \$100, \sigma_X^2 = 9{,}000,$$
$$\sigma_Y^2 = 15{,}000, \text{ and } \sigma_{XY} = 7{,}500.$$

If the weight of portfolio assets assigned to investment X is 0.4, compute the
a. portfolio expected return.
b. portfolio risk.

APPLYING THE CONCEPTS

5.10 The process of being served at a bank consists of two independent parts—the time waiting in line and the time it takes to be served by the teller. Suppose that the time waiting in line has an expected value of 4 minutes, with a standard deviation of 1.2 minutes, and the time it takes to be served by the teller has an expected value of 5.5 minutes, with a standard deviation of 1.5 minutes. Compute the
a. expected value of the total time it takes to be served at the bank.
b. standard deviation of the total time it takes to be served at the bank.

5.11 In the portfolio example in this section (see page 218), half the portfolio assets are invested in the Dow Jones fund and half in a weak-economy fund. Recalculate the portfolio expected return and the portfolio risk if
a. 30% of the portfolio assets are invested in the Dow Jones fund and 70% in a weak-economy fund.
b. 70% of the portfolio assets are invested in the Dow Jones fund and 30% in a weak-economy fund.
c. Which of the three investment strategies (30%, 50%, or 70% in the Dow Jones fund) would you recommend? Why?

SELF Test 5.12 You are trying to develop a strategy for investing in two different stocks. The anticipated annual return for a $1,000 investment in each stock under four different economic conditions has the following probability distribution:

		Returns	
Probability	Economic Condition	Stock X	Stock Y
0.1	Recession	−100	50
0.3	Slow growth	0	150
0.3	Moderate growth	80	−20
0.3	Fast growth	150	−100

Compute the
a. expected return for stock X and for stock Y.
b. standard deviation for stock X and for stock Y.
c. covariance of stock X and stock Y.
d. Would you invest in stock X or stock Y? Explain.

5.13 Suppose that in Problem 5.12 you wanted to create a portfolio that consists of stock X and stock Y. Compute the portfolio expected return and portfolio risk for each of the following percentages invested in stock X:
a. 30%
b. 50%
c. 70%
d. On the basis of the results of (a) through (c), which portfolio would you recommend? Explain.

5.14 You are trying to develop a strategy for investing in two different stocks. The anticipated annual return for a $1,000 investment in each stock under four different economic conditions has the following probability distribution:

		Returns	
Probability	Economic Condition	Stock X	Stock Y
0.1	Recession	−50	−100
0.3	Slow growth	20	50
0.4	Moderate growth	100	130
0.2	Fast growth	150	200

Compute the
a. expected return for stock X and for stock Y.
b. standard deviation for stock X and for stock Y.
c. covariance of stock X and stock Y.
d. Would you invest in stock X or stock Y? Explain.

5.15 Suppose that in Problem 5.14 you wanted to create a portfolio that consists of stock X and stock Y. Compute the portfolio expected return and portfolio risk for each of the following percentages invested in stock X:
a. 30%
b. 50%
c. 70%
d. On the basis of the results of (a) through (c), which portfolio would you recommend? Explain.

5.16 You plan to invest $1,000 in a corporate bond fund or in a common stock fund. The following information about the annual return (per $1,000) of each of these investments under different economic conditions is available, along with the probability that each of these economic conditions will occur:

Probability	Economic Condition	Corporate Bond Fund	Common Stock Fund
0.01	Extreme recession	−200	−999
0.09	Recession	−70	−300
0.15	Stagnation	30	−100
0.35	Slow growth	80	100
0.30	Moderate growth	100	150
0.10	High growth	120	350

Compute the
a. expected return for the corporate bond fund and for the common stock fund.

b. standard deviation for the corporate bond fund and for the common stock fund.
c. covariance of the corporate bond fund and the common stock fund.
d. Would you invest in the corporate bond fund or the common stock fund? Explain.
e. If you chose to invest in the common stock fund in (d), what do you think about the possibility of losing $999 of every $1,000 invested if there is an extreme recession?

5.17 Suppose that in Problem 5.16 you wanted to create a portfolio that consists of the corporate bond fund and the common stock fund. Compute the portfolio expected return and portfolio risk for each of the following situations:
a. $300 in the corporate bond fund and $700 in the common stock fund.
b. $500 in each fund.
c. $700 in the corporate bond fund and $300 in the common stock fund.
d. On the basis of the results of (a) through (c), which portfolio would you recommend? Explain.

5.3 Binomial Distribution

The next three sections use mathematical models to solve business problems.

> **MATHEMATICAL MODEL**
> A **mathematical model** is a mathematical expression that represents a variable of interest.

When a mathematical expression is available, you can compute the exact probability of occurrence of any particular outcome of the variable.

The **binomial distribution** is one of the most useful mathematical models. You use the binomial distribution when the discrete random variable is the number of events of interest in a sample of n observations. The binomial distribution has four basic properties:

- The sample consists of a fixed number of observations, n.
- Each observation is classified into one of two mutually exclusive and collectively exhaustive categories.
- The probability of an observation being classified as the event of interest, π, is constant from observation to observation. Thus, the probability of an observation being classified as not being the event of interest, $1 - \pi$, is constant over all observations.
- The outcome of any observation is independent of the outcome of any other observation.

Returning to the Saxon Home Improvement scenario presented on page 211 concerning the accounting information system, suppose the event of interest is defined as a tagged order form. You are interested in the number of tagged order forms in a given sample of orders.

What results can occur? If the sample contains four orders, there could be none, one, two, three, or four tagged order forms. No other value can occur because the number of tagged order forms cannot be more than the sample size, n, and cannot be less than zero. Therefore, the range of the binomial random variable is from 0 to n.

Suppose that you observe the following result in a sample of four orders:

First Order	Second Order	Third Order	Fourth Order
Tagged	Tagged	Not tagged	Tagged

What is the probability of having three tagged order forms in a sample of four orders in this particular sequence? Because the historical probability of a tagged order is 0.10, the probability that each order occurs in the sequence is

First Order	Second Order	Third Order	Fourth Order
$\pi = 0.10$	$\pi = 0.10$	$1 - \pi = 0.90$	$\pi = 0.10$

Each outcome is independent of the others because the order forms were selected from an extremely large or practically infinite population and each order form could only be selected once. Therefore, the probability of having this particular sequence is

$$\pi\pi(1 - \pi)\pi = \pi^3(1 - \pi)^1$$
$$= (0.10)^3(0.90)^1$$
$$= (0.10)(0.10)(0.10)(0.90)$$
$$= 0.0009$$

This result indicates only the probability of three tagged order forms (events of interest) from a sample of four order forms in a *specific sequence*. To find the number of ways of selecting x objects from n objects, *irrespective of sequence*, you use the **rule of combinations** given in Equation (5.10) and previously defined in Equation (4.14) on page 200.

[1] On many scientific calculators, there is a button labeled $_nC_r$ that allows you to compute the number of combinations. On these calculators, the symbol r is used instead of x.

COMBINATIONS

The number of combinations of selecting x objects[1] out of n objects is given by

$$_nC_x = \frac{n!}{x!(n-x)!} \qquad (5.10)$$

where

$$n! = (n)(n-1) \cdots (1) \text{ is called } n \text{ factorial. By definition, } 0! = 1.$$

With $n = 4$ and $x = 3$, there are

$$_nC_x = \frac{n!}{x!(n-x)!} = \frac{4!}{3!(4-3)!} = \frac{4 \times 3 \times 2 \times 1}{(3 \times 2 \times 1)(1)} = 4$$

such sequences. The four possible sequences are

Sequence 1 = *tagged, tagged, tagged, not tagged*, with probability
$$\pi\pi\pi(1 - \pi) = \pi^3(1 - \pi)^1 = 0.0009$$

Sequence 2 = *tagged, tagged, not tagged, tagged*, with probability
$$\pi\pi(1 - \pi)\pi = \pi^3(1 - \pi)^1 = 0.0009$$

Sequence 3 = *tagged, not tagged, tagged, tagged*, with probability
$$\pi(1 - \pi)\pi\pi = \pi^3(1 - \pi)^1 = 0.0009$$

Sequence 4 = *not tagged, tagged, tagged, tagged*, with probability
$$(1 - \pi)\pi\pi\pi = \pi^3(1 - \pi)^1 = 0.0009$$

Therefore, the probability of three tagged order forms is equal to

(Number of possible sequences) × (Probability of a particular sequence)
$$= (4) \times (0.0009) = 0.0036$$

You can make a similar, intuitive derivation for the other possible outcomes of the random variable—zero, one, two, and four tagged order forms. However, as n, the sample size, gets large, the computations involved in using this intuitive approach become time-consuming. Equation

(5.11) is the mathematical model that provides a general formula for computing any probability from the binomial distribution with the number of events of interest, x, given n and π.

BINOMIAL DISTRIBUTION

$$P(X = x \mid n, \pi) = \frac{n!}{x!(n-x)!} \pi^x (1 - \pi)^{n-x} \qquad (5.11)$$

where

$P(X = x \mid n, \pi)$ = probability that $X = x$ events of interest, given n and π

n = number of observations

π = probability of an event of interest

$1 - \pi$ = probability of not having an event of interest

x = number of events of interest in the sample ($X = 0, 1, 2, \cdots, n$)

$\dfrac{n!}{x!(n-x)!}$ = the number of combinations of x events of interest out of n observations

---

Equation (5.11) restates what was intuitively derived previously. The binomial variable X can have any integer value x from 0 through n. In Equation (5.11), the product

$$\pi^x (1 - \pi)^{n-x}$$

represents the probability of exactly x events of interest from n observations in a *particular sequence*.

The term

$$\frac{n!}{x!(n-x)!}$$

is the number of *combinations* of the x events of interest from the n observations possible. Hence, given the number of observations, n, and the probability of an event of interest, π, the probability of x events of interest is

$$P(X = x \mid n, \pi) = (\text{Number of combinations}) \times (\text{Probability of a particular combination})$$

$$= \frac{n!}{x!(n-x)!} \pi^x (1 - \pi)^{n-x}$$

Example 5.1 illustrates the use of Equation (5.11).

EXAMPLE 5.1

Determining $P(X = 3)$, Given $n = 4$ and $\pi = 0.1$

If the likelihood of a tagged order form is 0.1, what is the probability that there are three tagged order forms in the sample of four?

SOLUTION Using Equation (5.11), the probability of three tagged orders from a sample of four is

$$P(X = 3 \mid n = 4, \pi = 0.1) = \frac{4!}{3!(4-3)!}(0.1)^3 (1 - 0.1)^{4-3}$$

$$= \frac{4!}{3!(1)!}(0.1)^3 (0.9)^1$$

$$= 4(0.1)(0.1)(0.1)(0.9) = 0.0036$$

Examples 5.2 and 5.3 show the computations for other values of X.

EXAMPLE 5.2

Determining $P(X \geq 3)$, Given $n = 4$ and $\pi = 0.1$

If the likelihood of a tagged order form is 0.1, what is the probability that there are three or more (i.e., at least three) tagged order forms in the sample of four?

SOLUTION In Example 5.1, you found that the probability of *exactly* three tagged order forms from a sample of four is 0.0036. To compute the probability of *at least* three tagged order forms, you need to add the probability of three tagged order forms to the probability of four tagged order forms. The probability of four tagged order forms is

$$P(X = 4 \mid n = 4, \pi = 0.1) = \frac{4!}{4!(4-4)!}(0.1)^4(1-0.1)^{4-4}$$

$$= \frac{4!}{4!(0)!}(0.1)^4(0.9)^0$$

$$= 1(0.1)(0.1)(0.1)(0.1)(1) = 0.0001$$

Thus, the probability of at least three tagged order forms is

$$P(X \geq 3) = P(X = 3) + P(X = 4)$$

$$= 0.0036 + 0.0001$$

$$= 0.0037$$

There is a 0.37% chance that there will be at least three tagged order forms in a sample of four.

EXAMPLE 5.3

Determining $P(X < 3)$, Given $n = 4$ and $\pi = 0.1$

If the likelihood of a tagged order form is 0.1, what is the probability that there are fewer than three tagged order forms in the sample of four?

SOLUTION The probability that there are fewer than three tagged order forms is

$$P(X < 3) = P(X = 0) + P(X = 1) + P(X = 2)$$

Using Equation (5.11) on page 222, these probabilities are

$$P(X = 0 \mid n = 4, \pi = 0.1) = \frac{4!}{0!(4-0)!}(0.1)^0(1-0.1)^{4-0} = 0.6561$$

$$P(X = 1 \mid n = 4, \pi = 0.1) = \frac{4!}{1!(4-1)!}(0.1)^1(1-0.1)^{4-1} = 0.2916$$

$$P(X = 2 \mid n = 4, \pi = 0.1) = \frac{4!}{2!(4-2)!}(0.1)^2(1-0.1)^{4-2} = 0.0486$$

Therefore, $P(X < 3) = 0.6561 + 0.2916 + 0.0486 = 0.9963$. $P(X < 3)$ could also be calculated from its complement, $P(X \geq 3)$, as follows:

$$P(X < 3) = 1 - P(X \geq 3)$$

$$= 1 - 0.0037 = 0.9963$$

Computing binomial probabilities become tedious as n gets large. Figure 5.2 shows how binomial probabilities can be computed by Excel (left) and Minitab (right). Binomial probabilities can also be looked up in a table of probabilities, as discussed in the **Binomial** online topic available on this book's companion website. (See Appendix C to learn how to access the online topic files.)

FIGURE 5.2

Excel worksheet and Minitab results for computing binomial probabilities with $n = 4$ and $\pi = 0.1$

	A	B	
1	Binomial Probabilities		
2			
3	Data		
4	Sample size	4	
5	Probability of an event of interest	0.1	
6			
7	Statistics		
8	Mean	0.4	=B4 * B5
9	Variance	0.36	=B8 * (1 - B5)
10	Standard deviation	0.6	=SQRT(B9)
11			
12	Binomial Probabilities Table		
13	X	P(X)	
14	0	0.6561	=BINOMDIST(A14, $B$4, $B$5, FALSE)
15	1	0.2916	=BINOMDIST(A15, $B$4, $B$5, FALSE)
16	2	0.0486	=BINOMDIST(A16, $B$4, $B$5, FALSE)
17	3	0.0036	=BINOMDIST(A17, $B$4, $B$5, FALSE)
18	4	0.0001	=BINOMDIST(A18, $B$4, $B$5, FALSE)

Binomial with n = 4 and p = 0.1

x	P(X = x)
0	0.6561
1	0.2916
2	0.0486
3	0.0036
4	0.0001

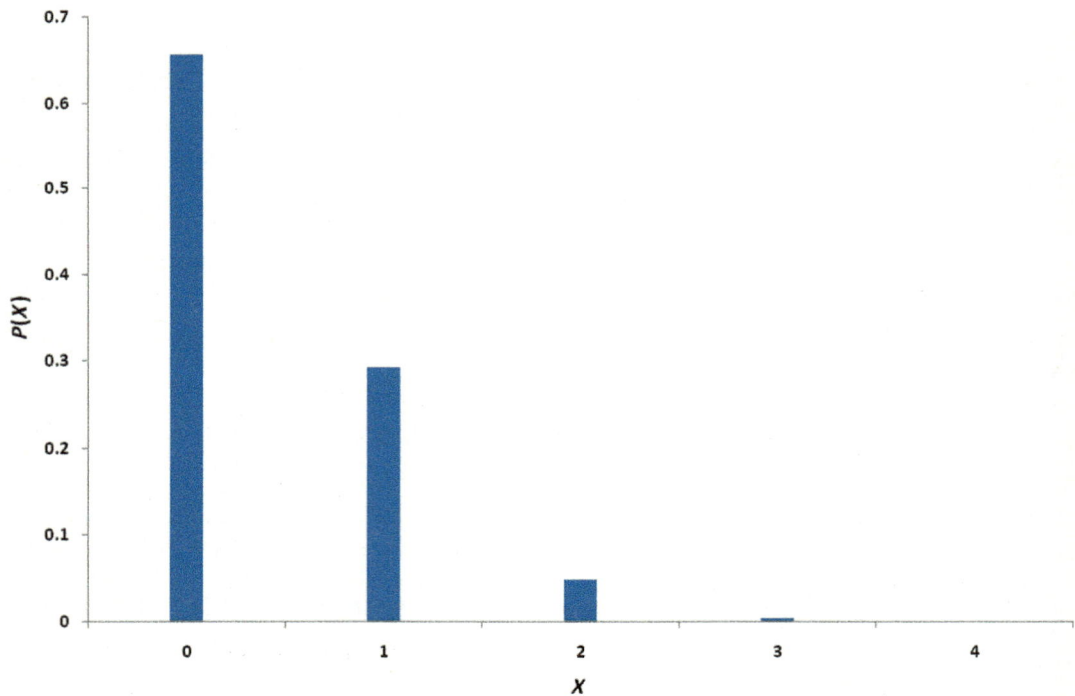

The shape of a binomial probability distribution depends on the values of n and π. Whenever $\pi = 0.5$, the binomial distribution is symmetrical, regardless of how large or small the value of n. When $\pi \neq 0.5$, the distribution is skewed. The closer π is to 0.5 and the larger the number of observations, n, the less skewed the distribution becomes. For example, the distribution of the number of tagged order forms is highly right skewed because $\pi = 0.1$ and $n = 4$ (see Figure 5.3).

FIGURE 5.3

Histogram of the binomial probability distribution with $n = 4$ and $\pi = 0.1$

Observe from Figure 5.3 that unlike the histogram for continuous variables in Section 2.6, the bars for the values are very thin, and there is a large gap between each pair of values. That is because the histogram represents a discrete variable. (Theoretically, the bars should have no width. They should be vertical lines.)

The mean (or expected value) of the binomial distribution is equal to the product of n and π. Instead of using Equation (5.1) on page 213 to compute the mean of the probability distribution, you can also use Equation (5.12) to compute the mean for variables that follow the binomial distribution.

Discrete Probability Distributions   **195**

> **MEAN OF THE BINOMIAL DISTRIBUTION**
>
> The mean, μ, of the binomial distribution is equal to the sample size, n, multiplied by the probability of an event of interest, π.
>
> $$\mu = E(X) = n\pi \qquad (5.12)$$

On the average, over the long run, you theoretically expect $\mu = E(X) = n\pi = (4)(0.1) = 0.4$ tagged order form in a sample of four orders.

The standard deviation of the binomial distribution can be calculated using Equation (5.13).

> **STANDARD DEVIATION OF THE BINOMIAL DISTRIBUTION**
>
> $$\sigma = \sqrt{\sigma^2} = \sqrt{Var(X)} = \sqrt{n\pi(1 - \pi)} \qquad (5.13)$$

The standard deviation of the number of tagged order forms is

$$\sigma = \sqrt{4(0.1)(0.9)} = 0.60$$

You get the same result if you use Equation (5.3) on page 214.

Example 5.4 applies the binomial distribution to service at a fast-food restaurant.

EXAMPLE 5.4

Computing Binomial Probabilities

Accuracy in taking orders at a drive-through window is important for fast-food chains. Periodically, *QSR Magazine* (data extracted from **http://www.qsrmagazine.com/reports/drive-thru_time_study/2009/2009_charts/whats_your_preferred_way_to_order_fast_food.html**) publishes the results of its surveys. Accuracy is measured as the percentage of orders that are filled correctly. Recently, the percentage of orders filled correctly at Wendy's was approximately 89%. Suppose that you go to the drive-through window at Wendy's and place an order. Two friends of yours independently place orders at the drive-through window at the same Wendy's. What are the probabilities that all three, that none of the three, and that at least two of the three orders will be filled correctly? What are the mean and standard deviation of the binomial distribution for the number of orders filled correctly?

SOLUTION Because there are three orders and the probability of a correct order is 0.89, $n = 3$ and $\pi = 0.89$ Using Equations (5.12) and (5.13),

$$\mu = E(X) = n\pi = 3(0.89) = 2.67$$
$$\sigma = \sqrt{\sigma^2} = \sqrt{Var(X)} = \sqrt{n\pi(1 - \pi)}$$
$$= \sqrt{3(0.89)(0.11)}$$
$$= \sqrt{0.2937} = 0.5419$$

Using Equation (5.11) on page 222,

$$P(X = 3 \mid n = 3, \pi = 0.89) = \frac{3!}{3!(3 - 3)!}(0.89)^3(1 - 0.89)^{3-3}$$
$$= \frac{3!}{3!(3 - 3)!}(0.89)^3(0.11)^0$$
$$= 1(0.89)(0.89)(0.89)(1) = 0.7050$$

$$P(X=0 \mid n=3, \pi=0.89) = \frac{3!}{0!(3-0)!}(0.89)^0(1-0.89)^{3-0}$$

$$= \frac{3!}{0!(3-0)!}(0.89)^0(0.11)^3$$

$$= 1(1)(0.11)(0.11)(0.11) = 0.0013$$

$$P(X=2 \mid n=3, \pi=0.89) = \frac{3!}{2!(3-2)!}(0.89)^2(1-0.89)^{3-2}$$

$$= \frac{3!}{2!(3-2)!}(0.89)^2(0.11)^1$$

$$= 3(0.89)(0.89)(0.11) = 0.2614$$

$$P(X \geq 2) = P(X=2) + P(X=3)$$

$$= 0.2614 + 0.7050$$

$$= 0.9664$$

The mean number of orders filled correctly in a sample of three orders is 2.67, and the standard deviation is 0.5419. The probability that all three orders are filled correctly is 0.7050, or 70.50%. The probability that none of the orders are filled correctly is 0.0013, or 0.13%. The probability that at least two orders are filled correctly is 0.9664, or 96.64%.

In this section, you have been introduced to the binomial distribution. The binomial distribution is an important mathematical model in many business situations.

Problems for Section 5.3

LEARNING THE BASICS

5.18 If $n = 5$ and $\pi = 0.40$, what is the probability that
a. $X = 4$?
b. $X \leq 3$?
c. $X < 2$?
d. $X > 1$?

5.19 Determine the following:
a. For $n = 4$ and $\pi = 0.12$, what is $P(X = 0)$?
b. For $n = 10$ and $\pi = 0.40$, what is $P(X = 9)$?
c. For $n = 10$ and $\pi = 0.50$, what is $P(X = 8)$?
d. For $n = 6$ and $\pi = 0.83$, what is $P(X = 5)$?

5.20 Determine the mean and standard deviation of the random variable X in each of the following binomial distributions:
a. $n = 4$ and $\pi = 0.10$
b. $n = 4$ and $\pi = 0.40$
c. $n = 5$ and $\pi = 0.80$
d. $n = 3$ and $\pi = 0.50$

APPLYING THE CONCEPTS

5.21 The increase or decrease in the price of a stock between the beginning and the end of a trading day is assumed to be an equally likely random event. What is the probability that a stock will show an increase in its closing price on five consecutive days?

5.22 The U.S. Department of Transportation reported that in 2009, Southwest led all domestic airlines in on-time arrivals for domestic flights, with a rate of 0.825. Using the binomial distribution, what is the probability that in the next six flights
a. four flights will be on time?
b. all six flights will be on time?
c. at least four flights will be on time?
d. What are the mean and standard deviation of the number of on-time arrivals?
e. What assumptions do you need to make in (a) through (c)?

5.23 A student is taking a multiple-choice exam in which each question has four choices. Assume that the student has no knowledge of the correct answers to any of the questions. She has decided on a strategy in which she will place four balls (marked $A, B, C,$ and D) into a box. She randomly selects one ball for each question and replaces the ball in the box. The marking on the ball will determine her answer to the question. There are five multiple-choice questions on the exam. What is the probability that she will get
a. five questions correct?
b. at least four questions correct?
c. no questions correct?
d. no more than two questions correct?

5.24 Investment advisors agree that near-retirees, defined as people aged 55 to 65, should have balanced portfolios. Most advisors suggest that the near-retirees have no more than 50% of their investments in stocks. However, during the huge decline in the stock market in 2008, 22% of near-retirees had 90% or more of their investments in stocks (P. Regnier, "What I Learned from the Crash," *Money*, May 2009, p. 114). Suppose you have a random sample of 10 people who would have been labeled as near-retirees in 2008. What is the probability that during 2008
a. none had 90% or more of their investment in stocks?
b. exactly one had 90% or more of his or her investment in stocks?
c. two or fewer had 90% or more of their investment in stocks?
d. three or more had 90% or more of their investment in stocks?

5.25 When a customer places an order with Rudy's On-Line Office Supplies, a computerized accounting information system (AIS) automatically checks to see if the customer has exceeded his or her credit limit. Past records indicate that the probability of customers exceeding their credit limit is 0.05. Suppose that, on a given day, 20 customers place orders. Assume that the number of customers that the AIS detects as having exceeded their credit limit is distributed as a binomial random variable.
a. What are the mean and standard deviation of the number of customers exceeding their credit limits?
b. What is the probability that zero customers will exceed their limits?
c. What is the probability that one customer will exceed his or her limit?
d. What is the probability that two or more customers will exceed their limits?

SELF Test 5.26 In Example 5.4 on page 225, you and two friends decided to go to Wendy's. Now, suppose that instead you go to Popeye's, which last month filled approximately 84.8% of orders correctly. What is the probability that
a. all three orders will be filled correctly?
b. none of the three will be filled correctly?
c. at least two of the three will be filled correctly?
d. What are the mean and standard deviation of the binomial distribution used in (a) through (c)? Interpret these values.

5.27 In Example 5.4 on page 225, you and two friends decided to go to Wendy's. Now, suppose that instead you go to McDonald's, which last month filled approximately 90.1% of the orders correctly. What is the probability that
a. all three orders will be filled correctly?
b. none of the three will be filled correctly?
c. at least two of the three will be filled correctly?
d. What are the mean and standard deviation of the binomial distribution used in (a) through (c)? Interpret these values.
e. Compare the result of (a) through (d) with those of Popeye's in Problem 5.26 and Wendy's in Example 5.4 on page 225.

5.4 Poisson Distribution

Many studies are based on counts of the times a particular event occurs in a given *area of opportunity*. An **area of opportunity** is a continuous unit or interval of time, volume, or any physical area in which there can be more than one occurrence of an event. Examples of variables that follow the Poisson distribution are the surface defects on a new refrigerator, the number of network failures in a day, the number of people arriving at a bank, and the number of fleas on the body of a dog. You can use the **Poisson distribution** to calculate probabilities in situations such as these if the following properties hold:

- You are interested in counting the number of times a particular event occurs in a given area of opportunity. The area of opportunity is defined by time, length, surface area, and so forth.
- The probability that an event occurs in a given area of opportunity is the same for all the areas of opportunity.
- The number of events that occur in one area of opportunity is independent of the number of events that occur in any other area of opportunity.
- The probability that two or more events will occur in an area of opportunity approaches zero as the area of opportunity becomes smaller.

Consider the number of customers arriving during the lunch hour at a bank located in the central business district in a large city. You are interested in the number of customers who arrive each minute. Does this situation match the four properties of the Poisson distribution given earlier? First, the *event* of interest is a customer arriving, and the *given area of opportunity* is defined as a one-minute interval. Will zero customers arrive, one customer arrive, two customers arrive, and so on? Second, it is reasonable to assume that the probability that a customer arrives during a particular one-minute interval is the same as the probability for all the other one-minute intervals. Third, the arrival of one customer in any one-minute interval has no effect on (i.e., is independent of) the arrival of any other customer in any other one-minute interval. Finally, the probability that two or more customers will arrive in a given time period approaches zero as the time interval becomes small. For example, the probability is virtually zero that two customers will arrive in a time interval of 0.01 second. Thus, you can use the Poisson distribution to determine probabilities involving the number of customers arriving at the bank in a one-minute time interval during the lunch hour.

The Poisson distribution has one characteristic, called λ (the Greek lowercase letter *lambda*), which is the mean or expected number of events per unit. The variance of a Poisson distribution is also equal to λ, and the standard deviation is equal to $\sqrt{\lambda}$. The number of events, X, of the Poisson random variable ranges from 0 to infinity (∞).

Equation (5.14) is the mathematical expression for the Poisson distribution for computing the probability of $X = x$ events, given that λ events are expected.

POISSON DISTRIBUTION

$$P(X = x \mid \lambda) = \frac{e^{-\lambda}\lambda^x}{x!} \tag{5.14}$$

where

$P(X = x \mid \lambda)$ = the probability that $X = x$ events in an area of opportunity given λ

λ = expected number of events

e = mathematical constant approximated by 2.71828

x = number of events ($x = 0, 1, 2, \ldots, \infty$)

To illustrate an application of the Poisson distribution, suppose that the mean number of customers who arrive per minute at the bank during the noon-to-1 P.M. hour is equal to 3.0. What is the probability that in a given minute, exactly two customers will arrive? And what is the probability that more than two customers will arrive in a given minute?

Using Equation (5.14) and $\lambda = 3$, the probability that in a given minute exactly two customers will arrive is

$$P(X = 2 \mid \lambda = 3) = \frac{e^{-3.0}(3.0)^2}{2!} = \frac{9}{(2.71828)^3(2)} = 0.2240$$

To determine the probability that in any given minute more than two customers will arrive,

$$P(X > 2) = P(X = 3) + P(X = 4) + \cdots + P(X = \infty)$$

Because in a probability distribution, all the probabilities must sum to 1, the terms on the right side of the equation $P(X > 2)$ also represent the complement of the probability that X is less than or equal to 2 [i.e., $1 - P(X \leq 2)$]. Thus,

$$P(X > 2) = 1 - P(X \leq 2) = 1 - [P(X = 0) + P(X = 1) + P(X = 2)]$$

Now, using Equation (5.14),

$$P(X > 2) = 1 - \left[\frac{e^{-3.0}(3.0)^0}{0!} + \frac{e^{-3.0}(3.0)^1}{1!} + \frac{e^{-3.0}(3.0)^2}{2!}\right]$$

$$= 1 - [0.0498 + 0.1494 + 0.2240]$$

$$= 1 - 0.4232 = 0.5768$$

Thus, there is a 57.68% chance that more than two customers will arrive in the same minute.

Discrete Probability Distributions   199

Computing Poisson probabilities can be tedious. Figure 5.4 shows how Poisson probabilities can be computed by Excel (left) and Minitab (right). Poisson probabilities can also be looked up in a table of probabilities, as discussed in the **Poisson** online topic available on this book's companion website. (See Appendix C to learn how to access online topics.)

FIGURE 5.4

Excel worksheet and Minitab results for computing Poisson probabilities with $\lambda = 3$

	A	B	C
1	Poisson Probabilities		
2			
3		Data	
4	Mean/Expected number of events of interest:		3
5			
6	Poisson Probabilities Table		
7	X	P(X)	
8	0	0.0498	=POISSON(A8, $E$4, FALSE)
9	1	0.1494	=POISSON(A9, $E$4, FALSE)
10	2	0.2240	=POISSON(A10, $E$4, FALSE)
11	3	0.2240	=POISSON(A11, $E$4, FALSE)
12	4	0.1680	=POISSON(A12, $E$4, FALSE)
13	5	0.1008	=POISSON(A13, $E$4, FALSE)
14	6	0.0504	=POISSON(A14, $E$4, FALSE)
15	7	0.0216	=POISSON(A15, $E$4, FALSE)
16	8	0.0081	=POISSON(A16, $E$4, FALSE)
17	9	0.0027	=POISSON(A17, $E$4, FALSE)
18	10	0.0008	=POISSON(A18, $E$4, FALSE)
19	11	0.0002	=POISSON(A19, $E$4, FALSE)
20	12	0.0001	=POISSON(A20, $E$4, FALSE)
21	13	0.0000	=POISSON(A21, $E$4, FALSE)
22	14	0.0000	=POISSON(A22, $E$4, FALSE)
23	15	0.0000	=POISSON(A23, $E$4, FALSE)
24	16	0.0000	=POISSON(A24, $E$4, FALSE)
25	17	0.0000	=POISSON(A25, $E$4, FALSE)
26	18	0.0000	=POISSON(A26, $E$4, FALSE)
27	19	0.0000	=POISSON(A27, $E$4, FALSE)
28	20	0.0000	=POISSON(A28, $E$4, FALSE)

Poisson with mean = 3

x	P(X = x)
0	0.049787
1	0.149361
2	0.224042
3	0.224042
4	0.168031
5	0.100819
6	0.050409
7	0.021604
8	0.008102
9	0.002701
10	0.000810
11	0.000221
12	0.000055
13	0.000013
14	0.000003
15	0.000001

EXAMPLE 5.5

Computing Poisson Probabilities

The number of work-related injuries per month in a manufacturing plant is known to follow a Poisson distribution with a mean of 2.5 work-related injuries a month. What is the probability that in a given month, no work-related injuries occur? That at least one work-related injury occurs?

SOLUTION Using Equation (5.14) on page 228 with $\lambda = 2.5$ (or Excel, Minitab, or a Poisson table lookup), the probability that in a given month no work-related injuries occur is

$$P(X = 0 | \lambda = 2.5) = \frac{e^{-2.5}(2.5)^0}{0!} = \frac{1}{(2.71828)^{2.5}(1)} = 0.0821$$

The probability that there will be no work-related injuries in a given month is 0.0821, or 8.21%. Thus,

$$P(X \geq 1) = 1 - P(X = 0)$$
$$= 1 - 0.0821$$
$$= 0.9179$$

The probability that there will be at least one work-related injury is 0.9179, or 91.79%.

Problems for Section 5.4

LEARNING THE BASICS

5.28 Assume a Poisson distribution.
a. If $\lambda = 2.5$, find $P(X = 2)$.
b. If $\lambda = 8.0$, find $P(X = 8)$.
c. If $\lambda = 0.5$, find $P(X = 1)$.
d. If $\lambda = 3.7$, find $P(X = 0)$.

5.29 Assume a Poisson distribution.
a. If $\lambda = 2.0$, find $P(X \geq 2)$.
b. If $\lambda = 8.0$, find $P(X \geq 3)$.
c. If $\lambda = 0.5$, find $P(X \leq 1)$.
d. If $\lambda = 4.0$, find $P(X \geq 1)$.
e. If $\lambda = 5.0$, find $P(X \leq 3)$.

5.30 Assume a Poisson distribution with $\lambda = 5.0$. What is the probability that
a. $X = 1$?
b. $X < 1$?
c. $X > 1$?
d. $X \leq 1$?

APPLYING THE CONCEPTS

5.31 Assume that the number of network errors experienced in a day on a local area network (LAN) is distributed as a Poisson random variable. The mean number of network errors experienced in a day is 2.4. What is the probability that in any given day
a. zero network errors will occur?
b. exactly one network error will occur?
c. two or more network errors will occur?
d. fewer than three network errors will occur?

SELF Test 5.32 The quality control manager of Marilyn's Cookies is inspecting a batch of chocolate-chip cookies that has just been baked. If the production process is in control, the mean number of chip parts per cookie is 6.0. What is the probability that in any particular cookie being inspected
a. fewer than five chip parts will be found?
b. exactly five chip parts will be found?
c. five or more chip parts will be found?
d. either four or five chip parts will be found?

5.33 Refer to Problem 5.32. How many cookies in a batch of 100 should the manager expect to discard if company policy requires that all chocolate-chip cookies sold have at least four chocolate-chip parts?

5.34 The U.S. Department of Transportation maintains statistics for mishandled bags per 1,000 airline passengers. In the first nine months of 2009, airlines had mishandled 3.89 bags per 1,000 passengers. What is the probability that in the next 1,000 passengers, airlines will have

a. no mishandled bags?
b. at least one mishandled bag?
c. at least two mishandled bags?

5.35 The U.S. Department of Transportation maintains statistics for consumer complaints per 100,000 airline passengers. In the first nine months of 2009, consumer complaints were 0.99 per 100,000 passengers. What is the probability that in the next 100,000 passengers, there will be
a. no complaints?
b. at least one complaint?
c. at least two complaints?

5.36 Based on past experience, it is assumed that the number of flaws per foot in rolls of grade 2 paper follows a Poisson distribution with a mean of 1 flaw per 5 feet of paper (0.2 flaw per foot). What is the probability that in a
a. 1-foot roll, there will be at least 2 flaws?
b. 12-foot roll, there will be at least 1 flaw?
c. 50-foot roll, there will be more than or equal to 5 flaws and fewer than or equal to 15 flaws?

5.37 J.D. Power and Associates calculates and publishes various statistics concerning car quality. The initial quality score measures the number of problems per new car sold. For 2009 model cars, Ford had 1.02 problems per car and Dodge had 1.34 problems per car (data extracted from S. Carty, "U.S. Autos Power Forward with Gains in Quality Survey," *USA Today*, June 23, 2009, p. 3B). Let the random variable X be equal to the number of problems with a newly purchased 2009 Ford.
a. What assumptions must be made in order for X to be distributed as a Poisson random variable? Are these assumptions reasonable?

Making the assumptions as in (a), if you purchased a 2009 Ford, what is the probability that the new car will have
b. zero problems?
c. two or fewer problems?
d. Give an operational definition for *problem*. Why is the operational definition important in interpreting the initial quality score?

5.38 Refer to Problem 5.37. If you purchased a 2009 Dodge, what is the probability that the new car will have
a. zero problems?
b. two or fewer problems?
c. Compare your answers in (a) and (b) to those for the Ford in Problem 5.37 (b) and (c).

5.39 Refer to Problem 5.37. Another article reported that in 2008, Ford had 1.12 problems per car and Dodge had 1.41 problems per car (data extracted from S. Carty, "Ford

Moves Up in Quality Survey," *USA Today*, June 5, 2008, p. 3B). If you purchased a 2008 Ford, what is the probability that the new car will have
a. zero problems?
b. two or fewer problems?
c. Compare your answers in (a) and (b) to those for the 2009 Ford in Problem 5.37 (b) and (c).

5.40 Refer to Problem 5.39. If you purchased a 2008 Dodge, what is the probability that the new car will have
a. zero problems?
b. two or fewer problems?
c. Compare your answers in (a) and (b) to those for the 2009 Dodge in Problem 5.38 (a) and (b).

5.41 A toll-free phone number is available from 9 A.M. to 9 P.M. for your customers to register complaints about a product purchased from your company. Past history indicates that an average of 0.8 calls is received per minute.
a. What properties must be true about the situation described here in order to use the Poisson distribution to calculate probabilities concerning the number of phone calls received in a one-minute period?

Assuming that this situation matches the properties discussed in (a), what is the probability that during a one-minute period
b. zero phone calls will be received?
c. three or more phone calls will be received?
d. What is the maximum number of phone calls that will be received in a one-minute period 99.99% of the time?

5.5 Hypergeometric Distribution

Both the binomial distribution and the **hypergeometric distribution** are concerned with the number of events of interest in a sample containing n observations. One of the differences in these two probability distributions is in the way the samples are selected. For the binomial distribution, the sample data are selected *with* replacement from a *finite* population or *without* replacement from an *infinite* population. Thus, the probability of an event of interest, π, is constant over all observations, and the outcome of any particular observation is independent of any other. For the hypergeometric distribution, the sample data are selected *without* replacement from a *finite* population. Thus, the outcome of one observation is dependent on the outcomes of the previous observations.

Consider a population of size N. Let A represent the total number of events of interest in the population. The hypergeometric distribution is then used to find the probability of X events of interest in a sample of size n, selected without replacement. Equation (5.15) represents the mathematical expression of the hypergeometric distribution for finding x events of interest, given a knowledge of n, N, and A.

HYPERGEOMETRIC DISTRIBUTION

$$P(X = x \mid n, N, A) = \frac{\binom{A}{x}\binom{N-A}{n-x}}{\binom{N}{n}} \qquad (5.15)$$

where

$P(X = x \mid n, N, A)$ = the probability of x events of interest, given knowledge of n, N, and A

n = sample size

N = population size

A = number of events of interest in the population

$N - A$ = number of events that are not of interest in the population

$$x = \text{number of events of interest in the sample}$$

$$\binom{A}{x} = {}_AC_x \text{ [see Equation (5.10) on page 221]}$$

$$x \leq A$$

$$x \leq n$$

Because the number of events of interest in the sample, represented by x, cannot be greater than the number of events of interest in the population, A, nor can x be greater than the sample size, n, the range of the hypergeometric random variable is limited to the sample size or to the number of events of interest in the population, whichever is smaller.

Equation (5.16) defines the mean of the hypergeometric distribution, and Equation (5.17) defines the standard deviation.

MEAN OF THE HYPERGEOMETRIC DISTRIBUTION

$$\mu = E(X) = \frac{nA}{N} \tag{5.16}$$

STANDARD DEVIATION OF THE HYPERGEOMETRIC DISTRIBUTION

$$\sigma = \sqrt{\frac{nA(N-A)}{N^2}}\sqrt{\frac{N-n}{N-1}} \tag{5.17}$$

In Equation (5.17), the expression $\sqrt{\frac{N-n}{N-1}}$ is a **finite population correction factor** that results from sampling without replacement from a finite population.

To illustrate the hypergeometric distribution, suppose that you are forming a team of 8 managers from different departments within your company. Your company has a total of 30 managers, and 10 of these people are from the finance department. If you are to randomly select members of the team, what is the probability that the team will contain 2 managers from the finance department? Here, the population of $N = 30$ managers within the company is finite. In addition, $A = 10$ are from the finance department. A team of $n = 8$ members is to be selected.

Using Equation (5.15),

$$P(X = 2 \mid n = 8, N = 30, A = 10) = \frac{\binom{10}{2}\binom{20}{6}}{\binom{30}{8}}$$

$$= \frac{\left(\frac{10!}{2!(8)!}\right)\left(\frac{(20)!}{(6)!(14)!}\right)}{\left(\frac{30!}{8!(22)!}\right)}$$

$$= 0.298$$

Thus, the probability that the team will contain two members from the finance department is 0.298, or 29.8%.

Computing hypergeometric probabilities can be tedious, especially as N gets large. Figure 5.5 shows how the hypergeometric probabilities for the team formation example can be computed by Excel (left) and Minitab (right).

FIGURE 5.5

Excel worksheet and Minitab results for the team member example

	A	B
1	Hypergeometric Probabilities	
2		
3	Data	
4	Sample size	8
5	No. of events of interest in population	10
6	Population size	30
7		
8	Hypergeometric Probabilities Table	
9	X	P(X)
10	0	0.0215 =HYPGEOMDIST(A10, $B$4, $B$5, $B$6)
11	1	0.1324 =HYPGEOMDIST(A11, $B$4, $B$5, $B$6)
12	2	0.2980 =HYPGEOMDIST(A12, $B$4, $B$5, $B$6)
13	3	0.3179 =HYPGEOMDIST(A13, $B$4, $B$5, $B$6)
14	4	0.1738 =HYPGEOMDIST(A14, $B$4, $B$5, $B$6)
15	5	0.0491 =HYPGEOMDIST(A15, $B$4, $B$5, $B$6)
16	6	0.0068 =HYPGEOMDIST(A16, $B$4, $B$5, $B$6)
17	7	0.0004 =HYPGEOMDIST(A17, $B$4, $B$5, $B$6)
18	8	0.0000 =HYPGEOMDIST(A18, $B$4, $B$5, $B$6)

Probability Density Function

Hypergeometric with N = 30, M = 10, and n = 8

x	P(X = x)
0	0.021523
1	0.132447
2	0.298005
3	0.317872
4	0.173836
5	0.049083
6	0.006817
7	0.000410
8	0.000008

Example 5.6 shows an application of the hypergeometric distribution in portfolio selection.

EXAMPLE 5.6

Computing Hypergeometric Probabilities

You are a financial analyst facing the task of selecting bond mutual funds to purchase for a client's portfolio. You have narrowed the funds to be selected to ten different funds. In order to diversify your client's portfolio, you will recommend the purchase of four different funds. Six of the funds are short-term corporate bond funds. What is the probability that of the four funds selected, three are short-term corporate bond funds?

SOLUTION Using Equation (5.15) with $X = 3, n = 4, N = 10,$ and $A = 6,$

$$P(X = 3 \mid n = 4, N = 10, A = 6) = \frac{\binom{6}{3}\binom{4}{1}}{\binom{10}{4}}$$

$$= \frac{\left(\frac{6!}{3!(3)!}\right)\left(\frac{(4)!}{(1)!(3)!}\right)}{\left(\frac{10!}{4!(6)!}\right)}$$

$$= 0.3810$$

The probability that of the four funds selected, three are short-term corporate bond funds is 0.3810, or 38.10%

Problems for Section 5.5

LEARNING THE BASICS

5.42 Determine the following:
a. If $n = 4, N = 10$, and $A = 5$, find $P(X = 3)$.
b. If $n = 4, N = 6$, and $A = 3$, find $P(X = 1)$.
c. If $n = 5, N = 12$, and $A = 3$, find $P(X = 0)$.
d. If $n = 3, N = 10$, and $A = 3$, find $P(X = 3)$.

5.43 Referring to Problem 5.42, compute the mean and standard deviation for the hypergeometric distributions described in (a) through (d).

APPLYING THE CONCEPTS

5.44 An auditor for the Internal Revenue Service is selecting a sample of 6 tax returns for an audit. If 2 or more of these returns are "improper," the entire population of 100 tax returns will be audited. What is the probability that the entire population will be audited if the true number of improper returns in the population is
a. 25?
b. 30?
c. 5?
d. 10?
e. Discuss the differences in your results, depending on the true number of improper returns in the population.

5.45 The dean of a business school wishes to form an executive committee of 5 from among the 40 tenured faculty members at the school. The selection is to be random, and at the school there are 8 tenured faculty members in accounting. What is the probability that the committee will contain
a. none of them?
b. at least 1 of them?
c. not more than 1 of them?
d. What is your answer to (a) if the committee consists of 7 members?

5.46 From an inventory of 30 cars being shipped to a local automobile dealer, 4 are SUVs. What is the probability that if 4 cars arrive at a particular dealership,
a. all 4 are SUVs?
b. none are SUVs?
c. at least 1 is an SUV?
d. What are your answers to (a) through (c) if 6 cars being shipped are SUVs?

5.47 A state lottery is conducted in which 6 winning numbers are selected from a total of 54 numbers. What is the probability that if 6 numbers are randomly selected,
a. all 6 numbers will be winning numbers?
b. 5 numbers will be winning numbers?
c. none of the numbers will be winning numbers?
d. What are your answers to (a) through (c) if the 6 winning numbers are selected from a total of 40 numbers?

5.48 In Example 5.6 on page 233, a financial analyst was facing the task of selecting bond mutual funds to purchase for a client's portfolio. Suppose that the number of funds had been narrowed to 12 funds instead of the ten funds (still with 6 short-term corporate funds) in Example 5.6. What is the probability that of the four funds selected,
a. exactly 1 is a short-term corporate bond funds?
b. at least 1 is a short-term corporate bond fund?
c. three are short-term corporate bond funds?
d. Compare the results of (c) to that of Example 5.6.

5.6 Online Topic: Using the Poisson Distribution to Approximate the Binomial Distribution

Under certain circumstances, you can use the Poisson distribution to approximate the binomial distribution. To study this topic, read the Section 5.6 online topic file that is available on this book's companion website. (See Appendix C to learn how to access the online topic files.)

USING STATISTICS @ Saxon Home Improvement Revisited

In the Saxon Home Improvement scenario at the beginning of this chapter, you were an accountant for the Saxon Home Improvement Company. The company's accounting information system automatically reviews order forms from online customers for possible mistakes. Any questionable invoices are tagged and included in a daily exceptions report. Knowing that the probability that an order will be tagged is 0.10, you were able to use the binomial distribution to determine the chance of finding a certain number of tagged forms in a sample of size four. There was a 65.6% chance that none of the forms would be tagged, a 29.2% chance that one would be tagged, and a 5.2% chance that two or more would be tagged. You were also able to determine that, on average, you would expect 0.4 forms to be tagged, and the standard deviation of the number of tagged order forms would be 0.6. Now that you have learned the mechanics of using the binomial distribution for a known probability of 0.10 and a sample size of four, you will be able to apply the same approach to any given probability and sample size. Thus, you will be able to make inferences about the online ordering process and, more importantly, evaluate any changes or proposed changes to the process.

SUMMARY

In this chapter, you have studied mathematical expectation and three important discrete probability distributions: the binomial, Poisson, and hypergeometric distributions. In the next chapter, you will study several important continuous distributions including the normal distribution.

To help decide what probability distribution to use for a particular situation, you need to ask the following questions:

- Is there a fixed number of observations, n, each of which is classified as an event of interest or not an event of interest? Or is there an area of opportunity? If there is a fixed number of observations, n, each of which is classified as an event of interest or not an event of interest, you use the binomial or hypergeometric distribution. If there is an area of opportunity, you use the Poisson distribution.
- In deciding whether to use the binomial or hypergeometric distribution, is the probability of an event of interest constant over all trials? If yes, you can use the binomial distribution. If no, you can use the hypergeometric distribution.

KEY EQUATIONS

Expected Value, μ, of a Discrete Random Variable

$$\mu = E(X) = \sum_{i=1}^{N} x_i P(X = x_i) \tag{5.1}$$

Variance of a Discrete Random Variable

$$\sigma^2 = \sum_{i=1}^{N} [x_i - E(X)]^2 P(X = x_i) \tag{5.2}$$

Standard Deviation of a Discrete Random Variable

$$\sigma = \sqrt{\sigma^2} = \sqrt{\sum_{i=1}^{N} [x_i - E(X)]^2 P(X = x_i)} \tag{5.3}$$

Covariance

$$\sigma_{XY} = \sum_{i=1}^{N} [x_i - E(X)][y_i - E(Y)] P(x_i y_i) \tag{5.4}$$

Expected Value of the Sum of Two Random Variables

$$E(X + Y) = E(X) + E(Y) \tag{5.5}$$

Variance of the Sum of Two Random Variables

$$Var(X + Y) = \sigma^2_{X+Y} = \sigma^2_X + \sigma^2_Y + 2\sigma_{XY} \tag{5.6}$$

Standard Deviation of the Sum of Two Random Variables

$$\sigma_{X+Y} = \sqrt{\sigma^2_{X+Y}} \tag{5.7}$$

Portfolio Expected Return

$$E(P) = wE(X) + (1 - w)E(Y) \qquad (5.8)$$

Portfolio Risk

$$\sigma_p = \sqrt{w^2\sigma_X^2 + (1-w)^2\sigma_Y^2 + 2w(1-w)\sigma_{XY}} \qquad (5.9)$$

Combinations

$$_nC_x = \frac{n!}{x!(n-x)!} \qquad (5.10)$$

Binomial Distribution

$$P(X = x \mid n, \pi) = \frac{n!}{x!(n-x)!}\pi^x(1-\pi)^{n-x} \qquad (5.11)$$

Mean of the Binomial Distribution

$$\mu = E(X) = n\pi \qquad (5.12)$$

Standard Deviation of the Binomial Distribution

$$\sigma = \sqrt{\sigma^2} = \sqrt{Var(X)} = \sqrt{n\pi(1-\pi)} \qquad (5.13)$$

Poisson Distribution

$$P(X = x \mid \lambda) = \frac{e^{-\lambda}\lambda^x}{x!} \qquad (5.14)$$

Hypergeometric Distribution

$$P(X = x \mid n, N, A) = \frac{\binom{A}{x}\binom{N-A}{n-x}}{\binom{N}{n}} \qquad (5.15)$$

Mean of the Hypergeometric Distribution

$$\mu = E(X) = \frac{nA}{N} \qquad (5.16)$$

Standard Deviation of the Hypergeometric Distribution

$$\sigma = \sqrt{\frac{nA(N-A)}{N^2}}\sqrt{\frac{N-n}{N-1}} \qquad (5.17)$$

KEY TERMS

area of opportunity
binomial distribution
covariance, σ_{XY}
expected value
expected value, μ, of a discrete random variable
expected value of the sum of two random variables
finite population correction factor
hypergeometric distribution
mathematical model
Poisson distribution
portfolio
portfolio expected return
portfolio risk
probability distribution for a discrete random variable
rule of combinations
standard deviation of a discrete random variable
standard deviation of the sum of two random variables
variance of a discrete random variable
variance of the sum of two random variables

CHAPTER REVIEW PROBLEMS

CHECKING YOUR UNDERSTANDING

5.49 What is the meaning of the expected value of a probability distribution?

5.50 What are the four properties that must be present in order to use the binomial distribution?

5.51 What are the four properties that must be present in order to use the Poisson distribution?

5.52 When do you use the hypergeometric distribution instead of the binomial distribution?

APPLYING THE CONCEPTS

5.53 Darwin Head, a 35-year-old sawmill worker, won $1 million and a Chevrolet Malibu Hybrid by scoring 15 goals within 24 seconds at the Vancouver Canucks National Hockey League game (B. Ziemer, "Darwin Evolves into an Instant Millionaire," *Vancouver Sun*, February 28, 2008, p. 1). Head said he would use the money to pay off his mortgage and provide for his children, and he had no plans to quit his job. The contest was part of the Chevrolet Malibu Million Dollar Shootout, sponsored by General Motors Canadian Division. Did GM-Canada risk the $1 million?

No! GM-Canada purchased event insurance from a company specializing in promotions at sporting events such as a half-court basketball shot or a hole-in-one giveaway at the local charity golf outing. The event insurance company estimates the probability of a contestant winning the contest, and for a modest charge, insures the event. The promoters pay the insurance premium but take on no added risk as the insurance company will make the large payout in the unlikely event that a contestant wins. To see how it works, suppose that the insurance company estimates that the probability a contestant would win a Million Dollar Shootout is 0.001, and that the insurance company charges $4,000.

a. Calculate the expected value of the profit made by the insurance company.
b. Many call this kind of situation a win–win opportunity for the insurance company and the promoter. Do you agree? Explain.

5.54 Between 1896 when the Dow Jones Index was created and 2009, the index rose in 64% of the years (data extracted from M. Hulbert, "What the Past Can't Tell Investors," *The New York Times*, January 3, 2010, p. BU2). Based on this information, and assuming a binomial distribution, what do you think is the probability that the stock market will rise
a. next year?
b. the year after next?
c. in four of the next five years?
d. in none of the next five years?
e. For this situation, what assumption of the binomial distribution might not be valid?

5.55 In late 2007, it was reported that 79% of U.S. adults owned a cell phone (data extracted from E. C. Baig, "Tips Help Navigate Tech-Buying Maze," *USA Today*, November 28, 2007, p. 5B). Suppose that by the end of 2009, that percentage was 85%. If a sample of 10 U.S. adults is selected, what is the probability that
a. 8 own a cell phone?
b. at least 8 own a cell phone?
c. all 10 own a cell phone?
d. If you selected the sample in a particular geographical area and found that none of the 10 respondents owned a cell phone, what conclusion might you reach about whether the percentage of cell phone owners in this area was 85%?

5.56 One theory concerning the Dow Jones Industrial Average is that it is likely to increase during U.S. presidential election years. From 1964 through 2008, the Dow Jones Industrial Average increased in 9 of the 12 U.S. presidential election years. Assuming that this indicator is a random event with no predictive value, you would expect that the indicator would be correct 50% of the time.
a. What is the probability of the Dow Jones Industrial Average increasing in 9 or more of the 12 U.S. presidential election years if the probability of an increase in the Dow Jones Industrial Average is 0.50?
b. What is the probability that the Dow Jones Industrial Average will increase in 9 or more of the 12 U.S. presidential election years if the probability of an increase in the Dow Jones Industrial Average in any year is 0.75?

5.57 Errors in a billing process often lead to customer dissatisfaction and ultimately hurt bottom-line profits. An article in *Quality Progress* (L. Tatikonda, "A Less Costly Billing Process," *Quality Progress*, January 2008, pp. 30–38) discussed a company where 40% of the bills prepared contained errors. If 10 bills are processed, what is the probability that
a. 0 bills will contain errors?
b. exactly 1 bill will contain an error?
c. 2 or more bills will contain errors?
d. What are the mean and the standard deviation of the probability distribution?

5.58 Refer to Problem 5.57. Suppose that a quality improvement initiative has reduced the percentage of bills containing errors to 20%. If 10 bills are processed, what is the probability that
a. 0 bills will contain errors?
b. exactly 1 bill will contain an error?
c. 2 or more bills will contain errors?
d. What are the mean and the standard deviation of the probability distribution?
e. Compare the results of (a) through (c) to those of Problem 5.57 (a) through (c).

5.59 A study by the Center for Financial Services Innovation showed that only 64% of U.S. income earners aged 15 and older had bank accounts (A. Carrns, "Banks Court a New Client," *The Wall Street Journal*, March 16, 2007, p. D1).
If a random sample of 20 U.S. income earners aged 15 and older is selected, what is the probability that
a. all 20 have bank accounts?
b. no more than 15 have bank accounts?
c. more than 10 have bank accounts?
d. What assumptions did you have to make to answer (a) through (c)?

5.60 One of the biggest frustrations for the consumer electronics industry is that customers are accustomed to returning goods for any reason (C. Lawton, "The War on Returns," *The Wall Street Journal*, May 8, 2008, pp. D1, D6). Recently, it was reported that returns for "no trouble found" were 68% of all the returns. Consider a sample of 20 customers who returned consumer electronics purchases. Use the binomial model to answer the following questions:
a. What is the expected value, or mean, of the binomial distribution?
b. What is the standard deviation of the binomial distribution?
c. What is the probability that 15 of the 20 customers made a return for "no trouble found"?
d. What is the probability that no more than 10 of the customers made a return for "no trouble found"?
e. What is the probability that 10 or more of the customers made a return for "no trouble found"?

5.61 Refer to Problem 5.60. In the same time period, 27% of the returns were for "buyer's remorse."
a. What is the expected value, or mean, of the binomial distribution?
b. What is the standard deviation of the binomial distribution?
c. What is the probability that none of the 20 customers made a return for "buyer's remorse"?
d. What is the probability that no more than 2 of the customers made a return for "buyer's remorse"?
e. What is the probability that 3 or more of the customers made a return for "buyer's remorse"?

5.62 One theory concerning the S&P 500 Index is that if it increases during the first five trading days of the year, it is likely to increase during the entire year. From 1950 through 2009, the S&P 500 Index had these early gains in 38 years. In 33 of these 38 years, the S&P 500 Index increased for the entire year. Assuming that this indicator is a random event with no predictive value, you would expect that the indicator would be correct 50% of the time. What is the probability of the S&P 500 Index increasing in 33 or more years if the true probability of an increase in the S&P 500 Index is
a. 0.50?
b. 0.70?
c. 0.90?
d. Based on the results of (a) through (c), what do you think is the probability that the S&P 500 Index will increase if there is an early gain in the first five trading days of the year? Explain.

5.63 *Spurious correlation* refers to the apparent relationship between variables that either have no true relationship or are related to other variables that have not been measured. One widely publicized stock market indicator in the United States that is an example of spurious correlation is the relationship between the winner of the National Football League Super Bowl and the performance of the Dow Jones Industrial Average in that year. The indicator states that when a team representing the National Football Conference wins the Super Bowl, the Dow Jones Industrial Average will increase in that year. When a team representing the American Football Conference wins the Super Bowl, the Dow Jones Industrial Average will decline in that year. Since the first Super Bowl was held in 1967 through 2009, the indicator has been correct 33 out of 43 times. Assuming that this indicator is a random event with no predictive value, you would expect that the indicator would be correct 50% of the time.
a. What is the probability that the indicator would be correct 33 or more times in 43 years?
b. What does this tell you about the usefulness of this indicator?

5.64 Approximately 300 million golf balls were lost in the United States in 2009. Assume that the number of golf balls lost in an 18-hole round is distributed as a Poisson random variable with a mean of 5 balls.

a. What assumptions need to be made so that the number of golf balls lost in an 18-hole round is distributed as a Poisson random variable?

Making the assumptions given in (a), what is the probability that
b. 0 balls will be lost in an 18-hole round?
c. 5 or fewer balls will be lost in an 18-hole round?
d. 6 or more balls will be lost in an 18-hole round?

5.65 According to a Virginia Tech survey, college students make an average of 11 cell phone calls per day. Moreover, 80% of the students surveyed indicated that their parents pay their cell phone expenses (J. Elliot, "Professor Researches Cell Phone Usage Among Students," **www.physorg.com**, February 26, 2007).
a. What distribution can you use to model the number of calls a student makes in a day?
b. If you select a student at random, what is the probability that he or she makes more than 10 calls in a day? More than 15? More than 20?
c. If you select a random sample of 10 students, what distribution can you use to model the proportion of students who have parents who pay their cell phone expenses?
d. Using the distribution selected in (c), what is the probability that all 10 have parents who pay their cell phone expenses? At least 9? At least 8?

5.66 Mega Millions is one of the most popular lottery games in the United States. Virtually all states participate in Mega Millions. Rules for playing and the list of prizes in most states are given below (see **megamillions.com**).

Rules:
- Select five numbers from a pool of numbers from 1 to 52 and one Mega Ball number from a second pool of numbers from 1 to 52.
- Each wager costs $1.

Prizes:
- Match all five numbers + Mega Ball—win jackpot (minimum of $12,000,000)
- Match all five numbers—win $250,000
- Match four numbers + Mega Ball—win $10,000
- Match four numbers—win $150
- Match three numbers + Mega Ball—win $150
- Match two numbers + Mega Ball—win $10
- Match three numbers—win $7
- Match one number + Mega Ball—win $3
- Match Mega Ball—win $2

Find the probability of winning
a. the jackpot.
b. the $250,000 prize. (Note that this requires matching all five numbers but not matching the Mega Ball.)
c. $10,000.
d. $150.

e. $10.
f. $7.
g. $3.
h. $2.
i. nothing.
j. All stores selling Mega Millions tickets are required to have a brochure that gives complete game rules and probabilities of winning each prize. (The probability of having a losing ticket is not given.) The slogan for all lottery games in the state of Ohio is "Play Responsibly. Odds Are, You'll Have Fun." Do you think Ohio's slogan and the requirement of making available complete game rules and probabilities of winning is an ethical approach to running the lottery system?

MANAGING ASHLAND MULTICOMM SERVICES

The Ashland MultiComm Services (AMS) marketing department wants to increase subscriptions for its *3-For-All* telephone, cable, and Internet combined service. AMS marketing has been conducting an aggressive direct-marketing campaign that includes postal and electronic mailings and telephone solicitations. Feedback from these efforts indicates that including premium channels in this combined service is a very important factor for both current and prospective subscribers. After several brainstorming sessions, the marketing department has decided to add premium cable channels as a no-cost benefit of subscribing to the *3-For-All* service.

The research director, Mona Fields, is planning to conduct a survey among prospective customers to determine how many premium channels need to be added to the *3-For-All* service in order to generate a subscription to the service. Based on past campaigns and on industry-wide data, she estimates the following:

Number of Free Premium Channels	Probability of Subscriptions
0	0.02
1	0.04
2	0.06
3	0.07
4	0.08
5	0.085

1. If a sample of 50 prospective customers is selected and no free premium channels are included in the *3-For-All* service offer, given past results, what is the probability that
   a. fewer than 3 customers will subscribe to the *3-For-All* service offer?
   b. 0 customers or 1 customers will subscribe to the *3-For-All* service offer?
   c. more than 4 customers will subscribe to the *3-For-All* service offer?

Suppose that in the actual survey of 50 prospective customers, 4 customers subscribe to the *3-For-All* service offer.

   d. What does this tell you about the previous estimate of the proportion of customers who would subscribe to the *3-For-All* service offer?

2. Instead of offering no premium free channels as in Problem 1, suppose that two free premium channels are included in the *3-For-All* service offer, Given past results, what is the probability that
   a. fewer than 3 customers will subscribe to the *3-For-All* service offer?
   b. 0 customers or 1 customer will subscribe to the *3-For-All* service offer?
   c. more than 4 customers will subscribe to the *3-For-All* service offer?
   d. Compare the results of (a) through (c) to those of **1**.

Suppose that in the actual survey of 50 prospective customers, 6 customers subscribe to the *3-For-All* service offer.

   e. What does this tell you about the previous estimate of the proportion of customers who would subscribe to the *3-For-All* service offer?
   f. What do the results in (e) tell you about the effect of offering free premium channels on the likelihood of obtaining subscriptions to the *3-For-All* service?

3. Suppose that additional surveys of 50 prospective customers were conducted in which the number of free premium channels was varied. The results were as follows:

Number of Free Premium Channels	Number of Subscriptions
1	5
3	6
4	6
5	7

How many free premium channels should the research director recommend for inclusion in the *3-For-All* service? Explain.

DIGITAL CASE

Apply your knowledge about expected value and the covariance in this continuing Digital Case from Chapters 3 and 4.

Open **BullsAndBears.pdf**, a marketing brochure from EndRun Financial Services. Read the claims and examine the supporting data. Then answer the following:

1. Are there any "catches" about the claims the brochure makes for the rate of return of Happy Bull and Worried Bear Funds?
2. What subjective data influence the rate-of-return analyses of these funds? Could EndRun be accused of making false and misleading statements? Why or why not?
3. The expected-return analysis seems to show that the Worried Bear Fund has a greater expected return than the Happy Bull Fund. Should a rational investor never invest in the Happy Bull Fund? Why or why not?

REFERENCES

1. Bernstein, P. L., *Against the Gods: The Remarkable Story of Risk* (New York: Wiley, 1996).
2. Emery, D. R., J. D. Finnerty, and J. D. Stowe, *Corporate Financial Management*, 3rd ed. (Upper Saddle River, NJ: Prentice Hall, 2007).
3. Kirk, R. L., ed., *Statistical Issues: A Reader for the Behavioral Sciences* (Belmont, CA: Wadsworth, 1972).
4. Levine, D. M., P. Ramsey, and R. Smidt, *Applied Statistics for Engineers and Scientists Using Microsoft Excel and Minitab* (Upper Saddle River, NJ: Prentice Hall, 2001).
5. *Microsoft Excel 2010* (Redmond, WA: Microsoft Corp., 2010).
6. Minitab *Release* 16 (State College, PA.: Minitab, Inc., 2010).
7. Moscove, S. A., M. G. Simkin, and N. A. Bagranoff, *Core Concepts of Accounting Information Systems*, 11th ed. (New York: Wiley, 2010).

CHAPTER 5 EXCEL GUIDE

EG5.1 THE PROBABILITY DISTRIBUTION FOR A DISCRETE RANDOM VARIABLE

In-Depth Excel Use the **COMPUTE worksheet** of the **Discrete Random Variable workbook** as a template for computing the expected value, variance, and standard deviation of a discrete random variable (see Figure EG5.1). The worksheet contains the data for the Section 5.1 example on page 212 involving the number of interruptions per day in a large computer network. For other problems, overwrite the X and $P(X)$ values in columns A and B, respectively. If a problem has more or fewer than six outcomes, select the cell range **A5:E5** and:
If the problem has more than six outcomes:

1. Right-click and click **Insert** from the shortcut menu.
2. If a dialog box appears, click **Shift cells down** and then click **OK**.
3. Repeat steps 1 and 2 as many times as necessary.
4. Select the formulas in cell range **C4:E4** and copy them down through the new table rows.
5. Enter the new X and $P(X)$ values in columns **A** and **B**.

If the problem has fewer than six outcomes, right-click and click **Delete** from the shortcut menu. If a dialog box appears, click **Shift cells up** and then click **OK**. Repeat as many times as necessary and then enter the new X and $P(X)$ values in columns **A** and **B**.

FIGURE EG5.1
Discrete random variable probability worksheet

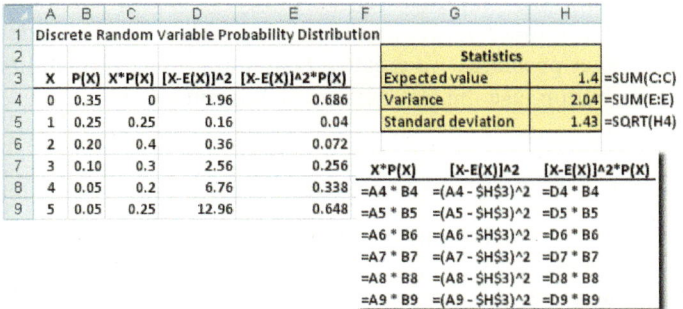

EG5.2 COVARIANCE AND ITS APPLICATION IN FINANCE

PHStat2 Use **Covariance and Portfolio Analysis** to perform portfolio analysis. For example, to create the portfolio analysis for the Section 5.2 investment example on page 216, select **PHStat → Decision-Making → Covariance and Portfolio Analysis**. In the procedure's dialog box (shown below):

1. Enter **5** as the **Number of Outcomes**.
2. Enter a **Title**, check **Portfolio Management Analysis**, and click **OK**.

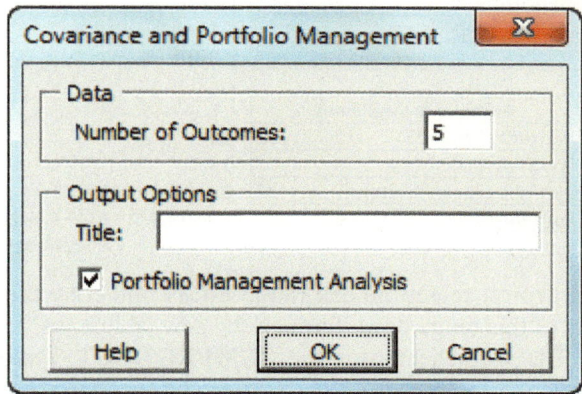

In the new worksheet (shown in Figure EG5.2 on page 242):

3. Enter the probabilities and outcomes in the table that begins in cell B3.
4. Enter **0.5** as the **Weight assigned to X**.

In-Depth Excel Use the **COMPUTE worksheet** of the **Portfolio workbook**, shown in Figure EG5.2, as a template for performing portfolio analysis. The worksheet contains the data for the Section 5.2 investment example on page 216. Overwrite the X and $P(X)$ values and the weight assigned to the X value when you enter data for other problems. If a problem has more or fewer than three outcomes, first select row **5**, right-click, and click **Insert** (or **Delete**) in the shortcut menu to insert (or delete) rows one at a time. If you

FIGURE EG5.2

Portfolio analysis worksheet

	A	B	C	D
1	Portfolio Expected Return and Risk			
2				
3	Probabilities & Outcomes:	P	X	Y
4		0.2	-300	200
5		0.5	100	50
6		0.3	250	-100
7				
8	Weight Assigned to X	0.5		
9				
10	Statistics			
11	E(X)	65	=SUMPRODUCT(B4:B6, C4:C6)	
12	E(Y)	35	=SUMPRODUCT(B4:B6, D4:D6)	
13	Variance(X)	37525	=SUMPRODUCT(B4:B6, H4:H6)	
14	Standard Deviation(X)	193.71	=SQRT(B13)	
15	Variance(Y)	11025	=SUMPRODUCT(B4:B6, I4:I6)	
16	Standard Deviation(Y)	105	=SQRT(B15)	
17	Covariance(XY)	-19275	=SUMPRODUCT(B4:B6, J4:J6)	
18	Variance(X+Y)	10000	=B13 + B15 + 2 * B17	
19	Standard Deviation(X+Y)	100	=SQRT(B18)	
20				
21	Portfolio Management			
22	Weight Assigned to X	0.5	=B8	
23	Weight Assigned to Y	0.5	=1-B22	
24	Portfolio Expected Return	50	=B22 * B11 + B23 * B12	
25	Portfolio Risk	50	=SQRT(B22^2 * B13 + B23^2 * B15 + 2 * B22 * B23 * B17)	

insert rows, select the cell range **B4:J4** and copy the contents of this range down through the new table rows.

The worksheet uses the **SUMPRODUCT** worksheet function to compute the sum of the products of corresponding elements of two cell ranges. The worksheet also contains a Calculations Area that contains various intermediate calculations. Open the **COMPUTE_FORMULAS** worksheet to examine all the formulas used in this area.

EG5.3 BINOMIAL DISTRIBUTION

PHStat2 Use **Binomial** to compute binomial probabilities. For example, to create a binomial probabilities table and histogram for Example 5.3 on page 223, similar to those in Figures 5.2 and 5.3, select **PHStat → Probability & Prob. Distributions → Binomial**. In the procedure's dialog box (shown in next column):

1. Enter **4** as the **Sample Size**.
2. Enter **0.1** as the **Prob. of an Event of Interest**.
3. Enter **0** as the **Outcomes From** value and enter **4** as the (Outcomes) **To** value.
4. Enter a **Title**, check **Histogram**, and click **OK**.

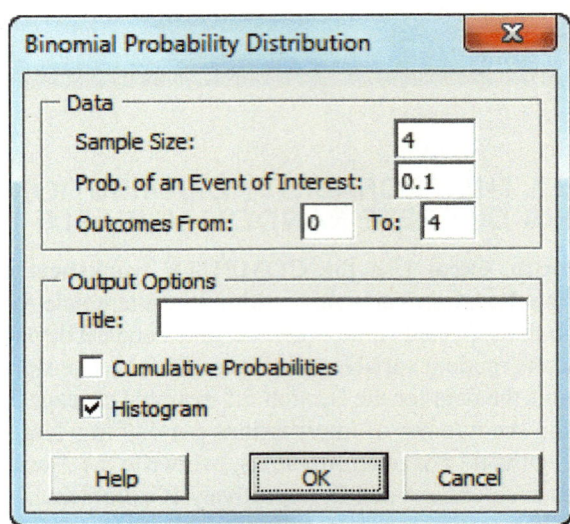

To add columns to the binomial probabilities table for $P(<=X), P(<X), P(>X)$, and $P(\geq X)$, check **Cumulative Probabilities** before clicking **OK** in step 4.

In-Depth Excel Use the **BINOMDIST** worksheet function to compute binomial probabilities. Enter the function as **BINOMDIST** (*X, sample size, π, cumulative*), where *X* is the number of events of interest, π is the probability of an event of interest, and *cumulative* is a **True** or **False** value. (When *cumulative* is **True**, the function computes the probability of *X* or fewer events of interest; when *cumulative* is **False**, the function computes the probability of exactly *X* events of interest.)

Use the **COMPUTE worksheet** of the **Binomial workbook**, shown in Figure 5.2 on page 224, as a template for computing binomial probabilities. The worksheet contains the data for the Section 5.3 tagged orders example. Overwrite these values and adjust the table of probabilities for other problems. To create a histogram of the probability distribution, use the instructions in Appendix Section F.5.

EG5.4 POISSON DISTRIBUTION

PHStat2 Use **Poisson** to compute Poisson probabilities. For example, to create a Poisson probabilities table similar to Figure 5.4 on page 229, select **PHStat → Probability & Prob. Distributions → Poisson**. In this procedure's dialog box (shown the top of the next page):

1. Enter **3** as the **Mean/Expected No. of Events of Interest**.
2. Enter a **Title** and click **OK**.

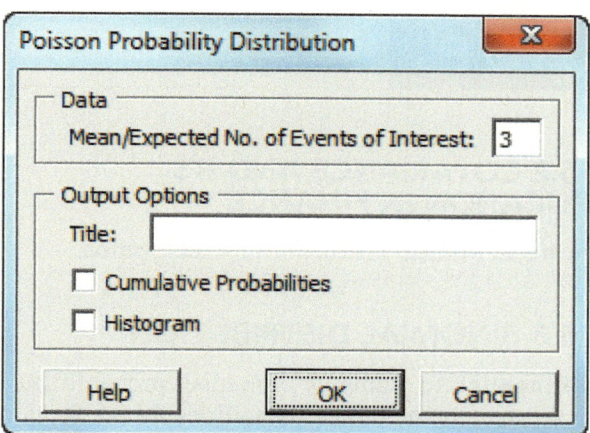

To add columns to the Poisson probabilities table for $P(<=X), P(<X), P(>X)$, and $P(\geq X)$, check **Cumulative Probabilities** before clicking **OK** in step 2. To create a histogram of the probability distribution on a separate chart sheet, check **Histogram** before clicking **OK** in step 2.

In-Depth Excel Use the **POISSON** worksheet function to compute Poisson probabilities. Enter the function as **POISSON**(*X, lambda, cumulative*), where *X* is the number of events of interest, *lambda* is the average or expected number of events of interest, and *cumulative* is a **True** or **False** value. (When *cumulative* is **True**, the function computes the probability of *X* or fewer events of interest; when *cumulative* is **False**, the function computes the probability of exactly *X* events of interest.)

Use the **COMPUTE worksheet** of the **Poisson workbook**, shown in Figure 5.4 on page 229, as a template for computing Poisson probabilities. The worksheet contains the entries for the bank customer arrivals problem of Section 5.4. To adapt this worksheet to other problems, change the **Mean/Expected number of events of interest value** in cell **E4**. To create a histogram of the probability distribution, use the instructions in Appendix Section F.5.

EG5.5 HYPERGEOMETRIC DISTRIBUTION

PHStat2 Use **Hypergeometric** to compute hypergeometric probabilities. For example, to create a hypergeometric probabilities table similar to Figure 5.5 on page 233, select **PHStat → Probability & Prob. Distributions → Hypergeometric**. In this procedure's dialog box (shown in the next column):

1. Enter **8** as the **Sample Size**.

2. Enter **10** as the **No. of Events of Interest in Pop.** (population).
3. Enter **30** as the **Population Size**.
4. Enter a **Title** and click **OK**.

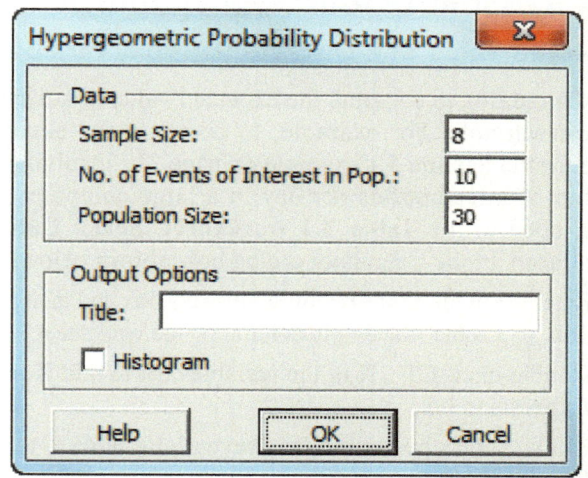

To create a histogram of the probability distribution on a separate chart sheet, check **Histogram** before clicking **OK** in step 4.

In-Depth Excel Use the **HYPGEOMDIST** function to compute hypergeometric probabilities. Enter the function as **HYPGEOMDIST**(*X, sample size, A, population size*), where *X* is the number of events of interest and *A* is the number of events of interest in the population.

Use the **COMPUTE worksheet** of the **Hypergeometric workbook**, shown in Figure 5.5 on page 233, as a template for computing hypergeometric probabilities. The worksheet contains the data for the Section 5.5 team-formation example. To create a histogram of the probability distribution, use the instructions in Appendix Section F.5.

To adapt this worksheet to other problems, change the sample size, the number of events of interest, and population size values in cells **B4**, **B5**, and **B6**, respectively. If a problem has a sample size other than 8, select row **11**, right-click, and click **Insert** (or **Delete**) in the shortcut menu to insert (or delete) rows one at a time. Then edit the *X* values in column A and if you inserted rows, select the cell **B10** formula, and copy it down through the new table rows.

CHAPTER 5 MINITAB GUIDE

MG5.1 THE PROBABILITY DISTRIBUTION FOR A DISCRETE RANDOM VARIABLE

Expected Value of a Discrete Random Variable

Use **Calculator** to compute the expected value of a discrete random variable. For example, to compute the expected value for the Section 5.1 example on page 212 involving the number of interruptions per day in a large computer network, open to the **Table_5.1 worksheet**. Select **Calc → Calculator**. In the Calculator dialog box (shown below):

1. Enter **C3** in the **Store result in variable** box and then press **Tab**. (C3 is the first empty column on the worksheet.)
2. Double-click **C1   X** in the variables list to add **X** to the **Expression** box.
3. Click ***** on the simulated keypad to add ***** to the **Expression** box.
4. Double-click **C2   P(X)** in the variables list to form the expression **X * 'P(X)'** in the **Expression** box.
5. Check **Assign as a formula**.
6. Click **OK**.

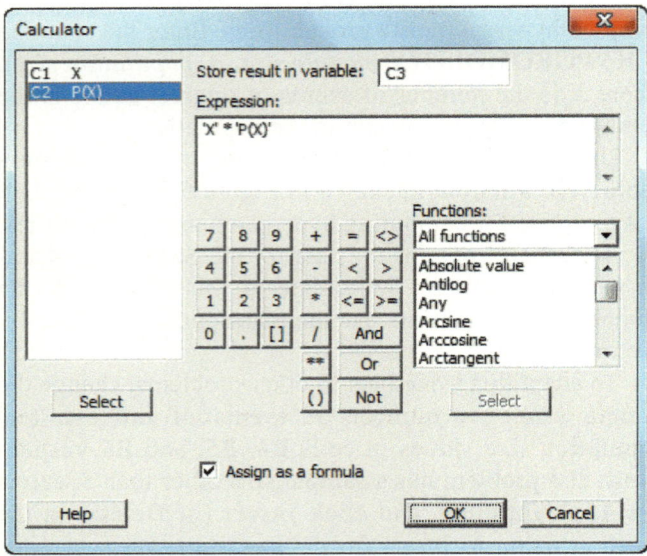

7. Enter **X*P(X)** as the name for column **C3**.
8. Reselect **Calc → Calculator**.

In the Calculator dialog box:

9. Enter **C4** in the **Store result in variable** box and then press **Tab**. (C4 is the first empty column on the worksheet.)
10. Enter **SUM(C3)** in the **Expression** box.
11. If necessary, clear **Assign as a formula**.
12. Click **OK**.

MG5.2 COVARIANCE AND ITS APPLICATION IN FINANCE

There are no Minitab instructions for this section.

MG5.3 BINOMIAL DISTRIBUTION

Use **Binomial** to compute binomial probabilities. For example, to compute these probabilities for the Section 5.3 tagged orders example on page 223, open to a new, blank worksheet and:

1. Enter **X** as the name of column **C1**.
2. Enter **0, 1, 2, 3,** and **4** in rows 1 to 5 of column **C1**.
3. Enter **P(X)** as the name of column **C2**.
4. Select **Calc → Probability Distributions → Binomial**.

In the Binomial Distribution dialog box (shown below):

5. Click **Probability** (to compute the probabilities of exactly *X* events of interest for all values of X).
6. Enter **4** (the sample size) in the **Number of trials** box.
7. Enter **0.1** in the **Event probability** box.
8. Click **Input column** and enter **C1** in its box.
9. Enter **C2** in the first **Optional storage** box.
10. Click **OK**.

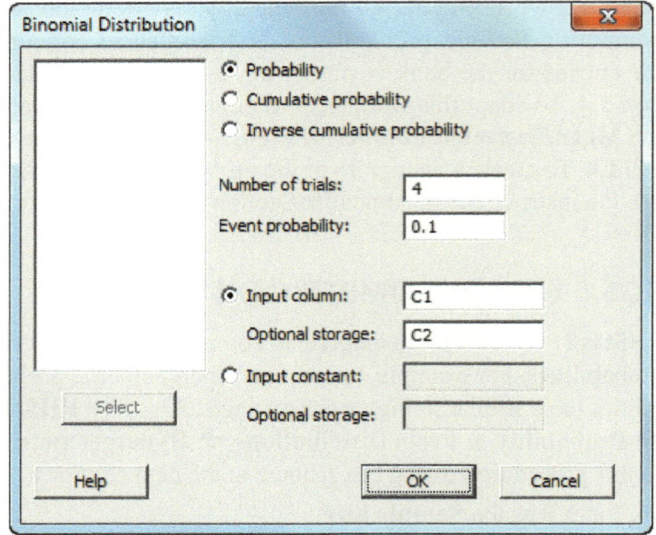

Skip step 9 to create the results shown in Figure 5.2 on page 224.

MG5.4 POISSON DISTRIBUTION

Use **Poisson** to compute Poisson probabilities. For example, to compute these probabilities for the Section 5.4 bank customer arrivals example on page 228, open to a new, blank worksheet and:

1. Enter **X** as the name of column **C1**.
2. Enter values **0** through **15** in rows 1 to 16 of column **C1**.
3. Enter **P(X)** as the name of column **C2**.
4. Select **Calc** → **Probability Distributions** → **Poisson**.

In the Poisson Distribution dialog box (shown below):

5. Click **Probability** (to compute the probabilities of exactly *X* events of interest for all values of X).
6. Enter **3** (the value) in the **Mean** box.
7. Click **Input column** and enter **C1** in its box.
8. Enter **C2** in the first **Optional storage** box.
9. Click **OK**.

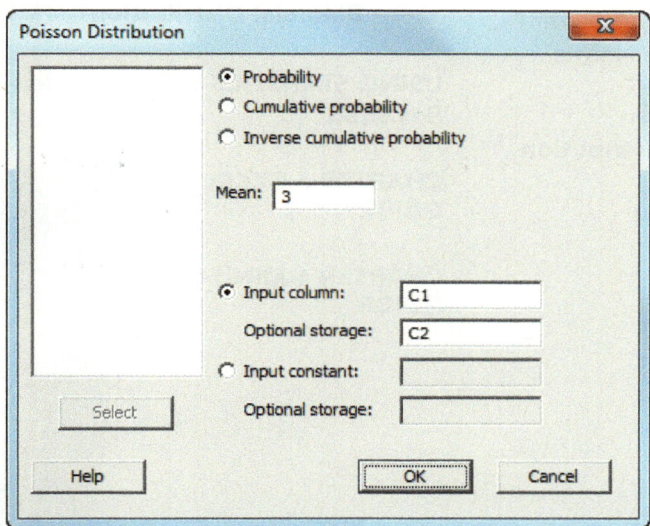

Skip step 8 to create the results shown in Figure 5.4 on page 229.

MG5.5 HYPERGEOMETRIC DISTRIBUTION

Use **Hypergeometric** to compute hypergeometric probabilities. For example, to compute these probabilities for the Section 5.5 team-formation example on page 232, open to a new, blank worksheet and:

1. Enter **X** as the name of column **C1**.
2. Enter the values **0** through **8** in rows 1 to 9 of column **C1**.
3. Enter **P(X)** as the name of column **C2**.
4. Select **Calc** → **Probability Distributions** → **Hypergeometric**.

In the Hypergeometric Distribution dialog box (shown below):

5. Click **Probability**.
6. Enter **30** in the **Population size (N)** box.
7. Enter **10** in the **Event count in population (M)** box.
8. Enter **8** in the **Sample size (n)** box.
9. Click **Input column** and enter **C1** in its box.
10. Enter **C2** in the first **Optional storage** box.
11. Click **OK**.

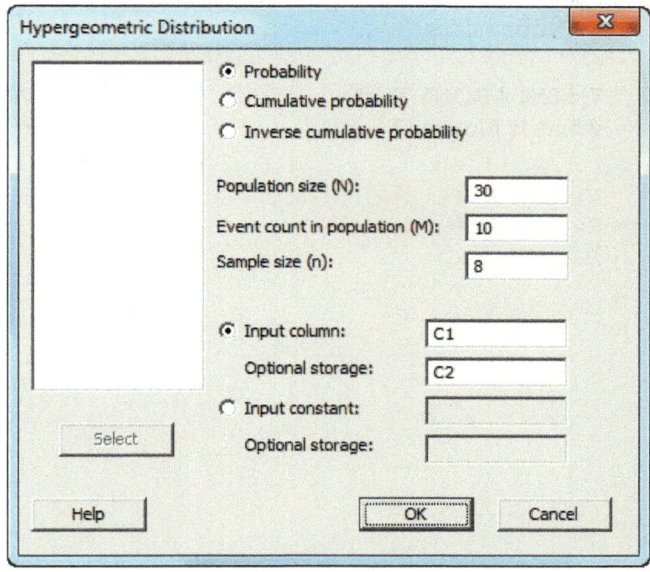

Skip step 10 to create the results shown in Figure 5.5 on page 233.

6 The Normal Distribution and Other Continuous Distributions

USING STATISTICS @ OurCampus!

6.1 Continuous Probability Distributions

6.2 The Normal Distribution
Computing Normal Probabilities

THINK ABOUT THIS: What Is Normal?

VISUAL EXPLORATIONS: Exploring the Normal Distribution

6.3 Evaluating Normality
Comparing Data Characteristics to Theoretical Properties
Constructing the Normal Probability Plot

6.4 The Uniform Distribution

6.5 The Exponential Distribution

6.6 *Online Topic:* The Normal Approximation to the Binomial Distribution

USING STATISTICS @ OurCampus! Revisited

CHAPTER 6 EXCEL GUIDE

CHAPTER 6 MINITAB GUIDE

Learning Objectives

In this chapter, you learn:

- To compute probabilities from the normal distribution
- How to use the normal distribution to solve business problems
- To use the normal probability plot to determine whether a set of data is approximately normally distributed
- To compute probabilities from the uniform distribution
- To compute probabilities from the exponential distribution

USING STATISTICS

@ OurCampus!

You are a designer for the OurCampus! website, a social networking site that targets college students. To attract and retain visitors to the site, you need to make sure that the exclusive-content daily videos can be quickly downloaded and played in a user's browser. Download time, the amount of time, in seconds, that passes from the first linking to the website home page until the first video is ready to play, is both a function of the streaming media technology used and the number of simultaneous users of the website.

To check how fast a video downloads, you open a web browser on a PC at the corporate offices of OurCampus! and measure the download time. Past data indicate that the mean download time is 7 seconds, and that the standard deviation is 2 seconds. Approximately two-thirds of the download times are between 5 and 9 seconds, and about 95% of the download times are between 3 and 11 seconds. In other words, the download times are distributed as a bell-shaped curve, with a clustering around the mean of 7 seconds. How could you use this information to answer questions about the download times of the first video?

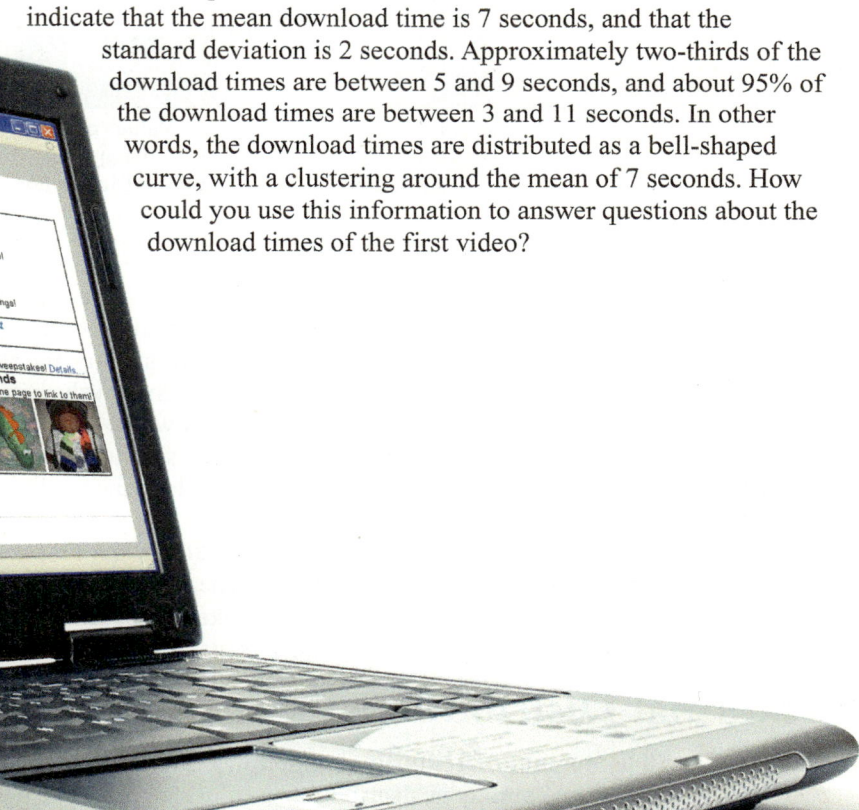

In Chapter 5, Saxon Home Improvement Company managers wanted to be able to answer questions about the number of tagged items in a given sample size. As an OurCampus! web designer, you face a different task, one that involves a continuous measurement because a download time could be any value and not just a whole number. How can you answer questions, such as the following, about this *continuous numerical variable*:

- What proportion of the video downloads take more than 9 seconds?
- How many seconds elapse before 10% of the downloads are complete?
- How many seconds elapse before 99% of the downloads are complete?
- How would enhancing the streaming media technology used affect the answers to these questions?

As in Chapter 5, you can use a probability distribution as a model. Reading this chapter will help you learn about characteristics of continuous probability distributions and how to use the normal, uniform, and exponential distributions to solve business problems.

6.1 Continuous Probability Distributions

A **probability density function** is a mathematical expression that defines the distribution of the values for a continuous random variable. Figure 6.1 graphically displays three probability density functions.

FIGURE 6.1
Three continuous probability distributions

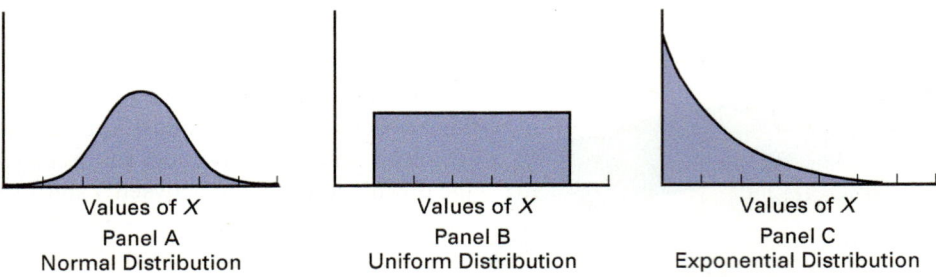

Panel A
Normal Distribution

Panel B
Uniform Distribution

Panel C
Exponential Distribution

Panel A depicts a *normal* distribution. The normal distribution is symmetrical and bell-shaped, implying that most values tend to cluster around the mean, which, due to the distribution's symmetrical shape, is equal to the median. Although the values in a normal distribution can range from negative infinity to positive infinity, the shape of the distribution makes it very unlikely that extremely large or extremely small values will occur.

Panel B shows a *uniform distribution* where each value has an equal probability of occurrence anywhere in the range between the smallest value and the largest value. Sometimes referred to as the *rectangular distribution*, the uniform distribution is symmetrical, and therefore the mean equals the median.

Panel C illustrates an *exponential distribution*. This distribution is skewed to the right, making the mean larger than the median. The range for an exponential distribution is zero to positive infinity, but the distribution's shape makes the occurrence of extremely large values unlikely.

6.2 The Normal Distribution

The **normal distribution** (sometimes referred to as the *Gaussian distribution*) is the most common continuous distribution used in statistics. The normal distribution is vitally important in statistics for three main reasons:

- Numerous continuous variables common in business have distributions that closely resemble the normal distribution.
- The normal distribution can be used to approximate various discrete probability distributions.
- The normal distribution provides the basis for *classical statistical inference* because of its relationship to the *central limit theorem* (which is discussed in Section 7.4).

The normal distribution is represented by the classic bell shape shown in Panel A of Figure 6.1. In the normal distribution, you can calculate the probability that values occur within certain ranges or intervals. However, because probability for continuous variables is measured as an area under the curve, the *exact* probability of a *particular value* from a continuous distribution such as the normal distribution is zero. As an example, time (in seconds) is measured and not counted. Therefore, you can determine the probability that the download time for a video on a web browser is between 7 and 10 seconds, or the probability that the download time is between 8 and 9 seconds, or the probability that the download time is between 7.99 and 8.01 seconds. However, the probability that the download time is *exactly* 8 seconds is zero.

The normal distribution has several important theoretical properties:

- It is symmetrical, and its mean and median are therefore equal.
- It is bell-shaped in appearance.
- Its interquartile range is equal to 1.33 standard deviations. Thus, the middle 50% of the values are contained within an interval of two-thirds of a standard deviation below the mean and two-thirds of a standard deviation above the mean.
- It has an infinite range ($-\infty < X < \infty$).

In practice, many variables have distributions that closely resemble the theoretical properties of the normal distribution. The data in Table 6.1 represent the amount of soft drink in 10,000 1-liter bottles filled on a recent day. The continuous variable of interest, the amount of soft drink filled, can be approximated by the normal distribution. The measurements of the amount of soft drink in the 10,000 bottles cluster in the interval 1.05 to 1.055 liters and distribute symmetrically around that grouping, forming a bell-shaped pattern.

TABLE 6.1

Amount of Fill in 10,000 Bottles of a Soft Drink

Amount of Fill (liters)	Relative Frequency
< 1.025	48/10,000 = 0.0048
1.025 < 1.030	122/10,000 = 0.0122
1.030 < 1.035	325/10,000 = 0.0325
1.035 < 1.040	695/10,000 = 0.0695
1.040 < 1.045	1,198/10,000 = 0.1198
1.045 < 1.050	1,664/10,000 = 0.1664
1.050 < 1.055	1,896/10,000 = 0.1896
1.055 < 1.060	1,664/10,000 = 0.1664
1.060 < 1.065	1,198/10,000 = 0.1198
1.065 < 1.070	695/10,000 = 0.0695
1.070 < 1.075	325/10,000 = 0.0325
1.075 < 1.080	122/10,000 = 0.0122
1.080 or above	48/10,000 = 0.0048
Total	1.0000

Figure 6.2 shows the relative frequency histogram and polygon for the distribution of the amount filled in 10,000 bottles.

FIGURE 6.2

Relative frequency histogram and polygon of the amount filled in 10,000 bottles of a soft drink

Source: Data are taken from Table 6.1.

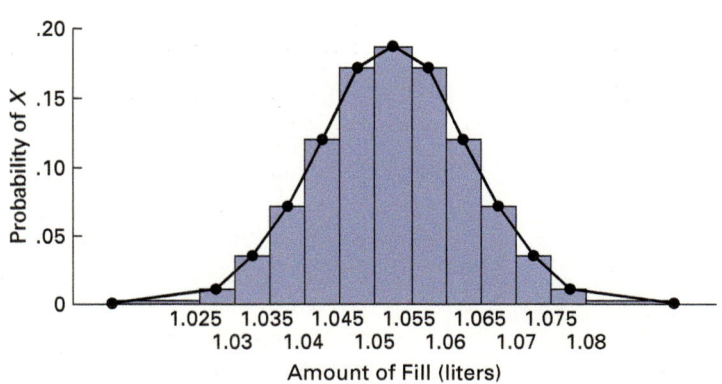

For these data, the first three theoretical properties of the normal distribution are approximately satisfied. However, the fourth one, having an infinite range, is not. The amount filled in a bottle cannot possibly be zero or below, nor can a bottle be filled beyond its capacity. From Table 6.1, you see that only 48 out of every 10,000 bottles filled are expected to contain 1.08 liters or more, and an equal number are expected to contain less than 1.025 liters.

The symbol $f(X)$ is used to represent a probability density function. The **probability density function for the normal distribution** is given in Equation (6.1).

NORMAL PROBABILITY DENSITY FUNCTION

$$f(X) = \frac{1}{\sqrt{2\pi}\sigma} e^{-(1/2)[(X-\mu)/\sigma]^2} \quad (6.1)$$

where

e = mathematical constant approximated by 2.71828

π = mathematical constant approximated by 3.14159

μ = mean

σ = standard deviation

X = any value of the continuous variable, where $-\infty < X < \infty$

Although Equation (6.1) may look complicated, because e and π are mathematical constants, the probabilities of the random variable X are dependent only on the two parameters of the normal distribution—the mean, μ, and the standard deviation, σ. Every time you specify particular values of μ and σ, a *different* normal probability distribution is generated. Figure 6.3 illustrates this principle. The distributions labeled A and B have the same mean (μ) but have different standard deviations. Distributions A and C have the same standard deviation (σ) but have different means. Distributions B and C have different values for both μ and σ.

FIGURE 6.3
Three normal distributions

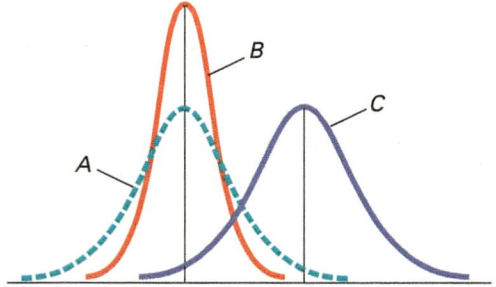

Computing Normal Probabilities

To compute normal probabilities, you first convert a normally distributed random variable, X, to a **standardized normal random variable**, Z, using the **transformation formula**, shown in Equation (6.2). Applying this formula allows you to look up values in a normal probability table and avoid the tedious and complex computations that Equation (6.1) would otherwise require.

THE TRANSFORMATION FORMULA

The Z value is equal to the difference between X and the mean, μ, divided by the standard deviation, σ.

$$Z = \frac{X - \mu}{\sigma} \quad (6.2)$$

The transformation formula computes a Z value that expresses the difference of the X value from the mean, μ, in units of the standard deviation (see Section 3.2 on page 131) called *standardized units*. While a random variable, X, has mean, μ, and standard deviation, σ, the standardized random variable, Z, always has mean $\mu = 0$ and standard deviation $\sigma = 1$.

Then you can determine the probabilities by using Table E.2, the **cumulative standardized normal distribution**. For example, recall from the Using Statistics scenario on page 247 that past data indicate that the time to download a video is normally distributed, with a mean $\mu = 7$ seconds and a standard deviation $\sigma = 2$ seconds. From Figure 6.4, you see that every measurement X has a corresponding standardized measurement Z, computed from Equation (6.2), the transformation formula. Therefore, a download time of 9 seconds is equivalent to 1 standardized unit (1 standard deviation) above the mean because

$$Z = \frac{9-7}{2} = +1$$

FIGURE 6.4
Transformation of scales

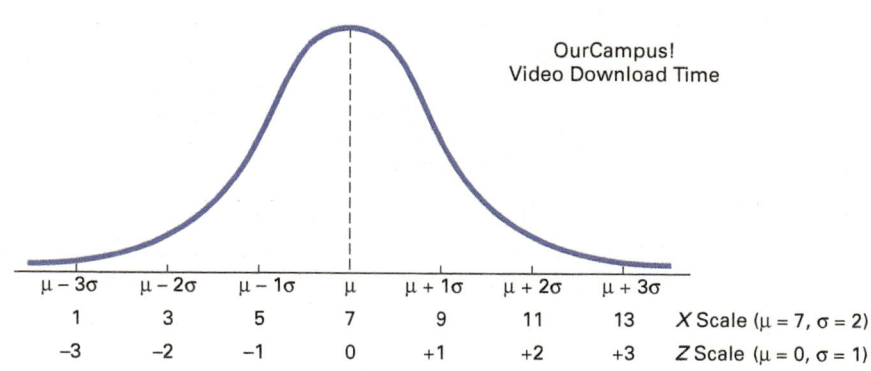

A download time of 1 second is equivalent to -3 standardized units (3 standard deviations) below the mean because

$$Z = \frac{1-7}{2} = -3$$

Figure 6.4 illustrates that the standard deviation is the unit of measurement. In other words, a time of 9 seconds is 2 seconds (1 standard deviation) higher, or *slower*, than the mean time of 7 seconds. Similarly, a time of 1 second is 6 seconds (3 standard deviations) lower, or *faster*, than the mean time.

To further illustrate the transformation formula, suppose that another website has a download time for a video that is normally distributed, with a mean $\mu = 4$ seconds and a standard deviation $\sigma = 1$ second. Figure 6.5 shows this distribution.

FIGURE 6.5
A different transformation of scales

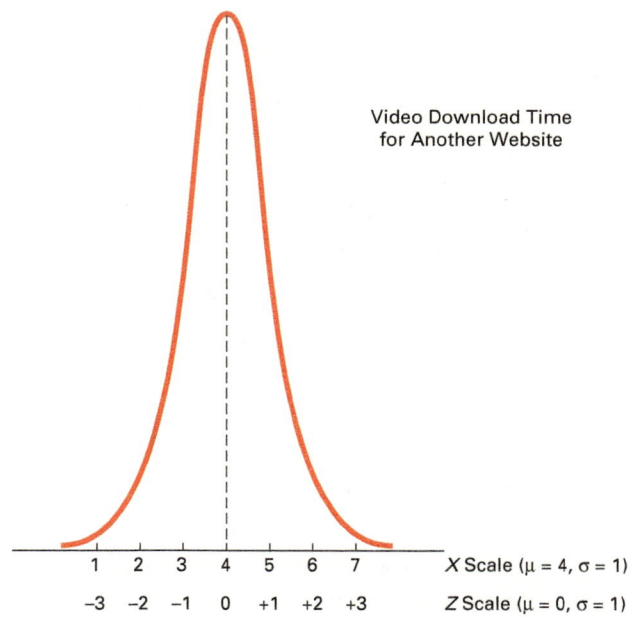

Comparing these results with those of the OurCampus! website, you see that a download time of 5 seconds is 1 standard deviation above the mean download time because

$$Z = \frac{5 - 4}{1} = +1$$

A time of 1 second is 3 standard deviations below the mean download time because

$$Z = \frac{1 - 4}{1} = -3$$

With the Z value computed, you look up the normal probability using a table of values from the cumulative standardized normal distribution, such as Table E.2 in Appendix E. Suppose you wanted to find the probability that the download time for the OurCampus! site is less than 9 seconds. Recall from page 251 that transforming $X = 9$ to standardized Z units, given a mean $\mu = 7$ seconds and a standard deviation $\sigma = 2$ seconds, leads to a Z value of $+1.00$.

With this value, you use Table E.2 to find the cumulative area under the normal curve less than (to the left of) $Z = +1.00$. To read the probability or area under the curve less than $Z = +1.00$, you scan down the Z column in Table E.2 until you locate the Z value of interest (in 10ths) in the Z row for 1.0. Next, you read across this row until you intersect the column that contains the 100ths place of the Z value. Therefore, in the body of the table, the probability for $Z = 1.00$ corresponds to the intersection of the row $Z = 1.0$ with the column $Z = .00$. Table 6.2, which reproduces a portion of Table E.2, shows this intersection. The probability listed at the intersection is 0.8413, which means that there is an 84.13% chance that the download time will be less than 9 seconds. Figure 6.6 graphically shows this probability.

TABLE 6.2

Finding a Cumulative Area Under the Normal Curve

Cumulative Probabilities

Z	.00	.01	.02	.03	.04	.05	.06	.07	.08	.09
0.0	.5000	.5040	.5080	.5120	.5160	.5199	.5239	.5279	.5319	.5359
0.1	.5398	.5438	.5478	.5517	.5557	.5596	.5636	.5675	.5714	.5753
0.2	.5793	.5832	.5871	.5910	.5948	.5987	.6026	.6064	.6103	.6141
0.3	.6179	.6217	.6255	.6293	.6331	.6368	.6406	.6443	.6480	.6517
0.4	.6554	.6591	.6628	.6664	.6700	.6736	.6772	.6808	.6844	.6879
0.5	.6915	.6950	.6985	.7019	.7054	.7088	.7123	.7157	.7190	.7224
0.6	.7257	.7291	.7324	.7357	.7389	.7422	.7454	.7486	.7518	.7549
0.7	.7580	.7612	.7642	.7673	.7704	.7734	.7764	.7794	.7823	.7852
0.8	.7881	.7910	.7939	.7967	.7995	.8023	.8051	.8078	.8106	.8133
0.9	.8159	.8186	.8212	.8238	.8264	.8289	.8315	.8340	.8365	.8389
1.0	.8413	.8438	.8461	.8485	.8508	.8531	.8554	.8577	.8599	.8621

Source: Extracted from Table E.2.

FIGURE 6.6

Determining the area less than Z from a cumulative standardized normal distribution

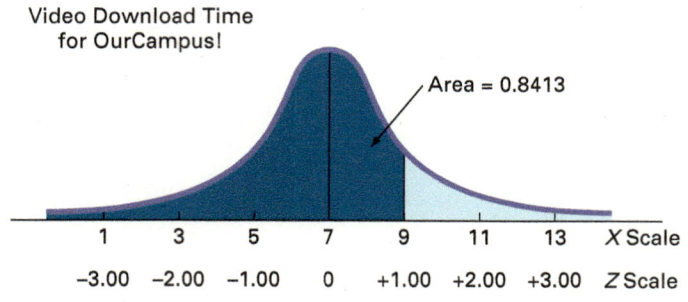

However, for the other website, you see that a time of 5 seconds is 1 standardized unit above the mean time of 4 seconds. Thus, the probability that the download time will be less

than 5 seconds is also 0.8413. Figure 6.7 shows that regardless of the value of the mean, μ, and standard deviation, σ, of a normally distributed variable, Equation (6.2) can transform the X value to a Z value.

FIGURE 6.7
Demonstrating a transformation of scales for corresponding cumulative portions under two normal curves

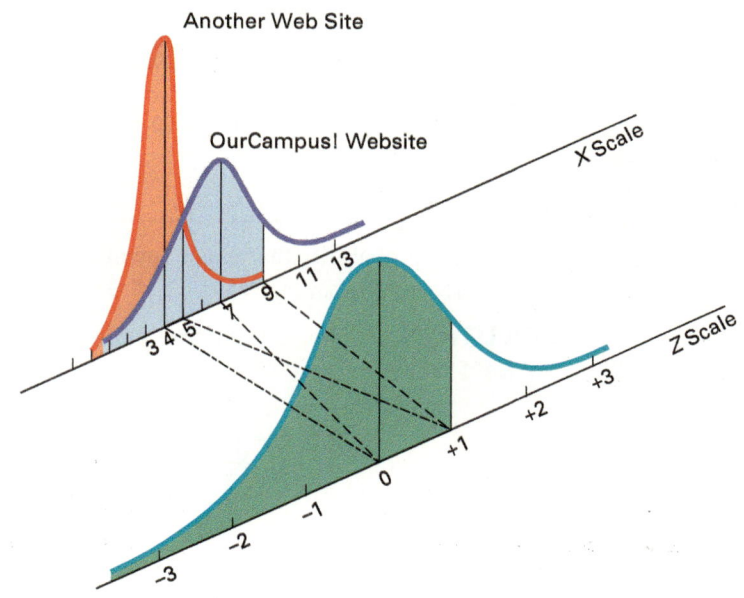

Now that you have learned to use Table E.2 with Equation (6.2), you can answer many questions related to the OurCampus! video download, using the normal distribution.

EXAMPLE 6.1

Finding $P(X > 9)$

What is the probability that the video download time for the OurCampus! website will be more than 9 seconds?

SOLUTION The probability that the download time will be less than 9 seconds is 0.8413 (see Figure 6.6 on page 252). Thus, the probability that the download time will be at least 9 seconds is the *complement* of less than 9 seconds, $1 - 0.8413 = 0.1587$. Figure 6.8 illustrates this result.

FIGURE 6.8
Finding $P(X > 9)$

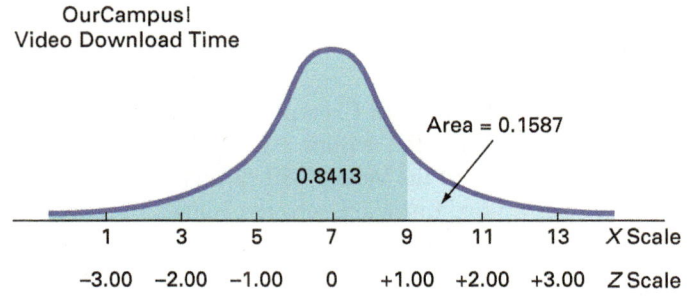

EXAMPLE 6.2

Finding $P(X < 7 \text{ or } X > 9)$

What is the probability that the video download time for the OurCampus! website will be under 7 seconds or over 9 seconds?

SOLUTION To find this probability, you separately calculate the probability of a download time less than 7 seconds and the probability of a download time greater than 9 seconds and then add these two probabilities together. Figure 6.9 on page 254 illustrates this result. Because the mean is 7 seconds, 50% of download times are under 7 seconds. From Example 6.1, you know that the probability that the download time is greater than 9 seconds is 0.1587. Therefore, the probability that a download time is under 7 or over 9 seconds, $P(X < 7 \text{ or } X > 9)$, is $0.5000 + 0.1587 = 0.6587$.

FIGURE 6.9
Finding $P(X < 7 \text{ or } X > 9)$

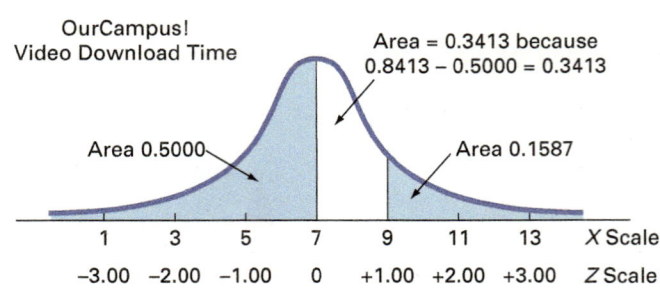

EXAMPLE 6.3

Finding $P(5 < X < 9)$

What is the probability that video download time for the OurCampus! website will be between 5 and 9 seconds—that is, $P(5 < X < 9)$?

SOLUTION In Figure 6.10, you can see that the area of interest is located between two values, 5 and 9.

FIGURE 6.10
Finding $P(5 < X < 9)$

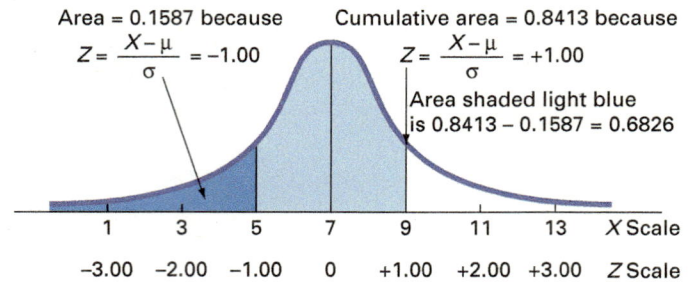

In Example 6.1 on page 253, you already found that the area under the normal curve less than 9 seconds is 0.8413. To find the area under the normal curve less than 5 seconds,

$$Z = \frac{5 - 7}{2} = -1.00$$

Using Table E.2, you look up $Z = -1.00$ and find 0.1587. Therefore, the probability that the download time will be between 5 and 9 seconds is $0.8413 - 0.1587 = 0.6826$, as displayed in Figure 6.10.

The result of Example 6.3 enables you to state that for any normal distribution, 68.26% of the values will fall within ± 1 standard deviation of the mean. From Figure 6.11, you can see that 95.44% of the values will fall within ± 2 standard deviations of the mean. Thus, 95.44% of the download times are between 3 and 11 seconds. From Figure 6.12, you can see that 99.73% of the values are within ± 3 standard deviations above or below the mean. Thus, 99.73% of the download times are between 1 and 13 seconds. Therefore, it is unlikely (0.0027, or only 27 in 10,000) that a download time will be so fast or so slow that it will take under 1 second or more than 13 seconds. In general, you can use 6σ (that is, 3 standard deviations below the mean to 3 standard deviations above the mean) as a practical approximation of the range for normally distributed data.

FIGURE 6.11
Finding $P(3 < X < 11)$

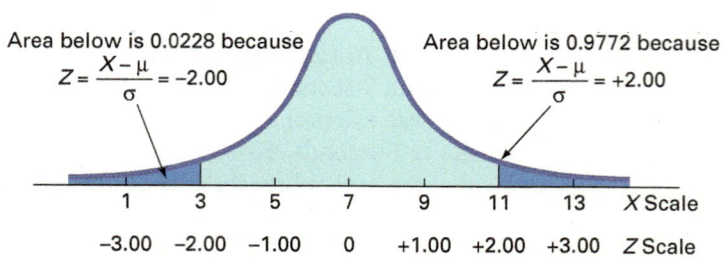

FIGURE 6.12
Finding $P(1 < X < 13)$

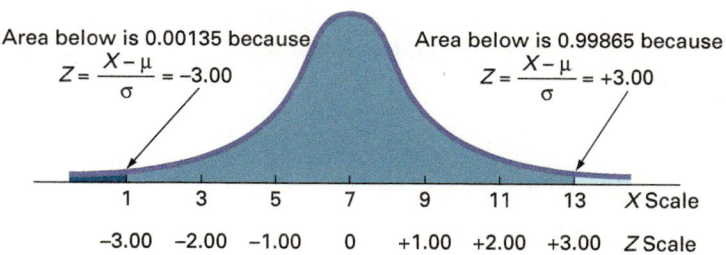

Figures 6.10, 6.11, and 6.12 illustrate that for any normal distribution,

- Approximately 68.26% of the values fall within ±1 standard deviation of the mean.
- Approximately 95.44% of the values fall within ±2 standard deviations of the mean
- Approximately 99.73% of the values fall within ±3 standard deviations of the mean.

This result is the justification for the empirical rule presented on page 152. The accuracy of the empirical rule improves as a data set follows the normal distribution more closely.

Examples 6.1 through 6.3 require you to use the normal distribution Table E.2 to find an area under the normal curve that corresponds to a specific X value. There are many circumstances in which you want to find the X value that corresponds to a specific area. Examples 6.4 and 6.5 illustrate such situations.

EXAMPLE 6.4

Finding the X Value for a Cumulative Probability of 0.10

How much time (in seconds) will elapse before the fastest 10% of the downloads of an Our-Campus! video are complete?

SOLUTION Because 10% of the videos are expected to download in under X seconds, the area under the normal curve less than this value is 0.1000. Using the body of Table E.2, you search for the area or probability of 0.1000. The closest result is 0.1003, as shown in Table 6.3 (which is extracted from Table E.2).

TABLE 6.3
Finding a Z Value Corresponding to a Particular Cumulative Area (0.10) Under the Normal Curve

Z	.00	.01	.02	.03	.04	.05	.06	.07	.08	.09
⋮	⋮	⋮	⋮	⋮	⋮	⋮	⋮	⋮	⋮	⋮
−1.5	.0668	.0655	.0643	.0630	.0618	.0606	.0594	.0582	.0571	.0559
−1.4	.0808	.0793	.0778	.0764	.0749	.0735	.0721	.0708	.0694	.0681
−1.3	.0968	.0951	.0934	.0918	.0901	.0885	.0869	.0853	.0838	.0823
−1.2	.1151	.1131	.1112	.1093	.1075	.0156	.0138	.1020	.1003	.0985

Source: Extracted from Table E.2.

Working from this area to the margins of the table, you find that the Z value corresponding to the particular Z row (−1.2) and Z column (.08) is −1.28 (see Figure 6.13).

FIGURE 6.13
Finding Z to determine X

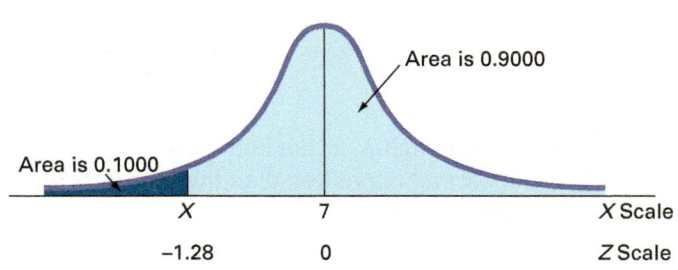

Once you find Z, you use the transformation formula Equation (6.2) on page 250 to determine the X value. Because

$$Z = \frac{X - \mu}{\sigma}$$

then

$$X = \mu + Z\sigma$$

Substituting $\mu = 7$, $\sigma = 2$, and $Z = -1.28$,

$$X = 7 + (-1.28)(2) = 4.44 \text{ seconds}$$

Thus, 10% of the download times are 4.44 seconds or less.

In general, you use Equation (6.3) for finding an X value.

FINDING AN X VALUE ASSOCIATED WITH A KNOWN PROBABILITY

The X value is equal to the mean, μ, plus the product of the Z value and the standard deviation, σ.

$$X = \mu + Z\sigma \qquad (6.3)$$

To find a *particular* value associated with a known probability, follow these steps:

1. Sketch the normal curve and then place the values for the mean and X on the X and Z scales.
2. Find the cumulative area less than X.
3. Shade the area of interest.
4. Using Table E.2, determine the Z value corresponding to the area under the normal curve less than X.
5. Using Equation (6.3), solve for X:

$$X = \mu + Z\sigma$$

EXAMPLE 6.5

Finding the X Values That Include 95% of the Download Times

What are the lower and upper values of X, symmetrically distributed around the mean, that include 95% of the download times for a video at the OurCampus! website?

SOLUTION First, you need to find the lower value of X (called X_L). Then, you find the upper value of X (called X_U). Because 95% of the values are between X_L and X_U, and because X_L and X_U are equally distant from the mean, 2.5% of the values are below X_L (see Figure 6.14).

FIGURE 6.14

Finding Z to determine X_L

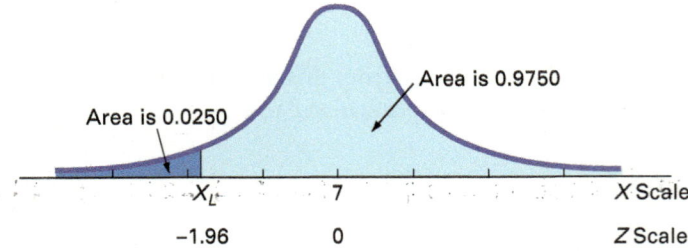

Although X_L is not known, you can find the corresponding Z value because the area under the normal curve less than this Z is 0.0250. Using the body of Table 6.4, you search for the probability 0.0250.

TABLE 6.4

Finding a Z Value Corresponding to a Cumulative Area of 0.025 Under the Normal Curve

					Cumulative Area					
Z	.00	.01	.02	.03	.04	.05	.06	.07	.08	.09
⋮	⋮	⋮	⋮	⋮	⋮	⋮	⋮	⋮	⋮	⋮
−2.0	.0228	.0222	.0217	.0212	.0207	.0202	.0197	.0192	.0188	.0183
−1.9	.0287	.0281	.0274	.0268	.0262	.0256	.0250	.0244	.0239	.0233
−1.8	.0359	.0351	.0344	.0336	.0329	.0232	.0314	.0307	.0301	.0294

Source: Extracted from Table E.2.

Working from the body of the table to the margins of the table, you see that the Z value corresponding to the particular Z row (−1.9) and Z column (.06) is −1.96.

Once you find Z, the final step is to use Equation (6.3) on page 256 as follows:

$$X = \mu + Z\sigma$$
$$= 7 + (-1.96)(2)$$
$$= 7 - 3.92$$
$$= 3.08 \text{ seconds}$$

You use a similar process to find X_U. Because only 2.5% of the video downloads take longer than X_U seconds, 97.5% of the video downloads take less than X_U seconds. From the symmetry of the normal distribution, you find that the desired Z value, as shown in Figure 6.15, is +1.96 (because Z lies to the right of the standardized mean of 0). You can also extract this Z value from Table 6.5. You can see that 0.975 is the area under the normal curve less than the Z value of +1.96.

FIGURE 6.15

Finding Z to determine X_U

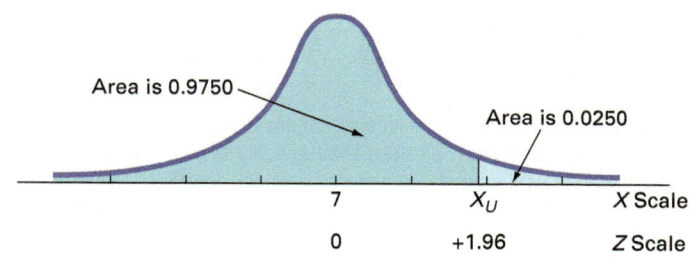

TABLE 6.5

Finding a Z Value Corresponding to a Cumulative Area of 0.975 Under the Normal Curve

					Cumulative Area					
Z	.00	.01	.02	.03	.04	.05	.06	.07	.08	.09
⋮	⋮	⋮	⋮	⋮	⋮	⋮	⋮	⋮	⋮	⋮
+1.8	.9641	.9649	.9656	.9664	.9671	.9678	.9686	.9693	.9699	.9706
+1.9	.9713	.9719	.9726	.9732	.9738	.9744	.9750	.9756	.9761	.9767
+2.0	.9772	.9778	.9783	.9788	.9793	.9798	.9803	.9808	.9812	.9817

Source: Extracted from Table E.2.

Using Equation (6.3) on page 256,

$$X = \mu + Z\sigma$$
$$= 7 + (+1.96)(2)$$
$$= 7 + 3.92$$
$$= 10.92 \text{ seconds}$$

Therefore, 95% of the download times are between 3.08 and 10.92 seconds.

Instead of looking up cumulative probabilities in a table, you can use Excel or Minitab to compute normal probabilities. Figure 6.16 is an Excel worksheet that computes normal probabilities for problems similar to Examples 6.1 through 6.4. Figure 6.17 shows Minitab results for Examples 6.1 and 6.4.

FIGURE 6.16
Excel worksheet for computing normal probabilities

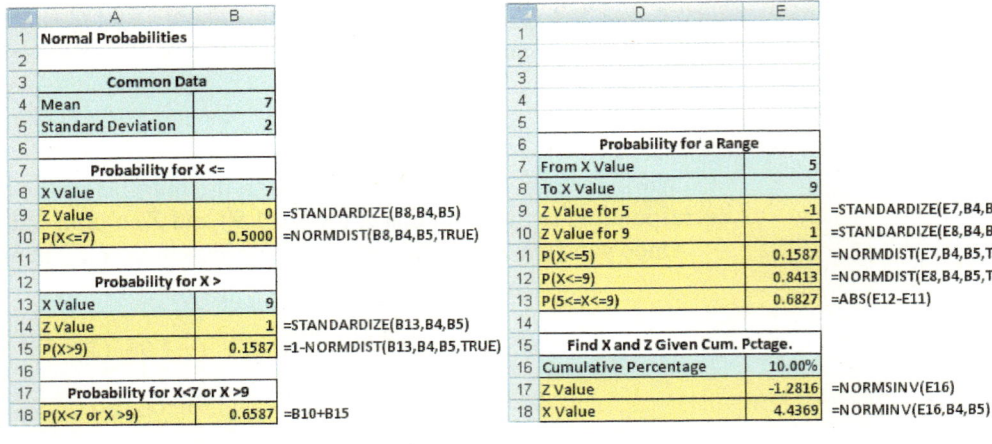

FIGURE 6.17
Minitab results for Examples 6.1 and 6.4

```
Cumulative Distribution Function
Normal with mean = 7 and standard deviation = 2
 x    P( X <= x )
 9      0.841345

Inverse Cumulative Distribution Function
Normal with mean = 7 and standard deviation = 2
P( X <= x )        x
    0.1        4.43690
```

THINK ABOUT THIS — What Is Normal?

Ironically, the statistician who popularized the use of "normal" to describe the distribution discussed in Section 6.2 was someone who saw the distribution as anything but the everyday, anticipated occurrence that the adjective *normal* usually suggests.

Starting with an 1894 paper, Karl Pearson argued that measurements of phenomena do not naturally, or "normally," conform to the classic bell shape. While this principle underlies statistics today, Pearson's point of view was radical to contemporaries who saw the world as standardized and normal. Pearson changed minds by showing that some populations are naturally *skewed* (coining that term in passing), and he helped put to rest the notion that the normal distribution underlies all phenomena.

Today, unfortunately, people still make the type of mistake that Pearson refuted. As a student, you are probably familiar with discussions about grade inflation, a real phenomenon at many schools. But, have you ever realized that a "proof" of this inflation—that there are "too few" low grades because grades are skewed toward A's and B's—wrongly implies that grades should be "normally" distributed. By the time you finish reading this book, you may realize that because college students represent small nonrandom samples, there are plenty of reasons to suspect that the distribution of grades would not be "normal."

Misunderstandings about the normal distribution have occurred both in business and in the public sector through the years. These misunderstandings have caused a number of business blunders and have sparked several public policy debates, including the causes of the collapse of large financial institutions in 2008. According to one theory, the investment banking industry's application of the normal distribution to assess risk may have contributed to the global collapse (see "A Finer Formula for Assessing Risks," *The New York Times*, May 11, 2010, p. B2). Using the normal distribution led these banks to overestimate the probability of having stable market conditions and underestimate the chance of unusually large market losses. According to this theory, the use of other distributions that have less area in the middle of their curves, and, therefore, more in the "tails" that represent unusual market outcomes, may have led to less serious losses.

As you study this chapter, make sure you understand the assumptions that must hold for the proper use of the "normal" distribution, assumptions that were not explicitly verified by the investment bankers. And, most importantly, always remember that the name *normal* distribution does not mean to suggest normal in the everyday (dare we say "normal"?!) sense of the word.

VISUAL EXPLORATIONS: Exploring the Normal Distribution

Use the Visual Explorations Normal Distribution procedure to see the effects of changes in the mean and standard deviation on the area under a normal distribution curve. Open the **Visual Explorations add-in workbook** (see Appendix Section D.4). Select **Add-ins → VisualExplorations → Normal Distribution**.

The add-in displays a normal curve for the OurCampus! download example and a floating control panel (see illustration at right). Use the control panel spinner buttons to change the values for the mean, standard deviation, and X value and note the effects of these changes on the probability of $X <$ value and the corresponding shaded area under the curve (see illustration at right). If you prefer to see the normal curve labeled with Z values, click **Z Values**.

Click the **Reset** button to reset the control panel values or click **Help** for additional information about the problem. Click **Finish** when you are done exploring.

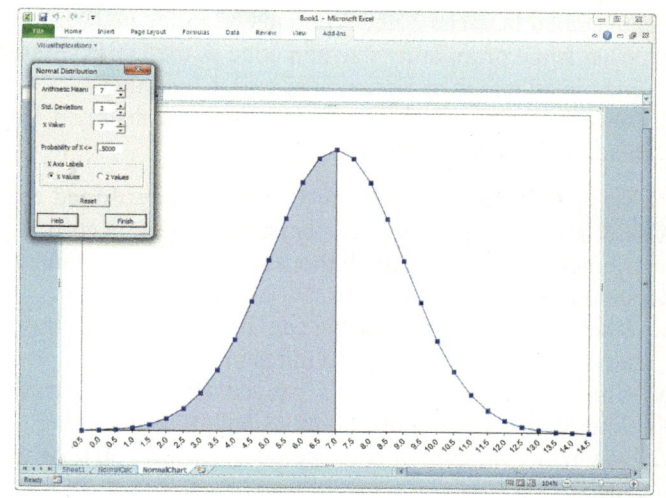

Problems for Section 6.2

LEARNING THE BASICS

6.1 Given a standardized normal distribution (with a mean of 0 and a standard deviation of 1, as in Table E.2), what is the probability that
a. Z is less than 1.57?
b. Z is greater than 1.84?
c. Z is between 1.57 and 1.84?
d. Z is less than 1.57 or greater than 1.84?

6.2 Given a standardized normal distribution (with a mean of 0 and a standard deviation of 1, as in Table E.2), what is the probability that
a. Z is between -1.57 and 1.84?
b. Z is less than -1.57 or greater than 1.84?
c. What is the value of Z if only 2.5% of all possible Z values are larger?
d. Between what two values of Z (symmetrically distributed around the mean) will 68.26% of all possible Z values be contained?

6.3 Given a standardized normal distribution (with a mean of 0 and a standard deviation of 1, as in Table E.2), what is the probability that
a. Z is less than 1.08?
b. Z is greater than -0.21?
c. Z is less than -0.21 or greater than the mean?
d. Z is less than -0.21 or greater than 1.08?

6.4 Given a standardized normal distribution (with a mean of 0 and a standard deviation of 1, as in Table E.2), determine the following probabilities:
a. $P(Z > 1.08)$
b. $P(Z < -0.21)$
c. $P(-1.96 < Z < -0.21)$
d. What is the value of Z if only 15.87% of all possible Z values are larger?

6.5 Given a normal distribution with $\mu = 100$ and $\sigma = 10$, what is the probability that
a. $X > 75$?
b. $X < 70$?
c. $X < 80$ or $X > 110$?
d. Between what two X values (symmetrically distributed around the mean) are 80% of the values?

6.6 Given a normal distribution with $\mu = 50$ and $\sigma = 4$, what is the probability that
a. $X > 43$?
b. $X < 42$?
c. 5% of the values are less than what X value?
d. Between what two X values (symmetrically distributed around the mean) are 60% of the values?

APPLYING THE CONCEPTS

6.7 In 2008, the per capita consumption of coffee in the United States was reported to be 4.2 kg, or 9.24 pounds (data extracted from **en.wikipedia.org/wiki/List_of_countries_by_coffee_consumption_per_capita**). Assume that the per capita consumption of coffee in the United States is approximately distributed as a normal random variable, with a mean of 9.24 pounds and a standard deviation of 3 pounds.

a. What is the probability that someone in the United States consumed more than 10 pounds of coffee in 2008?
b. What is the probability that someone in the United States consumed between 3 and 5 pounds of coffee in 2008?
c. What is the probability that someone in the United States consumed less than 5 pounds of coffee in 2008?
d. 99% of the people in the United States consumed less than how many pounds of coffee?

SELF Test 6.8 Toby's Trucking Company determined that the distance traveled per truck per year is normally distributed, with a mean of 50 thousand miles and a standard deviation of 12 thousand miles.
a. What proportion of trucks can be expected to travel between 34 and 50 thousand miles in a year?
b. What percentage of trucks can be expected to travel either below 30 or above 60 thousand miles in a year?
c. How many miles will be traveled by at least 80% of the trucks?
d. What are your answers to (a) through (c) if the standard deviation is 10 thousand miles?

6.9 Consumers spend an average of $21 per week in cash without being aware of where it goes (data extracted from "Snapshots: A Hole in Our Pockets," *USA Today*, January 18, 2010, p. 1A). Assume that the amount of cash spent without being aware of where it goes is normally distributed and that the standard deviation is $5.
a. What is the probability that a randomly selected person will spend more than $25?
b. What is the probability that a randomly selected person will spend between $10 and $20?
c. Between what two values will the middle 95% of the amounts of cash spent fall?

6.10 A set of final examination grades in an introductory statistics course is normally distributed, with a mean of 73 and a standard deviation of 8.
a. What is the probability that a student scored below 91 on this exam?
b. What is the probability that a student scored between 65 and 89?
c. The probability is 5% that a student taking the test scores higher than what grade?
d. If the professor grades on a curve (i.e., gives A's to the top 10% of the class, regardless of the score), are you better off with a grade of 81 on this exam or a grade of 68 on a different exam, where the mean is 62 and the standard deviation is 3? Show your answer statistically and explain.

6.11 A statistical analysis of 1,000 long-distance telephone calls made from the headquarters of the Bricks and Clicks Computer Corporation indicates that the length of these calls is normally distributed, with $\mu = 240$ seconds and $\sigma = 40$ seconds.
a. What is the probability that a call lasted less than 180 seconds?
b. What is the probability that a call lasted between 180 and 300 seconds?
c. What is the probability that a call lasted between 110 and 180 seconds?
d. 1% of all calls will last less than how many seconds?

6.12 In 2008, the per capita consumption of coffee in Sweden was reported to be 8.2 kg, or 18.04 pounds (data extracted from **en.wikipedia.org/wiki/List_of_countries_by_coffee_consumption_per_capita**). Assume that the per capita consumption of coffee in Sweden is approximately distributed as a normal random variable, with a mean of 18.04 pounds and a standard deviation of 5 pounds.
a. What is the probability that someone in Sweden consumed more than 10 pounds of coffee in 2008?
b. What is the probability that someone in Sweden consumed between 3 and 5 pounds of coffee in 2008?
c. What is the probability that someone in Sweden consumed less than 5 pounds of coffee in 2008?
d. 99% of the people in Sweden consumed less than how many pounds of coffee?

6.13 Many manufacturing problems involve the matching of machine parts, such as shafts that fit into a valve hole. A particular design requires a shaft with a diameter of 22.000 mm, but shafts with diameters between 21.990 mm and 22.010 mm are acceptable. Suppose that the manufacturing process yields shafts with diameters normally distributed, with a mean of 22.002 mm and a standard deviation of 0.005 mm. For this process, what is
a. the proportion of shafts with a diameter between 21.99 mm and 22.00 mm?
b. the probability that a shaft is acceptable?
c. the diameter that will be exceeded by only 2% of the shafts?
d. What would be your answers in (a) through (c) if the standard deviation of the shaft diameters were 0.004 mm?

6.3 Evaluating Normality

As discussed in Section 6.2, many continuous variables used in business closely follow a normal distribution. To determine whether a set of data can be approximated by the normal distribution, you either compare the characteristics of the data with the theoretical properties of the normal distribution or construct a normal probability plot.

Comparing Data Characteristics to Theoretical Properties

The normal distribution has several important theoretical properties:

- It is symmetrical; thus, the mean and median are equal.
- It is bell-shaped; thus, the empirical rule applies.
- The interquartile range equals 1.33 standard deviations.
- The range is approximately equal to 6 standard deviations.

Many continuous variables have characteristics that approximate these theoretical properties. However, other continuous variables are often neither normally distributed nor approximately normally distributed. For such variables, the descriptive characteristics of the data are inconsistent with the properties of a normal distribution. One approach that you can use to determine whether a variable follows a normal distribution is to compare the observed characteristics of the variable with what would be expected if the variable followed a normal distribution. To do so, you can

- Construct charts and observe their appearance. For small- or moderate-sized data sets, create a stem-and-leaf display or a boxplot. For large data sets, in addition, plot a histogram or polygon.
- Compute descriptive statistics and compare these statistics with the theoretical properties of the normal distribution. Compare the mean and median. Is the interquartile range approximately 1.33 times the standard deviation? Is the range approximately 6 times the standard deviation?
- Evaluate how the values are distributed. Determine whether approximately two-thirds of the values lie between the mean and ± 1 standard deviation. Determine whether approximately four-fifths of the values lie between the mean and ± 1.28 standard deviations. Determine whether approximately 19 out of every 20 values lie between the mean and ± 2 standard deviations.

For example, you can use these techniques to determine whether the returns in 2009 discussed in Chapters 2 and 3 (stored in Bond Funds) follow a normal distribution. Figures 6.18 and 6.19 display relevant Excel results for these data, and Figure 6.20 displays a Minitab boxplot for the same data.

FIGURE 6.18
Descriptive statistics for the 2009 returns

Return 2009	
Mean	7.1641
Standard Error	0.4490
Median	6.4000
Mode	6.0000
Standard Deviation	6.0908
Sample Variance	37.0984
Kurtosis	2.4560
Skewness	0.9085
Range	40.8000
Minimum	-8.8000
Maximum	32.0000
Sum	1318.2000
Count	184

FIGURE 6.19
Five-number summary and boxplot for the 2009 returns

Five-Number Summary	
Minimum	-8.8
First Quartile	3.4
Median	6.4
Third Quartile	10.8
Maximum	32

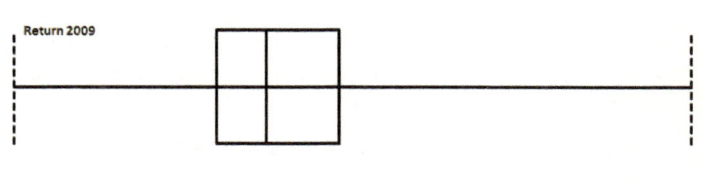

Boxplot for the Bond Funds 2009 Returns

FIGURE 6.20
Minitab boxplot

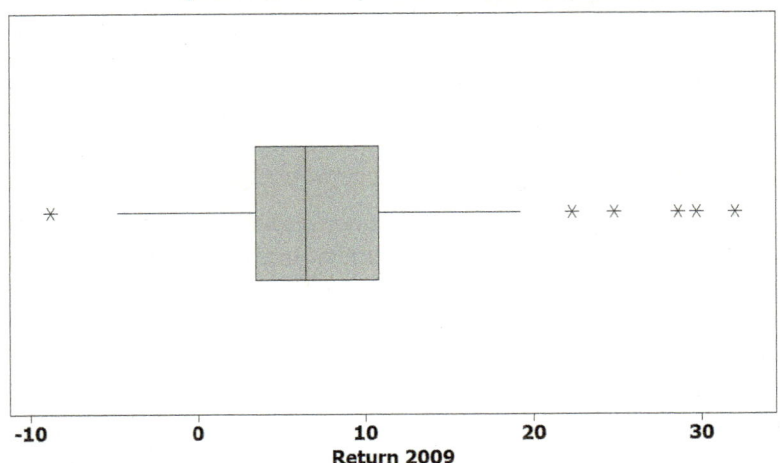

From Figures 6.18 through 6.20, and from an ordered array of the returns (not shown here), you can make the following statements:

- The mean of 7.1641 is greater than the median of 6.4. (In a normal distribution, the mean and median are equal.)
- The boxplot is very right-skewed, with a long tail on the right. (The normal distribution is symmetrical.)
- The interquartile range of 7.4 is approximately 1.21 standard deviations. (In a normal distribution, the interquartile range is 1.33 standard deviations.)
- The range of 40.8 is equal to 6.70 standard deviations. (In a normal distribution, the range is approximately 6 standard deviations.)
- 73.91% of the returns are within ±1 standard deviation of the mean. (In a normal distribution, 68.26% of the values lie within ±1 standard deviation of the mean.)
- 85.33% of the returns are within ±1.28 standard deviations of the mean. (In a normal distribution, 80% of the values lie within ±1.28 standard deviations of the mean.)
- 96.20% of the returns are within ±2 standard deviations of the mean. (In a normal distribution, 95.44% of the values lie within ±2 standard deviations of the mean.)
- The skewness statistic is 0.9085 and the kurtosis statistic is 2.456. (In a normal distribution, each of these statistics equals zero.)

Based on these statements and the criteria given on page 261, you can conclude that the 2009 returns are highly right-skewed and have somewhat more values within ±1 standard deviation of the mean than expected. The range is higher than what would be expected in a normal distribution, but this is mostly due to the single outlier at 32. Primarily because of the skewness, you can conclude that the data characteristics of the 2009 returns differ from the theoretical properties of a normal distribution.

Constructing the Normal Probability Plot

A **normal probability plot** is a visual display that helps you evaluate whether the data are normally distributed. One common plot is called the **quantile–quantile plot**. To create this plot, you first transform each ordered value to a Z value. For example, if you have a sample of $n=19$, the Z value for the smallest value corresponds to a cumulative area of $\dfrac{1}{n+1} = \dfrac{1}{19+1} = \dfrac{1}{20} = 0.05$.

The Z value for a cumulative area of 0.05 (from Table E.2) is -1.65. Table 6.6 illustrates the entire set of Z values for a sample of $n=19$.

TABLE 6.6
Ordered Values and Corresponding Z Values for a Sample of n = 19

Ordered Value	Z Value	Ordered Value	Z Value
1	−1.65	11	0.13
2	−1.28	12	0.25
3	−1.04	13	0.39
4	−0.84	14	0.52
5	−0.67	15	0.67
6	−0.52	16	0.84
7	−0.39	17	1.04
8	−0.25	18	1.28
9	−0.13	19	1.65
10	−0.00		

In a quantile–quantile plot, the Z values are plotted on the X axis, and the corresponding values of the variable are plotted on the Y axis. If the data are normally distributed, the values will plot along an approximately straight line.

Figure 6.21 illustrates the typical shape of the quantile–quantile normal probability plot for a left-skewed distribution (Panel A), a normal distribution (Panel B), and a right-skewed distribution (Panel C). If the data are left-skewed, the curve will rise more rapidly at first and then level off. If the data are normally distributed, the points will plot along an approximately straight line. If the data are right-skewed, the data will rise more slowly at first and then rise at a faster rate for higher values of the variable being plotted.

FIGURE 6.21
Normal probability plots for a left-skewed distribution, a normal distribution, and a right-skewed distribution

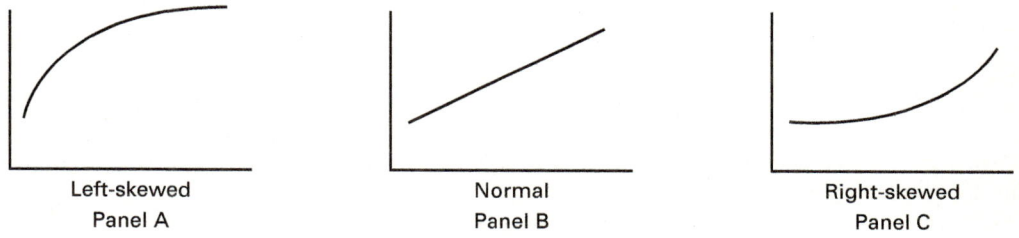

Figure 6.22 shows a normal probability plot for the 2009 returns as created using Excel (left results, a quantile–quantile plot) and Minitab (right results). The Excel quantile–quantile

FIGURE 6.22
Excel (quantile–quantile) and Minitab normal probability plots for 2009 returns

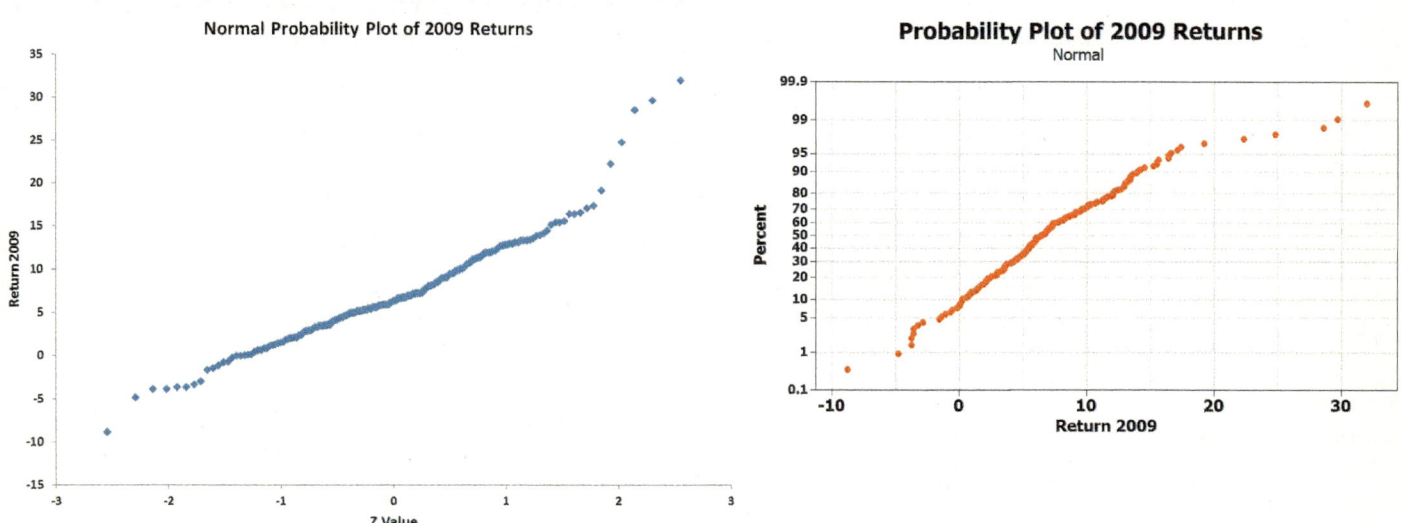

plot shows that the 2009 returns rise slowly at first and then rise more rapidly. Therefore, you can conclude that the 2009 returns are right-skewed.

The Minitab normal probability plot has the Return 2009 variable on the X axis and the cumulative percentage for a normal distribution on the Y axis. As is the case with the quantile–quantile plot, if the data are normally distributed, the points will plot along an approximately straight line. However, if the data are right-skewed, the curve will rise more rapidly at first and then level off. If the data are left-skewed, the data will rise more slowly at first and then rise at a faster rate for higher values of the variable being plotted. Observe that the values rise more rapidly at first and then level off, indicating a right-skewed distribution.

Problems for Section 6.3

LEARNING THE BASICS

6.14 Show that for a sample of $n = 39$, the smallest and largest Z values are -1.96 and $+1.96$, and the middle (i.e., 20th) Z value is 0.00.

6.15 For a sample of $n = 6$, list the six Z values.

APPLYING THE CONCEPTS

6.16 The file SUV contains the overall miles per gallon (MPG) of 2010 small SUVs ($n-26$):

24 23 22 21 22 22 18 18 26 26 26 19 19
19 21 21 21 21 21 18 19 21 22 22 16 16

Source: Data extracted from "Vehicle Ratings," *Consumer Reports*, April 2010, pp. 33–34.

Decide whether the data appear to be approximately normally distributed by
a. comparing data characteristics to theoretical properties.
b. constructing a normal probability plot.

6.17 As player salaries have increased, the cost of attending baseball games has increased dramatically. The file BBCost contains the cost of four tickets, two beers, four soft drinks, four hot dogs, two game programs, two baseball caps, and the parking fee for one car for each of the 30 Major League Baseball teams in 2009:

164, 326, 224, 180, 205, 162, 141, 170, 411, 187
185, 165, 151, 166, 114, 158, 305, 145, 161, 170
210, 222, 146, 259, 220, 135, 215, 172, 223, 216

Source: Data extracted from **teammarketing.com**, April 1, 2009.

Decide whether the data appear to be approximately normally distributed by
a. comparing data characteristics to theoretical properties.
b. constructing a normal probability plot.

6.18 The file PropertyTaxes contains the property taxes per capita for the 50 states and the District of Columbia. Decide whether the data appear to be approximately normally distributed by
a. comparing data characteristics to theoretical properties.
b. constructing a normal probability plot.

6.19 Thirty companies comprise the DJIA. Just how big are these companies? One common method for measuring the size of a company is to use its market capitalization, which is computed by multiplying the number of stock shares by the price of a share of stock. On March 29, 2010, the market capitalization of these companies ranged from Alcoa's $14.7 billion to ExxonMobil's $318.8 billion. The entire population of market capitalization values is stored in DowMarketCap.

Source: Data extracted from **money.cnn.com**, March 29, 2010.

Decide whether the market capitalization of companies in the DJIA appears to be approximately normally distributed by
a. comparing data characteristics to theoretical properties.
b. constructing a normal probability plot.
c. constructing a histogram.

6.20 One operation of a mill is to cut pieces of steel into parts that will later be used as the frame for front seats in an automotive plant. The steel is cut with a diamond saw, and the resulting parts must be within ± 0.005 inch of the length specified by the automobile company. The data come from a sample of 100 steel parts and are stored in Steel. The measurement reported is the difference, in inches, between the actual length of the steel part, as measured by a laser measurement device, and the specified length of the steel part. Determine whether the data appear to be approximately normally distributed by
a. comparing data characteristics to theoretical properties.
b. constructing a normal probability plot.

6.21 The file SavingsRate-MMCD contains the yields for a money market account and a five-year certificate of deposit (CD) for 25 banks in the United States, as of March 29, 2010.

Source: Data extracted from **www.Bankrate.com**, March 29, 2010.

For each type of investment, decide whether the data appear to be approximately normally distributed by
a. comparing data characteristics to theoretical properties.
b. constructing a normal probability plot.

6.22 The file `Utility` contains the electricity costs, in dollars, during July 2010 for a random sample of 50 one-bedroom apartments in a large city:

96	171	202	178	147	102	153	197	127	82
157	185	90	116	172	111	148	213	130	165
141	149	206	175	123	128	144	168	109	167
95	163	150	154	130	143	187	166	139	149
108	119	183	151	114	135	191	137	129	158

Decide whether the data appear to be approximately normally distributed by
a. comparing data characteristics to theoretical properties.
b. constructing a normal probability plot.

6.4 The Uniform Distribution

In the **uniform distribution**, a value has the same probability of occurrence anywhere in the range between the smallest value, a, and the largest value, b. Because of its shape, the uniform distribution is sometimes called the **rectangular distribution** (see Panel B of Figure 6.1 on page 248). Equation (6.4) defines the probability density function for the uniform distribution.

UNIFORM PROBABILITY DENSITY FUNCTION

$$f(X) = \frac{1}{b-a} \text{ if } a \leq X \leq b \text{ and 0 elsewhere} \quad (6.4)$$

where

a = minimum value of X
b = maximum value of X

Equation (6.5) defines the mean of the uniform distribution.

MEAN OF THE UNIFORM DISTRIBUTION

$$\mu = \frac{a+b}{2} \quad (6.5)$$

Equation (6.6) defines the variance and standard deviation of the uniform distribution.

VARIANCE AND STANDARD DEVIATION OF THE UNIFORM DISTRIBUTION

$$\sigma^2 = \frac{(b-a)^2}{12} \quad (6.6a)$$

$$\sigma = \sqrt{\frac{(b-a)^2}{12}} \quad (6.6b)$$

One of the most common uses of the uniform distribution is in the selection of random numbers. When you use simple random sampling (see Section 7.1), you assume that each random number comes from a uniform distribution that has a minimum value of 0 and a maximum value of 1.

Figure 6.23 illustrates the uniform distribution with $a = 0$ and $b = 1$. The total area inside the rectangle is equal to the base (1.0) times the height (1.0). Thus, the resulting area of 1.0 satisfies the requirement that the area under any probability density function equals 1.0.

FIGURE 6.23
Probability density function for a uniform distribution with $a = 0$ and $b = 1$

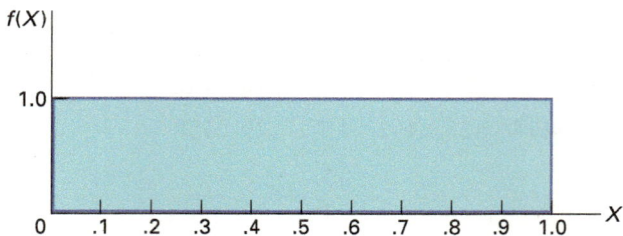

In this uniform distribution, what is the probability of getting a random number between 0.10 and 0.30? The area between 0.10 and 0.30, depicted in Figure 6.24, is equal to the base (which is $0.30 - 0.10 = 0.20$) times the height (1.0). Therefore,

$$P(0.10 < X < 0.30) = (\text{Base})(\text{Height}) = (0.20)(1.0) = 0.20$$

FIGURE 6.24
Finding $P(0.10 < X < 0.30)$ for a uniform distribution with $a = 0$ and $b = 1$

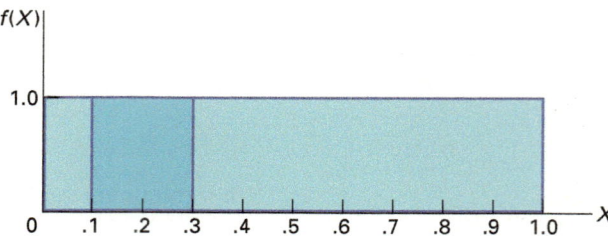

From Equations (6.5) and (6.6), the mean and standard deviation of the uniform distribution for $a = 0$ and $b = 1$ are computed as follows:

$$\mu = \frac{a+b}{2}$$
$$= \frac{0+1}{2} = 0.5$$

and

$$\sigma^2 = \frac{(b-a)^2}{12}$$
$$= \frac{(1-0)^2}{12}$$
$$= \frac{1}{12} = 0.0833$$
$$\sigma = \sqrt{0.0833} = 0.2887$$

Thus, the mean is 0.5, and the standard deviation is 0.2887.
Example 6.6 provides another application of the uniform distribution.

EXAMPLE 6.6

Computing Uniform Probabilities

In the Using Statistics scenario on page 247, the download time of videos was assumed to be normally distributed with a mean of 7 seconds. Suppose that the download time follows a uniform (instead of a normal) distribution between 4.5 and 9.5 seconds. What is the probability that a download time will take more than 9 seconds?

SOLUTION The download time is uniformly distributed from 4.5 to 9.5 seconds. The area between 9 and 9.5 seconds is equal to 0.5 seconds, and the total area in the distribution is 9.5 − 4.5 = 5 seconds. Therefore, the probability of a download time between 9 and 9.5 seconds is the portion of the area greater than 9, which is equal to 0.5/5.0 = 0.10. Because 9.5 is the maximum value in this distribution, the probability of a download time above 9 seconds is 0.10. In comparison, if the download time is normally distributed with a mean of 7 seconds and a standard deviation of 2 seconds (see Example 6.1 on page 253), the probability of a download time above 9 seconds is 0.1587.

Problems for Section 6.4

LEARNING THE BASICS

6.23 Suppose you select one value from a uniform distribution with $a = 0$ and $b = 10$. What is the probability that the value will be
a. between 5 and 7?
b. between 2 and 3?
c. What is the mean?
d. What is the standard deviation?

APPLYING THE CONCEPTS

6.24 The time between arrivals of customers at a bank during the noon-to-1 P.M. hour has a uniform distribution between 0 to 120 seconds. What is the probability that the time between the arrival of two customers will be
a. less than 20 seconds?
b. between 10 and 30 seconds?
c. more than 35 seconds?
d. What are the mean and standard deviation of the time between arrivals?

6.25 A study of the time spent shopping in a supermarket for a market basket of 20 specific items showed an approximately uniform distribution between 20 minutes and 40 minutes. What is the probability that the shopping time will be
a. between 25 and 30 minutes?
b. less than 35 minutes?
c. What are the mean and standard deviation of the shopping time?

6.26 How long does it take you to download a game for your iPod? According to Apple's technical support site, **www.apple.com/support/itunes**, downloading an iPod game using a broadband connection should take 3 to 6 minutes. Assume that the download times are uniformly distributed between 3 and 6 minutes. If you download a game, what is the probability that the download time will be
a. less than 3.3 minutes?
b. less than 4 minutes?
c. between 4 and 5 minutes?
d. What are the mean and standard deviation of the download times?

6.27 The scheduled commuting time on the Long Island Railroad from Glen Cove to New York City is 65 minutes. Suppose that the actual commuting time is uniformly distributed between 64 and 74 minutes. What is the probability that the commuting time will be
a. less than 70 minutes?
b. between 65 and 70 minutes?
c. greater than 65 minutes?
d. What are the mean and standard deviation of the commuting time?

6.5 The Exponential Distribution

The **exponential distribution** is a continuous distribution that is right-skewed and ranges from zero to positive infinity (see Panel C of Figure 6.1 on page 248). The exponential distribution is widely used in waiting-line (i.e., queuing) theory to model the length of time between arrivals in processes such as customers arriving at a bank's ATM, patients entering a hospital emergency room, and hits on a website.

The exponential distribution is defined by a single parameter, λ, the mean number of arrivals per unit of time. The probability density function for the length of time between arrivals is given by Equation (6.7).

EXPONENTIAL PROBABILITY DENSITY FUNCTION

$$f(X) = \lambda e^{-\lambda x} \text{ for } X > 0 \quad (6.7)$$

where

e = mathematical constant approximated by 2.71828

λ = mean number of arrivals per unit

X = any value of the continuous variable where $0 < X < \infty$

The mean time between arrivals, μ, is given by Equation (6.8).

MEAN TIME BETWEEN ARRIVALS

$$\mu = \frac{1}{\lambda} \quad (6.8)$$

The standard deviation of the time between arrivals, σ, is given by Equation (6.9).

STANDARD DEVIATION OF THE TIME BETWEEN ARRIVALS

$$\sigma = \frac{1}{\lambda} \quad (6.9)$$

The value $1/\lambda$ is equal to the mean time between arrivals. For example, if the mean number of arrivals in a minute is $\lambda = 4$, then the mean time between arrivals is $1/\lambda = 0.25$ minutes, or 15 seconds. Equation (6.10) defines the cumulative probability that the length of time before the next arrival is less than or equal to X.

CUMULATIVE EXPONENTIAL PROBABILITY

$$P(\text{arrival time} \leq X) = 1 - e^{-\lambda x} \quad (6.10)$$

To illustrate the exponential distribution, suppose that customers arrive at a bank's ATM at a rate of 20 per hour. If a customer has just arrived, what is the probability that the next customer will arrive within 6 minutes (i.e., 0.1 hour)? For this example, $\lambda = 20$ and $X = 0.1$. Using Equation (6.10),

$$P(\text{Arrival time} \leq 0.1) = 1 - e^{-20(0.1)}$$
$$= 1 - e^{-2}$$
$$= 1 - 0.1353 = 0.8647$$

Thus, the probability that a customer will arrive within 6 minutes is 0.8647, or 86.47%. Figure 6.25 shows this probability as computed by Excel (left results) and Minitab (right results).

FIGURE 6.25
Excel and Minitab results for finding exponential probabilities (mean = $1/\lambda$)

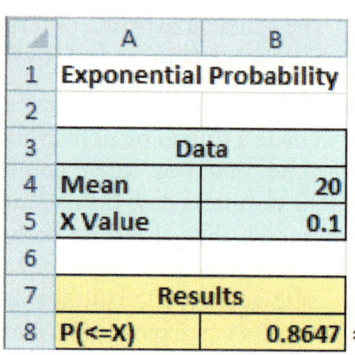

```
Cumulative Distribution Function

Exponential with mean = 0.05

  x    P( X <= x )
0.1       0.864665
```

EXAMPLE 6.6
Computing Exponential Probabilities

In the ATM example, what is the probability that the next customer will arrive within 3 minutes (i.e., 0.05 hour)?

SOLUTION For this example, $\lambda = 20$ and $X = 0.05$. Using Equation (6.10),

$$P(\text{Arrival time} \leq 0.05) = 1 - e^{-20(0.05)}$$
$$= 1 - e^{-1}$$
$$= 1 - 0.3679 = 0.6321$$

Thus, the probability that a customer will arrive within 3 minutes is 0.6321, or 63.21%.

Problems for Section 6.5

LEARNING THE BASICS

6.28 Given an exponential distribution with $\lambda = 10$, what is the probability that the arrival time is
a. less than $X = 0.1$?
b. greater than $X = 0.1$?
c. between $X = 0.1$ and $X = 0.2$?
d. less than $X = 0.1$ or greater than $X = 0.2$?

6.29 Given an exponential distribution with $\lambda = 30$, what is the probability that the arrival time is
a. less than $X = 0.1$?
b. greater than $X = 0.1$?
c. between $X = 0.1$ and $X = 0.2$?
d. less than $X = 0.1$ or greater than $X = 0.2$?

6.30 Given an exponential distribution with $\lambda = 5$, what is the probability that the arrival time is
a. less than $X = 0.3$?
b. greater than $X = 0.3$?
c. between $X = 0.3$ and $X = 0.5$?
d. less than $X = 0.3$ or greater than $X = 0.5$?

APPLYING THE CONCEPTS

6.31 Autos arrive at a toll plaza located at the entrance to a bridge at a rate of 50 per minute during the 5:00-to-6:00 P.M. hour. If an auto has just arrived,
a. what is the probability that the next auto will arrive within 3 seconds (0.05 minute)?
b. what is the probability that the next auto will arrive within 1 second (0.0167 minute)?
c. What are your answers to (a) and (b) if the rate of arrival of autos is 60 per minute?
d. What are your answers to (a) and (b) if the rate of arrival of autos is 30 per minute?

6.32 Customers arrive at the drive-up window of a fast-food restaurant at a rate of 2 per minute during the lunch hour. *(SELF Test)*
a. What is the probability that the next customer will arrive within 1 minute?
b. What is the probability that the next customer will arrive within 5 minutes?
c. During the dinner time period, the arrival rate is 1 per minute. What are your answers to (a) and (b) for this period?

6.33 Telephone calls arrive at the information desk of a large computer software company at a rate of 15 per hour.
a. What is the probability that the next call will arrive within 3 minutes (0.05 hour)?
b. What is the probability that the next call will arrive within 15 minutes (0.25 hour)?
c. Suppose the company has just introduced an updated version of one of its software programs, and telephone calls are now arriving at a rate of 25 per hour. Given this information, what are your answers to (a) and (b)?

6.34 An on-the-job injury occurs once every 10 days on average at an automobile plant. What is the probability that the next on-the-job injury will occur within
a. 10 days?
b. 5 days?
c. 1 day?

6.35 The time between unplanned shutdowns of a power plant has an exponential distribution with a mean of 20 days. Find the probability that the time between two unplanned shutdowns is
a. less than 14 days.
b. more than 21 days.
c. less than 7 days.

6.36 Golfers arrive at the starter's booth of a public golf course at a rate of 8 per hour during the Monday-to-Friday midweek period. If a golfer has just arrived,
a. what is the probability that the next golfer will arrive within 15 minutes (0.25 hour)?
b. what is the probability that the next golfer will arrive within 3 minutes (0.05 hour)?
c. The actual arrival rate on Fridays is 15 per hour. What are your answers to (a) and (b) for Fridays?

6.37 Some Internet companies sell a service that will boost a website's traffic by delivering additional unique visitors. Assume that one such company claims it can deliver 1,000 visitors a day. If this amount of website traffic is experienced, then the time between visitors has a mean of 1.44 minutes (or 0.6944 per minute). Assume that your website gets 1,000 visitors a day and that the time between visitors has an exponential distribution. What is the probability that the time between two visitors is
a. less than 1 minute?
b. less than 2 minutes?
c. more than 3 minutes?
d. Do you think it is reasonable to assume that the time between visitors has an exponential distribution?

6.6  *Online Topic:* The Normal Approximation to the Binomial Distribution

In many circumstances, you can use the normal distribution to approximate the binomial distribution. To study this topic, read the Section 6.6 online topic file that is available on this book's companion website. (See Appendix C to learn how to access the online topic files.)

USING STATISTICS @ OurCampus! Revisited

In the OurCampus! scenario, you were a designer for a social networking website. You sought to ensure that a video could be downloaded quickly for playback in the web browsers of site visitors. (Quick playback of videos would help attract and retain those visitors.) By running experiments in the corporate offices, you determined that the amount of time, in seconds, that passes from first linking to the website until a video is fully displayed is a bell-shaped distribution with a mean download time of 7 seconds and standard deviation of 2 seconds. Using the normal distribution, you were able to calculate that approximately 84% of the download times are 9 seconds or less, and 95% of the download times are between 3.08 and 10.92 seconds.

Now that you understand how to calculate probabilities from the normal distribution, you can evaluate download times of a video using different web page designs. For example, if the standard deviation remained at 2 seconds, lowering the mean to 6 seconds would shift the entire distribution lower by 1 second. Thus, approximately 84% of the download times would be 8 seconds or less, and 95% of the download times would be between 2.08 and 9.92 seconds. Another change that could reduce long download times would be reducing the variation. For example, consider the case where the mean remained at the original 7 seconds but the standard deviation was reduced to 1 second. Again, approximately 84% of the download times would be 8 seconds or less, and 95% of the download times would be between 5.04 and 8.96 seconds.

SUMMARY

In this and the previous chapter, you have learned about mathematical models called probability distributions and how they can be used to solve business problems. In Chapter 5, you used discrete probability distributions in situations where the outcomes come from a counting process (e.g., the number of courses you are enrolled in, the number of tagged order forms in a report generated by an accounting information system). In this chapter, you learned about continuous probability distributions where the outcomes come from a measuring process (e.g., your height, the download time of a video). Continuous probability distributions come in various shapes, but the most common and most important in business is the normal distribution. The normal distribution is symmetrical; thus, its mean and median are equal. It is also bell-shaped, and approximately 68.26% of its observations are within 1 standard deviation of the mean, approximately 95.44% of its observations are within 2 standard deviations of the mean, and approximately 99.73% of its observations are within 3 standard deviations of the mean. Although many data sets in business are closely approximated by the normal distribution, do not think that all data can be approximated using the normal distribution. In Section 6.3, you learned about various methods for evaluating normality in order to determine whether the normal distribution is a reasonable mathematical model to use in specific situations. In Sections 6.4 and 6.5, you studied continuous distributions that were not normally distributed—in particular, the uniform and exponential distributions.

Chapter 7 uses the normal distribution to develop the subject of statistical inference.

KEY EQUATIONS

Normal Probability Density Function

$$f(X) = \frac{1}{\sqrt{2\pi}\sigma} e^{-(1/2)[(X-\mu)/\sigma]^2} \tag{6.1}$$

Transformation Formula

$$Z = \frac{X - \mu}{\sigma} \tag{6.2}$$

Finding an X Value Associated with a Known Probability

$$X = \mu + Z\sigma \tag{6.3}$$

Uniform Probability Density Function

$$f(X) = \frac{1}{b - a} \tag{6.4}$$

Mean of the Uniform Distribution

$$\mu = \frac{a + b}{2} \tag{6.5}$$

Variance and Standard Deviation of the Uniform Distribution

$$\sigma^2 = \frac{(b - a)^2}{12} \tag{6.6a}$$

$$\sigma = \sqrt{\frac{(b - a)^2}{12}} \tag{6.6b}$$

Exponential Probability Density Function

$$f(X) = \lambda e^{-\lambda x} \text{ for } X > 0 \tag{6.7}$$

Mean Time Between Arrivals

$$\mu = \frac{1}{\lambda} \tag{6.8}$$

Standard Deviation of the Time Between Arrivals

$$\sigma = \frac{1}{\lambda} \tag{6.9}$$

Cumulative Exponential Probability

$$P(\text{arrival time} \leq X) = 1 - e^{-\lambda x} \tag{6.10}$$

KEY TERMS

cumulative standardized normal distribution
exponential distribution
normal distribution
normal probability plot
probability density function
probability density function for the normal distribution
quantile–quantile plot
rectangular distribution
standardized normal random variable
transformation formula
uniform distribution

CHAPTER REVIEW PROBLEMS

CHECKING YOUR UNDERSTANDING

6.38 Why is only one normal distribution table such as Table E.2 needed to find any probability under the normal curve?

6.39 How do you find the area between two values under the normal curve?

6.40 How do you find the X value that corresponds to a given percentile of the normal distribution?

6.41 What are some of the distinguishing properties of a normal distribution?

6.42 How does the shape of the normal distribution differ from the shapes of the uniform and exponential distributions?

6.43 How can you use the normal probability plot to evaluate whether a set of data is normally distributed?

6.44 Under what circumstances can you use the exponential distribution?

APPLYING THE CONCEPTS

6.45 An industrial sewing machine uses ball bearings that are targeted to have a diameter of 0.75 inch. The lower and upper specification limits under which the ball bearings can operate are 0.74 inch and 0.76 inch, respectively. Past experience has indicated that the actual diameter of the ball bearings is approximately normally distributed, with a mean of 0.753 inch and a standard deviation of 0.004 inch. What is the probability that a ball bearing is
a. between the target and the actual mean?
b. between the lower specification limit and the target?
c. above the upper specification limit?
d. below the lower specification limit?
e. Of all the ball bearings, 93% of the diameters are greater than what value?

6.46 The fill amount in 2-liter soft drink bottles is normally distributed, with a mean of 2.0 liters and a standard deviation of 0.05 liter. If bottles contain less than 95% of the listed net content (1.90 liters, in this case), the manufacturer may be subject to penalty by the state office of consumer affairs. Bottles that have a net content above 2.10 liters may cause excess spillage upon opening. What proportion of the bottles will contain
a. between 1.90 and 2.0 liters?
b. between 1.90 and 2.10 liters?
c. below 1.90 liters or above 2.10 liters?
d. At least how much soft drink is contained in 99% of the bottles?
e. 99% of the bottles contain an amount that is between which two values (symmetrically distributed) around the mean?

6.47 In an effort to reduce the number of bottles that contain less than 1.90 liters, the bottler in Problem 6.46 sets the filling machine so that the mean is 2.02 liters. Under these circumstances, what are your answers in Problem 6.46 (a) through (e)?

6.48 An orange juice producer buys all his oranges from a large orange grove. The amount of juice squeezed from each of these oranges is approximately normally distributed, with a mean of 4.70 ounces and a standard deviation of 0.40 ounce.
a. What is the probability that a randomly selected orange will contain between 4.70 and 5.00 ounces of juice?
b. What is the probability that a randomly selected orange will contain between 5.00 and 5.50 ounces of juice?
c. At least how many ounces of juice will 77% of the oranges contain?
d. 80% of the oranges contain between what two values (in ounces of juice), symmetrically distributed around the population mean?

6.49 The file **DomesticBeer** contains the percentage alcohol, number of calories per 12 ounces, and number of carbohydrates (in grams) per 12 ounces for 139 of the best-selling domestic beers in the United States. For each of the three variables, decide whether the data appear to be approximately normally distributed. Support your decision through the use of appropriate statistics and graphs.
Source: Data extracted from **www.Beer100.com**, March 18, 2010.

6.50 The evening manager of a restaurant was very concerned about the length of time some customers were waiting in line to be seated. She also had some concern about the seating times—that is, the length of time between when a customer is seated and the time he or she leaves the restaurant. Over the course of one week, 100 customers (no more than 1 per party) were randomly selected, and their waiting and seating times (in minutes) were recorded in **Wait**.
a. Think about your favorite restaurant. Do you think waiting times more closely resemble a uniform, an exponential, or a normal distribution?
b. Again, think about your favorite restaurant. Do you think seating times more closely resemble a uniform, an exponential, or a normal distribution?
c. Construct a histogram and a normal probability plot of the waiting times. Do you think these waiting times more closely resemble a uniform, an exponential, or a normal distribution?
d. Construct a histogram and a normal probability plot of the seating times. Do you think these seating times more closely resemble a uniform, an exponential, or a normal distribution?

6.51 All the major stock market indexes posted strong gains in 2009. The mean one-year return for stocks in the S&P 500, a group of 500 very large companies, was 23.45%. The mean one-year return for the NASDAQ, a group of 3,200 small and medium-sized companies, was 43.89%. Historically, the one-year returns are approximately normally distributed, the standard deviation in the S&P 500 is approximately 20%, and the standard deviation in the NASDAQ is approximately 30%.
a. What is the probability that a stock in the S&P 500 gained value in 2009?
b. What is the probability that a stock in the S&P 500 gained 10% or more?
c. What is the probability that a stock in the S&P 500 lost 20% or more in 2009?
d. What is the probability that a stock in the S&P 500 lost 40% or more?
e. Repeat (a) through (d) for a stock in the NASDAQ.
f. Write a short summary on your findings. Be sure to include a discussion of the risks associated with a large standard deviation.

6.52 The speed in which the home page of a website is downloaded is an important quality characteristic of that website. Suppose that the mean time to download the home page for the Internal Revenue Service is 1.2 seconds. Suppose that the download time is normally distributed, with a standard deviation of 0.2 second. What is the probability that a download time is
a. less than 2 seconds?
b. between 1.5 and 2.5 seconds?
c. above 1.8 seconds?
d. 99% of the download times are slower (higher) than how many seconds?
e. 95% of the download times are between what two values, symmetrically distributed around the mean?
f. Suppose that the download times are uniformly distributed between 0.45 and 1.95 seconds. What are your answers to (a) through (e)?

6.53 Suppose that the mean download time for a commercial tax preparation site is 2.0 seconds. Suppose that the download time is normally distributed, with a standard deviation of 0.5 second. What is the probability that a download time is
a. less than 2 seconds?
b. between 1.5 and 2.5 seconds?
c. above 1.8 seconds?
d. 99% of the download times are slower (higher) than how many seconds?
e. Suppose that the download times are uniformly distributed between 1.5 and 2.5 seconds. What are your answers to (a) through (e)?
f. Compare the results for the IRS site computed in Problem 6.52 to those of the commercial site.

6.54 (Class Project) According to Burton G. Malkiel, the daily changes in the closing price of stock follow a *random walk*—that is, these daily events are independent of each other and move upward or downward in a random manner—and can be approximated by a normal distribution. To test this theory, use either a newspaper or the Internet to select one company traded on the NYSE, one company traded on the American Stock Exchange, and one company traded on the NASDAQ and then do the following:
1. Record the daily closing stock price of each of these companies for six consecutive weeks (so that you have 30 values per company).
2. Record the daily changes in the closing stock price of each of these companies for six consecutive weeks (so that you have 30 values per company).

For each of your six data sets, decide whether the data are approximately normally distributed by
a. constructing the stem-and-leaf display, histogram or polygon, and boxplot.
b. comparing data characteristics to theoretical properties.
c. constructing a normal probability plot.
d. Discuss the results of (a) through (c). What can you say about your three stocks with respect to daily closing prices and daily changes in closing prices? Which, if any, of the data sets are approximately normally distributed?

Note: *The random-walk theory pertains to the daily changes in the closing stock price, not the daily closing stock price.*

TEAM PROJECT

The file **Bond Funds** contains information regarding eight variables from a sample of 184 bond mutual funds:
Type—Type of bonds comprising the bond mutual fund (intermediate government or short-term corporate)
Assets—In millions of dollars
Fees—Sales charges (no or yes)
Expense ratio—Ratio of expenses to net assets in percentage
Return 2009—Twelve-month return in 2009
Three-year return—Annualized return, 2007–2009
Five-year return—Annualized return, 2005–2009
Risk—Risk-of-loss factor of the mutual fund (below average, average, or above average)

6.55 For the expense ratio, three-year return, and five-year return, decide whether the data are approximately normally distributed by
a. comparing data characteristics to theoretical properties.
b. constructing a normal probability plot.

STUDENT SURVEY DATABASE

6.56 Problem 1.27 on page 44 describes a survey of 62 undergraduate students (stored in **UndergradSurvey**). For these data, for each numerical variable, decide whether the data are approximately normally distributed by
a. comparing data characteristics to theoretical properties.
b. constructing a normal probability plot.

6.57 Problem 1.27 on page 44 describes a survey of 62 undergraduate students (stored in **UndergradSurvey**).
a. Select a sample of undergraduate students and conduct a similar survey for those students.
b. For the data collected in (a), repeat (a) and (b) of Problem 6.56.
c. Compare the results of (b) to those of Problem 6.56.

6.58 Problem 1.28 on page 45 describes a survey of 44 MBA students (stored in **GradSurvey**). For these data, for each numerical variable, decide whether the data are approximately normally distributed by
a. comparing data characteristics to theoretical properties.
b. constructing a normal probability plot.

6.59 Problem 1.28 on page 45 describes a survey of 44 MBA students (stored in **GradSurvey**).
a. Select a sample of graduate students and conduct a similar survey for those students.
b. For the data collected in (a), repeat (a) and (b) of Problem 6.58.
c. Compare the results of (b) to those of Problem 6.58.

MANAGING ASHLAND MULTICOMM SERVICES

The AMS technical services department has embarked on a quality improvement effort. Its first project relates to maintaining the target upload speed for its Internet service subscribers. Upload speeds are measured on a standard scale in which the target value is 1.0. Data collected over the past year indicate that the upload speed is approximately normally distributed, with a mean of 1.005 and a standard deviation of 0.10. Each day, one upload speed is measured. The upload speed is considered acceptable if the measurement on the standard scale is between 0.95 and 1.05.

EXERCISES

1. Assuming that the distribution has not changed from what it was in the past year, what is the probability that the upload speed is
   a. less than 1.0?
   b. between 0.95 and 1.0?
   c. between 1.0 and 1.05?
   d. less than 0.95 or greater than 1.05?
2. The objective of the operations team is to reduce the probability that the upload speed is below 1.0. Should the team focus on process improvement that increases the mean upload speed to 1.05 or on process improvement that reduces the standard deviation of the upload speed to 0.075? Explain.

DIGITAL CASE

Apply your knowledge about the normal distribution in this Digital Case, which extends the Using Statistics scenario from this chapter.

To satisfy concerns of potential customers, the management of OurCampus! has undertaken a research project to learn the amount of time it takes users to load a complex video features page. The research team has collected data and has made some claims based on the assertion that the data follow a normal distribution.

Open **OC_QRTStudy.pdf**, which documents the work of a quality response team at OurCampus! Read the internal report that documents the work of the team and their conclusions. Then answer the following:

1. Can the collected data be approximated by the normal distribution?
2. Review and evaluate the conclusions made by the OurCampus! research team. Which conclusions are correct? Which ones are incorrect?
3. If OurCampus! could improve the mean time by five seconds, how would the probabilities change?

REFERENCES

1. Gunter, B., "Q-Q Plots," *Quality Progress* (February 1994), 81–86.
2. Levine, D. M., P. Ramsey, and R. Smidt, *Applied Statistics for Engineers and Scientists Using Microsoft Excel and Minitab* (Upper Saddle River, NJ: Prentice Hall, 2001).
3. *Microsoft Excel 2010* (Redmond, WA: Microsoft Corp., 2010).
4. Miller, J., "Earliest Known Uses of Some of the Words of Mathematics," http://jeff560.tripod.com/mathword.html.
5. *Minitab Release 16* (State College, PA: Minitab Inc., 2010).
6. Pearl, R., "Karl Pearson, 1857–1936," *Journal of the American Statistical Association*, 31 (1936), 653–664.
7. Pearson, E. S., "Some Incidents in the Early History of Biometry and Statistics, 1890–94," *Biometrika*, 52 (1965), 3–18.
8. Walker, H., "The Contributions of Karl Pearson," *Journal of the American Statistical Association*, 53 (1958), 11–22.

CHAPTER 6 EXCEL GUIDE

EG6.1 CONTINUOUS PROBABILITY DISTRIBUTIONS

There are no Excel Guide instructions for this section.

EG6.2 THE NORMAL DISTRIBUTION

PHStat2 Use **Normal** to compute normal probabilities. For example, to create the Figure 6.16 worksheet (see page 258) that computes probabilities for several Chapter 6 examples, select **PHStat → Probability & Prob. Distributions → Normal**. In this procedure's dialog box (shown below):

1. Enter **7** as the **Mean** and **2** as the **Standard Deviation**.
2. Check **Probability for:** $X <=$ and enter **7** in its box.
3. Check **Probability for:** $X >$ and enter **9** in its box.
4. Check **X for Cumulative Percentage** and enter **10** in its box.
5. Enter a **Title** and click **OK**.

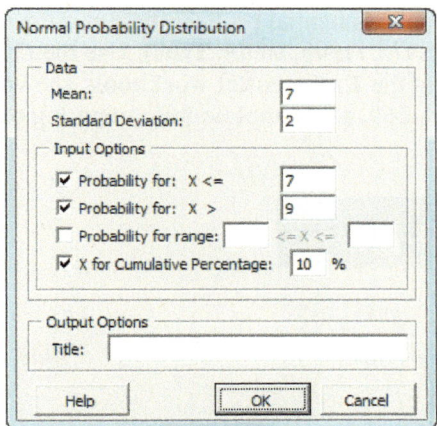

In-Depth Excel Use the **NORMDIST** worksheet function to compute normal probabilities. Enter the function as **NORMDIST**(*X value, mean, standard deviation*, **True**) to return the cumulative probability for less than or equal to the specified *X* value.

Use the **COMPUTE worksheet** of the **Normal workbook**, shown in Figure 6.16 on page 258, as a template for computing normal probabilities. The worksheet contains the data for solving the problems in Examples 6.1 through 6.4. Change the values for the **Mean, Standard Deviation, X Value, From X Value, To X Value**, and/or **Cumulative Percentage** to solve similar problems. To solve a problem that is similar to Example 6.5 on page 256, change the **Cumulative Percentage** cell twice, once to determine the lower value of *X* and the other time to determine the upper value of *X*.

The COMPUTE worksheet also uses the **STANDARDIZE** worksheet function to compute *Z* values, **NORMDIST** to compute the probability of less than or equal to the *X* value given, **NORMSINV** to compute the *Z* value for the cumulative percentage, and **NORMINV** to compute the *X* value for the given cumulative probability, mean, and standard deviation.

The worksheet also includes formulas that update probability labels when an *X* value is changed. Open to the **COMPUTE_FORMULAS worksheet** to examine all formulas.

EG6.3 EVALUATING NORMALITY

Comparing Data Characteristics to Theoretical Properties

Use instructions in Sections EG3.1 through EG3.3 in the Chapter 3 Excel Guide to compare data characteristics to theoretical properties.

Constructing the Normal Probability Plot

PHStat2 Use **Normal Probability Plot** to create a normal probability plot. For example, to create the Figure 6.22 normal probability plot for the 2009 returns on page 263, open to the **DATA worksheet** of the **Bond Funds workbook**. Select **PHStat → Probability & Prob. Distributions → Normal Probability Plot**. In the procedure's dialog box (shown below):

1. Enter **F1:F185** as the **Variable Cell Range**.
2. Check **First cell contains label**.
3. Enter a **Title** and click **OK**.

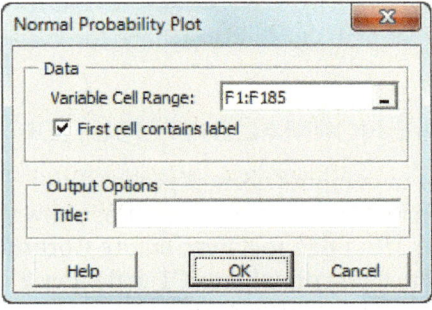

In addition to the chart sheet containing the normal probability plot, the procedure creates a worksheet of plot data that uses the **NORMSINV** function to compute the *Z* values used in the plot.

In-Depth Excel Create a normal probability plot by first creating a worksheet that computes *Z* values for the data to be plotted and then by creating a chart from that worksheet. Use the **PLOT_DATA worksheet** of the **NPP workbook** as a model for computing Z values. This worksheet contains columns for the rank, proportion, Z value, and the **Return 2009** variable and is the source of the data for the **NORMAL_PLOT chart sheet** that contains the Figure 6.22 normal probability plot (see page 263). For other problems, paste sorted variable data in column D, update the number of ranks in column A, and adjust the formulas in columns B and C. Column B formulas divide the column A cell by the quantity $n + 1$ (185 for the 2009 returns data) to compute cumulative percentages and column C formulas use the NORMSINV function to compute the Z values for those cumulative percentages. (Open to the **PLOT_FORMULAS worksheet** in the same workbook to examine these formulas.)

If you have fewer than 184 values, delete rows from the bottom up. If you have more than 184 values, insert rows from somewhere inside the body of the table to ensure that the normal probability plot is properly updated. To create your own normal probability plot for the Return 2009 variable, select the cell range **C1:D185**. Then select **Insert → Scatter** and select the first **Scatter** gallery choice (**Scatter with only Markers**). Relocate the chart to a chart sheet and adjust the chart formatting by using the instructions in Appendix F.

EG6.4 THE UNIFORM DISTRIBUTION

There are no Excel Guide instructions for this section.

EG6.5 THE EXPONENTIAL DISTRIBUTION

PHStat2 Use **Exponential** to compute an exponential probability. For example, to create the Figure 6.25 worksheet that computes the exponential probability for the bank ATM example (see page 269), select **PHStat → Probability & Prob. Distributions → Exponential**. In the procedure's dialog box (shown below):

1. Enter **20** as the **Mean per unit (Lambda)** and **0.1** as the **X Value**.
2. Enter a **Title** and click **OK**.

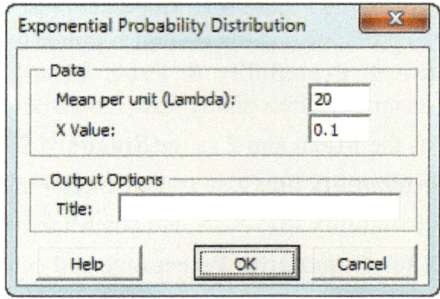

In-Depth Excel Use the **EXPONDIST** worksheet function to compute an exponential probability. Enter the function as **EXPONDIST(*X Value*, *mean*, True)**. Use the **COMPUTE worksheet** of the **Exponential workbook**, shown in Figure 6.25 on page 269, as a template for computing exponential probabilities.

CHAPTER 6 MINITAB GUIDE

MG6.1 CONTINUOUS PROBABILITY DISTRIBUTIONS

There are no Minitab Guide instructions for this section.

MG6.2 THE NORMAL DISTRIBUTION

Use **Normal** to compute normal probabilities. For example, to compute the normal probabilities shown in Figure 6.17 on page 258, open to a new, empty worksheet. Enter **X Value** as the name of column **C1** and enter **9** in the row 1 cell of column **C1**. Select **Calc → Probability Distributions → Normal**. In the Normal Distribution dialog box (shown in the next column):

1. Click **Cumulative probability**.
2. Enter **7** in the **Mean** box.
3. Enter **2** in the **Standard deviation** box.
4. Click **Input column** and enter **C1** in its box.
5. Click **OK**.

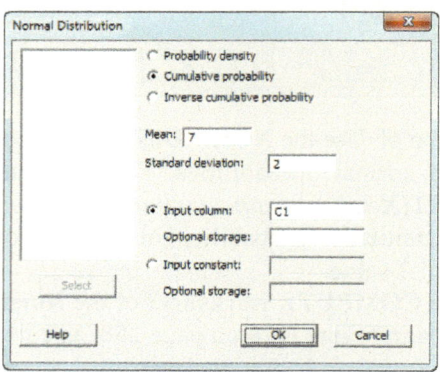

Minitab displays the Example 6.1 probability for a download time that is less than 9 seconds with $\mu = 7$ and $\sigma = 2$ (see in the left portion of Figure 6.17). To compute the normal probability for Example 6.4, enter **Cumulative Percentage** as the name of column **C2** and enter **0.1** in the row 1 cell of column C2. Again select **Calc → Probability Distributions → Normal**. In the Normal Distribution dialog box:

1. Click **Inverse cumulative probability**.
2. Enter **7** in the **Mean** box.

3. Enter **2** in the **Standard deviation** box.
4. Click **Input column** and enter **C2** in its box.
5. Click **OK**.

Minitab displays the Example 6.4 Z value corresponding to a cumulative area of 0.10 (see the right portion of Figure 6.17).

MG6.3 EVALUATING NORMALITY

Comparing Data Characteristics to Theoretical Properties

Use instructions in Sections MG3.1 through MG3.3 in the Chapter 3 Minitab Guide to compare data characteristics to theoretical properties.

Constructing the Normal Probability Plot

Use **Probability Plot** to create a normal probability plot. For example, to create the Figure 6.22 plot for the 2009 returns on page 263, open to the **Bond Funds worksheet**. Select **Graph → Probability Plot** and:

1. In the Probability Plots dialog box, click **Single** and then click **OK**.

In the Probability Plot - Single dialog box (shown below):

2. Double-click **C6 Return2009** in the variables list to add **'Return 2009'** to the **Graph variables** box.
3. Click **Distribution**.

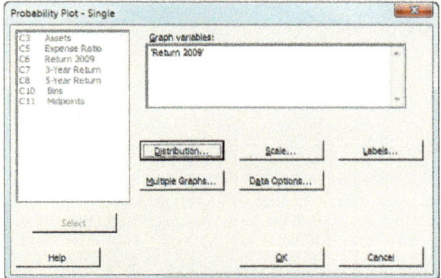

In the Probability Plot - Distribution dialog box:

4. Click the **Distribution** tab (shown at the top of the next column) and select **Normal** from the **Distribution** dropdown list.
5. Click the **Data Display** tab. Click **Symbols only** and clear the **Show confidence interval** check box.
6. Click **OK**.

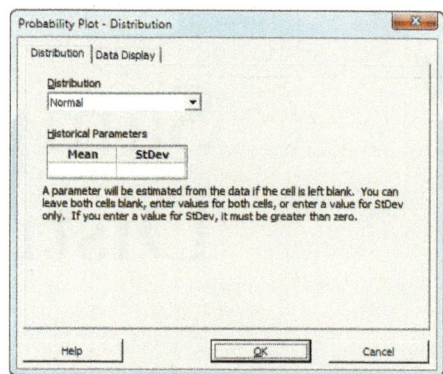

7. Back in the Probability Plot - Single dialog box, click **OK**.

MG6.4 THE UNIFORM DISTRIBUTION

There are no Minitab instructions for this section

MG6.5 THE EXPONENTIAL DISTRIBUTION

Use **Exponential** to compute an exponential probability. For example, to compute the exponential probability for the bank ATM example shown in Figure 6.25 worksheet on page 269, open to a new, blank worksheet. Enter **X Value** as the name of column **C1** and enter **0.1** in the row 1 cell of column **C1**. Select **Calc → Probability Distributions → Exponential**. In the Exponential Distribution dialog box (shown below):

1. Click **Cumulative probability**.
2. Enter **0.05** in the **Scale** box. (Minitab defines scale as the mean time *between* arrivals, $1/\lambda = 1/20 = 0.05$, not the mean number of arrivals, $\lambda = 20$.)
3. Leave the **Threshold** value as **0.0**.
4. Click **Input column** and enter **C1** in its box.
5. Click **OK**.

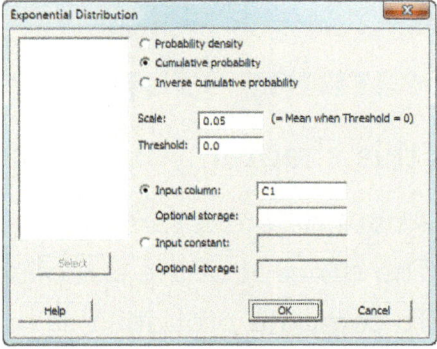

7 Sampling and Sampling Distributions

USING STATISTICS @ Oxford Cereals

7.1 Types of Sampling Methods
Simple Random Samples
Systematic Samples
Stratified Samples
Cluster Samples

7.2 Evaluating Survey Worthiness
Survey Error
Ethical Issues

THINK ABOUT THIS: New Media Surveys/Old Sampling Problems

7.3 Sampling Distributions

7.4 Sampling Distribution of the Mean
The Unbiased Property of the Sample Mean
Standard Error of the Mean
Sampling from Normally Distributed Populations
Sampling from Non-Normally Distributed Populations—The Central Limit Theorem

VISUAL EXPLORATIONS: Exploring Sampling Distributions

7.5 Sampling Distribution of the Proportion

7.6 Online Topic: Sampling from Finite Populations

USING STATISTICS @ Oxford Cereals Revisited

CHAPTER 7 EXCEL GUIDE

CHAPTER 7 MINITAB GUIDE

Learning Objectives

In this chapter, you learn:

- About different sampling methods
- The concept of the sampling distribution
- To compute probabilities related to the sample mean and the sample proportion
- The importance of the Central Limit Theorem

USING STATISTICS

@ Oxford Cereals

Oxford Cereals fills thousands of boxes of cereal during an eight-hour shift. As the plant operations manager, you are responsible for monitoring the amount of cereal placed in each box. To be consistent with package labeling, boxes should contain a mean of 368 grams of cereal. Because of the speed of the process, the cereal weight varies from box to box, causing some boxes to be underfilled and others overfilled. If the process is not working properly, the mean weight in the boxes could vary too much from the label weight of 368 grams to be acceptable.

Because weighing every single box is too time-consuming, costly, and inefficient, you must take a sample of boxes. For each sample you select, you plan to weigh the individual boxes and calculate a sample mean. You need to determine the probability that such a sample mean could have been randomly selected from a population whose mean is 368 grams. Based on your analysis, you will have to decide whether to maintain, alter, or shut down the cereal-filling process.

In Chapter 6, you used the normal distribution to study the distribution of video download times from the OurCampus! website. In this chapter, you need to make a decision about the cereal-filling process, based on the weights of a sample of cereal boxes packaged at Oxford Cereals. You will learn different methods of sampling and about sampling distributions and how to use them to solve business problems.

7.1 Types of Sampling Methods

In Section 1.3, a sample is defined as the portion of a population that has been selected for analysis. Rather than selecting every item in the population, statistical sampling procedures focus on collecting a small representative portion of the larger population. The results of the sample are then used to estimate characteristics of the entire population. There are three main reasons for selecting a sample:

- Selecting a sample is less time-consuming than selecting every item in the population.
- Selecting a sample is less costly than selecting every item in the population.
- Analyzing a sample is less cumbersome and more practical than analyzing the entire population.

The sampling process begins by defining the **frame**, a listing of items that make up the population. Frames are data sources such as population lists, directories, or maps. Samples are drawn from frames. Inaccurate or biased results can occur if a frame excludes certain portions of the population. Using different frames to generate data can lead to different conclusions.

After you select a frame, you draw a sample from the frame. As illustrated in Figure 7.1, there are two types of samples: nonprobability samples and probability samples.

FIGURE 7.1
Types of samples

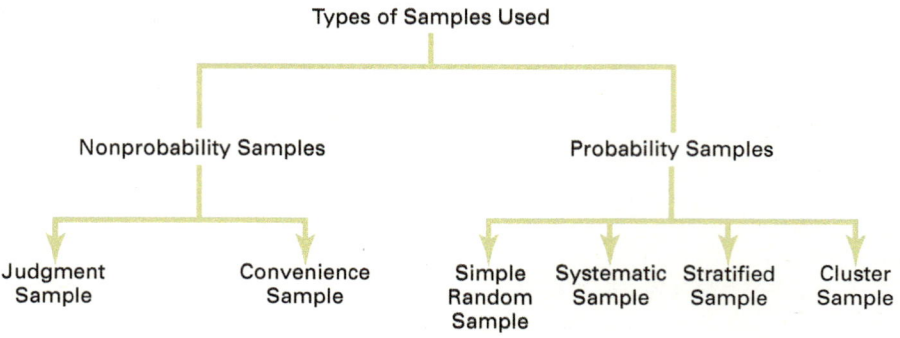

In a **nonprobability sample**, you select the items or individuals without knowing their probabilities of selection. Because of this, the theory of statistical inference that has been developed for probability sampling cannot be applied to nonprobability samples. A common type of nonprobability sampling is **convenience sampling**. In convenience sampling, items selected are easy, inexpensive, or convenient to sample. For example, if you were sampling tires stacked in a warehouse, it would be much more convenient to sample tires at the top of a stack than tires at the bottom of a stack. In many cases, participants in the sample select themselves. For example, many companies conduct surveys by giving visitors to their website the opportunity to complete survey forms and submit them electronically. The responses to these surveys can provide large amounts of data quickly and inexpensively, but the sample consists of self-selected web users. For many studies, only a nonprobability sample such as a judgment sample is available. In a **judgment sample**, you get the opinions of preselected experts in the subject matter. Although the experts may be well informed, you cannot generalize their results to the population.

Nonprobability samples can have certain advantages, such as convenience, speed, and low cost. However, their lack of accuracy due to selection bias and the fact that the results cannot be used for statistical inference more than offset these advantages.

In a **probability sample**, you select items based on known probabilities. Whenever possible, you should use probability sampling methods. Probability samples allow you to make inferences about the population of interest. The four types of probability samples most commonly used are simple random, systematic, stratified, and cluster samples. These sampling methods vary in their cost, accuracy, and complexity.

Simple Random Samples

In a **simple random sample**, every item from a frame has the same chance of selection as every other item. In addition, every sample of a fixed size has the same chance of selection as every other sample of that size. Simple random sampling is the most elementary random sampling technique. It forms the basis for the other random sampling techniques.

With simple random sampling, you use n to represent the sample size and N to represent the frame size. You number every item in the frame from 1 to N. The chance that you will select any particular member of the frame on the first selection is $1/N$.

You select samples with replacement or without replacement. **Sampling with replacement** means that after you select an item, you return it to the frame, where it has the same probability of being selected again. Imagine that you have a fishbowl containing N business cards, one card for each person. On the first selection, you select the card for Judy Craven. You record pertinent information and replace the business card in the bowl. You then mix up the cards in the bowl and select a second card. On the second selection, Judy Craven has the same probability of being selected again, $1/N$. You repeat this process until you have selected the desired sample size, n.

However, usually you do not want the same item to be selected again. **Sampling without replacement** means that once you select an item, you cannot select it again. The chance that you will select any particular item in the frame—for example, the business card for Judy Craven—on the first selection is $1/N$. The chance that you will select any card not previously chosen on the second selection is now 1 out of $N - 1$. This process continues until you have selected the desired sample of size n.

Regardless of whether you have sampled with or without replacement, "fishbowl" methods of sample selection have a major drawback—the ability to thoroughly mix the cards and randomly select the sample. As a result, fishbowl methods are not very useful. You need to use less cumbersome and more scientific methods of selection.

One such method uses a **table of random numbers** (see Table E.1 in Appendix E) for selecting the sample. A table of random numbers consists of a series of digits listed in a randomly generated sequence (see reference 8). Because the numeric system uses 10 digits (0, 1, 2, ..., 9), the chance that you will randomly generate any particular digit is equal to the probability of generating any other digit. This probability is 1 out of 10. Hence, if you generate a sequence of 800 digits, you would expect about 80 to be the digit 0, 80 to be the digit 1, and so on. Because every digit or sequence of digits in the table is random, the table can be read either horizontally or vertically. The margins of the table designate row numbers and column numbers. The digits themselves are grouped into sequences of five in order to make reading the table easier.

To use Table E.1 instead of a fishbowl for selecting the sample, you first need to assign code numbers to the individual items of the frame. Then you generate the random sample by reading the table of random numbers and selecting those individuals from the frame whose assigned code numbers match the digits found in the table. You can better understand the process of sample selection by studying Example 7.1.

EXAMPLE 7.1

Selecting a Simple Random Sample by Using a Table of Random Numbers

A company wants to select a sample of 32 full-time workers from a population of 800 full-time employees in order to collect information on expenditures concerning a company-sponsored dental plan. How do you select a simple random sample?

SOLUTION The company decides to conduct an e-mail survey. Assuming that not everyone will respond to the survey, you need to send more than 32 surveys to get the necessary 32 responses. Assuming that 8 out of 10 full-time workers will respond to such a survey (i.e., a response rate of 80%), you decide to send 40 surveys. Because you want to send the 40 surveys to 40 different individuals, you should sample without replacement.

The frame consists of a listing of the names and e-mail addresses of all $N = 800$ full-time employees taken from the company personnel files. Thus, the frame is a complete listing of the population. To select the random sample of 40 employees from this frame, you use a table of random numbers. Because the frame size (800) is a three-digit number, each assigned code number must also be three digits so that every full-time worker has an equal chance of selection. You assign a code of 001 to the first full-time employee in the population listing, a code of 002 to the second full-time employee in the population listing, and so on, until a code of 800 is assigned to the Nth full-time worker in the listing. Because $N = 800$ is the largest possible coded value, you discard all three-digit code sequences greater than 800 (i.e., 801 through 999 and 000).

To select the simple random sample, you choose an arbitrary starting point from the table of random numbers. One method you can use is to close your eyes and strike the table of random numbers with a pencil. Suppose you used this procedure and you selected row 06, column 05 of Table 7.1 (which is extracted from Table E.1) as the starting point. Although you can go in any direction, in this example you read the table from left to right, in sequences of three digits, without skipping.

TABLE 7.1

Using a Table of Random Numbers

Row	00000 12345	00001 67890	11111 12345	11112 67890	22222 12345	22223 67890	33333 12345	33334 67890
01	49280	88924	35779	00283	81163	07275	89863	02348
02	61870	41657	07468	08612	98083	97349	20775	45091
03	43898	65923	25078	86129	78496	97653	91550	08078
04	62993	93912	30454	84598	56095	20664	12872	64647
05	33850	58555	51438	85507	71865	79488	76783	31708
06	97340	03364	88472	04334	63919	36394	11095	92470
07	70543	29776	10087	10072	55980	64688	68239	20461
08	89382	93809	00796	95945	34101	81277	66090	88872
09	37818	72142	67140	50785	22380	16703	53362	44940
10	60430	22834	14130	96593	23298	56203	92671	15925
11	82975	66158	84731	19436	55790	69229	28661	13675
12	39087	71938	40355	54324	08401	26299	49420	59208
13	55700	24586	93247	32596	11865	63397	44251	43189
14	14756	23997	78643	75912	83832	32768	18928	57070
15	32166	53251	70654	92827	63491	04233	33825	69662
16	23236	73751	31888	81718	06546	83246	47651	04877
17	45794	26926	15130	82455	78305	55058	52551	47182
18	09893	20505	14225	68514	46427	56788	96297	78822
19	54382	74598	91499	14523	68479	27686	46162	83554
20	94750	89923	37089	20048	80336	94598	26940	36858
21	70297	34135	53140	33340	42050	82341	44104	82949
22	85157	47954	32979	26575	57600	40881	12250	73742
23	11100	02340	12860	74697	96644	89439	28707	25815
24	36871	50775	30592	57143	17381	68856	25853	35041
25	23913	48357	63308	16090	51690	54607	72407	55538

Begin selection (row 06, column 05)

Source: Data extracted from Rand Corporation, *A Million Random Digits with 100,000 Normal Deviates* (Glencoe, IL: The Free Press, 1955) and contained in Table E.1.

The individual with code number 003 is the first full-time employee in the sample (row 06 and columns 05–07), the second individual has code number 364 (row 06 and columns 08–10), and the third individual has code number 884. Because the highest code for any employee is 800, you discard the number 884. Individuals with code numbers 720, 433, 463, 363, 109, 592, 470, and 705 are selected third through tenth, respectively.

You continue the selection process until you get the required sample size of 40 full-time employees. If any three-digit sequence repeats during the selection process, you discard the repeating sequence because you are sampling without replacement.

Systematic Samples

In a **systematic sample**, you partition the N items in the frame into n groups of k items, where

$$k = \frac{N}{n}$$

You round k to the nearest integer. To select a systematic sample, you choose the first item to be selected at random from the first k items in the frame. Then, you select the remaining $n - 1$ items by taking every kth item thereafter from the entire frame.

If the frame consists of a listing of prenumbered checks, sales receipts, or invoices, taking a systematic sample is faster and easier than taking a simple random sample. A systematic sample is also a convenient mechanism for collecting data from telephone books, class rosters, and consecutive items coming off an assembly line.

To take a systematic sample of $n = 40$ from the population of $N = 800$ full-time employees, you partition the frame of 800 into 40 groups, each of which contains 20 employees. You then select a random number from the first 20 individuals and include every twentieth individual after the first selection in the sample. For example, if the first random number you select is 008, your subsequent selections are 028, 048, 068, 088, 108, . . . , 768, and 788.

Simple random sampling and systematic sampling are simpler than other, more sophisticated, probability sampling methods, but they generally require a larger sample size. In addition, systematic sampling is prone to selection bias. When using systematic sampling, if there is a pattern in the frame, you could have severe selection biases. To overcome the inefficiency of simple random sampling and the potential selection bias involved with systematic sampling, you can use either stratified sampling methods or cluster sampling methods.

Stratified Samples

In a **stratified sample**, you first subdivide the N items in the frame into separate subpopulations, or **strata**. A stratum is defined by some common characteristic, such as gender or year in school. You select a simple random sample within each of the strata and combine the results from the separate simple random samples. Stratified sampling is more efficient than either simple random sampling or systematic sampling because you are ensured of the representation of items across the entire population. The homogeneity of items within each stratum provides greater precision in the estimates of underlying population parameters.

EXAMPLE 7.2
Selecting a Stratified Sample

A company wants to select a sample of 32 full-time workers from a population of 800 full-time employees in order to estimate expenditures from a company-sponsored dental plan. Of the full-time employees, 25% are managers and 75% are nonmanagerial workers. How do you select the stratified sample in order for the sample to represent the correct percentage of managers and nonmanagerial workers?

SOLUTION If you assume an 80% response rate, you need to send 40 surveys to get the necessary 32 responses. The frame consists of a listing of the names and e-mail addresses of all $N = 800$ full-time employees included in the company personnel files. Because 25% of the full-time employees are managers, you first separate the frame into two strata: a subpopulation listing of all 200 managerial-level personnel and a separate subpopulation listing of all 600 full-time nonmanagerial workers. Because the first stratum consists of a listing of 200 managers, you assign three-digit code numbers from 001 to 200. Because the second stratum contains a listing of 600 nonmanagerial workers, you assign three-digit code numbers from 001 to 600.

To collect a stratified sample proportional to the sizes of the strata, you select 25% of the overall sample from the first stratum and 75% of the overall sample from the second stratum. You take two separate simple random samples, each of which is based on a distinct random starting point from a table of random numbers (Table E.1). In the first sample, you select 10 managers from the listing of 200 in the first stratum, and in the second sample, you select 30 nonmanagerial workers from the listing of 600 in the second stratum. You then combine the results to reflect the composition of the entire company.

Cluster Samples

In a **cluster sample**, you divide the N items in the frame into clusters that contain several items. **Clusters** are often naturally occurring designations, such as counties, election districts, city blocks, households, or sales territories. You then take a random sample of one or more clusters and study all items in each selected cluster.

Cluster sampling is often more cost-effective than simple random sampling, particularly if the population is spread over a wide geographic region. However, cluster sampling often requires a larger sample size to produce results as precise as those from simple random sampling or stratified sampling. A detailed discussion of systematic sampling, stratified sampling, and cluster sampling procedures can be found in reference 1.

Problems for Section 7.1

LEARNING THE BASICS

7.1 For a population containing $N = 902$ individuals, what code number would you assign for
a. the first person on the list?
b. the fortieth person on the list?
c. the last person on the list?

7.2 For a population of $N = 902$, verify that by starting in row 05, column 01 of the table of random numbers (Table E.1), you need only six rows to select a sample of $N = 60$ *without* replacement.

7.3 Given a population of $N = 93$, starting in row 29, column 01 of the table of random numbers (Table E.1), and reading across the row, select a sample of $N = 15$
a. *without* replacement.
b. *with* replacement.

APPLYING THE CONCEPTS

7.4 For a study that consists of personal interviews with participants (rather than mail or phone surveys), explain why simple random sampling might be less practical than some other sampling methods.

7.5 You want to select a random sample of $n = 1$ from a population of three items (which are called A, B, and C). The rule for selecting the sample is as follows: Flip a coin; if it is heads, pick item A; if it is tails, flip the coin again; this time, if it is heads, choose B; if it is tails, choose C. Explain why this is a probability sample but not a simple random sample.

7.6 A population has four members (called A, B, C, and D). You would like to select a random sample of $n = 2$, which you decide to do in the following way: Flip a coin; if it is heads, the sample will be items A and B; if it is tails, the sample will be items C and D. Although this is a random sample, it is not a simple random sample. Explain why. (Compare the procedure described in Problem 7.5 with the procedure described in this problem.)

7.7 The registrar of a college with a population of $N = 4,000$ full-time students is asked by the president to conduct a survey to measure satisfaction with the quality of life on campus. The following table contains a breakdown of the 4,000 registered full-time students, by gender and class designation:

	\multicolumn{4}{c}{Class Designation}			
Gender	Fr.	So.	Jr.	Sr.	Total
Female	700	520	500	480	2,200
Male	560	460	400	380	1,800
Total	1,260	980	900	860	4,000

The registrar intends to take a probability sample of $n = 200$ students and project the results from the sample to the entire population of full-time students.
a. If the frame available from the registrar's files is an alphabetical listing of the names of all $N = 4,000$ registered full-time students, what type of sample could you take? Discuss.
b. What is the advantage of selecting a simple random sample in (a)?
c. What is the advantage of selecting a systematic sample in (a)?
d. If the frame available from the registrar's files is a listing of the names of all $N = 4,000$ registered full-time students compiled from eight separate alphabetical lists, based on the gender and class designation breakdowns shown in the class designation table, what type of sample should you take? Discuss.
e. Suppose that each of the $N = 4,000$ registered full-time students lived in one of the 10 campus dormitories. Each dormitory accommodates 400 students. It is college policy to fully integrate students by gender and class designation in each dormitory. If the registrar is able to compile a listing of all students by dormitory, explain how you could take a cluster sample.

SELF Test 7.8 Prenumbered sales invoices are kept in a sales journal. The invoices are numbered from 0001 to 5000.
a. Beginning in row 16, column 01, and proceeding horizontally in Table E.1, select a simple random sample of 50 invoice numbers.
b. Select a systematic sample of 50 invoice numbers. Use the random numbers in row 20, columns 05–07, as the starting point for your selection.

c. Are the invoices selected in (a) the same as those selected in (b)? Why or why not?

7.9 Suppose that 5,000 sales invoices are separated into four strata. Stratum 1 contains 50 invoices, stratum 2 contains 500 invoices, stratum 3 contains 1,000 invoices, and stratum 4 contains 3,450 invoices. A sample of 500 sales invoices is needed.

a. What type of sampling should you do? Why?
b. Explain how you would carry out the sampling according to the method stated in (a).
c. Why is the sampling in (a) not simple random sampling?

7.2 Evaluating Survey Worthiness

Surveys are used to collect data. Nearly every day, you read or hear about survey or opinion poll results in newspapers, on the Internet, or on radio or television. To identify surveys that lack objectivity or credibility, you must critically evaluate what you read and hear by examining the worthiness of the survey. First, you must evaluate the purpose of the survey, why it was conducted, and for whom it was conducted.

The second step in evaluating the worthiness of a survey is to determine whether it was based on a probability or nonprobability sample (as discussed in Section 7.1). You need to remember that the only way to make valid statistical inferences from a sample to a population is through the use of a probability sample. Surveys that use nonprobability sampling methods are subject to serious, perhaps unintentional, biases that may make the results meaningless.

Survey Error

Even when surveys use random probability sampling methods, they are subject to potential errors. There are four types of survey errors:

- Coverage error
- Nonresponse error
- Sampling error
- Measurement error

Well-designed surveys reduce or minimize these four types of errors, often at considerable cost.

Coverage Error The key to proper sample selection is having an adequate frame. Remember that a frame is an up-to-date list of all the items from which you will select the sample. **Coverage error** occurs if certain groups of items are excluded from the frame so that they have no chance of being selected in the sample. Coverage error results in a **selection bias**. If the frame is inadequate because certain groups of items in the population were not properly included, any random probability sample selected will provide only an estimate of the characteristics of the frame, not the *actual* population.

Nonresponse Error Not everyone is willing to respond to a survey. In fact, research has shown that individuals in the upper and lower economic classes tend to respond less frequently to surveys than do people in the middle class. **Nonresponse error** arises from failure to collect data on all items in the sample and results in a **nonresponse bias**. Because you cannot always assume that persons who do not respond to surveys are similar to those who do, you need to follow up on the nonresponses after a specified period of time. You should make several attempts to convince such individuals to complete the survey. The follow-up responses are then compared to the initial responses in order to make valid inferences from the survey (see reference 1). The mode of response you use affects the rate of response. Personal interviews and telephone interviews usually produce a higher response rate than do mail surveys—but at a higher cost.

Sampling Error As discussed earlier, a sample is selected because it is simpler, less costly, and more efficient to examine than an entire population. However, chance dictates which individuals or items will or will not be included in the sample. **Sampling error** reflects the variation, or "chance differences," from sample to sample, based on the probability of particular individuals or items being selected in the particular samples.

When you read about the results of surveys or polls in newspapers or magazines, there is often a statement regarding a margin of error, such as "the results of this poll are expected to be within ±4 percentage points of the actual value." This **margin of error** is the sampling error. You can reduce sampling error by using larger sample sizes, although doing so increases the cost of conducting the survey.

Measurement Error In the practice of good survey research, you design a questionnaire with the intention of gathering meaningful information. But you have a dilemma here: Getting meaningful measurements is often easier said than done. Consider the following proverb:

A person with one watch always knows what time it is;

A person with two watches always searches to identify the correct one;

A person with ten watches is always reminded of the difficulty in measuring time.

Unfortunately, the process of measurement is often governed by what is convenient, not what is needed. The measurements you get are often only a proxy for the ones you really desire. Much attention has been given to measurement error that occurs because of a weakness in question wording (see reference 2). A question should be clear, not ambiguous. Furthermore, in order to avoid *leading questions*, you need to present questions in a neutral manner.

Three sources of **measurement error** are ambiguous wording of questions, the Hawthorne effect, and respondent error. As an example of ambiguous wording, several years ago, the U.S. Department of Labor reported that the unemployment rate in the United States had been underestimated for more than a decade because of poor questionnaire wording in the Current Population Survey. In particular, the wording had led to a significant undercount of women in the labor force. Because unemployment rates are tied to benefit programs such as state unemployment compensation, survey researchers had to rectify the situation by adjusting the questionnaire wording.

The *Hawthorne effect* occurs when a respondent feels obligated to please the interviewer. Proper interviewer training can minimize the Hawthorne effect.

Respondent error occurs as a result of an overzealous or underzealous effort by the respondent. You can minimize this error in two ways: (1) by carefully scrutinizing the data and then recontacting those individuals whose responses seem unusual and (2) by establishing a program of recontacting a small number of randomly chosen individuals in order to determine the reliability of the responses.

Ethical Issues

Ethical considerations arise with respect to the four types of potential errors that can occur when designing surveys: coverage error, nonresponse error, sampling error, and measurement error. Coverage error can result in selection bias and becomes an ethical issue if particular groups or individuals are *purposely* excluded from the frame so that the survey results are more favorable to the survey's sponsor. Nonresponse error can lead to nonresponse bias and becomes an ethical issue if the sponsor knowingly designs the survey so that particular groups or individuals are less likely than others to respond. Sampling error becomes an ethical issue if the findings are purposely presented without reference to sample size and margin of error so that the sponsor can promote a viewpoint that might otherwise be inappropriate. Measurement error becomes an ethical issue in one of three ways: (1) a survey sponsor chooses leading questions that guide the responses in a particular direction; (2) an interviewer, through mannerisms and tone, purposely creates a Hawthorne effect or otherwise guides the responses in a particular direction; or (3) a respondent willfully provides false information.

Ethical issues also arise when the results of nonprobability samples are used to form conclusions about the entire population. When you use a nonprobability sampling method, you need to explain the sampling procedures and state that the results cannot be generalized beyond the sample.

THINK ABOUT THIS New Media Surveys/Old Sampling Problems

Imagine that you are a software distributor and you decide to create a "customer experience improvement program" that records how your customers are using your products, with the goal of using the collected data to improve your products. Or say that you're the moderator of an opinion blog who decides to create an instant poll to ask your readers about important political issues. Or you're a marketer of products aimed at a specific demographic and decide to create a page in a social networking site through which you plan to collect consumer feedback. What might you have in common with a *dead-tree* publication that went out of business over 70 years ago?

By 1932, before there was ever an Internet—or even commercial television—a "straw poll" conducted by the magazine *Literary Digest* had successfully predicted five U.S. presidential elections in a row. For the 1936 election, the magazine promised its largest poll ever and sent about 10 million ballots to people all across the country. After receiving and tabulating more than 2.3 million ballots, the *Digest* confidently proclaimed that Alf Landon would be an easy winner over Franklin D. Roosevelt. As things turned out, FDR won in a landslide, with Landon receiving the fewest electoral votes in U.S. history. The reputation of the *Literary Digest* was ruined; the magazine would cease publication less than two years later.

The failure of the *Literary Digest* poll was a watershed event in the history of sample surveys and polls. This failure refuted the notion that the larger the sample is, the better. (Remember this the next time someone complains about a political survey's "small" sample size.) The failure opened the door to new and more modern methods of sampling—the theory and concepts this book discusses in Sections 7.1 and 7.2. Today's Gallup polls of political opinion (**www.gallup.com**) or Roper (now GfK Roper) Reports about consumer behavior (**www.gfkamerica.com/practice_areas/roper_consulting/roper_reports**) arose, in part, due to this failure. George Gallup, the "Gallup" of the poll, and Elmo Roper, of the eponymous reports, both first gained widespread public notice for their correct "scientific" predictions of the 1936 election.

The failed *Literary Digest* poll became fodder for several postmortems, and the reason for the failure became almost an urban legend. Typically, the explanation is coverage error: The ballots were sent mostly to "rich people," and this created a frame that excluded poorer citizens (presumably more inclined to vote for the Democrat Roosevelt than the Republican Landon). However, later analyses suggest that this was not true; instead, low rates of response (2.3 million ballots represented less than 25% of the ballots distributed) and/or nonresponse error (Roosevelt voters were less likely to mail in a ballot than Landon voters) were significant reasons for the failure (see reference 8).

When Microsoft introduced its new Office Ribbon interface with Office 2007, a program manager explained how Microsoft had applied data collected from its "Customer Experience Improvement Program" to the redesign of the user interface. This led others to speculate that the data were biased toward beginners—who might be less likely to *decline* participation in the program—and that, in turn, had led Microsoft to make decisions that ended up perplexing more experienced users. This was another case of nonresponse error!

The blog moderator's instant poll mentioned earlier is targeted to the moderator's community, and the social network–based survey is aimed at "friends" of a product; such polls can also suffer from nonresponse error, and this fact is often overlooked by users of these new media. Often, marketers extol how much they "know" about survey respondents, thanks to information that can be "mined" (see Sections 2.7 and 15.7) from a social network community. But no amount of information about the respondents can tell marketers who the nonresponders are. Therefore, new media surveys fall prey to the same old type of error that may have been fatal to *Literary Digest* way back when.

Today, companies establish formal surveys based on probability sampling and go to great lengths—and spend large sums—to deal with coverage error, nonresponse error, sampling error, and measurement error. Instant polling and tell-a-friend surveys can be interesting and fun, but they are not replacements for the methods discussed in this chapter.

Problems for Section 7.2

APPLYING THE CONCEPTS

7.10 A survey indicates that the vast majority of college students own their own personal computers. What information would you want to know before you accepted the results of this survey?

7.11 A simple random sample of $n = 300$ full-time employees is selected from a company list containing the names of all $N = 5,000$ full-time employees in order to evaluate job satisfaction.
a. Give an example of possible coverage error.
b. Give an example of possible nonresponse error.
c. Give an example of possible sampling error.
d. Give an example of possible measurement error.

7.12 Business Professor Thomas Callarman traveled to China more than a dozen times from 2000 to 2005. He warns people about believing everything they read about surveys conducted in China and gives two specific reasons: "First, things are changing so rapidly that what you hear today may not be true tomorrow. Second, the people who answer the surveys may tell you what they think you want to hear, rather than what they really believe" (T. E. Callarman, "Some Thoughts on China," *Decision Line*, March 2006, pp. 1, 43–44).
a. List the four types of survey error discussed in the paragraph above.
b. Which of the types of survey error in (a) are the basis for Professor Callarman's two reasons to question the surveys being conducted in China?

7.13 A recent survey of college freshmen investigated the amount of involvement their parents have with decisions concerning their education. When asked about the decision to go to college, 84% said their parents' involvement was about right, 10.3% said it was too much, and 5.7% said it was too little. When it came to selecting individual courses, 72.5% said their parents' involvement was about right, 3.5% said it was too much, and 24.0% said it was too little (M. B. Marklein, "Study: Colleges Shouldn't Fret Over Hands-on Parents," **www.usatoday.com**, January 23, 2008). What additional information would you want to know about the survey before you accepted the results of the study?

7.14 Recruiters are finding a wealth of unfiltered information about candidates on social-networking websites. A recent survey found that 83% of recruiters use search engines to learn more about candidates, and 43% eliminated candidates based on information they found (I. Phaneuf, "Who's Googling You?" *Job Postings*, Spring 2009, pp. 12–13). What additional information would you want to know about a survey before you accepted the results of the study?

7.3 Sampling Distributions

In many applications, you want to make inferences that are based on statistics calculated from samples to estimate the values of population parameters. In the next two sections, you will learn about how the sample mean (a statistic) is used to estimate the population mean (a parameter) and how the sample proportion (a statistic) is used to estimate the population proportion (a parameter). Your main concern when making a statistical inference is reaching conclusions about a population, *not* about a sample. For example, a political pollster is interested in the sample results only as a way of estimating the actual proportion of the votes that each candidate will receive from the population of voters. Likewise, as plant operations manager for Oxford Cereals, you are only interested in using the sample mean weight calculated from a sample of cereal boxes for estimating the mean weight of a population of boxes.

In practice, you select a single random sample of a predetermined size from the population. Hypothetically, to use the sample statistic to estimate the population parameter, you could examine *every* possible sample of a given size that could occur. A **sampling distribution** is the distribution of the results if you actually selected all possible samples. The single result you obtain in practice is just one of the results in the sampling distribution.

7.4 Sampling Distribution of the Mean

In Chapter 3, several measures of central tendency, including the mean, median, and mode, were discussed. Undoubtedly, the mean is the most widely used measure of central tendency. The sample mean is often used to estimate the population mean. The **sampling distribution of the mean** is the distribution of all possible sample means if you select all possible samples of a given size.

The Unbiased Property of the Sample Mean

The sample mean is **unbiased** because the mean of all the possible sample means (of a given sample size, n) is equal to the population mean, μ. A simple example concerning a population of four administrative assistants demonstrates this property. Each assistant is asked to apply the same set of updates to a human resources database. Table 7.2 presents the number of errors made by each of the administrative assistants. This population distribution is shown in Figure 7.2.

TABLE 7.2

Number of Errors Made by Each of Four Administrative Assistants

Administrative Assistant	Number of Errors
Ann	$X_1 = 3$
Bob	$X_2 = 2$
Carla	$X_3 = 1$
Dave	$X_4 = 4$

FIGURE 7.2

Number of errors made by a population of four administrative assistants

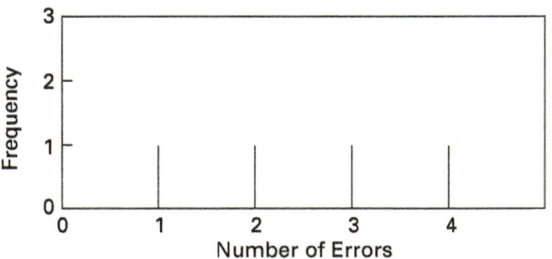

When you have the data from a population, you compute the mean by using Equation (7.1).

POPULATION MEAN

The population mean is the sum of the values in the population divided by the population size, N.

$$\mu = \frac{\sum_{i=1}^{N} X_i}{N} \tag{7.1}$$

You compute the population standard deviation, σ, by using Equation (7.2).

POPULATION STANDARD DEVIATION

$$\sigma = \sqrt{\frac{\sum_{i=1}^{N}(X_i - \mu)^2}{N}} \tag{7.2}$$

Thus, for the data of Table 7.2,

$$\mu = \frac{3 + 2 + 1 + 4}{4} = 2.5 \text{ errors}$$

and

$$\sigma = \sqrt{\frac{(3 - 2.5)^2 + (2 - 2.5)^2 + (1 - 2.5)^2 + (4 - 2.5)^2}{4}} = 1.12 \text{ errors}$$

If you select samples of two administrative assistants *with* replacement from this population, there are 16 possible samples ($N^n = 4^2 = 16$). Table 7.3 lists the 16 possible sample outcomes. If you average all 16 of these sample means, the mean of these values, is equal to 2.5, which is also the mean of the population, μ.

TABLE 7.3

All 16 Samples of $n = 2$ Administrative Assistants from a Population of $N = 4$ Administrative Assistants When Sampling with Replacement

Sample	Administrative Assistants	Sample Outcomes	Sample Mean
1	Ann, Ann	3, 3	$\bar{X}_1 = 3$
2	Ann, Bob	3, 2	$\bar{X}_2 = 2.5$
3	Ann, Carla	3, 1	$\bar{X}_3 = 2$
4	Ann, Dave	3, 4	$\bar{X}_4 = 3.5$
5	Bob, Ann	2, 3	$\bar{X}_5 = 2.5$
6	Bob, Bob	2, 2	$\bar{X}_6 = 2$
7	Bob, Carla	2, 1	$\bar{X}_7 = 1.5$
8	Bob, Dave	2, 4	$\bar{X}_8 = 3$
9	Carla, Ann	1, 3	$\bar{X}_9 = 2$
10	Carla, Bob	1, 2	$\bar{X}_{10} = 1.5$
11	Carla, Carla	1, 1	$\bar{X}_{11} = 1$
12	Carla, Dave	1, 4	$\bar{X}_{12} = 2.5$
13	Dave, Ann	4, 3	$\bar{X}_{13} = 3.5$
14	Dave, Bob	4, 2	$\bar{X}_{14} = 3$
15	Dave, Carla	4, 1	$\bar{X}_{15} = 2.5$
16	Dave, Dave	4, 4	$\bar{X}_{16} = 4$
			$\mu_{\bar{X}} = 2.5$

Because the mean of the 16 sample means is equal to the population mean, the sample mean is an unbiased estimator of the population mean. Therefore, although you do not know how close the sample mean of any particular sample selected comes to the population mean, you are assured that the mean of all the possible sample means that could have been selected is equal to the population mean.

Standard Error of the Mean

Figure 7.3 illustrates the variation in the sample means when selecting all 16 possible samples.

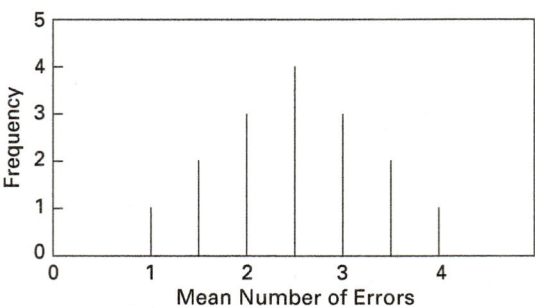

FIGURE 7.3
Sampling distribution of the mean, based on all possible samples containing two administrative assistants

Source: Data are from Table 7.3.

In this small example, although the sample means vary from sample to sample, depending on which two administrative assistants are selected, the sample means do not vary as much as the individual values in the population. That the sample means are less variable than the individual values in the population follows directly from the fact that each sample mean averages together all the values in the sample. A population consists of individual outcomes that can take on a wide range of values, from extremely small to extremely large. However, if a sample contains an extreme value, although this value will have an effect on the sample mean, the effect is reduced because the value is averaged with all the other values in the sample. As the sample size increases, the effect of a single extreme value becomes smaller because it is averaged with more values.

The value of the standard deviation of all possible sample means, called the **standard error of the mean**, expresses how the sample means vary from sample to sample. As the sample size increases, the standard error of the mean decreases by a factor equal to the square root of the sample size.

> **STANDARD ERROR OF THE MEAN**
>
> The standard error of the mean, $\sigma_{\bar{X}}$, is equal to the standard deviation in the population, σ, divided by the square root of the sample size, n.
>
> $$\sigma_{\bar{X}} = \frac{\sigma}{\sqrt{n}} \qquad (7.3)$$

Equation (7.3) defines the standard error of the mean when sampling *with* replacement or sampling *without* replacement from large or infinite populations.

Example 7.3 computes the standard error of the mean when the sample selected without replacement contains less than 5% of the entire population.

EXAMPLE 7.3

Computing the Standard Error of the Mean

Returning to the cereal-filling process described in the Using Statistics scenario on page 279, if you randomly select a sample of 25 boxes without replacement from the thousands of boxes filled during a shift, the sample contains much less than 5% of the population. Given that the standard deviation of the cereal-filling process is 15 grams, compute the standard error of the mean.

SOLUTION Using Equation (7.3) with $n = 25$ and $\sigma = 15$, the standard error of the mean is

$$\sigma_{\bar{X}} = \frac{\sigma}{\sqrt{n}} = \frac{15}{\sqrt{25}} = \frac{15}{5} = 3$$

The variation in the sample means for samples of $n = 25$ is much less than the variation in the individual boxes of cereal (i.e., $\sigma_{\bar{X}} = 3$, while $\sigma = 15$).

Sampling from Normally Distributed Populations

Now that the concept of a sampling distribution has been introduced and the standard error of the mean has been defined, what distribution will the sample mean, $\bar{X}$, follow? If you are sampling from a population that is normally distributed with mean, μ, and standard deviation, σ, then regardless of the sample size, n, the sampling distribution of the mean is normally distributed, with mean, $\mu_{\bar{X}} = \mu$, and standard error of the mean, $\sigma_{\bar{X}} = \sigma/\sqrt{n}$.

In the simplest case, if you take samples of size $n = 1$, each possible sample mean is a single value from the population because

$$\bar{X} = \frac{\sum_{i=1}^{n} X_i}{n} = \frac{X_1}{1} = X_1$$

Therefore, if the population is normally distributed, with mean μ and standard deviation σ, the sampling distribution $\bar{X}$ for samples of $n = 1$ must also follow the normal distribution, with mean $\mu_{\bar{X}} = \mu$ and standard error of the mean $\sigma_{\bar{X}} = \sigma/\sqrt{1} = \sigma$. In addition, as the sample size increases, the sampling distribution of the mean still follows a normal distribution, with $\mu_{\bar{X}} = \mu$, but the standard error of the mean decreases, so that a larger proportion of sample means are closer to the population mean. Figure 7.4 illustrates this reduction in variability. Note that 500 samples of size 1, 2, 4, 8, 16, and 32 were randomly selected from a normally distributed population. From the polygons in Figure 7.4, you can see that, although the sampling distribution of the mean is approximately[1] normal for each sample size, the sample means are distributed more tightly around the population mean as the sample size increases.

[1]Remember that "only" 500 samples out of an infinite number of samples have been selected, so that the sampling distributions shown are only approximations of the population distributions.

FIGURE 7.4
Sampling distributions of the mean from 500 samples of sizes $n = 1, 2, 4, 8, 16,$ and 32 selected from a normal population

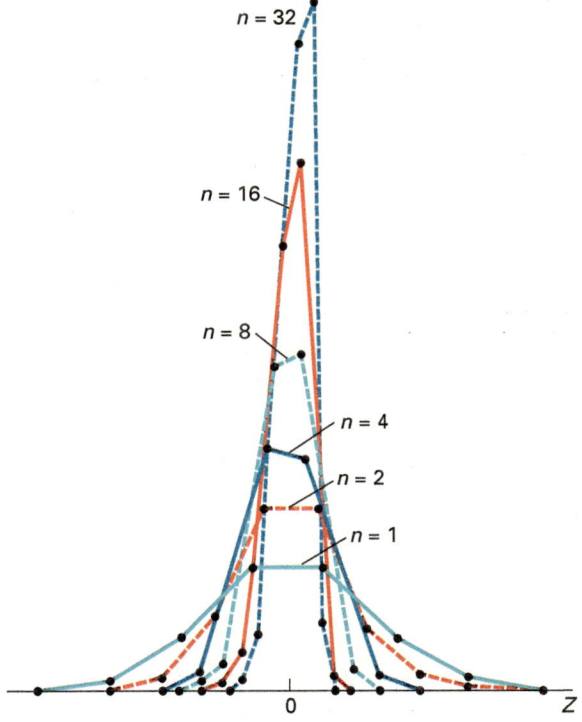

To further examine the concept of the sampling distribution of the mean, consider the Using Statistics scenario described on page 279. The packaging equipment that is filling 368-gram boxes of cereal is set so that the amount of cereal in a box is normally distributed, with a mean of 368 grams. From past experience, you know the population standard deviation for this filling process is 15 grams.

If you randomly select a sample of 25 boxes from the many thousands that are filled in a day and the mean weight is computed for this sample, what type of result could you expect? For example, do you think that the sample mean could be 368 grams? 200 grams? 365 grams?

The sample acts as a miniature representation of the population, so if the values in the population are normally distributed, the values in the sample should be approximately normally distributed. Thus, if the population mean is 368 grams, the sample mean has a good chance of being close to 368 grams.

How can you determine the probability that the sample of 25 boxes will have a mean below 365 grams? From the normal distribution (Section 6.2), you know that you can find the area below any value X by converting to standardized Z values:

$$Z = \frac{X - \mu}{\sigma}$$

In the examples in Section 6.2, you studied how any single value, X, differs from the population mean. Now, in this example, you want to study how a sample mean, $\bar{X}$, differs from the population mean. Substituting $\bar{X}$ for X, $\mu_{\bar{X}}$ for μ, and $\sigma_{\bar{X}}$ for σ in the equation above results in Equation (7.4).

> **FINDING Z FOR THE SAMPLING DISTRIBUTION OF THE MEAN**
>
> The Z value is equal to the difference between the sample mean, $\bar{X}$, and the population mean, μ, divided by the standard error of the mean, $\sigma_{\bar{X}}$.
>
> $$Z = \frac{\bar{X} - \mu_{\bar{X}}}{\sigma_{\bar{X}}} = \frac{\bar{X} - \mu}{\frac{\sigma}{\sqrt{n}}} \quad (7.4)$$

To find the area below 365 grams, from Equation (7.4),

$$Z = \frac{\bar{X} - \mu_{\bar{X}}}{\sigma_{\bar{X}}} = \frac{365 - 368}{\frac{15}{\sqrt{25}}} = \frac{-3}{3} = -1.00$$

The area corresponding to $Z = -1.00$ in Table E.2 is 0.1587. Therefore, 15.87% of all the possible samples of 25 boxes have a sample mean below 365 grams.

The preceding statement is not the same as saying that a certain percentage of *individual* boxes will contain less than 365 grams of cereal. You compute that percentage as follows:

$$Z = \frac{X - \mu}{\sigma} = \frac{365 - 368}{15} = \frac{-3}{15} = -0.20$$

The area corresponding to $Z = -0.20$ in Table E.2 is 0.4207. Therefore, 42.07% of the *individual* boxes are expected to contain less than 365 grams. Comparing these results, you see that many more *individual boxes* than *sample means* are below 365 grams. This result is explained by the fact that each sample consists of 25 different values, some small and some large. The averaging process dilutes the importance of any individual value, particularly when the sample size is large. Thus, the chance that the sample mean of 25 boxes is far away from the population mean is less than the chance that a *single* box is far away.

Examples 7.4 and 7.5 show how these results are affected by using different sample sizes.

EXAMPLE 7.4
The Effect of Sample Size, n, on the Computation of $\sigma_{\bar{X}}$

How is the standard error of the mean affected by increasing the sample size from 25 to 100 boxes?

SOLUTION If $n = 100$ boxes, then using Equation (7.3) on page 290:

$$\sigma_{\bar{X}} = \frac{\sigma}{\sqrt{n}} = \frac{15}{\sqrt{100}} = \frac{15}{10} = 1.5$$

The fourfold increase in the sample size from 25 to 100 reduces the standard error of the mean by half—from 3 grams to 1.5 grams. This demonstrates that taking a larger sample results in less variability in the sample means from sample to sample.

EXAMPLE 7.5
The Effect of Sample Size, n, on the Clustering of Means in the Sampling Distribution

If you select a sample of 100 boxes, what is the probability that the sample mean is below 365 grams?

SOLUTION Using Equation (7.4) on page 292,

$$Z = \frac{\bar{X} - \mu_{\bar{X}}}{\sigma_{\bar{X}}} = \frac{365 - 368}{\frac{15}{\sqrt{100}}} = \frac{-3}{1.5} = -2.00$$

From Table E.2, the area less than $Z = -2.00$ is 0.0228. Therefore, 2.28% of the samples of 100 boxes have means below 365 grams, as compared with 15.87% for samples of 25 boxes.

Sometimes you need to find the interval that contains a fixed proportion of the sample means. To do so, determine a distance below and above the population mean containing a specific area of the normal curve. From Equation (7.4) on page 292,

$$Z = \frac{\bar{X} - \mu}{\frac{\sigma}{\sqrt{n}}}$$

Solving for $\bar{X}$ results in Equation (7.5).

> **FINDING $\bar{X}$ FOR THE SAMPLING DISTRIBUTION OF THE MEAN**
>
> $$\bar{X} = \mu + Z\frac{\sigma}{\sqrt{n}} \tag{7.5}$$

Example 7.6 illustrates the use of Equation (7.5).

EXAMPLE 7.6
Determining the Interval That Includes a Fixed Proportion of the Sample Means

In the cereal-filling example, find an interval symmetrically distributed around the population mean that will include 95% of the sample means, based on samples of 25 boxes.

SOLUTION If 95% of the sample means are in the interval, then 5% are outside the interval. Divide the 5% into two equal parts of 2.5%. The value of Z in Table E.2 corresponding to an area of 0.0250 in the lower tail of the normal curve is -1.96, and the value of Z corresponding to a cumulative area of 0.9750 (i.e., 0.0250 in the upper tail of the normal curve) is $+1.96$. The lower value of $\bar{X}$ (called $\bar{X}_L$) and the upper value of $\bar{X}$ (called $\bar{X}_U$) are found by using Equation (7.5):

$$\bar{X}_L = 368 + (-1.96)\frac{15}{\sqrt{25}} = 368 - 5.88 = 362.12$$

$$\bar{X}_U = 368 + (1.96)\frac{15}{\sqrt{25}} = 368 + 5.88 = 373.88$$

Therefore, 95% of all sample means, based on samples of 25 boxes, are between 362.12 and 373.88 grams.

Sampling from Non-Normally Distributed Populations—The Central Limit Theorem

Thus far in this section, only the sampling distribution of the mean for a normally distributed population has been considered. However, in many instances, either you know that the population is not normally distributed or it is unrealistic to assume that the population is normally distributed. An important theorem in statistics, the Central Limit Theorem, deals with this situation.

> **THE CENTRAL LIMIT THEOREM**
>
> The **Central Limit Theorem** states that as the sample size (i.e., the number of values in each sample) gets *large enough*, the sampling distribution of the mean is approximately normally distributed. This is true regardless of the shape of the distribution of the individual values in the population.

What sample size is large enough? A great deal of statistical research has gone into this issue. As a general rule, statisticians have found that for many population distributions, when the sample size is at least 30, the sampling distribution of the mean is approximately normal. However, you can apply the Central Limit Theorem for even smaller sample sizes if the population distribution is approximately bell-shaped. In the case in which the distribution of a variable is extremely skewed or has more than one mode, you may need sample sizes larger than 30 to ensure normality in the sampling distribution of the mean.

Figure 7.5 illustrates the application of the Central Limit Theorem to different populations. The sampling distributions from three different continuous distributions (normal, uniform, and exponential) for varying sample sizes ($n = 2, 5, 30$) are displayed.

FIGURE 7.5
Sampling distribution of the mean for different populations for samples of $n = 2, 5,$ and 30

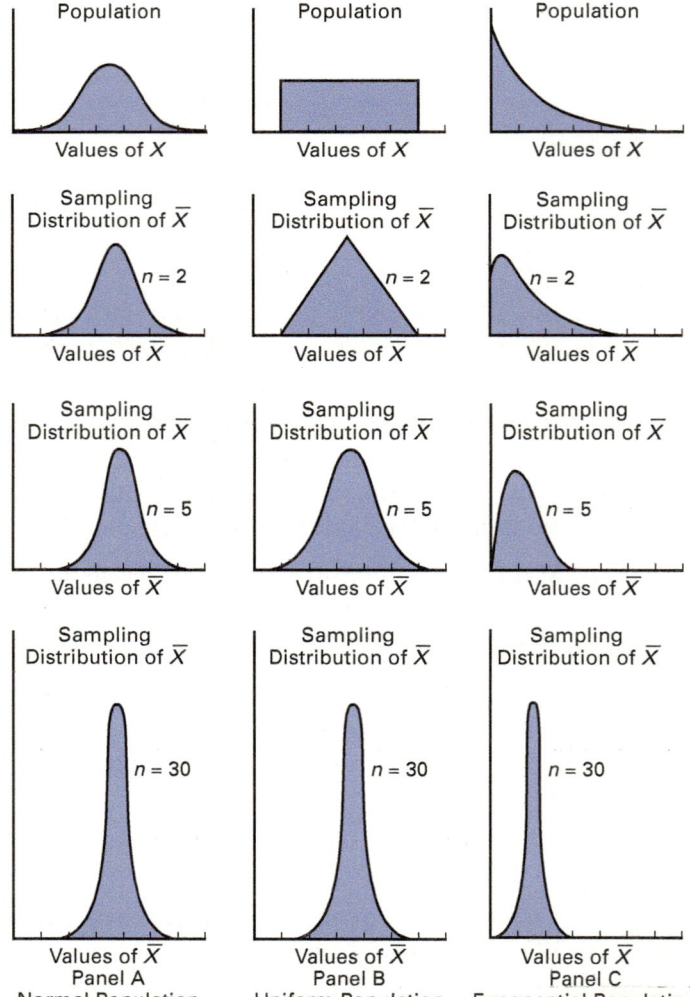

In each of the panels, because the sample mean is an unbiased estimator of the population mean, the mean of any sampling distribution is always equal to the mean of the population.

Panel A of Figure 7.5 shows the sampling distribution of the mean selected from a normal population. As mentioned earlier in this section, when the population is normally distributed, the sampling distribution of the mean is normally distributed for any sample size. [You can measure the variability by using the standard error of the mean, Equation (7.3), on page 290.]

Panel B of Figure 7.5 depicts the sampling distribution from a population with a uniform (or rectangular) distribution (see Section 6.4). When samples of size $n = 2$ are selected, there is a peaking, or *central limiting*, effect already working. For $n = 5$, the sampling distribution is bell-shaped and approximately normal. When $n = 30$, the sampling distribution looks very similar to a normal distribution. In general, the larger the sample size, the more closely the sampling distribution will follow a normal distribution. As with all other cases, the mean of each sampling distribution is equal to the mean of the population, and the variability decreases as the sample size increases.

Panel C of Figure 7.5 presents an exponential distribution (see Section 6.5). This population is extremely right-skewed. When $n = 2$, the sampling distribution is still highly right-skewed but less so than the distribution of the population. For $n = 5$, the sampling distribution is slightly right-skewed. When $n = 30$, the sampling distribution looks approximately normal. Again, the mean of each sampling distribution is equal to the mean of the population, and the variability decreases as the sample size increases.

Using the results from the normal, uniform, and exponential distributions, you can reach the following conclusions regarding the Central Limit Theorem:

- For most population distributions, regardless of shape, the sampling distribution of the mean is approximately normally distributed if samples of at least size 30 are selected.
- If the population distribution is fairly symmetrical, the sampling distribution of the mean is approximately normal for samples as small as size 5.
- If the population is normally distributed, the sampling distribution of the mean is normally distributed, regardless of the sample size.

The Central Limit Theorem is of crucial importance in using statistical inference to reach conclusions about a population. It allows you to make inferences about the population mean without having to know the specific shape of the population distribution.

VISUAL EXPLORATIONS | Exploring Sampling Distributions

Use the Visual Explorations **Two Dice Probability** procedure to observe the effects of simulated throws on the frequency distribution of the sum of the two dice. Open the **Visual Explorations add-in workbook** (see Appendix Section D.4) and:

1. Select **Add-Ins → VisualExplorations → Two Dice Probability**
2. Click the **Tally** button to tally a set of throws in the frequency distribution table and histogram. Optionally, click the spinner buttons to adjust the number of throws per tally (round).
3. Repeat step 2 as many times as necessary.
4. Click **Finish** to end the simulation.

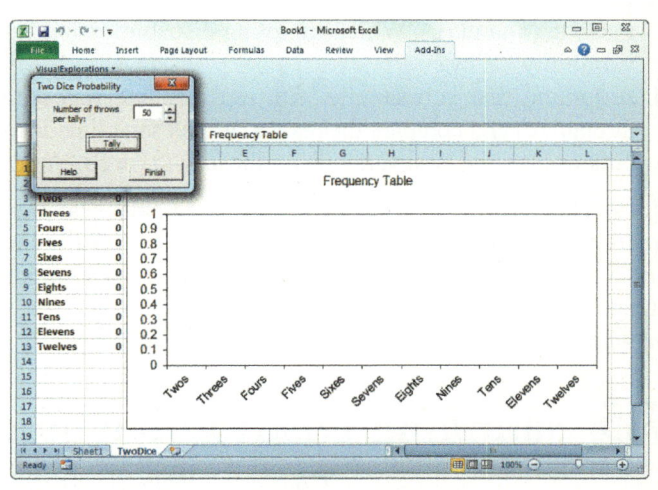

Problems for Section 7.4

LEARNING THE BASICS

7.15 Given a normal distribution with $\mu = 100$ and $\sigma = 10$, if you select a sample of $n = 25$, what is the probability that $\bar{X}$ is
a. less than 95?
b. between 95 and 97.5?
c. above 102.2?
d. There is a 65% chance that $\bar{X}$ is above what value?

7.16 Given a normal distribution with $\mu = 50$ and $\sigma = 5$, if you select a sample of $n = 100$, what is the probability that $\bar{X}$ is
a. less than 47?
b. between 47 and 49.5?
c. above 51.1?
d. There is a 35% chance that $\bar{X}$ is above what value?

APPLYING THE CONCEPTS

7.17 For each of the following three populations, indicate what the sampling distribution for samples of 25 would consist of:
a. Travel expense vouchers for a university in an academic year
b. Absentee records (days absent per year) in 2010 for employees of a large manufacturing company.
c. Yearly sales (in gallons) of unleaded gasoline at service stations located in a particular state.

7.18 The following data represent the number of days absent per year in a population of six employees of a small company:

1 3 6 7 9 10

a. Assuming that you sample without replacement, select all possible samples of $n = 2$ and construct the sampling distribution of the mean. Compute the mean of all the sample means and also compute the population mean. Are they equal? What is this property called?
b. Repeat (a) for all possible samples of $n = 3$.
c. Compare the shape of the sampling distribution of the mean in (a) and (b). Which sampling distribution has less variability? Why?
d. Assuming that you sample with replacement, repeat (a) through (c) and compare the results. Which sampling distributions have the least variability—those in (a) or (b)? Why?

7.19 The diameter of a brand of Ping-Pong balls is approximately normally distributed, with a mean of 1.30 inches and a standard deviation of 0.04 inch. If you select a random sample of 16 Ping-Pong balls,
a. what is the sampling distribution of the mean?
b. what is the probability that the sample mean is less than 1.28 inches?
c. what is the probability that the sample mean is between 1.31 and 1.33 inches?
d. The probability is 60% that the sample mean will be between what two values, symmetrically distributed around the population mean?

7.20 The U.S. Census Bureau announced that the median sales price of new houses sold in 2009 was $215,600, and the mean sales price was $270,100 (**www.census.gov/newhomesales**, March 30, 2010). Assume that the standard deviation of the prices is $90,000.
a. If you select samples of $n = 2$, describe the shape of the sampling distribution of $\bar{X}$.
b. If you select samples of $n = 100$, describe the shape of the sampling distribution of $\bar{X}$.
c. If you select a random sample of $n = 100$, what is the probability that the sample mean will be less than $300,000?
d. If you select a random sample of $n = 100$, what is the probability that the sample mean will be between $275,000 and $290,000?

7.21 Time spent using e-mail per session is normally distributed, with $\mu = 8$ minutes and $\sigma = 2$ minutes. If you select a random sample of 25 sessions,
a. what is the probability that the sample mean is between 7.8 and 8.2 minutes?
b. what is the probability that the sample mean is between 7.5 and 8 minutes?
c. If you select a random sample of 100 sessions, what is the probability that the sample mean is between 7.8 and 8.2 minutes?
d. Explain the difference in the results of (a) and (c).

SELF Test 7.22 The amount of time a bank teller spends with each customer has a population mean, μ, = 3.10 minutes and a standard deviation, σ, = 0.40 minute. If you select a random sample of 16 customers,
a. what is the probability that the mean time spent per customer is at least 3 minutes?
b. there is an 85% chance that the sample mean is less than how many minutes?
c. What assumption must you make in order to solve (a) and (b)?
d. If you select a random sample of 64 customers, there is an 85% chance that the sample mean is less than how many minutes?

7.5 Sampling Distribution of the Proportion

Consider a categorical variable that has only two categories, such as the customer prefers your brand or the customer prefers the competitor's brand. You are interested in the proportion of items belonging to one of the categories—for example, the proportion of customers that prefer your brand. The population proportion, represented by π, is the proportion of items in the entire population with the characteristic of interest. The sample proportion, represented by p, is the proportion of items in the sample with the characteristic of interest. The sample proportion, a statistic, is used to estimate the population proportion, a parameter. To calculate the sample proportion, you assign one of two possible values, 1 or 0, to represent the presence or absence of the characteristic. You then sum all the 1 and 0 values and divide by n, the sample size. For example, if, in a sample of five customers, three preferred your brand and two did not, you have three 1s and two 0s. Summing the three 1s and two 0s and dividing by the sample size of 5 results in a sample proportion of 0.60.

SAMPLE PROPORTION

$$p = \frac{X}{n} = \frac{\text{Number of items having the characteristic of interest}}{\text{Sample size}} \qquad (7.6)$$

The sample proportion, p, will be between 0 and 1. If all items have the characteristic, you assign each a score of 1, and p is equal to 1. If half the items have the characteristic, you assign half a score of 1 and assign the other half a score of 0, and p is equal to 0.5. If none of the items have the characteristic, you assign each a score of 0, and p is equal to 0.

In Section 7.4, you learned that the sample mean, $\bar{X}$ is an unbiased estimator of the population mean, μ. Similarly, the statistic p is an unbiased estimator of the population proportion, π. By analogy to the sampling distribution of the mean, whose standard error is $\sigma_{\bar{X}} = \frac{\sigma}{\sqrt{n}}$, the **standard error of the proportion**, σ_p, is given in Equation (7.7).

STANDARD ERROR OF THE PROPORTION

$$\sigma_p = \sqrt{\frac{\pi(1-\pi)}{n}} \qquad (7.7)$$

The **sampling distribution of the proportion** follows the binomial distribution, as discussed in Section 5.3 when sampling with replacement (or without replacement from extremely large populations). However, you can use the normal distribution to approximate the binomial distribution when $n\pi$ and $n(1-\pi)$ are each at least 5. In most cases in which inferences are made about the proportion, the sample size is substantial enough to meet the conditions for using the normal approximation (see reference 1). Therefore, in many instances, you can use the normal distribution to estimate the sampling distribution of the proportion.

Substituting p for $\bar{X}$, π for μ, and $\sqrt{\frac{\pi(1-\pi)}{n}}$ for $\frac{\sigma}{\sqrt{n}}$ in Equation (7.4) on page 292 results in Equation (7.8).

FINDING Z FOR THE SAMPLING DISTRIBUTION OF THE PROPORTION

$$Z = \frac{p - \pi}{\sqrt{\frac{\pi(1-\pi)}{n}}} \qquad (7.8)$$

To illustrate the sampling distribution of the proportion, suppose that the manager of the local branch of a bank determines that 40% of all depositors have multiple accounts at the bank. If you select a random sample of 200 depositors, because $n\pi = 200(0.40) = 80 \geq 5$ and

$n(1 - \pi) = 200(0.60) = 120 \geq 5$, the sample size is large enough to assume that the sampling distribution of the proportion is approximately normally distributed. Then, you can calculate the probability that the sample proportion of depositors with multiple accounts is less than 0.30 by using Equation (7.8):

$$Z = \frac{p - \pi}{\sqrt{\dfrac{\pi(1 - \pi)}{n}}}$$

$$= \frac{0.30 - 0.40}{\sqrt{\dfrac{(0.40)(0.60)}{200}}} = \frac{-0.10}{\sqrt{\dfrac{0.24}{200}}} = \frac{-0.10}{0.0346}$$

$$= -2.89$$

Using Table E.2, the area under the normal curve less than -2.89 is 0.0019. Therefore, if the population proportion of items of interest is 0.40, only 0.19% of the samples of $n = 200$ would be expected to have sample proportions less than 0.30.

Problems for Section 7.5

LEARNING THE BASICS

7.23 In a random sample of 64 people, 48 are classified as "successful."
a. Determine the sample proportion, p, of "successful" people.
b. If the population proportion is 0.70, determine the standard error of the proportion.

7.24 A random sample of 50 households was selected for a telephone survey. The key question asked was, "Do you or any member of your household own a cellular telephone that you can use to access the Internet?" Of the 50 respondents, 20 said yes and 30 said no.
a. Determine the sample proportion, p, of households with cellular telephones that can be used to access the Internet.
b. If the population proportion is 0.45, determine the standard error of the proportion.

7.25 The following data represent the responses (Y for yes and N for no) from a sample of 40 college students to the question "Do you currently own shares in any stocks?"

N N Y N N Y N Y N Y N N Y N Y Y N N N Y
N Y N N N N Y N N Y Y N N N Y N N Y N N

a. Determine the sample proportion, p, of college students who own shares of stock.
b. If the population proportion is 0.30, determine the standard error of the proportion.

APPLYING THE CONCEPTS

SELF Test 7.26 A political pollster is conducting an analysis of sample results in order to make predictions on election night. Assuming a two-candidate election, if a specific candidate receives at least 55% of the vote in the sample, that candidate will be forecast as the winner of the election. If you select a random sample of 100 voters, what is the probability that a candidate will be forecast as the winner when
a. the population percentage of her vote is 50.1%?
b. the population percentage of her vote is 60%?
c. the population percentage of her vote is 49% (and she will actually lose the election)?
d. If the sample size is increased to 400, what are your answers to (a) through (c)? Discuss.

7.27 You plan to conduct a marketing experiment in which students are to taste one of two different brands of soft drink. Their task is to correctly identify the brand tasted. You select a random sample of 200 students and assume that the students have no ability to distinguish between the two brands. (Hint: If an individual has no ability to distinguish between the two soft drinks, then the two brands are equally likely to be selected.)
a. What is the probability that the sample will have between 50% and 60% of the identifications correct?
b. The probability is 90% that the sample percentage is contained within what symmetrical limits of the population percentage?
c. What is the probability that the sample percentage of correct identifications is greater than 65%?
d. Which is more likely to occur—more than 60% correct identifications in the sample of 200 or more than 55% correct identifications in a sample of 1,000? Explain.

7.28 In a recent survey of full-time female workers ages 22 to 35 years, 46% said that they would rather give up some of their salary for more personal time. (Data extracted from "I'd Rather Give Up," *USA Today*, March 4, 2010, p. 1B.) Suppose you select a sample of 100 full-time female workers 22 to 35 years old.
a. What is the probability that in the sample, fewer than 50% would rather give up some of their salary for more personal time?
b. What is the probability that in the sample, between 40% and 50% would rather give up some of their salary for more personal time?
c. What is the probability that in the sample, more than 40% would rather give up some of their salary for more personal time?
d. If a sample of 400 is taken, how does this change your answers to (a) through (c)?

7.29 Companies often make flextime scheduling available to help recruit and keep female employees who have children. Other workers sometimes view these flextime schedules as unfair. An article in *USA Today* indicates that 25% of male employees state that they have to pick up the slack for moms working flextime schedules. (Data extracted from D. Jones, "Poll Finds Resentment of Flextime," **www.usatoday.com**, May 11, 2007.) Suppose you select a random sample of 100 male employees working for companies offering flextime.
a. What is the probability that 25% or fewer male employees will indicate that they have to pick up the slack for moms working flextime?
b. What is the probability that 20% or fewer male employees will indicate that they have to pick up the slack for moms working flextime?
c. If a random sample of 500 is taken, how does this change your answers to (a) and (b)?

7.30 According to Gallup's poll on consumer behavior, 36% of Americans say they will consider only cars manufactured by an American company when purchasing a new car. (Data extracted from *The Gallup Poll*, **www.gallup.com**, March 31, 2010.) If you select a random sample of 200 Americans,
a. what is the probability that the sample will have between 30% and 40% who say they will consider only cars manufactured by an American company when purchasing a new car?

b. the probability is 90% that the sample percentage will be contained within what symmetrical limits of the population percentage?
c. the probability is 95% that the sample percentage will be contained within what symmetrical limits of the population percentage?

7.31 The Agency for Healthcare Research and Quality reports that medical errors are responsible for injury to 1 out of every 25 hospital patients in the United States. (Data extracted from M. Ozan-Rafferty, "Hospitals: Never Have a Never Event," *The Gallup Management Journal*, **gmj.gallup.com**, May 7, 2009.) These errors are tragic and expensive. Preventable health care–related errors cost an estimated $29 billion each year in the United States. Suppose that you select a sample of 100 U.S. hospital patients.
a. What is the probability that the sample percentage reporting injury due to medical errors will be between 5% and 10%?
b. The probability is 90% that the sample percentage will be within what symmetrical limits of the population percentage?
c. The probability is 95% that the sample percentage will be within what symmetrical limits of the population percentage?
d. Suppose you selected a sample of 400 U.S. hospital patients. How does this change your answers in (a) through (c)?

7.32 A survey of 2,250 American adults reported that 59% got news both online and offline in a typical day. (Data extracted from "How Americans Get News in a Typical Day," *USA Today*, March 10, 2010, p. 1A.)
a. Suppose that you take a sample of 100 American adults. If the population proportion of American adults who get news both online and offline in a typical day is 0.59, what is the probability that fewer than half in your sample will get news both online and offline in a typical day?
b. Suppose that you take a sample of 500 American adults. If the population proportion of American adults who get news both online and offline in a typical day is 0.59, what is the probability that fewer than half in your sample will get news both online and offline in a typical day?
c. Discuss the effect of sample size on the sampling distribution of the proportion in general and the effect on the probabilities in (a) and (b).

7.6 *Online Topic*: Sampling from Finite Populations

In this section, sampling without replacement from finite populations is discussed. To study this topic, read the Section 7.6 online topic file that is available on this book's companion website. (See Appendix C to learn how to access the online topic files.)

USING STATISTICS @ Oxford Cereals Revisited

As the plant operations manager for Oxfords Cereals, you were responsible for monitoring the amount of cereal placed in each box. To be consistent with package labeling, boxes should contain a mean of 368 grams of cereal. Thousands of boxes are produced during a shift, and weighing every single box was determined to be too time-consuming, costly, and inefficient. Instead, a sample of boxes was selected. Based on your analysis of the sample, you had to decide whether to maintain, alter, or shut down the process.

Using the concept of the sampling distribution of the mean, you were able to determine probabilities that such a sample mean could have been randomly selected from a population with a mean of 368 grams. Specifically, if a sample of size $n = 25$ is selected from a population with a mean of 368 and standard deviation of 15, you calculated the probability of selecting a sample with a mean of 365 grams or less to be 15.87%. If a larger sample size is selected, the sample mean should be closer to the population mean. This result was illustrated when you calculated the probability if the sample size were increased to $n = 100$. Using the larger sample size, you determined the probability of selecting a sample with a mean of 365 grams or less to be 2.28%.

SUMMARY

You have learned that in many business situations, the population is so large that you cannot gather information on every item. Instead, statistical sampling procedures focus on selecting a small representative group of the larger population. The results of the sample are then used to estimate characteristics of the entire population. Selecting a sample is less time-consuming, less costly, and more practical than analyzing the entire population.

In this chapter, you studied four common probability sampling methods—simple random, systematic, stratified, and cluster sampling. You also studied the sampling distribution of the sample mean and the sampling distribution of the sample proportion and their relationship to the Central Limit Theorem. You learned that the sample mean is an unbiased estimator of the population mean, and the sample proportion is an unbiased estimator of the population proportion. In the next five chapters, the techniques of confidence intervals and tests of hypotheses commonly used for statistical inference are discussed.

KEY EQUATIONS

Population Mean

$$\mu = \frac{\sum_{i=1}^{N} X_i}{N} \tag{7.1}$$

Population Standard Deviation

$$\sigma = \sqrt{\frac{\sum_{i=1}^{N}(X_i - \mu)^2}{N}} \tag{7.2}$$

Standard Error of the Mean

$$\sigma_{\bar{X}} = \frac{\sigma}{\sqrt{n}} \tag{7.3}$$

Finding Z for the Sampling Distribution of the Mean

$$Z = \frac{\bar{X} - \mu_{\bar{X}}}{\sigma_{\bar{X}}} = \frac{\bar{X} - \mu}{\frac{\sigma}{\sqrt{n}}} \tag{7.4}$$

Finding $\bar{X}$ for the Sampling Distribution of the Mean

$$\bar{X} = \mu + Z \frac{\sigma}{\sqrt{n}} \tag{7.5}$$

Sample Proportion

$$p = \frac{X}{n} \tag{7.6}$$

Standard Error of the Proportion

$$\sigma_p = \sqrt{\frac{\pi(1-\pi)}{n}} \tag{7.7}$$

Finding Z for the Sampling Distribution of the Proportion

$$Z = \frac{p - \pi}{\sqrt{\frac{\pi(1-\pi)}{n}}} \tag{7.8}$$

KEY TERMS

Central Limit Theorem
cluster
cluster sample
convenience sampling
coverage error
frame
judgment sample
margin of error
measurement error
nonprobability sample
nonresponse bias
nonresponse error
probability sample
sampling distribution
sampling distribution of the mean
sampling distribution of the proportion
sampling error
sampling with replacement
sampling without replacement
selection bias
simple random sample
standard error of the mean
standard error of the proportion
strata
stratified sample
systematic sample
table of random numbers
unbiased

CHAPTER REVIEW PROBLEMS

CHECKING YOUR UNDERSTANDING

7.33 Why is the sample mean an unbiased estimator of the population mean?

7.34 Why does the standard error of the mean decrease as the sample size, n, increases?

7.35 Why does the sampling distribution of the mean follow a normal distribution for a large enough sample size, even though the population may not be normally distributed?

7.36 What is the difference between a population distribution and a sampling distribution?

7.37 Under what circumstances does the sampling distribution of the proportion approximately follow the normal distribution?

7.38 What is the difference between probability sampling and nonprobability sampling?

7.39 What are some potential problems with using "fishbowl" methods to select a simple random sample?

7.40 What is the difference between sampling *with* replacement versus sampling *without* replacement?

7.41 What is the difference between a simple random sample and a systematic sample?

7.42 What is the difference between a simple random sample and a stratified sample?

7.43 What is the difference between a stratified sample and a cluster sample?

APPLYING THE CONCEPTS

7.44 An industrial sewing machine uses ball bearings that are targeted to have a diameter of 0.75 inch. The lower and upper specification limits under which the ball bearing can operate are 0.74 inch (lower) and 0.76 inch (upper). Past experience has indicated that the actual diameter of the ball bearings is approximately normally distributed, with a mean of 0.753 inch and a standard deviation of 0.004 inch. If you select a random sample of 25 ball bearings, what is the probability that the sample mean is
a. between the target and the population mean of 0.753?
b. between the lower specification limit and the target?
c. greater than the upper specification limit?
d. less than the lower specification limit?
e. The probability is 93% that the sample mean diameter will be greater than what value?

7.45 The fill amount of bottles of a soft drink is normally distributed, with a mean of 2.0 liters and a standard deviation of 0.05 liter. If you select a random sample of 25 bottles, what is the probability that the sample mean will be
a. between 1.99 and 2.0 liters?
b. below 1.98 liters?
c. greater than 2.01 liters?
d. The probability is 99% that the sample mean amount of soft drink will be at least how much?
e. The probability is 99% that the sample mean amount of soft drink will be between which two values (symmetrically distributed around the mean)?

7.46 An orange juice producer buys oranges from a large orange grove that has one variety of orange. The amount of juice squeezed from these oranges is approximately normally distributed, with a mean of 4.70 ounces and a standard deviation of 0.40 ounce. Suppose that you select a sample of 25 oranges.
a. What is the probability that the sample mean amount of juice will be at least 4.60 ounces?
b. The probability is 70% that the sample mean amount of juice will be contained between what two values symmetrically distributed around the population mean?
c. The probability is 77% that the sample mean amount of juice will be greater than what value?

7.47 In Problem 7.46, suppose that the mean amount of juice squeezed is 5.0 ounces.
a. What is the probability that the sample mean amount of juice will be at least 4.60 ounces?
b. The probability is 70% that the sample mean amount of juice will be contained between what two values symmetrically distributed around the population mean?
c. The probability is 77% that the sample mean amount of juice will be greater than what value?

7.48 Junk bonds reported strong returns in 2009. The population of junk bonds earned a mean return of 57.5% in 2009. (Data extracted from *The Wall Street Journal*, January 4, 2010, p. R1.) Assume that the returns for junk bonds were distributed as a normal random variable, with a mean of 57.5 and a standard deviation of 20. If you selected a random sample of 16 junk bonds from this population, what is the probability that the sample would have a mean return
a. less than 50?
b. between 40 and 60?
c. greater than 40?

7.49 The article mentioned in Problem 7.48 reported that Treasury bonds had a mean return of −9.3% in 2009. Assume that the returns for the Treasury bonds were distributed as a normal random variable, with a mean of −9.3 and a standard deviation of 10. If you select an individual Treasury bond from this population, what is the probability that it would have a return
a. less than 0 (i.e., a loss)?
b. between −10 and −20?
c. greater than 5?
If you selected a random sample of four Treasury bonds from this population, what is the probability that the sample would have a mean return
d. less than 0—that is, a loss?
e. between −10 and −20?
f. greater than 5?
g. Compare your results in parts (d) through (f) to those in (a) through (c).

7.50 (Class Project) The table of random numbers is an example of a uniform distribution because each digit is equally likely to occur. Starting in the row corresponding to the day of the month in which you were born, use the table of random numbers (Table E.1) to take one digit at a time.

Select five different samples each of $n = 2, n = 5$, and $n = 10$. Compute the sample mean of each sample. Develop a frequency distribution of the sample means for the results of the entire class, based on samples of sizes $n = 2, n = 5$, and $n = 10$.

What can be said about the shape of the sampling distribution for each of these sample sizes?

7.51 (Class Project) Toss a coin 10 times and record the number of heads. If each student performs this experiment five times, a frequency distribution of the number of heads can be developed from the results of the entire class. Does this distribution seem to approximate the normal distribution?

7.52 (Class Project) The number of cars waiting in line at a car wash is distributed as follows:

Number of Cars	Probability
0	0.25
1	0.40
2	0.20
3	0.10
4	0.04
5	0.01

You can use the table of random numbers (Table E.1) to select samples from this distribution by assigning numbers as follows:
1. Start in the row corresponding to the day of the month in which you were born.
2. Select a two-digit random number.
3. If you select a random number from 00 to 24, record a length of 0; if from 25 to 64, record a length of 1; if from 65 to 84, record a length of 2; if from 85 to 94, record a length of 3; if from 95 to 98, record a length of 4; if 99, record a length of 5.

Select samples of $n = 2, n = 5$, and $n = 10$. Compute the mean for each sample. For example, if a sample of size 2 results in the random numbers 18 and 46, these would correspond to lengths 0 and 1, respectively, producing a sample mean of 0.5. If each student selects five different samples for each sample size, a frequency distribution of the sample means (for each sample size) can be developed from the results of the entire class. What conclusions can you reach concerning the sampling distribution of the mean as the sample size is increased?

7.53 (Class Project) Using Table E.1, simulate the selection of different-colored balls from a bowl, as follows:
1. Start in the row corresponding to the day of the month in which you were born.
2. Select one-digit numbers.
3. If a random digit between 0 and 6 is selected, consider the ball white; if a random digit is a 7, 8, or 9, consider the ball red.

Select samples of $n = 10, n = 25$, and $n = 50$ digits. In each sample, count the number of white balls and compute the proportion of white balls in the sample. If each student in the class selects five different samples for each sample size, a frequency distribution of the proportion of white balls (for each sample size) can be developed from the results of the entire class. What conclusions can you reach about the sampling distribution of the proportion as the sample size is increased?

7.54 (Class Project) Suppose that step 3 of Problem 7.53 uses the following rule: "If a random digit between 0 and 8 is selected, consider the ball to be white; if a random digit of 9 is selected, consider the ball to be red." Compare and contrast the results in this problem and those in Problem 7.53.

MANAGING ASHLAND MULTICOMM SERVICES

Continuing the quality improvement effort first described in the Chapter 6 Managing Ashland MultiComm Services case, the target upload speed for AMS Internet service subscribers has been monitored. As before, upload speeds are measured on a standard scale in which the target value is 1.0. Data collected over the past year indicate that the upload speeds are approximately normally distributed, with a mean of 1.005 and a standard deviation of 0.10.

EXERCISE

1. Each day, at 25 random times, the upload speed is measured. Assuming that the distribution has not changed from what it was in the past year, what is the probability that the upload speed is
   a. less than 1.0?
   b. between 0.95 and 1.0?
   c. between 1.0 and 1.05?
   d. less than 0.95 or greater than 1.05?
   e. Suppose that the mean upload speed of today's sample of 25 is 0.952. What conclusion can you reach about the upload speed today based on this result? Explain.
2. Compare the results of AMS1 (a) through (d) to those of AMS1. in Chapter 6 on page 274. What conclusions can you reach concerning the differences?

DIGITAL CASE

Apply your knowledge about sampling distributions in this Digital Case, which reconsiders the Oxford Cereals Using Statistics scenario.

The advocacy group Consumers Concerned About Cereal Cheaters (CCACC) suspects that cereal companies, including Oxford Cereals, are cheating consumers by packaging cereals at less than labeled weights. Recently, the group investigated the package weights of two popular Oxford brand cereals. Open **CCACC.pdf** to examine the group's claims and supporting data, and then answer the following questions:

1. Are the data collection procedures that the CCACC uses to form its conclusions flawed? What procedures could the group follow to make its analysis more rigorous?
2. Assume that the two samples of five cereal boxes (one sample for each of two cereal varieties) listed on the CCACC website were collected randomly by organization members. For each sample, do the following:
   a. Calculate the sample mean.
   b. Assume that the standard deviation of the process is 15 grams and the population mean is 368 grams. Calculate the percentage of all samples for each process that have a sample mean less than the value you calculated in (a).
   c. Again, assuming that the standard deviation is 15 grams, calculate the percentage of individual boxes of cereal that have a weight less than the value you calculated in (a).
3. What, if any, conclusions can you form by using your calculations about the filling processes for the two different cereals?
4. A representative from Oxford Cereals has asked that the CCACC take down its page discussing shortages in Oxford Cereals boxes. Is that request reasonable? Why or why not?
5. Can the techniques discussed in this chapter be used to prove cheating in the manner alleged by the CCACC? Why or why not?

REFERENCES

1. Cochran, W. G., *Sampling Techniques*, 3rd ed. (New York: Wiley, 1977).
2. Gallup, G. H., *The Sophisticated Poll-Watcher's Guide* (Princeton, NJ: Princeton Opinion Press, 1972).
3. Goleman, D., "Pollsters Enlist Psychologists in Quest for Unbiased Results," *The New York Times*, September 7, 1993, pp. C1, C11.
4. Hahn, G., and W. Meeker, *Statistical Intervals: A Guide for Practitioners* (New York: John Wiley and Sons, Inc., 1991).
5. "Landon in a Landslide: The Poll That Changed Polling," *History Matters: The U.S. Survey Course on the Web*, New York: American Social History Productions, 2005, downloaded at **http://historymatters.gmu.edu/d/5168/**.
6. *Microsoft Excel 2010* (Redmond, WA: Microsoft Corp., 2010).
7. *Minitab Release 16* (State College, PA: Minitab, Inc., 2010).
8. Rand Corporation, *A Million Random Digits with 100,000 Normal Deviates* (New York: The Free Press, 1955).
9. Squire, P., "Why the 1936 *Literary Digest* Poll Failed," *Public Opinion Quarterly 52*, 1988, pp.125–133.

CHAPTER 7 EXCEL GUIDE

EG7.1 TYPES OF SAMPLING METHODS

Simple Random Samples

PHStat2 Use **Random Sample Generation** to create a random sample *without replacement*. For example, to select the Example 7.1 sample of 40 workers on page 281, select **PHStat → Sampling → Random Sample Generation**. In the procedure's dialog box (shown below):

1. Enter **40** as the **Sample Size**.
2. Click **Generate list of random numbers** and enter **800** as the **Population Size**.
3. Enter a **Title** and click **OK**.

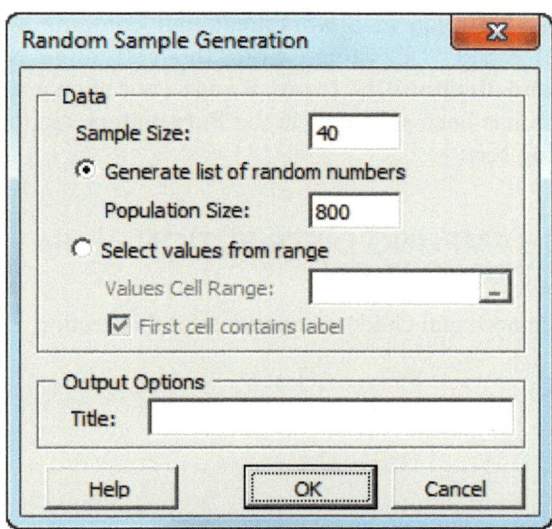

In-Depth Excel Use the **RANDBETWEEN** worksheet function to select a random integer that can be used to select an item from a frame. Enter the function as **RANDBETWEEN(1,** *population size***)**.

Use the **COMPUTE worksheet** of the **Random workbook** as a template for creating a random sample. This worksheet contains 40 copies of the formula **=RANDBETWEEN(1, 800)** in column B and provides an alternative way to selecting the sample desired in Example 7.1 on page 281. Because the RANDBETWEEN function samples *with replacement*, add additional copies of the formula in new column B rows until you have the sample size *without replacement* that Example 7.1 needs.

Analysis ToolPak Use **Sampling** to create a random sample *with replacement*. For example, to select a random sample of $n = 20$ from a cell range A1:A201 of 200 values that contains a column heading in cell A1, select **Data → Data Analysis**. In the Data Analysis dialog box, select **Sampling** from the **Analysis Tools** list and then click **OK**. In the procedure's dialog box (see below):

1. Enter **A1:A201** as the **Input Range** and check **Labels**.
2. Click **Random** and enter **20** as the **Number of Samples**.
3. Click **New Worksheet Ply** and then click **OK**.

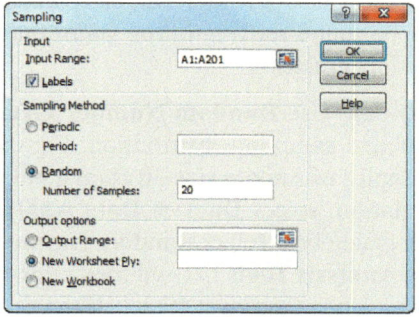

EG7.2 EVALUATING SURVEY WORTHINESS

There are no Excel Guide instructions for this section.

EG7.3 SAMPLING DISTRIBUTIONS

There are no Excel Guide instructions for this section.

EG7.4 SAMPLING DISTRIBUTION of the MEAN

PHStat2 Use **Sampling Distributions Simulation** to create a simulated sampling distribution. For example, to create 100 samples of $n = 30$ from a uniformly distributed population, select **PHStat → Sampling → Sampling Distributions Simulation**. In the procedure's dialog box (shown at the top of page 306):

1. Enter **100** as the **Number of Samples**.
2. Enter **30** as the **Sample Size**.
3. Click **Uniform**.
4. Enter a **Title** and click **OK**.

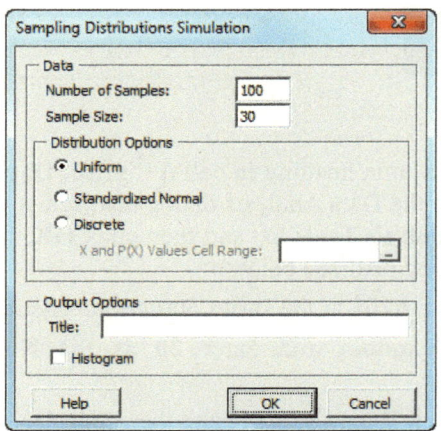
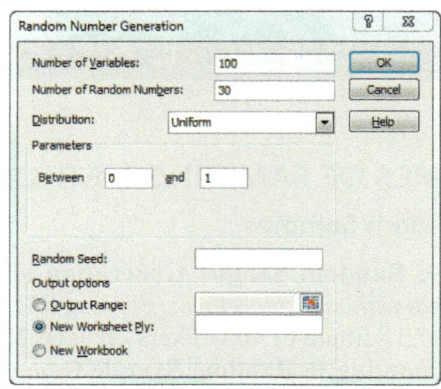

The sample means, overall mean, and standard error of the mean can be found starting in row 34 of the worksheet that the procedure creates.

Analysis ToolPak Use **Random Number Generation** to create a simulated sampling distribution. For example, to create 100 samples of sample size 30 from a uniformly distributed population, select **Data → Data Analysis**. In the Data Analysis dialog box, select **Random Number Generation** from the **Analysis Tools** list and then click **OK**. In the procedure's dialog box (shown at the top of the next column):

1. Enter **100** as the **Number of Variables**.
2. Enter **30** as the **Number of Random Numbers**.
3. Select **Uniform** from the **Distribution** drop-down list.
4. Keep the **Parameters** values as is.
5. Click **New Worksheet Ply** and then click **OK**.

Use the formulas that appear in rows 35 through 39 in the **SDS_FORMULAS worksheet** of the **SDS workbook** as models if you want to compute sample means, the overall mean, and the standard error of the mean.

If, for other problems, you select **Discrete** in step 3, you must be open to a worksheet that contains a cell range of X and $P(X)$ values. Enter this cell range as the **Value and Probability Input Range** (not shown when **Uniform** has been selected) in the **Parameters** section of the dialog box.

EG7.5 SAMPLING DISTRIBUTION of the PROPORTION

There are no Excel Guide instructions for this section.

CHAPTER 7 MINITAB GUIDE

MG7.1 TYPES OF SAMPLING METHODS

Simple Random Samples

Use **Sample From Columns** to create a random sample *with* or *without replacement*. For example, to select the Example 7.1 sample of 40 workers on page 281, first create the list of 800 employee numbers in column **C1**. Select **Calc → Make Patterned Data → Simple Set of Numbers**. In the Simple Set of Numbers dialog box (shown at right):

1. Enter **C1** in the **Store patterned data in** box.
2. Enter **1** in the **From first value** box.
3. Enter **800** in the **To last value** box.
4. Click **OK**.

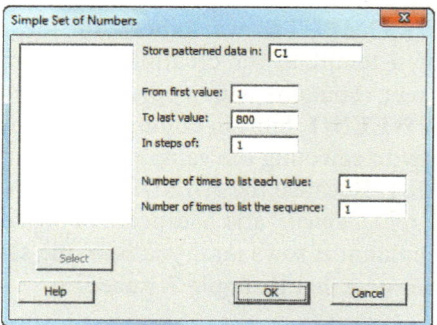

With the worksheet containing the column C1 list still open:

5. Select **Calc → Random Data → Sample from Columns**.

In the Sample From Columns dialog box (shown below):
6. Enter **40** in the **Number of rows to sample** box.
7. Enter **C1** in the **From columns** box.
8. Enter **C2** in the **Store samples in** box.
9. Click **OK**.

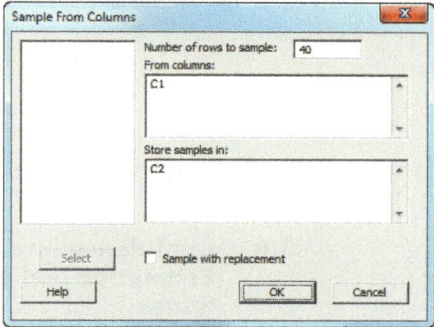

MG7.2 EVALUATING SURVEY WORTHINESS

There are no Minitab Guide instructions for this section.

MG7.3 SAMPLING DISTRIBUTIONS

There are no Minitab Guide instructions for this section.

MG7.4 SAMPLING DISTRIBUTION of the MEAN

Use **Uniform** to create a simulated sampling distribution from a uniformly distributed population. For example, to create 100 samples of $n = 30$ from a uniformly distributed population, open to a new, empty worksheet. Select **Calc → Random Data → Uniform**. In the Uniform Distribution dialog box (shown below):

1. Enter **100** in the **Number of rows of data to generate** box.
2. Enter **C1-C30** in the **Store in column(s)** box (to store the results in the first 30 columns).
3. Enter **0.0** in the **Lower endpoint** box.
4. Enter **1.0** in the **Upper endpoint** box.
5. Click **OK**.

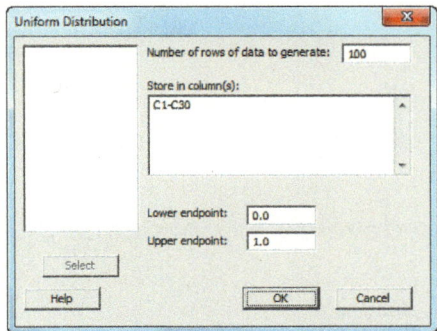

The 100 samples of $n = 30$ are entered *row-wise* in columns C1 through C30, an exception to the rule used in this book to enter data column-wise. (Row-wise data facilitates the computation of means.) While still opened to the worksheet with the 100 samples, enter **Sample Means** as the name of column **C31**. Select **Calc → Row Statistics**. In the Row Statistics dialog box (shown below):

6. Click **Mean**.
7. Enter **C1-C30** in the **Input variables** box.
8. Enter **C31** in the **Store result in** box.
9. Click **OK**.

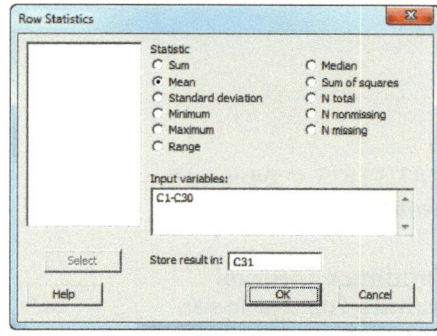

10. With the mean for each of the 100 row-wise samples in column C31, select **Stat → Basic Statistics → Display Descriptive Statistics**.
11. In the Display Descriptive Statistics dialog box, enter **C31** in the **Variables** box and click **Statistics**.
12. In the Display Descriptive Statistics - Statistics dialog box, select **Mean** and **Standard deviation** and then click **OK**.
13. Back in the Display Descriptive Statistics dialog box, click **OK**.

While still open to the worksheet created in steps 1 through 13, select **Graph → Histogram** and in the Histograms dialog box, click **Simple** and then click **OK**. In the Histogram - Simple dialog box:

1. Enter **C31** in the **Graph variables** box.
2. Click **OK**.

Sampling from Normally Distributed Populations

Use **Normal** to create a simulated sampling distribution from a normally distributed population. For example, to create 100 samples of $n = 30$ from a normally distributed population, open to a new, empty worksheet. Select **Calc → Random Data → Normal**. In the Normal Distribution dialog box:

1. Enter **100** in the **Number of rows of data to generate** box.
2. Enter **C1-C30** in the **Store in column(s)** box (to store the results in the first 30 columns).
3. Enter a value for μ in the **Mean** box.
4. Enter a value for σ in the **Standard deviation** box.
5. Click **OK**.

The 100 samples of $n = 30$ are entered row-wise in columns C1 through C30. To compute statistics, select **Calc → Row Statistics** and follow steps 6 through 13 from the set of instructions for a uniformly distributed population.

8 Confidence Interval Estimation

USING STATISTICS @ Saxon Home Improvement

8.1 Confidence Interval Estimate for the Mean (σ Known)
Can You Ever Know the Population Standard Deviation?

8.2 Confidence Interval Estimate for the Mean (σ Unknown)
Student's t Distribution
Properties of the t Distribution
The Concept of Degrees of Freedom
The Confidence Interval Statement

8.3 Confidence Interval Estimate for the Proportion

8.4 Determining Sample Size
Sample Size Determination for the Mean
Sample Size Determination for the Proportion

8.5 Applications of Confidence Interval Estimation in Auditing
Estimating the Population Total Amount
Difference Estimation
One-Sided Confidence Interval Estimation of the Rate of Noncompliance with Internal Controls

8.6 Confidence Interval Estimation and Ethical Issues

8.7 *Online Topic:* Estimation and Sample Size Determination for Finite Populations

USING STATISTICS @ Saxon Home Improvement Revisited

CHAPTER 8 EXCEL GUIDE

CHAPTER 8 MINITAB GUIDE

Learning Objectives

In this chapter, you learn:

- To construct and interpret confidence interval estimates for the mean and the proportion
- How to determine the sample size necessary to develop a confidence interval estimate for the mean or proportion
- How to use confidence interval estimates in auditing

USING STATISTICS

@ Saxon Home Improvement

Saxon Home Improvement distributes home improvement supplies in the northeastern United States. As a company accountant, you are responsible for the accuracy of the integrated inventory management and sales information system. You could review the contents of each and every record to check the accuracy of this system, but such a detailed review would be time-consuming and costly. A better approach is to use statistical inference techniques to draw conclusions about the population of all records from a relatively small sample collected during an audit. At the end of each month, you could select a sample of the sales invoices to estimate the following:

- The mean dollar amount listed on the sales invoices for the month
- The proportion of invoices that contain errors that violate the internal control policy of the warehouse
- The total dollar amount listed on the sales invoices for the month
- Any differences between the dollar amounts on the sales invoices and the amounts entered into the sales information system

How accurate are the results from the sample, and how do you use this information? Is the sample size large enough to give you the information you need?

In Section 7.4, you used the Central Limit Theorem and knowledge of the population distribution to determine the percentage of sample means that are within certain distances of the population mean. For instance, in the cereal-filling example used throughout Chapter 7 (see Example 7.6 on page 293), you can conclude that 95% of all sample means are between 362.12 and 373.88 grams. This is an example of *deductive* reasoning because the conclusion is based on taking something that is true in general (for the population) and applying it to something specific (the sample means).

Getting the results that Saxon Home Improvement needs requires *inductive* reasoning. Inductive reasoning lets you use some specifics to make broader generalizations. You cannot guarantee that the broader generalizations are absolutely correct, but with a careful choice of the specifics and a rigorous methodology, you can get useful conclusions. As a Saxon accountant, you need to use inferential statistics, which uses sample results (the "some specifics") to *estimate* (the making of "broader generalizations") unknown population parameters such as a population mean or a population proportion. Note that statisticians use the word *estimate* in the same sense of the everyday usage: something you are reasonably certain about but cannot flatly say is absolutely correct.

You estimate population parameters by using either point estimates or interval estimates. A **point estimate** is the value of a single sample statistic, such as a sample mean. A **confidence interval estimate** is a range of numbers, called an *interval*, constructed around the point estimate. The confidence interval is constructed such that the probability that the interval includes the population parameter is known.

Suppose you want to estimate the mean GPA of all the students at your university. The mean GPA for all the students is an unknown population mean, denoted by μ. You select a sample of students and compute the sample mean, denoted by $\bar{X}$, to be 2.80. As a *point estimate* of the population mean, μ, you ask how accurate is the 2.80 value as an estimate of the population mean, μ? By taking into account the variability from sample to sample (see Section 7.4, concerning the sampling distribution of the mean), you can construct a confidence interval estimate for the population mean to answer this question.

When you construct a confidence interval estimate, you indicate the confidence of correctly estimating the value of the population parameter, μ. This allows you to say that there is a specified confidence that μ is somewhere in the range of numbers defined by the interval.

After studying this chapter, you might find that a 95% confidence interval for the mean GPA at your university is $(2.75 \leq \mu \leq 2.85)$. You can interpret this interval estimate by stating that you are 95% confident that the mean GPA at your university is between 2.75 and 2.85.

In this chapter, you learn to construct a confidence interval for both the population mean and population proportion. You also learn how to determine the sample size that is necessary to construct a confidence interval of a desired width.

8.1 Confidence Interval Estimate for the Mean (σ Known)

In Section 7.4, you used the Central Limit Theorem and knowledge of the population distribution to determine the percentage of sample means that are within certain distances of the population mean. Suppose that in the cereal-filling example, you wished to estimate the population mean, using the information from a single sample. Thus, rather than taking $\mu \pm (1.96)(\sigma/\sqrt{n})$ to find the upper and lower limits around μ, as in Section 7.4, you substitute the sample mean, $\bar{X}$, for the unknown μ and use $\bar{X} \pm (1.96)(\sigma/\sqrt{n})$ as an interval to estimate the unknown μ. Although in practice you select a single sample of n values and compute the mean, $\bar{X}$, in order to understand the full meaning of the interval estimate, you need to examine a hypothetical set of all possible samples of n values.

Suppose that a sample of $n = 25$ boxes has a mean of 362.3 grams. The interval developed to estimate μ is $362.3 \pm (1.96)(15)/(\sqrt{25})$ or 362.3 ± 5.88. The estimate of μ is

$$356.42 \leq \mu \leq 368.18$$

Because the population mean, μ (equal to 368), is included within the interval, this sample results in a correct statement about μ (see Figure 8.1).

FIGURE 8.1
Confidence interval estimates for five different samples of $n = 25$ taken from a population where $\mu = 368$ and $\sigma = 15$

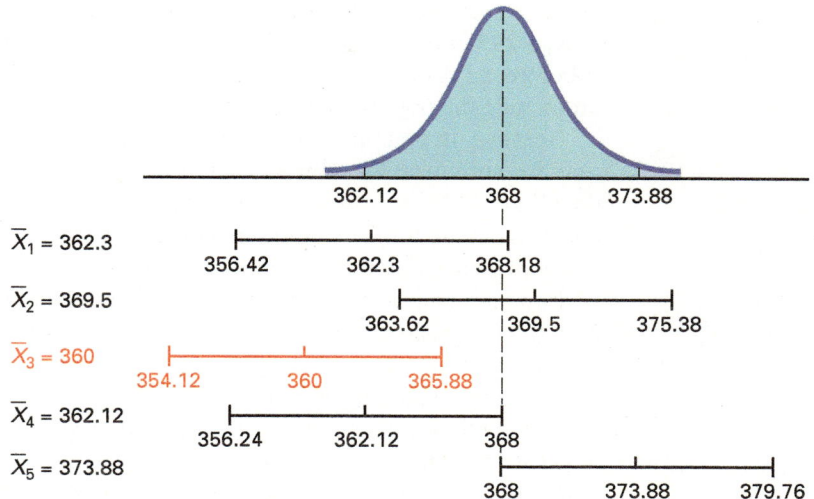

To continue this hypothetical example, suppose that for a different sample of $n = 25$ boxes, the mean is 369.5. The interval developed from this sample is

$$369.5 \pm (1.96)(15)/(\sqrt{25})$$

or 369.5 ± 5.88. The estimate is

$$363.62 \leq \mu \leq 375.38$$

Because the population mean, μ (equal to 368), is also included within this interval, this statement about μ is correct.

Now, before you begin to think that correct statements about μ are always made by developing a confidence interval estimate, suppose a third hypothetical sample of $n = 25$ boxes is selected and the sample mean is equal to 360 grams. The interval developed here is $360 \pm (1.96)(15)/(\sqrt{25})$, or 360 ± 5.88. In this case, the estimate of μ is

$$354.12 \leq \mu \leq 365.88$$

This estimate is *not* a correct statement because the population mean, μ, is not included in the interval developed from this sample (see Figure 8.1). Thus, for some samples, the interval estimate for μ is correct, but for others it is incorrect. In practice, only one sample is selected, and because the population mean is unknown, you cannot determine whether the interval estimate is correct. To resolve this problem of sometimes having an interval that provides a correct estimate and sometimes having an interval that does not, you need to determine the proportion of samples producing intervals that result in correct statements about the population mean, μ. To do this, consider two other hypothetical samples: the case in which $\bar{X} = 362.12$ grams and the case in which $\bar{X} = 373.88$ grams. If $\bar{X} = 362.12$, the interval is $362.12 \pm (1.96)(15)/(\sqrt{25})$, or 362.12 ± 5.88. This leads to the following interval:

$$356.24 \leq \mu \leq 368.00$$

Because the population mean of 368 is at the upper limit of the interval, the statement is correct (see Figure 8.1).

When $\bar{X} = 373.88$, the interval is $373.88 \pm (1.96)(15)/(\sqrt{25})$, or 373.88 ± 5.88. The interval estimate for the mean is

$$368.00 \leq \mu \leq 379.76$$

In this case, because the population mean of 368 is included at the lower limit of the interval, the statement is correct.

In Figure 8.1, you see that when the sample mean falls somewhere between 362.12 and 373.88 grams, the population mean is included *somewhere* within the interval. In Example 7.6 on page 293, you found that 95% of the sample means are between 362.12 and 373.88 grams. Therefore, 95% of all samples of $n = 25$ boxes have sample means that will result in intervals that include the population mean.

Because, in practice, you select only one sample of size n, and $\alpha/2$ is unknown, you never know for sure whether your specific interval includes the population mean. However, if you take all possible samples of n and compute their 95% confidence intervals, 95% of the intervals will include the population mean, and only 5% of them will not. In other words, you have 95% confidence that the population mean is somewhere in your interval.

Consider once again the first sample discussed in this section. A sample of $n = 25$ boxes had a sample mean of 362.3 grams. The interval constructed to estimate μ is

$$362.3 \pm (1.96)(15)/(\sqrt{25})$$

$$362.3 \pm 5.88$$

$$356.42 \leq \mu \leq 368.18$$

The interval from 356.42 to 368.18 is referred to as a *95% confidence interval*. The following contains an interpretation of the interval that most business professionals will understand. (For a technical discussion of different ways to interpret confidence intervals, see reference 3.)

"I am 95% confident that the mean amount of cereal in the population of boxes is somewhere between 356.42 and 368.18 grams."

To assist in your understanding of the meaning of the confidence interval, the following example concerns the order-filling process at a website. Filling orders consists of several steps, including receiving an order, picking the parts of the order, checking the order, packing, and shipping the order. The file **Order** contains the time, in minutes, to fill orders for a population of $N = 200$ orders on a recent day. Although in practice the population characteristics are rarely known, for this population of orders, the mean, μ, is known to be equal to 69.637 minutes, and the standard deviation, σ, is known to be equal to 10.411 minutes and the population is normally distributed. To illustrate how the sample mean and sample standard deviation can vary from one sample to another, 20 different samples of $n = 10$ were selected from the population of 200 orders, and the sample mean and sample standard deviation (and other statistics) were calculated for each sample. Figure 8.2 shows these results.

FIGURE 8.2
Sample statistics and 95% confidence intervals for 20 samples of $n = 10$ randomly selected from the population of $N = 200$ orders

Variable	Count	Mean	StDev	Minimum	Median	Maximum	Range	95% CI
Sample 1	10	74.15	13.39	56.10	76.85	97.70	41.60	(67.6973, 80.6027)
Sample 2	10	61.10	10.60	46.80	61.35	79.50	32.70	(54.6473, 67.5527)
Sample 3	10	74.36	6.50	62.50	74.50	84.00	21.50	(67.9073, 80.8127)
Sample 4	10	70.40	12.80	47.20	70.95	84.00	36.80	(63.9473, 76.8527)
Sample 5	10	62.18	10.85	47.10	59.70	84.00	36.90	(55.7273, 68.6327)
Sample 6	10	67.03	9.68	51.10	69.60	83.30	32.20	(60.5773, 73.4827)
Sample 7	10	69.03	8.81	56.60	68.85	83.70	27.10	(62.5773, 75.4827)
Sample 8	10	72.30	11.52	54.20	71.35	87.00	32.80	(65.8473, 78.7527)
Sample 9	10	68.18	14.10	50.10	69.95	86.20	36.10	(61.7273, 74.6327)
Sample 10	10	66.67	9.08	57.10	64.65	86.10	29.00	(60.2173, 73.1227)
Sample 11	10	72.42	9.76	59.60	74.65	86.10	26.50	(65.9673, 78.8727)
Sample 12	10	76.26	11.69	50.10	80.60	87.00	36.90	(69.8073, 82.7127)
Sample 13	10	65.74	12.11	47.10	62.15	86.10	39.00	(59.2873, 72.1927)
Sample 14	10	69.99	10.97	51.00	73.40	84.60	33.60	(63.5373, 76.4427)
Sample 15	10	75.76	8.60	61.10	75.05	87.80	26.70	(69.3073, 82.2127)
Sample 16	10	67.94	9.19	56.70	67.70	87.80	31.10	(61.4873, 74.3927)
Sample 17	10	71.05	10.48	50.10	71.15	86.20	36.10	(64.5973, 77.5027)
Sample 18	10	71.68	7.96	55.60	72.35	82.60	27.00	(65.2273, 78.1327)
Sample 19	10	70.97	9.83	54.40	70.05	84.60	30.20	(64.5173, 77.4227)
Sample 20	10	74.48	8.80	62.00	76.25	85.70	23.70	(68.0273, 80.9327)

From Figure 8.2, you can see the following:

- The sample statistics differ from sample to sample. The sample means vary from 61.10 to 76.26 minutes, the sample standard deviations vary from 6.50 to 14.10 minutes, the sample medians vary from 59.70 to 80.60 minutes, and the sample ranges vary from 21.50 to 41.60 minutes.
- Some of the sample means are greater than the population mean of 69.637 minutes, and some of the sample means are less than the population mean.
- Some of the sample standard deviations are greater than the population standard deviation of 10.411 minutes, and some of the sample standard deviations are less than the population standard deviation.
- The variation in the sample ranges is much more than the variation in the sample standard deviations.

The variation of sample statistics from sample to sample is called *sampling error*. Sampling error is the variation that occurs due to selecting a single sample from the population. The size of the sampling error is primarily based on the amount of variation in the population and on the sample size. Large samples have less sampling error than small samples, but large samples cost more to select.

The last column of Figure 8.2 contains 95% confidence interval estimates of the population mean order-filling time, based on the results of those 20 samples of $n = 10$. Begin by examining the first sample selected. The sample mean is 74.15 minutes, and the interval estimate for the population mean is 67.6973 to 80.6027 minutes. In a typical study, you would not know for sure whether this interval estimate is correct because you rarely know the value of the population mean. However, for this example *concerning the order-filling times*, the population mean is known to be 69.637 minutes. If you examine the interval 67.6973 to 80.6027 minutes, you see that the population mean of 69.637 minutes is located *between* these lower and upper limits. Thus, the first sample provides a correct estimate of the population mean in the form of an interval estimate. Looking over the other 19 samples, you see that similar results occur for all the other samples *except* for samples 2, 5, and 12. For each of the intervals generated (other than samples 2, 5, and 12), the population mean of 69.637 minutes is located *somewhere* within the interval.

For sample 2, the sample mean is 61.10 minutes, and the interval is 54.6473 to 67.5527 minutes; for sample 5, the sample mean is 62.18, and the interval is between 55.7273 and 68.6327; for sample 12, the sample mean is 76.26, and the interval is between 69.8073 and 82.7127 minutes. The population mean of 69.637 minutes is *not* located within any of these intervals, and the estimate of the population mean made using these intervals is incorrect. Although 3 of the 20 intervals did not include the population mean, if you had selected all the possible samples of $n = 10$ from a population of $N = 200$, 95% of the intervals would include the population mean.

In some situations, you might want a higher degree of confidence of including the population mean within the interval (such as 99%). In other cases, you might accept less confidence (such as 90%) of correctly estimating the population mean. In general, the **level of confidence** is symbolized by $(1 - \alpha) \times 100\%$, where α is the proportion in the tails of the distribution that is outside the confidence interval. The proportion in the upper tail of the distribution is $\alpha/2$, and the proportion in the lower tail of the distribution is $\alpha/2$. You use Equation (8.1) to construct a $(1 - \alpha) \times 100\%$ confidence interval estimate for the mean with σ known.

CONFIDENCE INTERVAL FOR THE MEAN (σ KNOWN)

$$\bar{X} \pm Z_{\alpha/2} \frac{\sigma}{\sqrt{n}}$$

or

$$\bar{X} - Z_{\alpha/2} \frac{\sigma}{\sqrt{n}} \leq \mu \leq \bar{X} + Z_{\alpha/2} \frac{\sigma}{\sqrt{n}} \tag{8.1}$$

where $Z_{\alpha/2}$ is the value corresponding to an upper-tail probability of $\alpha/2$ from the standardized normal distribution (i.e., a cumulative area of $1 - \alpha/2$).

The value of $Z_{\alpha/2}$ needed for constructing a confidence interval is called the **critical value** for the distribution. 95% confidence corresponds to an α value of 0.05. The critical Z value corresponding to a cumulative area of 0.975 is 1.96 because there is 0.025 in the upper tail of the distribution, and the cumulative area less than $Z = 1.96$ is 0.975.

There is a different critical value for each level of confidence, $1 - \alpha$. A level of confidence of 95% leads to a Z value of 1.96 (see Figure 8.3). 99% confidence corresponds to an α value of 0.01. The Z value is approximately 2.58 because the upper-tail area is 0.005 and the cumulative area less than $Z = 2.58$ is 0.995 (see Figure 8.4).

FIGURE 8.3
Normal curve for determining the Z value needed for 95% confidence

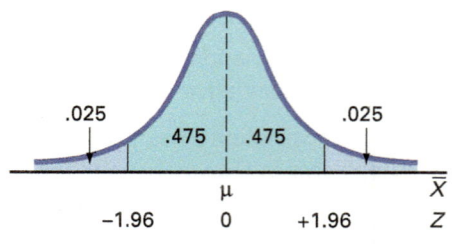

FIGURE 8.4
Normal curve for determining the Z value needed for 99% confidence

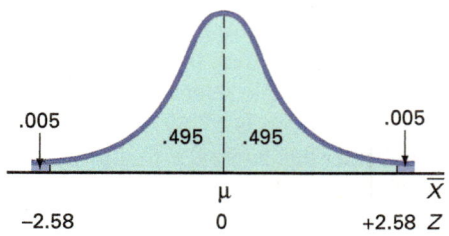

Now that various levels of confidence have been considered, why not make the confidence level as close to 100% as possible? Before doing so, you need to realize that any increase in the level of confidence is achieved only by widening (and making less precise) the confidence interval. There is no "free lunch" here. You would have more confidence that the population mean is within a broader range of values; however, this might make the interpretation of the confidence interval less useful. The trade-off between the width of the confidence interval and the level of confidence is discussed in greater depth in the context of determining the sample size in Section 8.4. Example 8.1 illustrates the application of the confidence interval estimate.

EXAMPLE 8.1

Estimating the Mean Paper Length with 95% Confidence

A paper manufacturer has a production process that operates continuously throughout an entire production shift. The paper is expected to have a mean length of 11 inches, and the standard deviation of the length is 0.02 inch. At periodic intervals, a sample is selected to determine whether the mean paper length is still equal to 11 inches or whether something has gone wrong in the production process to change the length of the paper produced. You select a random sample of 100 sheets, and the mean paper length is 10.998 inches. Construct a 95% confidence interval estimate for the population mean paper length.

SOLUTION Using Equation (8.1) on page 313, with $Z_{\alpha/2} = 1.96$ for 95% confidence,

$$\bar{X} \pm Z_{\alpha/2}\frac{\sigma}{\sqrt{n}} = 10.998 \pm (1.96)\frac{0.02}{\sqrt{100}}$$

$$= 10.998 \pm 0.0039$$

$$10.9941 \leq \mu \leq 11.0019$$

Thus, with 95% confidence, you conclude that the population mean is between 10.9941 and 11.0019 inches. Because the interval includes 11, the value indicating that the production process is working properly, you have no reason to believe that anything is wrong with the production process.

To see the effect of using a 99% confidence interval, examine Example 8.2.

EXAMPLE 8.2

Estimating the Mean Paper Length with 99% Confidence

Construct a 99% confidence interval estimate for the population mean paper length.

SOLUTION Using Equation (8.1) on page 313, with $Z_{\alpha/2} = 2.58$ for 99% confidence,

$$\bar{X} \pm Z_{\alpha/2}\frac{\sigma}{\sqrt{n}} = 10.998 \pm (2.58)\frac{0.02}{\sqrt{100}}$$

$$= 10.998 \pm 0.00516$$

$$10.9928 \leq \mu \leq 11.0032$$

Once again, because 11 is included within this wider interval, you have no reason to believe that anything is wrong with the production process.

As discussed in Section 7.4, the sampling distribution of the sample mean, $\bar{X}$, is normally distributed if the population for your characteristic of interest, X, follows a normal distribution. And, if the population of X does not follow a normal distribution, the Central Limit Theorem almost always ensures that $\bar{X}$ is approximately normally distributed when n is large. However, when dealing with a small sample size and a population that does not follow a normal distribution, the sampling distribution of $\bar{X}$ is not normally distributed, and therefore the confidence interval discussed in this section is inappropriate. In practice, however, as long as the sample size is large enough and the population is not very skewed, you can use the confidence interval defined in Equation (8.1) to estimate the population mean when σ is known. To assess the assumption of normality, you can evaluate the shape of the sample data by constructing a histogram, stem-and-leaf display, boxplot, or normal probability plot.

Can You Ever Know the Population Standard Deviation?

To solve Equation 8.1, you must know the value for σ, the population standard deviation. To know σ implies that you know all the values in the entire population. (How else would you know the value of this population parameter?) If you knew all the values in the entire population, you could directly compute the population mean. There would be no need to use the *inductive* reasoning of inferential statistics to *estimate* the population mean. In other words, if you knew σ, you really do not have a need to use Equation 8.1 to construct a "confidence interval estimate of the mean (σ known)."

More significantly, in virtually all real-world business situations, you would never know the standard deviation of the population. In business situations, populations are often too large to examine all the values. So why study the confidence interval estimate of the mean (σ known) at all? This method serves as an important introduction to the concept of a confidence interval because it uses the normal distribution, which has already been thoroughly discussed in Chapters 6 and 7. In the next section, you will see that constructing a confidence interval estimate when σ is not known requires another distribution (the t distribution) not previously mentioned in this book.

Because the confidence interval concept is a very important concept to understand when reading the rest of this book, review this section carefully to understand the underlying concept—even if you never have a practical reason to use the confidence interval estimate of the mean (σ known).

Problems for Section 8.1

LEARNING THE BASICS

8.1 If $\bar{X} = 85, \sigma = 8$, and $n = 64$, construct a 95% confidence interval estimate for the population mean, μ.

8.2 If $\bar{X} = 125, \sigma = 24$, and $n = 36$, construct a 99% confidence interval estimate for the population mean, μ.

8.3 Why is it not possible in Example 8.1 on page 314 to have 100% confidence? Explain.

8.4 Is it true in Example 8.1 on page 314 that you do not know for sure whether the population mean is between 10.9941 and 11.0019 inches? Explain.

APPLYING THE CONCEPTS

8.5 A market researcher selects a simple random sample of $n = 100$ customers from a population of 2 million customers. After analyzing the sample, she states that she has 95% confidence that the mean annual income of the 2 million customers is between $70,000 and $85,000. Explain the meaning of this statement.

8.6 Suppose that you are going to collect a set of data, either from an entire population or from a random sample taken from that population.
a. Which statistical measure would you compute first: the mean or the standard deviation? Explain.
b. What does your answer to (a) tell you about the "practicality" of using the confidence interval estimate formula given in Equation (8.1)?

8.7 Consider the confidence interval estimate discussed in Problem 8.5. Suppose that the population mean annual income is $71,000. Is the confidence interval estimate stated in Problem 8.5 correct? Explain.

8.8 You are working as an assistant to the dean of institutional research at your university. The dean wants to survey members of the alumni association who obtained their baccalaureate degrees 5 years ago to learn what their starting salaries were in their first full-time job after receiving their degrees. A sample of 100 alumni is to be randomly selected from the list of 2,500 graduates in that class. If the dean's goal is to construct a 95% confidence interval estimate for the population mean starting salary, why is it not possible that you will be able to use Equation (8.1) on page 313 for this purpose? Explain.

8.9 The manager of a paint supply store wants to estimate the actual amount of paint contained in 1-gallon cans purchased from a nationally known manufacturer. The manufacturer's specifications state that the standard deviation of the amount of paint is equal to 0.02 gallon. A random sample of 50 cans is selected, and the sample mean amount of paint per 1-gallon can is 0.995 gallon.
a. Construct a 99% confidence interval estimate for the population mean amount of paint included in a 1-gallon can.
b. On the basis of these results, do you think that the manager has a right to complain to the manufacturer? Why?
c. Must you assume that the population amount of paint per can is normally distributed here? Explain.
d. Construct a 95% confidence interval estimate. How does this change your answer to (b)?

SELF Test 8.10 The quality control manager at a light bulb factory needs to estimate the mean life of a large shipment of light bulbs. The standard deviation is 100 hours. A random sample of 64 light bulbs indicated a sample mean life of 350 hours.
a. Construct a 95% confidence interval estimate for the population mean life of light bulbs in this shipment.
b. Do you think that the manufacturer has the right to state that the light bulbs have a mean life of 400 hours? Explain.
c. Must you assume that the population light bulb life is normally distributed? Explain.
d. Suppose that the standard deviation changes to 80 hours. What are your answers in (a) and (b)?

8.2 Confidence Interval Estimate for the Mean (σ Unknown)

In the previous section, you learned that in most business situations, you do not know σ, the population standard deviation. This section discusses a method of constructing a confidence interval estimate of μ that uses the sample statistic S as an estimate of the population parameter σ.

Student's t Distribution

At the start of the twentieth century, William S. Gosset was working at Guinness in Ireland, trying to help brew better beer less expensively (see reference 4). As he had only small samples to study, he needed to find a way to make inferences about means without having to know σ. Writing under the pen name "Student,"[1] Gosset solved this problem by developing what today is known as the **Student's t distribution**, or the *t* distribution, for short.

If the random variable X is normally distributed, then the following statistic:

$$t = \frac{\bar{X} - \mu}{\frac{S}{\sqrt{n}}}$$

has a *t* distribution with $n - 1$ **degrees of freedom**. This expression has the same form as the Z statistic in Equation (7.4) on page 292, except that S is used to estimate the unknown σ.

[1] Guinness considered all research conducted to be proprietary and a trade secret. The firm prohibited its employees from publishing their results. Gosset circumvented this ban by using the pen name "Student" to publish his findings.

Properties of the t Distribution

The t distribution is very similar in appearance to the standardized normal distribution. Both distributions are symmetrical and bell-shaped, with the mean and the median equal to zero. However, the t distribution has more area in the tails and less in the center than does the standardized normal distribution (see Figure 8.5). This is due to the fact that because S is used to estimate the unknown σ, the values of t are more variable than those for Z.

FIGURE 8.5
Standardized normal distribution and t distribution for 5 degrees of freedom

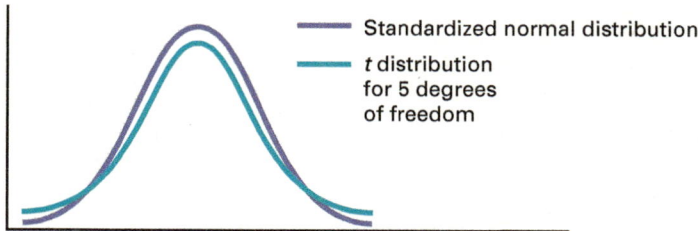

The degrees of freedom, $n - 1$, are directly related to the sample size, n. The concept of *degrees of freedom* is discussed further on page 318. As the sample size and degrees of freedom increase, S becomes a better estimate of σ, and the t distribution gradually approaches the standardized normal distribution, until the two are virtually identical. With a sample size of about 120 or more, S estimates σ closely enough so that there is little difference between the t and Z distributions.

As stated earlier, the t distribution assumes that the random variable X is normally distributed. In practice, however, when the sample size is large enough and the population is not very skewed, in most cases you can use the t distribution to estimate the population mean when σ is unknown. When dealing with a small sample size and a skewed population distribution, the confidence interval estimate may not provide a valid estimate of the population mean. To assess the assumption of normality, you can evaluate the shape of the sample data by constructing a histogram, stem-and-leaf display, boxplot, or normal probability plot. However, the ability of any of these graphs to help you evaluate normality is limited when you have a small sample size.

You find the critical values of t for the appropriate degrees of freedom from the table of the t distribution (see Table E.3). The columns of the table present the most commonly used cumulative probabilities and corresponding upper-tail areas. The rows of the table represent the degrees of freedom. The critical t values are found in the cells of the table. For example, with 99 degrees of freedom, if you want 95% confidence, you find the appropriate value of t, as shown in Table 8.1. The 95% confidence level means that 2.5% of the values (an area of 0.025) are in

TABLE 8.1
Determining the Critical Value from the t Table for an Area of 0.025 in Each Tail with 99 Degrees of Freedom

	Cumulative Probabilities					
	.75	.90	.95	.975	.99	.995
	Upper-Tail Areas					
Degrees of Freedom	.25	.10	.05	.025	.01	.005
1	1.0000	3.0777	6.3138	12.7062	31.8207	63.6574
2	0.8165	1.8856	2.9200	4.3027	6.9646	9.9248
3	0.7649	1.6377	2.3534	3.1824	4.5407	5.8409
4	0.7407	1.5332	2.1318	2.7764	3.7469	4.6041
5	0.7267	1.4759	2.0150	2.5706	3.3649	4.0322
⋮	⋮	⋮	⋮	⋮	⋮	⋮
96	0.6771	1.2904	1.6609	1.9850	2.3658	2.6280
97	0.6770	1.2903	1.6607	1.9847	2.3654	2.6275
98	0.6770	1.2902	1.6606	1.9845	2.3650	2.6269
99	0.6770	1.2902	1.6604	1.9842	2.3646	2.6264
100	0.6770	1.2901	1.6602	1.9840	2.3642	2.6259

Source: Extracted from Table E.3.

each tail of the distribution. Looking in the column for a cumulative probability of 0.975 and an upper-tail area of 0.025 in the row corresponding to 99 degrees of freedom gives you a critical value for t of 1.9842 (see Figure 8.6). Because t is a symmetrical distribution with a mean of 0, if the upper-tail value is $+1.9842$, the value for the lower-tail area (lower 0.025) is -1.9842. A t value of -1.9842 means that the probability that t is less than -1.9842 is 0.025, or 2.5%.

FIGURE 8.6
t distribution with 99 degrees of freedom

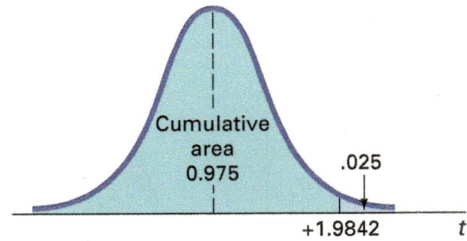

Note that for a 95% confidence interval, you will always have a cumulative probability of 0.975 and an upper-tail area of 0.025. Similarly, for a 99% confidence interval, you will have 0.995 and 0.005, and for a 90% confidence interval you will have 0.95 and 0.05.

The Concept of Degrees of Freedom

In Chapter 3, you learned that the numerator of the sample variance, S^2 [see Equation (3.6) on page 133], requires the computation

$$\sum_{i=1}^{n}(X_i - \bar{X})^2$$

In order to compute S^2, you first need to know $\bar{X}$. Therefore, only $n - 1$ of the sample values are free to vary. This means that you have $n - 1$ degrees of freedom. For example, suppose a sample of five values has a mean of 20. How many values do you need to know before you can determine the remainder of the values? The fact that $n = 5$ and $\bar{X} = 20$ also tells you that

$$\sum_{i=1}^{n} X_i = 100$$

because

$$\frac{\sum_{i=1}^{n} X_i}{n} = \bar{X}$$

Thus, when you know four of the values, the fifth one is *not* free to vary because the sum must be 100. For example, if four of the values are 18, 24, 19, and 16, the fifth value must be 23 so that the sum is 100.

The Confidence Interval Statement

Equation (8.2) defines the $(1 - \alpha) \times 100\%$ confidence interval estimate for the mean with σ unknown.

CONFIDENCE INTERVAL FOR THE MEAN (σ UNKNOWN)

$$\bar{X} \pm t_{\alpha/2} \frac{S}{\sqrt{n}}$$

or

$$\bar{X} - t_{\alpha/2} \frac{S}{\sqrt{n}} \leq \mu \leq \bar{X} + t_{\alpha/2} \frac{S}{\sqrt{n}} \tag{8.2}$$

where $t_{\alpha/2}$ is the critical value corresponding to an upper-tail probability of $\alpha/2$ (i.e., a cumulative area of $1 - \alpha/2$) from the t distribution with $n - 1$ degrees of freedom.

Confidence Interval Estimation

To illustrate the application of the confidence interval estimate for the mean when the standard deviation is unknown, recall the Saxon Home Improvement scenario presented on page 309. Using the Define, Collect, Organize, Visualize, and Analyze steps first discussed in Chapter 2, you define the variable of interest as the dollar amount listed on the sales invoices for the month. Your business objective is to estimate the mean dollar amount. Then, you collect the data by selecting a sample of 100 sales invoices from the population of sales invoices during the month. Once you have collected the data, you organize the data in a worksheet. You can construct various graphs (not shown here) to better visualize the distribution of the dollar amounts. To analyze the data, you compute the sample mean of the 100 sales invoices to be equal to $110.27 and the sample standard deviation to be equal to $28.95. For 95% confidence, the critical value from the t distribution (as shown in Table 8.1 on page 317) is 1.9842. Using Equation (8.2),

$$\bar{X} \pm t_{\alpha/2}\frac{S}{\sqrt{n}}$$

$$= 110.27 \pm (1.9842)\frac{28.95}{\sqrt{100}}$$

$$= 110.27 \pm 5.74$$

$$104.53 \leq \mu \leq 116.01$$

Figure 8.7 shows this confidence interval estimate of the mean dollar amount as computed by Excel (left results) and Minitab (right results).

FIGURE 8.7

Excel worksheet and Minitab confidence interval estimate for the mean sales invoice amount for the Saxon Home Improvement Company

	A	B	
1	Estimate for the Mean Sales Invoice Amount		
2			
3	Data		
4	Sample Standard Deviation	28.95	
5	Sample Mean	110.27	
6	Sample Size	100	
7	Confidence Level	95%	
8			
9	Intermediate Calculations		
10	Standard Error of the Mean	2.8950	=B4/SQRT(B6)
11	Degrees of Freedom	99	=B6 - 1
12	t Value	1.9842	=TINV(1 - B7, B11)
13	Interval Half Width	5.7443	=B12 * B10
14			
15	Confidence Interval		
16	Interval Lower Limit	104.53	=B5 - B13
17	Interval Upper Limit	116.01	=B5 + B13

One-Sample T

N	Mean	StDev	SE Mean	95% CI
100	110.27	28.95	2.90	(104.53, 116.01)

Thus, with 95% confidence, you conclude that the mean amount of all the sales invoices is between $104.53 and $116.01. The 95% confidence level indicates that if you selected all possible samples of 100 (something that is never done in practice), 95% of the intervals developed would include the population mean somewhere within the interval. The validity of this confidence interval estimate depends on the assumption of normality for the distribution of the amount of the sales invoices. With a sample of 100, the normality assumption is not overly restrictive (see the Central Limit Theorem on page 294), and the use of the t distribution is likely appropriate. Example 8.3 further illustrates how you construct the confidence interval for a mean when the population standard deviation is unknown.

EXAMPLE 8.3

Estimating the Mean Force Required to Break Electric Insulators

A manufacturing company produces electric insulators. Using the Define, Collect, Organize, Visualize, and Analyze steps first discussed in Chapter 2, you define the variable of interest as the strength of the insulators. If the insulators break when in use, a short circuit is likely. To test the strength of the insulators, you carry out destructive testing to determine how much force is required to break the insulators. You measure force by observing how many pounds are applied to the insulator before it breaks. You collect the data by selecting 30 insulators to be used in the experiment. You organize the data collected in a worksheet. Table 8.2 lists 30 values from this experiment, which are stored in Force. To analyze the data, you need to construct a 95% confidence interval estimate for the population mean force required to break the insulator.

TABLE 8.2

Force (in Pounds) Required to Break Insulators

1,870	1,728	1,656	1,610	1,634	1,784	1,522	1,696	1,592	1,662
1,866	1,764	1,734	1,662	1,734	1,774	1,550	1,756	1,762	1,866
1,820	1,744	1,788	1,688	1,810	1,752	1,680	1,810	1,652	1,736

SOLUTION To visualize the data, you construct a boxplot of the force, as displayed in Figure 8.8, and a normal probability plot, as shown in Figure 8.9. To analyze the data, you construct the confidence interval estimate shown in Figure 8.10. In each figure, Excel results are on the left and Minitab results are on the right.

FIGURE 8.8
Boxplots for the amount of force required to break electric insulators

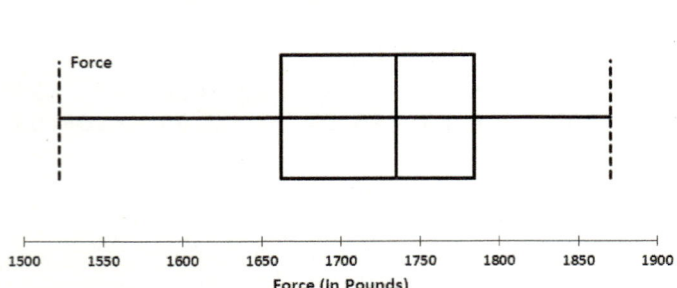
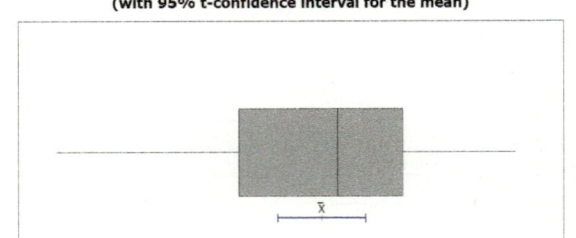

FIGURE 8.9
Normal probability plots for the amount of force required to break electric insulators

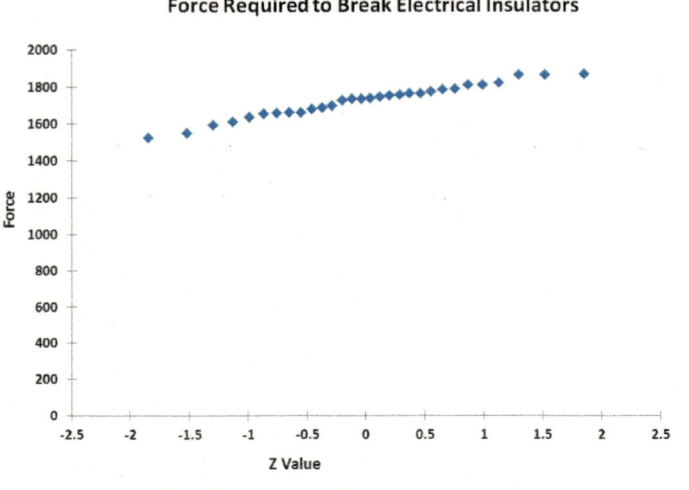
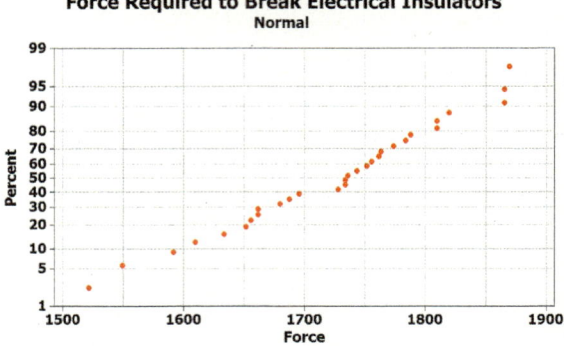

FIGURE 8.10
Confidence interval estimate for the mean amount of force required to break electric insulators

	A	B
1	Estimate for the Mean Amount of Force Required	
2		
3	**Data**	
4	Sample Standard Deviation	89.55
5	Sample Mean	1723.4
6	Sample Size	30
7	Confidence Level	95%
8		
9	**Intermediate Calculations**	
10	Standard Error of the Mean	16.3495 =B4/SQRT(B6)
11	Degrees of Freedom	29 =B6 - 1
12	t Value	2.0452 =TINV(1 - B7, B11)
13	Interval Half Width	33.4385 =B12 * B10
14		
15	**Confidence Interval**	
16	Interval Lower Limit	1689.96 =B5 - B13
17	Interval Upper Limit	1756.84 =B5 + B13

```
One-Sample T: Force
Variable   N    Mean   StDev   SE Mean        95% CI
Force     30  1723.4    89.6      16.3  (1690.0, 1756.8)
```

Figure 8.10 shows that the sample mean is $\bar{X} = 1,723.4$ pounds and the sample standard deviation is $S = 89.55$ pounds. Using Equation (8.2) on page 318 to construct the confidence interval, you need to determine the critical value from the t table, using the row for 29 degrees of freedom. For 95% confidence, you use the column corresponding to an upper-tail area of 0.025 and a cumulative probability of 0.975. From Table E.3, you see that $t_{\alpha/2} = 2.0452$. Thus, using $\bar{X} = 1,723.4$, $S = 89.55$, $n = 30$, and $t_{\alpha/2} = 2.0452$,

$$\bar{X} \pm t_{\alpha/2} \frac{S}{\sqrt{n}}$$

$$= 1,723.4 \pm (2.0452) \frac{89.55}{\sqrt{30}}$$

$$= 1,723.4 \pm 33.44$$

$$1,689.96 \leq \mu \leq 1,756.84$$

You conclude with 95% confidence that the mean breaking force required for the population of insulators is between 1,689.96 and 1,756.84 pounds. The validity of this confidence interval estimate depends on the assumption that the force required is normally distributed. Remember, however, that you can slightly relax this assumption for large sample sizes. Thus, with a sample of 30, you can use the t distribution even if the amount of force required is only slightly left-skewed. From the boxplot displayed in Figure 8.8 and the normal probability plot shown in Figure 8.9, the amount of force required appears only slightly left-skewed. Thus, the t distribution is appropriate for these data.

The interpretation of the confidence interval when σ is unknown is the same as when σ is known. To illustrate the fact that the confidence interval for the mean varies more when σ is unknown, return to the example concerning the order-filling times discussed in Section 8.1 on pages 312–313. Suppose that, in this case, you do *not* know the population standard deviation and instead use the sample standard deviation to construct the confidence interval estimate of the mean. Figure 8.11 on page 322 shows the results for each of 20 samples of $n = 10$ orders.

In Figure 8.11, observe that the standard deviation of the samples varies from 6.25 (sample 17) to 14.83 (sample 3). Thus, the width of the confidence interval developed varies from 8.94 in sample 17 to 21.22 in sample 3. Because you know that the population mean order time $\mu = 69.637$ minutes, you can see that the interval for sample 8 (69.68 − 85.48) and the interval for sample 10 (56.41 − 68.69) do not correctly estimate the population mean. All the other

FIGURE 8.11
Confidence interval estimates of the mean for 20 samples of $n = 10$, randomly selected from the population of $N = 200$ orders with σ unknown

Variable	N	Mean	Std Dev	SE Mean	95% CI
Sample 1	10	71.64	7.58	2.40	(66.22, 77.06)
Sample 2	10	67.22	10.95	3.46	(59.39, 75.05)
Sample 3	10	67.97	14.83	4.69	(57.36, 78.58)
Sample 4	10	73.90	10.59	3.35	(66.33, 81.47)
Sample 5	10	67.11	11.12	3.52	(59.15, 75.07)
Sample 6	10	68.12	10.83	3.43	(60.37, 75.87)
Sample 7	10	65.80	10.85	3.43	(58.03, 73.57)
Sample 8	10	77.58	11.04	3.49	(69.68, 85.48)
Sample 9	10	66.69	11.45	3.62	(58.50, 74.88)
Sample 10	10	62.55	8.58	2.71	(56.41, 68.69)
Sample 11	10	71.12	12.82	4.05	(61.95, 80.29)
Sample 12	10	70.55	10.52	3.33	(63.02, 78.08)
Sample 13	10	65.51	8.16	2.58	(59.67, 71.35)
Sample 14	10	64.90	7.55	2.39	(59.50, 70.30)
Sample 15	10	66.22	11.21	3.54	(58.20, 74.24)
Sample 16	10	70.43	10.21	3.23	(63.12, 77.74)
Sample 17	10	72.04	6.25	1.96	(67.57, 76.51)
Sample 18	10	73.91	11.29	3.57	(65.83, 81.99)
Sample 19	10	71.49	9.76	3.09	(64.51, 78.47)
Sample 20	10	70.15	10.84	3.43	(62.39, 77.91)

intervals correctly estimate the population mean. Once again, remember that in practice you select only one sample, and you are unable to know for sure whether your one sample provides a confidence interval that includes the population mean.

Problems for Section 8.2

LEARNING THE BASICS

8.11 If $\bar{X} = 75$, $S = 24$, and $n = 36$, and assuming that the population is normally distributed, construct a 95% confidence interval estimate for the population mean, μ.

8.12 Determine the critical value of t in each of the following circumstances:
a. $1 - \alpha = 0.95, n = 10$
b. $1 - \alpha = 0.99, n = 10$
c. $1 - \alpha = 0.95, n = 32$
d. $1 - \alpha = 0.95, n = 65$
e. $1 - \alpha = 0.90, n = 16$

8.13 Assuming that the population is normally distributed, construct a 95% confidence interval estimate for the population mean for each of the following samples:

Sample A: 1 1 1 1 8 8 8 8
Sample B: 1 2 3 4 5 6 7 8

Explain why these two samples produce different confidence intervals even though they have the same mean and range.

8.14 Assuming that the population is normally distributed, construct a 95% confidence interval for the population mean, based on the following sample of size $n = 7$:

1, 2, 3, 4, 5, 6, 20

Change the number 20 to 7 and recalculate the confidence interval. Using these results, describe the effect of an outlier (i.e., an extreme value) on the confidence interval.

APPLYING THE CONCEPTS

8.15 A stationery store wants to estimate the mean retail value of greeting cards that it has in its inventory. A random sample of 100 greeting cards indicates a mean value of $2.55 and a standard deviation of $0.44.
a. Assuming a normal distribution, construct a 95% confidence interval estimate for the mean value of all greeting cards in the store's inventory.
b. Suppose there are 2,500 greeting cards in the store's inventory. How are the results in (a) useful in assisting the store owner to estimate the total value of the inventory?

8.16 Southside Hospital in Bay Shore, New York, commonly conducts stress tests to study the heart muscle after a person has a heart attack. Members of the diagnostic imaging department conducted a quality improvement project with the objective of reducing the turnaround time for stress tests. Turnaround time is defined as the time from when a test is ordered to when the radiologist signs off on the test results. Initially, the mean turnaround time for a stress test was 68 hours. After incorporating changes into the stress-test process, the quality improvement team collected a sample of 50 turnaround times. In this sample, the mean turnaround time was 32 hours, with a standard deviation of 9 hours. (Data extracted from E. Godin, D. Raven, C. Sweetapple, and F. R. Del Guidice, "Faster Test Results," *Quality Progress*, January 2004, 37(1), pp. 33–39.)
a. Construct a 95% confidence interval estimate for the population mean turnaround time.
b. Interpret the interval constructed in (a).
c. Do you think the quality improvement project was a success?

8.17 The U.S. Department of Transportation requires tire manufacturers to provide tire performance information on the sidewall of a tire to better inform prospective customers as they make purchasing decisions. One very important measure of tire performance is the tread wear index, which indicates the tire's resistance to tread wear compared with a tire graded with a base of 100. A tire with a grade of 200 should last twice as long, on average, as a tire graded with a base of 100. A consumer organization wants to estimate the actual tread wear index of a brand name of tires that claims "graded 200" on the sidewall of the tire. A random sample of $n = 18$ indicates a sample mean tread wear index of 195.3 and a sample standard deviation of 21.4.
a. Assuming that the population of tread wear indexes is normally distributed, construct a 95% confidence interval estimate for the population mean tread wear index for tires produced by this manufacturer under this brand name.
b. Do you think that the consumer organization should accuse the manufacturer of producing tires that do not meet the performance information provided on the sidewall of the tire? Explain.
c. Explain why an observed tread wear index of 210 for a particular tire is not unusual, even though it is outside the confidence interval developed in (a).

8.18 The file **FastFood** contains the amount that a sample of nine customers spent for lunch ($) at a fast-food restaurant

4.20 5.03 5.86 6.45 7.38 7.54 8.46 8.47 9.87

a. Construct a 95% confidence interval estimate for the population mean amount spent for lunch ($) at a fast-food restaurant, assuming a normal distribution.
b. Interpret the interval constructed in (a).

8.19 The file **Sedans** contains the overall miles per gallon (MPG) of 2010 family sedans.

24 21 22 23 24 34 34 34 20 20
22 22 44 32 20 20 22 20 39 20

Source: Data extracted from "Vehicle Ratings," *Consumer Reports*, April 2010, p. 29.

a. Construct a 95% confidence interval estimate for the population mean MPG of 2010 family sedans, assuming a normal distribution.
b. Interpret the interval constructed in (a).
c. Compare the results in (a) to those in Problem 8.20(a).

8.20 The file **SUV** contains the overall miles per gallon (MPG) of 2010 small SUVs.

24 23 22 21 22 22 18 18 26 26 26 19 19
19 21 21 21 21 21 18 19 21 22 22 16 16

Source: Data extracted from "Vehicle Ratings," *Consumer Reports*, April 2010, pp. 33–34.

a. Construct a 95% confidence interval estimate for the population mean MPG of 2010 small SUVs, assuming a normal distribution.
b. Interpret the interval constructed in (a).
c. Compare the results in (a) to those in Problem 8.19(a).

8.21 Is there a difference in the yields of different types of investments? The file **SavingsRate-MMCD** contains the yields for a money market account and a five-year certificate of deposit (CD) for 25 banks in the United States, as of March 29, 2010.

Source: Data extracted from www.Bankrate.com, March 29, 2010.

a. Construct a 95% confidence interval estimate for the mean yield of money market accounts.
b. Construct a 95% confidence interval estimate for the mean yield of five-year certificates of deposits.
c. Compare the results of (a) and (b).

8.22 One of the major measures of the quality of service provided by any organization is the speed with which it responds to customer complaints. A large family-held department store selling furniture and flooring, including carpet, had undergone a major expansion in the past several years. In particular, the flooring department had expanded from 2 installation crews to an installation supervisor, a measurer, and 15 installation crews. The store had the business objective of improving its response to complaints. The variable of interest was defined as the number of days between when the complaint was made and when it was resolved. Data were collected from 50 complaints that were made in the last year. The data were stored in **Furniture**, and are as follows:

54   5 35 137 31 27 152   2 123 81 74 27
11 19 126 110 110 29 61 35 94 31 26   5
12   4 165 32 29 28 29 26 25   1 14 13
13 10   5 27   4 52 30 22 36 26 20 23
33 68

a. Construct a 95% confidence interval estimate for the population mean number of days between the receipt of a complaint and the resolution of the complaint.
b. What assumption must you make about the population distribution in order to construct the confidence interval estimate in (a)?
c. Do you think that the assumption needed in order to construct the confidence interval estimate in (a) is valid? Explain.
d. What effect might your conclusion in (c) have on the validity of the results in (a)?

8.23 In New York State, savings banks are permitted to sell a form of life insurance called savings bank life insurance (SBLI). The approval process consists of underwriting, which includes a review of the application, a medical information bureau check, possible requests for additional medical information and medical exams, and a policy compilation stage in which the policy pages are generated and sent to the bank for delivery. The ability to deliver approved policies to customers in a timely manner is critical to the profitability of this service to the bank. During a period of one month, a random sample of 27 approved policies was selected, and the total processing time, in days, was as shown below and stored in Insurance :

73 19 16 64 28 28 31 90 60 56 31 56 22 18
45 48 17 17 17 91 92 63 50 51 69 16 17

a. Construct a 95% confidence interval estimate for the population mean processing time.
b. What assumption must you make about the population distribution in order to construct the confidence interval estimate in (a)?
c. Do you think that the assumption needed in order to construct the confidence interval estimate in (a) is valid? Explain.

8.24 The file DarkChocolate contains the cost per ounce ($) for a sample of 14 dark chocolate bars:

0.68 0.72 0.92 1.14 1.42 0.94 0.77
0.57 1.51 0.57 0.55 0.86 1.41 0.90

Source: Data extracted from "Dark Chocolate: Which Bars Are Best?" *Consumer Reports*, September 2007, p. 8.

a. Construct a 95% confidence interval estimate for the population cost per ounce ($) of dark chocolate bars.
b. What assumption do you need to make about the population distribution to construct the interval in (a)?
c. Given the data presented, do you think the assumption needed in (a) is valid? Explain.

8.25 One operation of a mill is to cut pieces of steel into parts that are used in the frame for front seats in an automobile. The steel is cut with a diamond saw, and the resulting parts must be cut to be within ±0.005 inch of the length specified by the automobile company. The measurement reported from a sample of 100 steel parts (stored in Steel) is the difference, in inches, between the actual length of the steel part, as measured by a laser measurement device, and the specified length of the steel part. For example, the first observation, −0.002, represents a steel part that is 0.002 inch shorter than the specified length.
a. Construct a 95% confidence interval estimate for the population mean difference between the actual length of the steel part and the specified length of the steel part.
b. What assumption must you make about the population distribution in order to construct the confidence interval estimate in (a)?
c. Do you think that the assumption needed in order to construct the confidence interval estimate in (a) is valid? Explain.
d. Compare the conclusions reached in (a) with those of Problem 2.41 on page 85.

8.3 Confidence Interval Estimate for the Proportion

The concept of a confidence interval also applies to categorical data. With categorical data, you want to estimate the proportion of items in a population having a certain characteristic of interest. The unknown population proportion is represented by the Greek letter π. The point estimate for π is the sample proportion, $p = X/n$, where n is the sample size and X is the number of items in the sample having the characteristic of interest. Equation (8.3) defines the confidence interval estimate for the population proportion.

CONFIDENCE INTERVAL ESTIMATE FOR THE PROPORTION

$$p \pm Z_{\alpha/2}\sqrt{\frac{p(1-p)}{n}}$$

or

$$p - Z_{\alpha/2}\sqrt{\frac{p(1-p)}{n}} \leq \pi \leq p + Z_{\alpha/2}\sqrt{\frac{p(1-p)}{n}} \tag{8.3}$$

where

$$p = \text{sample proportion} = \frac{X}{n} = \frac{\text{Number of items having the characteristic}}{\text{sample size}}$$

π = population proportion
$Z_{\alpha/2}$ = critical value from the standardized normal distribution
n = sample size

Note: To use this equation for the confidence interval, the sample size n must be large enough to ensure that both X and $n - X$ are greater than 5.

You can use the confidence interval estimate for the proportion defined in Equation (8.3) to estimate the proportion of sales invoices that contain errors (see the Saxon Home Improvement scenario on page 309). Using the Define, Collect, Organize, Visualize, and Analyze steps, you define the variable of interest as whether the invoice contains errors (yes or no). Then, you collect the data from a sample of 100 sales invoices. The results, which you organize and store in a worksheet, show that 10 invoices contain errors. To analyze the data, you compute, for these data, $p = X/n = 10/100 = 0.10$. Since both X and $n - X$ are > 5, using Equation (8.3) and $Z_{\alpha/2} = 1.96$, for 95% confidence,

$$p \pm Z_{\alpha/2}\sqrt{\frac{p(1-p)}{n}}$$

$$= 0.10 \pm (1.96)\sqrt{\frac{(0.10)(0.90)}{100}}$$

$$= 0.10 \pm (1.96)(0.03)$$

$$= 0.10 \pm 0.0588$$

$$0.0412 \leq \pi \leq 0.1588$$

Therefore, you have 95% confidence that the population proportion of all sales invoices containing errors is between 0.0412 and 0.1588. This means that between 4.12% and 15.88% of all the sales invoices contain errors. Figure 8.12 shows a confidence interval estimate for this example. (Excel results are on the left and Minitab results are on the right.)

FIGURE 8.12
Confidence interval estimate for the proportion of sales invoices that contain errors

	A	B	
1	Proportion of In-Error Sales Invoices		
2			
3	Data		
4	Sample Size	100	
5	Number of Successes	10	
6	Confidence Level	95%	
7			
8	Intermediate Calculations		
9	Sample Proportion	0.1	=B5/B4
10	Z Value	-1.9600	=NORMSINV((1 - B6)/2)
11	Standard Error of the Proportion	0.03	=SQRT(B9 * (1 - B9)/B4)
12	Interval Half Width	0.0588	=ABS(B10 * B11)
13			
14	Confidence Interval		
15	Interval Lower Limit	0.0412	=B9 - B12
16	Interval Upper Limit	0.1588	=B9 + B12

Test and CI for One Proportion

```
Sample   X    N    Sample p         95% CI
1        10   100  0.100000   (0.041201, 0.158799)

Using the normal approximation.
```

Example 8.4 illustrates another application of a confidence interval estimate for the proportion.

EXAMPLE 8.4

Estimating the Proportion of Nonconforming Newspapers Printed

The operations manager at a large newspaper wants to estimate the proportion of newspapers printed that have a nonconforming attribute. Using the Define, Collect, Organize, Visualize, and Analyze steps, you define the variable of interest as whether the newspaper has excessive ruboff, improper page setup, missing pages, or duplicate pages. You collect the data by selecting a random sample of $n = 200$ newspapers from all the newspapers printed during a single day. You organize the results, which show that 35 newspapers contain some type of nonconformance, in a worksheet. To analyze the data, you need to construct and interpret a 90% confidence interval for the proportion of newspapers printed during the day that have a nonconforming attribute.

SOLUTION Using Equation (8.3),

$$p = \frac{X}{n} = \frac{35}{200} = 0.175, \text{ and with a 90\% level of confidence } Z_{\alpha/2} = 1.645$$

$$p \pm Z_{\alpha/2}\sqrt{\frac{p(1-p)}{n}}$$

$$= 0.175 \pm (1.645)\sqrt{\frac{(0.175)(0.825)}{200}}$$

$$= 0.175 \pm (1.645)(0.0269)$$

$$= 0.175 \pm 0.0442$$

$$0.1308 \leq \pi \leq 0.2192$$

You conclude with 90% confidence that the population proportion of all newspapers printed that day with nonconformities is between 0.1308 and 0.2192. This means that between 13.08% and 21.92% of the newspapers printed on that day have some type of nonconformance.

Equation (8.3) contains a Z statistic because you can use the normal distribution to approximate the binomial distribution when the sample size is sufficiently large. In Example 8.4, the confidence interval using Z provides an excellent approximation for the population proportion because both X and $n - X$ are greater than 5. However, if you do not have a sufficiently large sample size, you should use the binomial distribution rather than Equation (8.3) (see references 1, 2, and 7). The exact confidence intervals for various sample sizes and proportions of successes have been tabulated by Fisher and Yates (reference 2).

Problems for Section 8.3

LEARNING THE BASICS

8.26 If $n = 200$ and $X = 50$, construct a 95% confidence interval estimate for the population proportion.

8.27 If $n = 400$ and $X = 25$, construct a 99% confidence interval estimate for the population proportion.

APPLYING THE CONCEPTS

8.28 The telephone company has the business objective of wanting to estimate the proportion of households that would purchase an additional telephone line if it were made available at a substantially reduced installation cost. Data are collected from a random sample of 500 households. The results indicate that 135 of the households would purchase the additional telephone line at a reduced installation cost.
a. Construct a 99% confidence interval estimate for the population proportion of households that would purchase the additional telephone line.
b. How would the manager in charge of promotional programs concerning residential customers use the results in (a)?

8.29 In a survey of 1,200 social media users, 76% said it is okay to friend co-workers, but 56% said it is not okay to friend your boss. (Data extracted from "Facebook Etiquette at Work," *USA Today*, March 24, 2010, p. 1B.)
a. Construct a 95% confidence interval estimate for the population proportion of social media users who would say it is okay to friend co-workers.

b. Construct a 95% confidence interval estimate for the population proportion of social media users who would say it is not okay to friend their boss.
c. Write a short summary of the information derived from (a) and (b).

8.30 Have you ever negotiated a pay raise? According to an Accenture survey, 52% of U.S. workers have (J. Yang and K. Carter, "Have You Ever Negotiated a Pay Raise?" **www.usatoday.com**, May 22, 2009).
a. Suppose that the survey had a sample size of $n = 500$. Construct a 95% confidence interval for the proportion of all U.S. workers who have negotiated a pay raise.
b. Based on (a), can you claim that more than half of all U.S. workers have negotiated a pay raise?
c. Repeat parts (a) and (b), assuming that the survey had a sample size of $n = 5{,}000$.
d. Discuss the effect of sample size on confidence interval estimation.

8.31 In a survey of 1,000 airline travelers, 760 responded that the airline fee that is most unreasonable is additional charges to redeem points/miles. (Data extracted from "Which Airline Fee Is Most Unreasonable?" *USA Today*, December 2, 2008, p. B1.) Construct a 95% confidence interval estimate for the population proportion of airline travelers who think that the airline fee that is most unreasonable is additional charges to redeem points/miles.

8.32 In a survey of 2,395 adults, 1,916 reported that e-mails are easy to misinterpret, but only 1,269 reported that telephone conversations are easy to misinterpret. (Data extracted from "Open to Misinterpretation," *USA Today*, July 17, 2007, p. 1D.)
a. Construct a 95% confidence interval estimate for the population proportion of adults who report that e-mails are easy to misinterpret.
b. Construct a 95% confidence interval estimate for the population proportion of adults who report that telephone conversations are easy to misinterpret.
c. Compare the results of (a) and (b).

8.33 What are the most preferred forms of recognition in the workplace? In a survey by Office Arrow, 163 of 388 administrative professionals responded that verbal recognition is the most preferred form of recognition, and 74 responded that cash bonuses are most preferred. (Data extracted from "Most Preferred Forms of Recognition at Workplace," *USA Today*, May 4, 2009, p. 1B.)
a. Construct a 95% confidence interval estimate for the population proportion of administrative professionals who prefer verbal recognition.
b. Construct a 95% confidence interval estimate for the population proportion of administrative professionals who prefer cash bonuses.
c. Interpret the intervals in (a) and (b).
d. Explain the difference in the results in (a) and (b).

8.4 Determining Sample Size

In each confidence interval developed so far in this chapter, the sample size was reported along with the results, with little discussion of the width of the resulting confidence interval. In the business world, sample sizes are determined prior to data collection to ensure that the confidence interval is narrow enough to be useful in making decisions. Determining the proper sample size is a complicated procedure, subject to the constraints of budget, time, and the amount of acceptable sampling error. In the Saxon Home Improvement example, if you want to estimate the mean dollar amount of the sales invoices, you must determine in advance how large a sampling error to allow in estimating the population mean. You must also determine, in advance, the level of confidence (i.e., 90%, 95%, or 99%) to use in estimating the population parameter.

Sample Size Determination for the Mean

To develop an equation for determining the appropriate sample size needed when constructing a confidence interval estimate for the mean, recall Equation (8.1) on page 313:

$$\bar{X} \pm Z_{\alpha/2} \frac{\sigma}{\sqrt{n}}$$

The amount added to or subtracted from $\bar{X}$ is equal to half the width of the interval. This quantity represents the amount of imprecision in the estimate that results from sampling error.[2] The **sampling error**, e, is defined as

$$e = Z_{\alpha/2} \frac{\sigma}{\sqrt{n}}$$

[2] In this context, some statisticians refer to e as the **margin of error**.

Solving for n gives the sample size needed to construct the appropriate confidence interval estimate for the mean. "Appropriate" means that the resulting interval will have an acceptable amount of sampling error.

> **SAMPLE SIZE DETERMINATION FOR THE MEAN**
> The sample size, n, is equal to the product of the $Z_{\alpha/2}$ value squared and the standard deviation, σ, squared, divided by the square of the sampling error, e.
> $$n = \frac{Z_{\alpha/2}^2 \sigma^2}{e^2} \qquad (8.4)$$

To compute the sample size, you must know three factors:

1. The desired confidence level, which determines the value of $Z_{\alpha/2}$, the critical value from the standardized normal distribution[3]
2. The acceptable sampling error, e
3. The standard deviation, σ

[3] You use Z instead of t because, to determine the critical value of t, you need to know the sample size, but you do not know it yet. For most studies, the sample size needed is large enough that the standardized normal distribution is a good approximation of the t distribution.

In some business-to-business relationships that require estimation of important parameters, legal contracts specify acceptable levels of sampling error and the confidence level required. For companies in the food and drug sectors, government regulations often specify sampling errors and confidence levels. In general, however, it is usually not easy to specify the three factors needed to determine the sample size. How can you determine the level of confidence and sampling error? Typically, these questions are answered only by a subject matter expert (i.e., an individual very familiar with the variables under study). Although 95% is the most common confidence level used, if more confidence is desired, then 99% might be more appropriate; if less confidence is deemed acceptable, then 90% might be used. For the sampling error, you should think not of how much sampling error you would like to have (you really do not want any error) but of how much you can tolerate when reaching conclusions from the confidence interval.

In addition to specifying the confidence level and the sampling error, you need an estimate of the standard deviation. Unfortunately, you rarely know the population standard deviation, σ. In some instances, you can estimate the standard deviation from past data. In other situations, you can make an educated guess by taking into account the range and distribution of the variable. For example, if you assume a normal distribution, the range is approximately equal to 6σ (i.e., $\pm 3\sigma$ around the mean) so that you estimate σ as the range divided by 6. If you cannot estimate σ in this way, you can conduct a small-scale study and estimate the standard deviation from the resulting data.

To explore how to determine the sample size needed for estimating the population mean, consider again the audit at Saxon Home Improvement. In Section 8.2, you selected a sample of 100 sales invoices and constructed a 95% confidence interval estimate for the population mean sales invoice amount. How was this sample size determined? Should you have selected a different sample size?

Suppose that, after consulting with company officials, you determine that a sampling error of no more than $\pm\$5$ is desired, along with 95% confidence. Past data indicate that the standard deviation of the sales amount is approximately \$25. Thus, $e = \$5$, $\sigma = \$25$, and $Z_{\alpha/2} = 1.96$ (for 95% confidence). Using Equation (8.4),

$$n = \frac{Z_{\alpha/2}^2 \sigma^2}{e^2} = \frac{(1.96)^2(25)^2}{(5)^2}$$
$$= 96.04$$

Because the general rule is to slightly oversatisfy the criteria by rounding the sample size up to the next whole integer, you should select a sample of size 97. Thus, the sample of size $n = 100$ used on page 319 is slightly more than what is necessary to satisfy the needs of the company, based on the estimated standard deviation, desired confidence level, and sampling error. Because the calculated sample standard deviation is slightly higher than expected, $28.95 compared to $25.00, the confidence interval is slightly wider than desired. Figure 8.13 shows a worksheet solution for determining the sample size.

FIGURE 8.13
Worksheet for determining sample size for estimating the mean sales invoice amount for the Saxon Home Improvement Company

	A	B	
1	For the Mean Sales Invoice Amount		
2			
3	Data		
4	Population Standard Deviation	25	
5	Sampling Error	5	
6	Confidence Level	95%	
7			
8	Intemediate Calculations		
9	Z Value	-1.9600	=NORMSINV((1 - B6)/2)
10	Calculated Sample Size	96.0365	=((B9 * B4)/B5)^2
11			
12	Result		
13	Sample Size Needed	97	=ROUNDUP(B10, 0)

Example 8.5 illustrates another application of determining the sample size needed to develop a confidence interval estimate for the mean.

EXAMPLE 8.5

Determining the Sample Size for the Mean

Returning to Example 8.3 on page 320, suppose you want to estimate, with 95% confidence, the population mean force required to break the insulator to within ±25 pounds. On the basis of a study conducted the previous year, you believe that the standard deviation is 100 pounds. Determine the sample size needed.

SOLUTION Using Equation (8.4) on page 328 and $e = 25$, $\sigma = 100$, and $Z_{\alpha/2} = 1.96$ for 95% confidence,

$$n = \frac{Z_{\alpha/2}^2 \sigma^2}{e^2} = \frac{(1.96)^2(100)^2}{(25)^2}$$

$$= 61.47$$

Therefore, you should select a sample of 62 insulators because the general rule for determining sample size is to always round up to the next integer value in order to slightly oversatisfy the criteria desired. An actual sampling error slightly larger than 25 will result if the sample standard deviation calculated in this sample of 62 is greater than 100 and slightly smaller if the sample standard deviation is less than 100.

Sample Size Determination for the Proportion

So far in this section, you have learned how to determine the sample size needed for estimating the population mean. Now suppose that you want to determine the sample size necessary for estimating a population proportion.

To determine the sample size needed to estimate a population proportion, π, you use a method similar to the method for a population mean. Recall that in developing the sample size for a confidence interval for the mean, the sampling error is defined by

$$e = Z_{\alpha/2} \frac{\sigma}{\sqrt{n}}$$

When estimating a proportion, you replace σ with $\sqrt{\pi(1-\pi)}$. Thus, the sampling error is

$$e = Z_{\alpha/2}\sqrt{\frac{\pi(1-\pi)}{n}}$$

Solving for n, you have the sample size necessary to develop a confidence interval estimate for a proportion.

> **SAMPLE SIZE DETERMINATION FOR THE PROPORTION**
>
> The sample size n is equal to the product of $Z_{\alpha/2}$ squared, the population proportion, π, and 1 minus the population proportion, π, divided by the square of the sampling error, e.
>
> $$n = \frac{Z_{\alpha/2}^2 \pi(1-\pi)}{e^2} \qquad (8.5)$$

To determine the sample size, you must know three factors:

1. The desired confidence level, which determines the value of $Z_{\alpha/2}$, the critical value from the standardized normal distribution
2. The acceptable sampling error (or margin of error), e
3. The population proportion, π

In practice, selecting these quantities requires some planning. Once you determine the desired level of confidence, you can find the appropriate $Z_{\alpha/2}$ value from the standardized normal distribution. The sampling error, e, indicates the amount of error that you are willing to tolerate in estimating the population proportion. The third quantity, π, is actually the population parameter that you want to estimate! Thus, how do you state a value for what you are trying to determine?

Here you have two alternatives. In many situations, you may have past information or relevant experience that provides an educated estimate of π. Or, if you do not have past information or relevant experience, you can try to provide a value for π that would never *underestimate* the sample size needed. Referring to Equation (8.5), you can see that the quantity $\pi(1-\pi)$ appears in the numerator. Thus, you need to determine the value of π that will make the quantity $\pi(1-\pi)$ as large as possible. When $\pi = 0.5$, the product $\pi(1-\pi)$ achieves its maximum value. To show this result, consider the following values of π, along with the accompanying products of $\pi(1-\pi)$:

When $\pi = 0.9$, then $\pi(1-\pi) = (0.9)(0.1) = 0.09$.

When $\pi = 0.7$, then $\pi(1-\pi) = (0.7)(0.3) = 0.21$.

When $\pi = 0.5$, then $\pi(1-\pi) = (0.5)(0.5) = 0.25$.

When $\pi = 0.3$, then $\pi(1-\pi) = (0.3)(0.7) = 0.21$.

When $\pi = 0.1$, then $\pi(1-\pi) = (0.1)(0.9) = 0.09$.

Therefore, when you have no prior knowledge or estimate for the population proportion, π, you should use $\pi = 0.5$ for determining the sample size. Using $\pi = 0.5$ produces the largest possible sample size and results in the narrowest and most precise confidence interval. This increased precision comes at the cost of spending more time and money for an increased sample size. Also, note that if you use $\pi = 0.5$ and the proportion is different from 0.5, you will overestimate the sample size needed, because you will get a confidence interval narrower than originally intended.

Returning to the Saxon Home Improvement scenario on page 309, suppose that the auditing procedures require you to have 95% confidence in estimating the population proportion of sales invoices with errors to within ± 0.07. The results from past months indicate that the largest proportion has been no more than 0.15. Thus, using Equation (8.5) with $e = 0.07$, $\pi = 0.15$, and $Z_{\alpha/2} = 1.96$ for 95% confidence,

$$n = \frac{Z_{\alpha/2}^2 \pi(1-\pi)}{e^2}$$

$$= \frac{(1.96)^2(0.15)(0.85)}{(0.07)^2}$$

$$= 99.96$$

Because the general rule is to round the sample size up to the next whole integer to slightly oversatisfy the criteria, a sample size of 100 is needed. Thus, the sample size needed to satisfy the requirements of the company, based on the estimated proportion, desired confidence level, and sampling error, is equal to the sample size taken on page 325. The actual confidence interval is narrower than required because the sample proportion is 0.10, whereas 0.15 was used for π in Equation (8.5). Figure 8.14 shows a worksheet solution for determining the sample size.

FIGURE 8.14
Worksheet for determining sample size for estimating the proportion of sales invoices with errors for the Saxon Home Improvement Company

	A	B
1	For the Proportion of In-Error Sales Invoices	
2		
3	Data	
4	Estimate of True Proportion	0.15
5	Sampling Error	0.07
6	Confidence Level	95%
7		
8	Intermediate Calculations	
9	Z Value	-1.9600 =NORMSINV((1 - B6)/2)
10	Calculated Sample Size	99.9563 =(B9^2 * B4 * (1 - B4))/B5^2
11		
12	Result	
13	Sample Size Needed	100 =ROUNDUP(B10, 0)

Example 8.6 provides another application of determining the sample size for estimating the population proportion.

EXAMPLE 8.6

Determining the Sample Size for the Population Proportion

You want to have 90% confidence of estimating the proportion of office workers who respond to e-mail within an hour to within ± 0.05. Because you have not previously undertaken such a study, there is no information available from past data. Determine the sample size needed.

SOLUTION Because no information is available from past data, assume that $\pi = 0.50$. Using Equation (8.5) on page 330 and $e = 0.05$, $\pi = 0.50$, and $Z_{\alpha/2} = 1.645$ for 90% confidence,

$$n = \frac{Z_{\alpha/2}^2 \pi(1-\pi)}{e^2}$$

$$= \frac{(1.645)^2(0.50)(0.50)}{(0.05)^2}$$

$$= 270.6$$

Therefore, you need a sample of 271 office workers to estimate the population proportion to within ± 0.05 with 90% confidence.

Problems for Section 8.4

LEARNING THE BASICS

8.34 If you want to be 95% confident of estimating the population mean to within a sampling error of ±5 and the standard deviation is assumed to be 15, what sample size is required?

8.35 If you want to be 99% confident of estimating the population mean to within a sampling error of ±20 and the standard deviation is assumed to be 100, what sample size is required?

8.36 If you want to be 99% confident of estimating the population proportion to within a sampling error of ±0.04, what sample size is needed?

8.37 If you want to be 95% confident of estimating the population proportion to within a sampling error of ±0.02 and there is historical evidence that the population proportion is approximately 0.40, what sample size is needed?

APPLYING THE CONCEPTS

SELF Test 8.38 A survey is planned to determine the mean annual family medical expenses of employees of a large company. The management of the company wishes to be 95% confident that the sample mean is correct to within ±$50 of the population mean annual family medical expenses. A previous study indicates that the standard deviation is approximately $400.
a. How large a sample is necessary?
b. If management wants to be correct to within ±$25, how many employees need to be selected?

8.39 If the manager of a paint supply store wants to estimate, with 95% confidence, the mean amount of paint in a 1-gallon can to within ±0.004 gallon and also assumes that the standard deviation is 0.02 gallon, what sample size is needed?

8.40 If a quality control manager wants to estimate, with 95% confidence, the mean life of light bulbs to within ±20 hours and also assumes that the population standard deviation is 100 hours, how many light bulbs need to be selected?

8.41 If the inspection division of a county weights and measures department wants to estimate the mean amount of soft-drink fill in 2-liter bottles to within ±0.01 liter with 95% confidence and also assumes that the standard deviation is 0.05 liter, what sample size is needed?

8.42 A consumer group wants to estimate the mean electric bill for the month of July for single-family homes in a large city. Based on studies conducted in other cities, the standard deviation is assumed to be $25. The group wants to estimate, with 99% confidence, the mean bill for July to within ±$5.
a. What sample size is needed?
b. If 95% confidence is desired, how many homes need to be selected?

8.43 An advertising agency that serves a major radio station wants to estimate the mean amount of time that the station's audience spends listening to the radio daily. From past studies, the standard deviation is estimated as 45 minutes.
a. What sample size is needed if the agency wants to be 90% confident of being correct to within ±5 minutes?
b. If 99% confidence is desired, how many listeners need to be selected?

8.44 A growing niche in the restaurant business is gourmet-casual breakfast, lunch, and brunch. Chains in this group include EggSpectation and Panera Bread. Suppose that the mean per-person check for EggSpectation is approximately $12.50, and the mean per-person check for Panera Bread is $7.50.
a. Assuming a standard deviation of $2.00, what sample size is needed to estimate, with 95% confidence, the mean per-person check for EggSpectation to within ±$0.25?
b. Assuming a standard deviation of $2.50, what sample size is needed to estimate, with 95% confidence, the mean per-person check for EggSpectation to within ±$0.25?
c. Assuming a standard deviation of $3.00, what sample size is needed to estimate, with 95% confidence, the mean per-person check for EggSpectation to within ±$0.25?
d. Discuss the effect of variation on the sample size needed.

8.45 What proportion of Americans get most of their news from the Internet? According to a poll conducted by Pew Research Center, 40% get most of their news from the Internet. (Data extracted from "Drill Down," *The New York Times*, January 5, 2009, p. B3.)
a. To conduct a follow-up study that would provide 95% confidence that the point estimate is correct to within ±0.04 of the population proportion, how large a sample size is required?
b. To conduct a follow-up study that would provide 99% confidence that the point estimate is correct to within ±0.04 of the population proportion, how many people need to be sampled?
c. To conduct a follow-up study that would provide 95% confidence that the point estimate is correct to within ±0.02 of the population proportion, how large a sample size is required?
d. To conduct a follow-up study that would provide 99% confidence that the point estimate is correct to within ±0.02 of the population proportion, how many people need to be sampled?
e. Discuss the effects on sample size requirements of changing the desired confidence level and the acceptable sampling error.

8.46 A survey of 1,000 adults was conducted in March 2009 concerning "green practices." In response to the question of what was the most beneficial thing to do for the environment, 28% said buying renewable energy, 19% said using greener transportation, and 7% said selecting minimal or reduced packaging. (Data extracted from "Environmentally Friendly Choices," *USA Today*, March 31, 2009, p. D1.) Construct a 95% confidence interval estimate of the population proportion of who said that the most beneficial thing to do for the environment was
a. buy renewable energy.
b. use greener transportation.
c. select minimal or reduced packaging.
d. You have been asked to update the results of this study. Determine the sample size necessary to estimate, with 95% confidence, the population proportions in (a) through (c) to within ±0.02.

8.47 In a study of 500 executives, 315 stated that their company informally monitored social networking sites to stay on top of information related to their company. (Data extracted from "Checking Out the Buzz," *USA Today*, June 26, 2009, p. 1B.)
a. Construct a 95% confidence interval for the proportion of companies that informally monitored social networking sites to stay on top of information related to their company.
b. Interpret the interval constructed in (a).
c. If you wanted to conduct a follow-up study to estimate the population proportion of companies that informally monitored social networking sites to stay on top of information related to their company to within ±0.01 with 95% confidence, how many executives would you survey?

8.48 In response to the question "How do you judge a company?" 84% said the most important way was how a company responded to a crisis. (Data extracted from "How Do You Judge a Company?" *USA Today*, December 22, 2008, p. 1B.)
a. If you conduct a follow-up study to estimate the population proportion of individuals who said that the most important way to judge a company was how the company responded to a crisis, would you use a π of 0.84 or 0.50 in the sample size formula? Discuss.
b. Using your answer to (a), find the sample size necessary to estimate, with 95% certainty, the population proportion to within ±0.03.

8.49 There are many reasons adults use credit cards. A recent survey ("Why Adults Use Credit Cards," *USA Today*, October 18, 2007, p. 1D) found that 66% of adults used credit cards for convenience.
a. To conduct a follow-up study that would provide 99% confidence that the point estimate is correct to within ±0.03 of the population proportion, how many people need to be sampled?
b. To conduct a follow-up study that would provide 99% confidence that the point estimate is correct to within ±0.05 of the population proportion, how many people need to be sampled?
c. Compare the results of (a) and (b).

8.5 Applications of Confidence Interval Estimation in Auditing

Auditing is one of the areas in business that makes widespread use of probability sampling methods in order to construct confidence interval estimates.

> **AUDITING**
>
> **Auditing** is the collection and evaluation of evidence about information related to an economic entity, such as a sole business proprietor, a partnership, a corporation, or a government agency, in order to determine and report on how well the information corresponds to established criteria.

Auditors rarely examine a complete population of information. Instead, they rely on estimation techniques based on the probability sampling methods you have studied in this text. The following list contains some of the reasons sampling is used in auditing:

- Sampling is less time-consuming.
- Sampling is less costly.
- Sampling provides an objective way of estimating the sample size in advance.
- Sampling provides results that are objective and defensible. Because the sample size is based on demonstrable statistical principles, the audit is defensible before one's superiors and in a court of law.
- Sampling provides an estimate of the sampling error and therefore allows auditors to generalize their findings to the population with a known sampling error.

- Sampling is often more accurate than other methods for drawing conclusions about large populations. Examining every item in large populations is time-consuming and therefore often subject to more nonsampling error than is statistical sampling.
- Sampling allows auditors to combine, and then evaluate collectively, samples from different individuals.

Estimating the Population Total Amount

In auditing applications, you are often more interested in developing estimates of the population **total amount** than in the population mean. Equation (8.6) shows how to estimate a population total amount.

> **ESTIMATING THE POPULATION TOTAL**
>
> The point estimate for the population total is equal to the population size, N, times the sample mean.
>
> $$\text{Total} = N\bar{X} \tag{8.6}$$

Equation (8.7) defines the confidence interval estimate for the population total.

> **CONFIDENCE INTERVAL ESTIMATE FOR THE TOTAL**
>
> $$N\bar{X} \pm N(t_{\alpha/2})\frac{S}{\sqrt{n}}\sqrt{\frac{N-n}{N-1}} \tag{8.7}$$
>
> where $t_{\alpha/2}$ is the critical value corresponding to an upper-tail probability of $\alpha/2$ from the t distribution with $n-1$ degrees of freedom (i.e., a cumulative area of $1 - \alpha/2$).

To demonstrate the application of the confidence interval estimate for the population total amount, return to the Saxon Home Improvement scenario on page 309. In addition to estimating the mean dollar amount in Section 8.2 on page 319, one of the auditing tasks defined in the business problem is to estimate the total dollar amount of all sales invoices for the month. If there are 5,000 invoices for that month and $\bar{X} = \$110.27$, then using Equation (8.6),

$$N\bar{X} = (5,000)(\$110.27) = \$551,350$$

Since $n = 100$ and $S = \$28.95$, then using Equation (8.7) with $t_{\alpha/2} = 1.9842$ for 95% confidence and 99 degrees of freedom,

$$N\bar{X} \pm N(t_{\alpha/2})\frac{S}{\sqrt{n}}\sqrt{\frac{N-n}{N-1}} = 551,350 \pm (5,000)(1.9842)\frac{28.95}{\sqrt{100}}\sqrt{\frac{5,000-100}{5,000-1}}$$

$$= 551,350 \pm 28,721.295(0.99005)$$

$$= 551,350 \pm 28,435.72$$

$$\$522,914.28 \leq \text{Population total} \leq \$579,785.72$$

Therefore, with 95% confidence, you estimate that the total amount of sales invoices is between $522,914.28 and $579,785.72. Figure 8.15 shows a worksheet solution for constructing this confidence interval estimate.

Example 8.7 further illustrates the population total.

FIGURE 8.15
Worksheet for the confidence interval estimate of the total amount of all invoices for the Saxon Home Improvement Company

	A	B	
1	Total Amount of All Sales Invoices		
2			
3	Data		
4	Population Size	5000	
5	Sample Mean	110.27	
6	Sample Size	100	
7	Sample Standard Deviation	28.95	
8	Confidence Level	95%	
9			
10	Intermediate Calculations		
11	Population Total	551350.00	=B4 * B5
12	FPC Factor	0.9900	=SQRT((B4 - B6)/(B4 - 1))
13	Standard Error of the Total	14330.9521	=(B4 * B7 * B12)/SQRT(B6)
14	Degrees of Freedom	99	=B6 - 1
15	t Value	1.9842	=TINV(1 - B8, B14)
16	Interval Half Width	28435.72	=B15 * B13
17			
18	Confidence Interval		
19	Interval Lower Limit	522914.28	=B11 - B16
20	Interval Upper Limit	579785.72	=B11 + B16

EXAMPLE 8.7

Developing a Confidence Interval Estimate for the Population Total

An auditor is faced with a population of 1,000 vouchers and wants to estimate the total value of the population of vouchers. A sample of 50 vouchers is selected, with the following results:

$$\text{Mean voucher amount } (\overline{X}) = \$1{,}076.39$$
$$\text{Standard deviation } (S) = \$273.62$$

Construct a 95% confidence interval estimate of the total amount for the population of vouchers.

SOLUTION Using Equation (8.6) on page 334, the point estimate of the population total is

$$N\overline{X} = (1{,}000)(1{,}076.39) = \$1{,}076{,}390$$

From Equation (8.7) on page 334 a 95% confidence interval estimate of the population total amount is

$$(1{,}000)(1{,}076.39) \pm (1{,}000)(2.0096)\frac{273.62}{\sqrt{50}}\sqrt{\frac{1{,}000 - 50}{1{,}000 - 1}}$$

$$= 1{,}076{,}390 \pm 77{,}762.878\,(0.97517)$$

$$= 1{,}076{,}390 \pm 75{,}832$$

$$\$1{,}000{,}558 \leq \text{Population total} \leq \$1{,}152{,}222$$

Therefore, with 95% confidence, you estimate that the total amount of the vouchers is between $1,000,558 and $1,152,222.

Difference Estimation

An auditor uses **difference estimation** when he or she believes that errors exist in a set of items and he or she wants to estimate the magnitude of the errors based only on a sample. The following steps are used in difference estimation:

1. Determine the sample size required.
2. Calculate the differences between the values reached during the audit and the original values recorded. The difference in value i, denoted D_i, is equal to 0 if the auditor finds that the original value is correct, is a positive value when the audited value is larger than the original value, and is negative when the audited value is smaller than the original value.
3. Compute the mean difference in the sample, $\overline{D}$, by dividing the total difference by the sample size, as shown in Equation (8.8).

MEAN DIFFERENCE

$$\overline{D} = \frac{\sum_{i=1}^{n} D_i}{n} \qquad (8.8)$$

where D_i = Audited value − Original value

4. Compute the standard deviation of the differences, S_D, as shown in Equation (8.9). *Remember that any item that is not in error has a difference value of 0.*

STANDARD DEVIATION OF THE DIFFERENCE

$$S_D = \sqrt{\frac{\sum_{i=1}^{n}(D_i - \overline{D})^2}{n - 1}} \qquad (8.9)$$

5. Use Equation (8.10) to construct a confidence interval estimate of the total difference in the population.

CONFIDENCE INTERVAL ESTIMATE FOR THE TOTAL DIFFERENCE

$$N\overline{D} \pm N(t_{\alpha/2}) \frac{S_D}{\sqrt{n}} \sqrt{\frac{N - n}{N - 1}} \qquad (8.10)$$

where $t_{\alpha/2}$ is the critical value corresponding to an upper-tail probability of $\alpha/2$ from the t distribution with $n - 1$ degrees of freedom (i.e., a cumulative area of $1 - \alpha/2$).

The auditing procedures for Saxon Home Improvement require a 95% confidence interval estimate of the difference between the audited dollar amounts on the sales invoices and the amounts originally entered into the integrated inventory and sales information system. The data are collected by taking a sample of 100 sales invoices. The results of the sample are organized and stored in the Plumblnv workbook. There are 12 invoices in which the audited dollar amount on the sales invoice and the amount originally entered into the integrated inventory management and sales information system are different. These 12 differences are

$9.03 $7.47 $17.32 $8.30 $5.21 $10.80 $6.22 $5.63 $4.97 $7.43 $2.99 $4.63

The other 88 invoices are not in error. Each of their *differences* is 0. Thus, to analyze the data, you compute

$$\overline{D} = \frac{\sum_{i=1}^{n} D_i}{n} = \frac{90}{100} = 0.90$$

and[4]

$$S_D = \sqrt{\frac{\sum_{i=1}^{n}(D_i - \overline{D})^2}{n - 1}}$$

[4] In the numerator, there are 100 differences. Each of the last 88 is equal to $(0 - 0.9)^2$.

$$= \sqrt{\frac{(9.03 - 0.9)^2 + (7.47 - 0.9)^2 + \cdots + (0 - 0.9)^2}{100 - 1}}$$

$$S_D = 2.752$$

Using Equation (8.10), you construct the 95% confidence interval estimate for the total difference in the population of 5,000 sales invoices, as follows:

$$(5,000)(0.90) \pm (5,000)(1.9842)\frac{2.752}{\sqrt{100}}\sqrt{\frac{5,000 - 100}{5,000 - 1}}$$

$$= 4,500 \pm 2,702.91$$

$$\$1,797.09 \leq \text{Total difference} \leq \$7,202.91$$

Thus, the auditor estimates with 95% confidence that the total difference between the sales invoices, as determined during the audit, and the amount originally entered into the accounting system is between \$1,797.09 and \$7,202.91. Figure 8.16 shows the worksheet results for these data.

FIGURE 8.16
Worksheet for the total difference between the invoice amounts found during audit and the amounts entered into the accounting system for the Saxon Home Improvement Company

	A	B	
1	Total Difference In Actual and Entered		
2			
3	Data		
4	Population Size	5000	
5	Sample Size	100	
6	Confidence Level	95%	
7			
8	Intermediate Calculations		
9	Sum of Differences	90	=SUM(DIFFERENCES!A:A)
10	Average Difference in Sample	0.9	=B9/B5
11	Total Difference	4500	=B4 * B10
12	Standard Deviation of Differences	2.7518	=SQRT(E15)
13	FPC Factor	0.9900	=SQRT((B4 - B5)/(B4 - 1))
14	Standard Error of the Total Diff.	1362.2064	=(B4 * B12 * B13)/SQRT(B5)
15	Degrees of Freedom	99	=B5 - 1
16	t Value	1.9842	=TINV(1 - B6, B15)
17	Interval Half Width	2702.9129	=B16 * B14
18			
19	Confidence Interval		
20	Interval Lower Limit	1797.09	=B11 - B17
21	Interval Upper Limit	7202.91	=B11 + B17

In the previous example, all 12 differences are positive because the audited amount on the sales invoice is more than the amount originally entered into the accounting system. In some circumstances, you could have negative errors. Example 8.8 illustrates such a situation.

EXAMPLE 8.8

Difference Estimation

Returning to Example 8.7 on page 335, suppose that 14 vouchers in the sample of 50 vouchers contain errors. The values of the 14 errors are listed below and stored in **DiffTest**. Observe that two differences are negative:

$75.41 $38.97 $108.54   −$37.18 $62.75 $118.32   −$88.84
$127.74 $55.42 $39.03 $29.41 $47.99 $28.73 $84.05

Construct a 95% confidence interval estimate for the total difference in the population of 1,000 vouchers.

SOLUTION For these data,

$$\overline{D} = \frac{\sum_{i=1}^{n} D_i}{n} = \frac{690.34}{50} = 13.8068$$

and

$$S_D = \sqrt{\frac{\sum_{i=1}^{n}(D_i - \overline{D})^2}{n-1}}$$

$$= \sqrt{\frac{(75.41 - 13.8068)^2 + (38.97 - 13.8068)^2 + \cdots + (0 - 13.8068)^2}{50 - 1}}$$

$$= 37.427$$

Using Equation (8.10) on page 336, construct the confidence interval estimate for the total difference in the population, as follows:

$$(1,000)(13.8068) \pm (1,000)(2.0096)\frac{37.427}{\sqrt{50}}\sqrt{\frac{1,000 - 50}{1,000 - 1}}$$

$$= 13,806.8 \pm 10,372.4$$

$$\$3,434.40 \le \text{Total difference} \le \$24,179.20$$

Therefore, with 95% confidence, you estimate that the total difference in the population of vouchers is between \$3,434.40 and \$24,179.20.

One-Sided Confidence Interval Estimation of the Rate of Noncompliance with Internal Controls

Organizations use internal control mechanisms to ensure that individuals act in accordance with company guidelines. For example, Saxon Home Improvement requires that an authorized warehouse-removal slip be completed before goods are removed from the warehouse. During the monthly audit of the company, the auditing team is charged with the task of estimating the proportion of times goods were removed without proper authorization. This is referred to as the *rate of noncompliance with the internal control*. To estimate the rate of noncompliance, auditors take a random sample of sales invoices and determine how often merchandise was shipped without an authorized warehouse-removal slip. The auditors then compare their results with a previously established tolerable exception rate, which is the maximum allowable proportion of items in the population not in compliance. When estimating the rate of noncompliance, it is commonplace to use a **one-sided confidence interval**. That is, the auditors estimate an upper bound on the rate of noncompliance. Equation (8.11) defines a one-sided confidence interval for a proportion.

ONE-SIDED CONFIDENCE INTERVAL FOR A PROPORTION

$$\text{Upper bound} = p + Z_\alpha \sqrt{\frac{p(1-p)}{n}}\sqrt{\frac{N-n}{N-1}} \qquad (8.11)$$

where Z_α = the value corresponding to a cumulative area of $(1 - \alpha)$ from the standardized normal distribution (i.e., a right-tail probability of α).

If the tolerable exception rate is higher than the upper bound, the auditor concludes that the company is in compliance with the internal control. If the upper bound is higher than the tolerable exception rate, the auditor has failed to prove that the company is in compliance. The auditor may then request a larger sample.

Suppose that in the monthly audit, you select 400 sales invoices from a population of 10,000 invoices. In the sample of 400 sales invoices, 20 are in violation of the internal control.

If the tolerable exception rate for this internal control is 6%, what should you conclude? Use a 95% level of confidence.

The one-sided confidence interval is computed using $p = 20/400 = 0.05$ and $Z_\alpha = 1.645$. Using Equation (8.11),

$$\text{Upper bound} = p + Z_\alpha \sqrt{\frac{p(1-p)}{n}} \sqrt{\frac{N-n}{N-1}} = 0.05 + 1.645 \sqrt{\frac{0.05(1-0.05)}{400}} \sqrt{\frac{10{,}000 - 400}{10{,}000 - 1}}$$

$$= 0.05 + 1.645(0.0109)(0.98) = 0.05 + 0.0176 = 0.0676$$

Thus, you have 95% confidence that the rate of noncompliance is less than 6.76%. Because the tolerable exception rate is 6%, the rate of noncompliance may be too high for this internal control. In other words, it is possible that the noncompliance rate for the population is higher than the rate deemed tolerable. Therefore, you should request a larger sample.

In many cases, the auditor is able to conclude that the rate of noncompliance with the company's internal controls is acceptable. Example 8.9 illustrates such an occurrence.

EXAMPLE 8.9
Estimating the Rate of Noncompliance

A large electronics firm writes 1 million checks a year. An internal control policy for the company is that the authorization to sign each check is granted only after an invoice has been initialed by an accounts payable supervisor. The company's tolerable exception rate for this control is 4%. If control deviations are found in 8 of the 400 invoices sampled, what should the auditor do? To solve this, use a 95% level of confidence.

SOLUTION The auditor constructs a 95% one-sided confidence interval for the proportion of invoices in noncompliance and compares this to the tolerable exception rate. Using Equation (8.11) on page 338, $p = 8/400 = 0.02$, and $Z_\alpha = 1.645$ for 95% confidence,

$$\text{Upper bound} = p + Z_\alpha \sqrt{\frac{p(1-p)}{n}} \sqrt{\frac{N-n}{N-1}} = 0.02 + 1.645 \sqrt{\frac{0.02(1-0.02)}{400}} \sqrt{\frac{1{,}000{,}000 - 400}{1{,}000{,}000 - 1}}$$

$$= 0.02 + 1.645(0.007)(0.9998) = 0.02 + 0.0115 = 0.0315$$

The auditor concludes with 95% confidence that the rate of noncompliance is less than 3.15%. Because this is less than the tolerable exception rate, the auditor concludes that the internal control compliance is adequate. In other words, the auditor is more than 95% confident that the rate of noncompliance is less than 4%.

Problems for Section 8.5

LEARNING THE BASICS

8.50 A sample of 25 is selected from a population of 500 items. The sample mean is 25.7, and the sample standard deviation is 7.8. Construct a 99% confidence interval estimate for the population total.

8.51 Suppose that a sample of 200 (stored in **ItemErr**) is selected from a population of 10,000 items. Of these, 10 items are found to have the following errors:

13.76   42.87   34.65   11.09   14.54
22.87   25.52   9.81   10.03   15.49

Construct a 95% confidence interval estimate for the total difference in the population.

8.52 If $p = 0.04$, $n = 300$, and $N = 5{,}000$, calculate the upper bound for a one-sided confidence interval estimate for the population proportion, π, using the following levels of confidence:
a. 90%
b. 95%
c. 99%

APPLYING THE CONCEPTS

8.53 A stationery store wants to estimate the total retail value of the 1,000 greeting cards it has in its inventory. Construct a 95% confidence interval estimate for the population total value of all greeting cards that are in inventory if a random sample of 100 greeting cards indicates a mean value of $2.55 and a standard deviation of $0.44.

SELF Test **8.54** The personnel department of a large corporation employing 3,000 workers wants to estimate the family dental expenses of its employees to determine the feasibility of providing a dental insurance plan. A random sample of 10 employees (stored in the file **Dental**) reveals the following family dental expenses (in dollars) for the preceding year:

110 362 246 85 510 208 173 425 316 179

Construct a 90% confidence interval estimate for the total family dental expenses for all employees in the preceding year.

8.55 A branch of a chain of large electronics stores is conducting an end-of-month inventory of the merchandise in stock. There were 1,546 items in inventory at that time. A sample of 50 items was randomly selected, and an audit was conducted, with the following results:

Value of Merchandise

$\bar{X} = \$252.28$ $S = \$93.67$

Construct a 95% confidence interval estimate for the total value of the merchandise in inventory at the end of the month.

8.56 A customer in the wholesale garment trade is often entitled to a discount for a cash payment for goods. The amount of discount varies by vendor. A sample of 150 items selected from a population of 4,000 invoices at the end of a period of time (stored in **Discount**) revealed that in 13 cases, the customer failed to take the discount to which he or she was entitled. The amounts (in dollars) of the 13 discounts that were not taken were as follows:

6.45   15.32   97.36   230.63 104.18 84.92 132.76
66.12 26.55   129.43 88.32   47.81   89.01

Construct a 99% confidence interval estimate for the population total amount of discounts not taken.

8.57 Econe Dresses is a small company that manufactures women's dresses for sale to specialty stores. It has 1,200 inventory items, and the historical cost is recorded on a first-in, first-out (FIFO) basis. In the past, approximately 15% of the inventory items were incorrectly priced. However, any misstatements were usually not significant. A sample of 120 items was selected (see the **Fifo** file), and the historical cost of each item was compared with the audited value. The results indicated that 15 items differed in their historical costs and audited values. These values were as follows:

Sample Number	Historical Cost ($)	Audited Value ($)	Sample Number	Historical Cost ($)	Audited Value ($)
5	261	240	60	21	210
9	87	105	73	140	152
17	201	276	86	129	112
18	121	110	95	340	216
28	315	298	96	341	402
35	411	356	107	135	97
43	249	211	119	228	220
51	216	305			

Construct a 95% confidence interval estimate for the total population difference in the historical cost and audited value.

8.58 Tom and Brent's Alpine Outfitters conducts an annual audit of its financial records. An internal control policy for the company is that a check can be issued only after the accounts payable manager initials the invoice. The tolerable exception rate for this internal control is 0.04. During an audit, a sample of 300 invoices is examined from a population of 10,000 invoices, and 11 invoices are found to violate the internal control.
a. Calculate the upper bound for a 95% one-sided confidence interval estimate for the rate of noncompliance.
b. Based on (a), what should the auditor conclude?

8.59 An internal control policy for Rhonda's Online Fashion Accessories requires a quality assurance check before a shipment is made. The tolerable exception rate for this internal control is 0.05. During an audit, 500 shipping records were sampled from a population of 5,000 shipping records, and 12 were found that violated the internal control.
a. Calculate the upper bound for a 95% one-sided confidence interval estimate for the rate of noncompliance.
b. Based on (a), what should the auditor conclude?

8.6 Confidence Interval Estimation and Ethical Issues

Ethical issues related to the selection of samples and the inferences that accompany them can occur in several ways. The major ethical issue relates to whether confidence interval estimates are provided along with the point estimates. Providing a point estimate without also including the confidence interval limits (typically set at 95%), the sample size used, and an interpretation of the meaning of the confidence interval in terms that a person untrained in statistics can understand raises ethical issues. Failure to include a confidence interval estimate might mislead the user of the results into thinking that the point estimate is all that is needed to predict the population characteristic with certainty.

When media outlets publicize the results of a political poll, they often overlook including this information. Sometimes, the results of a poll include the sampling error, but the sampling error is often presented in fine print or as an afterthought to the story being reported. A fully ethical presentation of poll results would give equal prominence to the confidence levels, sample size, sampling error, and confidence limits of the poll.

When you prepare your own point estimates, always state the interval estimate in a prominent place and include a brief explanation of the meaning of the confidence interval. In addition, make sure you highlight the sample size and sampling error.

8.7 Online Topic: Estimation and Sample Size Determination for Finite Populations

In this section, confidence intervals are developed and the sample size is determined for situations in which sampling is done without replacement from a finite population. To study this topic, read the Section 8.7 online topic file that is available on this book's companion website. (See Appendix C to learn how to access the online topic files from the companion website.)

USING STATISTICS @ Saxon Home Improvement Revisited

In the Saxon Home Improvement scenario, you were an accountant for a distributor of home improvement supplies in the northeastern United States. You were responsible for the accuracy of the integrated inventory management and sales information system. You used confidence interval estimation techniques to draw conclusions about the population of all records from a relatively small sample collected during an audit.

At the end of the month, you collected a random sample of 100 sales invoices and made the following inferences:

- With 95% confidence, you concluded that the mean amount of all the sales invoices is between $104.53 and $116.01.
- With 95% confidence, you concluded that between 4.12% and 15.88% of all the sales invoices contain errors.
- With 95% confidence, you concluded that the total amount of all the sales invoices is between $522,914 and $579,786.
- With 95% confidence, you concluded that the total difference between the actual and audited amounts of sales invoices was between $1,797.09 and $7,202.91.

These estimates provide an interval of values that you believe contain the true population parameters. If these intervals are too wide (i.e., the sampling error is too large) for the types of decisions Saxon Home Improvement needs to make, you will need to take a larger sample. You can use the sample size formulas in Section 8.4 to determine the number of sales invoices to sample to ensure that the size of the sampling error is acceptable.

SUMMARY

This chapter discusses confidence intervals for estimating the characteristics of a population, along with how you can determine the necessary sample size. You learned how to apply these methods to numerical and categorical data. Table 8.3 on page 342 provides a list of topics covered in this chapter.

To determine what equation to use for a particular situation, you need to answer these questions:

- Are you constructing a confidence interval, or are you determining sample size?
- Do you have a numerical variable, or do you have a categorical variable?
- If you are constructing confidence intervals in auditing, are you trying to estimate the population total, the difference between an audited value and an actual value, or the rate of noncompliance?

The next four chapters develop a hypothesis-testing approach to making decisions about population parameters.

TABLE 8.3
Summary of Topics in Chapter 8

Type of Analysis	Type of Data	
	Numerical	Categorical
Confidence interval for a population parameter	Confidence interval estimate for the mean (Sections 8.1 and 8.2)	Confidence interval estimate for the proportion (Section 8.3)
	Confidence interval estimate for the total and mean difference (Section 8.5)	One-sided confidence interval estimate for the proportion (Section 8.5)
Determining sample size	Sample size determination for the mean (Section 8.4)	Sample size determination for the proportion (Section 8.4)

KEY EQUATIONS

Confidence Interval for the Mean (σ Known)

$$\bar{X} \pm Z_{\alpha/2}\frac{\sigma}{\sqrt{n}}$$

or

$$\bar{X} - Z_{\alpha/2}\frac{\sigma}{\sqrt{n}} \leq \mu \leq \bar{X} + Z_{\alpha/2}\frac{\sigma}{\sqrt{n}} \quad (8.1)$$

Confidence Interval for the Mean (σ Unknown)

$$\bar{X} \pm t_{\alpha/2}\frac{S}{\sqrt{n}}$$

or

$$\bar{X} - t_{\alpha/2}\frac{S}{\sqrt{n}} \leq \mu \leq \bar{X} + t_{\alpha/2}\frac{S}{\sqrt{n}} \quad (8.2)$$

Confidence Interval Estimate for the Proportion

$$p \pm Z_{\alpha/2}\sqrt{\frac{p(1-p)}{n}}$$

or

$$p - Z_{\alpha/2}\sqrt{\frac{p(1-p)}{n}} \leq \pi \leq p + Z_{\alpha/2}\sqrt{\frac{p(1-p)}{n}} \quad (8.3)$$

Sample Size Determination for the Mean

$$n = \frac{Z_{\alpha/2}^2 \sigma^2}{e^2} \quad (8.4)$$

Sample Size Determination for the Proportion

$$n = \frac{Z_{\alpha/2}^2 \pi(1-\pi)}{e^2} \quad (8.5)$$

Estimating the Population Total

$$\text{Total} = N\bar{X} \quad (8.6)$$

Confidence Interval Estimate for the Total

$$N\bar{X} \pm N(t_{\alpha/2})\frac{S}{\sqrt{n}}\sqrt{\frac{N-n}{N-1}} \quad (8.7)$$

Mean Difference

$$\bar{D} = \frac{\sum_{i=1}^{n} D_i}{n} \quad (8.8)$$

Standard Deviation of the Difference

$$S_D = \sqrt{\frac{\sum_{i=1}^{n}(D_i - \bar{D})^2}{n-1}} \quad (8.9)$$

Confidence Interval Estimate for the Total Difference

$$N\bar{D} \pm N(t_{\alpha/2})\frac{S_D}{\sqrt{n}}\sqrt{\frac{N-n}{N-1}} \quad (8.10)$$

One-Sided Confidence Interval for a Proportion

$$\text{Upper bound} = p + Z_{\alpha}\sqrt{\frac{p(1-p)}{n}}\sqrt{\frac{N-n}{N-1}} \quad (8.11)$$

KEY TERMS

auditing
confidence interval estimate
critical value
degrees of freedom
difference estimation
level of confidence
margin of error
one-sided confidence interval
point estimate
sampling error
Student's t distribution
total amount

CHAPTER REVIEW PROBLEMS

CHECKING YOUR UNDERSTANDING

8.60 Why can you never really have 100% confidence of correctly estimating the population characteristic of interest?

8.61 When are you able to use the t distribution to develop the confidence interval estimate for the mean?

8.62 Why is it true that for a given sample size, n, an increase in confidence is achieved by widening (and making less precise) the confidence interval?

8.63 Under what circumstances do you use a one-sided confidence interval instead of a two-sided confidence interval?

8.64 When would you want to estimate the population total instead of the population mean?

8.65 How does difference estimation differ from estimation of the mean?

APPLYING THE CONCEPTS

8.66 You work in the corporate office for a nationwide convenience store franchise that operates nearly 10,000 stores. The per-store daily customer count has been steady, at 900, for some time (i.e., the mean number of customers in a store in one day is 900). To increase the customer count, the franchise is considering cutting coffee prices by approximately half. The 12-ounce size will now be $0.59 instead of $0.99, and the 16-ounce size will be $0.69 instead of $1.19. Even with this reduction in price, the franchise will have a 40% gross margin on coffee. To test the new initiative, the franchise has reduced coffee prices in a sample of 34 stores, where customer counts have been running almost exactly at the national average of 900. After four weeks, the sample stores stabilize at a mean customer count of 974 and a standard deviation of 96. This increase seems like a substantial amount to you, but it also seems like a pretty small sample. Is there some way to get a feel for what the mean per-store count in all the stores will be if you cut coffee prices nationwide? Do you think reducing coffee prices is a good strategy for increasing the mean customer count?

8.67 What do Americans do to conserve energy? A survey of 500 adults (data extracted from "Going on an Energy Diet," *USA Today*, April 16, 2009, p. 1A) found the following percentages:

Turn off lights, power strips, unplug things: 73%
Recycle aluminum, plastic, newspapers, cardboard: 47%
Recycle harder-to-recycle products: 36%
Buy products with least packaging: 34%
Ride a bike or walk: 23%

a. Construct 95% confidence interval estimates for the population proportion of what adults do to conserve energy.
b. What conclusions can you reach concerning what adults do to conserve energy?

8.68 A market researcher for a consumer electronics company wants to study the television viewing habits of residents of a particular area. A random sample of 40 respondents is selected, and each respondent is instructed to keep a detailed record of all television viewing in a particular week. The results are as follows:
- Viewing time per week: $\bar{X} = 15.3$ hours, $S = 3.8$ hours.
- 27 respondents watch the evening news on at least three weeknights.

a. Construct a 95% confidence interval estimate for the mean amount of television watched per week in this area.
b. Construct a 95% confidence interval estimate for the population proportion who watch the evening news on at least three weeknights per week.

Suppose that the market researcher wants to take another survey in a different location. Answer these questions:

c. What sample size is required to be 95% confident of estimating the population mean viewing time to within ± 2 hours assuming that the population standard deviation is equal to five hours?
d. How many respondents need to be selected to be 95% confident of being within ± 0.035 of the population proportion who watch the evening news on at least three weeknights if no previous estimate is available?
e. Based on (c) and (d), how many respondents should the market researcher select if a single survey is being conducted?

8.69 The real estate assessor for a county government wants to study various characteristics of single-family houses in the county. A random sample of 70 houses reveals the following:
- Heated area of the houses (in square feet): $\bar{X} = 1,759, S = 380$.
- 42 houses have central air-conditioning.

a. Construct a 99% confidence interval estimate for the population mean heated area of the houses.
b. Construct a 95% confidence interval estimate for the population proportion of houses that have central air-conditioning.

8.70 The personnel director of a large corporation wishes to study absenteeism among clerical workers at the corporation's central office during the year. A random sample of 25 clerical workers reveals the following:
- Absenteeism: $\bar{X} = 9.7$ days, $S = 4.0$ days.
- 12 clerical workers were absent more than 10 days.

a. Construct a 95% confidence interval estimate for the mean number of absences for clerical workers during the year.
b. Construct a 95% confidence interval estimate for the population proportion of clerical workers absent more than 10 days during the year.

Suppose that the personnel director also wishes to take a survey in a branch office. Answer these questions:

c. What sample size is needed to have 95% confidence in estimating the population mean absenteeism to within ± 1.5 days if the population standard deviation is estimated to be 4.5 days?
d. How many clerical workers need to be selected to have 90% confidence in estimating the population proportion to within ± 0.075 if no previous estimate is available?
e. Based on (c) and (d), what sample size is needed if a single survey is being conducted?

8.71 The market research director for Dotty's Department Store wants to study women's spending on cosmetics. A survey of the store's customers is designed in order to estimate the proportion of women who purchase their cosmetics primarily from Dotty's Department Store and the mean yearly amount that women spend on cosmetics. A previous survey found that the standard deviation of the amount women spend on cosmetics in a year is approximately $18.

a. What sample size is needed to have 99% confidence of estimating the population mean amount spent to within $\pm$$5?
b. How many of the store's credit card holders need to be selected to have 90% confidence of estimating the population proportion to within ± 0.045?

8.72 The branch manager of a nationwide bookstore chain (located near a college campus) wants to study characteristics of her store's customers. She decides to focus on two variables: the amount of money spent by customers (on items other than textbooks) and whether the customers would consider purchasing educational DVDs related to graduate preparation exams, such as the GMAT, GRE, or LSAT. The results from a sample of 70 customers are as follows:
- Amount spent: $\bar{X} = \$28.52, S = \$11.39$.
- 28 customers stated that they would consider purchasing the educational DVDs.

a. Construct a 95% confidence interval estimate for the population mean amount spent in the bookstore.
b. Construct a 90% confidence interval estimate for the population proportion of customers who would consider purchasing educational DVDs.

Assume that the branch manager of another store in the chain (also located close to a college campus) wants to conduct a similar survey in his store. Answer the following questions:

c. What sample size is needed to have 95% confidence of estimating the population mean amount spent in this store to within $\pm$$2 if the standard deviation is assumed to be $10?
d. How many customers need to be selected to have 90% confidence of estimating the population proportion who would consider purchasing the educational DVDs to within ± 0.04?
e. Based on your answers to (c) and (d), how large a sample should the manager take?

8.73 The branch manager of an outlet (Store 1) of a nationwide chain of pet supply stores wants to study characteristics of her customers. In particular, she decides to focus on two variables: the amount of money spent by customers and whether the customers own only one dog, only one cat, or more than one dog and/or cat. The results from a sample of 70 customers are as follows:
- Amount of money spent: $\bar{X} = \$21.34, S = \$9.22$.
- 37 customers own only a dog.
- 26 customers own only a cat.
- 7 customers own more than one dog and/or cat.

a. Construct a 95% confidence interval estimate for the population mean amount spent in the pet supply store.
b. Construct a 90% confidence interval estimate for the population proportion of customers who own only a cat.

The branch manager of another outlet (Store 2) wishes to conduct a similar survey in his store. The manager does not have access to the information generated by the manager of Store 1. Answer the following questions:

c. What sample size is needed to have 95% confidence of estimating the population mean amount spent in this store to within $\pm$$1.50 if the standard deviation is estimated to be $10?
d. How many customers need to be selected to have 90% confidence of estimating the population proportion of customers who own only a cat to within ± 0.045?
e. Based on your answers to (c) and (d), how large a sample should the manager take?

8.74 Scarlett and Heather, the owners of an upscale restaurant in Dayton, Ohio, want to study the dining characteristics of their customers. They decide to focus on two variables: the amount of money spent by customers and whether customers order dessert. The results from a sample of 60 customers are as follows:
- Amount spent: $\bar{X} = \$38.54, S = \$7.26$.
- 18 customers purchased dessert.

a. Construct a 95% confidence interval estimate for the population mean amount spent per customer in the restaurant.
b. Construct a 90% confidence interval estimate for the population proportion of customers who purchase dessert.

Jeanine, the owner of a competing restaurant, wants to conduct a similar survey in her restaurant. Jeanine does not have access to the information that Scarlett and Heather have obtained from the survey they conducted. Answer the following questions:

c. What sample size is needed to have 95% confidence of estimating the population mean amount spent in her restaurant to within ±$1.50, assuming that the standard deviation is estimated to be $8?
d. How many customers need to be selected to have 90% confidence of estimating the population proportion of customers who purchase dessert to within ±0.04?
e. Based on your answers to (c) and (d), how large a sample should Jeanine take?

8.75 The manufacturer of Ice Melt claims that its product will melt snow and ice at temperatures as low as 0° Fahrenheit. A representative for a large chain of hardware stores is interested in testing this claim. The chain purchases a large shipment of 5-pound bags for distribution. The representative wants to know, with 95% confidence and within ±0.05, what proportion of bags of Ice Melt perform the job as claimed by the manufacturer.

a. How many bags does the representative need to test? What assumption should be made concerning the population proportion? (This is called *destructive testing*; i.e., the product being tested is destroyed by the test and is then unavailable to be sold.)
b. Suppose that the representative tests 50 bags, and 42 of them do the job as claimed. Construct a 95% confidence interval estimate for the population proportion that will do the job as claimed.
c. How can the representative use the results of (b) to determine whether to sell the Ice Melt product?

8.76 An auditor needs to estimate the percentage of times a company fails to follow an internal control procedure. A sample of 50 from a population of 1,000 items is selected, and in 7 instances, the internal control procedure was not followed.

a. Construct a 90% one-sided confidence interval estimate for the population proportion of items in which the internal control procedure was not followed.
b. If the tolerable exception rate is 0.15, what should the auditor conclude?

8.77 An auditor for a government agency needs to evaluate payments for doctors' office visits paid by Medicare in a particular zip code during the month of June. A total of 25,056 visits occurred during June in this area. The auditor wants to estimate the total amount paid by Medicare to within ±$5 with 95% confidence. On the basis of past experience, she believes that the standard deviation is approximately $30.

a. What sample size should she select?

Using the sample size selected in (a), an audit is conducted, with the following results:

Amount of Reimbursement

$\bar{X} = \$93.70 \quad S = \$34.55$

In 12 of the office visits, an incorrect amount of reimbursement was provided. For the 12 office visits in which there was an incorrect reimbursement, the differences between the amount reimbursed and the amount that the auditor determined should have been reimbursed were as follows (and stored in Medicare):

$17 $25 $14 −$10 $20 $40 $35 $30 $28 $22 $15 $5

b. Construct a 90% confidence interval estimate for the population proportion of reimbursements that contain errors.
c. Construct a 95% confidence interval estimate for the population mean reimbursement per office visit.
d. Construct a 95% confidence interval estimate for the population total amount of reimbursements for this geographic area in June.
e. Construct a 95% confidence interval estimate for the total difference between the amount reimbursed and the amount that the auditor determined should have been reimbursed.

8.78 A home furnishings store that sells bedroom furniture is conducting an end-of-month inventory of the beds (mattress, bed spring, and frame) in stock. An auditor for the store wants to estimate the mean value of the beds in stock at that time. She wants to have 99% confidence that her estimate of the mean value is correct to within ±$100. On the basis of past experience, she estimates that the standard deviation of the value of a bed is $200.

a. How many beds should she select?
b. Using the sample size selected in (a), an audit was conducted, with the following results:

$\bar{X} = \$1,654.27 \quad S = \$184.62$

Construct a 99% confidence interval estimate for the total value of the beds in stock at the end of the month if there were 258 beds in stock.

8.79 A quality characteristic of interest for a tea-bag-filling process is the weight of the tea in the individual bags. In this example, the label weight on the package indicates that the mean amount is 5.5 grams of tea in a bag. If the bags are underfilled, two problems arise. First, customers may not be able to brew the tea to be as strong as they wish. Second, the company may be in violation of the truth-in-labeling laws. On the other hand, if the mean amount of tea in a bag exceeds the label weight, the company is giving away product. Getting an exact amount of tea in a bag is problematic because of variation in the temperature and humidity inside the factory, differences in the density of the tea, and the extremely fast filling operation of the machine (approximately 170 bags per minute). The following data (stored in Teabags) are the weights, in grams, of a sample of 50 tea bags produced in one hour by a single machine:

```
5.65 5.44 5.42 5.40 5.53 5.34 5.54 5.45 5.52 5.41
5.57 5.40 5.53 5.54 5.55 5.62 5.56 5.46 5.44 5.51
5.47 5.40 5.47 5.61 5.53 5.32 5.67 5.29 5.49 5.55
5.77 5.57 5.42 5.58 5.58 5.50 5.32 5.50 5.53 5.58
5.61 5.45 5.44 5.25 5.56 5.63 5.50 5.57 5.67 5.36
```

a. Construct a 99% confidence interval estimate for the population mean weight of the tea bags.
b. Is the company meeting the requirement set forth on the label that the mean amount of tea in a bag is 5.5 grams?
c. Do you think the assumption needed to construct the confidence interval estimate in (a) is valid?

8.80 A manufacturing company produces steel housings for electrical equipment. The main component part of the housing is a steel trough that is made from a 14-gauge steel coil. It is produced using a 250-ton progressive punch press with a wipe-down operation that puts two 90-degree forms in the flat steel to make the trough. The distance from one side of the form to the other is critical because of weatherproofing in outdoor applications. The widths (in inches), shown below and stored in `Trough`, are from a sample of 49 troughs:

```
8.312 8.343 8.317 8.383 8.348 8.410 8.351 8.373 8.481 8.422
8.476 8.382 8.484 8.403 8.414 8.419 8.385 8.465 8.498 8.447
8.436 8.413 8.489 8.414 8.481 8.415 8.479 8.429 8.458 8.462
8.460 8.444 8.429 8.460 8.412 8.420 8.410 8.405 8.323 8.420
8.396 8.447 8.405 8.439 8.411 8.427 8.420 8.498 8.409
```

a. Construct a 95% confidence interval estimate for the mean width of the troughs.
b. Interpret the interval developed in (a).
c. Do you think the assumption needed to construct the confidence interval estimate in (a) in valid?

8.81 The manufacturer of Boston and Vermont asphalt shingles knows that product weight is a major factor in a customer's perception of quality. The last stage of the assembly line packages the shingles before they are placed on wooden pallets. Once a pallet is full (a pallet for most brands holds 16 squares of shingles), it is weighed, and the measurement is recorded. The file `Pallet` contains the weight (in pounds) from a sample of 368 pallets of Boston shingles and 330 pallets of Vermont shingles.
a. For the Boston shingles, construct a 95% confidence interval estimate for the mean weight.
b. For the Vermont shingles, construct a 95% confidence interval estimate for the mean weight.
c. Do you think the assumption needed to construct the confidence interval estimates in (a) and (b) is valid?
d. Based on the results of (a) and (b), what conclusions can you reach concerning the mean weight of the Boston and Vermont shingles?

8.82 The manufacturer of Boston and Vermont asphalt shingles provides its customers with a 20-year warranty on most of its products. To determine whether a shingle will last the entire warranty period, accelerated-life testing is conducted at the manufacturing plant. Accelerated-life testing exposes the shingle to the stresses it would be subject to in a lifetime of normal use via a laboratory experiment that takes only a few minutes to conduct. In this test, a shingle is repeatedly scraped with a brush for a short period of time, and the shingle granules removed by the brushing are weighed (in grams). Shingles that experience low amounts of granule loss are expected to last longer in normal use than shingles that experience high amounts of granule loss. In this situation, a shingle should experience no more than 0.8 grams of granule loss if it is expected to last the length of the warranty period. The file `Granule` contains a sample of 170 measurements made on the company's Boston shingles and 140 measurements made on Vermont shingles.
a. For the Boston shingles, construct a 95% confidence interval estimate for the mean granule loss.
b. For the Vermont shingles, construct a 95% confidence interval estimate for the mean granule loss.
c. Do you think the assumption needed to construct the confidence interval estimates in (a) and (b) is valid?
d. Based on the results of (a) and (b), what conclusions can you reach concerning the mean granule loss of the Boston and Vermont shingles?

REPORT WRITING EXERCISE

8.83 Referring to the results in Problem 8.80 concerning the width of a steel trough, write a report that summarizes your conclusions.

TEAM PROJECT

8.84 Refer to the team project on page 103 that uses the data in `Bond Funds`. Construct all appropriate confidence interval estimates of the population characteristics of below-average-risk, average-risk, and above-average-risk bond funds. Include these estimates in a report to the vice president for research at the financial investment service.

STUDENT SURVEY DATABASE

8.85 Problem 1.27 on page 44 describes a survey of 62 undergraduate students (stored in `UndergradSurvey`).
a. For these data, for each variable, construct a 95% confidence interval estimate for the population characteristic.
b. Write a report that summarizes your conclusions.

8.86 Problem 1.27 on page 44 describes a survey of 62 undergraduate students (stored in `UndergradSurvey`).
a. Select a sample of undergraduate students at your school and conduct a similar survey for those students.
b. For the data collected in (a), repeat (a) and (b) of Problem 8.85.
c. Compare the results of (b) to those of Problem 8.85.

8.87 Problem 1.28 on page 45 describes a survey of 44 MBA students (stored in `GradSurvey`).
a. For these data, for each variable, construct a 95% confidence interval estimate for the population characteristic.
b. Write a report that summarizes your conclusions.

8.88 Problem 1.28 on page 45 describes a survey of 44 MBA students (stored in GradSurvey).
a. Select a sample of graduate students in your MBA program and conduct a similar survey for those students.
b. For the data collected in (a), repeat (a) and (b) of Problem 8.87.
c. Compare the results of (b) to those of Problem 8.87.

MANAGING ASHLAND MULTICOMM SERVICES

The marketing department has been considering ways to increase the number of new subscriptions to the *3-For-All* cable/phone/Internet service. Following the suggestion of Assistant Manager Lauren Adler, the department staff designed a survey to help determine various characteristics of households who subscribe to cable television service from Ashland. The survey consists of the following 10 questions:

1. Does your household subscribe to telephone service from Ashland?
   (1) Yes   (2) No
2. Does your household subscribe to Internet service from Ashland?
   (1) Yes   (2) No
3. What type of cable television service do you have?
   (1) Basic
   (2) Enhanced
   (If Basic, skip to question 5.)
4. How often do you watch the cable television stations that are only available with enhanced service?
   (1) Every day
   (2) Most days
   (3) Occasionally or never
5. How often do you watch premium or on-demand services that require an extra fee?
   (1) Almost every day
   (2) Several times a week
   (3) Rarely
   (4) Never
6. Which method did you use to obtain your current AMS subscription?
   (1) AMS toll-free phone number
   (2) AMS website
   (3) Direct mail reply card
   (4) Good Tunes & More promotion
   (5) Other
7. Would you consider subscribing to the *3-For-All* cable/phone/Internet service for a trial period if a discount were offered?
   (1) Yes   (2) No
   (If no, skip to question 9.)
8. If purchased separately, cable, Internet, and phone services would currently cost $24.99 per week. How much would you be willing to pay per week for the *3-For-All* cable/phone/Internet service?
9. Does your household use another provider of telephone service?
   (1) Yes   (2) No
10. AMS may distribute Ashland Gold Cards that would provide discounts at selected Ashland-area restaurants for subscribers who agree to a two-year subscription contract to the *3-For-All* service. Would being eligible to receive a Gold Card cause you to agree to the two-year term?
    (1) Yes   (2) No

Of the 500 households selected that subscribe to cable television service from Ashland, 82 households either refused to participate, could not be contacted after repeated attempts, or had telephone numbers that were not in service. The summary results are as follows:

Household has AMS Telephone Service	Frequency
Yes	83
No	335
Household has AMS Internet Service	**Frequency**
Yes	262
No	156
Type of Cable Service	**Frequency**
Basic	164
Enhanced	254
Watches Enhanced Programming	**Frequency**
Every day	50
Most days	144
Occasionally or never	60
Watches Premium or On-Demand Services	**Frequency**
Almost every day	14
Several times a week	35
Almost never	313
Never	56
Method Used to Obtain Current AMS Subscription	**Frequency**
Toll-free phone number	230
AMS website	106
Direct mail	46
Good Tunes & More	10
Other	26
Would Consider Discounted Trial Offer	**Frequency**
Yes	40
No	378

Trial Weekly Rate ($) Willing to Pay (stored in AMS8)

23.00	20.00	22.75	20.00	20.00	24.50	17.50	22.25	18.00	21.00
18.25	21.00	18.50	20.75	21.25	22.25	22.75	21.75	19.50	20.75
16.75	19.00	22.25	21.00	16.75	19.00	22.25	21.00	19.50	22.75
23.50	19.50	21.75	22.00	24.00	23.25	19.50	20.75	18.25	21.50

Uses Another Phone Service Provider	Frequency
Yes	354
No	64

Gold Card Leads to Two-Year Agreement	Frequency
Yes	38
No	380

EXERCISE

1. Analyze the results of the survey of Ashland households that receive AMS cable television service. Write a report that discusses the marketing implications of the survey results for Ashland MultiComm Services.

DIGITAL CASE

Apply your knowledge about confidence interval estimation in this Digital Case, which extends the OurCampus! Digital Case from Chapter 6.

Among its other features, the OurCampus! website allows customers to purchase OurCampus! LifeStyles merchandise online. To handle payment processing, the management of OurCampus! has contracted with the following firms:

- **PayAFriend (PAF)** This is an online payment system with which customers and businesses such as OurCampus! register in order to exchange payments in a secure and convenient manner, without the need for a credit card.
- **Continental Banking Company (Conbanco)** This processing services provider allows OurCampus! customers to pay for merchandise using nationally recognized credit cards issued by a financial institution.

To reduce costs, management is considering eliminating one of these two payment systems. However, Lorraine Hildick of the sales department suspects that customers use the two forms of payment in unequal numbers and that customers display different buying behaviors when using the two forms of payment. Therefore, she would like to first determine the following:

- The proportion of customers using PAF and the proportion of customers using a credit card to pay for their purchases.
- The mean purchase amount when using PAF and the mean purchase amount when using a credit card.

Assist Ms. Hildick by preparing an appropriate analysis. Open **PaymentsSample.pdf**, read Ms. Hildick's comments, and use her random sample of 50 transactions as the basis for your analysis. Summarize your findings to determine whether Ms. Hildick's conjectures about OurCampus! customer purchasing behaviors are correct. If you want the sampling error to be no more than $3 when estimating the mean purchase amount, is Ms. Hildick's sample large enough to perform a valid analysis?

REFERENCES

1. Cochran, W. G., *Sampling Techniques*, 3rd ed. (New York: Wiley, 1977).
2. Fisher, R. A., and F. Yates, *Statistical Tables for Biological, Agricultural and Medical Research*, 5th ed. (Edinburgh: Oliver & Boyd, 1957).
3. Hahn, G., and W. Meeker, *Statistical Intervals, A Guide for Practitioners* (New York: John Wiley and Sons, Inc., 1991).
4. Kirk, R. E., ed., *Statistical Issues: A Reader for the Behavioral Sciences* (Belmont, CA: Wadsworth, 1972).
5. Larsen, R. L., and M. L. Marx, *An Introduction to Mathematical Statistics and Its Applications*, 4th ed. (Upper Saddle River, NJ: Prentice Hall, 2006).
6. *Microsoft Excel 2010* (Redmond, WA: Microsoft Corp., 2010).
7. *Minitab Release16* (State College, PA.: Minitab Inc., 2010).
8. Snedecor, G. W., and W. G. Cochran, *Statistical Methods*, 7th ed. (Ames, IA: Iowa State University Press, 1980).

CHAPTER 8 EXCEL GUIDE

EG8.1 CONFIDENCE INTERVAL ESTIMATE for the MEAN (σ KNOWN)

PHStat2 Use **Estimate for the Mean, sigma known** to compute the confidence interval estimate for the mean when σ is known. For example, to compute the estimate for the Example 8.1 mean paper length problem on page 314, select **PHStat → Confidence Intervals → Estimate for the Mean, sigma known**. In the procedure's dialog box (shown below):

1. Enter **0.02** as the **Population Standard Deviation**.
2. Enter **95** as the **Confidence Level** percentage.
3. Click **Sample Statistics Known** and enter **100** as the **Sample Size** and **10.998** as the **Sample Mean**.
4. Enter a **Title** and click **OK**.

For problems that use unsummarized data, click **Sample Statistics Unknown** and enter the **Sample Cell Range** in step 3.

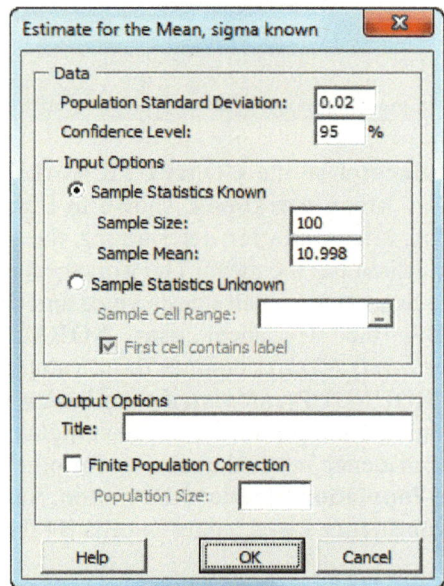

In-Depth Excel Use the **CONFIDENCE** worksheet function to compute the half-width of a confidence interval. Enter the function as **CONFIDENCE(1 − *confidence level*, *population standard deviation*, *sample size*)**.

Use the **COMPUTE** worksheet of the **CIE sigma known workbook** as a template for computing confidence interval estimates when σ is known. The worksheet also uses **NORMSINV(*cumulative percentage*)** to compute the Z value in cell B11 for one-half of the $(1 - \alpha)$ value.

The worksheet contains the data for the Example 8.1 mean paper length problem. To compute confidence interval estimates for other problems, change the **Population Standard Deviation, Sample Mean, Sample Size**, and **Confidence Level** values in cells B4 through B7, respectively. To examine all the formulas in the worksheet, open to the **COMPUTE_FORMULAS worksheet**.

EG8.2 CONFIDENCE INTERVAL ESTIMATE for the MEAN (σ UNKNOWN)

PHStat2 Use **Estimate for the Mean, sigma unknown** to compute the confidence interval estimate for the mean when σ is unknown. For example, to compute the Figure 8.7 estimate for the mean sales invoice amount (see page 319), select **PHStat → Confidence Intervals → Estimate for the Mean, sigma unknown**. In the procedure's dialog box (shown below):

1. Enter **95** as the **Confidence Level** percentage.
2. Click **Sample Statistics Known** and enter **100** as the **Sample Size**, **110.27** as the **Sample Mean**, and **28.95** as the **Sample Std. Deviation**.
3. Enter a **Title** and click **OK**.

For problems that use unsummarized data, click **Sample Statistics Unknown** and enter the **Sample Cell Range** in step 3.

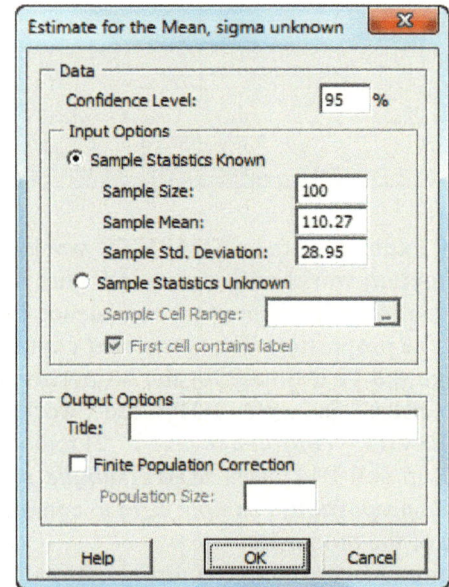

In-Depth Excel Use the **COMPUTE** worksheet of the **CIE sigma unknown workbook**, shown in Figure 8.7 on page 319, as a template for computing confidence interval estimates when σ is unknown. The worksheet contains the data for the Section 8.2 example for estimating the mean sales invoice amount. In cell B12, the worksheet uses **TINV(1 −** *confidence level*, *degrees of freedom*) to determine the critical value from the *t* distribution.

To compute confidence interval estimates for other problems, change the **Sample Standard Deviation**, **Sample Mean**, **Sample Size**, and **Confidence Level** values in cells B4 through B7, respectively.

EG8.3 CONFIDENCE INTERVAL ESTIMATE for the PROPORTION

PHStat2 Use **Estimate for the Proportion** to compute the confidence interval estimate for the proportion. For example, to compute the Figure 8.12 estimate for the proportion of in-error sales invoices (see page 325), select **PHStat → Confidence Intervals → Estimate for the Proportion**. In the procedure's dialog box (shown below):

1. Enter **100** as the **Sample Size**.
2. Enter **10** as the **Number of Successes**.
3. Enter **95** as the **Confidence Level** percentage.
4. Enter a **Title** and click **OK**.

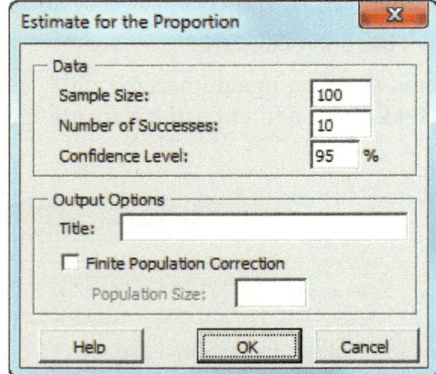

In-Depth Excel Use the **COMPUTE worksheet** of the **CIE Proportion workbook**, shown in Figure 8.12 on page 325, as a template for computing confidence interval estimates for the proportion. The worksheet contains the data for the Figure 8.12 estimate for the proportion of in-error sales invoices. In cell B10, the worksheet uses **NORMSINV((1 −** *confidence level*) **/ 2)** to compute the *Z* value and, in cell B11, uses **SQRT(***sample proportion* *** (1 −** *sample proportion*) **/** *sample size*) to compute the standard error of the proportion.

To compute confidence interval estimates for other problems, change the **Sample Size**, **Number of Successes**, and **Confidence Level** values in cells B4 through B6.

EG8.4 DETERMINING SAMPLE SIZE

Sample Size Determination for the Mean

PHStat2 Use **Determination for the Mean** to compute the sample size needed for estimating the mean. For example, to determine the sample size for the mean sales invoice amount, shown in Figure 8.13 on page 329, select **PHStat → Sample Size → Determination for the Mean**. In the procedure's dialog box (shown below):

1. Enter **25** as the **Population Standard Deviation**.
2. Enter **5** as the **Sampling Error**.
3. Enter **95** as the **Confidence Level** percentage.
4. Enter a **Title** and click **OK**.

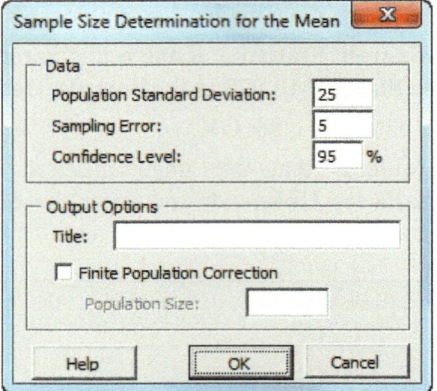

In-Depth Excel Use the **COMPUTE worksheet** of the **Sample Size Mean workbook**, shown in Figure 8.13 on page 329, as a template for determining the sample size needed for estimating the mean. The worksheet contains the data for the Section 8.4 mean sales invoice amount problem. In cell B9, the worksheet uses **NORMSINV((1 −** *confidence level*) **/ 2)** to compute the *Z* value and, in cell B13, uses **ROUNDUP(***calculated sample size*, **0)** to round up the calculated sample size to the next higher integer. To compute confidence interval estimates for other problems, change the **Population Standard Deviation**, **Sampling Error**, and **Confidence Level** values in cells B4 through B6.

Sample Size Determination for the Proportion

PHStat2 Use **Determination for the Proportion** to compute the sample size needed for estimating the proportion. For example, to determine the sample size for the proportion of in-error sales invoices, shown in Figure 8.14 on page 331, select **PHStat → Sample Size → Determination for the Proportion**. In the procedure's dialog box (shown on page 351):

1. Enter **0.15** as the **Estimate of True Proportion**.
2. Enter **0.07** as the **Sampling Error**.
3. Enter **95** as the **Confidence Level** percentage.
4. Enter a **Title** and click **OK**.

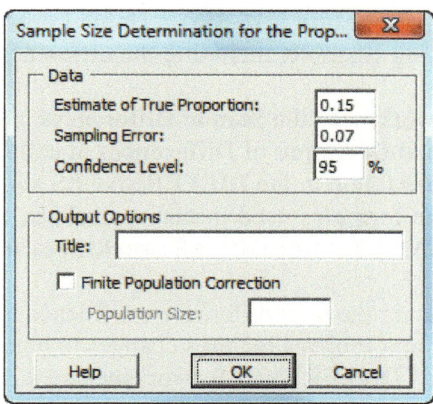

In-Depth Excel Use the **NORMSINV** and **ROUNDUP** functions to help determine the sample size needed for estimating the proportion. Enter **NORMSINV((1 − *confidence level*)/2)** to compute the *Z* value and enter **ROUNDUP(*calculated sample size*, 0)** to round up the calculated sample size to the next higher integer.

Use the **COMPUTE** worksheet of the **Sample Size Proportion workbook**, shown in Figure 8.14 on page 331, as a template for determining the sample size needed for estimating the proportion. The worksheet contains the data for the Section 8.4 in-error sales invoice problem. The worksheet uses the **NORMSINV** and **ROUNDUP** functions in the same way as discussed in the "Sample Size Determination for the Mean" *In-Depth Excel* instructions. To compute confidence interval estimates for other problems, change the **Estimate of True Proportion**, **Sampling Error**, and **Confidence Level** in cells B4 through B6.

EG8.5 APPLICATIONS of CONFIDENCE INTERVAL ESTIMATION in AUDITING

Estimating the Population Total Amount

PHStat2 Use **Estimate for the Population Total** to compute the confidence interval estimate for the population total. For example, to compute the Figure 8.15 estimate for the total of all sales invoices (see page 335), select **PHStat → Confidence Intervals → Estimate for the Population Total**. In the procedure's dialog box (shown in the right column):

1. Enter **5000** as the **Population Size**.
2. Enter **95** as the **Confidence Level** percentage.
3. Click **Sample Statistics Known** and enter **100** as the **Sample Size**, **110.27** as the **Sample Mean**, and **28.95** as the **Sample Standard Deviation**.
4. Enter a **Title** and click **OK**.

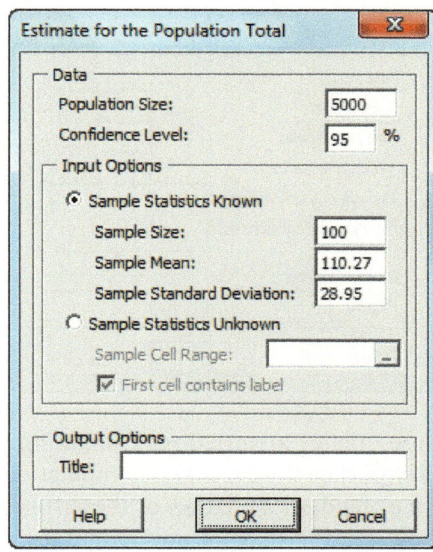

In-Depth Excel Use the **COMPUTE** worksheet of the **CIE Total workbook**, shown in Figure 8.15 on page 335, as a template for computing confidence interval estimates for the population total. The worksheet contains the data for the Figure 8.15 estimate for the total amount of all sales invoices. In cell B15, the worksheet uses **TINV(1 − *confidence level*, *degrees of freedom*)** to determine the *t* value. To compute confidence interval estimates for other problems, change the **Population Size**, **Sample Mean**, **Sample Size**, **Sample Standard Deviation**, and **Confidence Level** values in cells B4 through B8.

Difference Estimation

PHStat2 Use **Estimate for the Total Difference** to compute the confidence interval estimate for the total difference. For example, to compute the Figure 8.16 estimate for the total difference in the Saxon Home Improvement invoice auditing example (see page 337), open to the **DATA** worksheet of the **PlumbInv workbook**. Select **PHStat → Confidence Intervals → Estimate for the Total Difference**. In the procedure's dialog box (shown on page 352):

1. Enter **100** as the **Sample Size**.
2. Enter **5000** as the **Population Size**.
3. Enter **95** as the **Confidence Level** percentage.
4. Enter **A1:A13** as the **Differences Cell Range** and check **First cell contains label**.
5. Enter a **Title** and click **OK**.

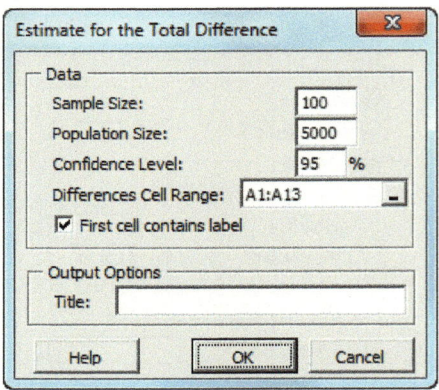

This procedure creates a worksheet containing the results and a second worksheet that contains computations that help to calculate the standard deviation of the differences. (The *In-Depth Excel* section that follows discusses contents of the second worksheet.)

In-Depth Excel Use the **COMPUTE worksheet** of the **CIE Total Difference workbook,** shown in Figure 8.16 on page 337, as a template for computing confidence interval estimates for the total difference. The worksheet contains the data for the Figure 8.16 Saxon Home Improvement invoice auditing example, including the difference data from PlumbInv.

In the worksheet, the **Sum of Differences** in cell B9 and the **Standard Deviation of Differences** in cell B12 rely on computations found in the **DIFFERENCES worksheet**. To examine the formulas used in that worksheet, open to the **DIFFERENCES_FORMULAS worksheet** in the same workbook.

Computing the total difference confidence interval estimate for other problems requires changes to both the COMPUTE and DIFFERENCES worksheets. First, in the COMPUTE worksheet, change the **Population Size, Sample Size,** and **Confidence Level** in cells B4 through B6, respectively. Then, in the DIFFERENCES worksheet, enter the differences in column A and adjust the column B formulas so that there is a column B formula for each difference listed. If there are more than 12 differences, select cell B13 and copy down through all the rows. If there are fewer than 12 differences, delete formulas in column B from the bottom up, starting with cell B13, until there are as many formulas as there are difference values.

CHAPTER 8 MINITAB GUIDE

MG8.1 CONFIDENCE INTERVAL ESTIMATE for the MEAN (σ KNOWN)

Use **1-Sample Z** to compute a confidence interval estimate for the mean when σ is known. For example, to compute the estimate for the Example 8.1 mean paper length problem on page 314, select **Stat → Basic Statistics → 1-Sample Z.** In the 1-Sample Z (Test and Confidence Interval) dialog box (shown below):

1. Click **Summarized data**.
2. Enter **100** in the **Sample size** box and **10.998** in the **Mean** box.
3. Enter **0.02** in the **Standard deviation** box.
4. Click **Options**.

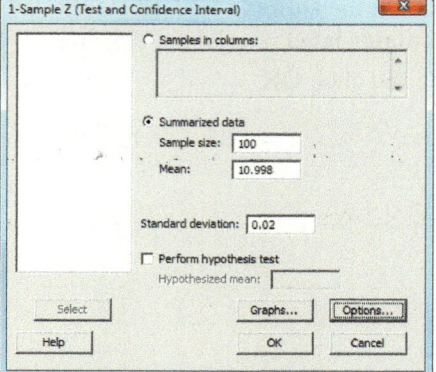

In the 1-Sample Z – Options dialog box (shown below):

5. Enter **95.0** in the **Confidence level** box.
6. Select **not equal** from the **Alternative** drop-down list.
7. Click **OK**.

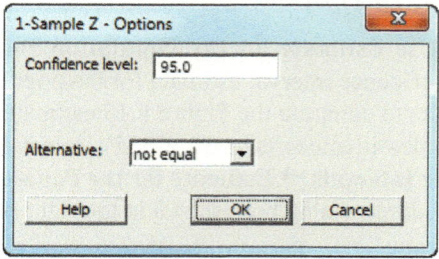

8. Back in the original dialog box, click **OK**.

For problems that use unsummarized data, click **Samples in columns** in step 1 and, in step 2, enter the name of the column that contains the data in the **Samples in columns** box.

MG8.2 CONFIDENCE INTERVAL ESTIMATE for the MEAN (σ UNKNOWN)

Use **1-Sample t** to compute a confidence interval estimate for the mean when σ is unknown. For example, to compute the Figure 8.7 estimate for the mean sales invoice amount (see page 319), select **Stat → Basic Statistics → 1-Sample t**. In the 1-Sample t (Test and Confidence Interval) dialog box (shown below):

1. Click **Summarized data**.
2. Enter **100** in the **Sample size** box, **110.27** in the **Mean** box, and **28.95** in the **Standard deviation** box.
3. Click **Options**.

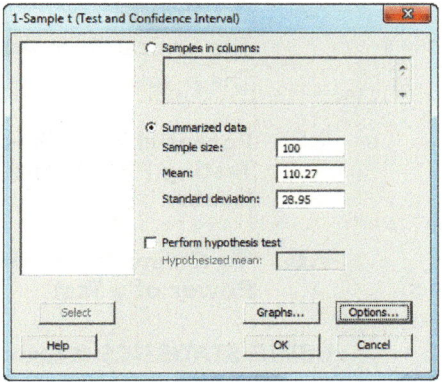

In the 1-Sample t - Options dialog box (similar to the 1-Sample Z - Options dialog box on page 352):

4. Enter **95.0** in the **Confidence level** box.
5. Select **not equal** from the **Alternative** drop-down list.
6. Click **OK**.
7. Back in the original dialog box, click **OK**.

For problems that use unsummarized data, click **Samples in columns** in step 1 and, in step 2, enter the name of the column that contains the data. To create a boxplot of the type shown in Figure 8.9 on page 320, replace step 7 with these steps 7 through 9:

7. Back in the original dialog box, click **Graphs**.
8. In the 1-Sample t - Graphs dialog box, check **Boxplot of data** and then click **OK**.
9. Back in the original dialog box, click **OK**.

MG8.3 CONFIDENCE INTERVAL ESTIMATE for the PROPORTION

Use **1 Proportion** to compute the confidence interval estimate for the population proportion. For example, to compute the Figure 8.12 estimate for the proportion of in-error sales invoices (see page 325), select **Stat → Basic Statistics → 1 Proportion**. In the 1 Proportion dialog box (shown below):

1. Click **Summarized data**.
2. Enter **10** in the **Number of events** box and **100** in the **Number of trials** box.
3. Click **Options**.

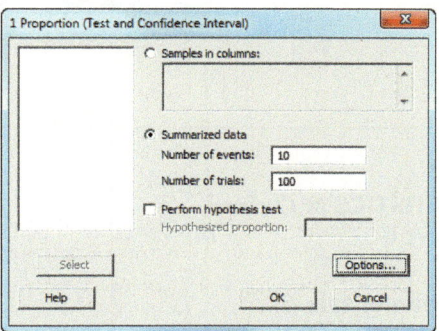

In the 1 Proportion - Options dialog box (shown below):

4. Enter **95.0** in the **Confidence level** box.
5. Select **not equal** from the **Alternative** drop-down list.
6. Check **Use test and interval based on normal distribution**.
7. Click **OK** (to return to the previous dialog box).

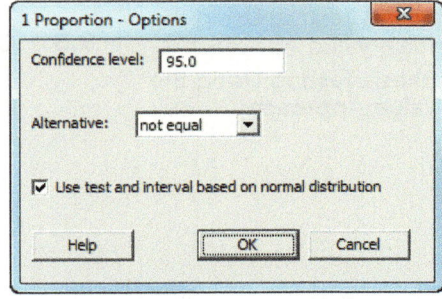

8. Back in the original dialog box, click **OK**.

For problems that use unsummarized data, click **Samples in columns** in step 1 and, in step 2, enter the name of the column that contains the data.

MG8.4 DETERMINING SAMPLE SIZE

There are no Minitab instructions for this section.

MG8.5 APPLICATIONS of CONFIDENCE INTERVAL ESTIMATION in AUDITING

There are no Minitab instructions for this section.

9 Fundamentals of Hypothesis Testing: One-Sample Tests

USING STATISTICS @ Oxford Cereals, Part II

9.1 Fundamentals of Hypothesis-Testing Methodology
The Null and Alternative Hypotheses
The Critical Value of the Test Statistic
Regions of Rejection and Nonrejection
Risks in Decision Making Using Hypothesis Testing
Hypothesis Testing Using the Critical Value Approach
Hypothesis Testing Using the *p*-Value Approach
A Connection Between Confidence Interval Estimation and Hypothesis Testing
Can You Ever Know the Population Standard Deviation?

9.2 *t* Test of Hypothesis for the Mean (σ Unknown)
The Critical Value Approach
The *p*-Value Approach
Checking the Normality Assumption

9.3 One-Tail Tests
The Critical Value Approach
The *p*-Value Approach

9.4 Z Test of Hypothesis for the Proportion
The Critical Value Approach
The *p*-Value Approach

9.5 Potential Hypothesis-Testing Pitfalls and Ethical Issues

9.6 *Online Topic:* The Power of a Test

USING STATISTICS @ Oxford Cereals, Part II Revisited

CHAPTER 9 EXCEL GUIDE

CHAPTER 9 MINITAB GUIDE

Learning Objectives

In this chapter, you learn:

- The basic principles of hypothesis testing
- How to use hypothesis testing to test a mean or proportion
- The assumptions of each hypothesis-testing procedure, how to evaluate them, and the consequences if they are seriously violated
- How to avoid the pitfalls involved in hypothesis testing
- Ethical issues involved in hypothesis testing

USING STATISTICS

@ Oxford Cereals, Part II

As in Chapter 7, you again find yourself as plant operations manager for Oxford Cereals. You are responsible for monitoring the amount in each cereal box filled. Company specifications require a mean weight of 368 grams per box. It is your responsibility to adjust the process when the mean fill weight in the population of boxes differs from 368 grams. How can you make the decision about whether to adjust the process when you are unable to weigh every single box as it is being filled? You begin by selecting and weighing a random sample of 25 cereal boxes. After computing the sample mean, how do you proceed?

In Chapter 7, you learned methods to determine whether the value of a sample mean is consistent with a known population mean. In this Oxford Cereals scenario, you want to use a sample mean to validate a claim about the population mean, a somewhat different problem. For this type of problem, you use an inferential method called **hypothesis testing**. Hypothesis testing requires that you state a claim unambiguously. In this scenario, the claim is that the population mean is 368 grams. You examine a sample statistic to see if it better supports the stated claim, called the *null hypothesis*, or the mutually exclusive alternative hypothesis (for this scenario, that the population mean is not 368 grams).

In this chapter, you will learn several applications of hypothesis testing. You will learn how to make inferences about a population parameter by *analyzing differences* between the results observed, the sample statistic, and the results you would expect to get if an underlying hypothesis were actually true. For the Oxford Cereals scenario, hypothesis testing allows you to infer one of the following:

- The mean weight of the cereal boxes in the sample is a value consistent with what you would expect if the mean of the entire population of cereal boxes is 368 grams.
- The population mean is not equal to 368 grams because the sample mean is significantly different from 368 grams.

9.1 Fundamentals of Hypothesis-Testing Methodology

Hypothesis testing typically begins with a theory, a claim, or an assertion about a particular parameter of a population. For example, your initial hypothesis in the cereal example is that the process is working properly, so the mean fill is 368 grams, and no corrective action is needed.

The Null and Alternative Hypotheses

The hypothesis that the population parameter is equal to the company specification is referred to as the null hypothesis. A **null hypothesis** is often one of status quo and is identified by the symbol H_0. Here the null hypothesis is that the filling process is working properly, and therefore the mean fill is the 368-gram specification provided by Oxford Cereals. This is stated as

$$H_0 : \mu = 368$$

Even though information is available only from the sample, the null hypothesis is stated in terms of the population parameter because your focus is on the population of all cereal boxes. You use the sample statistic to make inferences about the entire filling process. One inference may be that the results observed from the sample data indicate that the null hypothesis is false. If the null hypothesis is considered false, something else must be true.

Whenever a null hypothesis is specified, an alternative hypothesis is also specified, and it must be true if the null hypothesis is false. The **alternative hypothesis, H_1,** is the opposite of the null hypothesis, H_0. This is stated in the cereal example as

$$H_1 : \mu \neq 368$$

The alternative hypothesis represents the conclusion reached by rejecting the null hypothesis. The null hypothesis is rejected when there is sufficient evidence from the sample data that the null hypothesis is false. In the cereal example, if the weights of the sampled boxes are sufficiently above or below the expected 368-gram mean specified by Oxford Cereals, you reject the null hypothesis in favor of the alternative hypothesis that the mean fill is different from 368 grams. You stop production and take whatever action is necessary to correct the problem. If the null hypothesis is not rejected, you should continue to believe that the process is working correctly and therefore no corrective action is necessary. In this second circumstance, you have not proven that the process is working correctly. Rather, you have failed to prove that it is working incorrectly, and therefore you continue your belief (although unproven) in the null hypothesis.

In hypothesis testing, you reject the null hypothesis when the sample evidence suggests that it is far more likely that the alternative hypothesis is true. However, failure to reject the null hypothesis is not proof that it is true. You can never prove that the null hypothesis is correct because the decision is based only on the sample information, not on the entire population. Therefore, if you fail to reject the null hypothesis, you can only conclude that there is insufficient evidence to warrant its rejection. The following key points summarize the null and alternative hypotheses:

- The null hypothesis, H_0, represents the current belief in a situation.
- The alternative hypothesis, H_1, is the opposite of the null hypothesis and represents a research claim or specific inference you would like to prove.
- If you reject the null hypothesis, you have statistical proof that the alternative hypothesis is correct.
- If you do not reject the null hypothesis, you have failed to prove the alternative hypothesis. The failure to prove the alternative hypothesis, however, does not mean that you have proven the null hypothesis.
- The null hypothesis, H_0, always refers to a specified value of the population parameter (such as μ), not a sample statistic (such as $\bar{X}$).
- The statement of the null hypothesis always contains an equal sign regarding the specified value of the population parameter (e.g., $H_0: \mu = 368$ grams).
- The statement of the alternative hypothesis never contains an equal sign regarding the specified value of the population parameter (e.g., $H_1: \mu \neq 368$ grams).

EXAMPLE 9.1

The Null and Alternative Hypotheses

You are the manager of a fast-food restaurant. You want to determine whether the waiting time to place an order has changed in the past month from its previous population mean value of 4.5 minutes. State the null and alternative hypotheses.

SOLUTION The null hypothesis is that the population mean has not changed from its previous value of 4.5 minutes. This is stated as

$$H_0: \mu = 4.5$$

The alternative hypothesis is the opposite of the null hypothesis. Because the null hypothesis is that the population mean is 4.5 minutes, the alternative hypothesis is that the population mean is not 4.5 minutes. This is stated as

$$H_1: \mu \neq 4.5$$

The Critical Value of the Test Statistic

The logic of hypothesis testing involves determining how likely the null hypothesis is to be true by considering the data collected in a sample. In the Oxford Cereal Company scenario, the null hypothesis is that the mean amount of cereal per box in the entire filling process is 368 grams (the population parameter specified by the company). You select a sample of boxes from the filling process, weigh each box, and compute the sample mean. This statistic is an estimate of the corresponding parameter (the population mean, μ). Even if the null hypothesis is true, the statistic (the sample mean, $\bar{X}$) is likely to differ from the value of the parameter (the population mean, μ) because of variation due to sampling. However, you expect the sample statistic to be close to the population parameter if the null hypothesis is true. If the sample statistic is close to the population parameter, you have insufficient evidence to reject the null hypothesis. For example, if the sample mean is 367.9, you might conclude that the population mean has not changed (i.e., $\mu = 368$) because a sample mean of 367.9 is very close to the hypothesized value of 368. Intuitively, you think that it is likely that you could get a sample mean of 367.9 from a population whose mean is 368.

However, if there is a large difference between the value of the statistic and the hypothesized value of the population parameter, you might conclude that the null hypothesis is false. For example, if the sample mean is 320, you might conclude that the population mean is not 368 (i.e., $\mu \neq 368$) because the sample mean is very far from the hypothesized value of 368.

In such a case, you conclude that it is very unlikely to get a sample mean of 320 if the population mean is really 368. Therefore, it is more logical to conclude that the population mean is not equal to 368. Here you reject the null hypothesis.

However, the decision-making process is not always so clear-cut. Determining what is "very close" and what is "very different" is arbitrary without clear definitions. Hypothesis-testing methodology provides clear definitions for evaluating differences. Furthermore, it enables you to quantify the decision-making process by computing the probability of getting a certain sample result if the null hypothesis is true. You calculate this probability by determining the sampling distribution for the sample statistic of interest (e.g., the sample mean) and then computing the particular **test statistic** based on the given sample result. Because the sampling distribution for the test statistic often follows a well-known statistical distribution, such as the standardized normal distribution or t distribution, you can use these distributions to help determine whether the null hypothesis is true.

Regions of Rejection and Nonrejection

The sampling distribution of the test statistic is divided into two regions, a **region of rejection** (sometimes called the critical region) and a **region of nonrejection** (see Figure 9.1). If the test statistic falls into the region of nonrejection, you do not reject the null hypothesis. In the Oxford Cereals scenario, you conclude that there is insufficient evidence that the population mean fill is different from 368 grams. If the test statistic falls into the rejection region, you reject the null hypothesis. In this case, you conclude that the population mean is not 368 grams.

FIGURE 9.1
Regions of rejection and nonrejection in hypothesis testing

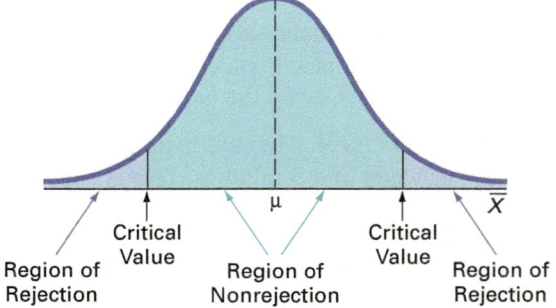

The region of rejection consists of the values of the test statistic that are unlikely to occur if the null hypothesis is true. These values are much more likely to occur if the null hypothesis is false. Therefore, if a value of the test statistic falls into this rejection region, you reject the null hypothesis because that value is unlikely if the null hypothesis is true.

To make a decision concerning the null hypothesis, you first determine the **critical value** of the test statistic. The critical value divides the nonrejection region from the rejection region. Determining the critical value depends on the size of the rejection region. The size of the rejection region is directly related to the risks involved in using only sample evidence to make decisions about a population parameter.

Risks in Decision Making Using Hypothesis Testing

Using hypothesis testing involves the risk of reaching an incorrect conclusion. You might wrongly reject a true null hypothesis, H_0, or, conversely, you might wrongly *not* reject a false null hypothesis, H_0. These types of risk are called Type I and Type II errors.

> **TYPE I AND TYPE II ERRORS**
>
> A **Type I error** occurs if you reject the null hypothesis, H_0, when it is true and should not be rejected. A Type I error is a "false alarm." The probability of a Type I error occurring is α.
> A **Type II error** occurs if you do not reject the null hypothesis, H_0, when it is false and should be rejected. A Type II error represents a "missed opportunity" to take some corrective action. The probability of a Type II error occurring is β.

In the Oxford Cereals scenario, you would make a Type I error if you concluded that the population mean fill is *not* 368 when it *is* 368. This error causes you to needlessly adjust the filling process (the "false alarm") even though the process is working properly. In the same scenario, you would make a Type II error if you concluded that the population mean fill *is* 368 when it is *not* 368. In this case, you would allow the process to continue without adjustment, even though an adjustment is needed (the "missed opportunity").

Traditionally, you control the Type I error by determining the risk level, α (the lowercase Greek letter *alpha*) that you are willing to have of rejecting the null hypothesis when it is true. This risk, or probability, of committing a Type I error is called the *level of significance* (α). Because you specify the level of significance before you perform the hypothesis test, you directly control the risk of committing a Type I error. Traditionally, you select a level of 0.01, 0.05, or 0.10. The choice of a particular risk level for making a Type I error depends on the cost of making a Type I error. After you specify the value for α, you can then determine the critical values that divide the rejection and nonrejection regions. You know the size of the rejection region because α is the probability of rejection when the null hypothesis is true. From this, you can then determine the critical value or values that divide the rejection and nonrejection regions.

The probability of committing a Type II error is called the β *risk*. Unlike a Type I error, which you control through the selection of α, the probability of making a Type II error depends on the difference between the hypothesized and actual values of the population parameter. Because large differences are easier to find than small ones, if the difference between the hypothesized and actual value of the population parameter is large, β is small. For example, if the population mean is 330 grams, there is a small chance (β) that you will conclude that the mean has not changed from 368. However, if the difference between the hypothesized and actual value of the parameter is small, β is large. For example, if the population mean is actually 367 grams, there is a large chance (β) that you will conclude that the mean is still 368 grams.

PROBABILITY OF TYPE I AND TYPE II ERRORS

The **level of significance (α)** of a statistical test is the probability of committing a Type I error.

The **β risk** is the probability of committing a Type II error.

The complement of the probability of a Type I error, $(1 - \alpha)$, is called the *confidence coefficient*. The confidence coefficient is the probability that you will not reject the null hypothesis, H_0, when it is true and should not be rejected. In the Oxford Cereals scenario, the confidence coefficient measures the probability of concluding that the population mean fill is 368 grams when it is actually 368 grams.

The complement of the probability of a Type II error, $(1 - \beta)$, is called the *power of a statistical test*. The power of a statistical test is the probability that you will reject the null hypothesis when it is false and should be rejected. In the Oxford Cereals scenario, the power of the test is the probability that you will correctly conclude that the mean fill amount is not 368 grams when it actually is not 368 grams. For an extended discussion of the power of a statistical test, read the **Section 9.6** online topic file that is available in on this book's companion website. (See Appendix C to learn how to access the online topic files.)

COMPLEMENTS OF TYPE I AND TYPE II ERRORS

The **confidence coefficient**, $(1 - \alpha)$, is the probability that you will not reject the null hypothesis, H_0, when it is true and should not be rejected.

The **power of a statistical test**, $(1 - \beta)$, is the probability that you will reject the null hypothesis when it is false and should be rejected.

Risks in Decision Making: A Delicate Balance Table 9.1 illustrates the results of the two possible decisions (do not reject H_0 or reject H_0) that you can make in any hypothesis test. You can make a correct decision or make one of two types of errors.

TABLE 9.1

Hypothesis Testing and Decision Making

Statistical Decision	Actual Situation	
	H_0 **True**	H_0 **False**
Do not reject H_0	Correct decision Confidence $= (1 - \alpha)$	Type II error $P(\text{Type II error}) = \beta$
Reject H_0	Type I error $P(\text{Type I error}) = \alpha$	Correct decision Power $= (1 - \beta)$

One way to reduce the probability of making a Type II error is by increasing the sample size. Large samples generally permit you to detect even very small differences between the hypothesized values and the actual population parameters. For a given level of α, increasing the sample size decreases β and therefore increases the power of the statistical test to detect that the null hypothesis, H_0, is false.

However, there is always a limit to your resources, and this affects the decision of how large a sample you can select. For any given sample size, you must consider the trade-offs between the two possible types of errors. Because you can directly control the risk of Type I error, you can reduce this risk by selecting a smaller value for α. For example, if the negative consequences associated with making a Type I error are substantial, you could select $\alpha = 0.01$ instead of 0.05. However, when you decrease α, you increase β, so reducing the risk of a Type I error results in an increased risk of a Type II error. However, to reduce β, you could select a larger value for α. Therefore, if it is important to try to avoid a Type II error, you can select α of 0.05 or 0.10 instead of 0.01.

In the Oxford Cereals scenario, the risk of a Type I error occurring involves concluding that the mean fill amount has changed from the hypothesized 368 grams when it actually has not changed. The risk of a Type II error occurring involves concluding that the mean fill amount has not changed from the hypothesized 368 grams when it actually has changed. The choice of reasonable values for α and β depends on the costs inherent in each type of error. For example, if it is very costly to change the cereal-filling process, you would want to be very confident that a change is needed before making any changes. In this case, the risk of a Type I error occurring is more important, and you would choose a small α. However, if you want to be very certain of detecting changes from a mean of 368 grams, the risk of a Type II error occurring is more important, and you would choose a higher level of α.

Now that you have been introduced to hypothesis testing, recall that in the Using Statistics scenario on page 355, the business problem facing Oxford Cereals is to determine whether the cereal-filling process is working properly (i.e., whether the mean fill throughout the entire packaging process remains at the specified 368 grams, and no corrective action is needed). To evaluate the 368-gram requirement, you select a random sample of 25 boxes, weigh each box, compute the sample mean, $\bar{X}$, and then evaluate the difference between this sample statistic and the hypothesized population parameter by comparing the sample mean weight (in grams) to the expected population mean of 368 grams specified by the company. The null and alternative hypotheses are

$$H_0: \mu = 368$$
$$H_1: \mu \neq 368$$

When the standard deviation, σ, is known (which rarely occurs), you use the **Z test for the mean** if the population is normally distributed. If the population is not normally distributed, you can still use the Z test if the sample size is large enough for the Central Limit Theorem to take effect (see Section 7.4). Equation (9.1) defines the Z_{STAT} test statistic for determining the difference between the sample mean, $\bar{X}$, and the population mean, μ, when the standard deviation, σ, is known.

Z TEST FOR THE MEAN (σ KNOWN)

$$Z_{STAT} = \frac{\bar{X} - \mu}{\frac{\sigma}{\sqrt{n}}} \tag{9.1}$$

In Equation (9.1), the numerator measures the difference between the observed sample mean, $\bar{X}$, and the hypothesized mean, μ. The denominator is the standard error of the mean, so Z_{STAT} represents the difference between $\bar{X}$ and μ in standard error units.

Hypothesis Testing Using the Critical Value Approach

The critical value approach compares the computed Z_{STAT} test statistic value from Equation (9.1) to critical values that divide the normal distribution into regions of rejection and nonrejection. The critical values are expressed as standardized Z values that are determined by the level of significance.

For example, if you use a level of significance of 0.05, the size of the rejection region is 0.05. Because the rejection region is divided into the two tails of the distribution, you divide the 0.05 into two equal parts of 0.025 each. For this **two-tail test**, a rejection region of 0.025 in each tail of the normal distribution results in a cumulative area of 0.025 below the lower critical value and a cumulative area of 0.975 $(1 - 0.025)$ below the upper critical value (which leaves an area of 0.025 in the upper tail). According to the cumulative standardized normal distribution table (Table E.2), the critical values that divide the rejection and nonrejection regions are -1.96 and $+1.96$. Figure 9.2 illustrates that if the mean is actually 368 grams, as H_0 claims, the values of the Z_{STAT} test statistic have a standardized normal distribution centered at $Z = 0$ (which corresponds to an $\bar{X}$ value of 368 grams). Values of Z_{STAT} greater than $+1.96$ or less than -1.96 indicate that $\bar{X}$ is sufficiently different from the hypothesized $\mu = 368$ that it is unlikely that such an $\bar{X}$ value would occur if H_0 were true.

FIGURE 9.2
Testing a hypothesis about the mean (σ known) at the 0.05 level of significance

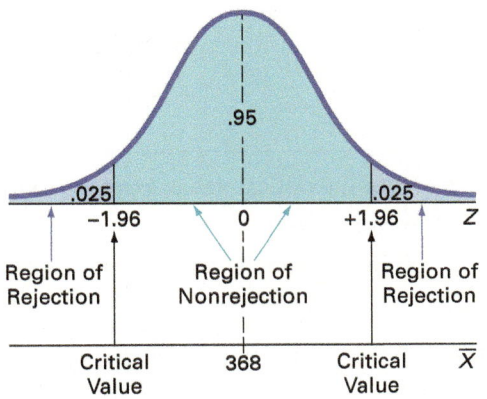

Therefore, the decision rule is

$$\text{Reject } H_0 \text{ if } Z_{STAT} > +1.96$$

$$\text{or if } Z_{STAT} < -1.96;$$

otherwise, do not reject H_0.

Suppose that the sample of 25 cereal boxes indicates a sample mean, $\bar{X}$ of 372.5 grams, and the population standard deviation, σ, is 15 grams. Using Equation (9.1) on page 360,

$$Z_{STAT} = \frac{\bar{X} - \mu}{\frac{\sigma}{\sqrt{n}}} = \frac{372.5 - 368}{\frac{15}{\sqrt{25}}} = +1.50$$

Because $Z_{STAT} = +1.50$ is between -1.96 and $+1.96$, you do not reject H_0 (see Figure 9.3). You continue to believe that the mean fill amount is 368 grams. To take into account the possibility of a Type II error, you state the conclusion as "there is insufficient evidence that the mean fill is different from 368 grams."

Exhibit 9.1 summarizes the critical value approach to hypothesis testing. Steps 1 though 4 correspond to the Define task, step 5 combines the Collect and Organize tasks, and step 6 corresponds to the Visualize and Analyze tasks of the business problem-solving methodology first introduced in Chapter 2.

FIGURE 9.3

Testing a hypothesis about the mean cereal weight (σ known) at the 0.05 level of significance

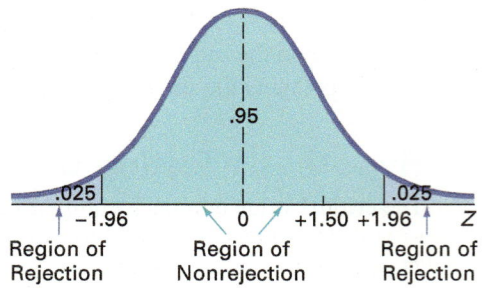

EXHIBIT 9.1 THE CRITICAL VALUE APPROACH TO HYPOTHESIS TESTING

1. State the null hypothesis, H_0, and the alternative hypothesis, H_1.
2. Choose the level of significance, α, and the sample size, n. The level of significance is based on the relative importance of the risks of committing Type I and Type II errors in the problem.
3. Determine the appropriate test statistic and sampling distribution.
4. Determine the critical values that divide the rejection and nonrejection regions.
5. Collect the sample data, organize the results, and compute the value of the test statistic.
6. Make the statistical decision and state the managerial conclusion. If the test statistic falls into the nonrejection region, you do not reject the null hypothesis. If the test statistic falls into the rejection region, you reject the null hypothesis. The managerial conclusion is written in the context of the real-world problem.

EXAMPLE 9.2
Applying the Critical Value Approach to Hypothesis Testing at Oxford Cereals

State the critical value approach to hypothesis testing at Oxford Cereals.

SOLUTION

Step 1: State the null and alternative hypotheses. The null hypothesis, H_0, is always stated as a mathematical expression, using population parameters. In testing whether the mean fill is 368 grams, the null hypothesis states that μ equals 368. The alternative hypothesis, H_1, is also stated as a mathematical expression, using population parameters. Therefore, the alternative hypothesis states that μ is not equal to 368 grams.

Step 2: Choose the level of significance and the sample size. You choose the level of significance, α, according to the relative importance of the risks of committing Type I and Type II errors in the problem. The smaller the value of α, the less risk there is of making a Type I error. In this example, making a Type I error means that you conclude that the population mean is not 368 grams when it is 368 grams. Thus, you will take corrective action on the filling process even though the process is working properly. Here, $\alpha = 0.05$ is selected. The sample size, n, is 25.

Step 3: Select the appropriate test statistic. Because σ is known from information about the filling process, you use the normal distribution and the Z_{STAT} test statistic.

Step 4: Determine the rejection region. Critical values for the appropriate test statistic are selected so that the rejection region contains a total area of α when H_0 is true and the nonrejection region contains a total area of $1 - \alpha$ when H_0 is true. Because $\alpha = 0.05$ in the cereal example, the critical values of the Z_{STAT} test statistic are -1.96 and $+1.96$. The rejection region is therefore $Z_{STAT} < -1.96$ or $Z_{STAT} > +1.96$. The nonrejection region is $-1.96 \leq Z_{STAT} \leq +1.96$.

Step 5: Collect the sample data and compute the value of the test statistic. In the cereal example, $\overline{X} = 372.5$, and the value of the test statistic is $Z_{STAT} = +1.50$.

Step 6: State the statistical decision and the managerial conclusion. First, determine whether the test statistic has fallen into the rejection region or the nonrejection region. For the cereal example, $Z_{STAT} = +1.50$ is in the region of nonrejection because

$-1.96 \leq Z_{STAT} = +1.50 \leq +1.96$. Because the test statistic falls into the nonrejection region, the statistical decision is to not reject the null hypothesis, H_0. The managerial conclusion is that insufficient evidence exists to prove that the mean fill is different from 368 grams. No corrective action on the filling process is needed.

EXAMPLE 9.3

Testing and Rejecting a Null Hypothesis

You are the manager of a fast-food restaurant. The business problem is to determine whether the population mean waiting time to place an order has changed in the past month from its previous population mean value of 4.5 minutes. From past experience, you can assume that the population is normally distributed, with a population standard deviation of 1.2 minutes. You select a sample of 25 orders during a one-hour period. The sample mean is 5.1 minutes. Use the six-step approach listed in Exhibit 9.1 on page 362 to determine whether there is evidence at the 0.05 level of significance that the population mean waiting time to place an order has changed in the past month from its previous population mean value of 4.5 minutes.

SOLUTION

Step 1: The null hypothesis is that the population mean has not changed from its previous value of 4.5 minutes:

$$H_0: \mu = 4.5$$

The alternative hypothesis is the opposite of the null hypothesis. Because the null hypothesis is that the population mean is 4.5 minutes, the alternative hypothesis is that the population mean is not 4.5 minutes:

$$H_1: \mu \neq 4.5$$

Step 2: You have selected a sample of $n = 25$. The level of significance is 0.05 (i.e., $\alpha = 0.05$).

Step 3: Because σ is assumed known, you use the normal distribution and the Z_{STAT} test statistic.

Step 4: Because $\alpha = 0.05$, the critical values of the Z_{STAT} test statistic are -1.96 and $+1.96$. The rejection region is $Z_{STAT} < -1.96$ or $Z_{STAT} > +1.96$. The nonrejection region is $-1.96 \leq Z_{STAT} \leq +1.96$.

Step 5: You collect the sample data and compute $\overline{X} = 5.1$. Using Equation (9.1) on page 360, you compute the test statistic:

$$Z_{STAT} = \frac{\overline{X} - \mu}{\frac{\sigma}{\sqrt{n}}} = \frac{5.1 - 4.5}{\frac{1.2}{\sqrt{25}}} = +2.50$$

Step 6: Because $Z_{STAT} = +2.50 > +1.96$, you reject the null hypothesis. You conclude that there is evidence that the population mean waiting time to place an order has changed from its previous value of 4.5 minutes. The mean waiting time for customers is longer now than it was last month. As the manager, you would now want to determine how waiting time could be reduced to improve service.

Hypothesis Testing Using the *p*-Value Approach

Using the *p*-value to determine rejection and nonrejection is another approach to hypothesis testing.

> **p-VALUE**
>
> The **p-value** is the probability of getting a test statistic equal to or more extreme than the sample result, given that the null hypothesis, H_0, is true. The *p*-value is also known as the *observed level of significance*.

The decision rules for rejecting H_0 in the *p*-value approach are

- If the *p*-value is greater than or equal to α, do not reject the null hypothesis.
- If the *p*-value is less than α, reject the null hypothesis.

Many people confuse these rules, mistakenly believing that a high *p*-value is reason for rejection. You can avoid this confusion by remembering the following:

> If the *p*-value is low, then H_0 must go.

To understand the *p*-value approach, consider the Oxford Cereals scenario. You tested whether the mean fill was equal to 368 grams. The test statistic resulted in a Z_{STAT} value of $+1.50$, and you did not reject the null hypothesis because $+1.50$ was less than the upper critical value of $+1.96$ and greater than the lower critical value of -1.96.

To use the *p*-value approach for the *two-tail test*, you find the probability of getting a test statistic Z_{STAT} that is equal to or *more extreme than* 1.50 standard error units from the center of a standardized normal distribution. In other words, you need to compute the probability of a Z_{STAT} value greater than $+1.50$, along with the probability of a Z_{STAT} value less than -1.50. Table E.2 shows that the probability of a Z_{STAT} value below -1.50 is 0.0668. The probability of a value below $+1.50$ is 0.9332, and the probability of a value above $+1.50$ is $1 - 0.9332 = 0.0668$. Therefore, the *p*-value for this two-tail test is $0.0668 + 0.0668 = 0.1336$ (see Figure 9.4). Thus, the probability of a test statistic equal to or more extreme than the sample result is 0.1336. Because 0.1336 is greater than $\alpha = 0.05$, you do not reject the null hypothesis.

FIGURE 9.4
Finding a *p*-value for a two-tail test

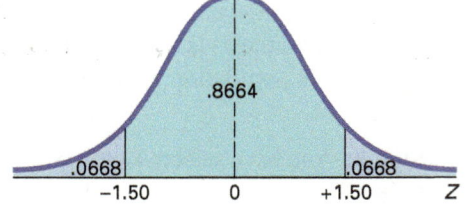

In this example, the observed sample mean is 372.5 grams, 4.5 grams above the hypothesized value, and the *p*-value is 0.1336. Thus, if the population mean is 368 grams, there is a 13.36% chance that the sample mean differs from 368 grams by at least 4.5 grams (i.e., is ≥ 372.5 grams or ≤ 363.5 grams). Therefore, even though 372.5 is above the hypothesized value of 368, a result as extreme as or more extreme than 372.5 is not highly unlikely when the population mean is 368.

Unless you are dealing with a test statistic that follows the normal distribution, you will only be able to approximate the *p*-value from the tables of the distribution. However, Excel and Minitab can compute the *p*-value for any hypothesis test, and this allows you to substitute the *p*-value approach for the critical value approach when you do hypothesis testing.

Figure 9.5 shows the results for the cereal-filling example discussed in this section, as computed by Excel (left results) and Minitab (right results). These results include the Z_{STAT} test statistic and critical values.

FIGURE 9.5
Excel and Minitab results for the Z test for the mean (σ known) for the cereal-filling example

	A	B	
1	Z Test for the Mean		
2			
3	**Data**		
4	Null Hypothesis μ=	368	
5	Level of Significance	0.05	
6	Population Standard Deviation	15	
7	Sample Size	25	
8	Sample Mean	372.5	
9			
10	**Intermediate Calculations**		
11	Standard Error of the Mean	3	=B6/SQRT(B7)
12	Z Test Statistic	1.5	=(B8 - B4)/B11
13			
14	**Two-Tail Test**		
15	Lower Critical Value	-1.9600	=NORMSINV(B5/2)
16	Upper Critical Value	1.9600	=NORMSINV(1 - B5/2)
17	*p*-Value	0.1336	=2 * (1 - NORMSDIST(ABS(B12)))
18	Do not reject the null hypothesis		=IF(B17 < B5, "Reject the null hypothesis", "Do not reject the null hypothesis")

One-Sample Z

Test of mu = 368 vs not = 368
The assumed standard deviation = 15

N	Mean	SE Mean	95% CI	Z	P
25	372.50	3.00	(366.62, 378.38)	1.50	0.134

Exhibit 9.2 summarizes the *p*-value approach to hypothesis testing.

> **EXHIBIT 9.2 THE *p*-VALUE APPROACH TO HYPOTHESIS TESTING**
> 1. State the null hypothesis, H_0, and the alternative hypothesis, H_1.
> 2. Choose the level of significance, α, and the sample size, n. The level of significance is based on the relative importance of the risks of committing Type I and Type II errors in the problem.
> 3. Determine the appropriate test statistic and the sampling distribution.
> 4. Collect the sample data, compute the value of the test statistic, and compute the *p*-value.
> 5. Make the statistical decision and state the managerial conclusion. If the *p*-value is greater than or equal to α, do not reject the null hypothesis. If the *p*-value is less than α, reject the null hypothesis. The managerial conclusion is written in the context of the real-world problem.

EXAMPLE 9.4

Testing and Rejecting a Null Hypothesis Using the *p*-Value Approach

You are the manager of a fast-food restaurant. The business problem is to determine whether the population mean waiting time to place an order has changed in the past month from its previous value of 4.5 minutes. From past experience, you can assume that the population standard deviation is 1.2 minutes and the population waiting time is normally distributed. You select a sample of 25 orders during a one-hour period. The sample mean is 5.1 minutes. Use the five-step *p*-value approach of Exhibit 9.2 to determine whether there is evidence that the population mean waiting time to place an order has changed in the past month from its previous population mean value of 4.5 minutes.

SOLUTION

Step 1: The null hypothesis is that the population mean has not changed from its previous value of 4.5 minutes:

$$H_0: \mu = 4.5$$

The alternative hypothesis is the opposite of the null hypothesis. Because the null hypothesis is that the population mean is 4.5 minutes, the alternative hypothesis is that the population mean is not 4.5 minutes:

$$H_1: \mu \neq 4.5$$

Step 2: You have selected a sample of $n = 25$, and you have chosen a 0.05 level of significance (i.e., $\alpha = 0.05$).

Step 3: Select the appropriate test statistic. Because σ is assumed known, you use the normal distribution and the Z_{STAT} test statistic.

Step 4: You collect the sample data and compute $\bar{X} = 5.1$. Using Equation (9.1) on page 360, you compute the test statistic as follows:

$$Z_{STAT} = \frac{\bar{X} - \mu}{\frac{\sigma}{\sqrt{n}}} = \frac{5.1 - 4.5}{\frac{1.2}{\sqrt{25}}} = +2.50$$

To find the probability of getting a Z_{STAT} test statistic that is equal to or more extreme than 2.50 standard error units from the center of a standardized normal distribution, you compute the probability of a Z_{STAT} value greater than +2.50 along with the probability of a Z_{STAT} value less than −2.50. From Table E.2, the probability of a Z_{STAT} value below −2.50 is 0.0062. The probability of a value below +2.50 is 0.9938. Therefore, the probability of a value above +2.50 is $1 - 0.9938 = 0.0062$. Thus, the *p*-value for this two-tail test is $0.0062 + 0.0062 = 0.0124$.

Step 5: Because the *p*-value $= 0.0124 < \alpha = 0.05$, you reject the null hypothesis. You conclude that there is evidence that the population mean waiting time to place an order has changed from its previous population mean value of 4.5 minutes. The mean waiting time for customers is longer now than it was last month.

A Connection Between Confidence Interval Estimation and Hypothesis Testing

This chapter and Chapter 8 discuss confidence interval estimation and hypothesis testing, the two major elements of statistical inference. Although confidence interval estimation and hypothesis testing share the same conceptual foundation, they are used for different purposes. In Chapter 8, confidence intervals estimated parameters. In this chapter, hypothesis testing makes decisions about specified values of population parameters. Hypothesis tests are used when trying to determine whether a parameter is less than, more than, or not equal to a specified value. Proper interpretation of a confidence interval, however, can also indicate whether a parameter is less than, more than, or not equal to a specified value. For example, in this section, you tested whether the population mean fill amount was different from 368 grams by using Equation (9.1) on page 360:

$$Z_{STAT} = \frac{\bar{X} - \mu}{\frac{\sigma}{\sqrt{n}}}$$

Instead of testing the null hypothesis that $\mu = 368$ grams, you can reach the same conclusion by constructing a confidence interval estimate of μ. If the hypothesized value of $\mu = 368$ is contained within the interval, you do not reject the null hypothesis because 368 would not be considered an unusual value. However, if the hypothesized value does not fall into the interval, you reject the null hypothesis because $\mu = 368$ grams is then considered an unusual value. Using Equation (8.1) on page 313 and the following data:

$$n = 25, \bar{X} = 372.5 \text{ grams}, \sigma = 15 \text{ grams}$$

for a confidence level of 95% (i.e., $\alpha = 0.05$),

$$\bar{X} \pm Z_{\alpha/2} \frac{\sigma}{\sqrt{n}}$$

$$372.5 \pm (1.96)\frac{15}{\sqrt{25}}$$

$$372.5 \pm 5.88$$

so that

$$366.62 \leq \mu \leq 378.38$$

Because the interval includes the hypothesized value of 368 grams, you do not reject the null hypothesis. There is insufficient evidence that the mean fill amount over the entire filling process is not 368 grams. You reached the same decision by using two-tail hypothesis testing.

Can You Ever Know the Population Standard Deviation?

The end of Section 8.1 on page 315 discussed how learning a confidence interval estimation method that required knowing σ, the population standard deviation, served as an effective introduction to the concept of a confidence interval. That passage then revealed that you would be unlikely to use that procedure for most practical applications for several reasons.

Likewise, for most practical applications, you are unlikely to use a hypothesis-testing method that requires knowing σ. If you knew the population standard deviation, you would also know the population mean and would not need to form a hypothesis about the mean and then test that hypothesis. So why study a hypothesis testing of the mean that requires that σ is known? Using such a test makes it much easier to explain the fundamentals of hypothesis testing. With a known population standard deviation, you can use the normal distribution and compute p-values using the tables of the normal distribution.

Because it is important that you understand the concept of hypothesis testing when reading the rest of this book, review this section carefully—even if you anticipate never having a practical reason to use the test represented by Equation (9.1).

Problems for Section 9.1

LEARNING THE BASICS

9.1 If you use a 0.05 level of significance in a (two-tail) hypothesis test, what will you decide if $Z_{STAT} = -0.76$?

9.2 If you use a 0.05 level of significance in a (two-tail) hypothesis test, what will you decide if $Z_{STAT} = +2.21$?

9.3 If you use a 0.10 level of significance in a (two-tail) hypothesis test, what is your decision rule for rejecting a null hypothesis that the population mean is 500 if you use the Z test?

9.4 If you use a 0.01 level of significance in a (two-tail) hypothesis test, what is your decision rule for rejecting $H_0: \mu = 12.5$ if you use the Z test?

9.5 What is your decision in Problem 9.4 if $Z_{STAT} = -2.61$?

9.6 What is the p-value if, in a two-tail hypothesis test, $Z_{STAT} = +2.00$?

9.7 In Problem 9.6, what is your statistical decision if you test the null hypothesis at the 0.10 level of significance?

9.8 What is the p-value if, in a two-tail hypothesis test, $Z_{STAT} = -1.38$?

APPLYING THE CONCEPTS

9.9 In the U.S. legal system, a defendant is presumed innocent until proven guilty. Consider a null hypothesis, H_0, that the defendant is innocent, and an alternative hypothesis, H_1, that the defendant is guilty. A jury has two possible decisions: Convict the defendant (i.e., reject the null hypothesis) or do not convict the defendant (i.e., do not reject the null hypothesis). Explain the meaning of the risks of committing either a Type I or Type II error in this example.

9.10 Suppose the defendant in Problem 9.9 is presumed guilty until proven innocent, as in some other judicial systems. How do the null and alternative hypotheses differ from those in Problem 9.9? What are the meanings of the risks of committing either a Type I or Type II error here?

9.11 Many consumer groups feel that the U.S. Food and Drug Administration (FDA) drug approval process is too easy and, as a result, too many drugs are approved that are later found to be unsafe. On the other hand, a number of industry lobbyists have pushed for a more lenient approval process so that pharmaceutical companies can get new drugs approved more easily and quickly. Consider a null hypothesis that a new, unapproved drug is unsafe and an alternative hypothesis that a new, unapproved drug is safe.
a. Explain the risks of committing a Type I or Type II error.
b. Which type of error are the consumer groups trying to avoid? Explain.
c. Which type of error are the industry lobbyists trying to avoid? Explain.
d. How would it be possible to lower the chances of both Type I and Type II errors?

9.12 As a result of complaints from both students and faculty about lateness, the registrar at a large university wants to determine whether the scheduled break between classes should be changed and, therefore, is ready to undertake a study. Until now, the registrar has believed that there should be 20 minutes between scheduled classes. State the null hypothesis, H_0, and the alternative hypothesis, H_1.

9.13 Do students at your school study more than, less than, or about the same as students at other business schools? *BusinessWeek* reported that at the top 50 business schools, students studied an average of 14.6 hours per week. (Data extracted from "Cracking the Books," Special Report/Online Extra, **www.businessweek.com**, March 19, 2007.) Set up a hypothesis test to try to prove that the mean number of hours studied at your school is different from the 14.6-hour-per-week benchmark reported by *BusinessWeek*.
a. State the null and alternative hypotheses.
b. What is a Type I error for your test?
c. What is a Type II error for your test?

9.14 The quality-control manager at a light bulb factory needs to determine whether the mean life of a large shipment of light bulbs is equal to 375 hours. The population standard deviation is 100 hours. A random sample of 64 light bulbs indicates a sample mean life of 350 hours.
a. At the 0.05 level of significance, is there evidence that the mean life is different from 375 hours?
b. Compute the p-value and interpret its meaning.
c. Construct a 95% confidence interval estimate of the population mean life of the light bulbs.
d. Compare the results of (a) and (c). What conclusions do you reach?

9.15 Suppose that in Problem 9.14, the standard deviation is 120 hours.
a. Repeat (a) through (d) of Problem 9.14, assuming a standard deviation of 120 hours.
b. Compare the results of (a) to those of Problem 9.14.

9.16 The manager of a paint supply store wants to determine whether the mean amount of paint contained in 1-gallon cans purchased from a nationally known manufacturer is actually 1 gallon. You know from the manufacturer's specifications that the standard deviation of the amount of paint is 0.02 gallon. You select a random sample of 50 cans, and the mean amount of paint per 1-gallon can is 0.995 gallon.
a. Is there evidence that the mean amount is different from 1.0 gallon? (Use $\alpha = 0.01$.)
b. Compute the p-value and interpret its meaning.

c. Construct a 99% confidence interval estimate of the population mean amount of paint.

d. Compare the results of (a) and (c). What conclusions do you reach?

9.17 Suppose that in Problem 9.16, the standard deviation is 0.012 gallon.

a. Repeat (a) through (d) of Problem 9.16, assuming a standard deviation of 0.012 gallon.

b. Compare the results of (a) to those of Problem 9.16.

9.2 *t* Test of Hypothesis for the Mean (σ Unknown)

In virtually all hypothesis-testing situations concerning the population mean, μ, you do not know the population standard deviation, σ. Instead, you use the sample standard deviation, S. If you assume that the population is normally distributed, the sampling distribution of the mean follows a t distribution with $n - 1$ degrees of freedom, and you use the ***t* test for the mean**. If the population is not normally distributed, you can still use the t test if the sample size is large enough for the Central Limit Theorem to take effect (see Section 7.4). Equation (9.2) defines the test statistic for determining the difference between the sample mean, $\overline{X}$, and the population mean, μ, when using the sample standard deviation, S.

> *t* TEST FOR THE MEAN (σ UNKNOWN)
>
> $$t_{STAT} = \frac{\overline{X} - \mu}{\frac{S}{\sqrt{n}}} \qquad (9.2)$$
>
> where the t_{STAT} test statistic follows a t distribution having $n - 1$ degrees of freedom.

To illustrate the use of the t test for the mean, return to the Chapter 8 Saxon Home Improvement scenario on page 309. The business objective is to determine whether the mean amount per sales invoice is unchanged from the $120 of the past five years. As an accountant for the company, you need to determine whether this amount changes. In other words, the hypothesis test is used to try to determine whether the mean amount per sales invoice is increasing or decreasing.

The Critical Value Approach

To perform this two-tail hypothesis test, you use the six-step method listed in Exhibit 9.1 on page 362.

Step 1 You define the following hypotheses:

$$H_0: \mu = \$120$$
$$H_1: \mu \neq \$120$$

The alternative hypothesis contains the statement you are trying to prove. If the null hypothesis is rejected, then there is statistical evidence that the population mean amount per sales invoice is no longer $120. If the statistical conclusion is "do not reject H_0," then you will conclude that there is insufficient evidence to prove that the mean amount differs from the long-term mean of $120.

Step 2 You collect the data from a sample of $n = 12$ sales invoices. You decide to use $\alpha = 0.05$.

Step 3 Because σ is unknown, you use the t distribution and the t_{STAT} test statistic. You must assume that the population of sales invoices is normally distributed because the sample size of 12 is too small for the Central Limit Theorem to take effect. This assumption is discussed on page 370.

Step 4 For a given sample size, n, the test statistic t_{STAT} follows a t distribution with $n - 1$ degrees of freedom. The critical values of the t distribution with $12 - 1 = 11$ degrees of freedom are found in Table E.3, as illustrated in Table 9.2 and Figure 9.6. The alternative hypothesis, $H_1: \mu \neq \$120$, has two tails. The area in the rejection region of the

t distribution's left (lower) tail is 0.025, and the area in the rejection region of the t distribution's right (upper) tail is also 0.025.

From the t table as given in Table E.3, a portion of which is shown in Table 9.2, the critical values are ± 2.2010. The decision rule is

$$\text{Reject } H_0 \text{ if } t_{STAT} < -2.2010$$

$$\text{or if } t_{STAT} > +2.2010;$$

otherwise, do not reject H_0.

TABLE 9.2
Determining the Critical Value from the t Table for an Area of 0.025 in Each Tail, with 11 Degrees of Freedom

	Cumulative Probabilities					
	.75	.90	.95	.975	.99	.995
	Upper-Tail Areas					
Degrees of Freedom	.25	.10	.05	.025	.01	.005
1	1.0000	3.0777	6.3138	12.7062	31.8207	63.6574
2	0.8165	1.8856	2.9200	4.3027	6.9646	9.9248
3	0.7649	1.6377	2.3534	3.1824	4.5407	5.8409
4	0.7407	1.5332	2.1318	2.7764	3.7469	4.6041
5	0.7267	1.4759	2.0150	2.5706	3.3649	4.0322
6	0.7176	1.4398	1.9432	2.4469	3.1427	3.7074
7	0.7111	1.4149	1.8946	2.3646	2.9980	3.4995
8	0.7064	1.3968	1.8595	2.3060	2.8965	3.3554
9	0.7027	1.3830	1.8331	2.2622	2.8214	3.2498
10	0.6998	1.3722	1.8125	2.2281	2.7638	3.1693
11	0.6974	1.3634	1.7959	2.2010	2.7181	3.1058

Source: Extracted from Table E.3.

FIGURE 9.6
Testing a hypothesis about the mean (σ unknown) at the 0.05 level of significance with 11 degrees of freedom

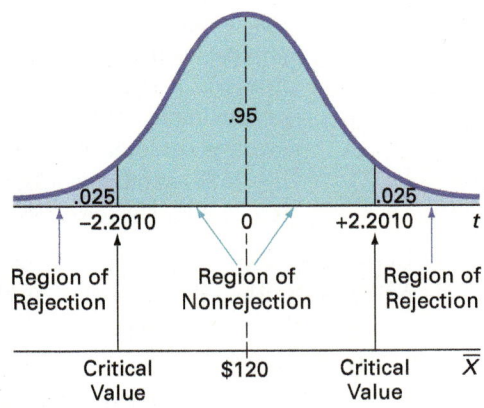

Step 5 You organize and store the data from a random sample of 12 sales invoices in Invoices:

108.98 152.22 111.45 110.59 127.46 107.26
93.32   91.97   111.56 75.71   128.58 135.11

Using Equations (3.1) and (3.7) on pages 127 and 133,

$$\bar{X} = \$112.85 \text{ and } S = \$20.80$$

From Equation (9.2) on page 368,

$$t_{STAT} = \frac{\bar{X} - \mu}{\frac{S}{\sqrt{n}}} = \frac{112.85 - 120}{\frac{20.80}{\sqrt{12}}} = -1.1908$$

Figure 9.7 shows the results for this test of hypothesis, as computed by Excel and Minitab.

FIGURE 9.7
Excel and Minitab results for the *t* test of sales invoices

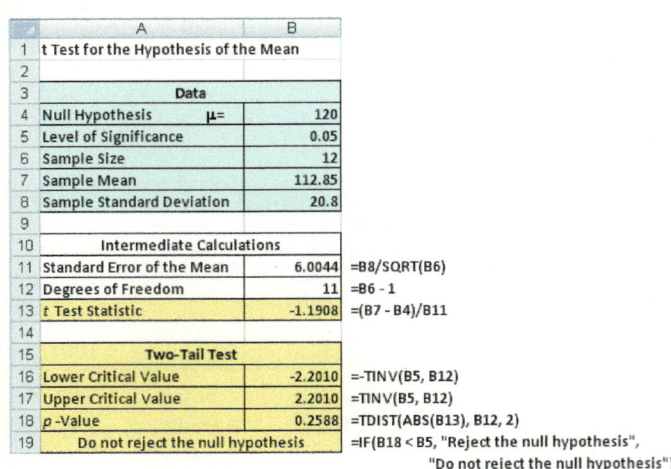

Step 6   Because $-2.2010 < t_{STAT} = -1.1908 < 2.2010$, you do not reject H_0. You have insufficient evidence to conclude that the mean amount per sales invoice differs from $120. The audit suggests that the mean amount per invoice has not changed.

The *p*-Value Approach

To perform this two-tail hypothesis test, you use the five-step method listed in Exhibit 9.2 on page 365.

Step 1–3   These steps are the same as in the critical value approach.
Step 4   From the Figure 9.7 results, the $t_{STAT} = -1.19$ and *p*-value $= 0.2588$.
Step 5   Because the *p*-value of 0.2588 is greater than $\alpha = 0.05$, you do not reject H_0. The data provide insufficient evidence to conclude that the mean amount per sales invoice differs from $120. The audit suggests that the mean amount per invoice has not changed. The *p*-value indicates that if the null hypothesis is true, the probability that a sample of 12 invoices could have a sample mean that differs by $7.15 or more from the stated $120 is 0.2588. In other words, if the mean amount per sales invoice is truly $120, then there is a 25.88% chance of observing a sample mean below $112.85 or above $127.15.

In the preceding example, it is incorrect to state that there is a 25.88% chance that the null hypothesis is true. Remember that the *p*-value is a conditional probability, calculated by *assuming* that the null hypothesis is true. In general, it is proper to state the following:

If the null hypothesis is true, there is a (*p*-value) × 100% chance of observing a test statistic at least as contradictory to the null hypothesis as the sample result.

Checking the Normality Assumption

You use the *t* test when the population standard deviation, σ, is not known and is estimated using the sample standard deviation, *S*. To use the *t* test, you assume that the data represent a random sample from a population that is normally distributed. In practice, as long as the sample size is not very small and the population is not very skewed, the *t* distribution provides a good approximation of the sampling distribution of the mean when σ is unknown.

There are several ways to evaluate the normality assumption necessary for using the *t* test. You can examine how closely the sample statistics match the normal distribution's theoretical properties. You can also construct a histogram, stem-and-leaf display, boxplot, or normal probability plot to visualize the distribution of the sales invoice amounts. For details on evaluating normality, see Section 6.3 on pages 260–264.

Figures 9.8 through 9.10 show the descriptive statistics, boxplot, and normal probability plot for the sales invoice data.

FIGURE 9.8
Excel and Minitab descriptive statistics for the sales invoice data

	A	B
1	**Invoice Amount**	
2		
3	Mean	112.8508
4	Standard Error	6.0039
5	Median	111.02
6	Mode	#N/A
7	Standard Deviation	20.7980
8	Sample Variance	432.5565
9	Kurtosis	0.1727
10	Skewness	0.1336
11	Range	76.51
12	Minimum	75.71
13	Maximum	152.22
14	Sum	1354.21
15	Count	12

Descriptive Statistics: Invoice Amount

Variable	Total Count	Mean	StDev	Variance	CoefVar	Minimum	Q1	Median
Invoice Amount	12	112.85	20.80	432.56	18.43	75.71	96.80	111.02

Variable	Q3	Maximum	Range	IQR	Skewness	Kurtosis
Invoice Amount	128.30	152.22	76.51	31.50	0.13	0.17

FIGURE 9.9
Excel and Minitab boxplots for the sales invoice data

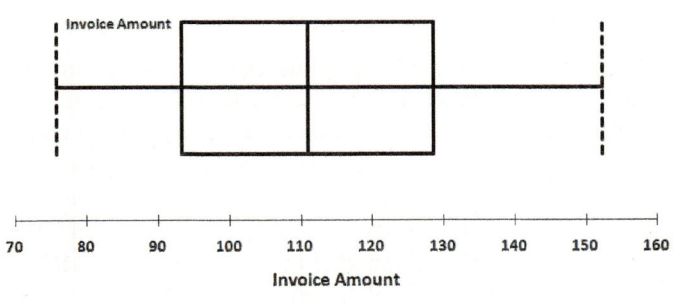
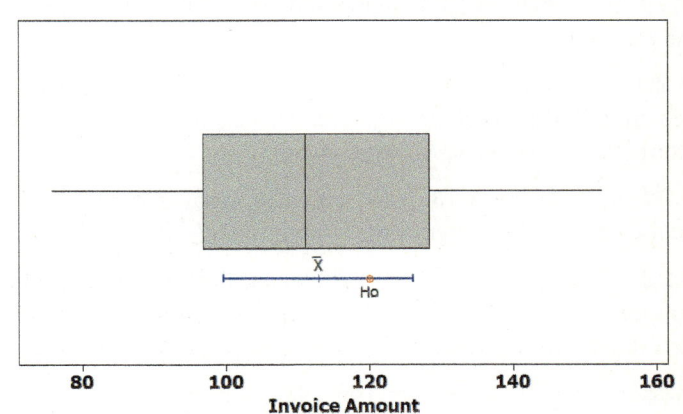

The mean is very close to the median, and the points on the normal probability plots on page 372 appear to be increasing approximately in a straight line. The boxplots appear to be approximately symmetrical. Thus, you can assume that the population of sales invoices is approximately normally distributed. The normality assumption is valid, and therefore the auditor's results are valid.

The t test is a **robust** test. A robust test does not lose power if the shape of the population departs somewhat from a normal distribution, particularly when the sample size is large enough to enable the test statistic t to be influenced by the Central Limit Theorem (see Section 7.4). However, you can reach erroneous conclusions and can lose statistical power if you use the t test incorrectly. If the sample size, n, is small (i.e., less than 30) and you cannot easily make the assumption that the underlying population is at least approximately normally distributed, then *nonparametric* testing procedures are more appropriate (see references 1 and 2).

FIGURE 9.10
Excel and Minitab normal probability plots for the sales invoice data

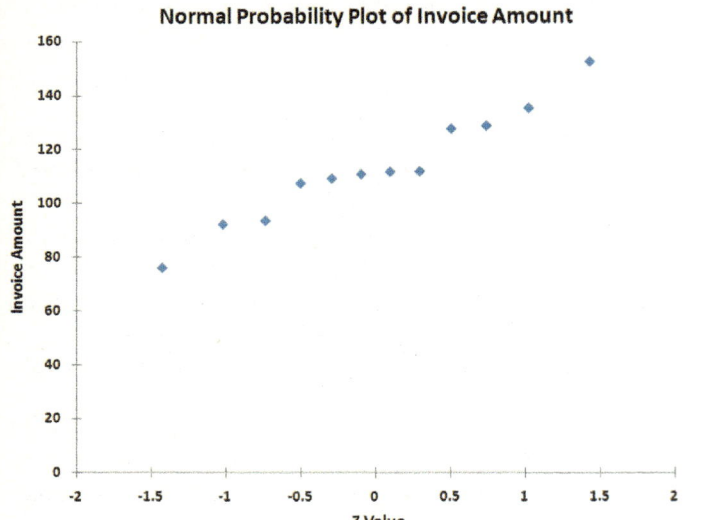
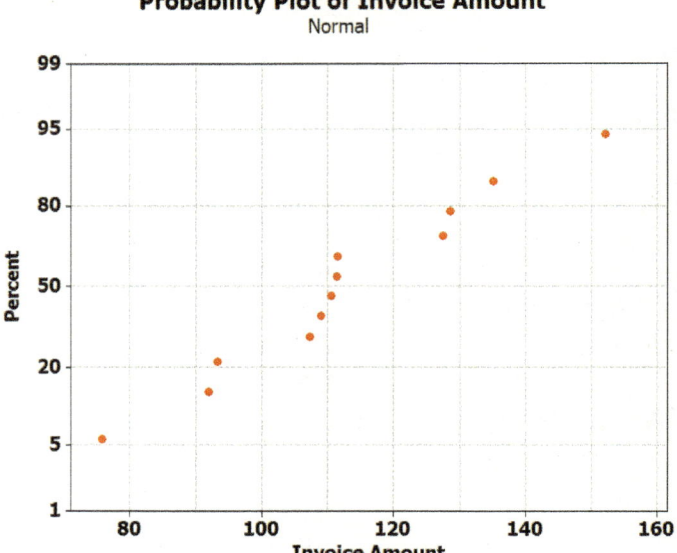

Problems for Section 9.2

LEARNING THE BASICS

9.18 If, in a sample of $n = 16$ selected from a normal population, $\bar{X} = 56$ and $S = 12$, what is the value of t_{STAT} if you are testing the null hypothesis $H_0: \mu = 50$?

9.19 In Problem 9.18, how many degrees of freedom does the t test have?

9.20 In Problems 9.18 and 9.19, what are the critical values of t if the level of significance, α, is 0.05 and the alternative hypothesis, H_1, is $\mu \neq 50$?

9.21 In Problems 9.18, 9.19, and 9.20, what is your statistical decision if the alternative hypothesis, H_1, is $\mu \neq 50$?

9.22 If, in a sample of $n = 16$ selected from a left-skewed population, $\bar{X} = 65$, and $S = 21$, would you use the t test to test the null hypothesis $H_0: \mu = 60$? Discuss.

9.23 If, in a sample of $n = 160$ selected from a left-skewed population, $\bar{X} = 65$, and $S = 21$, would you use the t test to test the null hypothesis $H_0: \mu = 60$? Discuss.

APPLYING THE CONCEPTS

✓SELF Test 9.24 You are the manager of a restaurant for a fast-food franchise. Last month, the mean waiting time at the drive-through window for branches in your geographical region, as measured from the time a customer places an order until the time the customer receives the order, was 3.7 minutes. You select a random sample of 64 orders. The sample mean waiting time is 3.57 minutes, with a sample standard deviation of 0.8 minute.

a. At the 0.05 level of significance, is there evidence that the population mean waiting time is different from 3.7 minutes?
b. Because the sample size is 64, do you need to be concerned about the shape of the population distribution when conducting the t test in (a)? Explain.

9.25 A manufacturer of chocolate candies uses machines to package candies as they move along a filling line. Although the packages are labeled as 8 ounces, the company wants the packages to contain a mean of 8.17 ounces so that virtually none of the packages contain less than 8 ounces. A sample of 50 packages is selected periodically, and the packaging process is stopped if there is evidence that the mean amount packaged is different from 8.17 ounces. Suppose that in a particular sample of 50 packages, the mean amount dispensed is 8.159 ounces, with a sample standard deviation of 0.051 ounce.

a. Is there evidence that the population mean amount is different from 8.17 ounces? (Use a 0.05 level of significance.)
b. Determine the p-value and interpret its meaning.

9.26 A stationery store wants to estimate the mean retail value of greeting cards that it has in its inventory. A random sample of 100 greeting cards indicates a mean value of $2.55 and a standard deviation of $0.44.

a. Is there evidence that the population mean retail value of the greeting cards is different from $2.50? (Use a 0.05 level of significance.)
b. Determine the p-value and interpret its meaning.

9.27 The U.S. Department of Transportation requires tire manufacturers to provide performance information on tire sidewalls to help prospective buyers make their purchasing decisions. One very important piece of information is the tread wear index, which indicates the tire's resistance to tread wear. A tire with a grade of 200 should last twice as long, on average, as a tire with a grade of 100.

A consumer organization wants to test the actual tread wear index of a brand name of tires that claims "graded 200" on the sidewall of the tire. A random sample of $n = 18$ indicates a sample mean tread wear index of 195.3 and a sample standard deviation of 21.4.

a. Is there evidence that the population mean tread wear index is different from 200? (Use a 0.05 level of significance.)
b. Determine the p-value and interpret its meaning.

9.28 The file **FastFood** contains the amount that a sample of nine customers spent for lunch ($) at a fast-food restaurant:

4.20 5.03 5.86 6.45 7.38 7.54 8.46 8.47 9.87

a. At the 0.05 level of significance, is there evidence that the mean amount spent for lunch is different from $6.50?
b. Determine the p-value in (a) and interpret its meaning.
c. What assumption must you make about the population distribution in order to conduct the t test in (a) and (b)?
d. Because the sample size is 9, do you need to be concerned about the shape of the population distribution when conducting the t test in (a)? Explain.

9.29 In New York State, savings banks are permitted to sell a form of life insurance called savings bank life insurance (SBLI). The approval process consists of underwriting, which includes a review of the application, a medical information bureau check, possible requests for additional medical information and medical exams, and a policy compilation stage in which the policy pages are generated and sent to the bank for delivery. The ability to deliver approved policies to customers in a timely manner is critical to the profitability of this service. During a period of one month, a random sample of 27 approved policies is selected, and the total processing time, in days, is recorded (and stored in **Insurance**):

73 19 16 64 28 28 31 90 60 56 31 56 22 18
45 48 17 17 17 91 92 63 50 51 69 16 17

a. In the past, the mean processing time was 45 days. At the 0.05 level of significance, is there evidence that the mean processing time has changed from 45 days?
b. What assumption about the population distribution is needed in order to conduct the t test in (a)?
c. Construct a boxplot or a normal probability plot to evaluate the assumption made in (b).
d. Do you think that the assumption needed in order to conduct the t test in (a) is valid? Explain.

9.30 The following data (in **Drink**) represent the amount of soft-drink filled in a sample of 50 consecutive 2-liter bottles. The results, listed horizontally in the order of being filled, were

2.109 2.086 2.066 2.075 2.065 2.057 2.052 2.044 2.036 2.038
2.031 2.029 2.025 2.029 2.023 2.020 2.015 2.014 2.013 2.014
2.012 2.012 2.012 2.010 2.005 2.003 1.999 1.996 1.997 1.992
1.994 1.986 1.984 1.981 1.973 1.975 1.971 1.969 1.966 1.967
1.963 1.957 1.951 1.951 1.947 1.941 1.941 1.938 1.908 1.894

a. At the 0.05 level of significance, is there evidence that the mean amount of soft drink filled is different from 2.0 liters?
b. Determine the p-value in (a) and interpret its meaning.
c. In (a), you assumed that the distribution of the amount of soft drink filled was normally distributed. Evaluate this assumption by constructing a boxplot or a normal probability plot.
d. Do you think that the assumption needed in order to conduct the t test in (a) is valid? Explain.
e. Examine the values of the 50 bottles in their sequential order, as given in the problem. Does there appear to be a pattern to the results? If so, what impact might this pattern have on the validity of the results in (a)?

9.31 One of the major measures of the quality of service provided by any organization is the speed with which it responds to customer complaints. A large family-held department store selling furniture and flooring, including carpet, had undergone a major expansion in the past several years. In particular, the flooring department had expanded from 2 installation crews to an installation supervisor, a measurer, and 15 installation crews. The store had the business objective of improving its response to complaints. The variable of interest was defined as the number of days between when the complaint was made and when it was resolved. Data were collected from 50 complaints that were made in the past year. The data, stored in **Furniture**, are as follows:

54   5   35 137 31 27 152   2 123 81 74 27
11 19 126 110 110 29   61 35   94 31 26   5
12   4 165   32   29 28   29 26   25   1 14 13
13 10   5   27   4 52   30 22   36 26 20 23
33 68

a. The installation supervisor claims that the mean number of days between the receipt of a complaint and the resolution of the complaint is 20 days. At the 0.05 level of significance, is there evidence that the claim is not true (i.e., that the mean number of days is different from 20)?
b. What assumption about the population distribution is needed in order to conduct the t test in (a)?
c. Construct a boxplot or a normal probability plot to evaluate the assumption made in (b).
d. Do you think that the assumption needed in order to conduct the t test in (a) is valid? Explain.

9.32 A manufacturing company produces steel housings for electrical equipment. The main component part of the housing is a steel trough that is made out of a 14-gauge steel coil. It is produced using a 250-ton progressive punch press with a wipe-down operation that puts two 90-degree forms in the flat steel to make the trough. The distance from one side of the form to the other is critical because of weatherproofing in outdoor applications. The company requires that the width of the trough be between 8.31 inches and 8.61 inches. The file **Trough** contains the widths of the troughs, in inches, for a sample of $n = 49$:

8.312 8.343 8.317 8.383 8.348 8.410 8.351 8.373 8.481 8.422
8.476 8.382 8.484 8.403 8.414 8.419 8.385 8.465 8.498 8.447
8.436 8.413 8.489 8.414 8.481 8.415 8.479 8.429 8.458 8.462
8.460 8.444 8.429 8.460 8.412 8.420 8.410 8.405 8.323 8.420
8.396 8.447 8.405 8.439 8.411 8.427 8.420 8.498 8.409

a. At the 0.05 level of significance, is there evidence that the mean width of the troughs is different from 8.46 inches?
b. What assumption about the population distribution is needed in order to conduct the t test in (a)?
c. Evaluate the assumption made in (b).
d. Do you think that the assumption needed in order to conduct the t test in (a) is valid? Explain.

9.33 One operation of a steel mill is to cut pieces of steel into parts that are used in the frame for front seats in an automobile. The steel is cut with a diamond saw and requires the resulting parts must be cut to be within ±0.005 inch of the length specified by the automobile company. The file **Steel** contains a sample of 100 steel parts. The measurement reported is the difference, in inches, between the actual length of the steel part, as measured by a laser measurement device, and the specified length of the steel part. For example, a value of −0.002 represents a steel part that is 0.002 inch shorter than the specified length.
a. At the 0.05 level of significance, is there evidence that the mean difference is not equal to 0.0 inches?
b. Construct a 95% confidence interval estimate of the population mean. Interpret this interval.
c. Compare the conclusions reached in (a) and (b).
d. Because $n = 100$, do you have to be concerned about the normality assumption needed for the t test and t interval?

9.34 In Problem 3.67 on page 165, you were introduced to a tea-bag-filling operation. An important quality characteristic of interest for this process is the weight of the tea in the individual bags. The file **Teabags** contains an ordered array of the weight, in grams, of a sample of 50 tea bags produced during an eight-hour shift.
a. Is there evidence that the mean amount of tea per bag is different from 5.5 grams? (Use $\alpha = 0.01$.)
b. Construct a 99% confidence interval estimate of the population mean amount of tea per bag. Interpret this interval.
c. Compare the conclusions reached in (a) and (b).

9.35 Although many people think they can put a meal on the table in a short period of time, an article reported that they end up spending about 40 minutes doing so. (Data extracted from N. Hellmich, "Americans Go for the Quick Fix for Dinner," *USA Today*, February 14, 2006.) Suppose another study is conducted to test the validity of this statement. A sample of 25 people is selected, and the length of time to prepare and cook dinner (in minutes) is recorded, with the following results (in **Dinner**):

44.0 51.9 49.7 40.0 55.5 33.0 43.4 41.3 45.2 40.7 41.1 49.1 30.9
45.2 55.3 52.1 55.1 38.8 43.1 39.2 58.6 49.8 43.2 47.9 46.6

a. Is there evidence that the population mean time to prepare and cook dinner is different from 40 minutes? Use the p-value approach and a level of significance of 0.05.
b. What assumption about the population distribution is needed in order to conduct the t test in (a)?
c. Make a list of the various ways you could evaluate the assumption noted in (b).
d. Evaluate the assumption noted in (b) and determine whether the t test in (a) is valid.

9.3 One-Tail Tests

In Section 9.1, hypothesis testing was used to examine the question of whether the population mean amount of cereal filled is 368 grams. The alternative hypothesis ($H_1 : \mu \neq 368$) contains two possibilities: Either the mean is less than 368 grams or the mean is more than 368 grams. For this reason, the rejection region is divided into the two tails of the sampling distribution of the mean. In Section 9.2, a two-tail test was used to determine whether the mean amount per invoice had changed from $120.

In contrast to these two examples, many situations require an alternative hypothesis that focuses on a *particular direction*. For example, the population mean is *less than* a specified value. One such situation involves the business problem concerning the service time at the drive-through window of a fast-food restaurant. The speed with which customers are served is of critical importance to the success of the service (see **www.qsrmagazine.com/reports/drive-thru_time_study**). In one past study, McDonald's had a mean service time of 174.22 seconds, which was only ninth best in the industry. Suppose that McDonald's began a quality improvement effort to reduce the service time by deploying an improved drive-through service process in a sample of 25 stores. Because McDonald's would want to institute the new process in all of its stores only if the test sample saw a *decreased* drive-through time, the entire rejection region is located in the lower tail of the distribution.

The Critical Value Approach

You wish to determine whether the new drive-through process has a mean that is less than 174.22 seconds. To perform this one-tail hypothesis test, you use the six-step method listed in Exhibit 9.1 on page 362.

Step 1 You define the null and alternative hypotheses:

$$H_0: \mu \geq 174.22$$

$$H_1: \mu < 174.22$$

The alternative hypothesis contains the statement for which you are trying to find evidence. If the conclusion of the test is "reject H_0," there is statistical evidence that the mean drive-through time is less than the drive-through time in the old process. This would be reason to change the drive-through process for the entire population of stores. If the conclusion of the test is "do not reject H_0," then there is insufficient evidence that the mean drive-through time in the new process is significantly less than the drive-through time in the old process. If this occurs, there would be insufficient reason to institute the new drive-through process in the population of stores.

Step 2 You collect the data by selecting a drive-through time sample of $n = 25$ stores. You decide to use $\alpha = 0.05$.

Step 3 Because σ is unknown, you use the t distribution and the t_{STAT} test statistic. You need to assume that the service time is normally distributed because only a sample of 25 drive-through times is selected.

Step 4 The rejection region is entirely contained in the lower tail of the sampling distribution of the mean because you want to reject H_0 only when the sample mean is significantly less than 174.22 seconds. When the entire rejection region is contained in one tail of the sampling distribution of the test statistic, the test is called a **one-tail test**, or **directional test**. If the alternative hypothesis includes the *less than* sign, the critical value of t is negative. As shown in Table 9.3 and Figure 9.11, because the entire rejection region is in the lower tail of the t distribution and contains an area of 0.05, due to the symmetry of the t distribution, the critical value of the t test statistic with $25 - 1 = 24$ degrees of freedom is -1.7109. The decision rule is

Reject H_0 if $t_{STAT} < -1.7109$;

otherwise, do not reject H_0.

TABLE 9.3

Determining the Critical Value from the t Table for an Area of 0.05 in the Lower Tail, with 24 Degrees of Freedom

	Cumulative Probabilities					
	.75	.90	.95	.975	.99	.995
	Upper-Tail Areas					
Degrees of Freedom	.25	.10	.05	.025	.01	.005
1	1.0000	3.0777	6.3138	12.7062	31.8207	63.6574
2	0.8165	1.8856	2.9200	4.3027	6.9646	9.9248
3	0.7649	1.6377	2.3534	3.1824	4.5407	5.8409
.	.	.	.	.	.	.
.	.	.	.	.	.	.
23	0.6853	1.3195	1.7139	2.0687	2.4999	2.8073
24	0.6848	1.3178	1.7109	2.0639	2.4922	2.7969
25	0.6844	1.3163	1.7081	2.0595	2.4851	2.7874

Source: Extracted from Table E.3.

FIGURE 9.11
One-tail test of hypothesis for a mean (σ unknown) at the 0.05 level of significance

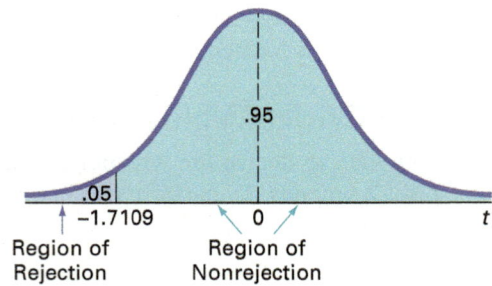

Step 5 From the sample of 25 stores you selected, you find that the sample mean service time at the drive-through equals 162.96 seconds and the sample standard deviation equals 20.2 seconds. Using $n = 25$, $\bar{X} = 162.96$, $S = 20.2$, and Equation (9.2) on page 368,

$$t_{STAT} = \frac{\bar{X} - \mu}{\frac{S}{\sqrt{n}}} = \frac{162.96 - 174.22}{\frac{20.2}{\sqrt{25}}} = -2.7871$$

Step 6 Because $t_{STAT} = -2.7871 < -1.7109$, you reject the null hypothesis (see Figure 9.11). You conclude that the mean service time at the drive-through is less than 174.22 seconds. There is sufficient evidence to change the drive-through process for the entire population of stores.

The p-Value Approach

Use the five steps listed in Exhibit 9.2 on page 365 to illustrate the t test for the drive-through time study using the p-value approach.

Step 1–3 These steps are the same as in the critical value approach on page 362.

Step 4 $t_{STAT} = -2.7871$ (see step 5 of the critical value approach). Because the alternative hypothesis indicates a rejection region entirely in the lower tail of the sampling distribution, to compute the p-value, you need to find the probability that the t_{STAT} test statistic will be less than –2.7871. Figure 9.12 shows that the p-value is 0.0051.

FIGURE 9.12
Excel and Minitab t test results for the drive-through time study

	A	B	
1	t Test for the Hypothesis of the Mean		
2			
3	Data		
4	Null Hypothesis μ=	174.22	
5	Level of Significance	0.05	
6	Sample Size	25	
7	Sample Mean	162.96	
8	Sample Standard Deviation	20.2	
9			
10	Intermediate Calculations		
11	Standard Error of the Mean	4.0400	=B8/SQRT(B6)
12	Degrees of Freedom	24	=B6 - 1
13	t Test Statistic	-2.7871	=(B7 - B4)/B11
14			
15	Lower-Tail Test		
16	Lower Critical Value	-1.7109	=-TINV(2 * B5, B12)
17	p-Value	0.0051	=IF(B13 < 0, E22, E23)
18	Reject the null hypothesis		=IF(B17 < B5, "Reject the null hypothesis", "Do not reject the null hypothesis")

Not shown
Cell E22: =TDIST(ABS(B13), B12, 1)
Cell E23: =1 - E22

One-Sample T
Test of mu = 174.22 vs < 174.22

N	Mean	StDev	SE Mean	95% Upper Bound	T	P
25	162.96	20.20	4.04	169.87	-2.79	0.005

Step 5 The p-value of 0.0051 is less than $\alpha = 0.05$ (see Figure 9.13). You reject H_0 and conclude that the mean service time at the drive-through is less than 174.22 seconds. There is sufficient evidence to change the drive-through process for the entire population of stores.

FIGURE 9.13
Determining the p-value for a one-tail test

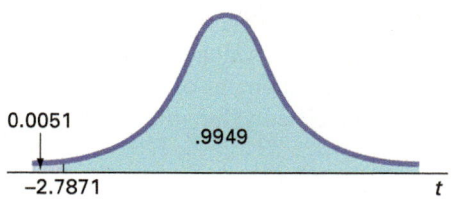

EXAMPLE 9.5

A One-Tail Test for the Mean

A company that manufactures chocolate bars is particularly concerned that the mean weight of a chocolate bar is not greater than 6.03 ounces. A sample of 50 chocolate bars is selected; the sample mean is 6.034 ounces, and the sample standard deviation is 0.02 ounces. Using the $\alpha = 0.01$ level of significance, is there evidence that the population mean weight of the chocolate bars is greater than 6.03 ounces?

SOLUTION Using the critical value approach, listed in Exhibit 9.1 on page 362,

Step 1 First, you define your hypotheses:

$$H_0: \mu \leq 6.03$$
$$H_1: \mu > 6.03$$

Step 2 You collect the data from a sample of $n = 50$. You decide to use $\alpha = 0.01$.

Step 3 Because σ is unknown, you use the t distribution and the t_{STAT} test statistic.

Step 4 The rejection region is entirely contained in the upper tail of the sampling distribution of the mean because you want to reject H_0 only when the sample mean is significantly greater than 6.03 ounces. Because the entire rejection region is in the upper tail of the t distribution and contains an area of 0.01, the critical value of the t distribution with $50 - 1 = 49$ degrees of freedom is 2.4049 (see Table E.3).

The decision rule is

$$\text{Reject } H_0 \text{ if } t_{STAT} > 2.4049;$$
$$\text{otherwise, do not reject } H_0.$$

Step 5 From your sample of 50 chocolate bars, you find that the sample mean weight is 6.034 ounces, and the sample standard deviation is 0.02 ounces. Using $n = 50$, $\overline{X} = 6.034$, $S = 0.02$, and Equation (9.2) on page 368,

$$t_{STAT} = \frac{\overline{X} - \mu}{\frac{S}{\sqrt{n}}} = \frac{6.034 - 6.03}{\frac{0.02}{\sqrt{50}}} = 1.414$$

Step 6 Because $t_{STAT} = 1.414 < 2.4049$, or using Microsoft Excel or Minitab, the p-value is $0.0818 > 0.01$, you do not reject the null hypothesis. There is insufficient evidence to conclude that the population mean weight is greater than 6.03 ounces.

To perform one-tail tests of hypotheses, you must properly formulate H_0 and H_1. A summary of the null and alternative hypotheses for one-tail tests is as follows:

- The null hypothesis, H_0, represents the status quo or the current belief in a situation.
- The alternative hypothesis, H_1, is the opposite of the null hypothesis and represents a research claim or specific inference you would like to prove.
- If you reject the null hypothesis, you have statistical proof that the alternative hypothesis is correct.
- If you do not reject the null hypothesis, you have failed to prove the alternative hypothesis. The failure to prove the alternative hypothesis, however, does not mean that you have proven the null hypothesis.
- The null hypothesis always refers to a specified value of the *population parameter* (such as μ), not to a *sample statistic* (such as $\overline{X}$).

- The statement of the null hypothesis *always* contains an equal sign regarding the specified value of the parameter (e.g., $H_0 : \mu \geq 174.22$).
- The statement of the alternative hypothesis *never* contains an equal sign regarding the specified value of the parameter (e.g., $H_1 : \mu < 174.22$).

Problems for Section 9.3

LEARNING THE BASICS

9.36 In a one-tail hypothesis test where you reject H_0 only in the *upper* tail, what is the *p*-value if $Z_{STAT} = +2.00$?

9.37 In Problem 9.36, what is your statistical decision if you test the null hypothesis at the 0.05 level of significance?

9.38 In a one-tail hypothesis test where you reject H_0 only in the *lower* tail, what is the *p*-value if $Z_{STAT} = -1.38$?

9.39 In Problem 9.38, what is your statistical decision if you test the null hypothesis at the 0.01 level of significance?

9.40 In a one-tail hypothesis test where you reject H_0 only in the *lower* tail, what is the *p*-value if $Z_{STAT} = +1.38$?

9.41 In Problem 9.40, what is the statistical decision if you test the null hypothesis at the 0.01 level of significance?

9.42 In a one-tail hypothesis test where you reject H_0 only in the *upper* tail, what is the critical value of the *t*-test statistic with 10 degrees of freedom at the 0.01 level of significance?

9.43 In Problem 9.42, what is your statistical decision if $t_{STAT} = +2.39$?

9.44 In a one-tail hypothesis test where you reject H_0 only in the *lower* tail, what is the critical value of the t_{STAT} test statistic with 20 degrees of freedom at the 0.01 level of significance?

9.45 In Problem 9.44, what is your statistical decision if $t_{STAT} = -1.15$?

APPLYING THE CONCEPTS

9.46 In a recent year, the Federal Communications Commission reported that the mean wait for repairs for Verizon customers was 36.5 hours. In an effort to improve this service, suppose that a new repair service process was developed. This new process, used for a sample of 100 repairs, resulted in a sample mean of 34.5 hours and a sample standard deviation of 11.7 hours.
a. Is there evidence that the population mean amount is less than 36.5 hours? (Use a 0.05 level of significance.)
b. Determine the *p*-value and interpret its meaning.

9.47 In a recent year, the Federal Communications Commission reported that the mean wait for repairs for AT&T customers was 25.3 hours. In an effort to improve this service, suppose that a new repair service process was developed. This new process, used for a sample of 100 repairs, resulted in a sample mean of 22.3 hours and a sample standard deviation of 8.3 hours.
a. Is there evidence that the population mean amount is less than 25.3 hours? (Use a 0.05 level of significance.)
b. Determine the *p*-value and interpret its meaning.

SELF Test 9.48 Southside Hospital in Bay Shore, New York, commonly conducts stress tests to study the heart muscle after a person has a heart attack. Members of the diagnostic imaging department conducted a quality improvement project with the objective of reducing the turnaround time for stress tests. Turnaround time is defined as the time from when a test is ordered to when the radiologist signs off on the test results. Initially, the mean turnaround time for a stress test was 68 hours. After incorporating changes into the stress-test process, the quality improvement team collected a sample of 50 turnaround times. In this sample, the mean turnaround time was 32 hours, with a standard deviation of 9 hours. (Data extracted from E. Godin, D. Raven, C. Sweetapple, and F. R. Del Guidice, "Faster Test Results," *Quality Progress*, January 2004, 37(1), pp. 33–39.)
a. If you test the null hypothesis at the 0.01 level of significance, is their evidence that the new process has reduced turnaround time?
b. Interpret the meaning of the *p*-value in this problem.

9.49 You are the manager of a restaurant that delivers pizza to college dormitory rooms. You have just changed your delivery process in an effort to reduce the mean time between the order and completion of delivery from the current 25 minutes. A sample of 36 orders using the new delivery process yields a sample mean of 22.4 minutes and a sample standard deviation of 6 minutes.
a. Using the six-step critical value approach, at the 0.05 level of significance, is there evidence that the population mean delivery time has been reduced below the previous population mean value of 25 minutes?
b. At the 0.05 level of significance, use the five-step *p*-value approach.
c. Interpret the meaning of the *p*-value in (b).
d. Compare your conclusions in (a) and (b).

9.50 The per-store daily customer count (i.e., the mean number of customers in a store in one day) for a nationwide convenience store chain that operates nearly 10,000 stores has been steady, at 900, for some time. To increase the customer count, the chain is considering cutting prices for coffee beverages by approximately half. The small size will now be $0.59 instead of $0.99, and the medium size will be $0.69 instead of $1.19. Even with this reduction in price, the chain will have a 40% gross margin on coffee. To test the new

initiative, the chain has reduced coffee prices in a sample of 34 stores, where customer counts have been running almost exactly at the national average of 900. After four weeks, the sample stores stabilize at a mean customer count of 974 and a standard deviation of 96. This increase seems like a substantial amount to you, but it also seems like a pretty small sample. Do you think reducing coffee prices is a good strategy for increasing the mean customer count?
a. State the null and alternative hypotheses.
b. Explain the meaning of the Type I and Type II errors in the context of this scenario.
c. At the 0.01 level of significance, is there evidence that reducing coffee prices is a good strategy for increasing the mean customer count?
d. Interpret the meaning of the p-value in (c).

9.51 The population mean waiting time to check out of a supermarket has been 10.73 minutes. Recently, in an effort to reduce the waiting time, the supermarket has experimented with a system in which there is a single waiting line with multiple checkout servers. A sample of 100 customers was selected, and their mean waiting time to check out was 9.52 minutes, with a sample standard deviation of 5.8 minutes.
a. At the 0.05 level of significance, using the critical value approach to hypothesis testing, is there evidence that the population mean waiting time to check out is less than 10.73 minutes?
b. At the 0.05 level of significance, using the p-value approach to hypothesis testing, is there evidence that the population mean waiting time to check out is less than 10.73 minutes?
c. Interpret the meaning of the p-value in this problem.
d. Compare your conclusions in (a) and (b).

9.4 Z Test of Hypothesis for the Proportion

In some situations, you want to test a hypothesis about the proportion of events of interest in the population, π, rather than test the population mean. To begin, you select a random sample and compute the **sample proportion**, $p = X/n$. You then compare the value of this statistic to the hypothesized value of the parameter, π, in order to decide whether to reject the null hypothesis. If the number of events of interest (X) and the number of events that are not of interest ($n - X$) are each at least five, the sampling distribution of a proportion approximately follows a normal distribution. You use the **Z test for the proportion** given in Equation (9.3) to perform the hypothesis test for the difference between the sample proportion, p, and the hypothesized population proportion, π.

Z TEST FOR THE PROPORTION

$$Z_{STAT} = \frac{p - \pi}{\sqrt{\frac{\pi(1 - \pi)}{n}}} \tag{9.3}$$

where

$$p = \text{Sample proportion} = \frac{X}{n} = \frac{\text{Number of events of interest in the sample}}{\text{Sample size}}$$

π = Hypothesized proportion of events of interest in the population

The Z_{STAT} test statistic approximately follows a standardized normal distribution when X and $(n - X)$ are each at least 5.

Alternatively, by multiplying the numerator and denominator by n, you can write the Z_{STAT} test statistic in terms of the number of events of interest, X, as shown in Equation (9.4).

Z TEST FOR THE PROPORTION IN TERMS OF THE NUMBER OF EVENTS OF INTEREST

$$Z_{STAT} = \frac{X - n\pi}{\sqrt{n\pi(1 - \pi)}} \tag{9.4}$$

The Critical Value Approach

To illustrate the Z test for a proportion, consider a survey conducted for American Express that sought to determine the reasons adults wanted Internet access while on vacation. (Data extracted from "Wired Vacationers," *USA Today*, June 4, 2010, p. 1A.) Of 2,000 adults, 1,540 said that they wanted Internet access so they could check personal e-mail while on vacation. A survey conducted in the previous year indicated that 75% of adults wanted Internet access so they could check personal e-mail while on vacation. Is there evidence that the percentage of adults who wanted Internet access to check personal e-mail while on vacation has changed from the previous year? To investigate this question, the null and alternative hypotheses are follows:

$H_0: \pi = 0.75$ (i.e., the proportion of adults who want Internet access to check personal email while on vacation has not changed from the previous year)

$H_1: \pi \neq 0.75$ (i.e., the proportion of adults who want Internet access to check personal email while on vacation has changed from the previous year)

Because you are interested in determining whether the population proportion of adults who want Internet access to check personal email while on vacation has changed from 0.75 in the previous year, you use a two-tail test. If you select the $\alpha = 0.05$ level of significance, the rejection and nonrejection regions are set up as in Figure 9.14, and the decision rule is

$$\text{Reject } H_0 \text{ if } Z_{STAT} < -1.96 \text{ or if } Z_{STAT} > +1.96;$$

otherwise, do not reject H_0.

FIGURE 9.14
Two-tail test of hypothesis for the proportion at the 0.05 level of significance

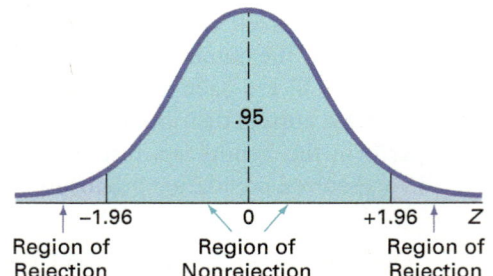

Because 1,540 of the 2,000 adults stated that they wanted Internet access to check personal email while on vacation,

$$p = \frac{1{,}540}{2{,}000} = 0.77$$

Since $X = 1{,}540$ and $n - X = 460$, each > 5, using Equation (9.3),

$$Z_{STAT} = \frac{p - \pi}{\sqrt{\dfrac{\pi(1-\pi)}{n}}} = \frac{0.77 - 0.75}{\sqrt{\dfrac{0.75(1-0.75)}{2{,}000}}} = \frac{0.02}{0.0097} = 2.0656$$

or, using Equation (9.4),

$$Z_{STAT} = \frac{X - n\pi}{\sqrt{n\pi(1-\pi)}} = \frac{1{,}540 - (2{,}000)(0.75)}{\sqrt{2{,}000(0.75)(0.25)}} = \frac{40}{19.3649} = 2.0656$$

Because $Z_{STAT} = 2.0656 > 1.96$, you reject H_0. There is evidence that the population proportion of all adults who want Internet access to check personal e-mail while on vacation has changed from 0.75 in the previous year. Figure 9.15 presents results for these data, as computed by Excel and Minitab.

FIGURE 9.15
Excel and Minitab results for the Z test for whether the proportion of adults who want Internet access to check personal email while on vacation has changed from the previous year

	A	B	
1	Z Test of Hypothesis for the Proportion		
2			
3	Data		
4	Null Hypothesis p=	0.75	
5	Level of Significance	0.05	
6	Number of Items of Interest	1540	
7	Sample Size	2000	
8			
9	Intermediate Calculations		
10	Sample Proportion	0.7700	=B6/B7
11	Standard Error	0.0097	=SQRT(B4*(1 - B4)/B7)
12	Z Test Statistic	2.0656	=(B10 - B4)/B11
13			
14	Two-Tail Test		
15	Lower Critical Value	-1.9600	=NORMSINV(B5/2)
16	Upper Critical Value	1.9600	=NORMSINV(1 - B5/2)
17	p-Value	0.0389	=2 * (1 - NORMSDIST(ABS(B12)))
18	Reject the null hypothesis		=IF(B17 < B5, "Reject the null hypothesis", "Do not reject the null hypothesis")

```
Test and CI for One Proportion
Test of p = 0.75 vs p not = 0.75

Sample    X     N   Sample p      95% CI             Z-Value  P-Value
1       1540  2000  0.770000  (0.751557, 0.788443)    2.07     0.039

Using the normal approximation.
```

The p-Value Approach

As an alternative to the critical value approach, you can compute the p-value. For this two-tail test in which the rejection region is located in the lower tail and the upper tail, you need to find the area below a Z value of −2.0656 and above a Z value of +2.0656. Figure 9.15 reports a p-value of 0.0389. Because this value is less than the selected level of significance ($\alpha = 0.05$), you reject the null hypothesis.

EXAMPLE 9.6
Testing a Hypothesis for a Proportion

A fast-food chain has developed a new process to ensure that orders at the drive-through are filled correctly. The business problem is defined as determining whether the new process can increase the percentage of orders processed correctly. The previous process filled orders correctly 85% of the time. Data are collected from a sample of 100 orders using the new process. The results indicate that 94 orders were filled correctly. At the 0.01 level of significance, can you conclude that the new process has increased the proportion of orders filled correctly?

SOLUTION The null and alternative hypotheses are

$H_0: \pi \leq 0.85$ (i.e., the population proportion of orders filled correctly using the new process is less than or equal to 0.85)
$H_1: \pi > 0.85$ (i.e., the population proportion of orders filled correctly using the new process is greater than 0.85)

Since $X = 94$ and $n - X = 6$, both > 5, using Equation (9.3) on page 379,

$$p = \frac{X}{n} = \frac{94}{100} = 0.94$$

$$Z_{STAT} = \frac{p - \pi}{\sqrt{\frac{\pi(1 - \pi)}{n}}} = \frac{0.94 - 0.85}{\sqrt{\frac{0.85(1 - 0.85)}{100}}} = \frac{0.09}{0.0357} = 2.52$$

The p-value for $Z_{STAT} > 2.52$ is 0.0059.

Using the critical value approach, you reject H_0 if $Z_{STAT} > 2.33$. Using the p-value approach, you reject H_0 if p-value < 0.01. Because $Z_{STAT} = 2.52 > 2.33$ or the p-value = 0.0059 < 0.01, you reject H_0. You have evidence that the new process has increased the proportion of correct orders above 0.85.

Problems for Section 9.4

LEARNING THE BASICS

9.52 If, in a random sample of 400 items, 88 are defective, what is the sample proportion of defective items?

9.53 In Problem 9.52, if the null hypothesis is that 20% of the items in the population are defective, what is the value of Z_{STAT}?

9.54 In Problems 9.52 and 9.53, suppose you are testing the null hypothesis $H_0: \pi = 0.20$ against the two-tail alternative hypothesis $H_1: \pi \neq 0.20$ and you choose the level of significance $\alpha = 0.05$. What is your statistical decision?

APPLYING THE CONCEPTS

9.55 The U.S. Department of Education reports that 46% of full-time college students are employed while attending college. (Data extracted from "The Condition of Education 2009," *National Center for Education Statistics*, **nces.ed.gov**.) A recent survey of 60 full-time students at Miami University found that 29 were employed.
a. Use the five-step *p*-value approach to hypothesis testing and a 0.05 level of significance to determine whether the proportion of full-time students at Miami University is different from the national norm of 0.46.
b. Assume that the study found that 36 of the 60 full-time students were employed and repeat (a). Are the conclusions the same?

9.56 Online magazines make it easy for readers to link to an advertiser's website directly from an advertisement placed in the digital magazine. A recent survey indicated that 56% of online magazine readers have clicked on an advertisement and linked directly to the advertiser's website. The survey was based on a sample size of $n = 6,403$. (Data extracted from "Metrics," *EContent*, January/February, 2007, p. 20.)
a. Use the five-step *p*-value approach to try to determine whether there is evidence that more than half of all the readers of online magazines have linked to an advertiser's website. (Use the 0.05 level of significance.)
b. Suppose that the sample size was only $n = 100$, and, as before, 56% of the online magazine readers indicated that they had clicked on an advertisement to link directly to the advertiser's website. Use the five-step *p*-value approach to try to determine whether there is evidence that more than half of all the readers of online magazines have linked to an advertiser's website. (Use the 0.05 level of significance.)
c. Discuss the effect that sample size has on hypothesis testing.
d. What do you think are your chances of rejecting any null hypothesis concerning a population proportion if a sample size of $n = 20$ is used?

9.57 One of the issues facing organizations is increasing diversity throughout the organization. One of the ways to evaluate an organization's success at increasing diversity is to compare the percentage of employees in the organization in a particular position with a specific background to the percentage in a particular position with that specific background in the general workforce. Recently, a large academic medical center determined that 9 of 17 employees in a particular position were female, whereas 55% of the employees for this position in the general workforce were female. At the 0.05 level of significance, is there evidence that the proportion of females in this position at this medical center is different from what would be expected in the general workforce?

9.58 Of 1,000 respondents aged 24 to 35, 65% reported that they preferred to "look for a job in a place where I would like to live" rather than "look for the best job I can find, the place where I live is secondary." (Data extracted from L. Belkin, "What Do Young Jobseekers Want? (Something Other Than a Job)," *The New York Times*, September 6, 2007, p. G2.) At the 0.05 level of significance, is there evidence that the proportion of all young jobseekers aged 24 to 35 who preferred to "look for a job in a place where I would like to live" rather than "look for the best job I can find, the place where I live is secondary" is different from 60%?

9.59 The telephone company wants to investigate the desirability of beginning a marketing campaign that would offer customers the right to purchase an additional telephone line at a substantially reduced installation cost. The campaign will be initiated if there is evidence that more than 20% of the customers would consider purchasing an additional telephone line if it were made available at a substantially reduced installation cost. A random sample of 500 households is selected. The results indicate that 135 of the households would purchase the additional telephone line at a reduced installation cost.
a. At the 0.05 level of significance, is there evidence that more than 20% of the customers would purchase the additional telephone line?
b. How would the manager in charge of promotional programs concerning residential customers use the results in (a)?

9.60 A study by the Pew Internet and American Life Project (**pewinternet.org**) found that Americans had a complex and ambivalent attitude toward technology. (Data extracted from M. Himowitz, "How to Tell What Kind of Tech User You Are," *Newsday*, May 27, 2007, p. F6.) The study reported that 8% of the respondents were "Omnivores" who are gadget lovers, text messengers, and online gamers (often with their own blogs or web pages), video makers, and YouTube posters. You believe that the percentage of students at your school who are Omnivores is greater than 8%, and you plan to carry out a study to prove that this is so.
a. State the null and alternative hypotheses.
b. You select a sample of 200 students at your school and find that 30 students can be classified as Omnivores. Use either the six-step critical value hypothesis-testing approach or the five-step *p*-value approach to determine at the 0.05 level of significance whether there is evidence that the percentage of Omnivores at your school is greater than 8%.

9.5 Potential Hypothesis-Testing Pitfalls and Ethical Issues

To this point, you have studied the fundamental concepts of hypothesis testing. You have used hypothesis testing to analyze differences between sample statistics and hypothesized population parameters in order to make business decisions concerning the underlying population characteristics. You have also learned how to evaluate the risks involved in making these decisions.

When planning to carry out a hypothesis test based on a survey, research study, or designed experiment, you must ask several questions to ensure that you use proper methodology. You need to raise and answer questions such as the following in the planning stage:

- What is the goal of the survey, study, or experiment? How can you translate the goal into a null hypothesis and an alternative hypothesis?
- Is the hypothesis test a two-tail test or one-tail test?
- Can you select a random sample from the underlying population of interest?
- What types of data will you collect in the sample? Are the variables numerical or categorical?
- At what level of significance should you conduct the hypothesis test?
- Is the intended sample size large enough to achieve the desired power of the test for the level of significance chosen?
- What statistical test procedure should you use and why?
- What conclusions and interpretations can you reach from the results of the hypothesis test?

Failing to consider these questions early in the planning process can lead to biased or incomplete results. Proper planning can help ensure that the statistical study will provide objective information needed to make good business decisions.

Statistical Significance Versus Practical Significance

You need to make a distinction between the existence of a statistically significant result and its practical significance in a field of application. Sometimes, due to a very large sample size, you may get a result that is statistically significant but has little practical significance. For example, suppose that prior to a national marketing campaign focusing on a series of expensive television commercials, you believe that the proportion of people who recognize your brand is 0.30. At the completion of the campaign, a survey of 20,000 people indicates that 6,168 recognized your brand. A one-tail test trying to prove that the proportion is now greater than 0.30 results in a p-value of 0.0047, and the correct statistical conclusion is that the proportion of consumers recognizing your brand name has now increased. Was the campaign successful? The result of the hypothesis test indicates a statistically significant increase in brand awareness, but is this increase practically important? The population proportion is now estimated at $6,168/20,000 = 0.3084$, or 30.84%. This increase is less than 1% more than the hypothesized value of 30%. Did the large expenses associated with the marketing campaign produce a result with a meaningful increase in brand awareness? Because of the minimal real-world impact that an increase of less than 1% has on the overall marketing strategy and the huge expenses associated with the marketing campaign, you should conclude that the campaign was not successful. On the other hand, if the campaign increased brand awareness from 30% to 50%, you could conclude that the campaign was successful.

Reporting of Findings

In conducting research, you should document both good and bad results. You should not just report the results of hypothesis tests that show statistical significance but omit those for which there is insufficient evidence in the findings. In instances in which there is insufficient evidence to reject H_0, you must make it clear that this does not prove that the null hypothesis is true. What the result does indicate is that with the sample size used, there is not enough information to *disprove* the null hypothesis.

Ethical Issues

You need to distinguish between poor research methodology and unethical behavior. Ethical considerations arise when the hypothesis-testing process is manipulated. Some of the areas where ethical issues can arise include the use of human subjects in experiments, the data collection method, the type of test (one-tail or two-tail test), the choice of the level of significance, the cleansing and discarding of data, and the failure to report pertinent findings.

9.6 Online Topic: The Power of a Test

Section 9.1 defines Type I and Type II errors and the power of a test. To examine the power of a test in greater depth, read the **Section 9.6** online topic file that is available on this book's companion website. (See Appendix C to learn how to access the online topic files.)

USING STATISTICS @ Oxford Cereals, Part II Revisited

As the plant operations manager for Oxford Cereals, you were responsible for the cereal-filling process. It was your responsibility to adjust the process when the mean fill weight in the population of boxes deviated from the company specification of 368 grams. Because weighing all the cereal boxes would be too time-consuming and impractical, you needed to select and weigh a sample of boxes and conduct a hypothesis test.

You determined that the null hypothesis should be that the population mean fill was 368 grams. If the mean weight of the sampled boxes were sufficiently above or below the expected 368-gram mean specified by Oxford Cereals, you would reject the null hypothesis in favor of the alternative hypothesis that the mean fill was different from 368 grams. If this happened, you would stop production and take whatever action is necessary to correct the problem. If the null hypothesis was not rejected, you would continue to believe in the status quo—that the process was working correctly—and therefore take no corrective action.

Before proceeding, you considered the risks involved with hypothesis tests. If you rejected a true null hypothesis, you would make a Type I error and conclude that the population mean fill was not 368 when it actually was 368. This error would result in adjusting the filling process even though the process was working properly. If you did not reject a false null hypothesis, you would make a Type II error and conclude that the population mean fill was 368 when it actually was not 368. Here, you would allow the process to continue without adjustment even though the process was not working properly.

After collecting a random sample of 25 cereal boxes, you used the six-step critical value approach to hypothesis testing. Because the test statistic fell into the nonrejection region, you did not reject the null hypothesis. You concluded that there was insufficient evidence to prove that the mean fill differed from 368 grams. No corrective action on the filling process was needed.

SUMMARY

This chapter presented the foundation of hypothesis testing. You learned how to perform tests on the population mean and on the population proportion. The chapter developed both the critical value approach and the *p*-value approach to hypothesis testing.

In deciding which test to use, you should ask the following question: Does the test involve a numerical variable or a categorical variable? If the test involves a numerical variable, use the *t* test for the mean. If the test involves a categorical variable, use the *Z* test for the proportion. Table 9.4 provides a list of hypothesis tests covered in the chapter.

TABLE 9.4
Summary of Topics in Chapter 9

Type of Analysis	Type of Data	
	Numerical	Categorical
Hypothesis test concerning a single parameter	*t* test of hypothesis for the mean (Section 9.2)	*Z* test of hypothesis for the proportion (Section 9.4)

KEY EQUATIONS

Z Test for the Mean (σ Known)

$$Z_{STAT} = \frac{\bar{X} - \mu}{\frac{\sigma}{\sqrt{n}}} \quad (9.1)$$

t Test for the Mean (σ Unknown)

$$t_{STAT} = \frac{\bar{X} - \mu}{\frac{S}{\sqrt{n}}} \quad (9.2)$$

Z Test for the Proportion

$$Z_{STAT} = \frac{p - \pi}{\sqrt{\frac{\pi(1-\pi)}{n}}} \quad (9.3)$$

Z Test for the Proportion in Terms of the Number of Events of Interest

$$Z_{STAT} = \frac{X - n\pi}{\sqrt{n\pi(1-\pi)}} \quad (9.4)$$

KEY TERMS

alternative hypothesis (H_1)
β risk
confidence coefficient
critical value
directional test
hypothesis testing
level of significance (α)
null hypothesis (H_0)
one-tail test
p-value
power of a statistical test
region of nonrejection
region of rejection
robust
sample proportion
t test for the mean
test statistic
two-tail test
Type I error
Type II error
Z test for the mean
Z test for the proportion

CHAPTER REVIEW PROBLEMS

CHECKING YOUR UNDERSTANDING

9.61 What is the difference between a null hypothesis, H_0, and an alternative hypothesis, H_1?

9.62 What is the difference between a Type I error and a Type II error?

9.63 What is meant by the power of a test?

9.64 What is the difference between a one-tail test and a two-tail test?

9.65 What is meant by a *p*-value?

9.66 How can a confidence interval estimate for the population mean provide conclusions for the corresponding two-tail hypothesis test for the population mean?

9.67 What is the six-step critical value approach to hypothesis testing?

9.68 What is the five-step p-value approach to hypothesis testing?

APPLYING THE CONCEPTS

9.69 An article in *Marketing News* (T. T. Semon, "Consider a Statistical Insignificance Test," *Marketing News*, February 1, 1999) argued that the level of significance used when comparing two products is often too low—that is, sometimes you should be using an α value greater than 0.05. Specifically, the article recounted testing the proportion of potential customers with a preference for product 1 over product 2. The null hypothesis was that the population proportion of potential customers preferring product 1 was 0.50, and the alternative hypothesis was that it was not equal to 0.50. The p-value for the test was 0.22. The article suggested that, in some cases, this should be enough evidence to reject the null hypothesis.
a. State, in statistical terms, the null and alternative hypotheses for this example.
b. Explain the risks associated with Type I and Type II errors in this case.
c. What would be the consequences if you rejected the null hypothesis for a p-value of 0.22?
d. Why do you think the article suggested raising the value of α?
e. What would you do in this situation?
f. What is your answer in (e) if the p-value equals 0.12? What if it equals 0.06?

9.70 La Quinta Motor Inns developed a computer model to help predict the profitability of sites that are being considered as locations for new hotels. If the computer model predicts large profits, La Quinta buys the proposed site and builds a new hotel. If the computer model predicts small or moderate profits, La Quinta chooses not to proceed with that site. (Data extracted from S. E. Kimes and J. A. Fitzsimmons, "Selecting Profitable Hotel Sites at La Quinta Motor Inns," *Interfaces*, Vol. 20, March–April 1990, pp. 12–20.) This decision-making procedure can be expressed in the hypothesis-testing framework. The null hypothesis is that the site is not a profitable location. The alternative hypothesis is that the site is a profitable location.
a. Explain the risks associated with committing a Type I error in this case.
b. Explain the risks associated with committing a Type II error in this case.
c. Which type of error do you think the executives at La Quinta Motor Inns want to avoid? Explain.
d. How do changes in the rejection criterion affect the probabilities of committing Type I and Type II errors?

9.71 Webcredible, a UK-based consulting firm specializing in websites, intranets, mobile devices, and applications, conducted a survey of 1,132 mobile phone users between February and April 2009. The survey found that 52% of mobile phone users are now using the mobile Internet. (Data extracted from "Email and Social Networking Most Popular Mobile Internet Activities," **www.webcredible.co.uk**, May 13, 2009.) The authors of the article imply that the survey proves that more than half of all mobile phone users are now using the mobile Internet.
a. Use the five-step p-value approach to hypothesis testing and a 0.05 level of significance to try to prove that more than half of all mobile phone users are now using the mobile Internet.
b. Based on your result in (a), is the claim implied by the authors valid?
c. Suppose the survey found that 53% of mobile phone users are now using the mobile Internet. Repeat parts (a) and (b).
d. Compare the results of (b) and (c).

9.72 The owner of a gasoline station wants to study gasoline purchasing habits of motorists at his station. He selects a random sample of 60 motorists during a certain week, with the following results:
- The amount purchased was $\bar{X} = 11.3$ gallons, $S = 3.1$ gallons.
- Eleven motorists purchased premium-grade gasoline.

a. At the 0.05 level of significance, is there evidence that the population mean purchase was different from 10 gallons?
b. Determine the p-value in (a).
c. At the 0.05 level of significance, is there evidence that less than 20% of all the motorists at the station purchased premium-grade gasoline?
d. What is your answer to (a) if the sample mean equals 10.3 gallons?
e. What is your answer to (c) if 7 motorists purchased premium-grade gasoline?

9.73 An auditor for a government agency is assigned the task of evaluating reimbursement for office visits to physicians paid by Medicare. The audit was conducted on a sample of 75 of the reimbursements, with the following results:
- In 12 of the office visits, there was an incorrect amount of reimbursement.
- The amount of reimbursement was $\bar{X} = \$93.70$, $S = \$34.55$.

a. At the 0.05 level of significance, is there evidence that the population mean reimbursement was less than $100?
b. At the 0.05 level of significance, is there evidence that the proportion of incorrect reimbursements in the population was greater than 0.10?
c. Discuss the underlying assumptions of the test used in (a).
d. What is your answer to (a) if the sample mean equals $90?
e. What is your answer to (b) if 15 office visits had incorrect reimbursements?

9.74 A bank branch located in a commercial district of a city had the business objective of improving the process for serving customers during the noon-to-1:00 P.M. lunch period. The waiting time (defined as the time the customer enters the line until he or she reaches the teller window) of all customers during this hour is recorded over a period of a week. Data were collected from a random sample of 15 customers, and the results are organized (and stored in Bank1) as follows:

| 4.21 | 5.55 | 3.02 | 5.13 | 4.77 | 2.34 | 3.54 | 3.20 |
| 4.50 | 6.10 | 0.38 | 5.12 | 6.46 | 6.19 | 3.79 | |

a. At the 0.05 level of significance, is there evidence that the population mean waiting time is less than 5 minutes?
b. What assumption about the population distribution is needed in order to conduct the t test in (a)?
c. Construct a boxplot or a normal probability plot to evaluate the assumption made in (b).
d. Do you think that the assumption needed in order to conduct the t test in (a) is valid? Explain.
e. As a customer walks into the branch office during the lunch hour, she asks the branch manager how long she can expect to wait. The branch manager replies, "Almost certainly not longer than 5 minutes." On the basis of the results of (a), evaluate this statement.

9.75 A manufacturing company produces electrical insulators. If the insulators break when in use, a short circuit is likely to occur. To test the strength of the insulators, destructive testing is carried out to determine how much force is required to break the insulators. Force is measured by observing the number of pounds of force applied to the insulator before it breaks. The following data (stored in Force) are from 30 insulators subjected to this testing:

1,870	1,728	1,656	1,610	1,634	1,784	1,522	1,696	1,592	1,662
1,866	1,764	1,734	1,662	1,734	1,774	1,550	1,756	1,762	1,866
1,820	1,744	1,788	1,688	1,810	1,752	1,680	1,810	1,652	1,736

a. At the 0.05 level of significance, is there evidence that the population mean force is greater than 1,500 pounds?
b. What assumption about the population distribution is needed in order to conduct the t test in (a)?
c. Construct a histogram, boxplot, or normal probability plot to evaluate the assumption made in (b).
d. Do you think that the assumption needed in order to conduct the t test in (a) is valid? Explain.

9.76 An important quality characteristic used by the manufacturer of Boston and Vermont asphalt shingles is the amount of moisture the shingles contain when they are packaged. Customers may feel that they have purchased a product lacking in quality if they find moisture and wet shingles inside the packaging. In some cases, excessive moisture can cause the granules attached to the shingle for texture and coloring purposes to fall off the shingle, resulting in appearance problems. To monitor the amount of moisture present, the company conducts moisture tests. A shingle is weighed and then dried. The shingle is then reweighed, and, based on the amount of moisture taken out of the product, the pounds of moisture per 100 square feet are calculated. The company would like to show that the mean moisture content is less than 0.35 pound per 100 square feet. The file Moisture includes 36 measurements (in pounds per 100 square feet) for Boston shingles and 31 for Vermont shingles.
a. For the Boston shingles, is there evidence at the 0.05 level of significance that the population mean moisture content is less than 0.35 pound per 100 square feet?
b. Interpret the meaning of the p-value in (a).
c. For the Vermont shingles, is there evidence at the 0.05 level of significance that the population mean moisture content is less than 0.35 pound per 100 square feet?
d. Interpret the meaning of the p-value in (c).
e. What assumption about the population distribution is needed in order to conduct the t tests in (a) and (c)?
f. Construct histograms, boxplots, or normal probability plots to evaluate the assumption made in (a) and (c).
g. Do you think that the assumption needed in order to conduct the t tests in (a) and (c) is valid? Explain.

9.77 Studies conducted by the manufacturer of Boston and Vermont asphalt shingles have shown product weight to be a major factor in the customer's perception of quality. Moreover, the weight represents the amount of raw materials being used and is therefore very important to the company from a cost standpoint. The last stage of the assembly line packages the shingles before the packages are placed on wooden pallets. Once a pallet is full (a pallet for most brands holds 16 squares of shingles), it is weighed, and the measurement is recorded. The file Pallet contains the weight (in pounds) from a sample of 368 pallets of Boston shingles and 330 pallets of Vermont shingles.
a. For the Boston shingles, is there evidence that the population mean weight is different from 3,150 pounds?
b. Interpret the meaning of the p-value in (a).
c. For the Vermont shingles, is there evidence that the population mean weight is different from 3,700 pounds?
d. Interpret the meaning of the p-value in (c).
e. In (a) through (d), do you have to worry about the normality assumption? Explain.

9.78 The manufacturer of Boston and Vermont asphalt shingles provides its customers with a 20-year warranty on most of its products. To determine whether a shingle will last through the warranty period, accelerated-life testing is conducted at the manufacturing plant. Accelerated-life testing exposes the shingle to the stresses it would be subject to in a lifetime of normal use in a laboratory setting via an experiment that takes only a few minutes to conduct. In this test, a shingle is repeatedly scraped with a brush for a short period of time, and the shingle granules removed by the brushing are weighed (in grams). Shingles that experience low amounts of granule loss are expected to last longer in normal use than shingles that experience high amounts of granule loss. The file `Granule` contains a sample of 170 measurements made on the company's Boston shingles and 140 measurements made on Vermont shingles.

a. For the Boston shingles, is there evidence that the population mean granule loss is different from 0.50 grams?
b. Interpret the meaning of the *p*-value in (a).
c. For the Vermont shingles, is there evidence that the population mean granule loss is different from 0.50 grams?
d. Interpret the meaning of the *p*-value in (c).
e. In (a) through (d), do you have to worry about the normality assumption? Explain.

REPORT WRITING EXERCISE

9.79 Referring to the results of Problems 9.76 through 9.78 concerning Boston and Vermont shingles, write a report that evaluates the moisture level, weight, and granule loss of the two types of shingles.

MANAGING ASHLAND MULTICOMM SERVICES

Continuing its monitoring of the upload speed first described in the Chapter 6 Managing Ashland MultiComm Services case on page 274, the technical operations department wants to ensure that the mean target upload speed for all Internet service subscribers is at least 0.97 on a standard scale in which the target value is 1.0. Each day, upload speed was measured 50 times, with the following results (stored in `AMS9`).

0.854 1.023 1.005 1.030 1.219 0.977 1.044 0.778 1.122 1.114
1.091 1.086 1.141 0.931 0.723 0.934 1.060 1.047 0.800 0.889
1.012 0.695 0.869 0.734 1.131 0.993 0.762 0.814 1.108 0.805
1.223 1.024 0.884 0.799 0.870 0.898 0.621 0.818 1.113 1.286
1.052 0.678 1.162 0.808 1.012 0.859 0.951 1.112 1.003 0.972

Calculate the sample statistics and determine whether there is evidence that the population mean upload speed is less than 0.97. Write a memo to management that summarizes your conclusions.

DIGITAL CASE

Apply your knowledge about hypothesis testing in this Digital Case, which continues the cereal-fill-packaging dispute first discussed in the Digital Case from Chapter 7.

In response to the negative statements made by the Concerned Consumers About Cereal Cheaters (CCACC) in the Chapter 7 Digital Case, Oxford Cereals recently conducted an experiment concerning cereal packaging. The company claims that the results of the experiment refute the CCACC allegations that Oxford Cereals has been cheating consumers by packaging cereals at less than labeled weights.

Open **OxfordCurrentNews.pdf**, a portfolio of current news releases from Oxford Cereals. Review the relevant press releases and supporting documents. Then answer the following questions:

1. Are the results of the experiment valid? Why or why not? If you were conducting the experiment, is there anything you would change?
2. Do the results support the claim that Oxford Cereals is not cheating its customers?
3. Is the claim of the Oxford Cereals CEO that many cereal boxes contain *more* than 368 grams surprising? Is it true?
4. Could there ever be a circumstance in which the results of the Oxford Cereals experiment *and* the CCACC's results are both correct? Explain

REFERENCES

1. Bradley, J. V., *Distribution-Free Statistical Tests* (Upper Saddle River, NJ: Prentice Hall, 1968).
2. Daniel, W., *Applied Nonparametric Statistics*, 2nd ed. (Boston: Houghton Mifflin, 1990).
3. *Microsoft Excel 2010* (Redmond, WA: Microsoft Corp., 2007).
4. *Minitab Release 16* (State College, PA: Minitab Inc., 2010).

CHAPTER 9 EXCEL GUIDE

EG9.1 FUNDAMENTALS of HYPOTHESIS-TESTING METHODOLOGY

PHStat2 Use **Z Test for the Mean, sigma known** to perform the Z test for the mean when σ is known. For example, to perform the Z test for the Figure 9.5 cereal-filling example on page 364, select **PHStat → One-Sample Tests → Z Test for the Mean, sigma known**. In the procedure's dialog box (shown below):

1. Enter **368** as the **Null Hypothesis**.
2. Enter **0.05** as the **Level of Significance**.
3. Enter **15** as the **Population Standard Deviation**.
4. Click **Sample Statistics Known** and enter **25** as the **Sample Size** and **372.5** as the **Sample Mean**.
5. Click **Two-Tail Test**.
6. Enter a **Title** and click **OK**.

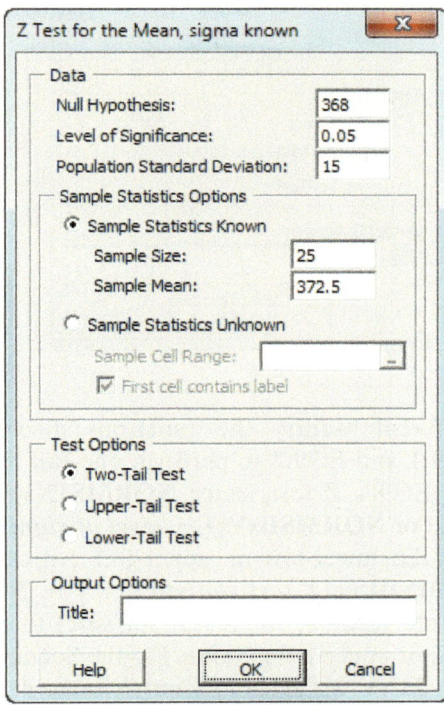

For problems that use unsummarized data, click **Sample Statistics Unknown** in step 4 and enter the cell range of the unsummarized data as the **Sample Cell Range**.

In-Depth Excel Use the **COMPUTE worksheet** of the **Z Mean workbook**, shown in Figure 9.5 on page 364, as a template for performing the two-tail Z test. The worksheet contains the data for the Section 9.1 cereal-filling example. For other problems, change the values in cells B4 through B8 as necessary.

In cells B15 and B16, **NORMSINV**(*level of significance / 2*) and **NORMSINV**(1 - *level of significance / 2*) computes the lower and upper critical values. The expression 2 * (1 − NORMSDIST (*absolute value of the Z test statistic*)) computes the *p*-value for the two-tail test in cell B17. In cell A18, **IF**(*p-value < level of significance, display reject message, display do not reject message*) determines which message to display in the cell.

EG9.2 *t* TEST of HYPOTHESIS for the MEAN (σ UNKNOWN)

PHStat2 Use *t* **Test for the Mean, sigma unknown** to perform the *t* test for the mean when σ is unknown. For example, to perform the *t* test for the Figure 9.7 sales invoice example on page 370, select **PHStat → One-Sample Tests → t Test for the Mean, sigma unknown**. In the procedure's dialog box (shown on the top of page 390):

1. Enter **120** as the **Null Hypothesis**.
2. Enter **0.05** as the **Level of Significance**.
3. Click **Sample Statistics Known** and enter **12** as the **Sample Size**, **112.85** as the **Sample Mean**, and **20.8** as the **Sample Standard Deviation**.
4. Click **Two-Tail Test**.
5. Enter a **Title** and click **OK**.

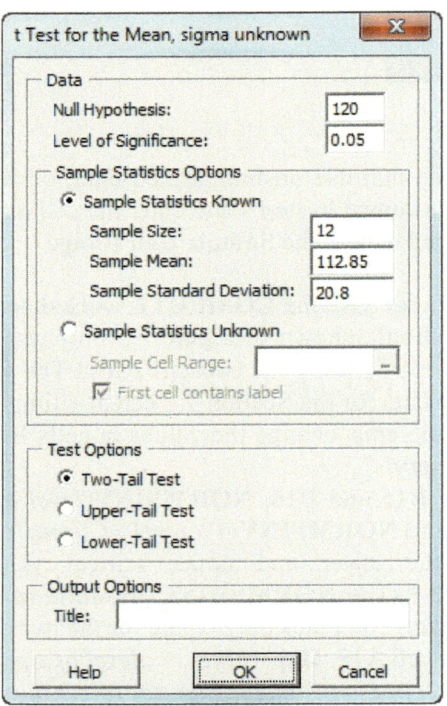

Tests → **t Test for the Mean, sigma unknown**. In the procedure's dialog box (shown below):

1. Enter **174.22** as the **Null Hypothesis**.
2. Enter **0.05** as the **Level of Significance**.
3. Click **Sample Statistics Known** and enter **25** as the **Sample Size**, **162.96** as the **Sample Mean**, and **20.2** as the **Sample Standard Deviation**.
4. Click **Lower-Tail Test**.
5. Enter a **Title** and click **OK**.

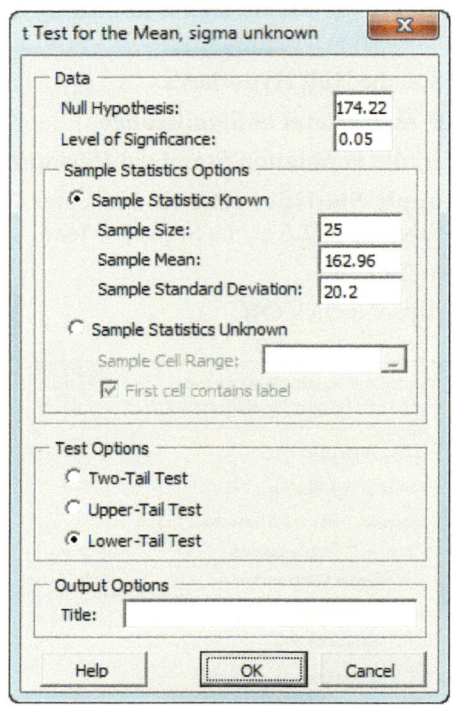

For problems that use unsummarized data, click **Sample Statistics Unknown** in step 3 and enter the cell range of the unsummarized data as the **Sample Cell Range**.

In-Depth Excel Use the **COMPUTE worksheet** of the **T mean workbook**, shown in Figure 9.7 on page 370, as a template for performing the two-tail *t* test. The worksheet contains the data for the Section 9.2 sales invoice example. For other problems, change the values in cells B4 through B8 as necessary.

In cells B16 and B17, the worksheet uses the expressions **-TINV**(*level of significance*, *degrees of freedom*) and **TINV**(*level of significance*, *degrees of freedom*) to compute the lower and upper critical values, respectively. In cell B18, the worksheet uses **TDIST**(*absolute value of the t test statistic*, *degrees of freedom*, **2**) to compute the *p*-value. The worksheet also uses an **IF** function to determine which message to display in cell A19.

EG9.3 ONE-TAIL TESTS

PHStat2 Click either **Lower-Tail Test** or **Upper-Tail Test** in the procedure dialog boxes discussed in Sections EG9.1 and EG9.2 to perform a one-tail test. For example, to perform the Figure 9.12 one-tail test for the drive-through time study example on page 376, select **PHStat → One-Sample**

In-Depth Excel Modify the functions discussed in Section EG9.1 and EG9.2 to perform one-tail tests. For the Section EG9.1 *Z* test, enter **NORMSINV**(*level of significance*) or **NORMSINV**(**1** − *level of significance*) to compute the lower-tail or upper-tail critical value. Enter **NORMSDIST**(*Z test statistic*) or **1** − **NORMSDIST**(*absolute value of the Z test statistic*) to compute the lower-tail or upper-tail *p*-value. For the Section EG9.2 *t* test, enter **-TINV**(**2** * *level of significance*, *degrees of freedom*) or **TINV**(**2** * *level of significance*, *degrees of freedom*) to compute the lower-tail or upper-tail critical values.

Computing *p*-values is more complex. If the *t* test statistic is less than zero, the lower-tail *p*-value is equal to **TDIST**(*absolute value of the t test statistic*, *degrees of* *freedom*, **1**), and the upper-tail *p*-value is equal to **1 − TDIST**(*absolute value of the t test statistic*, *degrees of freedom*, **1**). If the *t* test statistic is greater than or equal to zero, the values are reversed.

Use the **COMPUTE_LOWER worksheet** or the **COMPUTE_UPPER worksheet** of the **Z Mean workbook** or the **T mean workbook** as a template for performing one-tail *t* tests. Open the **COMPUTE_ALL_FORMULAS worksheet** of either workbook to examine all formulas.

EG9.4 Z TEST of HYPOTHESIS for the PROPORTION

PHStat2 Use **Z Test for the Proportion** to perform the *Z* test of hypothesis for the proportion. For example, to perform the *Z* test for the Figure 9.15 vacation Internet access study example on page 381, select **PHStat → One-Sample Tests → Z Test for the Proportion**. In the procedure's dialog box (shown in the right column):

1. Enter **0.75** as the **Null Hypothesis**.
2. Enter **0.05** as the **Level of Significance**.
3. Enter **1540** as the **Number of Items of Interest**.
4. Enter **2000** as the **Sample Size**.
5. Click **Two-Tail Test**.
6. Enter a **Title** and click **OK**.

In-Depth Excel Use the **COMPUTE worksheet** of the **Z Proportion workbook**, shown in Figure 9.15 on page 381, as a template for performing the two-tail *Z* test. The worksheet contains the data for the Section 9.4 vacation Internet

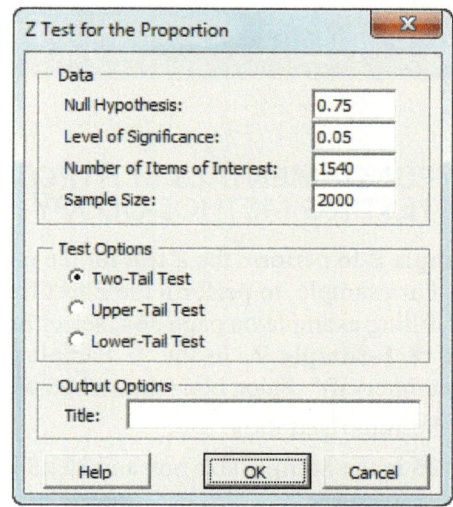

access study example. For other problems, change the values in cells B4 through B7 as necessary.

The worksheet uses **NORMSINV**(*level of significance / 2*) and **NORMSINV(1 - *level of significance / 2*)** to compute the lower and upper critical values in cells B15 and B16. In cell B17, the worksheet uses the expression **2 * (1 − NORMSDIST**(*absolute value of the Z test statistic*) to compute the *p*-value. The worksheet also uses an **IF** function to determine which message to display in cell A18.

Use the **COMPUTE_LOWER worksheet** or **COMPUTE_UPPER worksheet** as a template for performing one-tail tests. Open to the **COMPUTE_ALL_FORMULAS worksheet** to examine all formulas in the one-tail test worksheets.

CHAPTER 9 MINITAB GUIDE

MG9.1 FUNDAMENTALS of HYPOTHESIS-TESTING METHODOLOGY

Use **1-Sample Z** to perform the Z test for the mean when σ is known. For example, to perform the Z test for the Figure 9.5 cereal-filling example on page 364, select **Stat → Basic Statistics → 1-Sample Z**. In the "1-Sample Z (Test and Confidence Interval)" dialog box (shown below):

1. Click **Summarized data**.
2. Enter **25** in the **Sample size** box and **372.5** in the **Mean** box.
3. Enter **15** in the **Standard deviation** box.
4. Check **Perform hypothesis test** and enter **368** in the **Hypothesized mean** box.
5. Click **Options**.

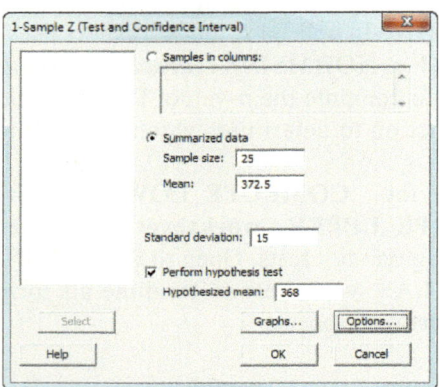

In the 1-Sample Z - Options dialog box:

6. Enter **95.0** in the **Confidence level** box.
7. Select **not equal** from the **Alternative** drop-down list.
8. Click **OK**.
9. Back in the original dialog box, click **OK**.

For problems that use unsummarized data, open the worksheet that contains the data and replace steps 1 and 2 with these steps:

1. Click **Samples in columns**.
2. Enter the name of the column containing the unsummarized data in the **Samples in column** box.

MG9.2 *t* TEST of HYPOTHESIS for the MEAN (σ UNKNOWN)

Use ***t* Test for the Mean, sigma unknown** to perform the *t* test for the mean when σ is unknown. For example, to perform the *t* test for the Figure 9.7 sales invoice example on page 370, select **Stat → Basic Statistics → 1-Sample t**.

In the 1-Sample t (Test and Confidence Interval) dialog box (shown below):

1. Click **Summarized data**.
2. Enter **12** in the **Sample size** box, **112.85** in the **Mean** box, and **20.8** in the **Standard deviation** box.
3. Check **Perform hypothesis test** and enter **120** in the **Hypothesized mean** box.
4. Click **Options**.

In the 1-Sample t - Options dialog box:

5. Enter **95.0** in the **Confidence level** box.
6. Select **not equal** from the **Alternative** drop-down list.
7. Click **OK**.
8. Back in the original dialog box, click **OK**.

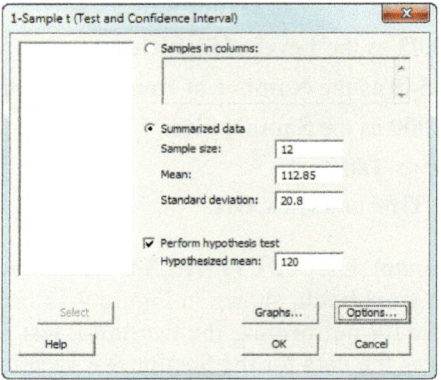

For problems that use unsummarized data, open the worksheet that contains the data and replace steps 1 and 2 with these steps:

1. Click **Samples in columns**.
2. Enter the name of the column containing the unsummarized in the **Samples in column** box.

To create a boxplot of the unsummarized data, replace step 8 with the following steps 8 through 10:

8. Back in the original dialog box, click **Graphs**.
9. In the 1-Sample t - Graphs dialog box, check **Boxplot of data** and then click **OK**.
10. Back in the original dialog box, click **OK.**

MG9.3 ONE-TAIL TESTS

To perform a one-tail test for **1-Sample Z**, select **less than** or **greater than** from the drop-down list in step 7 of the Section MG9.1 instructions.

To perform a one-tail test for **1-Sample t**, select **less than** or **greater than** from the drop-down list in step 6 of the Section MG9.2 instructions.

MG9.4 Z TEST of HYPOTHESIS for the PROPORTION

Use **1 Proportion** to perform the Z test of hypothesis for the proportion. For example, to perform the Z test for the Figure 9.15 vacation Internet access study example on page 381, select **Stat → Basic Statistics → 1 Proportion**. In the 1 Proportion (Test and Confidence Interval) dialog box (shown below):

1. Click **Summarized data**.
2. Enter **1540** in the **Number of events** box and **2000** in the **Number of trials** box.
3. Check **Perform hypothesis test** and enter **0.75** in the **Hypothesized proportion** box.
4. Click **Options**.

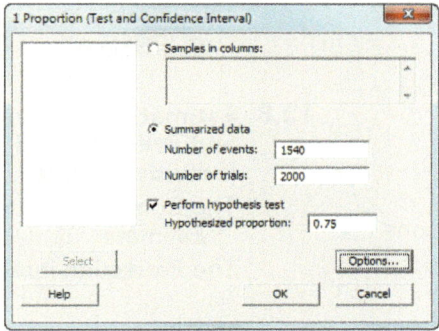

In the 1-Proportion - Options dialog box (shown in right column):

5. Enter **95.0** in the **Confidence level** box.
6. Select **not equal** from the **Alternative** drop-down list.
7. Check **Use test and interval based on normal distribution**.
8. Click **OK**.

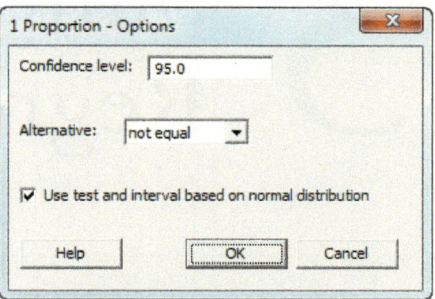

9. Back in the original dialog box, click **OK**.

To perform a one-tail test, select **less than** or **greater than** from the drop-down list in step 6. For problems that use unsummarized data, open the worksheet that contains the data and replace steps 1 and 2 with these steps:

1. Click **Samples in columns**.
2. Enter the name of the column containing the unsummarized in the **Samples in column** box.

13 Simple Linear Regression

USING STATISTICS @ Sunflowers Apparel

13.1 Types of Regression Models

13.2 Determining the Simple Linear Regression Equation
The Least-Squares Method
Predictions in Regression Analysis: Interpolation Versus Extrapolation
Computing the Y Intercept, b_0, and the Slope, b_1

VISUAL EXPLORATIONS: Exploring Simple Linear Regression Coefficients

13.3 Measures of Variation
Computing the Sum of Squares
The Coefficient of Determination
Standard Error of the Estimate

13.4 Assumptions

13.5 Residual Analysis
Evaluating the Assumptions

13.6 Measuring Autocorrelation: The Durbin-Watson Statistic
Residual Plots to Detect Autocorrelation
The Durbin-Watson Statistic

13.7 Inferences About the Slope and Correlation Coefficient
t Test for the Slope
F Test for the Slope
Confidence Interval Estimate for the Slope
t Test for the Correlation Coefficient

13.8 Estimation of Mean Values and Prediction of Individual Values
The Confidence Interval Estimate
The Prediction Interval

13.9 Pitfalls in Regression

Think About This: By Any Other Name

USING STATISTICS @ Sunflowers Apparel Revisited

CHAPTER 13 EXCEL GUIDE

CHAPTER 13 MINITAB GUIDE

Learning Objectives

In this chapter, you learn:

- How to use regression analysis to predict the value of a dependent variable based on an independent variable
- The meaning of the regression coefficients b_0 and b_1
- How to evaluate the assumptions of regression analysis and know what to do if the assumptions are violated
- How to make inferences about the slope and correlation coefficient
- How to estimate mean values and predict individual values

USING STATISTICS

@ Sunflowers Apparel

The sales for Sunflowers Apparel, a chain of upscale clothing stores for women, have increased during the past 12 years as the chain has expanded the number of stores. Until now, Sunflowers managers selected sites based on subjective factors, such as the availability of a good lease or the perception that a location seemed ideal for an apparel store. As the new director of planning, you need to develop a systematic approach that will lead to making better decisions during the site-selection process. As a starting point, you believe that the size of the store significantly contributes to store sales, and you want to use this relationship in the decision-making process. How can you use statistics so that you can forecast the annual sales of a proposed store based on the size of that store?

In this chapter and the next two chapters, you learn how **regression analysis** enables you to develop a model to predict the values of a numerical variable, based on the value of other variables.

In regression analysis, the variable you wish to predict is called the **dependent variable**. The variables used to make the prediction are called **independent variables**. In addition to predicting values of the dependent variable, regression analysis also allows you to identify the type of mathematical relationship that exists between a dependent variable and an independent variable, to quantify the effect that changes in the independent variable have on the dependent variable, and to identify unusual observations. For example, as the director of planning, you might want to predict sales for a Sunflowers store based on the size of the store. Other examples include predicting the monthly rent of an apartment based on its size and predicting the monthly sales of a product in a supermarket based on the amount of shelf space devoted to the product.

This chapter discusses **simple linear regression**, in which a *single* numerical independent variable, X, is used to predict the numerical dependent variable Y, such as using the size of a store to predict the annual sales of the store. Chapters 14 and 15 discuss *multiple regression models*, which use *several* independent variables to predict a numerical dependent variable, Y. For example, you could use the amount of advertising expenditures, price, and the amount of shelf space devoted to a product to predict its monthly sales.

13.1 Types of Regression Models

In Section 2.6, you used a **scatter plot** (also known as a **scatter diagram**) to examine the relationship between an X variable on the horizontal axis and a Y variable on the vertical axis. The nature of the relationship between two variables can take many forms, ranging from simple to extremely complicated mathematical functions. The simplest relationship consists of a straight-line relationship, or **linear relationship**. Figure 13.1 illustrates a straight-line relationship.

FIGURE 13.1
A straight-line relationship

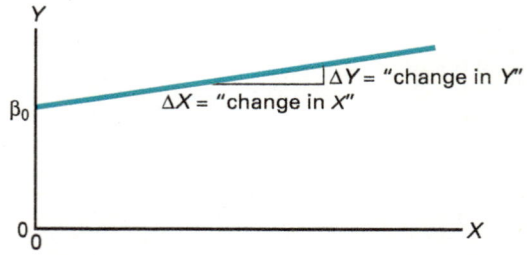

Equation (13.1) represents the straight-line (linear) model.

SIMPLE LINEAR REGRESSION MODEL

$$Y_i = \beta_0 + \beta_1 X_i + \varepsilon_i \qquad (13.1)$$

where

$\beta_0 = Y$ intercept for the population
$\beta_1 = $ slope for the population
$\varepsilon_i = $ random error in Y for observation i
$Y_i = $ dependent variable (sometimes referred to as the **response variable**) for observation i
$X_i = $ independent variable (sometimes referred to as the predictor, or **explanatory variable**) for observation i

The $Y_i = \beta_0 + \beta_1 X_i$ portion of the simple linear regression model expressed in Equation (13.1) is a straight line. The **slope** of the line, β_1, represents the expected change in Y per unit change in X. It represents the mean amount that Y changes (either positively or negatively) for a one-unit change in X. The **Y intercept**, β_0, represents the mean value of Y when X equals 0. The last component of the model, ε_i, represents the random error in Y for each observation, i. In other words, ε_i is the vertical distance of the actual value of Y_i above or below the expected value of Y_i on the line.

The selection of the proper mathematical model depends on the distribution of the X and Y values on the scatter plot. Figure 13.2 illustrates six different types of relationships.

FIGURE 13.2
Six types of relationships found in scatter plots

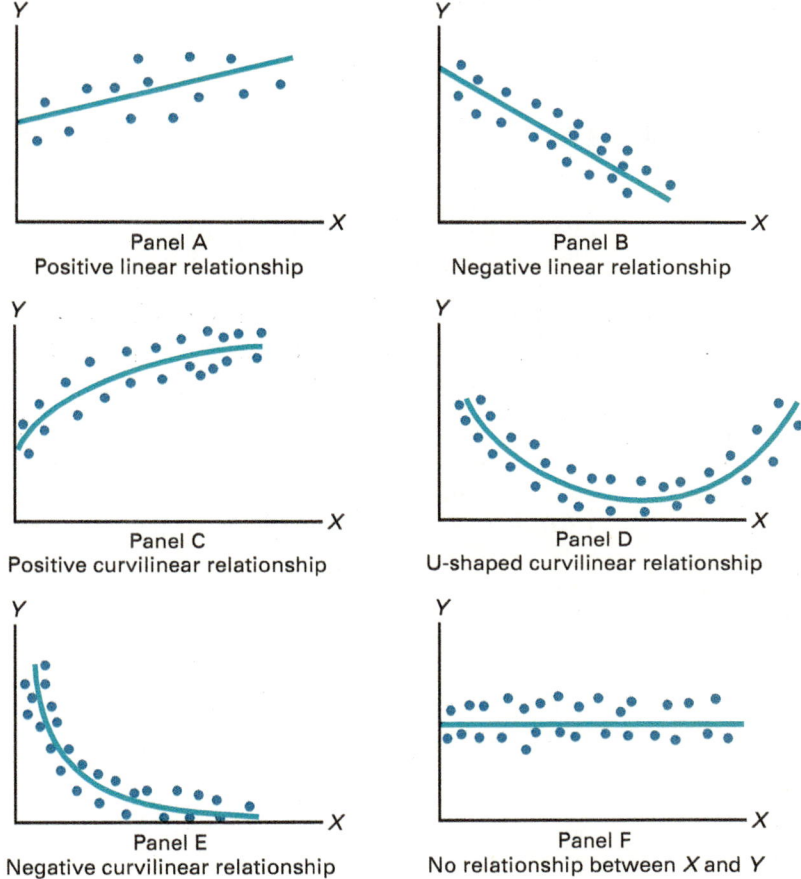

In Panel A, the values of Y are generally increasing linearly as X increases. This panel is similar to Figure 13.3 on page 554, which illustrates the positive relationship between the square footage of the store and the annual sales at branches of the Sunflowers Apparel women's clothing store chain.

Panel B is an example of a negative linear relationship. As X increases, the values of Y are generally decreasing. An example of this type of relationship might be the price of a particular product and the amount of sales.

Panel C shows a positive curvilinear relationship between X and Y. The values of Y increase as X increases, but this increase tapers off beyond certain values of X. An example of a positive curvilinear relationship might be the age and maintenance cost of a machine. As a machine gets older, the maintenance cost may rise rapidly at first but then level off beyond a certain number of years.

Panel D shows a U-shaped relationship between X and Y. As X increases, at first Y generally decreases; but as X continues to increase, Y not only stops decreasing but actually increases above its minimum value. An example of this type of relationship might be the number of errors per hour at a task and the number of hours worked. The number of errors per hour decreases as the individual becomes more proficient at the task, but then it increases beyond a certain point because of factors such as fatigue and boredom.

Panel E illustrates an exponential relationship between X and Y. In this case, Y decreases very rapidly as X first increases, but then it decreases much less rapidly as X increases further. An example of an exponential relationship could be the value of an automobile and its age. The value drops drastically from its original price in the first year, but it decreases much less rapidly in subsequent years.

Finally, Panel F shows a set of data in which there is very little or no relationship between X and Y. High and low values of Y appear at each value of X.

Although scatter plots are useful in visually displaying the mathematical form of a relationship, more sophisticated statistical procedures are available to determine the most appropriate model for a set of variables. The rest of this chapter discusses the model used when there is a *linear* relationship between variables.

13.2 Determining the Simple Linear Regression Equation

In the Sunflowers Apparel scenario on page 551, the business objective of the director of planning is to forecast annual sales for all new stores, based on store size. To examine the relationship between the store size in square feet and its annual sales, data were collected from a sample of 14 stores. Table 13.1 shows the organized data, which are stored in Site.

Figure 13.3 displays the scatter plot for the data in Table 13.1. Observe the increasing relationship between square feet (X) and annual sales (Y). As the size of the store increases,

TABLE 13.1

Square Footage (in Thousands of Square Feet) and Annual Sales (in Millions of Dollars) for a Sample of 14 Branches of Sunflowers Apparel

Store	Square Feet (Thousands)	Annual Sales (in Millions of Dollars)	Store	Square Feet (Thousands)	Annual Sales (in Millions of Dollars)
1	1.7	3.7	8	1.1	2.7
2	1.6	3.9	9	3.2	5.5
3	2.8	6.7	10	1.5	2.9
4	5.6	9.5	11	5.2	10.7
5	1.3	3.4	12	4.6	7.6
6	2.2	5.6	13	5.8	11.8
7	1.3	3.7	14	3.0	4.1

FIGURE 13.3

Scatter plot for the Sunflowers Apparel data

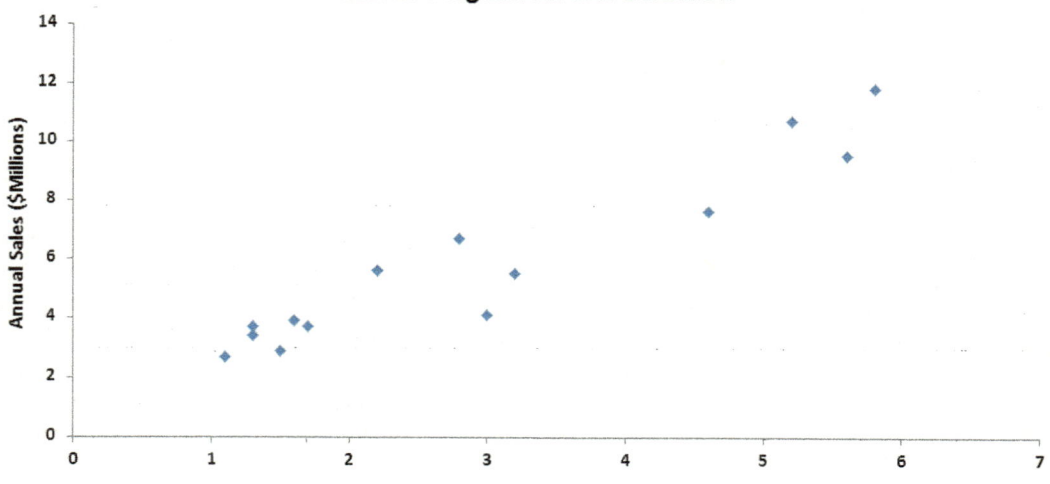

annual sales increase approximately as a straight line. Thus, you can assume that a straight line provides a useful mathematical model of this relationship. Now you need to determine the specific straight line that is the *best* fit to these data.

The Least-Squares Method

In the preceding section, a statistical model is hypothesized to represent the relationship between two variables, square footage and sales, in the entire population of Sunflowers Apparel stores. However, as shown in Table 13.1, the data are collected from a random sample of stores. If certain assumptions are valid (see Section 13.4), you can use the sample Y intercept, b_0, and the sample slope, b_1, as estimates of the respective population parameters, β_0 and β_1. Equation (13.2) uses these estimates to form the **simple linear regression equation**. This straight line is often referred to as the **prediction line**.

SIMPLE LINEAR REGRESSION EQUATION: THE PREDICTION LINE

The predicted value of Y equals the Y intercept plus the slope multiplied by the value of X.

$$\hat{Y}_i = b_0 + b_1 X_i \qquad (13.2)$$

where

$\hat{Y}_i$ = predicted value of Y for observation i
X_i = value of X for observation i
b_0 = sample Y intercept
b_1 = sample slope

Equation (13.2) requires you to determine two **regression coefficients**—b_0 (the sample Y intercept) and b_1 (the sample slope). The most common approach to finding b_0 and b_1 is using the least-squares method. This method minimizes the sum of the squared differences between the actual values (Y_i) and the predicted values ($\hat{Y}_i$) using the simple linear regression equation [i.e., the prediction line; see Equation (13.2)]. This sum of squared differences is equal to

$$\sum_{i=1}^{n}(Y_i - \hat{Y}_i)^2$$

Because $\hat{Y}_i = b_0 + b_1 X_i$,

$$\sum_{i=1}^{n}(Y_i - \hat{Y}_i)^2 = \sum_{i=1}^{n}[Y_i - (b_0 + b_1 X_i)]^2$$

Because this equation has two unknowns, b_0 and b_1, the sum of squared differences depends on the sample Y intercept, b_0, and the sample slope, b_1. The **least-squares method** determines the values of b_0 and b_1 that minimize the sum of squared differences around the prediction line. Any values for b_0 and b_1 other than those determined by the least-squares method result in a greater sum of squared differences between the actual values (Y_i) and the predicted values ($\hat{Y}_i$). Figure 13.4[1] presents the simple linear regression model for the Table 13.1 Sunflowers Apparel data.

[1]The equations used to compute these results are shown in Examples 13.3 and 13.4 on pages 558–560 and 565–566. You should use software to do these computations for large data sets, given the complex nature of the computations.

FIGURE 13.4
Excel and Minitab simple linear regression models for the Sunflowers Apparel data

	A	B	C	D	E	F	G	H	I
1	Simple Linear Regression								
2									
3	Regression Statistics								
4	Multiple R	0.9509							
5	R Square	0.9042							
6	Adjusted R Square	0.8962							
7	Standard Error	0.9664							
8	Observations	14							
9									
10	ANOVA								
11		df	SS	MS	F	Significance F			
12	Regression	1	105.7476	105.7476	113.2335	0.0000			
13	Residual	12	11.2067	0.9339					
14	Total	13	116.9543						
15									
16		Coefficients	Standard Error	t Stat	P-value	Lower 95%	Upper 95%	Lower 95.0%	Upper 95.0%
17	Intercept	0.9645	0.5262	1.8329	0.0917	-0.1820	2.1110	-0.1820	2.11095
18	Square Feet	1.6699	0.1569	10.6411	0.0000	1.3280	2.0118	1.3280	2.01177

```
Regression Analysis: Annual Sales versus Square Feet
The regression equation is
Annual Sales = 0.964 + 1.67 Square Feet

Predictor      Coef    SE Coef       T      P
Constant     0.9645     0.5262    1.83  0.092
Square Feet  1.6699     0.1569   10.64  0.000

S = 0.966380    R-Sq = 90.4%    R-Sq(adj) = 89.6%

Analysis of Variance
Source          DF       SS       MS       F      P
Regression       1   105.75   105.75  113.23  0.000
Residual Error  12    11.21     0.93
Total           13   116.95

Predicted Values for New Observations
New Obs    Fit   SE Fit      95% CI           95% PI
    1    7.644   0.309   (6.971, 8.317)   (5.433, 9.854)

Values of Predictors for New Observations
              Square
New Obs        Feet
    1          4.00
```

In Figure 13.4, observe that $b_0 = 0.9645$ and $b_1 = 1.6699$. Using Equation (13.2) on page 555, the prediction line for these data is

$$\hat{Y}_i = 0.9645 + 1.6699 X_i$$

The slope, b_1, is $+1.6699$. This means that for each increase of 1 unit in X, the predicted value of Y is estimated to increase by 1.6699 units. In other words, for each increase of 1.0 thousand square feet in the size of the store, the predicted annual sales are estimated to increase by 1.6699 millions of dollars. Thus, the slope represents the portion of the annual sales that are estimated to vary according to the size of the store.

The Y intercept, b_0, is $+0.9645$. The Y intercept represents the predicted value of Y when X equals 0. Because the square footage of the store cannot be 0, this Y intercept has little or no practical interpretation. Also, the Y intercept for this example is outside the range of the observed values of the X variable, and therefore interpretations of the value of b_0 should be made cautiously. Figure 13.5 displays the actual values and the prediction line. To illustrate a situation in which there is a direct interpretation for the Y intercept, b_0, see Example 13.1.

FIGURE 13.5
Scatter plot and prediction line for Sunflowers Apparel data

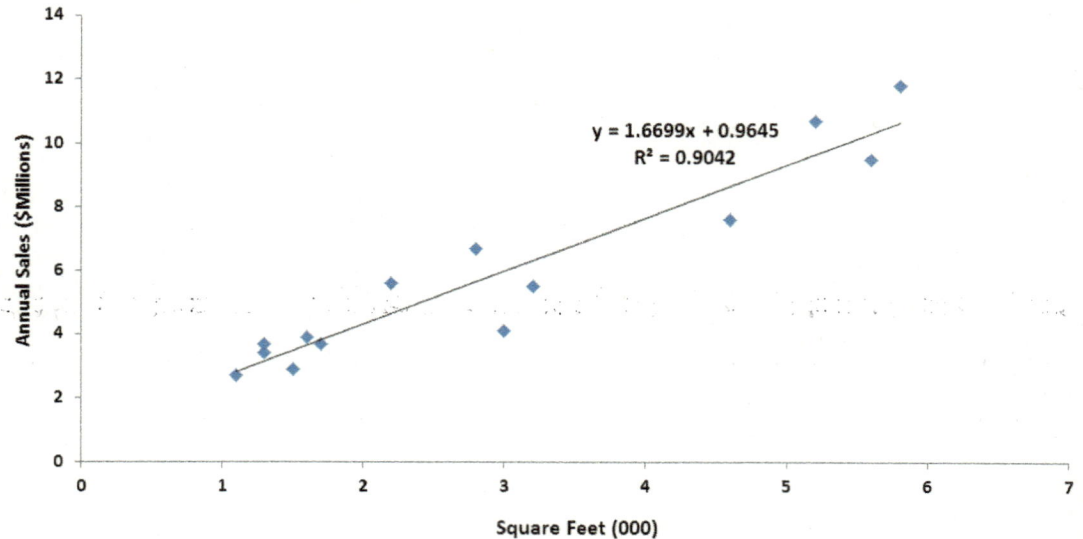

Simple Linear Regression

EXAMPLE 13.1

Interpreting the Y Intercept, b_0, and the Slope, b_1

A statistics professor wants to use the number of hours a student studies for a statistics final exam (X) to predict the final exam score (Y). A regression model was fit based on data collected from a class during the previous semester, with the following results:

$$\hat{Y}_i = 35.0 + 3X_i$$

What is the interpretation of the Y intercept, b_0, and the slope, b_1?

SOLUTION The Y intercept $b_0 = 35.0$ indicates that when the student does not study for the final exam, the predicted final exam score is 35.0. The slope $b_1 = 3$ indicates that for each increase of one hour in studying time, the predicted change in the final exam score is $+3.0$. In other words, the final exam score is predicted to increase by a mean of 3 points for each one-hour increase in studying time.

Return to the Sunflowers Apparel scenario on page 551. Example 13.2 illustrates how you use the prediction line to predict the annual sales.

EXAMPLE 13.2

Predicting Annual Sales Based on Square Footage

Use the prediction line to predict the annual sales for a store with 4,000 square feet.

SOLUTION You can determine the predicted value by substituting $X = 4$ (thousands of square feet) into the simple linear regression equation:

$$\hat{Y}_i = 0.9645 + 1.6699X_i$$
$$\hat{Y}_i = 0.9645 + 1.6699(4) = 7.644 \text{ or } \$7,644,000$$

Thus, a store with 4,000 square feet has predicted annual sales of $7,644,000.

Predictions in Regression Analysis: Interpolation Versus Extrapolation

When using a regression model for prediction purposes, you should consider only the **relevant range** of the independent variable in making predictions. This relevant range includes all values from the smallest to the largest X used in developing the regression model. Hence, when predicting Y for a given value of X, you can interpolate within this relevant range of the X values, but you should not extrapolate beyond the range of X values. When you use the square footage to predict annual sales, the square footage (in thousands of square feet) varies from 1.1 to 5.8 (see Table 13.1 on page 554). Therefore, you should predict annual sales *only* for stores whose size is between 1.1 and 5.8 thousands of square feet. Any prediction of annual sales for stores outside this range assumes that the observed relationship between sales and store size for store sizes from 1.1 to 5.8 thousand square feet is the same as for stores outside this range. For example, you cannot extrapolate the linear relationship beyond 5,800 square feet in Example 13.2. It would be improper to use the prediction line to forecast the sales for a new store containing 8,000 square feet because the relationship between sales and store size may have a point of diminishing returns. If that is true, as square footage increases beyond 5,800 square feet, the effect on sales may become smaller and smaller.

Computing the Y Intercept, b_0, and the Slope, b_1

For small data sets, you can use a hand calculator to compute the least-squares regression coefficients. Equations (13.3) and (13.4) give the values of b_0 and b_1, which minimize

$$\sum_{i=1}^{n}(Y_i - \hat{Y}_i)^2 = \sum_{i=1}^{n}[Y_i - (b_0 + b_1 X_i)]^2$$

COMPUTATIONAL FORMULA FOR THE SLOPE, b_1

$$b_1 = \frac{SSXY}{SSX} \tag{13.3}$$

where

$$SSXY = \sum_{i=1}^{n}(X_i - \bar{X})(Y_i - \bar{Y}) = \sum_{i=1}^{n}X_i Y_i - \frac{\left(\sum_{i=1}^{n}X_i\right)\left(\sum_{i=1}^{n}Y_i\right)}{n}$$

$$SSX = \sum_{i=1}^{n}(X_i - \bar{X})^2 = \sum_{i=1}^{n}X_i^2 - \frac{\left(\sum_{i=1}^{n}X_i\right)^2}{n}$$

COMPUTATIONAL FORMULA FOR THE Y INTERCEPT, b_0

$$b_0 = \bar{Y} - b_1 \bar{X} \tag{13.4}$$

where

$$\bar{Y} = \frac{\sum_{i=1}^{n} Y_i}{n}$$

$$\bar{X} = \frac{\sum_{i=1}^{n} X_i}{n}$$

EXAMPLE 13.3

Computing the Y Intercept, b_0, and the Slope, b_1

Compute the Y intercept, b_0, and the slope, b_1, for the Sunflowers Apparel data.

SOLUTION In Equations (13.3) and (13.4), five quantities need to be computed to determine b_1 and b_0. These are n, the sample size; $\sum_{i=1}^{n} X_i$, the sum of the X values; $\sum_{i=1}^{n} Y_i$, the sum of the Y values; $\sum_{i=1}^{n} X_i^2$, the sum of the squared X values; and $\sum_{i=1}^{n} X_i Y_i$, the sum of the product of X and Y. For the Sunflowers Apparel data, the number of square feet (X) is used to predict the annual sales (Y) in a store. Table 13.2 presents the computations of the sums needed for the site selection problem. The table also includes $\sum_{i=1}^{n} Y_i^2$, the sum of the squared Y values that will be used to compute SST in Section 13.3.

TABLE 13.2

Computations for the Sunflowers Apparel Data

Store	Square Feet (X)	Annual Sales (Y)	X^2	Y^2	XY
1	1.7	3.7	2.89	13.69	6.29
2	1.6	3.9	2.56	15.21	6.24
3	2.8	6.7	7.84	44.89	18.76
4	5.6	9.5	31.36	90.25	53.20
5	1.3	3.4	1.69	11.56	4.42
6	2.2	5.6	4.84	31.36	12.32
7	1.3	3.7	1.69	13.69	4.81
8	1.1	2.7	1.21	7.29	2.97
9	3.2	5.5	10.24	30.25	17.60
10	1.5	2.9	2.25	8.41	4.35
11	5.2	10.7	27.04	114.49	55.64
12	4.6	7.6	21.16	57.76	34.96
13	5.8	11.8	33.64	139.24	68.44
14	3.0	4.1	9.00	16.81	12.30
Totals	40.9	81.8	157.41	594.90	302.30

Using Equations (13.3) and (13.4), you can compute b_0 and b_1:

$$SSXY = \sum_{i=1}^{n}(X_i - \bar{X})(Y_i - \bar{Y}) = \sum_{i=1}^{n}X_iY_i - \frac{\left(\sum_{i=1}^{n}X_i\right)\left(\sum_{i=1}^{n}Y_i\right)}{n}$$

$$SSXY = 302.3 - \frac{(40.9)(81.8)}{14}$$
$$= 302.3 - 238.97285$$
$$= 63.32715$$

$$SSX = \sum_{i=1}^{n}(X_i - \bar{X})^2 = \sum_{i=1}^{n}X_i^2 - \frac{\left(\sum_{i=1}^{n}X_i\right)^2}{n}$$

$$= 157.41 - \frac{(40.9)^2}{14}$$
$$= 157.41 - 119.48642$$
$$= 37.92358$$

Therefore,

$$b_1 = \frac{SSXY}{SSX}$$
$$= \frac{63.32715}{37.92358}$$
$$= 1.6699$$

And,

$$\bar{Y} = \frac{\sum_{i=1}^{n}Y_i}{n} = \frac{81.8}{14} = 5.842857$$

$$\bar{X} = \frac{\sum_{i=1}^{n}X_i}{n} = \frac{40.9}{14} = 2.92143$$

Therefore,

$$b_0 = \bar{Y} - b_1 \bar{X}$$
$$= 5.842857 - (1.6699)(2.92143)$$
$$= 0.9645$$

VISUAL EXPLORATIONS: Exploring Simple Linear Regression Coefficients

Use the Visual Explorations Simple Linear Regression procedure to create a prediction line that is as close as possible to the prediction line defined by the least-squares solution. Open the **Visual Explorations** add-in workbook (see Appendix Section D.4) and select **Add-ins → VisualExplorations → Simple Linear Regression**.

In the Simple Linear Regression dialog box (shown below):

1. Click for the spinner buttons for **b1 slope** (the slope of the prediction line), and **b0 intercept** (the Y intercept of the prediction line) to change the prediction line.
2. Using the visual feedback of the chart, try to create a prediction line that is as close as possible to the prediction line defined by the least-squares estimates. In other words, try to make the **Difference from Target SSE** value as small as possible. (See page 563 for an explanation of SSE.)

At any time, click **Reset** to reset the b_1 and b_0 values or **Solution** to reveal the prediction line defined by the least-squares method. Click **Finish** when you are finished with this exercise.

Using Your Own Regression Data

Select **Simple Linear Regression with your worksheet data** from the VisualExplorations menu to explore the simple linear regression coefficients using data you supply from a worksheet. In the procedure's dialog box, enter the cell range of your Y variable as the **Y Variable Cell Range** and the cell range of your X variable as the **X Variable Cell Range**. Click **First cells in both ranges contain a label**, enter a **Title**, and click **OK**. After the scatter plot appears onscreen, continue with the step 1 and step 2 instructions.

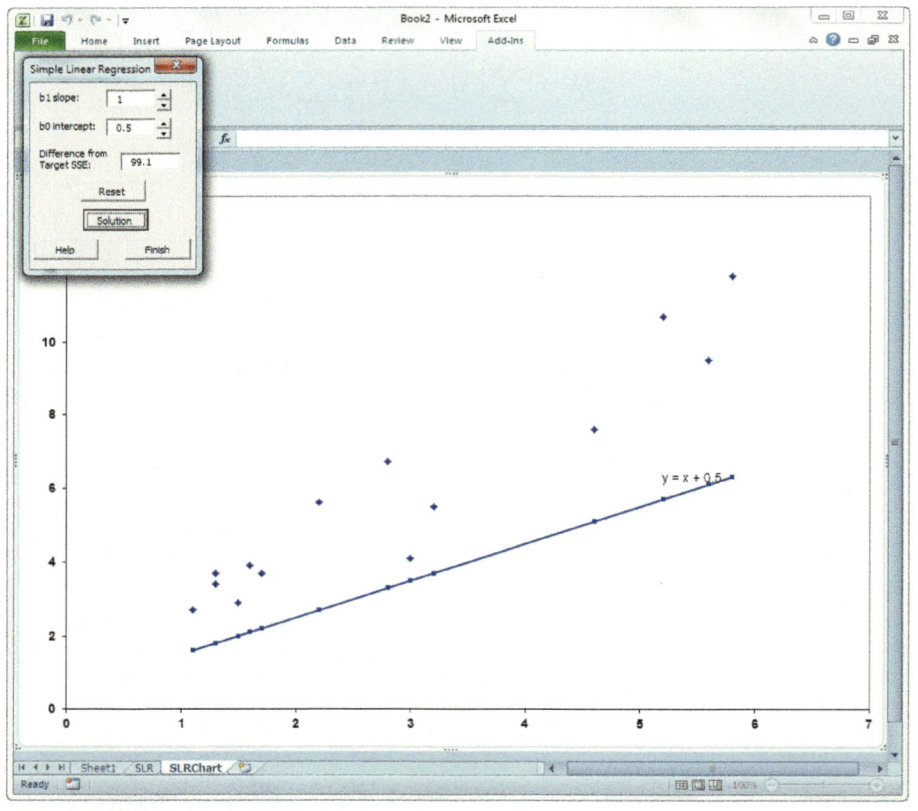

Problems for Section 13.2

LEARNING THE BASICS

13.1 Fitting a straight line to a set of data yields the following prediction line:

$$\hat{Y}_i = 2 + 5X_i$$

a. Interpret the meaning of the Y intercept, b_0.
b. Interpret the meaning of the slope, b_1.
c. Predict the value of Y for $X = 3$.

13.2 If the values of X in Problem 13.1 range from 2 to 25, should you use this model to predict the mean value of Y when X equals
a. 3?
b. −3?
c. 0?
d. 24?

13.3 Fitting a straight line to a set of data yields the following prediction line:

$$\hat{Y}_i = 16 - 0.5X_i$$

a. Interpret the meaning of the Y intercept, b_0.
b. Interpret the meaning of the slope, b_1.
c. Predict the value of Y for $X = 6$.

APPLYING THE CONCEPTS

SELF Test 13.4 The marketing manager of a large supermarket chain would like to use shelf space to predict the sales of pet food. A random sample of 12 equal-sized stores is selected, with the following results (stored in **Petfood**):

Store	Shelf Space (X) (Feet)	Weekly Sales (Y) ($)
1	5	160
2	5	220
3	5	140
4	10	190
5	10	240
6	10	260
7	15	230
8	15	270
9	15	280
10	20	260
11	20	290
12	20	310

a. Construct a scatter plot.
For these data, $b_0 = 145$ and $b_1 = 7.4$.
b. Interpret the meaning of the slope, b_1, in this problem.
c. Predict the weekly sales of pet food for stores with 8 feet of shelf space for pet food.

13.5 Zagat's publishes restaurant ratings for various locations in the United States. The file **Restaurants** contains the Zagat rating for food, décor, service, and the cost per person for a sample of 100 restaurants located in New York City and in a suburb of New York City. Develop a regression model to predict the price per person, based on a variable that represents the sum of the ratings for food, décor, and service.
Sources: Extracted from *Zagat Survey 2010, New York City Restaurants;* and *Zagat Survey 2009–2010, Long Island Restaurants.*

a. Construct a scatter plot.
For these data, $b_0 = -28.1975$ and $b_1 = 1.2409$.
b. Assuming a linear cost relationship, use the least-squares method to compute the regression coefficients b_0 and b_1.
c. Interpret the meaning of the Y intercept, b_0, and the slope, b_1, in this problem.
d. Predict the cost per person for a restaurant with a summated rating of 50.

13.6 The owner of a moving company typically has his most experienced manager predict the total number of labor hours that will be required to complete an upcoming move. This approach has proved useful in the past, but the owner has the business objective of developing a more accurate method of predicting labor hours. In a preliminary effort to provide a more accurate method, the owner has decided to use the number of cubic feet moved as the independent variable and has collected data for 36 moves in which the origin and destination were within the borough of Manhattan in New York City and in which the travel time was an insignificant portion of the hours worked. The data are stored in **Moving**.
a. Construct a scatter plot.
b. Assuming a linear relationship, use the least-squares method to determine the regression coefficients b_0 and b_1.
c. Interpret the meaning of the slope, b_1, in this problem.
d. Predict the labor hours for moving 500 cubic feet.

13.7 A critically important aspect of customer service in a supermarket is the waiting time at the checkout (defined as the time the customer enters the line until he or she is served). Data were collected during time periods in which a constant number of checkout counters were open. The total number of customers in the store and the waiting times (in minutes) were recorded. The results are stored in **Supermarket**.
a. Construct a scatter plot.
b. Assuming a linear relationship, use the least-squares method to determine the regression coefficients b_0 and b_1.
c. Interpret the meaning of the slope, b_1, in this problem.
d. Predict the waiting time when there are 20 customers in the store.

13.8 The value of a sports franchise is directly related to the amount of revenue that a franchise can generate. The file **BBRevenue** represents the value in 2010 (in millions of dollars) and the annual revenue (in millions of dollars) for the 30 major league baseball franchises. (Data extracted from **www.forbes.com/2010/04/07/most-valuable-baseball-teams-business-sportsmoney-baseball-valuations-10_values.html**.) Suppose you want to develop a simple linear regression model to predict franchise value based on annual revenue generated.

a. Construct a scatter plot.
b. Use the least-squares method to determine the regression coefficients b_0 and b_1.
c. Interpret the meaning of b_0 and b_1 in this problem.
d. Predict the value of a baseball franchise that generates $150 million of annual revenue.

13.9 An agent for a residential real estate company in a large city would like to be able to predict the monthly rental cost for apartments, based on the size of an apartment, as defined by square footage. The agent selects a sample of 25 apartments in a particular residential neighborhood and gathers the following data (stored in Rent).

Rent ($)	Size (Square Feet)
950	850
1,600	1,450
1,200	1,085
1,500	1,232
950	718
1,700	1,485
1,650	1,136
935	726
875	700
1,150	956
1,400	1,100
1,650	1,285
2,300	1,985
1,800	1,369
1,400	1,175
1,450	1,225
1,100	1,245
1,700	1,259
1,200	1,150
1,150	896
1,600	1,361
1,650	1,040
1,200	755
800	1,000
1,750	1,200

a. Construct a scatter plot.
b. Use the least-squares method to determine the regression coefficients b_0 and b_1.
c. Interpret the meaning of b_0 and b_1 in this problem.
d. Predict the monthly rent for an apartment that has 1,000 square feet.
e. Why would it not be appropriate to use the model to predict the monthly rent for apartments that have 500 square feet?
f. Your friends Jim and Jennifer are considering signing a lease for an apartment in this residential neighborhood. They are trying to decide between two apartments, one with 1,000 square feet for a monthly rent of $1,275 and the other with 1,200 square feet for a monthly rent of $1,425. Based on (a) through (d), which apartment do you think is a better deal?

13.10 A company that holds the DVD distribution rights to movies previously released only in theaters wants to estimate sales revenue of DVDs based on box office success. The box office gross (in $millions) for each of 22 movies in the year that they were released and the DVD revenue (in $millions) in the following year are shown below and stored in Movie.

Title	Gross	DVD Revenue
Bolt	109.92	81.60
Madagascar: Escape 2 Africa	177.02	107.54
Quantum of Solace	166.82	44.41
Beverly Hills Chihuahua	93.78	60.21
Marley and Me	106.66	62.82
High School Musical 3 Senior Year	90.22	58.81
Bedtime Stories	85.54	48.79
Role Models	66.70	38.78
Pineapple Express	87.34	44.67
Eagle Eye	101.40	34.88
Fireproof	33.26	31.05
Momma Mia!	144.13	33.14
Seven Pounds	60.15	27.12
Australia	46.69	28.16
Valkyrie	60.73	26.43
Saw V	56.75	26.10
The Curious Case of Benjamin Button	79.30	42.04
Max Payne	40.68	25.03
Body of Lies	39.32	21.45
Nights in Rodanthe	41.80	17.51
Lakeview Terrace	39.26	21.08
The Spirit	17.74	18.78

Sources: Data extracted from **www.the-numbers.com/market/movies2008.php**; and **www.the-numbers.com/dvd/charts/annual/2009.php**.

For these data,
a. construct a scatter plot.
b. assuming a linear relationship, use the least-squares method to determine the regression coefficients b_0 and b_1.
c. interpret the meaning of the slope, b_1, in this problem.
d. predict the sales revenue for a movie DVD that had a box office gross of $75 million.

13.3 Measures of Variation

When using the least-squares method to determine the regression coefficients for a set of data, you need to compute three measures of variation. The first measure, the **total sum of squares** (**SST**), is a measure of variation of the Y_i values around their mean, $\bar{Y}$. The **total variation**, or total sum of squares, is subdivided into **explained variation** and **unexplained variation**. The explained variation, or **regression sum of squares (SSR)**, represents variation that is explained by the relationship between X and Y, and the unexplained variation, or **error sum of squares** (**SSE**), represents variation due to factors other than the relationship between X and Y. Figure 13.6 shows these different measures of variation.

FIGURE 13.6
Measures of variation

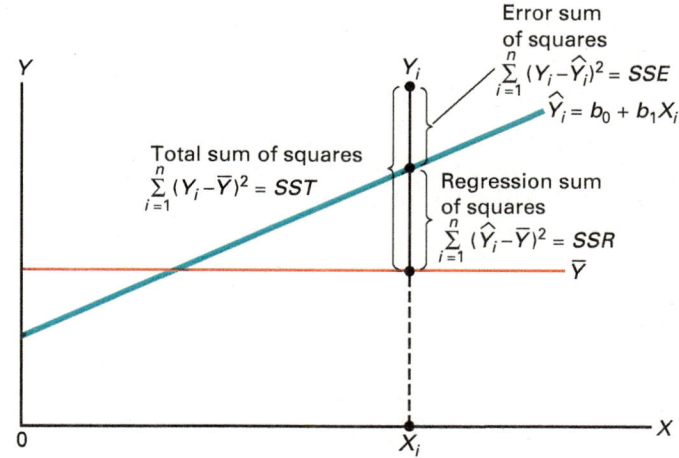

Computing the Sum of Squares

The regression sum of squares (SSR) is based on the difference between $\hat{Y}_i$ (the predicted value of Y from the prediction line) and $\bar{Y}$ (the mean value of Y). The error sum of squares (SSE) represents the part of the variation in Y that is not explained by the regression. It is based on the difference between Y_i and $\hat{Y}_i$ Equations (13.5), (13.6), (13.7), and (13.8) define these measures of variation and the total sum of squares (SST).

> **MEASURES OF VARIATION IN REGRESSION**
>
> The total sum of squares is equal to the regression sum of squares (SSR) plus the error sum of squares (SSE).
>
> $$SST = SSR + SSE \tag{13.5}$$

> **TOTAL SUM OF SQUARES (SST)**
>
> The total sum of squares (SST) is equal to the sum of the squared differences between each observed value of Y and the mean value of Y.
>
> $$SST = \text{Total sum of squares}$$
> $$= \sum_{i=1}^{n}(Y_i - \bar{Y})^2 \tag{13.6}$$

REGRESSION SUM OF SQUARES (SSR)

The regression sum of squares (SSR) is equal to the sum of the squared differences between each predicted value of Y and the mean value of Y.

$$SSR = \text{Explained variation or regression sum of squares}$$

$$= \sum_{i=1}^{n} (\hat{Y}_i - \bar{Y})^2 \qquad (13.7)$$

ERROR SUM OF SQUARES (SSE)

The error sum of squares (SSE) is equal to the sum of the squared differences between each observed value of Y and the predicted value of Y.

$$SSE = \text{Unexplained variation or error sum of squares}$$

$$= \sum_{i=1}^{n} (Y_i - \hat{Y}_i)^2 \qquad (13.8)$$

Figure 13.7 shows the sum of squares portion of the Figure 13.4 results for the Sunflowers Apparel data. The total variation, SST, is equal to 116.9543. This amount is subdivided into the sum of squares explained by the regression (SSR), equal to 105.7476, and the sum of squares unexplained by the regression (SSE), equal to 11.2067. From Equation (13.5) on page 563:

$$SST = SSR + SSE$$

$$116.9543 = 105.7476 + 11.2067$$

FIGURE 13.7
Excel and Minitab sum of squares portion for the Sunflowers Apparel data

	A	B	C	D	E	F
10	ANOVA					
11		df	SS	MS	F	Significance F
12	Regression	1	105.7476	105.7476	113.2335	0.0000
13	Residual	12	11.2067	0.9339		
14	Total	13	116.9543			

```
Analysis of Variance
Source          DF      SS      MS       F       P
Regression       1   105.75  105.75  113.23   0.000
Residual Error  12    11.21    0.93
Total           13   116.95
```

The Coefficient of Determination

By themselves, SSR, SSE, and SST provide little information. However, the ratio of the regression sum of squares (SSR) to the total sum of squares (SST) measures the proportion of variation in Y that is explained by the independent variable X in the regression model. This ratio, called the coefficient of determination, r^2, is defined in Equation (13.9).

COEFFICIENT OF DETERMINATION

The coefficient of determination is equal to the regression sum of squares (i.e., explained variation) divided by the total sum of squares (i.e., total variation).

$$r^2 = \frac{\text{Regression sum of squares}}{\text{Total sum of squares}} = \frac{SSR}{SST} \qquad (13.9)$$

The **coefficient of determination** measures the proportion of variation in Y that is explained by the variation in the independent variable X in the regression model.

For the Sunflowers Apparel data, with $SSR = 105.7476$, $SSE = 11.2067$, and $SST = 116.9543$,

$$r^2 = \frac{105.7476}{116.9543} = 0.9042$$

Therefore, 90.42% of the variation in annual sales is explained by the variability in the size of the store as measured by the square footage. This large r^2 indicates a strong linear relationship between these two variables because the regression model has explained 90.42% of the variability in predicting annual sales. Only 9.58% of the sample variability in annual sales is due to factors other than what is accounted for by the linear regression model that uses square footage.

Figure 13.8 presents the regression statistics table portion of the Figure 13.4 results for the Sunflowers Apparel data. This table contains the coefficient of determination (labeled R Square in Excel and R-Sq in Minitab).

FIGURE 13.8 Excel and Minitab regression statistics for the Sunflowers Apparel data

	A	B
3	**Regression Statistics**	
4	Multiple R	0.9509
5	R Square	0.9042
6	Adjusted R Square	0.8962
7	Standard Error	0.9664
8	Observations	14

```
Predictor      Coef     SE Coef       T        P
Constant     0.9645     0.5262     1.83    0.092
Square Feet  1.6699     0.1569    10.64    0.000

S = 0.966380    R-Sq = 90.4%    R-Sq(adj) = 89.6%
```

EXAMPLE 13.4
Computing the Coefficient of Determination

Compute the coefficient of determination, r^2, for the Sunflowers Apparel data.

SOLUTION You can compute SST, SSR, and SSE, which are defined in Equations (13.6), (13.7), and (13.8) on pages 563 and 564, by using Equations (13.10), (13.11), and (13.12).

COMPUTATIONAL FORMULA FOR SST

$$SST = \sum_{i=1}^{n}(Y_i - \bar{Y})^2 = \sum_{i=1}^{n} Y_i^2 - \frac{\left(\sum_{i=1}^{n} Y_i\right)^2}{n} \tag{13.10}$$

COMPUTATIONAL FORMULA FOR SSR

$$SSR = \sum_{i=1}^{n}(\hat{Y}_i - \bar{Y})^2$$

$$= b_0 \sum_{i=1}^{n} Y_i + b_1 \sum_{i=1}^{n} X_i Y_i - \frac{\left(\sum_{i=1}^{n} Y_i\right)^2}{n} \tag{13.11}$$

COMPUTATIONAL FORMULA FOR SSE

$$SSE = \sum_{i=1}^{n}(Y_i - \hat{Y}_i)^2 = \sum_{i=1}^{n} Y_i^2 - b_0 \sum_{i=1}^{n} Y_i - b_1 \sum_{i=1}^{n} X_i Y_i \tag{13.12}$$

Using the summary results from Table 13.2 on page 559,

$$SST = \sum_{i=1}^{n}(Y_i - \bar{Y})^2 = \sum_{i=1}^{n}Y_i^2 - \frac{\left(\sum_{i=1}^{n}Y_i\right)^2}{n}$$

$$= 594.9 - \frac{(81.8)^2}{14}$$

$$= 594.9 - 477.94571$$

$$= 116.95429$$

$$SSR = \sum_{i=1}^{n}(\hat{Y}_i - \bar{Y})^2$$

$$= b_0\sum_{i=1}^{n}Y_i + b_1\sum_{i=1}^{n}X_iY_i - \frac{\left(\sum_{i=1}^{n}Y_i\right)^2}{n}$$

$$= (0.9645)(81.8) + (1.6699)(302.3) - \frac{(81.8)^2}{14}$$

$$= 105.74726$$

$$SSE = \sum_{i=1}^{n}(Y_i - \hat{Y}_i)^2$$

$$= \sum_{i=1}^{n}Y_i^2 - b_0\sum_{i=1}^{n}Y_i - b_1\sum_{i=1}^{n}X_iY_i$$

$$= 594.9 - (0.9645)(81.8) - (1.6699)(302.3)$$

$$= 11.2067$$

Therefore,

$$r^2 = \frac{105.74726}{116.95429} = 0.9042$$

Standard Error of the Estimate

Although the least-squares method produces the line that fits the data with the minimum amount of prediction error, unless all the observed data points fall on a straight line, the prediction line is not a perfect predictor. Just as all data values cannot be expected to be exactly equal to their mean, neither can all the values in a regression analysis be expected to fall exactly on the prediction line. Figure 13.5 on page 556 illustrates the variability around the prediction line for the Sunflowers Apparel data. Observe that many of the actual values of Y fall near the prediction line, but none of the values are exactly on the line.

The **standard error of the estimate** measures the variability of the actual Y values from the predicted Y values in the same way that the standard deviation in Chapter 3 measures the variability of each value around the sample mean. In other words, the standard error of the estimate is the standard deviation *around* the prediction line, whereas the standard deviation in Chapter 3 is the standard deviation *around* the sample mean. Equation (13.13) defines the standard error of the estimate, represented by the symbol S_{YX}.

> **STANDARD ERROR OF THE ESTIMATE**
>
> $$S_{YX} = \sqrt{\frac{SSE}{n-2}} = \sqrt{\frac{\sum_{i=1}^{n}(Y_i - \hat{Y}_i)^2}{n-2}} \quad (13.13)$$
>
> where
> Y_i = actual value of Y for a given X_i
> $\hat{Y}_i$ = predicted value of Y for a given X_i
> SSE = error sum of squares

From Equation (13.8) and Figure 13.4 or Figure 13.7 on pages 556 or 534, $SSE = 11.2067$. Thus,

$$S_{YX} = \sqrt{\frac{11.2067}{14-2}} = 0.9664$$

This standard error of the estimate, equal to 0.9664 millions of dollars (i.e., $966,400), is labeled Standard Error in the Figure 13.8 Excel results and S in the Minitab results. The standard error of the estimate represents a measure of the variation around the prediction line. It is measured in the same units as the dependent variable Y. The interpretation of the standard error of the estimate is similar to that of the standard deviation. Just as the standard deviation measures variability around the mean, the standard error of the estimate measures variability around the prediction line. For Sunflowers Apparel, the typical difference between actual annual sales at a store and the predicted annual sales using the regression equation is approximately $966,400.

Problems for Section 13.3

LEARNING THE BASICS

13.11 How do you interpret a coefficient of determination, r^2, equal to 0.80?

13.12 If $SSR = 36$ and $SSE = 4$, determine SST, then compute the coefficient of determination, r^2, and interpret its meaning.

13.13 If $SSR = 66$ and $SST = 88$, compute the coefficient of determination, r^2, and interpret its meaning.

13.14 If $SSE = 10$ and $SSR = 30$, compute the coefficient of determination, r^2, and interpret its meaning.

13.15 If $SSR = 120$, why is it impossible for SST to equal 110?

APPLYING THE CONCEPTS

 13.16 In Problem 13.4 on page 561, the marketing manager used shelf space for pet food to predict weekly sales (stored in Petfood). For those data, $SSR = 20,535$ and $SST = 30,025$.
a. Determine the coefficient of determination, r^2, and interpret its meaning.
b. Determine the standard error of the estimate.
c. How useful do you think this regression model is for predicting sales?

13.17 In Problem 13.5 on page 561, you used the summated rating to predict the cost of a restaurant meal (stored in Restaurants). For those data, $SSR = 6,951.3963$ and $SST = 15,890.11$
a. Determine the coefficient of determination, r^2, and interpret its meaning.
b. Determine the standard error of the estimate.
c. How useful do you think this regression model is for predicting audited sales?

13.18 In Problem 13.6 on page 561, an owner of a moving company wanted to predict labor hours, based on the

cubic feet moved (stored in Moving). Using the results of that problem,
a. determine the coefficient of determination, r^2, and interpret its meaning.
b. determine the standard error of the estimate.
c. How useful do you think this regression model is for predicting labor hours?

13.19 In Problem 13.7 on page 561, you used the number of customers to predict the waiting time at the checkout line in a supermarket (stored in Supermarket). Using the results of that problem,
a. determine the coefficient of determination, r^2, and interpret its meaning.
b. determine the standard error of the estimate.
c. How useful do you think this regression model is for predicting the waiting time at the checkout line in a supermarket?

13.20 In Problem 13.8 on page 561, you used annual revenues to predict the value of a baseball franchise (stored in BBRevenue). Using the results of that problem,
a. determine the coefficient of determination, r^2, and interpret its meaning.
b. determine the standard error of the estimate.

c. How useful do you think this regression model is for predicting the value of a baseball franchise?

13.21 In Problem 13.9 on page 562, an agent for a real estate company wanted to predict the monthly rent for apartments, based on the size of the apartment (stored in Rent). Using the results of that problem,
a. determine the coefficient of determination, r^2, and interpret its meaning.
b. determine the standard error of the estimate.
c. How useful do you think this regression model is for predicting the monthly rent?
d. Can you think of other variables that might explain the variation in monthly rent?

13.22 In Problem 13.10 on page 562, you used box office gross to predict DVD revenue (stored in Movie). Using the results of that problem,
a. determine the coefficient of determination, r^2, and interpret its meaning.
b. determine the standard error of the estimate.
c. How useful do you think this regression model is for predicting DVD revenue?
d. Can you think of other variables that might explain the variation in DVD revenue?

13.4 Assumptions

When hypothesis testing and the analysis of variance were discussed in Chapters 9 through 12, the importance of the assumptions to the validity of any conclusions reached was emphasized. The assumptions necessary for regression are similar to those of the analysis of variance because both are part of the general category of *linear models* (reference 4).

The four **assumptions of regression** (known by the acronym LINE) are as follows:

- Linearity
- Independence of errors
- Normality of error
- Equal variance

The first assumption, **linearity**, states that the relationship between variables is linear. Relationships between variables that are not linear are discussed in Chapter 15.

The second assumption, **independence of errors**, requires that the errors (ε_i) are independent of one another. This assumption is particularly important when data are collected over a period of time. In such situations, the errors in a specific time period are sometimes correlated with those of the previous time period.

The third assumption, **normality**, requires that the errors (ε_i) are normally distributed at each value of X. Like the t test and the ANOVA F test, regression analysis is fairly robust against departures from the normality assumption. As long as the distribution of the errors at each level of X is not extremely different from a normal distribution, inferences about β_0 and β_1 are not seriously affected.

The fourth assumption, **equal variance**, or **homoscedasticity**, requires that the variance of the errors (ε_i) be constant for all values of X. In other words, the variability of Y values is the same when X is a low value as when X is a high value. The equal-variance assumption is important when making inferences about β_0 and β_1. If there are serious departures from this assumption, you can use either data transformations or weighted least-squares methods (see reference 4).

13.5 Residual Analysis

Sections 13.2 and 13.3 developed a regression model using the least-squares method for the Sunflowers Apparel data. Is this the correct model for these data? Are the assumptions presented in Section 13.4 valid? **Residual analysis** visually evaluates these assumptions and helps you to determine whether the regression model that has been selected is appropriate.

The **residual**, or estimated error value, e_i, is the difference between the observed (Y_i) and predicted ($\hat{Y}_i$) values of the dependent variable for a given value of X_i. A residual appears on a scatter plot as the vertical distance between an observed value of Y and the prediction line. Equation (13.14) defines the residual.

> **RESIDUAL**
>
> The residual is equal to the difference between the observed value of Y and the predicted value of Y.
>
> $$e_i = Y_i - \hat{Y}_i \qquad (13.14)$$

Evaluating the Assumptions

Recall from Section 13.4 that the four assumptions of regression (known by the acronym LINE) are linearity, independence, normality, and equal variance.

Linearity To evaluate linearity, you plot the residuals on the vertical axis against the corresponding X_i values of the independent variable on the horizontal axis. If the linear model is appropriate for the data, you will not see any apparent pattern in the plot. However, if the linear model is not appropriate, in the residual plot, there will be a relationship between the X_i values and the residuals, e_i.

You can see such a pattern in Figure 13.9. Panel A shows a situation in which, although there is an increasing trend in Y as X increases, the relationship seems curvilinear because the upward trend decreases for increasing values of X. This quadratic effect is highlighted in Panel B, where there is a clear relationship between X_i and e_i. By plotting the residuals, the linear trend of X with Y has been removed, thereby exposing the lack of fit in the simple linear model. Thus, a quadratic model is a better fit and should be used in place of the simple linear model. (See Section 15.1 for further discussion of fitting curvilinear models.)

FIGURE 13.9
Studying the appropriateness of the simple linear regression model

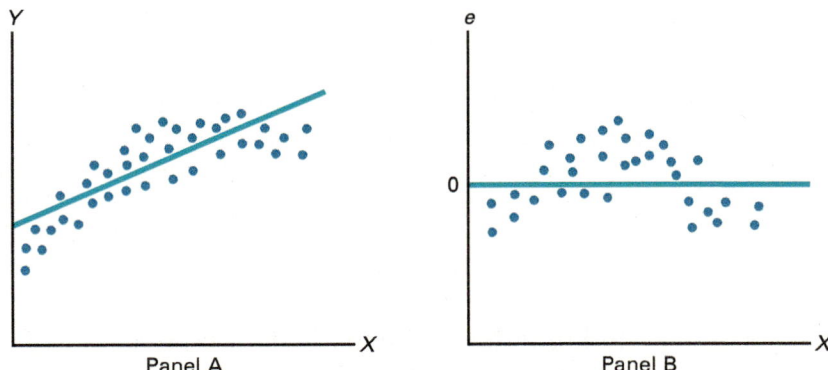

To determine whether the simple linear regression model is appropriate, return to the evaluation of the Sunflowers Apparel data. Figure 13.10 displays the predicted annual sales values and residuals.

FIGURE 13.10
Table of residuals for the Sunflowers Apparel data

Observation	Square Feet	Predicted Annual Sales	Annual Sales	Residuals
1	1.7	3.803239598	3.7	0.103239598
2	1.6	3.636253367	3.9	-0.263746633
3	2.8	5.640088147	6.7	-1.059911853
4	5.6	10.31570263	9.5	0.815702635
5	1.3	3.135294672	3.4	-0.264705328
6	2.2	4.638170757	5.6	-0.961829243
7	1.3	3.135294672	3.7	-0.564705328
8	1.1	2.801322208	2.7	0.101322208
9	3.2	6.308033074	5.5	0.808033074
10	1.5	3.469267135	2.9	0.569267135
11	5.2	9.647757708	10.7	-1.052242292
12	4.6	8.645840318	7.6	1.045840318
13	5.8	10.6496751	11.8	-1.150324902
14	3.0	5.974060611	4.1	1.874060611

To assess linearity, the residuals are plotted against the independent variable (store size, in thousands of square feet) in Figure 13.11. Although there is widespread scatter in the residual plot, there is no clear pattern or relationship between the residuals and X_i. The residuals appear to be evenly spread above and below 0 for different values of X. You can conclude that the linear model is appropriate for the Sunflowers Apparel data.

FIGURE 13.11
Plot of residuals against the square footage of a store for the Sunflowers Apparel data

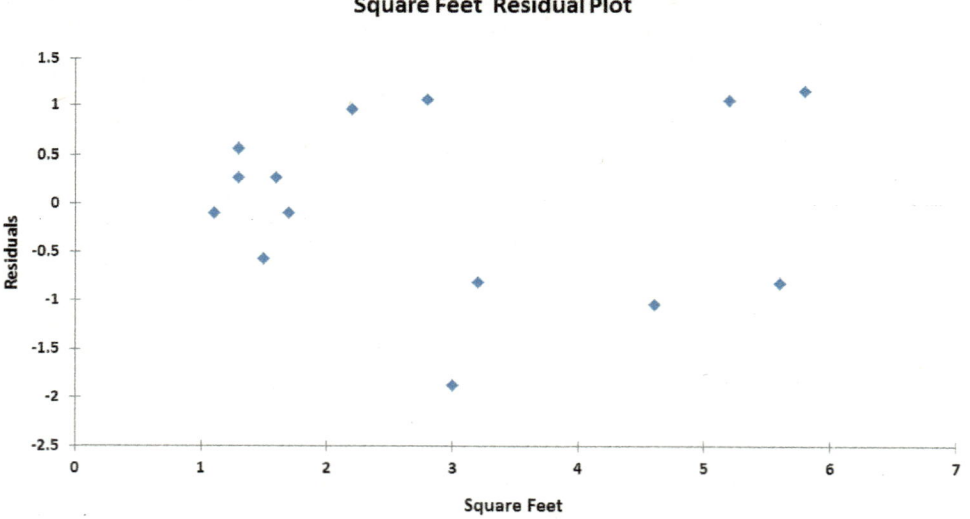

Independence You can evaluate the assumption of independence of the errors by plotting the residuals in the order or sequence in which the data were collected. If the values of Y are part of a time series (see Section 2.6), one residual may sometimes be related to the previous residual. If this relationship exists between consecutive residuals (which violates the assumption of independence), the plot of the residuals versus the time in which the data were collected will often show a cyclical pattern. Because the Sunflowers Apparel data were collected during the same time period, you do not need to evaluate the independence assumption for these data.

Normality You can evaluate the assumption of normality in the errors by organizing the residuals into a frequency distribution as shown in Table 13.3. You cannot construct a meaningful histogram because the sample size is too small. And with such a small sample size ($n = 14$), it can be difficult to evaluate the normality assumption by using a stem-and-leaf display (see Section 2.5), a boxplot (see Section 3.3), or a normal probability plot (see Section 6.3).

TABLE 13.3

Frequency Distribution of 14 Residual Values for the Sunflowers Apparel Data

Residuals	Frequency
−2.25 but less than −1.75	1
−1.75 but less than −1.25	0
−1.25 but less than −0.75	3
−0.75 but less than −0.25	1
−0.25 but less than +0.25	2
+0.25 but less than +0.75	3
+0.75 but less than +1.25	4
	14

From the normal probability plot of the residuals in Figure 13.12, the data do not appear to depart substantially from a normal distribution. The robustness of regression analysis with modest departures from normality enables you to conclude that you should not be overly concerned about departures from this normality assumption in the Sunflowers Apparel data.

FIGURE 13.12

Excel and Minitab normal probability plots of the residuals for the Sunflowers Apparel data

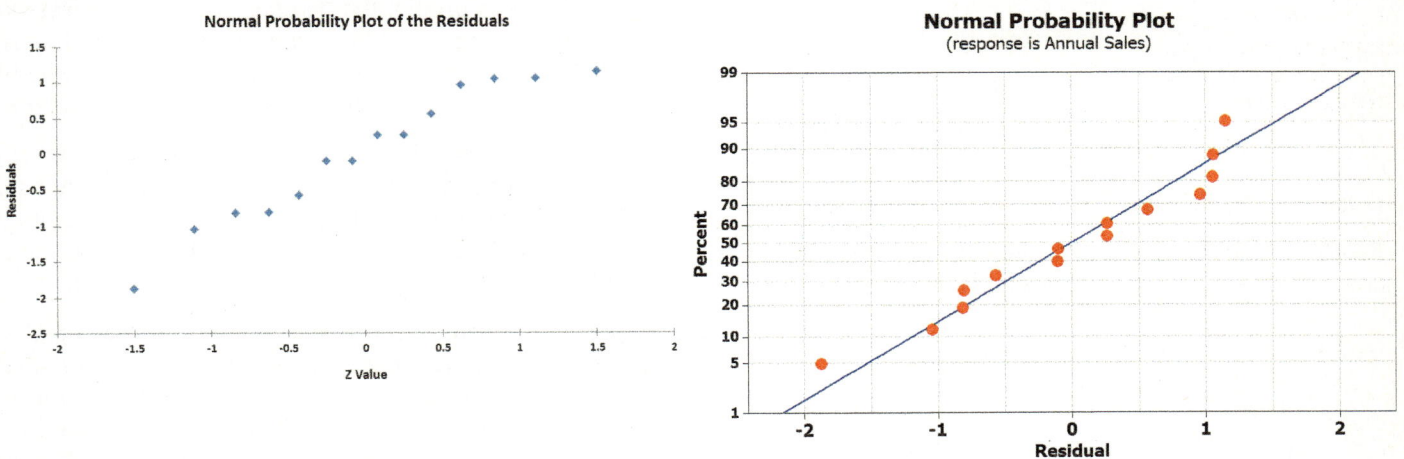

Equal Variance You can evaluate the assumption of equal variance from a plot of the residuals with X_i. For the Sunflowers Apparel data of Figure 13.11 on page 570, there do not appear to be major differences in the variability of the residuals for different X_i values. Thus, you can conclude that there is no apparent violation in the assumption of equal variance at each level of X.

To examine a case in which the equal-variance assumption is violated, observe Figure 13.13, which is a plot of the residuals with X_i for a hypothetical set of data. This plot is fan shaped because the variability of the residuals increases dramatically as X increases. Because this plot shows unequal variances of the residuals at different levels of X, the equal-variance assumption is invalid.

FIGURE 13.13
Violation of equal variance

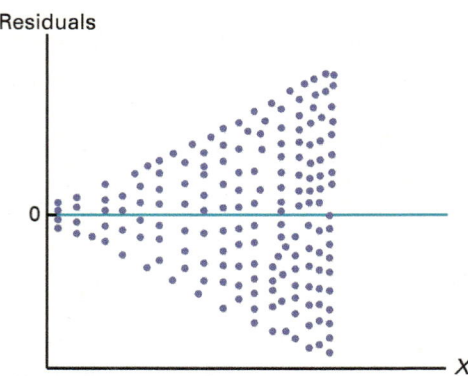

Problems for Section 13.5

LEARNING THE BASICS

13.23 The following results provide the X values, residuals, and a residual plot from a regression analysis:

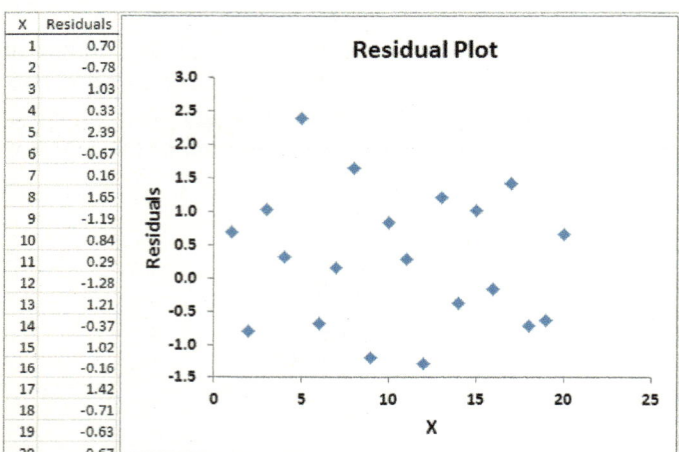

Is there any evidence of a pattern in the residuals? Explain.

13.24 The following results show the X values, residuals, and a residual plot from a regression analysis:

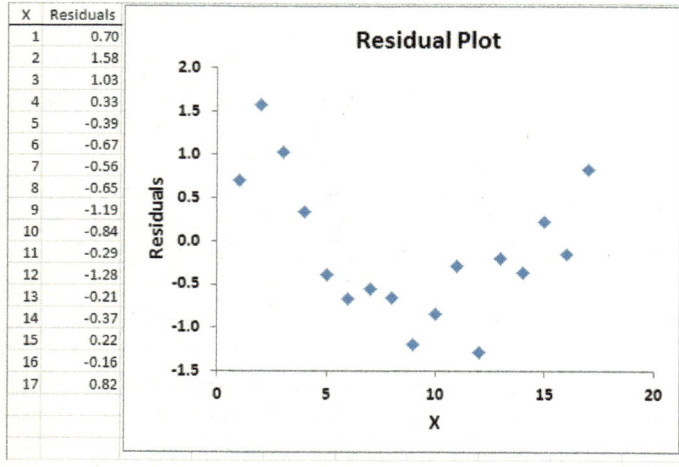

Is there any evidence of a pattern in the residuals? Explain.

APPLYING THE CONCEPTS

13.25 In Problem 13.5 on page 561, you used the summated rating to predict the cost of a restaurant meal. Perform a residual analysis for these data (stored in **Restaurants**). Evaluate whether the assumptions of regression have been seriously violated.

SELF Test 13.26 In Problem 13.4 on page 561, the marketing manager used shelf space for pet food to predict weekly sales. Perform a residual analysis for these data (stored in **Petfood**). Evaluate whether the assumptions of regression have been seriously violated.

13.27 In Problem 13.7 on page 561, you used the number of customers to predict the waiting time at a supermarket checkout. Perform a residual analysis for these data (stored in **Supermarket**). Based on these results, evaluate whether the assumptions of regression have been seriously violated.

13.28 In Problem 13.6 on page 561, the owner of a moving company wanted to predict labor hours based on the cubic feet moved. Perform a residual analysis for these data (stored in **Moving**). Based on these results, evaluate whether the assumptions of regression have been seriously violated.

13.29 In Problem 13.9 on page 562, an agent for a real estate company wanted to predict the monthly rent for apartments, based on the size of the apartments. Perform a residual analysis for these data (stored in **Rent**). Based on these results, evaluate whether the assumptions of regression have been seriously violated.

13.30 In Problem 13.8 on page 561, you used annual revenues to predict the value of a baseball franchise. Perform a residual analysis for these data (stored in **BBRevenue**). Based on these results, evaluate whether the assumptions of regression have been seriously violated.

13.31 In Problem 13.10 on page 562, you used box office gross to predict DVD revenue. Perform a residual analysis for these data (stored in **Movie**). Based on these results, evaluate whether the assumptions of regression have been seriously violated.

13.6 Measuring Autocorrelation: The Durbin-Watson Statistic

One of the basic assumptions of the regression model is the independence of the errors. This assumption is sometimes violated when data are collected over sequential time periods because a residual at any one time period may tend to be similar to residuals at adjacent time periods. This pattern in the residuals is called **autocorrelation**. When a set of data has substantial autocorrelation, the validity of a regression model is in serious doubt.

Residual Plots to Detect Autocorrelation

As mentioned in Section 13.5, one way to detect autocorrelation is to plot the residuals in time order. If a positive autocorrelation effect exists, there will be clusters of residuals with the same sign, and you will readily detect an apparent pattern. If negative autocorrelation exists, residuals will tend to jump back and forth from positive to negative to positive, and so on. This type of pattern is very rarely seen in regression analysis. Thus, the focus of this section is on positive autocorrelation. To illustrate positive autocorrelation, consider the following example.

The business problem faced by the manager of a package delivery store is to predict weekly sales. In approaching this problem, she has decided to develop a regression model to use the number of customers making purchases as an independent variable. Data are collected for a period of 15 weeks. Table 13.4 organizes the data (stored in CustSale).

TABLE 13.4

Customers and Sales for a Period of 15 Consecutive Weeks

Week	Customers	Sales ($Thousands)	Week	Customers	Sales ($Thousands)
1	794	9.33	9	880	12.07
2	799	8.26	10	905	12.55
3	837	7.48	11	886	11.92
4	855	9.08	12	843	10.27
5	845	9.83	13	904	11.80
6	844	10.09	14	950	12.15
7	863	11.01	15	841	9.64
8	875	11.49			

Because the data are collected over a period of 15 consecutive weeks at the same store, you need to determine whether autocorrelation is present. Figure 13.14 presents results for these data.

FIGURE 13.14

Excel and Minitab regression results for the Table 13.4 package delivery store data

	A	B	C	D	E	F	G
1	Package Delivery Store Sales Analysis						
2							
3	*Regression Statistics*						
4	Multiple R	0.8108					
5	R Square	0.6574					
6	Adjusted R Square	0.6311					
7	Standard Error	0.9360					
8	Observations	15					
9							
10	ANOVA						
11		df	SS	MS	F	Significance F	
12	Regression	1	21.8604	21.8604	24.9501	0.0002	
13	Residual	13	11.3901	0.8762			
14	Total	14	33.2506				
15							
16		Coefficients	Standard Error	t Stat	P-value	Lower 95%	Upper 95%
17	Intercept	-16.0322	5.3102	-3.0192	0.0099	-27.5041	-4.5603
18	Customers	0.0308	0.0062	4.9950	0.0002	0.0175	0.0441

```
Regression Analysis: Sales versus Customers
The regression equation is
Sales = - 16.0 + 0.0308 Customers

Predictor      Coef    SE Coef       T       P
Constant    -16.032      5.310   -3.02   0.010
Customers  0.030760   0.006158    5.00   0.000


S = 0.936037    R-Sq = 65.7%    R-Sq(adj) = 63.1%

Analysis of Variance
Source          DF       SS       MS       F       P
Regression       1   21.860   21.860   24.95   0.000
Residual Error  13   11.390    0.876
Total           14   33.251

Durbin-Watson statistic = 0.883003
```

From Figure 13.14, observe that r^2 is 0.6574, indicating that 65.74% of the variation in sales is explained by variation in the number of customers. In addition, the Y intercept, b_0, is -16.0322, and the slope, b_1, is 0.0308. However, before using this model for prediction, you must perform a residual analysis. Because the data have been collected over a consecutive period of 15 weeks, in addition to checking the linearity, normality, and equal-variance assumptions, you must investigate the independence-of-errors assumption. To do this, you plot the residuals versus time in Figure 13.15 to help examine whether a pattern exists. In Figure 13.15, you can see that the residuals tend to fluctuate up and down in a cyclical pattern. This cyclical pattern provides strong cause for concern about the existence of autocorrelation in the residuals and, therefore, a violation of the independence-of-errors assumption.

FIGURE 13.15
Residual plot for the Table 13.4 package delivery store data

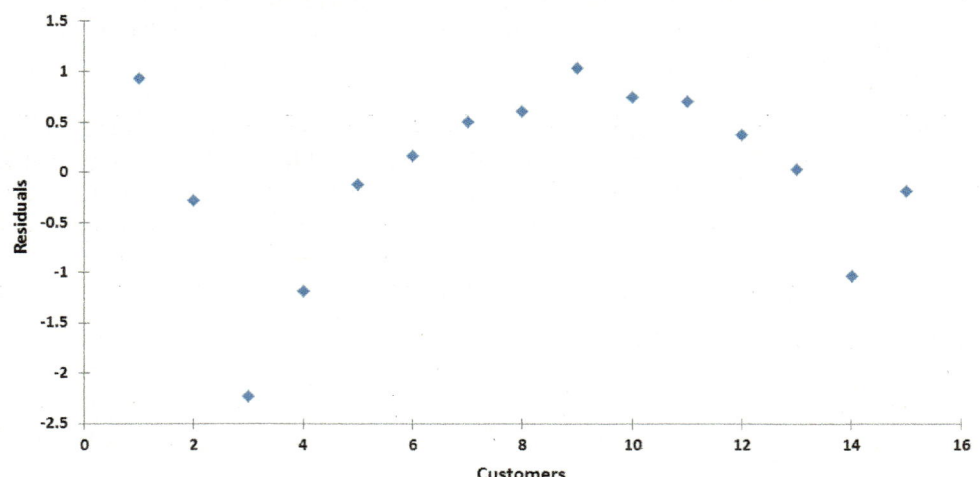

The Durbin-Watson Statistic

The **Durbin-Watson statistic** is used to measure autocorrelation. This statistic measures the correlation between each residual and the residual for the previous time period. Equation (13.15) defines the Durbin-Watson statistic.

DURBIN-WATSON STATISTIC

$$D = \frac{\sum_{i=2}^{n}(e_i - e_{i-1})^2}{\sum_{i=1}^{n} e_i^2} \qquad (13.15)$$

where

e_i = residual at the time period i

In Equation (13.15), the numerator, $\sum_{i=2}^{n}(e_i - e_{i-1})^2$, represents the squared difference between two successive residuals, summed from the second value to the nth value and the denominator, $\sum_{i=1}^{n} e_i^2$, represents the sum of the squared residuals. This means that value of the Durbin-Watson statistic, D, will approach 0 if successive residuals are positively autocorrelated. If the residuals are not correlated, the value of D will be close to 2. (If the residuals are negatively autocorrelated, D will be greater than 2 and could even approach its maximum value of 4.) For the package delivery store data, the Durbin-Watson statistic, D, is 0.8830. (See the Figure 13.16 Excel results below or the Figure 13.14 Minitab results on page 573.)

FIGURE 13.16
Excel Durbin-Watson statistic worksheet for the package delivery store data

Minitab reports the Durbin-Watson statistic as part of its regression results. See Section MG13.6 for more information.

	A	B	
1	Durbin-Watson Statistics		
2			
3	Sum of Squared Difference of Residuals	10.0575	=SUMXMY2(RESIDUALS!E3:E16, RESIDUALS!E2:E15)
4	Sum of Squared Residuals	11.3901	=SUMSQ(RESIDUALS!E2:E16)
5			
6	Durbin-Watson Statistic	0.8830	=B3/B4

You need to determine when the autocorrelation is large enough to conclude that there is significant positive autocorrelation. After computing D, you compare it to the critical values of the Durbin-Watson statistic found in Table E.8, a portion of which is presented in Table 13.5. The critical values depend on α, the significance level chosen, n, the sample size, and k, the number of independent variables in the model (in simple linear regression, $k = 1$).

TABLE 13.5
Finding Critical Values of the Durbin-Watson Statistic

	$\alpha = .05$									
	$k = 1$		$k = 2$		$k = 3$		$k = 4$		$k = 5$	
n	d_L	d_U	d_L	d_U	d_L	d_U	d_L	d_U	d_L	d_U
15	1.08	1.36	.95	1.54	.82	1.75	.69	1.97	.56	2.21
16	1.10	1.37	.98	1.54	.86	1.73	.74	1.93	.62	2.15
17	1.13	1.38	1.02	1.54	.90	1.71	.78	1.90	.67	2.10
18	1.16	1.39	1.05	1.53	.93	1.69	.82	1.87	.71	2.06

In Table 13.5, two values are shown for each combination of α (level of significance), n (sample size), and k (number of independent variables in the model). The first value, d_L, represents the lower critical value. If D is below d_L, you conclude that there is evidence of positive autocorrelation among the residuals. If this occurs, the least-squares method used in this chapter is inappropriate, and you should use alternative methods (see reference 4). The second value, d_U, represents the upper critical value of D, above which you would conclude that there is no evidence of positive autocorrelation among the residuals. If D is between d_L and d_U, you are unable to arrive at a definite conclusion.

For the package delivery store data, with one independent variable ($k = 1$) and 15 values ($n = 15$), $d_L = 1.08$ and $d_U = 1.36$. Because $D = 0.8830 < 1.08$, you conclude that there is positive autocorrelation among the residuals. The least-squares regression analysis of the data is inappropriate because of the presence of significant positive autocorrelation among the residuals. In other words, the independence-of-errors assumption is invalid. You need to use alternative approaches, discussed in reference 4.

Problems for Section 13.6

LEARNING THE BASICS

13.32 The residuals for 10 consecutive time periods are as follows:

Time Period	Residual	Time Period	Residual
1	−5	6	+1
2	−4	7	+2
3	−3	8	+3
4	−2	9	+4
5	−1	10	+5

a. Plot the residuals over time. What conclusion can you reach about the pattern of the residuals over time?
b. Based on (a), what conclusion can you reach about the autocorrelation of the residuals?

13.33 The residuals for 15 consecutive time periods are as follows:

Time Period	Residual	Time Period	Residual
1	+4	9	+6
2	−6	10	−3
3	−1	11	+1
4	−5	12	+3
5	+2	13	0
6	+5	14	−4
7	−2	15	−7
8	+7		

a. Plot the residuals over time. What conclusion can you reach about the pattern of the residuals over time?
b. Compute the Durbin-Watson statistic. At the 0.05 level of significance, is there evidence of positive autocorrelation among the residuals?
c. Based on (a) and (b), what conclusion can you reach about the autocorrelation of the residuals?

APPLYING THE CONCEPTS

13.34 In Problem 13.4 on page 561 concerning pet food sales, the marketing manager used shelf space for pet food to predict weekly sales.
a. Is it necessary to compute the Durbin-Watson statistic in this case? Explain.
b. Under what circumstances is it necessary to compute the Durbin-Watson statistic before proceeding with the least-squares method of regression analysis?

13.35 What is the relationship between the price of crude oil and the price you pay at the pump for gasoline? The file **Oil & Gas** contains the price ($) for a barrel of crude oil (Cushing, Oklahoma spot price) and a gallon of gasoline (New York Harbor Conventional spot price) for 104 weeks ending June 25, 2010. (Data extracted from Energy Information Administration, U.S. Department of Energy, **www.eia.doe.gov.**)
a. Construct a scatter plot with the price of oil on the horizontal axis and the price of gasoline on the vertical axis.
b. Use the least-squares method to develop a simple linear regression equation to predict the price of a gallon of gasoline using the price of a barrel of crude oil as the independent variable.
c. Interpret the meaning of the slope, b_1, in this problem.
d. Plot the residuals versus the time period.
e. Compute the Durbin-Watson statistic.
f. At the 0.05 level of significance, is there evidence of positive autocorrelation among the residuals?
g. Based on the results of (d) through (f), is there reason to question the validity of the model?

SELF Test 13.36 A mail-order catalog business that sells personal computer supplies, software, and hardware maintains a centralized warehouse for the distribution of products ordered. Management is currently examining the process of distribution from the warehouse and is interested in studying the factors that affect warehouse distribution costs. Currently, a small handling fee is added to the order, regardless of the amount of the order. Data that indicate the warehouse distribution costs and the number of orders received have been collected over the past 24 months and stored in **Warecost**. The results are

Months	Distribution Cost ($Thousands)	Number of Orders
1	52.95	4,015
2	71.66	3,806
3	85.58	5,309
4	63.69	4,262
5	72.81	4,296
6	68.44	4,097
7	52.46	3,213
8	70.77	4,809
9	82.03	5,237
10	74.39	4,732
11	70.84	4,413
12	54.08	2,921
13	62.98	3,977
14	72.30	4,428
15	58.99	3,964
16	79.38	4,582
17	94.44	5,582
18	59.74	3,450
19	90.50	5,079
20	93.24	5,735
21	69.33	4,269
22	53.71	3,708
23	89.18	5,387
24	66.80	4,161

a. Assuming a linear relationship, use the least-squares method to find the regression coefficients b_0 and b_1.
b. Predict the monthly warehouse distribution costs when the number of orders is 4,500.
c. Plot the residuals versus the time period.
d. Compute the Durbin-Watson statistic. At the 0.05 level of significance, is there evidence of positive autocorrelation among the residuals?
e. Based on the results of (c) and (d), is there reason to question the validity of the model?

13.37 A freshly brewed shot of espresso has three distinct components: the heart, body, and crema. The separation of these three components typically lasts only 10 to 20 seconds. To use the espresso shot in making a latte, a cappuccino, or another drink, the shot must be poured into the beverage during the separation of the heart, body, and crema. If the shot is used after the separation occurs, the drink becomes excessively bitter and acidic, ruining the final drink. Thus, a longer separation time allows the drink-maker more time to pour the shot and ensure that the beverage will meet expectations. An employee at a coffee shop hypothesized that the harder the espresso grounds were tamped down into the portafilter before brewing, the longer the separation time would be. An experiment using 24 observations was conducted to test this relationship. The independent variable Tamp measures the distance, in inches, between the espresso grounds and the top of the portafilter (i.e., the harder the tamp, the larger the distance). The dependent variable Time is the number of seconds the heart, body, and crema are separated (i.e., the amount of time after the shot is poured before it must be used for the customer's beverage). The data are stored in Espresso and are shown below:
a. Use the least-squares method to develop a simple regression equation with Time as the dependent variable and Tamp as the independent variable.
b. Predict the separation time for a tamp distance of 0.50 inch.
c. Plot the residuals versus the time order of experimentation. Are there any noticeable patterns?
d. Compute the Durbin-Watson statistic. At the 0.05 level of significance, is there evidence of positive autocorrelation among the residuals?

Shot	Tamp (Inches)	Time (Seconds)	Shot	Tamp (Inches)	Time (Seconds)
1	0.20	14	13	0.50	18
2	0.50	14	14	0.50	13
3	0.50	18	15	0.35	19
4	0.20	16	16	0.35	19
5	0.20	16	17	0.20	17
6	0.50	13	18	0.20	18
7	0.20	12	19	0.20	15
8	0.35	15	20	0.20	16
9	0.50	9	21	0.35	18
10	0.35	15	22	0.35	16
11	0.50	11	23	0.35	14
12	0.50	16	24	0.35	16

e. Based on the results of (c) and (d), is there reason to question the validity of the model?

13.38 The owner of a chain of ice cream stores has the business objective of improving the forecast of daily sales so that staffing shortages can be minimized during the summer season. The owner has decided to begin by developing a simple linear regression model to predict daily sales based on atmospheric temperature. A sample of 21 consecutive days is selected, and the results are stored in IceCream. (Hint: Determine which are the independent and dependent variables.)
a. Assuming a linear relationship, use the least-squares method to compute the regression coefficients b_0 and b_1.
b. Predict the sales for a day in which the temperature is 83°F.
c. Plot the residuals versus the time period.
d. Compute the Durbin-Watson statistic. At the 0.05 level of significance, is there evidence of positive autocorrelation among the residuals?
e. Based on the results of (c) and (d), is there reason to question the validity of the model?

13.7 Inferences About the Slope and Correlation Coefficient

In Sections 13.1 through 13.3, regression was used solely for descriptive purposes. You learned how the least-squares method determines the regression coefficients and how to predict Y for a given value of X. In addition, you learned how to compute and interpret the standard error of the estimate and the coefficient of determination.

When residual analysis, as discussed in Section 13.5, indicates that the assumptions of a least-squares regression model are not seriously violated and that the straight-line model is appropriate, you can make inferences about the linear relationship between the variables in the population.

t Test for the Slope

To determine the existence of a significant linear relationship between the X and Y variables, you test whether β_1 (the population slope) is equal to 0. The null and alternative hypotheses are as follows:

$H_0: \beta_1 = 0$ [There is no linear relationship (the slope is zero).]

$H_1: \beta_1 \neq 0$ [There is a linear relationship (the slope is not zero).]

If you reject the null hypothesis, you conclude that there is evidence of a linear relationship. Equation (13.16) defines the test statistic.

TESTING A HYPOTHESIS FOR A POPULATION SLOPE, β_1, USING THE t TEST

The t_{STAT} test statistic equals the difference between the sample slope and hypothesized value of the population slope divided by the standard error of the slope.

$$t_{STAT} = \frac{b_1 - \beta_1}{S_{b_1}} \qquad (13.16)$$

where

$$S_{b_1} = \frac{S_{YX}}{\sqrt{SSX}}$$

$$SSX = \sum_{i=1}^{n}(X_i - \bar{X})^2$$

The t_{STAT} test statistic follows a t distribution with $n - 2$ degrees of freedom.

Return to the Sunflowers Apparel scenario on page 551. To test whether there is a significant linear relationship between the size of the store and the annual sales at the 0.05 level of significance, refer to the t test results shown in Figure 13.17.

FIGURE 13.17
Excel and Minitab t test results for the slope for the Sunflowers Apparel data

	A	B	C	D	E	F	G	H	I
16		Coefficients	Standard Error	t Stat	P-value	Lower 95%	Upper 95%	Lower 95.0%	Upper 95.0%
17	Intercept	0.9645	0.5262	1.8329	0.0917	-0.1820	2.1110	-0.1820	2.11095
18	Square Feet	1.6699	0.1569	10.6411	0.0000	1.3280	2.0118	1.3280	2.01177

```
Predictor      Coef    SE Coef       T       P
Constant     0.9645     0.5262    1.83   0.092
Square Feet  1.6699     0.1569   10.64   0.000
```

From Figure 13.17,

$$b_1 = +1.6699 \quad n = 14 \quad S_{b_1} = 0.1569$$

and

$$t_{STAT} = \frac{b_1 - \beta_1}{S_{b_1}}$$

$$= \frac{1.6699 - 0}{0.1569} = 10.6411$$

Using the 0.05 level of significance, the critical value of t with $n - 2 = 12$ degrees of freedom is 2.1788. Because $t_{STAT} = 10.6411 > 2.1788$ or because the p-value is approximately 0, which is less than $\alpha = 0.05$, you reject H_0 (see Figure 13.18). Hence, you can conclude that there is a significant linear relationship between mean annual sales and the size of the store.

FIGURE 13.18
Testing a hypothesis about the population slope at the 0.05 level of significance, with 12 degrees of freedom

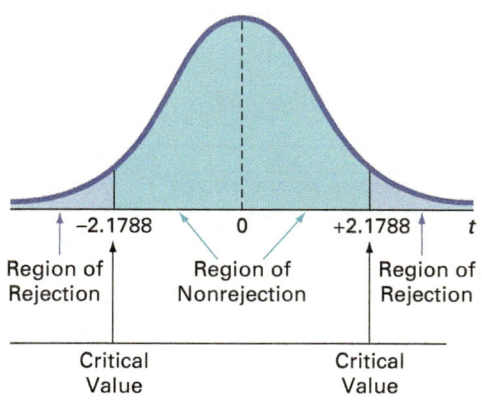

F Test for the Slope

As an alternative to the *t* test, in simple linear regression, you can use an *F* test to determine whether the slope is statistically significant. In Section 10.4, you used the *F* distribution to test the ratio of two variances. Equation (13.17) defines the *F* test for the slope as the ratio of the variance that is due to the regression (MSR) divided by the error variance ($MSE = S_{YX}^2$).

TESTING A HYPOTHESIS FOR A POPULATION SLOPE, β_1, USING THE *F* TEST

The F_{STAT} test statistic is equal to the regression mean square (MSR) divided by the mean square error (MSE).

$$F_{STAT} = \frac{MSR}{MSE} \qquad (13.17)$$

where

$$MSR = \frac{SSR}{1} = SSR$$

$$MSE = \frac{SSE}{n-2}$$

The F_{STAT} test statistic follows an *F* distribution with 1 and $n - 2$ degrees of freedom.

Using a level of significance α, the decision rule is

$$\text{Reject } H_0 \text{ if } F_{STAT} > F_\alpha;$$

otherwise, do not reject H_0.

Table 13.6 organizes the complete set of results into an analysis of variance (ANOVA) table.

TABLE 13.6
ANOVA Table for Testing the Significance of a Regression Coefficient

Source	df	Sum of Squares	Mean Square (Variance)	F
Regression	1	SSR	$MSR = \frac{SSR}{1} = SSR$	$F_{STAT} = \frac{MSR}{MSE}$
Error	$n - 2$	SSE	$MSE = \frac{SSE}{n-2}$	
Total	$n - 1$	SST		

Figure 13.19, a completed ANOVA table for the Sunflowers sales data, shows that the computed F_{STAT} test statistic is 113.2335 and the *p*-value is approximately 0.

FIGURE 13.19
Excel and Minitab F test results for the Sunflowers Apparel data

	A	B	C	D	E	F
10	ANOVA					
11		df	SS	MS	F	Significance F
12	Regression	1	105.7476	105.7476	113.2335	0.0000
13	Residual	12	11.2067	0.9339		
14	Total	13	116.9543			

```
Analysis of Variance
Source           DF      SS       MS       F        P
Regression        1   105.75   105.75   113.23   0.000
Residual Error   12    11.21     0.93
Total            13   116.95
```

Using a level of significance of 0.05, from Table E.5, the critical value of the F distribution, with 1 and 12 degrees of freedom, is 4.75 (see Figure 13.20). Because $F_{STAT} = 113.2335 > 4.75$ or because the p-value $= 0.0000 < 0.05$, you reject H_0 and conclude that there is a significant linear relationship between the size of the store and annual sales. Because the F test in Equation (13.17) on page 579 is equivalent to the t test in Equation (13.16) on page 578, you reach the same conclusion.

FIGURE 13.20
Regions of rejection and nonrejection when testing for the significance of the slope at the 0.05 level of significance, with 1 and 12 degrees of freedom

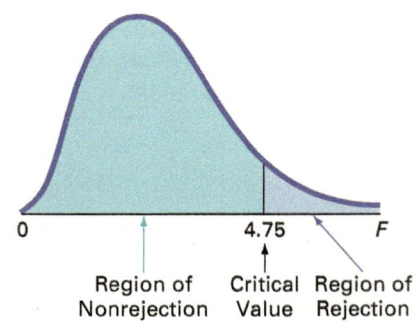

Confidence Interval Estimate for the Slope

As an alternative to testing for the existence of a linear relationship between the variables, you can construct a confidence interval estimate of β_1 using Equation (13.18).

> **CONFIDENCE INTERVAL ESTIMATE OF THE SLOPE, β_1**
>
> The confidence interval estimate for the population slope can be constructed by taking the sample slope, b_1, and adding and subtracting the critical t value multiplied by the standard error of the slope.
>
> $$b_1 \pm t_{\alpha/2} S_{b_1}$$
> (or)
> $$b_1 - t_{\alpha/2} S_{b_1} \leq \beta_1 \leq b_1 + t_{\alpha/2} S_{b_1} \qquad (13.18)$$
>
> where
>
> $t_{\alpha/2}$ = critical value corresponding to an upper-tail probability of $\alpha/2$ from the t distribution with $n - 2$ degrees of freedom (i.e., a cumulative area of $1 - \alpha/2$).

From the Figure 13.17 results on page 578,

$$b_1 = 1.6699 \quad n = 14 \quad S_{b_1} = 0.1569$$

To construct a 95% confidence interval estimate, $\alpha/2 = 0.025$, and from Table E.3, $t_{\alpha/2} = 2.1788$. Thus,

$$b_1 \pm t_{\alpha/2} S_{b_1} = 1.6699 \pm (2.1788)(0.1569)$$
$$= 1.6699 \pm 0.3419$$
$$1.3280 \leq \beta_1 \leq 2.0118$$

Therefore, you estimate with 95% confidence that the population slope is between 1.3280 and 2.0118. Because these values are both above 0, you conclude that there is a significant linear relationship between annual sales and the size of the store. Had the interval included 0, you would have concluded that no significant relationship exists between the variables. The confidence interval indicates that for each increase of 1,000 square feet, predicted annual sales are estimated to increase by at least $1,328,000 but no more than $2,011,800.

t Test for the Correlation Coefficient

In Section 3.5 on page 157, the strength of the relationship between two numerical variables was measured using the **correlation coefficient**, r. The values of the coefficient of correlation range from -1 for a perfect negative correlation to $+1$ for a perfect positive correlation. You can use the correlation coefficient to determine whether there is a statistically significant linear relationship between X and Y. To do so, you hypothesize that the population correlation coefficient, ρ, is 0. Thus, the null and alternative hypotheses are

$$H_0: \rho = 0 \text{ (no correlation)}$$

$$H_1: \rho \neq 0 \text{ (correlation)}$$

Equation (13.19) defines the test statistic for determining the existence of a significant correlation.

TESTING FOR THE EXISTENCE OF CORRELATION

$$t_{STAT} = \frac{r - \rho}{\sqrt{\dfrac{1 - r^2}{n - 2}}} \qquad (13.19a)$$

where

$$r = +\sqrt{r^2} \text{ if } b_1 > 0$$
$$r = -\sqrt{r^2} \text{ if } b_1 < 0$$

The t_{STAT} test statistic follows a t distribution with $n - 2$ degrees of freedom. r is calculated as follows:

$$r = \frac{\text{cov}(X,Y)}{S_X S_Y} \qquad (13.19b)$$

where

$$\text{cov}(X, Y) = \frac{\sum_{i=1}^{n}(X_i - \overline{X})(Y_i - \overline{Y})}{n - 1}$$

$$S_X = \sqrt{\frac{\sum_{i=1}^{n}(X_i - \overline{X})^2}{n - 1}}$$

$$S_Y = \sqrt{\frac{\sum_{i=1}^{n}(Y_i - \overline{Y})^2}{n - 1}}$$

In the Sunflowers Apparel problem, $r^2 = 0.9042$ and $b_1 = +1.6699$ (see Figure 13.4 on page 556). Because $b_1 > 0$, the correlation coefficient for annual sales and store size is the positive square root of r^2, that is, $r = +\sqrt{0.9042} = +0.9509$. Using Equation (13.19a) to test the null hypothesis that there is no correlation between these two variables results in the following observed t statistic:

$$t_{STAT} = \frac{r - 0}{\sqrt{\frac{1 - r^2}{n - 2}}}$$

$$= \frac{0.9509 - 0}{\sqrt{\frac{1 - (0.9509)^2}{14 - 2}}} = 10.6411$$

Using the 0.05 level of significance, because $t_{STAT} = 10.6411 > 2.1788$, you reject the null hypothesis. You conclude that there is a significant association between annual sales and store size. This t_{STAT} test statistic is equivalent to the t_{STAT} test statistic found when testing whether the population slope, β_1, is equal to zero.

Problems for Section 13.7

LEARNING THE BASICS

13.39 You are testing the null hypothesis that there is no linear relationship between two variables, X and Y. From your sample of $n = 10$, you determine that $r = 0.80$.
a. What is the value of the t test statistic t_{STAT}?
b. At the $\alpha = 0.05$ level of significance, what are the critical values?
c. Based on your answers to (a) and (b), what statistical decision should you make?

13.40 You are testing the null hypothesis that there is no linear relationship between two variables, X and Y. From your sample of $n = 18$, you determine that $b_1 = +4.5$ and $S_{b_1} = 1.5$.
a. What is the value of t_{STAT}?
b. At the $\alpha = 0.05$ level of significance, what are the critical values?
c. Based on your answers to (a) and (b), what statistical decision should you make?
d. Construct a 95% confidence interval estimate of the population slope, β_1.

13.41 You are testing the null hypothesis that there is no linear relationship between two variables, X and Y. From your sample of $n = 20$, you determine that $SSR = 60$ and $SSE = 40$.
a. What is the value of F_{STAT}?
b. At the $\alpha = 0.05$ level of significance, what is the critical value?
c. Based on your answers to (a) and (b), what statistical decision should you make?
d. Compute the correlation coefficient by first computing r^2 and assuming that b_1 is negative.
e. At the 0.05 level of significance, is there a significant correlation between X and Y?

APPLYING THE CONCEPTS

SELF Test 13.42 In Problem 13.4 on page 561, the marketing manager used shelf space for pet food to predict weekly sales. The data are stored in Petfood. From the results of that problem, $b_1 = 7.4$ and $S_{b_1} = 1.59$.
a. At the 0.05 level of significance, is there evidence of a linear relationship between shelf space and sales?
b. Construct a 95% confidence interval estimate of the population slope, β_1.

13.43 In Problem 13.5 on page 561, you used the summated rating of a restaurant to predict the cost of a meal. The data are stored in Restaurants. Using the results of that problem, $b_1 = 1.2409$ and $S_{b_1} = 0.1421$.
a. At the 0.05 level of significance, is there evidence of a linear relationship between the summated rating of a restaurant and the cost of a meal?
b. Construct a 95% confidence interval estimate of the population slope, β_1.

13.44 In Problem 13.6 on page 561, the owner of a moving company wanted to predict labor hours, based on the number of cubic feet moved. The data are stored in Moving. Use the results of that problem.
a. At the 0.05 level of significance, is there evidence of a linear relationship between the number of cubic feet moved and labor hours?
b. Construct a 95% confidence interval estimate of the population slope, β_1.

13.45 In Problem 13.7 on page 561, you used the number of customers to predict the waiting time on the checkout line. The data are stored in Supermarket. Use the results of that problem.

a. At the 0.05 level of significance, is there evidence of a linear relationship between the number of customers and the waiting time on the checkout line?
b. Construct a 95% confidence interval estimate of the population slope, β_1.

13.46 In Problem 13.8 on page 561, you used annual revenues to predict the value of a baseball franchise. The data are stored in `BBRevenue`. Use the results of that problem.
a. At the 0.05 level of significance, is there evidence of a linear relationship between annual revenue and franchise value?
b. Construct a 95% confidence interval estimate of the population slope, β_1.

13.47 In Problem 13.9 on page 562, an agent for a real estate company wanted to predict the monthly rent for apartments, based on the size of the apartment. The data are stored in `Rent`. Use the results of that problem.
a. At the 0.05 level of significance, is there evidence of a linear relationship between the size of the apartment and the monthly rent?
b. Construct a 95% confidence interval estimate of the population slope, β_1.

13.48 In Problem 13.10 on page 562, you used box office gross to predict DVD revenue. The data are stored in `Movie`. Use the results of that problem.
a. At the 0.05 level of significance, is there evidence of a linear relationship between box office gross and DVD revenue?
b. Construct a 95% confidence interval estimate of the population slope, β_1.

13.49 The volatility of a stock is often measured by its beta value. You can estimate the beta value of a stock by developing a simple linear regression model, using the percentage weekly change in the stock as the dependent variable and the percentage weekly change in a market index as the independent variable. The S&P 500 Index is a common index to use. For example, if you wanted to estimate the beta for Disney, you could use the following model, which is sometimes referred to as a *market model*:

$$(\% \text{ weekly change in Disney}) = \beta_0$$
$$+ \beta_1(\% \text{ weekly change in S \& P 500 index}) + \varepsilon$$

The least-squares regression estimate of the slope b_1 is the estimate of the beta value for Disney. A stock with a beta value of 1.0 tends to move the same as the overall market. A stock with a beta value of 1.5 tends to move 50% more than the overall market, and a stock with a beta value of 0.6 tends to move only 60% as much as the overall market. Stocks with negative beta values tend to move in the opposite direction of the overall market. The following table gives some beta values for some widely held stocks as of July 7, 2010:
a. For each of the six companies, interpret the beta value.
b. How can investors use the beta value as a guide for investing?

Company	Ticker Symbol	Beta
Procter & Gamble	PG	0.53
AT&T	T	0.65
Disney	DIS	1.25
Apple	AAPL	1.43
eBay	EBAY	1.75
Ford	F	2.75

Source: Data extracted from **finance.yahoo.com**, July 7, 2010.

13.50 Index funds are mutual funds that try to mimic the movement of leading indexes, such as the S&P 500 or the Russell 2000. The beta values (as described in Problem 13.49) for these funds are therefore approximately 1.0, and the estimated market models for these funds are approximately

$$(\% \text{ weekly change in index fund}) =$$
$$0.0 + 1.0(\% \text{ weekly change in the index})$$

Leveraged index funds are designed to magnify the movement of major indexes. Direxion Funds is a leading provider of leveraged index and other alternative-class mutual fund products for investment advisors and sophisticated investors. Two of the company's funds are shown in the following table. (Data extracted from **www.direxionfunds.com**, July 7, 2010.)

Name	Ticker Symbol	Description
Daily Small Cap 3x Fund	TNA	300% of the Russell 2000 Index
Daily India Bull 2x Fund	INDL	200% of the Indus India Index

The estimated market models for these funds are approximately

$$(\% \text{ weekly change in TNA}) = 0.0 + 3.0$$
$$(\% \text{ weekly change in the Russell 2000})$$
$$(\% \text{ weekly change in INDL}) = 0.0 + 2.0$$
$$(\% \text{ weekly change in the Indus India Index})$$

Thus, if the Russell 2000 Index gains 10% over a period of time, the leveraged mutual fund TNA gains approximately 30%. On the downside, if the same index loses 20%, TNA loses approximately 60%.
a. The objective of the Direxion Funds Large Cap Bull 3x fund, BGU, is 300% of the performance of the Russell 1000 Index. What is its approximate market model?
b. If the Russell 1000 Index gains 10% in a year, what return do you expect BGU to have?
c. If the Russell 1000 Index loses 20% in a year, what return do you expect BGU to have?
d. What type of investors should be attracted to leveraged index funds? What type of investors should stay away from these funds?

13.51 The file **Cereals** contains the calories and sugar, in grams, in one serving of seven breakfast cereals:

Cereal	Calories	Sugar
Kellogg's All Bran	80	6
Kellogg's Corn Flakes	100	2
Wheaties	100	4
Nature's Path Organic Multigrain Flakes	110	4
Kellogg's Rice Krispies	130	4
Post Shredded Wheat Vanilla Almond	190	11
Kellogg Mini Wheats	200	10

a. Compute and interpret the coefficient of correlation, r.
b. At the 0.05 level of significance, is there a significant linear relationship between calories and sugar?

13.52 Movie companies need to predict the gross receipts of an individual movie once the movie has debuted. The following results (stored in **PotterMovies**) are the first weekend gross, the U.S. gross, and the worldwide gross (in $millions) of the six Harry Potter movies that debuted from 2001 to 2009:

Title	First Weekend	U.S. Gross	Worldwide Gross
Sorcerer's Stone	90.295	317.558	976.458
Chamber of Secrets	88.357	261.988	878.988
Prisoner of Azkaban	93.687	249.539	795.539
Goblet of Fire	102.335	290.013	896.013
Order of the Phoenix	77.108	292.005	938.469
Half-Blood Prince	77.836	301.460	934.601

Source: Data extracted from www.the-numbers.com/interactive/comp-Harry-Potter.php.

a. Compute the coefficient of correlation between first weekend gross and the U.S. gross, first weekend gross and the worldwide gross, and the U.S. gross and worldwide gross.
b. At the 0.05 level of significance, is there a significant linear relationship between first weekend gross and the U.S. gross, first weekend gross and the worldwide gross, and the U.S. gross and worldwide gross?

13.53 College basketball is big business, with coaches' salaries, revenues, and expenses in millions of dollars. The file **College Basketball** contains the coaches' salary and revenue for college basketball at 60 of the 65 schools that played in the 2009 NCAA men's basketball tournament. (Data extracted from "Compensation for Division I Men's Basketball Coaches," *USA Today*, April 2, 2010, p. 8C; and C. Isadore, "Nothing but Net: Basketball Dollars by School," **money.cnn.com/2010/03/18/news/companies/basketball_profits/**.)

a. Compute and interpret the coefficient of correlation, r.
b. At the 0.05 level of significance, is there a significant linear relationship between a coach's salary and revenue?

13.54 College football players trying out for the NFL are given the Wonderlic standardized intelligence test. The file **Wonderlic** lists the average Wonderlic scores of football players trying out for the NFL and the graduation rates for football players at the schools they attended. (Data extracted from S. Walker, "The NFL's Smartest Team," *The Wall Street Journal*, September 30, 2005, pp. W1, W10.)

a. Compute and interpret the coefficient of correlation, r.
b. At the 0.05 level of significance, is there a significant linear relationship between the average Wonderlic score of football players trying out for the NFL and the graduation rates for football players at selected schools?
c. What conclusions can you reach about the relationship between the average Wonderlic score of football players trying out for the NFL and the graduation rates for football players at selected schools?

13.8 Estimation of Mean Values and Prediction of Individual Values

In Chapter 8, you studied the concept of the confidence interval estimate of the population mean. In Example 13.2 on page 557, you used the prediction line to predict the mean value of Y for a given X. The annual sales for stores with 4,000 square feet was predicted to be 7.644 millions of dollars ($7,644,000). This estimate, however, is a *point estimate* of the population mean. This section presents methods to develop a confidence interval estimate for the mean response for a given X and for developing a prediction interval for an individual response, Y, for a given value of X.

The Confidence Interval Estimate

Equation (13.20) defines the **confidence interval estimate for the mean response** for a given X.

Simple Linear Regression

> **CONFIDENCE INTERVAL ESTIMATE FOR THE MEAN OF Y**
>
> $$\hat{Y}_i \pm t_{\alpha/2} S_{YX} \sqrt{h_i}$$
>
> $$\hat{Y}_i - t_{\alpha/2} S_{YX} \sqrt{h_i} \leq \mu_{Y|X=X_i} \leq -\hat{Y}_i + t_{\alpha/2} S_{YX} \sqrt{h_i} \qquad (13.20)$$
>
> where
>
> $$h_i = \frac{1}{n} + \frac{(X_i - \bar{X})^2}{SSX}$$
>
> $\hat{Y}_i$ = predicted value of Y; $\hat{Y}_i = b_0 + b_1 X_i$
>
> S_{YX} = standard error of the estimate
>
> n = sample size
>
> X_i = given value of X
>
> $\mu_{Y|X=X_i}$ = mean value of Y when $X = X_i$
>
> $$SSX = \sum_{i=1}^{n}(X_i - \bar{X})^2$$
>
> $t_{\alpha/2}$ = critical value corresponding to an upper-tail probability of $\alpha/2$ from the t distribution with $n - 2$ degrees of freedom (i.e., a cumulative area of $1 - \alpha/2$).

The width of the confidence interval in Equation (13.20) depends on several factors. Increased variation around the prediction line, as measured by the standard error of the estimate, results in a wider interval. As you would expect, increased sample size reduces the width of the interval. In addition, the width of the interval varies at different values of X. When you predict Y for values of X close to $\bar{X}$, the interval is narrower than for predictions for X values further away from $\bar{X}$.

In the Sunflowers Apparel example, suppose you want to construct a 95% confidence interval estimate of the mean annual sales for the entire population of stores that contain 4,000 square feet ($X = 4$). Using the simple linear regression equation,

$$\hat{Y}_i = 0.9645 + 1.6699 X_i$$
$$= 0.9645 + 1.6699(4) = 7.6439 \text{ (millions of dollars)}$$

Also, given the following:

$$\bar{X} = 2.9214 \quad S_{YX} = 0.9664$$

$$SSX = \sum_{i=1}^{n}(X_i - \bar{X})^2 = 37.9236$$

From Table E.3, $t_{\alpha/2} = 2.1788$. Thus,

$$\hat{Y}_i \pm t_{\alpha/2} S_{YX} \sqrt{h_i}$$

where

$$h_i = \frac{1}{n} + \frac{(X_i - \bar{X})^2}{SSX}$$

so that

$$\hat{Y}_i \pm t_{\alpha/2} S_{YX} \sqrt{\frac{1}{n} + \frac{(X_i - \bar{X})^2}{SSX}}$$

$$= 7.6439 \pm (2.1788)(0.9664)\sqrt{\frac{1}{14} + \frac{(4 - 2.9214)^2}{37.9236}}$$

$$= 7.6439 \pm 0.6728$$

so

$$6.9711 \leq \mu_{Y|X=4} \leq 8.3167$$

Therefore, the 95% confidence interval estimate is that the mean annual sales are between $6,971,100 and $8,316,700 for the population of stores with 4,000 square feet.

The Prediction Interval

In addition to constructing a confidence interval for the mean value of Y, you can also construct a prediction interval for an individual value of Y. Although the form of this interval is similar to that of the confidence interval estimate of Equation (13.20), the prediction interval is predicting an individual value, not estimating a mean. Equation (13.21) defines the **prediction interval for an individual response, Y,** at a given value, X_i, denoted by $Y_{X=X_i}$.

PREDICTION INTERVAL FOR AN INDIVIDUAL RESPONSE, Y

$$\hat{Y}_i \pm t_{\alpha/2} S_{YX} \sqrt{1 + h_i} \tag{13.21}$$

$$\hat{Y}_i - t_{\alpha/2} S_{YX} \sqrt{1 + h_i} \leq Y_{X=X_i} \leq \hat{Y}_i + t_{\alpha/2} S_{YX} \sqrt{1 + h_i}$$

where

$Y_{X=X_i}$ = future value of Y when $X = X_i$
$t_{\alpha/2}$ = critical value corresponding to an upper-tail probability of $\alpha/2$ from the t distribution with $n - 2$ degrees of freedom (i.e., a cumulative area of $1 - \alpha/2$)

In addition, h_i, $\hat{Y}_i$, S_{YX}, n, and X_i are defined as in Equation (13.20) on page 585.

To construct a 95% prediction interval of the annual sales for an individual store that contains 4,000 square feet ($X = 4$), you first compute $\hat{Y}_i$. Using the prediction line:

$$\hat{Y}_i = 0.9645 + 1.6699 X_i$$
$$= 0.9645 + 1.6699(4)$$
$$= 7.6439 \text{ (millions of dollars)}$$

Also, given the following:

$$\bar{X} = 2.9214 \quad S_{YX} = 0.9664$$

$$SSX = \sum_{i=1}^{n}(X_i - \bar{X})^2 = 37.9236$$

From Table E.3, $t_{\alpha/2} = 2.1788$. Thus,

$$\hat{Y}_i \pm t_{\alpha/2} S_{YX} \sqrt{1 + h_i}$$

where

$$h_i = \frac{1}{n} + \frac{(X_i - \bar{X})^2}{\sum_{i=1}^{n}(X_i - \bar{X})^2}$$

so that

$$\hat{Y}_i \pm t_{\alpha/2} S_{YX} \sqrt{1 + \frac{1}{n} + \frac{(X_i - \bar{X})^2}{SSX}}$$

$$= 7.6439 \pm (2.1788)(0.9664)\sqrt{1 + \frac{1}{14} + \frac{(4 - 2.9214)^2}{37.9236}}$$

$$= 7.6439 \pm 2.2104$$

so

$$5.4335 \leq Y_{X=4} \leq 9.8543$$

Therefore, with 95% confidence, you predict that the annual sales for an individual store with 4,000 square feet is between $5,433,500 and $9,854,300.

Figure 13.21 presents results for the confidence interval estimate and the prediction interval for the Sunflowers Apparel data. If you compare the results of the confidence interval estimate and the prediction interval, you see that the width of the prediction interval for an individual store is much wider than the confidence interval estimate for the mean. Remember that there is much more variation in predicting an individual value than in estimating a mean value.

FIGURE 13.21
Excel and Minitab confidence interval estimate and prediction interval results for the Sunflowers Apparel data

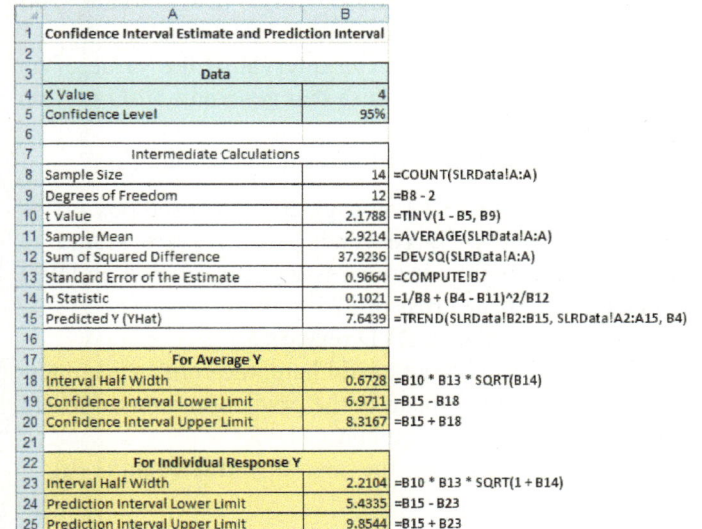

Problems for Section 13.8

LEARNING THE BASICS

13.55 Based on a sample of $n = 20$, the least-squares method was used to develop the following prediction line: $\hat{Y}_i = 5 + 3X_i$.
In addition,

$$S_{YX} = 1.0 \quad \bar{X} = 2 \quad \sum_{i=1}^{n}(X_i - \bar{X})^2 = 20$$

a. Construct a 95% confidence interval estimate of the population mean response for $X = 2$.
b. Construct a 95% prediction interval of an individual response for $X = 2$.

13.56 Based on a sample of $n = 20$, the least-squares method was used to develop the following prediction line: $\hat{Y}_i = 5 + 3X_i$.
In addition,

$$S_{YX} = 1.0 \quad \bar{X} = 2 \quad \sum_{i=1}^{n}(X_i - \bar{X})^2 = 20$$

a. Construct a 95% confidence interval estimate of the population mean response for $X = 4$.
b. Construct a 95% prediction interval of an individual response for $X = 4$.

c. Compare the results of (a) and (b) with those of Problem 13.55 (a) and (b). Which intervals are wider? Why?

APPLYING THE CONCEPTS

13.57 In Problem 13.5 on page 561, you used the summated rating of a restaurant to predict the cost of a meal. The data are stored in Restaurants. For these data, $S_{YX} = 9.5505$ and $h_i = 0.026844$ when $X = 50$.
a. Construct a 95% confidence interval estimate of the mean cost of a meal for restaurants that have a summated rating of 50.
b. Construct a 95% prediction interval of the cost of a meal for an individual restaurant that has a summated rating of 50
c. Explain the difference in the results in (a) and (b).

SELF Test 13.58 In Problem 13.4 on page 561, the marketing manager used shelf space for pet food to predict weekly sales. The data are stored in Petfood. For these data, $S_{YX} = 30.81$ and $h_i = 0.1373$ when $X = 8$.
a. Construct a 95% confidence interval estimate of the mean weekly sales for all stores that have 8 feet of shelf space for pet food.
b. Construct a 95% prediction interval of the weekly sales of an individual store that has 8 feet of shelf space for pet food.
c. Explain the difference in the results in (a) and (b).

13.59 In Problem 13.7 on page 561, you used the total number of customers in the store to predict the waiting time at the checkout counter. The data are stored in Supermarket.
a. Construct a 95% confidence interval estimate of the mean waiting time for all customers when there are 20 customers in the store.
b. Construct a 95% prediction interval of the waiting time for an individual customer when there are 20 customers in the store.
c. Why is the interval in (a) narrower than the interval in (b)?

13.60 In Problem 13.6 on page 561, the owner of a moving company wanted to predict labor hours based on the number of cubic feet moved. The data are stored in Moving.
a. Construct a 95% confidence interval estimate of the mean labor hours for all moves of 500 cubic feet.
b. Construct a 95% prediction interval of the labor hours of an individual move that has 500 cubic feet.
c. Why is the interval in (a) narrower than the interval in (b)?

13.61 In Problem 13.9 on page 562, an agent for a real estate company wanted to predict the monthly rent for apartments, based on the size of an apartment. The data are stored in Rent.
a. Construct a 95% confidence interval estimate of the mean monthly rental for all apartments that are 1,000 square feet in size.
b. Construct a 95% prediction interval of the monthly rental for an individual apartment that is 1,000 square feet in size.
c. Explain the difference in the results in (a) and (b).

13.62 In Problem 13.8 on page 561, you predicted the value of a baseball franchise, based on current revenue. The data are stored in BBRevenue.
a. Construct a 95% confidence interval estimate of the mean value of all baseball franchises that generate $200 million of annual revenue.
b. Construct a 95% prediction interval of the value of an individual baseball franchise that generates $200 million of annual revenue.
c. Explain the difference in the results in (a) and (b).

13.63 In Problem 13.10 on page 562, you used box office gross to predict DVD revenue. The data are stored in Movie. The company is about to release a movie on DVD that had a box office gross of $75 million.
a. What is the predicted DVD revenue?
b. Which interval is more useful here, the confidence interval estimate of the mean or the prediction interval for an individual response? Explain.
c. Construct and interpret the interval you selected in (b).

13.9 Pitfalls in Regression

Some of the pitfalls involved in using regression analysis are as follows:

- Lacking awareness of the assumptions of least-squares regression
- Not knowing how to evaluate the assumptions of least-squares regression
- Not knowing what the alternatives are to least-squares regression if a particular assumption is violated
- Using a regression model without knowledge of the subject matter
- Extrapolating outside the relevant range
- Concluding that a significant relationship identified in an observational study is due to a cause-and-effect relationship

The widespread availability of spreadsheet and statistical applications has made regression analysis much more feasible today than it once was. However, many users with access to such applications do not understand how to use regression analysis properly. Someone who is not familiar with either the assumptions of regression or how to evaluate the assumptions cannot be expected to know what the alternatives to least-squares regression are if a particular assumption is violated.

The data in Table 13.7 (stored in **Anscombe**) illustrate the importance of using scatter plots and residual analysis to go beyond the basic number crunching of computing the Y intercept, the slope, and r^2.

TABLE 13.7
Four Sets of Artificial Data

Data Set A		Data Set B		Data Set C		Data Set D	
X_i	Y_i	X_i	Y_i	X_i	Y_i	X_i	Y_i
10	8.04	10	9.14	10	7.46	8	6.58
14	9.96	14	8.10	14	8.84	8	5.76
5	5.68	5	4.74	5	5.73	8	7.71
8	6.95	8	8.14	8	6.77	8	8.84
9	8.81	9	8.77	9	7.11	8	8.47
12	10.84	12	9.13	12	8.15	8	7.04
4	4.26	4	3.10	4	5.39	8	5.25
7	4.82	7	7.26	7	6.42	19	12.50
11	8.33	11	9.26	11	7.81	8	5.56
13	7.58	13	8.74	13	12.74	8	7.91
6	7.24	6	6.13	6	6.08	8	6.89

Source: Data extracted from F. J. Anscombe, "Graphs in Statistical Analysis," *The American Statistician*, 27 (1973), 17–21.

Anscombe (reference 1) showed that all four data sets given in Table 13.7 have the following identical results:

$$\hat{Y}_i = 3.0 + 0.5X_i$$

$$S_{YX} = 1.237$$

$$S_{b_1} = 0.118$$

$$r^2 = 0.667$$

$$SSR = \text{Explained variation} = \sum_{i=1}^{n}(\hat{Y}_i - \bar{Y})^2 = 27.51$$

$$SSE = \text{Unexplained variation} = \sum_{i=1}^{n}(Y_i - \hat{Y}_i)^2 = 13.76$$

$$SST = \text{Total variation} = \sum_{i=1}^{n}(Y_i - \bar{Y})^2 = 41.27$$

If you stopped the analysis at this point, you would fail to observe the important differences among the four data sets.

From the scatter plots of Figure 13.22 and the residual plots of Figure 13.23 on page 590, you see how different the data sets are. Each has a different relationship between X and Y. The only data set that seems to approximately follow a straight line is data set A. The residual plot for data set A does not show any obvious patterns or outlying residuals. This is certainly not true for data sets B, C, and D. The scatter plot for data set B shows that a curvilinear regression model is more appropriate. This conclusion is reinforced by the residual plot for data set B. The scatter plot and the residual plot for data set C clearly show an outlying observation. In this case, one approach used is to remove the outlier and reestimate the regression model (see reference 4). The scatter plot for data set D represents a situation in which the model is heavily dependent on the outcome of a single data point ($X_8 = 19$ and $Y_8 = 12.50$). Any regression model with this characteristic should be used with caution.

FIGURE 13.22
Scatter plots for four data sets

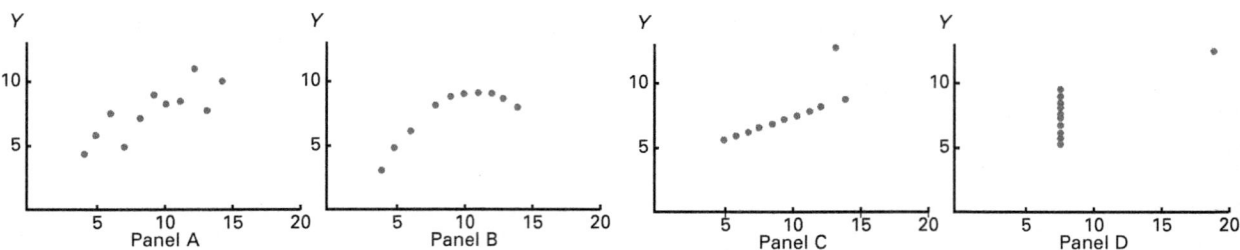

FIGURE 13.23
Residual plots for four data sets

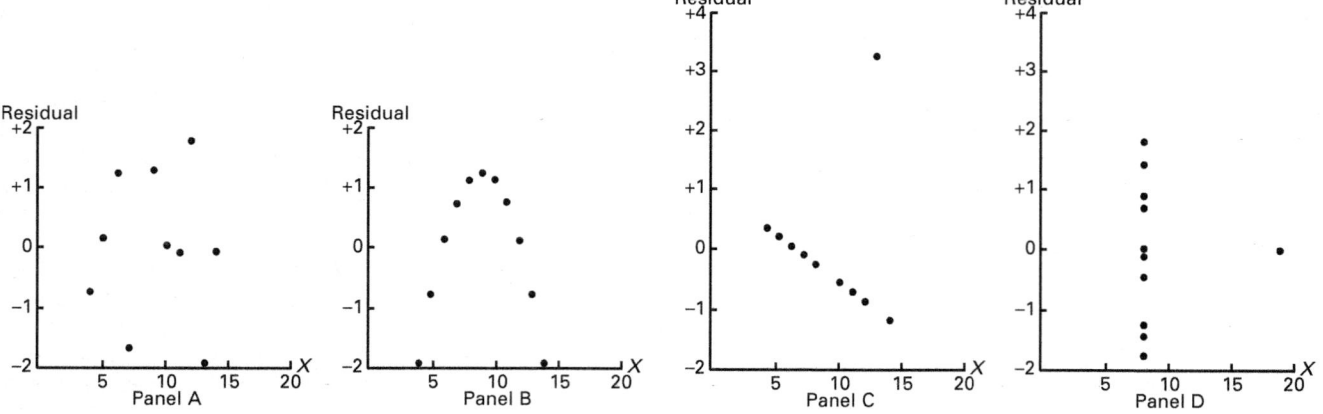

In summary, scatter plots and residual plots are of vital importance to a complete regression analysis. The information they provide is so basic to a credible analysis that you should always include these graphical methods as part of a regression analysis. Thus, a strategy you can use to help avoid the pitfalls of regression is as follows:

1. Start with a scatter plot to observe the possible relationship between X and Y.
2. Check the assumptions of regression (**l**inearity, **i**ndependence, **n**ormality, **e**qual variance) by performing a residual analysis that includes the following:
   a. Plotting the residuals versus the independent variable to determine whether the linear model is appropriate and to check for equal variance
   b. Constructing a histogram, stem-and-leaf display, boxplot, or normal probability plot of the residuals to check for normality
   c. Plotting the residuals versus time to check for independence (this step is necessary only if the data are collected over time)
3. If there are violations of the assumptions, use alternative methods to least-squares regression or alternative least-squares models (see reference 4).
4. If there are no violations of the assumptions, carry out tests for the significance of the regression coefficients and develop confidence and prediction intervals.
5. Avoid making predictions and forecasts outside the relevant range of the independent variable.

6. Keep in mind that the relationships identified in observational studies may or may not be due to cause-and-effect relationships. Remember that, although causation implies correlation, correlation does not imply causation.

THINK ABOUT THIS: By Any Other Name

You may not have frequently heard the phrase "regression model" outside a classroom, but the basic concepts of regression can be found under a variety of names in many sectors of the economy:

- **Advertising and marketing** Managers use econometric models (in other words, regression models) to determine the effect of an advertisement on sales, based on a set of factors. In one recent example, the number of tweets that mention specific products was used to make accurate prediction of sales trends. (See H. Rui, A. Whinston, and E. Winkler, "Follow the Tweets," *The Wall Street Journal*, November 30, 2009, p. R4.) Also, managers use data mining to predict patterns of behavior of what customers will buy in the future, based on historic information about the consumer.
- **Finance** Any time you read about a financial "model," you should assume that some type of regression model is being used. For example, a *New York Times* article on June 18, 2006, titled "An Old Formula That Points to New Worry" by Mark Hulbert (p. BU8), discusses a market timing model that predicts the returns of stocks in the next three to five years, based on the dividend yield of the stock market and the interest rate of 90-day Treasury bills.
- **Food and beverage** Enologix, a California consulting company, has developed a "formula" (a regression model) that predicts a wine's quality index, based on a set of chemical compounds found in the wine. (See D. Darlington, "The Chemistry of a 90+ Wine," *The New York Times Magazine*, August 7, 2005, pp. 36–39.)
- **Government** The Bureau of Labor Statistics uses hedonic models, a type of regression model, to adjust and manage its consumer price index ("Hedonic Quality Adjustment in the CPI," *Consumer Price Index*, **stat.bls.gov/cpi/cpihqaitem.htm**).
- **Transportation** Bing Travel uses data mining and predictive technologies to objectively predict airfare pricing. (See C. Elliott, "Bing Travel's Crean: We Save the Average Couple $50 per Trip," *Elliott Blog*, **www.elliott.org/first-person/bing-travel-we-save-the-average-couple-50-per-trip/**.)
- **Real estate** Zillow.com uses information about the features contained in a home and its location to develop estimates about the market value of the home, using a "formula" built with a proprietary model.

In a more general way, regression models are part of the "quants" movement that revolutionized Wall Street investing before moving on to other fields (see S. Baker, "Why Math Will Rock Your World: More Math Geeks Are Calling the Shots in Business. Is Your Industry Next?" *BusinessWeek*, January 23, 2006, pp. 54–62). While the methods, including advanced regression models, that the quants used in Wall Street operations have been seen by some as the cause of the 2007 economic meltdown (see S. Patterson, *The Quants: How a New Breed of Math Whizzes Conquered Wall Street and Nearly Destroyed It*, New York: Crown Business, 2010), the rise of quants reflects a growing use of regression and other statistical techniques in business.

In his landmark 2006 *BusinessWeek* article, Baker predicted that statistics and probability will become core skills for businesspeople and consumers. He claimed that those who would become successful would know how to use statistics, whether they are building financial models or making marketing plans. More recent articles, including S. Lohr's "For Today's Graduate, Just One Word: Statistics" (*The New York Times*, August 6, 2009, pp. A1, A3) confirm Baker's prediction and discussed how statistics is being used to "mine" large data sets to discover patterns, often using regression models. Hal Varian, the chief economist at Google, is quoted in that article as saying, "I keep saying that the sexy job in the next ten years will be statisticians."

USING STATISTICS: @Sunflowers Apparel Revisited

In the Sunflowers Apparel scenario, you were the director of planning for a chain of upscale clothing stores for women. Until now, Sunflowers managers selected sites based on factors such as the availability of a good lease or a subjective opinion that a location seemed like a good place for a store. To make more objective decisions, you developed a regression model to analyze the relationship between the size of a store and its annual sales. The model indicated that about 90.4% of the variation in sales was explained by the size of the store. Furthermore, for each increase of 1,000 square feet, mean annual sales were estimated to increase by $1.67 million. You can now use your model to help make better decisions when selecting new sites for stores as well as to forecast sales for existing stores.

SUMMARY

As you can see from the chapter roadmap in Figure 13.24, this chapter develops the simple linear regression model and discusses the assumptions and how to evaluate them. Once you are assured that the model is appropriate, you can predict values by using the prediction line and test for the significance of the slope. In Chapter 14, regression analysis is extended to situations in which more than one independent variable is used to predict the value of a dependent variable.

FIGURE 13.24
Roadmap for simple linear regression

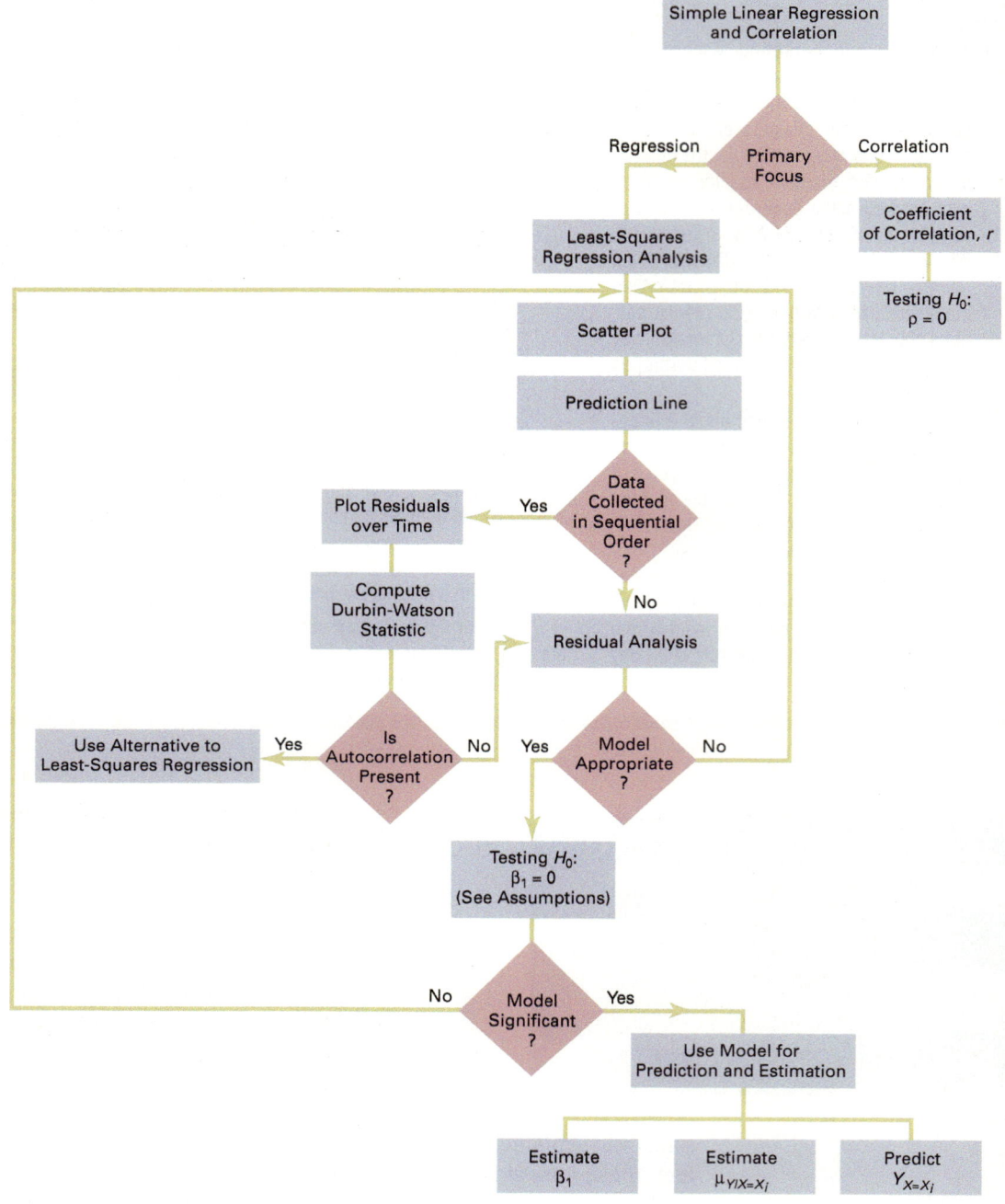

KEY EQUATIONS

Simple Linear Regression Model
$$Y_i = \beta_0 + \beta_1 X_i + \varepsilon_i \tag{13.1}$$

Simple Linear Regression Equation: The Prediction Line
$$\hat{Y}_i = b_0 + b_1 X_i \tag{13.2}$$

Computational Formula for the Slope, b_1
$$b_1 = \frac{SSXY}{SSX} \tag{13.3}$$

Computational Formula for the Y Intercept, b_0
$$b_0 = \bar{Y} - b_1 \bar{X} \tag{13.4}$$

Measures of Variation in Regression
$$SST = SSR + SSE \tag{13.5}$$

Total Sum of Squares (SST)
$$SST = \text{Total sum of squares} = \sum_{i=1}^{n}(Y_i - \bar{Y})^2 \tag{13.6}$$

Regression Sum of Squares (SSR)
$$SSR = \text{Explained variation or regression sum of squares}$$
$$= \sum_{i=1}^{n}(\hat{Y}_i - \bar{Y})^2 \tag{13.7}$$

Error Sum of Squares (SSE)
$$SSE = \text{Unexplained variation or error sum of squares}$$
$$= \sum_{i=1}^{n}(Y_i - \hat{Y}_i)^2 \tag{13.8}$$

Coefficient of Determination
$$r^2 = \frac{\text{Regression sum of squares}}{\text{Total sum of squares}} = \frac{SSR}{SST} \tag{13.9}$$

Computational Formula for SST
$$SST = \sum_{i=1}^{n}(Y_i - \bar{Y})^2 = \sum_{i=1}^{n}Y_i^2 - \frac{\left(\sum_{i=1}^{n}Y_i\right)^2}{n} \tag{13.10}$$

Computational Formula for SSR
$$SSR = \sum_{i=1}^{n}(\hat{Y}_i - \bar{Y})^2$$
$$= b_0 \sum_{i=1}^{n} Y_i + b_1 \sum_{i=1}^{n} X_i Y_i - \frac{\left(\sum_{i=1}^{n} Y_i\right)^2}{n} \tag{13.11}$$

Computational Formula for SSE
$$SSE = \sum_{i=1}^{n}(Y_i - \hat{Y}_i)^2 = \sum_{i=1}^{n} Y_i^2 - b_0 \sum_{i=1}^{n} Y_i - b_1 \sum_{i=1}^{n} X_i Y_i \tag{13.12}$$

Standard Error of the Estimate
$$S_{YX} = \sqrt{\frac{SSE}{n-2}} = \sqrt{\frac{\sum_{i=1}^{n}(Y_i - \hat{Y}_i)^2}{n-2}} \tag{13.13}$$

Residual
$$e_i = Y_i - \hat{Y}_i \tag{13.14}$$

Durbin-Watson Statistic
$$D = \frac{\sum_{i=2}^{n}(e_i - e_{i-1})^2}{\sum_{i=1}^{n} e_i^2} \tag{13.15}$$

Testing a Hypothesis for a Population Slope, β_1, Using the t Test
$$t_{STAT} = \frac{b_1 - \beta_1}{S_{b_1}} \tag{13.16}$$

Testing a Hypothesis for a Population Slope, β_1, Using the F Test
$$F_{STAT} = \frac{MSR}{MSE} \tag{13.17}$$

Confidence Interval Estimate of the Slope, β_1
$$b_1 \pm t_{\alpha/2} S_{b_1}$$
$$b_1 - t_{\alpha/2} S_{b_1} \leq \beta_1 \leq b_1 + t_{\alpha/2} S_{b_1} \tag{13.18}$$

Testing for the Existence of Correlation

$$t_{STAT} = \frac{r - \rho}{\sqrt{\frac{1-r^2}{n-2}}} \quad (13.19a)$$

$$r = \frac{cov(X,Y)}{S_X S_Y} \quad (13.19b)$$

Confidence Interval Estimate for the Mean of Y

$$\hat{Y}_i \pm t_{\alpha/2} S_{YX} \sqrt{h_i}$$

$$\hat{Y}_i - t_{\alpha/2} S_{YX} \sqrt{h_i} \leq \mu_{Y|X=X_i} \leq \hat{Y}_i + t_{\alpha/2} S_{YX} \sqrt{h_i} \quad (13.20)$$

Prediction Interval for an Individual Response, Y

$$\hat{Y}_i \pm t_{\alpha/2} S_{YX} \sqrt{1 + h_i}$$

$$\hat{Y}_i - t_{\alpha/2} S_{YX} \sqrt{1 + h_i} \leq Y_{X=X_i} \leq \hat{Y}_i + t_{\alpha/2} S_{YX} \sqrt{1 + h_i} \quad (13.21)$$

KEY TERMS

- assumptions of regression
- autocorrelation
- coefficient of determination
- confidence interval estimate for the mean response
- correlation coefficient
- dependent variable
- Durbin-Watson statistic
- equal variance
- error sum of squares (SSE)
- explained variation
- explanatory variable
- homoscedasticity
- independence of errors
- independent variable
- least-squares method
- linearity
- linear relationship
- normality
- prediction interval for an individual response, Y
- prediction line
- regression analysis
- regression coefficient
- regression sum of squares (SSR)
- relevant range
- residual
- residual analysis
- response variable
- scatter diagram
- scatter plot
- simple linear regression
- simple linear regression equation
- slope
- standard error of the estimate
- total sum of squares (SST)
- total variation
- unexplained variation
- Y intercept

CHAPTER REVIEW PROBLEMS

CHECKING YOUR UNDERSTANDING

13.64 What is the interpretation of the Y intercept and the slope in the simple linear regression equation?

13.65 What is the interpretation of the coefficient of determination?

13.66 When is the unexplained variation (i.e., error sum of squares) equal to 0?

13.67 When is the explained variation (i.e., regression sum of squares) equal to 0?

13.68 Why should you always carry out a residual analysis as part of a regression model?

13.69 What are the assumptions of regression analysis?

13.70 How do you evaluate the assumptions of regression analysis?

13.71 When and how do you use the Durbin-Watson statistic?

13.72 What is the difference between a confidence interval estimate of the mean response, $\mu_{Y|X=X_i}$, and a prediction interval of $Y_{X=X_i}$?

APPLYING THE CONCEPTS

13.73 Researchers from the Pace University Lubin School of Business conducted a study on Internet-supported courses. In one part of the study, four numerical variables were collected on 108 students in an introductory management course that met once a week for an entire semester. One variable collected was *hit consistency*. To measure hit consistency, the researchers did the following: If a student did not visit the Internet site between classes, the student was given a 0 for that time period. If a student visited the Internet site one or more times between classes, the student was given a 1 for that time period. Because there were 13 time periods, a student's score on hit consistency could range from 0 to 13.

The other three variables included the student's course average, the student's cumulative grade point average (GPA), and the total number of hits the student had on the Internet site supporting the course. The following table gives the correlation coefficient for all pairs of variables. Note that correlations marked with an * are statistically significant, using $\alpha = 0.001$:

Variable	Correlation
Course Average, Cumulative GPA	0.72*
Course Average, Total Hits	0.08
Course Average, Hit Consistency	0.37*
Cumulative GPA, Total Hits	0.12
Cumulative GPA, Hit Consistency	0.32*
Total Hits & Hit Consistency	0.64*

Source: Data extracted from D. Baugher, A. Varanelli, and E. Weisbord, "Student Hits in an Internet-Supported Course: How Can Instructors Use Them and What Do They Mean?" *Decision Sciences Journal of Innovative Education*, 1 (Fall 2003), 159–179.

a. What conclusions can you reach from this correlation analysis?
b. Are you surprised by the results, or are they consistent with your own observations and experiences?

13.74 Management of a soft-drink bottling company has the business objective of developing a method for allocating delivery costs to customers. Although one cost clearly relates to travel time within a particular route, another variable cost reflects the time required to unload the cases of soft drink at the delivery point. To begin, management decided to develop a regression model to predict delivery time based on the number of cases delivered. A sample of 20 deliveries within a territory was selected. The delivery times and the number of cases delivered were organized in the following table (and stored in Delivery):

Customer	Number of Cases	Delivery Time (Minutes)	Customer	Number of Cases	Delivery Time (Minutes)
1	52	32.1	11	161	43.0
2	64	34.8	12	184	49.4
3	73	36.2	13	202	57.2
4	85	37.8	14	218	56.8
5	95	37.8	15	243	60.6
6	103	39.7	16	254	61.2
7	116	38.5	17	267	58.2
8	121	41.9	18	275	63.1
9	143	44.2	19	287	65.6
10	157	47.1	20	298	67.3

a. Use the least-squares method to compute the regression coefficients b_0 and b_1.
b. Interpret the meaning of b_0 and b_1 in this problem.
c. Predict the delivery time for 150 cases of soft drink.
d. Should you use the model to predict the delivery time for a customer who is receiving 500 cases of soft drink? Why or why not?
e. Determine the coefficient of determination, r^2, and explain its meaning in this problem.
f. Perform a residual analysis. Is there any evidence of a pattern in the residuals? Explain.
g. At the 0.05 level of significance, is there evidence of a linear relationship between delivery time and the number of cases delivered?
h. Construct a 95% confidence interval estimate of the mean delivery time for 150 cases of soft drink and a 95% prediction interval of the delivery time for a single delivery of 150 cases of soft drink.

13.75 Measuring the height of a California redwood tree is a very difficult undertaking because these trees grow to heights of over 300 feet. People familiar with these trees understand that the height of a California redwood tree is related to other characteristics of the tree, including the diameter of the tree at the breast height of a person. The data in Redwood represent the height (in feet) and diameter (in inches) at the breast height of a person for a sample of 21 California redwood trees.
a. Assuming a linear relationship, use the least-squares method to compute the regression coefficients b_0 and b_1. State the regression equation that predicts the height of a tree based on the tree's diameter at breast height of a person.
b. Interpret the meaning of the slope in this equation.
c. Predict the height for a tree that has a breast diameter of 25 inches.
d. Interpret the meaning of the coefficient of determination in this problem.
e. Perform a residual analysis on the results and determine the adequacy of the model.
f. Determine whether there is a significant relationship between the height of redwood trees and the breast height diameter at the 0.05 level of significance.
g. Construct a 95% confidence interval estimate of the population slope between the height of the redwood trees and breast diameter.

13.76 You want to develop a model to predict the selling price of homes based on assessed value. A sample of 30 recently sold single-family houses in a small city is selected to study the relationship between selling price (in thousands of dollars) and assessed value (in thousands of dollars). The houses in the city were reassessed at full value one year prior to the study. The results are in House1 . (Hint: First, determine which are the independent and dependent variables.)

a. Construct a scatter plot and, assuming a linear relationship, use the least-squares method to compute the regression coefficients b_0 and b_1.
b. Interpret the meaning of the Y intercept, b_0, and the slope, b_1, in this problem.
c. Use the prediction line developed in (a) to predict the selling price for a house whose assessed value is $170,000.
d. Determine the coefficient of determination, r^2, and interpret its meaning in this problem.
e. Perform a residual analysis on your results and evaluate the regression assumptions.
f. At the 0.05 level of significance, is there evidence of a linear relationship between selling price and assessed value?
g. Construct a 95% confidence interval estimate of the population slope.

13.77 You want to develop a model to predict the assessed value of houses, based on heating area. A sample of 15 single-family houses in a city is selected. The assessed value (in thousands of dollars) and the heating area of the houses (in thousands of square feet) are recorded; the results are stored in House2 . (Hint: First, determine which are the independent and dependent variables.)
a. Construct a scatter plot and, assuming a linear relationship, use the least-squares method to compute the regression coefficients b_0 and b_1.
b. Interpret the meaning of the Y intercept, b_0, and the slope, b_1, in this problem.
c. Use the prediction line developed in (a) to predict the assessed value for a house whose heating area is 1,750 square feet.
d. Determine the coefficient of determination, r^2, and interpret its meaning in this problem.
e. Perform a residual analysis on your results and evaluate the regression assumptions.
f. At the 0.05 level of significance, is there evidence of a linear relationship between assessed value and heating area?

13.78 The director of graduate studies at a large college of business would like to predict the grade point average (GPA) of students in an MBA program based on Graduate Management Admission Test (GMAT) score. A sample of 20 students who have completed two years in the program is selected. The results are stored in GPIGMAT . (Hint: First, determine which are the independent and dependent variables.)
a. Construct a scatter plot and, assuming a linear relationship, use the least-squares method to compute the regression coefficients b_0 and b_1.
b. Interpret the meaning of the Y intercept, b_0, and the slope, b_1, in this problem.
c. Use the prediction line developed in (a) to predict the GPA for a student with a GMAT score of 600.
d. Determine the coefficient of determination, r^2, and interpret its meaning in this problem.
e. Perform a residual analysis on your results and evaluate the regression assumptions.
f. At the 0.05 level of significance, is there evidence of a linear relationship between GMAT score and GPA?
g. Construct a 95% confidence interval estimate of the mean GPA of students with a GMAT score of 600 and a 95% prediction interval of the GPA for a particular student with a GMAT score of 600.
h. Construct a 95% confidence interval estimate of the population slope.

13.79 An accountant for a large department store would like to develop a model to predict the amount of time it takes to process invoices. Data are collected from the past 32 working days, and the number of invoices processed and completion time (in hours) are stored in Invoice . (Hint: First, determine which are the independent and dependent variables.)
a. Assuming a linear relationship, use the least-squares method to compute the regression coefficients b_0 and b_1.
b. Interpret the meaning of the Y intercept, b_0, and the slope, b_1, in this problem.
c. Use the prediction line developed in (a) to predict the amount of time it would take to process 150 invoices.
d. Determine the coefficient of determination, r^2, and interpret its meaning.
e. Plot the residuals against the number of invoices processed and also against time.
f. Based on the plots in (e), does the model seem appropriate?
g. Based on the results in (e) and (f), what conclusions can you make about the validity of the prediction made in (c)?

13.80 On January 28, 1986, the space shuttle *Challenger* exploded, and seven astronauts were killed. Prior to the launch, the predicted atmospheric temperature was for freezing weather at the launch site. Engineers for Morton Thiokol (the manufacturer of the rocket motor) prepared charts to make the case that the launch should not take place due to the cold weather. These arguments were rejected, and the launch tragically took place. Upon investigation after the tragedy, experts agreed that the disaster occurred because of leaky rubber O-rings that did not seal properly due to the cold temperature. Data indicating the atmospheric temperature at the time of 23 previous launches and the O-ring damage index are stored in O-Ring .

Note: Data from flight 4 is omitted due to unknown O-ring condition.
Sources: Data extracted from *Report of the Presidential Commission on the Space Shuttle Challenger Accident,* Washington, DC, 1986, Vol. II (H1–H3); and Vol. IV (664), and *Post Challenger Evaluation of Space Shuttle Risk Assessment and Management,* Washington, DC, 1988, pp. 135–136.

a. Construct a scatter plot for the seven flights in which there was O-ring damage (O-ring damage index $\neq 0$). What conclusions, if any, can you reach about the relationship between atmospheric temperature and O-ring damage?

b. Construct a scatter plot for all 23 flights.
c. Explain any differences in the interpretation of the relationship between atmospheric temperature and O-ring damage in (a) and (b).
d. Based on the scatter plot in (b), provide reasons why a prediction should not be made for an atmospheric temperature of 31°F, the temperature on the morning of the launch of the *Challenger*.
e. Although the assumption of a linear relationship may not be valid for the set of 23 flights, fit a simple linear regression model to predict O-ring damage, based on atmospheric temperature.
f. Include the prediction line found in (e) on the scatter plot developed in (b).
g. Based on the results in (f), do you think a linear model is appropriate for these data? Explain.
h. Perform a residual analysis. What conclusions do you reach?

13.81 Crazy Dave, a well-known baseball analyst, would like to study various team statistics for the 2009 baseball season to determine which variables might be useful in predicting the number of wins achieved by teams during the season. He has decided to begin by using a team's earned run average (ERA), a measure of pitching performance, to predict the number of wins. The data for the 30 Major League Baseball teams are stored in BB2009 . (Hint: First, determine which are the independent and dependent variables.)
a. Assuming a linear relationship, use the least-squares method to compute the regression coefficients b_0 and b_1.
b. Interpret the meaning of the Y intercept, b_0, and the slope, b_1, in this problem.
c. Use the prediction line developed in (a) to predict the number of wins for a team with an ERA of 4.50.
d. Compute the coefficient of determination, r^2, and interpret its meaning.
e. Perform a residual analysis on your results and determine the adequacy of the fit of the model.
f. At the 0.05 level of significance, is there evidence of a linear relationship between the number of wins and the ERA?
g. Construct a 95% confidence interval estimate of the mean number of wins expected for teams with an ERA of 4.50.
h. Construct a 95% prediction interval of the number of wins for an individual team that has an ERA of 4.50.
i. Construct a 95% confidence interval estimate of the population slope.
j. The 30 teams constitute a population. In order to use statistical inference, as in (f) through (i), the data must be assumed to represent a random sample. What "population" would this sample be drawing conclusions about?
k. What other independent variables might you consider for inclusion in the model?

13.82 Can you use the annual revenues generated by National Basketball Association (NBA) franchises to predict franchise values? Figure 2.15 on page 87 shows a scatter plot of revenue with franchise value, and Figure 3.10 on page 159, shows the correlation coefficient. Now, you want to develop a simple linear regression model to predict franchise values based on revenues. (Franchise values and revenues are stored in NBAValues .)
a. Assuming a linear relationship, use the least-squares method to compute the regression coefficients b_0 and b_1.
b. Interpret the meaning of the Y intercept, b_0, and the slope, b_1, in this problem.
c. Predict the value of an NBA franchise that generates $150 million of annual revenue.
d. Compute the coefficient of determination, r^2, and interpret its meaning.
e. Perform a residual analysis on your results and evaluate the regression assumptions.
f. At the 0.05 level of significance, is there evidence of a linear relationship between the annual revenues generated and the value of an NBA franchise?
g. Construct a 95% confidence interval estimate of the mean value of all NBA franchises that generate $150 million of annual revenue.
h. Construct a 95% prediction interval of the value of an individual NBA franchise that generates $150 million of annual revenue.
i. Compare the results of (a) through (h) to those of baseball franchises in Problems 13.8, 13.20, 13.30, 13.46, and 13.62 and European soccer teams in Problem 13.83.

13.83 In Problem 13.82 you used annual revenue to develop a model to predict the franchise value of National Basketball Association (NBA) teams. Can you also use the annual revenues generated by European soccer teams to predict franchise values? (European soccer team values and revenues are stored in SoccerValues .)
a. Repeat Problem 13.82 (a) through (h) for the European soccer teams.
b. Compare the results of (a) to those of baseball franchises in Problems 13.8, 13.20, 13.30, 13.46, and 13.62 and NBA franchises in Problem 13.82.

13.84 During the fall harvest season in the United States, pumpkins are sold in large quantities at farm stands. Often, instead of weighing the pumpkins prior to sale, the farm stand operator will just place the pumpkin in the appropriate circular cutout on the counter. When asked why this was done, one farmer replied, "I can tell the weight of the pumpkin from its circumference." To determine whether this was really true, a sample of 23 pumpkins were measured for circumference and weighed; the results are stored in Pumpkin .
a. Assuming a linear relationship, use the least-squares method to compute the regression coefficients b_0 and b_1.
b. Interpret the meaning of the slope, b_1, in this problem.

c. Predict the weight for a pumpkin that is 60 centimeters in circumference.
d. Do you think it is a good idea for the farmer to sell pumpkins by circumference instead of weight? Explain.
e. Determine the coefficient of determination, r^2, and interpret its meaning.
f. Perform a residual analysis for these data and evaluate the regression assumptions.
g. At the 0.05 level of significance, is there evidence of a linear relationship between the circumference and weight of a pumpkin?
h. Construct a 95% confidence interval estimate of the population slope, β_1.

13.85 Can demographic information be helpful in predicting sales at sporting goods stores? The file **Sporting** contains the monthly sales totals from a random sample of 38 stores in a large chain of nationwide sporting goods stores. All stores in the franchise, and thus within the sample, are approximately the same size and carry the same merchandise. The county or, in some cases, counties in which the store draws the majority of its customers is referred to here as the customer base. For each of the 38 stores, demographic information about the customer base is provided. The data are real, but the name of the franchise is not used, at the request of the company. The data set contains the following variables:

Sales—Latest one-month sales total (dollars)
Age—Median age of customer base (years)
HS—Percentage of customer base with a high school diploma
College—Percentage of customer base with a college diploma
Growth—Annual population growth rate of customer base over the past 10 years
Income—Median family income of customer base (dollars)

a. Construct a scatter plot, using sales as the dependent variable and median family income as the independent variable. Discuss the scatter plot.
b. Assuming a linear relationship, use the least-squares method to compute the regression coefficients b_0 and b_1.
c. Interpret the meaning of the Y intercept, b_0, and the slope, b_1, in this problem.
d. Compute the coefficient of determination, r^2, and interpret its meaning.
e. Perform a residual analysis on your results and determine the adequacy of the fit of the model.
f. At the 0.05 level of significance, is there evidence of a linear relationship between the independent variable and the dependent variable?
g. Construct a 95% confidence interval estimate of the population slope and interpret its meaning.

13.86 For the data of Problem 13.85, repeat (a) through (g), using Age as the independent variable.

13.87 For the data of Problem 13.85, repeat (a) through (g), using HS as the independent variable.

13.88 For the data of Problem 13.85, repeat (a) through (g), using College as the independent variable.

13.89 For the data of Problem 13.85, repeat (a) through (g), using Growth as the independent variable.

13.90 The file **CEO-Compensation** includes the total compensation (in $) of CEOs of 197 large public companies and their investment return in 2009.
Source: Data extracted from D. Leonard, "Bargains in the Boardroom," *The New York Times,* April 4, 2010, pp. BU1, BU7, BU10, BU11.

a. Compute the correlation coefficient between compensation and the investment return in 2009.
b. At the 0.05 level of significance, is the correlation between compensation and the investment return in 2009 statistically significant?
c. Write a short summary of your findings in (a) and (b). Do the results surprise you?

13.91 Refer to the discussion of beta values and market models in Problem 13.49 on page 583. The S&P 500 Index tracks the overall movement of the stock market by considering the stock prices of 500 large corporations. The file **StockPrices** contains 2009 weekly data for the S&P 500 and three companies. The following variables are included:

WEEK—Week ending on date given
S&P—Weekly closing value for the S&P 500 Index
GE—Weekly closing stock price for General Electric
DISC—Weekly closing stock price for Discovery Communications
AAPL—Weekly closing stock price for Apple

Source: Data extracted from **finance.yahoo.com**, June 3, 2010.

a. Estimate the market model for GE. (Hint: Use the percentage change in the S&P 500 Index as the independent variable and the percentage change in GE's stock price as the dependent variable.)
b. Interpret the beta value for GE.
c. Repeat (a) and (b) for Discovery.
d. Repeat (a) and (b) for Apple.
e. Write a brief summary of your findings.

REPORT WRITING EXERCISE

13.92 In Problems 13.85 through 13.89, you developed regression models to predict monthly sales at a sporting goods store. Now, write a report based on the models you developed. Append to your report all appropriate charts and statistical information.

MANAGING ASHLAND MULTICOMM SERVICES

To ensure that as many trial subscriptions to the *3-For-All* service as possible are converted to regular subscriptions, the marketing department works closely with the customer support department to accomplish a smooth initial process for the trial subscription customers. To assist in this effort, the marketing department needs to accurately forecast the monthly total of new regular subscriptions.

A team consisting of managers from the marketing and customer support departments was convened to develop a better method of forecasting new subscriptions. Previously, after examining new subscription data for the prior three months, a group of three managers would develop a subjective forecast of the number of new subscriptions. Livia Salvador, who was recently hired by the company to provide expertise in quantitative forecasting methods, suggested that the department look for factors that might help in predicting new subscriptions.

Members of the team found that the forecasts in the past year had been particularly inaccurate because in some months, much more time was spent on telemarketing than in other months. Livia collected data (stored in AMS13) for the number of new subscriptions and hours spent on telemarketing for each month for the past two years.

EXERCISES

1. What criticism can you make concerning the method of forecasting that involved taking the new subscriptions data for the prior three months as the basis for future projections?

2. What factors other than number of telemarketing hours spent might be useful in predicting the number of new subscriptions? Explain.

3. a. Analyze the data and develop a regression model to predict the number of new subscriptions for a month, based on the number of hours spent on telemarketing for new subscriptions.
   b. If you expect to spend 1,200 hours on telemarketing per month, estimate the number of new subscriptions for the month. Indicate the assumptions on which this prediction is based. Do you think these assumptions are valid? Explain.
   c. What would be the danger of predicting the number of new subscriptions for a month in which 2,000 hours were spent on telemarketing?

DIGITAL CASE

Apply your knowledge of simple linear regression in this Digital Case, which extends the Sunflowers Apparel Using Statistics scenario from this chapter.

Leasing agents from the Triangle Mall Management Corporation have suggested that Sunflowers consider several locations in some of Triangle's newly renovated lifestyle malls that cater to shoppers with higher-than-mean disposable income. Although the locations are smaller than the typical Sunflowers location, the leasing agents argue that higher-than-mean disposable income in the surrounding community is a better predictor than store size of higher sales. The leasing agents maintain that sample data from 14 Sunflowers stores prove that this is true.

Open **Triangle_Sunflower.pdf** and review the leasing agents' proposal and supporting documents. Then answer the following questions:

1. Should mean disposable income be used to predict sales based on the sample of 14 Sunflowers stores?
2. Should the management of Sunflowers accept the claims of Triangle's leasing agents? Why or why not?
3. Is it possible that the mean disposable income of the surrounding area is not an important factor in leasing new locations? Explain.
4. Are there any other factors not mentioned by the leasing agents that might be relevant to the store leasing decision?

REFERENCES

1. Anscombe, F. J., "Graphs in Statistical Analysis," *The American Statistician*, 27 (1973), 17–21.
2. Hoaglin, D. C., and R. Welsch, "The Hat Matrix in Regression and ANOVA," *The American Statistician*, 32 (1978), 17–22.
3. Hocking, R. R., "Developments in Linear Regression Methodology: 1959–1982," *Technometrics*, 25 (1983), 219–250.
4. Kutner, M. H., C. J. Nachtsheim, J. Neter, and W. Li, *Applied Linear Statistical Models*, 5th ed. (New York: McGraw-Hill/Irwin, 2005).
5. *Microsoft Excel 2010* (Redmond, WA: Microsoft Corp., 2010).
6. *Minitab Release 16* (State College, PA: Minitab, Inc., 2010).

CHAPTER 13 EXCEL GUIDE

EG13.1 TYPES of REGRESSION MODELS

There are no Excel Guide instructions for this section.

EG13.2 DETERMINING the SIMPLE LINEAR REGRESSION EQUATION

PHStat2 Use **Simple Linear Regression** to perform a simple linear regression analysis. For example, to perform the Figure 13.4 analysis of the Sunflowers Apparel data on page 556, open to the **DATA worksheet** of the **Site workbook**. Select **PHStat → Regression → Simple Linear Regression**. In the procedure's dialog box (shown below):

1. Enter **C1:C15** as the **Y Variable Cell Range**.
2. Enter **B1:B15** as the **X Variable Cell Range**.
3. Check **First cells in both ranges contain label**.
4. Enter **95** as the **Confidence level for regression coefficients**.
5. Check **Regression Statistics Table** and **ANOVA and Coefficients Table**.
6. Enter a **Title** and click **OK**.

The procedure creates a worksheet that contains a copy of your data as well as the worksheet shown in Figure 13.4.

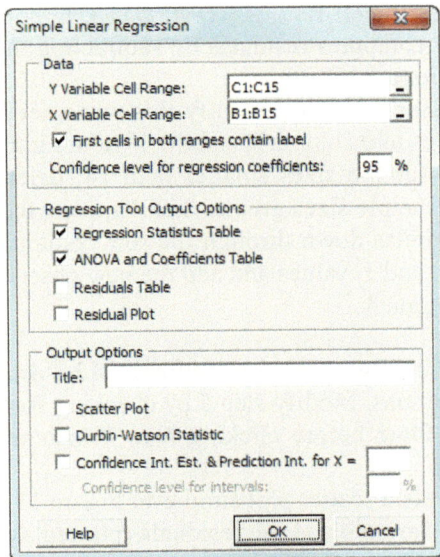

For more information about these worksheets, read the following *In-Depth Excel* section.

To create a scatter plot that contains a prediction line and regression equation similar to Figure 13.5 on page 556, modify step 6 by checking the **Scatter Plot** output option before clicking **OK**.

In-Depth Excel Use the **COMPUTE worksheet** of the **Simple Linear Regression workbook**, shown in Figure 13.4 on page 556, as a template for performing simple linear regression. Columns A through I of this worksheet duplicate the visual design of the Analysis ToolPak regression worksheet. The worksheet uses the regression data in the **SLRDATA worksheet** to perform the regression analysis for the Table 13.1 Sunflowers Apparel data.

Not shown in Figure 13.4 is the Calculations area in columns K through M. This area contains an array formula in the cell range L2:M6 that contains the expression **LINEST(**cell range of Y variable, cell range of X variable, **True, True)** to compute the b_1 and b_0 coefficients in cells L2 and M2, the b_1 and b_0 standard errors in cells L3 and M3, r^2 and the standard error of the estimate in cells L4 and M4, the F test statistic and error df in cells L5 and M5, and SSR and SSE in cells L6 and M6. In cell L9, the expression **TINV(1 − confidence level, Error degrees of freedom)** computes the critical value for the t test.

To perform simple linear regression for other data, paste the regression data into the SLRDATA worksheet. Paste the values for the X variable into column A and the values for the Y variable into column B. Open to the COMPUTE worksheet. First, enter the confidence level in cell L8. Then edit the array formula: Select the cell range L2:M6, edit the cell ranges in the formulas, and then, while holding down the **Control** and **Shift** keys (or the **Apple** key on a Mac), press the **Enter** key. (Open the **COMPUTE_FORMULAS worksheet** to examine all the formulas in the worksheet, some of which are discussed in later sections of this Excel Guide.)

To create a scatter plot that contains a prediction line and regression equation similar to Figure 13.5 on page 556, first use the Section EG2.6 *In-Depth Excel* scatter plot instructions with the Table 13.1 Sunflowers Apparel data to create a basic plot. Then select the plot and:

1. Select **Layout → Trendline** and select **More Trendline Options** from the Trendline gallery.

In the Format Trendline dialog box (shown on page 602):

2. Click **Trendline Options** in the left pane. In the Trendline Options pane on the right, click **Linear**, check **Display Equation on chart**, check **Display R-squared value on chart**, and then click **Close**.

For scatter plots of other data, if the X axis does not appear at the bottom of the plot, right-click the Y axis and

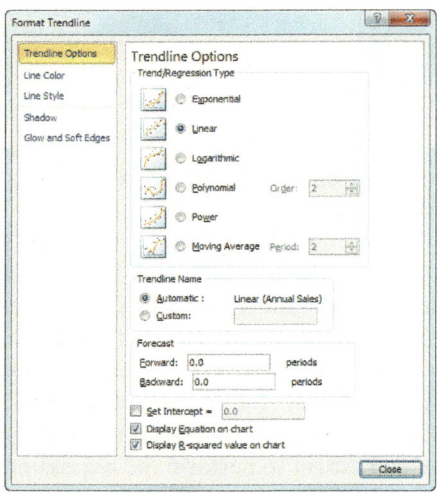

click **Format Axis** from the shortcut menu. In the Format Axis dialog box, click **Axis Options** in the left pane. In the Axis Options pane on the right, click **Axis value** and in its box enter the value shown in the dimmed **Minimum** box at the top of the pane. Then click **Close**.

Analysis ToolPak Use **Regression** to perform simple linear regression. For example, to perform the Figure 13.4 analysis of the Sunflowers Apparel data (see page 556), open to the **DATA worksheet** of the **Site workbook** and:

1. Select **Data → Data Analysis**.
2. In the Data Analysis dialog box, select **Regression** from the **Analysis Tools** list and then click **OK**.

In the Regression dialog box (see below):

3. Enter **C1:C15** as the **Input Y Range** and enter **B1:B15** as the **Input X Range**.
4. Check **Labels** and check **Confidence Level** and enter **95** in its box.
5. Click **New Worksheet Ply** and then click **OK**.

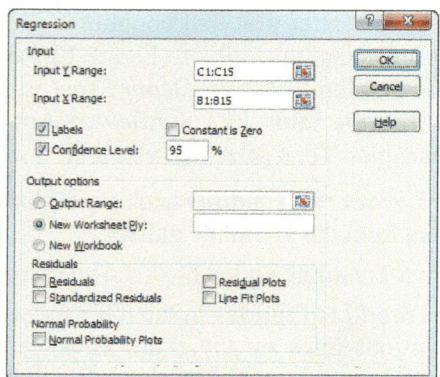

EG13.3 MEASURES of VARIATION

The measures of variation are computed as part of creating the simple linear regression worksheet using the Section EG13.2 instructions.

If you use either Section EG13.2 *PHStat2* or *In-Depth Excel* instructions, formulas used to compute these measures are in the **COMPUTE worksheet** that is created. Formulas in cells B5, B7, B13, C12, C13, D12, and E12 copy values computed by the array formula in cell range L2:M6. The cell F12 formula, in the form =**FDIST(*F test statistic*, 1, *error degrees of freedom*)**, computes the *p*-value for the *F* test for the slope, discussed in Section 13.7.

EG13.4 ASSUMPTIONS

There are no Excel Guide instructions for this section.

EG13.5 RESIDUAL ANALYSIS

PHStat2 Use the Section EG13.2 *PHStat2* instructions. Modify step 5 by checking **Residuals Table** and **Residual Plot** in addition to checking **Regression Statistics Table** and **ANOVA and Coefficients Table**.

In-Depth Excel Use the **RESIDUALS worksheet** of the **Simple Linear Regression workbook**, shown in Figure 13.10 on page 570, as a template for creating a residuals worksheet. This worksheet computes the residuals for the regression analysis for the Table 13.1 Sunflowers Apparel data. In column C, the worksheet computes the predicted Y values (labeled Predicted Annual Sales in Figure 13.10) by first multiplying the X values by the b_1 coefficient in cell B18 of the **COMPUTE worksheet** and then adding the b_0 coefficient (in cell B17 of COMPUTE). In column E, the worksheet computes residuals by subtracting the predicted Y values from the Y values.

For other problems, modify this worksheet by pasting the X values into column B and the Y values into column D. Then, for sample sizes smaller than 14, delete the extra rows. For sample sizes greater than 14, copy the column C and E formulas down through the row containing the last pair and X and Y values and add the new observation numbers in column A.

Analysis ToolPak Use the Section EG13.2 *Analysis Tool-Pak* instructions. Modify step 5 by checking **Residuals** and **Residual Plots** before clicking **New Worksheet Ply** and then **OK**.

To create a scatter plot similar to Figure 13.11, use the original X variable and the residuals (plotted as the Y variable) as the chart data.

EG13.6 MEASURING AUTOCORRELATION: the DURBIN-WATSON STATISTIC

PHStat2 Use the *PHStat2* instructions at the beginning of Section EG13.2. Modify step 6 by checking the **Durbin-Watson Statistic** output option before clicking **OK**.

In-Depth Excel Use the **DURBIN_WATSON worksheet** of the **Simple Linear Regression workbook**, similar to the worksheet shown in Figure 13.16 on page 575, as a template for computing the Durbin-Watson statistic. The worksheet computes the statistic for the package delivery simple linear regression model. In cell B3, the worksheet uses the expression **SUMXMY2**(*cell range of the second through last residual, cell range of the first through the second-to-last residual*) to compute the sum of squared difference of the residuals, the numerator in Equation (13.15) on page 574, and in cell B4 uses **SUMSQ**(*cell range of the residuals*) to compute the sum of squared residuals, the denominator in Equation (13.15).

To compute the Durbin-Watson statistic for other problems, first create the simple linear regression model and the RESIDUALS worksheet for the problem, using the instructions in Sections EG13.2 and EG13.5. Then open the DURBIN_WATSON worksheet and edit the formulas in cell B3 and B4 to point to the proper cell ranges of the new residuals.

EG13.7 INFERENCES ABOUT the SLOPE and CORRELATION COEFFICIENT

The t test for the slope and F test for the slope are included in the worksheet created by using the Section EG13.2 instructions. The t test computations in the worksheets created by using the *PHStat2* and *In-Depth Excel* instructions are discussed in Section EG13.2. The F test computations are discussed in Section EG13.3.

EG13.8 ESTIMATION of MEAN VALUES and PREDICTION of INDIVIDUAL VALUES

PHStat2 Use the Section EG13.2 *PHStat2* instructions but replace step 6 with these steps 6 and 7:

6. Check **Confidence Int. Est. & Prediction Int. for X =** and enter **4** in its box. Enter **95** as the percentage for **Confidence level for intervals**.

7. Enter a **Title** and click **OK**.

The additional worksheet created is discussed in the following *In-Depth Excel* instructions.

In-Depth Excel Use the **CIEandPI worksheet** of the **Simple Linear Regression workbook**, shown in Figure 13.21 on page 587, as a template for computing confidence interval estimates and prediction intervals. The worksheet contains the data and formulas for the Section 13.8 examples that use the Table 13.1 Sunflowers Apparel data. The worksheet uses the expression **TINV(1 −** *confidence level, degrees of freedom*) to compute the t critical value in cell B10 and the expression **TREND**(*Y variable cell range, X variable cell range, X value*) to compute the predicted Y value for the X value in cell B15. In cell B12, the expression **DEVSQ**(*X variable cell range*) computes the *SSX* value that is used, in turn, to help compute the h statistic.

To compute a confidence interval estimate and prediction interval for other problems:

1. Paste the regression data into the **SLRData worksheet**. Use column A for the X variable data and column B for the Y variable data.
2. Open to the **CIEandPI worksheet**.

In the CIEandPI worksheet:

3. Change values for the **X Value** and **Confidence Level**, as is necessary.
4. Edit the cell ranges used in the cell B15 formula that uses the TREND function to refer to the new cell ranges for the Y and X variables.

To create a scatter plot similar to Figure 13.11 on page 570, use the original X variable and the residuals (plotted as the Y variable) as the chart data.

CHAPTER 13 MINITAB GUIDE

MG13.1 TYPES of REGRESSION MODELS

There are no Minitab Guide instructions for this section.

MG13.2 DETERMINING the SIMPLE LINEAR REGRESSION EQUATION

Use **Regression** to perform a simple linear regression analysis. For example, to perform the Figure 13.4 analysis of the Sunflowers Apparel data on page 556, open to the **Site** worksheet. Select **Stat → Regression → Regression**. In the Regression dialog box (shown below):

1. Double-click **C3   Annual Sales** in the variables list to add '**Annual Sales**' to the **Response** box.
2. Double-click **C2   Square Feet** in the variables list to add '**Square Feet**' to the **Predictors** box.
3. Click **Graphs**.

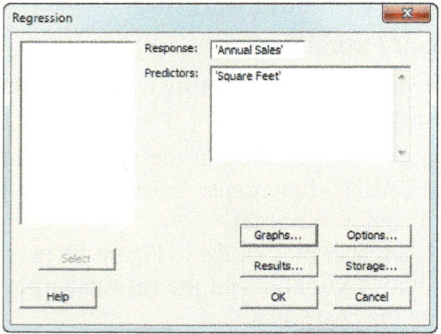

In the Regression - Graphs dialog box (shown below):

4. Click **Regular** (in Residuals for Plots) and **Individual Plots** (in Residual Plots).
5. Check **Histogram of residuals, Normal plot of residuals, Residuals versus fits**, and **Residuals versus order** and then press **Tab**.
6. Double-click **C2   Square Feet** in the variables list to add '**Square Feet**' in the **Residuals versus the variables** box.
7. Click **OK**.

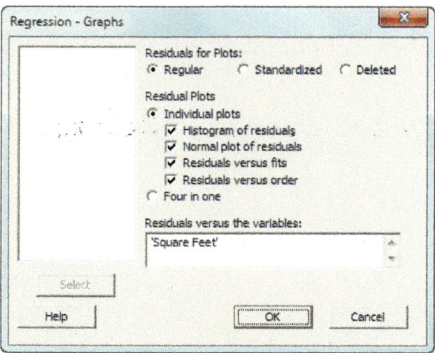

8. Back in the Regression dialog box, click **Results**.

In the Regression - Results dialog box (not shown):

9. Click **Regression equation, table of coefficients, s, R-squared, and basic analysis of variance** and then click **OK**.
10. Back in the Regression dialog box, click **Options**.

In the Regression - Options dialog box (shown below):

11. Check **Fit Intercept**.
12. Clear all the **Display** and **Lack of Fit Test** check boxes.
13. Enter **4** in the **Prediction intervals for new observations** box.
14. Enter **95** in the **Confidence level** box.
15. Click **OK**.
16. Back in the Regression dialog box, click **OK**.

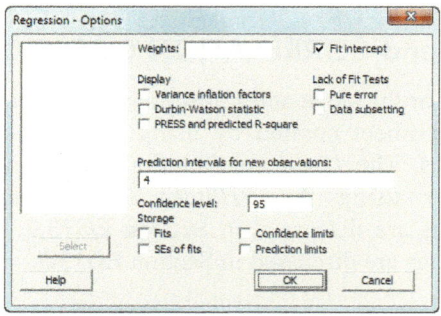

To create a scatter plot that contains a prediction line and regression equation similar to Figure 13.5 on page 556, use the Section MG2.6 scatter plot instructions with the Table 13.1 Sunflowers Apparel data.

MG13.3 MEASURES of VARIATION

The measures of variation are computed in the Analysis of Variance table that is part of the simple linear regression results created using the Section MG13.2 instructions.

MG13.4 ASSUMPTIONS

There are no Minitab Guide instructions for this section.

MG13.5 RESIDUAL ANALYSIS

Selections in step 5 of the Section MG13.2 instructions create the residual plots and normal probability plots necessary for residual analysis. To create the list of residual values similar to column E in Figure 13.10 on page 570, replace step

15 of the Section MG13.2 instructions with these steps 15 through 17:

15. Click **Storage**.
16. In the Regression - Storage dialog box, check **Residuals** and then click **OK**.
17. Back in the Regression dialog box, click **OK**.

MG13.6 MEASURING AUTOCORRELATION: the DURBIN-WATSON STATISTIC

To compute the Durbin-Watson statistic, use the Section MG13.2 instructions but check **Durbin-Watson statistic** (in the Regression - Options dialog box) as part of step 12.

MG13.7 INFERENCES ABOUT the SLOPE and CORRELATION COEFFICIENT

The t test for the slope and F test for the slope are included in the results created by using the Section MG13.2 instructions.

MG13.8 ESTIMATION of MEAN VALUES and PREDICTION of INDIVIDUAL VALUES

The confidence interval estimate and prediction interval are included in the results created by using the Section MG13.2 instructions.

CHAPTER 11
Simple Interest and Simple Discount

18 Months Same as Cash Financing on New TVs*

Radhika had just received mail for the first time in her new apartment, and there it was in big bold letters: 18 MONTHS SAME AS CASH FINANCING*. The ad read: The minimum monthly payment for this purchase does not include interest charges during the promotional period. You'll pay no interest for 18 months. Simply pay at least the total minimum monthly payment due as indicated on your billing statement. There's no prepayment penalty, and this offer provides you with the flexibility you need to meet your specific budget and purchasing requirements.

It sounded like a great deal. She really wanted to buy a flat panel TV and was short on cash. But Radhika had some concerns. First, she didn't know much about financing or how interest was computed; and second, she knew that the asterisk would probably mean trouble. After reading further, she found the following:

*The 18-month promotion is for televisions with a minimum value of $499.99. The 12-month promotion requires a minimum purchase of $299.99. These are "same as cash" promotions. If the balance on these purchases is paid in full before the expiration of the promotional period indicated on your billing statement and your account is kept current, then accrued finance charges will not be imposed on these purchases. If the balance on these purchases is not paid in full, finance charges will be assessed from the purchase date at the annual simple interest rate of 24.99%. For accounts not kept current, the default simple interest rate of 27.99% will be applied to all balances on your account. Minimum monthly payments are required. The minimum finance charge is $2.00. Certain rules apply to the allocation of payments and finance charges on your promotional purchase if you make more than one purchase on your account.

Wow! That was a lot to digest. Radhika had her heart set on a TV that cost about $800, and she was hoping to keep her payments under $20 per month. Would that be enough to pay the account in full in 18 months? And if she came up short by a few hundred dollars, would she still be charged all of that interest? If so, how much would 24.99% cost her during that time? What was simple interest, anyway? None of this sounded simple to her. And the late penalties—she didn't even want to think about those.

Radhika took a deep breath. Maybe this wasn't such a good idea, she thought as she reached for her keys. But she really wanted that TV.

LEARNING OUTCOMES

11-1 The Simple Interest Formula
1. Find simple interest using the simple interest formula.
2. Find the maturity value of a loan.
3. Convert months to a fractional or decimal part of a year.
4. Find the principal, rate, or time using the simple interest formula.

11-2 Ordinary and Exact Interest
1. Find the exact time.
2. Find the due date.
3. Find the ordinary interest and the exact interest.
4. Make a partial payment before the maturity date.

11-3 Promissory Notes
1. Find the bank discount and proceeds for a simple discount note.
2. Find the true or effective interest rate of a simple discount note.
3. Find the third-party discount and proceeds for a third-party discount note.

A corresponding Business Math Case Video for this chapter, *The Real World: Video Case: Should I Buy New Equipment Now?* can be found online at www.pearsonhighered.com\cleaves.

Interest: an amount paid or earned for the use of money.

Simple interest: interest when a loan or investment is repaid in a lump sum.

Principal: the amount of money borrowed or invested.

Rate: the percent of the principal paid as interest per time period.

Time: the number of days, months, or years that the money is borrowed or invested.

Every business and every person at some time borrows or invests money. A person (or business) who borrows money must pay for the use of the money. A person who invests money must be paid by the person or firm who uses the money. The price paid for using money is called **interest**.

In the business world, we encounter two basic kinds of interest, *simple* and *compound*. **Simple interest** applies when a loan or investment is repaid in a lump sum. The person using the money has use of the full amount of money for the entire time of the loan or investment. Compound interest, which is explained in Chapter 13, most often applies to savings accounts, installment loans, and credit cards.

Both types of interest take into account three factors: the principal, the interest rate, and the time period involved. **Principal** is the amount of money borrowed or invested. **Rate** is the percent of the principal paid as interest per time period. **Time** is the number of days, months, or years that the money is borrowed or invested.

11-1 THE SIMPLE INTEREST FORMULA

LEARNING OUTCOMES
1. Find simple interest using the simple interest formula.
2. Find the maturity value of a loan.
3. Convert months to a fractional or decimal part of a year.
4. Find the principal, rate, or time using the simple interest formula.

1 Find simple interest using the simple interest formula.

The interest formula $I = PRT$ shows how interest, principal, rate, and time are related and gives us a way of finding one of these values if the other three values are known.

HOW TO Find simple interest using the simple interest formula

1. Identify the principal, rate, and time.
2. Multiply the principal by the rate and time.

$$\text{Interest} = \text{principal} \times \text{rate} \times \text{time}$$
$$I = PRT$$

The rate of interest is a percent for a given time period, usually one year. The time in the interest formula must be expressed in the same unit of time as the rate. If the rate is a percent per year, the time must be expressed in years or a decimal or fractional part of a year. Similarly, if the rate is a percent per month, the time must be expressed in months.

EXAMPLE 1 Find the interest paid on a loan of $1,500 for one year at a simple interest rate of 9% per year.

$I = PRT$ Use the simple interest formula. Principal P is $1,500, rate R is 9% per year, and time T is one year.

$I = (\$1,500)(9\%)(1)$ Write 9% as a decimal. Multiply.
$I = (\$1,500)(0.09)(1)$
$I = \$135$

The interest on the loan is $135.

EXAMPLE 2 Kanette's Salon borrowed $5,000 at $8\frac{1}{2}$% per year simple interest for two years to buy new hair dryers. How much interest must be paid?

$I = PRT$ Use the simple interest formula. Principal P is $5,000, rate R is $8\frac{1}{2}$% per year, and time T is two years.

$I = (\$5,000)(8\frac{1}{2}\%)(2)$
$I = (\$5,000)(0.085)(2)$ Write $8\frac{1}{2}$% as a decimal. Multiply.
$I = \$850$

Kanette's Salon will pay $850 interest.

Simple Interest and Simple Discount

Prime interest rate (prime), reference rate, or base lending rate: the lowest rate of interest charged by banks for short-term loans to their most creditworthy customers.

A loan that is made using simple interest is to be repaid in a lump sum at the end of the time of the loan. Banks and lending institutions make loans at a variety of different rates based on factors such as prime interest rate and the amount of risk that the loan will be repaid. The **prime interest rate** is the lowest rate of interest charged by banks for short-term loans to their most creditworthy customers. Banks establish the rate of a loan based on the current prime rate and the likelihood that it will not change significantly over the time of the loan. Some banks may refer to the prime lending rate as the **reference rate** or the **base lending rate**.

Loans are made at the prime rate or higher, often significantly higher. Investments such as savings accounts and certificates of deposit earn interest at a rate less than prime. Lending institutions make a profit based on the difference between the rate of interest charged for loans and the rate of interest given for investments.

> **DID YOU KNOW?**
>
> **Banks Lend Money to Other Banks?**
>
> Yes, these loans are short term (usually overnight) and made through the Federal Reserve at a rate that is lower than prime. This rate is referred to as the **federal funds rate**. Each bank establishes its own prime rate, but this rate is almost always the same among the major banks. Changes to the prime rate are usually made at the same time as a change in the federal funds rate is made. There is no scheduled time that these changes occur.

STOP AND CHECK

1. Find the interest paid on a loan of $38,000 for one year at a simple interest rate of 10.5%.

2. A loan of $17,500 for six years has a simple interest rate of 7.75%. Find the interest.

3. The 7th Inning borrowed $6,700 at 9.5% simple interest for three years. How much interest is paid?

4. Find the interest on a $38,500 loan at a simple interest rate of 12.3% for five years.

2 Find the maturity value of a loan.

Maturity value: the total amount of money due at the end of a loan period—the amount of the loan and the interest.

The *total* amount of money due at the end of a loan period—the amount of the loan *and* the interest—is called the **maturity value** of the loan. When the principal and interest of a loan are known, the maturity value is found by adding the principal and the interest. The maturity value can also be found directly from the principal, rate, and time.

> **HOW TO** Find the maturity value of a loan
>
> 1. If the principal and interest are known, add them.
>
> $$\text{Maturity value} = \text{principal} + \text{interest}$$
> $$MV = P + I$$
>
> 2. If the principal, rate, and time are known, use either of the formulas:
>   (a) Maturity value = principal + (principal × rate × time)
> $$MV = P + PRT$$
>   (b) Maturity value = principal (1 + rate × time)
> $$MV = P(1 + RT)$$

Both variations of the formula for finding the maturity value when the principal, rate, and time are known require that the operations be performed according to the standard order of operations. To review briefly, when more than one operation is to be performed, perform operations within parentheses first. Perform multiplications and divisions before additions and subtractions. Perform additions and subtractions last. For a more detailed discussion of the order of operations, review Chapter 1, Section 3, Learning Outcome 2.

EXAMPLE 3

In Example 2 on page 390, we found that Kanette's Salon would pay $850 interest on a $5,000 loan. How much money will Kanette's Salon pay at the end of two years?

Maturity value = principal + interest P and I are known.
$MV = P + I$ Substitute known values.
$= \$5,000 + \$850 = \$5,850$

Kanette's Salon will pay $5,850 at the end of the loan period.

EXAMPLE 4

Marcus Logan can purchase furniture with a two-year simple interest loan at 9% interest per year. What is the maturity value for a $2,500 loan?

Maturity value = principal $(1 + \text{rate} \times \text{time})$ P, R, and T are known.
$MV = P(1 + RT)$ Substitute $P = \$2,500$,
                                                                    $R = 9\%$ or 0.09,
                                                                    $T = 2$ years.
$MV = \$2,500(1 + 0.09 \times 2)$ Multiply in parentheses.
$MV = \$2,500(1 + 0.18)$ Add in parentheses.
$MV = \$2,500(1.18)$ Multiply.
$MV = \$2,950$

Marcus will pay $2,950 at the end of two years.

TIP

Does a Calculator Know the Proper Order of Operations? Some Do, Some Don't.

Using a basic calculator, you enter calculations as they should be performed according to the standard order of operations.

[AC] .09 [×] 2 [=][+] 1 [=] [×] 2500 [=] ⇒ 2950

Using a business or scientific calculator with parentheses keys allows you to enter values for the maturity value formula as they appear. The calculator is programmed to perform the operations in the standard order. The calculator has special keys for entering parentheses, [(] and [)].

[AC] 2500 [×] [(] 1 [+] .09 [×] 2 [)] [=] ⇒ 2950

✓ STOP AND CHECK

1. How much is paid at the end of two years for a loan of $8,000 if the total interest is $660?

2. A loan of $7,250 is to be repaid in three years and has a simple interest rate of 12%. How much is paid after the three years?

3. Find the maturity value of a $1,800 loan made for two years at $9\frac{3}{4}\%$ simple interest per year.

4. Find the maturity value of a three-year, simple interest loan at 11% per year in the amount of $7,275.

---

3 Convert months to a fractional or decimal part of a year.

Not all loans or investments are made for a whole number of years; but, as the interest rate is most often given per year, the time must also be expressed in the same unit of time as the rate.

HOW TO   Convert months to a fractional or decimal part of a year

1. Write the number of months as the numerator of a fraction.
2. Write 12 as the denominator of the fraction.
3. Reduce the fraction to lowest terms if using the fractional equivalent.
4. Divide the numerator by the denominator to get the decimal equivalent of the fraction.

Simple Interest and Simple Discount

EXAMPLE 5
Convert (a) 5 months and (b) 15 months to years, expressed in both fraction or mixed-number and decimal form.

(a) 5 months = $\frac{5}{12}$ year ⟶ 5 months equal $\frac{5}{12}$ year.

$12\overline{)5.0000000}$ = 0.4166666 year = 0.42 year

To write the fraction as a decimal, divide the number of months (the numerator) by the number of months in a year (the denominator).

5 months = $\frac{5}{12}$ year or 0.42 year (rounded)

(b) 15 months = $\frac{15}{12}$ years = $\frac{5}{4}$ or $1\frac{1}{4}$ years ⟶ 15 months equal $\frac{15}{12}$ years.

$12\overline{)15.00}$ = 1.25 years
  12.00
  ───
   3 0
   2 4
   ───
    60
    60
    ──
     0

To write the fraction as a decimal, divide the number of months (the numerator) by the number of months in a year (the denominator).

15 months = $1\frac{1}{4}$ years or 1.25 years

EXAMPLE 6
To save money for a shoe repair shop, Stan Wright invested $2,500 for 45 months at $3\frac{1}{2}$% simple interest per year. How much interest did he earn?

$T = 45$ months $= \frac{45}{12}$ years $= 3\frac{3}{4}$ or 3.75 years   Write the time in terms of years.

$I = PRT$ Use the simple interest formula.

$I = \$2{,}500(0.035)(3.75)$ Principal P is \$2,500, rate R is 0.035, and time T is $\frac{45}{12}$ or 3.75. Multiply.

$I = \$328.13$ Round to the nearest cent.

Stan Wright earned \$328.13 in interest.

TIP
Check Calculations by Estimating

As careful as we are, there will always be times that we hit an incorrect key or use an improper sequence of steps and produce an incorrect solution. You can catch most of these mistakes by first anticipating what a reasonable answer should be.

In Example 6, 1% interest for one year would be \$25. At that rate the interest for four years would be \$100. The actual rate is $3\frac{1}{2}$ times one percent and the time is less than four years, so a reasonable estimate would be \$350.

TIP
So Many Choices!

When time is expressed in months, the calculator sequence is the same as when time is expressed in years, except that you do not enter a whole number for the time. Months can be changed to years in the sequence rather than as a separate calculation. All other steps are the same. To solve the equation in Example 6 using a calculator without the percent key, use the decimal equivalent of $3\frac{1}{2}$% and the fraction for the time.

[AC] 2500 [×] .035 [×] 45 [÷] 12 [=] ⟹ 328.125

It is not necessary to find the decimal equivalent of $\frac{45}{12}$ or to reduce $\frac{45}{12}$. However, you will get the same result if you use 3.75 or $\frac{15}{4}$.

[AC] 2500 [×] .035 [×] 3.75 [=] ⟹ 328.125

[AC] 2500 [×] .035 [×] 15 [÷] 4 [=] ⟹ 328.125

 STOP AND CHECK

1. Change eight months to years, expressed in fraction and decimal form. Round to the nearest millionth.

2. Change 15 months to years, expressed in both fraction and decimal form.

3. Carrie made a \$1,200 loan for 18 months at 9.5% simple interest. How much interest was paid?

4. Find the maturity value of a loan of \$1,750 for 28 months at 9.8% simple interest.

4 Find the principal, rate, or time using the simple interest formula.

So far in this chapter, we have used the formula $I = PRT$ to find the simple interest on a loan. However, sometimes you need to find the principal or the rate or the time instead of the interest. You can remember the different forms of this formula with a circle diagram (see Figure 11-1) like the one used for the percentage formula. Cover the unknown term to see the form of the simple interest formula needed to find the missing value.

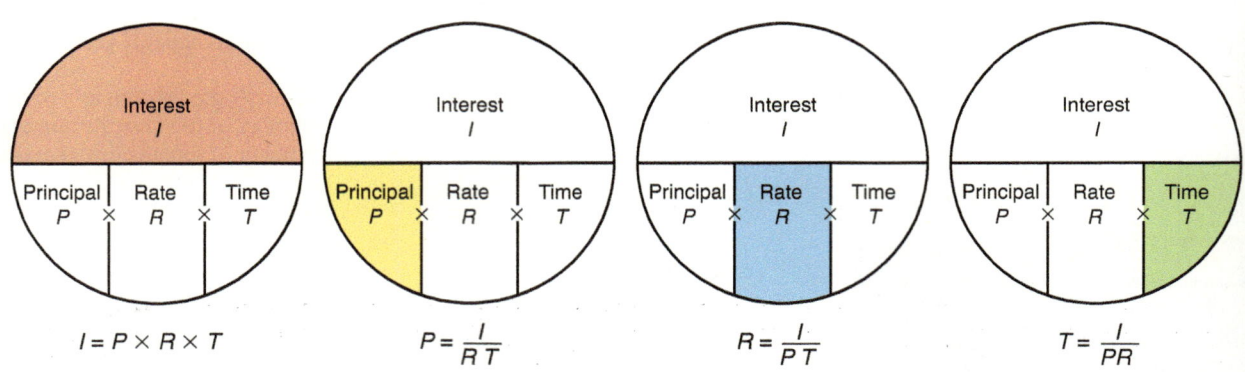

FIGURE 11-1
Various Forms of the Simple Interest Formula

> **HOW TO**   Find the principal, rate, or time using the simple interest formula
>
> 1. Select the appropriate form of the formula.
>   (a) To find the principal, use
> $$P = \frac{I}{RT}$$
>   (b) To find the rate, use
> $$R = \frac{I}{PT}$$
>   (c) To find the time, use
> $$T = \frac{I}{PR}$$
> 2. Replace letters with known values and perform the indicated operations.

EXAMPLE 7   To buy a food preparation table for his restaurant, the owner of the 7th Inning borrowed $1,800 for $1\frac{1}{2}$ years and paid $202.50 simple interest on the loan. What rate of interest did he pay?

$R = \dfrac{I}{PT}$ R is unknown. Select the correct form of the simple interest formula. Replace letters with known values: I is $202.50, P is $1,800, T is 1.5 years. Perform the operations.

$R = \dfrac{\$202.50}{(\$1,800)(1.5)}$

$R = 0.075$ Write the rate in percent form by moving the decimal point two places to the right and attaching a % symbol.

$R = 7.5\%$

The owner paid 7.5% interest.

EXAMPLE 8

Phyllis Cox wanted to borrow some money to expand her photography business. She was told she could borrow a sum of money for 18 months at 6% simple interest per year. She thinks she can afford to pay as much as $540 in interest charges. How much money could she borrow?

$P = \dfrac{I}{RT}$ P is unknown. Select the correct form of the simple interest formula.

$I = \$540$

$R = 6\% = 0.06$ Write the percent as a decimal equivalent.

$T = 18 \text{ months} = \dfrac{18}{12}$ The interest rate is per year, so write 18 months as 1.5 years.

$ = 1.5 \text{ years}$ Replace letters with known values: I is $540, R is 0.06, T is 1.5.

$P = \dfrac{\$540}{0.06(1.5)}$ Perform the operations.

$P = \$6{,}000$

The principal is $6,000.

TIP

Numerator Divided by Denominator

When a series of calculations has fractions and a calculation in the denominator, the numerator must be divided by the entire denominator. You can do this three ways:

1. With a basic calculator and using memory, multiply 0.06×1.5, store the result in memory and clear the display, and divide 540 by the stored product:

   $\boxed{AC}$ .06 $\boxed{\times}$ 1.5 $\boxed{=}$ $\boxed{M^+}$ CE/C 540 $\boxed{\div}$ MRC $\boxed{=}$ $\Rightarrow$ 6000

2. Using repeated division, divide 540 by both .06 and 1.5:

   $\boxed{AC}$ 540 $\boxed{\div}$ .06 $\boxed{\div}$ 1.5 $\boxed{=}$ $\Rightarrow$ 6000

3. With a business or scientific calculator and parentheses, group the calculation in the denominator using parentheses:

   $\boxed{AC}$ 540 $\boxed{\div}$ $\boxed{(}$ .06 $\boxed{\times}$ 1.5 $\boxed{)}$ $\boxed{=}$ $\Rightarrow$ 6000

EXAMPLE 9

The 7th Inning borrowed $2,400 at 7% simple interest per year to buy new tables for Brubaker's Restaurant. If it paid $420 interest, what was the duration of the loan?

$T = \dfrac{I}{PR}$ T is unknown. Select the correct form of the simple interest formula. Replace letters with known values: $I = \$420$, $P = \$2{,}400$, $R = 0.07$.

$T = \dfrac{\$420}{\$2{,}400(0.07)} = 2.5 \text{ years}$ Perform the operations.

The duration of the loan is 2.5 years.

TIP

Is the Answer Reasonable?

Suppose in the previous example we had mistakenly made the following calculations:

$$420 \div 2400 \times 0.07 = \Rightarrow 0.01225$$

Is it reasonable to think that $420 in interest would be paid on a $2,400 loan that is made for such a small portion of a year? The interest on a 10% loan for one year would be $240. The interest on a 10% loan for two years would be $480. This type of reasoning draws attention to an unreasonable answer.

You can reexamine your steps to discover that you should have used your memory function, repeated division, or your parentheses keys.

STOP AND CHECK

1. What is the simple interest rate of a loan of $2,680 for $2\frac{1}{2}$ years if $636.50 interest is paid?

2. Find the simple interest rate of a loan of $5,000 that is made for three years and requires $1,762.50 in interest.

3. How much money is borrowed if the interest rate is $9\frac{1}{4}\%$ simple interest and the loan is made for 3.5 years and has $904.88 interest?

4. A loan of $16,840 is borrowed at 9% simple interest and is repaid with $4,167.90 interest. What is the duration of the loan?

11-1 SECTION EXERCISES

SKILL BUILDERS

1. Find the interest paid on a loan of $2,400 for one year at a simple interest rate of 11% per year.

2. Find the interest paid on a loan of $800 at $8\frac{1}{2}\%$ annual simple interest for two years.

3. How much interest will have to be paid on a loan of $7,980 for two years at a simple interest rate of 6.2% per year?

4. Find the total amount of money (maturity value) that the borrower will pay back on a loan of $1,400 at $12\frac{1}{2}\%$ annual simple interest for three years.

5. Find the maturity value of a loan of $2,800 after three years. The loan carries a simple interest rate of 7.5% per year.

6. Susan Duke borrowed $20,000 for four years to purchase a car. The simple interest loan has a rate of 8.2% per year. What is the maturity value of the loan?

Convert to years, expressed in decimal form to the nearest hundredth.

7. 9 months

8. 40 months

9. A loan is made for 18 months. Convert the time to years.

10. Express 28 months as years in decimal form.

APPLICATIONS

11. Alexa May took out a $42,000 construction loan to remodel a house. The loan rate is 8.3% simple interest per year and will be repaid in six months. How much is paid back?

12. Madison Duke needed start-up money for her bakery. She borrowed $1,200 for 30 months and paid $360 simple interest on the loan. What interest rate did she pay?

13. Raul Fletes needed money to buy lawn equipment. He borrowed $500 for seven months and paid $53.96 in interest. What was the rate of interest?

14. Linda Davis agreed to lend money to Alex Luciano at a special interest rate of 9% per year, on the condition that he borrow enough that he would pay her $500 in interest over a two-year period. What was the minimum amount Alex could borrow?

15. Jake McAnally needed money for college. He borrowed $6,000 at 12% simple interest per year. If he paid $360 interest, what was the duration of the loan?

16. Keaton Smith borrowed $25,000 to purchase stock for his baseball card shop. He repaid the simple interest loan after three years. He paid interest of $6,750. What was the interest rate?

11-2 ORDINARY AND EXACT INTEREST

LEARNING OUTCOMES
1. Find the exact time.
2. Find the due date.
3. Find the ordinary interest and the exact interest.
4. Make a partial payment before the maturity date.

Sometimes the time period of a loan is indicated by the beginning date and the due date of the loan rather than by a specific number of months or days. In such cases, you must first determine the time period of the loan.

1 Find the exact time.

Exact time: time that is based on counting the exact number of days in a time period.

In Chapter 8, Section 3, Learning Outcome 1 we found the exact days in each month of a year. The exact number of days in a time period is called **exact time**.

EXAMPLE 1
Find the exact time of a loan made on July 12 and due on September 12.

Days in July	$31 - 12 = 19$	July has 31 days.
Days in August	$= 31$	August has 31 days.
Days in September	$= 12$	
Total days	62	

The exact time from July 12 to September 12 is 62 days.

Another way to calculate exact time is by using a table or calendar that assigns each day of the year a numerical value. See Table 11-1.

HOW TO

Find the exact time of a loan using the sequential numbers table (Table 11-1)

1. If the beginning and due dates of the loan fall within the same year, subtract the beginning date's sequential number from the due date's sequential number.
2. If the beginning and due dates of the loan do not fall within the same year:
   (a) Subtract the beginning date's sequential number from 365.
   (b) Add the due date's sequential number to the difference from step 2a.
3. If February 29 is between the beginning and due dates, add 1 to the difference from step 1 or the sum from step 2b.

From May 15 to Oct. 15
288 − 135 = 153 days

From May 15 to March 15
365 − 135 = 230

230 + 74 = 304 days (non-leap year)
304 + 1 = 305 days (leap year)

EXAMPLE 2

Find the exact time of a loan from July 12 to September 12.

```
  255    Sequence number for September 12
− 193    Sequence number for July 12
  62 days
```

TABLE 11-1
Sequential Numbers for Dates of the Year

Day of Month	Jan.	Feb.	Mar.	Apr.	May	June	July	Aug.	Sept.	Oct.	Nov.	Dec.
1	1	32	60	91	121	152	182	213	244	274	305	335
2	2	33	61	92	122	153	183	214	245	275	306	336
3	3	34	62	93	123	154	184	215	246	276	307	337
4	4	35	63	94	124	155	185	216	247	277	308	338
5	5	36	64	95	125	156	186	217	248	278	309	339
6	6	37	65	96	126	157	187	218	249	279	310	340
7	7	38	66	97	127	158	188	219	250	280	311	341
8	8	39	67	98	128	159	189	220	251	281	312	342
9	9	40	68	99	129	160	190	221	252	282	313	343
10	10	41	69	100	130	161	191	222	253	283	314	344
11	11	42	70	101	131	162	192	223	254	284	315	345
12	12	43	71	102	132	163	193	224	255	285	316	346
13	13	44	72	103	133	164	194	225	256	286	317	347
14	14	45	73	104	134	165	195	226	257	287	318	348
15	15	46	74	105	135	166	196	227	258	288	319	349
16	16	47	75	106	136	167	197	228	259	289	320	350
17	17	48	76	107	137	168	198	229	260	290	321	351
18	18	49	77	108	138	169	199	230	261	291	322	352
19	19	50	78	109	139	170	200	231	262	292	323	353
20	20	51	79	110	140	171	201	232	263	293	324	354
21	21	52	80	111	141	172	202	233	264	294	325	355
22	22	53	81	112	142	173	203	234	265	295	326	356
23	23	54	82	113	143	174	204	235	266	296	327	357
24	24	55	83	114	144	175	205	236	267	297	328	358
25	25	56	84	115	145	176	206	237	268	298	329	359
26	26	57	85	116	146	177	207	238	269	299	330	360
27	27	58	86	117	147	178	208	239	270	300	331	361
28	28	59	87	118	148	179	209	240	271	301	332	362
29	29	*	88	119	149	180	210	241	272	302	333	363
30	30		89	120	150	181	211	242	273	303	334	364
31	31		90		151		212	243		304		365

*For centennial years (those at the turn of the century), leap years occur only when the number of the year is divisible by 400. Thus, 2000 was a leap year (2000/400 divides exactly), but 1700, 1800, and 1900 were not leap years.

Simple Interest and Simple Discount 431

EXAMPLE 3
A loan made on September 5 is due July 5 of the *following year*. Find (a) the exact time for the loan in a non-leap year and (b) the exact time in a leap year.

(a) *Exact time in a non-leap year*

From Table 11-1, September 5 is the 248th day.

$$\begin{array}{r}365\\-248\\\hline 117\end{array}\text{ days}$$

Subtract 248 from 365.
Days from September 5 through December 31

July 5 is the 186th day.
117 + 186 = 303 days   Add 117 and 186 to find the exact time of the loan.

(b) *Exact time in a leap year*

303 + 1 = 304 days   Because Feb. 29 is between the beginning and due dates, add 1 to the non-leap year total.

Exact time is 303 days in a non-leap year and 304 days in a leap year.

STOP AND CHECK

1. Find the exact time of a loan made on April 15 and due on October 15.

2. Find the exact time of a loan made on March 20 and due on September 20.

3. Find the exact number of days of a loan made on October 14 and due on December 21.

4. A loan made on November 1 is due on March 1 of the following year. How many days are in the loan using exact time?

2 Find the due date.

Sometimes the beginning date of a loan and the time period of the loan are known and the due date must be determined.

HOW TO Find the due date of a loan given the beginning date and the time period in days

1. Add the sequential number of the beginning date to the number of days in the time period.
2. If the sum is less than or equal to 365, find the date (Table 11-1) corresponding to the sum.
3. If the sum is more than 365, subtract 365 from the sum. Then find the date (Table 11-1) in the following year corresponding to the difference.
4. Adjust for February 29 in a leap year if appropriate by *subtracting* 1 from the result in step 2 or 3.

60-day loan beginning on July 1:
July 1 = Day 182
182 + 60 = 242
242nd day = August 30

EXAMPLE 4
Find the due date for a 90-day loan made on November 15.

From Table 11-1, November 15 is the 319th day.

$$\begin{array}{r}319\\+\ 90\\\hline 409\end{array}$$

Add 319 to 90 days in the time period.

409 is greater than 365, so the loan is due in the following year.

$$\begin{array}{r}409\\-365\\\hline 44\end{array}$$

Subtract 365 from 409.

In Table 11-1, day 44 corresponds to February 13.

The loan is due February 13 of the following year.

STOP AND CHECK

1. Find the due date for a 120-day loan made on June 12.

2. What is the due date for a loan made on July 17 for 150 days?

3. Use exact time and find the due date of a $3,200 loan made on January 29 for 90 days.

4. Use exact time and find the due date of a $2,582 loan made on November 22 for 120 days.

3 Find the ordinary interest and the exact interest.

An interest rate is normally given as a rate *per year*. But if the time period of the loan is in days, then using the simple interest formula requires that the rate *also* be expressed as a rate *per day*. We convert a rate per year to a rate per day in two different ways, depending on whether the rate per day is to be an **ordinary interest** or an **exact interest**. Ordinary interest assumes 360 days per year; exact interest assumes 365 days per year.

Ordinary interest: assumes 360 days per year.

Exact interest: assumes 365 days per year.

HOW TO   Find the ordinary interest and the exact interest

1. To find the ordinary interest, use 360 as the number of days in a year.
2. To find the exact interest, use 365 as the number of days in a year.

EXAMPLE 5
Find the ordinary interest for a loan of $500 at a 7% annual interest rate. The loan was made on March 15 and is due May 15.

Exact time = $135 - 74 = 61$ days	Find each date's sequential number in Table 11-1 and subtract.
$I = PRT$	Replace with known values.
$I = \$500(0.07)\left(\dfrac{61}{360}\right)$	Perform the operations.
$I = \$5.93$	Round to the nearest cent.

The interest is $5.93.

EXAMPLE 6
Find the exact interest on the loan in Example 5.

Exact time = 61 days	
$I = PRT$	Replace with known values.
$I = \$500(0.07)\left(\dfrac{61}{365}\right)$	Perform the operations.
$I = \$5.85$	Round to the nearest cent.

The interest is $5.85.

TIP

Make Comparisons Quickly by Storing Common Portions of Problems

The two preceding examples can be calculated and compared using the memory function of a calculator.

Be sure memory is clear or equal to 0 before you begin. Store the first calculation (500 × 0.07) in memory.

AC 500 × .07 = M⁺
AC MR × 61 ÷ 360 = ⇒ 5.930555556
AC MR × 61 ÷ 365 = ⇒ 5.849315068

Simple Interest and Simple Discount   433

Note that the interest varies in the two cases. The first method illustrated, *ordinary interest*, is most often used by bankers when they are *lending* money because it yields a slightly higher amount of interest. It is sometimes called the **banker's rule**. On the other hand, when bankers *pay* interest on savings accounts, they normally use a 365-day year—exact interest—which yields the most accurate amount of interest but is less than the amount yielded by the banker's rule.

Banker's rule: calculating interest on a loan based on ordinary interest—which yields a slightly higher amount of interest.

EXAMPLE 7

Borrowing money to pay cash for large purchases is sometimes profitable when a cash discount is allowed on the purchases. For her consulting firm, Joann Jimanez purchased a computer, printer, copier, and fax machine that regularly sold for $5,999. A special promotion offered the equipment for $5,890, with cash terms of 3/10, n/30. She does not have the cash to pay the bill now, but she will within the next three months. She finds a bank that will loan her the money for the equipment at 10% (using ordinary interest) for 90 days. Should she take out the loan to take advantage of the special promotion and cash discount?

What You Know	What You Are Looking For	Solution Plan
Regular price: $5,999 Special price: $5,890 Cash discount rate: 0.03 Exact term of loan: 90 days Ordinary interest uses 360 days.	Should Joann Jimanez take out the loan? Cash discount on special price, compared with interest on loan	Cash discount = special price × discount rate Ordinary interest on loan = principal × rate × time The principal of the loan is the net amount Joann would pay, once the cash discount is allowed on the special price, or 97% of the cash price.

Solution

$$\begin{aligned}
\text{Cash discount} &= \$5{,}890(0.03) \\
&= \$176.70 \\
\text{Principal} &= \$5{,}890(0.97) \\
&= \$5{,}713.30 \\
\text{Interest on loan} &= \$5{,}713.30(0.1)\left(\frac{90}{360}\right) \\
&= \$142.83 \\
\text{Difference} &= \$176.70 - \$142.83 \\
&= \$33.87
\end{aligned}$$

Conclusion

The interest on the loan is $142.83, which is $33.87 less than the cash discount of $176.70. Because the cash discount is more than the interest on the loan, Joann will not lose money by borrowing to take advantage of the discount terms of the sale. But other factors—the time she spends to take out the loan, for example—should be considered.

✓ STOP AND CHECK

1. Find the ordinary interest on a loan of $1,350 at 6.5% annual interest rate if the loan is made on March 3 and due on September 3.

2. Find the exact interest for the loan in Exercise 1.

3. Compare the interest amounts from the two methods. Which method would you guess bankers offer to borrowers?

4. Use the banker's rule to find the maturity value of a loan of $4,250 made on April 12 and repaid on October 12. The interest rate is 7.2% simple interest.

4 Make a partial payment before the maturity date.

Simple interest loans are intended to be paid with a lump sum payment at the maturity date. To save some interest, a borrower may decide to make one or more partial payments before the maturity date. The most common method for properly crediting a partial payment is to first apply the loan payment to the accumulated interest. The remainder of the partial payment is applied to the principal. This process is called the **U.S. Rule**.

Some states have passed legislation that forbids a lender from charging interest on interest. That means if the partial payment does not cover the accumulated interest, the principal for calculating the interest cannot be increased by the unpaid interest.

U.S. rule: any partial loan payment first covers any interest that has accumulated. The remainder of the partial payment reduces the loan principal.

Adjusted principal: the remaining principal after a partial payment has been properly credited.

Adjusted balance due at maturity: the remaining balance due at maturity after one or more partial payments have been made.

> **HOW TO** Find the adjusted principal and adjusted balance due at maturity for a partial payment made before the maturity date
>
> 1. Determine the exact time from the date of the loan to the first partial payment.
> 2. Calculate the interest using the time found in step 1.
> 3. Subtract the amount of interest found in step 2 from the partial payment.
> 4. Subtract the remainder of the partial payment (step 3) from the original principal. This is the **adjusted principal**.
> 5. Repeat the process with the adjusted principal if additional partial payments are made.
> 6. At maturity, calculate the interest from the last partial payment. Add this interest to the adjusted principal from the last partial payment. This is the **adjusted balance due at maturity**.

EXAMPLE 8 Tony Powers borrows $5,000 on a 10%, 90-day note. On the 30th day, Tony pays $1,500 on the note. If ordinary interest is applied, what is Tony's adjusted principal after the partial payment? What is the adjusted balance due at maturity?

$\$5{,}000(0.1)\left(\dfrac{30}{360}\right) = \$41.67$	Calculate the ordinary interest on 30 days.
$\$1{,}500 - \$41.67 = \$1{,}458.33$	Amount of partial payment applied to principal
$\$5{,}000 - \$1{,}458.33 = \$3{,}541.67$	Adjusted principal
$\$3{,}541.67(0.1)\left(\dfrac{60}{360}\right) = \$59.03$	Interest on adjusted principal
$\$3{,}541.67 + \$59.03 = \$3{,}600.70$	Adjusted balance due at maturity

The adjusted principal after 30 days is $3,541.67 and the adjusted balance due at maturity is $3,600.70.

EXAMPLE 9 How much interest was saved by making the partial payment in Example 8?

$\$41.67 + \$59.03 = \$100.70$	Total interest paid with partial payment
$\$5{,}000(0.1)\left(\dfrac{90}{360}\right) = \$125$	Interest if no partial payment is made
$\$125 - \$100.70 = \$24.30$	Interest saved

The interest saved by making a partial payment is $24.30.

STOP AND CHECK

1. James Ligon borrowed $10,000 at 9% for 270 days with ordinary interest applied. On the 60th day he paid $3,000 on the note. What is the adjusted balance due at maturity?

2. Jennifer Raymond borrowed $5,800 on a 120-day note that required ordinary interest at 7.5%. Jennifer paid $2,500 on the note on the 30th day. How much interest did she save by making the partial payment?

3. Tatiana Jacobs borrowed $8,500 on a 9%, 180-day note. On the 60th day, Tatiana paid $3,000 on the note. If ordinary interest is applied, find Tatiana's adjusted principal on the loan after the partial payment.

4. Find the adjusted balance due at maturity on Tatiana's loan (Exercise 3).

11-2 SECTION EXERCISES

SKILL BUILDERS

1. Find the exact interest on a loan of $32,400 at 8% annually for 30 days.

2. Find the exact interest on a loan of $12,500 at 7.75% annually for 45 days.

3. Find the exact interest on a loan of $6,000 at 8.25% annually for 50 days.

4. Find the exact interest on a loan of $9,580 at 8.5% annually for 40 days.

5. A loan made on March 10 is due September 10 of the *following year.* Find the exact time for the loan in a non-leap year and a leap year.

6. Find the exact time of a loan made on March 25 and due on November 15 of the same year.

7. A loan is made on January 15 and has a due date of October 20 during a leap year. Find the exact time of the loan.

8. Find the due date for a loan made on October 15 for 120 days.

9. A loan is made on March 20 for 180 days. Find the due date.

10. Find the due date of a loan that is made on February 10 of a leap year and is due in 60 days.

APPLICATIONS

Exercises 11 and 12: A loan for $3,000 with a simple annual interest rate of 15% was made on June 15 and was due on August 15.

11. Find the exact interest.

12. Find the ordinary interest.

13. Find the adjusted balance due at maturity for a 90-day note of $15,000 at 13.8% ordinary interest if a partial payment of $5,000 is made on the 60th day of the loan.

14. Raul Fletes borrowed $8,500 on a 300-day note that required ordinary interest at 11.76%. Raul paid $4,250 on the note on the 60th day. How much interest did he save by making the partial payment?

11-3 PROMISSORY NOTES

LEARNING OUTCOMES
1. Find the bank discount and proceeds for a simple discount note.
2. Find the true or effective interest rate of a simple discount note.
3. Find the third-party discount and proceeds for a third-party discount note.

Promissory note: a legal document promising to repay a loan.

Maker: the person or business that borrows the money.

Payee: the person or business loaning the money.

Term: the length of time for which the money is borrowed.

Maturity date: the date on which the loan is due to be repaid.

Face value: the amount borrowed.

When a business or individual borrows money, it is customary for the borrower to sign a legal document promising to repay the loan. The document is called a **promissory note**. The note includes all necessary information about the loan. The **maker** is the person borrowing the money. The **payee** is the person loaning the money. The **term** of the note is the length of time for which the money is borrowed; the **maturity date** is the date on which the loan is due to be repaid. The **face value** of the note is the amount borrowed.

1 Find the bank discount and proceeds for a simple discount note.

If money is borrowed from a bank at a simple interest rate, the bank sometimes collects the interest, which is also called the **bank discount**, at the time the loan is made. Thus, the maker receives the face value of the loan minus the bank discount. This difference is called the **proceeds**. Such a loan is called a **simple discount note**. Loans of this type allow the bank or payee of the loan to receive all fees and interest at the time the loan is made. This increases the yield on the loan because the interest and fees can be reinvested immediately. Besides increased yields, a bank may require this type of loan when the maker of the loan has an inadequate or poor credit history. This decreases the amount of risk to the bank or lender.

HOW TO Find the bank discount and proceeds for a simple discount note

1. For the bank discount, use:

$$\text{Bank discount} = \text{face value} \times \text{discount rate} \times \text{time}$$
$$I = PRT$$

2. For the proceeds, use:

$$\text{Proceeds} = \text{face value} - \text{bank discount}$$
$$A = P - I$$

EXAMPLE 1 Find the (a) bank discount and (b) proceeds using ordinary interest on a promissory note to Mary Fisher for $4,000 at 8% annual simple interest from June 5 to September 5.

(a) Exact days = 248 − 156 = 92   Subtract sequential numbers (Table 11-1).
Bank discount = PRT

Bank discount = $\$4{,}000(0.08)\left(\dfrac{92}{360}\right)$ Multiply.

Bank discount = **$81.78**   Rounded to the nearest cent.

The bank discount is $81.78.

Simple Interest and Simple Discount   437

(b) Proceeds = A = P − I
Proceeds = $4,000 − $81.78
Proceeds = $3,918.22

Subtract the bank discount from the face value of the note.

The proceeds are $3,918.22.

Undiscounted note: another term for a simple interest note.

The difference between the simple interest note—which is also called an **undiscounted note**—and the simple discount note is the amount of money the borrower has use of for the length of the loan, and the maturity value of the loan—the amount owed at the end of the loan term. Interest is paid on the same amount for the same period of time in both cases. In the simple interest note, the borrower has use of the full principal of the loan, but the maturity value is principal plus interest. In the simple discount note, the borrower has use of only the proceeds (face value − discount), but the maturity value is just the face value, as the interest (the discount) was paid "in advance."

Suppose Bill borrows $5,000 with a discount (interest) rate of 10%. The discount is 10% ($5,000), or $500, so he gets the use of only $4,500, although the bank charges interest on the full $5,000. The maturity value is $5,000.

Here is a comparison of simple interest notes versus simple discount notes:

	Simple interest note	Simple discount note
Principal or face value	$5,000	$5,000
Interest or discount	500	500
Amount available to borrower or proceeds	5,000	4,500
Amount to be repaid or maturity value	5,500	5,000

STOP AND CHECK

1. Find the bank discount and proceeds using ordinary interest for a loan to Michelle Anders for $7,200 at 8.25% annual simple interest from August 8 to November 8.

2. Find the bank discount and proceeds using ordinary interest for a loan to Andre Peters for $9,250 at 7.75% annual simple interest from January 17 to July 17.

3. Find the bank discount and proceeds using ordinary interest for a loan to Megan Anders for $3,250 at 8.75% annual simple interest from February 23 to November 23.

4. Frances Johnson is making a bank loan for $32,800 at 7.5% annual simple interest from May 10 to July 10. Find the bank discount and proceeds using ordinary interest.

2 Find the true or effective interest rate of a simple discount note.

For a simple interest note, the borrower uses the full face value of the loan for the entire period of the loan. In a simple discount note, the borrower only uses the proceeds of the loan for the period of the loan. Because the proceeds are less than the face value of the loan, the stated discount rate is not the true or effective rate of interest of the note. To find the **effective interest rate of a simple discount note**, the proceeds of the loan is used as the principal in the interest formula.

Effective interest rate for a simple discount note: the actual interest rate based on the proceeds of the loan.

HOW TO   Find the true or effective interest rate of a simple discount note

1. Find the bank discount (interest).

$$I = PRT$$

2. Find the proceeds.

$$\text{Proceeds} = \text{principal} - \text{bank discount}$$

3. Find the effective interest rate.

$$R = \frac{I}{PT} \text{ using the proceeds as the principal.}$$

EXAMPLE 2

What is the effective interest rate of a simple discount note for $5,000, at an ordinary bank discount rate of 12%, for 90 days? Round to the nearest tenth of a percent.

Find the bank discount:

$I = PRT$

$I = \$5{,}000(0.12)\left(\dfrac{90}{360}\right)$

$I = \$150$ Bank discount

Find the proceeds:

Proceeds = principal − bank discount
Proceeds = $5,000 − $150
Proceeds = $4,850

Find the effective interest rate:

$R = \dfrac{I}{PT}$ Substitute proceeds for principal.

$R = \dfrac{\$150}{\$4{,}850\left(\dfrac{90}{360}\right)}$

$R = \dfrac{\$150}{\$1{,}212.50}$

$R = 0.1237113402$

$R = 12.4\%$ Effective interest rate

The effective interest rate for a simple discount note of $5,000 for 90 days is 12.4%.

STOP AND CHECK

1. What is the effective interest rate of a simple discount note for $8,000, at an ordinary bank discount rate of 11%, for 120 days? Round to the nearest tenth of a percent.

2. What is the effective interest rate of a simple discount note for $22,000, at an ordinary bank discount rate of 8.36%, for 90 days? Round to the nearest tenth of a percent.

3. Ebbe Wojtek needs to calculate the effective interest rate of a simple discount note for $18,000, at an ordinary bank discount rate of 9.6%, for 270 days. Find the effective rate rounded to the nearest tenth.

4. Ole Christian Borgesen needs to calculate the effective interest rate of a simple discount note for $16,000, at an ordinary bank discount rate of 8.4%, for 210 days. Find the effective rate rounded to the nearest tenth.

3 Find the third-party discount and proceeds for a third-party discount note.

Third party: an investment group or individual that assumes a note that was made between two other parties.

Third-party discount note: a note that is sold to a third party (usually a bank) so that the original payee gets the proceeds immediately and the maker pays the third party the original amount at maturity.

Discount period: the amount of time that the third party owns the third-party discounted note.

Many businesses agree to be the payee for a promissory note as payment for the sale of goods. If these businesses in turn need cash, they may sell such a note to an investment group or person who is the **third party** of the note. Selling a note to a third party in return for cash is called *discounting* a note. The note is called a **third-party discount note**.

When the third party discounts a note, it gives the business owning the note the maturity value of the note minus a third-party discount. The discount is based on how long the third party holds the note, called the **discount period**. The third party receives the full maturity value of the note from the maker when it comes due. From the standpoint of the note maker (the borrower), the term of the note is the same because the maturity (due) date is the same, and the maturity value is the same.

The following diagram shows how the discount period is determined.

Original date of loan	Date loan is discounted	Maturity date
July 14	Aug. 3	Sept. 12

                           Discount period

Simple Interest and Simple Discount

HOW TO Find the third-party discount and proceeds for a third-party discount note

1. For the third-party discount, use:

    Third-party discount = maturity value of original note × discount rate × discount period

    $I = PRT$

2. For the proceeds to the original payee, use:

    Proceeds = maturity value of original note − third-party discount

    $A = P - I$

EXAMPLE 3 Alpine Pleasures, Inc., delivers ski equipment to retailers in July but does not expect payment until mid-September, so the retailers agree to sign promissory notes for the equipment. These notes are based on exact interest, with a 10% annual simple interest rate. One promissory note held by Alpine is for $8,000, was made on July 14, and is due September 12. Alpine needs cash, so it takes the note to an investment group. On August 3, the group agrees to buy the note at a 12% discount rate using the banker's rule (ordinary interest). Find the proceeds for the note.

A table can help you organize the facts:

Date of original note	Principal of note	Simple interest rate	Date of discount note	Third-party discount rate	Maturity date
July 14	$8,000	10%	Aug. 3	12%	Sept. 12

Calculate the time and maturity value of the original note.

255	September 12 (Table 11-1)
− 195	July 14 (Table 11-1)
60 days	Exact days of the original loan

$I = PRT$ Use the simple interest formula to find exact interest.

$I = \$8,000(0.1)\left(\dfrac{60}{365}\right)$ Use 365 days in a year.

$I = \$131.51$ (rounded)

The simple interest for the original loan is $131.51.

To find the maturity value, add the principal and interest.

Maturity value = principal + interest
Maturity value = $8,000 + $131.51
Maturity value = $8,131.51

The maturity value of the original loan is $8,131.51.

Now calculate the discount period.

Discount period = number of days from August 3 to September 12

August 3 is the 215th day.

255	September 12
− 215	August 3
40 days	Exact days of discount period

The discount period for the discount note is 40 days.

Now calculate the third-party discount based on the banker's rule (ordinary interest).

Third-party discount = maturity value × third-party discount rate × discount period

Third-party discount = $8,131.51(0.12)\left(\dfrac{40}{360}\right)$ Use 360 days in a year.

Third-party discount = $108.42

The third-party discount is $108.42.

Now calculate the proceeds that will be received by Alpine.

$$\text{Proceeds} = \text{maturity value} - \text{third-party discount}$$
$$\text{Proceeds} = \$8{,}131.51 - \$108.42$$
$$\text{Proceeds} = \$8{,}023.09$$

The proceeds to Alpine are $8,023.09.

> **TIP**
>
> **Interest-Free Money**
>
> A non-interest-bearing note is very uncommon but sometimes available. This means that you borrow a certain amount and pay that same amount back later. The note itself carries no interest, and the maturity value of the note is the same as the face value or principal. The payee or person loaning the money only wants the original amount of money at the maturity date.
>
> What happens if a non-interest-bearing note is discounted? Use the information from Example 1, without the simple interest on the original loan.
>
> Third-party discount = maturity value × discount rate × discount period
>
> Third-party discount = $\$8{,}000(0.12)\left(\dfrac{40}{360}\right)$ The maturity value is the face value, or $8,000, rather than $8,131.51, which included interest.
>
> Third-party discount = $106.67
>
> The third-party discount is $106.67.
>
> Proceeds = maturity value − third-party discount
>
> Proceeds = $8,000 − $106.67   The maturity value is $8,000.
>
> Proceeds = $7,893.33
>
> The proceeds are $7,893.33.
>
> The original payee loans $8,000 and receives $7,893.33 in cash from the third party.

⛔ STOP AND CHECK

1. Hugh's Trailers delivers trailers to retailers in February and expects payment in July. The retailers sign promissory notes based on exact interest with 8.25% annual simple interest. One promissory note held by Hugh's for $19,500 was made on February 15 and is due July 20. On May 5 a third party buys the note at a 10% discount using the banker's rule. Find the maturity exact time of the original note.

2. Find the maturity value of the original note in Exercise 1.

3. Find the third-party discount for the note in Exercise 1.

4. Find the proceeds to Hugh's Trailers for the discounted note in Exercise 1.

11-3 SECTION EXERCISES

SKILL BUILDERS

Use the banker's rule unless otherwise specified.

1. José makes a simple discount note with a face value of $2,500, a term of 120 days, and a 9% discount rate. Find the discount.

2. Find the proceeds for Exercise 1.

3. Find the discount and proceeds on a $3,250 face-value note for six months if the discount rate is 9.2%.

4. Find the maturity value of the undiscounted promissory note shown in Figure 11-2.

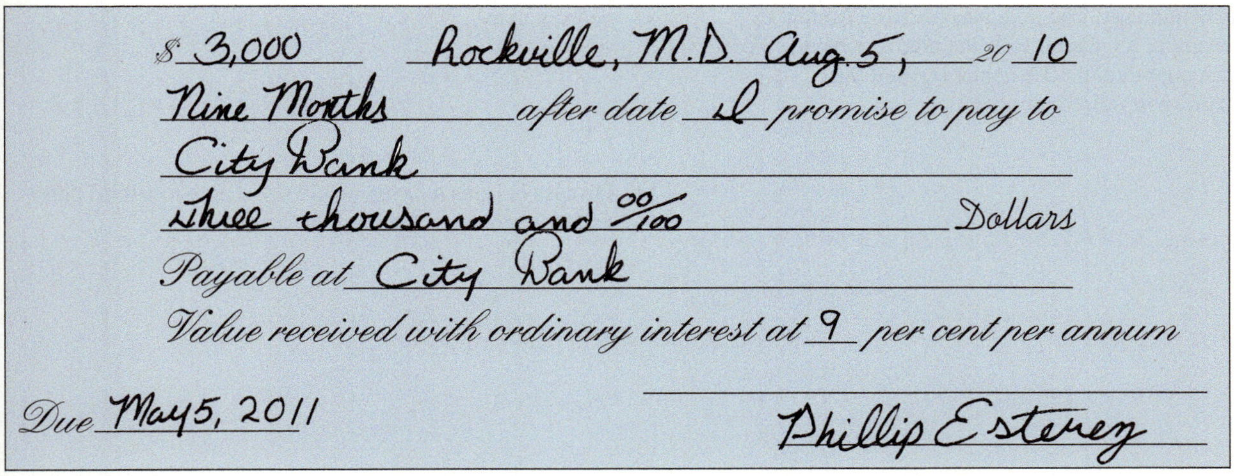

$3,000   Rockville, M.D. Aug. 5, 20 10

Nine Months after date I promise to pay to

City Bank

Three thousand and 00/100 Dollars

Payable at City Bank

Value received with ordinary interest at 9 per cent per annum

Due May 5, 2011

Phillip Esterey

FIGURE 11-2
Promissory Note

5. Roland Clark has a simple discount note for $6,500, at an ordinary bank discount rate of 8.74%, for 60 days. What is the effective interest rate? Round to the nearest tenth of a percent.

6. What is the effective interest rate of a simple discount note for $30,800, at an ordinary bank discount rate of 14%, for 20 days? Round to the nearest tenth of a percent.

7. Shanquayle Jenkins needs to calculate the effective interest rate of a simple discount note for $19,750, at an ordinary bank discount rate of 7.82%, for 90 days. Find the effective rate rounded to the nearest hundredth of a percent.

8. Matt Crouse needs to calculate the effective interest rate of a simple discount note for $12,800, at an ordinary bank discount rate of 8.75%, for 150 days. Find the effective rate rounded to the nearest tenth of a percent.

9. Carter Manufacturing holds a note of $5,000 that has an interest rate of 11% annually. The note was made on March 18 and is due November 13. Carter sells the note to a bank on June 13 at a discount rate of 10% annually. Find the proceeds on the third-party discount note.

10. Discuss reasons a payee might agree to a non-interest-bearing note.

11. Discuss reasons a payee would sell a note to a third party and lose money in the process.

SUMMARY

CHAPTER 11

Learning Outcomes | What to Remember with Examples

Section 11-1

1 Find simple interest using the simple interest formula. (p. 388)

1. Identify the principal, rate, and time.
2. Multiply the principal by the rate and time.

$$\text{Interest} = \text{principal} \times \text{rate} \times \text{time}$$
$$I = PRT$$

Find the interest paid on a loan of $8,400 for one year at $9\frac{1}{2}\%$ annual simple interest rate.	Find the interest paid on a loan of $4,500 for two years at a simple interest rate of 12% per year.
Interest = principal × rate × time = $8,400(0.095)(1) = $798	Interest = principal × rate × time = $4,500(0.12)(2) = $1,080

2 Find the maturity value of a loan. (p. 389)

1. If the principal and interest are known, add them.

$$\text{Maturity value} = \text{principal} + \text{interest}$$
$$MV = P + I$$

2. If the principal, rate, and time are known, use either of the formulas:
   (a) Maturity value = principal + (principal × rate × time)
   $$MV = P + PRT$$
   (b) Maturity value = principal (1 + rate × time)
   $$MV = P(1 + RT)$$

Find the maturity value of a loan of $8,400 with $798 interest.	Find the maturity value of a loan of $4,500 for two years at a simple interest rate of 12% per year.
$MV = P + I$ $MV = \$8,400 + \$798$ $MV = \$9,198$	$MV = P(1 + RT)$ $MV = \$4,500[1 + 0.12(2)]$ $MV = \$4,500(1.24)$ $MV = \$5,580$

3 Convert months to a fractional or decimal part of a year. (p. 390)

1. Write the number of months as the numerator of a fraction.
2. Write 12 as the denominator of the fraction.
3. Reduce the fraction to lowest terms if using the fractional equivalent.
4. Divide the numerator by the denominator to get the decimal equivalent of the fraction.

Convert 42 months to years.	Convert 3 months to years.
$\dfrac{42}{12} = \dfrac{7}{2} = 3.5$ years	$\dfrac{3}{12} = \dfrac{1}{4} = 0.25$ years

4 Find the principal, rate, or time using the simple interest formula. (p. 392)

1. Select the appropriate form of the formula.

   (a) To find the principal, use $P = \dfrac{I}{RT}$

   (b) To find the rate, use $R = \dfrac{I}{PT}$

   (c) To find the time, use $T = \dfrac{I}{PR}$

2. Replace letters with known values and perform the indicated operations.

Nancy Jeggle borrowed $6,000 for $3\frac{1}{2}$ years and paid $2,800 simple interest. What was the annual interest rate?	R is unknown. $R = \dfrac{I}{PT}$ $R = \dfrac{\$2,800}{(\$6,000)(3.5)}$ $R = 0.1333333333$ $R = 13.3\%$ annually (rounded)

444   Quantitative Methods for Business

Donna Ruscitti paid $675 interest on an 18-month loan at 10% annual simple interest. What was the principal?	P is unknown. $P = \dfrac{I}{RT}$ $\dfrac{18}{12} = \dfrac{3}{2} = 1.5$ $P = \dfrac{\$675}{0.10(1.5)}$ $P = \$4,500$
Ashish Paranjape borrowed $1,500 at 8% annual simple interest. If he paid $866.25 interest, what was the time period of the loan?	T is unknown. $T = \dfrac{I}{PR}$ $T = \dfrac{\$866.25}{\$1,500(0.08)}$ $T = 7.2$ years (rounded)

Section 11-2

1 Find the exact time. (p. 395)

Change months and years to exact time in days.

1 month = exact number of days in the month; 1 year = 365 days (or 366 days in a leap year)

Find the exact time of a loan made October 1 and due May 1 (non-leap year).

October, December, January, and March have 31 days. November and April have 30 days. February has 28 days.

$4(31) + 2(30) + 28 = 212$ days

Find the exact time of a loan using the sequential numbers table (Table 11-1).

1. If the beginning and due dates of the loan fall within the same year, subtract the beginning date's sequential number from the due date's sequential number.
2. If the beginning and due dates of the loan do not fall within the same year:
   (a) Subtract the beginning date's sequential number from 365.
   (b) Add the due date's sequential number to the difference from step 2a.
3. If February 29 is between the beginning and due dates, add 1 to the difference from step 1 or to the sum from step 2b.

Find the exact time of a loan made on March 25 and due on October 10.	Find the exact time of a loan made on June 7 and due the following March 7 in a non-leap year.
October 10 = day 283 March 25 = day 84 199 days The loan is made for 199 days.	December 31 = day 365 June 7 = day 158 207 days March 7 = + 66 days 273 days The loan is made for 273 days in all.

2 Find the due date. (p. 397)

Find the due date of a loan given the beginning date and the time period in days.

1. Add the sequential number of the beginning date to the number of days in the time period.
2. If the sum is less than or equal to 365, find the date (Table 11-1) corresponding to the sum.
3. If the sum is more than 365, subtract 365 from the sum. Then find the date (Table 11-1) in the following year corresponding to the difference.
4. Adjust for February 29 in a leap year if appropriate by subtracting 1 from the result in step 2 or 3.

Figure the due date for a 60-day loan made on August 12.

August 12 = day 224
              + 60
              284   Day 284 is October 11.

Simple Interest and Simple Discount 445

3 Find the ordinary interest and the exact interest. (p. 398)

1. To find the ordinary interest, use 360 as the number of days in a year.
2. To find the exact interest, use 365 as the number of days in a year.

On May 15, Roberta Krech borrowed $6,000 at 12.5% annual simple interest. The loan was due on November 15. Find the ordinary interest due on the loan.

Use Table 11-1 to find exact time. November 15 is day 319. May 15 is day 135. So time is $319 - 135 = 184$ days.

$$I = PRT$$
$$I = (\$6,000)(0.125)\left(\frac{184}{360}\right)$$
$$I = \$383.33$$

Find the exact interest due on Roberta's loan (see above).

$$I = PRT$$
$$I = (\$6,000)(0.125)\left(\frac{184}{365}\right)$$
$$I = \$378.08$$

4 Make a partial payment before the maturity date. (p. 400)

1. Determine the exact time from the date of the loan to the first partial payment.
2. Calculate the interest using the time found in step 1.
3. Subtract the amount of interest found in step 2 from the partial payment.
4. Subtract the remainder of the partial payment (step 3) from the original principal. This is the **adjusted principal**.
5. Repeat the process with the adjusted principal if additional partial payments are made.
6. At maturity, calculate the interest from the last partial payment. Add this interest to the adjusted principal from the last partial payment. This is the **adjusted balance due at maturity**.

Tony Powers borrows $7,000 on a 12%, 90-day note. On the 60th day, Tony pays $1,500 on the note. If ordinary interest is applied, what is Tony's adjusted principal after the partial payment? What is the adjusted balance due at maturity?

$\$7,000(0.12)\left(\frac{60}{360}\right) = \$140$ Calculate the ordinary interest on 60 days.

$\$1,500 - \$140 = \$1,360$ Amount of partial payment applied to principal
$\$7,000 - \$1,360 = \$5,640$ Adjusted principal

$\$5,640(0.12)\left(\frac{30}{360}\right) = \$56.40$ Interest on adjusted principal

$\$5,640 + \$56.40 = \$5,696.40$ Adjusted balance due at maturity

The adjusted principal after 90 days is $5,640 and the adjusted balance due at maturity is $5,696.40.

Section 11-3

1 Find the bank discount and proceeds for a simple discount note. (p. 402)

1. For the bank discount, use:

$$\text{Bank discount} = \text{face value} \times \text{discount rate} \times \text{time}$$
$$I = PRT$$

2. For the proceeds, use:

$$\text{Proceeds} = \text{face value} - \text{bank discount}$$
$$A = P - I$$

The bank charged Robert Milewsky a 11.5% annual discount rate on a bank note of $1,500 for 120 days. Find the proceeds of the note using the banker's rule.

First find the discount, and then subtract the discount from the face value of $1,500.

$$\text{Discount} = I = PRT$$
$$\text{Discount} = \$1,500(0.115)\left(\frac{120}{360}\right) \quad \text{Ordinary interest}$$
$$\text{Discount} = \$57.50$$
$$\text{Proceeds} = A = P - I$$
$$\text{Proceeds} = \$1,500 - \$57.50$$
$$\text{Proceeds} = \$1,442.50$$

2 Find the true or effective interest rate of a simple discount note. (p. 403)

1. Find the bank discount (interest).
$$I = PRT$$
2. Find the proceeds.
$$\text{Proceeds} = \text{principal} - \text{bank discount}$$
3. Find the effective interest rate.
$$R = \frac{I}{PT} \qquad \text{Use the proceeds as the principal.}$$

Larinda Temple has a simple discount note for $5,000, at an ordinary bank discount rate of 8%, for 90 days. What is the effective interest rate? Round to the nearest tenth of a percent.

Find the bank discount:

$I = PRT$

$I = \$5,000(0.08)\left(\dfrac{90}{360}\right)$

$I = \$100$

$R = \dfrac{I}{PT}$

$R = \dfrac{\$100}{\$4,900\left(\dfrac{90}{360}\right)}$

$R = \dfrac{\$100}{\$1,225}$

$R = 0.0816326531$

$R = 8.2\%$

Proceeds = principal − bank discount
Proceeds = $5,000 − $100
Proceeds = $4,900

The effective interest rate for a simple discount note of $5,000 for 90 days is 8.2%.

---

3 Find the third-party discount and proceeds for a third-party discount note. (p. 404)

1. For the third-party discount, use:

Third-party discount = maturity value of original note × discount rate × discount period
$$I = PRT$$

2. For the proceeds to the original payee, use:

Proceeds = maturity value of original note − third-party discount
$$A = P - I$$

Mihoc Trailer Sales made a note of $10,000 with Darcy Mihoc, company owner, at 9% simple interest based on exact interest. The note is made on August 12 and due on November 10. However, Mihoc Trailer Sales needs cash, so the note is taken to a third party on September 5. The third party agrees to accept the note with a 13% annual discount rate using the banker's rule. Find the proceeds of the note to the original payee.

To find the proceeds, we find the maturity value of the original note and then find the third-party discount. Exact time is 90 days (314 − 224).

$$\text{Maturity value} = P(1 + RT)$$

$$\text{Maturity value} = \$10,000\left(1 + 0.09\left(\dfrac{90}{365}\right)\right) \qquad \text{Exact interest}$$

$$\text{Maturity value} = \$10,221.92$$

Exact time of the discount period is 66 days (314 − 248). Use the banker's rule.

$$\text{Third-party discount} = I = PRT$$

$$\text{Third-party discount} = \$10,221.92(0.13)\left(\dfrac{66}{360}\right) \qquad \text{Ordinary interest}$$

Third-party discount = $243.62
Proceeds = A = P − I
Proceeds = $10,221.92 − $243.62
Proceeds = $9,978.30

EXERCISES SET A — CHAPTER 11

SKILL BUILDERS

Find the simple interest. Round to the nearest cent when necessary.

	Principal	Annual rate	Time	Interest
1.	$500	12%	2 years	_____
2.	$3,575	11%	3 years	_____

3. Capco, Inc., borrowed $4,275 for three years at 12% interest. (a) How much simple interest did the company pay? (b) What is the maturity value?

Find the rate of annual simple interest in each of the following problems.

	Principal	Interest	Time	Rate
4.	$800	$124	1 year	_____
5.	$175	$31.50	2 years	_____

Find the time period of the loan using the formula for simple interest.

	Principal	Annual rate	Interest	Time
6.	$450	10%	$135	_____
7.	$1,500	$8\frac{1}{2}$%	$478.13	_____

In each of the following problems, find the principal, based on simple interest.

	Interest	Annual rate	Time	Principal
8.	$300	3%	2 years	_____
9.	$90	3.2%	1 year	_____

10. A loan for three years with an annual simple interest rate of 9% costs $486 interest. Find the principal.

Write a fraction expressing each amount of time as a part of a year (12 months = 1 year).

11. 7 months

12. 16 months

APPLICATIONS

13. Carol Stoy invested $500 at 2% annually for six months. How much interest did she receive?

14. Use the banker's rule to find the interest paid on a loan of $1,200 for 60 days at a simple interest rate of 6% annually.

15. Use the banker's rule to find the interest paid on a loan of $800 for 120 days at a simple interest rate of 6% annually.

16. Interest figured using 360 days per year is called what kind of interest?

Use Table 11-1 to find the exact time from the first date to the second date for non-leap years unless a leap year is identified.

17. March 15 to July 10

18. January 27, 2008, to September 30, 2008

If a loan is made on the given date, find the date it is due.

19. January 10 for 210 days

20. August 12 for 60 days

For Exercise 21, find (a) the exact interest and (b) the ordinary interest. Round answers to the nearest cent.

21. A loan of $1,200 at 10% annually made on October 15 and due on March 20 of the following non-leap year

22. Find the discount (ordinary interest) and proceeds on a promissory note for $2,000 made by Barbara Jones on February 10, 2011, and payable to First State Bank on August 10, 2011, with a discount rate of 9%.

23. MAK, Inc., accepted an interest-bearing note for $10,000 with 9% annual ordinary interest. The note was made on April 10 and was due December 6. MAK needed cash and took the note to First United Bank, which offered to buy the note at a discount rate of $12\frac{1}{2}$%. The transaction was made on July 7. How much cash did MAK receive for the note?

24. Malinda Levi borrows $12,000 on a 9.5%, 90-day note. On the 30th day, Malinda pays $4,000 on the note. If ordinary interest is applied, what is Malinda's adjusted principal after the partial payment? What is the adjusted balance due at maturity?

25. Shameka Bonner has a simple discount note for $11,000, at an ordinary bank discount rate of 11%, for 120 days. What is the effective interest rate? Round to the nearest tenth of a percent.

Simple Interest and Simple Discount   449

NAME _____   DATE _____

EXERCISES SET B

CHAPTER 11

SKILL BUILDERS

Find the simple interest. Round to the nearest cent when necessary.

	Principal	Annual rate	Time	Interest
EL 1.	$1,000	$9\frac{1}{2}\%$	3 years	_____
EL 2.	$2,975	$12\frac{1}{2}\%$	2 years	_____

3. Legan Company borrowed $15,280 at $10\frac{1}{2}\%$ for 12 years. How much simple interest did the company pay? What was the total amount paid back?

Find the rate of annual simple interest in each of the following problems.

	Principal	Interest	Time	Rate
4.	$1,280	$256	2 years	_____
5.	$40,000	$32,000	10 years	_____

Find the time period of the loan using the formula for simple interest.

	Principal	Annual rate	Interest	Time
6.	$700	6%	$84	_____
7.	$3,549	9.2%	$979.52	_____

In each of the following problems, find the principal, based on simple interest.

	Interest	Annual rate	Time	Principal
8.	$56.25	$2\frac{1}{2}\%$	3 years	_____
9.	$20	1.25%	2 years	_____

10. An investor earned $1,170 interest on funds invested at $9\frac{3}{4}\%$ annual simple interest for four years. How much was invested?

Write a fraction expressing each amount of time as a part of a year (12 months = 1 year).

11. 18 months

12. 9 months

APPLICATIONS

13. Alpha Hodge borrowed $500 for three months and paid $12.50 interest. What was the annual rate of interest?

14. Find the ordinary interest paid on a loan of $2,100 for 90 days at a simple interest rate of 4% annually.

15. Find the ordinary interest paid on a loan of $15,835 for 45 days at a simple interest rate of 8.1% annually.

16. When the exact number of days in a year is used to figure time, it is called what kind of interest?

Use Table 11-1 to find the exact time from the first date to the second date for non-leap years unless a leap year is identified.

17. April 12 to November 15

18. November 12 to April 15 of the next year

19. February 3, 2012, to August 12, 2012

If a loan is made on the given date, find the date it is due.

20. May 30 for 240 days

21. June 13 for 90 days

22. A loan of $8,900 at 7.75% annually is made on September 10 and due on December 10. Find (a) the exact interest and (b) the ordinary interest. Round answers to the nearest cent.

23. Find the discount and proceeds using the banker's rule on a promissory note for $1,980 at 8% made by Alexa Green on January 30, 2012, and payable to Enterprise Bank on July 30, 2012.

24. Find the exact interest on a loan of $2,100 at 7.75% annual interest for 40 days.

25. Allan Stojanovich can purchase an office desk for $1,500 with cash terms of 2/10, n/30. If he can borrow the money at 12% annual simple ordinary interest for 20 days, will he save money by taking advantage of the cash discount offered?

26. Shaunda Sanders borrows $16,000 on a 10.8%, 120-day note. On the 60th day, Shaunda pays $10,000 on the note. If ordinary interest is applied, what is Shaunda's adjusted principal after the partial payment? What is the adjusted balance due at maturity?

27. Bam Doyen has a simple discount note for $6,250, at an ordinary bank discount rate of 9%, for 90 days. What is the effective interest rate? Round to the nearest tenth of a percent.

PRACTICE TEST — CHAPTER 11

Simple Interest and Simple Discount

NAME _____ **DATE** _____

1. Find the simple interest on $500 invested at 4% annually for three years.

2. How much money was borrowed at 12% annually for 6 months if the interest was $90?

3. A loan of $3,000 was made for 210 days. If ordinary interest is $218.75, find the rate.

4. A loan of $5,000 at 12% annually requires $1,200 interest. For how long is the money borrowed?

5. Find the exact time from February 13 to November 27 in a non-leap year.

6. Find the exact time from October 12 to March 28 of the following year (a leap year).

7. Find the exact time from January 28, 2012, to July 5, 2012.

8. Sondra Davis borrows $6,000 on a 10%, 120-day note. On the 60th day, Sondra pays $2,000 on the note. If ordinary interest is applied, what is Sondra's adjusted principal after the partial payment? What is the adjusted balance due at maturity?

9. Find the ordinary interest on a loan of $2,800 at 10% annually made on March 15 for 270 days.

10. A bread machine with a cash price of $188 can be purchased with a one-year loan at 10% annual simple interest. Find the total amount to be repaid.

11. A copier that originally cost $3,000 was purchased with a loan for 12 months at 15% annual simple interest. What was the *total* cost of the copier?

12. Find the exact interest on a loan of $850 at 11% annually. The loan was made January 15 and was due March 15.

13. Michael Denton has a simple discount note for $2,000, at an ordinary bank discount rate of 12%, for 240 days. What is the effective interest rate? Round to the nearest tenth of a percent.

14. Find the duration of a loan of $3,000 if the loan required interest of $213.75 and was at a rate of $9\frac{1}{2}$% annual simple interest.

15. Find the rate of simple interest on a $1,200 loan that requires the borrower to repay a total of $1,302 after one year.

16. A promissory note using the banker's rule has a face value of $5,000 and is discounted by the bank at the rate of 14%. If the note is made for 180 days, find the amount of the discount.

17. Find the ordinary interest paid on a loan of $1,600 for 90 days at a simple interest rate of 13% annually.

18. Jerry Brooks purchases office supplies totaling $1,890. He can take advantage of cash terms of 2/10, n/30 if he obtains a short-term loan. If he can borrow the money at $10\frac{1}{2}$% annual simple ordinary interest for 20 days, will he save money if he borrows to take advantage of the cash discount? How much will he save?

19. Find the exact interest on a loan of $25,000 at $8\frac{1}{2}$% annually for 21 days.

20. Find the exact interest on a loan of $1,510 at $7\frac{3}{4}$% annual interest for 27 days.

CRITICAL THINKING — CHAPTER 11

Simple Interest and Simple Discount

1. In applying most formulas involving a rate, a fractional or decimal equivalent of the rate is used. Explain how a rate can be mentally changed to a decimal equivalent.

2. When solving problems, one should devise a method to estimate the solution. Describe a strategy for estimating the interest in the first example of Section 11-1 on page 388.

3. Explain how the rate can be estimated in Example 7 on page 392.

4. Use the formula $I = P\left(R \times \dfrac{D}{365}\right)$ to find the exact interest on $100 for 30 days and 7.50%.

5. Find the exact interest on $1,000 for 60 days at 5.3% annual interest rate.

6. The ordinary interest using exact time (banker's rule) will always be higher than exact interest using exact time. Explain why this is true.

7. Show how the formulas $I = PRT$ and $MV = P + I$ lead to the formula $MV = P(1 + RT)$.

8. The maturity value for a loan of $2,000 at 9% interest for two years was found to be $4,360. Examine the solution to identify the incorrect mathematical process. Explain the correct process and rework the problem correctly.

$$MV = P(1 + RT)$$
$$MV = \$2{,}000(1 + 0.09 \times 2)$$
$$MV = \$2{,}000(1.09 \times 2)$$
$$MV = \$2{,}000(2.18)$$
$$MV = \$4{,}360$$

Challenge Problem

A simple interest loan with a final "balloon payment" can be a good deal for both the consumer and the banker. For the banker, this loan reduces the rate risk, because the loan rate is locked in for a short period of time. For the consumer, this loan allows lower monthly payments.

You borrow $5,000 at 13% simple interest rate for a year.

For 12 monthly payments:

$$\$5{,}000(13\%)(1) = \$650 \text{ interest per year}$$

$$\dfrac{\$5{,}000 + \$650}{12} = \dfrac{\$5{,}650}{12} = \$470.83 \text{ monthly payment}$$

Your banker offers to make the loan as if it is to be extended over five years but with interest for only one year, or 60 monthly payments, but with a final balloon payment on the 12th payment. This means a much lower monthly payment.

For 60 monthly payments:

$$\frac{\$5{,}650}{60} = \$94.17 \text{ monthly payment}$$

The lower monthly payment is tempting! The banker will expect you to make these lower payments for *one* year. You will actually make 11 payments of $94.17: $94.17(11) = $1,035.87, which is the amount paid during the first 11 months.

The 12th and final payment, the *balloon payment,* is the *remainder* of the loan.

$$\$5{,}650 - \$1{,}035.87 = \$4{,}614.13$$

At this time you are expected to pay the balance of the loan in the balloon payment shown above. Don't panic! Usually the loan is refinanced for another year. But beware—you may have to pay a higher interest rate for the next year.

a. Find the monthly payment for a $2,500 loan at 12% interest for one year, extended over a three-year period with a balloon payment at the end of the first year.

b. What is the amount of the final balloon payment for a $1,000 loan at 10% interest for one year, extended over five years?

c. You need a loan of $5,000 at 10% interest for one year. What is the amount of the monthly payment?

d. Compare the monthly payment and final balloon payment of the loan in part c if the loan is extended over two years.

CASE STUDIES

11-1 90 Days Same as Cash!

Sara had just rented her first apartment starting December 1 before beginning college in January. The apartment had washer and dryer hook-ups, so Sara wanted to buy the appliances to avoid trips to the laundromat. The Saturday newspaper had an advertisement for a local appliance store offering "90 days, same as cash!" financing. Sara asked how the financing worked and learned that she could pay for the washer and dryer anytime during the first 90 days for the purchase price plus sales tax. If she waited longer, she would have to pay the purchase price, plus sales tax, plus 26.8% annual simple interest for the first 90 days, plus 3% simple interest per month (or any part of a month) on the unpaid balance after 90 days. Together, the washer and dryer cost $699 plus the 8.25% sales tax. Sara knew that her tax refund from the IRS would be $1,000 so she bought the washer and dryer confident that she could pay off the balance within the 90 days.

1. If Sara pays off the balance within 90 days, how much will she pay?

2. If Sara bought the washer and dryer on December 15, using the exact interest, what is her deadline for paying no interest in a non-leap year? In a leap year? Is the finance company likely to use exact or ordinary interest and why?

3. If Sara's IRS refund does not come until April 1, what is her payoff amount? (Assume ordinary interest and a non-leap year.)

4. How much did it cost her to pay off this loan 17 days late? What annual simple interest rate does this amount to?

11-2 The Price of Money

James wants to buy a flat screen television for his new apartment. He has saved $700, but still needs $500 more. The bank where he has a checking and savings account will loan him $500 at 12% annual interest using a 90-day promissory note. James also visited the PayDay Loan store to compare the cost of borrowing. The manager told James that he could borrow $500 at 12% for two weeks. If James needed more time to repay the loan, he would be charged 16% on the balance due for each additional week. He wondered how much it would cost to pay the loan back in 12 weeks so he could compare the cost to the bank's lending rate. He recognized that 12 weeks is a few days less than 90 days.

1. Calculate the total cost (principal plus interest) for the 90-day promissory note from the bank.

2. How much will James pay if he gets the loan from the PayDay Loan store and pays the balance back in two weeks?

3. How much will it cost if James gets his loan from the PayDay Loan store and pays it back in 12 weeks (nearly 90 days)?

4. James wondered how PayDay Loan can stay in business unless its customers neglect to determine how much they owe before agreeing to borrow. What do you think? When would a PayDay loan be an appropriate choice?

11-3 Quality Photo Printing

As a professional photographer, Jillian had seen a significant shift in customer demand for digital technologies in photography. Many customers, attempting to save a few dollars, had invested in low-end digital cameras (and even lower-end printers) to avoid processing fees typically associated with printing photographs. The end result, for most customers, was a bounty of digital photographic images but with limited options for creating quality printed digital photographs. Jillian was hoping to tap into this underserved market by offering customers superior quality digital printing using advanced pigment inks to produce exquisite color prints. To provide this service, Jillian needs to purchase a state-of-the-art photo printer she found listed through a photography supply company for $8,725, plus sales tax of 5.5%. The supply company is offering cash terms of 3/15, n/30, with a 1.5% service charge on late payments, or 90 days same as cash financing if Jillian will apply and is approved for a company credit card. If she is unable to pay within 90 days under the second option, she would have to pay 24.9% annual simple interest for the first 90 days, plus 2% simple interest per month on the unpaid balance after 90 days. Jillian has an excellent credit rating, but is not sure what to do.

1. If Jillian took the cash option and was able to pay off the printer within the 15-day discount period, how much would she save? How much would she owe?

2. If Jillian takes the 90 days same as cash option and purchases the printer on December 30 to get a current-year tax deduction, using exact time, what is her deadline for paying no interest in a non-leap year? In a leap year? Find the dates in ordinary time. Is the finance company likely to use exact or ordinary interest and why?

3. If Jillian takes the 90 days same as cash and pays within 90 days, what is her payoff amount? If she can't pay until April 30, how much additional money would she owe? (Assume ordinary interest and exact time and a non-leap year.)

4. Jillian finds financing available through a local bank. Find the bank discount and proceeds using ordinary interest and ordinary time for a 90-day promissory note for $9,200 at 8% annual simple interest. Is this enough money for Jillian to cover the purchase price of the printer? Is this a better option for Jillian to pursue, and why or why not?

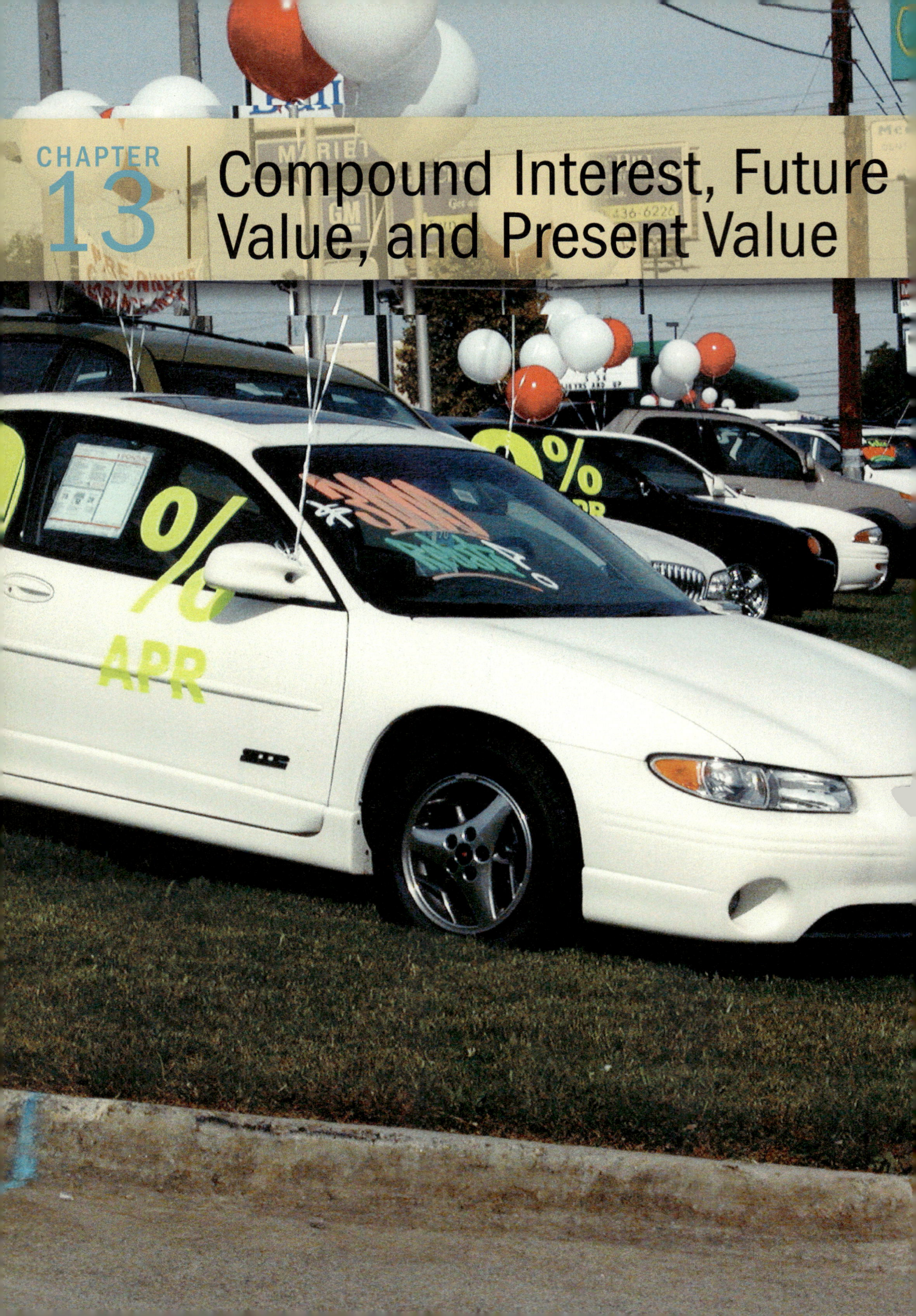
CHAPTER 13
Compound Interest, Future Value, and Present Value

Auto Loans: When Is 4% APR Better Than 0% APR?

What could possibly be wrong with a zero percent auto loan? Nothing could be more enticing than free money, and that's exactly what zero-percent finance deals seem to offer. With an auto loan, zero-percent financing may cost more than you think. Before taking on any loan, there are many things to consider. Compound interest—one of the topics you'll learn about in Chapter 13, is of special concern. With compound interest, you will actually pay more interest than you expect. Look for the annual percentage rate (APR) on your loan information. The APR tells you the effective interest rate that you will actually pay for the term of your loan. Does that mean a lower interest rate is the best deal? Not always. Here are a few things you should know about this special financing arrangement.

Anyone who purchases a vehicle with a cash rebate gets the rebate. But only about 5 percent of all consumers qualify for zero percent financing. You must have an excellent credit rating and a certain amount of income to qualify. Most zero-percent loans have short payback terms, which mean higher monthly payments. You may have to make a large down payment and be subject to prepayment penalties. Also, most zero percent financing applies only to certain makes and models of vehicles or those already on the lot.

Want to make the best deal? Consider rebates instead of special financing. Rebates are simply a form of discount, or savings, which may be greater than the amount you would save with zero percent financing. The table below shows a comparison of zero percent financing versus a rebate. In the table, the rebate deals saved money compared to the zero percent financing—more than $800 savings over the life of the loan. Do the math ahead of time to find out whether the rebate or the special financing would save you more money.

Financing a $20,000 New Car				
Loan terms	**36 Months**		**60 Months**	
APR	0%	4.0%	2.9%	5.6%
Price of new car	$20,000.00	$20,000.00	$20,000.00	$20,000.00
Less dealer rebate	$0	$2,000.00	$0	$2,000.00
Amount to finance	$20,000.00	$18,000.00	$20,000.00	$18,000.00
Monthly payment	$555.56	$531.43	$358.49	$344.65
Total financing cost	$20,000.00	$19,131.48	$21,509.40	$20,679.00
Savings		$868.52		$830.40

LEARNING OUTCOMES

13-1 Compound Interest and Future Value
1. Find the future value and compound interest by compounding manually.
2. Find the future value and compound interest using a $1.00 future value table.
3. Find the future value and compound interest using a formula or a calculator application (optional).
4. Find the effective interest rate.
5. Find the interest compounded daily using a table.

13-2 Present Value
1. Find the present value based on annual compounding for one year.
2. Find the present value using a $1.00 present value table.
3. Find the present value using a formula or a calculator application (optional).

 A corresponding Business Math Case Video for this chapter, *The Real World: Video Case: Should I Invest in Elvis?* can be found online at www.pearsonhighered.com\cleaves.

For some loans made on a short-term basis, interest is computed once, using the simple interest formula. For other loans, interest may be *compounded:* Interest is calculated more than once during the term of the loan or investment and this interest is added to the principal. This sum (principal + interest) then becomes the principal for the next calculation of interest, and interest is charged or paid on this new amount. This process of adding interest to the principal before interest is calculated for the next period is called *compounding interest.*

13-1 COMPOUND INTEREST AND FUTURE VALUE

LEARNING OUTCOMES
1. Find the future value and compound interest by compounding manually.
2. Find the future value and compound interest using a $1.00 future value table.
3. Find the future value and compound interest using a formula or a calculator application (optional).
4. Find the effective interest rate.
5. Find the interest compounded daily using a table.

Interest period: the amount of time after which interest is calculated and added to the principal.

Compound interest: the total interest that accumulated after more than one interest period.

Future value, maturity value, compound amount: the accumulated principal and interest after one or more interest periods.

Whether the interest rate is simple or compound, interest is calculated for each **interest period**. When simple interest is calculated, the entire period of the loan or investment is the interest period. When the interest is compounded, there are two or more interest periods, each of the same duration. The interest period may be one day, one week, one month, one quarter, one year, or some other designated period of time. The greater the number of interest periods in the time period of the loan or investment, the greater the total interest that accumulates during the time period. The total interest that accumulates is the **compound interest**. The sum of the compound interest and the original principal is the **future value** or **maturity value** or **compound amount** in the case of an investment, or the compound amount in the case of a loan. In this chapter we use the term *future value* to mean future value *or* compound amount, depending on whether the principal is an investment or a loan.

1 Find the future value and compound interest by compounding manually.

We can calculate the future value of the principal using the simple interest formula method. The terms of a loan or investment indicate the annual number of interest periods and the annual interest rate. Dividing the annual interest rate by the annual number of interest periods gives us the **period interest rate** or interest rate per period. We can use the period interest rate to calculate the interest that accumulates for each period using the familiar simple interest formula: $I = PRT$. I is the interest for the period, P is the principal at the beginning of the period, R is the period interest rate, and T is one period. As the value of T in the formula is one period, the formula is simplified to $I = PR(1)$, or $I = PR$. The value of P is different for each period in turn because the principal at the beginning of each period includes the original principal and all the interest so far accumulated. We can find the end-of-period principal directly by using $1 + R$ for the rate.

Period interest rate: the rate for calculating interest for one interest period—the annual interest rate divided by the number of interest periods per year.

> **HOW TO**   Find the period interest rate
>
> Divide the annual interest rate by the number of interest periods per year.
>
> $$\text{Period interest rate} = \frac{\text{annual interest rate}}{\text{number of interest periods per year}}$$

> **HOW TO**   Find the future value using the simple interest formula method
>
> 1. Find the first end-of-period principal: Multiply the original principal by the sum of 1 and the period interest rate.
>
>   First end-of-period principal = original principal × (1 + period interest rate)
>
> $A = P(1 + R)$
>
> 2. For each remaining period in turn, find the next end-of-period principal: Multiply the previous end-of-period principal by the sum of 1 and the period interest rate.
>
>   End-of-period principal = previous end-of-period principal × (1 + period interest rate)

3. Identify the last end-of-period principal as the future value.

$$\text{Future value} = \text{last end-of-period principal}$$

The future value is calculated before the amount of the compound interest can be calculated.

HOW TO   Find the compound interest

Subtract the original principal from the future value.

$$\text{Compound interest} = \text{future value} - \text{original principal}$$
$$I = A - P$$

EXAMPLE 1   Susan Riddle Duke's Photography secured a small business loan of $8,000 for three years, compounded annually. If the interest rate was 9%, find (a) the future value (compound amount) and (b) the compound interest paid on the loan. (c) Compare the compound interest with simple interest for the same loan period, original principal, and annual interest rate.

$$\text{Period interest rate} = \frac{\text{rate per year}}{\text{number of interest periods per year}}$$

(a) Because the loan is compounded annually, there is one interest period per year. So the period interest rate is 0.09. There are three interest periods, one for each of the three years.

First end-of-period principal = $8,000(1 + 0.09)$ $8,000(1.09) = 8,720$
= **$8,720**

Next end-of-period principal = **$8,720**$(1 + 0.09)$ $8,720(1.09) = 9,504.8$
= **$9,504.80**

Third end-of-period principal = **$9,504.80**$(1 + 0.09)$ $9,504.80(1.09) = 10,360.232$
= $10,360.23

The future value is $10,360.23.

(b) Compound interest is the future value (compound amount) minus the original principal.

$10,360.23   Future value
− 8,000.00   Original principal
$ 2,360.23   Compound interest

The compound interest is $2,360.23.

(c) Use the simple interest formula to find the simple interest on $8,000 at 9% annually for three years.

$$I = PRT$$
$$I = \$8,000(0.09)(3)$$
$$I = \$2,160.00 \quad \text{Simple interest}$$

Difference: $2,360.23 − $2,160.00 = $200.23

The simple interest is $2,160.00, which is $200.23 less than the compound interest.

EXAMPLE 2   Find the future value of a $10,000 investment at 2% annual interest compounded semiannually for three years.

$$\text{Period interest rate} = \frac{2\% \text{ annually}}{2 \text{ periods annually}} = \frac{0.02}{2} = 0.01 \text{ or } 1\%$$

Number of periods = years(2) = 3(2) = 6

First end-of-period principal = $10,000(1 + 0.01)$ $10,000(1.01) = 10,100$
= $10,100

Second end-of-period principal = $10,100(1 + 0.01)$ $10,100(1.01) = 10,201$
= $10,201

Third end-of-period principal = $10,303.01 $10,201(1.01) = 10,303.01$
Fourth end-of-period principal = $10,406.04 $10,303.01(1.01) = 10,406.04$

Fifth end-of-period principal = $10,510.10   10,406.04(1.01) = 10,510.10
Sixth end-of-period principal = $10,615.20   10,510.10(1.01) = 10,615.20

The future value is $10,615.20.

> ### TIP
> **Calculator Shortcut for Compounding**
>
> Many calculators keep the result of a calculation in the calculator and allow the next calculation to begin with this amount.
>
> Examine the calculator steps that can be used for Example 2.
>
> 10000 ⊠ 1.01 ⊟ ⟹ 10100   Record display as first end-of-period principal.
>
> Do not clear the calculator.
>
> ⊠ 1.01 ⊟ ⟹ 10,201   Record display as second end-of-period principal.
>
> Continue without clearing the calculator.
>
> ⊠ 1.01 ⊟ ⟹ 10,303.01   Record display as third end-of-period principal.
> ⊠ 1.01 ⊟ ⟹ 10,406.0401   Record display as fourth end-of-period principal.
> ⊠ 1.01 ⊟ ⟹ 10,510.1005   Record display as fifth end-of-period principal.
> ⊠ 1.01 ⊟ ⟹ 10,615.20151   Record display as sixth end-of-period principal.

🛑 STOP AND CHECK

1. Find the monthly interest rate on a loan that has an annual interest rate of 9.2%. Round to thousandths.

2. A loan of $2,950 at 8% is made for two years compounded annually. Find the future value (compound amount) of the loan. Find the amount of interest paid on the loan.

3. Find the future value of a $20,000 investment at 3.5% annual interest compounded semiannually for two years.

4. Find the future value of a $15,000 money market investment at 2.8% annual interest compounded semiannually for three years.

2   Find the future value and compound interest using a $1.00 future value table.

As you may have guessed from the previous examples, compounding interest for a large number of periods is very time-consuming. This task is done more quickly by using other methods. One method is to use a compound interest table, as shown in Table 13-1.

Table 13-1 gives the future value of $1.00, depending on the number of interest periods per year and the interest rate per period.

> **HOW TO**   Find the future value and compound interest using a $1.00 future value table
>
> 1. Find the number of interest periods: Multiply the number of years by the number of interest periods per year.
>
>   Interest periods = number of years × number of interest periods per year
>
> 2. Find the period interest rate: Divide the annual interest rate by the number of interest periods per year.
>
> $$\text{Period interest rate} = \frac{\text{annual interest rate}}{\text{number of interest periods per year}}$$
>
> 3. Using Table 13-1, select the periods row corresponding to the number of interest periods.
> 4. Select the rate-per-period column corresponding to the period interest rate.
> 5. Locate the value in the cell where the periods row intersects the rate-per-period column. This value is sometimes called the *i-factor*.
> 6. Multiply the original principal by the value from step 5 to find the future value or compound amount.
>
>   Future value = principal × table value
>
> 7. To find the compound interest,
>
>   Compound interest = future value − original principal

TABLE 13-1
Future Value or Compound Amount of $1.00

Periods	0.50%	1.00%	1.50%	2.00%	2.50%	3.00%	3.50%	4.00%	4.50%	5.00%	5.50%
1	1.00500	1.01000	1.01500	1.02000	1.02500	1.03000	1.03500	1.04000	1.04500	1.05000	1.05500
2	1.01003	1.02010	1.03023	1.04040	1.05063	1.06090	1.07123	1.08160	1.09203	1.10250	1.11303
3	1.01508	1.03030	1.04568	1.06121	1.07689	1.09273	1.10872	1.12486	1.14117	1.15763	1.17424
4	1.02015	1.04060	1.06136	1.08243	1.10381	1.12551	1.14752	1.16986	1.19252	1.21551	1.23882
5	1.02525	1.05101	1.07728	1.10408	1.13141	1.15927	1.18769	1.21665	1.24618	1.27628	1.30696
6	1.03038	1.06152	1.09344	1.12616	1.15969	1.19405	1.22926	1.26532	1.30226	1.34010	1.37884
7	1.03553	1.07214	1.10984	1.14869	1.18869	1.22987	1.27228	1.31593	1.36086	1.40710	1.45468
8	1.04071	1.08286	1.12649	1.17166	1.21840	1.26677	1.31681	1.36857	1.42210	1.47746	1.53469
9	1.04591	1.09369	1.14339	1.19509	1.24886	1.30477	1.36290	1.42331	1.48610	1.55133	1.61909
10	1.05114	1.10462	1.16054	1.21899	1.28008	1.34392	1.41060	1.48024	1.55297	1.62889	1.70814
11	1.05640	1.11567	1.17795	1.24337	1.31209	1.38423	1.45997	1.53945	1.62285	1.71034	1.80209
12	1.06168	1.12683	1.19562	1.26824	1.34489	1.42576	1.51107	1.60103	1.69588	1.79586	1.90121
13	1.06699	1.13809	1.21355	1.29361	1.37851	1.46853	1.56396	1.66507	1.77220	1.88565	2.00577
14	1.07232	1.14947	1.23176	1.31948	1.41297	1.51259	1.61869	1.73168	1.85194	1.97993	2.11609
15	1.07768	1.16097	1.25023	1.34587	1.44830	1.55797	1.67535	1.80094	1.93528	2.07893	2.23248
16	1.08307	1.17258	1.26899	1.37279	1.48451	1.60471	1.73399	1.87298	2.02237	2.18287	2.35526
17	1.08849	1.18430	1.28802	1.40024	1.52162	1.65285	1.79468	1.94790	2.11338	2.29202	2.48480
18	1.09393	1.19615	1.30734	1.42825	1.55966	1.70243	1.85749	2.02582	2.20848	2.40662	2.62147
19	1.09940	1.20811	1.32695	1.45681	1.59865	1.75351	1.92250	2.10685	2.30786	2.52695	2.76565
20	1.10490	1.22019	1.34686	1.48595	1.63862	1.80611	1.98979	2.19112	2.41171	2.65330	2.91776
21	1.11042	1.23239	1.36706	1.51567	1.67958	1.86029	2.05943	2.27877	2.52024	2.78596	3.07823
22	1.11597	1.24472	1.38756	1.54598	1.72157	1.91610	2.13151	2.36992	2.63365	2.92526	3.24754
23	1.12155	1.25716	1.40838	1.57690	1.76461	1.97359	2.20611	2.46472	2.75217	3.07152	3.42615
24	1.12716	1.26973	1.42950	1.60844	1.80873	2.03279	2.28333	2.56330	2.87601	3.22510	3.61459
25	1.13280	1.28243	1.45095	1.64061	1.85394	2.09378	2.36324	2.66584	3.00543	3.38635	3.81339
26	1.13846	1.29526	1.47271	1.67342	1.90029	2.15659	2.44596	2.77247	3.14068	3.55567	4.02313
27	1.14415	1.30821	1.49480	1.70689	1.94780	2.22129	2.53157	2.88337	3.28201	3.73346	4.24440
28	1.14987	1.32129	1.51722	1.74102	1.99650	2.28793	2.62017	2.99870	3.42970	3.92013	4.47784
29	1.15562	1.33450	1.53998	1.77584	2.04641	2.35657	2.71188	3.11865	3.58404	4.11614	4.72412
30	1.16140	1.34785	1.56308	1.81136	2.09757	2.42726	2.80679	3.24340	3.74532	4.32194	4.98395

Periods	6.00%	6.50%	7.00%	7.50%	8.00%	8.50%	9.00%	9.50%	10.00%	11.00%	12.00%
1	1.06000	1.06500	1.07000	1.07500	1.08000	1.08500	1.09000	1.09500	1.10000	1.11000	1.12000
2	1.12360	1.13423	1.14490	1.15563	1.16640	1.17723	1.18810	1.19903	1.21000	1.23210	1.25440
3	1.19102	1.20795	1.22504	1.24230	1.25971	1.27729	1.29503	1.31293	1.33100	1.36763	1.40493
4	1.26248	1.28647	1.31080	1.33547	1.36049	1.38586	1.41158	1.43766	1.46410	1.51807	1.57352
5	1.33823	1.37009	1.40255	1.43563	1.46933	1.50366	1.53862	1.57424	1.61051	1.68506	1.76234
6	1.41852	1.45914	1.50073	1.54330	1.58687	1.63147	1.67710	1.72379	1.77156	1.87041	1.97382
7	1.50363	1.55399	1.60578	1.65905	1.71382	1.77014	1.82804	1.88755	1.94872	2.07616	2.21068
8	1.59385	1.65500	1.71819	1.78348	1.85093	1.92060	1.99253	2.06687	2.14359	2.30454	2.47596
9	1.68948	1.76257	1.83846	1.91724	1.99900	2.08386	2.17189	2.26322	2.35795	2.55804	2.77308
10	1.79085	1.87714	1.96715	2.06103	2.15892	2.26098	2.36736	2.47823	2.59374	2.83942	3.10585
11	1.89830	1.99915	2.10485	2.21561	2.33164	2.45317	2.58043	2.71366	2.85312	3.15176	3.47855
12	2.01220	2.12910	2.25219	2.38178	2.51817	2.66169	2.81266	2.97146	3.13843	3.49845	3.89598
13	2.13293	2.26749	2.40985	2.56041	2.71962	2.88793	3.06580	3.25375	3.45227	3.88328	4.36349
14	2.26090	2.41487	2.57853	2.75244	2.93719	3.13340	3.34173	3.56285	3.79750	4.31044	4.88711
15	2.39656	2.57184	2.75903	2.95888	3.17217	3.39974	3.64248	3.90132	4.17725	4.78459	5.47357
16	2.54035	2.73901	2.95216	3.18079	3.42594	3.68872	3.97031	4.27195	4.59497	5.31089	6.13039
17	2.69277	2.91705	3.15882	3.41935	3.70002	4.00226	4.32763	4.67778	5.05447	5.89509	6.86604
18	2.85434	3.10665	3.37993	3.67580	3.99602	4.34245	4.71712	5.12217	5.55992	6.54355	7.68997
19	3.02560	3.30859	3.61653	3.95149	4.31570	4.71156	5.14166	5.60878	6.11591	7.26334	8.61276
20	3.20714	3.52365	3.86968	4.24785	4.66096	5.11205	5.60441	6.14161	6.72750	8.06231	9.64629
21	3.39956	3.75268	4.14056	4.56644	5.03383	5.54657	6.10881	6.72507	7.40025	8.94917	10.80385
22	3.60354	3.99661	4.43040	4.90892	5.43654	6.01803	6.65860	7.36395	8.14027	9.93357	12.10031
23	3.81975	4.25639	4.74053	5.27709	5.87146	6.52956	7.25787	8.06352	8.95430	11.02627	13.55235
24	4.04893	4.53305	5.07237	5.67287	6.34118	7.08457	7.91108	8.82956	9.84973	12.23916	15.17863
25	4.29187	4.82770	5.42743	6.09834	6.84848	7.68676	8.62308	9.66836	10.83471	13.58546	17.00006
26	4.54938	5.14150	5.80735	6.55572	7.39635	8.34014	9.39916	10.58626	11.91818	15.07986	19.04007
27	4.82235	5.47570	6.21387	7.04739	7.98806	9.04955	10.24508	11.59261	13.10999	16.73865	21.32488
28	5.11169	5.83162	6.64884	7.57595	8.62711	9.81822	11.16714	12.69391	14.42099	18.57990	23.88387
29	5.41839	6.21067	7.11426	8.14414	9.31727	10.65277	12.17218	13.89983	15.86309	20.62369	26.74993
30	5.74349	6.61437	7.61226	8.75496	10.06266	11.55825	13.26768	15.22031	17.44940	22.89230	29.95992

Table shows future value (FV) of $1.00 compounded for N periods at R rate per period.
Table values can be generated using the formula $FV = \$1(1 + R)^N$.

EXAMPLE 3

Use Table 13-1 to compute the compound interest on a $5,000 loan for six years compounded annually at 8%.

Interest periods = number of years × interest periods per year
= 6(1) = 6 periods

Period interest rate = $\dfrac{\text{annual interest rate}}{\text{interest periods per year}}$

= $\dfrac{8\%}{1}$ = 8%

Find period row 6 of the table and the 8% rate column. The value in the intersecting cell is 1.58687. This means that $1 would be worth $1.58687, or $1.59 rounded, compounded annually at the end of six years.

$5,000(1.58687) = **$7,934.35**   The loan is for $5,000, so multiply $5,000 by 1.58687 to find the future value of the loan.

The future value is $7,934.35.

$7,934.35 − $5,000 = $2,934.35   The future value minus the principal is the compound interest.

The compound interest on $5,000 for six years compounded annually at 8% is $2,934.35.

EXAMPLE 4

An investment of $3,000 at 4% annually is compounded *quarterly* (four times a year) for three years. Find the future value and the compound interest.

Interest periods = number of years × number of interest periods per year
= 3(4) = 12   The investment is compounded four times a year for three years.

Period interest rate = $\dfrac{\text{annual interest rate}}{\text{number of interest periods per year}}$ Divide the annual rate of 8% by the number of periods per year to find the period interest rate.

= $\dfrac{4\%}{4}$ = 1%

Future value of $1 = **1.12683**   Find the 12 periods row in Table 13-1. Move across to the 1% column.

$3,000(**1.12683**) = $3,380.49   The principal times the future value per dollar equals the total future value. Round to the nearest cent.

$3,380.49 is the future value.

Compound interest = future value − original principal
= $3,380.49 − $3,000
= $380.49

The compound interest is $380.49.

STOP AND CHECK

1. Use Table 13-1 to compute the compound interest on $2,890 for five years compounded annually at 4%.

2. A loan of $2,982 is repaid in three years. Find the amount of interest paid on the loan if it is compounded quarterly at 10%.

3. Andre Castello owns a savings account that is paying 2.5% interest compounded annually. His current balance is $7,598.42. How much interest will he earn over five years if the rate remains constant?

4. Natalie Bradley invested $25,000 at 2% for three years compounded semiannually. Find the future value at the end of three years using Table 13-1.

3 Find the future value and compound interest using a formula or a calculator application (optional).

Table values are most often generated with a formula. When the table does not include the rate you need or does not have as many periods as you need, the equivalent table value can be found by using the formula. The formula for finding the future value or the compound interest will require a calculator or electronic spreadsheet that has a power function. A business or scientific calculator or an electronic spreadsheet, such as Excel, is normally used.

> **HOW TO** Find the future value and the compound interest using formulas
>
> The future value formula is
>
> $$FV = P(1 + R)^N$$
>
> where FV is the future value, P is the principal, R is the period interest rate, and N is the number of periods.
>
> The compound interest formula is
>
> $$I = P(1 + R)^N - P$$
>
> where I is the amount of compound interest, P is the principal, R is the period rate, and N is the number of periods.

Business calculators, scientific calculators, and electronic spreadsheets impose a standard order of operations when making calculations. However, it is helpful to make some of the calculations in a formula mentally or before you begin the evaluation of the formula. For instance, in the future value formula you can find the period interest rate and the number of periods first. Also, you can change the period interest rate to a decimal equivalent and add 1.00 mentally.

> **TIP**
>
> **Power Key on a Calculator**
>
> A scientific, graphing, or business calculator has a special key for entering exponents. This key is referred to as the *general power key*.
> One common key label is $\boxed{\wedge}$. The exponent is entered after pressing this key.
> Another common key label is $\boxed{x^y}$. The exponent is entered after pressing this key.

EXAMPLE 5 Find the future value of a three-year investment of $5,000 that earns 6% compounded monthly.

Find the period interest rate:

$R = \dfrac{6\%}{12} = \dfrac{0.06}{12} = 0.005$ Change the annual rate to a decimal equivalent and divide by 12.

Find the number of periods:

$N = 3(12) = 36$ Multiply the number of years by 12.

Evaluate the future value formula:

$FV = P(1 + R)^N$ Substitute known values.
$FV = 5,000(1 + 0.005)^{36}$ Mentally add inside parentheses.
$FV = 5,000(1.005)^{36}$ Evaluate using a calculator or spreadsheet.
5000 $\boxed{(}$ 1.005 $\boxed{)}$ $\boxed{\wedge}$ 36 $\boxed{=}$ $\Rightarrow$ 5983.402624
$FV = \$5,983.40$ Rounded

EXAMPLE 6 Find the compound interest earned on a four-year investment of $3,500 at 4.5% compounded monthly.

Find the period interest rate:

$R = \dfrac{4.5\%}{12} = \dfrac{0.045}{12} = 0.00375$ Change the annual rate to a decimal equivalent and divide by 12.

Find the number of periods:

$N = 4(12) = 48$ Multiply the number of years by 12.

Evaluate the compound interest formula:

$I = P(1 + R)^N - P$ Substitute known values.
$I = 3,500(1 + 0.00375)^{48} - 3,500$ Mentally add inside parentheses.

$$I = 3{,}500(1.00375)^{48} - 3{,}500$$

3500 `(` 1.00375 `)` `^` 48 `=` `-` 3500 `=` ⇒

$I = \$688.85$

Evaluate using a calculator or spreadsheet.
688.850321
Rounded

Business and graphing calculators have financial applications that already have the formulas entered. To use these applications, you enter amounts for the known variables and solve for the unknown variables. For our illustrations we will use the BA II Plus™ and the TI-84 Plus™ by Texas Instruments.

Let's rework Example 5 using calculator applications.

EXAMPLE 7
Rework Example 5 using the calculator applications of the BA II Plus and the TI-84 Plus calculators.

BA II Plus:

	Keys to press	Display shows
Set decimals to two places if necessary.	2nd [FORMAT] 2 ENTER	DEC= 2.00
Set all variables to defaults.	2nd [RESET] ENTER	RST 0.00 ◁
Enter number of periods/payments.	36 N	N= 36.00 ◁
Enter interest rate per period (as a %).	.5 I/Y	I/Y= 0.50 ◁
Enter beginning amount as a negative.	5000 +/− PV	PV= −5,000.00 ◁
Compute future value.	CPT FV	FV= 5,983.40 *
Set the calculator back to normal mode.	2nd QUIT	

The symbol ◁ shown above a number indicates that the value in the display has been assigned to the indicated variable.

The symbol * shown above the number indicates that the value in the display is the result of a calculation.

TI-84:

Change to 2 fixed decimal places.	MODE ↓ → → → ENTER
Select Finance Application.	Press APPS 1:Finance ENTER
Select TVM Solver, which is already highlighted.	ENTER

Use the arrow keys to move cursor to appropriate variables and enter amounts. Enter 0 for unknowns.

Press 36 ENTER to store 36 months to N. Press 6 ENTER to store 6% per year to I%.

Press (−) 5000 ENTER to store 5,000 to PV. Press 0 ENTER to leave PMT unassigned. When you are *making payments* the present value (PV) is negative, so it is important to enter the negative sign in front of 5000. When you are *receiving* payments, as in an annuity, the present value will be positive.

Press 0 ENTER to leave FV unassigned.

Press 12 ENTER to store 12 payments/periods per year to P/Y and C/Y will automatically change to 12 also.

PMT at the bottom of the screen should have END highlighted.

Use up arrow to move cursor up to FV. Press ALPHA [SOLVE] to solve for future value. The future value is calculated and replaces the 0 at the blinking cursor.

```
N=         36.00
I%=         6.00
PV=     −5000.00
PMT=        0.00
■FV=     5983.40
P/Y=       12.00
C/Y=       12.00
PMT:END BEGIN
```

EXAMPLE 8
Joe Gallegos can invest $10,000 at 8% compounded quarterly for two years. Or he can invest the same $10,000 at 8.2% compounded annually for the same two years. If all other conditions (such as early withdrawal penalty, and so on) are the same, which deal should he take?

> **DID YOU KNOW?**
>
> Calculator instruction books sometimes are not easy to follow, so we have given you the keystrokes for some examples to help you get started. Descriptions that are displayed *on* the calculator keys are shown in rectangular boxes—for example, ENTER. Descriptions displayed *above* the calculator keys are shown with brackets—for example, [RESET]. Some calculators use color to coordinate the keys. For example, with the TI-84 Plus Silver Edition, the ALPHA key is green and the alpha characters above the keys that are used with this function key are also green.

> **DID YOU KNOW?**
>
> The calculator menu choices 1:Finance and 1:TVM Solver are displayed on the calculator screen. Pressing ENTER selects the choice that is highlighted on the screen that is displayed. To select another choice from the screen menu, use the cursor to move up or down to highlight the desired choice then press ENTER. You can also select your choice from the menu by pressing the number in front of the description. For example, to select Finance, you can press 1.

Compound Interest, Future Value, and Present Value

What You Know	What You Are Looking For
Principal: $10,000 Time period: 2 years Deal 1 annual rate: 8% Deal 1 interest periods per year: 4 Deal 2 annual rate: 8.2% Deal 2 interest periods per year: 1	Which deal should Joe take? Future value for each investment

Solution Plan

Number of interest periods = number of years × number of interest periods per year
Deal 1 interest periods = 2(4) = 8   Deal 2 interest periods = 2(1) = 2

$$\text{Period interest rate} = \frac{\text{annual interest rate}}{\text{number of interest periods per year}}$$

Deal 1 period interest rate = $\frac{8\%}{4}$ = 2%   Deal 2 period interest rate = $\frac{8.2\%}{1}$ = 8.2%

Solution

Deal 1: Using the future value formula for $10,000 at 2% per period for 8 periods

$FV = P(1 + R)^N$	Substitute known values.
$FV = \$10{,}000(1 + 0.02)^8$	Mentally add inside parentheses.
$FV = 10{,}000(1.02)^8$	Evaluate using a calculator or spreadsheet.
10000 [(] 1.02 [)] [^] 8 [=] ⇒	11716.59381
$FV = \$11{,}716.59$	Future value for Deal 1

Deal 2: Using the future value formula for $10,000 at 8.2% per period for 2 periods

$FV = P(1 + R)^N$	Substitute known values.
$FV = \$10{,}000(1 + 0.082)^2$	Mentally add inside parentheses.
$FV = 10{,}000(1.082)^2$	Evaluate using a calculator or spreadsheet.
10000 [(] 1.082 [)] [^] 2 [=] ⇒	11707.24
$FV = \$11{,}707.24$	Future value for Deal 2

Conclusion

Deal 1, the lower interest rate of 8% compounded more frequently (quarterly), is a slightly better deal because it yields the greater future value.

TIP
Using Calculator Applications for Example 8.

TI BA II Plus:
Set decimal to two places if necessary.

Deal 1	Deal 2
2nd [RESET] ENTER	2nd [RESET] ENTER
8 N	2 N
2 I/Y	8.2 I/Y
10000 +/− PV	10000 +/− PV
CPT FV	CPT FV
$11,716.59	$11,707.24

TI-84
APPS 1:Finance ENTER 1:TVM Solver ENTER

Enter the appropriate amounts.

Deal 1	Deal 2
N=8.00	N=2.00
I%=8.00	I%=8.20
PV=−10000.00	PV=−10000.00
PMT=0.00	PMT=0.00
FV=0.00	FV=0.00
P/Y=4.00	P/Y=1.00
C/Y=4.00	C/Y=1.00
PMT:**END** BEGIN	PMT:**END** BEGIN

Move cursor up to FV.   ALPHA [SOLVE]

The future value is calculated and replaces the 0 at the blinking cursor.

$11,716.59 $11,707.24

STOP AND CHECK

1. Kellen Davis invested $20,000 that earns 2.4% compounded monthly for four years. Find the future value of Kellen's investment.

2. Jonathan Vergues invested $17,500 that earns 1.2% compounded semiannually for 2 years. What is the future value of the investment after 2 years?

3. Lunetha Pryor has a $18,200 certificate of deposit (CD) that earns 2.25% interest compounded quarterly for 5 years. Find the compound interest after 5 years.

4. Susan Bertrees can invest $12,000 at 2% interest compounded twice a year or compounded quarterly. If either investment is for five years, which investment results in more interest? How much more interest is yielded by the better investment?

4 Find the effective interest rate.

If the investment in Example 4 on page 460 is compounded annually instead of quarterly for three years—three periods at 4% per period—the future value is $3,374.58 using table value 1.12486, and the compound interest is $374.58. The simple interest at the end of three years is $3,000 × 4% × 3, or $360. $3,000 at 4% for 3 years:

$360	$374.58	$380.49
Simple interest	Compounded annually using table value	Compounded quarterly using table value

You can see from these comparisons that a loan or investment with an interest rate of 4% compounded quarterly carries higher interest than a loan with an interest rate of 4% compounded annually or a loan with an annual simple interest rate of 4%. When you compare interest rates, you need to know the actual or **effective rate** of interest. The effective rate of interest equates compound interest rates to equivalent simple interest rates so that comparisons can be made.

The effective rate of interest is also referred to as the **annual percentage yield (APY)** when identifying the rate of earnings on an investment. It is referred to as the **annual percentage rate (APR)** when identifying the rate of interest on a loan.

Effective rate: the simple interest rate that is equivalent to a compound rate.

Annual percentage yield (APY): effective rate of interest for an investment.

Annual percentage rate (APR): effective rate of interest for a loan.

> **HOW TO** Find the effective interest rate of a compound interest rate
>
> **Using the manual compound interest method:** Divide the compound interest for the first year by the principal.
>
> $$\text{Effective annual interest rate} = \frac{\text{compound interest for first year}}{\text{principal}} \times 100\%$$
>
> **Using the table method:** Find the future value of $1.00 by using the future value table, Table 13-1. Subtract $1.00 from the future value of $1.00 after one year and divide by $1.00 to remove the dollar sign.
>
> $$\text{Effective annual interest rate} = \frac{\text{future value of \$1.00 after 1 year} - \$1.00}{\$1.00} \times 100\%$$

EXAMPLE 9 Marcia borrowed $6,000 at 10% compounded semiannually. What is the effective interest rate?

Using the manual compound interest method:

Period interest rate = $\frac{10\%}{2}$ = 5% = 0.05

First end-of-period principal = $6,000(1 + 0.05)
= $6,300

Second end-of-period principal = $6,300(1 + 0.05)
= $6,615

Compound interest after first year = $6,615 − $6,000 = $615

Compound Interest, Future Value, and Present Value   469

$$\text{Effective annual interest rate} = \frac{\$615}{\$6,000}(100\%)$$
$$= 0.1025(100\%)$$
$$= 10.25\%$$

Using the table method:

10% compounded semiannually means two periods in the first (and every) year and a period interest rate of 5%. The Table 13-1 value is 1.10250. Subtract 1.00.

$$\text{Effective annual interest rate} = (1.10250 - 1.00)(100\%)$$
$$= 0.10250(100\%)$$
$$= 10.25\%$$

The effective interest rate is 10.25%.

STOP AND CHECK

1. Willy Spears borrowed $2,800 at 8% compounded semiannually. Use the manual compound interest method to find the effective interest rate.

2. Use Table 13-1 to find the effective interest rate on Willy Spears' loan in Exercise 1. Compare the rate using the table with the rate found manually.

3. Mindi Lancaster invested $82,500 at 2% compounded semiannually. Use Table 13-1 to find the APY for her investment.

4. Una Sircy invested $5,000 at 3% compounded semiannually. Use Table 13-1 to find the APY for her investment.

5 Find the interest compounded daily using a table.

Some banks compound interest daily and others use continuous compounding to compute interest on savings accounts. There is no significant difference in the interest earned on money using interest compounded daily and interest compounded continuously. A computer is generally used in calculating interest if either daily or continuous compounding is used.

Table 13-2 gives compound interest for $100 compounded daily (using 365 days as a year). Notice that this table gives the *compound interest* rather than the future value of the principal, as is given in Table 13-1.

Using Table 13-2 is exactly like using Table 12-1, which gives the *simple* interest on $100.

HOW TO Find the compounded daily interest using a table

1. Determine the amount of money the table uses as the principal ($1, $100, or $1,000).
2. Divide the loan principal by the table principal.
3. Using Table 13-2, select the days row corresponding to the time period (in days) of the loan.
4. Select the interest rate column corresponding to the interest rate of the loan.
5. Locate the value in the cell where the interest column intersects the days row.
6. Multiply the quotient from step 2 by the value from step 5.

TIP

Examine Table Title and Footnote Carefully!

All tables are not alike! Different reference sources may approach finding the same information using different methods.

In working with compound interest, you may more frequently want to know the accumulated amount than the accumulated interest, or vice versa. A table can be designed to give a factor for finding either amount directly.

- Determine whether the table will help you find the compound amount or the compound interest. Table 13-1 finds the compound amount and Table 13-2 finds the compound interest. Also, the principal that is used to determine the table value may be $1, $10, $100, or some other amount.

- Determine the principal amount used in calculating table values. Table 13-1 uses $1 as the principal and Table 13-2 uses $100 as the principal.

TABLE 13-2
Compound Interest on $100, Compounded Daily (365 Days) (Exact Time, Exact Interest Basis)

Days	\multicolumn{9}{c}{Annual rate for selected rates}								
	0.50%	0.75%	1.00%	1.25%	1.50%	1.75%	2.00%	2.25%	2.50%
1	0.001370	0.002055	0.002740	0.003425	0.004110	0.004795	0.005479	0.006164	0.006849
2	0.002740	0.004110	0.005480	0.006849	0.008219	0.009589	0.010959	0.012329	0.013699
3	0.004110	0.006165	0.008219	0.010274	0.012329	0.014384	0.016439	0.018494	0.020549
4	0.005480	0.008219	0.010959	0.013699	0.016439	0.019179	0.021920	0.024660	0.027400
5	0.006850	0.010274	0.013699	0.017124	0.020550	0.023975	0.027400	0.030826	0.034251
6	0.008219	0.012329	0.016439	0.020550	0.024660	0.028771	0.032881	0.036992	0.041103
7	0.009589	0.014384	0.019180	0.023975	0.028771	0.033566	0.038362	0.043159	0.047955
8	0.010959	0.016440	0.021920	0.027401	0.032881	0.038363	0.043844	0.049326	0.054808
9	0.012329	0.018495	0.024660	0.030826	0.036992	0.043159	0.049326	0.055493	0.061661
10	0.013699	0.020550	0.027401	0.034252	0.041103	0.047956	0.054808	0.061661	0.068514
11	0.015070	0.022605	0.030141	0.037678	0.045215	0.052752	0.060290	0.067829	0.075368
12	0.016440	0.024660	0.032882	0.041104	0.049326	0.057549	0.065773	0.073998	0.082223
13	0.017810	0.026716	0.035622	0.044530	0.053438	0.062347	0.071256	0.080167	0.089078
14	0.019180	0.028771	0.038363	0.047956	0.057550	0.067144	0.076740	0.086336	0.095933
15	0.020550	0.030826	0.041104	0.051382	0.061662	0.071942	0.082223	0.092506	0.102789
16	0.021920	0.032882	0.043845	0.054809	0.065774	0.076740	0.087707	0.098676	0.109645
17	0.023290	0.034937	0.046586	0.058235	0.069886	0.081538	0.093192	0.104846	0.116502
18	0.024660	0.036993	0.049327	0.061662	0.073998	0.086337	0.098676	0.111017	0.123359
19	0.026031	0.039048	0.052068	0.065089	0.078111	0.091135	0.104161	0.117188	0.130217
20	0.027401	0.041104	0.054809	0.068515	0.082224	0.095934	0.109646	0.123360	0.137075
21	0.028771	0.043160	0.057550	0.071942	0.086337	0.100733	0.115132	0.129532	0.143934
22	0.030141	0.045215	0.060291	0.075370	0.090450	0.105533	0.120617	0.135704	0.150793
23	0.031512	0.047271	0.063033	0.078797	0.094563	0.110332	0.126103	0.141877	0.157653
24	0.032882	0.049327	0.065774	0.082224	0.098677	0.115132	0.131590	0.148050	0.164513
25	0.034252	0.051383	0.068516	0.085652	0.102790	0.119932	0.137076	0.154224	0.171374
26	0.035623	0.053438	0.071257	0.089079	0.106904	0.124732	0.142563	0.160398	0.178235
27	0.036993	0.055494	0.073999	0.092507	0.111018	0.129533	0.148051	0.166572	0.185096
28	0.038363	0.057550	0.076741	0.095935	0.115132	0.134334	0.153538	0.172746	0.191958
29	0.039734	0.059606	0.079483	0.099363	0.119247	0.139134	0.159026	0.178921	0.198821
30	0.041104	0.061662	0.082224	0.102791	0.123361	0.143936	0.164514	0.185097	0.205684
31	0.042474	0.063718	0.084966	0.106219	0.127476	0.148737	0.170003	0.191273	0.212547
32	0.043845	0.065774	0.087708	0.109647	0.131591	0.153539	0.175491	0.197449	0.219411
33	0.045215	0.067831	0.090451	0.113076	0.135706	0.158341	0.180981	0.203625	0.226275
34	0.046586	0.069887	0.093193	0.116504	0.139821	0.163143	0.186470	0.209802	0.233140
35	0.047956	0.071943	0.095935	0.119933	0.143936	0.167945	0.191960	0.215980	0.240005
40	0.054809	0.082225	0.109648	0.137078	0.164515	0.191960	0.219412	0.246872	0.274339
45	0.061662	0.092508	0.123362	0.154226	0.185099	0.215981	0.246873	0.277774	0.308684
50	0.068516	0.102791	0.137078	0.171377	0.205686	0.240008	0.274341	0.308685	0.343041
55	0.075370	0.113076	0.150796	0.188530	0.226278	0.264040	0.301816	0.339606	0.377410
60	0.082225	0.123362	0.164516	0.205687	0.246875	0.288078	0.329299	0.370536	0.411790
90	0.123363	0.185101	0.246876	0.308689	0.370540	0.432429	0.494355	0.556319	0.618321
120	0.164518	0.246877	0.329304	0.411797	0.494358	0.576987	0.659683	0.742446	0.825276
150	0.205689	0.308691	0.411799	0.515011	0.618330	0.721753	0.825282	0.928917	1.032658
180	0.246878	0.370544	0.494362	0.618332	0.742453	0.866728	0.991154	1.115733	1.240465
240	0.329306	0.494364	0.659692	0.825291	0.991161	1.157303	1.323717	1.490404	1.657364
360	0.494365	0.742461	0.991168	1.240487	1.490419	1.740967	1.992132	2.243915	2.496318
365	0.501249	0.752812	1.005003	1.257823	1.511275	1.765360	2.020078	2.275432	2.531424
730	1.005010	1.511291	2.020106	2.531468	3.045390	3.561884	4.080963	4.602641	5.126930
1095	1.511296	2.275480	3.045411	3.821133	4.602689	5.390124	6.183480	6.982803	7.788138
1825	2.531494	3.821160	5.127038	6.449332	7.788249	9.143998	10.516789	11.906838	13.314360
3650	5.127074	7.788332	10.516940	13.314603	16.183066	19.124122	22.139607	25.231403	28.401442

Table shows interest (I) on $100 compounded daily for N days at an annual rate of R. Table values can be generated using the formula $I = 100(1 + R/365)^N - 100$.

TABLE 13-2
Compound Interest on $100, Compounded Daily (365 Days) (Exact Time, Exact Interest Basis)—Continued

	Annual rate for selected rates									
Days	5.00%	5.25%	5.75%	6.00%	6.75%	7.25%	7.50%	8.25%	8.50%	9.00%
1	0.013699	0.014384	0.015753	0.016438	0.018493	0.019863	0.020548	0.022603	0.023288	0.024658
2	0.027399	0.028769	0.031509	0.032879	0.036990	0.039730	0.041100	0.045211	0.046581	0.049321
3	0.041102	0.043157	0.047268	0.049323	0.055490	0.059601	0.061657	0.067824	0.069879	0.073991
4	0.054806	0.057547	0.063029	0.065770	0.073993	0.079476	0.082217	0.090442	0.093183	0.098667
5	0.068512	0.071938	0.078792	0.082219	0.092500	0.099355	0.102782	0.113065	0.116493	0.123348
6	0.082220	0.086332	0.094558	0.098671	0.111010	0.119237	0.123351	0.135693	0.139807	0.148036
7	0.095930	0.100728	0.110326	0.115125	0.129524	0.139124	0.143924	0.158327	0.163128	0.172730
8	0.109642	0.115126	0.126097	0.131583	0.148041	0.159015	0.164502	0.180965	0.186453	0.197431
9	0.123355	0.129527	0.141870	0.148043	0.166562	0.178909	0.185084	0.203609	0.209784	0.222137
10	0.137071	0.143929	0.157646	0.164505	0.185085	0.198808	0.205670	0.226257	0.233121	0.246849
11	0.150788	0.158333	0.173424	0.180971	0.203613	0.218710	0.226260	0.248911	0.256463	0.271568
12	0.164507	0.172739	0.189205	0.197439	0.222144	0.238617	0.246854	0.271570	0.279810	0.296292
13	0.178229	0.187148	0.204988	0.213910	0.240678	0.258527	0.267453	0.294234	0.303163	0.321023
14	0.191952	0.201558	0.220774	0.230383	0.259216	0.278442	0.288056	0.316904	0.326521	0.345759
15	0.205677	0.215971	0.236562	0.246859	0.277757	0.298360	0.308663	0.339578	0.349885	0.370502
16	0.219403	0.230385	0.252353	0.263338	0.296301	0.318282	0.329274	0.362258	0.373254	0.395251
17	0.233132	0.244802	0.268146	0.279820	0.314849	0.338208	0.349890	0.384942	0.396629	0.420006
18	0.246863	0.259221	0.283942	0.296304	0.333400	0.358139	0.370510	0.407632	0.420009	0.444767
19	0.260595	0.273642	0.299740	0.312791	0.351955	0.378073	0.391134	0.430327	0.443394	0.469534
20	0.274329	0.288065	0.315540	0.329281	0.370514	0.398011	0.411762	0.453027	0.466785	0.494308
21	0.288066	0.302490	0.331344	0.345774	0.389075	0.417953	0.432395	0.475732	0.490182	0.519087
22	0.301804	0.316917	0.347149	0.362269	0.407640	0.437899	0.453031	0.498442	0.513583	0.543873
23	0.315544	0.331346	0.362957	0.378767	0.426209	0.457849	0.473672	0.521158	0.536991	0.568664
24	0.329286	0.345777	0.378768	0.395267	0.444781	0.477803	0.494318	0.543878	0.560403	0.593462
25	0.343029	0.360210	0.394581	0.411771	0.463356	0.497761	0.514967	0.566604	0.583822	0.618266
26	0.356775	0.374646	0.410397	0.428277	0.481935	0.517723	0.535621	0.589335	0.607245	0.643076
27	0.370522	0.389083	0.426215	0.444785	0.500517	0.537688	0.556279	0.612071	0.630674	0.667892
28	0.384272	0.403523	0.442035	0.461297	0.519103	0.557658	0.576941	0.634812	0.654109	0.692714
29	0.398023	0.417964	0.457858	0.477811	0.537692	0.577632	0.597608	0.657558	0.677549	0.717542
30	0.411776	0.432408	0.473684	0.494328	0.556285	0.597610	0.618279	0.680309	0.700994	0.742377
31	0.425531	0.446854	0.489512	0.510848	0.574881	0.617592	0.638954	0.703066	0.724445	0.767217
32	0.439288	0.461302	0.505342	0.527370	0.593480	0.637577	0.659633	0.725827	0.747902	0.792064
33	0.453047	0.475752	0.521175	0.543895	0.612083	0.657567	0.680316	0.748594	0.771363	0.816917
34	0.127683	0.134071	0.146849	0.153238	0.630690	0.677561	0.701004	0.771366	0.794831	0.841776
35	0.131441	0.138017	0.151171	0.157749	0.649299	0.697558	0.721696	0.794143	0.818304	0.866641
40	0.549411	0.576959	0.632077	0.659646	0.742400	0.797606	0.825220	0.908106	0.935749	0.991059
45	0.618300	0.649313	0.711367	0.742408	0.835587	0.897753	0.928850	1.022197	1.053332	1.115630
50	0.687235	0.721718	0.790719	0.825237	0.928859	0.997999	1.032586	1.136418	1.171052	1.240354
55	0.756218	0.794176	0.870134	0.908134	1.022219	1.098345	1.136430	1.250768	1.288909	1.365233
60	0.825248	0.866686	0.949612	0.991099	1.115664	1.198791	1.240380	1.365247	1.406903	1.490265
90	1.240422	1.302841	1.427794	1.490327	1.678155	1.803565	1.866327	2.054844	2.117759	2.243705
120	1.657306	1.740883	1.908241	1.992022	2.243775	2.411953	2.496145	2.749132	2.833599	3.002739
150	2.075907	2.180819	2.390964	2.496197	2.812542	3.023977	3.129857	3.448144	3.554457	3.767407
180	2.496231	2.622657	2.875973	3.002864	3.384472	3.639658	3.767486	4.151911	4.280368	4.537753
240	3.342080	3.512073	3.852895	4.023725	4.537896	4.882081	5.054597	5.573842	5.747491	6.095642
360	5.054775	5.314097	5.834658	6.095900	6.883491	7.411788	7.676912	8.476207	8.743951	9.281418
365	5.126750	5.389858	5.918047	6.183131	6.982358	7.518507	7.787585	8.598855	8.870629	9.416214
730	10.516335	11.070222	12.186328	12.748573	14.452250	15.602292	16.181634	17.937113	18.528139	19.719080
1095	16.182231	17.056750	18.825568	19.719965	22.443716	24.293858	25.229377	28.078354	29.042331	30.992085
1825	28.400343	30.015193	33.306041	34.982553	40.139588	43.686550	45.493537	51.051913	52.951474	56.822519
3650	64.866481	69.039503	77.705005	82.202895	96.391041	106.458246	111.683692	128.166805	133.941534	145.933026

Table shows interest (I) on $100 compounded daily for N days at an annual rate of R. Table values can be generated using the formula $I = 100(1 + R/365)^N - 100$.

> **EXAMPLE 10** Find the interest on $800 at 7.5% annually, compounded daily, for 28 days.
>
> $800 ÷ $100 = 8   Find the number of $100 units in the principal.
> Find the 28 days row in Table 13-2. Move across to the 7.5% column and find the interest for $100.
>
> 8($0.576941) = $4.615528   Multiply the table value by 8, the number of $100 units.
>
> **The interest is $4.62.**

STOP AND CHECK

1. Find the interest on $1,850 at 7.25% annually, compounded daily for 60 days.

2. Find the interest on $3,050 at 6% annually, compounded daily for 365 days.

3. Find the interest on $10,000 at 6.75% annually, compounded daily for 730 days.

4. Bob Weaver has $20,000 invested for three years at a 5.25% annual rate compounded daily. How much interest will he earn?

13-1 SECTION EXERCISES

SKILL BUILDERS

Find the future value and compound interest. Use Table 13-1 or the future value and compound interest formula.

1. A loan of $5,000 at 6% compounded semiannually for two years

2. A loan of $18,500 at 6% compounded quarterly for four years

3. An investment of $7,000 at 2% compounded semiannually for six years

4. A loan of $500 at 5% compounded semiannually for five years

5. A loan of $1,000 at 12% compounded monthly for two years

6. An investment of $2,000 at 1.5% compounded annually for ten years

APPLICATIONS

Use the simple interest formula method for Exercises 7 to 10.

7. Thayer Farm Trust made a farmer a loan of $1,200 at 16% for three years compounded annually. Find the future value and the compound interest paid on the loan. Compare the compound interest with simple interest for the same period.

8. Maeola Killebrew invests $3,800 at 2% compounded semiannually for two years. What is the future value of the investment, and how much interest will she earn over the two-year period?

9. Carolyn Smith borrowed $6,300 at $8\frac{1}{2}$% for three years compounded annually. What is the compound amount of the loan and how much interest will she pay on the loan?

10. Margaret Hillman invested $5,000 at 1.8% compounded quarterly for one year. Find the future value and the interest earned for the year.

Use Table 13-1 or the appropriate formula for Exercises 11–16.

11. First State Bank loaned Doug Morgan $2,000 for four years compounded annually at 8%. How much interest was Doug required to pay on the loan?

12. A loan of $8,000 for two acres of woodland is compounded quarterly at an annual rate of 6% for five years. Find the compound amount and the compound interest.

13. Compute the compound amount and the interest on a loan of $10,500 compounded annually for four years at 10%.

14. Find the future value of an investment of $10,500 if it is invested for four years and compounded semiannually at an annual rate of 2%.

15. You have $8,000 that you plan to invest in a compound-interest-bearing instrument. Your investment agent advises you that you can invest the $8,000 at 8% compounded quarterly for three years or you can invest the $8,000 at $8\frac{1}{4}$% compounded annually for three years. Which investment should you choose to receive the most interest?

16. Find the future value of $50,000 at 6% compounded semiannually for ten years.

474 Quantitative Methods for Business

17. Find the effective interest rate for a loan for four years compounded semiannually at an annual rate of 2%. Use the table method.

18. What is the effective interest rate for a loan of $5,000 at 10% compounded semiannually for three years? Use the simple interest formula method.

19. Ross Land has a loan of $8,500 compounded quarterly for four years at 6%. What is the effective interest rate for the loan? Use the table method.

20. What is the effective interest rate for a loan of $20,000 for three years if the interest is compounded quarterly at a rate of 12%?

Use Table 13-2 for Exercises 21 to 24.

21. Find the compound interest on $2,500 at 0.75% compounded daily by Leader Financial Bank for 20 days.

22. How much compound interest is earned on a deposit of $1,500 at 0.5% compounded daily for 30 days?

23. John McCormick has found a short-term investment opportunity. He can invest $8,000 at 0.5% interest for 15 days. How much interest will he earn on this investment if the interest is compounded daily?

24. What is the compound interest on $8,000 invested at 1.25% for 180 days if it is compounded daily?

13-2 PRESENT VALUE

LEARNING OUTCOMES
1 Find the present value based on annual compounding for one year.
2 Find the present value using a $1.00 present value table.
3 Find the present value using a formula or a calculator application (optional).

In Section 1 of this chapter we learned how to find the future value of money invested at the present time. Sometimes businesses and individuals need to know how much to invest at the present time to yield a certain amount at some specified future date. For example, a business may want to set aside a lump sum of money to provide pensions for employees in years to come. Individuals may want to set aside a lump sum of money now to pay for a child's college education or for a vacation. You can use the concepts of compound interest to determine the amount of money that must be set aside at present and compounded periodically to yield a certain amount of money at some specific time in the future. The amount of money set aside now is called *present value*. See Figure 13-1.

Compound Interest, Future Value, and Present Value   475

Present value: the amount that must be invested now and compounded at a specified rate and time to reach a specified future value.

1 Find the present value based on annual compounding for one year.

Finding the present value of $100 means finding the *principal* that we must invest today so that $100 is its future value. We know that the future value of principal depends on the period interest rate and the number of interest periods. Just as calculating future value by hand is time-consuming when there are many interest periods, so is calculating **present value** by hand. A present value table is more efficient. For now, we find present value based on the simplest case—annual compounding for one year. In this case, the number of interest periods is 1, and the period interest rate is the annual interest rate. In this case,

$$\text{Future value} = \text{principal}(1 + \text{annual interest rate}) \text{ or } FV = P(1 + R)$$

If we know the future value and want to know the present value,

$$\text{Principal(present value)} = \frac{\text{future value}}{1 + \text{annual interest rate}} \text{ or } PV = \frac{FV}{1 + R}$$

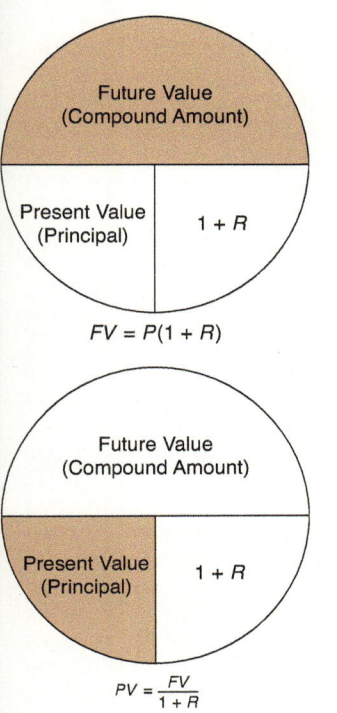

HOW TO   Find the present value based on annual compounding for one year

Divide the future value by the sum of 1 and the decimal equivalent of the annual interest rate.

$$\text{Present value(principal)} = \frac{\text{future value}}{1 + \text{annual interest rate}} \text{ or } PV = \frac{FV}{1 + R}$$

FIGURE 13-1
Relationship Between Future Value and Present Value

EXAMPLE 1
Find the amount of money that the 7th Inning needs to set aside today to ensure that $10,000 will be available to buy a new large-screen plasma television in one year if the annual interest rate is 4% compounded annually.

$1 + 0.04 = 1.04$ Convert the annual interest rate to a decimal and add to 1.

$\dfrac{\$10,000}{1.04} = \$9,615.38$ Divide the future value by 1.04 to get the present value.

An investment of $9,615.38 at 4% would have a value of $10,000 in one year.

✓ STOP AND CHECK

1. How much money needs to be set aside today to have $15,000 in one year if the annual interest rate is 2% compounded annually?

2. How much should be set aside today to have $15,000 in one year if the annual interest rate is 4% compounded annually?

3. Greg Karrass should set aside how much money today to have $30,000 in one year if the annual interest rate is 2.8% compounded annually?

4. Jamie Puckett plans to purchase real estate in one year that costs $148,000. How much should be set aside today at an annual interest rate of 3.46% compounded annually?

2 Find the present value using a $1.00 present value table.

If the interest in the preceding example had been compounded more than once a year, you would have to make calculations for each time the money was compounded. One method for finding the present value when the principal is compounded for more than one period is to use Table 13-3, which shows the present value of $1.00 at different interest rates for different periods. Table 13-3 is used like Table 13-1, which gives the future value of $1.00.

TABLE 13-3
Present Value of $1.00

					Rate per period							
Periods	0.5%	1%	1.5%	2%	2.5%	3%	4%	5%	6%	8%	10%	12%
1	0.99502	0.99010	0.98522	0.98039	0.97561	0.97087	0.96154	0.95238	0.94340	0.92593	0.90909	0.89286
2	0.99007	0.98030	0.97066	0.96117	0.95181	0.94260	0.92456	0.90703	0.89000	0.85734	0.82645	0.79719
3	0.98515	0.97059	0.95632	0.94232	0.92860	0.91514	0.88900	0.86384	0.83962	0.79383	0.75131	0.71178
4	0.98025	0.96098	0.94218	0.92385	0.90595	0.88849	0.85480	0.82270	0.79209	0.73503	0.68301	0.63552
5	0.97537	0.95147	0.92826	0.90573	0.88385	0.86261	0.82193	0.78353	0.74726	0.68058	0.62092	0.56743
6	0.97052	0.94205	0.91454	0.88797	0.86230	0.83748	0.79031	0.74622	0.70496	0.63017	0.56447	0.50663
7	0.96569	0.93272	0.90103	0.87056	0.84127	0.81309	0.75992	0.71068	0.66506	0.58349	0.51316	0.45235
8	0.96089	0.92348	0.88771	0.85349	0.82075	0.78941	0.73069	0.67684	0.62741	0.54027	0.46651	0.40388
9	0.95610	0.91434	0.87459	0.83676	0.80073	0.76642	0.70259	0.64461	0.59190	0.50025	0.42410	0.36061
10	0.95135	0.90529	0.86167	0.82035	0.78120	0.74409	0.67556	0.61391	0.55839	0.46319	0.38554	0.32197
11	0.94661	0.89632	0.84893	0.80426	0.76214	0.72242	0.64958	0.58468	0.52679	0.42888	0.35049	0.28748
12	0.94191	0.88745	0.83639	0.78849	0.74356	0.70138	0.62460	0.55684	0.49697	0.39711	0.31863	0.25668
13	0.93722	0.87866	0.82403	0.77303	0.72542	0.68095	0.60057	0.53032	0.46884	0.36770	0.28966	0.22917
14	0.93256	0.86996	0.81185	0.75788	0.70773	0.66112	0.57748	0.50507	0.44230	0.34046	0.26333	0.20462
15	0.92792	0.86135	0.79985	0.74301	0.69047	0.64186	0.55526	0.48102	0.41727	0.31524	0.23939	0.18270
16	0.92330	0.85282	0.78803	0.72845	0.67362	0.62317	0.53391	0.45811	0.39365	0.29189	0.21763	0.16312
17	0.91871	0.84438	0.77639	0.71416	0.65720	0.60502	0.51337	0.43630	0.37136	0.27027	0.19784	0.14564
18	0.91414	0.83602	0.76491	0.70016	0.64117	0.58739	0.49363	0.41552	0.35034	0.25025	0.17986	0.13004
19	0.90959	0.82774	0.75361	0.68643	0.62553	0.57029	0.47464	0.39573	0.33051	0.23171	0.16351	0.11611
20	0.90506	0.81954	0.74247	0.67297	0.61027	0.55368	0.45639	0.37689	0.31180	0.21455	0.14864	0.10367
21	0.90056	0.81143	0.73150	0.65978	0.59539	0.53755	0.43883	0.35894	0.29416	0.19866	0.13513	0.09256
22	0.89608	0.80340	0.72069	0.64684	0.58086	0.52189	0.42196	0.34185	0.27751	0.18394	0.12285	0.08264
23	0.89162	0.79544	0.71004	0.63416	0.56670	0.50669	0.40573	0.32557	0.26180	0.17032	0.11168	0.07379
24	0.88719	0.78757	0.69954	0.62172	0.55288	0.49193	0.39012	0.31007	0.24698	0.15770	0.10153	0.06588
25	0.88277	0.77977	0.68921	0.60953	0.53939	0.47761	0.37512	0.29530	0.23300	0.14602	0.09230	0.05882
26	0.87838	0.77205	0.67902	0.59758	0.52623	0.46369	0.36069	0.28124	0.21981	0.13520	0.08391	0.05252
27	0.87401	0.76440	0.66899	0.58586	0.51340	0.45019	0.34682	0.26785	0.20737	0.12519	0.07628	0.04689
28	0.86966	0.75684	0.65910	0.57437	0.50088	0.43708	0.33348	0.25509	0.19563	0.11591	0.06934	0.04187
29	0.86533	0.74934	0.64936	0.56311	0.48866	0.42435	0.32065	0.24295	0.18456	0.10733	0.06304	0.03738
30	0.86103	0.74192	0.63976	0.55207	0.47674	0.41199	0.30832	0.23138	0.17411	0.09938	0.05731	0.03338

The table shows the lump sum amount of money, present value (PV), that should be invested now so that the accumulated amount will be $1.00 after a specified number of periods, N, at a specified rate per period, R. Table values can be generated using the formula $PV = \dfrac{\$1.00}{(1+R)^N}$.

HOW TO   Find the present value using a $1.00 present value table

1. Find the number of interest periods: Multiply the time period, in years, by the number of interest periods per year.

   Interest periods = number of years × number of interest periods per year

2. Find the period interest rate: Divide the annual interest rate by the number of interest periods per year.

   $$\text{Period interest rate} = \dfrac{\text{annual interest rate}}{\text{number of interest periods per year}}$$

3. Using Table 13-3, select the periods row corresponding to the number of interest periods.
4. Select the rate-per-period column corresponding to the period interest rate.
5. Locate the value in the cell where the periods row intersects the rate-per-period column.
6. Multiply the future value by the value from step 5.

EXAMPLE 2
The Absorbent Diaper Company needs $20,000 in five years to buy a new diaper edging machine. How much must the firm invest at the present if it receives 5% interest compounded annually?

$R = 5\%$ and $N = 5$ years

Table value = 0.78353

The money is to be compounded for 5 periods, so we find periods row 5 in Table 13-3 and the 5% rate column to find the present value of $1.00.

Compound Interest, Future Value, and Present Value   477

$20,000(0.78353) = $15,670.60   Multiply the present value factor times the desired future value to find the amount that must be invested at the present.

The Absorbent Diaper Company should invest $15,670.60 today to have $20,000 in five years.

TIP
Which Table Do I Use?

Tables 13-1 and 13-3 have entries that are reciprocals. Except for minor rounding discrepancies, the product of corresponding entries is 1. And 1 divided by a table value equals its comparable table value in the other table.

Look at period row 1 at 1% on each table.

Table 13-1: 1.01000 $1 \div 1.01000 = 0.99010$ (rounded)   Table 13-3: 0.99010

Look at period row 16 at 4% on each table.

Table 13-1: 1.87298 $1 \div 1.87298 = 0.53391$ (rounded)   Table 13-3: 0.53391

One way to select the appropriate table is to anticipate whether you expect a larger or smaller amount. You expect a future value to be larger than what you start with. All entries in Table 13-1 are greater than 1 and produce a larger product.

You expect a present value to require a smaller investment to reach a desired amount. All entries in Table 13-3 are less than 1 and produce a smaller product.

FV table factors > 1
PV table factors < 1

STOP AND CHECK

1. The 7th Inning needs $35,000 in four years to buy new framing equipment. How much should be invested at 4% interest compounded annually?

2. How much should be invested now to have $15,000 in two years if interest is 4% compounded quarterly?

3. How much should be invested now to have $15,000 in four years if interest is 4% compounded quarterly?

4. How much should be invested now to have $15,000 in six years if interest is 4% compounded quarterly? Compare your results for Exercises 2–4.

---

3 Find the present value using a formula or a calculator application (optional).

A formula for finding the present value can be found by solving the future value formula for the (original) principal.

$FV = P(1 + R)^N$ Divide both sides of the equations by $(1 + R)^N$.

$\dfrac{FV}{(1 + R)^N} = \dfrac{P(1 + R)^N}{(1 + R)^N}$ Reduce.

$\dfrac{FV}{(1 + R)^N} = P$ Rewrite with P on the left side of the equation.

$P = \dfrac{FV}{(1 + R)^N}$ Original principal is present value.

$PV = \dfrac{FV}{(1 + R)^N}$ Now use PV for P.

HOW TO: Find the present value using a formula.

The present value formula is

$$PV = \frac{FV}{(1+R)^N}$$

where PV is the present value, FV is the future value, R is the interest rate per period, and N is the number of periods.

EXAMPLE 3

The Holiday Boutique would like to put away some of the holiday profits to save for a planned expansion. A total of $8,000 is needed in three years. How much money in a 5.2% three-year certificate of deposit that is compounded monthly must be invested now to have the $8,000 in three years?

Period interest rate $= \dfrac{5.2\%}{12} = \dfrac{0.052}{12} = 0.0043333333$

Number of periods $= 3(12) = 36$

$PV = \dfrac{FV}{(1+R)^N}$ Substitute known values.

$PV = \dfrac{8{,}000}{(1 + 0.0043333333)^{36}}$ Mentally add inside parentheses.

$PV = \dfrac{8{,}000}{(1.0043333333)^{36}}$ Evaluate using a calculator.

8000 ÷ ((1.0043333333) ^ 36 = ⇒ 6846.78069

$PV = \$6{,}846.78$ Rounded

The Holiday Boutique must invest $6,846.78 now at 5.2% interest for three years, compounded monthly to have $8,000 at the end of the three years.

EXAMPLE 4

Rework Example 3 using the calculator applications of the BA II Plus and the TI-84 Plus calculators. See p. 462 for more detailed instruction.

BA II Plus:
2nd [FORMAT] 2 ENTER
2nd [RESET] ENTER
36 N
.4333333333 I/Y
8000 +/− FV
CPT PV
⇒ **6846.78**

TI-84:
APPS ENTER ENTER
36 ENTER 5.2 ENTER
0 ENTER 0 ENTER
(−) 8000 ENTER
12 ENTER
Be sure PMT has **END** highlighted. Use up arrow to move cursor up to PV. Press ALPHA [SOLVE].
PV = **6846.78**

STOP AND CHECK

Use the present value formula or a calculator application.

1. Mary Kaye Keller needs $30,000 in seven years. How much must she set aside today at 4.8% compounded monthly?

2. How much should a family invest now at $2\frac{3}{4}\%$ compounded annually to have a $7,000 house down payment in four years?

3. If you were offered $700 today or $800 in two years, which would you accept if the $700 can be invested at 2.4% annual interest compounded monthly?

4. Bridgett Smith inherited some money and needs $45,000 in 15 years for her child's college fund. How much of the inheritance should she invest now at 2.8% compounded quarterly?

13-2 SECTION EXERCISES

SKILL BUILDERS

Find the amount that should be set aside today to yield the desired future amount; use Table 13-3 or the appropriate formula.

	Future amount needed	Interest rate	Compounding period	Investment time
1.	$4,000	3%	semiannually	2 years
2.	$7,000	2.5%	annually	20 years
3.	$10,000	4%	quarterly	4 years
4.	$5,000	3%	semiannually	6 years

APPLICATIONS

5. Compute the amount of money to be set aside today to ensure a future value of $2,500 in one year if the interest rate is 2.5% annually, compounded annually.

6. How much should Linda Bryan set aside now to buy equipment that costs $8,500 in one year? The current interest rate is 0.95% annually, compounded annually.

7. Ronnie Cox has just inherited $27,000. How much of this money should he set aside today to have $21,000 to pay cash for a Ventura Van, which he plans to purchase in one year? He can invest at 1.9% annually, compounded annually.

8. Shirley Riddle received a $10,000 gift from her mother and plans a minor renovation to her home. She also plans to make an investment for one year, at which time she plans to take a trip projected to cost $6,999. The current interest rate is 2.3% annually, compounded annually. How much should be set aside today for her trip?

9. Rosa Burnett needs $2,000 in three years to make the down payment on a new car. How much must she invest today if she receives 1.5% interest annually, compounded annually? Use Table 13-3.

10. Use Table 13-3 to calculate the amount of money that must be invested now at 4% annually, compounded quarterly, to obtain $1,500 in three years.

11. Dewey Sykes plans to open a business in four years when he retires. How much must he invest today to have $10,000 when he retires if the bank pays 2% annually, compounded quarterly?

12. Charlie Bryant has a child who will be college age in five years. How much must he set aside today to have $20,000 for college tuition in five years if he gets 1.5% annually, compounded annually?

SUMMARY

CHAPTER 13

Compound Interest, Future Value, and Present Value

Learning Outcomes

Section 13-1

1 Find the future value and compound interest by compounding manually. (p. 456)

What to Remember with Examples

Find the period interest rate: Divide the annual interest rate by the number of interest periods per year.

$$\text{Period interest rate} = \frac{\text{annual interest rate}}{\text{number of interest periods per year}}$$

Find the future value using the simple interest formula method:

1. Find the first end-of-period principal: Multiply the original principal by the sum of 1 and the period interest rate.

   First end-of-period principal = original principal × (1 + period interest rate)

2. For each remaining period in turn, find the next end-of-period principal: Multiply the previous end-of-period principal by the sum of 1 and the period interest rate.

   End-of-period principal = previous end-of-period principal × (1 + period interest rate)

3. Identify the last end-of-period principal as the future value.

   Future value = last end-of-period principal

Find the compound interest: Subtract the original principal from the future value.

Compound interest = future value − original principal

Find the compound amount and compound interest on $5,000 at 7% compounded annually for two years.

($5,000)(1 + 0.07) = $5,350 end-of-first-period principal
($5,350)(1 + 0.07) = $5,724.50 end-of-last-period principal (future value)
Compound amount = $5,724.50
Compound interest = $5,724.50 − $5,000 = $724.50

Find the compound amount (future value) and compound interest on $1,500 at 8% compounded semiannually for two years.

Number of interest periods = 2(2) = 4 periods

$$\text{Period interest rate} = \frac{8\%}{2} = 4\% \text{ or } 0.04 \text{ per period}$$

$1,500(1 + 0.04) = $1,560 (first period)
$1,560(1 + 0.04) = $1,622.40 (second period)
$1,622.40(1 + 0.04) = $1,687.30 (third period)
$1,687.30(1 + 0.04) = $1,754.79 (fourth period)
Compound amount = $1,754.79
Compound interest = $1,754.79 − $1,500 = $254.79

---

2 Find the future value and compound interest using a $1.00 future value table. (p. 458)

1. Find the number of interest periods: Multiply the number of years by the number of interest periods per year.

   Interest periods = number of years × number of interest periods per year

2. Find the period interest rate: Divide the annual interest rate by the number of interest periods per year.

   $$\text{Period interest rate} = \frac{\text{annual interest rate}}{\text{number of interest periods per year}}$$

3. Using Table 13-1, select the periods row corresponding to the number of interest periods.
4. Select the rate-per-period column corresponding to the period interest rate.
5. Locate the value in the cell where the periods row intersects the rate-per-period column.
6. Multiply the original principal by the value from step 5 to find future value or compound amount.

   Future value = principal × table value

482 Quantitative Methods for Business

7. To find the compound interest:

$$\text{Compound interest} = \text{future value} - \text{original principal}$$

Find the future value of $2,000 at 12% compounded semiannually for four years.	Find the compound interest on $800 at 8% compounded annually for four years for 4 periods.
4(2) = 8 periods	Annually indicates one period per year. Period interest rate is 8%.
$\dfrac{12\%}{2} = 6\%$ period interest rate.	Find periods row 4 in Table 13-1.
Find periods row 8 in Table 13-1 and move across to the 6% rate column: 1.59385.	Move across to the 8% rate column and find the compound amount per dollar of principal: 1.36049.
$2,000(1.59385) = $3,187.70 future value or compound amount	800(1.36049) = $1,088.39 compound amount
	$1,088.39 compound amount or future value
	−800.00 principal
	$288.39 compound interest

3 Find the future value and compound interest using a formula or a calculator application (optional). (p. 461)

The future value formula is

$$FV = P(1 + R)^N$$

where FV is the future value, P is the principal, R is the period interest rate, and N is the number of periods.

Find the future value of a three-year investment of $3,500 that earns 5.4% compounded monthly.

Find the period interest rate:

$R = \dfrac{5.4\%}{12} = \dfrac{0.054}{12} = 0.0045$ Change the annual rate to a decimal equivalent and divide by 12.

Find the number of periods:

$N = (3)(12) = 36$ Multiply the number of years by 12.

Evaluate the future value formula:

$FV = P(1 + R)^N$ Substitute known values.
$FV = 3,500(1 + 0.0045)^{36}$ Mentally add inside parentheses.
$FV = 3,500(1.0045)^{36}$ Evaluate using a calculator or spreadsheet.

3500 × (1.0045) ^ 36 = ⇒ 4114.015498

$FV = \$4,114.02$ Rounded

To solve using a calculator application with the TI BA II Plus or TI-84, see Example 7 on p. 462 and in the Tip following Example 8 on pp. 462–463.

The compound interest formula is

$$I = P(1 + R)^N - P$$

where I is the amount of compound interest, P is the principal, R is the period rate, and N is the number of periods.

Find the compound interest earned on a four-year investment of $6,500 at 5.5% compounded monthly.

Find the period interest rate:

$R = \dfrac{5.5\%}{12} = \dfrac{0.055}{12} = 0.0045833333$ Change the annual rate to a decimal equivalent and divide by 12.

Find the number of periods:

$N = (4)(12) = 48$ Multiply the number of years by 12.

Compound Interest, Future Value, and Present Value

Evaluate the compound interest formula:

$I = P(1 + R)^N - P$ Substitute known values.
$I = 6{,}500(1 + 0.0045833333)^{48} - 6{,}500$ Mentally add inside parentheses.
$I = 6{,}500(1.0045833333)^{48} - 6{,}500$ Evaluate using a calculator or spreadsheet.
6500 [(1.0045833333)] [^] 48 [=] [−] 6500 [=] ⇒ 1,595.428696
$I = \$1{,}595.43$ Rounded

4 Find the effective interest rate. (p. 464)

Using the manual compound interest method: Divide the compound interest for the *first year* by the principal.

$$\text{Effective annual interest rate} = \frac{\text{compound interest for first year}}{\text{principal}} \times 100\%$$

Using the table method: Use Table 13-1 to find the future value of $1.00 of the investment. Subtract $1.00 from the future value of $1.00 after one year and divide by $1.00 to remove the dollar sign.

$$\text{Effective interest rate} = \frac{\text{future value of \$1.00 after 1 year} - \$1.00}{\$1.00} \times 100\%$$

Betty Padgett earned $247.29 interest on a one-year investment of $3,000 at 8% annually, compounded quarterly. Find the effective interest rate.

Using the simple interest formula method:

$$\text{Effective interest} = \frac{\$247.29}{\$3{,}000}(100\%) = 0.08243(100\%) = 8.24\%$$

Using Table 13-1: Periods per year = 4

$$\text{Rate per period} = \frac{8\%}{4} = 2\%$$

Table value = 1.08243 (from Table 13-1)

Effective interest rate = 1.08243 − 1.00 = 0.08243 = 8.24%

5 Find the interest compounded daily using a table. (p. 465)

1. Determine the amount of money the table uses as the principal. (A typical table principal is $1, $100, or $1,000.)
2. Divide the loan principal by the table principal.
3. Using Table 13-2, select the days row corresponding to the time period (in days) of the loan.
4. Select the interest rate column corresponding to the interest rate of the loan.
5. Locate the value in the cell where the interest column intersects the days row.
6. Multiply the quotient from step 2 by the value from step 5.

Find the interest on a $300 loan borrowed at 9% compounded daily for 21 days.
Select the 21 days row of Table 13-2; then move across to the 9% rate column. The table value is 0.519087.

$$\frac{\$300}{100}(0.519087) = \$1.56$$

The interest on $300 is $1.56.

Section 13-2

1 Find the present value based on annual compounding for one year. (p. 471)

Divide the future value by the sum of 1 and the decimal equivalent of the annual interest rate.

$$\text{Present value (principal)} = \frac{\text{future value}}{1 + \text{annual interest rate}}$$

Find the amount of money that must be invested to produce $4,000 in one year if the interest rate is 7% annually, compounded annually.

$$\text{Present value} = \frac{\$4{,}000}{1 + 0.07} = \frac{\$4{,}000}{1.07} = \$3{,}738.32$$

How much must be invested to produce $30,000 in one year if the interest rate is 6% annually, compounded annually?

$$\text{Present value} = \frac{\$30{,}000}{1 + 0.06} = \frac{\$30{,}000}{1.06} = \$28{,}301.89$$

484 Quantitative Methods for Business

2 Find the present value using a $1.00 present value table. (p. 471)

1. Find the number of interest periods: Multiply the time period, in years, by the number of interest periods per year.

$$\text{Interest periods} = \text{number of years} \times \text{number of interest periods per year}$$

2. Find the period interest rate: Divide the annual interest rate by the number of interest periods per year.

$$\text{Period interest rate} = \frac{\text{annual interest rate}}{\text{number of interest periods per year}}$$

3. Using Table 13-3, select the periods row corresponding to the number of interest periods.
4. Select the rate-per-period column corresponding to the period interest rate.
5. Locate the value in the cell where the periods row intersects the rate-per-period column.
6. Multiply the future value by the value from step 5.

Find the amount of money that must be deposited to ensure $3,000 at the end of three years if the investment earns 6% compounded semiannually.

$(3)(2) = 6$ periods

$\dfrac{6\%}{2} = 3\%$ rate per period

Find periods row 6 in Table 13-3 and move across to the 3% rate column: 0.83748.

$\$3,000(0.83748) = \$2,512.44$

The amount that must be invested now to have $3,000 in three years is $2,512.44.

---

3 Find the present value using a formula or a calculator application (optional). (p. 473)

Present Value Formula:

$$PV = \frac{FV}{(1+R)^N}$$

where PV is the present value, FV is the future value, R is the interest rate per period, and N is the number of periods.

Ezell Allen has saved some money that he wants to put away for a down payment on a home in five years. He can invest the money in a 5.4% five-year certificate of deposit that is compounded monthly. How much of his money should he set aside now for a down payment of $10,000 in 5 years?

$$\text{Period interest rate} = \frac{5.4\%}{12} = \frac{0.054}{12} = 0.0045$$

Number of periods $= 5(12) = 60$

$PV = \dfrac{FV}{(1+R)^N}$ Substitute known values.

$PV = \dfrac{10{,}000}{(1+0.0045)^{60}}$ Mentally add inside parentheses.

$PV = \dfrac{10{,}000}{(1.0045)^{60}}$ Evaluate using a calculator.

10000 ÷ ((1.0045)) ^ 60 = ⇒ 7638.420009
$PV = \$7{,}638.42$ Rounded

Ezell must invest $7,638.42 now at 5.4% interest for five years, compounded monthly to have $10,000 at the end of the five years.

To solve using a calculator application with the TI BA II Plus or TI-84, see Example 4 on p. 474.

EXERCISES SET A

CHAPTER 13

Use Table 13-1 or the appropriate formula for Exercises 1–4.

	Principal	Term (years)	Rate of compound interest	Compounded	Compound amount	Compound interest
1.	$2,000	3	3%	semiannually	_____	_____
2.	$5,000	4	4%	quarterly	_____	_____
3.	$10,000	2	2.5%	annually	_____	_____
4.	$8,000	4	1%	semiannually	_____	_____

Find the amount that should be set aside today to yield the desired future amount. Use Table 13-3 or the present value formula.

	Future amount needed	Interest rate	Compounding	Investment time (years)		Future amount needed	Interest rate	Compounding	Investment time (years)
EXCEL 5.	$20,000	4%	semiannually	5	EXCEL 6.	$8,000	6%	quarterly	6
EXCEL 7.	$9,800	2%	semiannually	12	EXCEL 8.	$14,700	3%	annually	20

9. Manually calculate the compound interest on a loan of $1,000 at 8%, compounded annually for two years.

10. Manually calculate the compound interest on a 13% loan of $1,600 for three years if the interest is compounded annually.

11. Use Table 13-1 or the appropriate formula to find the future value of an investment of $3,000 made by Ling Lee for five years at 3% annual interest compounded semiannually.

12. Use Table 13-1 or the appropriate formula to find the interest on a certificate of deposit (CD) of $10,000 for five years at 4% compounded semiannually.

13. Find the future value of an investment of $8,000 compounded quarterly for seven years at 2%.

14. Find the compound interest on a loan of $5,000 for two years if the interest is compounded quarterly at 12%.

15. Mario Piazza was offered $900 now for one of his salon photographs or $1,100 in one year for the same photograph. Which would give Mr. Piazza a greater yield if he could invest the $900 for one year at 4% compounded quarterly? Use Table 13-1.

16. Lauren McAnally invests $2,000 at 2% compounded semiannually for two years, and Inez Everett invests an equal amount at 2% compounded quarterly for 18 months. Use Table 13-1 to determine which investment yields the greater interest.

17. Use Table 13-2 to find the compound interest and the compound amount on an investment of $2,000 if it is invested for 21 days at 0.75% compounded daily.

18. Use Table 13-2 to find the amount of interest on $100 invested for 10 days at 8.5% compounded daily.

In the following exercises, find the amount of money that should be invested (present value) at the stated interest rate to yield the given amount (future value) after the indicated amount of time. Use Table 13-3 or the appropriate formula.

19. $1,500 in three years at 2.5% compounded annually

20. $1,000 in seven years at 8% compounded quarterly

21. $4,000 in two years at 2% annual interest compounded quarterly

22. $500 in 15 years at 4% annual interest compounded semiannually

23. Find the amount that should be invested today to have $1,800 in one year at 6% annual interest compounded monthly.

24. Myrna Lewis wishes to have $4,000 in four years to tour Europe. How much must she invest today at 6% annual interest compounded quarterly to have $4,000 in four years?

NAME _____ DATE _____

EXERCISES SET B

CHAPTER 13

Use Table 13-1 for Exercises 1–4.

Principal	Term (years)	Rate of compound interest	Compounded	Compound amount	Compound interest
1. $5,000	5	5%	semiannually	_____	_____
2. $12,000	7	4%	quarterly	_____	_____
3. $7,000	10	2%	semiannually	_____	_____
4. $2,985	8	3%	annually	_____	_____

Find the amount that should be set aside today to yield the desired future amount. Use Table 13-3 or the present value formula.

	Future amount needed	Interest rate	Compounding	Investment time (years)		Future amount needed	Interest rate	Compounding	Investment time (years)
EXCEL 5.	$3,000	6%	quarterly	5	EXCEL 6.	$46,000	2.5%	annually	25
EXCEL 7.	$17,000	3%	semiannually	8	EXCEL 8.	$11,200	4%	quarterly	3

9. Manually calculate the compound interest on a loan of $200 at 6% compounded annually for four years.

10. Manually calculate the compound interest on a loan of $6,150 at $11\frac{1}{2}$% annual interest compounded annually for three years.

11. EZ Loan Company loaned $500 at 8% annual interest compounded quarterly for one year. Use Table 13-1 or the appropriate formula to calculate the amount the loan company will earn in interest.

12. Use Table 13-2 to find the daily interest on $2,500 invested for 21 days at 2.25% compounded daily.

13. Find the factor for compounding an amount for 25 periods at 8% per period.

14. Find the compound interest on a loan of $5,000 for two years if the interest is compounded semiannually at 12%.

15. An investment of $1,000 is made for two years and is compounded semiannually at 5%. Find the compound amount and compound interest at the end of the two years.

16. Carlee McNally invests $5,000 at 6% compounded semiannually for one year, and Jake McNally invests an equal amount at 6% compounded quarterly for one year. Use Table 13-1 to determine the interest for each investment. Find the effective rate to the nearest hundredth percent for each investment.

17. Use Table 13-2 to find the compound interest and the compound amount on an investment of $24,982 if it is invested for 28 days at 2.25% compounded daily.

18. Use Table 13-2 to find the accumulated daily interest on an investment of $5,000 invested for 120 days at 2.5%.

In the following exercises, find the amount of money that should be invested (present value) at the stated interest rate to yield the given amount (future value) after the indicated amount of time. Use Table 13-3 or the appropriate formula.

19. $2,000 in five years at 3% compounded semiannually

20. $3,500 in 12 years at 2% compounded annually

21. $10,000 in seven years at 4% annual interest compounded quarterly

22. $800 in four years at 3% annual interest compounded annually

23. Find the amount that should be invested today to have $700 in six years at 6% annual interest compounded quarterly.

24. Louis Banks was offered $25,000 cash now or $29,500 to be paid after two years for a resort cabin. If money can be invested in today's market for 4% annual interest compounded quarterly, which offer should Louis accept?

PRACTICE TEST — CHAPTER 13

1. Manually calculate the compound interest on a loan of $2,000 at 7% compounded annually for three years.

2. Manually calculate the compound interest on a 6.25% annual interest loan of $3,000 for four years if interest is compounded annually.

3. Use Table 13-1 or the appropriate formula to find the interest on a loan of $5,000 for six years at 10% annual interest if interest is compounded semiannually.

4. Use Table 13-1 to find the future value on an investment of $12,000 for seven years at 6% annual interest compounded quarterly.

5. An investment of $1,500 is made for two years at 2% annual interest compounded semiannually. Find the compound amount and the compound interest at the end of two years.

6. Use Table 13-1 to find the compound interest on a loan of $3,000 for one year at 12% annual interest if the interest is compounded quarterly.

7. Find the effective interest rate for the loan described in Exercise 6.

8. Use Table 13-2 to find the interest compounded on an investment of $2,000 invested at 5.75% for 28 days compounded daily.

9. Use Tables 13-1 and 13-2 to compare the interest on an investment of $3,000 that is invested at 8% annual interest compounded quarterly and daily, respectively, for one year.

Find the amount that should be invested today (present value) at the stated interest rate to yield the given amount (future value) after the indicated amount of time for Exercises 10–13.

10. $3,400 in four years at 4% annual interest compounded annually

11. $5,000 in eight years at 3% annual interest compounded semiannually

12. $8,000 in 12 years at 5% annual interest compounded annually

13. $6,000 in six years at 4% annual interest compounded quarterly

14. Jamie Juarez needs $12,000 in 10 years for her daughter's college education. How much must be invested today at 2% annual interest compounded semiannually to have the needed funds?

15. If you were offered $600 today or $680 in one year, which would you accept if money can be invested at 2% annual interest compounded semiannually?

16. Derek Anderson plans to buy a house in four years. He will make an $8,000 down payment on the property. How much should he invest today at 6% annual interest compounded quarterly to have the required amount in four years?

17. Which of the two options yields the greatest return on your investment of $2,000?
    Option 1: 8% annual interest compounded quarterly for four years
    Option 2: $8\frac{1}{4}$% annual interest compounded annually for four years

18. If you invest $2,000 today at 6% annual interest compounded quarterly, how much will you have after three years? (Table 13-1)

19. If you invest $1,000 today at 5% annual interest compounded daily, how much will you have after 20 days? (Table 13-2)

20. How much money should Bryan Trailer Sales set aside today to have $15,000 in one year to purchase a forklift if the interest rate is 2.95% compounded annually?

CRITICAL THINKING

CHAPTER 13

1. The compound amount or future value can be found using two formulas: $I = PR$ (assuming $T = 1$) and $A = P + I$. Show how these two formulas relate to the single formula $A = P(1 + R)$.

2. Because the entries in the present value table (Table 13-3) are reciprocals of the corresponding entries in the future value table (Table 13-1), how can Table 13-3 be used to find the future value of an investment?

3. In finding a future value, how will your result compare in size to your original investment?

4. In finding a present value, how will your result compare in size to your desired goal (future value)?

5. How can the future value table (Table 13-1) be used to find the present value of a desired goal?

6. Banking regulations require that the effective interest rate (APR or APY) be stated on all loan or investment contracts. Why?

7. Illustrate the procedure described in Exercise 5 to find the present value of an investment if you want to have $500 at the end of two years. The investment earns 8% compounded quarterly. Check your result using the present value table.

8. How does the effective interest rate compare with the compounded rate on a loan or investment? Illustrate your answer with an example that shows the compounded rate and the effective rate.

Challenge Problem

One real estate sales technique is to encourage customers or clients to buy today because the value of the property will probably increase during the next few years. "Buy this lot today for $28,000. In two years, I project it will sell for $32,500." The buyer has a CD worth $30,000 now, which earns 4% compounded annually and will mature in 2 years. Cashing in the CD now requires the buyer to pay an early withdrawal penalty of $600.

a. Should the buyer purchase the land now or in two years?

b. What are some of the problems with waiting to buy land?

c. What are some of the advantages of waiting?

d. Lots in a new subdivision sell for $15,600. Assuming that the price of the lot does not increase, how much would you need to invest today at 8% compounded quarterly to buy the lot in one year?

e. 1. You have inherited $60,000 and plan to buy a home. If you invest the $60,000 today at 5%, compounded annually, how much could you spend on the house in one year?
   2. If you intend to spend $60,000 on a house in one year, how much of your inheritance should you invest today at 5%, compounded annually? How much do you have left to spend on a car?

CASE STUDIES

13.1 How Fast Does Your Money Grow?

Barry heard in his Personal Finance class that he should start investing as soon as possible. He had always thought that it would be smart to start investing after he finishes college and when his salary is high enough to pay the bills and to have money left over. He projects that will be 5–10 years from now. Barry wants to compare the difference between investing now and investing later. A financial planner who spoke to the class suggested that a Roth IRA (Individual Retirement Account) would be a more profitable investment over the long term than a regular IRA, so Barry wants to seriously consider the Roth IRA.

When table values do not include the information you need, use the formula $FV = \$1(1 + R)^N$ where R is the period rate and N is the number of periods.

1. If Barry purchases a $2,000 Roth IRA when he is 25 years old and expects to earn an average of 6% per year compounded annually over 35 years (until he is 60), how much will accumulate in the investment?

2. If Barry doesn't put the money in the IRA until he is 35 years old, how much money will accumulate in the account by the time he is 60 years old? How much less will he earn because he invested 10 years later?

3. Interest rate is critical to the speed at which your investment grows. If $1 is invested at 2% compounded annually, it takes approximately 34.9 years to double. If $1 is invested at 5% compounded annually, it takes approximately 14.2 years to double. Use Table 13-1 to determine how many years it takes $1 to double if invested at 10% compounded annually; at 12% compounded annually.

4. At what interest rate would you need to invest to have your money double in 10 years if it is compounded annually?

13.2 Planning: The Key to Wealth

Abdol Akhim has just come from a Personal Finance class where he learned that he can determine how much his savings will be worth in the future. Abdol is completing his two-year business administration degree this semester and has been repairing computers in his spare time to pay for his tuition and books. Abdol got out his savings records and decided to apply what he had learned. He has a balance of $1,000 in a money market account at First Savings Bank, and he considers this to be an emergency fund. His instructor says that he should have 3–6 months of his total bills in an emergency fund. His bills are currently $700 a month. He also has a checking account and a regular savings account at First Savings Bank, and he will shift some of his funds from those accounts into the emergency fund. One of Abdol's future goals is to buy a house. He wants to start another account to save the $8,000 he needs for a down payment.

1. How much interest will Abdol receive on $1,000 in a 365-day year if he keeps it in the money market account earning 2.25% compounded daily?

2. How much money must Abdol shift from his other accounts to his emergency fund to have four times his monthly bills in the account by the end of the year?

3. Abdol realizes he needs to earn more interest than his current money market can provide. Using annual compounding on an account that pays 5.5% interest annually, find the amount Abdol needs to invest to have the $8,000 down payment for his house in 5 years.

13.3 Future Value/Present Value

At 45 years of age, Seth figured he wanted to work only 10 more years. Being a full-time landlord had a lot of advantages: cash flow, free time, being his own boss—but it was time to start thinking towards retirement. The real estate investments that he had made over the last 15 years had paid off handsomely. After selling a duplex and a four-unit and paying the associated taxes, Seth had $350,000 in the bank and was debt-free. With only 10 years before retirement, Seth wanted to make solid financial decisions that would limit his risk exposure. Fortunately, he had located another property that seemed to meet his needs—an older, but well maintained four-unit apartment. The price tag was $250,000, well within his range, and the apartment would require no remodeling. Seth figured he could invest the other $100,000, and between the two hoped to have $1 million to retire on by age 55.

1. Seth read an article in the local newspaper stating the real estate in the area had appreciated by 5% per year over the last 30 years. Assuming the article is correct, what would the future value of the $250,000 apartment be in 10 years?

2. Seth's current bank offers a 1-year certificate of deposit account paying 2% compounded semiannually. A competitor bank is also offering 2%, but compounded daily. If Seth invests the $100,000, how much more money will he have in the second bank after one year, due to the daily compounding?

3. A friend of Seth's who is a real estate developer needs to borrow $80,000 to finish a development project. He is desperate for cash and offers Seth 18%, compounded monthly, for $2\frac{1}{2}$ years. Find the future value of the loan using the future value table. Does this loan meet Seth's goals of low risk? How could he reduce the risk associated with this loan?

4. After purchasing the apartment, Seth receives a street, sewer, and gutter assessment for $12,500 due in 2 years. How much would he have to invest today in a CD paying 2%, compounded semiannually, to fully pay the assessment in 2 years?

CHAPTER 14
Annuities and Sinking Funds

Is Social Security in Crisis?

Will Social Security be there when you need it? Social Security payroll taxes currently produce more revenue than is needed to pay benefits to current retirees. Social Security projections are that benefits will begin to exceed revenues in 2017. By 2040, the trust fund will be exhausted, and will be unable to pay the full benefits that have been promised to older Americans.

So started the formal Social Security debate, which has dominated most of the past decade, and has since become largely a political fight. But what was the original purpose of Social Security? And what are the implications for you today?

Social Security provided a critical foundation of income for retired and disabled workers. For one-third of Americans over 65, Social Security benefits represent 90% of their total income. It was originally structured to resemble private-sector pensions (retirement plans). The retirement benefit was based on a worker's wages and years of service. In most plans, the monthly lifetime benefit after 35 years of service would be at least half of the income earned in the final working year.

Congress expected that company pensions would eventually replace Social Security benefits. But pension coverage peaked at 40% in the 1960s. Today, approximately only 15% of private-sector workers are covered by defined-benefit pensions.

So how can you avoid relying on Social Security when you retire? One of the best things you can do is start a supplemental retirement program right now with an annuity. Annuities may be single- or flexible-payment; fixed or variable; deferred or immediate. No matter the type, annuities are financial contracts with an insurance company that are designed to be a source of retirement income. The very best plans are systematic and enable the investor to make regular and consistent payments into the annuity fund, which compounds interest. And these plans are not expensive; many require as little as $25 a month, or $300 annually to get started. Let's say you're age 25. By investing $300 annually for 40 years at 7%, you would end up with $59,890.50 at age 65. Not a bad investment for $25 a month—about the same price as dinner and a movie.

Will Social Security still be there when you retire? It's impossible to say. Better to get started investing with an annuity now (or soon), rather than find out later when it's too late.

LEARNING OUTCOMES

14-1 Future Value of an Annuity
1. Find the future value of an ordinary annuity using the simple interest formula method.
2. Find the future value of an ordinary annuity with periodic payments using a $1.00 ordinary annuity future value table.
3. Find the future value of an annuity due with periodic payments using the simple interest formula method.
4. Find the future value of an annuity due with periodic payments using a $1.00 ordinary annuity future value table.
5. Find the future value of a retirement plan annuity.
6. Find the future value of an ordinary annuity or an annuity due using a formula or a calculator application.

14-2 Sinking Funds and the Present Value of an Annuity
1. Find the sinking fund payment using a $1.00 sinking fund payment table.
2. Find the present value of an ordinary annuity using a $1.00 ordinary annuity present value table.
3. Find the sinking fund payment or the present value of an annuity using a formula or a calculator application.

Annuity: a contract between a person (the annuitant) and an insurance company (the insurer) for receiving and disbursing money for the annuitant or the beneficiary of the annuitant.

Accumulation phase of an annuity: the time when money is being paid into the fund and earnings are being added to the fund.

Liquidation or payout phase of an annuity: the time when the annuitant or beneficiary is receiving money from the fund.

So far we have discussed interest accumulated from one *lump-sum* amount of money. Another type of investment option is an annuity. An **annuity** is a contract between you (the **annuitant**) and an insurance company (the **insurer**) for receiving and disbursing money for the annuitant or the beneficiary of the annuitant. An annuity has two phases—the accumulation phase and the liquidation phase. The **accumulation phase of an annuity** is the period during which you are paying money into the fund. The **liquidation or payout phase of an annuity** is the period during which you are receiving money from the fund. During both phases of the annuity, the fund balance may earn compound interest. An annuity is purchased by making either a single lump-sum payment or a series of periodic payments. Under the terms of the contract, the insurer agrees to make a lump-sum payment or periodic payments to you beginning at some future date. This investment option is a long-term investment option that is commonly used for retirement planning or as a college fund for small children. Penalties are normally applied if funds are withdrawn before a time specified in the agreement.

There are many options to consider when purchasing an annuity. You can choose how the money is invested (stocks, bonds, money market instruments, or a combination of these) and the level of risk of the investment. High-risk options have the potential to earn a high rate of return but the investment may be at risk. Low-risk options normally earn a lower rate of interest but the risk is also lower. A guaranteed rate of interest has no risk at all on the principal and guarantees a specific interest rate.

You can choose to invest with pre-taxed money or with taxed money. If pre-taxed money is invested, the tax on the entire fund is deferred until you begin receiving payments. If taxed money is invested, only the tax on the earnings is deferred until you begin receiving payments. In our study of annuities, we will examine only some basic interest-based options. Other options can be investigated by contacting insurance agencies or brokers or the Office of Investor Education and Assistance with the U.S. Securities and Exchange Commission (*http://www.sec.gov/investor/pubs/varannty.htm*).

14-1 FUTURE VALUE OF AN ANNUITY

LEARNING OUTCOMES

1. Find the future value of an ordinary annuity using the simple interest formula method.
2. Find the future value of an ordinary annuity with periodic payments using a $1.00 ordinary annuity future value table.
3. Find the future value of an annuity due with periodic payments using the simple interest formula method.
4. Find the future value of an annuity due with periodic payments using a $1.00 ordinary annuity future value table.
5. Find the future value of a retirement plan annuity.
6. Find the future value of an ordinary annuity or an annuity due using a formula or a calculator application.

Annuity certain: an annuity paid over a guaranteed number of periods.

Contingent annuity: an annuity paid over an uncertain number of periods.

Ordinary annuity: an annuity for which payments are made at the end of each period.

Annuity due: an annuity for which payments are made at the beginning of each period.

An annuity paid out over a guaranteed number of periods is an **annuity certain**. An annuity paid out over an uncertain number of periods is a **contingent annuity**.

We can also categorize annuities according to when payment is made into the fund. For an **ordinary annuity**, payment is made at the *end* of the period. For an **annuity due**, payment is made at the *beginning* of the period.

1 Find the future value of an ordinary annuity using the simple interest formula method.

Finding the future value of an annuity into which periodic payments are made means finding the amount of the annuity at the end of the accumulation phase. This is similar to finding the future value of a lump sum. The significant difference is that for each interest period, more principal—the annuity payment—is added to the amount on which interest is earned. The simple interest formula $I = PRT$ is still the basis of calculating interest for each period of the annuity.

> **HOW TO** Find the future value of an ordinary annuity in the accumulation phase with periodic payments using the simple interest formula method
>
> 1. Find the first end-of-period principal.
>
>   First end-of-period principal = annuity payment
>
> 2. For each remaining period in turn, find the next end-of-period principal.
>   (a) Multiply the previous end-of-period principal by the sum of 1 and the decimal equivalent of the period interest rate.

(b) Add the product from step 2a and the annuity payment.

End-of-period principal = previous end-of-period principal ×
(1 + period interest rate) + annuity payment

3. Identify the last end-of-period principal as the future value.

Future value = last end-of-period principal

For an ordinary annuity, no interest accumulates on the annuity payment during the period in which it is paid because the payment is made at the *end* of the period. For the first period, this means no interest accumulates at all.

EXAMPLE 1

What is the future value of an ordinary annuity with annual payments of $1,000 after three years at 4% annual interest?

The period interest rate is 0.04. The annuity is $1,000.
End-of-year value = (previous end-of-year value)(1 + 0.04) + $1,000

End-of-year 1 = $1,000.00   No interest is earned the first year.
End-of-year 2 = $1,000.00(1.04) + $1,000.00
= $1,040.00 + $1,000.00
= $2,040.00

End-of-year 3 = $2,040.00(1.04) + $1,000.00
= $2,121.60 + $1,000.00
= $3,121.60

The future value is $3,121.60.

HOW TO   Find the total interest earned on an annuity

1. Find the total amount invested:

Total invested = payment amount × number of payments

2. Find the total interest:

Total interest = future value of annuity − total invested

EXAMPLE 2

Find the total interest earned on the annuity in the preceding example.

Total invested = $1,000(3)   Payment = $1,000
                                       Number of payments = 3
= $3,000

Total interest = $3,121.60 − $3,000   Future value = $3,121.60
= $121.60

The total interest earned is $121.60.

A lump-sum investment earns more interest than an annuity. Compare the earnings of a $3,000 lump-sum investment (Figure 14-1) and an annuity of the same accumulated investment (Figure 14-2).

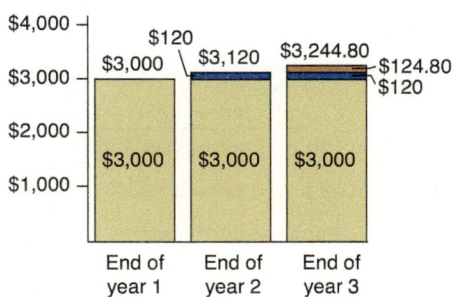

FIGURE 14-1
Lump-Sum Investment of $3,000

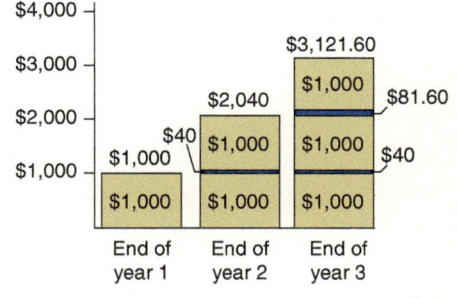

FIGURE 14-2
Three-Year Ordinary Annuity of $1,000 per Year

STOP AND CHECK

1. Find the future value and total interest of an ordinary annuity with annual payments of $5,000 at 2.9% annual interest after four years.

2. Find the future value and total interest of an ordinary annuity with annual payments of $3,500 at 3.42% annual interest after three years.

3. Find the value of an ordinary annuity after two years of $1,500 invested semiannually at 4% annual interest.

4. What is the value after 2 years of an ordinary annuity of $300 paid semiannually at 3% annual interest?

2 Find the future value of an ordinary annuity with periodic payments using a $1.00 ordinary annuity future value table.

Calculating the future value of an ordinary annuity with periodic payments can become quite tedious if the number of periods is large. For example, a monthly annuity such as a monthly savings plan running for five years has 60 periods and 60 calculation sequences. For this reason, most businesspeople rely on prepared tables, calculators, or computers.

HOW TO Find the future value of an ordinary annuity with periodic payments using a $1.00 ordinary annuity future value table

Using Table 14-1:

1. Select the periods row corresponding to the number of interest periods.
2. Select the rate-per-period column corresponding to the period interest rate.
3. Locate the value in the cell where the periods row intersects the rate-per-period column.
4. Multiply the annuity payment by the table value from step 3.

$$\text{Future value} = \text{annuity payment} \times \text{table value}$$

EXAMPLE 3 Use Table 14-1 to find the future value of a semiannual ordinary annuity of $6,000 for five years at 6% annual interest compounded semiannually.

$$5 \text{ years} \times 2 \text{ periods per year} = 10 \text{ periods}$$

$$\frac{6\% \text{ annual interest rate}}{2 \text{ periods per year}} = 3\% \text{ period interest rate}$$

The Table 14-1 value for 10 periods at 3% is 11.464.

$$\begin{aligned}\text{Future value of annuity} &= \text{annuity payment} \times \text{table value} \\ &= \$6{,}000(11.464) \\ &= \$68{,}784\end{aligned}$$

The future value of the ordinary annuity is $68,784.

EXAMPLE 4
Find the total interest earned on the annuity in Example 1.

Total invested = $6,000(10)
                 = $60,000

Total interest = $68,784 − $60,000
               = $8,784

Payment = $6,000
Number of payments = 10

Future value = $68,784

The total interest earned is $8,784.

TABLE 14-1
Future Value of $1.00 Ordinary Annuity

Periods	0.25%	0.50%	0.75%	1.00%	1.50%	2.00%	2.50%	3.00%	3.50%	4.00%
1	1.000	1.000	1.000	1.000	1.000	1.000	1.000	1.000	1.000	1.000
2	2.002	2.005	2.008	2.010	2.015	2.020	2.025	2.030	2.035	2.040
3	3.008	3.015	3.023	3.030	3.045	3.060	3.076	3.091	3.106	3.122
4	4.015	4.030	4.045	4.060	4.091	4.122	4.153	4.184	4.215	4.246
5	5.025	5.050	5.076	5.101	5.152	5.204	5.256	5.309	5.362	5.416
6	6.038	6.076	6.114	6.152	6.230	6.308	6.388	6.468	6.550	6.633
7	7.053	7.106	7.159	7.214	7.323	7.434	7.547	7.662	7.779	7.898
8	8.070	8.141	8.213	8.286	8.433	8.583	8.736	8.892	9.052	9.214
9	9.091	9.182	9.275	9.369	9.559	9.755	9.955	10.159	10.368	10.583
10	10.113	10.228	10.344	10.462	10.703	10.950	11.203	11.464	11.731	12.006
11	11.139	11.279	11.422	11.567	11.863	12.169	12.483	12.808	13.142	13.486
12	12.166	12.336	12.508	12.683	13.041	13.412	13.796	14.192	14.602	15.026
13	13.197	13.397	13.601	13.809	14.237	14.680	15.140	15.618	16.113	16.627
14	14.230	14.464	14.703	14.947	15.450	15.974	16.519	17.086	17.677	18.292
15	15.265	15.537	15.814	16.097	16.682	17.293	17.932	18.599	19.296	20.024
16	16.304	16.614	16.932	17.258	17.932	18.639	19.380	20.157	20.971	21.825
17	17.344	17.697	18.059	18.430	19.201	20.012	20.865	21.762	22.705	23.698
18	18.388	18.786	19.195	19.615	20.489	21.412	22.386	23.414	24.500	25.645
19	19.434	19.880	20.339	20.811	21.797	22.841	23.946	25.117	26.357	27.671
20	20.482	20.979	21.491	22.019	23.124	24.297	25.545	26.870	28.280	29.778
21	21.533	22.084	22.652	23.239	24.471	25.783	27.183	28.676	30.269	31.969
22	22.587	23.194	23.822	24.472	25.838	27.299	28.863	30.537	32.329	34.248
23	23.644	24.310	25.001	25.716	27.225	28.845	30.584	32.453	34.460	36.618
24	24.703	25.432	26.188	26.973	28.634	30.422	32.349	34.426	36.667	39.083
25	25.765	26.559	27.385	28.243	30.063	32.030	34.158	36.459	38.950	41.646
26	26.829	27.692	28.590	29.526	31.514	33.671	36.012	38.553	41.313	44.312
27	27.896	28.830	29.805	30.821	32.987	35.344	37.912	40.710	43.759	47.084
28	28.966	29.975	31.028	32.129	34.481	37.051	39.860	42.931	46.291	49.968
29	30.038	31.124	32.261	33.450	35.999	38.792	41.856	45.219	48.911	52.966
30	31.113	32.280	33.503	34.785	37.539	40.568	43.903	47.575	51.623	56.085
35	36.529	38.145	39.854	41.660	45.592	49.994	54.928	60.462	66.674	73.652
40	42.013	44.159	46.446	48.886	54.268	60.402	67.403	75.401	84.550	95.026
45	47.566	50.324	53.290	56.481	63.614	71.893	81.516	92.720	105.782	121.029
50	53.189	56.645	60.394	64.463	73.683	84.579	97.484	112.797	130.998	152.667
55	58.882	63.126	67.769	72.852	84.530	98.587	115.551	136.072	160.947	191.159
60	64.647	69.770	75.424	81.670	96.215	114.052	135.992	163.053	196.517	237.991
65	70.484	76.582	83.371	90.937	108.803	131.126	159.118	194.333	238.763	294.968
70	76.394	83.566	91.620	100.676	122.364	149.978	185.284	230.594	288.938	364.290
75	82.379	90.727	100.183	110.913	136.973	170.792	214.888	272.631	348.530	448.631
80	88.439	98.068	109.073	121.672	152.711	193.772	248.383	321.363	419.307	551.245
85	94.575	105.594	118.300	132.979	169.665	219.144	286.279	377.857	503.367	676.090
90	100.788	113.311	127.879	144.863	187.930	247.157	329.154	443.349	603.205	827.983
95	107.080	121.222	137.822	157.354	207.606	278.085	377.664	519.272	721.781	1012.785
100	113.450	129.334	148.145	170.481	228.803	312.232	432.549	607.288	862.612	1237.624

Table values show the future value, or accumulated amount of the investment and interest, of a $1.00 investment for a given number of periods at a given rate per period.

Table values can be generated using the formula FV of $1.00 per period = $\dfrac{(1 + R)^N - 1}{R}$, where FV is the future value, R is the interest rate per period, and N is the number of periods.

TABLE 14-1
Future Value of $1.00 Ordinary Annuity—Continued

Periods	4.50%	5.00%	5.50%	6.00%	6.50%	7.00%	8.00%	9.00%	10.00%	12.00%
1	1.000	1.000	1.000	1.000	1.000	1.000	1.000	1.000	1.000	1.000
2	2.045	2.050	2.055	2.060	2.065	2.070	2.080	2.090	2.100	2.120
3	3.137	3.153	3.168	3.184	3.199	3.215	3.246	3.278	3.310	3.374
4	4.278	4.310	4.342	4.375	4.407	4.440	4.506	4.573	4.641	4.779
5	5.471	5.526	5.581	5.637	5.694	5.751	5.867	5.985	6.105	6.353
6	6.717	6.802	6.888	6.975	7.064	7.153	7.336	7.523	7.716	8.115
7	8.019	8.142	8.267	8.394	8.523	8.654	8.923	9.200	9.487	10.089
8	9.380	9.549	9.722	9.897	10.077	10.260	10.637	11.028	11.436	12.300
9	10.802	11.027	11.256	11.491	11.732	11.978	12.488	13.021	13.579	14.776
10	12.288	12.578	12.875	13.181	13.494	13.816	14.487	15.193	15.937	17.549
11	13.841	14.207	14.583	14.972	15.372	15.784	16.645	17.560	18.531	20.655
12	15.464	15.917	16.386	16.870	17.371	17.888	18.977	20.141	21.384	24.133
13	17.160	17.713	18.287	18.882	19.500	20.141	21.495	22.953	24.523	28.029
14	18.932	19.599	20.293	21.015	21.767	22.550	24.215	26.019	27.975	32.393
15	20.784	21.579	22.409	23.276	24.182	25.129	27.152	29.361	31.772	37.280
16	22.719	23.657	24.641	25.673	26.754	27.888	30.324	33.003	35.950	42.753
17	24.742	25.840	26.996	28.213	29.493	30.840	33.750	36.974	40.545	48.884
18	26.855	28.132	29.481	30.906	32.410	33.999	37.450	41.301	45.599	55.750
19	29.064	30.539	32.103	33.760	35.517	37.379	41.446	46.018	51.159	63.440
20	31.371	33.066	34.868	36.786	38.825	40.995	45.762	51.160	57.275	72.052
21	33.783	35.719	37.786	39.993	42.349	44.865	50.423	56.765	64.002	81.699
22	36.303	38.505	40.864	43.392	46.102	49.006	55.457	62.873	71.403	92.503
23	38.937	41.430	44.112	46.996	50.098	53.436	60.893	69.532	79.543	104.603
24	41.689	44.502	47.538	50.816	54.355	58.177	66.765	76.790	88.497	118.155
25	44.565	47.727	51.153	54.865	58.888	63.249	73.106	84.701	98.347	133.334
26	47.571	51.113	54.966	59.156	63.715	68.676	79.954	93.324	109.182	150.334
27	50.711	54.669	58.989	63.706	68.857	74.484	87.351	102.723	121.100	169.374
28	53.993	58.403	63.234	68.528	74.333	80.698	95.339	112.968	134.210	190.699
29	57.423	62.323	67.711	73.640	80.164	87.347	103.966	124.135	148.631	214.583
30	61.007	66.439	72.435	79.058	86.375	94.461	113.283	136.308	164.494	241.333
35	81.497	90.320	100.251	111.435	124.035	138.237	172.317	215.711	271.024	431.663
40	107.030	120.800	136.606	154.762	175.632	199.635	259.057	337.882	442.593	767.091
45	138.850	159.700	184.119	212.744	246.325	285.749	386.506	525.859	718.905	1358.230
50	178.503	209.348	246.217	290.336	343.180	406.529	573.770	815.084	1163.909	2400.018
55	227.918	272.713	327.377	394.172	475.880	575.929	848.923	1260.092	1880.591	4236.005
60	289.498	353.584	433.450	533.128	657.690	813.520	1253.213	1944.792	3034.816	7471.641
65	366.238	456.798	572.083	719.083	906.786	1146.755	1847.248	2998.288	4893.707	13173.937
70	461.870	588.529	753.271	967.932	1248.069	1614.134	2720.080	4619.223	7887.470	23223.332
75	581.044	756.654	990.076	1300.949	1715.656	2269.657	4002.557	7113.232	12708.954	40933.799
80	729.558	971.229	1299.571	1746.600	2356.291	3189.063	5886.935	10950.574	20474.002	72145.693
85	914.632	1245.087	1704.069	2342.982	3234.016	4478.576	8655.706	16854.800	32979.690	127151.714
90	1145.269	1594.607	2232.731	3141.075	4436.576	6287.185	12723.939	25939.184	53120.226	224091.119
95	1432.684	2040.694	2923.671	4209.104	6084.188	8823.854	18701.507	39916.635	85556.760	394931.472
100	1790.856	2610.025	3826.702	5638.368	8341.558	12381.662	27484.516	61422.675	137796.123	696010.548

Table values show the future value, or accumulated amount of the investment and interest, of a $1.00 investment for a given number of periods at a given rate per period.

Table values can be generated using the formula FV of $1.00 per period = $\dfrac{(1 + R)^N - 1}{R}$, where FV is the future value, R is the interest rate per period, and N is the number of periods.

STOP AND CHECK

1. Use Table 14-1 to find the accumulation phase future value and total interest of an ordinary annuity of $4,000 for eight years at 2% annual interest.

2. Use Table 14-1 to find the accumulated amount and total interest of an ordinary annuity with semiannual payments of $6,000 for five years at 4% annual interest.

3. John Crampton put $1,200 in an ordinary annuity account every quarter of the accumulation phase for five years at a 2% annual rate compounded quarterly. What is the future value of the annuity?

4. Tiffany Evans created an ordinary annuity with $2,500 payments made semiannually at 6% annually. Find her annuity value at the end of six years.

3 Find the future value of an annuity due with periodic payments using the simple interest formula method.

Because an annuity due is paid at the *beginning* of each period rather than at the end, the annuity due payment earns interest throughout the period in which it is paid. The future value of an annuity due, then, is greater than the future value of the corresponding ordinary annuity, given the same number of periods, the same period interest rate, and the same annuity payment. The difference in the future value of an ordinary annuity and an annuity due is exactly one additional period's worth of interest.

> **HOW TO** Find the future value of an annuity due with periodic payments using the simple interest formula method
>
> 1. Find the first end-of-period principal: Multiply the annuity payment by the sum of 1 and the decimal equivalent of the period interest rate.
>
>   First end-of-period principal = annuity payment × (1 + period interest rate)
>
> 2. For each remaining period in turn, find the next end-of-period principal:
>   (a) Add the previous end-of-period principal and the annuity payment.
>   (b) Multiply the sum from step 2a by the sum of 1 and the period interest rate.
>
>   End-of-period principal = (previous end-of-period principal + annuity payment) × (1 + period interest rate)
>
> 3. Identify the last end-of-period principal as the future value.
>
>   Future value = last end-of-period principal

TIP
Ordinary Annuity versus Annuity Due

The difference between an ordinary annuity and an annuity due is whether you make the first payment immediately or at the end of the first period.

If you are establishing your own annuity plan through a savings account, you begin your annuity with your first payment or deposit (annuity due).

If you are entering a payroll deduction plan, a 401(k) plan, or an annuity plan with an insurance company, you may complete the paperwork to establish the plan, and the first payment will be made at a later time.

EXAMPLE 5 What is the future value of an annuity due with an annual payment of $1,000 for three years at 4% annual interest? Find the total investment and the total interest earned.

The annuity payment is $1,000; the period interest rate is 4%.
End-of-year value = (previous end-of-year + $1,000)(1 + 0.04)

End-of-year 1	= $1,000(1.04)	The annuity due earns interest
	= $1,040	during the first period.
End-of-year 2	= ($1,040 + $1,000)(1.04)	Second payment is made.
	= ($2,040)(1.04)	
	= $2,121.60	
End-of-year 3	= ($2,121.60 + $1,000)(1.04)	Third payment is made.
	= ($3,121.60)(1.04)	
	= $3,246.46	Future value of annuity due
Total investment	= investment per period × total periods	
	= $1,000(3)	
	= $3,000	
Total interest earned	= future value − total investment	
	= $3,246.46 − $3,000	
	= $246.46	

The future value of the annuity due is $3,246.46, the total investment is $3,000, and the total interest earned is $246.46.

In the three-year ordinary annuity (Figure 14-3, repeated from Figure 14-2 for comparison purposes) the total interest earned is $121.60. In the annuity due (Figure 14-4) the first $1,000 payment earns interest during the first period and then interest is earned on that interest throughout the duration of the annuity. The total interest earned is $246.46 or $124.86 more than an ordinary annuity.

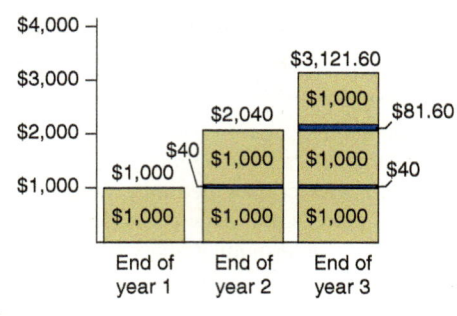

FIGURE 14-3
Three-Year Ordinary Annuity of $1,000 per Year

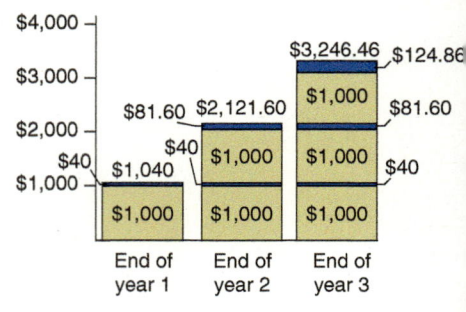

FIGURE 14-4
Three-Year Annuity Due of $1,000 per Year

 **STOP AND CHECK**

1. Manually calculate the future value of an annuity due that sets aside $1,500 annually for four years at 3.75% annual interest compounded anually. How much interest is earned?

2. Manually calculate the value of an annuity due after two years of $4,000 payments at 4.25% compounded annually.

3. DeMarco receives $5,000 semiannually from his grandmother's estate. He invests the money at 3.8% compounded semiannually. How much will he have after two years investing as an annuity due?

4. If you make six monthly payments of $50 to an annuity due and receive 3% annual interest compounded monthly, how much will you accumulate?

4 Find the future value of an annuity due with periodic payments using a $1.00 ordinary annuity future value table.

Because the future value of an annuity due is so closely related to the future value of the corresponding ordinary annuity, we can also use Table 14-1 to find the future value of an annuity due. An annuity due accumulates interest one period more than does the ordinary annuity, but has the same number of payments. Thus, we adjust Table 14-1 values by multiplying by the sum of 1 and the period interest rate. This applies interest for the first payment, which is made at the beginning of the first period, for the entire time of the annuity.

HOW TO Find the future value of an annuity due with a periodic payment using a $1.00 ordinary annuity future value table

Use Table 14-1:

1. Select the periods row corresponding to the number of interest periods.
2. Select the rate-per-period column corresponding to the period interest rate.
3. Locate the value in the cell where the periods row intersects the rate-per-period column.
4. Multiply the annuity payment by the table value from step 3. This is equivalent to an *ordinary annuity.*
5. Multiply the amount that is equivalent to an ordinary annuity by the sum of 1 and the period interest rate to adjust for the extra interest that is earned on an annuity due.

Future value = annuity payment × table value × (1 + period interest rate)

EXAMPLE 6 Use Table 14-1 to find the future value of a quarterly annuity due of $2,800 for four years at 4% annual interest compounded quarterly.

$$4 \text{ years} \times 4 \text{ periods per year} = 16 \text{ periods}$$

$$\frac{4\% \text{ annual interest rate}}{4 \text{ periods per year}} = 1\% \text{ period interest rate}$$

The Table 14-1 value for 16 periods at 1% is 17.258.

Annuities and Sinking Funds 503

Future value = annuity payment × table value × (1 + period interest rate)
= $2,800(17.258)(1.01)   Future value for ordinary annuity
= $48,322.40(1.01)   Adjustment for annuity due
= $48,805.62   Future value for annuity due

The future value is $48,805.62.

EXAMPLE 7
What is the total interest earned on the annuity due in the Example 6?

Total invested = $2,800(16)   Payment = $2,800
              = $44,800   Number of payments = 16
Total interest = $48,805.62 − $44,800
              = $4,005.62

The total interest earned is $4,005.62.

EXAMPLE 8
Sarah Smith wants to select the best annuity plan. She plans to invest a total of $40,000 over ten years' time at 8% annual interest. Annuity 1 is a quarterly ordinary annuity of $1,000; interest is compounded quarterly. Annuity 2 is a semiannual ordinary annuity of $2,000; interest is compounded semiannually. Annuity 3 is a quarterly annuity due of $1,000; interest is compounded quarterly. Annuity 4 is a semiannual annuity due of $2,000; interest is compounded semiannually. Which annuity yields the greatest future value?

What You Know	What You Are Looking For	Solution Plan
Annuity 1: Ordinary annuity of $1,000 quarterly for ten years at 8% annual interest compounded quarterly Annuity 2: Ordinary annuity of $2,000 semiannually for ten years at 8% annual interest compounded semiannually Annuity 3: Annuity due of $1,000 quarterly for ten years at 8% annual interest compounded quarterly Annuity 4: Annuity due of $2,000 semiannually for ten years at 8% annual interest compounded semiannually.	Which annuity yields the greatest future value? Future value of each annuity	Number of periods = years × periods per year Period interest rate = $\dfrac{\text{annual interest rate}}{\text{periods per year}}$ Future value of ordinary annuity = annuity payment × Table 14-1 value Future value of annuity due = annuity payment × Table 14-1 value × (1 + period interest rate)

Solution

Annuity 1
Number of periods = years × periods per year
                 = 10(4) = 40

Period interest rate = $\dfrac{\text{annual interest rate}}{\text{periods per year}}$
                    = $\dfrac{8\%}{4}$ = 2%

Table value = 60.402
Future value = annuity payment × table value
Future value = ($1,000)(60.402)
            = $60,402

Annuity 2
= 10(2) = 20

= $\dfrac{8\%}{2}$ = 4%

= 29.778

= $2,000(29.778)
= $59,556

Annuity 3
The number of periods and period interest rate are the same as those for annuity 1.
Future value = annuity payment × table value × (1 + period interest rate)
            = $1,000(60.402)(1.02)
            = $61,610.04

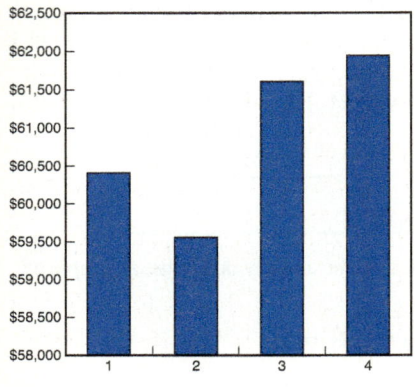

FIGURE 14-5
Four Two-Year Annuities at 8% Annual Interest

Annuity 4
The number of periods and period interest rate are the same as those for annuity 2.
Future value = annuity payment × table value × (1 + period interest rate)
= $2,000(29.778)(1.04)
= $61,938.24

> **Conclusion**
>
> **Annuity 4, with the larger annuity due payment, yields the greatest future value.** Notice that the ordinary annuity with fewer periods per year yields the least future value of all four annuities. If the total investment is the same, the number of years is the same, and the annual rate of interest is the same, any annuity due yields a larger future value than any corresponding ordinary annuity. The annuity due with the largest payment is the most profitable, while the ordinary annuity paid most frequently is the most profitable ordinary annuity. See Figure 14-5.

STOP AND CHECK

1. Use Table 14-1 to find the future value of an annual annuity due of $3,000 for ten years at 2%.

2. Use Table 14-1 to find the future value of a semiannual annuity due of $1,000 for five years at 6% annually compounded semiannually.

3. Use Table 14-1 to find the future value of a quarterly annuity due of $500 invested at 2% annually compounded quarterly for five years.

4. Use Table 14-1 to find the future value of a semiannual annuity due of $1,000 for five years invested at 2% annually compounded semiannually. Compare the interest earned on this annuity with the interest earned on the annuity in Exercise 3.

5 Find the future value of a retirement plan annuity.

A retirement plan is an arrangement to provide people with an income during retirement when they are no longer earning a steady income from employment. Employment-based retirement plans or **pensions** may be classified as **defined benefit** or **defined contribution**, according to how the benefits are determined. A defined benefit plan guarantees a certain payout at retirement, according to a fixed formula that usually depends on the member's salary and the number of years' membership in the plan. A defined contribution plan will provide a payout at retirement that is dependent on the amount of money contributed and the performance of the investment vehicles utilized.

Over the last 20 years, there has been a notable shift in corporate America away from pensions and defined benefit plans. Defined contribution plans have gained in popularity, mostly because they are governed by fewer rules, are simpler to administer, and unlike defined benefit plans, do not require firms to pay for pension insurance to protect them. They also reflect a movement toward the individual choice and responsibility of the employee. The version that corporations offer to their employees, **401(k) plans**, are the most common type of defined contribution plan, followed by **403(b) plans**, designed for employees of public education entities and most other nonprofit organizations. Both are named for sections of the Internal Revenue Service code that defines these plans.

All defined contribution plans work basically the same way. You decide what percentage of your salary you would like to contribute, and your employer makes regular contributions into your individual account on your behalf, through payroll deduction. Your contributions are deducted *before* taxes are calculated. Your employer's plan will have a limited selection of investment options from which to choose, and you decide in which option to invest your money. When you leave your job, you still maintain ownership over your account. Many employers also match all or part of an employee's contribution.

Beyond the retirement plan options available through your employer, individuals who receive taxable compensation during the year are also eligible to set up an **individual retirement arrangement (IRA)**. Contributions to a **traditional IRA** are often tax-deductible—money is deposited *before tax*, that is, contributions are made *with pre-tax assets* and withdrawals at retirement are taxed as income. Currently, the most that can be contributed to your traditional IRA generally is the smaller of $5,000 ($6,000 if you are age 50 or older) or your taxable compensation for the year. If neither you nor your spouse was covered for any part of the year by an

Pension: an arrangement to provide people with an income when they are no longer earning a regular income from employment, typically provided by an employer.

Defined benefit plan: a plan that guarantees a certain payout at retirement, according to a fixed formula that usually depends on the member's salary and the number of years' membership in the plan.

Defined contribution plan: a plan that provides a payout at retirement that is dependent on the amount of money contributed and the performance of the investment vehicles utilized.

401(k) plan: a defined contribution retirement plan for individuals working for private-sector companies.

403(b) plan: a defined contribution retirement plan designed for employees of public education entities and most other nonprofit organizations.

Traditional IRA: an individual retirement arrangement is a personal savings plan that allows you to set aside money for retirement. Contributions are typically tax-deductible in the year of the contribution, and taxes are deferred until contributions are withdrawn.

Roth IRA: an IRA where contributions are not tax-deductible, but qualified distributions are tax free when withdrawn.

employer retirement plan, you can take an income tax deduction for total contributions to one or more of your traditional IRAs for those same amounts. For example, a 45-year-old individual making $35,000 who is not covered by an employer-sponsored plan would be eligible to contribute (and deduct from taxable income) $5,000 to a traditional IRA. You can withdraw or use your traditional IRA assets at any time. However, a 10% additional tax (in addition to regular income tax) generally applies if you withdraw or use IRA assets before you are age 59½—unless the funds are used towards significant medical expenses, costs for higher education, and first-time home expenses, among others. See IRS Publications for additional details.

Another popular type of IRA is a **Roth IRA**, which is generally subject to the same rules that apply to a traditional IRA. One notable exception is that, unlike a traditional IRA, you do not get an income tax deduction for contributions to a Roth IRA. However, a major advantage to a Roth IRA is that if you satisfy all requirements, qualified distributions (defined in IRS Publication 590) will be tax free.

Regular contributions made to either form of IRA or to a defined contribution retirement plan constitute an annuity. The future value of the annuity is determined using the same methods found earlier in this chapter. Payments made at the end of each period signify an ordinary annuity, while payments made at the beginning of each period signify an annuity due.

EXAMPLE 9

Ethan Thomas, who is currently 20 years old, wants to plan for retirement by contributing $5,000 each year to a Roth IRA. He has an option that earns 4% per year. How much will he have in his retirement fund at age 60 when he can withdraw funds without a penalty? He will not make a contribution at age 60, so he will have made 40 payments.

A Roth IRA contribution is made as the fund is established, so it is an annuity due.

Number of periods = 40
Rate per period = 4%
Annuity payment = $5,000
Table 14-1 value = 95.026

Future value of annuity due = annuity payment × table value × 1.04
= $5,000(95.026)(1.04)
= $494,135.20

Ethan will have $494,135.20 in a 4% Roth IRA fund at age 60.

EXAMPLE 10

Tyson Smithey has the opportunity to contribute to a payroll deduction 401(k) plan at work. He selects an option that averages 6% per year and contributes $500 per month. How much should he have in the account in 5 years?

A payroll-deduction plan is considered to be an ordinary annuity.

Number of periods = 5(12) = 60   Rate per period = $\frac{6\%}{12}$ = 0.5%

Annuity payment = $500   Table 14-1 value = 69.770

Future value of the ordinary annuity = annuity payment × table value
= $500(69.770) = $34,885

Tyson will have $34,885 in his 401(k) plan after 5 years.

EXAMPLE 11

In Example 10 if Tyson's employer will match the first $100 per month of his contribution, how much will this increase his fund after 5 years?

Number of periods = 5(12) = 60   Rate per period = $\frac{6\%}{12}$ = 0.5%

Annuity payment = $500 + $100 match = $600   Table 14-1 value = 69.770

Future value of the ordinary annuity = annuity payment × table value
= $600(69.770) = $41,862

Tyson will have $41,862 in his 401(k) plan with his employer's matching funds, which is an increase of $6,977 over what he contributes.

6 Find the future value of an ordinary annuity or an annuity due using a formula or a calculator application.

Using tables to find the future value of an annuity can be limiting. Annuity rates may not be stated as whole number percents. Evaluating an annuity formula requires a business, scientific or graphing calculator or computer software like Excel. Many of the calculator or software features can be used to facilitate these calculations. Be sure to apply the *order of operations*. For more details, review Chapter 5, Section 1, Learning Outcome 5.

> **HOW TO** Find the future value of an ordinary annuity or an annuity due using a formula:
>
> 1. Identify the period rate R as a decimal equivalent, the number of periods N, and the amount of the annuity payment PMT.
> 2. Substitute the values from step 1 into the appropriate formula.
>
> $$FV_{\text{ordinary annuity}} = PMT\left(\frac{(1+R)^N - 1}{R}\right)$$
>
> $$FV_{\text{annuity due}} = PMT\left(\frac{(1+R)^N - 1}{R}\right)(1+R)$$
>
> 3. Evaluate the formula.

EXAMPLE 12
Find the future value of an ordinary annuity of $100 paid monthly at 5.25% for 10 years.

$R = \dfrac{5.25\%}{12} = \dfrac{0.0525}{12} = 0.004375$ Periodic interest rate

$N = 10(12) = 120$ Number of payments

$PMT = \$100$

$FV_{\text{ordinary annuity}} = \$100\left(\dfrac{(1 + 0.004375)^{120} - 1}{0.004375}\right)$ Mentally add within the innermost parentheses.

$FV_{\text{ordinary annuity}} = \$100\left(\dfrac{(1.004375)^{120} - 1}{0.004375}\right)$

Calculator sequence: 100 [×] [(] 1.004375 [^] 120 [−] 1 [)] [÷] 0.004375 [=] ⇒ 15737.69632

The future value of the ordinary annuity is $15,737.70.

EXAMPLE 13
Find the future value of an annuity due of $50 monthly at 5.75% for 5 years.

$R = \dfrac{5.75\%}{12} = \dfrac{0.0575}{12} = 0.0047916667$ Periodic interest rate

$N = 5(12) = 60$ Number of payments

$PMT = \$50$

$FV_{\text{annuity due}} = \$50\left(\dfrac{(1 + 0.0047916667)^{60} - 1}{0.0047916667}\right)(1 + 0.0047916667)$ Mentally add within the parentheses.

$FV_{\text{annuity due}} = \$50\left(\dfrac{(1.0047916667)^{60} - 1}{0.0047916667}\right)(1.0047916667)$

Calculator sequence: 50 [×] [(] 1.0047916667 [^] 60 [−] 1 [)] [÷] 0.0047916667 [=] [ANS] [×] 1.0047916667 [)] [=] ⇒ 3482.788889

The future value of the annuity due is $3,482.79.

Calculator applications are also available for calculating annuities. The steps are similar to those used in calculating future value of a lump sum. You key in different known and unknown values. The default setting on most calculators is for an ordinary annuity.

Annuities and Sinking Funds   507

EXAMPLE 14
Rework Example 12 using a TI BA II Plus and TI-84 calculator.

BA II Plus:

	Keys to press	Display shows
Set decimals to two places if necessary.	2ND [FORMAT] 2 ENTER	DEC= 2.00
Set all variables to defaults.	2ND [RESET] ENTER	RST 0.00
Enter number of periods/payments.	120 N	N= 120.00 ◁
Enter interest rate per period (as a %).	.4375 I/Y	I/Y= 0.44 ◁
Enter payment amount as a negative.	100 +/− PMT	PMT= −100.00 ◁
Compute future value.	CPT FV	FV= 15,737.70*

TI-84:

Change to 2 fixed decimal places.	MODE ↓ → → → ENTER
Select Finance Application.	Press APPS 1:Finance ENTER
Select TVM Solver.	1:TVM Solver ENTER

Use the arrow keys to move cursor to appropriate variables and enter amounts. Enter 0 for unknowns.

Press 120 ENTER to store 120 months to N. Press 5.25 ENTER to store 5.25% per year to I%.
Press 0 ENTER to leave PV unassigned.
Press (−) 100 ENTER to store $100 to PMT.
Press 0 ENTER to leave FV unassigned.
Press 12 ENTER to store 12 payments/periods per year to P/Y and C/Y (number of compounding periods per year) will automatically change to 12 also.
PMT: END should be highlighted.

Use up arrow to move cursor up to FV. Press ALPHA [SOLVE] to solve for future value.

Your calculator screen should look like the one below with a ■ beside FV=15737.70 showing the calculated future value.

```
N=          120.00
I%=           5.25
PV=           0.00
PMT=       −100.00
■FV=      15737.70
P/Y=         12.00
C/Y=         12.00
PMT:END BEGIN
```

The future value $15,737.70 is the same result as was found in Example 12.

For an annuity due on the TI BA II Plus, change the setting by pressing 2nd [BGN] 2nd [SET]. Then return to calculator mode by pressing 2nd [QUIT]. On the TI-84, at the bottom of the TMV Solver screen, change PMT to BEGIN.

> **DID YOU KNOW?**
>
> **Annuity Functions and Other Financial Functions Are Available in Excel™.**
>
> To access these functions, select the Formulas tab and then Insert Function. You can search for the function by name and the available functions will appear. Select the function that represents the unknown that you are trying to find.
>
> Once you highlight a function, the syntax (the sequence for entering the known values) and a brief description of what this function will do is shown. If you need more information, you can select *Help on the function* at the bottom of the box.

EXAMPLE 15
Rework Example 13 using a TI BA II Plus and TI-84 calculator.

BA II Plus:

2ND [FORMAT] 2 ENTER
2ND [RESET] ENTER 60 N
.47916667 I/Y
50 +/− PMT
2ND [BGN] 2ND [SET]
2ND [QUIT]
CPT FV ⇒ 3,482.79

TI-84:

APPS ENTER ENTER

Use the arrows keys to move cursor to appropriate variables and enter amounts. Enter 0 for unknowns.

60 ENTER 5.75 ENTER
0 ENTER (−) 50 ENTER
0 ENTER
12 ENTER ↓ highlight **BEGIN** ENTER
↑↑↑ ALPHA [SOLVE] ⇒ 3,482.79

The future value $3,482.79 is the same result as was found in Example 13.

STOP AND CHECK

1. Use the formula to find the future value of an ordinary annuity of $250 paid monthly at 4.62% for 25 years.

2. Use the formula to find the future value of an ordinary annuity of $30 paid weekly at 5.2% for 15 years.

3. Use the formula to find the future value of an annuity due of $200 monthly at 1.35% for 14 years.

4. Marquita is creating an annuity due of $25 every two weeks at 6% for 35 years. Find the future value of her annuity due.

5. Doris Pallandino contributes $3,500 each year to a Roth IRA that earns 3% per year. Use a calculator to determine how much she will have at the end of 35 years?

6. Ernie Prather contributes $400 per month to a 401(k) retirement plan at work. The plan averages 5% per year. Use a calculator to find the amount he can expect to have in 10 years.

14-1 SECTION EXERCISES

SKILL BUILDERS

Use Table 14-1 to find the future value of the annuities.

	Annuity type	Periodic payment	Annual interest rate	Payment paid	Years
1.	Ordinary annuity	$1,000	5%	Annually	8
2.	Ordinary annuity	$ 500	4%	Semiannually	4
3.	Ordinary annuity	$2,000	8%	Quarterly	3
4.	Annuity due	$3,000	6%	Semiannually	3
5.	Annuity due	$5,000	3%	Annually	4
6.	Annuity due	$ 800	7%	Annually	5

7. Manually find the future value of an ordinary annuity of $300 paid annually at 5% for three years. Verify your result by using the table method.

8. Manually find the future value of an annuity due of $500 paid semiannually for two years at 6% annual interest compounded semiannually. Verify your result by using the table method.

APPLICATIONS

Use the simple interest formula method for Exercises 9–12.

9. Find the future value of an ordinary annuity of $3,000 annually after two years at 3.8% annual interest. Find the total interest earned.

10. Len and Sharron Smith are saving money for their daughter Heather to attend college. They set aside an ordinary annuity of $4,000 annually for ten years at 7% annual interest. How much will Heather have for college after two years? Find the total interest earned.

11. Harry Taylor plans to pay an ordinary annuity of $5,000 annually for ten years. The annual rate of interest is 3.8%. How much will Harry have at the end of three years? How much interest will he earn on the investment after three years?

12. Scott Martin is planning to establish a retirement annuity. He is committed to an ordinary annuity of $3,000 annually at 3.6% annual interest. How much will Scott have accumulated after three years? How much interest will he earn?

Use Table 14-1 or the appropriate formula for Exercises 13–17.

13. Find the future value of an ordinary annuity of $6,500 semiannually for seven years at 6% annual interest compounded semiannually. How much was invested? How much interest was earned?

14. Pat Lechleiter pays an ordinary annuity of $2,500 quarterly at 8% annual interest compounded quarterly to establish supplemental income for retirement. How much will Pat have available at the end of five years?

15. Latanya Brown established an ordinary annuity of $1,000 annually at 7% annual interest. What is the future value of the annuity after 15 years? How much of her own money will Latanya have invested during this time period? By how much will her investment have grown?

16. You invest in an ordinary annuity of $500 annually at 8% annual interest. Find the future value of the annuity at the end of ten years. How much have you invested? How much interest has your annuity earned?

17. You invest in an ordinary annuity of $2,000 annually at 8% annual interest. What is the future value of the annuity at the end of five years? How much have you invested? How much interest has your annuity earned?

18. Make a chart comparing your results for Exercises 16 and 17. Use these headings: Years, Total Investment, Total Interest. What general conclusion might you draw about effective investment strategy?

Use the simple interest formula method for Exercises 19–22:

19. Find the future value of an annuity due of $12,000 annually for three years at 3% annual interest. How much was invested? How much interest was earned?

20. Bernard McGhee has decided to establish an annuity due of $2,500 annually for 15 years at 7.2% annual interest. How much is the annuity due worth after two years? How much was invested? How much interest was earned?

21. Find the future value of an annuity due of $7,800 annually for two years at 8.1% annual interest. Find the total amount invested. Find the interest.

22. Find the future value of an annuity due of $400 annually for two years at 6.8% annual interest compounded annually.

Use Table 14-1 or the appropriate formula for Exercises 23–26.

23. Find the future value of a quarterly annuity due of $4,400 for three years at 8% annual interest compounded quarterly. How much was invested? How much interest was earned?

24. Find the future value of an annuity due of $750 semiannually for four years at 8% annual interest compounded semiannually. What is the total investment? What is the interest?

25. Which annuity earns more interest: an annuity due of $300 quarterly for one year at 8% annual interest compounded quarterly, or an annuity due of $600 semiannually for one year at 8% annual interest compounded semiannually?

26. You have carefully examined your budget and determined that you can manage to set aside $250 per year. So you set up an annuity due of $250 annually at 7% annual interest. How much will you have contributed after 20 years? What is the future value of your annuity after 20 years? How much interest will you earn?

27. June Watson is contributing $3,000 each year to a Roth IRA. The IRA earns 3.2% per year. How much will she have at the end of 25 years?

28. Marvin Murphy contributes $400 per month to a payroll deduction 401(k) at work. His employer matches his contribution up to $200 per month. If the fund averages 5.4% per year, how much will be in the account in 10 years?

14-2 SINKING FUNDS AND THE PRESENT VALUE OF AN ANNUITY

LEARNING OUTCOMES
1. Find the sinking fund payment using a $1.00 sinking fund payment table.
2. Find the present value of an ordinary annuity using a $1.00 ordinary annuity present value table.
3. Find the sinking fund payment or the present value of an annuity using a formula or a calculator application.

Businesses and individuals often use sinking funds to accumulate a desired amount of money by the end of a certain period of time to pay off a financial obligation, to use for a retirement or college fund, or to reach a specific goal such as retiring a bond issue or paying for equipment replacement and modernization. Essentially, a **sinking fund** is payment into an ordinary annuity to yield a desired future value. That is, the future value is known and the payment amount is unknown.

Sinking fund: payment into an ordinary annuity to yield a desired future value.

	Payment	Future Value
Sinking Fund	Unknown	Known
Accumulation Phase of an Annuity	Known	Unknown

1 Find the sinking fund payment using a $1.00 sinking fund payment table.

A sinking fund payment is made at the *end* of each period, so a sinking fund payment is an ordinary annuity payment. These payments, along with the interest, accumulate over a period of time to provide the desired future value.

To calculate the *payment* required to yield a desired future value, use Table 14-2. The procedure for locating a value in Table 14-2 is similar to the procedure used for Table 14-1.

TABLE 14-2
$1.00 Sinking Fund Payments

Periods	\multicolumn{7}{c}{Rate per period}
	1%	2%	3%	4%	6%	8%	12%
1	1.0000000	1.0000000	1.0000000	1.0000000	1.0000000	1.0000000	1.0000000
2	0.4975124	0.4950495	0.4926108	0.4901961	0.4854369	0.4807692	0.4716981
3	0.3300221	0.3267547	0.3235304	0.3203485	0.3141098	0.3080335	0.2963490
4	0.2462811	0.2426238	0.2390270	0.2354900	0.2285915	0.2219208	0.2092344
5	0.1960398	0.1921584	0.1883546	0.1846271	0.1773964	0.1704565	0.1574097
6	0.1625484	0.1585258	0.1545975	0.1507619	0.1433626	0.1363154	0.1232257
7	0.1386283	0.1345120	0.1305064	0.1266096	0.1191350	0.1120724	0.0991177
8	0.1206903	0.1165098	0.1124564	0.1085278	0.1010359	0.0940148	0.0813028
9	0.1067404	0.1025154	0.0984339	0.0944930	0.0870222	0.0800797	0.0676789
10	0.0955821	0.0913265	0.0872305	0.0832909	0.0758680	0.0690295	0.0569842
11	0.0864541	0.0821779	0.0780774	0.0741490	0.0667929	0.0600763	0.0484154
12	0.0788488	0.0745596	0.0704621	0.0665522	0.0592770	0.0526950	0.0414368
13	0.0724148	0.0681184	0.0670295	0.0601437	0.0529601	0.0465218	0.0356772
14	0.0669012	0.0626020	0.0585263	0.0546690	0.0475849	0.0412969	0.0308712
15	0.0621238	0.0578255	0.0537666	0.0499411	0.0429628	0.0368295	0.0268242
16	0.0579446	0.0536501	0.0496108	0.0458200	0.0389521	0.0329769	0.0233900
17	0.0542581	0.0499698	0.0459525	0.0421985	0.0354448	0.0296294	0.0204567
18	0.0509820	0.0467021	0.0427087	0.0389933	0.0323565	0.0267021	0.0179373
19	0.0480518	0.0437818	0.0398139	0.0361386	0.0296209	0.0241276	0.0157630
20	0.0454153	0.0411567	0.0372157	0.0335818	0.0271846	0.0218522	0.0138788
25	0.0354068	0.0312204	0.0274279	0.0240120	0.0182267	0.0136788	0.0075000
30	0.0287481	0.0246499	0.0210193	0.0178301	0.0126489	0.0088274	0.0041437
40	0.0204556	0.0165558	0.0132624	0.0105235	0.0064615	0.0038602	0.0013036
50	0.0155127	0.0118232	0.0088655	0.0065502	0.0034443	0.0017429	0.0004167

Table values show the sinking fund payment earning a given rate for a given number of periods so that the accumulated amount at the end of the time will be $1.00. The formula for generating the table values is $TV = \dfrac{R}{(1+R)^N - 1}$, where TV is the table value, R is the rate per period, and N is the number of periods or payments.

HOW TO
Find the sinking fund payment using a $1.00 sinking fund payment table

Use Table 14-2:
1. Select the periods row corresponding to the number of interest periods.
2. Select the rate-per-period column corresponding to the period interest rate.
3. Locate the value in the cell where the periods row intersects the rate-per-period column.
4. Multiply the table value from step 3 by the desired future value.

Sinking fund payment = future value × Table 14-2 value

EXAMPLE 1
Use Table 14-2 to find the annual sinking fund payment required to accumulate $140,000 in 12 years at 6% annual interest.

12 years × 1 period per year = 12 periods

$$\dfrac{6\% \text{ annual interest rate}}{1 \text{ period per year}} = 6\% \text{ period interest rate}$$

The Table 14-2 value for 12 periods at 6% is 0.0592770

Sinking fund payment = desired future value × table factor
= $140,000(0.0592770)
= $8,298.78

A sinking fund payment of **$8,298.78** is required at the end of each year for 12 years at 6% to yield the desired $140,000.

EXAMPLE 2

Find the total interest earned on the sinking fund in the previous example.

$FV = \$140,000$ Number of payments = 12
Total investment = amount of payment × 12
= $8,298.78(12)
= $99,585.36
Total interest earned = $140,000 − $99,585.36
= **$40,414.64**

STOP AND CHECK

1. Use Table 14-2 to find the annual sinking fund payment needed to accumulate $12,000 in six years at 4% annual interest.

2. What is the total amount paid and the interest on the sinking fund in Exercise 1?

3. Use Table 14-2 to find the quarterly sinking fund payment needed to accumulate $25,000 in ten years at 4% annual interest compounded quarterly.

4. What is the amount paid and the interest on the sinking fund in Exercise 3?

2 Find the present value of an ordinary annuity using a $1.00 ordinary annuity present value table.

In the liquidation or payout phase of an annuity, a common option is for periodic payments to be made to the annuitant or beneficiary for a certain period of time. The future value of the *accumulation phase* of the annuity becomes the present value of the *liquidated or payout phase* of the annuity. Figure 14-6 shows the accumulation phase or future value growth of an annuity. The **present value of an annuity** is the amount needed in a fund to pay out a specific periodic payment over a specified period of time during the liquidation or payout phase. The balance that is in the fund continues to earn interest while payouts are being made, but the balance is steadily declining. At the end of the specified time of the liquidation phase, the balance will be zero. See Figure 14-7.

Present value of an annuity: the amount needed in a fund so that the fund can pay out a specified regular payment for a specified amount of time.

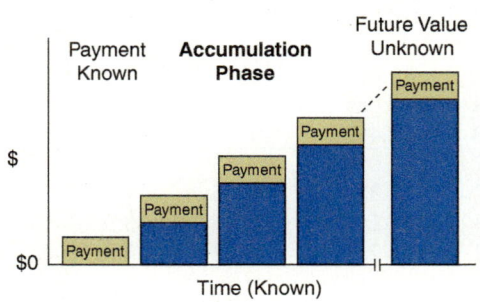

FIGURE 14-6
Future Value of an Annuity

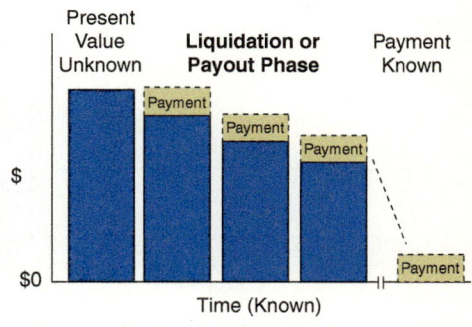

FIGURE 14-7
Present Value of an Annuity

DID YOU KNOW?

When you set your calculator to *display* two decimal places as you did in finding annuities, the calculator retains calculated values that have as many decimal places as the capacity of the calculator, so the internal calculations are often more accurate than calculations made with table values rounded to as few as three decimal places. For example, if you use a calculator (the **BA II Plus** or the **TI-84**) to find the present value of the annuity in Example 3, the present value would be $33,888.22—which is $0.22 more than the result using the table value.

HOW TO Find the present value of an annuity using a table value

Use Table 14-3:

1. Locate the table value for the given number of payout periods and the given rate per period.
2. Multiply the table value times the periodic annuity payment.

Present value of annuity = periodic annuity payment × table value

EXAMPLE 3

Use Table 14-3 to find the present value of an ordinary annuity in the payout phase with semiannual payments of $3,000 for seven years at 6% annual interest compounded semiannually.

7 years × 2 periods per year = 14 periods

$$\frac{6\% \text{ annual interest}}{2 \text{ periods per year}} = 3\% \text{ period interest rate}$$

The Table 14-3 value for 14 periods at 3% is 11.296.

Present value of annuity = annuity payment × table factor
= $3,000(11.296)
= $33,888

A fund of **$33,888** is needed now at 6% interest compounded semiannually to receive an annuity payment of $3,000 twice a year for seven years.

TABLE 14-3
Present Value of a $1.00 Ordinary Annuity

Periods	2%	3%	4%	5%	6%	7%	8%	9%	10%	12%
1	0.980	0.971	0.962	0.952	0.943	0.935	0.926	0.917	0.909	0.893
2	1.942	1.913	1.886	1.859	1.833	1.808	1.783	1.759	1.736	1.690
3	2.884	2.829	2.775	2.723	2.673	2.624	2.577	2.531	2.487	2.402
4	3.808	3.717	3.630	3.546	3.465	3.387	3.312	3.240	3.170	3.037
5	4.713	4.580	4.452	4.329	4.212	4.100	3.993	3.890	3.791	3.605
6	5.601	5.417	5.242	5.076	4.917	4.767	4.623	4.486	4.355	4.111
7	6.472	6.230	6.002	5.786	5.582	5.389	5.206	5.033	4.868	4.564
8	7.325	7.020	6.733	6.463	6.210	5.971	5.747	5.535	5.335	4.968
9	8.162	7.786	7.435	7.108	6.802	6.515	6.247	5.995	5.759	5.328
10	8.983	8.530	8.111	7.722	7.360	7.024	6.710	6.418	6.145	5.650
11	9.787	9.253	8.760	8.306	7.887	7.499	7.139	6.805	6.495	5.938
12	10.575	9.954	9.385	8.863	8.384	7.943	7.536	7.161	6.814	6.194
13	11.348	10.635	9.986	9.394	8.853	8.358	7.904	7.487	7.103	6.424
14	12.106	11.296	10.563	9.899	9.295	8.745	8.244	7.786	7.367	6.628
15	12.849	11.938	11.118	10.380	9.712	9.108	8.559	8.061	7.606	6.811
16	13.578	12.561	11.652	10.838	10.106	9.447	8.851	8.313	7.824	6.974
17	14.292	13.166	12.166	11.274	10.477	9.763	9.122	8.544	8.022	7.120
18	14.992	13.754	12.659	11.690	10.828	10.059	9.372	8.756	8.201	7.250
19	15.678	14.324	13.134	12.085	11.158	10.336	9.604	8.950	8.365	7.366
20	16.351	14.877	13.590	12.462	11.470	10.594	9.818	9.129	8.514	7.469
25	19.523	17.413	15.622	14.094	12.783	11.654	10.675	9.823	9.077	7.843
30	22.396	19.600	17.292	15.372	13.765	12.409	11.258	10.274	9.427	8.055
40	27.355	23.115	19.793	17.159	15.046	13.332	11.925	10.757	9.779	8.244
50	31.424	25.730	21.482	18.256	15.762	13.801	12.233	10.962	9.915	8.304

Table values show the present value of a $1.00 ordinary annuity, or the lump sum amount that, invested now, yields the same compounded amount as an annuity of $1.00 at a given rate per period for a given number of periods. The formula for generating the table values is $TV = \frac{(1 + R)^N - 1}{R(1 + R)^N}$, where TV is the table value, R is the rate per period, and N is the number of periods.

STOP AND CHECK

1. Use Table 14-3 to find the present value of an ordinary annuity with an annual payout of $5,000 for five years at 4% interest compounded annually.

2. What is the present value of an ordinary annuity with an annual payout of $20,000 at 7% annual interest for 20 years?

3. What lump sum must be set aside today at 8% annual interest compounded quarterly to provide quarterly payments of $7,000 to Demetrius Ball for the next ten years?

4. Tim Warren is setting up an ordinary annuity and wants to receive $10,000 semiannually for the next 20 years. How much should he set aside at 6% annual interest compounded semiannually?

3 Find the sinking fund payment or the present value of an annuity using a formula or a calculator application.

As with future value, tables do not always have the values that you need to find a sinking fund payment or a present value of an annuity. A formula allows you the flexibility of using any interest rate or any number of periods.

HOW TO Find the sinking fund payment or present value of an ordinary annuity using a formula

1. Identify the period rate R as a decimal equivalent, the number of periods N, and the future value FV of the annuity.
2. Substitute the values from step 1 in the appropriate formula.

$$PMT_{\text{ordinary annuity}} = FV\left(\frac{R}{(1+R)^N - 1}\right)$$

$$PV_{\text{ordinary annuity}} = PMT\left(\frac{(1+R)^N - 1}{R(1+R)^N}\right)$$

3. Evaluate the formula.

EXAMPLE 4
Debbie Bennett wants to have $100,000 in a retirement fund to supplement her retirement. She plans to work for 20 more years and has found an annuity fund that earns 5.5% annual interest. How much does she need to contribute to the fund each month to reach her goal?

$R = \dfrac{5.5\%}{12} = \dfrac{0.055}{12} = 0.0045833333$ Periodic interest rate

$N = 20(12) = 240$ Number of payments

$FV = \$100{,}000$

Formula:

$$PMT_{\text{ordinary annuity}} = \$100{,}000\left(\frac{0.0045833333}{(1 + 0.0045833333)^{240} - 1}\right)$$

100000 × .0045833333 ÷ ((1.0045833333 ^ 240 − 1) = ⇒

$PMT = 229.5539756$ (round to nearest cent)

BA II Plus:	TI-84:
2ND [FORMAT] 2 ENTER	APPS ENTER ENTER
2ND [RESET] ENTER	240 ENTER 5.5 ENTER
240 N	0 ENTER 0 ENTER
.45833333 I/Y	100000 ENTER
100000 FV	12 ENTER highlight END ENTER ↑↑↑↑
CPT PMT ⇒ −229.55	ALPHA [SOLVE] ⇒ −229.55

The payment that Debbie should make into the sinking fund each month is $229.55.

EXAMPLE 5

At retirement Debbie Bennett will begin drawing a payment each month from her retirement fund. How much does she need in a fund that pays 5.5% interest to receive a $700 per month payment for 20 years?

$$R = \frac{5.5\%}{12} = \frac{0.055}{12} = 0.0045833333 \quad \text{Periodic interest rate}$$

$$N = 20(12) = 240 \quad \text{Number of payments}$$

$$PMT = \$700$$

Formula:

$$PV_{\text{ordinary annuity}} = \$700\left(\frac{(1 + 0.0045833333)^{240} - 1}{0.0045833333(1 + 0.0045833333)^{240}}\right)$$

700 (1.0045833333 ^ 240 − 1) ÷
(.0045833333 × 1.0045833333 ^ 240) = ⇒

$PV = 101760.8545$ Round to nearest cent.

BA II Plus:	TI-84:
2ND [FORMAT] 2 ENTER	APPS ENTER ENTER
2ND [RESET] ENTER	240 ENTER 5.5 ENTER
240 N	0 ENTER (−) 700 ENTER
.45833333 I/Y	0 ENTER 12 ENTER ENTER
700 +/− PMT	↓ highlight END ENTER
CPT PV ⇒ 101,760.85	↑↑↑↑↑ ALPHA [SOLVE] ⇒ 101760.85

Debbie needs to have $101,760.85 in the fund to receive an annuity payment of $700 each month for 20 years.

STOP AND CHECK

1. Shameka plans to have $350,000 in a retirement fund at her retirement. She plans to work for 26 years and has found a sinking fund that earns 4.85% annual interest compounded monthly. How much does she need to contribute to the fund each month to reach her goal?

2. At retirement Mekisha will begin drawing a payment each month from her retirement fund. Use the formula to determine the amount she needs in a fund that pays 5.25% interest to receive a $2,000 per month payment for 25 years.

14-2 SECTION EXERCISES

SKILL BUILDERS

1. What semiannual sinking fund payment would be required to yield $48,000 nine years from now? The annual interest rate is 6% compounded semiannually.

2. The Bamboo Furniture Company manufactures rattan patio furniture. It has just purchased a machine for $13,500 to cut and glue the pieces of wood. The machine is expected to last five years. If the company establishes a sinking fund to replace this machine, what annual payments must be made if the annual interest rate is 8%?

3. Tristin and Kim Denley are establishing a college fund for their 1-year-old daughter, Chloe. They want to save enough now to pay college tuition at the time she enters college (17 years from now). If her tuition is projected to be $35,000 for a two-year degree, what annual sinking fund payment should they establish if the annual interest is 8%?

4. Kathy and Patrick Mowers have a 12-year-old daughter and are now in a financial position to begin saving for her college education. What annual sinking fund payment should they make to have her entire college expenses paid at the time she enters college six years from now? Her college expenses are projected to be $30,000 and the annual interest rate is 6%.

5. Matthew Bennett recognizes the value of saving part of his income. He has set a goal to have $25,000 in cash available for emergencies. How much should he invest semiannually to have $25,000 in ten years if the sinking fund he has selected pays 8% annually, compounded semiannually?

6. Stein and Company has established a sinking fund to retire a bond issue of $500,000, which is due in ten years. How much is the quarterly sinking fund payment if the account pays 8% annual interest compounded quarterly?

7. Find the present value of an ordinary annuity with annual payments of $680 at 9% annual interest for 25 years?

8. Erin Calipari plans to have a stream of $2,500 payments each year for two years at 8% annual interest. How much should she set aside today?

9. Emily Bennett is setting up an annuity for a memorial scholarship. What lump sum does she need to set aside today at 7% annual interest to have the scholarship pay $3,000 annually for 10 years?

10. Kristin Bennett, a nationally recognized philanthropist, set up an ordinary annuity of $1,600 for ten years at 9% annual interest. How much does Bennett have to deposit today to pay the stream of annual payments?

11. Ken and Debbie Bennett have agreed to pay for their granddaughter's college education and need to know how much to set aside so annual payments of $15,000 can be made for five years at 3% annual interest.

12. Janice and Terry Van Dyke have decided to establish a quarterly ordinary annuity of $3,000 for the next ten years at 8% annual interest compounded quarterly. How much should they invest in a lump sum now to provide the stream of payments?

SUMMARY CHAPTER 14

Learning Outcomes

Section 14-1

1 Find the future value of an ordinary annuity using the simple interest formula method. (p. 492)

What to Remember with Examples

1. Find the first end-of-period principal.

    First end-of-period principal = annuity payment

2. For each remaining period in turn, find the next end-of-period principal:
    (a) Multiply the previous end-of-period principal by the sum of 1 and the decimal equivalent of the period interest rate.
    (b) Add the product from step 2a and the annuity payment.

    End-of-period principal = previous end-of-period principal ×
    (1 + period interest rate) + annuity payment

3. Identify the last end-of-period principal as the future value.

    Future value = last end-of-period principal

Find the future value of an annual ordinary annuity of $2,000 for two years at 4% annual interest.

$$\text{End-of-year 1} = \$2{,}000$$
$$\text{End-of-year 2} = \$2{,}000(1.04) + \$2{,}000$$
$$= \$2{,}080 + \$2{,}000$$
$$= \$4{,}080$$

The future value is $4,080.

Find the future value of a semiannual ordinary annuity of $300 for one year at 5% annual interest, compounded semiannually.

$$\frac{5\% \text{ annual interest rate}}{2 \text{ periods per year}} = 2.5\% = 0.025 \text{ period interest rate}$$
$$\text{End-of-period 1} = \$300$$
$$\text{End-of-period 2} = \$300(1.025) + \$300$$
$$= \$307.50 + \$300$$
$$= \$607.50$$

The future value is $607.50.

Find the total interest earned on an annuity:

1. Find the total amount invested:

    Total invested = payment amount × number of payments

2. Find the total interest:

    Total interest = future value of annuity − total invested

---

Find the total interest earned on the semiannual ordinary annuity in the previous example.

Total invested = $300(2)   Payment = $300
              = $600   Number of payments = 2
Total interest = $607.50 − $600   Future value = $607.50
              = $7.50

---

2 Find the future value of an ordinary annuity with periodic payments using a $1.00 ordinary annuity future value table. (p. 494)

Using Table 14-1:

1. Select the periods row corresponding to the number of interest periods.
2. Select the rate-per-period column corresponding to the period interest rate.
3. Locate the value in the cell where the periods row intersects the rate-per-period column.
4. Multiply the annuity payment by the table value from step 3.

    Future value = annuity payment × table value

Annuities and Sinking Funds

Find the future value of an ordinary annuity of $5,000 semiannually for four years at 4% annual interest compounded semiannually.

$$4 \text{ years} \times 2 \text{ periods per year} = 8 \text{ periods}$$
$$\frac{4\% \text{ annual interest rate}}{2 \text{ periods per year}} = 2\% \text{ period interest rate}$$

The Table 14-1 value for eight periods at 2% is 8.583.

$$\text{Future value} = \$5,000(8.583)$$
$$= \$42,915$$

The future value is $42,915.

3 Find the future value of an annuity due with periodic payments using the simple interest formula method. (p. 497)

1. Find the first end-of-period principal: Multiply the annuity payment by the sum of 1 and the decimal equivalent of the period interest rate.

    First end-of-period principal = annuity payment × (1 + period interest rate)

2. For each remaining period in turn, find the next end-of-period principal:
    (a) Add the previous end-of-period principal and the annuity payment.
    (b) Multiply the sum from step 2a by the sum of 1 and the period interest rate.

    End-of-period principal = (previous end-of-period principal + annuity payment) × (1 + period interest rate)

3. Identify the last end-of-period principal as the future value.

    Future value = last end-of-period principal

Find the future value of an annual annuity due of $3,000 for two years at 5% annual interest.

$$\text{End-of-year 1} = \$3,000(1.05)$$
$$= \$3,150$$
$$\text{End-of-year 2} = (\$3,150 + \$3,000)(1.05)$$
$$= \$6,150(1.05)$$
$$= \$6,457.50$$

The future value is $6,457.50.

Find the future value and the total interest earned of a semiannual annuity due of $400 for one year at 4% annual interest compounded semiannually.

$$\frac{4\% \text{ annual interest rate}}{2 \text{ periods per year}} = 2\% = 0.02 \text{ period interest rate}$$
$$\text{End-of-period 1} = \$400(1.02)$$
$$= \$408$$
$$\text{End-of-period 2} = (\$408 + \$400)(1.02)$$
$$= (\$808)(1.02)$$
$$= \$824.16$$

The future value is $824.16.

Find the total interest earned on the semiannual annuity:

Total invested = $400(2)   Payment = $400
              = $800   Number of payments = 2
Total interest = $824.16 − $800   Future value = $824.16
              = $24.16

The total interest is $24.16.

4 Find the future value of an annuity due with periodic payments using a $1.00 ordinary annuity future value table. (p. 498)

Use Table 14-1:

1. Select the periods row corresponding to the number of interest periods.
2. Select the rate-per-period column corresponding to the period interest rate.
3. Locate the value in the cell where the periods row intersects the rate-per-period column.

4. Multiply the annuity payment by the table value from step 3. This is equivalent to an ordinary annuity.
5. Multiply the product from step 4 by the sum of 1 and the period interest rate to adjust for the extra interest that is earned on an annuity due.

Future value = annuity payment × table value × (1 + period interest rate)

Find the future value of a quarterly annuity due of $1,500 for three years at 8% annual interest compounded quarterly.

$$3 \text{ years} \times 4 \text{ periods per year} = 12 \text{ periods}$$

$$\frac{8\% \text{ annual interest rate}}{4 \text{ periods per year}} = 2\% \text{ period interest rate}$$

The Table 14-1 value for 12 periods at 2% is 13.412.

$$\text{Future value} = \$1,500(13.412)(1.02)$$
$$= \$20,520.36$$

The future value is $20,520.36.

---

5 Find the future value of a retirement plan annuity. (p. 500)

Various retirement plan options are available from employers or from individual retirement arrangements. Retirement plans are generally annuities. In most instances, individual retirement arrangements are annuity due plans and employment-based plans (through payroll deductions) are ordinary annuities.

Campbell Johnson has the opportunity to contribute to a payroll deduction 401(k) plan at work. She selects an option that averages 3% per year and contributes $200 per month. How much should she have in the account in 5 years?

A payroll-deduction plan is considered to be an ordinary annuity.

$$\text{Number of periods} = 5(12) = 60$$

$$\text{Rate per period} = \frac{3\%}{12} = 0.25\%$$

$$\text{Annuity payment} = \$200$$

$$\text{Table 14-1 value} = 64.647$$

$$\text{Future value of ordinary annuity} = \text{annuity payment} \times \text{table value}$$
$$= \$200(64.647)$$
$$= \$12,929.40$$

Campbell will have $12,929.40 in her 401(k) plan after 5 years.

---

6 Find the future value of an ordinary annuity or an annuity due using a formula or a calculator application. (p. 502)

Find the future value of an ordinary annuity or an annuity due using the formula.

1. Identify the period rate R as a decimal equivalent, the number of periods N, and the amount of the annuity payment PMT.
2. Substitute the values from step 1 into the appropriate formula.

$$FV_{\text{ordinary annuity}} = PMT\left(\frac{(1+R)^N - 1}{R}\right)$$

$$FV_{\text{annuity due}} = PMT\left(\frac{(1+R)^N - 1}{R}\right)(1+R)$$

3. Evaluate the formula.

Use the formula to find the future value of an ordinary annuity of $50 paid monthly at 5% for 20 years.

$R = \dfrac{5\%}{12} = \dfrac{0.05}{12} = 0.0041666667$ Periodic interest rate

$N = 20(12) = 240$ Number of payments

$PMT = \$50$

$$FV_{\text{ordinary annuity}} = \$50\left(\frac{(1 + 0.0041666667)^{240} - 1}{0.0041666667}\right) \quad \text{Mentally add within innermost parentheses.}$$

$$FV_{\text{ordinary annuity}} = \$50\left(\frac{(1.0041666667)^{240} - 1}{0.0041666667}\right)$$

Annuities and Sinking Funds   **521**

Calculator sequence:

50 (1.0041666667 ^ 240 − 1) ÷ 0.0041666667 = ⇒ 20551.68352

The future value of the ordinary annuity is $20,551.68.

Refer to Example 14 (p. 503) and Example 15 (p. 503) for using calculator applications on the TI BA II Plus and TI-84.

Section 14-2

1 Find the sinking fund payment using a $1.00 sinking fund payment table. (p. 508)

Use Table 14-2:

1. Select the periods row corresponding to the number of interest periods.
2. Select the rate-per-period column corresponding to the period interest rate.
3. Locate the value in the cell where the periods row intersects the rate-per-period column.
4. Multiply the table value from step 3 by the desired future value.

$$\text{Sinking fund payment} = \text{future value} \times \text{table value}$$

Find the quarterly sinking fund payment required to yield $15,000 in five years if interest is 8% compounded quarterly.

$$5 \text{ years} \times 4 \text{ periods per year} = 20 \text{ periods}$$

$$\frac{8\% \text{ annual interest rate}}{4 \text{ periods per year}} = 2\% \text{ period interest rate}$$

The Table 14-2 value for 20 periods at 2% is 0.0411567.

$$\text{Sinking fund payment} = \$15,000(0.0411567)$$
$$= \$617.35$$

The required quarterly payment is $617.35.

2 Find the present value of an ordinary annuity using a $1.00 ordinary annuity present value table. (p. 509)

Use Table 14-3:

1. Locate the table value for the given number of payout periods and the given rate per period.
2. Multiply the table value by the periodic annuity payment.

$$\text{Present value of annuity} = \text{periodic annuity payment} \times \text{table value}$$

Find the lump sum required today earning 6% annual interest compounded semiannually to yield the same as a semiannual ordinary annuity payment of $2,500 for 15 years.

$$15 \text{ years} \times 2 \text{ periods per year} = 30 \text{ periods}$$

$$\frac{6\% \text{ annual interest rate}}{2 \text{ periods per year}} = 3\% \text{ period interest rate}$$

The Table 14-3 value for 30 periods at 3% is 19.600.

$$\text{Present value} = \$2,500(19.600)$$
$$= \$49,000$$

The lump sum required for deposit today is $49,000.

3 Find the sinking fund payment or the present value of an annuity using a formula or a calculator application. (p. 511)

Find the sinking fund payment or present value of an ordinary annuity using a formula:

1. Identify the period rate R as a decimal equivalent, the number of periods N, and the future value FV of the annuity.
2. Substitute the values from step 1 in the appropriate formula.

$$PMT_{\text{ordinary annuity}} = FV\left(\frac{R}{(1+R)^N - 1}\right)$$

$$PV_{\text{ordinary annuity}} = PMT\left(\frac{(1+R)^N - 1}{R(1+R)^N}\right)$$

3. Evaluate the formula.

> Camesa plans to have $500,000 in her retirement fund when she retires in 23 years. She is investigating a sinking fund that earns 4.75% annual interest. How much does she need to contribute to the fund each month to reach her goal?
>
> $R = \dfrac{4.75\%}{12} = \dfrac{0.0475}{12} = 0.0039583333$ Periodic interest rate
>
> $N = 23(12) = 276$ Number of payments
>
> $FV = \$500{,}000$
>
> $PMT_{\text{ordinary annuity}} = \$500{,}000 \left(\dfrac{0.0039583333}{(1 + 0.0039583333)^{276} - 1} \right)$
>
> 500000 $\boxed{\times}$ 0.0039583333 $\boxed{\div}$ $\boxed{(}$ 1.0039583333 $\boxed{\wedge}$ 276 $\boxed{-}$ 1 $\boxed{)}$ $\boxed{=}$
>
> $PMT = 1{,}001.959664$ (round to next cent)
>
> Camesa should make monthly payments of $1,001.96 into the sinking fund.

Refer to Example 4 (p. 511) and Example 5 (p. 512) for using calculator applications on the TI BA II Plus and TI-84.

EXERCISES SET A

CHAPTER 14

Use Table 14-1 to complete the following table.

Annuity payment	Annual rate	Annual interest	Years	Type of annuity	Future value of annuity
1. $1,400	3%	Compounded annually	5	Ordinary	_____
2. $2,900	8%	Compounded quarterly	10	Ordinary	_____
3. $1,250	6%	Compounded semiannually	$1\frac{1}{2}$	Annuity due	_____
4. $800	5%	Compounded annually	15	Annuity due	_____

Use Table 14-2 to find the sinking fund payment.

	Desired future value	Annual interest rate	Years	Frequency of payments
EL 5.	$240,000	6%	15	Annually
EL 6.	$3,000	4%	10	Semiannually
EL 7.	$50,000	4%	5	Quarterly
EL 8.	$45,000	3%	8	Annually

Use Table 14-3 to find the amount that needs to be invested today to provide a stream of payments in the annuity liquidation phase.

Payment amount	Annual interest rate	Years	Frequency of payments
9. $10,000	4%	20	Annually
10. $12,000	4%	10	Semiannually
11. $5,000	8%	4	Quarterly
12. $1,000	3%	15	Annually

13. Roni Sue deposited $1,500 at the beginning of each year for three years at an annual interest rate of 9%. Find the future value manually.

Use Table 14-1.

14. Barry Michael plans to deposit $2,000 at the end of every six months for the next five years to save up for a boat. If the interest rate is 6% annually, compounded semiannually, how much money will Barry have in his boat fund after five years?

15. Bob Paris opens a retirement income account paying 5% annually. He deposits $3,000 at the beginning of each year.
    (a) How much will be in the account after ten years?
    (b) When Bob retires at age 65, in 19 years, how much will be in the account?

16. The Shari Joy Corporation decided to set aside $3,200 at the beginning of every six months to provide donation funds for a new Little League baseball field scheduled to be built in 18 months. If money earns 4% annual interest compounded semiannually, how much will be available as a donation for the field?

Use Table 14-2 for Exercises 17 and 20.

17. How much must be set aside at the end of each six months by the Fabulous Toy Company to replace a $155,000 piece of equipment at the end of eight years if the account pays 6% annual interest compounded semiannually?

18. Lausanne Private School System needs to set aside funds for a new computer system. What quarterly sinking fund payment would be required to amount to $45,000, the approximate cost of the system, in $1\frac{1}{2}$ years at 4% annual interest compounded quarterly?

19. Ernie Wroten contributes $1,750 each year to a Roth IRA. The IRA earns 2.67% per year. How much will he have at the end of 15 years?

20. Jasmine Naylor contributes $100 per month to a payroll deduction 401(k) at work. Her employer matches her contribution up to $50 per month. If the fund averages 4.2% per year, how much will be in the account in 25 years?

EXERCISES SET B — CHAPTER 14

Annuities and Sinking Funds

Use Table 14-1 to complete the table below.

	Annuity payment	Annual rate	Annual interest	Years	Type of annuity	Future value of annuity
1.	$1,900	8%	Compounded quarterly	3	Ordinary	_____
2.	$5,000	5%	Compounded annually	20	Ordinary	_____
3.	$2,150	7%	Compounded annually	8	Annuity due	_____
4.	$600	6%	Compounded semiannually	5	Annuity due	_____

Use Table 14-2 to find the sinking fund payment.

	Desired future value	Annual interest rate	Years	Frequency of payments	Sinking fund payment
5.	$24,000	6%	10	Semiannually	_____
6.	$45,000	8%	4	Quarterly	_____
7.	$8,000	6%	17	Annually	_____
8.	$10,000	4%	19	Annually	_____

Use Table 14-3 to find the amount that needs to be invested today to receive payments for the specified length of time.

	Payment amount	Annual interest rate	Years	Frequency of payments
9.	$7,000	2%	30	Annually
10.	$20,000	6%	15	Semiannually
11.	$10,000	8%	5	Quarterly
12.	$6,000	5%	10	Annually

13. Manually find the future value of an annuity due of $1,100 deposited annually for three years at 5% interest.

14. Sam and Jane Crawford had a baby in 1998. At the end of that year they began putting away $2,000 a year at 10% annual interest for a college fund. How much money will be in the account when the child is 18 years old?

15. A business deposits $4,500 at the end of each quarter in an account that earns 8% annual interest compounded quarterly. What is the value of the annuity in five years?

16. University Trailers is setting aside $800 at the beginning of every quarter to purchase a forklift in 30 months. The annual interest will be 8% compounded quarterly. How much will be available for the purchase?

Use Table 14-2 for Exercises 17 and 20.

17. Tasty Food Manufacturers, Inc., has a bond issue of $1,400,000 due in 30 years. If it wants to establish a sinking fund to meet this obligation, how much must be set aside at the end of each year if the annual interest rate is 6%?

18. Zachary Alexander owns a limousine that will need to be replaced in four years at a cost of $65,000. How much must he put aside each year in a sinking fund at 8% annual interest to purchase the new limousine?

19. Randy Tolar contributes $250 each year to a Roth IRA. The IRA earns 2.45% per year. How much will he have at the end of 10 years?

20. Jennifer Guyton contributes $75 per month to a payroll deduction 401(k) at work. Her employer contributes $25 per month. If the fund averages 4.8% per year, how much will be in the account in 17 years?

PRACTICE TEST

CHAPTER 14

1. Manually find the future value of an ordinary annuity of $9,000 per year for two years at 3.25% annual interest.

2. Manually find the future value of an annuity due of $2,700 per year for three years at 4.5% annual interest.

3. What is the future value of an annuity due of $5,645 paid every six months for three years at 6% annual interest compounded semiannually?

4. What is the future value of an ordinary annuity of $300 every three months for four years at 8% annual interest compounded quarterly?

5. What is the sinking fund payment required at the end of each year to accumulate $125,000 in 16 years at 4% annual interest?

6. What is the present value of an ordinary annuity of $985 paid out every six months for eight years at 8% annual interest compounded semiannually?

7. Mike's Sport Shop deposited $3,400 at the end of each year for 12 years at 7% annual interest. How much will Mike have in the account at the end of the time period?

8. How much would the annuity amount to in Exercise 7 if Mike had deposited the money at the beginning of each year instead of at the end of each year?

9. How much must be set aside at the end of each year by the Caroline Cab Company to replace four taxicabs at a cost of $90,000? The current interest rate is 6% annually. The existing cabs will wear out in three years.

10. How much must Johnny Williams invest today to have an amount equivalent to investing $2,800 at the end of every six months for the next 15 years if interest is earned at 8% annually compounded semiannually?

11. Maurice Eftink owns a lawn design business. His lawnmower cost $7,800 and should last for six years. How much must he set aside each year at 6% annual interest to have enough money to buy a new mower?

12. Reed and Sondra Davis want to know how much they must deposit in a retirement savings account today to have payments of $1,500 every six months for 15 years. The retirement account is paying 8% annual interest compounded semiannually.

13. Morris Stocks has a Roth IRA with $2,200 payments each year for 11 years in an account paying 7% annual interest. What is the future value of the annuity due at the end of this period of time?

14. Maura Helba is saving for her college expenses. She sets aside $175 at the beginning of each three months in an account paying 8% annual interest compounded quarterly. How much will Maura have accumulated in the account at the end of four years?

15. What is the present value of a semiannual ordinary annuity of $2,500 for seven years at 6% annual interest compounded semiannually?

16. How much will you need to invest today to have quarterly payments of $800 for ten years? The interest rate is 8% annually, compounded quarterly.

17. Goldie's Department Store has a fleet of delivery trucks that will last for three years of heavy use and then need to be replaced at a cost of $75,000. How much must they set aside every three months in a sinking fund at 8% annual interest, compounded quarterly, to have enough money to replace the trucks?

18. Linda Zuk wants to save $25,000 for a new boat in six years. How much must be put aside in equal payments each year in an account earning 6% annual interest for Linda to be able to purchase the boat?

19. What is the present value of an ordinary annuity of $3,400 at 5% annual interest for seven years?

20. An annual ordinary annuity of $2,500 for five years at 5% annual interest requires what lump-sum payment now?

21. Danny Lawrence Properties, Inc., has a bond issue that will mature in 25 years for $1 million. How much must the company set aside each year in a sinking fund at 8% annual interest to meet this future obligation?

22. How much money needs to be set aside today at 10% annual interest compounded semiannually to pay $500 for five years?

23. You are starting an ordinary annuity of $680 for 25 years at 5% annual interest. What lump-sum amount would have to be set aside today for this annuity?

24. Your parents are retiring and want to set aside a lump sum earning 8% annual interest compounded quarterly to pay out $5,000 quarterly for ten years. What lump sum should your parents set aside today?

25. Ted Davis has set the goal of accumulating $80,000 for his son's college fund, which will be needed 18 years in the future. How much should he deposit each year in a sinking fund that earns 8% annual interest? How much should he deposit each year if he waits until his son starts school (at age six) to begin saving? Compare the two payment amounts.

CRITICAL THINKING

CHAPTER 14

1. Select three table values from Table 14-1 and verify them using the formula

$$FV = \frac{(1 + R)^N - 1}{R}$$

2. To find the future value of an annuity due, you multiply the future value of an ordinary annuity by the sum of 1 + the period interest rate. Explain why this is the same as adding the simple interest earned on the first payment for the entire length of the annuity.

3. In Example 8 on page 499, we found that the annuity due with semi-annual payments had the greater future value. Also, the ordinary annuity with the quarterly payments was more than the ordinary annuity with semiannual payments. Why?

4. How are future value of a lump sum and future value of an annuity similar?

5. How are future value of a lump sum and future value of an annuity different?

6. How are the present value of a lump sum and the periodic payment of a sinking fund similar? How are they different?

7. How are annuities and sinking funds similar? How are they different?

8. Select three table values from Table 14-2 and verify them using the formula

$$TV = \frac{R}{(1 + R)^N - 1}$$

9. Select three table values from Table 14-3 and verify them using the formula

$$TV = \frac{(1 + R)^N - 1}{R(1 + R)^N}$$

10. Explain the difference in an ordinary annuity and an annuity due.

Challenge Problem

Carolyn Ellis is setting up an annuity for her retirement. She can set aside $2,000 at the end of each year for the next 20 years and it will earn 6% annual interest. What lump sum will she need to set aside today at 6% annual interest to have the same retirement fund available 20 years from now? How much more will Carolyn need to invest in periodic payments than she will if she makes a lump sum payment if she intends to accumulate the same retirement balance?

CASE STUDIES

14-1 Annuities for Retirement

Naomi Dexter is 20 years old and attends Southwest Tennessee Community College. Her Business English instructor asked her to write a report detailing her plans for retirement. Naomi decided she would investigate several ways to accumulate $1 million by the time she retires. She also thinks she would like to retire early when she is 50 years old so she can travel around the world. She is considering a long-term certificate of deposit (CD) that pays 3% annually, and an annuity that returns 6% annually. She also did a little research and learned that the average long-term return from stock market investments is between 10% and 12%. Now she needs to calculate how much money she will need to deposit each year to accumulate $1 million.

1. If Naomi wants to accumulate $1,000,000 by investing money every year into her CD at 3% for 30 years until retirement, how much does she need to deposit each year?

2. If she decides to invest in an annuity that returns at 6% interest, how much will she need to deposit annually to accumulate the $1,000,000?

3. If Naomi invests in a stock portfolio, her returns for 10 or more years will average 10%–12%. Naomi realizes that the stock market has higher returns because it is a more risky investment than a savings account or a CD. She wants her calculations to be conservative, so she decides to use 8% to calculate possible stock market earnings. How much will she need to invest annually to accumulate $1,000,000 in the stock market?

4. After looking at the results of her calculations, Naomi has decided to aim for $500,000 savings by the time she retires. She expects to have a starting salary after college of $25,000 to $35,000 and she has taken into account all of the living expenses that will come out of her salary. What will Naomi's annual deposits need to be to accumulate $500,000 in an investment at 6%?

5. If Naomi decides that she will invest $3,000 per year in a 6% annuity for the first ten years, $6,000 for the next ten years, and $9,000 for the next ten years, how much will she accumulate? Treat each ten-year period as a separate annuity. After the ten years of an annuity, then it will continue to grow at compound interest for the remaining years of the 30 years.

14-2 Accumulating Money

Joseph reads a lot about people who are success oriented. He loves to learn about courage, risk taking, and as he describes it, "the road less traveled." His local bookstore has a large business section where he has found biographies of entrepreneurs and maverick corporate leaders. He also finds fascinating some of the books he has seen on financial planning and ways to accumulate wealth. One interesting savings plan he read about challenges the reader to put aside one full paycheck at the end of the year as a "holiday present to yourself." Joseph had never thought about saving in that way, and wondered if it would really accumulate much savings.

1. He decided to test the numbers by seeing how much money he would accumulate by a retirement age of 65 if he put one paycheck away at the end of each year. Right now that would mean depositing $1,000 at year-end for the next 35 years. Assuming he makes one yearly deposit of $1,000 at 5% compounded annually, how much interest would he earn?

2. Joseph was surprised at how large the sum would be and then realized that he would be able to put more money away in future years because most likely, his salary would go up. He also thought that he could invest the money over the long term at a higher interest rate, so he redid the calculations with a $1,500 annual year-end deposit, at 8% for 35 years. What was his result?

3. Joseph was amazed at how much he could save in this manner and decided to design a detailed savings plan based on projected yearly increases. He realized that he could not start depositing $1,500 now, but that he would be able to deposit more than that in the future. If he were able to deposit $1,000 at the end of each year for the next 5 years at 8% compounded annually, $1,500 at the end of years 6–10 at 8% compounded annually, and $2,000 at the end of years 11–35 at 5% compounded annually, how much would he accumulate at the end of 35 years? Assume that any balances from earlier depositing periods would continue to earn the same rate of annual interest. Use the tables for future value of annuities and compound amount.

4. By how much does the result differ from the amount calculated above for $1,500 deposited for 35 years? What accounts for the difference?

5. If Joseph decided that he wanted to have $300,000 accumulated in 30 years by making an annual payment at the end of each year that would earn 12% compounded annually, what would his sinking fund payment be? Use the appropriate table to determine the answer.

14-3 Certified Financial Planner

After completing his Certified Financial Planner designation (CFP), Andre was excited about the prospects of working with small business owners and their employees regarding retirement planning. Andre wanted to show the value of an annuity program as one of the viable investment options in a salary reduction retirement plan. In addition, he wanted to demonstrate the substantial tax benefits that annuities can provide. For instance, qualified annuities (by definition) not only reduce your current taxable salary, they also accumulate earnings on a tax-deferred basis—meaning you don't pay taxes on the earnings until they are withdrawn. Andre was developing a spreadsheet to show the way that annuities could grow using various rates of return.

1. If an individual put the equivalent of $50 per month, or $600 annually into an ordinary annuity, how much money would accumulate in 20 years at 3% compounded annually? How much at 5%?

2. Using the same information from Exercise 1 and assuming a 25% tax bracket, what would be the net effect of investing at 8% for 20 years if taxes on the earnings were paid from the investment fund each year? How would this compare if no taxes had to be paid, such as in a tax-deferred annuity at 8% for 20 years?

3. Jessica, a 25-year-old client of Andre's, wants to retire by age 65 with $1,000,000. How much would she have to invest annually assuming a 6% rate of return?

4. Jessica decides that 40 years is just too long to work, and she thinks that she can do much better than 6%. She decides that she wants to accumulate $1,000,000 by age 55 using a variable annuity earning 12%. How much will she have to invest annually to achieve this goal? Do you think that 12% is a reasonable interest rate to use? Why or why not?

CHAPTER 16 | Mortgages

Real Estate Tax Benefits

For most individuals, owning an affordable home is the American dream, but did you know that borrowing to pay for one is a taxpayer's dream? Home mortgage interest is deductible on your income taxes if you itemize deductions. You can deduct the interest on up to $1 million of home mortgage debt, whether it is used to purchase a first or a second home. You can also deduct the interest on up to $100,000 of home equity debt, even if you don't use the money for home improvements. What could the home mortgage deduction mean to you? What follows is an example of the potential tax savings for Devin, age 27.

Devin rents a home at a cost of $1,200 per month. He is single with no children and takes the standard deduction on his income taxes. His adjusted gross income is $50,000. He has $3,500 in state income tax withheld from his paychecks throughout the year, but doesn't qualify for any other itemized deductions. Devin's federal income tax liability for 2011 will look something like this:

Adjusted gross income:	$50,000
Less standard deduction (single):	$5,700
Less personal exemption:	$3,650
Taxable income	$40,650

Devin's 2011 federal income tax is $6,356

However, if Devin purchases a home with a monthly mortgage payment of $1,200, his tax liability is lowered. At the end of the year Devin will receive a Form 1098 from his mortgage company that shows how much of his mortgage payments for the year went to mortgage interest. In this case, Devin's 1098 for the year 2011 shows that he paid $11,400 in mortgage interest. Devin also paid $2,500 in real estate taxes on his home in 2011. His federal income tax liability for 2011 will look something like this:

Adjusted gross income:	$50,000
Less itemized deduction (state taxes):	$3,500
Less itemized deduction (real estate taxes):	$2,500
Less itemized deduction (mortgage interest):	$11,400
Less personal exemption:	$3,650
Taxable income	$28,950

Devin's 2011 federal income tax is $3,929

In this example, Devin saves $2,427 in federal income taxes, nearly enough to pay for his real estate taxes of $2,500. In addition, his monthly housing cost stays the same and he owns his home rather than renting. Good deal, Devin!

LEARNING OUTCOMES

16-1 Mortgage Payments
1. Find the monthly mortgage payment.
2. Find the total interest on a mortgage and the PITI.

16-2 Amortization Schedules and Qualifying Ratios
1. Prepare a partial amortization schedule of a mortgage.
2. Calculate qualifying ratios.

A corresponding Business Math Case Video for this chapter, *The Real World: Video Case: Should I Buy a House?* can be found online at www.pearsonhighered.com\cleaves.

16-1 MORTGAGE PAYMENTS

LEARNING OUTCOMES
1 Find the monthly mortgage payment.
2 Find the total interest on a mortgage and the PITI.

The purchase of a home is one of the most costly purchases individuals or families make in a lifetime. A home is a type of "real" property. **Real estate** or **real property** is land plus any permanent improvements to the land. The improvements can be water or sewage systems, homes, commercial buildings, or any type of structure. Most individuals must borrow money to pay for the real property. These loans are referred to as **mortgages** because the lending agency requires that the real property be held as **collateral**. If the payments are not made as scheduled, the lending agency can take possession of the property and sell it to pay against the loan.

As a home buyer makes payments on a mortgage, the home buyer builds equity in the home. The home buyer's **equity** is the difference between the expected selling price of a home or **market value** and the balance owed on the home. A home may increase or decrease in value as a result of economic changes and average prices of other homes in the neighborhood. This change in value also changes the owner's equity in the home.

A home buyer may select from several types of first mortgages. A **first mortgage** is the primary mortgage on a home and is ordinarily made at the time of purchase of the home. The agency holding the first mortgage has the first right to the proceeds up to the amount of the mortgage and settlement fees from the sale of the home if the homeowner fails to make required payments.

One type of first mortgage is the **conventional mortgage**. Money for a conventional mortgage is usually obtained through a mortgage lender or a bank. These loans are not insured by a government program. Two types of conventional mortgages are the *fixed-rate mortgage* (FRM) and the *adjustable-rate mortgage* (ARM). The rate of interest on the loan for a **fixed-rate mortgage** remains the same for the entire time of the loan. Fixed-rate mortgages have several payment options. The number of years of the loan may vary, but 15- and 30-year loans are the most common. The home buyer makes the same payment (principal plus interest) each month of the loan. Another option is the **biweekly mortgage**. The home buyer makes 26 equal payments each year rather than 12. This method builds equity more quickly than the monthly payment method.

Another option for fixed-rate loans is the **graduated payments mortgage**. The home buyer makes small payments at the beginning of the loan and larger payments at the end. Home buyers who expect their income to rise may choose this option.

The rate of interest on a loan for an **adjustable-rate mortgage** may escalate (increase) or de-escalate (decrease) during the time of the loan. The rate of an adjustable-rate mortgage depends on the prime lending rate of most banks.

Several government agencies insure the repayment of first mortgage loans. Loans with this insurance include those made under the **Federal Housing Administration (FHA)** and the **Veterans Administration (VA)**. These loans may be obtained through a savings and loan institution, a bank, or a mortgage lending company and are insured by a government program.

Interest paid on home loans is an allowable deduction on personal federal income tax under certain conditions. For this reason, many homeowners choose to borrow money for home improvements, college education, and the like by making an additional loan using the real property as collateral. This type of loan is a **second mortgage** or an **equity line of credit** and is made against the equity in the home. In the case of a loan default, the second mortgage lender has rights to the proceeds of the sale of the home *after* the first mortgage has been paid.

1 Find the monthly mortgage payment.

The repayment of a loan in equal installments that are applied to principal and interest over a specific period of time is called the **amortization** of the loan. To calculate the **monthly mortgage payment**, it is customary to use a table, a formula, a business or financial calculator that has the formula programmed into the calculator, or computer software. The monthly payment table gives the factor that is multiplied by the dollar amount of the loan in thousands to give the total monthly payment, including principal and interest. A portion of a monthly payment table is shown in Table 16-1.

The interest rate for first mortgages has fluctuated between 3% and 8% for the past few years. Second mortgage rates are generally higher than first mortgage rates.

Real estate or real property: land plus any permanent improvements to the land.

Mortgage: a loan in which real property is used to secure the debt.

Collateral: the property that is held as security on a mortgage.

Equity: the difference between the expected selling price and the balance owed on property.

Market value: the expected selling price of a property.

First mortgage: the primary mortgage on a property.

Conventional mortgage: mortgage that is not insured by a government program.

Fixed-rate mortgage: the interest rate for the mortgage remains the same for the entire loan.

Biweekly mortgage: payment is made every two weeks for 26 payments per year.

Graduated payments mortgage: payments at the beginning of the loan are smaller and they increase during the loan.

Adjustable-rate mortgage: the interest rate may change during the time of the loan.

Federal Housing Administration (FHA): a governmental agency within the U.S. Department of Housing and Urban Development (HUD) that insures residential mortgage loans. To receive an FHA loan, specific construction standards must be met and the lender must be approved.

Veterans Administration (VA): a governmental agency that guarantees the repayment of a loan made to an eligible veteran. The loans are also called GI loans.

Second mortgage: a mortgage in addition to the first mortgage that is secured by the real property.

Equity line of credit: a revolving, open-end account that is secured by real property.

Amortization: the process for repaying a loan through equal payments at a specified rate for a specific length of time.

Monthly mortgage payment: the amount of the equal monthly payment that includes interest and principal.

TABLE 16-1
Monthly Payment of Principal and Interest per $1,000 of Amount Financed

Years financed	4.00%	4.25%	4.50%	4.75%	5.00%	5.25%	5.50%	5.75%	6.00%	6.25%	6.50%	6.75%	7.00%	7.25%	7.50%	7.75%
10	10.12	10.24	10.36	10.48	10.61	10.73	10.85	10.98	11.10	11.23	11.35	11.48	11.61	11.74	11.87	12.00
12	8.76	8.88	9.00	9.12	9.25	9.37	9.50	9.63	9.76	9.89	10.02	10.15	10.28	10.42	10.55	10.69
15	7.40	7.52	7.65	7.78	7.91	8.04	8.17	8.30	8.44	8.57	8.71	8.85	8.99	9.13	9.27	9.41
17	6.76	6.89	7.02	7.15	7.29	7.42	7.56	7.69	7.83	7.97	8.11	8.25	8.40	8.54	8.69	8.83
20	6.06	6.19	6.33	6.46	6.60	6.74	6.88	7.02	7.16	7.31	7.46	7.60	7.75	7.90	8.06	8.21
22	5.70	5.84	5.97	6.11	6.25	6.39	6.54	6.68	6.83	6.98	7.13	7.28	7.43	7.59	7.75	7.90
25	5.28	5.42	5.56	5.70	5.85	5.99	6.14	6.29	6.44	6.60	6.75	6.91	7.07	7.23	7.39	7.55
30	4.77	4.92	5.07	5.22	5.37	5.52	5.68	5.84	6.00	6.16	6.32	6.49	6.65	6.82	6.99	7.16
35	4.43	4.58	4.73	4.89	5.05	5.21	5.37	5.54	5.70	5.87	6.04	6.21	6.39	6.56	6.74	6.92

Table values show the monthly payment of a $1,000 mortgage for the given number of years at the given annual interest rate if the interest is compounded monthly. Table values can be generated by using the formula: $M = (\$1,000R)/(1 - (1 + R)^{-N})$, where M = monthly payment, R = the monthly interest rate, and N = total number of payments of the loan.

HOW TO
Find the monthly mortgage payment of principal and interest using a per-$1,000 monthly payment table

1. Find the amount financed: Subtract the down payment from the purchase price.
2. Find the number of $1,000 units in the amount financed: Divide the amount financed (from step 1) by $1,000.
3. Locate the table value for the number of years financed and the annual interest rate.
4. Multiply the table value from step 3 by the number of $1,000 units from step 2.

$$\text{Monthly mortgage payment} = \frac{\text{amount financed}}{\$1,000} \times \text{table value}$$

EXAMPLE 1

Lunelle Miller is purchasing a home for $212,000. Home Federal Savings and Loan has approved her loan application for a 30-year fixed-rate loan at 6% annual interest. If Lunelle agrees to pay 20% of the purchase price as a down payment, calculate the monthly payment.

$212,000(0.20) = \$42,400$ Down payment
$212,000 - \$42,400 = \$169,600$ Amount to be financed
$169,600 \div \$1,000 = 169.6$ $1,000 units

Use Table 16-1 to find the factor for financing a loan for 30 years with a 6% annual interest rate. This factor is 6.00.

Multiply the number of thousands times the factor.

$$169.6(6.00) = \$1,017.60$$

The monthly payment of $1,017.60 includes the principal and interest.

HOW TO
Find the monthly mortgage payment of principal and interest using a formula

1. Identify the monthly rate (R) as a decimal equivalent, the number of months (N), and the loan principal (P).
2. Substitute the values from step 1 in the formula.

$$M = P\left(\frac{R}{1 - (1 + R)^{-N}}\right)$$

3. Evaluate the formula.

EXAMPLE 2

Use the monthly payment of principal and interest formula to find the monthly payment for Lunelle Miller's loan from Example 1.

$R = \dfrac{6\%}{12} = \dfrac{0.06}{12} = 0.005$ Monthly interest rate

$N = 30(12) = 360$ Total number of payments

$P = \$169{,}600$ Amount financed

$M = P\left(\dfrac{R}{1 - (1 + R)^{-N}}\right)$ Substitute known values.

$M = \$169{,}600\left(\dfrac{0.005}{1 - (1 + 0.005)^{-360}}\right)$

$M = \$169{,}600\left(\dfrac{0.005}{1 - (1.005)^{-360}}\right)$

$M = \$169{,}600\left(\dfrac{0.005}{1 - (0.166041928)}\right)$

$M = \$169{,}600\left(\dfrac{0.005}{0.833958072}\right)$

$M = \$169{,}600(0.0059955053)$

$M = \$1016.837691$

$M = \$1{,}016.84$

Calculator sequence:

169600 [(] .005 [)] [÷] [(] 1 [−] [(] 1 [+] .005 [)] [^] [(] [(−)] 360 [)] [)]
[ENTER] ⇒ 1016.837691

On many calculators entering a negative number like −360 requires using a special key [(−)].

The monthly payment of $1,016.84 includes the principal and interest.

Note that the monthly payment using the table value of 6.00 compared to the formula calculation of 0.0059955053 times 1,000 or 5.9955053 causes a variation in the monthly payment.

HOW TO

Find the monthly payment of principal and interest using a calculator application

Values for Example 1 are used for illustration.

TI BA II Plus:

	Keys:	Display:	
Set decimals to two places if necessary.	2nd [FORMAT] 2 ENTER	DEC=	2.00
Reset TMV variables.	2nd [RESET] ENTER	RST	0.00
Set payments per year to 12.	2nd [P/Y] 12 ENTER	P/Y=	12.00
Return to standard calculator mode.	2nd [QUIT]		0.00
Enter number of years. using payment multiplier.	30 2nd [xP/Y] N	N=	360.00
Enter interest rate.	6 I/Y	I/Y=	6.00
Enter loan amount.	169600 PV	PV=	169,600.00
Compute payment.	CPT PMT	PMT=	−1,016.84

The monthly payment is $1,016.84. Recall that *amounts paid out* are given as negative amounts.

The discrepancy in the table calculations and the calculator calculations is from table values being rounded to the nearest cent.

TI-84:

Change to 2 fixed decimal places.	MODE [↓] [→] [→] [→] ENTER
Select Finance Application.	APPS 1:Finance ENTER
Select TVM Solver.	ENTER

Use the arrows keys to move cursor to appropriate variables and enter amounts. Enter 0 for unknowns.

Press 360 ENTER to store 360 months to N.
Press 6 ENTER to store 6% per year to I%.
Press 169600 ENTER to store $169,600 to PV.
Press 0 ENTER to leave PMT unassigned.
Press 0 ENTER to leave FV unassigned.
Press 12 ENTER to store 12 payments/periods per year to P/Y and C/Y will automatically change to 12.
PMT: **END** should be highlighted.

Use up arrow to move cursor up to PMT in the middle of the screen. Press ALPHA [SOLVE] to solve for the monthly payment.

```
N=          360.00
I%=           6.00
PV=      169600.00
■PMT=     −1016.84
FV=           0.00
P/Y=         12.00
C/Y=         12.00
PMT:END BEGIN
```

✓ STOP AND CHECK

Use Table 16-1, the formula, or a calculator application.

1. Natalie Bradley is purchasing a home for $148,500 and has been preapproved for a 30-year fixed-rate loan of 5.75% annual interest. If Natalie pays 20% of the purchase price as a down payment, what will her principal-plus-interest payment be?

2. Find the monthly payment for a home loan of $160,000 using a 20-year fixed-rate mortgage at 5.5%.

3. Find the monthly payment for a home loan of $160,000 using a 25-year fixed-rate mortgage at 5.5%.

4. Find the monthly payment for a home loan of $160,000 using a 30-year fixed-rate mortgage at 5.5%.

2 Find the total interest on a mortgage and the PITI.

Often, a buyer wants to know the total amount of interest that will be paid during the entire loan.

HOW TO   Find the total interest on a mortgage

1. Find the total of the payments: Multiply the number of payments by the amount of the payment (principal + interest).
2. Subtract the amount financed from the total of the payments.

Total interest = number of payments × amount of payment − amount financed

EXAMPLE 3

Calculate the total interest paid on the fixed-rate loan of $169,600 for 30 years at 6% interest rate using the payment amount found in Example 1.

Total interest = number of payments × amount of payment − amount financed
= 30(12)($1,017.60) − $169,600
= $366,336.00 − $169,600
= $196,736.00

The total interest is $196,736.00.

540 Quantitative Methods for Business

Points: a one-time payment to the lender made at closing that is a percentage of the total loan.

Mortgage closing costs: fees charged for services that must be performed to process and close a home mortgage loan.

Good faith estimate: an estimate of the mortgage closing costs that lenders are required to provide to the buyer in writing prior to the loan closing date.

Escrow: an account for holding the part of a monthly payment that is to be used to pay taxes and insurance. The amount accumulates and the lender pays the taxes and insurance from this account as they are due.

PITI: the adjusted monthly payment that includes the principal, interest, taxes, and insurance.

The three preceding examples show how to calculate the monthly payment and the total interest for a mortgage loan. There are other costs associated with purchasing a home. Lending companies may require the borrower to pay **points** at the time the loan is made or closed. Payment of points is a one-time payment of a percentage of the loan that is an additional cost of making the mortgage. One point is 1%, two points is 2%, and so on.

Fees charged for services that must be performed to process and close a home mortgage loan are called **mortgage closing costs**. Examples of these costs include credit reports, surveys, inspections, appraisals, legal fees, title insurance, and taxes. Even though these fees are paid when the loan is closed, lenders are required by law to disclose to the buyer in writing the estimated mortgage closing costs prior to the closing date. This estimate is known as the **good faith estimate**. Some fees are paid by the buyer and some by the seller. Average closing costs for most home purchases are about 6% of the loan amount.

Because the lending agency must be assured that the property taxes and insurance are paid on the property, the annual costs of these items may be prorated each year and added to the monthly payment for that year. These funds are held in **escrow** until the taxes or insurance payment is due, at which time the lending agency makes the payment for the homeowner. These additional costs make the monthly payment more than just the principal and interest payment we found in the preceding examples. The adjusted monthly payment that includes the principal, interest, taxes, and insurance is abbreviated as **PITI**.

HOW TO Find the total PITI payment

1. Find the principal and interest portion of the monthly payment.
2. Find the monthly taxes by dividing the annual taxes by 12.
3. Find the monthly insurance by dividing the annual insurance by 12.
4. Find the sum of the monthly principal, interest, taxes, and insurance.

EXAMPLE 4

Find the total PITI payment for Lunelle Miller's loan from Example 1 if her annual taxes are $1,985 and her annual homeowner's insurance is $960.

$1,017.60	Monthly principal and interest found in Example 1
$1,985 ÷ 12 = $165.4166667	Monthly taxes
$960 ÷ 12 = $80.00	Monthly insurance

PITI = $1,017.60 + $165.42 + $80.00
     = $1,263.02

The total PITI payment is $1,263.02.

EXAMPLE 5

Qua Wau is trying to determine whether to accept a 25-year 6.5% mortgage or a 20-year 6% mortgage on the house he is planning to buy. He needs to finance $125,700 and has planned to budget $1,000 monthly for his payment of principal and interest. Which mortgage should Qua choose?

What You Know	What You Are Looking For
Amount financed: $125,700 Annual interest rate: 6.5% for 25 years and 6% for 20 years Monthly budget allowance for payment: $1,000	Monthly payment and total cost for 25-year mortgage and monthly payment and total cost for 20-year mortgage. Which mortgage should Qua choose?

Solution Plan

Number of $1,000 units of amount financed = amount financed ÷ $1,000
Monthly payment = number of $1,000 units of amount financed × table value
Total cost = monthly payment × 12 × number of years financed

Solution

Number of $1,000 units financed = $125,700 ÷ $1,000
                                = 125.7

DID YOU KNOW?

You should shop for a home mortgage just as you would shop for an automobile. Many factors go into determining the interest rate and other terms of a mortgage. Mortgages over longer periods of time usually have higher interest rates but the monthly payment will be lower. However, you will pay much more interest for mortgages of longer periods of time. Your credit rating and score are important factors in determining the interest rate of your mortgage. Sometimes adjustable rate mortgages have lower interest rates to begin than fixed rate mortgages but the interest rate can change over time, thus changing your monthly payment amounts. It pays to shop for a home mortgage and learn all of your options before shopping for a home.

25-Year Mortgage
The Table 16-1 value for 25 years and 6.5% is $6.75.

Monthly payment = number of $1,000 units financed × table value
= 125.7($6.75)
= $848.48

Total cost = monthly payment × 12 × number of years financed
= $848.48(12)(25)
= $254,544.00

20-Year Mortgage
The Table 16-1 value for 20 years and 6% is $7.16.

Monthly payment = number of $1,000 units financed × table value
= 125.7($7.16)
= $900.01

Total cost = monthly payment × 12 × years financed
= $900.01(12)(20)
= $216,002.40

The monthly payment for the 25-year mortgage is $848.48 for a total cost of $254,544.00. The monthly payment for the 20-year mortgage is $900.01 for a total cost of $216,002.40.

Conclusion

Qua's budget of $1,000 monthly can cover either monthly payment. He would save $38,541.60 over the 20-year period if he chooses the 20-year plan. That is the plan he should choose. Other considerations that could impact his decision would be the return on an investment of the difference in the monthly payments ($51.53) if an annuity were started with the difference. Also, will the addition of the taxes and insurance to the monthly payment (PITI) be more than he can manage?

STOP AND CHECK

1. Find the monthly payment on a home mortgage of $195,000 at 4.25% annual interest for 17 years.

2. How much interest is paid on the mortgage in Exercise 1?

3. The annual insurance premium on the home in Exercise 1 is $1,080 and the annual property tax is $1,252. Find the adjusted monthly payment including principal, interest, taxes, and insurance (PITI).

4. Marcella Cannon can budget $1,200 monthly for a house note (not including taxes and insurance). The home she has fallen in love with would have a $185,400 mortgage. She can finance the loan for 15 years at 5.75% or 30 years at 6.25%. Which terms should she choose to best fit her budget?

16-1 SECTION EXERCISES

SKILL BUILDERS

Find the indicated amounts for the fixed-rate mortgages.

	Purchase price of home	Down payment	Mortgage amount	Interest rate	Years	Monthly payment per $1,000	Mortgage payment	Total paid for mortgage	Interest paid
1.	$100,000	$0		4.75%	30				
2.	$183,000	$13,000		5.50%	30				
3.	$95,000	$8,000		5.75%	25				
4.	$125,500	20%		4.25%	20				
5.	$495,750	18%		5.00%	35				
6.	$83,750	15%		6%	22				

APPLICATIONS

7. Stephen Black has just purchased a home for $155,000. Northridge Mortgage Company has approved his loan application for a 30-year fixed-rate loan at 5.00%. Stephen has agreed to pay 25% of the purchase price as a down payment. Find the down payment, amount of mortgage, and monthly payment.

8. Find the total interest Stephen will pay if he pays the loan on schedule.

9. If Stephen made the same loan for 20 years, how much interest would he save?

10. How much would Stephen's monthly payment increase for a 20-year mortgage over a 30-year mortgage?

11. The annual insurance premium on Maria Snyder's home is $2,074 and the annual property tax is $1,403. If her monthly principal and interest payment is $1,603, find the adjusted monthly payment including principal, interest, taxes, and insurance (PITI).

12. Susan Blair has a 25-year home mortgage of $208,917 at 4.75% interest and will pay $1,798 annual insurance premium. Her annual property tax will be $2,106. Find her monthly PITI payment.

13. Use the formula or a calculator application to find the monthly payment on a home mortgage of $276,834 at 4.776% interest for 25 years.

14. Use the formula or a calculator application to find the monthly payment on a home mortgage of $192,050 at 5.125% interest for 30 years.

16-2 AMORTIZATION SCHEDULES AND QUALIFYING RATIOS

LEARNING OUTCOMES
1. Prepare a partial amortization schedule of a mortgage.
2. Calculate qualifying ratios.

1 Prepare a partial amortization schedule of a mortgage.

Amortization schedule: a table that shows the balance of principal and interest for each payment of the mortgage.

Homeowners are sometimes given an **amortization schedule** that shows the amount of principal and interest for each payment of the loan. With some loan arrangements, extra amounts paid with the monthly payment are credited against the principal, allowing for the mortgage to be paid sooner.

HOW TO Prepare an amortization schedule of a mortgage

1. For the first month:
   (a) Find the interest portion of the first monthly payment (principal and interest portion only):

   Interest portion of the first monthly payment = original principal × monthly interest rate

   (b) Find the principal portion of the monthly payment:

   Principal portion of the first monthly payment = monthly payment − interest portion of the first monthly payment

   (c) Find the first end-of-month principal:

   First end-of-month principal = original principal − principal portion of the first monthly payment

2. For the interest portion, principal portion, and end-of-month principal for each remaining month in turn:
   (a) Find the interest portion of the monthly payment:

   Interest portion of the monthly payment = previous end-of-month principal × monthly interest rate

   (b) Find the principal portion of the monthly payment:

   Principal portion of the monthly payment = monthly payment − interest portion of the monthly payment

   (c) Find the end-of-month principal:

   End-of-month principal = previous end-of-month principal − principal portion of the monthly payment

EXAMPLE 1

Complete the first two rows of the amortization schedule for Lunelle's mortgage of $69,600 at 7% annual interest for 30 years. The monthly payment for interest and principal was found to be $462.84.

First month

$$\text{Interest portion of monthly payment} = \text{original principal} \times \text{monthly rate}$$
$$= \$69{,}600 \left(\frac{0.07}{12}\right)$$
$$= \$406.00$$

Principal portion of monthly payment = monthly payment (without insurance and taxes) − interest portion of monthly payment
= $462.84 − $406.00 = $56.84

End-of-month principal = previous end-of-month principal − principal portion of monthly payment
= $69,600 − $56.84 = $69,543.16

Second month

$$\text{Interest portion of monthly payment} = \$69{,}543.16\left(\frac{0.07}{12}\right) = \$405.67$$

Principal portion of monthly payment = $462.84 − $405.67 = $57.17
End-of-month principal = $69,543.16 − $57.17 = $69,485.99

The first two rows of an amortization schedule for this loan are shown in the following chart.

Portion of payment applied to:

Month	Monthly payment	Interest [previous end-of-month principal × monthly rate]	Principal [monthly payment − interest portion]	End-of-month principal [previous end-of-month principal − principal portion]
1	$462.84	$406.00	$56.84	$69,543.16
2	$462.84	$405.67	$57.17	$69,485.99

DID YOU KNOW?

Calculator applications can build an amortization schedule one line at a time. However, computer software such as Excel™ is often used to generate an amortization schedule that shows the interest and principal breakdown for each payment of the loan.

STOP AND CHECK

1. Complete two rows of an amortization schedule for Natalie's home mortgage of $118,800 at 5.75% for 30 years if the monthly payment is $693.79.

2. Complete two rows of an amortization schedule for a home mortgage of $160,000 for 20 years at 5.5% with a monthly payment of $1,100.80.

3. Complete three rows of an amortization schedule for a home mortgage of $160,000 at 5.5% for 25 years if the monthly payment is $982.40.

4. Complete rows 4–6 of an amortization schedule for a home mortgage of $160,000 at 5.5% for 30 years if the year 4 beginning principal owed is $159,471.18 and the monthly payment is $908.80.

2 Calculate qualifying ratios.

qualifying ratio: a ratio that lenders use to determine an applicant's capacity to repay a loan.

loan-to-value (LTV) ratio: the amount mortgaged divided by the appraised value of the property.

housing or front-end ratio: monthly housing expenses (PITI) divided by the gross monthly income.

debt-to-income (DTI) or back-end ratio: total fixed monthly expenses divided by the gross monthly income.

Mortgage **qualifying ratios** are the most important factors, after your credit report, that lending institutions examine to determine loan applicants' capacity to repay a loan. The **loan-to-value ratio (LTV)** is found by dividing the amount mortgaged by the appraised value of the property. If this ratio, when expressed as a percent, is more than 80%, the borrower may be required to purchase private mortgage insurance (PMI). The **housing ratio** or **front-end ratio** is found by dividing the monthly housing expenses (PITI) by your gross monthly income. In most cases the housing ratio should not exceed 28%.

The **debt-to-income ratio (DTI)** or **back-end ratio** is found by dividing your fixed monthly expenses by your gross monthly income. The debt-to-income ratio should be no more than 36%. Fixed monthly expenses are monthly housing expenses (PITI plus any other expenses directly associated with home ownership), monthly installment loan payments, monthly revolving credit line payments, alimony and child support, and other fixed monthly expenses. Monthly income includes income from employment, including overtime and commissions, self-employment income, alimony, child support, Social Security, retirement or VA benefits, interest and dividend income, income from trusts, partnerships, and so on.

HOW TO Find the qualifying ratio for a mortgage

1. Select the formula for the desired qualifying ratio.

$$\text{Loan-to-value ratio} = \frac{\text{amount mortgaged}}{\text{appraised value of property}}$$

$$\text{Housing ratio} = \frac{\text{total mortgage payment (PITI)}}{\text{gross monthly income}}$$

$$\text{Debt-to-income ratio} = \frac{\text{total fixed monthly expenses}}{\text{gross monthly income}}$$

2. Evaluate the formula.

EXAMPLE 2
Find the loan-to-value ratio for a home appraised at $250,000 that the buyer will purchase for $248,000. The buyer plans to make a down payment of $68,000.

Amount mortgaged = $248,000 − $68,000 = $180,000
Appraised value = $250,000

$$\text{Loan-to-value ratio} = \frac{\text{Amount mortgaged}}{\text{Appraised value of property}} \quad \text{Substitute values in the formula.}$$

$$\text{Loan-to-value ratio} = \frac{\$180{,}000}{\$250{,}000} \qquad \text{Divide.}$$

Loan-to-value ratio = 0.72 or 72%

The loan-to-value ratio is 72%.

✓ STOP AND CHECK

1. Reed Davis has $84,000 for a down payment on a home and has identified a property that can be purchased for $386,000. The appraised value of the property is $395,000. What is the loan-to-value ratio?

2. If Sheri Rieth has total gross monthly earnings of $5,893 and the total PITI for the loan she wants is $1,482, what is the housing ratio? How does this ratio compare with the desired acceptable ratio?

3. Emily Harrington has $1,675 total fixed monthly expenses and gross monthly income of $4,975. What is the debt-to-income ratio she would use in purchasing a home?

4. Pam Cox expects to pay monthly $1,845 in principal and interest, $74 in homeowner's insurance, and $104 in real estate tax for her home mortgage. Her gross monthly salary is $5,798 and she receives alimony of $200 per month. Find the housing ratio she would have when purchasing the home. Is her ratio favorable?

16-2 SECTION EXERCISES

SKILL BUILDERS

Make an amortization table to show the first two payments for the mortgages in Exercises 1–6.

	Amount of mortgage	Annual interest rate	Years	Monthly payment		Amount of mortgage	Annual interest rate	Years	Monthly payment
1.	$100,000	5.75%	30	$584	2.	$180,000	5.5%	30	$1,022.4

Amount of mortgage	Annual interest rate	Years	Monthly payment		Amount of mortgage	Annual interest rate	Years	Monthly payment
$87,000	5.75%	25	$547.23	4.	$100,400	4.25%	20	$621.48

Amount of mortgage	Annual interest rate	Years	Monthly payment		Amount of mortgage	Annual interest rate	Years	Monthly payment
$406,515	5%	35	$2,052.90	6.	$71,187.50	6%	22	$486.21

APPLICATIONS

7. Justin Wimmer is financing $169,700 for a home at 5.25% interest with a 20-year fixed-rate loan. Find the interest paid and principal paid for each of the first two months of the loan and find the principal owed at the end of the second month.

8. Heike Drechsler is financing $84,700 for a home in the mountains. The 17-year fixed-rate loan has an interest rate of 6%. Create an amortization schedule for the first two months of the loan.

9. Conchita Martinez has made a $210,300 loan for a home near Albany, New York. Her 20-year fixed-rate loan has an interest rate of 5.50%. Create an amortization schedule for the first two payments.

10. Jake Drewrey is financing $142,500 for a ten-year fixed-rate mortgage at 5.75%. Create an amortization schedule for the first two payments.

11. Conchita Martinez will have a monthly interest and principal payment of $1,825.40. Her monthly real estate taxes will be $58.93 and her monthly homeowner's payments will be $84.15. If her gross monthly income is $6,793, find the housing ratio.

12. Jake Drewrey has total fixed monthly expenses of $1,340 and his gross monthly income is $3,875. What is his debt-to-income ratio? How does his ratio compare to the desired ratio?

Mortgages 549

SUMMARY

CHAPTER 16

Learning Outcomes

Section 16-1

1 Find the monthly mortgage payment. (p. 564)

What to Remember with Examples

Find the monthly mortgage payment of principal and interest using a per-$1,000 monthly payment table.

1. Find the amount financed: Subtract the down payment from the purchase price.
2. Find the number of $1,000 units in the amount financed: Divide the amount financed (from step 1) by $1,000.
3. Locate the table value in Table 16-1 for the number of years financed and the annual interest rate.
4. Multiply the table value from step 3 by the number of $1,000 units from step 2.

$$\text{Monthly mortgage payment} = \frac{\text{amount financed}}{\$1,000} \times \text{table value}$$

> Find the monthly payment for a home selling for $90,000 if a 10% down payment is made, payments are made for 30 years, and the annual interest rate is 5.5%.
>
> $90,000(0.1) = $9,000 down payment
> $90,000 − $9,000 = $81,000 mortgage amount
> $81,000 ÷ $1,000 = 81 units of $1,000
>
> The table value for 30 years and 5.5% is $5.68.
> Payment = 81($5.68) = $460.08

Find the monthly mortgage payment of principal and interest using a formula.

1. Identify the monthly rate (R) as a decimal equivalent, the number of months (N), and the loan principal (P).
2. Substitute the values from step 1 in the formula.

$$M = P\left(\frac{R}{1 - (1 + R)^{-N}}\right)$$

3. Evaluate the formula.

> Find the monthly payment for the loan in the previous example.
>
> $R = 0.055/12 = 0.0045833333; N = 360; P = \$81,000$
>
> $$M = P\left(\frac{R}{1 - (1 + R)^{-N}}\right)$$
>
> $$M = 81,000\left(\frac{0.0045833333}{1 - (1 + 0.0045833333)^{-360}}\right)$$
>
> Calculator sequence:
>
> 81000 (.0045833333) ÷ (1 − (1 + .0045833333) ^ ((−) 360))
> ENTER
>
> Display: 459.9090891
> The monthly payment is $459.91.
>
> See pp. 566–567 for instructions for the TI BAII Plus and TI-84.

2 Find the total interest on a mortgage and the PITI. (p. 567)

1. Find the total of the payments: Multiply the number of payments by the amount of the payment (principal + interest).
2. Subtract the amount financed from the total of the payments.

$$\text{Total interest} = \text{number of payments} \times \text{amount of payment} - \text{amount financed}$$

Find the total interest on the mortgage in the preceding example.

$$\begin{aligned}\text{Total interest} &= 30(12)(\$459.91) - \$81{,}000 \\ &= \$165{,}567.60 - \$81{,}000 \\ &= \$84{,}567.60\end{aligned}$$

To find the total PITI payment:

1. Find the principal and interest portion of the monthly payment.
2. Find the monthly taxes by dividing the annual taxes by 12.
3. Find the monthly insurance by dividing the annual insurance by 12.
4. Find the sum of the monthly principal, interest, taxes, and insurance.

Find the total PITI payment for a loan that has monthly principal and interest payments of $2,134, annual taxes of $1,085, and annual homeowners insurance of $1,062.

$2,134   Monthly principal and interest
$1,085 ÷ 12 = $90.41666667   Monthly taxes
$1,062 ÷ 12 = $88.50   Monthly insurance
PITI = $2,134 + $90.42 + $88.50 = $2,312.92

The total PITI payment is $2,312.92.

Section 16-2

1 Prepare a partial amortization schedule of a mortgage. (p. 571)

1. For the first month:
   (a) Find the interest portion of the first monthly payment (principal and interest only):

   Interest portion of the first monthly payment = original principal × monthly interest rate

   (b) Find the principal portion of the monthly payment:

   Principal portion of the first monthly payment = monthly payment − interest portion of first monthly payment

   (c) Find the first end-of-month principal:

   First end-of-month principal = original principal − principal portion of the first monthly payment

2. For each remaining month in turn:
   (a) Find the interest portion of the monthly payment:

   Interest portion of the monthly payment = previous end-of-month principal × monthly interest rate

   (b) Find the principal portion of the monthly payment:

   Principal portion of the monthly payment = monthly payment − interest portion of the monthly payment

   (c) Find the end-of-month principal:

   End-of-month principal = previous end-of-month principal − principal portion of the monthly payment

Complete an amortization schedule for three months of payments on a $90,000 mortgage at 4.25% for 30 years.

$$\begin{aligned}\text{Monthly payment} &= \frac{\$90{,}000}{\$1{,}000} \times \text{table value} \\ &= 90(\$4.92) \\ &= \$442.80\end{aligned}$$

Month 1

$$\text{Interest portion} = \$90{,}000\left(\frac{0.0425}{12}\right)$$
$$= \$318.75$$

$$\text{Principal portion} = \$442.80 - \$318.75$$
$$= \$124.05$$

$$\text{End-of-month principal} = \$90{,}000 - \$124.05$$
$$= \$89{,}875.95$$

Month 2

$$\text{Interest portion} = \$89{,}875.95\left(\frac{0.0425}{12}\right)$$
$$= \$318.31$$

$$\text{Principal portion} = \$442.80 - \$318.31$$
$$= \$124.49$$

$$\text{End-of-month principal} = \$89{,}875.95 - \$124.49$$
$$= \$89{,}751.46$$

Month 3

$$\text{Interest portion} = \$89{,}751.46\left(\frac{0.0425}{12}\right)$$
$$= \$317.87$$

$$\text{Principal portion} = \$442.80 - \$317.87$$
$$= \$124.93$$

$$\text{End-of-month principal} = \$89{,}751.46 - \$124.93$$
$$= \$89{,}626.53$$

Portion of payment applied to:

Month	Monthly payment	Interest	Principal	End-of-month principal
1	$442.80	$318.75	$124.05	$89,875.95
2	$442.80	318.31	124.49	89,751.46
3	$442.80	317.87	124.93	89,626.53

2 Calculate qualifying ratios. (p. 573)

Find the qualifying ratio for a mortgage.

1. Select the formula for the desired qualifying ratio.

$$\text{Loan-to-value ratio} = \frac{\text{amount mortgaged}}{\text{appraised value of property}}$$

$$\text{Housing ratio} = \frac{\text{total mortgage payment (PITI)}}{\text{gross monthly income}}$$

$$\text{Debt-to-income ratio} = \frac{\text{total fixed monthly expenses}}{\text{gross monthly income}}$$

2. Evaluate the formula.

Find the loan-to-value ratio for a home appraised at $398,400 that the buyer will purchase for $398,000. The buyer plans to make a down payment of $100,000.

Amount mortgaged = $398,000 − $100,000 = $298,000

Appraised value = $398,400

$$\text{Loan-to-value ratio} = \frac{\text{amount mortgaged}}{\text{appraised value of property}} \quad \text{Substitute values in the formula.}$$

$$\text{Loan-to-value ratio} = \frac{\$298{,}000}{\$398{,}400} \quad \text{Divide.}$$

Loan-to-value ratio = 0.7479919679 or 75%

EXERCISES SET A

CHAPTER 16

Find the monthly payment.

Mortgage amount	Annual percentage rate	Years
1. $287,500	5.75%	20
2. $146,800	5.25%	30
3. $152,300	6.25%	25
4. $113,400	5%	15

EXCEL 5. Find the total interest paid for the mortgage in Exercise 1.

EXCEL 6. Find the total interest paid for the mortgage in Exercise 2.

EXCEL 7. Find the total interest paid for the mortgage in Exercise 3.

EXCEL 8. Find the total interest paid for the mortgage in Exercise 4.

9. Create an amortization schedule for the first two months' payments on a mortgage of $487,700 with an interest rate of 6% and monthly payment of $2,926.20.

10. Louise Grantham is buying a home for $198,500 with a 20% down payment. She has a 5.75% loan for 25 years. Create an amortization schedule for the first two months of her loan.

11. James Author's monthly principal plus interest payment is $1,565.74 and his annual homeowner's insurance premium is $1,100. His annual real estate taxes total $1,035. Find his PITI payment.

12. Find the loan-to-value ratio for a home appraised at $583,620 that the buyer will purchase for $585,000. The buyer plans to make a down payment of $175,000.

13. Find James Author's housing ratio if his PITI is $1,743.66 and his gross monthly income is $6,310.

14. Find Julia Rholes' debt-to-income ratio if her fixed monthly expenses are $1,836 and her gross monthly income is $4,934.

15. Use the formula or a calculator application to find the monthly payment on a home mortgage of $645,730 at 4.862% interest for 20 years.

16. Use the formula or a calculator application to find the monthly payment on a home mortgage of $219,275 at 5.265% interest for 30 years.

EXERCISES SET B

CHAPTER 16

Find the monthly payment.

Mortgage amount	Annual percentage rate	Years
1. $487,700	6%	30
2. $212,983	6.75%	15
3. $82,900	4.5%	35
4. $179,500	4.0%	17

5. Find the total interest paid for the mortgage in Exercise 1.

6. Find the total interest paid for the mortgage in Exercise 2.

7. Find the total interest paid for the mortgage in Exercise 3.

8. Find the total interest paid for the mortgage in Exercise 4.

9. Create a partial amortization schedule for the first two payments on a mortgage of $152,300 at 6.25% that has a monthly payment of $1,005.18 and is financed for 25 years.

10. Mary Starnes is paying $14,000 down on a house that costs $138,200 and she has a 6% loan for 30 years. Create a partial amortization table for the first two months of her mortgage.

11. Jerry Corless' monthly principal plus interest payment is $2,665.45 and his annual homeowner's insurance premium is $1,320. His annual real estate taxes total $1,325. Find his PITI payment.

12. Find the loan-to-value ratio for a home appraised at $135,230 that the buyer will purchase for $135,000. The buyer plans to make a down payment of $25,000.

13. Find Jerry Corless' housing ratio if his PITI is $2,885.87 and his gross monthly income is $8,310.

14. Find Elizabeth Herrington's debt-to-income ratio if her fixed monthly expenses are $1,236 and her gross monthly income is $4,194.

15. Use the formula or a calculator application to find the monthly payment on a home mortgage of $315,200 at 4.658% interest for 25 years.

16. Use the formula or a calculator application to find the monthly payment on a home mortgage of $327,790 at 5.402% interest for 35 years.

PRACTICE TEST — CHAPTER 16

Mortgages

1. Find the table value for a 25-year mortgage at 6%.

2. Find the monthly payment on a mortgage of $230,000 for 30 years at 7.5%.

3. Find the total amount of interest that will be paid on the mortgage in Exercise 2.

4. What percent of the mortgage in Exercise 2 is the interest paid?

Hullett Houpt is purchasing a home for $197,000. He will finance the mortgage for 15 years and pay 7% interest on the loan. He makes a down payment that is 20% of the purchase price. Use Table 16-1 as needed.

5. Find the down payment.

6. Find the amount of the mortgage.

7. If Hullett is required to pay two points for making the loan, how much will the points cost?

8. Find the monthly payment that includes principal and interest.

9. Find the total interest Hullett will pay over the 15-year period.

10. Calculate the monthly payment and the total interest Hullett would have to pay if he decided to make the loan for 30 years instead of 15 years.

11. How much interest can be saved by paying for the home in 15 years rather than 30 years?

12. Find the interest portion and principal portion for the first payment of Hullett's 15-year loan.

13. Make an amortization schedule for the first three payments of the 15-year loan Hullett could make.

14. Make an amortization schedule for the first three payments of the 30-year loan Hullett could make.

15. Find Leshaundra's debt-to-income ratio if her fixed monthly expenses are $1,972 and her gross monthly income is $5,305.

16. Use the formula or a calculator application to find the monthly payment on a home mortgage of $249,500 at 5.389% interest for 30 years.

CRITICAL THINKING

CHAPTER 16

1. How does a mortgage relate to a sinking fund?

2. For a mortgage of a given amount and rate, what happens to the total amount of interest paid if the number of years in the mortgage increases?

3. How can you reduce your monthly payment on a home mortgage?

4. Describe the process for finding the monthly payment for a mortgage of a given amount at a given rate for a given period.

Challenge Problem

Bob Owen is closing a real estate transaction on a farm in Yocona, Mississippi, for $385,900. His mortgage holder requires a 25% down payment and he also must pay $60.00 to record the deed, $100 in attorney's fees for document preparation, and $350 for an appraisal report. Bob will also have to pay a 1.5% loan origination fee. Bob chooses a 35-year mortgage at 7%. (a) How much cash will Bob need to close on the property? (b) How much will Bob's mortgage be? (c) What is Bob's monthly payment on the property?

CASE STUDIES

16.1 Home Buying: A 30-Year Commitment?

Shantel and Kwamie are planning to buy their first home. Although they are excited about the prospect of being homeowners, they are also a little frightened. A mortgage payment for the next 30 years sounds like a huge commitment. They visited a few new developments and scanned the real estate listings of preowned homes, but they really have no idea how much a mortgage payment would be on a $150,000, $175,000, or $200,000 loan. They have come to you for advice.

1. After you explain to them that they can borrow money at different rates and for different amounts of time, Shantel and Kwamie ask you to complete a chart indicating what the monthly mortgage payment would be under some possible interest rates and borrowing periods. They also want to know what their total interest would be on each if they chose a 25-year loan at 5% interest. Complete the chart.

Amount borrowed	4.5% 15 year	4.75% 20 year	5.0% 25 year	5.25% 30 year	Total interest paid on 25-year loan
$150,000					
$175,000					
$200,000					

2. If Shantel and Kwamie made a down payment of $20,000 on a $175,000 home, what would be their monthly mortgage payment assuming they finance for 25 years at 5.0%? How much would they save on each monthly payment by making the down payment? How much interest would they save over the life of the loan?

16.2 Investing in Real Estate

Jacob had finally found the house that he was looking for, and was anxious to make an offer. He knew that one of the keys to successful real estate investing was to purchase properties for at least 30% below market value. He had done his research, and with an asking price of only $124,500, this 2-bedroom ranch-style home was a bargain and well within his price range. The house, though, needed a number of repairs including paint, carpet, appliances, and a new wall to turn an open area into another bedroom. After contacting several contractors, he felt confident that the work could be completed for $12,000. With that figure in mind, Jacob decided that the total cost of the house would be $140,000 or less, including any settlement charges. He just needed to finalize some of the payment details to make sure the house was right for him.

1. By putting 20% down on the house, Jacob can get a 30-year fixed-rate mortgage for 5.25%. Based on a purchase price of $140,000, compute the down payment, and the principal and interest payment for the loan.

2. Although Jacob hopes to have the house sold within a few months, he knows there is a possibility that it will not sell quickly. In that case, he would likely end up keeping it as a rental property. Using the information from Exercise 1 find the total amount of interest that Jacob will pay on the mortgage if he keeps it for the full 30 years.

3. Jacob finds a lender that will offer him 100% financing using an adjustable-rate mortgage based on a 30-year amortization, with a 5-year interest lock at 5.0%. The loan, however, would include a prepayment penalty, which is applied as follows: prepayment penalty is 80% of the balance of the first mortgage, times the interest rate, divided by 2. Compute the new mortgage payment, along with the maximum prepayment penalty. Is it a good idea for Jacob to take this loan? Why or why not?

4. Jacob decides that the 30-year fixed-rate mortgage in Exercise 1 is the best for him. Construct an amortization table for the first three payments of the mortgage. The monthly payment will be $618.24.

CHAPTER 19 | Insurance

The Price of Disaster

Until now, it had been a beautiful summer day. Angela finished work, did some shopping, and was returning from day care with her two young children when she noticed storm clouds approaching. These clouds looked more ominous and threatening than usual. After arriving at home, Angela and the children (Jacob, 10, and Emily, 8) scrambled out and into the house. Angela heard the faint sound of a siren. Straining to hear better, she headed back outside and saw the unimaginable—a massive tornado had formed and was heading straight toward her neighborhood. Dropping her groceries, Angela rushed into the house and had both her children in the shelter of the basement in less than a minute.

The tornado wasn't far behind. Smashing through the neighborhood in a matter of seconds, the full force of the F-3 twister narrowly missed them, resulting only in minor damage to the roof of their house—but left a large limb on top of their car. The twister was gone as quickly as it came. Angela and the children were unharmed, and were able to walk out a lower-level door with little difficulty. It wasn't until they were outside that they realized the devastation to their neighborhood and how truly fortunate they were to be alive!

After the immediate shock subsided, Angela's first thought was about insurance, or more appropriately, her lack of insurance. Money had always been tight and paying for insurance just had not been a priority. Now, it seemed like the most important thing in the world. Angela had homeowners insurance on the house, but had no idea for how much or whether it covered tornadoes. She had liability coverage on the car, but had dropped the collision/comprehensive coverage. And life insurance? She had only the $10,000 policy provided by her employer. Angela knew that she was lucky to be alive. Who would provide for her children if she died? Could she afford to repair her house? Could she replace her car? What should she do next?

LEARNING OUTCOMES

19-1 Life Insurance
1. Estimate life insurance premiums using a rate table.
2. Apply the extended term nonforfeiture option to a cancelled whole-life policy.

19-2 Property Insurance
1. Estimate renters insurance premiums using a rate table.
2. Estimate homeowners insurance premiums using a rate table.
3. Find the compensation with a coinsurance clause.

19-3 Motor Vehicle Insurance
1. Find automobile insurance premiums using rate tables.

Insurance: a form of protection against unexpected financial loss.

Comprehensive policy: insurance policy that protects the insured against several risks.

Insured (policyholder): the individual, organization, or business that carries the insurance or financial protection against loss.

Insurer (underwriter): the insurance company that insures for a specific loss according to contract provisions.

Policy: the contract between the insurer and the insured.

Premium: the amount paid by the insured for the protection provided by the policy.

Face value: the maximum amount of insurance provided by the policy.

Beneficiary: the individual, organization, or business to whom the proceeds of the policy are payable.

Insurance is a form of protection against unexpected financial loss. Businesses and individuals need insurance to help bear the burden of accidents, acts of God that result in large financial losses, and loss of life. Insurance helps distribute the burden of financial loss among those who share the same type of risk. Many types of insurance are available, such as fire, life, homeowners, health, accident, and automobile. Many insurance companies offer a **comprehensive policy** that protects the insured against several risks. The combined rate for a comprehensive policy is usually lower than if each type of protection is purchased separately.

Before we can discuss specific types of insurance, we need to understand some important terms used in the insurance field.

Insured (policyholder)	The individual, organization, or business that carries the insurance or financial protection against loss
Insurer (underwriter)	The insurance company that assures payment for a specific loss according to contract provisions
Policy	The contract between the insurer and the insured
Premium	The amount paid by the insured for the protection provided by the policy
Face value	The maximum amount of insurance provided by the policy
Beneficiary	The individual, organization, or business to whom the proceeds of the policy are payable

19-1 LIFE INSURANCE

LEARNING OUTCOMES

1. Estimate life insurance premiums using a rate table.
2. Apply the extended term nonforfeiture option to a cancelled whole-life policy.

Life insurance: an insurance policy that pays a specified amount to the beneficiary of the policy upon the death of the insured.

Income shortfall: the difference in the total living expenses of a family and the amount of income a family would have after the death of the insured. This shortfall can be used to project the amount of insurance needed by the family.

Life insurance provides financial assistance to the designated beneficiary, surviving spouse, or dependents of the insured in the event of the insured person's death. Knowing the right amount of life insurance to carry is as important as understanding the type of insurance to carry. Life insurance is usually purchased for the purpose of providing income for a family upon the death or disability of the insured person. Some financial planners suggest life insurance coverage should be seven to ten times annual income. Another way to determine the amount of life insurance needed by a family is to determine the difference in the total expenses of a family and the amount of income the family would have after the death of the insured. This difference is sometimes called **income shortfall**.

Although anyone may purchase life insurance, companies often insure the lives of their employees as a fringe benefit of employment. In partnerships, the beneficiary is often the surviving partner. Several types of life insurance policies are available, some of which even function as savings programs. In this section, we look at three types of life insurance policies in common use: *term*, *whole-life*, and *universal life*.

Term insurance: insurance purchased for a certain period of time. At the end of the time period, the policy has no cash value and the insurance ends. If the premium stays the same for the entire term of the insurance, it is called *level* term.

Term insurance is purchased for a certain period of time such as 5, 10, or 20 years. For example, those insured under a 10-year term policy pay premiums for 10 years or until they die, whichever occurs first. If the insured dies during the 10-year period, the beneficiary of the policy receives the face value of the policy. If the insured is still living at the end of the 10-year period, the insurance ends and the policy has no cash value. The insured would then be required to reapply for a new policy, with no guarantee of insurability under the new contract. Term insurance, however, often provides for convertibility to a policy with permanent protection, such as whole-life or universal life. This convertibility option typically does not last for the entire coverage period. The advantage of conversion is that the new policy would be issued at the same rate class as the original term policy, even after a change in insurability. The major advantage of term insurance is that it is the least expensive type of life insurance.

Whole-life (ordinary life) insurance: the insured pays premiums for his or her entire life. At the death of the insured, the beneficiary receives the face value of the policy. If the policy is cancelled, the insured is paid the cash value of the policy.

People who take out **whole-life (ordinary life) insurance** policies agree to pay premiums for their entire lives. At the time of the insured's death, a beneficiary receives the face value of the policy. This type of policy also builds up a cash value. Policyholders who cancel their policy are entitled to a certain sum of money back, depending on the amount that was paid in.

Universal life: provides permanent insurance coverage with flexibility in premium payment, and death benefit options.

Another popular form of life insurance coverage is **universal life**, often referred to as flexible premium life. Universal life provides permanent insurance coverage with greater flexibility in premium payment and the potential for cash accumulation. A universal life policy includes a cash account, which is increased with each premium payment. Interest is paid within the policy (credited) on the account at a rate specified by the company. Mortality charges and administrative costs are then charged against (reduce) the cash account. The surrender value of the policy is the amount remaining in the cash account less applicable surrender charges, if any.

When compared to whole-life coverage, universal life has two major advantages: (1) The internal rate of return of a universal life policy can be higher because it moves with prevailing interest rates (interest sensitive) or the financial markets (equity indexed universal life and variable universal life); and (2) universal life policies provide for greater flexibility, because the owner can discontinue or adjust premiums if the cash value allows it; and death benefits can be increased/decreased, subject to the limitations of the policy.

1 Estimate life insurance premiums using a rate table.

Life insurance rates are typically determined by the age, gender, and health of the insured and the type of policy. Therefore, rate quotes are generally made on an individual basis. Many rate calculators are available on the Internet that can be used for personalized rate quotes. Table 19-1 gives some typical annual premiums for fixed-rate term, whole-life, and universal life insurance that can be used to estimate an annual premium.

DID YOU KNOW?

Life insurance companies use several factors to determine your rate classification. The primary determinants are tobacco/nicotine use, your weight/height ratio, and your family health history. Your driving record and any dangerous vocations or avocations (pilot/hang glider/sky diver) may also play a part in your rate classification. Only those individuals that meet an insurer's strictest standards are eligible for the very best (preferred) rates—typically less than 25% of all applicants.

TABLE 19-1
Estimated Annual Life Insurance Premium Rates per $1,000 of Face Value

| Age | 10-Year Level Term | | | | | | Age | 20-Year Level Term | | | | | |
| | Male | | | Female | | | | Male | | | Female | | |
	PREF	NT	T	PREF	NT	T		PREF	NT	T	PREF	NT	T
20	0.87	1.27	2.28	0.75	1.10	1.88	20	1.09	1.50	2.86	0.91	1.31	2.56
25	0.87	1.27	2.28	0.75	1.10	1.88	25	1.09	1.50	2.86	0.91	1.31	2.56
30	0.87	1.36	2.49	0.75	1.16	2.06	30	1.12	1.61	3.24	0.96	1.42	2.67
35	0.87	1.44	2.73	0.75	1.26	2.23	35	1.17	1.73	3.62	1.02	1.53	2.78
40	1.13	1.96	3.78	1.00	1.57	2.93	40	1.49	2.36	5.38	1.26	2.00	3.77
45	1.51	2.69	5.33	1.38	2.12	4.08	45	2.23	3.73	8.42	1.75	2.92	5.57
50	2.03	3.76	8.08	1.72	2.98	5.78	50	3.45	5.99	12.90	2.59	4.40	8.02
55	2.95	5.61	12.48	2.27	4.44	8.33	55	5.38	9.52	19.15	3.96	6.66	11.45
60	4.61	9.07	20.07	3.46	6.95	12.57	60	8.46	15.15	29.14	6.17	10.36	16.74

| Age | Whole Life | | | | | | Age | Universal Life | | | | | |
| | Male | | | Female | | | | Male | | | Female | | |
	PREF	NT	T	PREF	NT	T		PREF	NT	T	PREF	NT	T
20	8.39	9.02	10.55	7.55	8.12	9.95	20	5.25	5.78	7.17	4.53	4.65	5.97
25	9.51	10.22	12.70	8.65	9.30	11.59	25	6.21	6.69	8.61	5.37	5.61	7.17
30	10.86	11.68	14.77	9.82	10.56	13.48	30	7.41	8.13	10.29	6.45	6.81	8.73
35	12.37	13.30	16.59	10.97	11.80	14.85	35	9.09	9.93	12.69	7.89	8.25	10.77
40	14.42	15.50	19.31	12.54	13.48	16.69	40	11.25	12.33	15.69	9.69	10.17	13.41
45	17.65	18.98	24.03	15.14	16.28	20.43	45	14.01	15.45	19.65	12.09	12.69	16.77
50	22.45	24.14	30.65	19.09	20.53	25.39	50	17.61	19.17	24.45	15.09	16.05	21.33
55	28.67	30.82	39.00	24.11	25.92	30.97	55	22.41	24.57	31.41	18.93	20.25	26.97
60	36.06	38.77	49.39	29.75	31.99	37.25	60	28.77	34.53	43.65	23.97	28.29	37.53

PREF = preferred; NT = non-tobacco; T = tobacco usage

> **HOW TO** Estimate an annual life insurance premium using a rate table
>
> 1. Locate the estimated annual rate in Table 19-1 according to type of policy, age, sex, and rate class.
> 2. Divide the policy face value by $1,000 and multiply the quotient by the rate from step 1.
>
> $$\text{Estimated annual premium} = \frac{\text{face value}}{\$1{,}000} \times \text{rate}$$

EXAMPLE 1 Estimate the annual premium of an insurance policy with a preferred rate class and a face value of $100,000 for a 30-year-old male for (a) a 10-year level term policy; (b) 20-year level term policy; (c) a whole-life policy; (d) a universal life policy.

$$\text{Estimated annual premium} = \frac{\text{face value}}{\$1{,}000} \times \text{rate}$$
$$= \frac{\$100{,}000}{\$1{,}000} \times \text{rate} \quad \text{The face value is \$100,000.}$$
$$= 100 \times \text{rate}$$

Look at Table 19-1 to find the rate for each type of policy.

(a) A 10-year level term policy: 100($0.87) = $87
(b) 20-year level term policy: 100($1.12) = $112
(c) A whole-life policy: 100($10.86) = $1,086
(d) A universal life policy: 100($7.41) = $741

The estimated annual premium for a $100,000 10-year level term policy is $87; for a 20-year level term policy is $112; for a whole-life policy is $1,086; and for a universal life policy is $741.

Since it is often inconvenient to make lump-sum annual payments, most companies allow payments to be made semiannually (twice a year), quarterly (every three months), or monthly for slightly higher rates than would apply on an annual basis. Table 19-2 shows some typical rates for periods of less than one year.

EXAMPLE 2 Use Tables 19-1 and 19-2 to estimate the (a) semiannual, (b) quarterly, and (c) monthly premiums for a $250,000 whole-life policy on a 40-year-old female, using a non-tobacco rate.

$$\text{Annual premium} = \frac{\text{amount of coverage}}{\$1{,}000} \times \text{rate}$$
$$= \left(\frac{\$250{,}000}{\$1{,}000}\right)(\$13.48) \quad \text{The face value is \$250,000. The annual rate, according to Table 19-1, is \$13.48.}$$
$$= 250(\$13.48) = \$3{,}370$$

Find the period rates using Table 19-2.

(a) Semiannual premium: Annual premium × semiannual rate = semiannual premium
$3,370 (51%)
= $3,370 (0.51) = $1,718.70

(b) Quarterly premium: Annual premium × quarterly rate = quarterly premium
$3,370 (26%)
= $3,370 (0.26) = $876.20

(c) Monthly premium   Annual premium × monthly rate = monthly premium
$3,370 (8.75%)
= $3,370 (0.0875) = $294.88

The semiannual premium is $1,718.70, quarterly is $876.20, and monthly is $294.88.

TABLE 19-2
Premium Rates for Periods Less than One Year

Period	Percent of Annual Premium
Semiannually	51.00
Quarterly	26.00
Monthly	8.75

Fixed-time payment insurance: a policy with a specified face value for the insured's entire life with premium payment made for a fixed period of time.

Other types of life insurance are fixed-time payment insurance, fixed-time endowment, and variable life policies. A **fixed-time payment insurance** policy gives a specified face value for the insured's entire life, but premium payments are made only for a fixed period of time. At the

Insurance 567

paid-up insurance: insurance that continues after premiums are no longer paid.

fixed-time endowment insurance: a policy that is a combination insurance and savings plan that is paid for a fixed period of time.

variable life: a policy that builds up a cash reserve that you can invest in any of the choices offered by the insurance company, based on how well those investments are doing.

end of the fixed time, the insured has **paid-up insurance**, that is, the insurance continues after premiums are no longer paid. A **fixed-time endowment insurance** policy is a combination insurance and savings plan. The insured has term insurance protection for the face value of the policy for the fixed time of the policy. At the end of the fixed time, the insured receives the face value of the policy and the insurance ends. The premiums for fixed-term payment and fixed-term endowment policies are significantly higher than the premiums for term or straight-life policies.

Another popular form of permanent life insurance protection is **variable life**. This type of life insurance is "variable" because it allows you to allocate a portion of your premium dollars to a separate account comprised of various investment funds within the insurance company's portfolio, such as an equity fund, a money market fund, a bond fund, or some combination thereof. Hence, the value of the death benefit and the cash value may fluctuate up or down, depending on the performance of the investment portion of the policy.

Which life insurance policy you choose depends on a number of factors, among the most important being the level of coverage needed and affordability. It's difficult to apply a rule of thumb because the amount of life insurance you need depends on factors such as your other sources of income, how many dependents you have, your debts, and your lifestyle. As mentioned at the beginning of this chapter, the general guideline is between seven and ten times your annual salary. What you can afford is based largely on your budget. If you are on a limited budget, then term insurance is probably the best choice for you. If you would like to build cash value but need flexibility, universal life would be best. If you are concerned with guaranteed coverage and can afford the premiums, then whole life is an excellent option. If your salary is important to supporting your family, paying the mortgage or other recurring bills, or sending your kids to college, then purchasing adequate life insurance coverage is an important means to ensure that these financial obligations are covered in the event of your death.

STOP AND CHECK

1. Estimate the annual premium of a 10-year level term insurance policy with a face value of $200,000 for a 20-year-old female using a non-tobacco rate.

2. Use Tables 19-1 and 19-2 to estimate the (a) semiannual, (b) quarterly, and (c) monthly premiums for a $500,000 whole-life insurance policy on a 50-year-old male using a non-tobacco rate.

3. Estimate the monthly premium on a 20-year level term insurance policy of $300,000 for a 60-year-old male who uses tobacco.

4. Estimate the quarterly premium on a universal-life insurance policy for a 30-year-old female who gets a preferred rate. The face value of the policy is $600,000.

2 Apply the extended term nonforfeiture option to a cancelled whole-life policy.

Lapse: the loss of insurance coverage due to nonpayment of premiums.

Nonforfeiture options: the options that are available to a policyholder when payments are discontinued.

Most types of life insurance policies except term insurance build up cash value. If a policyholder decides to cancel a policy or to allow it to **lapse** by not making the required payments, the insured normally has three choices, called **nonforfeiture options**:

1. **Cash Value or Surrender Option.** A policyholder can choose to surrender (give up) a policy and receive its cash value. If the insured wants to maintain the insurance coverage but use the cash value, a loan can be made for the amount of the cash value. The loan must be repaid with interest, or the amount of the loan and interest is deducted from the face value of the policy.

2. **Paid-Up Insurance.** The cash value of the policy is applied to a reduced amount of paid-up insurance. The reduced insurance continues for the entire life of the insured and no additional premiums are paid.

3. **Extended Term Insurance.** The cash value of the policy is applied to a term policy for the same face value as the original policy. The term policy will last as long a time period as the cash value will purchase. If the insured stops paying a policy and does not choose a nonforfeiture option, in most cases this option will be automatically implemented.

568 Quantitative Methods for Business

> **HOW TO** Apply the extended term nonforfeiture option to a cancelled whole-life policy.
>
> 1. Identify the cash value of the cancelled policy.
> 2. Estimate the annual premium for a term policy of the same face value. Use a fixed rate in Table 19-1.
> 3. Determine the number of years of paid-up term insurance.
>
> $$\text{Years of paid-up term insurance} = \frac{\text{cash value of surrendered policy}}{\text{annual premium of term policy}}$$

EXAMPLE 3 Eleanor McLeod, a smoker, started a $100,000 whole-life insurance policy when she was 30 years old. At age 50, she determines that she has a cash value of $20,200 and wants to convert to extended term for the same face value. Using the 20-year level term rates, estimate how long her extended term insurance will last.

Estimated annual term premium: $8.02 per $1,000   50-year-old female; 20-year level term rate

$$\frac{\$100,000}{\$1,000} = 100 \text{ units} \quad \text{Number of insurance units}$$

$$\$8.02(100) = \$802 \quad \text{Annual term rate}$$

$$\text{Years of paid-up term insurance:} \frac{\text{cash value of surrendered policy}}{\text{annual premium of term policy}}$$

$$\frac{\$20,200}{\$802} = 25.18703242 \text{ years}$$

The paid-up term insurance will extend for 25 years.

1. Juanna Makhloufi started a whole-life insurance policy for $300,000 when she was 20 years old. At age 50, the policy has a cash value of $19,340 and Juanna decides to convert the policy to extended term for the same face value. Using 20-year level term non-tobacco rates, estimate the number of years her extended term insurance will last.

2. Byron Johnson, who gets a preferred rate, started a whole-life insurance policy for $500,000 when he was 38 years old. At age 60, the policy has a cash value of $13,208 and Bryon plans to convert the policy to extended term for the same face value. Use 10-year level term rates to estimate the number of years of extended coverage he will have.

3. Frances Johnson, who smokes, started a $250,000 whole-life insurance policy at age 32. Her policy has a cash value of $20,915 at age 50. Use 10-year level term rates to estimate the number of years of extended term coverage she can expect.

4. At age 60, Norman McLeod, who uses tobacco, wants to convert a $300,000 whole-life insurance policy to extended term with the same face value. Use 20-year level term rates to estimate the number of years of extended term coverage his cash value of $31,390 will buy.

19-1 SECTION EXERCISES

SKILL BUILDERS

Use Tables 19-1 and 19-2.

1. Find the annual premium for a 10-year level term insurance policy with a face value of $45,000 for a 35-year-old female using a non-tobacco rate.

2. Find the annual premium for a whole-life insurance policy with a face value of $75,000 for a 45-year-old female who smokes.

3. What are the quarterly payments on a $100,000 whole-life insurance policy for a 30-year-old male with a preferred rate?

4. What are the monthly payments on a $200,000 universal-life insurance policy for a 50-year-old male using a non-tobacco rate?

5. Compare the premiums for a 10-year level term policy for $75,000 for a 40-year-old male to the same policy for a 40-year-old female. Use a non-tobacco rate.

6. Compare the premiums for a 20-year level term policy for $500,000 for a 60-year-old male to the same policy for a 60-year-old female. Both use tobacco.

APPLICATIONS

7. Compare the annual life insurance premium of Jenny Davis who is 35 years old, and purchases a $250,000, 20-year level term policy using a non-tobacco rate to the premium paid by Chloe Levine, her friend who is the same age as Jenny and purchases exactly the same policy. Chloe is a smoker.

8. Compare the annual life insurance premium of Garrett Townse who is 30 years old, and purchases a $100,000, 10-year level term policy using a non-tobacco rate to the premium paid by Edward Collins, his business partner who is the same age as Garrett and purchases exactly the same policy and uses tobacco.

9. Cindy Franklin started a whole-life insurance policy for $250,000 when she was 23 years old. At age 50, the policy has a cash value of $12,606 and Cindy converts the policy to extended term insurance for the same face value. Use 20-year level term rates to estimate the number of years of extended term insurance she has using a non-tobacco rate.

10. Parker Water's $200,000 whole-life insurance policy has a cash value of $11,288. Parker is 60 years old, smokes, and is converting to an extended term policy for the same face value. Use 10-year level term rates to estimate the number of years of extended term insurance she has.

19-2 PROPERTY INSURANCE

LEARNING OUTCOMES
1. Estimate renters insurance premiums using a rate table.
2. Estimate homeowners insurance premiums using a rate table.
3. Find the compensation with a coinsurance clause.

Businesses, homeowners, and renters need insurance to protect them from financial loss if their property is damaged or destroyed. Some types of perils that might cause damage or loss to property are fire, storms, burglary, and vandalism. Many types of comprehensive policies are available to cover property damage or loss, medical expenses for injuries on the property, loss of income when damage/peril causes a business to be closed for a period of time, rental expense when a peril causes a home to be unlivable, and injury or damage to the property of others. Because premiums for a comprehensive business insurance policy are based on numerous factors specific to the nature of an individual business, we will illustrate property insurance by focusing on renters and homeowners insurance.

1 Estimate renters insurance premiums using a rate table.

Take a good look around your home or apartment. If everything you own was destroyed by a natural disaster, would you be able to afford to replace it all? If any of your valuable personal property was stolen or vandalized, would you be able to afford to pay for it out of your own pocket? Do you have the cash on hand to replace your computer, laptop, iPod, DVD player, TV, stereo, jewelry, clothing, furniture, or appliances? If the answer to any of those questions was no, then **renters insurance** would be a wise investment. Renters insurance is a necessity for anyone renting or subletting a home or apartment. Whether you live in a single-family home, duplex, townhome, condo, loft, studio, or apartment, you need to have renters insurance to protect your belongings and personal liability.

Property owners or landlords are required to carry property coverage, which protects the actual structure of the house or apartment. Most renters, however, aren't aware that all their personal property inside the dwelling will be covered only if they have renters insurance. In fact, today many landlords throughout America require tenants to purchase renters insurance when they sign a lease. The good news is that a renters insurance policy is typically very affordable and easy to obtain.

Rates for renters insurance vary according to a few factors, including the coverage and liability limits. One of the most important determinants, though, is your credit score. A poor credit score not only affects your ability to borrow money, it also increases your renters insurance premium! Even an occasional late payment past 30 days will have an effect, so make sure that all of your bills are always paid in a timely manner.

As you can see from Table 19-3, renters insurance rates are expressed in annual premiums, depending on the property coverage limit, the amount of liability coverage, the deductible selected, and the credit rating category of the applicant. In addition to the base coverage, options can be added including: identity theft/fraud protection—$20/year; sewer/sump pump backup protection (for property located in a basement)—$75/year. Extended coverage endorsements beyond the maximum coverage amounts can also be added for specific personal property: jewelry, watches, and furs—$0.85/$100/year; camera equipment—$1.35/$100/year; computer equipment—$0.95/$100/year; fine art and collectibles—$1.10/$100/year; firearms and accessories—$1.45/$100/year; and portable tools—$3.25/$100/year.

Renters insurance: provides both property and liability protection for the covered policyholder, as well as certain additional benefits.

DID YOU KNOW?
A slash in a rate expression is read as "per." For example, $0.85/$100/year is read as "eighty-five cents per hundred dollars per year."

TABLE 19-3
Estimated Annual Renters Insurance Premium Rates

| Liability | $20,000 Policy Limit |||||| $40,000 Policy Limit ||||||
| | $500 Deductible ||| $1,000 Deductible ||| $500 Deductible ||| $1,000 Deductible |||
	GOOD	OCC	BAD	GOOD	OCC	BAD	GOOD	OCC	BAD	GOOD	OCC	BAD
$300,000	141	226	253	126	203	227	195	312	349	174	280	313
$500,000	149	239	268	134	215	241	206	330	370	185	297	333
$1,000,000	169	270	303	154	246	276	233	373	418	213	339	381

GOOD = good credit; OCC = occasional payments past 30 days; BAD = judgments, collection, bankruptcy

HOW TO
Estimate an annual renters insurance premium using a rate table

1. Locate the base annual premium in Table 19-3 according to maximum policy coverage limit, liability limit, deductible, and credit score rating for the applicant.
2. Add the additional cost for any options selected.
3. Compute the annual cost for extended coverage endorsements.

$$\text{Cost} = \left(\frac{\text{coverage desired}}{\$100}\right)(\text{rate for endorsement})$$

4. Add the premiums from *steps 1 to 3*.

Total annual premium = base annual premium + cost for each option + cost for each extended coverage endorsement

EXAMPLE 1
Kirsten Lewen wants to buy renters insurance for her new apartment. She has excellent credit, and wants to find the most affordable policy. She also decides to add the identity theft/fraud protection, and an additional $2,000 of computer equipment coverage. Find the annual premium for a $20,000 policy, with the minimum liability offered, using a $1,000 deductible.

The annual base premium for a $20,000 policy, $300,000 liability, and $1,000 deductible is $126.

The cost for the identity theft/fraud protection is $20.

Cost for additional computer coverage $= \dfrac{\$2,000}{\$100}(\$0.95) = \$19$

Total annual premium $= \$126 + \$20 + \$19 = \$165$

The annual premium for the renters insurance policy is $165.

STOP AND CHECK

1. Lars Pacheco needs a $40,000 renters insurance policy and has selected the $500,000 liability with $1,000 deductible. The insurance company has determined his credit is excellent and given him the "good" credit rate. If he adds an endorsement to insure $7,000 of jewelry and the option of identity theft, find his annual premium.

2. Fred Rayburn is a renter who has a renters insurance policy for $20,000 of household goods and has selected the maximum liability with $500 deductible. His credit is rated as occasional payments after 30 days. If Fred also adds an endorsement of $2,500 for firearms he keeps at his condo, how much is his annual premium?

3. Beth Grubbs rents an apartment in New York and has renters insurance to cover $20,000 of her personal belongings. She selects the minimum liability with a deductible of $500 for each claim. Beth's credit is rated as bad as she has a recent bankruptcy on her record. Find her annual premium.

4. Barbara Hensley is moving into a loft apartment and is required to have renters insurance to protect her personal property. She has an excellent credit rating and elects to purchase a policy that will cover $40,000 in personal property and $500,000 in liability. She will have a deductible of $1,000. Barbara also selects an endorsement for her $8,500 engagement ring and $2,000 for her camera equipment. Find her annual renters insurance premium.

2 Estimate homeowners insurance premiums using a rate table.

Homeowners insurance: provides property coverage for both the covered dwelling and additional structures, and liability protection for the covered policyholder, as well as certain additional benefits.

As the old adage goes—home is where your heart is—along with a healthy chunk of your net worth. For most individuals, the purchase of a home will be one the most significant investments of their life. And let's face it, disasters happen. Fires, hurricanes, earthquakes, tornadoes, and floods are all too often a part of life today. Natural disasters and man-made accidents are not just a possibility, but an eventuality—so be sure to protect the investment in your home with a homeowners insurance policy. A **homeowners insurance** policy covers both property and liability. It protects your home, personal property, and other structures on your property in case of damage or total loss. It is designed to pay homeowners for damages to their home and its contents, but can also protect them from financial liability if someone is injured on their property, or elsewhere.

What Does Homeowners Insurance Protect? Each home insurance policy is different, but standard policies usually provide the following:

- Broad coverage for damage to your house and any permanent structures on your property (unless the cause of the damage is specifically excluded in your policy).
- Damage to your personal property from causes specified in your policy.
- Limited coverage, which is available for items like stolen jewelry or cash. Coverage amounts vary depending on your state of residence.
- Additional coverage for valuable items and additional supplementary liability coverage, which can be purchased through endorsements to your homeowners policy.

Typical exclusions to a homeowners policy include damage from flooding, earthquake, normal wear and tear, war, intentional damage, or buildings used for business. Flood and earthquake coverage generally must be purchased separately. Make sure you recognize what your needs are, what is covered, and what is excluded in any policy before you buy.

Rates for homeowners insurance vary according to several factors, such as type of dwelling, location, proximity to the fire station, rating of the fire department, water supply, and fire hazards. Most states have developed a system for classifying rates according to these factors. In addition, the credit rating category of the policyholder and/or spouse has a major impact on homeowners insurance rates. In the case of spouses with different credit ratings, the lower credit classification will determine the rate category. Table 19-4 shows a sample classification system for two of the primary home construction styles—frame regular, and masonry—along with different zone ratings representing access to fire protection.

TABLE 19-4
Estimated Annual Homeowners Insurance Premium Rates per $100 of Face Value

Deductible	Frame Regular						Masonry					
	Zone 1			Zone 2			Zone 1			Zone 2		
	GOOD	OCC	BAD	GOOD	OCC	BAD	GOOD	OCC	BAD	GOOD	OCC	BAD
$1,000	0.29	0.38	0.75	0.34	0.46	0.92	0.27	0.36	0.71	0.32	0.43	0.86
$1,500	0.27	0.36	0.71	0.32	0.44	0.87	0.25	0.34	0.67	0.30	0.41	0.81

GOOD = good credit; OCC = occasional payments past 30 days; BAD = judgments, collection, bankruptcy

As you can see from Table 19-4, homeowners insurance rates are expressed as an annual amount per $100 of coverage, based on the construction type, fire protection zone, credit rating category, and deductible selected. To find the annual premium, divide the amount of coverage by $100 and multiply the result by the rate in the table. In addition, options can be added to the base coverage including the following: identity theft/fraud protection—$20/year; sewer/sump pump backup protection—$75/year. Extended coverage endorsements beyond the maximum coverage amounts can also be added for specific personal property. Endorsements can be added for: jewelry, watches, and furs—$0.85/$100/year; camera equipment—$1.35/$100/year; computer equipment—$0.95/$100/year; fine art and collectibles—$1.10/$100/year; firearms and accessories—$1.45/$100/year; and portable tools—$3.25/$100/year.

HOW TO Estimate an annual homeowners insurance premium using a rate table

1. Locate the base annual rate in Table 19-4 according to construction type, zone, deductible, and credit score rating for the applicant(s).

$$\text{Base annual premium} = \left(\frac{\text{dwelling coverage}}{\$100}\right)(\text{rate from table})$$

2. Add the additional cost for any options selected.
3. Compute the annual cost for extended coverage endorsements.

$$\text{Cost} = \left(\frac{\text{coverage desired}}{\$100}\right)(\text{rate for endorsement})$$

4. Add the premiums from steps 1 to 3.

$$\text{Total annual premium} = \text{base annual premium} + \text{cost for each option} + \text{cost for each extended coverage endorsement}$$

EXAMPLE 2 Eric and Angela are in the process of buying a new home and need homeowners insurance. Their credit history, as provided by the bank, shows that they both occasionally make payments past 30 days, but with no other major problems. They need to insure their masonry home for $150,000, which is located in fire protection zone 1, and decide to go with a $1,000 deductible. They also decide to add the identity theft/fraud protection and the sewer/sump pump backup coverage, and an additional $3,000 of protection for jewelry, watches, and furs. Find the annual premium for their homeowners policy.

$$\text{Annual premium for dwelling} = \left(\frac{\text{dwelling amount}}{\$100}\right)(\text{rate}) \quad \text{rate for dwelling is \$0.36 per \$100}$$

$$= \frac{\$150,000}{\$100}(\$0.36) = \$540$$

The cost for the identity theft/fraud protection is $20 and the cost for sewer backup is $75.

$$\text{Cost for additional coverage for jewelry, watches, and furs} = \frac{\$3,000}{\$100}(\$0.85) = \$25.50$$

Total annual premium = $540 + $20 + $75 + $25.50 = $660.50

The annual premium for the homeowners insurance policy is $660.50.

STOP AND CHECK

1. Paul and Vanessa Herndon have their masonry home insured for $600,000. The home is in zone 1. Find the annual premium for the home if they have a good credit rating and select a $1,000 deductible.

2. Stewart Ungo insures his frame home for $350,000 and chooses a $1,500 deductible. The home is located in zone 1. Find the annual homeowners premium if his credit rating is good.

3. Larry Byrd insures his frame home for $265,000 and includes an endorsement for jewelry worth $5,000. What is the annual premium for his home located in zone 2 if his credit is OCC and his deductible is $1,000?

4. Kim Kiser's masonry home is insured for $328,000 with a $1,500 deductible. The home is located in zone 1. Find the annual premium if Kim's credit is rated BAD.

3 Find the compensation with a coinsurance clause.

One of the most important protection considerations with your homeowners insurance has to do with replacement cost. Most homeowners policies issued by quality insurance carriers today provide personal property replacement coverage; if not as standard coverage, it is typically available as an endorsement to your policy. Without this important protection, your policy would provide only actual cash value coverage. Actual cash value is the replacement cost of your property minus depreciation. For example, using actual cash value, a three-year-old television stolen from your home that originally sold for $1,000 might result in a settlement of only 40% of the original purchase price. That's a $600 difference! Full replacement cost coverage on personal property would compensate you for the full replacement of the television, even if it cost more to purchase today.

The concept of replacement cost applies to your dwelling as well, not just the contents. Most of today's standardized homeowners policies provide replacement cost coverage for your dwelling, up to your policy's dollar limits. Replacement cost is what you would pay to rebuild or repair your home, based on current construction costs. Replacement cost is different from market value. It does not include the value of your land. To assist you in determining the amount it would cost to rebuild your home, your company or agent usually has construction cost tables to help you figure the cost. To encourage homeowners to take out full replacement coverage, insurance companies offer plans that include a **coinsurance clause**. Such a clause means that to receive full protection or compensation up to the value of the policy for a partial loss, such as a storm-damaged roof, you must insure your dwelling for at least 80% of its replacement cost. If you insure your dwelling for less than 80% of the full replacement cost, the insurance company will pay only part of the expense of a partial loss.

Coinsurance clause: property must be insured for at least 80% of the replacement cost for full compensation for a loss.

HOW TO Find the compensation with a coinsurance clause

1. Find the face value required by the 80% coinsurance clause for full compensation: Multiply 0.8 by the replacement value of the property.
2. Find the compensation for the loss if the insurance is less than 80% of the replacement value:

Compensation (up to amount of loss)

= amount of loss (up to the face value) × $\dfrac{\text{face value of policy}}{80\% \text{ of replacement value of property}}$

EXAMPLE 3
Cassandra Brighton owns a home with a replacement value of $200,000. She has a homeowners insurance policy with an 80% coinsurance clause and a face value of $130,000. There is a fire, and the building damage is figured to be $50,000. What will the insurance company pay as compensation?

Does Cassandra carry as much insurance as its coinsurance clause requires for full protection?

0.8($200,000) = $160,000   80% of replacement value

Cassandra has a policy worth only $130,000, so she does *not* get full compensation for the loss. Find the compensation:

$$\text{Compensation} = \text{loss} \times \frac{\text{face value of policy}}{80\% \text{ of replacement value}}$$

$$\text{Compensation} = \$50,000 \left(\frac{\$130,000}{\$160,000} \right) = \$40,625$$

Cassandra receives $40,625 compensation for her loss of $50,000.

If Cassandra had carried a policy for 80% of the replacement value of her property, she would have gotten the full $50,000 compensation for the loss.

TIP

Maximum Compensation for a Loss

When calculating the compensation an insurance company will pay, if the policy has a coinsurance clause, the compensation for the amount of loss can be *no more than the face value of the policy*, regardless of the actual dollar value of the loss.

EXAMPLE 4

John Worthy's home is insured for 80% of the replacement value. The replacement value of the home is $105,000. A fire causes $90,000 worth of damage to the property. How much compensation will John receive from the insurance company?

0.8($105,000) = $84,000 face value of policy   Compensation cannot exceed the face value of the policy.

Compensation = $84,000

The loss compensation is $84,000.

In the preceding example, the $90,000 loss can only be compensated at $84,000 because the face value of the policy is only $84,000.

STOP AND CHECK

1. Audrey Boles owns a home with a replacement value of $650,000. Its homeowners insurance policy has an 80% coinsurance clause and a face value of $400,000. Damage from a fire is estimated to be $82,000. What compensation will the insurance company pay?

2. Maggie Mallette owns a home with a replacement value of $492,000. The homeowners insurance policy has an 80% coinsurance clause and a face value of $350,000. Damage caused by a storm costs $43,790 to repair. What compensation will the insurance company pay?

3. Max McLeod owns a home with a replacement value of $798,500. His homeowners insurance policy has an 80% coinsurance clause and a face value of $600,000. Damage caused by a hurricane costs $590,000. How much will Max's insurance company pay?

4. Tim Akers has insured his home for $550,000. The replacement value of the home is $690,000 with an 80% coinsurance clause. Repairs from a fire cost $38,588. How much will the insurance company pay?

19-2 SECTION EXERCISES

SKILL BUILDERS

Use Table 19-3 and the information on page 668 to find the total annual renters insurance premiums in Exercises 1–4.

1. Tim Navholtz needs a $20,000 renters insurance policy and has selected the $1,000,000 liability with $1,000 deductible. The insurance company has determined his credit is excellent and has given him the "good" credit rate. If he adds an endorsement to ensure $12,000 of jewelry and the options of identity theft/protection and sewer/sump pump backup protection for his basement, find his annual premium.

Insurance   575

2. Margaret Davis has a renters insurance policy for $40,000 of household goods and has selected $500,000 liability with $1,000 deductible. Her credit is rated as occasional payments after 30 days. If Margaret also adds an endorsement of $18,500 to insure her collectible antiques and $5,000 to insure the jewelry she keeps at her condo, how much is her annual premium?

3. Shay Manning rents an apartment in Chicago and carries $20,000 insurance on her personal belongings. She selects the minimum liability with a deductible of $1,000 for each claim and carries identity theft/fraud protection. Shay's credit is rated as bad as she has a recent bankruptcy on her record. Find her annual premium.

4. Nevelyn Smith is moving into a loft apartment and is required to have renters insurance to protect her personal property. She has an excellent credit rating and elects to purchase a policy that will cover $20,000 in personal property, cover $300,000 in liability, and have a deductible of $1,000. Nevelyn also selects an endorsement for her $8,500 engagement ring and $2,000 for her camera equipment. Find her annual renters insurance premium.

5. Find the annual homeowners insurance premium on a masonry home located in zone 2 if the home is insured for $275,000. The owner chooses a $1,500 deductible and has good credit.

6. A frame home and its contents are located in zone 1 and are insured for $150,000. Find the total annual insurance premium if the insured has a credit rating of OCC and chooses a deductible of $1,000.

7. If a 2% charge is added to the annual premium of $1,021.80 when payments are made semiannually, how much would semiannual payments be?

8. Chandler Burford owns a masonry home located in zone 2. What is the annual homeowners insurance premium if the home is insured for $350,000, the owner has an OCC credit rating and chooses a deductible of $1,000. The homeowner also has endorsements for a $2,000 watch and portable tools valued at $3,500.

9. Alice Lee owns a masony home in zone 1. The home is insured for $200,000 and the computer equipment endorsement is added for $8,000. Alice has excellent credit and her deductible is $1,500. A 3% charge is added to the annual premium because she pays quarterly. Find her quarterly payment.

APPLICATIONS

10. The market value of a home is $255,000. It has been insured for $204,000 in a homeowners insurance policy with an 80% coinsurance clause. What part of a loss due to fire will the insurance company pay?

11. If a fire causes damage valued at $75,000, what is the amount of compensation to the owner of the home in Exercise 10?

12. A home valued at $295,000 is insured in a policy that contains an 80% coinsurance clause. The face value of the policy is $100,000. If the home is a total loss, what is the amount of compensation?

13. Marjorie Mays owns a home that has a replacement value of $395,000. How much insurance is required on the property for coverage up to the face value of the policy if an 80% coinsurance clause exists?

14. Marjorie (Exercise 13) had a fire that resulted in a loss valued at $83,000. How much compensation is the insurance company obligated to pay if the home is insured for $220,000?

15. How much compensation is the insurance company obligated to pay Marjorie if she has the $83,000 loss shown in Exercise 14 but the property is insured for $300,000?

19-3 MOTOR VEHICLE INSURANCE

LEARNING OUTCOME
1. Find automobile insurance premiums using rate tables.

Motor vehicle insurance: liability, comprehensive, and collision insurance for a motor vehicle.

Liability insurance: protection for the owner of a vehicle if an accident causes personal injury or damage to someone else's property and is the fault of the driver of the insured vehicle.

Comprehensive insurance: protection for the owner of a vehicle for damage to the vehicle typically caused by a nonaccident incident such as fire, water, theft, vandalism, or other risks.

Collision insurance: protection for the owner of a vehicle for damages (both personal and property) from an accident that is the insured driver's fault.

No-fault insurance: protection for the owner of a vehicle for damage to the insured vehicle when the amount of damage is within the no-fault limits imposed by state law.

Deductible: the dollar amount the insured pays for each automobile insurance claim. The insurance company pays the remainder of the cost of each covered loss up to the limits of the policy.

Motor vehicle insurance is a major expense item for individuals and businesses because of the high risk of personal injury or death and damage to property. Insurance for motor vehicles may be purchased to protect the individual or business from several risks. These include liability for personal injury and property damage; damage to or loss of the insured vehicle and its occupants caused by a collision; and damage or loss to the insured vehicle caused by theft, fire, flood, storms, and other incidents that may not be related to a collision. These types of insurance generally fall into three types: liability, comprehensive, and collision.

Liability insurance protects the insured from losses incurred in a vehicle accident resulting in personal injury or damage to someone else's property if the accident is the fault of the insured or a designated driver.

Comprehensive insurance protects the insured's vehicle from damage caused by fire, theft, vandalism, wildlife, and other risks, such as falling debris, storm damage, or road hazards such as rocks.

Collision insurance protects the insured's vehicle from damage (both personal and property) caused by an automobile accident in which the driver of the insured vehicle is *also* at fault. This type of insurance is also used when the driver of another vehicle who is at fault does not have insurance coverage.

Some states have **no-fault insurance** programs. In these states, all parties involved in an accident submit a claim for personal and property damages to their own insurance company if the amount is under a certain stated maximum. However, a person can still pursue legal action for additional compensation if the damage is above the stated maximum.

All auto insurance policies have a deductible. The **deductible** is the portion of the policy the policyholder is responsible for paying if a claim is filed. The amount the insured is required to pay for damages depends on the policy. Deductibles vary, but they are most often amounts of $100, $250, $500, or $1,000. For example, if you are at fault in a vehicle crash that causes $3,500 worth of damage to your vehicle and your deductible is $1,000, you are required to pay the first $1,000 and the insurance company will pay the remaining amount up to the amount of the policy, or $2,500 in this example. Deductibles are paid each and every time the insured requires the insurance company to cover damages. The insurance premium you pay, or the price of your total annual coverage, can be reduced by choosing a higher deductible. In other words, if you are willing to pay a larger amount of each and every claim, you can reduce the total cost of your insurance.

1 Find automobile insurance premiums using rate tables.

Factors that affect the cost of automobile insurance include the primary location of the vehicle (large city, small town, rural area); the total distance traveled per year and the distance traveled to work each day; the types of use (such as pleasure, traveling to and from work, strictly business); the driving record and training of the insured driver(s); the academic grades of drivers who are still in school; the age, sex, and marital status of the insured driver(s); the type and age of the vehicle; and the amount of coverage desired. Similar to both renters and homeowners insurance, the credit rating category of the policyholder has a major impact on automobile insurance rates. Accident statistics and

TABLE 19-5
Annual Automobile Liability Insurance Premiums

Liability Limits*	Territory 1			Territory 2		
	GOOD	OCC	BAD	GOOD	OCC	BAD
50/100/50	385	600	846	354	552	778
100/300/100	425	682	961	391	627	884
250/500/250	460	750	1036	423	690	953
500/1000/500	530	843	1208	488	776	1111

GOOD = good credit; OCC = occasional payments past 30 days; BAD = judgments, collection, bankruptcy
*Bodily injury maximum for one person/Total bodily injury coverage per accident/Property damage

---

Uninsured or under insured motorist coverage: protection for the owner of a vehicle when damages are incurred in an accident that is not the owner's fault but the other driver has no or insufficient insurance.

Medical expenses: provides payment to the driver and each passenger in the insured's vehicle of 100% of any medical bills up to the coverage limit arising from a collision.

Liability limits: the maximum amount that an insurance company will pay for a single accident based on coverage selected by the insured.

Bodily injury: personal injury of a person other than the insured or members of the insured's household that is sustained in an accident.

Property damage: damage to the property of others in an accident.

Territory: the type of area in which the car is kept and driven.

---

probabilities involving these factors are also used in determining appropriate insurance rates. Many companies offer **uninsured or under insured motorist coverage**, which compensates the insured person when the accident is the fault of a motorist who has no or insufficient insurance.

Table 19-5 shows a hypothetical annual rate schedule for liability insurance, including uninsured/underinsured motorist bodily injury and property damage protection, as well as $10,000 of **medical expense** coverage. Using **liability limits** of 50/100/50 as an example, the first number is the maximum dollar limit (expressed in thousands) the company will pay for the **bodily injury** per person in an accident—in this case $50,000. The second number, 100, is the maximum dollar limit the company will pay for *all* bodily injuries combined in any one accident—in this case $100,000. The third number, 50, refers to the maximum dollar limit the company will pay others for **property damage**, including other vehicles or property such as fences, buildings, utility poles, etc.—in this case $50,000.

The uninsured/underinsured motorist protection included in Table 19-5 includes the same coverage maximums provided by the bodily injury/total bodily injury/property damage liability limits chosen by the insured, in this example 50/100/50. This means that in the event an at-fault driver has no or insufficient coverage, the coverage limits provided by one's own uninsured/underinsured motorist protection per accident would be $50,000 per bodily injury/$100,000 bodily injury maximum/$50,000 property damage.

Notice that there are several columns of information. The **territory** refers to the type of area in which the car is kept and driven. Under each territory are three credit rating categories which refer to the credit rating of the insured. In fact, credit history is becoming one of the major factors in determining auto insurance rates. In the case of spouses with different credit ratings and one vehicle, the lower credit classification will determine the rate category. If there are two vehicles covered under one auto policy, then each spouse (and their individual credit rating classifications) will be assigned to the vehicle they each primarily drive.

Two other components of the motor vehicle insurance premium are premiums for comprehensive and collision coverage. Comprehensive and collision premiums are based on the *model class* (compact, luxury, SUV, truck, etc.), the *vehicle age*, the *credit rating*, and the amount of the *deductible*. Table 19-6 gives sample rates for comprehensive and collision premiums.

In addition to the base premiums for liability, comprehensive, and collision coverage, several discounts and surcharges may apply to your automobile insurance coverage, including: 25% good student discount for full-time students between the ages of 16 and 24 with at least a "B" average or 3.0 grade point average; 5% accident free for 3 years discount; 10% multivehicle discount; $60/year ticket surcharge for any moving violation issued during the past 3 years (maximum $120/year); and a $150 accident surcharge for each at-fault accident during the past 3 years (maximum $300/year).

HOW TO Find an annual automobile insurance premium using table values

1. Locate the bodily injury and property damage premium according to territory, credit rating, and per person/per accident bodily injury and property damage coverage (Table 19-5).
2. Locate the comprehensive premium according to model class, vehicle age, territory, credit rating, and deductible.
3. Locate the collision premium according to model class, vehicle age, territory, credit rating, and deductible.
4. Add the premiums from steps 1 to 3 to find the base annual premium.
5. Multiply any applicable discounts by the base premium and subtract.
6. Add any ticket or accident surcharges.

Total annual premium = bodily injury/property damage premium + comprehensive premium + collision premium − discounts + surcharges

TABLE 19-6
Annual Auto Insurance Premium Rates for Comprehensive and Collision

Model Class	Vehicle Age	Territory 1 Comprehensive $0 Deductible GOOD	OCC	BAD	$250 Deductible GOOD	OCC	BAD	Collision $500 Deductible GOOD	OCC	BAD	$1,000 Deductible GOOD	OCC	BAD
1	0–1	584	934	1129	393	628	759	535	855	1279	471	753	1126
	2–3	520	831	1005	350	559	676	449	718	1074	396	633	946
	4–5	397	635	768	267	427	516	396	633	946	349	557	833
	6+	374	598	723	252	402	486	332	530	793	292	467	698
2	0–1	502	803	971	338	540	653	503	804	1202	443	708	1058
	2–3	447	715	864	301	481	581	417	667	998	367	587	879
	4–5	342	546	660	230	367	444	367	587	878	323	517	773
	6+	321	514	621	216	346	418	297	474	709	261	418	624
3	0–1	472	755	913	318	508	614	478	764	1142	421	672	1006
	2–3	420	672	812	283	452	546	392	627	938	345	552	826
	4–5	321	513	621	216	345	417	342	547	818	301	481	720
	6+	302	483	584	203	325	393	277	442	661	244	389	582

Model Class	Vehicle Age	Territory 2 Comprehensive $0 Deductible GOOD	OCC	BAD	$250 Deductible GOOD	OCC	BAD	Collision $500 Deductible GOOD	OCC	BAD	$1,000 Deductible GOOD	OCC	BAD
1	0–1	514	822	994	346	553	668	492	787	1177	433	693	1036
	2–3	457	732	884	308	492	594	413	661	988	364	582	870
	4–5	349	559	676	235	376	454	364	582	871	321	513	767
	6+	329	526	636	221	354	427	305	488	730	269	430	642
2	0–1	442	707	854	297	475	574	463	739	1106	407	651	974
	2–3	393	629	760	265	423	511	384	614	918	338	540	808
	4–5	301	481	581	202	323	391	338	540	807	297	475	711
	6+	283	452	547	190	304	368	273	436	653	240	384	575
3	0–1	415	664	803	280	447	540	440	702	1051	387	619	925
	2–3	370	591	715	249	398	481	361	577	863	318	508	760
	4–5	283	452	546	190	304	367	315	503	752	277	443	662
	6+	266	425	514	179	286	346	255	407	608	224	358	536

GOOD = good credit; OCC = occasional payments past 30 days; BAD = judgments, collection, bankruptcy

EXAMPLE 1
Use Tables 19-5 and 19-6 to find the annual premium for an automobile liability insurance policy in which the insured lives in territory 1, has good credit, and wishes to have 50/100/50 coverage. The vehicle is a three-year-old, model class 2 vehicle with a deductible for comprehensive of $250 and $500 for collision. The driver has been accident and ticket free for the last three years.

Liability premium = $385	Territory 1, good credit, 50/100/50.
Comprehensive premium = $301	Model class 2, age 3, $250 deductible, good credit.
Collision premium = $417	Model class 2, age 3, $500 deductible, good credit.
Base annual premium = $1,103	Sum.
$1,103 × 0.05 = $55.15	5% accident-free discount

Total annual premium = $385 + $301 + $417 − $55.15 = $1,047.85

TIP
What If Damages Exceed the Book Value of the Vehicle?

As vehicles age, they generally decrease in value. The value of a particular year, make, and model of a vehicle is published for car dealers and insurance companies. This value is referred to as the **book value** of a vehicle. If the damages resulting from an accident exceed the book value, the insurance company will only pay for the book value. When this situation occurs, the vehicle is commonly said to be **totaled**.

For example, if the vehicle *books* for $14,500 and the damages to the vehicle are $16,000, the vehicle is *totaled* and the vehicle owner receives $14,500.

Book value: the value of a specific model and year of a used vehicle that is based on the estimated resale value of the vehicle.

Totaled: when damages to a vehicle exceed the book value, the insurance covers the damages up to the book value.

Claim compensation: money paid by the insurance company to persons as a result of an automobile crash when the insured is at fault. The money may be for bodily injury or for property damage. The insured must pay any amounts that exceed the amount of coverage of the policy.

While the insured pays insurance premiums, the insurance company must pay when the insured is involved in an automobile crash or if something happens to the insured automobile. These payments or claims are called **compensation**.

EXAMPLE 2

Margo Mahler has 50/100/50 insurance. She has $500 deductible collision and $250 deductible comprehensive. Margo crashed into a vehicle (failed to yield). Three persons, Leslie, Jim, and Ursala, were injured. Leslie's medical care was $21,000, Jim's medical care was $68,754, Ursala had no injuries, and their car required $3,895 to repair. Margo's vehicle damage amounted to $5,093, but she had no injuries. How much will the insurance company need to pay and to whom? Will Margo need to pay anything? If so, how much?

Liability: Margo's insurance pays up to $50,000 per person. Leslie's $21,000 medical care will be paid by the insurance company. The insurance company will pay the limit, $50,000, for Jim's medical care. Margo will need to pay the difference $68,754 − $50,000 = $18,754. The insurance company will pay $3,895 to Ursala for vehicle repair and $5,093 − $500 = $4,593 to Margo for vehicle repairs.

STOP AND CHECK

1. Use Tables 19-5 and 19-6 to find the annual premium for an automobile insurance policy in which the insured lives in territory 1, has good credit, and buys 100/300/100 coverage. The vehicle is a 5-year-old, model class 3 vehicle and both comprehensive and collision are carried with a $500 deductible on collision and a $250 deductible on comprehensive.

2. Use Tables 19-5 and 19-6 to find the annual premium for an automobile insurance policy for Megan Anders, who lives in territory 2, has good credit, and buys 50/100/50 coverage. The vehicle is 7 years old, model class 2, and both comprehensive and collision are carried with a $250 deductible on comprehensive and a $1,000 deductible on collision.

3. Margaret Davis has an automobile insurance policy with OCC credit rating and she lives in territory 2. She buys 100/300/100 coverage. Her vehicle is new, in model class 1, and she elects a $250 deductible on comprehensive and a $1,000 deductible on collision. What is her annual premium?

4. Find the annual auto insurance premium for Reed Davis if he has a good credit rating and lives in territory 1. Reed buys 50/100/50 liability coverage and $250 deductible comprehensive and $1,000 deductible collision coverage. Reed's truck is 2 years old and falls in model class 2.

19-3 SECTION EXERCISES

SKILL BUILDERS

Find the total annual automobile insurance premium.

	Territory	Credit rating	Model class	Vehicle age	Liability coverage	Comprehensive deductible	Collision deductible
1.	1	GOOD	1	New	50/100/50	$250	$500
2.	1	OCC	2	3 years	250/500/250	$0	$500
3.	2	BAD	3	4 years	100/300/100	$0	$500
4.	2	GOOD	2	6 years	100/300/100	$250	$1,000
5.	1	OCC	1	1 year	50/100/50	$250	$1,000
6.	2	BAD	3	2 years	50/100/50	$0	$1,000

7. Find the annual auto insurance premium for Dontae Knight if he has good credit and lives in territory 2. Dontae has 50/100/50 liability coverage and a $250 comprehensive deductible and a $500 collision deductible. His vehicle is new and is in model class 1.

8. What is the annual vehicle insurance premium for Shanté Banks if she has good credit and lives in territory 1? Shanté has 100/300/100 liability coverage and a $250 deductible on comprehensive coverage and $1,000 deductible on collision. Her vehicle is 30 months old and is in model class 1.

APPLICATIONS

9. Find the annual premium for an automobile insurance policy if the insured lives in territory 2 and is classified OCC. The policy contains 250/500/250 liability coverage. The vehicle is 3 years old and in model class 3, the deductible for collision is $500, and the deductible for comprehensive is $250.

10. Find the annual premium on a 50/100/50 liability policy for a driver in territory 1 if the vehicle is 4.5 years old and in model class 2. The insured selects a comprehensive deductible of $250 and a collision deductible of $500. The insured's credit is good.

11. What are the monthly payments on an automobile insurance policy for a driver in territory 1 with 50/100/50 liability coverage? The 8-year-old vehicle is in model class 1; the comprehensive deductible is $250 and the collision deductible is $1,000. The insured has a recent bankruptcy on his credit report. Assume no additional fee is required for the monthly payment option.

12. How much will the liability portion of the automobile insurance policy pay an injured person with medical expenses of $8,362 if the insured has a policy with 50/100/50 coverage and is liable for his or her injuries?

Insurance 581

SUMMARY

CHAPTER 19

Learning Outcomes

Section 19-1

What to Remember with Examples

1 Estimate life insurance premiums using a rate table. (p. 663)

1. Locate the estimated annual rate in Table 19-1 according to type of policy, age, sex and rate class.
2. Divide the policy face value by $1,000 and multiply the quotient by the rate from step 1.

$$\text{Estimated annual premium} = \frac{\text{face value}}{\$1,000} \times \text{rate}$$

Use Table 19-1 to find the annual premium for a 40-year-old male who uses tobacco for a $50,000 (a) 10-year level term policy and (b) whole-life policy.

(a) 10-year level term policy: $\left(\frac{\$50,000}{\$1,000}\right)(\$3.78) = \$189$

(b) Whole-life policy: $\left(\frac{\$50,000}{\$1,000}\right)(\$19.31) = \$965.50$

Use Tables 19-1 and 19-2 to find the quarterly premium for a $50,000 whole-life policy on a 30-year-old female using a preferred rate classification.

$$\begin{pmatrix}\text{Monthly, quarterly,}\\ \text{or semiannual}\\ \text{premium}\end{pmatrix} = \begin{pmatrix}\text{annual}\\ \text{premium}\end{pmatrix} \times \begin{pmatrix}\text{rate from}\\ \text{Table 19-2}\end{pmatrix}$$

$$\text{Annual premium} = \left(\frac{\$50,000}{\$1,000}\right)(\$9.82) = \$491$$

$$\text{Quarterly premium} = (\$491)(0.26) = \$127.66$$

2 Apply the extended term nonforfeiture option to a cancelled whole-life policy. (p. 665)

1. Identify the cash value of the cancelled policy.
2. Estimate the annual premium for a term policy of the same face value. Use a fixed rate in Table 19-1.
3. Determine the number of years of paid-up term insurance.

$$\text{Years of paid-up term insurance} = \frac{\text{cash value of surrendered policy}}{\text{annual premium of term policy}}$$

Craig Schmaling got a non-tobacco rate and started a $200,000 whole-life insurance policy at age 45. At age 60, he decides to use the $13,278 cash value for paid-up 10-year term insurance for the same face value. How many years of paid-up insurance will he have?

$9.07 per $1,000 from Table 19-1

$$\frac{\$200,000}{\$1,000} = 200 \text{ units}$$

$$\text{Estimated annual term premium} = 200(\$9.07) = \$1,814$$

$$\text{Years of paid-up term insurance} = \frac{\text{cash value of surrendered policy}}{\text{annual premium of term policy}}$$

$$= \frac{\$13,278}{\$1,814} = 7.32 \text{ years}$$

Section 19-2

1 Estimate renters insurance premiums using a rate table. (p. 668)

1. Locate the base annual premium in Table 19-3 according to maximum policy coverage limit, liability limit, deductible, and credit score rating for the applicant.
2. Add the additional cost for any options selected.
3. Compute the annual cost for extended coverage endorsements.

$$\text{Cost} = \left(\frac{\text{coverage desired}}{\$100}\right)(\text{rate for endorsement})$$

4. Add the premiums from steps 1 through 3.

$$\text{Total annual premium} = \text{base annual premium} + \text{cost for each option} + \text{cost for each extended coverage endorsement}$$

Suzette Cannon wants to buy renters insurance for her new condominium. She has excellent credit, and decides she needs a $40,000 policy with $500,000 liability and $1,000 deductible. She also decides to add the identity theft/fraud protection and an additional $4,000 of coverage for her engagement ring. Find Suzette's total annual premium for her renters insurance if she has a good credit rating.

The base annual premium for a $40,000 policy, $500,000 liability, and $1,000 deductible with good credit is $185.

The cost for the identity theft/fraud protection is $20

$$\text{Cost for additional jewelry coverage} = \left(\frac{\$4,000}{\$100}\right)(\$0.85) = \$34$$

Total annual premium = $185 + $20 + $34 = $239

The annual premium for the renters insurance policy is $239.

2 Estimate homeowners insurance premiums using a rate table. (p. 669)

1. Locate the base annual rate in Table 19-4 according to construction type, zone, deductible, and credit score rating for the applicant(s).

$$\text{Base annual premium} = \left(\frac{\text{dwelling coverage}}{\$100}\right)(\text{rate from table})$$

2. Add the additional cost for any options selected.
3. Compute the annual cost for extended coverage endorsements.

$$\text{Cost} = \left(\frac{\text{coverage desired}}{\$100}\right)(\text{rate for endorsement})$$

4. Add the premiums from steps 1 through 3.

$$\text{Total annual premium} = \text{base annual premium} + \text{cost for each option} + \text{cost for each extended coverage endorsement}$$

Use Table 19-4 to find the annual premium for a masonry home if it is insured for $350,000. The building is in zone 2 and the owner's credit rating is BAD. A $1,000 deductible is selected. The owner also adds an endorsement for $8,000 in firearms.

$$\text{Annual premium for dwelling} = \left(\frac{\$350,000}{\$100}\right)(\$0.86) = \$3,010$$

$$\text{Cost of additional firearms coverage} = \left(\frac{\$8,000}{\$100}\right)(\$1.45) = \$116$$

Total annual premium = $3,010 + $116 = $3,126

3 Find the compensation with a coinsurance clause. (p. 671)

1. Find the face value required by the 80% coinsurance clause for full compensation: Multiply 0.8 by the replacement value of the property.
2. Find the compensation for the loss if the insurance is less than 80% of the replacement value.

$$\frac{\text{Compensation (up to amount of loss)}}{} = \frac{\text{amount of loss}}{\text{(up to face value)}} \times \frac{\text{face value of policy}}{80\% \text{ of replacement value of property}}$$

A property valued at $325,000 is insured with a policy that contains an 80% coinsurance clause. The face value of the policy is $200,000. What is the amount of compensation if a fire results in a total loss of the property?

$$\text{Compensation} = \$200,000\left(\frac{\$200,000}{0.8 \times \$325,000}\right)$$

$$= \$200,000\left(\frac{\$200,000}{\$260,000}\right)$$

$$\text{Compensation} = \$200,000(0.7692307692) = \$153,846.15$$

Even though the fire caused damages valued at $325,000, the insured receives only $153,846.15 in compensation.

Section 19-3

1 Find automobile insurance premiums using rate tables. (p. 774)

1. Locate the bodily injury and property damage premium according to territory, credit rating, and per person/per accident bodily injury and property damage coverage (Table 19-5).
2. Locate the comprehensive premium according to model class, vehicle age, territory, credit rating, and deductible.
3. Locate the collision premium according to model class, vehicle age, territory, credit rating, and deductible.
4. Add the premiums from steps 1 to 3 to find the base annual premium.
5. Multiply any applicable discounts by the base premium and subtract.
6. Add any ticket or accident surcharges.

$$\begin{aligned}\text{Total annual premium} = &\text{ bodily injury/property damage premium} \\ &+ \text{ comprehensive premium} + \text{ collision premium} \\ &- \text{ discounts} + \text{ surcharges}\end{aligned}$$

Use Tables 19-5 and 19-6 to find the annual premium for an automobile policy in which the insured lives in territory 2, makes occasional payments over 30 days, has a 4-year-old model class 2 vehicle, and wishes to have 100/300/100 liability coverage, a comprehensive deductible of $0, and a collision deductible of $1,000. The insured was accident free for the last three years, but received one moving violation during that time.

The cost of 100/300/100 bodily injury and property damage coverage for territory 2, OCC credit is $627 (Table 19-5).

The cost of comprehensive coverage with a $0 deductible is $481.

The cost of collision coverage with a $1,000 deductible is $475.

Base annual premium = $627 + $481 + $475 = $1,583

The 5% accident-free discount = $1,583(0.05) = $79.15

The surcharge for one ticket during the last three years is $60.

Total annual premium = $627 + $481 + $475 − $79.15 + $60 = $1,563.85.

EXERCISES SET A

CHAPTER 19

Using Table 19-3 and the option/endorsement rates on p. 668, find the annual renters insurance premium for each of the following.

	Policy limit	Deductible	Credit rating	Liability	Endorsement or option	Base Premium	Endorsement or option premium	Total annual premium
1.	$20,000	$500	GOOD	$300,000	$18,500 (computer)			
2.	$40,000	$1,000	OCC	$500,000	$25,000 (art and collectibles)			
3.	$40,000	$1,000	BAD	$300,000	none			

Use Table 19-4 and the information that follows the table when necessary to solve the following problems.

4. Linda Kodama owns a frame home in zone 2 valued at $95,000. The building is insured for $60,000 and the policy has an 80% coinsurance clause. How much will Linda receive from her policy if a fire causes $38,000 in damages?

5. Robyn Presley insures her masonry home located in zone 2 for $260,000 and adds an endorsement for $16,000 in antique collectibles. She has excellent credit and selects a deductible of $1,000. Find the total annual insurance premium.

6. Frank Hopkins has a homeowners policy for his brick (masonry) home located in zone 2 for its appraised value of $528,900 and selects a deductible of $1,500. If Frank has excellent credit, find his total annual homeowners premium.

Use Tables 19-5 and 19-6 and the information that follows the tables to find the total annual premium for each of the following automobile liability insurance policies.

	Territory	Credit rating	Liability coverage	Model class	Vehicle age	Comprehensive deductible	Collision deductible
7.	1	GOOD	250/500/250	3	New	$250	$500
8.	1	OCC	100/300/100	2	4 years	$0	$500
9.	2	BAD	50/100/50	1	3 years	$250	$1,000

10. The company car for the Greenwood Rental Agency in territory 2 for a driver is insured with 50/100/50 coverage. The car is model class 1, is 3 years old, and has a comprehensive deductible of $0 and a collision deductible of $500. What is the annual insurance premium if the credit rating is good?

586 Quantitative Methods for Business

11. Sally Greenspan has 100/300/100 liability coverage and lives in territory 2. She has a good credit rating and carries a comprehensive deductible of $250 and a collision deductible of $500. Her 4-year-old vehicle falls in model class 3. Find her annual insurance premium.

12. A driver in territory 1, Laura Jansky is buying an auto insurance policy with 100/300/100 liability coverage. She has a comprehensive deductible of $250 and a collision deductible of $1,000. Her new vehicle is in model class 2. Find her annual premium if her credit rating is OCC.

13. Cheuk NamLam lives in territory 1. He has auto liability insurance with 50/100/50 coverage. He has a $250 deductible for comprehensive and $500 for collision. His 8-year-old vehicle is in model class 2. Find his annual premium if his credit is BAD.

Use Table 19-1 to find the annual premium of each of the following life insurance policies:

	Sex	Age	Policy type	Rate classification	Face value	Annual premium
14.	Male	25	20-year level term	T	$150,000	
15.	Female	30	Whole-life	NT	$200,000	

Use Tables 19-1 and 19-2 to find the following premiums:

	Sex	Age	Policy type	Rate classification	Face value	Annual premium	Monthly premium	Quarterly premium
16.	Female	60	Whole-life	NT	$350,000			
17.	Female	35	10-year level term	PREF	$480,000			

18. a. Find the annual premium paid by Sara Cushion, age 45, on a universal-life insurance policy for $500,000 if Sara smokes.
    b. Find the semiannual premium Sara would pay on the universal-life policy.

19. A whole-life policy purchased at age 50 by Thomas Wimberly costs how much more per $1,000 than the same policy for a male age 60? Use a non-tobacco rate.

20. How much are the total quarterly payments paid by Erich Shultz, age 40, and his wife Demetria, age 35, if each has a 20-year level term insurance policy for $300,000 and both use tobacco?

21. Marguerite Jones is 40 years old, uses tobacco, and decides to convert her $500,000 whole-life insurance policy to extended term insurance. Use 20-year level term rates to estimate the number of years of extended term life insurance her cash value of $27,879 will buy.

22. Marquesha Long at age 55 wants to convert her $200,000 whole-life insurance policy to extended term insurance with the same face value. Use 20-year level term rates to estimate the number of years of coverage her cash value of $14,053 will buy using a non-tobacco rate.

NAME _____   DATE _____

EXERCISES SET B   CHAPTER 19

Using Table 19-3 and the option/endorsement rates on p. 668, find the annual renters insurance premium for each of the following:

	Policy limit	Deductible	Credit rating	Liability	Endorsement or option	Base premium	Endorsement or option premium	Total annual premium
1.	40,000	$500	OCC	$500,000	$4,200 camera equipment			
2.	20,000	$500	GOOD	$300,000	identity theft protection			
3.	20,000	1,000	BAD	$300,000	$5,000 portable tools			

Use Table 19-4 and the information that follows the table when necessary to solve the following.

4. What part of the damages will Hampton Insurance Company pay on a home with $18,000 damage by fire if the market value is $86,000 and it is insured for $65,000? The policy contains an 80% coinsurance clause.

5. In zone 1, a frame dwelling is insured for $305,000 and the insured has good credit and selects a $1,500 deductible. If no extra charge is added for semiannual payments, find the premium paid every six months.

6. Shaniqua Dunlap has a homeowners policy for his brick (masonry) home located in zone 1 for its appraised value of $248,500 and selects a deductible of $1,000. If Shaniqua has excellent credit, find her total annual homeowners premium.

Use Tables 19-5 and 19-6 and the information that follows the tables to find the total annual premium for each of the following automobile liability insurance policies.

	Territory	Credit rating	Total coverage	Model class	Vehicle age	Comprehensive deductible	Collision deductible
7.	2	OCC	50/100/50	1	1 year	$0	$500
8.	2	BAD	50/100/50	3	4 years	$0	$500
9.	1	GOOD	100/300/100	2	New	$250	$1,000

588 Quantitative Methods for Business

10. Aggawal Montoya has a good credit rating and lives in territory 1. He has automobile insurance on his 3-year-old vehicle with 100/300/100 coverage. The vehicle is in model class 1 and has a $250 deductible for comprehensive and $1,000 for collision. Find his annual premium.

11. Larry Tremont has an insurance policy with a $1,000 deductible clause for collision and a $250 deductible clause for comprehensive. Larry's liability coverage on his 5-year-old, model class 2 vehicle is 50/100/50. Find his annual premium if he lives in territory 2 and has an OCC credit rating.

12. Fred Case has an auto insurance policy with 500/1000/500 liability coverage. He lives in territory 2 and has good credit. His vehicle is in model class 3 and is 26 months old. His deductible for comprehensive is $250 and for collision is $500. Find his annual premium.

13. John Malinowsky has auto insurance with 100/300/100 liability coverage. His vehicle is 12 years old and is in model class 2. John lives in territory 1. Find his annual premium if he has a $250 deductible on comprehensive and a $500 deductible on collision and has good credit.

Use Table 19-1 to find the annual premium of the following life insurance policies:

	Sex	Age	Policy type	Rate classification	Face value	Annual premium
14.	Male	30	10-year level term	NT	$300,000	$408
15.	Female	50	Whole-life	T	$100,000	$2,539

Use Tables 19-1 and 19-2 to find the premiums.

	Sex	Age	Policy type	Rate classification	Face value	Annual premium	Monthly premium	Quarterly premium
16.	Female	20	Universal-life	PREF	$350,000			
17.	Male	40	20-year level term	T	$100,000			

18. Sam Molla has a 10-year level term life insurance policy with a value of $250,000. How much is his semiannual premium if he is 40 years old with a non-tobacco rate?

19. Find the annual premium paid on a whole-life insurance policy for $375,000 taken out at age 30 by a male who has the preferred rate.

20. Find the monthly premium of a $450,000 universal-life insurance policy purchased by a 25-year-old female, who gets the preferred rate.

21. At 30 years old, Jaime Dawson finds the need to convert his whole-life insurance policy of $500,000 to extended term coverage with the same face value. Use 10-year level term rates to estimate the number of years of extended term coverage his cash value of $1,095 will provide using a non-tobacco rate.

22. Tancia Brown is 55 years old, has a non-tobacco rate, and is converting her $450,000 whole-life insurance policy to extended term insurance with the same face value. Use 10-year level term rates to estimate the number of years of coverage her cash value of $13,826 will buy.

PRACTICE TEST

CHAPTER 19

1. Find the annual premium on a $300,000 whole-life insurance policy for a 40-year-old male using a non-tobacco rate.

2. Find the annual premium on an automobile insurance policy with liability limits of 50/100/50 in territory 2 for a person who has a 2-year-old car in model class 2. The comprehensive deductible is $250 and the collision deductible is $1,000. The insured person has good credit.

3. Find the annual premium for a homeowners policy on a masonry home insured at $287,500 in zone 2. The owner has excellent credit, chooses a $1,500 deductible, and insures $3,000 in jewelry.

4. Find the annual premium on a 100/300/100 liability limits automobile insurance policy for a driver in territory 2. The vehicle is 5 years old, in model class 2. The comprehensive deductible is $250 and the collision deductible is $1,000. The insured has good credit.

5. Find the annual premium on a 10-year level term life insurance policy for $150,000 for a 30-year-old male who uses tobacco.

6. Find the annual premium on an automobile insurance policy for a driver in territory 1 with 100/300/100 liability limits. The new car is in model class 3 and has a $500 collision deductible and a $250 comprehensive deductible. The insured has OCC credit rating.

7. A frame home is insured for $178,000. Find the total annual premium if the home is in zone 1 and the owner chooses $1,000 deductible and the optional identity theft protection. The owner also adds an endorsement to insure camera equipment valued at $3,700 and has an OCC credit rating.

8. Compare the cost per year of a whole-life insurance policy for $200,000 to a 20-year level term policy for a 60-year-old male using a non-tobacco rate.

9. How much does a 45-year-old female using a non-tobacco rate pay in monthly premiums for a $250,000 whole-life insurance policy?

10. Find the quarterly payments on a 10-year level term life insurance policy for $150,000 on a 40-year-old male with a non-tobacco rate.

11. The market value of a home is $72,500. It is insured for $50,000 with an 80% coinsurance clause. If a fire causes $62,000 in damages, how much of the damages will the policy cover?

12. Find the annual premium for a 50/100/50 automobile liability insurance policy for a driver in territory 2 with a 12-year-old car in model class 3. Collision has a $500 deductible and comprehensive has a $250 deductible. The insured has an OCC credit rating.

590   Quantitative Methods for Business

13. Mary Lynne Winston is 55 years old, has a non-tobacco rate, and decides to convert her $100,000 whole-life insurance policy to extended term coverage with the same face value. How many years of 10-year level term insurance will she have if her cash value is $1,856?

Use Table 19-3 and the information on page 668 to find the total annual renters insurance premiums in Exercises 14–18.

14. Brett Smyly needs a $40,000 renters insurance policy and has selected the $500,000 liability with $1,000 deductible. The insurance company has determined his credit is excellent and has given him the "good" credit rate. If he adds an endorsement to ensure $6,500 of jewelry and the option of identity theft/protection coverage, find his annual premium.

15. Duke Schmidt has a renters insurance policy for $20,000 of household goods, has selected $300,000 liability with $1,000 deductible, and his credit is rated as occasional payments past 30 days. If Duke also adds an endorsement of $12,500 to insure his gun collection and $3,500 to insure the jewelry he keeps at his condo, how much is his annual premium?

16. Tashundra Bolsinger rents an apartment in St. Louis and carries $40,000 insurance on her personal belongings. She selects the maximum liability with a deductible of $1,000 for each claim and carries identity theft/fraud protection. Tashundra's credit is rated as OCC because she has a couple of late payments on her record. Find her annual premium.

17. Laquita Marbut lives in a condo and is required to have renters insurance to protect her personal property. She has an excellent credit rating and elects to purchase a policy that will cover $20,000 in personal property and $300,000 in liability. She will have a deductible of $1,000. Laquita also selects an endorsement of $3,800 for her computer and $1,500 for her camera equipment and the identity theft protection option. Find her annual renters insurance premium.

18. Laura Bains lives in an apartment in San Francisco and her landlord requires her to have renters insurance to protect her personal property. She has an OCC credit rating and elects to purchase a policy that will cover $40,000 in personal property and $500,000 in liability. She will have a deductible of $1,000. Laura also selects an endorsement of $3,000 for jewelry and $2,500 for her collectibles. Find her annual renters insurance premium.

CRITICAL THINKING

CHAPTER 19

1. The formula for finding the estimated annual life insurance premium rate using a table with rates per $1,000 of face value (Table 19-1) is given on page 663. Another source may have a table giving rates per $100 of face value. How will the formula change when using the rate per $100 of face value?

2. Examine Table 19-1 and compare the annual life insurance premium rates per $1,000 of face value for non-tobacco users with the rate for persons who use tobacco.

3. If Claudia McLeod had a homeowners policy insurance to cover 60% of the property's value, and fire damages were 40% of the property value, what percent will the insurance company with an 80% coinsurance clause pay for the loss?

4. If Payten Pastner had homeowners insurance to cover 80% of the property's value, and fire damages were 90% of the total value, what percent will the insurance company with an 80% coinsurance clause pay for the loss?

5. If a car rental agency charges $15.50 per day for a liability, comprehensive, and collision waiver, this would be equivalent to what annual premium? Why do you suppose no difference is made for territory or driver class?

6. Why is whole-life insurance more expensive than level term life insurance?

7. Justify why life insurance premiums are higher for males than for females who are in the same age category.

8. The formula given for using Table 19-1 is

$$\text{Annual premium} = \frac{\text{face value}}{\$1,000} \times \text{rate}.$$

Is the formula

$$\text{Annual premium} = \text{face value} \times \frac{\text{rate}}{\$1,000}$$

equivalent? Why or why not?

Challenge Problem

Manny Bober has a homeowners insurance policy with a value of $500,000. His masonry home is located in zone 2. Use the rates in Table 19-4 to compare the cost of his annual premium based on which deductible he selects if his credit rating is GOOD.

CASE STUDIES

19-1 How Much Is Enough?

Alex and Christa are married and have two teenage children. Alex works full-time as an electrical engineer and Christa works part-time as a floral designer. They own a modest 3-bedroom, 2-bath home on a ¼-acre lot and have two cars, and both have excellent credit. They recently attended a financial planning seminar that highlighted a number of issues, such as saving, investing, insuring, and tax and estate planning. Alex and Christa have decided to reassess their insurance needs to determine what portion of their budget should be designated for insurance premiums.

They decide to review their auto insurance first. According to the literature they picked up, they live in territory 1. They own two cars, one of which is 2 years old and considered model class 1; the other is 6 years old and considered model class 2. They feel they should have $100/$300 bodily injury coverage, and $100,000 of property damage coverage. They decide to purchase comprehensive coverage with $0 deductible and collision coverage with a $1,000 deductible on their newer vehicle, but they decide to forego comprehensive and collision coverage on their older vehicle. They both have excellent driving records, with no moving violations or at-fault accidents during the past 3 years. Their insurance company allows a 5% discount for being accident free for 3 years and a 10% discount for insuring multiple vehicles.

1. What amount should Alex and Christa plan to spend annually on their automobile insurance? Use the tables provided in this chapter.

Coverage	Car 1: 2 years old	Car 2: 6 years old
Body injury/property damage		
Comprehensive		
Collision		

2. The market value of their home is approximately $180,000. Their insurance policy contains a coinsurance clause. How much insurance should Alex and Christa carry to meet the coinsurance requirement and how much should they anticipate for an annual insurance premium for that level of coverage if their home is in zone 1, is masonry construction, and they choose a $1,000 deductible?

3. Alex is also thinking about purchasing additional life insurance. His employer provides some life insurance coverage, but the financial planner at the seminar they attended suggested he carry insurance to represent an amount 5 to 15 times his annual earnings. Alex earns $75,000 a year and his employer provides $75,000 of life insurance. If Alex decides to purchase enough insurance to cover 10 times his earnings, how much more insurance should he purchase? If he is a 40-year-old male, preferred rate class, and selects 20-year level term insurance, how much should he plan to spend annually on life insurance?

4. Considering the auto insurance, the property insurance, and the life insurance, how much should Alex and Christa plan to pay each year in premiums? What percentage of Alex's gross pay does the total premium represent?

19-2 Soul Food Catering

Amaya left the doctor's office with a strange feeling that seemed to be a combination of euphoria and apprehension. As if moving her catering business to a new location wasn't enough, her family was also moving into a new home. Now she felt apprehension at being a first-time mom at age 30 while running a successful business. But she also felt euphoria about the new addition to the family. Amaya couldn't wait to tell her husband that they were expecting a baby. This was going to mean big changes. Her first thought was child care—but for now, that could wait. Her most pressing concern was insurance. With the move to a new home valued at $250,000, certainly the cost for property insurance was going up. By adding two brand new delivery vans for her catering business at $17,500 each, the cost for automobile insurance would, at minimum, double. And now with a baby on the way, life insurance was more important than ever. After her husband, the next call was going to be to their insurance agent. Thank goodness she and her husband had maintained their excellent credit ratings, but there was a lot of planning to do.

1. Amaya's agent states that a good rule of thumb for life insurance is to purchase 5 to 7 times your annual income. Amaya's income averages $50,000 annually, but she would like to have the house paid off as well in the event of her death, so she decides $600,000 is the face amount she would like to have. Using the life insurance table, make a comparison of 10-year, 20-year, whole-life, and universal life annual rates for $600,000 of face amount using a preferred rate class.

2. Given your answers to question 1, which coverage would you recommend that Amaya take? What incentive does she have to take a higher-priced premium? Explain.

3. Because of the higher replacement cost, Amaya's agent recommends insuring the new home at $275,000. The dwelling is a regular frame home located in zone 2. Using homeowners insurance rates per $100 of face value in Table 19-4, find the annual premium for the dwelling using a $1,500 deductible.

4. Even though there have been no accidents or tickets during the past 3 years, Amaya is very concerned about the liability on the new vans, so she decides to go with 100/300/100 liability coverage. Use Table 19-5 to find the annual premium for automobile liability insurance using territory 2, and Table 19-6 to find the comprehensive and collision rates using territory 2, model class 1, with a $250 deductible for comprehensive and a $1,000 deductible for collision. Allow discounts of 5% for being accident free for three years and 10% for insuring multiple vehicles.